CAMBRIDGE LIBRARY COLLECTION
Books of enduring scholarly value

History

The books reissued in this series include accounts of historical events and movements by eye-witnesses and contemporaries, as well as landmark studies that assembled significant source materials or developed new historiographical methods. The series includes work in social, political and military history on a wide range of periods and regions, giving modern scholars ready access to influential publications of the past.

Official Catalogue of the Great Exhibition of the Works of Industry of All Nations 1851

Copper from Cornwall, a hand-drill from Hampshire, elephant teeth from Sudan, and snuff-boxes from Switzerland. The Great Exhibition of 1851 included some 13,000 natural and man-made objects in the largest collection of materials and inventions the world had ever seen. This single-volume catalogue lists all the items on show with their origin and location. With the aid of its maps and lists, visitors were able to navigate the Crystal Palace with ease, despite its immense size. In 'The Catalogue's Account of Itself', included at the end of the book, Charles Dickens describes with great verve the complex compilation process of the catalogue, completed just hours before the Exhibition opened. New arrivals necessitated several corrected printings, and this is the fourth edition. A truly fascinating record of the state of the world seen through material objects in the mid-nineteenth century, this volume will delight both the curious browser and the scholar.

Cambridge University Press has long been a pioneer in the reissuing of out-of-print titles from its own backlist, producing digital reprints of books that are still sought after by scholars and students but could not be reprinted economically using traditional technology. The Cambridge Library Collection extends this activity to a wider range of books which are still of importance to researchers and professionals, either for the source material they contain, or as landmarks in the history of their academic discipline.

Drawing from the world-renowned collections in the Cambridge University Library, and guided by the advice of experts in each subject area, Cambridge University Press is using state-of-the-art scanning machines in its own Printing House to capture the content of each book selected for inclusion. The files are processed to give a consistently clear, crisp image, and the books finished to the high quality standard for which the Press is recognised around the world. The latest print-on-demand technology ensures that the books will remain available indefinitely, and that orders for single or multiple copies can quickly be supplied.

The Cambridge Library Collection will bring back to life books of enduring scholarly value (including out-of-copyright works originally issued by other publishers) across a wide range of disciplines in the humanities and social sciences and in science and technology.

Official Catalogue of the Great Exhibition of the Works of Industry of All Nations 1851

ANONYMOUS

CAMBRIDGE
UNIVERSITY PRESS

CAMBRIDGE UNIVERSITY PRESS

Cambridge, New York, Melbourne, Madrid, Cape Town,
Singapore, São Paolo, Delhi, Tokyo, Mexico City

Published in the United States of America by Cambridge University Press, New York

www.cambridge.org
Information on this title: www.cambridge.org/9781108029995

This edition first published 1851
This digitally printed version 2011

ISBN 978-1-108-02999-5 Paperback

By Authority of the Royal Commission.

OFFICIAL  CATALOGUE

OF THE

GREAT EXHIBITION

OF THE

WORKS OF INDUSTRY OF ALL NATIONS,

1851.

THE EARTH IS THE LORD'S, AND ALL THAT THEREIN IS:
THE COMPASS OF THE WORLD AND THEY THAT DWELL THEREIN.

FOURTH CORRECTED AND IMPROVED EDITION, 15th September, 1851.

LONDON:
SPICER BROTHERS, WHOLESALE STATIONERS; W. CLOWES & SONS, PRINTERS;
Contractors to the Royal Commission,
29 NEW BRIDGE STREET, BLACKFRIARS, AND AT THE EXHIBITION BUILDING, HYDE PARK.

NE NOSTRA, ISTA QUÆ INVENIMUS, DIXERIS: SAY NOT THE DISCOVERIES WE MAKE ARE OUR OWN :
INSITA SUNT NOBIS OMNIUM ARTIUM SEMINA,   THE GERMS OF EVERY ART ARE IMPLANTED WITHIN US.
MAGISTERQUE EX OCCULTO DEUS PRODUCIT INGENIA.   AND GOD OUR INSTRUCTOR, FROM HIDDE SOURCES, DEVELOPS THE
                                                  FACULTIES OF INVENTION.

HUMANI GENERIS PROGRESSUS,   THE PROGRESS OF THE HUMAN RACE,
EX COMMUNI OMNIUM LABORE ORTUS,   RESULTING FROM THE COMMON LABOUR OF ALL MEN,
UNISCUJUSQUE INDUSTRLÆ DEBET ESSE FINIS :   OUGHT TO BE THE FINAL OBJECT OF THE EXERTION OF EACH INDIVIDUAL.
HOC ADJUVANDO,   IN PROMOTING THIS END,
DEI OPT : MAX : VOLUNTATEM EXSEQUIMUR.   WE ARE ACCOMPLISHING THE WILL OF THE GREAT AND BLESSED GOD.

ARRANGEMENT.

ALTHOUGH the plan adopted in the arrangement of the Catalogue is exceedingly simple, the great extent of the Exhibition, and the variety of its contents, may render a few preparatory remarks acceptable.

ARRANGEMENT IN THE BUILDING.—The western half of the building is occupied by Great Britain and her Dependencies.

The productions of the United Kingdom are arranged in thirty classes, and each class is indicated by a red banner.

The Colonies are also marked in the same manner.

The eastern half of the building is filled with the productions of foreign countries, whose names are inscribed on similar banners suspended over the various divisions.

The Plan (see pp. 12 and 13) will assist in determining the position of Countries and Classes in the building.

ARRANGEMENT OF THE CATALOGUE.—The British productions are entered in the Catalogue in the order of the classes, and the Foreign in alphabetical order of the countries; the title and number of the class, and the name of each colony and foreign country, are printed conspicuously at the top of the page.

EXHIBITORS' NUMBERS.—Each class as well as each foreign collection has its own distinct set of numbers; and labels are appended to the various articles, showing where the descriptions are to be found in the Catalogue.

The most convenient method of using the Catalogue will be to ascertain the Country or Class, and the Number of the Exhibitor, as given by the card appended to the object, and to refer to the same Country or Class, and Number in the Catalogue.

Many numbers will be found wanting in the Catalogue, but these, from various causes, are also vacant in the Exhibition itself.

Since the publication of the former Catalogue a large number of articles have arrived from India, Russia, Turkey, and France, notices of which are included in this edition. Great pains have been taken to render the present issue as correct as possible; and it is particularly requested that any inaccuracies which have escaped notice, may be immediately communicated to the Contractors, Messrs. SPICER & CLOWES, at the Catalogue Office, in the Exhibition Building, with a note of the Class and Number under which they occur.

G. W. YAPP, *Compiler.*

ABBREVIATIONS USED IN THE WORK.—Inv. Inventor; Des. Designer; Mod. Modeller; Sculp. Sculptor, Carver, or Engraver; Exec. Executed by; Prod. Producer; Manu. Manufacturer; Imp. Importer; Prop. Proprietor; Pat. Patent Reg. Registered; Impr. Improver; Pro. Reg. Provisionally Registered.

LONDON: PRINTED BY W. CLOWES AND SONS, STAMFORD STREET, AND CHARING CROSS.

CONTENTS.

The following Table has been arranged in the order which it is believed will be found most convenient for examining the various departments of the Exhibition; and reference has been made at the end of each Class to that which follows next in the order of the arrangement.

UNITED KINGDOM.—West End of Building.

PAGE

Articles exhibited by Her Majesty the Queen, H.R.H. the Prince Albert, and H.R.H. the Prince of Wales . 5

Objects exhibited outside the Building, including Granite, Marbles, Stones, Slate, Coal, Cements, large Pottery, Anchors, Life-boats, &c. . . . 7

Statuary and other objects of interest placed in the Transept and Main Avenue; a few of these are placed in the Eastern or Foreign end of the Nave . . 8

Plan of the Building, showing the relative position of the various Classes and Countries 12

Ground Floor—South Side.
(Commencing at the West End.)

Gems and Ornamental Stones, Fossils, Clays, Marbles, Stones, Coal, Peat, Models of Coal Mines, &c. (Class 1, Nos. 1 to 277) 14

Ores, Metals, Models of Mining machinery, &c. (Class 1, No. 400 to end) 19

On the South and West Walls are specimens of House Decorations, Imitation Marbles, &c. (Class 26) . 136

Also Specimens of Woods, Ivory, &c. (Class 4, Nos. 134, 135) 29

Sculpture Court (Class 30) 154

Agricultural and Horticultural Machines and Implements (Class 9) 54

General Hardware, Locks, Grates, &c. (Class 22) . 109

Sheffield Cutlery, &c. (Class 22, Nos. 102 to 240) . 110

Birmingham Goods (Class 22, Nos. 249 to 374) . 114

Mediæval Court, containing Church Furniture, Decorations, &c. 136

Furniture, Upholstery, Paper-hangings, Papier Maché, Japanned Goods, Decorative Ceilings, &c. (Class 26) 129

Woollen, Worsted, and Mixed Fabrics, Shawls, &c. (Classes 12 and 15) 74

Flax and Hemp Manufactures (Class 14) . . 83

Dyed and printed Fabrics (Class 18) . . . 95

Ground Floor, North Side.
(Commencing at the West End by Main Avenue.)

Cotton Fabrics (Class 11) 73

Leather, Saddlery and Harness, Boots and Shoes, Skins, Furs, and Feathers (Class 16) . . . 85

Mineral Manufactures for Buildings or Decorations (Class 27) 137

Ceilings, &c. (Class 26) 136

Paper, Printing, and Bookbinding (Class 17) . 91

Fine Art Court—Sculpture, Modelling, Mosaics, Enamels, &c. (Class 30) 147

Hydraulic Press, Steam Hammer, Fire Engines, Marine Engines, Locomotives, and Railway Apparatus, Carriages, &c. (Class 5) 30

PAGE

Machinery in Motion, in Four Divisions.
First Division at North-west Corner of the Building.

Cotton Machinery from Oldham and Manchester. (Class 6) 38

Machinery from the United States of America.—*See* America 184

On the Wall are Specimens of Woods, &c.—(*See* Class 4, Nos. 136, 137, 138) 29

Second Division, behind Western Refreshment Room.

Cotton and Woollen Machinery, Power Looms, &c. (Class 6) 38

On the Walls are Specimens of Plaids. (Classes 12 and 15) 81

Third and largest Division.

Flax, Silk, Lace, and Hemp Machinery, Lathes and Engineering Machinery and Tools, Mills, &c. (Class 6) 33

Fourth Division, behind the Fine Art Court.

Railway and Steam Machinery. (Class 5) . . 30

Printing and other Machinery. (Class 6) . . 38

Building Contrivances, &c. (Class 7) . . 43

Naval Models, &c. (Class 8, Nos. 181 to 197) . 50

French Machinery in Motion.—See France. . 220

South Transept Gallery.
(By stairs near Switzerland, corner of Main Avenue, East.)

Clothing, ready for immediate use, Hats, Hosiery, &c. (Class 20) 103

Shawls, Woollens, and Mixed Fabrics. (Classes 12 and 15, Nos. 275 to 313) 80

Organs and Electric Clock (Class 10) . . 60

Silk and Velvet Fabrics (Class 13) . . . 81

South Gallery.

Chemical and Pharmaceutical Products (Class 2) . 22

Substances used as Food (Class 3) . . . 24

Vegetable and Animal Substances used in Manufactures (Class 4) 27

Military Arms, Models, &c. (Class 8) . . 47

Against the wall, a State Bed, and Specimens of Embroidery (Class 19) 97

West Gallery.

Naval Architecture, Arms, &c. (Class 8) . . 47

North Gallery.

Civil Engineering, Architecture, and Building Contrivances (Class 7) 43

Surgical Apparatus, Anatomical Models, &c. (Class 10) 60

Cutlery, Edge and Hand Tools, &c. (Class 21) . 108

Manufactures from Animal and Vegetable Substances not woven or felted (Class 28) . . . 139

North Transept Gallery.

	PAGE
China, Porcelain, earthenware, &c. (Class 25) .	128
Organs (Class 10) .	60
Bee-hives, Bees at work, &c. (Class 9, Nos. 290 & 291).	59
Miscellaneous Manufactures and Small Wares (Class 29)	142

North Central Gallery.

	PAGE
Glass (Class 24) .	125
Musical and Philosophical Instruments, &c. (Class 10)	60

West Gallery.

	PAGE
Globes, Maps, Orreries, Clocks, Aerial Machines, &c. (Class 10) .	60

South Central Gallery.

	PAGE
Clock and Watch work, &c. (Class 10) .	60
Plate, Jewellery, &c. (Class 23) .	122
Tapestry, Carpets, Floor Cloth, Lace, Embroidery, &c. (Class 19) .	97

NOTE. The larger articles are suspended from the girders of the galleries throughout the building.

BRITISH DEPENDENCIES.

The productions of India and the Colonies are arranged on each side of the Main Avenue, close to the Transept.

	PAGE		PAGE		PAGE
India, &c. .	156	Newfoundland .	170	British Guiana .	172
Jersey and Guernsey .	162	New Brunswick .	171	Bahamas .	174
Ceylon .	163	St. Helena .	171	Trinidad .	174
Ionian Islands .	163	Mauritius .	171	Falkland Islands .	176
Gibraltar .	164	Grenada .	171	Bermudas .	176
Malta .	164	Montserrat .	171	New South Wales .	176
Cape of Good Hope .	165	Jamaica .	171	South Australia .	177
Western Africa .	166	St. Kitt's .	171	Van Diemen's Land .	177
Gold Coast and Ashantee .	167	Barbadoes .	171	New Zealand .	183
Canada .	168	Antigua .	172	Labuan, and other parts of the Eastern Archipelago .	183
Nova Scotia .	170	St. Vincent. .	172		

FOREIGN STATES.—East End of Building.

Main Avenue, East.

	PAGE
Sculpture and other objects of interest placed opposite the various countries to which they belong	10

Ground Floor.

(*Commencing at the Transept and proceeding towards the East.*)

	PAGE
China .	214
Tunis .	314
Brazil .	214
Chili .	214
Mexico .	288
New Granada .	291
Society Islands .	302
St. Domingo (with the Colonies) .	307
Persia .	291
Greece .	285
Turkey .	316
Egypt .	217
Spain .	302
Portugal and Madeira .	291
Switzerland .	309
Italy :—	
Rome .	295
Sardinia .	301
Tuscany .	318
France .	220
Belgium .	206
Netherlands .	288
Austria .	193

	PAGE
Germany.—*States of the Zollverein.*	
1. Prussia, Baden, and United States of Northern Germany.	
a. Provinces of Brandenburg, Silesia, Posen, and Pomerania .	253
b. Grand Duchy of Baden ; Southern parts of the West Provinces of Prussia and Electoral Hesse .	260
c. Provinces of Prussia and Lithuania .	262
d. Northern Parts of Electoral Hesse, and of the Prussian West Provinces ; Principality of Lippe .	263
e. Grand Duchy of Saxony, Prussian Saxony, Brunswick, Anhalt, and States of Thuringia.	268
2. Bavaria .	273
3. Saxony .	275
4. Wurtemburg .	279
5. Frankfort-on-the-Maine .	281
6. Grand Duchy of Hesse .	282
7. Luxemburg .	284
8. Nassau .	284
Hanse Town and North Germany :—	
Hanover .	288
Mecklenburg-Strelitz .	288
Mecklenburg-Schwerin .	288
Nuremburg .	288
Oldenburg .	291
Hamburgh .	286
Lubeck and Bremen .	288

	PAGE
Denmark .	216
Sweden and Norway .	308
Russia .	296
United States of America .	184

South and South-Central Galleries.

(*Commencing from Swiss Staircase.*)

	PAGE
France :— Silks, Velvets, Lace, Prints, Flowers, Linen, Harness, &c.	220
Austria :—Lace, Silks, &c. .	193
France :—Surgical Apparatus, Anatomical Models, Furniture, &c.	220
Zollverein :—Musical and Philosophical Instruments, Silks, Linens, &c. .	253

North Central Gallery.

	PAGE
United States of America .	184
Russia .	296
Zollverein (North and North-Central Galleries).	253
Austria .	193
Belgium .	206

North Gallery

Stained Glass Windows, &c. :—

	PAGE
British (Class 24) .	127
French .	220
Belgian .	206
Austrian .	193

United Kingdom.

ARTICLES EXHIBITED BY HER MAJESTY THE QUEEN.

MAIN AVENUE, EAST.

96 Portrait of Her Majesty on Sèvres china, size of life, half length, by A. Ducluzeau, after a portrait by F. Winterhalter. Painted in 1846. (Class 30.)

97 Portrait of H.R.H. Prince Albert, on Sèvres china, size of life, half length, painted by A. Bezanget, after a portrait by F. Winterhalter. These portraits are exhibited jointly by Her Majesty and H.R.H. Prince Albert.
(Class 30.)

140 The Great Diamond of Runjeet Singh, called "Koh-i-Noor," or Mountain of Light. (Class 23.)

MAIN AVENUE, WEST.

140 Jewel case, in the cinque-cento style, designed by L. Gruner, Esq., and executed at the manufactory of Mr. Henry Elkington, at Birmingham. The material is bronze, gilt and silvered by electro-type process; upon this case are portraits on china of Her Majesty, H.R.H. Prince Albert, and H.R.H. the Prince of Wales, copied from miniatures by R. Thorburn, Esq., A.R.A. The small medallions, representing profiles of their R.H. the Princes and Princesses, were modelled from life by Leonard Wyon, Esq.
(Class 23.)

CLASS 23.—CENTRAL SOUTH GALLERY.

1 Table of gold and silver electro-plate, manufactured by Messrs. Elkington. The top of the table is an electro-type reproduction of a plate of fine workmanship, obtained and copied for Mr. H. Elkington under the direction of the Chevalier de Schlick. The eight subjects in bas-relief represent Minerva, Astrologia, Geometrica, Arithmetica, Musica, Rhetorica. The centre figure represents Temperance surrounded by the four elements. At he bottom of this plate is an inscription pointing to the artist. The table is designed by George Stanton, a young artist in the employ of Mr. H. Elkington, and a student n the Birmingham School of Design.

CLASS 30.—FINE ART COURT.

353 A cradle, carved in Turkey boxwood by W. G. Rogers, and designed by his son, symbolising the union of the Royal House of England with that of Saxe-Coburg and Gotha. One end exhibits in the centre the armorial bearings of Her Majesty the Queen, surrounded by masses of foliage, natural flowers and birds; on the rocker, beneath, is seen the head of "Nox," represented as a beautiful sleeping female, crowned with a garland of poppies, supported upon bats' wings, and surrounded by the seven planets.

The other end, or the back of the head of the cradle, is devoted to the arms of H.R.H. Prince Albert; the shield occupies the centre, and round it, among the arabesque foliage, the six crests of the Prince are scattered, with the motto "Treu und Fest." Below, on the rocker. is discovered a head of "Somnus" with closed eyes, and over the chin a wimple, which, on each side, terminates in poppies.

In the interior of the head of the cradle, guardian angels are introduced; and above, the royal crown is found embedded in foliage. The friezes, forming the most important part of the sides of the body of the cradle, are composed of roses, poppies, conventional foliage, butterflies, and birds, while beneath them rise a variety of pinks, studied from nature. The edges and the insides of the rockers are enriched with the insignia of royalty and emblems repose.

CLASS 24.—CENTRAL NORTH GALLERY, I. 27.

20 A pair of richly cut crystal glass candelabra, 8 feet high, carrying 15 lights each. The shaft composed of prisms upwards of 3 feet in length. Designed and manufactured by F. and C. Osler, of Birmingham, and 44 Oxford St. London.

CLASS 19.—CENTRAL NORTH GALLERY, I. 36.

156 Axminster carpet, designed by L. Gruner, Esq., and manufactured at Glasgow, for Mr. Dowbiggen.

379 A Berlin-wool carpet executed by one hundred and fifty ladies of Great Britain. The dimensions of this carpet are thirty feet in length, and twenty in breadth.

The carpet has been produced under the management of a Committee. The design by Mr. J. W. Papworth; the patterns were painted and the work executed under the superintendence of Mr. W. B. Simpson.

CLASS 19.—SOUTH GALLERY, P. 15 to 17.

337 Axminster carpet, designed by L. Gruner, Esq., and manufactured by Messrs. Blackmore Brothers, at Wilton for Messrs. Watson, Bell, & Co.

IN INDIAN DEPARTMENT.

Presented to Her Majesty by the Nawab Nazim of Bengal.

A splendid reception-seat, with canopy of purple velvet, embroidered in gold, supported on silver pillars, with two "moarchals," or emblems of dignity, used by the princes of India upon state occasions, made of pure gold, and containing feathers of the birds of paradise.—A state palanquin of ivory, with canopy of gold embroidered cloth.—A purdah, or canopy, used only by persons of the highest rank.—A nalkee, a palanquin of ivory, used only when the sun is below the horizon.—A howdah, or palanquin, with trappings, to be borne on the back of an elephant.—State harness and ornaments for horses and camels.

HIS ROYAL HIGHNESS PRINCE ALBERT.

CLASS 30.—SOUTH TRANSEPT.

15 Group in marble, "Theseus and Amazons," executed at Rome by Joseph Engel, Esq., from Hungary, pupil of the Royal Academy.

CLASS 3.

107 Three samples of grain grown on the royal farms at Windsor, consisting of wheat, oats, and beans, one bushel of each.

CLASSES 12 & 15.—MAIN AVENUE, WEST.

500 Two brocaded dresses manufactured by T. Gregory and Brothers, Shelf, near Halifax, Yorkshire. The weft of cashmere wool shorn from goats kept by H.R.H. Prince Albert, in Windsor Park. The warp is of silk.

Two shawls and a specimen of coarse cloth, manufactured by J. Haley and Son, Bramley, near Leeds. The whole of the material is of the cashmere wool as above described.

The cashmere goats' wool, of which these articles are manufactured, consists of two distinct materials called wool and kemp. The wool is beautifully rich and soft to the touch, and is probably superior in this respect to the finest Continental lambs' wool, and equal in richness to the Thibet wool. It is also divisible into qualities. The kemp presents the appearance of a coarse, rough hair, which would deteriorate the appearance of even common fabrics by its inferiority and harshness.

The two materials, as shorn from the goat, are closely intermingled, and present the appearance of coarse hairy wool of a very low character; but a minute inspection snows that part of it is of a very fine quality. The separation is effected entirely by hand, fibre by fibre; no machinery having as yet been applied to this purpose. The process is both difficult and tedious, one person not being able to separate more than half an ounce in twelve hours.

After the separation of the qualities, it is desirable further to divide it, in order to make a warp yarn for fabrics like the shawls; but this was impossible in the present instance, owing to the small quantity produced, otherwise the fabric would have been much finer. In the dresses this was achieved, the warp being of silk, and the quantity required for the weft not therefore so great in proportion.

Specimen of coarse cloth manufactured entirely of the coarse hair or kemp, which is generally considered worthless.

CLASS 27.

140 A block of Parrot coal from West Wemyss colliery, Kirkaldy, Fifeshire, partly polished.

141 Garden seat, designed by L. Gruner, Esq., and executed in Fifeshire by Thomas Williams Waun, of Parrot or cannel coal, from the estate of Rear-Admiral Wemyss.

CLASS 30.

350 Two slabs for tables, designed by L. Gruner, Esq., in the cinque-cento style, executed by Mr. Thomas Woodruff at Bakewell, in Derbyshire stones, in imitation of the Florentine mosaic.

351 Candelabrum in the cinque-cento style, designed by L. Gruner, Esq., modelled by Ant. Trentanove, and executed in scagliola in imitation of giallo antico, by L. Romoli.

At the CAVALRY BARRACKS opposite the Exhibition.

Model houses for four families of the class of manufacturing and mechanical operatives, intended to convey practical information for the improvement of the dwellings of the working classes. Built with hollow bricks and of fireproof construction, from the designs of Henry Roberts, Esq. F.S.A.

HIS ROYAL HIGHNESS PRINCE ALBERT,

ON BEHALF OF

H.R.H. THE PRINCE OF WALES.

CLASS 30.—MAIN AVENUE, EAST.

98 Shield presented by His Majesty the King of Prussia to His Royal Highness the Prince of Wales, in commemoration of the baptism of the infant Prince, for whom His Majesty acted as sponsor.

The pictorial embellishments of the shield, the general plan for which was given by the king himself, were designed by Doctor Peter Von Cornelius, and the architectural ornaments by Counsellor Stüler. The execution of the remaining portions—goldsmiths' work, enamel, &c., was performed by M. G. Hossauer; the modelling by M. A Fischer; the chasing by M. A Mertens; and the lapidary work by M. Calandrelli.

In the centre of the shield is a head of our Saviour. The middle compartment, surrounded by a double line of ornamental work, is divided by a cross into four smaller compartments, which contain emblematic representations of the two Sacraments, Baptism and the Lord's Supper, with their Old Testament types—the opening of the fountain in the rock by Moses, and the fall of manna. At the extremities of the arms of the cross are represented the Evangelists, noting down what they have seen and heard in the Gospels, which are to communicate to all futurity the plan of man's salvation, and prove inexhaustible sources of divine revelation and doctrine.

On the extreme points of the arabesques that rise above the Evangelists, are represented the Christian virtues of Faith, Hope, and Charity, and of Christian Righteousness. Around the entire centre stand in a circle the twelve Apostles. Peter is seen under Faith represented in the arabesque; on the right and left of him are Philip and Andrew; under Hope is James; on either side are Bartholomew and Simon; John is placed beneath the figure of Charity; on either side are James the younger and Thomas; under Righteousness is Paul; on the right and left are Matthew and Judas Thaddeus, going forth into the world to teach and to baptize, and to propagate the kingdom of the Redeemer.

The relievo which surrounds the edge of the shield, represents the betrayal, the redeeming atonement of Christ, and his resurrection. Another portion represents our Lord's triumphant entry into Jerusalem; a third portion the descent of the Holy Ghost, the preaching of the Gospel, and the formation of the Church. The fourth and principal compartment contains an allegorical representation of the birth of the Prince of Wales and of the visit of the king of Prussia, accompanied by Baron Humboldt, General von Natzmer, and the Count von Stolberg, and welcomed by His Royal Highness Prince Albert and the Duke of Wellington: a knight of St. George being represented on the beach standing upon a dragon.

The shield has been denominated the Buckler of Faith. The inscription on the shield runs thus:

"FRIDERICUS GULIELMUS REX BORUSSORUM,
ALBERTO EDUARDO, PRINCIPI WALLIÆ,
IN MEMORIAM DIEI BAPT. XXV. JAN. A. MDCCCXLII."

ZOLLVEREIN, OCTAGON ROOM, No. 836.

COUNT ERNEST OF COBURG-GOTHA.

Fruit stones of various sizes, carved with a penknife.

OBJECTS OUTSIDE THE BUILDING.

(Principally belonging to Class I.)

WESTERN END.
SOUTH ENCLOSURE.

1 ORGAN, J. Penzance, Prod.—Block of serpentine from the Lizard, Cornwall, partly polished.

2 BOARD, —. (J. Donohue, New Rd. Agent).—Two figures in artificial stone.

3 TEAGLE, R. & W. 24 Hertford St. Chelsea, Inv. and Manu.—A figure of Lazarus, in artificial stone, cast from an original carved wood figure, said to be brought from Rome.

4 RAYSDALE, W.—Blocks of gypsum used in the manufacture of plaster.

5 ROBINS, ASPDIN, & COX, Northfleet and Great Scotland Yard, Manu.—Illustrations of Portland cement.

6 MORPHET, J. Studford, near Settle, Prod.—Blue flagstone, obtained from Horton Wood quarries, which have been worked probably about 100 years.

7 GREAVES, R. Warwick, Prod.—Blue lias limestone. Models in lias, Portland, and improved Roman cement, &c.

8 OLD DELABOLE SLATE Co. (by J. Carter), Camelford, Prop.—Slate slab, as raised from the quarries at Delabole. Slate cistern.

9 STIRLING, J. jun. Belvidere rd. Lambeth, Des. Inv. & Manu.—Specimens of slate.

10 WHITE & SONS, Westminster, Manu.—Illustrations of the strength of cement.

11 SEELEY, J. Keppel row, New rd. Manu.—Mercury, after Giov. da Bologna, in artificial stone.

12 WELSH SLATE Co. 1 New Boswell Court (W. H. B. Barwis, Secretary).—Slate from Festiniog, Merionethshire.

13 SINCLAIR, J. Forss, Thurso, Scotland, Manu.—A cistern or bath of Forss-Rockhill flag. Samples of the stone, showing the natural surface, the half-rubbed and the full-rubbed surface, &c.

14 FREEMAN, W. & J. Millbank St. Westminster, Prod.—An obelisk in granite. Sundry large slabs and blocks of stone.

16 STRUTHERS, W. S. 7 Holywell St. Westminster, Manu.—Slate filter, the water being filtered in its ascent.

17 Specimens of Irish flagging.

18 SHARP, S. Commercial Rd. Lambeth, Agent to A. ADAM, Wick, Caithness-shire, Scotland.—Rockhill paving-stone, from the original quarries.

19 FURSE, T. W. 96 High St. Whitechapel, Inv. and Manu.—Waterproof artificial stone, for sewers and drains of large dimensions; for flooring churches. Drains for railways, &c.

20 CARNEGIE, W. F. L. Kinblethmont, Arbroath, Scotland, Prop.—Flag-stones and freestones known as Arbroath pavement, from Leysmill Quarries, dressed by Hunter's stone-planing machine.

22 HAYWOOD, J. Ardsley, near Barnsley, Prod.—Grind-stones from the Ardsley Oaks Quarry, Barnsley.

23 DOVE, D. Nitshill, Hurlet, near Glasgow, Prod.—Freestone block, from Nitshill Quarry. Grindstone from the same quarry, three feet in diameter by six inches thick.

24 BEDFORD, BONSON, DRAKE, & Co. Oaks Quarry, near Barnsley, Prod.—Grindstones from the Oaks Quarry, near Barnsley, 9 feet 7 inches in diameter and 14¼ inches thick, for grinding machinery, &c.

25 RAYNES, LUPTON, & Co. Liverpool, Prod.—Specimens of pure limestone, from Pentregwyddel quarries, near Abergele, Denbighshire, used as a lithographic stone, &c. Specimens of stone, from Graig-lwyd quarries (Penmaen-Mawr, Carnarvonshire).

26 PENZANCE SERPENTINE Co.—A block of rough serpentine.

27 TOWLER, E. Market Rasen.—Blue lias, hydraulic cement, and polished stones, from Kirton Lindseys Tunnel Stone Works.

28 FRANKLIN, P. S. Galway, Ireland, Prop.—Block of stone, partly polished. Block of marble and paving-stones.

29 BROWN, RUSBY, & BOOTH, Sheffield, Prod. and Manu.—Flags and steps. Block of sandstone: weight four tons.

30 LOCAL COMMITTEE, FALMOUTH AND PENRYN.—Sundry paving stones.

34 OAKELEY, E. Coed Talon, near Mold, Flintshire, Wales.—Steam-coal from Coed Talon and Leeswood collieries, near Mold, North Wales; a single block weighing 16 tons.

35 BUCKINGHAM, J. 13 Judd Pl. East, New Rd. Agent to Messrs. Myers & Co. Bonville's Court Collieries.—Anthracite coal, from Tenby, South Wales. Specimens of patented artificial coal.

36 ROUND, D. G. Hange Colliery, Tipton, near Birmingham, Prod.—Specimens of South Staffordshire coal, 19 feet in circumference, and five tons in weight. Specimens of iron ore.

37 JAMES & AUBREY, Swansea, Prod.—Block of anthracite, or stone coal, from Cwmllynfell, in the Swansea valley.

38 INCE HALL COAL & CANNEL Co. Wigan.—Blocks of Arley and Pemberton coal.

39 CAMERON'S COALBROOK STEAM COAL AND SWANSEA AND LOUGHOR RAILWAY Co. 2 Moorgate St.—Steam coal, from Loughor, South Wales.

40 HAINES & SONS, Denbigh Hall, Tipton, Staffordshire, Prop.—Large specimen of the Staffordshire thick, or ten-yard coal; weight 13 tons. Raised from a depth of 165 yards by the ordinary steam-engine, with no other apparatus than that generally in use.

41 BARROW, R. Staveley Works, near Chesterfield, Derbyshire.—Coal, from the mines of Staveley, county of Derby, raised from a shaft 459 feet deep. The block is estimated to weigh 24 tons.

42 JONES, SELLS, & Co. 55 Bankside, Southwark, Agents.—Anthracite coal, from Llanelly, South Wales.

43 DAVIS, D. Hirwain, near Merthyr Tydvil, Wales, Prop.—The Blaengwawr steam coal, from Aberdare.

44 NEATH ABBEY COAL Co.—Brynddwey coal, from between the vales of Neath and Swansea. Anthracite coal from the western side of the vale of Neath.

45 PRICE, T. P. & D. Tillery Colliery, near Newport, Monmouthshire. Prod.—Steam coal, the produce of a newly opened colliery. The coal may be brought up in masses of fifty tons weight.

47 THE BRYMBO Co. Wrexham, Wales, Prod.—Block of coal, from Brymbo, near Wrexham, North Wales.

48 FITZWILLIAM, The Earl.—Pillar exhibiting a complete section of the Barnsley thick bed of coal, from the Elsicot colliery.

49 ABERCARN COAL Co.—Block of steam coal.

50 GILMOUR, A. and Co. Kilmarnock.—Steam coal.

52 CRUTTWELL, ALLIES, & Co. Abergavenny, Manu.—Fossil tree from the coal measures.

53 BAGNALL & JESSON, West Bromwich, near Birmingham, Prod.—Column of South Staffordshire thick coal—showing the different working seams as they exist in vertical section.

WESTERN END.
NORTH ENCLOSURE.

54 CHEESEWRING GRANITE Co.—Agent in London, E. Turner, Belvidere Rd. Lambeth.—Granite column and pedestal, 30 feet high, from the Cheesewring granite quarries, near Liskeard, Cornwall.

55 RODGER, Lieut. W. R.N. Inv. & Pat.—Large anchor, manufactured by Fox, Henderson, & Co.

57 LONGRIDGE & Co.—Large anchor.

58 BROWN, Sir S. LENOX, & Co.—Large anchor.

59 BATEMAN, —.—Two life boats.

60 YOUNG, C. & Co., Edinburgh, Inv. and Manu.—Simultaneously-acting level crossing gates for railways.

61 DENCH.—Two greenhouses on a new construction.

62 KENT, A. Chichester.—New mode of glazing greenhouses.

63 PHILLIPS, C. Weston-super-Mare, Manu.—Flowerpots, &c. of superior clay. Flower guards and seed basins, strawberry tiles, striking pans, &c.

64 DOULTON & Co. Lambeth, Manu.—Large pipe in stone ware and other articles.

65 SINGER & Co. Vauxhall Pottery, Manu.—A still and other articles in stone ware.

66 FERGUSON, MILLER, & Co. Heathfield, near Glasgow, Manu.—Pipes and other large stone ware.

67 GREEN, S. & Co.—Large stone ware.

68 GRANGEMOUTH COAL COMPANY, Grangemouth, Sunderland, Manu.—Sundry objects in stone ware.

69 GARNKIRK COMPANY (Sprot, M. and T.)—Sundry articles in stone ware.

70 RAMSAY, G. H. Derwent Haugh, Newcastle, Inv.—Fire-clay goods.

71 FRANCIS & SONS, Nine Elms, Manu.—Drain pipes manufactured by machinery.

75 HOSKEN, R. Penryn, Cornwall, Manu.—Granite obelisk and base, 20 feet high, weighing about 15 tons, of Cornish granite, from the quarries at Carnseu, near Penryn.

76 At some distance from the western extremity of the building is a colossal equestrian statue of Richard Cœur de Lion, by the BARON MAROCHETTI.

The paving in the south enclosure at this end of the building is laid by three exhibitors, Mr. SINCLAIR, Caithness; Messrs. BROWN, RUSBY, and Co. Yorkshire; and Mr. FRANKLIN, Ireland.

EASTERN END.

100 Monument of granite in form of a cross, cut out of a single block, remarkably fine grained.—Kullgrin (Sweden).

101 STANDISH & NOBLE, Bagshot, Imp. and Prod.—*Cupressus funebris,* or weeping cypress, 30 feet in height, from the green-tea country, Wheychow (Hwuychow), in the north of China. Specimens of the wood polished.—(China.)

102 Life-boat, as at present in use in the French navy.—(France.)

103 LEGLER, Paris.—Ornamental fountain in cast-iron bronze, with figures, statuettes, &c.—(France.)

104 Tent, the material manufactured at the Jubulpore School of Industry in India, by Thugs.—(India.)

The pavement at the eastern entrance is laid by the SEYSSEL ASPHALTE COMPANY in their prepared asphalte.

The pavement at the south, or trancept entrance, consists of slate slabs from Festiniog, North Wales.

LIST OF STATUARY AND OTHER OBJECTS OF INTEREST PLACED IN THE MAIN AVENUES OF THE BUILDING.

SOUTH TRANSEPT.

1 Fighting horses.
2 Jealousy of Oberon.
3 Ariel. } LOUGH, J. G.
4 Puck.
5 Titania.
6 A Nymph preparing for the Bath. } BAILY, E. H.,
7 A Youth resting after the Chase. } R.A., F.R.S.
8 Satan tempting Eve.
9 Satan vanquished by the Archangel:—" And he laid hold on the dragon, that old serpent, which is the devil and Satan, and bound him a thousand years," Rev. xx.—STEPHENS, E. B.
10 Statue of Victory, modelled by Professor Rauch, of Berlin. In Carrara marble.—W. Walton, Carrara. Agents, JOHN WRIGHT, Pimlico; TOOTAL & BROWNE, Pimlico, and 73 Piccadilly.
11 "The archangel Michael having subdued Satan," Milton.—LOUGH, J. G.
12 The Jealousy of Medea.
13 Alfred the Great receiving from his Mother the book of Saxon poetry.
14 Her Majesty on her favourite charger Hammon.—THORNYCROFT.
15 Group in marble. An episode in the history of the war between the Amazons and the Argonauts.—ENGEL, J., 27 Berners St. Oxford St.
16 Colossal group of Virginius and Daughter, marble.—MACDOWELL, P., R. A.
17 Young Girl at the Spring.—WOODINGTON, W. F.
18 The Suppliant. } WEEKES, H.
19 Statue of the Marquis Wellesley. }

20 Resting after a run.
21 A Sleeping Child and Dog. } WEEKES, H.
22 Cupid, statue in marble. }
23 Eve, a model. } MACDOWELL, P., R.A.
24 Girl praying. }
25 Dante's Beatrice. " Guardami ben; ben son, ben son Beatrice."—HANCOCK, J.
25A Dancing girl reposing.—W. MARSHALL, A.R.A.
698 Pair of cast-iron park-gates.—COTTAM & HALLEN. (Class 22.)
128 Patent electro-magnetic clock. The Works to be seen in the Gallery.—SHEPHERD, C. (Class 10.)
410 Two fire engines.—SHAND & MASON. (Class 5.)
682 Two bells.—J. TAYLOR & SONS, Loughborough (Class 22.)

At the intersection of the Main Avenue and Transept.

20 Large fountain, in cut crystal glass, 27 feet high.—OSLER, F. & C. (Class 24.)

NORTH TRANSEPT.

26 Equestrian statues of Her Majesty and of H.R.H. Prince Albert, full size, designed for bronze.—WYATT, J.
146 Model of H. M. ship " Queen," 116 guns. Designed by Sir W. SYMONDS.—THE ADMIRALTY. (Class 8.)
28 Model for statue of Lord Falkland, executed in marble for the New Palace, Westminster.—BELL, J.
29 A Deer-stalker.—STEPHENS, E. B.
30 Group, Abel and Thirza.—EARLE, T.
31 Adam.—PHYSICK, E. J.
32 A colossal group: The Murder of the Innocents.—HOLLINS, P.

33 Statue in plaster of Paris : The Forsaken. — FORREST, A. H.

34 Samson bursting his Bonds.—LEGREW, J.

35 The dying Shipwrecked Sea-boy.—SIBSON, H. Douro Cottages, St. John's Wood.

36 Plaster cast of Apollo Belvedere, from the original, to imitate marble.—BRUCCIANI, D.

37 Group in plaster : Rizpah watching over the dead bodies of her Sons.—2 Samuel, xxi. 10.—LEIFCHILD, H. S.

38 Deer-stalking, and colossal head of a horse.— M'CARTHY, H.

39 Statue in plaster : Prometheus chained to the Rock. —WOOD, S.

40 Model of a colossal statue of the Duke of Wellington. —MILNES, T.

41 Youthful Athlete.—RICHARDSON, E.

42 Group : Milton and his Daughters.—LEGREW, J.

43 Model, life size: Figure with torch, &c.—ADAMS, G. G.

44 Model, Jacob and Rachel. } EARLE, T.
45 Sin Triumphant. }

45A Statue in terra cotta.—DOULTON & WATT, Lambeth.

46 Model for a statue of Hampden, executed in marble for the New Palace of Westminster.

47 Youth at a Stream.—FOLEY, J. H., A.R.A.

462 Fountain and hydraulic ram. — FREEMAN ROE & HANSON. (Class 5.)

320 Collection of stuffed birds and animals.—HANCOCK, J. (Class 29.)

A collection of palms and other tropical plants.— LODDIGES, C. & SONS, Hackney.

48 Ornamental fountain of cast-iron, bronzed; Cupid and the Swan.—COALBROOK DALE Co. (from the original design by John Bell.)

Rustic chair formed of knots of wood.

49 Ornamental park entrance of cast-iron, bronzed, consisting of a pair of principal gates, and two side gates, hung on iron pillars of new construction ; each of the four gates was cast in one piece.—COALBROOK DALE Co. (from the original design by Charles Crookes.)

50 Large vase for flowers, designed by Baron Marochetti, in terra-cotta. Encaustic and other tiles. Flower-pots, &c. with Parian bas-reliefs, after Thorwaldsen.—MINTON, H. & Co.

664 Closed cases of exotic ferns, cacti, and other plants. —WARD, N. B. Esq. (Class 10.)

4 Plate glass, manufactured by R. Swinburne, Shields. —G. DONNE, Leadenhall Street. (Class 24.)

798 Three church bells.—WARNER & SONS, 8 Crescent, Jewin Street. (Class 22.)

390 Carpet loom at work ; rug designed by Lawson.— JACKSON & GRAHAM. (Class 19.)

248AModel of conservatory.—WEEKS & Co., Chelsea. (Class 9.)

A Jardiniere.—PUGIN.

MAIN AVENUE, WEST.

51 Venus and Cupid.—DAVIS, E.

52 Bronze figure : Youth at the Stream, after Foley.— HATFIELD, J. A.

53 Cast, in bronze: The Eagle Slayer.—COALBROOK DALE Co. (from the original model by John Bell.)

1 Silk trophy.—KEITH & Co. Wood St. Cheapside. (Class 13.)

408 Two looking glasses, each upwards of 12 feet high. —BRITISH PLATE GLASS Co. (Class 26.)

54 Group, in bronze : The Horse and Dragon.— WYATT, M. C.

56 Bronze statue of the Duke of Rutland, for the market-place at Leicester.—DAVIS, E.

57 Sir William Follett ; colossal statue by BEHNES.

Large collection of specimens of Canadian and Van Diemen's Land timber. Lower jawbone of sperm whale.

97 Large silver candelabrum. — HUNT & ROSKILL. (Class 23.)

58 Group and pedestal, mosaic sculpture : " The faithful friend of man trampling under foot his most insidious enemy." Bell from Montreal. (Canada.)

58A Model of the interior of Her Majesty's Theatre.— DEIGHTON, —.

59 Madonna and Child.—DAVIS, E.

60 Restoration of the monument of Phillippa of Hainault, Queen of Edward III. in Westminster Abbey, executed in English alabaster from drawings by G. G. Scott. Statuettes and angels by J. Philip.—CUNDY, S.

61 Gothic monument and Purbeck marble tablet, with emblazoned inscription in early English character.— MATHER, A. A.

386 Large looking-glass and console table, ornamented and gilt.—M'LEAN, CHARLES. (Class 26.)

62 Monumental brass for an altar tomb: The story of the good Samaritan.—WALLER & Co.

63 Spandril from Hereford Cathedral, designed by N. J. Cottingham ; carved by Boulton and Swales. Statuettes, &c. Brass lectern for Hereford Cathedral, designed by Cottingham ; executed by T. Potter.

64 Gothic monument, of the decorated style, period fourteenth century.—PURDY, C. W.

65 Monumental tablet in brass, to the memory of the officers of Lord Hardinge's staff, who fell in the battles of the Sutleje ; produced by direction of Lord Hardinge, and intended to be sent to India.—ARCHER, J. W.

66 Monumental brass.—GOULD.

38 Model of the orchestra of the Sacred Harmonic Society, Exeter Hall, executed by Mr. Phidias Clarke.— SACRED HARMONIC SOCIETY. (Class 7.)

220 Model of the New County Assize Courts, erected at Cambridge by Messrs. Wyatt and Brandon ; the principal front of Whitby stone, and the fittings of the interior of oak ; modelled by S. Salter. Model in card of the new church of St. Mary and St. Nicholas, at Wilton. Erected by Wyatt and Brandon. (Class 7.)

107 Models by Salter of cast-iron bridge over the River Aire, and suspension aqueduct over the River Calder at Stanley, Yorkshire; designed by J. W. LEATHER. (Class 7.)

221 St. Nicholas Church, Hamburg, now being rebuilt by G. G. Scott, of London. (Class 7.)

224 Railway bridge across the Ouse at Selby, Yorkshire. Erected by Messrs. Walker & Burgess. (Class 7.)

222 Dinting Vale viaduct on the Sheffield and Manchester Railway. Built by A. S. Jee. (Class 7.)

67 Statue of Rosamonda.—THOMAS, JOHN.

68 A Fountain :—Acis and Galatea.—THOMAS, J.

158 Polished columns of Madrepore marble, with Caen stone capitals. Various specimens of marbles, rough, polished, and manufactured.—CHAMPERNOWNE, H. (Class 1.)

79 MONUMENTAL CROSS, executed in Caen stone by the Hon. Mrs. Ross, of Bladensburg.

518 A grand pianoforte in ornamental case.—BROADWOOD & SONS. (Class 10.)

80 Specimens of Jordan's machine carving : Altar screen designed by W. Harris, chairs, carved trophy of birds, foliage, statuettes, &c.

187 " Multum in Uno," forming loo, bagatelle, and chess table. Cottage piano, &c.—JENNENS & BETTRIDGE. (Class 26.)

81 Eldon and Stowell group, representing John, first Earl of Eldon, and William Baron Stowell, 29 years Judge of the High Court of Admiralty. Des. and mod. by the late M. Watson, and executed by G. Nelson.—EARL of ELDON.

135 Large slab of Honduras mahogany.—ROBERT FAUNTLEROY & SONS. (Class 4.)

B 3

18 Large specimens of crystallized alum.—PATTIN-SON, W. W. (Class 2.)

6 Large specimen of crystallized alum.—WILSON, J., Glasgow. (Class 2.)

10 Sulphate of copper, &c.—HATMEL & ELLIS, Manchester. (Class 2.)

29 Large crystallized mass of refined spermaceti.—MILLER & SONS. (Class 4.)

17 Large specimens of crystallized alum.—MOBERLY, W. Landsend, near Whitby. (Class 2.)

8 Specimens of bichromate of potash.—DENTITH, W. Manchester. (Class 2.)

55 Large church clock.—DENT, E. I. (Class 10.)

683 Large bell, cast in tune.—JOHN MURPHY, Dublin. (Class 22.)

26 Patent pressure filter and fountain.—FORSTER, J. Liverpool. (Class 7.)

157 Corinthian capital, in papier-maché.—BIELEFELD, C. F. (Class 26.)

690 Octagon glass case, containing specimens of cutlery. —RODGERS & SONS, Sheffield. (Class 22.)

106 Polished iron radiating stove.—JOBSON & CO. Sheffield. (Class 22.)

82 Chimney-piece in white marble, with or-molu ornaments. Statuettes.—THOMAS, J.

276 Polished steel stove, or-molu mountings.—FEETHAM & CO. (Class 22.)

237 Swedish ventilating stove grate. — JEAKES, W. (Class 22.)

805 Improved open fire pedestal stove, with candelabrum for gas.—BAILEY, W. & SONS. (Class 22.)

83 Unfinished statue of Shakspeare, from the Stratford bust.—BELL, J.

641 Ornamental rustic dome of cast-iron, bronzed, 20 feet in diameter by 30 feet high; adapted for glazing, from the design by C. Crookes and J. Bell; iron casting of the Eagle-slayer, and a statuette of Æolus, by J. Bell. Garden-seats, chairs, &c.—COALBROOK DALE CO. (Class 22.)

168 Grand pianoforte.—COLLARD & CO. (Class 10.)

84 The Mourners.—LOUGH, J. G.

157 Improved patent catatoptric apparatus for a light-house, manufactured by W. C. Wilkins and J. Letourneur. Dioptric apparatus of the fourth class. Parabolic reflecting lamp.—WILKINS, W. C. (Class 7.)

85 Vase and pedestal, in cast-iron, coloured and gilt.—HANDYSIDE, A. Derby.

86 Chimneypiece.—BRINE BROTHERS & T. SHARP.

254 Astronomical telescope, the object-glass 11½ inches diameter, mounted on a stand, having equatorial movements and complete adjustments. Improved microscopes, and photographic camera obscura.—ROSS, A. (Class 10.)

254A Solid astronomical eye-glass made by A. ROSS.—READE, Rev. J. B. (Class 10.)

301 Talbotypes taken by Ross's photographic camera.—BUCKLE, S. Peterborough. (Class 30.)

301 A large collection of skins and furs.—NICHOLAY & SON; HUDSON'S BAY COMPANY; BEVINGTONS & MORRIS; SMITH, G. & SONS; LAMPSON, C. M.; MEYER, S. & M.; CLARKE, R. & SONS. (Class 16.)

323 Large collection of ostrich and other feathers, birds of Paradise, &c. Court plumes, as used from the beginning of the present century. Specimens of dying ostrich and marabout feathers and birds of Paradise, with a variety of colours on the same feathers.—ADCOCK & CO. (Class 16.)

87 Font, executed in marble.—PEYMAN, H. P.

223 A model of a decorated Gothic church, at Lever Bridge, Bolton, Lancashire, designed by E. Sharpe, architect. The church is almost entirely built of terra cotta. —WILLOCK, E. P. & CO. Manchester. (Class 7.)

19 Model fountain, with small engine for working it JAMES, J. (Class 7.)

140. Her Majesty's Jewel-case, in cinque-cento style, designed by L. GRUNER. (Class 23.)

500 Cashmere wool and fabrics, exhibited by H.R.H. Prince Albert. (Class 12, 15.)

106 Model of Britannia Suspension Bridge, on a scale of one-eighth of an inch to the foot; R. Stephenson, engineer; model by Jabez James. (Class 7.)

9 Model of wrought-iron bridge on the South Western Railway, over the Wye, at Chepstow, designed by I. K. Brunel, C.E., now in course of construction by Finch and Willey, of Liverpool. (Class 7.)

105 Model of the wrought-iron bar-chain suspension bridge at Kieff (Russia), now erecting across the River Dnieper; the largest work of the kind hitherto executed.—VIGNOLES, C. (Class 7.)

88 Fountain, in artificial limestone, designed for a market place, by J. W. Papworth.—SEELEY, J.

89 Clay model, an original design, Liberation of Caractacus.—PANORMO, C., A.R.S.D.

256 Irish poplin Jacquard loom, at work. (Class 12.)

90 Models of 3,000 square miles of England, shewing portions of various counties.—CARRINGTON, F. A.

169 Model of the Lord Mayor's state barge.—SEARLE & SONS. (Class 8.)

179 Boots and shoes.—GILBERT. (Class 16.)

180 Patent boots and shoes.—DOWIE. (Class 16.)

181 Patent boots and shoes.—TAYLOR & BOWLEY. (Cl.16.)

192 Boots and shoes.—HICKSON & SONS. (Class 16.)

91 Trigonometrical model of the Undercliff, Isle of Wight, from a trigonometrical survey, the vertical heights being on the same scale as the base.—IBBETSON, Capt. L. L. B.

192 Transit circle. Westbury circle. — TROUGHTON & SIMMS. (Class 10.)

Instruments by DOLLAND. (Class 10.)

165 SMITH, W. H. 1 Royal Exchange Buildings, Inv.—Recoil breakwater and lighthouse, said to combine economy, strength, and general applicability to all depths and situations. (Class 7.)

22 Dioptric revolving lighthouse of the first order.—CHANCE BROTHERS & CO. Birmingham. (Class 24.)

28 Limestone model of the breakwater in Plymouth Sound, with silver lighthouse and beacon, made for the Exhibition under the direction of the Lords of the Admiralty. The breakwater was constructed agreeably to a report of the late John Rennie, and of Joseph Whidby, Master, R.N.; the lighthouse designed by Walker and Burgess; with sectional and other models, &c.—STUART, W. (Class 7.)

92 Colossal head of a horse, modelled by the Baron Marochetti.—Electro deposit by ELKINGTON & CO.

93, 94 Bust of Prince Albert, Duke of Wellington, and the late Sir R. Peel, Bart.—ELKINGTON & CO.

95 Model of the docks and commercial portion of the town of Liverpool, exhibiting a river front of five miles. —LIVERPOOL LOCAL COMMITTEE.

399 Large specimens of plate glass.—THAMES PLATE GLASS WORKS. (Class 26.)

684 Spherical bell.—MEARS & CO. Whitechapel. (Cl.22.)

MAIN AVENUE, EAST.

530 Gold ore from California.—MARRIOTT, Mrs. F.

96 Portrait of Her Majesty on Sèvres china, half length, by A. Ducluzeau, after a portrait by F. Winterhalter.

97 Portrait of H.R.H. Prince Albert, on Sèvres china, half length, painted by A. Bazanget, after a portrait by F. Winterhalter.

27 Andromeda and pedestal, bronze.—The COALBROOK DALE CO. (the original model by John Bell.)

140 The great diamond of Runjeet Singh, "Koh-i-Noor." (Class 23.)

98 Shield presented by His Majesty the King of Prussia

to H. R. H. the Prince of Wales, in commemoration of the baptism of the infant Prince.

531 Large quartz crystal.—Duke of Devonshire. (Cl. 1.)

98A The Orphans.—MILLER, F. M.

99 Zephyr and Aurora.—MARSHALL, W., A.R.A.

100 Model for a statue of Dr. Jenner.

101 Model of a colossal statue of the late Marquis of Bute. —THOMAS, J. E.

102 Statue of Dr. Goodhall, provost of Eton.—WEEKES.

2 Mass of native silver from Atacama.—(Chili.)

51 Large earthen wine jar, manufactured in the village of Toboso, in La Mancha.—(Spain.)

262 Howitzer and mortars of wrought-iron. From the Royal Ordnance Office, Onate (Spain).

263 Howitzer, from Royal Cannon Foundry, Seville.

1098 Large earthern olive jar, from Portugal.

A large mosaic: "Ruins of Pæstum," by Rinaldi (Rome).

19 Large tazza of Oriental alabaster, of the diameter of 3½ English feet, by Moda, Tommaso Della (Rome.)

103 The nymph "Glycera" and a nymph; statues in marble, by the late R. J. Wyatt, of Rome. Capt. LEYLAND.

16 Cupid and Psyche (Rome). } Exhibited by Capt.
29 Rinaldi and Armeda (Rome). } Leyland.

437 Statue of Her Majesty the Queen, cast in zinc by the Vieille Montagne Mining Company. (Class 1.)

1053 Iron fountain, cast by André, of Val D'Osne (France).

173 Church-organ, by Ducroquet, P. A. Rue St. Maur, St. Germain, Paris (France).

1215 Group in plaster. Bas-reliefs in marble, The Medici, and Francesca da Rimini, by Etex.

Bas-relief in bronze: The Raft.

923 Large iron tazza.—MATIFAT, Paris.

45 Pilgrim Boy, by Jaen de Bay.

187 St. Michael and the Dragon, colossal group in plaster, by J. B. Du Seigneur, 86 rue de l'Ouest (France).

586 Bust in marble: "Fiat Volentas Tua," and Head of Christ, by H. Lemaire. (France.)

The Dancing Faun, by E. E. L. Lequesne (France).

1215 Group in plaster, by Etex (France).

573 Two groups: Children & Dogs. Group: Drowned Mother, Child, and Eagle, carved glass frame—LECHESNE (France).

Bronze group: Death of the Stag.—J. DE BAY. (France).

779 Two large vases, zinc bronzed (France).

464 Equestrian statue of Godfrey of Bouillon. The Happy and Unhappy Child, by E. Simonis (Belgium).

455 The Infant Moses.—DE CUYPE (Belgium).

465 The Cradle of Love, and the Captive Love, by Fraiken (Belgium).

466 Paul and Virginia—G. GEEFS (Belgium).

466A A plaster group: The Lion in Love; and a small marble statue of Cupid; by S. Geefs, Schaerbeck (Belgium).

463 Mother and Child.—L. JEHOTTE (Belgium).

450 Carvings in wood, by C. Geertz (Belgium).

409 Carvings in wood (Belgium).

454 Christ crucified, carving in wood (Belgium).

465 Psyche calling on Love for help, by C. A. Fraiken, Schaerbeck, near Brussels (Belgium).

456 The Young Shepherd—Giotto's first Trial at Drawing, by J. Tuerlincks (Rome).

461 Venus and Cupid disarmed.—S. JAQUET (Belgium).

464 Truth.—SIMONIS (Belgium).

451 Girl and Dove, by S. Geefs (Belgium).

463 Statue: The Torments of Cain, by L. Jehotte, St. Jotheten-Noode, near Brussels (Belgium).

455 Canadian Woman weeping the loss of her Child, by Cuyper (Belgium).

95 Castings in zinc: Stag at Rest (Netherlands).

720 Group in marble: Mazeppa, by G. Pierotti, of Milan. Jewels and precious stones.—H. T. HOPE, M.P.

Group in marble: The Anglers, by R. Monti, of Milan.

710 The wounded Achilles, by Fraccaroli, of Verona.

737 Painted window, representing Dante and some of his Ideas, by G. Bertini, Milan (Austria).

430 Statuettes, by Ferncorn, cast in iron; candelabrum by Bernardo de Bernardis; and statue, Field Marshal Radetzky—from the Prince of Salm's Foundry (Austria).

712 Statuette in marble, and models in wax, by D. Gaudolfi.

267 Castings in zinc, by Geiss of Berlin (Prussia.)

Coil of flat iron-wire rope, made by Felten of Cologne.

279 Group, in zinc, bronzed, representing an Amazon on horseback attacked by a tiger—modelled by Professor A. Kiss, and cast in zinc and bronzed by M. Geiss, of Berlin.

840 Table ornament of oxydized silver, by Albert Wagner (Prussia).

194 Large globe, in relief (Prussia).

90 Two statues, seven feet high, modelled by Schwanthaler, cast in bronze and unchased, but matted. Libussa, Queen of the Bohemians, anno 700; and George I. of Bohemia (Bavaria).

285 Boy with a Swan, in bronze, by Schwanthaler, the property of the King of Prussia.

235 Marble pedestal; table-tops of marble and red-granite; large vase with pedestal, by Cantian, of Berlin.

90 Colossal Lion, fifteen feet long and nine feet high, by Müller, of Munich (Bavaria.)

271 Group of figures in cast-iron; the Warwick vase; the Athenian vase; the Alexander vase, the border decorated with reliefs after Thorwaldsen, from the Royal Prussian Iron Foundry, Berlin (Prussia).

Gothic vase in terra cotta.

852 Tigress, by Julius Haenel.

299 The Muse Polyhymnia, after an antique in the Royal Museum, Berlin, by Kesseler, of Greifswald (Prussia).

273 Cast of a part of the pedestal of the monument of Fred. William III. of Prussia, by Prof. F. Drake, Berlin.

289 Newfoundland Dog in bronze, after the model of Moeller, by L. Fribel, of Berlin.—(Prussia).

431 Statue: Arminius, Prince of the Cheruskers, a hostage at Rome, by C. Cauer, of Creuznach.—(Prussia).

Girl at Well, in bronze, by Einsiedelsches, of Lauchhammer.

240 A fountain, with group of children, &c. by E. March, Thiergartenfelde, near Charlottenburg, Prussia.

105 Models of two groups, representing the breaking-in of horses, by Von Hofer, of Stuttgard.—(Wurtemberg)

37 A bell of brass, 383 kilogr. weight, with iron clapper and tackle, by F. Gruhl, Kleinwelka, near Bautzen, Saxony.

837 Four tables and pedestal of inlaid marble (Prussia). Large candelabra.—(Russia).

39 Adam and Eve, in plaster, by Jerichau—(Denmark).

38 Orestes, a statue, by Bissen.—(Denmark).

Vases of Swedish porphyry, presented by the King of Sweden to the late Gen. Sir R. Wilson.—Capt. WALLIS, R.N.

Model of the Falls of Niagara, by G. Catlin.

166 Mass of zinc ore weighing 16,400 lbs., taken from near the surface in Sussex county, New Jersey, U. S.

522 Statue in marble: The Greek Slave, by Hiram Powers, United States.—(America).

547 Statue in marble: The Fisher Boy.—HIRAM POWERS-Specimens of newspapers, published in America.

511 Railway bridge of simple construction, United States.

467 Statue: The Wounded Indian, by Stephenson, of Boston, Massachusetts, U. S. America.

428 Large spherical bell of union metal. — MORRIES STIRLING (Class 1).

61 Model of a glasshouse, with eight-pot furnace. Large melting-pot weighing one ton. Specimens of sheet and plate glass, ruby and other coloured glass, &c. Exhibited by J. Hartley & Co., of Sunderland, Durham (*in the United States department, south-east corner*). (Class 24.) B 4

33 34 35 36 37 38 39

| 25. China, &c. | Pottery | * Organs. * Curtains, &c |
| China. | | |

NORTH GALLERY.

1 2 3 4 5 6 7 8 9 10 11 12 13 14 15 16 17 18 19 20 21 22 23 24 25 26 27 28 29 30 31 32

7. *Civil Engineering, Architectural and Building, Models, &c.* | 10. *Anatomical.* | *Cutlery* | 28. *Animal & Vegetable Manuf.*

25. *China and Pottery.*

10. *Philosophical Instruments.* | 10. *Musical Instruments.* | *Musical* | 24. *Glass, Chandeliers, Decorations, &c.* | 25. *China.* | *

NORTH CENTRAL GALLERY.

19. *Carpets, Table Covers, Tapestries, Oil Cloths, &c., suspended from the Girders in the Gallery, and against the Walls of the Building.*

* *Two Carpets and large Chandelier exhibited by Her Majesty.*

SOUTH CENTRAL GALLERY.

10. *Clocks, &c* | 23. *Jewellery, Plate, &c.* | 19. *Lace and Embroidery* | 13. *Silks, Shawls, &c.*

8. *Military, Arms, Models, &c.* | 4. *Raw Materials.* | 3. *Substances used as Food.* | 2. *Chemicals.* | 13. *Silk*

1 2 3 4 5 6 7 8 9 10 11 12 13 14 15 16 17 18 19 20 21 22 23 24 25 26 27 28 29 30 31 32

SOUTH GALLERY.

Naval Architecture, Arms, Maps, &c. | *Globes, &c.* | *Organs, &c.* | *Clocks, &c* | *Paisley Shawls* | *Silks & Shawls.*

[The Building is divided into areas (spaces of 24 feet square, between 4 columns) which are marked on the plan by letters at each corner of the square, and by numbers along the sides ; these letters and numbers are marked on every column in the Building in white characters at about 7 feet from the ground.]

Organs
12. *Shawls* | *Tartans*

33 34 35 36 37 38 39
SOUTH.

NORTH SIDE.
Exit. N *Exit* O *Exit*

10 11 12 13 14 15 16 17 N 19 20 21 22 23 24 25 26 28 29 30 31 32 33 34 35 36 37 38 39

Plaids, &c. (on Wall). | *Canvass, &c. (on Wall).* | *Printing and French Machinery.* | 8. *Naval Models, &c.* | *Ladies.* | Queen's Robing Room.

6. *Machinery in Motion.* *Cotton, Woollen, Power Looms, &c.*

Refreshment Court.

1 2 3 4 5 6 7 8 9

Specimens of Woods, &c. (on Wall). | 6. *Machinery in Motion.* | *Coalbrookdale Gates and Fountain.*

6. *Machines in Motion.* | *Western* | *Flax, Silk and Lace, Rope Making,* | 5. *Railway & Steam Machinery in motion.*

Cotton, Oldham. | *American Machinery.* | *Cotton, Manchester.* | *Ladies.* | *Refreshment Court.* | *Gents.* | *Lathes and Tools, Mills.* | 7. *Building Contrivances, &c.* | *India.*

Tropical Plants. Roe's

5. *LOCOMOTIVES AND RAILWAY APPARATUS.*

Fountain. H.M Ship Queen.

5. *Carriages.* | 5. *Carriages.* | 27. *Mineral Manufactures.* | 5. *Marine Engines.* | *Hydraulic Press, Steam Hammer, Fire Engines, &c.* | 30. *Fine Arts Court.* | *India.* | *The Queen.*

NORTH TRANSEPT.

11. *Cotton Fabrics.* | 16. *Leather, Furs, Hair.* | 27. *Minerals* | 26. *Furniture, Ceilings.* | 17. *Paper.* | *Jersey.* | *Ceylon.* | *Malta.* | *India.*

Osler's Crystal Fountain.

18. *Printing and Dyeing.* | 14. *Flax* | 15. *Shawls.* | 12. *Woollen Fabrics.* | 22 *Hardware* | 26. *Furniture.* | 22. *Hardware.* | *Cape.* | *Africa.* | *India.*

MAIN AVENUE, WEST. | *Prince Albert.*

SOUTH TRANSEPT.

18. *Printed Fabrics Manchester, London, and Glasgow.* | *Flax.* | 12 & 15. *Woollen and Mixed Fabrics, and Shawls.* | *Sheffield.* | 26. *Furniture.* | *Birmingham* | *Medi-eval Court.* | *Canada.* | *India.*

Statue of the Queen.

22. *General Hardware, Brass and Iron work of all kinds, Locks and Grates, &c.*

Park Gates

9. *Agricultural and Horticultural Machines and Implements.*

30. *Sculpture Court.* | *Australia.* | *West Indies, &c.* | *Offices.* | *India.*

* 1. *Gems—Clays—Stones.* | 1. *Coal—Coke—Models.* | 1. *Iron—Copper—Lead—Models.* | *N.S. Wales.* | *Offices.*

Decorations & Glass. | *Carlisle on Sofa (on Wall)* | *Bell. Looking Glass, Liverpool Model* | *Large Electrolysis Plymouth Breakwater Lighthouse. Isle of Wight and other Models.* | *Seeley's* | *Fountain. Models of Bridges, &c. Cashmere wool from Windsor Architectural Models.* | *Skins, Furs, and Feathers. Astronomical Telescope. Lighthouse. The Mourners. Coalbrookdale Dome.* | *Shakspere. Cutlery. Filter and* | *Fountain. Dent's Clock. Bell. Chemical Specimens. Statuary. Machine Carving. Stone Cross. Marble Pillars.* | *Thoma's* | *Fountain, &c. Church Decoration, &c. Large Glass, McLean. Monument of Hullmandel, Canadian Timber. Horse & Dragon. Silk Trophy. Eagle Slayer. Youth at Stream. Venus and Cupid.* | *India.* | *India.* | *Statuary* | *Statuary.*

1 2 3 4 5 6 7 8 9 10 11 12 13 14 15 16 17 N 19 20 21 22 23 24 25 26 G 28 29 30 31 32 33 34 35 36 37 38 39
Exit. *Exit.* *Exit.*

SOUTH SIDE.

On South Wall, Decorations, Specimens of Natural Woods, &c., Imitation Marbles, Woods, &c.

I E S.

40 41 42 43

Fishing, &c.

NORTH GALLERY.

44 45 46 47 48 49 50 51 52 53 54 55 56 57 58 59 60 61 62 63 64 65 66 67 68 69 70 71 72 73 74 75 76 77

29 | 24. Stained Glass, | British | French | Belgian, | Austrian, and British. | Prussia | and | Bavaria. | British Papers.

29. Wax Flowers, &c | Italy. | Belgium. | Austria | Zollverein. | Prussia | Russia | United States. | England.

NORTH CENTRAL GALLERY.

19. Carpets, Table Covers, Tapestries, Oil Cloths, &c., suspended from the Girders in the Gallery, and against the Walls of the Building.

SOUTH CENTRAL GALLERY.

Switzerland | France. Silks, Velvets, Lace, &c. | Austria. Lace, Silks, &c. | Zollverein. Musical Instruments, Apparatus, Silks, Linens, &c.

France. Prints, Flowers, Lace, Linen, Silk, Harness, &c. | Austria | British Naval, Furniture, &c. | France, Surgical, &c.

44 45 46 47 48 49 50 51 52 53 54 55 56 57 58 59 60 61 62 63 64 65 66 67 68 69 70 71 72 73 74 75 76 77

SOUTH GALLERY.

20. Hosiery, &c.

[The Articles are divided into Classes and Nations, and the Names of such Classes and Nations are given on the Plan, and indicated by banners in the Building. The size of the Plan to the Building is as 1 foot to 1851 feet.]

40 41 42 43

FLOOR.

40 41 42 43 44 45 46 47 48

Gents. | Dining Room for Exhibitors. | France. China, Tapestry, &c.

NORTH SIDE.

50 51 52 53 54 55 56 57 59 60 61 62 63 64 65 66 67 68 69 70 71 72 73 74 75 76 77

France. | Belgium. | Austria. | Zollv. | Gents. | Refreshment Room. | Ladies.

Musical Instruments, Chemicals, &c. | Machinery, Arms, &c. | Machinery, &c. | Machinery, Furniture, &c. | Machinery, &c. | Open Court. | Open Court. | Open Court. | Workshop.

English Paper Hangings

Turkey and Egypt. | Italy and Sardinia. | Machinery, Arms, Instruments, &c. | Furniture & Carpets | Furniture, &c. | Octagon Room, China, &c. | Hanse Towns. | Malachite Vases, China, &c. | United States. Machinery, &c.

Persia. | Greece. | Italy. | France. | Belgium | Austria. | Zollverein. | N. Germany | Russia. | United States.

Portraits of the Queen and Prince Albert on Porcelain. | The Koh-i-noor Diamond. | Andromeda. | Prince of Wales' Shield. | The Orphans. | Statuary. | Large Wine Jar. | Statues by Wyatt of Rome. | Alabaster Tazza. | Statue of the Queen in Zinc. | Fountain. | French Organ | French Electric and other Clocks | St. Michael and Dragon. | Godfrey de Bouillon. | Children and Dogs. | Stag at Rest. | Mazeppa Group. | The Wounded Achilles. | Painted Window | Berlin Castings. | Amazon and Tiger. | Globe in relief. | Bronzes. | Bavarian Lion. | Stuttgardt Horses. | Brass Bell. | Russian Candelabra. | Adam and Eve. | Vases of Swedish Porphyry. | Falls of Niagara. | Mass of Zinc. 16,400 lbs. | The Fisher Boy and Greek Slave | American Bridge. | The Wounded Indian. | Large Bell. | Catalogue Office

China Tunis | Switzerland. | France | France. | Belgium. | Austria | Zollverein. | Denmark. | Sweden | United States of America.

China and Tunis. | China. | Switzerland | Jewellery, &c | Plate, Bronzes, China, &c. | Belgium. | Fabrics | Saxony | Prussia Fabrics | Zollverein. | Russia. | Musical Instruments, &c.

Offices. | Tunis.19 | Offices. | Switzerland | Lace, Gloves, &c. | Furniture, Carpets, &c. | Belgium. | Toys, &c. | Pipes, &c. | Wurtemburg | Prussia Cloths, &c. | Prussia, Cloths, Hats Carpets, &c. | Russia. | United States. Raw Produce, Oil Cloth, Hardware.

Offices. | France, Printing, Decorations, &c. | Belgium. | Austria | Saxony | Zollv. | Russia. | France

40 41 42 43 44 45 46 47 48 50 51 52 53 54 55 56 57 59 60 61 62 63 64 65 66 67 68 69 70 71 72 73 74 75 76 77

SOUTH SIDE.

a Toledo Swords, &c.   b Queen of Spain's Jewels.   c Mr. Hope's Jewels.

Section I.—RAW MATERIALS.

Class 1.   MINING AND MINERAL PRODUCTS.

—— South Side—Areas S. 1 to S. 27. ——

1 Fossil fish from the old red sandstone (*Cephalaspis*).

2 POWELL, W. J. Tisbury, Wilts, Prop.—Specimens of polished flint from the oolites of Tisbury.

3 CARTER, J. Delabole, near Camelford, Cornwall, Prop.—Two specimens of rock crystals, taken from the slate quarries at Delabole, near Camelford; used for jewellery.

4 BONITTO, J. Nelson; BALLERAS, G. E., of London, Exhib.; and PARIS, E. Prod.—Specimens of emerald in the matrix from the mine of Muso, New Granada.

5 LENTAIGNE, J. Tallaght House, Dublin, Prop.—Limestone inclosing granite.

6 Block of carboniferous limestone containing shells of *Productus*.

7 BREADALBANE, Marquis of.—Specimens of copper, silver-lead, and lead ores; granite, porphyry, &c. from Perthshire and Argyllshire.

8 LEESON, Dr. H. B. Greenwich, Inv.—Models, crystalline minerals, and engravings.

9 MITCHELL, Rev. W. St. Bartholomew's Hospital, Des. and Inv.—Models of all the primary and secondary forms of crystals, &c.

10 DYER, W. Little Hampton, near Arundel, Inv.—Sussex coast agates, found on the sea-beach.

11 SLATER & WRIGHT, Whitby, Manu.—Specimens of rough jet, and articles manufactured from jet for ornamental purposes.

12 WEBB, Mr. Calcot Farm, Reading.—Portion of a fossil silicified tree from the sand. The horn of an ox dug up from the peat.

13 ELLIS, R. Harrowgate.—Collection of the different mineral waters of Harrowgate and their analyses.

14 TENNANT, J. 149 Strand.—Four cases of minerals and fossils for educational, scientific, and ornamental purposes. Large crystal emerald, &c., the property of the Duke of Devonshire.

15 NELIS, J. Omagh, Co. Tyrone. — Case of pearls, found in the deepest parts of the river Strule, at Omagh.

16 COWIE & RAE, Ellon, Scotland, Pro.—Pearls from the river Ythan, Aberdeenshire.

17 HORNE, —, Camberwell.—Petrified eggs and nest from Goree Island, W. Coast of N. America, lat. 63° 13′.

18 MAYO & Co. 17 Silver St. Wood St. Cheapside.—Glass pipes for the conveyance of aqueous and aeriform fluids, connected by Mayo's patented joints.

18A LOWRY, J. W.—Diagrams of fossils.

19 COOK, A. Prop.—A large crystal of black quartz. (Batten, A. agent.)

20 MACDONALD, Major, C. Prop.—A large series of torquoises in the matrix, in unpolished fragments, and manufactured into various ornaments.

20A WATKINS, Rev. C. F. Brixworth.—Siliceous fossils from the chalk beds of south Wilts, in quartz, agates, calcedony, &c.

21 OLDFIELD, Rev. —, Dublin, Prop. — Crystalline quartz adapted for various useful and ornamental purposes.

22 TOLAN, W.—A collection of polished agates from the Isle of Wight.

23 HIGHLEY, S. jun. 32 Fleet St.—Native sulphur, from Sicily, with products.

23A BRAIDLEY, Mrs. J. 36 Ladbroke Sq. Notting Hill.—Specimens of amethyst and quartz from Brazils.

24 THISTLETHWAYTE, H. F. The Vine House, Sevenoaks, Kent.—A collection of gems and precious stones, mostly collected by Mr Hertz, to show the great variety of shades of colour in each species, and the connexion of some of the classes.

25 JAMIESON, G. 107 Union St. Aberdeen, Prop.—Cairngorm stones and Aberdeen and Peterhead granite, cut and mounted. A ram's head mounted. Pearls found in the rivers Don, Ythan, and Ugie.

26 CASSELS, A. Edinburgh, Prop.—Two curling stones used in Scotland in the national game of curling, made of the rock of the Ailsa Craig, in the Firth of Clyde, &c.

27 KAY, J. Hayhill, Ochiltree, Manu.—Curling stone, made of greenstone trap.

28 MAJENDIE, Ashhurst, Esq.—White topazes from Van Diemen's Land. Rough and cut.

29 HOWARD, T., C.E. Bristol.—Sands, clays, building stones, and marbles; coals, minerals, and metals, from the Bristol basin. Maps and sections of the strata, &c.

30 FAHIE, J. K. Tipperary, Ireland, Prod.—Copper ore. Clay. Artificial cement and stucco, prepared from gypsum found near Tipperary. Anthracite coal. Draining tiles and pipes. Felspar, from Cork. Hydraulic and building limestone. Marbles from Cloyne. Lead ore found at Oola.

31 A collection of Labrador felspar.

32 A collection of minerals from the Mendip Hills, Somersetshire.

33 TALLING, —, Truro.—Sundry minerals from Truro.

34 Minerals from Liskeard, Cornwall.

35 IPSWICH MUSEUM COMMITTE, by the Rev. J. Henslow, President.—Minerals from the neighbourhood of Ipswich, and used in the arts, for manure, cement, &c.

36 PAINE, J. M. Farnham, Prod.—Phosphoric fossils and marls from the upper greensand, the gault, and the upper part of the lower greensand, geological formations. Hops grown upon the same.

37 LANCE, E. J. Frimley, Bagshot, Surrey.—Specimens of minerals, used as manures; of cultivated soils or earths, arranged from London to Cornwall. Specimens of corn, in illustration of the above mineral collection, &c.

38 GILL, W. E. Truro, Inv.—Normal guano, prepared from the refuse of the fisheries, as a superior fertilizer.

39 GOULD, Rev. J. Rector of Beaconsfield.—Clay and chalk. Silicious and other sands.

40 SWEETMAN, J. Sutton, Dublin Co. Ireland, Prop.—Blue limestone. Dolomite. Cement from dolomite. Quartz rock. Steatite. Brown hæmatite iron ore. Black oxide of manganese. Umber. Yellow and brown ochre, &c.

41 TESCHEMACHER, E. F. 4 Park Terrace, Highbury, Exhib.—Collection of mineral and other manures.

42 HARRIS, J. 2 Hart St. Mark Lane.—Deodorized fæcal manure.

43 Silt, sand, turf, &c., from the Isle of Ely.

44 RAMSAY, G. H. Newcastle, (Agent, A. Hurst, 65 Mark Lane.)—Artificial manure, bone dust, and superphosphate of lime.

45 MITCHELL, W. B. Sheffield. —Minerals from the neighbourhood of Sheffield.

46 NESBITT, J. C. Kennington.—Phosphate fossils for manure.

47 CAWLEY, J. Pendell, Blechingley, Prod. and Manu.

—Fuller's earth in the raw state, and dried and prepared for use in the manufacture of woollens. Stone and spar found in the same strata, at the Cockley pits in Nutfield, Surrey.

48 GAWKROGER & HYNAM, 7 Prince's Sq. Finsbury, Manu.—Fuller's earth, from Reigate and Nutfield, in Surrey.

49 WILSON, Sir T. MARYON, Charlton, near Blackheath. —Specimens of sands and loams for casting, from Charlton, and sands used for glass and house purposes from Hampstead.

50 ROCK, J. jun. Hastings.—Coal found in the summit tunnel of the Hastings and Ashford railway, 300 feet above the sea level. Claystone, said to contain oxide of chromium. Fine white sand, from Hastings cliffs, &c.

51 ROSS, T. Claremont, Hastings.—Iron ore and Tilgate stone, from Hastings. Hastings granite, clay, and hone stone.

52 Specimen of fossil orthoceratite.

53 WHITTAKER, J. Wirksworth, Derbyshire, Prop.— Specimens of marble, and marble vase. White sand. White lead ore, and stalactite.

54 BRODIE, P. E. Down Hatherley, Gloucester, Prod. —Limestone, applicable to purposes of lithography, &c. Ironstone, septaria, iron pyrites, hard limestone, bone bed, from Wiltshire, Gloucestershire, Somersetshire, &c.

55 RIDDELL, Sir J. M. Bart. Strontian, Prop.—Hexahedral prismatic calcareous and other spars. Crystallized carbonate of strontia. Sulphates of barytes with phosphate of lead. Gneiss. Gneiss passing into granite. Gneiss with red felspar, &c. Porphyritic granite. Granite studded with garnets, from the summit of Ben Resipole. Sulphurets of lead and zinc, &c.

56 DANN, T. Reigate, Prod.—Grey-stone lime, from lime-works, Reigate Hill.

57 WORTHINGTON, W. Northwich, Cheshire, Prop.— Rock salt, from Northwich; refined salt for curing fish. Fine high-dried and Malvern salt, for table use. Large grained bay salt.

58 HILL, J. Ringsend, Dublin, Manu.—Basket and pink salt for table use; Irish fine, or butter salt, and coarse or provision salt.

59 Brassington, Derbyshire.—Wad and white-lead ore.

60 ROAKE, J. W. Newbury, Berkshire.—Specimens of soils which surround Newbury, with their applications. Samples of bricks, tiles, and pottery.

62 DYER, W. B. Mold, Prop.—White lead ore, carbonate lead ore, from Jamaica mine.

63 CAIRNS, J. jun. 96 Charlotte St. Manchester.—Carbonate of barytes from Anglezark Moor, Lancashire.

64 BROOKMAN & LANGDON, 28 Great Russell St.— Cumberland graphite and other minerals.

65 BROCKEDON, W. 29 Devonshire St. Queen Sq. Pat. and Manu.—Native black lead from Cumberland, India, Ceylon, Greenland, Spain, Bohemia, &c. Cumberland lead in powder, purified and condensed into blocks, for pencilmakers. Samples of S. Mordan's and other points and pencils.

66 REEVES & SONS, 113 Cheapside, Inv. and Manu.— Drawing pencils, crayons, &c.

67 ADAIR, R. Maryport, Manu.—Materials used in black-lead pencil making, with a pencil in the several processes from the grooving to the finishing.

68 WOLFF, E. & SON, 23 Church street, Spitalfields, Manu.—Native Cumberland, East India and Spanish blacklead; the same purified in blocks; and manufactured pencils.

69 BANKS, SON & Co. Greta Pencil Works, Keswick. —Black-lead and other manufactured pencils.

70 ROGERS, S. S. Douglas, Isle of Man.—Specimens of the earths and sands of the Isle of Man.

71 TENNANTS, C. & Co. Manchester, Manu.—Large groups of crystals of sulphate of copper.

72 THOMPSON, J. Northwich.—Crystalline block of rock salt.

73 CLAXTON, J.—Sands from Alum Bay, Isle of Wight.

74 SQUIRE, J. & W. Yarmouth, Isle of Wight.—Specimen of pure white sand, for the manufacture of best flint glass, from Alum Bay, near the Needles, Isle of Wight.

75 COLLINSON, C. Mansfield, Prop.—Red casting-sand; found only at Mansfield, and used for the finest castings.

76 RELF, S. Reigate, Surrey, Prod.—White sand, from the Tunnel Caves, at Reigate, usually called silver sand.

77 MORRISON, G. Agent of Earl SOMERS, Reigate.— Sand from the common called Reigate Heath, which, from its fine sharp grit, is valued in the manufacture of glass.

78 LONG, J. Limerick.—Sands and earths from the river Shannon.

79 ROUSE, Capt. and WHITLEY, N. Truro.—Sands from Cornwall for building, agricultural, and other purposes.

80 FLATHER & HADEN, 1 Castle Mills, and 2 Broad Lane, Sheffield.—Prepared Trent sand, or wharpe, and Welch rotten-stone. Prepared lime, for polishing Britannia metal, brass, copper, German silver, and silver goods.

81 SOLOMON, T. Truro.—Varieties of hone-stones.

82 SCRAMPTON, —, Leicester. Specimens of Whittle Hill hones and whetstones.

84 MEINIG, C. 103 Leadenhall St. Manu.—Circular grindstones, for glass, mineral teeth, fine tools, &c. Grinding lathe, &c. Circular and flat oilstones.

85 SNOW, W. P.—Specimen of rock from the Arctic regions.

86 Figure in terra cotta, from the Bank Park Pyropolite Works.

87 POTTER & Co. 87 Aldgate, and Cromford, Derbyshire, Prop. and Manu.—Derbyshire spar, white-lead ore, lead ore, barytes, &c.

88 FALMOUTH LOCAL COMMITTEE. — Quartz, pebbles, and sand, from Swan Pool, near Falmouth.

89 NICHOLLS, J. Truro.—Fire-clay, for stopping furnaces.

90 WHITEWAY, WATTS, & Co. Wareham, Dorset, also of Kingsteignton, Devon, Prod.—Tobacco-pipe, top and alumine clay; also black or carbonaceous clay used in the potteries; from the pits at Kingsteignton. Blue clay used in potteries, from the Furzebrook pits, near Wareham Dorset.

91 KING & Co. Stourbridge.—Stourbridge fire-clay and various raw and burnt articles manufactured from it. Model of a glass-house in Stourbridge.

92 JENKINS & BEER, Truro, Prod.—Lump and powdered ochre, from Penwethers, near Truro, used chiefly by painters, paper-stainers, and paper-makers.

93 JENKINS & COURTNEY, Truro, Prod.—Specimens of Cornish china-stone, with its natural fracture; from Great Bodilla China-stone Quarries, St. Stephen's, Cornwall, much used in manufacturing the finer descriptions of china and earthenware.

94 THRISCUTT, C. St. Austell.—China-clay as dug out of the earth, from Caudle Down Clay-works, prepared, burned, and calcined.

95 WHITLEY, N. Truro.—Clays of the district.

96 Various clays and ochres.

97 MINTON, H. & Co.—Raw materials used in the manufacture of porcelain.

98 HIGHLEY, S. jun. 32 Fleet St. Imp.—Rocks and fossils, to illustrate works on geology, from Dr. Krantz, at Bonn.

99 GREAVES, R. Warwick, Prod. — Two busts of Shakspeare in cement.

100 FAYLE & Co. Old Swan Lane, Upper Thames St. Prop.—Norden blue clay, from the Isle of Purbeck.

101 PHILLIPS, W. Morley Works, near Plympton, Prod. —Disintegrated granite. Prepared china clay, or decomposed felspar. Clay for fire-bricks and crucibles. Plymouth porcelain made by Cookworthy. Pottery and china, made from the china clay.

102 PIKE, W. & J. Wareham, Isle of Purbeck, Prod.— Potter's or blue clay. Stoneware clay, used for stoneware and drain-pipes. Pipe and alum clay.

103 WEST OF ENGLAND CHINA STONE & CLAY Co. St. Austell, Cornwall.—China stone and china clay.

104 TRUSCOTT, C. St. Austell, Cornwall.—China stone and china clay, native and calcined; in a state for porcelain; and for bleaching and paper-making.

105 GRIMSLEY, H. Oxford, Des. and Mod.—Terra-cotta statue, in clay from Shotover Hill, near Oxford. Clay, sand, and ochre, from ditto with fourteen different strata.

106 BURNETT, N. Black Hedley, Gateshead, Newcastle-upon-Tyne.—Specimen of clay, found near Black Hedley; and articles made from that clay, by Fell and Co. Newcastle.

107 MARTYN, E. St. Austell, Prod. and Manu.—China clay. French kaolin used in the Staffordshire potteries, in bleaching, and in paper-making. China stone.

108 WHEELER, PHILIP, & Co. St. Austell, Prop.—Samples of clays. China. Bleaching used in cotton and paper. Clay, used in the manufacture of alum and china stone ware.

109 BROWNE, W. St. Austell, Prop.—Specimen of china clay, derived from the decomposition of felspar.

110 MICHELL, SARAH, St. Austell.—White china clay, for manufacturing china and earthenware, also for bleaching paper, calico, &c.

111 WANDESFORDE, Hon. C. Prop.—Anthracite coal. Iron-stone. Fire-clay. Slate-clay, &c. Clay for making draining-tiles. Sand, for fire-bricks and moulding.

111A Specimens of china stone and china clay.

112 BEAMISH.—Carbonate of barytes in lump and powdered.

112A Specimens of fire clay.

113 PHIPPARD, T. Wareham, Prop.—Potter's, or pipe or brown clay, from Carey pits, with ware and tobacco pipes made therefrom; also siliceous sand, for the manufacture of glass.

115 KING, G. Demidge Lodge, Gazeley, near Newmarket, Manu.—Red brick earth, as dug from the pit. Red building pamment, and coping bricks made from it.

116 ENNISKILLEN, the Earl of, Florence Court.—Two kinds of clay, and drain pipes and tiles made of them.

117 SQUIRES & SONS, Stourbridge.—Model of a glasshouse furnace, with pots of fire-clay, showing one in a working state; and of a pot, in which the glass is melted.

118 ANSTEY, S. 10 Devonshire St. Hoxton Fields.— Pots for melting brass, iron, gold, silver, antimony, &c.

119 FISHER, F. Woolpit, Suffolk, Manu.—Specimens of Woolpit brick-earth. White building bricks. Pamment bricks and draining pipes.

120 WALKER, R. Victoria Works, Beverley.—Carbonate of lime, and Paris white manufactured from it.

121 DEERING, J. Middleton, Co. of Cork, Ireland, Prod. —Various minerals obtained at Rostellan, and articles of earthenware and glass, manufactured from them.

122 PEASE, J. Darlington.—Coal, from Pease's West Collieries; coke made from the above. Fire-clay, fire-bricks, drain-pipes, coping, ridge-tiles, &c.

123 HODSON, Sir G. Bart. Hollybrooke, Bray, County Wicklow, Ireland, Prop.—Specimens of porcelain clay, from Sugarloaf mountain.

123A LONG, J. E. E. Co. Roscommon.—Specimens of drain-pipes.

124 SMEDLEY, T. Well St. Holywell.—Sand for glass-making, and clay from Landidno.

124A JOHNSTONE, W. Co. Leitrim.—Specimens of drain-pipes.

125 LEE, J. LL.D. Hartwell near Aylesbury, Prop.— Samples of fine washed sand, from Stone, near Aylesbury, and glass prisms and spheres made from it.

125A LANCE, T. I. Frimley, Bagshot.—Geological map of the British Isles.

126 METHVEN & SONS, Kirkaldy.—Specimens of drain-pipes, tiles, and pottery.

127 NORTH DEVON POTTERY Co. Annery, near Bideford, Manu.—Raw clay, as raised from the pit. Gravel or sand, from the River Torridge. Sewerage pipes, hollow brick, ridge and garden tiles, &c., made from the same.

127A Pipe-clay, pipes, and sand for glass-making.

128 BULLER, T. W. Bovey Tracey Pottery.—Materials and produce from Bovey Tracey. Pottery manufactured with the lignite of that neighbourhood, &c.

128A GORE, C. Moreton in Marsh.—Samples of ochre.

129 FAHIE, J. K. Tipperary, Ireland, Prod.—White and black clay. Draining tiles and pipes. Felspar, from Cork.

129A COOPER, S.—Specimens of drain-pipes from the River Shannon.

130 WHITE & SONS, Westminster, Manu.—Specimens of cements and plasters used for building purposes, illustrated by panels, pavements, skirtings, &c. Also trials showing resistance of Portland cement. Specimens of concrete blocks.

130A PIPER, T. & W., and WHITE & SONS, Imp. and Manu.—Wall panel in French plaster, as an application in place of lime rendering.

131 BLYTH & JACOBS, 44 and 45 Baldwin's Gardens, Gray's Inn Lane.—Gypsum; the same calcined; also prepared for manure. Plaster of Paris, with articles of the same.

131A MAC ANASPIE, P. & J.—Specimens of cements.

131B DYER, C. K.—Patent metallic cement.

131C Block of gypsum, from Co. Monaghan, Ireland.

132 GOWANS, J. Edinburgh, Prop.—Group and statue in freestone; A. H. Ritchie, des. and sculp., 92 Princes Street, Edinburgh. Stone from Redhall and Binny quarries; Binny bitumen candles, &c. Model and drawing of steam cranes. Drawing of boring machine.

133 FRESTON, W. Hawthorn Cottage, Stroud.—Building stone from Painswick Quarries, from Sheepscombe, and from Nailworth Quarries.

134 MAXWELL, W. Munches, Dalbeattie, Scotland, Pro. —Slab of granite from Craignair quarry, near Dalbeattie.

135 VOSS, J. Woodyhide, Corfe Castle, Prop.—Purbeck marble, used in decorating the interior of the Temple Church, London, &c.; from Woodyhide, Corfe Castle.

136 KING, T. Morpeth.—Ornamental carving in stone, from a quarry at Hartford Bridge belonging to the Earl of Carlisle.

137 SIM, W. Inverary, Scotland, Manu.—Specimens of granite, from Inverary, Bonan, Loch Etive, and Mull.

138 LENTAIGNE, Dr. Dublin, Prop.—Various specimens of Irish marble.

139 GELLING, F. L. Castletown, Isle of Man, Prod.— Gelling marble, from Coshnahawin and Skillicore, Isle of Man; red porphyry, and agate or pebble.

140 COLLES, A. Marble Works, Kilkenny, Ireland, Manu.—Bust pedestal of Kilkenny marble, from the Black Quarry.

141 MEREDITH, J. H. Powey, Cornwall, Prop.—Slabs of black, red, and green porphyry. Tessellated porphyry table, containing 54 specimens of native stones from Withiel.

142 ROSSMORE, Lord, Rossmore Park, Monaghan, Ireland, Prop.—Specimens of green granite from Rossmore Park, county Monaghan.

143 COURTOWN, Lord.—Block of jasper.

144 FRANKLIN, P. L. Galway, Ireland.—Column of black Irish marble, partly polished, from Lough Corrib.

Class 1.
MINING and MINERAL PRODUCTS.

145 Malahide, Lord Talbot de, Malahide Castle, Londonderry.—Specimen of Irish verd antique.

146 Hall, J. & T. Marble Works, Derby, Manu.—Series of pieces of Derbyshire black marble. White marble, exhibiting T. Hall's new method of ornamenting, by depositing on the surface malachite or green carbonate of copper.

147 Long, J. C. E.—Building of ornamental stones, from Ireland.

148 Manderson, W.—Marbles of Ireland.

149 Damon, T. Weymouth, Prop.—Two polished slabs of septaria or turtle stone, from the Oxford clay formation, Weymouth, Dorset.

150 Monteiro, L. A. 2 Upper Phillimore Pl. Kensington.—Specimen of stalagmite or pure Oriental alabaster, veined in colours, from Granada.

151 Quilliam & Creer, Castletown, Isle of Man, Prod.—Slabs of Poolvash black marble, inlaid with red and yellow composition, to imitate encaustic tiles; invented and designed by the Rev. J. G. Cumming, &c.

152 Building material found in Sussex.

153 Specimens of Irish building stones.

153a Trenchard, T. J.—Specimens of stone from Raxwell Quarry, near Weymouth.

154 Sparks, W. Crewkerne, Collector.—Specimens of stone from the counties of Dorset, Somerset, and Devon: Greensand, Purbeck marble, blue lias limestone, white lias, new red sandstone, millstone grit, carboniferous limestone, and granite.

155 Slab of green Connemara marble from the D'Arcy estate.

156 Mountain limestone from Weardale.

157 Cumming, Rev. J. G.—White carbonate of barytes from South Barrule, and carboniferous limestone from the Isle of Man.

158 Champernowne, H.—Cubes of polished Devonshire marbles. (Main Avenue, West.)

159 Tennant, J. Strand.—The maps of the Ordnance Survey geologically coloured by the officers of the Geological Survey of the United Kingdom.

160 Freeman, W. & J. Millbank St. Westminster, Prod.—Specimens of granite, Portland stone, slate stone, Purbeck marble, Bath stone, fire-stone, Galway marble, and Caen stone, from all parts of the United Kingdom.

161 Hutchison, John, Monyray, near Peterhead, Prop.—Bust and pedestal in blue Peterhead granite.

162 Nicholls, J. Trekenning St. Colomb, Prop.—Block of porphyry or elvan stone, raised near Newquay, Cornwall; resisting the action of the weather.

163 Falmouth and Penryn Committee.—Stone, from Porkellis, Wendron; from Forest-gate, Stithians; from Church Town; from Mylor, near Penryn; and from Wendron. Specimens of building stone, granite stone for road making, porphyry, quartz, sand, and magnetic iron ore, from the neighbourhood. (See Outside, No. 30.)

164 Hicks, T. Truro.—Porphyry for various purposes.

165 Whitley, N. Truro.—Varieties of porphyry.

166 St. Austell Committee.—Specimens of building material.

167 Liskeard Committee.—Specimens of building material.

169 Rodd, T. H. Trebantha Hall, near Launceston, Prop.—Varieties of porphyry for ornamental and building purposes.

170 Jenkins & Stick, Truro.—Varieties of porphyry, from Tremone, in Withiel.

170a Specimens of limestone, glazed.

171 Sowden, M. Burley, near Leeds, Prod.—Hard delf-stone grit, suitable for headstones, steps, &c.

172 Freeman, S. Cromweld Bottom, near Halifax, Prod.

—Laminated flag-stone; black stone, from Ringby, and from the Elland Edge Quarry; sand-stone from the quarries at Greetland, near Halifax, Yorkshire.

173 Set of dressed blocks of oolitic freestone.

174 Haigh, J. Godley Cottage, near Halifax, Prod.—Freestone, from Northowram Quarries, near Halifax, rough and dressed. Flag, for causeways, &c. Millstone grit.

175 Johnstone, G. Craigleith, Edinburgh, Prop.—Stone from Carlingnose Quarry, North Queensferry, Scotland, used at dockyards, &c.; stone from Barnton Mount Quarry, and Craigleith Quarry, near Edinburgh.

176 Luard, Beedham, & Co. Rotherhithe, Prop.—Specimens of Caen and Aubigny stone. Specimens of Scotch granites and Rainville stone.

177 Smith, T. Vine Hall, Hurst Green, Prop.—Limestone, from Mountfield, Sussex. Two blocks of concrete, formed with the Mountfield stone-lime.

178 Barry & Barry, Mawgan St. Columb, Prod.—Firestone, a soft grained elvan or porphyry, from near Newquay.

179 Kirk & Parry, Sleaford, Lincolnshire, Prop.—Specimen of Ancaster stone, quarried from the lower oolite formation, at Wilsford, near Sleaford, Lincolnshire.

180 Foot, J. Abingdon St. Westminster, Prop.—Specimens of Portland stone, with specimens of workmanship; to be used for internal and external work.

181 Staple, T. Stoke-under-Hamdon, nr. Yeovil, Prod.—Blocks of Ham-hill stone (oolite), partially worked.

182 Rutherford, J. Wingerworth, near Chesterfield, Prod.—Stone from Wingerworth, Lion and Bramley-Fall Quarry, near Chesterfield; used for docks, bridges, &c.

183 Walsh, J. E. Executors of, Leeds, Prop.—Sandstone, used for docks, bridges, locks, engine beds, &c. Potternewton stone, used for landings, sills, &c.

184 Price, J. High St. Gateshead, Newcastle-upon-Tyne, Prop.—Freestone, from a quarry in Gateshead, used for building furnaces for glass-houses.

185 Grissell, T. 11 New Palace Yd. Westminster, Prod.—Specimen of magnesian limestone, used in the construction of the New Houses of Parliament, from quarries at Anston, in Yorkshire.

186 Townsend, R. Clearwell, near Monmouth.—Forest stone for steps, coping, &c. Ashlar blocks for paving, gravestones, &c. from the Forest of Dean.

187 Lindley, C. Mansfield, Prop.—Magnesian limestone, or dolomite, from the Mansfield Woodhouse Quarries, reopened 1840, after a lapse of several centuries, for the supply of materials for the new houses of Parliament at Westminster. White calcareous sandstone. Red calcareous sandstone from quarries in work 400 years.

188 Stocks, M. Shebden Hall, near Halifax, Prop.—Specimens of ashlar building stone, from the Shebden-head quarries, near Halifax.

189 Bell, J. 25 Buckingham Pl. Fitzroy Sq. Des. and Manu.—Specimens of oolite limestone, from the Oreton Bank Works, Shropshire; marble, &c.

190 Clark, G. H. Rotherhithe, Agent.—Granite, from Haytor Rocks, South Devon. Bramley Fall stone, from Yorkshire and Berwick-on-Tweed. Specimen of Spanish marble, polished.

190a Smith, C.—Oolite limestone and blue granite.

191 Williams, W. 1 Wellington St. Cardiff, Wales, Prop.—Free-stone from the Quarrella quarry, near Bridgend, Glamorganshire.

192 Seymour, Z. Shut, near Glastonbury, Prod.—Model of stone steps from the blue lias stone; and specimens.

193 Porphyritic granite from Wexford.

194 Jennings, B. Hereford, Prop.—Specimen of sandstone, from the Three Elms Quarries near Hereford, very durable.

195 Cumming, Rev. J. G. Castletown, Isle of Man.—

Class 1.
MINING and MINERAL PRODUCTS.

Specimens of flagstone, marble, freestone, granite, porphyrite, greenstone, iron ore, &c., from the Isle of Man.

196 Stones used at Liverpool for building purposes.

197 POWELL, F. Knaresborough, Yorkshire, Collector.—Building stones, from quarries near Knaresborough.

197A RAYNES, LUPTON & Co. Liverpool. — Specimens of limestone for lithographing, from Pentregwyddel, Abergele.

198 CARNEGIE, W. F. Lindsay, Arbroath, Manu.—Flagstones, various, from Arbroath quarries.

199 LONG, W.—Flags from County Clare.

200 HILL, J., C.E.—Building material from Kilrush.

201 TAYLOR, J. Stamford.—Marble, sandstones, slate, limestone, &c. obtained within seven miles of Stamford.

202 POWELL, W. J. Tisbury, near Hindon, Wilts. Prod.—Hard and soft varieties of building stone, flint, and chert. A fossil fish and tree from the oolite formations at Tisbury.

203 DRIVER, W. 4 Lyon's Inn, Strand, Middlesex, Prod.—Specimens from the Chevin stone quarry, Otley, York.

204 STANHOPE LIMESTONE QUARRIES.—Specimens of the cockle strata in the "Great Mountain limestone" from Weardale, in the county of Durham.

205 Slab of sawn slate from Glanmore, County Wicklow, Ireland.

206 SINCLAIR, J. Forss, Thurso, Scotland, Prod.—A slab of paving stone from Forss Rock Hill Quarries.

207 ROYAL DUBLIN SOCIETY.—Valencia flags.

208 DAWBARN & Co.—Manufactured slate.

209 STIRLING, T. jun. Belvidere Rd. Lambeth, Des. Inv. and Manu.—Slate cabinet, exhibiting the various applications of slate. Patent filters. Ornamental loo-table top. Sofa and side-table ornamental tops. Chess or ladies' work-table tops. Roofing slates from the Bangor quarries, &c.

210 GREAVES, J. W. Port Madoc, Carnarvon, Wales, Prop.—Slabs and slates from the quarry at Festiniog, with tools used in manufacturing the same. Blue lias lime.

211 BREADALBANE, Marquis of.—Slates from the quarries of Easdale, &c., in Argyllshire.

212 LIMERICK LOCAL COMMITTEE.—Roofing slates.

213 GEORGE, J. 43 Edgware Rd. Inv. Pat. and Manu. Model of a house; built with wrought iron and slate slabs, glass, &c., intended to secure stability, durability, and freedom from damp and vermin, to save space and improve temperature and ventilation.

214 DELABOLE SLATE COMPANY.—Cistern and ridge of slate. Sundry slates.

215 WILLIAMS, D. Bangor.—Patent slate ridges from Bangor, Wales.

216 Patent corrugated galvanised iron.

217 CADDEL, —. Dalkeith.—Specimens of coal, showing the strata of the Mid Lothian coal fields.

218 PENNOCK, T.—Specimens of carbonate of barytes.

219 HUNTER, L.—Model of a coal mine.

220 LANDALE, D. 6 Forth St. Edinburgh.—Sections of the Scotch coal field, with specimens of the coals and ironstones of Fifeshire and Ayrshire.

221 BITUMINOUS SHALE Co. 145 Upper Thames St. and Wareham, Dorset, Manu. and Prod.—Bituminous shale, with its products.

222 CAHILL, M. Ballyconra House, County Kilkenny, Ireland.—Peat charcoal, for deodorizing, mixing with manure, smelting, &c.

223 TURNER, S. Orchard Pl. East India Docks, Manu.—Coal and its products. Products of caoutchouc and wood.

224 AZULAY, B. Rotherhithe, Pat.—Artificial fuel, made from pressure by coal-dust. Charcoal, from refuse tan.

225 OXLAND, R. Buckland St. Plymouth, Inv. and Manu.—Specimens of Dartmoor peat, and the products obtained by its destructive distillation in cast-iron retorts; peat charcoal, pyroxylic spirit, chloroform, &c.

226 LYON & Co. Swansea.—Two bricks of patent fuel.

227 EVANS, G. Melbury Ter. Regent's Pk. Prop.—Peat and its products. Illustrations of Stone's inventions. Patent peat coke and fuel. Patent manure, &c.

228 COBBOLD, E. 1 High St. Kensington, Inv.—Condensed peat fuel. Various products obtained from peat.

229 SEYSSEL ASPHALTE Co.—Raw material, and various products of asphalte.

230 PATENT FUEL Co. 15 St. Mary Axe, Manu.—Warlich's patent fuel.

231 GREAT PEAT-WORKING COMPANY OF IRELAND; offices, 1 Agar St. Strand.—Samples of their condensed peat, prepared by Gwynne and Hay's patent.

232 PARSONS, J. 2 Wharf, Eagle Wharf Rd. New North Rd.—Blocks of patent fuel, and a number of fire revivers.

240 ROGERS, J.—Peat, compressed peat, and charcoal prepared from peat.

241 Diagram of a group of coal plants.

242 THE BIDEFORD ANTHRACITE MINING Co. Bideford, Devon. — Anthracite coal. Compressed fuel, in blocks. Mineral black paint, in powder, and with oil or coal tar.

242A FITZGERALD, Rev. R. Clare Vein, Tarbert, County Kerry, Ireland.—Small specimen of pearl in its natural state.

243 MALLET, R. C. E.—Anthracite coal, from Castle Comer, Ireland.

244 BAGOT, C. 12 Charlemont Pl. Ireland.—Turf, or peat. Anthracite, or stone coal, from Kilkenny.

247 BUTLER, J. L. Liverpool, Prop.—Coal, cannel-coal, and coke, from different seams, at Ince, near Wigan.

248 O'BYRNE, W. C. 7 Montague St. Portman Sq. Prop.—Specimen of Slievardagh (O'Byrne) coal.

249 RUSSELL & SON, Bathgate, Stirling.—Specimen of cannel or gas coal, from Boghead, near Bathgate, Scotland, chiefly used for the production of gas.

252 WYLAM'S PATENT FUEL COMPANY.—Patent fuel.

253 POWELL, T. Gaer, near Newport, Monmouthshire, Prop.—Specimens of Powell's Duffryn steam coal, from Aberdare, in Glamorganshire. Bituminous coal from the Monythusloyne vein, raised at Lispentwyn. Model of apparatus used for shipment of coals from boats or waggons at Cardiff dock.

254 BUCKINGHAM, J. 13 Judd Pl. East, New Road, Prod. and Imp.—Anthracite, from Boniville's Court Colliery, Pembrokeshire, South Wales.

255 BARROW, R. Staveley Works, near Chesterfield.—Coal cut to show the use of Staveley coal as ballast.

258 JONES, SELLS, & Co. 55 Bankside, Southwark. Agents for anthracite, from Llanelly. (See Outside, 43.)

259 LLANGENNECH COAL Co. Port of Llanelly, and 6 Coal Exchange, Prod.—Woody and sparry specimens of free-burning, smokeless, steam-coal, from the same vein.

260 WESTERN GAS LIGHT Co. 9 Holles St. Cavendish Sq.—Newcastle cannel coal, from which the gas supplied to the building of the Great Exhibition is made. Coke.

261 ATKINSON, J. Coleford, Gloucester.—A complete set of specimens of the workable seams of coal and veins of iron ore, from Her Majesty's Forest of Dean, in compartments.

262 DAY & TWIBELL, Barnsley, Prop.—A column of coal, three feet square at the base, showing the entire thickness, and the different qualities of the seams or beds which are found together, and generally known by the name of the Barnsley thick coal, from the Mount Osborne Collieries.

263 FIELD, COOPERS, & FAULDS, Worsbro' Dale, Barnsley, Prop.—Silkstone Main house coal, from the Silkstone bed. Worsbro' Park hard or steam coal, and soft or house coal, from the Barnsley bed.

264 FIRTH, BARBER, & Co. Oaks Colliery, Barnsley Prod.—Coal for steam ships, for converting iron into steel for smelting iron, from the Oaks Colliery.

265 CORY, W. & W. jun. Commercial Rd. Manu.—London burnt coke, for locomotives and foundries.

266 CLARKE, R. C. Exors. of, Silkstone, near Barnsley, Prod.—Coal, from the old Silkstone Colliery, Yorkshire.

267 NIXON, J. & Co. Cardiff, Prod.—Merthyr and Cardiff steam coal, from the Werfa colliery, near Aberdare and Merthyr Tydvil.

268 INCE HALL COAL & CANNEL Co. Wigan cannel, Arley and Lemberton coal, with various articles manufactured of cannel coal. (See Outside, 38.)

269 RAMSAY, G. H. Derwent Haugh, Newcastle, Inv.—Cannel coal, with carved specimens. Coke and sample of coal from which it is made. Samples of prepared manure for different crops.

270 MITCHELL, Rev. W. A.M. Woolwich, Inv. and Manu.—Specimens of coal recently discovered near Edinburgh, with ornamental articles made of the same.

271 RUSSELL, J. Risca, near Newport, Monmouthshire, Prop.—Specimen of Risca black-vein coal, South Wales. Specimen of new black-vein coal, raised at Cwm Tilery. Argillaceous iron ores from Risca. Fire-bricks.

272 MORGAN & SONS, Llanelly, Wales, Prod.—Stone coal, or anthracite, from Cwm Amman, Llanelly, Gelly Ceidrim.

273 COAL TRADE OF NORTHUMBERLAND AND DURHAM, Newcastle-upon-Tyne.—Map, section, synopsis, working plan, and specimen of the fossil plants, coals, rocks, &c. of the coal-field of Durham and Northumberland; with models of machinery.

274 BRYMBO Co. Wrexham, Wales, Prod.—Minerals and coal from Brymbo, &c.

275 RANDALL, J. Coalport, Salop, Prop.—Minerals, and their associated fossils, used in the manufacture of Shropshire iron. Also specimens of clays, pottery, brick, tile, &c. Cement from the curl-stone, manufactured by M. Brosely.

276 WATNEY, A. Llanelly, Wales Prod. and Manu.—Specimens of pure anthracite coal, from Gwendraeth, Llanelly. Models of anthracite blast furnace, &c.

277 CLIVE, J. W.—Raw and calcined specimens of a stratum of mineral substance found among the shaly iron ores of Clanway Colliery, Tunstall, Staffordshire.

400 BUTTERLEY IRON Co. Alfreton, Prod.—Specimens of coal and iron-stone, and of organic remains in connexion with the Derbyshire coal-field. Iron in its different stages of manufacture, including pig-iron, refined metal, puddled, and merchant bar iron, &c.

401 BAUGH-DEELEY & Co.—Iron chains used in coal mines. Improved vice.

402 CRUTWELL, ALLIES, & Co.—Iron and iron ores.

403 CAWLEY, P. Soho, near Birmingham, Inv.—Complete model and section of a Staffordshire coal-pit, with apparatus for preventing explosions in coal mines.

404 BRUNTON, W.—Model of plan proposed for ventilating mines and diagrams.

405 HARRISON, AINSLIE, & Co. Newland Furnace, Ulverston.—Hæmatite iron ore, from Lindal Moor, in Furness. Charcoal pig-iron and furnace cinder, from Newland, Backbarrow, Duddon, and Lorn Furnaces, said to be the only charcoal furnaces in Britain.

406 FARNLEY Co.—Coal. Coke. Iron-stone.

407 DICKINSON, T. F. Newcastle-upon-Tyne, Prod.—Specimen of hæmatite, or kidney ore, used to mix with poorer iron-stone.

408 MOORE, J. M.D. 10 Saville Row, Prop.—Iron ore, with its products, limestone rock, fire-clay, moulding sand, coal, peat-turf, &c. from the Arigna mines, Roscommon.

409 SCHNEIDER, H. W. Ulverstone, Manu.—Iron ore; Scotch pig-iron; blister, cast, and shear steel.

410 SOLLY & Co. Leabrook Iron and Steel Works, Tipton, Staffordshire.—Iron and manufactured steel, with specimens of tools and cutlery.

411 BIRD & Co. 5 Martin's Lane, Cannon St. City, Prop.—Specimens of pig, bar, and refined iron, Staffordshire

bar iron, Pentwyn rails, lap-welled boiler tubes. enamelled corrugated sheets, tin and term plates, &c.

412 The EBBW VALE Co. near Abergavenny, and 83 Upper Thames St. Prod.— Coal, ironstone, &c. from the Ebbw Vale and Coalbrook Dale. Maps and models of the mineral fields and workings.

413 SUTCLIFFE, J. C. Barnsley, Yorkshire, Manu.—Model of Honey Well coal mine.

413A JAMES, J. Blaina, near Abergavenny, Wales, Inv.—Model of a close top blast furnace for smelting iron ore, &c.

414 DICKINSON, J. F.G.S. Birmingham, Prod.—Section of the strata in the coal and ironstone mines at Dowlais and Merthyr Tydvil, South Wales.

415 BEECROFT, BUTLER, & Co., Leeds, and 8 Pancras Lane, London, Manu.—Railway tire-bars and double fagoted axles in forged state, cut and broken to show mode of manufacture and fibre. Railway tire-bars and axles, bent cold to show toughness. Double worked cable chain iron, twisted and cut. Various other specimens of best Kirkstall bar iron.

416 WINGERWORTH IRON Co. Chesterfield, Derbyshire.—Iron ore and pig iron. Specimens of castings, wrought iron and steel made from the same.

417 BIDDULPH, J.—Cwm Avon Works, Tailbach, Glamorganshire, Manu.—Bar and sheet iron, tin plates, naptha, and minerals.

418 MILLS, R. Foxhole Colliery, near Swansea, Inv.—Model for opening and closing doors, for mining purposes, by a reversion of levers, without the aid of boys.

419 THOMAS, J. T. Coleford. — Iron ores, from the Forest of Dean.

420 ULVERSTON MINING Co. Stainton.—Furness iron ore, hæmatite, produced from mines of the Earl of Burlington, and used for mixing with inferior iron ores.

421 MONTAGUE, A. Lydney, Gloucestershire, Prop.—Specimens of the iron ore from the mines of the Forest of Dean, with pig-iron, &c.

422 AINSWORTH, T. Cleator, near Whitehaven, Manu.—Iron ore, from mines in Cleator. Pig iron, from hæmatite ore only.

423 BEWICK, J. Grosmont, near Whitby, Agent —Calcareous ironstone from the valley of the Esk. Sandstone from Fairhead, near Grosmont. Petrified shells, &c.

424 BICKFORD, SMITH, & DAVEY, Tuckingmill, Cornwall, Inv. and Manu.—Several kinds of safety fuze, adapted to convey fire to the charge in blasting rocks or ice, or in submarine operations.

425 PAGE, J. R. Athenæum Club House, Prop.—Ironstone, from the Leitrim coal and iron basin, rough and washed, with iron, from the same.

426 MONKLAND IRON AND STEEL Co. (W. MURRAY, 33 West George St. Glasgow).—Specimens of coal, ironstone, fire-clay, and Roman cement, from the mineral field of Lanarkshire, with illustrations of their value, in malleable iron, &c.

427 BLACKWELL, S. H. Dudley.—A collection of all the iron ores of the United Kingdom.

428 STIRLING (MORRIES), J. D. F.R.S.E. 13 Great Cumberland St. Hyde Park.—Improved cast iron, called toughened cast iron. Improved wrought iron. Hardened iron for tops of rails. Various alloys of iron. New bell metals, containing iron. New gun metal, bearing metal sheathing, &c.—Pat.

429 BANKART & SONS, Red Jacket Copper Works, near Neath, South Wales, Inv. and Manu.—Various stages of the process of copper smelting, as practised at Red Jacket Works. Rees' patent fuel. Pure native carbon, found in the collieries of Penrose and Starbuck, Vale of Neath, and electrodes made from it.

430 ABERCARN AND GWYTHEN COLLIERIES Co. Newport, Monmouthshire, Prop.—Block of Abercarn stone, very hard and durable. Blocks of Abercarn and Gwythen charcoal vein coal, and of Abercarn rock vein coal. Apparatus, &c.

431 WALES, J. Newcastle.—Models of coal mine, old flint wheel, and of Davy-lamps.

432 WOOD, H. L. Newcastle.—Underground working of coal.

434 TAYLOR, R. London, Pro.—Model machinery and apparatus used for dressing the inferior copper ores called halvans, at the Tywarnhaile mines, the property of H.R.H. the Prince of Wales. Specimens of the mineral in its several states of preparation, and of the clean ore.

435 RUEL, W. H. Holborn.—Crucibles for assaying, &c.

436 MOREWOOD & ROGERS, Steel Yard Wharf, Upper Thames St.—Patent galvanized tinned iron, ferric sheet lead, plumbic zinc, wire of compound metals, &c.

437 VIEILLE MONTAGNE ZINC MINING Co.—Busts of Her Majesty and H.R.H. Prince Albert, life size. Statuette of Sir Robert Peel. Eos, a favourite greyhound of H.R.H. Prince Albert, cast in zinc by Schroeder, London. Models of vessels, bolted with zinc bolts, sheathed with zinc, and painted with zinc paint. Statue of Her Majesty (in Main Avenue, East).

437A JACK, C. 8 & 9 Tottenham Court New Rd. and 80 Upper Thames St.—Specimens of perforated zinc of various patterns. Mouldings, blinds, &c. of zinc manufacture.

438 GLOVER, T. Clerkenwell.—Meters; and the large gas-meter for measuring the gas supplied to the building.

439 BERGER, F. 12 Cornhill.—Copper ores, from Trenance mines, Cornwall. Native copper from Serpentine. (Under N.W. Stairs.)

440 BOLITHO, E. Penzance.—Model of a reverberatory tin-smelting furnace, &c. Specimens of ores and products.

441 LONGMAID, W. London, Manu.—Rock salt, ores, &c., from Cornwall and Devon. Chemical preparations.

441A RICHARDS, A.—A sectional model of East Pool Mine.

442 BREADALBANE, Marquis.—Copper ore.

443 REDRUTH LOCAL COMMITTEE, Redruth, Collectors. —Specimens of copper ore from various mines in Cornwall, showing the various processes it undergoes.

444 GRYLLS, S. & REDRUTH COMMITTEE.—A large mass of copper pyrites.

445 LEAN, J. West Caradon Mine, Liskeard.—Grey and native copper ore.

446 PUCKEY, J. St. Blazey, St. Austell, Agent.—Mass of copper ore, about 1,500 lbs. weight, from Par. Consols mine, St. Blazey, Cornwall.

447 WELLBORNE, W. Bodmin.—Iron-ore.

448 TAYLOR, J. Cornwall—Iron ores from Restormel.

449 DREW, J. St. Austell.—Iron ores from the Trerank mine. Red hæmatite, from Treverbyn mine, &c.

450 BENNETT, CARR, & Co. Moorgate St. London.— Copper ores, gossan, &c. St. Breuard, Cornwall.

451 TAYLOR, R.—Mining tools, as used in the Cornish mines.

452 DUCHY OF CORNWALL.—Sections of Cornish copper mines.

453 DEVON GT. CONSOL. COPPER MINING Co. Tavistock. —Specimens of copper ore.

454 SECCOMBE, S. Phœnix Mines, Liskeard, Prod.—Tin and copper ore, and gozzan, copal, &c. from Phœnix mines. Fire-bricks. Native copper, from West Caradon mine.

455 WELLBORNE, W. Bodmin.—Tin ore and tin.

456 READWIN, T. A. Winchester Buildings.—Tin-stone, from Wheal Augusta, St. Just.

457 DIAMOND, J. Tavistock.—Tin ore, from Wheal Mary.

457A BIRD, J. Wallwyd, Merioneth, Wales, Prop.—Specimen of silver lead-ore, 350 lbs., from the Cowarch mine.

458 COLLETT, W. R. Gort.—Cahirglissaun silver lead-ore, found in carbonate of lime between Gort and Kinvara, Galway county, Ireland.

459 BLEE, R. Redruth, Inv.—Safety bucket for mines, having guides to run in grooves.

460 POLKINGHORNE, W. Fowey Consols Mine, Tyewardreath, Inv.—Synopsis exhibiting the standard, produce, price, and quantity of Cornwall and Swansea copper ores.

461 MICHELL, F.—Pick for dressing granite.

462 ARTHUR, J.—Apparatus for lifting pumps from mines full of water.

463 EDDY, J.—Apparatus for lifting pumps.

464 TRESIZE, T. Perran Foundry.—Model of improved smelting furnace.

465 VINCENT, T. Redruth.—Model of a steam-engine, by a working miner.

466 HOSKING, R. Perran Foundry, Falmouth.—Model of compound valve for pumps.

467 THE TRURO LOCAL COMMITTEE.—Articles illustrating lead, from East Wheal Rose, near Truro, Pentire Glaze, near Wadebridge, and other Cornish mines.

468 THE TRURO LOCAL COMMITTEE.—Articles illustrating tin, from various Cornish mines.

469 LOCAL COMMITTEE, St. Austell, Collectors.—Alluvium, in which stream tin ore is found. The ore as prepared for sale. Specimens of pebbles of tin ore. Building stone from the vicinity of St. Austell.

470 WELBORNE, J. W. St. Austell, and 38 Albemarle St. Manager.—Slab of rosin tin ore, from the Par. Consols mine. Stone of the magnetic oxide of iron, from Roche Rock iron mine. Sulphuret of copper, or yellow copper ore.

471 WHITE & GRANT, Glasgow.—Patent safety cage.

472 HOSKING, R. Perran, Cornwall.—Reversing apparatus for horse whim and stamping machinery.

473 SWANSEA COMMITTEE, Swansea, Manu.—Specimens of copper ore, and of calcined ore, blistered and refined copper, &c.

474 TAYLOR, JOHN, London.—Collection of rare and extraordinary metalliferous minerals.

475 THORNE, W. Barnstaple, Prop.—Iron and copper lead ores, &c., from Tavistock, Combmartin, and Perranzabuloe. Hydraulic cement and raw mineral paint. Ashlarstone, hone-stone, &c., near Barnstaple.

476 GOODHALE & REEVES, for the Ringeridge Nickel Works, Vigersund, viâ Drammen, Norway.—Nickel ore, from mines in the district of Ringeridge.

477 JOHNSON & MATTHEY, 79 Hatton Garden, Manu.— Metals and compounds: Platinum, palladium, iridium, rhodium, uranium, &c.

478 PIMM, H & Co. 29 Newhall St. Birmingham, Manu. —Gold and silver leaf and bronze powders.

479 MATHISON, G. F. Royal Mint Refinery.—Sulphuric acid process of separating gold, silver, and copper.

480 PATTINSON, H. L. Newcastle-upon-Tyne, Inv.— Illustrations of Pattinson's process for the separation of silver from lead.

481 HALLETT, G. Broadwall, Blackfriars, Manu. — Antimony ore from Sarawak, Borneo, Leghorn, Tuscany, and Algeria. Refined metallic antimony.

482 HUNT, J.—Machine for washing poor slimy ores, employed in Brittany.

483 A COLLECTION of MINERALS contributed by Agents and Workmen connected with the Lead Mines of Allendale, Alston Moor, Weardale, Caldbeck, and Keswick.

484 SOPWITH, T. F.R.S. Allenheads, Northumberland. —Specimens of lead ore and lead manufacture, and of silver extracted in the process.

485 OXLAND, R.—Separation of wolfram from tin.

486 BRUCCIANI, D.—Facsimile of the largest piece of gold found in California.

Class 1.

MINING and MINERAL PRODUCTS.

486A IBBETSON, CAPT.— Model of the Isle of Wight, in metal.

487 JORDAN, C. 37 Chapman St. Manchester.—Specimens of metals and their alloys.

488 GARLAND, T. Fairfield, Redruth, Manu.—Impure oxide of arsenic, obtained from tin ores. Commercial oxide of arsenic, and lump arsenic, obtained from the preceding.

489 LOW, J. 30 Gracechurch St. part Prop.—Copper, from Low's patent works, Penclawdd.

490 ROWLANDSON, T. 7 Esher St. Kennington, Pat.— Specimens of ores and products from the Isle of Anglesea, the Vale of Ovoca, Wicklow, and the Cwmhusian Gold Mine, Merionethshire.

491 HARRISON, J. Bakervale, Derbyshire.—Lead ore from Mogshaw mine, Bakervale.

492 ROWE, R. Laxey Glen, Douglas, Isle of Man, Joint Prop.—Silver lead ore, and blende ore.

492A COATES, W.—Specimens of lead ore, from Tullyratty mine, Strangford, Ireland, the property of Lord de Ros.

493 CUMMING, J. G. Isle of Man.—Argentiferous galena, from the Foxdale Mines.

494 BYERS, J. Stockton-on-Tees, Durham, Prod. and Manu.—Lead ore, silver, and litharge, from Grasshill Mine, Teesdale. Refined, common, and slag lead, sheet, and pipe.

495 BURR, T. W. & G. Shrewsbury, Prod. and Manu.— Mineral specimen, raised at the Snailbeach lead mines, Shrewsbury, weighing 12 cwt.

496 DEVONSHIRE, The Duke of, and his Agent, Captain EDDY, Grassington.—Specimen of Devonshire lode, gritstone, &c. Transverse section of the Devonshire lode.

497 PATTINSON & CAIN, Newcastle-upon-Tyne, Prod.— Specimens of arsenio-phosphate of lead. From Drygill Mine, near Hesket New Market, Cumberland.

498 BENNETT, T. 11 Woodbridge St. Clerkenwell, Manu. —Leaf-gold, made by steam-machinery.

499 SMITH, R. Blockford, Perth.—Minerals of Scotland. Chemicals from unusual sources.

500 PHILLIPS, SMITH, & Co. Llanelly.—Specimens of iron and tin plate.

501 DOWNMAN, H. H.—Wood impregnated with block tin.

502 JENKINS, H. W. Truro.—Specimens of arsenic, wolfram, from various tin-mines in Cornwall, used as a mordant in dyeing calicoes. Varieties of mundics and rarer minerals, from various parts of Cornwall.

503 DAVEY, S. Redruth, Miner.—Specimens of ores of zinc.

504 COLE, E. J.—Rich specimen of tin ore. Black tin, from Risehill Mine, near Tavistock.

505 WILLIAMS & SONS, County Wicklow Ireland.—Sulphur ore ; manganese ore, from Glandore Mining Company.

506 GREY, J. Dilston, Corbridge, Agent.—Blende and calamine from Alston Moor, Cumberland ; spelter from them.

507 MINING Co. FOR IRELAND, 2 Burgh Quay, Dublin, Prod.—Silver-lead ore, from Shallee mines. Silvery-copper ore, from Gurtnadyne. Copper ore, from Ballynoe, and Lackamore, all Co. Tipperary, rough and dressed.

508 ROYAL DUBLIN SOCIETY OF IRELAND.—Specimens of lead ore in its various stages ; lead, lead-pipe ; patent shot ; sheet of copper.

509 BUCCLEUCH, Duke of.—Model of furnaces for separating pure silver from lead ore. A block of pure silver. Specimens of lead. Crystals of lead. Model of a lead vapour condensing apparatus. Collection of minerals.

510 WALLACE, W. & COWPER, T. Nenthead, Alston, Prop.—Carbonate of lead, from Little Eggleshope Lead Mine, in Teesdale, Durham. Minerals from Alston.

511 BARRETT, Capt. — Cobalt and copper ores from Conniston mines, near Kendal, Lancaster.

512 BLEE, R. Redruth.—Cobalt ores, from Cornwall.

513 LISKEARD COMMITTEE.—Iron pyrites ; hornblende ; antimony.

514 MUSCHAMP, W. Derwent Lodge, Sunderland.— Copper ores.

515 DUBLIN SOCIETY.—Copper ore, from Knockmahon mines, Waterford.

516 TENNANT, J. Strand.—Copper ore from Lake Superior.

517 GRAHAM, J. Barrhead, near Glasgow.—Greenstone, showing native copper ; native copper, as found in the fissures of the rock, from Boyleston quarry, Renfrewshire.

518 BERGER, J. Native copper, from the Lizard.

519 BRUNTON, W. Cornwall.—Safety fuse for blasting.

520 COPELAND, G. A. Pendennis, Falmouth, Inv. and Manu.—Safety blasting cartridges.

521 OFFLAHERTIE, H.—Lead ore, from Glengola mines.

521A MURCHISON, J. H.—Specimens of copper ore from the Island of Kawaw, New Zealand. Specimens of the matrix of the silver lead ore at Beevalston, Devonshire.

522 FORBES, Dr.—Cinnabar, from California, and 5,160 grains of mercury distilled from 7,560 grains of the cinnabar.

523 DAVIES & TAYLOR, Aberystwyth.—Lead ores.

524 HUNT, R.—Mining map of Cornwall.

525 ARKANSAS MINING Co.—Sample of lead ore as cut from the vein, containing portions of copper and iron ores and sulphuret of zinc, coated with quartz and barytes.

526 HAWKE, E. H., Scorrier, Cornwall.—Specimens of safety fuse.

529 KNIFE, J. A. Clapham, Surrey, Des. & Prop.— Geological map of the British Isles, sites of the minerals, &c. Geological and mineralogical map of England and Wales, with parts of Scotland, Ireland, and France.

530 MARRIOTT, Mrs. Frederick, 3 Eastbourne Terrace, Hyde Park.—Specimen of gold ore from the Mariposa Mine, California, estimated to contain 45¾ per cent. of gold. Another specimen. (Main Avenue, East.)

531 DEVONSHIRE, Duke of. — Large quartz crystal. (Main Avenue, East.)

532 ERSKINE, J. Scotland, Prod.—Specimens of lead ore, from the Black Craig mines.

533 WEBB, —, Islington.—Soda-water pipe, and diagram of London strata. (South Wall.)

534 SAMUEL, M. A. 23 Netland Square, Notting Hill, Prod.—Sulphate of iron, from Shakspeare's Cliff, Dover.

(See also Objects outside the Building, pages 7 and 8.)

Proceed to Sculpture Court, page 154.

Class 2. CHEMICAL AND PHARMACEUTICAL PRODUCTS.
—— South Gallery. ——

1 PONTIFEX & WOOD, Shoe Lane.—Various chemicals, including crystals of nitric acid, tartaric acid, sulphate of copper. Rochelle salts.

2 MELINCRYTHAN CHEMICAL Co. Neath, Wales, Manu. —Sugar of lead, or acetate of lead.

3 BUTTON, C. 146 Holborn Bars, Manu.—Chemical products.

3A READE, Rev. J B. Stone Vicarage, Aylesbury, Inv. —Soluble Prussian-blue, &c.

4 BUCKLEY, J., the Trustees of the late, Manchester, Manu.—Crystals of copperas, or sulphate of iron.

5 EVANS, F. J.—Napthalim, from coal.

6 WILSON, J. Glasgow, Manu.—Alum slate, raw and manufactured. Iron pyrites and sulphate of iron. Sulphate of ammonia obtained from the distillation of coal. A rare specimen of naphthaline.

7 SPENCE, P. Pendleton Alum Works, Manchester, Inv. and Manu.—Iron pyrites and its products. Shale or schist, and alum produced from it. Patent zinc cement, or hydraulic mortar; and specimens of the waste materials from which the cement is manufactured.

7A TENNANTS, C. & Co. Manchester, Manu.—Salts of copper, zinc, and tin, potash, soda, &c. used in calico dyeing and printing.

7B YOUNG, J. Ardwick Bridge, Manchester, Inv. — Mineral oil. Paraffine. Stannates, with models of apparatus.

7C BROWN & Co.—Muriates and sulphates of ammonia.

7D DICK & Co., Burg Chemical Works, Carlisle.—Copperas, manufactured by Spence's patent process.

8 DENTITH W. & Co. Manchester, Manu. — Ornaments of bichromate of potash, and of nitrate of lead (in Main Avenue, West). Mineral colours, &c. used by calico-printers and dyers, china and earthenware manufacturers.

9 KURTZ & SCHMERSAHL, Cornbrook Works, Manchester, Manu.—New colouring matters, and preparations for printing and dyeing in cotton, linen, silk, and wool; with specimens. Ultramarine, of various qualities.

10 HATMEL & ELLIS, 9 Sugar Lane, Manchester, Manu.—Specimens of sulphate of copper, nitrate of lead, &c. (In Main Avenue, West). Sulphur. Orchella weed.

11 HOWARDS & KENT, Stratford, Essex, Manu.— Quinine and cinchonine, with materials and salts. Nectandria radiæi, or green-heart bark, and its alkaloid beberine. Camphor, borax, tartaric and citric acid, antimony, silver, bismuth, iron, mercury, magnesia, potassium, iodine, zinc, opium, and their preparations.

12 BELL, J: L. Washington Chemical Works, Newcastle-upon-Tyne, Manu.—Specimens of Pattinson's patent oxichloride of lead, and landscapes painted with colours prepared from it.

13 KING, J. Glasgow, Manu. (Sole partner of the HURLET & CAMPSIE ALUM Co.)—Alum. Red and yellow prussiates of potash.

14 MAY & BAKER, Battersea, Surrey, Manu.—Chemical preparations.

15 COOK, T. A. Newcastle-upon-Tyne, Manu.—Crystallized carbonate of soda, manufactured by the Walker Alkali Company.

16 LINDSAY, G. Sunderland, Manu.—Green vitriol, or copperas of commerce, extensively used in dyeing silks, woollens and cottons, making writing inks, Venetian red, &c.

17 MOBERLEY, W. Mulgrave Alum Works, Landsend, near Whitby, Prod. and Manu.—Crystallised alum (in Main Avenue), raw alum shale, calcined shale, alum meal, and finished alum. Sulphate of magnesia, rough and refined. Ammonia and magnesia, for manure

18 PATTINSON, W. W. Gateshead, Newcastle-upon-Tyne, Manu.—Specimens of crystallized alum (in Main Avenue), pure sulphate of alumina, called in commerce concentrated alum, and bicarbonate of soda.—Manufactured at the Felling Chemical Works.

19 RICHARDSON BROTHERS & Co. Manu.—Refined saltpetre from the East Indies, &c.

20 STEVENSON, W. Jarrow Chemical Works, South Shields, Manu.—Crystals of soda converted into bicarbonate by exposure to carbonic acid gas.

21 TULLOCH, A. Waltham Abbey, Prod.—Saltpetre, charcoal, and sulphur, used in the manufacture of gunpowder at the Waltham Abbey Mills.

22 MASON & SON, 11 Munster St. Regent's Park, Manu. —Royal premier blacking. French varnish, and waterproof varnish.

23 HILLS, F. C. Deptford, Pat. and Manu.—Nitrate of potash, made by patent process. Sal-ammoniac and smelling salts, derived from the ammoniacal liquid of gas works.

24 HEMINGWAY, A. W. Portman St.—Double salts of iron.

25 PONTING, T. C. 32 High St. Bristol, Inv. and Manu. —Marking ink. Shaving cream. Medicinal vegetable fluid extracts, made with cold water.

26 CLIFFORD, G. 5 Inner Temple Lane.—Specimens: deeds, writings, engravings, &c., injured by fire, water, age, dirt, smoke, &c. in a restored and unrestored state.

27 BRAMWELL, T. & Co. Heworth Chemical Works, Newcastle-upon-Tyne, Manu.—Crystals of prussiate of potass of commerce. Ferrocyanide of potassium of chemists, used for dyeing blue in place of indigo.

28 WINSOR & NEWTON, 38 Rathbone Pl. Manu.—Artists' pigment. Brushes and pencils for drawing and painting. Canvas palettes, &c.

29 FAWCETT, B. 73 Snow Hill and 7 Somner St. Southwark.—Graining and flatting with the innoxious paragon paint.

30 CHESHIRE, J. jun. Northwich, Manu.—Specimens of best table salt, and other salt.

31 SPENCER, J. A. 9 Westbourne Pl. Hyde Park, Manu. —Chemical preparations: Naphthaline, caffeine, quinine, &c.

32 WATT, W. Glasgow, Manu.—Sea-weed, with its chemical products: Kelp, sulphate of potash, chloride of potassium, carbonate of soda, and iodine.

33 PICCIOTTO, M. H. 8 Crosby Sq. Inv. and Manu.— Gumarabic, purified by a patent process. Hochstaetter ultramarine blue. Mannite prepared in Italy. Italian flax.

34 BULLOCK, J. L. 22 Conduit St. Manu.—Chemical principles from substances used as food or medicine.

35 NAYLOR, W. 56 James St. Oxford St. Manu.—Varnishes. Wood, stained without sizing.

36 NISSEN & PARKER, 43 Mark Lane, Inv.—Tinted paper, chemically prepared pulp for bank checks.

37 BULLOCK, E. & Co. Galway. Ireland.—Arran kelp. Potash. Sulphate of soda, iodine, and other preparations from sea-weed.

38 SPURGIN, T. Saffron Walden, Prod.—Root, stem, flower, and stigmata of saffron..

39 HAWTHORNE, J. 77 Charrington St. Inv.—A new ink for staining oak and mahogany. Stained specimens.

40 HALL, J. Queenborough, Prod.—Specimen of copperas, from the works at Queenborough, Isle of Sheppey, with specimens of pyrites and copperas in a granulated form.

41 HOPKIN & WILLIAMS, 5 New Cavendish St. Manu.— Pure tannin. Crystallized chromic acid. Benzoate of ammonia. Biniodide of mercury. Pure aconitine, and other chemicals.

42 BOWER, J. Hunslet, Leeds, Manu.—Carbonate of soda, particularly adapted for scouring wood or woollens.

43 JENKINS, W. H. Truro, Inv.—Arsenical compound:

a general preventive of foulness, barnacles, &c. on ships' bottoms, buoys, &c. and of dry-rot in buildings.

44 Fox & BARRINGTON, Manchester.—Chemicals.

45 BARNES, J. B. 143 New Bond St. Manu.—Valerianic acid and valerianates.

46 PARROTT, W. 7 Cleaveland St. Prod.—Semi-transparent brown colour from the smut of corn.

47 WOOD & BEDFORD, Leeds, Manu.—Specimens of the varieties of lichen used in the manufacture of cudbear, orchil, and litmus, and of the substances obtained from them.

48 BLUNDELL, SPENCE, & Co. Hull, and 9 Upper Thames St. Inv. and Manu.—Colours for oil painting and paper staining. White oxichloride of lead : pat. White zinc paint. New drying oil. Anti-corrosion and stucco paint. Patent dryer. Composition for ships' bottoms. Oils, &c.

49 BANKART, F. Swansea.—Crystals of sulphate of iron.

50 GODSON, S. H. Tenbury, Worcestershire, and Rutland Gate, London, Prop.—Native mineral waters. Concentrated acid tested, to show the bromine constituents, &c.

51 DINNEFORD & Co. 172 New Bond St. Inv. and Manu.—Magnesian minerals and chemicals.

52 SCHILLING & SUTTON, Brighton, Manu.—Samples of soda, Seltzer, and Fachingen water. Effervescing lemonade.

52A STRUVE & Co. Brighton.—Artificial mineral waters.

53 KANE, W. J. Dublin, Manu.—Specimen of sulphate of soda, made in brick furnaces, and of bleaching powder (chloride of lime). Specimens of sulphur pyrites and manganese ore.

54 WARD, SMITH, & Co. Glasgow, Manu.—Iodine. Muriate of potash. Sulphate of potash. Alkali salt.

55 FOWLER, J. 35 Bedford St. Covent Garden.—Pure enzoic acid.

56 LAWRENCE, W. 163 Sloane St. Manu.—Specimens of cod liver oil.

57 BROWN, F. 12 Eccleston Pl. Pimlico, Pat. and Manu.—Innoxious colours manufactured from the oxide of zinc.

58 ELLAM, JONES, & Co., Markeaton Mills, Derby, Manu.—Emery: Granular rhombohedral corundum-stone, from Naxos, in Asia Minor. Mineral and vegetable colours, native and manufactured.

59 RUSSELL & ROBERTSON, Omoa Foundry, Holytown, Lanarkshire, Inv.—White carbonate of lead or ceruse, yellow chromate of lead, and red dichromate of lead ; manufactured by a new process.

60 JOHNSON, J. R. 12 Bankside, Inv.—Calico printed and dyed with munjeet and madder. Illustrations of printing in chintz, eight fast colours.

61 SCOTT, L. 41 Moorgate St. Manu.—Patent white oxide of zinc, an innoxious substitute for white lead in artistic and house painting, &c. produced from spelter by destructive distillation.

62 DAVY, MACKMURDO, & Co. Bermondsey, Manu.—Chemical preparations.

63 DAUPTAIN, GORTON, & Co. 17 Wharf Road, City Road, Manu.—Samples of ultramarine.

64 ESTCOURT, S. 2 Green Ter. New River Head, Inv. and Manu.—Refined Indian blue.

65 COPPOCK, J. Bridport, Inv.—A chemical liquid for imparting a mahogany and rose-wood colour to common woods, with specimens.

66 BELL & Co. 2 Wellington St. Goswell St.—Mineral paints, which will dry under water, or on metals exposed to extreme heat : for ships' bottoms, damp walls, &c.

68 MARSHALL, J. Leeds, Manu.—Samples of indigo, carmine, orchil, cudbear, lac dyes, and turmeric.

69 LEE, C. 119 Lower Thames St. City, Imp.—Newly invented black dyeing material, for dyeing silk.

70 DAVIES, J. Cross St. King St. Manchester, Inv. and Manu.—Preserved size, for any climate.

71 LAMPLOUGH, H. 88 Snow Hill, Inv.—Aloes, opium, myrrh, Russian castoreine, ipecacuanha, rhubarb, &c.

72 COULSON, JUKES, & Co. 12 Clements Lane, Lombard St. Prop.—Mineral black for paint.

73 PEACOCK, G. Southampton Docks. — Wood preserved by a superior composition.

73A SHRUBSOLE, W. High Street, Dorking.—A case of artificial crystals.

74 STEPHENS, H. 54 Lower Stamford St. Blackfriars, Inv.—Stains for wood. Patent ever-pointed pencils. Fountain ink-holders. Ink-holders. Patent fountain pens.

75 HAYES, P. & Co. Salford.—Resins and varnishes.

76 DUNCAN, W. L. Sydenham, Kent, Inv.—Sample of cotton waste cleansed after being used by engineers.

77 MASON, Mrs. B. 38 Doughty St.—Pooloo's Chinese cement. Agent, T. J. Blofeld, 6 Middle Row, Holborn.

78 HUMFREY, C. Farnham Pl. Southwark, Inv. and Manu.—Colours produced by fatty acids with metallic oxides and peroxides. Candles and refined fatty matters.

79 DICKSON, G. & Co. 46 Dundas St. Edinburgh, Manu.—Medicinal cod, ling, and skate liver oil. Cod liver ointment.

80 BREAREY, W. A. Douglas, Isle of Man, Inv.—Refined oil. Pure oleine, for fine machinery, and instruments.

81 ROBERTSON, W. Banff, Scotland, Manu.—Cod-liver and skate-liver oil, extracted by steam-heat. Sulphate of baryta and chloride of barium.

82 LINKLATER, J. 5 Sidney St.—Cod-liver oil.

83 OWEN, C. Edinburgh, Manu.—Pure cod-liver oil.

84 KING, W. W. Soho St. Liverpool, Manu.—Effervescent citrate of magnesia.

85 BURT, S. J. 26 Farringdon St. Prop.—Cantharides. Cantharidine and its compounds.

86 HUSKISSON, J. W. & H. 77 Swinton St. Gray's Inn Road, Manu.—Chemical preparations of soda, iodine, mercury, potash, lead, citric and tartaric acids, iron, and zinc.

87 MURRAY, Sir J. M.D. Monktown, Dublin, Inv.—Bicarbonate of magnesia, dissolved in distilled water. Fluid camphor and magnesia. Carbonate of magnesia in crystals.

88 STURGES, J. Kettering, Inv.—Preparation for preserving the turnip plant from the fly. Proposed remedy for the smut in wheat.

89 WARD, J. County Donegal, Ramelton.—Kelp manufactured from sea-weed, and specimens of iodine, muriate of potash, sulphate of potash, &c. made from kelp.

90 KENT, J. H. Stanton, near Bury St. Edmonds, Prod.—Dried pharmaceutical indigenous plants, with extracts.

91 TRUMAN & HANBURY, Winch Lane and Spitalfields.—Specimens illustrating the manufacture of beer.

92 GODFREY & COOKE, 31 Southampton St. Covent Garden, and 30 Conduit St. Manu.—Carmine. Lake. Bismuth oxide. Ammonia. Oil of amber. Salt of amber. Artificial musk. Watchmaker's oil. Essence of ambergris, &c.

93 SQUIRE, P. 277 Oxford St. Inv. and Manu.—Pharmaceutical extracts. Chloroform and other inhalers. Apparatus for preparing infusions.

94 SMITH, T. & H. 21 Duke St. Edinburgh, Manu.—Specimens of aloine, the cathartic principle of the aloes, of gallic acid, of crystallized mannite, and of cantharidine.

95 BASS, J. 81 Hatton Garden, Inv.—Concentrated medicinal infusions and decoctions.

96 McCULLOCH, C. Covent Garden Market.—English and American herbs and roots.

97 TUSTIAN, J. Melcombe, near Banbury, Manu.—Petals and confection of the red rose. Extract of henbane.

98 TUSTIAN & USHER, Melcombe, near Banbury, Manu.—English rhubarb, trimmed and untrimmed, and in powder.

99 JENNINGS, H. C. 97 Leadenhall St. — Starch, gums, and a vegetable wax from potatoes and wheat.

100 HOPWOOD, H. Richmond.—Large crystals of sugar of milk.

CHEMICAL and PHARMACEUTICAL PRODUCTS.

101 TENNANT, M. B. Brighton.—A chemical production for labels or artist's designs, a product of a silvery hue, to be thrown over drawings by means of chemical agency.

102 KEATING, T. 79 St. Paul's Churchyard. — Jalap root and hay saffron, from Asia Minor; kousso, from Abyssinia; sarsaparilla root, from Paraguay.

103 WATTS, J. 107 Edgware Road, Manu.—Pharmaceutical extracts.

104 DUNCAN, FLOCKHART, & Co. Edinburgh, Manu.—Chloroform.

105 LEA, A. 150 Oxford St. Inv.—Myrrhine aids to the digestive organs.

106 MORSON, T. & SON, Southampton Row and Hornsey Rd.—Specimens of crystallized salts of morphine, strichnine, cinchonie, of pure aconita and veratric, gallic, tannic, and meconic acids, pyro-gallic and pyro-meconic acids, &c.

107 MACFARLAN, J. F. & Co. 17 North Bridge, Edinburgh, Manu.—Series illustrative of the manufacture of the salts of morphia. Specimens of gallic and tannic acids. Specimens of sulphate of bebeerin and its alkaloid.

108 POUND, M. 198 Oxford St. Imp. and Manu.—Imports from Calcutta; Indian bael; fruit of the Bengal quince. Wine of bael. Bark of the root of the bael tree. Soap berries, the fruit of the Sapindus. Jujube fruit, imported from Paris. Flaked cold cream, &c.

109 COLLINS, R. N. Oxford St. Cannon St. Inv. and Manu.—Disinfecting powder.

110 HATTERSLEY, W. Elixir of sarsaparilla prepared without heat.

111 DAVENPORT, J. T. 33 Russell St. Bloomsbury.—Chemical preparations.

112 NIXEY, W. G. 22 Moor St. Soho.—Cement.

113 OYLER, S. 2 York St. Camden Town.—Lint.

114 AUSTIN, J. B. Banbury, Manu.—Decoctions and infusions of medical substances. Superphosphate of lime. Sulphate of lime or gypsum. Fine white sand, found at Todmarton, near Banbury.

115 SAVORY & MOORE.—Kousso, sumbul, or musk-root.

116 BELL, J. — Cod-liver oil, stearine, sarsaparilla, juice of taraxacum, otto of roses, &c. Salt, from the Droitwich Patent Salt Works.

117 THE LONDON DRUGGISTS.—Balsams, barks, beetles, extracts, expressed oils, essential oils, roots, seeds, woods, spices, peppers, &c. Fruits, gums and resins, leaves, mosses, &c.

118 COPNEY, W. Plough Ct. Lombard St.—Crystals of citric acid, sulphate of copper, sulphate of magnesia, and octahedra of alum.

119 STURGE, J. E. Birmingham.—Crystal of chlorate of potash and amorphous phosphorus.

120 OXLAND, J. & R. Plymouth.—Samples of sugar, produced by a process of refining without blood.

121 PINTO, PEREZ, & Co. Limehouse.—Specimens of acetate of lead in crystals.

122 STEVENSON, J. C. Jarrow, South Shields.—Large crystal of soda.

123 RILEY, E. Museum of Practical Geology, Piccadilly.—Specimens of hippuric acid peculiarly prepared.

124 GREENISH, T. 20 New St. Dorset Sq. Manu.—Specimens of various syrups. Superphosphate of iron. Tincture of Columba. Tincture of hops.

125 TRIX, T. Exeter, Manu.—Extract of henbane from the wild herb.

126 DIXON, SON, & Co. Newton Heath, Manchester.—Models of matches made with Schrotter's amorphous phosphorus. A. Albright, Patentee.

Proceed to Class 3.

Class 3. SUBSTANCES USED AS FOOD.

—— South Gallery. ——

1 LIGHTON, J. Frampton, near Boston, Prod.—Glass of honey, 19 lbs., produced under an improved system.

2 DOUBLEDAY, H. Coggeshall, Essex, Prod.—Fine specimen of honeycomb.

3 CARLETON, E. Blaris, Lisburn, Ireland.—Camomile flowers.

4 BENTLEY, J. F. Stamford, Lincoln, Prod.—Specimens of honey in the comb, free from pollen and brood cells, collected under Nutt's system.

5 KITCHENER, W. C. Newmarket, Cambridgeshire, Prod. and Inv.—Two specimens of honey. Apparatus for obtaining honey without impurity.

6 DUTTON, R. W. 146 Fleet St. Prop.—Honey in the comb.

7 HILLS & UNDERWOOD, Eastcheap, Inv. and Manu.—Vinegar manufactured from malt.

11 COPLAND, BARNES, & Co. 46 Botolph Lane, Eastcheap.—Tart fruits, jams, jellies, &c. hermetically sealed, which retain for years their flavour and quality.

12 GAMBLE, J. H. 33 Royal Exchange, Manu.—Preserved provisions. Canister of boiled meat, supplied to the Arctic Expedition in 1824, and found by Captain Sir James Ross in Prince Regent's Inlet in 1849, in a perfect state of preservation, &c.

13 Colquhoun, J. N. Lt.-Col. R.A. Woolwich.—Fruit of the plantain, dried in the sun, from Jalisco (Guadalasara) Mexico.

14 SMITH, M. Copper Alley, Dublin. (Agent in London, J. Kendall, 8 Harp Lane, Great Tower St).—Preserved pig.

15 RITCHIE & McCALL, 137 Hounsditch.—" Goldner's Patent." Preserved animal and vegetable substances.

16 BROCCHIERE, P. 21 Rue Louis le Grand, Paris.—Concentrated forms of food prepared from blood of cattle.

17 CLAY, J. Edgeley, Stockport.—Specimen of prepared maize or Indian corn.

20 LEONARD, J. & T. P. Hull, Prop.—Beef, prepared, cured, and rolled, so as to keep good for any length of time. The process of curing and mode of preparing invented by J. Tupling.

21 WARRINER, G. & SOYER, A. 7 Upper St. Martin's Lane.—Osmazome, or essence of meat, &c.

22 PAYNE & SON, 328 Regent St. Imp. and Manu.—Indian curry powder; Delhi, Chusnee, and Indian curry sauce, &c.

23 UNDERWOOD, G. H. Pendleton, Manchester, Inv.—Meats, preserved without the use of salt.

24 LINKLATER, J. 5 Sidney St. Commercial Rd.—Smoked mutton.

26 WHITNEY, J. Calver Hill, Hereford, Inv.—Beef preserved in a dry state, peculiarly adapted for the use of sailors, being free from salt.

27 WEATHERLEY, H. 54 Theobald's Rd.—Specimens of honey-drops.

27A WHEELER, F. Rochester.—Specimens of free-labour produce.

28 SNOWDEN, R. City Rd. and East Rd. Inv. and Pat.—Coffee raw, and prepared by patent process. Samples of the processes of cleansing and purifying the coffee berry previous to roasting and grinding.

29 LEBAIGUE, 10 Little Titchfield St. Imp. and Manu.—Chocolate and cocoa, the in various stages of manufacture.

30 PARIS CHOCOLATE COMPANY, 252 Regent St.—Chocolate, &c.

31 FRY & SONS, Bristol. — Trunk of cocoa-tree, and specimens of leaves, flowers, pods, and nuts, from the West Indies, and manufactured cocoa and chocolate.

32 WHITE, G. B. 147 Shoreditch, Imp. and Manu.—Cocoa and chocolate, raw and manufactured.

33 SHINTON, R. 29 Spencer St. St. George's East.—Samples of cocoa.

34 MONTEIRO, L. A. 2 Upper Phillimore Pl. Kensington.—Chocolate manufactured.

35 LANE, W. R. 226 Strand, Manu.—Essence of coffee, manufactured by a machine invented by the exhibitor.

36 GRUT, B. 1 Sambrook Ct. Imp.—Caracas cocoa, from New Granada.

37 BUDD, J. T. 82 Mount St. Grosvenor Sq. Manu.—Extract of cocoa.

38 BENHAM, W. A. Cross St. Queen's Sq. Bloomsbury.—Samples of Trinidad cocoa, raw, and in the various stages of manufacture.

39 BENSON, W. 133 Oxford St. Imp.—Flor de Cabanas, Martinez, Havannah cigars, and samples of tobacco.

40 LAMBERT & BUTLER, 141, 142 Drury Lane.—Tobacco from America, Havannah, Holland, &c.

41 BREMNER & TILL, 60 Fenchurch St.—Tobacco.

42 JONAS BROTHERS, 42 and 43 Leman St. Whitechapel, Manu.—Cigars and tobacco.

43 JONES & Co. 39 Brunswick Sq. Imp.—Cigars, foreign and British.

44 LUNDY FOOT & Co. Dublin, Inv. and Manu.—Snuff, made solely from the leaf and stalk of Virginia tobacco.

45 TAYLOR, T. G. Hackney, Grower and Manu.—Tobacco of English growth and manu. and snuff.

46 HYAMS, M. 79 Long Lane, Manu.—Cigars of British manufacture. Samples of tobacco.

47 SALES, POLLARD, & Co. 57 Red Cross St. Cripplegate, Manu.—Cigars of Yara tobacco.

48 BUCKLAND & TOPLISS, Barrington Cres. Brixton, Inv. and Manu.—The cigarilla.

49 COHEN & ORR, 41 St. James's St. Im.—Raw tobacco and cigars.

50 GOODES, G. & S. 12 Prince's St. Spitalfields, Manu.—British cigars.

52 RICHARDSON BROTHERS, Edinburgh, Manu.—Tobacco, imported from Virginia into Leith, raw and manufactured. Snuffs, &c.

53 THE LONDON SPICE TRADE, Imp.—Samples of spices, including mace, nutmegs, cloves, cinnamon, cassia, pimento, black and white pepper, ginger, and carrawayseeds.

54 FAULKNER, R. & C. 44 Jermyn St. St. James's, Manu.—Preserved fruits.

55 FORTNUM, MASON, & Co. 182 Piccadilly, Imp.—Preserved and dried fruits, and edible seeds, from various countries. Varieties of honey.

56 CLEMENS, J. 25 Mincing Lane, and Malagar, Pro.—Jordan almonds. Raisins.

58 SPUR, G. Boston, Manu.—Specimens of linseed-cake from English linseed.

58AGRACE, D. Brighton.—Patent mushroom spawn.

59 RICHARDSON & SONS, 6 Duke St. Southwark, Prop.—Golding hops, grown in "the Hill," in Mid-Kent, in East Kent, and in the heart of Mid-Kent. Jones's hops, from Kent and Sussex. Grape hops, Colgate hops, &c.

60 ASHBURNHAM, The Dowager Lady, Broomham, near Hastings, Prod.—A bag of hops, grown within three miles of the sea, in the parish of Guestling, Sussex.

61 ATTFIELD, C. Farnham, Prod.—Pocket of hops.

62 PAINE, J. M. Farnham, Surrey.—Samples of choice white-bines and true Golding hops.

63 GOLDING, R. Hunton, Maidstone, Manu.—Pocket of Mid-Kent hops.

64 PLOMLEY, F. Maidstone, Des.—Magnified view of the formation and growth of the hop fungus, from its earliest to its latest stage.

65 MASTERS, A. Tonbridge, Prop.—Four branches of dried hops. Samples of the same.

66 PETERSON, T. Trinity Chambers, Water Lane, Tower St. Agent.—Oil cakes. Vegetable oils and manures.

68 BURN, R. North Merchiston House, Edinburgh, Imp. Des. and Manu.—Cotton seed (seed cotton), with oil, and oil-cake made from them, imported from the colonies.

70 SHEPPARD, A. Ipswich, Prop.—Eggshell white wheat, and Chevalier malting barley, grown in Suffolk. Malt manufactured at Ipswich.

71 THE TRURO LOCAL COMMITTEE.—Specimens of Cornish agricultural grains, Indian corn, &c.

72 WEBB, R. Calcot Farm, Reading, Prod.—Mummy Talavera wheat. Free trade wheat. Wellington apple, famous for keeping, &c.

73 RAYNBIRD, R. Hengrave, near Bury St. Edmunds, Prod.—Kessingland wheat, grown upon a light soil, at Hengrave, Suffolk. Chevalier barley, grown at Hengrave. Tick beans with white eyes, grown at Hengrave.

74 RAYNBIRD, H. Laverstoke, Andover Rd. Hampshire, Prod.—Specimens of wheat produced by hybridization, and of Hopetown and Piper's thickset wheat, from which the hybrids were obtained.

75 KENDALL, J. Treverlin, Truro, Cornwall.—Sheaf of white wheat, named "The giant straw wheat."

77 TAYLOR & SON, Bishop Stortford, Herts, Manu.—Varieties of malt: amber coloured, white and brown.

78 WELLSMAN, J. Moulton, near Newmarket, Manu.—Sample of pale malt, manufactured from Chevalier barley.

79 MAUND, B. F.L.S. Bromsgrove, Prod.—Specimens of wheat, artificially hybridized, showing that its exterior form can be modified.

80 WRENCH, J. and SONS, London Bridge.—Samples of grain most familiar in the London market.

82 PAYNE, H. Birdbrook Moat, near Halstead.—Varieties of grain.

83 STRANGE, B. Banbury.—Stiff clay soil, &c. Sample of beans, growth 1850, as per statement annexed.

85 MILNE, W. Rhynie, Scotland, Inv.—One quarter of Scotch barley oats.

86 WALKER, W. Mossat, near Aberdeen, Prod.—Sample of Kildrummie oats.

88 COUSENS, S. Great Bentley, near Colchester, Prod.—White wheat, new variety; weight of imp. bush. 64 lbs. net.

90 FOX, J. J. Devizes, Prop.—Specimens of red straw-white Essex wheat, and of Nursery, Lammas, and Talavera red wheat, grown in Wiltshire.

90A CAHILL, M. Ballyraggit, Kilkenny, Prod.—Samples of wheat, oats, and barley, grown at Grove, Kilkenny.

91 STEVENS, R. Stamford, Prod.—Sample of wheat Collyweston white.

92 CROUGHTON, W. P. Tenterden, Kent, Prod.—Hoary white wheat; produce, over five quarts per acre. Golden pod beans; produce, over four quarters six bushels per acre.

93 ASPREY, J. Sandleford, near Newbury, Berks, Prod.—White trump wheat, grown on very poor soil; weigh 67 lbs. per bushel.

94 FORDHAM, T. Snelsmore Hill East, near Newbury, Prod.—Samples of hybrydized white wheat; weight 66¼ lbs. per bushel. Prolific beans; weight 70 lbs. per bushel.

95 JUSON, W. Red Hill, Shrewsbury.—Samples of grain and fine flower.

98 KEENE, W. 42 Cornhill, Prop.—Forty-day maize from the Pyrenees.

99 IRWIN, ELIZABETH, Ballymore, Boyle, Roscommon,

SUBSTANCES USED AS FOOD.

Prod.—Black barley, grown at Ballymore, in the county of Roscommon, Ireland, from African seed.

100 BEXLEY, Lord, by J. BESWICK, Footscray, Kent, Prod.—Bushel of white chittim wheat.

101 MOSES, H. E. & M. 87 Tower Hill.—Fresh preserved meats from the Camperdown establishments, Sydney, New South Wales, having undergone a voyage of 16,000 miles, and remaining in a perfectly fresh state.

102 GIBSON, C. Pitlochry, Perth, Prod.—Samples of English barley, grown near Pitlochry, about 600 feet above the level of the sea.

103 GUILLEREZ, A. F. 37 Castle St. Edinburgh, Prod.—Lentils cultivated at South Queensferry, near Edinburgh.

103ASADLER, W. J. Swindon, Wilts.—Lawrance's prolixus crystal wheat, 66½ lbs. to the bushel.

104 GIBBS & Co. Half-Moon St. Piccadilly, Imp. and Prod.—Dried grasses and seeds, wheat, barley, &c.

105 LAWSON P. & SON, Edinburgh, Prop.—Vegetable products of Scotland; substances used for food for man and domestic animals, in the chemical arts, in medicine, in manufactures, and in house and ship building.

106 JONES, G. Redland, Bristol.—Specimen of wheat, grown by spade culture and dibbling.

107 H. R. H. PRINCE ALBERT.—Three samples of grain grown on the Royal farm at Windsor, consisting of wheat, oats, and beans, one bushel of each.

107A WRIGHT, H. Antingham, near North Walsham, Manu.—Malt, as manufactured from barley grown by Rev. C. Cremer, of Beeston, near Cromer, Norfolk.

108 GENTILE, J. P. Harbertonford Works, near Totnes, Devon, Manu.—Macaroni and Italian pastes. Chocolate. Vegeto-animal food; a compound of the most nutritious principles of meat and wheat, &c.

110 WATT, G. Upper Balfour, Banchory, Scotland.—Sample of barley, grown after turnips, in a five-course rotation, with the ordinary farm-yard manure.

112 SUTTON, J. & SONS, Reading.—Specimens of grain. Skinless chevalier barley, a new variety. Purple-topped yellow hybrid turnip, valuable for late sowing, as a substitute for swedes. Lincolnshire red turnip.

114 M'KILLICAN, J. Piperhill, Cawdor, Scotland, Prod.—Perennial rye-grass seeds raised on the farm of Piperhill, Nairnshire. Samples of white wheat. The land from which, previous to its improvement, was not worth 1s. per acre.

115 ILLINGWORTH, A. Banchory Ternan, Scotland, Prod.—English barley, weighing 59¼ lbs. per bushel. Scotch Birley oats, weighing 44 lbs. per bushel. Perennial rye-grass seeds, weighing 30½ lbs. per bushel.

116 BATTY & FEAST, 15 and 16 Pavement, Finsbury Sq. Inv. and Manu.—Preserves, pickles, &c.

117 COLMAN, J. & J. 9 College Hill, City, Manu.—Starch from wheat and rice, mustard, British gum, indigo blue, &c.

118 NOAK, W. & J. Droitwich, Manu.—Sample bottle of brine, obtained from springs at a depth of 173 feet, at Droitwich, with specimens of the salt.

119 DEWAR, T. Newcastle-upon-Tyne, Manu.—Mustard and specimens of brown and white mustard seed, from which mustard for table use is made.

120 LEVY, W. 2 White Row, Spitalfields, Manu.—Samples of Taganrog wheat, macaroni, vermicelli, &c.

121 TUCKER, R. G. Lenton, near Nottingham, Manu.—Starch, used by lace-dressers. Gum substitute, used by cotton, silk, woollen, and wall-paper printers. Adhesive, or label gum, &c.

122 TUCKER, E. Belfast, Ireland.—Starch, produced at Belfast.

123 BROWN & POLSON, Thrushcraig, near Paisley, Manu.—Patent starch, manufactured from sago flour and potato flour. Patent wheat starch. Arrowroot.

124 WOTHERSPOON, R. Glenfield Starch Works, Maxwelton, near Paisley, Manu.—Specimen of Glenfield patent powder starch, made from sago; a new material from which the starch is made.

125 RECKITT & SON, Hull, Manu.—Starch, &c. from wheat, potato, and sago.

126 SHAND & MUCKART, Montrose.—Samples of starch.

127 MILLER, D. & W. Musselburgh, near Edinburgh, Prod.—Starch: household white, bleachers' wheaten, Royal blue, and sago flour. Scotch farina. Arrowroot.

128 JONES, O. & Co. Battersea, Inv. Pat. and Manu.—Starch, hair powder, and gluten from rice.

129 PIESSE, S. 43 Molyneux St. Marylebone, Inv. and Manu.—Lactine, or artificial milk. Pestachio nuts, and powder. Patchonly.

130 BERGER, S. Bromley, Middlesex, Manu.—Berger's patent rice starch.

132 M'GARRY & SONS, Palmerstown and Ashtown Mills, Manu.—Linseed and rape oils and cakes, and Irish mustard.

133 M'CULLUM, M. 12 Cannon St. Leith, Discoverer.—Specimens of the rhizome, or creeping stem, of *Typho latifolia*, or large red mace. Samples of the meal, &c.

134 EDWARDS, H. 32 Great Windmill St. Haymarket. Inv. and Manu.—Custard powder.

138 ST. ETIENNE, Madame D. Harberton Ford, Totnes.—Specimens of gluten from wheat, potato-flour, &c. Specimens of vegeto-animal substance for long voyages, &c. Specimens of chocolate, biscuits, starch, imitation of sago, tapioca, arrowroot, &c. Potato-flour and starch-gums, &c.

139 MOORE, E. D. Ranton Abbey, Eccleshall, Stafford, Pat.—Essence of milk; samples combined with chocolate, cocoa, and coffee.

140 FADEUILHE, V. B. 19 Newington Cres. Inv. Pat. and Manu.—Consolidated milk.

141 GLASS, G. M. Brandon St. Walworth, Inv. and' Manu.—Gelatine.

142 GARDNER, J. M.D. 51 Mortimer St. Discoverer.—Coffee leaves prepared for use as a beverage tea. Pat.

143 ASSAM Co.—Samples of tea, the produce of Assam, and entirely manufactured by natives of India.

144 SAUNDERS & GATCHILL, Dublin, Agents.—Chicory in all its stages, from the kiln-dried root to the ground dust, fit for use.

146 POOLE, SARAH R. Kingston-on-Thames. — Patent crystallized malt, the substance converted into sugar.

149 PERKINS, H. Hanworth Park, Surrey.—A small loaf of sugar made from sugar-canes grown by the exhibitor in the county of Surrey.

150 KIDD & PODGER, Isleworth, Middlesex, Manu.—Flour from English and Australian wheat dressed through Swiss silk machines.

152 MARRIAGE, E. Colchester.—Samples of flour.

153 M'CANN, J. Beamond Mill, Drogheda, Manu.—Coarse cut oatmeal, used for making stirabout in Ireland.

154 STENHOUSE, A. Farina Works, Dunning, Perth, and 43 Molyneux St. Bryanstone Sq.—Farina used as food.

157 STYLES, T. 148 Upper Thames St. Manu.—Ashby's prepared groats, &c.

159 CHITTY, E. Guildford, Manu.—Flour.

160 FITCH, F. C. Steeple Bumstead, Essex, Prod.—Fine wheaten flour, manufactured from Essex wheat.

161 SMITH, J. Hare Craig, Dundee.—Patent oat flour. (Agent in London, W. J. Robertson, 48 Devonshire St. and 35 Walbrook, City.)

162 BUCK & SON, Danby Mills, near Middleham, Bradford, Prod.—Double superfine flour; wheat meal and oatmeal. Exhibited for colour and quality.

Proceed to Class 4.

Class 4.   VEGETABLE and ANIMAL SUBSTANCES used in MANUFACTURES.

—— South Gallery. ——

1 GRIGOR, J. & Co. Nurseries, Forres, Scotland.— Varieties of larch and native Scotch pines. Weeping birch, one year old, from seeds produced by native trees on the banks of the Findhorn, Morayshire, sown 20th April, 1850.

2 KING, EMMA, Church St. Edmonton, Prod.—Anatomized plants.

2A COOKE, E. W. "The Ferns," Victoria Rd. Kensington.—Preserved pitcher plants.

3 STEVENS, W. 1 Rock Pl. Tottenham Rd. Kingsland. Preserved flowers, retaining their natural form, for botanical illustrations.

3A CROWCHER, C. jun. Chapel Pl. Liverpool Rd.— Specimen of calcined straw.

4 PURSEY, W. H. Spring St. Paddington.—Imitations of flowers cut in vegetables and chemically preserved.

5 ROCK, MARY, Stratford Place, Hastings.—Mosses and pebbles from Hastings.

5A TILLEY, Lieut. Fivehead, Taunton.—Anatomized leaves, &c.

6 HARRISON, R. & J. Hull.—Varieties of British and foreign woods.

7 BURNETT, Sir W.,M.D., K.C.B., F.R.S.—Specimens of Burnettized and un-Burnettized timber, canvas, cotton, and woollen cloth, and raw hides, tested to demonstrate the efficacy of the process. Antiseptic and disinfecting solutions.

8 FITCH, F. C. Steeple Bumpstead, Chelmsford.— Specimens of English woods.

8A AULDJO, Mrs. Richardson, Noel House, Kensington.—A table made from a block of wood, found in 1835 in excavating a Roman villa near Pompeii, destroyed A.D. 79. The pedestal is copied from a bronze candelabrum in the museum at Naples.

9 SAUNDERS, W. W. Wandsworth, Prop.—Collection of woods, arranged geographically, with specimens of veneers, &c.

9A EVANS, W. Castle St. Swansea, Inv.—Piece of Welsh oak, prepared by a peculiar process, as a substitute for fancy wood. Cannon lock on a new principle.

10 STOWE, H. Buckingham, Inv.—Specimens of wood, stained without heat or moisture; the process being equally applicable to carved wood.

14 HOLTZAPFFEL & Co. 64 Charing Cross, and 127 Long Acre, Prop.—Specimens of woods commonly employed in England for turnery.

15 GILLOW & Co. 176 Oxford St. and Lancaster.— Specimen of St. Domingo mahogany.

16 ENDERSON, H. J. 140 Praed St. Paddington, Prod. —Specimens of graining, &c.

19 SCOTT, E. & Co. 83 Dean St. Soho.—Walnut and rosewood veneers.

20 NEWTON, C. H. Plough Bridge, Rotherhithe, Surrey, Manu.—Specimen to illustrate the patent desiccating process for seasoning wood in a few weeks.

21 BETHELL, J. 8 Parliament St. Westminster, Inv. and Pat.—Wood, saturated with oil of tar.

21A SAMUELS, D. 71 Lebon St. West Ham, Essex, Inv. and Manu.—Picture frame of various English woods.

22 CLASSON, J. Industrial Depôt, Northumberland Buildings, Dublin.—Calenders, &c. made of bog-yew, bog-oak, and other fancy woods, the growth of Ireland. Specimens of Irish woods, peat, and peat charcoal. Scouring powders.

23 BROTHERTON & Co. Hungerford Wharf, Imp. and Manu.—Rape seed and olive oil, and almond oil.

24 BARCLAY & SON, 170 Regent St. Manu.—Bleached wax Wax candles, night lights, &c.

25 FREEMAN, Messrs. 3 Wigmore St. Cavendish Sq. Manu.—Fine transparent wax and spermaceti lights, with plaited wicks, and other candles and night lights. Materials in the unmanufactured state. Refined oils, &c.

26 BAUWENS, L. F. Grease Works, Wakefield, Manu. —Products of various patent processes used in extracting pure oils and greases from the refuse soap-suds of woollen, silk, and other manufactures.

27 ROSE, W. A. 66 Upper Thames St. Manu.—Palm-oil. White and liquid grease. Clarified machinery and burning oil. Varnishes. Samples of the paints supplied to Messrs. Fox, Henderson and Co. for decorating the Exhibition building.

28 HILLAS, F. 5 Ordnance Row, Lewisham Rd. Inv.— Purified animal, vegetable, and fish oil.

29 MILLER, T. J. Dorset Wharf, Westminster, Imp. and Manu.—Spermaceti oil, from the South Seas. Spermaceti, rough, filtered, and refined. Crystallized mass of refined spermaceti. (Main Avenue, West.)

30 EWEN, J. 17 Garlick Hill, City, Manu.—Clarified fats, for pharmaceutical, culinary, and perfumery purposes.

31 DURANT, R. jun. 11 Copthall Court, Prop.—Samples of raw silk from Italy, China, India, Turkey, &c.

32 DODGE, Mrs. CATHERINE, Godalming, Surrey, Prod. —Silk produced by the silkworm, fed upon the leaves of the white mulberry at Godalming, Surrey, with specimens manufactured.

34 HANDS & LEAVESLEY, Coventry, Silk Dyers.—Specimens of dyed silks.

35 DOXAT & Co. Bishopsgate St. Without, Imp.— Sample of Italian raw silk

36 HOWE, J. & Co. Coventry, Dyers.—Specimens of self-colours dyed from thrown silk; yellow gum; specimens of shade dyeing, &c.: said to show permanency of colour.

37 JAQUEMOT, J. M. 36 Old Broad St. Imp.—Skeins of raw silk, the produce of a filature, near Geneva, Switzerland.

39 OLIVER, W. 89 John St. Fitzroy Sq.—A slab of bird's-eye maple.

40 SECTIONAL COMMITTEE ON VEGETABLE KINGDOM.— Samples of the ordinary flax and hemp of commerce: French, Flemish, Dutch, Friesland, Archangel, Riga, English, Egyptian, and New Zealand flax. Petersburgh, Riga, American, Egyptian, India, Manilla, Italian hemp and Jute.

41 TRENT, E. W. Park Hemp Works, Old Ford.— New Zealand flax as imported; the same cleansed by machinery invented by artist: fishing lines; tow, rope, &c.

42 WRIGHT, L. W. & Co. 75 Cheapside, Inv. and Manu. —China grass and flax, raw and manufactured. Wheat straw paper, &c.

43 DONLAN, M. J. J. 4 St. Peter's Sq. Hammersmith, Inv.—The seeds of flax and hemp chemically prepared. Samples of flax straw, and of the flax in different stages of preparation, &c. Samples of sail-cloth. Samples of the phormium tenax, or New Zealand flax, in different stages of preparation, with specimens manufactured.

44 GILLMAN, E. Twickenham, Agent for Tao Nui, a New Zealand Chief.—Specimens of New Zealand woods, gums, and barks. Flax, and flax manufactures.

45 HIVES & ATKINSON, Leeds, Imp. and Manu.—Sam-

VEGETABLE and ANIMAL SUBSTANCES

ples of flax, from the Courtrai and Lokeren districts, Belgium. Yellow flax, from Trimingham, Norfolk. Blue flax, grown in Yorkshire. Chinese reed and China grass, raw and manufactured.

46 CATOR, NELSON, & Co. Selby, Manu.—Flax grown in Yorkshire, raw and manufactured.

47 LONG, J. C.E.—Specimens of Irish wood.

49 ADAMS, —, Ballyderitt, Coleraine.—Sample of flax.

51 ROBERTSON, H. 7 Salisbury St. Strand, Prod.—British vegetable fibre, for the manufacture of thread and paper.

53 PICCIOTTO, M. H. 3 Dean St. Finsbury.—Italian flax.

54 MASON, G. Prod. — 1 Flax grown, steeped, and prepared for market at Yately, North Hants. 2 Produced in South Hants. 3 Produced at Cobham, Surrey. 4 Flax grown and scutched at the Farnborough workhouse. 5 Flax scutched by prisoners in county gaol, Winchester. 6 Refuse tow and flax manufactured at Yately. 7 Coarse tow and flax. 8 Models of tools used.

55 MARSHALL & Co. Leeds, Imp. and Manu.—China grass and Courtrai flax, dressed and manufactured.

56 BARSHAM, J. Kingston-on-Thames, Inv. and Manu.—Cocoa-nut fibre, natural and manufactured.

57 NIGHTINGALE, W. & C. 64 Wardour St. Soho, Imp. and Manu.—Bed feathers and downs. Horse and other hair mattresses. Eider-down quilt.

58 MORRELL, H. 149 Fleet St. Manu.—Quills, lead pencils, sealing-wax, and wafers, in the various stages of manufacture, with their materials.

59 HEAL & SONS, Tottenham Ct. Rd. Imp. &c.—Bed feathers, steamed and dressed. Russian down. Greenland eider-down. Dorset of the same, covered with embroidery. Eider-down quilt.

60 BLYTH, HAMILTON, & BLYTH, 52 Little Britain, London, and Liverpool, Imp. and Manu.—Goose bed feathers, dressed and purified. English horse-hair, raw, curled, and manufactured.

61 ENGLISH'S PATENT CAMPHINE Co. Hull.—Samples of varnishes, seeds, &c.

62 BARKER & Co. Breams Buildings, Chancery Lane, Inv. and Manu.—Mastic varnish for paintings. Essential oils. Hair dyes, essences, extracts, and perfumes.

63 MANNING, J. 18 Coles Ter. Barnsbury Rd. Islington.—Varnish, made without the aid of heat.

64 PENNEY, H. 4 York Pl. Baker St. Manu.—Colourless linseed oil and copal varnish.

65 SMITH, B. T. & C. 12 Church St. Mile End New Town, Manu.—Specimens of colours.

66 JEWESBURY & Co. Mincing Lane.—Varieties of cochineal and lac dye.

68 SMITH & SON, 14 Corbet Court, Spitalfields. — Archil and cudbear, lichens, &c. from which they are derived; and specimens of fabrics and leathers dyed and printed with archil and cudbear.

70 COONEY, C. 60 Back Lane, Dublin.—Samples of Irish manufacture in starch, indigo, blues, vegetable gums, and blacking.

71 SAUNDERS & GATCHILL, Dublin.—Pastel, or imitation woad, made from the chicory plant, used in the dye vat for fixing colours in woollen cloths.

72 ROBINSON, J. & Co. Huddersfield, Inv. and Manu.—Archil paste and cudbear, patent process. Liquid archil for dyeing and printing. Samples of worsted yarn dyed in best cudbear.

73 HALLIDAY & Co. Quay St. Salford.—Post-office label gums, &c.

74 BRUCE, G. 52 Nelson St. Liverpool, Inv.—Black varnish, for wood and iron-work, either for land or marine

purposes. Blue, red, green, and stone-coloured composition. Spirit varnish.

75 LONG & REYNOLDS, Hackney, Manu.—Safflower for dyeing, with specimens.

76 SADLER, T. Gloucester Ter. Regent's Park.—Cochineal, produce of Oaxacor, Mexico.

77 BURCH, W. Sewardstone Mill, Woodford, Essex, Manu.—A series of substances and combinations used in the art of dyeing. Colours used in oil painting and printing, &c. with illustrative specimens.

78 MOORE, J. Littlecott Farm, Pewsey, Wilts, Prop.—Pure South-down ewe, stuffed, seven years old, and which never was shorn. Length of the wool, 25 inches; weight, 36 lbs.

80 HENDERSON, R. Wooler, Northumberland, Prod.—Fleeces of cheviot wool, grown at an elevation of 2,600 feet.

81 DORRIEN, C. Chichester.—Samples of Merino wool from two-years-old sheep; weight of fleece nearly 8 lbs.

83 PRICE'S PATENT CANDLE Co. Vauxhall, Manu.—Specimens of candles, vegetable tallow, palm oil, &c.

84 REBOW, J. G. Wivenhoe Park, near Colchester, Pro.—South-down sheep's wool.

85 MILLNER, R. Dublin, Prop.—Fleeces, long wool, grown in the counties Meath and Galway. Fleeces, long and short wool mountain, grown in the county Wicklow.

85A SECTIONAL COMMITTEE ON ANIMAL KINGDOM.—Various kinds of wool.

86 MANINGS, G. Wedhampton, near Devizes, Manu.—Diamond teg matching wool, for combing; and diamond clothing wool, from South-down fleeces, from Wilts.

88 SANDS, W. & Co. Mortimer St. Leeds.—Specimens of "burry" wool in the original state, with specimens of the same cleaned by machinery.

91 PRELLER, C. A. 31 Abchurch Lane, Pat. and Manu.—English wool. Mohair and fine Australian wool, with samples combed, without oil.

91A CAHILL, M. Ballyraggit, Kilkenny, Prod.—Fleece of Leicester wool, from Grove, County Kilkenny.

94 IRVING G. VERE, Newton by Leadhills, Lanarkshire, Prod.—Fleece of an aged ewe of the black-faced Highland breed, unlaid.

95 GOOD, FLOODMAN, & Co. Hull, Imp.—White Iceland wool.

95A BREADALBANE, Marquis of, Prod.—Specimens of woollen yarn, made from the wool of the bison.

97 LIPPERT, D. 66 Albion St. Leeds, Imp.—Fleeces of German wool.

101A SMITHSON, T. Bramley, Leeds.—Samples of wool.

103 HORAN, H. 7 Stud St. Islington, Manu.—Prepared Greenland whalebone of different colours, for covering whip handles, walking sticks, and telescopes, with portions of black and white whalebone, as cut from the fin.

104 WESTALL & Co. 69 Aldersgate St.—Samples of whalebone and manufactures from the same.

105 CLAUSSEN, P. 26 Gresham St. Inv. and Pat.—Samples of flax in all its stages, from straw to cloth, prepared by the exhibitor's process. Cloths produced from flax; flax cotton, flax cloth, flax silk, flax wool. Hemp and other fibrous plants, prepared either in whole or part, as above.

106 ROYAL BELFAST FLAX IMPROVEMENT SOCIETY.—Specimens of flax.

107 ROYLE, Dr. J. F. Acton Green.—Specimens of cotton.

108 PUCKRIDGE, F. 5 and 6 Kingsland Pl. Manu.—Gold-beater's skin, raw and prepared, and flexible fine gold, silver, and other metals, for ornamental purposes.

109 STAIGHT, T. 12 Walbrook, Manu.—Turning and carving in ivory. Carved ivory chessmen, the Crusaders.—Reg. Carvings in pearl.

USED IN MANUFACTURES.

111 TEBBITT, W. North Crescent, Bedford Sq. Manu.— Card box of mother-o'-pearl, &c. Specimen of pierced work, for the cover of a drawing-room table book, &c.

114 MARKWICK, M. 32 King William St. Manu.— Patent epithems for medical, surgical, and veterinary purposes. " Impermeable spongio-piline," for applying heated fluids to the body, in lieu of poultices and fomentations. Water-dressing, and piline.

115 GRANVILLE & Co. 9 Gresham St. West, Prop.; BURKE, W. H. Tottenham, Manu. — India-rubber manufactures.

116 REA, E. 117 Wardour St. Manu.—Lac, lacquers, polish, varnishes, sealing-wax, gums, varnishes, &c.

117 SIMPSON, HUMPHREY, & VICKERS, 23 Little Britain, Imp. and Manu.—Isinglass, cut and uncut.

118 DAWSON & MORRIS, 96 Fenchurch St. Imp. and Manu.—Samples of isinglass.

119 SWINBORNE, T. C. & G. & Co. Coggeshall, and 1 Gt. Tower St. London, Manu.—Refined isinglass, gelatines, and glues.

120 WATT & SON, Dumfries, Scotland, Manu.—Glue made from pieces of hides and skins, principally used by cabinet-makers and joiners.

121 ABBOTT & WRIGHT, Needham Market, Suffolk, Manu.—Crown glue, made from the hides and feet of cattle.

122 NIMMO, T. & Co. Linlithgow, Scotland, Manu.— Specimens of glue, for the use of joiners and paper-makers, &c.; refined gelatine.

124 TUCKER, E. Belfast.—Specimens of glue.

125 DUFAVILLE, W. Broughton House, Islington.— Culinary articles: fish, crystal, brilliant, and various other gelatines. British isinglass, &c., loose, and in gelatine wrappers.

125A MULLER, F. Hackney.—Gelatine and glue.

126 CURTIS BROTHERS & Co. Coleman St.—Substances used for tanning leather.

126A KITCHIN, J. Commercial Sale Rooms, Mincing Lane.

—Shumac, in the leaf, and ground, from Palermo, used in tanning sheep and calf skins, moroccos, &c.

127 FRENCH, B. 51 Crutched Friars, Imp. and Manu.— Cork, raw and manufactured by hand.

128 HOLT, E. 24 White Rock Pl. Hastings, Inv. and Manu.—Mosses, from East Sussex. Sea-weeds, zoophytes, and corallines, from Hastings and St. Leonards, in frame.

130 FIELD, J. C. & J. 12 Wigmore St. Cavendish Sq. Manu.—Samples of stearine, produced entirely from tallow.

131 GROVES, N. 58 Watling St. Dublin, Manu.—Parchment and glue, Irish manufacture.

132 PEET, T. 6 Frederic St. Regent's Park.—Corks solely of British manufacture, cut by hand.

----

134 BREADALBANE, Marquis of.—Specimens of woods grown in Perthshire and Argyllshire, and of veneer from the Scotch fir, dug from a peat bog in Glenorchy, Argyllshire. (Ground Floor, South-west Corner, Areas A. 34 and C. 3.)

135 FAUNTLEROY, R. & SONS, Potters Fields, Tooley St.— An extensive collection of foreign hard and fancy woods. An elephant's head, with tusks and grinders. A variety of elephants', hippopotamus', and walrus' teeth, and sea unicorns' horns. Mother-o'-pearl shells. Corozo nuts, or vegetable ivory, coquilla nuts, &c. (Ground Floor, South Wall, S. 11 to 14.)

A circular slab of Honduras mahogany. (In the Main Avenue, West.)

136 CROSS, S. 57 Bunhill Row, Prop.—Collection of English woods. (Ground Floor, North side, C. No. 2.)

137 MURRAY, Sir W. Bart. Dunnottar, Stonehaven, Prop.—Plank of Scotch fir, and section of Scotch elm. (Ground Floor, North side, C. No. 5.)

138 DILLON, Viscount C. H. Prop.—Slabs of yew, oak, and fir, from trees found in the bogs. (Ground Floor, North side, C. No. 3.)

139 PAYNE'S PATENT TIMBER PRESERVING COMPANY Whitehall Wharf.—English woods. (South Wall.)

Proceed to Class 8, page 47.

SECTION II.—MACHINERY.

Class 5.   MACHINES FOR DIRECT USE, INCLUDING CARRIAGES, RAILWAY AND MARINE MECHANISM.

Areas A. B. 10 to 34; C. D. E. 1 to 10, & 19 to 33; F. 1 to 32; G. H. 1 to 13, & 19 to 26.

1 ATHERTON, C. Dockyard, Devonport, Inv.—Pair of marine steam-engines of 25-horse power, planned with a view to apply the sway-beam principle of construction to driving the submerged screw propeller. Model of expansion slide.

2 POWELL, E. J. 11 Hartland Ter. Camden Town, Des.—Drawings of the various forms of patent screw propellers.

3 SMITH, F. P. Greenwich.—Several screw propellers.

4 STOTHERT, SLAUGHTER, & Co. Bristol, Inv. and Manu. —Marine engine, intended to meet the assumed requirements of machinery for propulsion by screw, in which it is imperative to drive the propeller shaft at a speed unsuited to the speed of the vacuum apparatus.

5 TAPLIN, R. 7 Upper Woodland Terrace, Woolwich, Inv.—Model of a telescopic funnel or chimney for marine boilers.

6 WATT, JAMES, & Co. 18 London St. London, and Soho, Birmingham, Des. and Manu.—Marine-engines, of the collective power of 700 horses, designed for driving the screw propeller by direct action. Models made in 1785, showing the early application of steam power to locomotion, &c.

7 ROUGHTON, R. Dockyard, Woolwich.—Improved slide valve.

8 PENN & SON, Greenwich, Manu.—Pair of marine oscillating engines, and of patent marine engines on the trunk principle, for the driving of screw-propellers direct. Working models of marine oscillating engines, and of patent trunk engines. An auxiliary or "donkey" engine.

10 FOSSICK & HACKWORTH, Stockton-on-Tees, Manu. and Inv.—High-pressure steam-engine boiler, with increased size of the fire-tube. Locomotive and carriage, buffer and draw spring.

11 HAWTHORN & Co. Leith, Manu.—High-pressure oscillating steam-engine, of simple construction, without slide, valves, eccentrics, or gearing.

12 EDWARDS, T. Islington Foundry, Birmingham, Manu.—Patent five-horse power, direct action, high-pressure steam-engine.

13 HICK, B. and SON, Bolton.—Steam-engine driving Hibbert and Platt's cotton machinery.

14 SIMPSON & SKIPTON, Trafford St. Manchester.—Improved reciprocating high-pressure steam-engine, driving Parr, Curtiss, & Madely's cotton machinery.

16 DAVIES, J. & G. Albion Foundry, Tipton, Staffordshire, Inv.—Pair of patent elliptic revolving steam-engines. Steam regulating self-acting damper. Feed nozzle, valves, patent revolving blowing apparatus, &c.

20 JOYCE, W. Greenwich, Manu.—Pendulous steam-engine.

22 McNAUGHT, W. 26 Robertson St. Glasgow, Inv.— Patent double cylinder steam-engine, a modification of Woolf's double cylinder engine. Montgomery's self-acting break for railway carriages. (See also Class 6.)

24 LYNCH & INGLIS, Garratt Rd. Manchester, Manu. and Des.—One-horse portable steam engine, for driving agricultural or other machinery.

25 CROSSKILL, W. Beverley.—A steam-engine.

26 FAIRBAIRN, W. & SONS, Manchester, Inv. and Manu.—Six-horse steam-engine.

28 MACINTOSH, J. 5 Gray's Inn Sq. Inv.—Improved rotatory or revolving steam-pumps or engines for agricultural and other mills, marine engines, and locomotives. —Patented.

29 HODGE and BATLEY, 9 Adam St. Adelphi.—Steam-engine.

30 RANSOMES & MAY, Ipswich, Inv. and Manu.—A five-horse power steam-engine.

34 BUTTERLEY Co. Alfreton, near Derby. — Eight-horse oscillating steam-engine.

35 CARRETT, W. E. 13 Rockingham St. Leeds, Inv. and Pat.—A steam-pump, combining a high-pressure engine and an improved suction and force pump. A portable high-pressure boiler.

37 EVANS & SON, 104 Wardour St. Soho, Manu.— Steam-engine, six-horse power, simple in construction, portable and economical in working. Want & Vernum, Pat.

38 MAUDSLAY, SONS, & FIELD, Lambeth, Des. and Manu.—A small double cylinder direct-acting high-pressure steam-engine. Connecting-rod adapted to marine steam-engines, of the collective power of 800 horses. Models of patent marine steam-engines for driving screw propellers, &c. Model of a patent gun-metal screw propeller. (See also Class 6, No. 228.)

39 CLAYTON, SHUTTLEWORTH, & Co. Lincoln, Manu.— An oscillating steam-engine, arrangements simple and compact, suitable for working corn mills, sawing machinery, &c.

40 POPE & SON, 81 Edgeware Rd. and Lisson Grove, Manu. and Des. — Improved oscillating cylinder steam-engine.

41 NASMYTH, J. Manchester.—A steam-engine.

42 DONKIN, B. & Co. Bermondsey, Manu. and part Inv.—Patent disc water-metre, disc engine, and disc pump.

44 ARMSTRONG, W. G. Newcastle-upon-Tyne.—Model of hydraulic crane, steam-engine, accumulator, corn-lift, and hydraulic machine for unshipping coals.

45 LLOYD, E. Glyndwrdu, near Corwen, Wales, Inv.— Patent steam-engine, on the double cylinder expansion principle.

46 SIEMENS, C. W. Birmingham, Inv.—Working model of a patent chronometric governor. Model of a variable expansion valve. Model of a surface condenser. Water-meter. Regenerative condenser. Working model of a regenerative evaporator.

48 BUNNETT, J. & Co. 26 Lombard St. City, and Deptford, Kent, Inv. Pat. and Manu.—Patent concentric reciprocating steam-engine for high or low pressure.

49 COLLINGE, C. & Co. 65 Bridge St. Lambeth.—Portable high-pressure steam-engine.

52 RENNIE, G. & Sir J. Holland St. Manu. and Licensees.—Model of Bishop's patent disc engine, fitted as an auxiliary power to drive a screw propeller.

53 GREEN, E. Phœnix Foundry, Wakefield, Inv. and Manu.—Patent fuel economiser, applicable to steam-boilers. Warm-air apparatus.

56 WATKINS & HILL, 5 Charing Cross, Manu.—Improved barometric vacuum gauge. Sectional models of steam engines.

(Several French machines exhibited here.)

MACHINES for DIRECT USE, including CARRIAGES, &c.

57 FITZ MAURICE, The Hon. W. E. Hamilton Lodge, Prince's Gate, Inv.—Patent rotatory steam-engine. A model steam-engine, illustrating a new method of converting rectilinear into rotatory motion, by the Rev. J. Booth. Patented. Constructed by J. Aspinall, 261 High Holborn.

58 WHITELAW, J. Johnstone, Renfrewshire, Scotland, Inv. — Models, &c. Centrifugal atmospheric churn and pump.

60 WILDING, W. H. 2 Chesterfield St. King's Cross, Inv.—Patent steam-engine, exhibiting a new method of converting reciprocating rectilinear motion into rotatory motion. Model of a patent submerged paddle-wheel.

61 LEIGH, E. Miles Platting, Manchester, Inv.—Patent steam-engine.

63 WILLIAMS, D Thornhill, Llandilo, Inv.—Furnace for burning anthracite coal.

64 DODDS & SON, Rotherham, Inv. and Manu.—Four-horse portable steam-engine, for thrashing, &c. Model of locomotive engine, without boiler, fitted with Dodds' patent wedge motion. Jessop's patent steeled tyre-bar and railway-bar. Model railway-bar straigthtening press, on truck.

65 SURMON & Co. New North Rd. Hoxton, Manu.— Jukes's patent smoke-consuming furnaces.

66 REDMOND, A. F. Birmingham, Imp. and Inv.— Working model of a steam-engine, with three kinds of side valves.

67 EBBW VALE Co. 83, Upper Thames St. and Abergavenny.—An improved double cylinder steam-engine, one horse-power. Inv. and des. by Evan William, a blind man.

68 CLAY, J. Edgeley, Stockport.—Smoke-consuming furnace.

69 WHITNEY, J. Calver Hill, Hereford.—Fusible metal plate for steam boilers.

70 CONSTABLE, W. 57 Marine Parade, Brighton, Inv.— Model of invention for converting into a uniform force the fluctuating force of reciprocating steam-engines. Prov. reg.

76 CRADDOCK, T. Ranelagh Works, Pimlico, Inv. and Manu.—Patent high-pressure, expansive, and condensing steam-engine, with tubular boiler and regulating damper.

78 FERGUSON, D. Kilkenny, Ireland, Inv.—Registered boat-propeller and water-wheel.

82 MORRELL, G. 149 Fleet St. Inv.—Rotatory engine.

88 JENKINS, G. 4 Nassau St. Soho, Inv. and Pat.— Hydro-pneumatic engine.

90 READ, S. K. 50 Paradise St. Rotherhithe, Inv. and Manu.—Domestic pump and fire-engine.

91 REED, J. H. Westbourne Lodge, Harrow Rd. Inv. —Model of a new patent propeller.

92 PHILLIPS, W. H. 16 York Ter. Camberwell New Rd. Inv. and Pat.—Patent portable fire annihilator.

92A FIRE ANNIHILATOR Co. 105 Leadenhall St.—Patent street engine.

94 HILL, W. Blackheath Rd. Greenwich, Inv. and Manu. — Improved flue-boiler and furnace, for hot-water apparatus. Registered.

96 SIMONS, W. V. South Shields. — Electro-magnetic machine.

97 RHONE, E. Cooper's Gardens, Hackney.—Model of revolving blade paddle-wheel.

98 SCOTT, M. 6 John Street, Adelphi.—Hydraulic machine.

100 ERSKINE, D. Clerk St. Edinburgh, Inv. and Manu. —New self-reversing and other beam engines, for planing machines. Silver locomotive and railway. Circulating steam-boiler, for lectures. New hydraulic locomotive. Horizontal water wheel.

101 WHYTEHEAD, W. K. Cornhill.—McNaught's steam-engine indicators; oil-testing machines, &c.

102 POTTS, J. Stockton-on-Tees, Manu. — Working model of a high-pressure steam-engine, with glass cylinder.

103 HODGES, B. J. Grove House Lodge, Outer Circle, Regent's Park.—Sectional model of a marine condensing steam-engine for the use of schools.

104 SHARP, W. D. Swindon, Wilts, Inv.—Steam-engine, with improved valves, valve-gear, &c.

105 BEVAN, H. Llanelly.—Plan of a locomotive steam carriage for common roads.

106 BECKETT, E. G. 3 Joynson St. Strangeways, Manchester, Manu.—High-pressure steam engine, suitable where small power is required.

108 WEBSTER, B. 5 Stracey St. Stepney, near Commercial Rd. East, Maker.—Model of oscillating engines of 300 horse-power, with eccentric paddle-wheels.

112 PERRY, H. Bromley Bow, Manu.—Model of a condensing engine and boiler.

113 SHAW, B. L. Newhouse, Huddersfield.—Model of Whitham's patent hydraulic engine.

116 LINTON, J. Selby, Yorkshire, Inv. and Manu.— Model of an improved engine, working high-pressure steam expansively.

118 FITT, W. Ponder's End, Des.—Model of convertible wind, water, or steam power, of improved construction.

119 FIRTH, T. & J. Elizabeth St. Belfast.—Registered hollow fire-bars.

122 HURRY, H. C. 81 King St. Manchester, Inv.— Model showing patent improvements in lubricating.

124 GALLOWAY, W. & J. Manchester, Manu.—Patent lifting jacks. Patent steam-engine boilers.

125 FLYNN, W. P. 16 Summer Hill South, Cork.—Improved paddle-wheel, combining the action of the screw with that of the wheel. Prov. reg.

126 TERRETT, R. 2 Homer St. Lambeth, Inv.—Improved feathering paddle-wheel, and feathering windmill.

127 VALLANCE, P. 1 Davies St. Berkeley Sq. — Horizontal windmill.

128 WILLISON, R. Alloa, Scotland.—Double lift and force pump.

129 Model copper boiler.

130 JUDGE, T. Hampstead, Inv. and Manu.—Cranks for steam-engines and turret clocks, gas-soot consumer, self-adjusting spirit level, &c.

131 BICKLE, W. 18 Reading St. Swindon, Des. and Manu.—Working model of a pair of non-condensing steam-engines, standing within the compass of a shilling, and weighing three drachms.

132 ECCLESHALL, T. 2 Gt. Ruston St. North, Birmingham, Inv.—Submarine propeller for steam vessels. Atmospheric propeller for navigation.

133 DAY, H. J. 80 Rahere St. Clerkenwell. — Small model of a pair of oscillating engines.

134 HEMMING, G. 44 Lucas St. Commercial Road East. —Two drawings of marine engines in perspective.

136 STEVENS, J. L. 3 Copthall Buildings, Inv.—Models of surface-propeller water-wheel, and omnibus ventilator. Prov. reg. Robinson's safety-plug for boats, &c. Reg.

138 RICHARDS, T. 2 Kidd St. Woolwich, Manu. and Des.—Model apparatus for connecting engines and paddle wheels. Models of propellers.

140 KEASLEY, W. H. 7 Smithfield Bars, Inv.—Archimedean screw for hand propulsion, creating no swell.

141 SMITH, G. 49 Lime St.—Improved method of feathering the float of paddle-wheels.

143 HODGSON, R. Ewell, near Epsom, Inv.—Patent parabolic submarine propeller, for steam-ships.

148 PATERSON, T. 15 Rupert St. Haymarket, Inv.— Model of a rotatory steam-engine. Prov. reg.

151 HAYCRAFT, W. T. Greenwich.—Model of the "anhydrous" steam-engine.

152 ELDER, D. Royal Adelaide Steamer, Leith.—Model of oscillating marine engine.

MACHINES for DIRECT USE, including

154 SCOTT, G. 22A Winchester St. City.—Boiler cleanser.

156 JONES, W. Tabernacle Sq. Finsbury.—Model of an improved paddle-wheel.

158 DEANE, C. A. 7 Henry St. Hampstead Rd.—Model of pedestal engine.

160 PYM, J. 52 Threadneedle St.—Model of a submerged paddle-wheel, to work wholly or partially under water.

162 COLEGRAVE, Round Hill House, Brighton, Inv.—A model of a patent equilibrium slide-valve and cylinder.

200 TUCK, J. H. 22 Pall Mall, Manu.—Pneumatic governor for regulating the speed of steam-engines. Lariviere's patent.

201 CARNELL & HOSKING, R. Perran Foundry, near Truro.—Treble-beat hydraulic valves and seats.

202 ASHBY, J. Croydon Common.—Screw friction-clutch.

204 LEES, T.—Water-gauge, alarm-valve, &c.

205 NEWCOMBE, T. East Lane, Walworth.—Models of a furnace for steam-engines, and a machine for rolling hides.

206 HASKETH, —. Redruth.—Lubricator.

208 GADD & BIRD, Manchester.—Expansive piston.

300 LLOYD, G. 70 Gt. Guildford St. Southwark, Inv. and Manu.—Centrifugal disc blowing-machine.

301 NAPIER, J. R. Vulcan Foundry, Glasgow.—Portable forge.

304 KENNEDY, M. 3 George St. Camden Town, Des. and Manu.—Improved blast-fan, for forges, furnaces, ventilating and fumigating.

305 WHEELER, E. Finsbury Circus.—Equilibrium slide valves.

400 DALY, J. Limerick.—Improved pump and bell.

401 MERRYWEATHER, M. 63 Long Acre, Manu.—Merryweather's powerful fire-engines. Garden engines. Leather hose. Firemen's helmets, tools, &c. Fire escapes, &c.

402 SHALDERS, W. jun. Bank Pl. Norwich, Des. and Manu.—Patent fountain pumps, engines, and hydraulic work.

403 STOTHERT, RAYNO, & PITT, Newark Foundry, Bath, Imp. and Manu.—Improved iron crane for a dock or wharf.

403A STOTHERT, H. Bath, Inv.—Model of a plan for removing the sewage of London without disturbing the present arrangement of drains.

404 FOX, HENDERSON, & Co.—Derrick crane and model. Proving press and patent pipes.

405 BERRIEDALE, LORD, 17 Hill St. Berkeley Sq.—A double acting fire-engine for private houses.

406 FOURDRINIER, E. N. 38 Barclay St. Sunderland, Inv.—Patent safety apparatus, for preventing loss of life and property when a rope or chain breaks in shafts of mines and collieries.

407 BEGG, W. G. 20 Market St. Edinburgh, Inv. and Manu.—Safety cages, for mine shafts, to prevent the loss of life and destruction of property in mine shafts, when the rope or chain snaps.

408 EASTON & AMOS, Grove, Southwark, Manu. &c.—Improved patent hydraulic ram.

409 BADDELEY, W. 29 Alfred St. Islington, Inv. and Manu.—Farmers' fire-engines and force-pumps.

410 SHAND & MASON (late TILLEY & Co.), 245 Blackfriars Rd. Manu.—Fire engines, fire pumps, garden engines, patent hose and suction pipes, fire cocks, series of jet pipes, &c. (North Transept.)

411 JAMES & Co. 24 Leadenhall St. Pat.—Crane for raising and weighing at one operation; and weighing machines.

412 The BANK QUAY FOUNDRY Co. Warrington, Manu.—Large hydraulic press, used in raising the Britannia tubular bridge.

413 HOWARD & RAVENHILL, Rotherhithe, Inv. Pat. and Manu.—Links for suspension bridge.

414 GOSSAGE, J. 71 Florence Rd. Deptford.—Improved portable engine-pump; designed for the use of ships.

415 GREATOREX, D. 8 Desborough Ter. Harrow Rd. Paddington, Inv. and Manu.—Hoisting machine.

416 BELLHOUSE, E. T. & Co. Eagle Foundry, Manchester, Inv.—Hydraulic press for packing cotton, &c. Fireproof hoist for mills and warehouses. Iron model cottage. Brick-pressing machine.

417 FAIRBAIRN, W. Manchester.—Wrought-iron tubular crane.

418 DEVON GT. CONSOL COPPER MINING Co.—Models of two water-wheels of 140 horse-power each, erected at the mines for pumping water.

420 APPOLD, J. G. 23 Wilson St. Finsbury, Inv.—Centrifugal pump for draining marshes for a tide pump, without valves.

421 BESSEMER, H. Baxter House, Old St. Pancras Road, Pat. and Manu.—Centrifugal disc pump for draining land, discharging 20 tons per minute. Patent pump for steam ships. Centrifugal disc pump for locomotive engines.

422 STOCKER, S. & G. 4 Arthur St. New Oxford St. Manu. and Pat.—Beer machines, counters, spirit tap, lift pumps, &c. Air-tight bottles, indestructible pewter pots.

423 SLACK, J. 46 Commercial Rd. Lambeth, Inv.—Polished slate cistern, with an improved patent rapid purifier, calculated to produce 3,000 gallons per day.

424 WARNER & SONS, 8 Crescent, Jewin St. Manu.—Overshot water-wheel, with three pumps. Horsewheel, double and treble barrel pumps. Patent standard iron lift and other improved pumps. Garden engine with reg. spreader. Fire-engine with folding handles.

425 CLARK, D. G. 12 London St. Greenwich, Inventor's Agent.—Water filter, with self-acting regulator or water-meter.

426 DEANE, J. Cross Wall, Dover.—Diving apparatus.

427 BYWATER, W. 99 Piccadilly.—Water meter.

428 TURNER, E. W. K. 31 Praed St. Paddington.—Model of an invention for improving the water supply.

429 BOTTEN, C. Crawford Passage, Ray St. Clerkenwell.—Appold's self-regulating friction break. Labour machine for prisons.

434 M'NICOLL & VERNON, Liverpool.—Patent steam travelling crane for railways, for loading and discharging the cargoes of vessels, &c. J. M'Nicoll, Inv. and Pat.

436 TEBAY, J. Aldine Chambers, Paternoster Row, Inv. and Manu.—Patent water-meter.

438 FELL, R. 33 Nicholas Lane, Inv.—Sea-water regenerator. Patent self-cleaning filter. New motive power, by compressed air, &c.

440 SIEBE, A. 5 Denmark St. Soho.—Improved self-pressure cock for steam-boilers.

444 FLETCHER, P. 161 Westgate St. Gloucester.—Improved slide-tap and apparatus for supplying fire-engines or jets with water, from street plugs.

445 SUMPTION, J. Ebury Sq. Pimlico.—Fire-plug and cock-box, on a new principle.

447 BROUGHTON, R. A. Park St. Brighouse.—Pump for supplying boilers.

448 CHEAVIN, S. Spalding, Inv.—Floating filtering pump. Specimens of metallic paste or cement, for preventing damp in walls, and keeping out wet.

449 SMITH, R. & SON, St. Mary Cray, Kent.—New high-pressure fire-engine. Model of a newly-invented double-motion pump, with transparent glass tubes, showing the moveable parts of the inside of the pump.

450 NEVILL, J. P. 8 Crutched Friars, Inv.—Machine for discharging loose cargo.

452 SELFE, H. Kingston, Surrey, Manu. and Inv.—Common pump with reserve-chamber. Model of a confla-

gration. Common pump on an improved principle; the syphon illustrated.

462 FREEMAN ROE, & HANSON, 70 Strand, Manu.—Hydraulic ram. Fountain basins of iron, for pleasure grounds. (North Transept.)

466 KEITH, 36 G. Piccadilly.—Liquid meter.

467 BEERE, G. Gallaway House, Bath, Manu.—Archimedean screw for raising fluids.

468 BILLINTON, W. C.E. 31 Regent St. Prop.—Patent improved water-meter.

471 BURGESS, D. Glasgow.—Hydrostatic press.

472 FIRTH, T. Huddersfield.—Hydrostatic press.

474 DOWNTON, J. 4 Conant Pl. Commercial Road, Limehouse.—Pump.

475 CLUNES, T. 100 Lock St. Aberdeen.—Pumps.

476 LITTLE, R. J. Major, Woolwich Common, Des.—Improved water or steam cock, for connecting pipes without breaking joints in its repair. Sectional drawings. Manufactured by Frost, Noakes, and Vincent, 195 Brick Lane, Whitechapel.

478 LAMBERT & SON, Short St. Lambeth.—Locomotive and steam fittings.

480 WIGHT, J. 95 Nelson St. Tradeston, Glasgow.—Model of catenary water-wheel.

482 COLLINGE & Co. 65 Bridge St. Lambeth.—Patent traversing screw lifting jacks.

484 ENGLAND, G. Hatcham, New Cross.—Traversing jack.

485 BAYMAN, H. Old Gravel Lane.—Lifting jacks.

486 HALEY, —. Frome St. Somerset.—Lifting jacks.

488 GLADSTONE, J. jun. & Co. Liverpool.—Lifting jacks.

490 THORNTON & SONS, Bradford St. Birmingham, Manu.—Patent couplings for railway waggons. Patent shaft carriage axles. Hydraulic lifting jack. Patent steam-engine piston. Improved crown-head lifting screw jack. Improved double bar wrench for locomotive purposes. Railway shovels, improved shapes.

501 GT. WESTERN RAILWAY Co.—Railway traversing frame and permanent way.

502 BROTHERHOOD, R. Chippenham.—Railway signal and stops, and patent tilt wagon.

503 BECKERS, G. E. Great Western Railway, Paddington.—Self-acting siding stop for railways.

506 GT. WESTERN RAILWAY Co.—Locomotive engine and tender, constructed at the Company's works at Swindon. One of the ordinary class of engines constructed by this Company for passenger-traffic, since 1847. [It is capable of taking a passenger-train, of 120 tons, at an average speed of 60 miles per hour, upon easy gradients. The evaporation of the boiler, when in full work, is equal to 1,000 horse-power, of 33,000 lbs. per horse—the effective power as measured by a dynamometer is equal to 743 horse-power. The weight of the engine, empty, is 31 tons; coke and water, 4 tons—engine, in working order, 35 tons. Tender empty, 9 tons; water, 1,000 gallons, 7 tons 3 cwt.; coke, 1 ton 10 cwt.—total 17 tons 13 cwt. The heating surfaces are, fire-box 156 feet; 305 tubes 1,759 feet. Diameter of cylinder, 18 inches; length of stroke, 24 inches; diameter of driving-wheel, 8 feet; maximum pressure of steam, 120 lbs. The actual consumption of fuel in practice, with an average load of 90 tons, and an average speed of 29 miles, including stoppages (ordinary mail train), has averaged 20·8 lbs. of coke per mile.]

507 LEE, J. 103 Long Acre, Inv. and Pat.—Patent breaks and axle-box, of improved construction.

508 CRAMPTON, T R. South Eastern Railway Co. 15 Buckingham St. Adelphi.—London and Paris express locomotive engine the "Folkstone," Crampton's patent. This engine is suspended on three points, and has a separate cranked axle.

509 ENGLAND, G. Hatcham Iron Works, New Cross, Inv. and Manu. — Improved locomotive engine for light traffic, and express trains.

510 ADAMS, W. B. 1 Adam St. Adelphi, Pat. and Des —Light locomotive engine on four wheels. Double railway carriage for first and second-class passengers. Patent spring, grease-tight axle-box, &c.

512 LONDON AND NORTH WESTERN RAILWAY COMP. C. Stewart, Sec. Euston Sq. London.—Express locomotive engine "Liverpool," Crampton's patent, 15 Buckingham St. Adelphi. [This engine contains 2,285 feet of heating surface, being 270 feet more than the largest engine on the broad gauge. Diameter of cylinder 18 inches, length of stroke 24 inches, diameter of driving wheels 8 feet. The weight of the engine empty (weighed in the Exhibition), is 32 tons; coke and water 4 tons; the evaporation of the boiler at full work is equal to 1,140 horses power; pressure of steam 120 lbs. on the square inch. The engine has a very low boiler, and the greatest weight is on the extreme wheels, which ensure steadiness.]

513 LONDON AND NORTH WESTERN RAILWAY COMP.—Narrow-gauge express engine, the "Cornwall," designed by Mr. Trevethick.

514 KNOX, G. Tottenhall, near Wolverhampton.—Railway break carriage.

522 FAIRBAIRN, W. Manchester. — Locomotive tank engine.

526 WILSON, E. B. & Co. Leeds, and 2 Poet's Corner, Westminster, Manu.—Locomotive double boiler tank engine, and screw moorings.

530 WILLIAMS, C. C. Glasshouse Yd. Goswell St. Inv. and Manu.—Railway carriage, made of East India Moulmein teak, unpainted.

532 HENSON, H. H. Pinner, near Watford, Inv.—Patent improved covered waggon, for the conveyance of merchandise by railway, fire and water proof.

534 KITSON, THOMPSON, & HEWITSON, Leeds, Manu.—Locomotive tank engine, length of stroke 22 in.; diameter of cylinder 11 in., of driving wheel 6 ft., of fore and hind wheels 3 ft. 8 in.

536 HAWTHORN, R. & W. Newcastle-upon-Tyne, Manu.—First-class patent passenger locomotive engine.

539 McCONNEL, I. E. Wolverton, Railway passenger carriage.

541 HADDAN, J. C. 29 Bloomsbury Sq. Inv.—Patent railway carriage, with papier-maché panels. Patent railway wheels, with wrought-iron naves.

543 PATENT SHAFT and AXLETREE Co. Brunswick Iron Works, Wednesbury, Birmingham, Manu.—Patent railway carriage and other axles, with illustrations of the processes of manufacture. Patent link for suspension bridges, rolled into form at one heat.

550 ROBERTS, J. C. Holywell, Wales.—Electric railway whistle.

552 DE BERGUE, C. 9 Dowgate Hill, Inv. and Manu.—Specimens of patent vulcanized India-rubber buffers for railway carriages. Patent station buffer.

554 SANDFORD, OWEN, & WATSON, Rotherham.—Railway wheels.

555 SPENCER, T. Tipton, Staffordshire, Manu.—Chambers' patent wrought-iron wheel.

556 LACY, H. C. M.P. Richmond.—Patent railway sleepers.

557 CRESTADORA, A. Manchester.—Patent impulsoria.

558 WARREN, P. Foley Fenton, Staffordshire Potteries. —Model of a driving-wheel for railway engines, devised to prevent slipping when going up inclines. Two pair of couplings for railway carriages. Model of an improved crane, weighing and lifting at the same time.

C

MACHINES for DIRECT USE, including

559 PIZZIE, W. Albourne Mills, Marlborough.—Railway break which can be instantly applied to every wheel in the train.

560 DILLON, J. 28 Upper Buckingham St. Dublin.—Railway break.

561 COOLEY, J. Spalding, Inv.—Railway signal.

562 PERRY, H. J. 3 Greenwich Road, Greenwich.—Railway model.

564 TENNANT, M. B. Trafalgar House, Brighton, Inv.—Brass models of five patent railway carriages linked together, with auxiliary safety-wheels, and traverse bolts and socket buffers. Model of permanent flat roofing.

566 MURRAY, W. 20 University St. Bedford Sq.—Railway couplings.

568 CLARKSON, T. C. 111 Strand.—Railway buffers.

570 SANDERSON, C. Baker St. Reading.—Instrument for setting out railway curves for sidings and crossings.

572 STEVENS, J. St. Leonard Station, Edinburgh.—Railway signal.

574 HEMMINGWAY, A. Halton, nr. Leeds, and 12 Denham St. Vauxhall, London.—Model locomotive.

576 CRIPPS, W. N. 352 Bell Barn Road, Birmingham.—Railway carriage model.

580 DODDS & SON, Rotherham.—Model locomotive.

581 FOURNESS, W. Leeds.—Railway whistle.

582 LOCKYER, J. H. Leicester.—Self-acting railway signal.

586 MACBAY, W. Royal Artillery Barracks, Woolwich.—Model railway carriage, with self-acting collision and atmospheric breaks. Model of London, with design for railways in the streets. Model of buildings, with self-acting fire extinguisher.

588 SNOWDEN, W. F. St. Thomas's St. Weymouth, and King's Cross, London.—Models of a new mode of assisting carriages up and down hills on railways and common roads.

591 PARSEY, A. 455 Oxford St. Inv. and Pat.—Compressed air-engine, for locomotive and stationary purposes.

600 YOUNG, C. & Co. Edinburgh, Inv. and Manu.—Simultaneously-acting level-crossing gates for railways. (N.B. These gates are placed outside the building, at the west end.)

601 BARLOW, P. W. Blackheath, Inv.—Model of cast-iron permanent way. Sleepers for points and crossings for railways.

602 BARLOW, W. H. Derby, Inv. and Pat.—Wrought iron permanent way for railways.

609 STEVENS & SON, Darlington Works, Southwark Bridge Rd. Manu. and Pat.—Model of railway junction semaphore signals and double station signal.

610 DE FONTAINE, M. P. A. 4 South St. Finsbury.—Vidie's patent railway warner.

614 HOBY, J. W. Renfrew, near Glasgow, Inv. and Manu.—Patent system of permanent way for railways, &c.

615 GREAVES, H. 4 Ordsall Ter. Manchester, Inv.—Iron surface-packed railway sleepers, with rails.

616 SAMUEL, J. C.E. 3 Duke St. Adelphi, Inv. and Pat.—Patent cast-iron timber-bedded wedge-trough permanent way for railways. Patent fish-chair, or improved joint-chair. Patent improved donkey-engine. Sectional model of double cylinder continuous expansion steam-engine.

618 DUNN, T. Windsor Bridge, near Manchester, Inv. and Manu.—Apparatus for removing carriages from one set of rails to another. Traversing machine, &c. Drawings of machinery, &c. Dunn's patent letter-copying press.

624 ORMEROD, R. & SON, St. George's Foundry, Manchester, Pat. and Manu.—Patent traversing machine. Dunn's patent turn-table.

628 CUBITT, J. Great George St.—Permanent way of the Great Northern Railway, with Ransomes and May's patent chairs, tree-nails, and wedges.

636 THORNEYCROFT, G. B. & Co. Wolverhampton, Inv. and Manu.—Specimens of Brigg's patent compound railway axle. Patent axle. Patent charcoal tire for railway wheels and patent charcoal rails.

637 WORSDELL, G. & Co. Warrington, Manu.—Railway axle-forge, hammered, showing process of manufacture; bent cold, and having borne a pressure of 84 tons. Railway wheel-tire. Patent railway axle-box.

638 EBBW VALE Co., 83 Upper Thames St. London and Abergavenny.—Section of every description of railway bars used on different railways.

639 POTIER, W. 33 Green St. Wellington St. Blackfriars.—Gut wheel-bands.

640 RANSOMES & MAY, Ipswich, Manu.—Barlow and Heald's railway turn-table. Wild's railway turn-table and switch. Barlow's iron-sleeper. Registered water-crane. Patent compressed treenails and wedges for railways. Patent compressed ship treenails. Leggatt's Queen press, with self-inking apparatus. Chilled cast-iron pedestal, or axle bearing.

641 COALBROOK DALE Co. Shropshire.—Square, round, flat, half-round, oval, bar iron; angle T and girder iron; sash bar and moulding iron, tire iron, engine floor and foot plate iron.

642 PARSONS, P. M. C.E. 6 Duke St. Adelphi, Des. and Pat.—Patent switches and crossing for railways. Normanville's patent axle-box. Patent machine for dressing millstones.

643 BAINES, W. Birmingham, Inv.—An improved railway-switch. Improved joint and intermediate chairs.

644 KENNARD, R. W. Falkirk Iron Works, Scotland, and 67 Upper Thames St. London, Manu. — Various switches.

645 BIDDULPH, J. Cwm Avon Works, Tailbach, South Wales —Large and small flanch rails.

646 BEECROFT, BUTLER, & Co. Leeds.—Entire wrought-iron railway wheels, with solid wrought-iron bosses, forged in one piece, tyres and axles bent cold. Imp. pat. axletrees reg. imp. moveable eccentric tumbler, &c.

647 DERWENT IRON Co. Newcastle-on-Tyne.—Specimens of rolled iron plates used in the construction of marine engines and the building of iron ships, 17 feet to 20 feet long. Rolled keel iron, a railway bar, measuring 66 feet 9 inches in length.

648 RICHARDSON, J. 9 Woburn Buildings, Tavistock Sq.—Table of weights of wrought iron.

649 MERSEY IRON Co. Liverpool.—Samples of patent rolled iron.

650 LEADBETTER, J. G. Gordan St. Glasgow.—Patent canal-lift, or hydro-pneumatic elevator; a substitute for canal-locks, slip-docks, &c. Railway turn-table, or weighing-machine. Swivel-bridge elevator, &c.

651 RICHARDSON, R. 39 Moorgate St. Inv. and Pat.—Patent fish-joint for rails. Iron fishing pieces.

652 GOMPERTZ, L. Kennington Oval, Inv.—Railway trains constructed to prevent collision. Square carriage wheels, termed *scrapers*, to advance by steps and without jolting.

654 CUNNINGHAM & CARTER, Addison Rd. Kensington and Sydenham, Inv. and Pat —Model of a new atmospheric railway and carriages.

655 HARLOW & YOUNG, Paradise St. Rotherhithe, Inv. and Pat.—Patent atmospheric railway, with metal valves and discs.

656 JONES, T. M. Southampton Chambers, 53 Chancery Lane, Inv.—Model of a railway train and breaks, showing an invention for stopping trains quickly and safely; also for connecting and steadying the carriages.

659 CRUTWELL & Co. Newport.—Permanent way.

660 BOYDELL, J. 54 Threadneedle St. Inv. and Manu.—Mode of facilitating the draught of heavily-laden carriages.

661 STANTON, R. 73 Shoe Lane, Inv. and Manu.—Electro-magnetic engine. Locomotive steam-engine.

662 LONG, C. A. 1 King St. Portman Sq. Inv.—Railway signal, worked by the agency of electricity; intended to obviate the danger of one train overtaking another.

666 BANKS & CHAMBERS, German St. Manchester, Manu.—Railway carriage wheel, upon Banks' patent principle of inserting steel segments in that part of the tire which is most exposed to friction.

668 COPLING, J. jun. The Grove, Hackney, Inv.—Railway signal, for instant communication between the guards, passengers, and engine-driver.

670 LIPSCOMBE, F. 233 Strand, Inv. and Pat.—A contrivance for preventing vibration in an iron railway wheel, and thus causing it to run without noise. Portable fountains, for drawing-room tables, conservatories, &c.

672 EASTWOOD & FROST, Morledge Iron Works, Derby, Manu.—Iron wheels, and rolled and bar iron from which they are made.

674 DICKER, J. 2 Clarence Ter. Rotherfield St. Islington, Inv.—Apparatus for transferring mail-bags, &c. on railways.

681 TABOR, J. A. Colchester, Inv.—Improved application of the whistle to locomotive engines, and proposed application thereof to steam-boats.

682 JACKSON, P. R. Salford Rolling Mills, Manchester, Manu.—Locomotive and carriage tires. Spur-wheel, moulded by a patent machine. Registered stench-trap, easy to clean out. Model of a powerful hydraulic press, which will lift upwards of 3,000 tons. Patented.

684 CHABOT, C. 9A Skinner St. Snow Hill, Improver.—Models of three railway carriages, with rotatory and self-acting break. Locked buffers. An economical spring, &c.

686 McNAUGHT, W. 26 Robertson St. Glasgow.—Montgomery's self-acting railway-break.

690 HANDLEY, W. 26 Gt. Earl St. Seven Dials, Inv.—Patent break for railway trains.

691 CHESSHIRE, E. Birmingham, Inv.—Model of an invention for lessening the danger of collisions on railways.

692 HARVEY, W. 3 Cumming Pl. Pentonville Hill.—A locomotive, with patent safety machine.

693 WALKER, W. Shrewsbury, Inv.—Railway-break.

694 GRAY, G. 42 Woodcock St. Birmingham.—Improved railway-break and signal vans. Improved composite rail-block breaks. Prov. reg.

697 WILSON, C. Leeds—Model of locomotive.

698 GREENWAY, C. Southport, Inv.—Patent turn-table for railways. Patent anti-friction axle. Patent castor, for furniture.

699 COWPER, E. A. 9 Kensington Park Rd. Notting Hill, Inv.—Detonating fog and accident signal for railways.

700 LESTER, T. 15 Ure Place, Glasgow.—Elevation of an outside cylinder passenger tank engine and first-class carriage, for the Glasgow, Paisley, and Greenock Railway.

701 HATTERSLEY, W. 107 St. George's St, St. George's East, Inv.—Passengers' signal for railway and other carriages, for ready communication with drivers, guards, &c.

702 ELLIOTT, T. Stockton-on-Tees.—Model of a rotatory locomotive.

703 JACKSON, J. 5 Victoria Grove, Bayswater, Inv.—Model of a railroad with stationary engine for propelling carriages by compressed air.

704 GREEN, W. 28 Frederick St. Hampstead Rd. Manu.—First-class railway carriage, showing the framing complete.

705 STOY, H. Ann St. York Rd. Lambeth.—Railway break.

706 SQUIRE, J. & Co. 5 Barge Yd. City, Manu.—Dewrance's patent metal: Locomotive axle and connecting rod. Shaft bearings. Carriage-axle bearings, &c. Carriage-axle bearings, crank-shaft bearings, &c. of Babbitt's patent metal. Meads' patent gas-meter. Model of steam-engine and sugar-mill. Sample of patent metal machinery for cotton weft.

707 TIDMARSH, R. 3 Jamaica Row, Bermondsey, Manu.—Torrop's patent railway and steam-boat time signal.

708 MELLING, R. jun. 5 Coupland St. Green Heys, Manu.—Model of a royal state railway carriage, broad gauge, with promenade round the outside.

709 PEARCE, T. B. 93 Newman St. Oxford St.—A railway revolving fog signal light.

710 HOY, J. 6 Pickering Pl. Paddington, Inv. and Manu.—Railway signal, for day and night.

711 ALLAN, A. Crewe, Cheshire, Inv.—Model of hydrostatic or floating turn-table for railways. Model of improved crane.

712 WATSON, T. 79 Provost St. City Rd. Inv.—A day or night signal for railways, &c.

713 WHARTON, W. Euston Station, Inv.—Wharton's patent railway wheel.

714 HINITT, J. 22 Vauxhall Row, Vauxhall, Inv.—Working model of a locomotive.

715 MANSELL, R. C. Ashford, Kent, Inv.—Safety wheel for railway purposes, having its tire so secured that, in the event of a breakage, no part can leave the wheel; manufactured by Fox and Henderson, Birmingham, and others.

716 ANGUS, F. J. 21 King St. Bath St. City Rd. Inv.—Railway-accident detector; applicable also to buildings. Model life-boat.

726 FAURE, T. 2 Little Argyll St. Regent St. Inv.—Snow-sweeping engine for railways and common roads.

728 SHAW, J. & Co. 91 Paddock, near Huddersfield, Inv.—Patent signals and points or switches on railways.

732 FAIRBAIRN, W. Manchester.—Model locomotive.

739 ASHBURY, —.—Model railway truck.

750 WATTS, T. 3 Pelham Pl. Inv.—Model of a suspension bridge for a railway between England and France.

752 BARBER-BEAUMONT, G. D. Twickenham, Inv.—Patent locomotive machinery, for working up or down steep inclines from or to wharfs, &c. This model only shows the principle of bite for steep inclines; the same principle with different construction of leverage is adapted to common roads, and has been worked by locomotive steam engines.

753 BURSILL, G. H. 9 York Ter. Queen's Rd. Hornsey Rd. Holloway, Manu.—Improved pressure guage.

754 GUNN, J. 3 Ebenezer Ter. Turner St. London Hospital, Inv.—Machine to be propelled by hand-power.

756 BOWLER, J. Birmingham, Inv.—Model of a carriage to run on the rim of the wheels instead of the axle. The propelling wheel does not touch the rail or road.

758 DRURY, F. 26 Albert Ter. Barnsbury Rd. Inv. Des. and Manu.—First model of a church bell forged from one ingot of cast steel. Reg.

764 MORRIS, W. 2 Priory Pl. Dover, Inv.—Model of a self-acting machine for weighing and discharging, indicating, computing, and registering.

765 SLIGHT, J. 35 Leith-Walk, Edinburgh, Manu.—Model of Henderson's Derrick crane.

766 CADELL, H. Thorneybank, Dalkeith.—Weighing-machine.

770 NICHOLL & Co. 16 Aldersgate St. Manu.—Scale-beams, weighing-machines, Excheq. standard scales, weights, and measures, &c.

771 OLLIFFE, C. R. Ramsgate, Inv.—Private secretary, or fraud preventor, for indicating the number of people entering a public vehicle, or exhibition room.

772 DAY & MILLWARD, 118 Suffolk St. Birmingham,

MACHINES for DIRECT USE, including

Manu. and Inv.—Patent weighing-machines. Druggist's scale for counter, fishing reels, &c.

774 DAVIDSON, J. & Co. Barony St. Edinburgh, Inv. and Manu.—Steelyards or weighing-machines, the under levers, beams, &c. made of malleable iron, with welded steel centres, the bearers lined with welded steel, &c.

775 RICHMOND, J. Bow, Middlesex, Inv. and Manu.—Improved engine counter, applicable also to turnstiles for bridges, &c.

776 CRAIG, J. 51 Cornwallis St. Liverpool, Des. and Manu.—Portable weighing-machine. Cotton sack, or bale weighing-machine. Library weighing and measuring-machine. Chimney-arch and smoke damper, to prevent chimneys smoking.

777 YATES, W. Bromley, near Bow, Middlesex, Inv.—An indicator, for registering and detecting change of speed of steam-engines or machinery.

778 GOODFELLOW, J. 4 James St. West, Devonport, Inv. —Gauge for showing the height of water in steam boilers, in which talc is substituted for glass.|

779 HOWE, G. 119 Gt. Guildford St. Southwark, Inv. and Manu.—Water gauge for steam boilers.

780 MEDHURST, T. 465 Oxford St. Manu.—Improved portable compound lever weighing-machine.

782 DONBAVAND, W. 95 Gt. Ancoat St. Manchester, Manu.—Bright steel box and scale beam, mounted upon a brass pillar.

784 POOLEY, H. Liverpool, Inv. and Manu.—Patent locomotive engine weighing tables, with drawings, &c. Drawing of a patent engine, for weighing canal boats and their cargoes, &c. Drawings, in plan and detail, of the first large establishment in England, of baths and wash-houses for the poor, erected by the Corporation of Liverpool, 1845-6. Architect, Joseph Franklin; Engineer, Henry Pooley.

801 ANDERSON, J. Elgin, Scotland, Inv. and Manu.—Victoria car, made with light springs, high wheels, and low seats, to avoid danger from accidents.

802 ANDREWS, R. Southampton, Manu.—Light outside car, with imitation caning, on a new principle.

803 ANDREWS, J. 42 Great Brunswick St. Dublin.—Irish car.

804 BASKCOMB, G. H. Chislehurst, Des. — Model carriage, with four wheels: indicates the distance of ground it travels over. Model curricle, or single horse dog-cart. Improved registered dog-cart.

805 BISHOP, J. 343 Strand, Inv.—Model of improved public conveyance.

806 BLACK, H. & Co. 1 Berners St. Manu.—A spheroid-back Brougham.

807 PARSONS, —. Islington.—Model omnibus.

808 CABLE, G.—Model of coach.

809 BOOKER, E. & SONS, 13 & 14 Mount St. Grosvenor Sq. Des. and Manu.—Improved "sociable," forming an open or close carriage at pleasure.

810 WHEATLEY, J. Greenwich.—Model of omnibus.

811 BRIGGS, G. & Co. 45 Wigmore St. Cavendish Sq. Des. and Manu.—Town-travelling chariot and mail phaeton.

812 BROWN, MARSHALL, & Co. Birmingham, Manu.—Improved safety cab, Aiken's patent iron suspension wheels. New light cab phaeton. Aiken's patent cart wheel, with part of axle.

813 BROWN, OWEN, & Co. Lichfield St. Birmingham.—Park phaeton of light construction.

814 BROWNE, W. 39 Grafton St. Dublin, Inv.—Irish jaunting cars, common and improved.

815 COATES & BLIZARD, Park Lane.—A Brougham.

816 COOK, ROWLEY, & Co. King St. Regent's St. Manu.—Patent Brougham, and patent park phaeton, with inverted double C springs, &c. Models of a patent cabriolet to carry

five persons, and of an omnibus divided into compartments, invented by J. A. Franklinski.

817 COLLINGE & Co. Bridge Rd. Lambeth.—Patent axletrees.

818 CORBEN & SONS, 30 and 31 Gt. Queen St. Lincoln's Inn, Manu.—Registered carriage.

819 CHAND & MUNRO, Bristol.—A Cobourg conveyance.

820 COUSINS & SON, Oxford, Inv. and Manu.—Light two-wheeled sporting carriage, adapted to carry two or four persons.

824 CROALL, W. jun. & Co. Greenside Pl. Edinburgh, Des. and Builders.—Oriental demi-cabriolet, hung on a new principle.

826 CROSSKILL, E. Vauxhall Wheel Works, Liverpool.—Improved patent wheels. Liverpool town float, lorrie, and coal cart. Specimen of a sporting cart, mounted upon Crosskill's new patent wheels and axles, with model horse, handsome harness, lamps, &c., by Messrs. Puckering and Houlgate, Beverley. (See also Class 9.)

828 DAVIES, D. 15 Wigmore St. Inv. — Basterna Brougham and other improved carriages. Model of improved patent railway-carriage break. New single wheel revolving carriage, &c. Patented. Carriage, with automatic steps, &c. New carriage with dome roof. Basterna Brougham, light summer carriage, for hot climates, with patent canopy, &c. Improved railway-carriage break, &c.

830 DAWSON, F. W. 19 York St. North Polygon, Bath, Inv. and Manu.—Newly-invented wheel chair for the use of invalids, and pedemotive, or self-propelling carriage.

842 DRABBLE & Co. 8 Pancras Lane, Inv. and Manu.—Patent conical arms and axletrees.

843 FOWLER & FRY, Bristol.—Dog-cart.

844 DUFFIELD, J. E. & Co. 114 Aldersgate St. Manu.—Highly-finished light phaeton and harness. Best quilted Somerset saddle and Weymouth bridle.

845 FULLER, G. & T. Bath, Manu.—Landau carriage, with improvements.

846 GEARY, S. 19 Euston Pl. Euston Sq. Inv.—Model of a patent street-watering cart, with fire-engine combined.

848 GIBSON, T. 8 and 9 Weaman St. Birmingham, Manu.—Railway bearing-spring. Registered elliptic spring with India-rubber bearings. Grasshopper spring with scroll irons. Elliptic spring. Patent mail and Collinge's axletree. Coach ironmongery.

849 DART & SON, 12 Bedford St. Covent Garden.—Laces for linings of carriages.

856 GREVILLE, J. 36 Mary St. Dublin, Manu.—Irish jaunting car.

858 GRISDALE, J. E. 289 Strand, Inv.—Working model of spring carriage wheel.

860 HADLEY. J. London Rd. Worcester, Inv. and Manu. —Basterna Clarence and Brougham, with furniture of Worcester china.

862 HALLMARKE, ALDEBERT, & HALLMARKE 57 and 58 Long Acre, Inv. and Manu.—Underspring step-piece barouche. New park phaeton. Drawings of a state carriage, Demi-state carriage. State railway carriage, &c.

864 HARDING, W. & Co. 68 Long Acre, Des. and Manu. —Specimens of carriage laces, linings, and carpets, showing the progressive improvements in their manufacture; also of tassels, bullions, fringes, and other upholstery ornaments.

868 HEATH, J. 4 Broad St. Bath, Inv. and Manu.—Light open park wheel chair, with glass panels, &c. Newly-invented reclining and elevating spinal bed wheel chair, &c.

872 HOLMES, HERBERT, & ARTHUR, Derby, Manu.—Light park phaeton. Dog-cart, or sporting buggy. Set of buggy harness. Winter shoes for horses. Drawings of modern carriage.

874 HOOPER, G. 28 Haymarket, Inv. Des. and Manu.—Improved Brougham carriage. Improved barouche landau.

Designs of new and improved forms of carriages, chiefly prov. reg. Working model of a Brougham carriage, by W. Hooper, jun.

880 HORNE, W. 93 Long Acre.—A patent segmental Brougham of improved construction. A patent segmental chariot, with all the improvements of the patent Brougham.

882 HUTTLY, F. 10 Lamb's Conduit. St. Manu.—Coach lace patterns, silk vellum, cut on terry lace, drawn on terry, and relief, cut on terry. Figured silk-ground lace. Reg. des.

884 HUTTON & SONS, Summerhill, Dublin.—Improved carriages, including a clarence, brougham, park phæton, &c.

888 JORDAN, W. H. Cumberland Basin, Clifton, near Bristol, Des. and Manu.—Invalid three-wheel chairs.

892 KENT, R. Saffron Walden, Essex, Des. and Manu.—Carriage with low body, forming an invalid's pony chaise.

894 KESTERTON, E. 80 Long Acre, Des. and Manu.—Carriage of novel design for summer and winter.

895 KINDER & WHEELER, Granby Pl. Leicester, Des. and Inv.—An Albert phaeton either for one or a pair of ponies, with an improved fore-carriage.

896 KINGS, W. 101 Long Acre, Des. and Manu.—Cabriolet domestique.

898 KINROSS W. & Co. Stirling, Scotland, Manu.—City omnibus, to carry nineteen passengers inside, with abundant ventilation, &c.

902 LEWIS, C. B. 14 King Street, St. James', Inv.—Omnibus improvement.

908 MARKS, J. I. Langham Pl. Cavendish Sq. Manu.—Noiseless wheels. Inv. and Pat. R. W. Thomson.

910 MASON, W. H. Kingsland Rd.—Pony carriage.

912 MENZIES, A. Glasgow, Prop.—Model of an omnibus, with three horses abreast.

913 RAWORTH, B. P. Sheffield.—Carriage axles, &c.

914–916 MIDDLETON, W. & C. 40 Long Acre, Manu. and Inv.—Improved convenable carriage. Centripetal plate.

918 MITCHELL, Rev. G. (LL.D) Whitburn, Linlithgow-shire, Inv.—Model of a safety carriage, which can be stopped from the inside; described in fifty different languages.

919 MITCHELL, Rev. W. A. M. Woolwich.—Model of railway engine, carriages, &c., with plan to prevent accidents.

922 MULLINER, F. Northampton, Manu. and part Inv — Improved pilentum, suspended on elliptic springs and patent axletrees.

924 MULLINER, H. Leamington Spa. Manu.—Four-wheeled carriage, commonly called a Brougham. Drawings of an improved curricle, dog-carts, Buchan sociables, &c.

926 NEWHAM, J. Market Harborough, Leicestershire, Manu.—Pony carriage, of an entirely new description.

928 NEWNHAM, B. 19 Broad St. Bath, Manu.—Bath wheel chair.

932 NURSE & Co. 43 Crawford St. and 200 Regent St. Inv. and Manu.—Curricle and cabriolet Brougham, for one or two horses.

934 OFFORD, R. 79 Wells St. Oxford St. Inv. and Manu.—Four-wheel carriage. A new carriage.

936 PATERNOSTER, T. 13 Charlotte St. Fitzroy Sq. Des. and Manu.—Lace, in thread, worsted, and silk, for carriages.

938 PETERS & SONS, Park St. Grosvenor Sq. Manu.—Light park barouche, with lee and under springs.

940 QUAN & SONS, 10 Talbot St. Dublin.—Improved Irish jaunting cars.

948 HARVEY, J. 41 Bridge Rd. Lambeth, Des. and Pat.—The patent Richmond car.

950 ROBINSON & Co. 12 Mount St. Grosvenor Sq. Des. Inv. and Manu.—Britannia phaeton of new design, with registered lock or wheel-plate, &c.

952 ROCK, J. jun. Hastings, Sussex, Inv. and Manu.—Improved carriage-spring, with a testing machine.

954 ROCK & GOWAR, Hastings.—Omnibus for the conveyance of passengers, of novel construction. Patented.

956 ROCK & SON, Hastings, Inv. Des. and Manu.—Patent dioropha, combining a Clarence or pilentum coach, a barouche, and an open carriage. Patent pony carriage.

958 SAUNDERS, C. New Yard, Gt. Queen St. Inv.—Double lever wheel-plate, to shorten the carriage. Improved brougham.

960 SAWYER, W. St. James's St. Dover, Inv. and Manu.—A velocipede.

962 SHANKS, R. H. 4 Gt. Queen St. Manu.—Step-piece landau, on elliptic springs.

964 SHILLIBEER, G. 1 and 2 Commercial Pl. City Rd. Inv. Pat. and Manu.—Patent expanding funeral carriage.

965 CLARKE & WILLIAMS, 447 West Strand.—Spring propeller.

966 SHILTON, T. Baddersley Ensor, near Atherstone, Inv. and Manu.—Wheel of improved construction of spoke, giving elasticity and ease in the motion of the carriage, &c.

968 SILK & BROWN, 8 Long Acre, Des. and Manu.—Barouche, hung upon improved horizontal springs. A highly-finished carriage; hung upon a swan-neck perch, lee and under-springs.

970 HILL & STONE, 21 Little Moorfields, Inv.—A park phaeton, with adjusting head.

971 SHUFF, W. 1 Dover St. Islington.—Carriage retarder.

972 SMITH, O. H. Pimlico Wheel Works, Upper Belgrave Pl. Prop.—Wheels for gun carriages, &c. (wood), made by machinery, inv. by Youngs Parfrey.

978 THOMSON, G. Stirling, Scotland, Manu.—Four-seated gig, not liable to duty.

979 THORN, W. & F. 10 John St. Oxford St. Inv. and Manu.—Brougham, æquimotive springs, invisible step, &c.

982 THRUPP, C. J. 269 Oxford St. Des. and Manu.—Landaulet Brougham and shamrock car.

984 TILBURY, J. 35 Gloucester Pl. New Rd. Manu.—Light sporting phæton, with patent noiseless wheels.

988 VEZEY, R. & E. Long Acre, Bath, Inv. and Manu.—Newly-designed sovereign sociable, with registered springs and axles, and India-rubber bearings.

989 WALKERS & GILDER, 16 White Lion St. Norton Folgate, Inv. and Manu.—Registered single Brougham carriage, with additional front. Improved lamp-irons. Prepared rubber round-robins to hind springs.

990 WARD, J. 41 Paris St. Exeter, Manu.—A cab park-phaeton, with leather robbins and Collinge's axles.

991 WATTS, C. Parkhurst, Isle of Wight, Inv. and Manu. —Velocipede, consisting of three wheels.

992 WILLOUGHBY, J. 1 John St. Oxford St.—Invalid bed carriage.

993 FULJAMES & Co. 4 Brownlow Mews, Gray's Inn Rd.—A carriage jack.

995 WILSON, J. 26 Portland St. Walworth, Des.—Improved velocipede, constructed principally of iron.

996 WYBURN, MELLER, & TURNER, 121 Long acre, Manu.—Dress chariot.

997 WARD, J. 5 and 6 Leicester Sq. Des. and Manu.—Four-wheeled pleasure-ground Victoria chair, lined wit satin, des. and woven by Draper, Holborn. Recumbent and portable folding chairs, for invalids.

998 DUNN, J. Rainton Colliery, Durham.—Model of a railway for reversing engine without turn-table. (South-East corner, in the United States department.)

999 THE EARL OF DURHAM.—Improved coal drop (with the above).

1000 TUNSTALL & WILLIAMS, Bath.—Self-acting invalid chair.

Proceed to Class 6, next page.

Class 6. MANUFACTURING MACHINES AND TOOLS.

—— Areas A. B. 10 to 31; C. D. E. 1 to 10, & 19 to 33: G. H. 25, 26. ——

1 HIBBERT, PLATT & SONS, Hartford Works, Oldham, Inv. and Manu.—An extensive series of improved machines for the manufacture of cotton. Machines used for opening and cleaning cotton. Machinery used in the manufacture of cotton yarn. Patent looms for weaving cotton cloth, worked by J. Whittaker & Sons, Hurst, near Ashton-under-Lyne. The steam engine, mill gearing, and framing are made and exhibited by Hick & Son, Bolton.

2 BOOTH & Co. Preston, Lancashire, Manu.—Mule spindles, for spinning cotton and silk. Throstle spindle and fly, for cotton, silk, flax, or worsted. Roving spindle and fly, with Iver's patent spring, &c.

3 CRABTREE, T. Godley, near Halifax, Manu.—Card-setting machine for producing the complete card from the wire and leather, or cloth, in operation by Messrs. Sykes and Brothers, of Lindley, near Huddersfield.

4 DALTON, J. Mottram-in-Longendale, Inv.—Machine for printing calicoes, de laines, and other textile fabrics; to print, by one process, patterns on each side.

5 PRESTON, F. Manchester, Manu. — Spindles and flyers used in preparing, spinning, and doubling cotton, silk, worsted, woollen, and flax.

(Several American machines exhibited here.)

6 PARR, CURTIS, & MADELEY, Manchester, Manu. and Pat. — Carding engine. Drawing frame. Slubbing and roving frame. Patent self-acting mules. Planing machine for metals. General shaping machine. Slide and screw-cutting lathe. Drilling machine.

7 LEACH, T. Rochdale.—Doffing and cleaning plates, and springs for cotton and wool machinery. Springs and under clearers for throstles and mules.

8 WILD, W. 26 Broughton Rd. Salford.—A cask made by machinery.

10 MASON, J. Rochdale, near Manchester, joint Inv. and Manu.—Hand-mule. Slubbing frame. Roving frame. Patent power-loom, lathe chucks.

14 HIGGINS & SONS, King St. Salford, Manu. and part Inv.—Cotton machinery: patent roving frame, and double self-acting radial mule. Long-line flax machinery: drawing, roving, and spinning frame.

15 SHARP BROTHERS, Manchester.—Danforth-throstle, for spinning.

16 MATHER, W. & C. Salford Iron Works, Manu.—Calico-printing machine, for printing eight colours at one operation, with drying apparatus. Sewing machine, and patent pistons.

17 SAXON, A. Manchester.—Metallic bobbins.

18 HARRISON, J. Bank Foundry, Blackburn, Manu.—Power-loom adapted for fabrics of light materials, in cotton, wool, and flax. Power-loom, adapted for heavy and tweeled goods. Power-loom, made fifty or sixty years ago.

19 GIBSON & Co. Glasgow.—Case of shuttles.

20 HORNBY & KENWORTHY, Blackburn, Inv. and Manu. —Patent sizing or dressing machine, with a peculiar arrangement for laying out the yarn, &c. Model of patent warping-machine, with a self-acting backing-off motion.

21 BULLOUGH, J. Blackburn, Inv. and Manu.—Model of patent power loom, which stops the motion when the weft thread breaks.

22 SMITH, M. Heywood, near Manchester, Inv. and Manu.—Loom for weaving naval canvas, Dutch and Venetian carpets, &c. Loom for weaving strong fustians, &c. Loom for weaving plaids, &c. Loom for weaving silks.

23 TAYLOR & SON, Halifax.—Jacquard loom.

24 MACINDOE, G. P. George Sq. Glasgow.—Spinning mule.

25 M'NAUGHT, W. Robertson St. Glasgow.—Coat's patent bobbin making machine. Patented.

27 CALVERT, F. A. 32 Cannon St. Manchester, Inv. and Pat.—Patent machines for wool-burring and cotton-cleaning, &c. Patent method of constructing burring and carding cylinders.

28 PATERSON, T. L. Glasgow, Inv. and Pat.—Model of a patent machine for winding yarn from the hank, upon the shuttlecope or pern.

29 JORDAN, W. 43 Hilton St. Manchester.—Warping creel and heck.

30 DE FONTAINE MOREAU, 4 South St. Finsbury.—Novel apparatus for the working of spindles without straps or cords, &c. Patented. Apparatus for dispensing with cards in the Jacquard machine. Patented.

32 CHALMERS, D. Manchester Wire Works, Inv. — New damask power-loom. Railway-break, calculated to prevent collision, and to act without shock.

35 CRICHTON, D. 165 Bradford Rd. Manchester, Inv.—Model loom, exhibiting a new principle of mechanical action on the yarn and cloth rollers, &c.

36 CRICHTON & Co. Great Bridgewater St. Manchester. —Cotton-opener, on Hardacre's patent principle. Drawing of double-beater lap machine, with fan.

37 NIMMO & SON, 211 Cowgate, Edinburgh, Manu.—Spinning-wheel, for fine flax. A check reel, standard measure of Scotland. A model wheel, for producing fine yarn or twisted thread.

38 MILLIGAN, W. Bradford, Yorkshire, Inv.—Power-loom made by Hodgson and Haley, to show the taking-up motion. Patented.

39 M'KENZIE, D. 52 Burton St. Tavistock Sq. — A reader for the Jacquard loom and frames, &c.

40 DONISTHORPE, G. E. Leeds, Inv. — Double wool-combing machine.

41 BARLOW, C. 89 Chancery Lane, Imp.—Patent sewing machine, with two threads.·

42 SUTCLIFFE, R. Idle, near Bradford, Inv. —Patent spinning frame, for spinning and doubling cotton, &c.

43 HENNING, J. Cambray House, Waringstown, County Down, Ireland.—Cambric loom. Damask loom. Machine for weaving damask or other figured fabrics on the Jacquard principle.

44 SANDEMAN, H. Tulloch Bleachfield, Perth, Manu.—Machine for stretching cloth after it has shrunk in the processes of bleaching, scouring, dyeing, printing, &c.

45 DE BERGUE, C. 9 Dowgate Hill, Inv. and Manu.—Specimens of dents, and reeds or combs, complete, for weaving every description of fabrics, manufactured by patent machinery.

46 MASON, J. Rochdale.—Two carding machines, mule loom grinding-frame, vice; the patent driving bands made by J. H. Whitehead, Saddleworth.

47 MARSLAND & Co. Blackfriars, Manchester.— Cotton winding machine.

48 BERRY, B. & SONS, Bowling, near Bradford.—Machinery for the manufacture of worsted yarns, exhibited in operation.

49 HUNT, E. Nailsworth, Inv. and Manu.—A gig-mill on an improved principle, for dressing cloth; finishing with teasles, without removing the cloth from the machine.

50 ELLIOTT & HEYS, 93 Mill St. Manchester, Inv. and Pat.—Improved loom.

51 TAYLOR, J. Victoria Rd. Leeds.—Heckles.

52 JUDKINS, C. T. Manchester, Pat.—Patent heald machine, for producing healds or weavers' harness, &c. Sewing machine, capable of sewing 500 stitches per minute. Patent self-acting machine, for closing metals upon the eyes or loops of heald.

53 PLENTY, J. & E. P. Newbury, Berks. Inv. and Manu.—Machine for tarring yarn.

54 ROBINSON, R. Belfast, Ireland, Inv. Des. and Manu. —Flax seeding machine, which may also be used for crushing linseed, corn, or beans for feeding. Flax straw, grown in the county Down, Ireland.

55 BINNS, W. Bradford, Manu.—Six-pitch wool combs, used in the preparation of wool for the worsted silt trade.

56 BROWN, T. B. Hampen Andover's Ford, Chelten-ham, Gloucestershire.—Loom for sail cloth. Tarpauling without seam. Flax tube sacks of mixed flax and hemp, wove without seam. Flax coats, perfectly waterproof.

57, 58 GAIMES, SANDERS, & NICHOL, Birchin Lane, Cornhill, Manu.—Mode of making silk hats on cork and linen bodies, and felt caps. Model of a hat factory.

59 SMITH, J. Orchard St. Galston, Ayrshire, Scotland, Inv.—Improved spelf-machine, applicable to fabrics of small design, out of the range of traddles.

60 GATENBY & PASS, Manchester, Manu.—Reeds or combs applied for weaving textile fabrics, manufactured by steam power.

61 ILES, C. Bardesley Works, Birmingham, Inv. and Manu.—Machine for sticking pins in circular tablets.

62 DICKINS, T. Middleton, Lancashire, Inv.—Working model of a mill, or apparatus for warping silk.

63 RIGGE & Co. Kendal, Manu.—Sheets of card, of different qualities, used for carding wool.

64 CROSS, C. 19 Gutter Lane, Cheapside.—Model looms.

65 SEARLE, H. Hoxton Old Town, Manu.—Lint ma-chine: the material in process of manufacture.

66 WATKINS, W. & T. Bridge St. Bradford, Inv.— Ironstone porcelain guides, used in the roving and spinning of worsted, silk, cotton, flax, &c.

67 VICTORY, J. St. Leonards, Hastings.—Lathe tools.

68 JAQUIN, C. A. 68 New St. Bishopsgate St., Des. and Manu.—Fly-press, lever-press, and tools, used in making metal buttons, &c. Loop for label made by machinery.

69 SLATE, J.—Twine-reels.

70 STEANE, J. Burgess, Nottingham.—Machine for carding trimmings.

71 THOM, J.—Sulphuring apparatus.

72 TAYLOR, E. Kinghorn. — Specimens of superior heckles for linen manufacture.

73 SMITH, J. W. 48 Fleet St. Leicester.—Needles for stocking frames.

74 PLUMMER, R. Newcastle-upon-Tyne, Inv.—Patent machinery used in the manufacture of flax, hemp, &c. Raw materials and manufactures in illustration.

75 LAWSON & SONS, Leeds, Inv. and Manu.—Machinery for the preparation and spinning of flax.

77 PARKER, C. E. & C. Dundee, Scotland, Inv. and Manu.—Parker's patent mathematical power-loom for weav-ing navy-sail-cloth, and other heavy fabrics.

78 CRAWHALL, J. Newcastle-upon-Tyne, Inv. — Im-proved patent machine for manufacturing ropes.

80 DAVENPORT, J. L. Derby, Manu.—Silk-throwing machinery, made by W. Abell. Winding and cleaning en-gine. Spinning or twisting mill. Doubling frame. Reeling machine. Dramming apparatus.

82 BARLOW, A. 26 Bread St. Inv.—Patent double ac-tion Jacquard loom, with two cylinders and two sets of cards.

84 FROST, J. Macclesfield, Inv.—Models of improved silk-winding machine and cleaning frame; of a spinning and doubling machine; of a throwing-mill, with spindles turned by friction: to be patented.

85 REED, T. S. Siddal's Lane Mills, Derby, Inv.— Patent power-loom, for making fringes and like fabrics without the use of shuttles

86 CLAUSSEN, P. 26 Gresham St. Pat. and partly Inv.— Circular hand-loom, for weaving looped fabrics, elastic cloth, &c. Manlove and Alliot, Prop.

87 GARDNER & BAZLEY, Nottingham.—A 48-spindles doubling-frame, for the production of lace thread.

88 HUDSON & BOTTOM, Nottingham.—Lace dressing frame.

89 CARVER, T. & T. G. Nottingham.—Stocking-frame.

90 BALL, DUNNICLIFF, & Co. Nottingham, Manu.— Warp-lace machine, making plain blonde.

91 COWSLADE & LOVEJOY, Reading, Berkshire, Inv.— Printing press, with improved inking apparatus.

92 SEWELL, T. R. Carrington, near Nottingham, Inv. and Manu.—Machine for making bobbin-net lace. Figured and plain net, made by the machine.

94 BIRKIN, R. Nottingham, Manu.—Machine for the production of bobbin-net lace, &c.

95 FUSSELL, F. R. School of Design, Nottingham.— Paintings illustrating the manufacture of lace.

96 BURTON & EAMES, Lenton Works, nr. Nottingham. Prop.—Patent gassing machine, for singeing the loose fibre from lace, muslins, &c.

100 FOURDRINIER, G. H. Hanley, Inv. and Manu.— Patent steam press, for printing the impressions to be trans ferred on to earthenware or china. Patent oscillating double-piston steam-engine, with potters' flint and colour mill. Original model of Fourdrinier's paper-machine; with specimen of pottery tissue paper, 2¼ miles long.

102 HARDING, PULLEIN, & JOHNSON, Guildhall Chambers, Prop.—Machines for making printing type from copper, zinc, or other metal.

103 UNDERWOOD, T. Birmingham.—Lithographic colour press.

104 SHERWIN, COPE, & Co. 5 Cumberland St. Shoreditch, Inv. and Manu.—Printing press, exhibiting a simple com-bination of levers, &c. Arming press, for bookbinders.

108 TIDCOMBE, G. Watford, Manu.—Machine for cut-ting paper in the continuous sheet.

110 SHAW, W. 8 Bachelor's Walk, Dublin, Manu.—Im-proved machine for ruling paper.

112 WILSON, G. 27 St. Martin's Ct. Leicester Sq. Inv. and Pat.—Paper and mill-board cutting machines.

114 GREIG, D. & J. Lothian Rd. Edinburgh, Des. and Manu.—Iron lithographic press, with frame, for registering coloured printing, &c. Copper-plate press, with single motion. Portable fanners for cooling apartments in hot climates, suggested by Capt. Davidson, 18th Bombay In-fantry.

116 MARRIOTT, W. Leeds Rd. Huddersfield.—Regis-tered machine for packing dry substances, and for printing labels.

118 COOKE, H. 127 High St. Oxford, Inv.—Printing apparatus of new construction, designed to give increased facilities to the compositor.

120 NELSON, T. jun. Hope Park End, Edinburgh, Inv. —Working model of a new printing machine. Illuminated book-titles.

121 ULLMER, Fetter Lane, London.—Self-inking press.

122 INGRAM, H. 198 Strand, Prop.—A printing machine on the vertical principle, as used at the "Times" office (invented by Mr. Applegath). The machine which is erected in the Exhibition is made to print circular wood-cuts and type in the best manner.

124 CLYMER & DIXON, 10 Finsbury St. Finsbury Sq. Pat. and Manu.—Columbian printing press.

128 REDMOND, A. Birmingham, Imp. and Inv.—Working model of patent machine for dry-cementing envelopes.

130 DONKIN, B. & Co. Bermondsey, Manu. and part Inv.—Model of improved paper-making machine.

132 BREWER, JANE, 19 Surrey Pl. Old Kent Rd. Manu. —Endless brass wire cloth, rollers, moulds, &c. used in making paper.

134 COWPER, E. F.R.S. 9 Kensington Park Rd. Notting Hill, Inv. and Pat.—Model by T. B. Winter, Esq. student in King's College, London, of the printing-machine now in general use. The Catalogue of the Exhibition is printed by these machines.

135 CHURCH & GODDARD, Birmingham, Manu.—Machine for cutting card-boards into cards for printing and other purposes. Machine to cut, print, number, count, and pack tickets. Machine for dating railway tickets.

136 TAYLOR, W. Nottingham, Des. and Manu.—Machine for forming hemispherical paper-shades from flat discs of paper Ornamental paper work, &c.

138 BLACK, J. Edin. Manu.—Patent folding machine.

140 WHITAKER, R. Bury St. Edmund's.—Bookbinders' press.

142 STRAKER, S. 80 Bishopsgate St. Within, Manu.— Side-lever lithographic press, with improved registering-machine, for colour printing.

144 BREWER, C. & W. Malcolm Works, Larkhall Lane, Inv. and Manu.—Rollers, moulds, &c. for paper-making, with illustrations. Patented.

146 RANSOMES & MAY, of Ipswich, Manu.—Model of patent excavator, for railways or canals. Models of improved apparatus and machinery, for preparing timber with creosote, &c.

148 POPE, T. & C. 56 St. Paul's Sq. Birmingham.— Copying and other presses.

150 COBE, T. 19 Portugal St. Lincoln's Inn, Manu.— Model of improved printing press.

151 HARRIS, C. Shalford, Guildford.—Fly press for embossing.

152 LIGHTFOOT, T. M. South Shields.—Rag-beating engine.

154 JARRETT, G. 45 Lee St. Kingsland Rd.—Improved embossing presses.

155 COLLETT, C. 8 Great Cambridge St. Hackney Rd.— Embossing presses.

156 SULLIVAN, T. Foots' Cray, Kent, Inv. and Manu.— Models of rollers for producing the water-mark, &c. in machine-laid paper.

157 HARRILD & SONS, 10 and 11 Great Distaff Lane, Friday St.—Printing presses and plough cutting machine.

158 NAPIER & SON, Lambeth, Inv. and Manu.—Compass which registers on paper the compass course which a vessel has been steered for 24 hours. Perfecting printing machine (worked by H. Silverlock, printer). Pat. self-feeding and discharging centrifugal apparatus, suited for the separation of molasses from the crystal and other purposes.

160 MCCLURE & Co. Bow Churchyard, London.—Lithographic press.

162 HOPKINSON & COPE, 14 New North St. Finsbury, Inv. and Manu.—Albion printing press. Holm's patent, Scandinavian printing machine, worked by H. Silverlock, printer, Doctors Commons.

164 WATERLOW & SONS, London Wall.—Printing machine. Patent self-feeding envelope machine, producing envelopes folded, gummed, and embossed. Machine for numbering bank notes. Patent autographic press.

165 WATSON, H. Newcastle.—Pulp-strainer for paper making, and hydro-electric machine. Patent valve.

166 COWAN & SONS, 45 Upper Thames St.—Patent paper pulp meter.

168 SCHLESINGER & Co. 8 Old Jewry.—Paging and numbering machine. Ticket-printing machine. Machine for printing bank notes.

200 FAIRBAIRN, W. & SONS, Manchester.—Rivetting machine.

201 WHITWORTH, J. & Co. Manchester, Manu.—Self-acting lathes, planing, slotting, drilling and boring, screwing, cutting, and dividing, punching and shearing, machines. Patent knitting machine. Patent screw stocks, with dies and taps. Measuring machine, and standard yard, &c.

202 FOSTER, T. Manchester, Inv.—Method of applying etching ground copper rollers.

203 LYONS, M. 143 Suffolk St. Birmingham, Inv.—Apparatus and specimens to illustrate the process of bright electro-plating, gilding, electro-engraving, and deposition of copper for the formation of tubes, particularly suitable for embossed works of art.

204 SHARP BROTHERS, Manchester.—Lathe, slotting, and self-acting planing machines.

205 MORDAN, SAMPSON, & Co. City Rd. Manu.—Bright steel fire-proof jewel-box, with or molu ornaments. Elegant carved and inlaid pearl inkstand, &c. Gold pens. Complex self-acting rose-engine and tracing-machine. Combination copying and seal press.

206 MUIR, W. Salford, Manu.—Amateur foot lathe, with joiner's bench, tool-chest, &c. Patent coffee-mills. Screw embossing press, with specimens, &c. Copying presses. Screw-stocks, taps, &c. Oil-testing machine. Inv. by E. Thomas, of Manchester. Registered theodolite. Des. by H. Goss, of Salford. Soap-cutting-machine. Inv. by W. Storey, of Manchester.

208 GARFORTH, W. J. & J. Dukinfield, near Ashton-under-Lyne.—Steam rivetting machine, direct action.

209 LEWIS & SONS, Manchester, Manu.—Wheel cutting and dividing engine. Model of Lewis Mac Lardy's patent roving and slab spindle, &c.

210 SHANKS, A. 6 Robert St. Adelphi, Inv. and Manu.— Bolt screwing machine. Improved high-pressure engine. Detail planing machines, one being for hand power.

212 JOHNSON, R. & BROTHER, Dale St. Manchester, Manu.—Wire-drawing benches, showing the process of drawing strong and fine sizes of iron wire, with specimens.

213 PARR, CURTIS, & MADELEY, Manchester.—Planing-machine, lathes, &c.

214 TAYLOR, W. 33 Little Queen St. Holborn.—Press for striking medals.

215 BENNETT, J. 1 Thistle St. Oldham.—Drawing of an engineer's lathe.

218 HICK & SON, Bolton, Des. and Manu.—Radial drilling machine. Ball safety-valve. Punchings, showing the power of Hick's compound hydraulic press. Portable smith's hearth or forge. High-pressure oscillating steam-engine. Models of steam-engines. Machine for cleaning and preparing grain. Improved mandrils.

219 GLASGOW, J. Manchester.—Improved screwing machine, with dies, taps, chucks, &c. complete.

220 SHEPHERD, HILL, & SPINK, Hunsted Rd. Leeds, Manu.—Self-acting side lathe, with screw-cutting apparatus, self-acting surface and improved disengaging motion.

221 COTTAM & HALLEN, 2 Winsley St. Inv. and Manu. —Hydrostatic press for proving girders, with dial index and dead hand.

222 RYDER, W. Bolton, Inv. and Pat.—Forging machine for small articles up to two inches, round or square, with specimen Slubbing, roving, and throstle spindles and flys, and all kinds of rollers for cotton machinery.

223 SANDFORD, OWEN, & WATSON, Phœnix Iron Works,

Rotherham, Inv. Des. and Manu.—Improved screw-cutting lathe, of very simple construction.

224 EADES & SON, Birmingham, Manu.—A small four-feet screw-cutting and slide and other lathes, on iron stands, with apparatus complete. Set of screw stocks, dies, taps, &c.

226 DALGETY, A. Deptford, Inv. and Manu.—Self-acting surfacing and screw-cutting lathe, self-adjusting chucks, &c.

228 MAUDSLAY, SONS, & FIELD, Cheltenham Pl. Lambeth.—Coining press, acting by an eccentric.

230 SMITH, BEACOCK, & TANNETT, Leeds, Manu.—Self-acting side lathe, with bed 18 feet long, head stock 15 inches, centres, self-acting surfacing and screw-cutting motion, &c. Self-acting drilling and planing machine.

232 HOLTZAPFFEL & Co. 64 Charing Cross, and 127 Long Acre, Manu.—A centre lathe for amateur ornamental turning. Eccentric, oval, spherical, geometric, and other chucks; compound sliding rest; drilling instrument; sets of turning tools, &c., in ivory and hardwood. Specimens of turning by amateurs in ivory, and other materials; cannel coal, &c.

234 WILLIAMS, J. Westlake Buildings, Bath, Des. and Manu.—One horse power portable steam-engine for amateurs, designed by Rev. C. R. Davy. A self-acting foot power slide and screw-cutting lathe. Foot-power drilling machine, &c. Model of private doors. Ornamental cutting apparatus for lathes. Bolt and nut shaping machine. Ornamental screw lifting-jack, made and designed by Rev. C. R. Davy.

236 NASMYTH, J. Manchester.—Steam hammer.

238 STEWART, D. Y. & Co. Glasgow, Manu.—Model of patent mould-making machine for cast-iron pipes; pipes 44 inches diameter, cast in moulds made by the machine. Machine for testing the strength of cast-iron.

240 MORRALL, A. Studley Works, Warwickshire, Inv. and Manu.—Knitting pins. Steel, gilt and plated bodkins. Needles in the different stages of manufacture. Specimens of machinery for making needles. Stamp press, or eyeing machine; filing, heading, and curing machine.

242 VAUGHAN, G. Westmoreland St. Marylebone.—Machine for setting the teeth of saws.

244 CHURCH, J. Chelmsford, Manu.—Model lathes, with vice attached.

246 CAMPBELL, G. Charlton, Woolwich, Inv.—Portable steam forge, with blowing apparatus.

301 BEART, R. Godmanchester, near Huntingdon, Inv.—Patent brick and tile machines. Model of a patent apparatus for boring Artesian wells. Patent apparatus for boring stone, and for cutting thin plates of sand or other stone. Sandstone filter, containing 5,000 superficial inches of sawn surface.

304 BRUNTON, W. jun.—Machine for washing ores.

305 WARING, C. H. Neath Abbey, Glamorganshire, Inv. and Manu.—Machines for cutting or working coal, &c. Provisionally registered.

306 CLAUDET & HOUGHTON, 89 High Holborn.—Two machines for cutting glass shades, the invention of Mr. Claudet; one for cutting round, oval, or Syrian glass shades of any sizes, the other for cutting round shades only.

308 HART, J. Seymour Pl. Bryanstone Sq.—Portable brick and tile machines. Patented.

310 BRADLEY, R. & Co. Wakefield, Inv. and Manu.—A machine for moulding bricks. A working model of a colliery.

312 HUNTER, J. Leysmill, Arbroath, Scotland, Inv.—Model of Hunter's stone-planing machine, with specimens of planed stones from Leysmill Quarries, near Arbroath.

314 MACKENZIE, J. S. Newark-upon-Trent, Inv. and Manu.—Mackenzie's triturator, consisting of a mortar, in a frame, and pestle, to which a rotatory motion is given.

317 MARSDEN, —, Leeds.—Washing machine.

324 RANDELL & SAUNDERS, 14 Orange Grove, Bath, Inv.—Patent machines for driving saws, for the purpose of cutting stone in its natural beds. Traversing steam crane for underground quarries. Patent saw frame for cutting blocks of stone, &c.

328 RADCLIFFE, A. 67 St. John St. Road.—Model of steam trigger. Improved shifting quarry-boards. Glaziers' diamonds, &c.

330 SPELLER, W. 14 York St. Blackfriars Rd. Manu.—Well-boring implements.

400 BESSEMER, H. Baxter House, Old St. Pancras Rd. Pat. and Manu.—Vacuum slate table for holding plate-glass during grinding and polishing. Centrifugal machine for separating molasses from crystals of sugar.

401 FURNESS, W Liverpool, Pat.—Patent machines for working in wood. Power and foot-mortising machines. Tenoning and planing machines. Moulding machine.

402 SCHIELE, C. Manchester, Inv. and Manu.—Specimens of the construction of revolving rubbing surfaces by a patent rule, &c. Spindle joint, for locomotive regulators. Self-acting feed regulator. Screws and nuts, &c.

403 FAIRBAIRN, W. Manchester.—Corn mill.

404 CROSSKILL, W. Iron Works, Beverley, Pat. and Manu.—Patent mills for grinding all kinds of mineral and vegetable substances, pottery flints, cropolites, corn, paints, &c Portable and fixture steam engines.

405 ROTCH & FINZEL, 2 Furnival's Inn.—Centrifugal machine for separating molasses from sugar. Manlove and Alliott, manu.

406 BIRCH, J. Edward St. Regent's Park, Inv.—Machine for cutting sash and roof bars, &c.

407 MAIDLOW, J. Queen's Ter. St. John's Wood.—Improved bench screw for carpenters.

408 DAKIN & Co. St. Paul's Churchyard.—Patent apparatus for roasting coffee in silver.

410 BARRETT & Co. Reading.—Biscuit making machine.

412 WASLEY, J. Redruth, Cornwall.—Machine for setting up mitred frames. A trammel for striking spiral lines

414 HURWOOD, G. Ipswich, Inv. and Pat.—Various patent metal mills for grinding corn, pulse, spices, &c. Plate showing grinding surface of a mill. Stone case, with apparatus for supplying air to the grinding surfaces of mill-stones.

416 CORCORAN, B. & Co. 36 Mark Lane, Des. and Manu.—Model of an improved drying kiln for malt, &c. Flour-dressing machine. Woven wire of various textures, for machines, &c. Millstones for grinding wheat. Portable corn-mill for emigrants, &c.

417 BARKER, C. M. 22 Portsmouth Pl. Kennington Lane, Inv. Pat. and Manu.—Curvilinear sawing machine for ships' timbers, &c. Circular sawing, or rack bench.

418 ROBINSONS & RUSSELL, Mill Wall Works.—Patent portable steam sugar-cane mill.

420 BLUNDEL & Co. Hull and Upper Thames St.—Linseed presses.

421 FAIRBAIRN & Co. Manchester.—A flour-mill.

422 HUNT, J. Botley Mill, near Orford, Inv. and Manu.—Flour-dressing machine, on a new principle.

424 GUTTA PERCHA Co.—Printing, folding, and cutting machinery, for working from gutta percha castings.

426 BEDFORD, J. Mill Hill, Leeds, Manu.—Flour-dressing machine, complete.

428 BLACKMORE, W. Wandsworth, Prop.—Model of an improved bolting mill, showing the mode of dressing flour through patent bolting cloths without seams: improved by J. Ayton, of Norwich, &c.

429 ADAMS, S. & C. Oldbury, near Birmingham, Inv. Pat. and Manu.—Patent durable steel hand-mill, for grinding flour for colonial and domestic uses.

430 THOMSON, W. Shott's Foundry, Edinburgh, Des. and Manu.—Planing machine of novel construction. Tool for cleaning off flooring-boards and deck-planking.

432 COLLINGE & Co. 65 Bridge Rd. Lambeth.—Patent horizontal sugar mill.

436 SPILLER, J. Battersea.—Flour-dressing machine.

438 SHORE, Thos. City Rd.—Flour-dressing machine.

440 SHARP, S. Stamford.—A sugar cutter.

441 WEATHERLEY, H. Inv. and Manu. 54 Theobald's Rd.—A machine for dressing currants.

442 WESTRUP, W. 282 Wapping, Inv.—Patent corn mill, made by Middleton, Southwark.

443 FIELDHOUSE, G. & Co. Wolverhampton.—Mills on pillar stand for grinding coffee and pepper.

444 COOMBE, B. & Co. 30 Mark Lane, Manu.—A smut-machine and corn-screen combined ; (of friction that it can bear without breaking or injuring the grain ; also fanning it at the same time, scouring the fibrous end off, and all that adheres to it, effectually cleaning the wheat from all dirt, clods, smut, &c. ; the best wheat is considerably improved by passing through this machine, of simple construction.) A model of a flour-dressing machine, with registered fan-brushes and flanges complete. Specimens of wove and twist wire in brass and copper.

445 GRAHAM, WEST, & Co. 304 Wapping, Manu.—Model of a horizontal mill, for crushing sugar-canes with five rollers. Model of the old vertical sugar-cane mill. Model of a set of evaporating pans.

446 HUXHAMS & BROWN, Exeter, Inv. and Manu.—Mill to grind bark for tanners, making but little dust. Emigrant's or hand flour-mill. Mill-stones for grinding wheat.

447 GILBERT, J. 79 Wardour St. Soho, Inv.—Guillotine cutting machine, for cutting end joints, and for mouldings and other work in joinery and cabinet-making, &c.

448 ADORNO, J. N. 6 Golden Sq.—Machines for making cigarettes and cigars.

449 SQUIRE & Co. Great Dover St. Borough.—Direct acting sugar mill.

450 GATTI & BOLLA, 129 Holborn Hill.—Chocolate apparatus ; and model of a steam-engine for the manufacture of French and Italian chocolate.

454 MANLOVE, ALLIOTT, & SEYRIG, Lenton Works, Nottingham, Inv.—Centrifugal machines for washing and drying clothes ; for drying starch, &c. and purifying sugar.

455 STAIGHT & SONS, 35 Charles St. Prop.—Ivory comb-cutting machine. Illustrations of improved mode of cutting ivory.

456 PROSSER & HADLEY, 20½ Clipstone St. Manu.—Patent ornamental sawing machine, capable of performing curvilinear cuttings, both in outline and perforation.

457 TOMS, G. B. & Co. East India Chambers, Imp. and Agents.—French mill-stones, made at La Ferté-sous-Jouarre, to which is applied Hanon-Valcke's patent aërator.

458 SAVAGE, A. 43 Eastcheap, Manu.—Mills for grinding and bruising wheat, malt, coffee, drugs, &c. Roasters, &c. for coffee, chocolate, malt, &c.

459 HUGHES & SONS, 1 and 8 Great Dover Rd. Borough. Manu.—Two millstones of a superior manufacture for grinding wheat.

460 LAW, W. 31 St. Andrew's Sq. Edinburgh, Inv.—Machine for roasting coffee.

462 MILLINGTON, B. & E. Newark-upon-Trent, Inv. and Manu.—Patent smut machine, for cleaning corn.

466 RANKIN, R. & J. Liverpool, Manu.—Patent vertical smut machine and corn screen, with separator attached, for extracting sand, seeds, and small grain ; and registered portable driving apparatus.

467 SQUIRE, C. 20 Old Fish St. Doctor's Commons.—Timber-preserving apparatus.

468 BURT, H. P. 238 Blackfriars Rd.—Timber-seasoning apparatus.

470 ASHBY, W. 8 Prospect Pl. Sheffield, Inv.—Upright flour-dressing machine.

472 HALL, W. Castlecomer, Ireland.—Model of grinding mill.

501 PERRY, H. J. Greenwich.—A sausage chopper.

502 MANSELL, T. 94 Bull St. Birmingham, Inv. and Manu.— Patent fly-press for cutting with steel tools or knives on an even surface of steel, with accuracy. Patent boot-blocking machine.

503 THOMPSON, W. King's Coll.—Hair-working machine.

504 WAIT, J. 12 Duke St. Portland Pl.—Boot and shoe machine.

506 BIERTUMPFEL, H. Albany St. Manu.—Candle-mould frame.

508 GILBERTSON, J. Hertford.—Model of furnace for preventing effluvia in boiling fat, &c.

602 PONTIFEX & WOOD, Shoe Lane, Fleet St.—Sugar apparatus, pumps, &c. in copper and brass.

604 LAWRENCE, J. sen. Colnbrook, Slough, Des. and Inv.—Distributor, with six outlets. Patent refrigerator. Pat. store cask or vat, with tinned-copper attemperating pan.

605 TYLER, H. & Co. 85 Upper White Cross St. St. Luke's, Inv. and Manu. — A patent double soda-water machine

606 TYLOR & SON, Warwick Lane, Newgate St.—Soda-water machinery. Bottling or corking machine, &c.

608 COX, W. Manchester, Pat.—Improved apparatus for the manufacture of aerated waters ; also an improved construction of cock or tap.

609 SADDINGTON, S. & W. 63 Wood St. Cheapside, Manu.—Drum sieve, for druggists, &c. Straining sieve, of silk lawn, for starch, colours, &c.

610 BOURRA, L. A. 31 Rathbone Pl. Inv. and Pat.—Patent colour-extractor apparatus.

611 ASKEW, C. 27½ Charles St. Hampstead Rd. Inv. and Manu.—Model refrigerator, for cooling beer.

612 DAWSON, J. Distiller, Green Park, Linlithgow, Inv.—New distiller or rectifier's recording close safe.

613 BARLOW, H. B. Manchester, for LE FORESTIER AIME, Havre, Prop.—Model of a press for making wine, with improved gearing. For Hervot, L., Havre, Inv.—Cask for excluding the air and registering the contents.

615 COFFEY, T. 4 Providence Row, Finsbury Sq. Inv.—Refrigerator for cooling worts or condensing steam.

617 HALLIDAY, A. P. 6 Bank Pl. Salford, Manchester, Inv. — Apparatus for the manufacture of pyroligneous acid.

618 HULLS, J. High Wycombe, Manu. — Wheeler's patent refrigerator. Wheeler's patent condenser.

619 HILL, EVANS & Co. Worcester, Prop.—Model of a patent vinegar apparatus, fer acetification without sulphuric, pyroligneous, or other foreign acid.

621 MASTERMANN, J. & T. 38 Broad St. Ratcliff, Inv. and Pat.—Apparatus for bottling and corking bottles.

623 THOMSON, YOUNGER, & Co. Des. and Inv.—Apparatus for the heating and cooling of worts in the process of fermentation.

624 COOPER & BURSILL, Eastbourne, Sussex, and 9 York Terr. Queen's Rd. Hornsey Rd. Prop.—Patent aerating machine ; a carbonating machine, adapted to draught purposes.

630 TIZZARD, W. L. High St. Aldgate.—Model brewery.

631 PLIMSOLL, S. Sheffield.—Improved warming apparatus.

Proceed to Class 20, page 103.

Class 7. CIVIL ENGINEERING, ARCHITECTURE, AND BUILDING CONTRIVANCES.

—— North Gallery, and with Classes 5 & 6. ——

1 SIEBE, A. 5 Denmark St. Soho. Inv. and Manu.— A three motion diving machine. Air pump with a figure of a man in diving dress and helmet.

2 GEARY, S. 19 Euston Pl. Euston Sq. Inv.—Model of a patent stationary fire-engine, to be fitted up within the pedestal of a lamp or other post, &c. Improved Venetian perforated blind. New mode of paving streets, &c. by trams. Models of improved railway carriages, parish water-cart and fire-engine combined, &c. &c.

3 GREEN, B. Arcade, Newcastle-upon-Tyne, Des.— Model of arch of the Newcastle and North Shields Railway, &c. Models of monuments erected to the late Earl Durham and Earl Grey. Geometrical drawings of design for the proposed high-level bridge at Newcastle-upon-Tyne.

4 M'KIRDY, J. G. Birkwood, Lesmahago, Scotland, Prod.—Model of wooden bridge for foot passengers.

5 ASSER, L. 147 Regent St. Inv.—Blocks for building to cause equal distribution of pressure.

6 RIDDELL, T. 1 Market Terrace, Southgate Rd. Islington.—Model of a building showing how talc may be used instead of glass.

7 TURNER, R. Hammersmith, Dublin.—Models of the Great Palm House, at Kew; of the Winter Garden in the Regent's Park Botanical Gardens; of the iron roof over the railway station, Lime Street, Liverpool; of a winter garden; of an iron roof for a wet dock, to permit a man-of-war in full sail to enter; of an iron roof for another dock; wooden model for exhibition structure, and sections of same, &c. (With Class 6.)

8 CLARK, G. D. 12 London St. Greenwich, Inv. (Agent).—Iron castings for architectural purposes, in combination with, or in lieu of, bricks or stone.

9 FINCH & WILLEY, Windsor Foundry, Liverpool, Manu.—Model of a wrought-iron bridge to carry the South Wales Railway over the river Wye at Chepstow. Designed by I. K. Brunel, C.E. (In Central Avenue.)

10 OATES, W. Mirfield, Inv.—Self-acting cloughs.

11 COLES, W. 3 Charing Cross.— Two anti-friction pulleys. Two models of anti-friction railway carriages.

12 REDMAN, J. B. 5 New Palace Yard, Westminster, Des.—Model of the royal terrace pier at Milton, erected by means of cast-iron cylinders.

13 BERMINGHAM, T. Clarendon Lodge, Sandymount, Dublin, Imp.—A box of Désiré Lebrun compasses, for all drawing purposes, with pen, invented by Elliot, of London. A model of moveable flood-gates or lifts (called hauses), inv. by M. Thénard, of Paris, to render rivers navigable.

14 JEFFREY, R. Upper North Pl. Gray's Inn Rd.— Railway tunnel signal. Life protector. Safety disc.

15 HAMMOND, R. C. 45 Baldwin's Gardens, Leather Lane, Holborn, Inv. and Manu.—Model of a convex-chain suspension bridge.

16 PRATT, Major, 7 Upper Area, Hungerford Market, Inv.—Moveable steps for tidal rivers. New self-acting trap for street drains.

17 GREEN, J. Caledonian Rd. Inv.—Model of moveable dam for river operations; and of a new plan of shifting a dam, &c.

18 CLARK, C. C.E. Sea-side Hotel, Hastings.—Model of the proposed ship canal through the isthmus of Suez.

19 JAMES, J.—Model fountain with small engine for working it. (Main Avenue, West.)

20 WATT, W. Glasgow, Manu.—Hydro-pneumatic lift, for canal locks. Hydro-pneumatic elevators. Patent hydro-pneumatic ship-lift. Application of compressed air for the prevention of vessels from sinking.

21 WEST & GREGSON, Union St. Oldham, Des. and Manu.—Model station-meter for gas-works. Experimental meter and consumers' gas-meter.

24 MORTON, S. & H. Leith Walk, Edinburgh, Inv. and Manu.—Model of a patent slip for hauling up ships, of the largest class, for repairs—a cheap substitute for dry docks —with model of a frigate.

25 MARTIN, J. Lindsey House, Chelsea, Des. and Inv.—Application of town sewage to agricultural purposes. Sewer traps. Patent junctions for pipes. Ventilation of coal mines. Life boat. Drawings of laminated beams, bridges, harbours, piers, lighthouses, &c.

26 FORSTER J., South John St. Liverpool, Inv. and Patentee.—Fountain, with pressure-filter attached. Household filters. Manufactured by Cochrane & Co. Woodside Iron Works, Dudley. (Central Avenue.)

27 RENCZYNSKI, Capt. G. A. 31 Tonbridge Pl. New Rd.—A philosophical quadrant stand. Models of a self-supporting suspension bridge, hand-power locomotive and steam-engine. (With locomotives, &c.)

28 STUART, W. Breakwater, Plymouth, Devon. Des.— Limestone model of the breakwater in Plymouth Sound, with silver lighthouse and beacon, made for the exhibition under the directions of the Lords of the Admiralty. The breakwater was constructed agreeably to a report of the late John Rennie and of Joseph Whiaby, master R.N.; the lighthouse designed by Walker and Burgess: with sectional and other models, &c. (Central Avenue.)

29 THE ROYAL SCOTTISH SOCIETY OF ARTS, Edinburg.—A bar of iron, of superior quality, $2\frac{1}{4}$ inches square, twisted into a spiral form by the action of the steam-engine while boring. Model of a suspension bridge, to prevent vertical oscillation. Model of a steam-boat.

30 ROEBUCK, J. J. Huddersfield, Prod.—Model and drawings of No. 4 skew arch of the Huddersfield viaduct, built in stone, over the Bradford Road, &c.

31 HURWOOD, G. Ipswich, Suffolk, Inv. and Pat.— Window made to open and close in one or in several parts by the application of the patented apparatus. Used for ventilating the Exhibition building. Various models showing the mode of applying the invention to different windows. Patent ship-lights and scuttles. Model and drawing of a breakwater.

32 SANKEY, W. H. V. Inv. and Manu.—Drawings of an improved tubular bridge, called the "compound hollow girder bridge." Model of the "compound hollow girder bridge." Improved form of piers for bridges, &c. Drawing of improved railway carriage. Drawing of improved method of building stone bridges.

33 LOWE, W. Belton, near Grantham, Inv.—Model of a portable bridge, for the use of an army in crossing rivers.

34 BAIN, C. Morden St. Greenwich, Inv.—Radial gauge cock for steam-boilers. Elevating machine, to be used in the construction and repair of towers, chimneys, &c. Compound and tubular bridges.

35 GANDELL, E. F. 3 Princes St. Westminster, Des. —Model for a lighthouse on the Goodwin Sands.

36 BYNE, R. H. Engineer, 10 Eccleston St. South, Pimlico, Modeller.—Model of a design for an iron-girder railway bridge.

37 HUNT & GANDELL, 3 Princes St. Westminster, Des.

C 4

—Model of a proposed bridge over the Thames at Westminster.

38 SACRED HARMONIC SOCIETY, Office No. 6, in Exeter Hall.—Model of the orchestra of the Sacred Harmonic Society, Exeter Hall, by Mr. P. Clarke. (Central Avenue.)

39 TOWNLEY, W. 99 Holborn Hill, Inv.—Model of the surface or superstructure of London Bridge, with machinery, &c. New system for washing and watering streets, &c. (With Classes 5 and 6.)

40 NICHOLSON, G. jun. 1 Harcourt St. Marylebone, Inv. —Model of railway spring-buffer carriage, with self-acting spring life preserve; scaffolding for building purposes; fire-escape; watering and sweeping machine, &c.

41 CLIVE, J. H. 12 Stanhope Pl. Hyde Park, and Tunstall, Staffordshire, Inv.—Model of a bar-trellis suspension bridge, to make a cheap road-way over rivers, without obstructing the navigation by high masted vessels.

42 WOODS, F. F. 5 Pelham Ter. Brompton, Manu. Inv. and Pat.—Patent union paving, designed to create less noise than on stone-paved roads, than roads made with loose stones, and less mud, less slippery than wood paving, better foothold for horses, and more durable. (Outside, West End.)

43 BODLEY, —. 2 Queen Square Place, Westminster. —Revolving window sash. (With Classes 5 and 6.)

44 TEASDEL, W. Great Yarmouth, Inv. and Des.— A coffer dam.

45 CHAPMAN, J. Frome, Des. and Manu.—Model of a bridge across the Wylye, at Upton Lovel, Wilts, each parapet formed by trussing a beam of red pine, on the system of Herr Laves, of Hanover.

46 DONKIN, B. & Co. Bermondsey. — Model of the frame inv. by the late M. J. Brunel, and used in the construction of the Thames Tunnel.

47 GROUT, A. 8 Shepherd St. Tenter Ground, Spitalfields, Inv. and Manu.—Wire bridge for parks, &c.; all the weight borne by the hand-rail.

48 ASKEW, C. 27½ Charles St. Hampstead Rd. Inv.— Improved and ornamental shutters, either in metal or wood, adapted for shops and private houses. Patent filter. Paddle wheels.

49 BRUFF, P. Ipswich, Des.—Model for a proposed national harbour of refuge on the east coast of England.

50 GARDNER, H. 3 Essex St. Islington, Inv. — Double cone blocks, or artificial hollow stones for building in water to any depth without damming, the cavities to be filled in with cement or concrete.

51 BEADON, W. 1 Crescent, Taunton; and Otterhead, Honiton, Inv.—Patent door and lock. New patent imperishable eaves-gutter for security against drip, made of clay. New patent barge brick and water-shoot coping.

52 TODD, C. Leeds, Inv. and Des.—Model of a girder, or vertebral arch, originally invented and designed for a bridge to cross the river Mersey, at Runcorn Gap, in one span of 1,263 feet. (With Classes 5 and 6.)

53 HEINKE, C. E. Inv. and Manu.—Patent submarine helmet, dress, and other diving apparatus.

54 DEVEY, G. 16 Gt. Marlborough St. Inv.—Proposed method of carrying off smoke by underground drainage.

55 BANKS, L. 23 Parliament St. Hull, Des. and Manu. —Twin geometric staircase.

56 BOYDELL, J. 54 Threadneedle St. Inv. and Manu.— New method of joining iron joists and rafters to wood, &c. Fire-proof door. Method of casting iron ships with wood, without bolts, or rivets, &c. New method of framing the sides of iron ships. (With Classes 5 and 6.)

57 DORR, W. 2 Hewell Place, Southampton St. Camberwell. — Chimney-sweeping apparatus. (With Classes 5 and 6.)

58 GRISDALE, J. E. 289 Strand, Inv.—Model of a wind-guard for smoky chimneys.

59 MORRELL, G. 149 Fleet St.—Iron abutments and tension rods on piers.—Reg.

60 HERRING, C. 177 High Holborn.—Patent window and model. A new and simple invention for taking out both sashes to clean, &c.

61 SADLER, J. H. Leeds, Inv. and Pat.—A bridge for railway or other purposes, composed of a series of girders balanced upon piers.

62 LOWE, A. & Co. Salford, Manchester. — Patent effluvia traps, as used in model cottages, erected by Prince Albert opposite the Exhibition.

63 BELL, W. 40 Pickering Pl. Paddington, Inv.—Suspension-bridges for railway purposes and for northern rivers thickly frozen in winter, so as not to impede floating ice.

64 NAYLOR, W. 56 James's St. Oxford St.—New glass registered ventilator.

65 OLIVER, O. 68 John St. Tottenham Court Rd. Inv. —Registered ventilator and chimney-pot. Fire-escape, applicable to all the stories of a building at the same time.

66 HURST, G. High St. Bedford, Des. and Inv.—Model of a partition, to rise from, and sink into the floor.

67 HORN, A. 39 Baker St. Pentonville, Inv.—Self-acting iron shutter.

68 HILL, S. Clifton, York, Inv.—Model of window, with six panes to open and shut separately, with Venetian blinds for sun shades, and as security against burglars. Fire-place with ventilating air chamber, &c.

69 BATES, T. 9 Domingo St. Old St. Inv. and Manu.— Model of sash-frame and sashes, to open inwards, for being cleaned.

70 REMINGTON, G. W. & J. 138 Sloane St. Inv.— Models of reciprocating engines. Iron breakwater. Breakwater for harbours of refuge.

71 GILES, A. 9 Adelphi Ter. Des.—Model of a curved timber roof. Model of repairing or dry dock.

72 M'LEAN, C. 110 Fleet St.—Models for shop fronts.

73 BOUCH, T. Edinburgh, Inv. and Des.—Model of an apparatus for shipping and unshipping the trains of the Edinburgh, Perth, and Dundee railway.

74 HARRIS, J. C. Bristol.—Model of a shop front.

75 JACKSON & CLAY, 21 Homer St. Lambeth, Inv.— Fire-escape, in form of a table, self-acting. Prov. reg.

76 SPURGIN, J. Guildford St. Inv.—Endless ladder and crane. Patent paddle apparatus. Patent jointed bridge.

77 PEILE, J. J. & Co. 74 Market Place, Whitehaven, Inv. and Manu.—Ship screws.

78 RUSSELL, H. H. 20 George St. Adelphi, Inv. and Des.—Tidal staircase. A speedy Louis for hoisting light stones. Model of a suspension bridge. Registered improvement on Taaffe's patent slating. Design for a new bridge at Westminster and Cologne.

79 SHIELD, —.—Model of shot tower.

80 HOOKE, T. 80 New Cut, Lambeth, Inv. and Manu. —Registered portable bed-room fire-escape.

81 NAYLOR, M. 121 Radnor St. Hulme, Prod.—Illustration of sewering, paving, &c. at Manchester.

82 WELLS, G. Admiralty Office, Inv. — Telegraphic lighthouse, intended to prevent mistake as to identity.

84 LAVANCKY, J. B. 9 Richmond Buildings, Dean St. Soho.—Model of a portable drawbridge.

86 HAWKS, CRAWSHAY, & Co. Gateshead, Newcastle-upon-Tyne, Manu.—Model of the high-level bridge at Newcastle-upon-Tyne. Samples of naval cable and other chain.

90 DUNHILL, T. C.E. 19 Fortess Terrace, Kentish Town, Projector.—Model of metropolitan cattle and carcase market, abattoir, &c. to accommodate 6,000 oxen, and 40,000 sheep.

91 HADLEY, C.—Model of patent paving.

92 TIPLER, T. W. Rugby.—Model of fire escape.

93 LEGRAS, L. N 2 Tenison St. York Road.—Various inventions in connection with sewerage, &c.

94 ELL, G. 3 Tottenham Court, New Road, Inv. and Improver.—Adjustable scaffold observatory or fire-escape. Adjustable ladder. Wheelbarrow. Folding steps, &c.

95 BREMNER, J. D. & A., C.E. Invs.—Model of an apparatus for building sea-walls in deep water. Models of lifeboats. Models of the means used for raising the iron steamship Great Britain. Models of cranes, &c.

96 SMITH, B. Bron Seiont, Carnarvon, Wales, Inv.—Models of four-rail mixed gauge railway, tunnels, railway carriages, &c.

97 WILSON, M. Whitehaven, Inv.—Governor-paddles to obviate the back water in water wheels.

98 RENNIE, G. 21 Whitehall Pl.—Models of stone bridges. Model of an asylum harbour for Dover, by G. B. Rennie, jun.; and of a wrought-iron girder bridge proposed over the Rhine, at Cologne.

99 THE COMMISSIONERS OF NORTHERN LIGHTHOUSES, Edinburgh, Mr. Alan Stevenson, Engineer.—Revolving dioptric apparatus of the first order (same as that at Skerryvore). Fixed dioptric apparatus of the first order, invented by M Fresnel (same as that at the Isle of May, with various improvements). Model of the Bell Rock Lighthouse, lighted in 1811: executed according to the design and under the superintendence of the late Robert Stevenson Model of the Skerryvore Lighthouse: executed according to the design and under the superintendence of Alan Stevenson. Model of balance crane, designed by the late Robert Stevenson, and used by him in the erection of the Bell Rock Lighthouse. Model of the apparatus of an intermittent light: designed by the late Robert Stevenson, and introduced by him at the lights of Tarbetness, Barrahead, and Mull of Galloway, on the coast of Scotland. Model of a lighthouse lantern, on the diagonal arrangement: designed by Alan Stevenson. Mechanical lamp of four wicks, in which the oil is kept continually overflowing by the means of pumps, which raise it from the cistern below. Holophotal arrangement of lighthouse apparatus, prepared by Thomas Stevenson.

100 STEVENSON, T. 84 George St. Edinburgh, Inv.—Revolving light, with axial rotation. Ordinary parabolic reflector rendered holophotal (where the entire light is parallelized) by a portion of the catadioptric annular lens. Holophotal catadioptric annular lens apparatus. Small model of holophotal apparatus, acting by refraction and total reflection only. Holophotal apparatus, with parabolic strips.

101 TUCKEY, R. Hamp. Ct. Palace —Proposed fire-escape.

102 MAXWELL, J. Dumfries.—Iron skylights and iron sashes.

104 HOPKINSON, Jos. sen. Huddersfield.—Bobbin ladder for vessels in port or distress, and suitable for a fire-escape.

105 VIGNOLES, C. 4 Trafalgar Sq. Des.—Model of the wrought-iron bar-chain suspension bridge at Kieff (Russia), now erecting across the river Dnieper; the largest work of the kind hitherto executed. (Central Avenue.)

106 CLARK, E. 448 West Strand.—Model of the Britannia Bridge, and of the apparatus used in floating and raising the tubes. Engineer, R. Stephenson; model executed for C Mare, Esq. by J. James. (Central Avenue.)

107 LEATHER, J. W. Des.—Models by Salter of cast-iron bridge over the river Aire, and suspension aqueduct over the Calder, at Stanley, Yorkshire. (Central Avenue.)

109 WILLIAMS, C.—Models of foot bridge, and of various engineering inventions.

110 CROGGON & Co. 2 Dowgate Hill.—Patent asphalte roofing felt; boiler felt for preventing radiation of heat; ship-sheathing felt, and inodorous felt for damp walls.

111 WILLETT, F. 5 Edward St. Portman Sq. Prop.—Models, with diagram, to show the principle of Taaffe's patent for roofing houses, &c.

112 THOMPSON, F. jun. C. E. Water-works Chambers, Orange St. Leicester Sq. Inv.—New apparatus for economising the consumption of gas. and increasing the light.

113 WILSON, T. H. Twickenham, Inv.—Slides for excluding the wet and the cold from hall doors, shutters, hatchways, and port-holes. Invention for securing carriage gates and coach-house doors.

114 DOBSON, J. Newcastle-upon-Tyne, Des.—Model of the roofs erected at the Newcastle-upon-Tyne Central Railway Station, &c. Model of a rolling machine, designed by T. Charlton, used in rolling iron for the same.

115 PRATT, H. St. Swithin St. Worcester, Inv.—Design of a mill and new power machine for the manu. of bread.

116 McCLELLAND, 3 Palace New Road, Lambeth.—Roof of 100 feet span. Scale ½ inch to a foot.

117 BARCLAY, J. Tongue, by Goldspie, Scotland, Des. and Inv.—A portable pressing-machine. Model of a wooden float bridge, for narrow straits or rivers.

118 TUTTON, J. 20 South Audley St. Grosvenor Sq. Inv. and Pat.—Models of patent improvements in the arrangement of the window spaces of dwelling-houses.

119 WALKER, E. Cardington St. Hampstead Rd.—Patent wire window blinds.

119A SMITH, J. Bartholomew Close.—Model of a door.

120 EVERY, S. F. Quordon, near Derby, Inv. and Manu.—Patent Vulcan chimney-sweeper. Circular and oblong chimney-sweeping machines.

121 NEALE, W. J. 30 Basinghall St. (Hon. Sec. to Com. for awarding medals for the best Chimney-sweeping Machinery.)—Prize machinery. Prize plans and estimates for altering awkward chimneys.

122 ALLAN, J. sen. Glasgow, Manu.—Portable apparatus for making gas from rosin, cooking food for cattle, &c. Gas candelabrum, of cast-iron.

123 NESS, MARY, 24 Mold Green, Huddersfield, Inv.—Window-cleaner, for the protection of female servants.

124 HILL, O. & J. 37 Gt. George St. Westminster, Imp.—Modification of Dr. Arnott's ventilating curtain-pump, arranged so as to be worked by a weight, and to be portable.

125 MACKENZIE, J. S. Newark-upon-Trent, Inv.—The vulcan spring, for closing doors, &c.

126 MACKIE, W. 141 Lower Bagot St. Dublin, Inv.—Patent safety window fittings.

127 ROBERTS, B. E. 2 Nelson Pl. Clifton, near Bristol, Inv.—Newly-invented safety window-sash, which may be cleaned from within.

128 WILLIAMS, L. 14 Upper Marylebone St. Portland Pl. Inv. and Manu.—Man-help for painting ships, houses, &c. Concave-bottom tea-kettle. Safety cot.

129 BRAMHALL, T. 1 Union St. St. George's Rd. Southwark, Inv. and Manu.—Iron and zinc plate work: the anti-Boreas guard.

130 BROWN, R. Sheffield.—Model of a magnetic lightning conductor (half size).

131 BAYLISS, T. 273 Strand.—Fire escapes

132 HOLLAND, T. 40 South Audley St. Inv.—Improved brass cock for kitchen boilers, &c., for giving out hot and cold water, and filling itself. Improved shop shutters. Almanac.

133 ENGLISH PATENT CAMPHINE Co.—Model apparatus for generating heat from bituminous substances without smoke.

134 BOOTH, G. R. 9 Portland Pl. Wandsworth Rd. Inv. and Manu.—Vegetable gas apparatus.

137 SAMPSON, T. Landore, Swansea, Inv.—A high-pressure steam-boiler, with self-feeding apparatus and still.

139 VAUGHAN, W. Maidstone, Inv.—Machine to facilitate the construction of marble, stone, slate, or other chimney-pieces

140 FARRELL, I. 210 Gt. Brunswick St. Dublin, Manu.—Model of a registered circular window.

CIVIL ENGINEERING, ARCHITECTURE,

141 HARPER, T. 15 Upper Seymour St. West, Inv.—Model of a window to serve for an entrance to a garden or pleasure ground. Presented to the Royal Dublin Society by the Exhibitor.

142 M'NEILL, F. & Co. Bunhill Row, Finsbury, Manu.—Waterproof bituminous felt for lining damp walls, &c. ; patent asphalted roofing felt ; patent thin ship sheathing felt, for use under copper, &c.

143 ROCK, J. jun. Hastings.—Model of street barricade.

144 ANDERSON, G. Rothbury, Northumberland, Inv. and Manu.—Model of an improved window.

145 LOWE, G. G. 2 High St. Portland Town, Inv.—Self-cleaning sanitary cistern.

146 QUINCEY, H. 82 Hatton Garden, Inv. and Pat.—Revolving iron safety shutters, perforated metal and dwarf Venetian blinds. Self-supplying pedestal coal vase, &c.

147 THEOBALD, J. 21 Brunswick St. Blackfriars Rd. Inv.—Improved window-sash, with alarm and fire-escape.

148 WALBY, J. 59 Greek St. Soho Sq. Inv.—Universal fire-escape.

150 IRISH ENGINEERING Co.—Finch and Willey's patent safety railway wheel, the skeleton imbedded in the tyre, rendering bolts or other fastenings unnecessary.

151 ALLEN, T. Clifton, near Bristol, Inv. and Manu.—Model of registered fire-proof iron roof, showing the principle applied to a roof of 60 feet span.

152 BUNNETT, J. & Co. 26 Lombard St. City, and Deptford, Kent, Inv. Pat. and Manu.—New patent iron safety shutters. Patent ventilating sashes, &c.

155 TROTMAN, S. Clarendon Rd. Notting Hill, Inv. and Manu —Mechanical fountain. Night dial.

156 WHYTOCK, A. 494 New Oxford St. Manu.—Model of emigrant's house, made of Morewood and Rogers' patent galvanized tinned iron.

157 WILKINS, W. C. 24 Long Acre, Inv. and Manu.—Lantern and revolving apparatus for floating light. Reciprocating dioptric apparatus for lighthouse. (Main Avenue.)

158 COCHRANE, A. 17 Bryanstone St. Bryanstone Sq. Inv.—Patent lock, to be entitled the "Catch-key lock." Smoke condenser, air conductor, &c.

159 RETTIE, R. Edinburgh, Inv.—Railway and marine lamps, signals, life-boats, fire-extinguisher, breakwater, &c. Mining and ventilating apparatus.

160 KING, W. 8 Woodstock St. Bond St. Inv. and Manu.—Models of a floating breakwater and foundation for a lighthouse or place of refuge on the Goodwin Sands.

162 PERKES, S. & Co. Emerson St. Southwark Bridge.—Bearers for principal beams in buildings. Models of patent combination bridges, &c.

163 ROVERE, F. P. C.E. 2 New Inn, St.Clement's, Des.—Design for a wrought-iron girderbridge at Westminster.

164 MAPLIN, —.—Model of a lighthouse, from designs by Messrs. Walker and Burgess, C.E., founded on Mitchell's screw piles (in locomotive passage).

165 SMITH, W. H. 1 Royal Exchange Buildings, Inv.—Recoil breakwater and lighthouse, said to combine economy, strength, and general applicability to all depths and situations. Tubular suspension girder bridge, to prevent vibratory action. Plan for a suspension tunnel.

166 FOX & BARRETT, Thames Chambers, 12 George St. Adelphi, Prop.—Specimens of patent fire-proof flooring or roofing.

169 NASMYTH, G. 7 Park Rd. Kensington, Inv. and Pat.—Two models of wrought-iron girders. (With Classes 5 & 6.)

170 NEWNHAM, T. G. Newtown, Montgomeryshire, Wales.—Model of a portion of the roof of Dolfor church. Model of open roof, of terra cotta. Model of sliding sashes.

171 YOUNG, J. Gas Works, Selkirk, Scotland.—Model of coal-gas apparatus, constructed on a new arrangement.

172 METROPOLITAN ASSOCIATION FOR IMPROVING THE

DWELLINGS OF THE INDUSTRIOUS CLASSES.—Model of dwellings for artizans in Albert Street, Mile End New Town.

173 MACKRORY, F. 4 Milton Ter. Vauxhall Bridge Rd. Pimlico, Inv. and Manu.—Improved window to prevent the entrance of dust and wet.

174 NIXON, T. Kettering, Inv. Des. and Manu.—Design for a self-ventilating garden-light or sky-light, perfectly water-tight. Registered.

175 REMINGTON, ANNE, 138 Sloane St. Chelsea, Inv.—Improved roasting apparatus, with self-acting baster, and heat reflector.

176 HOLMES, J. East Ham, Essex, Des. &c.—Two cottages in one.

177 FREEMAN, J. 19 Artillery Pl. Finsbury.—Model of skew bridge, crossing Westminster Bridge Rd.

178 MOORSOM, Capt. 17A Gt. George St. Westminster, Des. and Superintendent.—Model of a railway viaduct over the Nore, near Kilkenny. Model of prize design for the great bridge over the Rhine, to be erected at Cologne.

180 ROSE, J. T. Regent St. Leith, Des.—Design for a timber viaduct of great span.

181 McLACHLAN, J. Mount Pleasant, Douglas, Isle of Man.—Model of a house, and plans showing sanatory improvements.

182 DANIELL, W. Truro, Inv.—A fire-escape.

183 BERGIN, M. O. 8 George St. Cork, Ireland, Inv.—Working model of a registered self-acting fire-extinguisher.

184 HENDY, J. 1 Bouverie St. Fleet St. Inv.—Model for a new national fire-escape.

185 WEBSTER, W. BULLOCK, 2 St. James's Pl. Hampstead Rd. Inv. and Manu.—Model of a fire-escape, available for a long range or block of houses, of different heights.

186 GREEN, I. 3 Vittoria Pl. Euston Sq. Inv.—Wind guards for chimney-tops.

187 NUNN, ALICIA, 2A Welbeck St. Cavendish Sq.—Self-cleaning solid pulp blotting roller for drying writing.

188 WILSON, T. H. Twickenham, Inv.—Slides for excluding the wet and cold from doors and shutters, hatchways and portholes, &c. Self-acting stop and bolts.

189 STAFFORD, D. 3 Sloane Ter. Sloane St. Chelsea.—" The interceptor cowl," a protection against gusts of wind.

190 MUDGE, J. 78 Tottenham Ct. Rd. Inv.—Private fire-escape, which can be worked from the street or the room.

191 BEESTON, J. 5 Swaile's Cottages, Cambridge Road, Hammersmith.—Treble ventilating chimney.

192 ADCOCK, T. jun. Penkridge, Staffordshire, Inv.—Simultaneous gates for railway crossings, planned for safety, economy, and despatch.

193 STUCKEY, W. Mitre Chambers, Fenchurch St. Inv.—Carriage, crane, and portable fire-escape combined.

194 TAYLOR, HY. 6 John St. West, Barnsbury Rd. Islington.—Machine for sweeping chimneys.

195 WILSON & WOODFIN, Hull. — Various traps for drains.

196 HOOPER, W H. 12 Gt. Cumberland Pl. Hyde Park, Inv.—Model of a rotatory floating breakwater.

197 BAIN, W. 141 High Holborn, Inv.—System of pipes in case of fire. Machine for saving life and property from shipwreck on the coast.

198 BOULANGER, C. T. Alice St. Bermondsey New Rd. Inv.—A fumigator, with refrigerant or cooler, applicable to the destruction of insects in tender plants, in animals, &c.

199 INGLIS, A. Park St. South Shields. Model of a ventilating machine.

201 JACKSON, H. 62 Westbourne St. Pimlico, Inv. and Manu.— Fire-escape dressing-table.

202 BROWN, J. 71 Leadenhall St. Inv. and Manu.—Model of a navigable balloon.

203 FRIARSON, M. 20 Westbourne Park Rd. Paddington Inv.—Registered ventilating shield-cowl.

204 Dunn, M. Newcastle-upon-Tyne, Inv.—Fire-escape.
205 Hearder, J. H. 34 George St. Plymouth.—Rarefying apparatus, for producing a draught in chimneys, &c.
206 Lamb, J. Sunderland.—Tapered tubular gas apparatus for warming. (South east corner.)
215 Taylor, J. W., Rear-Admiral.—Models of patent breakwater; life and anchor boats.
216 Stafford, D. 3 Sloane Terrace, Sloane St. Chelsea.—Patent interceptor cowl.
217 Teagle, R. & W. Chelsea. — Patent chimney-sweeping apparatus.

In Main Avenue, West.

220 Wyatt & Brandon.—Model of the new County

Assize Courts at Cambridge, erected by the exhibitors: modelled by S. Salter. Model in card, of the new church of St. Mary and St. Nicholas, at Wilton.
221 Scott, G. G.—Model of St. Nicholas church, Hamburg.
222 Jee, A. S.—Model of the Dinting Vale viaduct on the Sheffield and Manchester Railway.
223 Willock, E. P. & Co. Manchester.—Model of a decorated Gothic church, at Lever Bridge, Bolton, Lancashire: des. by E. Sharpe.
224 Walker & Bourgess.—Railway bridge across the Ouse.

Also Nos. 9, 19, 26, 28, 38, 105, 106, 107, and 157.

Proceed to Class 21, page 108.

Class 8. **NAVAL ARCHITECTURE, MILITARY ENGINEERING, GUNS, WEAPONS, ETC.**

—— West End Gallery, and South West Gallery. ——

1 Clayton, R. 9 Gresham St. Inv.—The swimming-glove, designed and formed after the web-footed shape.
2 Clarkson, T. C. 111 Strand.—Life boats, of cork, &c.
3 Exall, W. Reading. Inv. and Manu.—Anchor without beam or stock, and having three flukes or grapples, all of which will lay hold at the same time.
4 Murray, J.—Harpoon-gun.
5 Light, E. 216 High St. Wapping, Inv. and Des.—Life belts and buoys. Life boats. Yachting jackets to support the body in the water, &c.
6 Reekes, T. Chelsea.—Nautical cap.
7 Foster, J. R.N.—Specimen of wood and Indian-rubber joinings.
8 Vickers, W. R. 32 Baker St. Portman Sq. Des.—Geometrical floating life-belt, stuffed with cork.
9 Holbrook, J. N. Remington St. City Rd Inv.—Polar and captain's life preservers. Rafts to be carried on board ship. Floaters, life-boats, &c. Fishing stand. Ladies' bathing machine, &c.
10 Lee, T. 4 Bread St. Hill, Des. and Manu.—Improved life-preserver, or swimming belt.
11 Spencer, E. 116 Fenchurch St. Manu.—Watertight trunk, capable of sustaining 15 persons in the water
13 Hely, A. A. 16 Manchester Buildings, Westminster, Inv.—Patent cork-driving apparatus and vent-bottle. Lifefloat, composed of waterproof canvas cases, filled with bedding, provisions, &c. Salvage-boat, life-girdle, &c.
14 Bell, H. Baltic Wharf, Millbank, Westminster, Inv.—Water grapnel, or deep-sea anchor. Submarine boat. Diving-bell adapted for locomotion. Life-boat for the beach.
15 Royal Humane Society, Prop.—Ice-boat, presented to the Society by the one established at Hamburgh. Breaker ladder; ice sledge, drags, and other apparatus.
16 Hatt, C. Lowestoft, Suffolk.—Life-boat.
17 Sparke, W. Exeter, Devon.—Life-boat.
18 Robertson, J. Limehouse Hole, Poplar, Manu.—Cordage of Russian and Manilla hemp, and New Zealand flax (in Classes 5 and 6). Fog or alarm signals. Rapson's slide tiller.
19 King, P. H. F. Sydney Cottage, Hewlett Pl. Cheltenham.—Marine table for preventing breakages at sea.
20 Holtum, W. Walmer, Deal, Inv.—Model of an apparatus for propelling a line to a vessel in distress at a distance from the shore, with wicker boat to travel on a hawser from the shore to the vessel, &c.
21 Jerningham (Commander).—Anchor and mortar for shipwreck purposes.
22 Manby, G. W. Great Yarmouth. — Life-boat and mortar apparatus.

23 Ayckbourn, F. 129 Strand, Inv. and Manu.—Patent float, or invisible life-preserver, and swimming-belt. Models of life-boats and portable boats.
25 Offord, D. Gt. Yarmouth, Inv.—Grapnell shot, to assist the hauling of life-boats, &c. off the beach through heavy surfs.
26 Offord, D. & Bradbeer, S. Gt. Yarmouth, Invs.—Rock life-preserving apparatus.
27 Leftwich, W. H. 43 Cumberland Market, Regent's Park.—Model of a heavy armed cutter, constructed from portions of various old men-of-war and of other oak from places of notoriety.
28 Purser, J. 73 Shaftesbury St. New North Rd. Hoxton.—Fire escape. Bomb shell.
29 Carte, A. G. Citadel, Hull, Inv. and Manu.—Pocket apparatus and sea-service rocket apparatus, for throwing a line to a stranded ship. Self-acting life-buoy, by means of which the lives of nearly 400 persons have been saved since 1838. Self-adjusting cork life-belt. Alarm-signal, for the protection of houses, &c.
30 Ditchburn, T. J. Blackwall, Des. and Manu.—Models of river, coasting, sea-going, and war steam-vessels, "Vladimere," built for the Emperor of Russia; H. M. screw steam-vessel "Sharpshooter;" steam-packet "Wonder;" iron cutter-yacht "Mystery;" "Earl Spencer," one of the last pas enger sailing-packets that plied between London and Gravesend, built 1796; H.M. "Fairy" screw steam-yacht; a schooner sailing-yacht; wrought-iron caissoon, to supersede entrance gates to the new docks at Woolwich.
31 Lavars, J. Bridge St. Bristol, Inv.—Models of a floating buoyant settee, for the deck of passenger steamers.
32 Sloggett, R. Devonport, Des. and Prod.—Specimen of naval architectural drawing, representing the profile and bow of a war steam-ship of 500 horse power.
33 Simons, W. Greenock, Scotland, Des. and Manu.—Model of a screw frigate. Model of a yacht.
34 Walters, H. Monmouth Ct. Dorset Pl. Pall Mall.—Fire escape and scaling ladder.
35 Moore, W. F. Plymouth, Devon, Manu.—Half model of cutter yacht, Pixey, and of schooner yacht, Halcyon.
36 White, J. East Cowes, Isle of Wight, Des. and Manu.—Design for a new 90-gun ship. Models of H. M. S. Victory, Phaeton, steam-ship Termagant, and brigs Waterwitch, Daring, and Contest. Models of a schooner and a cutter-yacht, Victoria yacht, built for the Emperor of Russia, &c.
36a White, T. J. & R. West Cowes, Isle of Wight, Inv. Des. and Manu.—Model of the steam-ship Vassitei Tigaret, built for the Turkish Government. Designed for a 50-gun frigate, and for the first transatlantic steam-ship; Medina

steam-ship. Design for an ocean steam-ship of 3,000 tons. Steam-ship Vectis, built for the Peninsular and Oriental Company. Models of life-boats. Screw, steam, and sailing-ships of 2,500 tons, &c.

37 TOVELL, G. R. Mistley, Manningtree, Essex, Inv.—Model of a ship's hull, of parabolical form.

38 MURRAY, W. 20 John St. Adelphi, Manu. and Licensee.—A harpoon gun, Tucker's tapping-up apparatus for propelling, and Normanville's ship scrubber.

39 AZULAY, B. Rotherhithe, Inv.—Model of a sailing vessel, with auxiliary screw-propeller, worked by the men on board. It has also a backward motion.

40 DEANS, W. 9 America Sq.—Two models of triangular bottomed ships' hulls.

41 GIBSON, A. 2 Exmouth Pl. Cheltenham.—Steam-ship, with improved endless-chain paddles.

42 GEORDESON, J.—Method of reefing the sails by lowering the masts.

45 ERSKINE, D. Clerk St. Edinburgh.—Life-boats.

46 RICHARDSON, H. T.—Life-boat.

47 ACHESON, J. 102 Leadenhall St.—Life-boat.

49 BONNEY, W. W. Claremont Villa, St. John's, Fulham.—Life-boat.

50 HODSON, J. Sunderland.—Life-boat.

51 ALLAN, J. H.—Life-boat.

52 WHITE, T. jun. Cowes, Isle of Wight, Des. Inv. and Manu.—Four models for the entire navy, from one design. Frigate and corvette upon parabolic sections. Heaving-up slip. Work on naval architecture illustrative of the whole.

53 HAWKSWORTH, A.—Life-boat

54 REED, J. Silver St. Stockton-on-Tees, Inv.—A life-boat, righting itself under all circumstances, without the aid of an iron keel or deadweight of any kind.

55 TREDWEN, R.—Life-boat.

56 WIGRAM, MONEY & SONS, Blackwall.—Half models of ships, &c.

57 ROBSON, J. Gateshead, Newcastle, Prop.—Model of an iron steam-tug or passenger-steamer.

58 PETLEY, T. 7 Gt. Hermitage St.—Model of iron steam-tug.

59 GREENER, W. Birmingham, Inv. and Manu.—Double guns and rifles; harpoon guns; rocket gun and lines for use in shipwrecks; patent stanchion gun for wild-fowl shooting: military musket, and rifle. Laminated steel, &c.

60 DYNE, W. 17 Basing Pl. Kingsland Rd. and Brighton Station, London Bridge, Inv.—Patent life-launch. Life-boat and rafts. "Stone life-boat." "Stone buoy," &c.

61 BROWN, LENOX, & Co. 8 Billiter Sq.—Inv. and Manu.—The largest and smallest anchors and cables used in the Royal Navy. Patent windlass purchase. Registered pit chain. Patent malleable cast-iron blocks.

62 FAWCETT, F. Mount Pleasant, Douglas.—Isle of Man life-boats.

63 BETTELEY, J. Liverpool, Manu.—Model of ship's windlass, with patent propeller. Patent anti-friction sheaves.

64 BAILLIE, B. 118 Wardour St. Soho, Inv.—Model of a vessel, with improved rigging, mast, and sails for a fore-and-aft rigged vessel.

65 PEARSON, J. W. Mill Dam. South Shields.—Model of an oar.

66 THOMPSON, T. Commander, R.N. 3 George St. Leith, Inv.—Safety-plug, for boats and vessels, constructed of gun-metal or brass.

67 PARKER, C. Newark, Notts, Inv.—A screw valve, intended to supersede the present plug in ship's boats.

68 HOPWOOD and ARMSTRONG, 184 St. George St. Wellclose Sq.—Brass registered side scuttles, for light and ventilation of ships, &c.

69 GREGORY, 54 St. George St. East, Inv.—Safety-plate, to cover the aperture of a ship's scuttle.—Registered.

71 LONG, J. & J. & Co.—Improved steering wheel.

72 DENHAM, Capt. H. M. R.N., F.R.S., United Service Club, Inv.—Model, with drawing and description, of Denham's Jury Tiller. Cooper and Maclean, 12 Billiter Square, agents.

73 HALL, W. E. Moreton, Bideford, and 55 Gt. Marylebone St. Inv.—Apparatus for the application of the Catenarian curve to the line of ships. Model of an 18-gun brig or corvette. Series of diagrams, illustrating a theory of naval architecture.

74 BAIRD, J. R. 210 Strand, Inv.—Method of lowering a ship's boat.

75 ORR, M. Greenock, Scotland, Inv.—Model, drawing, and explanation of angulated jibs. Treatise on the area of sails for open boats.

76 WATSON, T. 79 Provost St. Hoxton—Model of a plan for the correct measurement of tonnage in ships.

77 POOLE, J. jun. Copper House, Cornwall.—Paddle wheel.

78 SLATER, W. 332 High St. Wapping, Prop.—Improved patent copper powder-barrel, which preserves gunpowder in perfect safety against fire and damp.

79 GALE, G. H. Swansea.—Life-boat.

80 LADD, C. P. Lieut. R.N. 10 Walcot Pl. Lambeth, Des. and Inv.—Marine swing table to prevent breakage of glass and spilling of liquids at sea in rough weather.

81 MASON, E. Brompton Post Office, Inv. and Des.—Models of improved double-action screw steam boat, and of a self-acting life-boat. Section of ship's deck, with concealed fastenings.

82 CORYTON, J. Erectheum Club, St. James's Sq. Inv. and Prop.—Life-boat, and new propeller, &c.

83 BREMNER, J. Wick, Scotland.—Life-boat.

84 FERGUSON, C. A & T. Poplar.—Gun-carriage.

85 ALLAN, J. H. 2 Leadenhall St. Prop.—Model of a South Shields coble. Model of truss-work, introduced by Sir R. Seppings for the internal fastening of ships, and on the same principle as the girders of the Exhibition Building.

86 LYONS, G. 8 Britain St. Portsea, Inv. and Manu.—Screw propelling rudder.

87 MARGARY, —.—Specimens of patent canvas. Various pieces of prepared and unprepared canvas in different stages of perfection.

88 PARSEY, W. 455 Oxford St. Inv.—Bell buoy for warning vessels of danger.

89 KINCAID, T. Greenock, Scotland, Inv.—Models of fan propeller, variously applied.

90 BEADON, G. Creechbarrow Taunton, Somersetshire, Inv.—"Prince Albert's mirror," upon a nautical adjustment. Universal rowlocks. Whale gun. Boat safety reel. Life raft. Mast clamp. Gun elevator, &c. Indicating or filter cock. Phaeton hood lifter. Improved door, obviating draughts, &c. Universal tractor.

91 CLARK, J. 10 Parliament St. Westminster, Inv.—Model of the bunk life-boat: to be used as a cot. Model of a flexible life-boat.

92 YOUNG, DOWSON, & Co. Poplar, Manu.—Improved rudder fastenings, which can be refitted on board.

93 GRANTHAM, J. Orange Ct. Liverpool, Inv.—Model of the section of an iron ship, wood sheathing, &c.

94 SMALE, W. 13 Charlton Ter. Woolwich, Inv.—Anchor, which can be taken to pieces and stowed in one-third less room than an ordinary anchor.

95 HONIBALL, J 42 Cornhill, Pat.—Porter's patent anchors, which have been tested by order of the Right Hon. the Lords Commissioners of the Admiralty.

97 BETTELEY & Co. Brunswick Dock, Liverpool.—Windlass.

98 COTTEW, J. E. 19 South St. Lambeth, Inv.—Windlass to raise ships' anchors.

99 INGLEFIELD, E. A., R.N. 9 Portsea Pl. Connaught Sq. Inv.—Model of H.M. brig "Flying-Fish," fitted with a screw propelled, to be worked by the capstern ; also gearing for connecting the screw-shaft with the chain-pumps. An anchor without a stock, both flukes taking the ground, when in use.

100 ROBINSON, J. 6 Pattison St. Stepney, Inv.—Boats to save life from shipwreck. Patent steering-machines, with a reboundable rudder. Patent machines for raising weights, weighing anchor, &c. Improved pumping-machine.

101 MUNTZ, G. F. M.P. Limehouse, Inv.—Patent ships' sheathing metal and ships' fastenings.

102 WOOD & Co. Liverpool, and 275 Wapping, London. Manu.—Patent windlass purchase and spindles; patent winch, steering barrel and anchor; chain cable iron, &c.

103 BROWNING, S. J. 66 High St. Portsmouth, Inv. and Manu.—Brass urn-shaped binnacle of entirely new construction, with newly invented compass, &c. Binnacle, invented by S. J. Browning for H.M. yacht Victoria and Albert. Marine target, &c.

104 BERTHON, Rev. E. L. Fareham, Hants, Inv.—Perpetual log, for indicating the speed and leeway of ships: patented. Clinometer, for showing the list and trim of ships: patented. Collapsible life-boat.

105 TAYLOR, JANET, 104 Minories, Manu.—A bronze binnacle, with compass, designed from the water lily.

106 HEMSLEY, T. 11 King St. Tower Hill, Inv. and Manu.—Improved ship's binnacle, with reflecting lamp, which can also be used as a signal-light.

108 PARKES, H. P. Dudley, Inv. Pat. and Manu.—Wrought-iron stud chain, as adopted by the sub-marine committee, Liverpool. A patent flat pit chain or band.

109 WEST, Commander, 1 James' St. Adelphi.—Marine compass on a new principle, controlling the oscillation of the magnetic needle.

110 SOULBY, J. 126, High St. Wapping, Manu.—Safety windlass Captain Cook's quadrant and compass, the identical instrument used by that celebrated mariner in his voyage round the world.

111 JENKINS, J. 2 Union Row, Minories, Manu.—Boat binnacle, containing compass and lamp.

112 FYER & ROBINSON.—Steering wheel.

113 SCOULLER, J. 65 Argyle St. Glasgow, Inv.—Fog signal-light, for shore and ship signals.

114 HASTINGS, J. 24 Billiter St. City, Prop.—Models of a windlass and capstan, fitted with Johnstone's patent double-action lever purchase. Model of a ship's capstan and rim or cable-holder, and Gryll's patent whelps.

115 ALLISON, E. W. 36 Nottingham Pl. Stepney, Inv.—Improved steering wheel to prevent accidents at sea.

116 SALTER, J. West St. Commercial Rd. Inv. and Manu.—Model of improved ship's capstan.

117 SPENCELEY, J. Whitstable, near Canterbury, Inv.—Patent pillar and screw apparatus, for preventing ships from logging, and for restoring logged ships to their original shear. Patented.

119 MATHEWS, T. 83 Berwick St. Soho.—Paddle-wheel.

120 GILBERT, E. Falmouth.—Registered marine signal lamp, which yields a light equal to a blue light.

121 CHAPMAN, J. T. 328 Wapping, Inv. and Pat.—Pair of shroud blocks and portable screw winch, for setting up a ship's rigging and raising weights.

123 BURGESS, F. 18 Salisbury St. Strand, Prop.—Model of splicing main and top masts, by small pieces of wood.

124 SIMMENS, J.—Mounts Bay fishing-boat.

125 SMITH, S. Ship Yard, Waterford, Des.—Spring machine for modelling ships of any form or dimensions

126 ESDAILES & MARGRAVE, City Saw Mills, Regent's Canal, Manu. — Bothway's internal iron-strapped ships' blocks.—Tested block and other specimens, in use.

127 RUSSELL, T. S. 37 Gt. George St. Westminster, Inv.—Model of ships constructed on the wave principle : War steamer, with paddle-wheels, constructed by Robinson and Russell, at Millwall, showing the new patent system of armament. Sailing corvette, on the wave principle, proposed by Captain Fishbourne, and constructed by Dr. Phipps, &c.

128 ORDNANCE SURVEY DEPARTMENTS.—Ordnance maps of England and Wales, city of Dublin, county of Lancaster, town of Liverpool &c.

129 ELLIS, F. A. Commander, R.N. Gt. Yarmouth.—Model of a yacht with a silding keel, to enable her to go up shallow rivers and over bar-harbours. A method of lowering the mast. A projecting bow, &c.

130 MACNAB, J. 25 York Pl. Edinburgh.—Model of an improved first-class sea-going steam-ship.

131 GREEN, Richard, Blackwall.—Model of the "Owen Glendower" East Indiaman, built at Blackwall.

132 HOWE, J. Newcastle-upon-Tyne.—Model of a clipper merchant schooner, complete and in working order.

133 DOWNS, H. Mile Town, Sheerness, Des.—Model of a corvette of 20 guns, regularly built, fitted, armed, and rigged.

134 LAMPORT, C. Workington, Des.—Model of one of Lindsay & Co.'s line of ships to Calcutta, 800 tons register.

135 CLARKE, J. A. 7 Hamilton Sq. Birkenhead, Des.—Model of an improved steam vessel intended to possess all the qualities desirable in a good sea-boat, and for carrying weight at an increased speed.

136 NORTHUMBERLAND LIFE BOAT COMMITTEE.—Models of life-boats competing for the prize. Communicated by Capt. Washington, R.N. F.R.S.

Names of Competitors.

1 Ainsworth, John	28 Houten, William Va
2 Anderson, Thomas	29 Jones, Josiah, jun.
3 Beeching, James	30 Lee, George
4 Bertram, James	31 Lyons, George
5 Blair, Robert	32 Milburn, George
6 Bosch, P. Van Den	33 Orton, Reginald
7 Bremner, James	34 Palmer, George
8 Bromley, Gilbee	35 Patterson, William
9 Browne, John Harcourt	36 Plenty, James, & Edw. Pellew
10 Costain, Thomas	37 Robinson, Alexander
11 Edmond, John	38 Robinson, Daniel
12 Falkingbridge, William	39 Robinson, William Wharton
13 Farrow, George	40 Saxby & Brain
14 Francis, Joseph	41 Semmens, J.
15 Gale, John & Robert	42 Severn, Henry Augustus
16 Gale, G. Hamlyn	43 Sharpe, Benjamin
17 Gaze, Thomas	44 Sinclair, Duncan
18 Grant, William	45 Slater and Wright
19 Greener, William	46 Sparke, William
20 Gurr, Charles	47 Teasdel, William
21 Hall, Messrs.	48 Thompson, John
22 Harding, J. & J.	49 Tredwen, Richard
23 Harvey, T., & Son	50 Turner, George
24 Hatt, Cyprian	51 Wake, Thomas, & Son
25 Hay, the Rt. Hon. Lord J.	52 W. M. & R. F.
26 Hinks, Henry	53 Whettam, James
27 Hodgson, Joseph	54 White, Thomas and John

136A HAWKS, W. R. Robin Hood's Bay, nr. Whitby, Inv. and Manu.—Model of life-boat, emptying itself in a few seconds, by means of two apertures in the bottom.

137 FAWENS, G. Inv.—A life-boat, of wood and cork, lined with gutta percha.

138 MILBURN, G. Blyth, Northumberland.—Life-boat.

139 M'LAREN, W. 74 High St. Camden Town, Manu.—Model of an 80-gun ship, fully rigged, &c.

140 CONSTABLE, H. Brighton.—Model of Trafalgar (the battle of).

141 BILBE & Co. Nelson Dock, Rotherhithe, Inv.—Model of a merchant ship, with diagonal frame timbers

142 COLEGRAVE, F. E. Round Hill House, Brighton, Inv.—A model of a brigantine fitted with anchor, cable, and lanyard springs.

143 BROOKES, H. 46 Mornington Pl. Hampstead Rd. Prop.—Patent steam-tug, for hauling vessels on canals or narrow rivers, having neither paddles, wheels, nor screw propeller.

144 MUMFORD, W. T. 19 Edward St. Deptford, Inv.—A model of the paddle-box of a steam frigate of 600 horse-power, with wheel and paddle-box boat. Model of a carriage for working a gun at a bow, broadside, or sternport.

145 ADMIRALTY, SOMERSET HOUSE.—Series of half-models of ships-of-war, fitted with screw-propellers.

146 ADMIRALTY, SOMERSET HOUSE.—Series of half-models of sailing ships. Series of half-models of experimental frigates. Series of half-models of experimental brigs. Whole models; and models of bows, sterns, and transverse sections.

147 CAMPBELL, A. F. Great Plumstead, Norwich.—Model of a screw steamer.

148 TWYMAN, H. Ramsgate, Manu.—Model of a lugger used on this coast for rendering assistance to vessels in distress.

149 MARE, C. J. & Co. Orchard Yd. Blackwall, Manu. and Des.—1 Model of Her Majesty's iron screw steam-yacht, "Fairy." 2 Model of iron steam-vessels built for the Emperor of Russia, the Viceroy of Egypt, &c.

150 HARRIS, Sir W. S. Plymouth, Inv.—Practical models, illustrative of the system of lightning conductors employed in Her Majesty's ships.

151 HUSBAND, J. Mylor, Falmouth, Inv.—Model of a new life-boat. A new fastening for ships.

152 ALDEBERT, I. 57 Long Acre, Inv.—Model of a first-class frigate.

153 TURNBULL, R. South Shields, Des.—Model of the hull of a merchant ship, of 867 tons O. M., built according to Lloyd's.

154 TURNBULL, E. Whitby, Yorkshire, Manu.—Models of a 74-gun ship, of the time of Lord Nelson, and of the steam-ship Phœnix.

156 HALL, J. Bromley, Bow, Middlesex, Prop.—Models of a ship's rudder, and a plan for wearing a ship without a rudder.

157 BELL, H. Baltic Wharf, Milbank.—Life-boat.

158 BROWNE, W. C. Totnes, Devon, Des. and Inv.—Model of Princess Royal, 120-gun ship, made of wood and card-board.

159 HARVEY, D. 3 Cumming Pl. Pentonville Hill.—Models of the "Victoria and Albert," and "Fairy" yachts, and a 46-gun frigate.

160 GRAY, J. Newhaven, Sussex, Builder.—Mechanical model of a South Sea whaling fishery ship, on a scale of ¼ inch to a foot.

161 HORN, H. Victoria Cottage, Kingston, Portsea.—Model of a 12-gun brig on a slip for launching.

162 WHITE, —.—Model of the ship " Enderby."

163 MILLER, RAVENHILL, & Co. Ratcliffe and Blackwall, Builder.—Model of the Jupiter steam-boat, running between London and Gravesend. Des. by E. Pascoe.

164 ROSE, J. T. Regent St. Leith, Des.—Model of a Roman war-galley (Quadrireme), illustrative of Mr. Howell's theory of the Polycrots, that the "banks" were reckoned in the direction of the galley's length, and not from the number of tiers.

165 SMITH, H. 208 Rotherhithe St. Rotherhithe, Manu.—A built model of the barque " Ealing Grove." Models of equestrian figures.

166 HOLL, J. & Co. Vauxhall Wharf.—Model of a barge.

*** FROM 167 TO 180 IN SOUTH GALLERY AT EAST END.

167 WENTZELL, A. Lambeth, Manu.—Racing boat, built of mahogany and maple. Light gig, built of mahogany, maple, and chesnut. Registered life-boat.

168 FORSTER, J. & T. Streatham, Inv.—Boat, built of wood, coated on both sides with a compound of gutta percha and India-rubber. Accoutrements made of the above, and of a waterproof japanned fabric.

169 SEARLE & SONS, Stangate, Lambeth, Manu.—Model of the state barge of the Lord Mayor of London. (Main Avenue, West.) Pair-oared gig.

169A BROWN, J. 71 Leadenhall St. Inv. and Manu.—Portable raft for shipwreck, &c. Double-action sofa bed, to prevent sea sickness. Fire-escape scaffold.

170 LAPTHORN, J. Gosport, Hants, Maker of Sails.—Model of a brig yacht, 450 tons, spars and sails.

171 RUTHVEN, M. W. New St. Edinburgh, Inv. and Pat.—Model of a steam vessel, with improvements in propelling and navigating.

172 SHULDHAM, M. Melton, Woodbridge, Inv.—Revolving masts, &c. with an improved method of securing the masts by an open octagonal pyramid, rising from the vessel's deck. Method of ballasting vessels with the revolving rig.

173 PENRICE, Lieut. R.E. Ordnance Survey, Hull, Inv. and Prop.—Model of the stern of a vessel, with a new propeller and machinery, the object being to obtain a more direct reaction, less slip, and greater velocity of stroke.

174 DEMPSTER, H. 1 Cannon St. Hamburgh Pl. Leith.—Drawing of a simple telegraph, being a system of sea signals by means of colours. Mast with model flag.

175 LONG, J. P. Gt. Yarmouth, Inv.—Model of a new plan for paddle-wheels of steam-vessels. Improvement for adjusting the rigging of vessels, &c.

176 PILKINGTON, J. Goole, Leeds, Inv.—A wrought-iron keelson for wood-built ships : being tubular and water-tight, assists in ballasting vessels when clear of cargo, by opening a valve to admit water, &c.

177 CORTE, —.—Rocket apparatus.

178 NOULTON & WYLD, Fore St. Lambeth, Manu.—London outrigger sculling boat, for racing ; the body in one plank, from head to stern, without a join or reel. Model of an eight-oared shallop, with awnings.

179 BIFFEN, W. Hammersmith, Inv. and Builder—A rigged portable expansive boat.

180 HUBBARD, C. Dickleburgh, near Scole, Norfolk, Inv.—Gutta percha portable boat, for crossing detached inland waters. Miniature working model of a portable wince, for climbing precipices. Case of ornithological specimens.

*** FROM 181 TO 197 WITH CLASSES V. AND VI. GROUND FLOOR, NORTH SIDE.

181 BROOKER, J. Maryport, Des.—Figure-head: Ceres, picking up the veil of her daughter Proserpine.

182 GLADSTONE, J. jun. & Co. Liverpool.—Model of ship's windlass purchase.

184 FERGUSON, C. A. & T. Mast House, Mill Wall, Poplar, Inv. and Manu.—Models of masts made with small timber. Improved fid. Caselli's improved gun. Gun-carriages. Blocks, &c.

185 ANSELL, C. Tottenham, Des. — Sailing gunning

punt, with water-tight bulk heads, for wild-fowl shooting on the coast. Stanchion gun, with improved vulcanised India-rubber recoil spring.

186 WELD, J. Lulworth Castle, Wareham, Des.—Model of a 12-gun brig of war, on peculiar scientific principles, calculated to insure fast sailing.

187 ANDERSON, J. North Shields.—A life-boat.

188 JEFFERY, WALSH, & Co. Limehouse, Inv.—Specimen of patent marine glue, showing its utility in naval architecture, and its durability and cleanliness. In the construction of made-masts, it admits of small seasoned Dantzic, or northern timber, being used instead of yellow pine.

189 O'CONNER, H. Limerick.—A rotatory boat-pump.

190 ANDERSON, R. Westoe, South Shields, Inv.—Small pattern life-boat, clinker-built, fitted with air-tight ceiling, feathered and grooved up to her gunwales; she has a well holding 44 gallons of water for ballast.

191 TRAIL, A. 8 Upper East Smithfield, Inv. and Pat.—Patent storm sails.

192 ADDISON & GILBERT, Emmet St. Poplar.—Models of patent sails.

193 ROBINSON & RUSSELL.—Model of Prussian war steamer.

194 CARPENTER, Capt. United Service Club.—Duplex rudder and screw-propeller.

195 LAURIE, R. W. 8 Carlton Pl. Laurieston, Glasgow, Inv. and Pat.—Various articles for the preservation of life at sea. Buoyant mattrasses, cushions, bolsters, portmanteaus, &c. Life floats and belts. Model of a life-boat, &c.

197 TAYLOR, F. 6 Laurie St. Leith, Inv. and Manu.—Marine chair. Deck seat, &c. convertible into life raft. Camp stool. Models of life-boats, &c.

199 NAYLOR I. Monk Bretton, near Barnsley, Inv.—Patent alarm-gun for the protection of property and game.

200 WILKINSON & SON, 27 Pall Mall, Manu.—Gun, with spiral recoil spring, for wild-fowl shooting. Fowling pieces. Rifle. Silver-gilt scimetar, ornamented with precious stones, &c. Regulation swords, &c. Highland claymore. Illustrations of the manufacture of gun barrels and sword blades.

201 JENNENS & Co. 56 Conduit Street, Manu.—Specimens of military officers' cap-plates, breast-plates, and buttons; and naval fancy and livery buttons.

202 ALLEN & Co. 124 New Bond St.—A new ventilating hat; the ventilation is in the lower crown. For hot climates it allows a current of air between the sun and head. For cold climates, it acts as a ventilator without exposing the head to the weather.

203 WITTON, DAW, & Co. 57 Threadneedle St. Manu.—Rifles for India and Africa. Fowling piece. Duelling pistols.

204 LANDON & MORLAND, 17 Jermyn St. St. James's Des. and Inv.—Officers' infantry helmet of papier-maché. Privates' helmets.

205 HAWKER, Col. P. Longparish House, near Whitchurch, Hants, Inv.—A stanchion gun, with improved waterproof ignition, forged and stocked on a new principle. Models of two-handed punts containing gun, gear, &c. for wild-fowl shooting.

206 BRAZIER, J. & R. Wolverhampton, Manu.—Specimens of gun manufacture. Double gun-tube locks; double rifle-locks; musket percussion-locks, &c.

207 POTTS, T. H. Haydon Sq. Minories, Inv. and Manu.—Double-barrel guns, with improved breeches, bolted triggers, &c. Instrument for drawing the breeches.

208 COX, N. F. Gt. Peter St. Westminster, Manu.—Fencing implements.

209 MOORE & GREY, 78 Edgware Rd. Manu.—Double fowling-pieces, two-grooved rifles, and pistols.

210 POWELL, R. 28 Poland St. Oxford St. Des.—Design for a military cloak coat.

211 FIRMIN & SONS, 153 Strand, and 13 Conduit St. Bond St. Manu.—Specimens of military and other buttons. Orders, in enamel and silver. Plates for military shoulder-belts, shakos, &c. Swords, Highland dirk, &c.

212 HAWKES & Co. 14 Piccadilly, Inv. and Manu.—Military and other head dresses. English military accoutrements. Embroidered banner.

213 BERINGTON, J. Hoxton.—Improved military knapsack, belt, and pouch.

214 ROBINSON, A. 41 Whitcomb St. Haymarket.—Best Damascus gun barrels.

215 GIBBS, G. Clare St. Bristol, Inv. and Manu.—Improved reg. double-barrel gun, with protector against wet.

216 BEATTIE, J. 205 Regent St. Manu.—Two-groove rifle, double guns, duelling pistols, small double holsters, set of best double gun furniture, hogskin flasks, shot pouches, loading rod, with swivel.

217 MANTON & SON, 6 Dover St. Piccadilly, Manu.—Double guns, double rifle, and duelling pistols, and apparatus.

218 NEEDHAM, W. & J. 26 Piccadilly, Prop.—Patent self-priming gun. Self-priming musket, to use the military flange cap. Safety stop-lock gun. Game registers, double and single guns to load at the breech. Self-loading carbine.

219 BOSS, T. 73 St. James' St. Manu.—A central fire double and other guns. Specimen of the manufacture of a gun barrel, &c.

220 BECKWITH, H. 58 Skinner St. Snowhill, Manu.—Fowling-pieces, blunderbusses, and other fire-arms.

221 BENTLEY & SON, 12 South Castle St. Liverpool, Inv. and Manu.—Double patent central fire percussion guns.

222 TRULOCK & SON, 9 Dawson St. Dublin, Manu.—Double-bar. guns. Centripetal double gun. Pistols. Barrel and lock manufacture.

223 DEANE, ADAMS, & DEANE, 30 King William St. London Bridge.—Patent spiral raised rib rifles. Patent safety stop lock guns. Patent gun locks: fowling-pieces, Indian and African rifles, pistols, &c.

223A DEANE, G. & J. 30 King Wm. St. London Bridge.—Guns, rifles, pistols, &c.

224 PARKER, FIELD, & SONS, 233 Holborn, Manu.—Fowling and rifle guns. Pistols. Air-gun. Musket. Fusil. Carbine. Manacles, &c.

225 ELEY, W. & C. 38 Broad St. Golden Sq. Inv. and Manu.—Illustrations of the manufacture of patent wire cartridges and percussion caps. Gun wadding.

226 LANG, J. 7 Haymarket, Manu.—Guns, rifles, pistols. and revolvers. Patent walking-stick gun, with rifle and shot barrels, &c.

227 INSKIP, H. Hertford, Inv.—United service powder and shot flask. Prov. Reg. Improved egg boiler.

228 GOLDING, W. 27 Davies St. Berkeley Sq. Inv. and Manu.—Double sporting gun, with improvements.

229 WOOLFIELD, T. Hertford, Inv. and Manu.—Simple constructed single gun for countries where there are no gun-makers.

230 WOODWARD, J. 64 St. James's St.—Fowling piece, with detached waterproof lock.

231 YEOMANS & SON, 67 Chamber St. Goodman's Fields.—An assortment of muskets.

232 EGG, H. 1 Piccadilly, Manu.—Self-priming and barrel copper cap fowling pieces.

233 FAIRMAN, J. 68 Jermyn St. near St. James's St. Manu.—Double cross-eyed gun. Double gun in soft state. Single gun. Single rifle two grooved. Improved game markers, caps, and chemically prepared waddings:

234 OSBORNE, C. 1 Lichfield St. Birmingham, Manu.—Improved central-fire double guns with chain-twist barrels; bar-slide, double, and single guns; tube single gun; large single gun, with Col. Hawker's improved ignition; improved alarm gun, pistols, &c.

235 GODDARD, S. A. Birmingham, Manu.—Fowling guns; American ducking gun. Pattern, and common African musket. California protector gun. Invented by the exhibitor. Gun barrels, partially finished.

236 RIGBY, W. & J. 24 Suffolk St. Dublin, Manu.—Guns and rifles, double and single; rifle and revolving pistols. Parts of guns in unfinished state, &c.

237 REILLY, E. M. New Oxford St. Manu.—Improved guns, rifles, pistols, air guns, &c.

238 DAVIDSON, D. Captain, Bombay Army (per C. H. Davidson, Haddington), Inv.—Rifles and pistols, with telescopic sights, and bored for grooved bullets.

238A WATKINS & HILL, Charing Cross.—Rifle, with telescope.

239 BULL, J. Bedford, Manu.—Double-barrel gun, with the modern improvements.

240 RICHARDS, WESTLEY, & SON, Birmingham, Manu.—Rifles, double tiger guns, pistols, &c. Registered improved corkscrews and carving forks.

241 COOPER, J. R. & Co. 24 Legge St. Birmingham, Manu.—Patent self-cocking pocket-pistol, revolving pistols, ladies' pistols, &c.

242 WALKER, R. Graham St. and Broad St. Birmingham, Manu. and Pat.—Specimen of percussion caps; metallic gun-wadding.

243 TOWNSEND, J. 11 and 12 Sand St. Birmingham, Manu.—Improved rifle and walking-stick air-guns.

244 REEVES, GREAVES, & Co. 28 Bartholomew St. Birmingham, Manu.—Officers' dress sabres and field-swords.

245 HART, H. 54 New Canal St. Birmingham, Manu.—Guns and pistols. Specimens of gun-barrel manufacture in every state, from the old horse-nail stubs of earliest period to the latest improvements.

246 BROOKES & SON, 28 Russell St. Birmingham, Manu.—Fowling-pieces. Rifles. Revolving gun. Military guns. South American (Buenos Ayres) and Spanish carbines. African trading guns. Dane guns. Pistols, &c.

247 TIPPING & LAWDEN, Birmingham, Manu.—Illustration of gun-barrel manufacture; rifles, guns, pistols, air-guns, &c.

248 MOLE, R. Broad St. Birmingham, Manu.—Gilt mounted sword, blade of finest cast steel; highly mounted Mamaluke sword; officers' regulation swords. Matchets of best cast steel for America, West Indies, &c.

249 POWELL & SON, Carr's Lane, Birmingham, Manu.—Double-barrelled rifle and gun; pistols; improved safety trigger guard; pair of lock actions, &c.

250 WINTON, H. 53 Cleveland St. Birmingham, Inv. and Manu.—Improved safety guns.

251 CARRON, W. Birmingham.—Alarm gun.

251A BAYLIS & SON, 8 St. Mary's Row, Birmingham.—Gun implements.

252 HOSKINS, J. 31 Frith St, Soho Sq. Inv. and Manu.—Double gun, with safety; on a new and simple principle.

253 DAVIS, J. 1 Duke St. North Parade, Bath, Inv. and Manu.—Soldier's musket, substituting the blade of the bayonet for the ramrod.

254 SHAW, J. Glossop, Inv. and Pat.—India rubber air-gun; the requisite pressure of air for one discharge being procured instantly at the pull of the trigger. Patent valve-bugle: the valves applicable to all brass instruments: the patent is now being worked by J. Köhler, Henrietta Street, Covent Garden.

255 FLETCHER, T. 161 Westgate St. Gloucester.—Two double guns, with various improvements.

256 FORSYTH & Co. Leicester St. Leicester Sq. Inv. and Manu.—Patent safety gun, &c. Original percussion gun, as invented by Forsyth, containing a reservoir of powder.

257 ERSKINE, J. Newton Stewart, Scotland, Inv. and Manu.—Two guns, newly invented to prevent accidental discharge, with complete waterproof for the cap.

258 RIPPINGILLE, E. 81 King St. Manchester, and 87 Albany St. Regent's Park, London, Inv.—An improved gun-lock, with stock.

259 HASWELL, R. 12 Upper Ashby St. Prop.—Air pistol on a new principle.

260 NEEDHAM, H. 4 Vine St. Regent St.—Self-priming fowling-piece.

261 BRIDER, J. 4 Clifton Cottages, Denmark St. Camberwell, Inv. and Manu. — Telescope loading rod for fire-arms.

262 BRIDER, G. 30 Bow St. Covent Garden, Inv. and Manu.—Rifle mallet for hot climates.

263 BAKER, T. K. 88 Fleet St. Inv. and Manu.—Improved patent gun-lock for preventing accidents from fire-arms.

264 GOLDEN & SON, Huddersfield, Manu.—Bentley's patent double gun, with improved locks, &c.

265 WEBSTER, W. Hampstead Rd.—Fuzee musket.

266 SHORMAN, J. 6 Gt. Pulteney St. Golden Sq. Prod.—Specimens of inlaying and engraving on the iron work of guns, &c.

267 MORTIMER, T. E. 97 George St. Edinburgh, Manu.—Double rifle. Fowling-piece. Highland pistols. Improved conical and other balls. Gun-case, with fittings.

268 STAINES, E. Salisbury Pl.—Fortification plans.

269 HODGES R. E. 44 Southampton Row, Russell Sq.—Patent application of India-rubber to projectile purposes.

270 PARSONS, W. Swaffham, Norfolk, Manu.—Improved double guns. Loading rod and socket, &c.

271 HALL, Lieut.-Col. R.E. Southampton.—The Tower of London, after the destruction of the Armoury, modelled by R. Davis.

272 MOULIN, C. 24 Stanley St. Chelsea.—Model of a fortified town.

273 LILLYWHITE, J. Frederick St. Portsea, Manu.—Metal model of a gun of 95 cwt. with carriage and slide.

274 BEARFOOT, R. 11 Warwick St. Woolwich, Inv.—Two magazines for the resistance of water, applicable for powder, or any maritime purpose.

275 TYLDEN, R. A. Capt. Woolwich, Manu.—Models of British ordnance.

276 FERGUSSON, J. 20 Langham Pl. Inv.—Model, showing eight different modes of fortification on a new system.

277 JOYCE, F. & Co. 57 Upper Thames St. Inv. and Manu.—Improved anti-corrosive waterproof percussion gun-caps. Percussion tube primers. Chemically-prepared gun waddings. Patent wire cartridges, &c.

278 GRAINGER, J. Wolverhampton, Manu.—Tube and bar-action gun and rifle gun-locks.

280 GARDNER, W. T. 22 Mead Row, Lambeth, Inv. and Manu.—Model of a ship's gun loaded at the breech.

281 KING, T. J. 16 Whiskin St. Des.—Pistols inlaid with gold and silver. Small iron scent-bottle, inlaid with silver.

282 MUNRO, J. jun. 4 High St. Lambeth, Manu.—Models of brass guns, gun-carriages, and limbers.

283 FITZMAURICE, Hon. W. E. Hamilton Lodge, Princes Gate.—Model of a gun and mortar.

284 WALKER, SARAH, & Co. 12 Legge St. Birmingham, Manu.—Specimens illustrative of the manufacture of percussion-caps and patent metallic gun-wadding.

285 RICHARDSON, R. 21 Tonbridge Pl. New Rd. Manu.—Models of tents, marquees, and rick cloth.

286 SYMINGTON, W. 41 Gracechurch St. Inv.—Gun wads.

287 SQUIRES, W. Cottage Grove, Mile End, Inv. and Manu.—New rifle, calculated to project a ball to a great distance with a small charge.

288 M'GETTRICK, F. 81½ Philip St. Kingsland Rd. Des. and Inv.—Model of a war-engine, able to fire 10,900 charges of ball-cartridges in ten minutes.

289 TRUSCOTT, J. 111 Fore St. Devonport, Inv.—Rotatory sprinkler, for watering roads and streets, or using liquid manure. Portable life-boat or raft, applicable to vessels which carry many passengers.

290 RHIND, W. G. Ross, Herefordshire, Inv.—Model of marine life-preserving deck seat, so constructed that in three minutes it can be changed into a safety raft, capable of sustaining eight people on the water.

291 RIGMAIDEN, J. Lieut. R.N. 6 Harley Pl. Inv. and Manu.—Model of lanyard-plates, to set up standing rigging of ships, in lieu of rope lanyards and dead-eyes.

292 ALLEN, J. Greenock, Scotland, Inv.—New patent safety anchor.

293 BENNETT, E. 2 Victoria Place, Woolwich.—Nine pieces of wood, each forming a universal wedge.

294 ROYAL THAMES YACHT CLUB.—Models of various yachts.

295 HAUGHTER, V.—Traversing gun on platform. Model life boat.

296 HITT, T. Bridport, Inv. and Manu.—Life-boot, (one of a pair) for enabling a person to sustain himself in water.

297 CHERRETT, D. Grosvenor Mews, Berkeley Sq.—An improved two-groove rifled pistol, with invisible lock, throws a ball 250 yards, and can be used as a pistol, or from the shoulder.

298 SCAMP, W. Admiralty, Somerset House.—Models. Great Preservative Dry Dock for the Royal Navy, for laying up ships of all classes, dry, without dismantling them, or removing the machinery; for examining, repairing, and refitting ships, and selecting from the reserve for commission with certainty, and with the greatest facility, despatch, and economy; for building ships, seasoned and dry; and also for laying up ships in frame for seasoning, having been advanced on existing ships.

299 WILSON, J. Stratford, Essex.—Model life-boats.

302 EDGINGTON, B. 2 Duke St. London Bridge, Inv. and Manu.—Tents. Stoves and cooking apparatus for tents. Trophy of flag.

303 BLAIR, J. Irvine, Ayrshire, N. B. Inv.—Portable camp-cot, combining a tent, bedstead, and couch.

304 CROID, R.—Model of a life-boat.

305 SMITH, T. & W. Newcastle-upon-Tyne, Prop. — Model of the merchant frigate Blenheim, built at St. Peter's Dockyard, Newcastle-upon-Tyne.

306 TRIGENZA, R.—Two Falmouth fishing-boats.

307 HEDLEY, G. Yorke St. Monkwearmouth, Sunderland, Manu.—Model of a merchant-vessel of the first class, to rank A 1 at Lloyd's, fitted with Hughes's new windlass and steering apparatus, &c.

308 SWALLOW, J. C.—Model of a life-boat.

309 NATIONAL INSTITUTION FOR THE PRESERVATION OF LIFE FROM SHIPWRECK.—Model of life-boat, and specimens of gold and silver medals.

309A COLLARS, J. B.—Model of a life-boat.

310 MARINERS' FRIEND SOCIETY, 58 Fenchurch St. Invs. —Models of stations for affording assistance in case of wreck. Life belt, &c.

312 SLATER & WRIGHT, Whitby, Inv.—A life-boat and carriage, not liable to upset on being struck by a sea on one side. Jet, from Boulty Alum Works, for making brooches, bracelets, necklaces, rings, &c.

313 SPARROW, R. Wexford.—Life-boat model on an improved principle.

314 WILLIAMS, W.—Model of a life-boat.

315 LAING, J. Sunderland.—Model of the ship "Vimiera," 1,020 tons, belonging to D. Dunbar and Sons, of London, built by J. Laing; model made by T. Hardy.

316 HODGSON, M. 6 Moor St. Sunderland, Manu.—Model of a pilot coble, such as ply out of the port of Sunderland, with its oars, sail, and other appointments.

317 MONTEAGLE, The Right Hon. Lord, 7 Park St. Westminster.—Model of a curragh (curabus), or light row-boat, portable by one man; used for fishing on the north-west coast of Ireland.

317A WARNER, Captain.—Bomb-shells, &c.

318 HUGHES, J. Sunderland, Inv. — Model steering apparatus. Model of masting-shears, capable of lifting a boiler of 20 tons weight, and adapted to put masts into ships.

320 ROOK, G. H. Landport, Portsmouth, Working Shipwright.—Model of H.M. steam yacht tender, Fairy, with her entire fittings on the deck, masts, rigging, &c. (In Class 6.)

322 DRUERY, J. Hartlepool, Inv.—Model and plan of a ship and shore sheet-iron life-boat, to recover herself when upset; provided with a cabin, water tight.

323 GALE, G. H. 38 Wind St. Swansea, Inv.—Hydrostatic apparatus for life-boats, ships, &c. made of gutta percha. A life or surf-raft or boat, &c.

324 BEE, B.—Model of a life-boat.

325 BOWEN, A. F. Botley, Inv.—Clear anchor.

327 ETRICK, A. High Barnes, near Sunderland, Inv.—Model exhibiting a new method of launching a long-boat of a merchant or other vessel. Portable punching, slotting, and stamping apparatus, of novel construction Bogie, or timber-lifting apparatus. Improved travelling bag or portmanteau, registered.

329 MACDONALD, J. 13 Henry St. Vauxhall, Inv.—Binnacle and ship's compass. Ship engine pump. Water-closet. Steam chest and valve. Lantern and lamp for ship's head, &c.

330 PEARCE, T. B. 93 Newman St. Inv.—Railway fog-signal lamp. Fishing tackle. Improved walking-stick, &c.

332 WILLIAMS, T. Red Lion St. Clerkenwell, Inv.—Self-acting ship pump.

333 LONGRIDGE & Co. 4 Mansion House Pl.—The largest and the smallest anchor used in the British Navy, made by the Badlington Iron Company, Northumberland.

334 BROWN, Capt. Sir S., R.N. Vanbrugh Lodge, Blackheath, Inv.—Twisted and other chain cables. Stay pins and improved welding 1810 to 1812. Picture of Union Bridge over the Tweed, 1820. Model of Brighton pier. Model of a naval arsenal floating dock, and plan of drawing up ships. Model of a brass column and lighthouse. Model of railway and railway carriages. Model of a pair of midship timbers or ribs of a line-of-battle ship. Model of submarine ship propellers. Model of improved mariner's compass. Model of an equipoise bed.

SOME OF THE FOLLOWING OBJECTS ARE OUTSIDE THE BUILDING AT THE WEST END.

335 BATEMAN, J. 101 Upper St. Islington, Inv. and Pat. —Patent life-boats for 30 persons, and for six persons.

336 RODGER, Lieut. R.N. 9 Shawfield St. King's Rd. Chelsea, Inv.—Patent small palmed anchors, with improved iron stock. Manufactured by Fox, Henderson, and Co.

337 STURDEE, A. B. Woolwich.—Working model of a twin-stern steam ship. (In Class 5.)

338 HUDSON, J. 12 Hanover Sq.—Model of the steamship "Medea."

339 FAIRLY, E.—Method of raising a stranded vessel.

340 WARD, —.—Model of a steam vessel (in Class 5).
341 M'CRAE, J.—Model of a life-boat.
342 RICKARDS, C.—Steerman's indicator.
343 MARCUARD, C. R.—Model of an 18-gun brig.
344 JONES, T.—Propeller for canal navigation.
345 EGG, D.—Pistols, inlaid with gold and silver.
346 LANCASTER, C.—Guns and rifles, smooth-bored.
348 SEARS, M. W.—Patent needle-gun.

349 HALL, H. W., Lieut. R.N.—Model of an anchor.
350 REID, Captain J. H.—Model of a fan-propeller.
351 RANKINE, A. Lancefield Foundry, Kirkcudbright
Inv.—Working model of an iron-planked war-steamer, with
screw-propeller.
352 BAYLEY, J. Middle St. Deal, Manu.—Model of a
Deal lugger, 20 tons.
353 PUGH, E. Whitstable.—Apparatus for water ballast.

Proceed to Class 7, page 43.

Class 9. AGRICULTURAL AND HORTICULTURAL MACHINES AND IMPLEMENTS.

—— On the South Side: Areas N. O. 1; P. Q. R. 1 to 27. ——

1 STANLEY, W. P. Market Pl. Peterborough, Manu.
—A two-horse portable steam-engine. The farmers' registered steam cooking apparatus. Cake-breaker, for sheep,
cattle, and manure. Registered roller-mill. Chaff-engine.
Turnip-cutter, &c.
3 GUEST, J. Bedford, Inv. and Manu.—Steerage drill,
for turnips or mangel-wurzel, with manure. Eight-row cup
drill, for corn and seed.
4 DEAN, T. Wishaw, Scotland, Inv.—Cutlery apparatus attached to a tile and pipe-machine, for forming over-
laps in tiles and pipes. The machine will be worked.
4A SMITH, A. K. Exminster, Inv. and Maker.—Rotatory screening machine.
11 CROSSKILL, E. Liverpool.—Cart, waggon, and patent wheels.
13 HARDING, E. Oldsprings, Market Drayton, Inv.—
One-horse cart, with revolving axle. Set of whippletrees.
15 BUSBY, W. Newton-le-Willows, Bedale, Manu.—
Carts for farming purposes. A light horse-hoe, for ridge
work, improved by the exhibitor. Ploughs, drills, &c.
16 HARVEYS & TAIT, Strathaven, Scotland, Inv. and
Manu.—Clydesdale tilt-cart, for farm use. Farm kitchen
fire-place crane.
17 CAMPBELL, A. F. Gt. Plumstead, Norfolk.—Patent
four-wheel parallel motion harrow.
17A GREGORY, R. Beverley, Inv. and Manu.—Model of
a draining-machine.
18 STENT, W. Stockwith, Gainsborough, Inv. and
Manu.—New pea supporter.
20 NICHOLLS, R. H. 11 Elizabeth St. Eaton Sq. Inv.—
Patent locomotive dibble, for planting corn. Machine for
giving motion to rotatory machinery.
21 WILKIE, J. & Co. Uddingston, near Glasgow, Scotland.—Parallel drill grubber. Turn wrist plough; two-horse
sowing plough; subsoil plough, invented by Mr. Smith;
friction-wheel plough.
21A REVIS, T. 8 Cleave Pl. Larkhall Lane, Stockwell,
Surrey, Inv.—Single seed planter. Single seed dibbler.
22 EATON, J. Woodford, near Thrapstone, Inv. and
Manu.—A patent seed-dibbler for wheat, &c. An ornamental sheep-crib for hay, roots, cake, &c. invented and
registered by W. Knight, Esq. of Titchmarsh.
23 HARKES, D. Mere, near Knutsford, Inv. and Manu.
—Plough, with welded joints. Parallel expanding horse-
hoe. Cheese and cider press. Machine for screening
clay.
24 BRABY and SONS, Duke St. Upper Stamford St.—
New application of springs to a waggon.
25 WINDSOR, J. Oswestry, Manu.—Winnowing-machine. Clover seed drill, for grass seeds and turnips.

25A ALSOP, D. 6 Boone St. Lee, Kent, Inv. and Manu.
—Sulphurator and fumigator, to diffuse powdered sulphur
more uniformly than can be done by the dredge-box, &c.
25B KINGSWELL, F. 6 Upper St. Martin's Lane.—Model
waggon.
25C GINGELL, W. J. Nelson St. Bristol.—Model of a
corn or seed meter.
26 ROBERTSON, G. Stonehaven.—Model cart, with
sliding axle.
27 ALCOCK, T. Radcliffe, near Nottingham, Inv. and
Manu.—Chaff-cutter, with improved rising roller. Improved
two-wheeled iron, and swing iron plough.
28 LOWCOCK, H. St. Peter's St. Tiverton, Inv. and
Pat.—Lowcock's patent turn-wrist plough, &c. manufactured
by R. Adams, of Marldon.
28A FOWLER, J. Bristol, Inv.—Draining-plough, for horse
or steam power, on a new system. Windlass, or capstan, for
applying horse-power to the plough.
28B FOWLER & FRY, Bristol, Des. and Manu.—Farm
cart, adapted for harvest and winter purposes.
29 ELLS, —, 3 & 6 Tottenham Court Road.—Wheel
barrow on an improved principle.
30 CARPENTER, W. Banbury, Inv. — Anti-attrition
thrashing-machine.
31 SAWNEY, W. Beverley.—Winnowing-machine. Iron
model bridge.
32 BENDALL, J. Woodbridge, Manu.—A universal self-
adjusting cultivator, for skimming, cleaning, pulverizing, or
subsoiling land: pat. A corn-crushing machine: pat.
33 BLACKHALL, J. 22 Upper Gray St. Edinburgh, Inv.
—Model of high-pressure boiler, for steaming bones, flax,
and food for cattle. Specimen of steamed bone-manure.
34 BEART, R. Godmanchester, Huntingdonshire.—
Patent scarifier or land cultivator.
35 MARSHALL, Lt.-Col. W. Newfield Cottage, Craigel-
lachie, Inv.—Cereal seed-planting and simultaneously-ope-
rating machine, to show the advantage of thin seeding.
36 WINDUS, T. F.S.A. Stamford Hill, Inv. (J. Rendall,
Maker, Stamford Hill).—Two centripetal barrows.
37 BURRELL, C. Thetford, Norfolk, Des. and Manu.—
A six-horse power portable steam-engine, adapted for driving agricultural machinery. Reg. machine for making gates.
Reg. gorse-cutting and bruising machine.
38 STEEVENS, W. D. 157 High Holborn.—Model of new
portable railway, without steam.
38A ARMITAGE and Co. Mousehole Forge, Sheffield.—
An improved plough.
38B MURPHY, D. I. Chamber of Commerce, Cork.—
Model of Archimedean agricultural machine.
41 ELLIOTT, J. Southampton, Inv.—A poor man's

closet. Models of farm buildings and of cottages for la-bourers. Draining level. Specimens of clay tubes, for building roofs and walls of cottages, &c.

41A FYFE, W. W. 30 Hamilton Pl. Edinburgh, Inv.—Syphon apparatus, for the washing of sheep, and improving the growth of wool by the copious application of pure water.

42 SLIGHT, J. 34 Leith Walk, Edinburgh, Manu.—Sub-soil trench plough; an improvement on Read's by the Mar-quis of Tweeddale. The Tweeddale trench plough. Model of Henderson's patent Derrick crane.

43 STARKEY, T. Farthinghoe, Brackley, Northampton-shire, Inv. and Manu.—Clod-crusher. Telescope ladder. Propeller for a ship, very simple, but of great power. Table convertible into a bed, chest of drawers, &c. Two tables, as specimens of British woods. Seat, to shut up, for the pocket.

44 RACE, E. Beverley, Inv. and Manu.—Model of a new tipping waggon.

45 GOLDING, R. Hunton, Maidstone.—A beehive.

45A GOLDING, E. Hurstborne Priors, Andover Rd. Inv. and Manu.—Improved rolling barley chumper.

46 DAVIS, T. Guy St. Nicholas, Warwick.—Drum part of a registered thrashing machine, worked by steam or horse.

47 CLAYTON, H. Atlas Works, near Dorset Sq. Inv. and Manu.—Machinery and tools for the manufacture of drain-age pipes, and for making drains, drawings of kilns, drying sheds, &c.

48 MORRISON & SON, Banff, Scotland, Prod.—Samples of yellow turnip and seed, cultivated in Banffshire and Aber-deenshire; Aberdeenshire, or Gordon yellow turnip, and seed; Williamson's Swedish turnip, and seed; Birchromb yellow turnip, and seed.

48A PALMER, R. Bideford, Devon, Inv. and Manu.—Machine for cutting, and reducing to a pulp, turnips, carrots, mangold-wurzel, potatoes, apples, &c.

49 DRUMMOND & SONS, Stirling, Prop.—A grubber or cultivator, made by L. Potter, Bothkennar, near Stirling. A two-horse iron swing plough, made by J. Barrowman, of Saline, Fifeshire.

50 NICHOLSON, W. N. Newark-on-Trent, Inv. and Manu.—Oil-cake breaking machines; mill for grinding barley, beans, &c. Improved double blast corn-dressing or winnowing machine.

51 SEAWARD, W. Oulton, Wakefield, Des.—Tree-remover, for transplanting large shrubs and trees. Conifera supporter, to prevent cypresses, arbor-vitæ, &c. from being broken down by snow, &c.

52 JONES, E. 138 Leadenhall St. Inv.—Airish mow, adapted to the preservation of corn in the harvest-time of rainy seasons.

53 COOCH, J. Harleston, near Northampton, Inv. and Manu.—Patent winnowing or dressing-machine. Barley hummeller. Patent sack-holder, invented by H. Gilbert, of St. Leonard's-on-Sea.

55 ABBOTT, W. Bideford, Devon, Inv. — Common plough, with wheel behind. Improved machine or apparatus for drying malt.

56 CHENERY, S. March Cambs, Inv.—Land-presser, particularly adapted for fen-land.

56A EBBS, B. 9 Lower Ter. Islington, Des.—Lady's garden rake, consisting of a hoe, spud, and rake, all in one.

57 NEWBERRY, W. Hooknorton, Chippingnorton, Oxon.—Five-row dibbling machine.

58 ROYCE, G. Fletland, Market Deeping, Inv.—Patent self-acting reeing-sieve for corn and seeds. Patent smut-machine, and general corn-cleaner.

59 WHISHAW, F. John St. Adelphi.—Feeding trough for poultry.

60 BECKFORD, T. & GOSLING, W. Highfield Farm, War-grave, Henley-on-Thames, Inv. and Manu.—Model circular mowing and tedding machine, to be drawn by one horse.

61 RODENHURST, W. & J. Market Drayton, Manu.—Compound screw and lever cheese-press. Hay or straw cutting machine.

62 GILL and WARD, Oxford, Manu.—Improved por-table copper steam generator. Two iron vessels for boiling or steaming food.

63 WATT, J. Biggar, Scotland, Imp. and Manu.—Im-proved broad-cast sowing-machine, for grain and grass seeds.

65 BIGG, T. Leicester House, Great Dover St. South-wark, Inv. and Manu.—Improved apparatus for sheep-dip-ping.

66 GREEN, T. 97 North St. Leeds, Manu.—Wire aviary and ornamental seat.

66A AMOS, J. King St. Bristol, Manu.—Improved barrel churn.

67 SHANKS and SON, Arbroath, Forfar.—Grass and hay-cutting machines.

68 WHITFIELD, J. A. Pelaw Staith, near Gateshead, Inv.—Improved grappling or dredging-iron, for drawing from the water the bodies of persons apparently drowned.

69 JOLLY, J. Vale of Aylesbury, Manu.—Churn and stand; milk-pails; butter-tub; butter prints and boards; milk-strainer.

70 JENNISON, J. Frodingham, Duffield, Yorkshire, Inv.—York's corn stacks. Stack-level, to assist the stack-builder. Hedge models, &c.

72 HART, C. Wantage.—A registered universal portable mill, for splitting or grinding all sorts of farm produce into fine meal.

72A PHILLIPS, G. Harrow-on-the-Hill, Manu. — Im-proved collateral beehive, made of wood, glass, and zinc.

73 FRANCE, A. Stirling, Manu. and Des.—A drill-plough for green crops. A green-crop grubber.

74 SHERIFF, T. West Carns, near Dunbar, N.B.—A machine for sowing grain, being an improved drill. A ma-chine for dressing grain, or improved winnowing machine.

75 BENNETT, H. Liverpool, Manu.—Model of a self-cleaning clod crusher and roller. Mill for mixing provender and preparing manure for drill sowing. Machine for pre-paring gorse or furze for food for cattle. Mill for kibbling or crushing beans, oats, &c. Oilcake crusher, &c.

76 WOODBOURNE, J. Kingsley, near Alton, Manu.—Machine for bagging hops by pressure.

77 PEARCE, W. Poole, Dorset.—Clod crusher, cider mill, gorse cutting and bruising machine, ploughs, &c.

78 GILLETT, J. Brailes, near Shipston-on-Stour, Inv. and Manu.—Chaff engines. Model rick ventilator: patent. Mill for splitting, bruising, and grinding beans, oats, and barley. Self-acting alarum gun.

80 SWAN, R. F. Boxford, Suffolk, Inv. and Manu.—Model of a tipping waggon.

81 MACKAY, W. H. Swansea, Inv.—Machine for mow-ing hay or cutting corn.

82 WOODS, J. Stowmarket, Suffolk, Inv. and Manu.—New universal farmers' crushing and grinding mill: re-gistered.

83 CORNES, J. Burbridge, near Nantwich, Chester, Inv. and Manu.—A chaff-cutting machine, with three knives, makes five different lengths of chaff. Chaff-cutting ma-chine, with two knives.

84 ROE, FREEMAN, & HANSON, 70 Strand, Manu.—Four-horse portable steam-engine, for agricultural and other purposes.

85 SELLAR & SON, Huntly, near Aberdeen, Inv. and Manu.—Double mould, or drill plough, with improved mould-boards. Swing plough.

86 JAMES, J. & Co. 24 Leadenhall St. Manu.—Paten weighing machines, and weigh-bridge.

87 Rowley, J. J. Rowthorne, near Chesterfield.—Improved machine for dropping peat, bone-dust, turnip, rape, or mangold seed, &c.: patent. Improved corn-dressing machine: registered.

88 Drummond, P. R. Perth, Inv. and Manu.—Anti-metallic table churns, with six actions.

89 Read, R. 35 Regent Circus, Inv.—New patent watering engine. Horticultural machine, and syringe, &c. New patent stomach pump. Aperitive fountain. Injecting instruments for removing obstructions of the bowels of animals. Improved hollow probang for relieving hoven or choked bullocks, &c.

89A Blaikie, J. 71 Stockwell St. Glasgow.—Model reaping and mowing machine.

90 Wood, G. Alnwick, Northumberland.—Improved cottage beehive.

90A Holmes, J. 1 Wellington ter. Newcastle-on-Tyne.—Garden seat and plant stands.

91 Brown, D. S. 2 Alexandrian Lodge, Old Kent Rd. Imp.—Patent instruments for fumigating plants, to destroy insects, &c.

91A Jordan, T. Billericay, Essex, Inv. and Manu.—Improved plough.

92 Pettit, W. J. Sudbury, Suffolk, Inv. and Manu.—Temple and collateral beehives.

93 Marychurch, J. Haverfordwest, South Wales, Manu.—Winnowing-machine. Chaff-cutter. Turnip-cutter formed of a cylindrical barrel.

94 Law, R. Shettleston, Glasgow.—A farm cart, iron plough, model turn wrist plough.

96 Crowley & Sons, Newport Pagnell Bucks, Inv. and Manu.—One-horse cart, with newly invented tipping apparatus. Hames. One-horse universal hoe.

98 Brodie, W. Airdrie, Scotland.—Brodie's registered drain-tile and pipe-machine.

99 Clark, J. Kirkton Blantyre, by Hamilton, Scotland, Manu.—Plough.

100 Istance, R. Carmarthen.—Beehive ventilator.

101 Epps, W. J. Maidstone, Inv.—Sulphurator, for throwing flour of sulphur in a diffused state upon grapes, hops, peas, roses, &c. for the purpose of destroying the mould or mildew.

103 Briggs, T. Denley Pottery, Derbyshire, Manu.—Improved beehive.

104 Ponton, G. Grangefoot, Linlithgow, Scotland, Inv. Imp. and Manu.—Improved swing-ploughs; drill plough; bean-sowing machine.

105 Thompson, G. 18 Gt. George St. Westminster, Inv.—Patent machine for digging and turning over earth, which may also be used as a cultivator or scarifier.

106 Halstead & Sons, Chichester, Inv. and Manu.—Improved iron ploughs, and oil-cake breaker.

107 Sewell & Co. Longtown, Cumberland, and 30 Spring St. Hyde Park, London.—Netherby plough for cutting, displacing, and leaving in proper position furrows of various widths and depths, on moderately stiff soils, requiring for stiff clays another form of mould-plate.

108 Reeves, T. R. & J. Bratton, Westbury, Wilts. Manu.—Liquid manure distributing cart, and liquid manure drop-drill, invented and patented by T. Chandler, of Aldbourne, Hungerford, Berks.

109 Maynard, R. Whittlesford, Cambridge, Manu.—Universal oil-cake breakers and weighing machines. Engine for drawing clover and trefoil seed, inv. by Mr. Constable, Cambridge.

109A Cottam & Hallen, Oxford St. Manu—Chaff-cutter, winnowing machine, draining tools, tile machine, liquid manure and force pump, various ploughs, and other agricultural implements. Enamelled stable fittings, &c.

110 Carson, H. Warminster, Wilts, Manu.—Scarifier, invented by H. Carson. Patent turnip-cutter, patented by E. Moody, of Maiden Bradley. Cheese press, with double lever. A set of six harrows, particularly adapted for wet lands.

112 Parsons, J. Craven Farm, Stamford Hill, Inv. and Manu.—Model of a digging-machine.

114 Hayward, G. Crewkerne, Inv. and Manu.—Plough, with drilling-machine attached, for sowing all kinds of corn, and turnip seed, with or without dry manure, &c.

115 Butlin, W. Northampton, Des. and Manu.—Four-horse power steam-engine, simple in design, economical in fuel, low in price.

116 Hodges & Sons, 16 Westmoreland St. Dublin, Manu.—Improved safety kettles, and improved steaming apparatus.

117 Hayes, J. Elton, Huntingdonshire, Des. Inv. and Manu.—Grinding-mill, to grind barley into soft meal for pigs, and to split beans.

119 Hunter, W. & J. Samuelston, Haddington, Scotland, Inv. and Manu.—Lever grain drilling-machine.

120 Sholl, J. 33 Lamb St. Spital Sq. Inv.—Castle beehive, as in use at the royal farm, Windsor; observatory beehive; specimens of honey, &c.

121 Glover, W. Warwick, Manu.—One-horse cart for general purposes.

122 Maynard & Son, Bedford, Des. and Manu.—Improved Bedfordshire one-horse cart, mounted on an improved iron axle.

122A Service, W. 8 Rutland Ter. Hornsey Rd. Holloway, Inv.—Archimedean sifting machine.

123 Weir, E. 351 Oxford St. Inv. and Manu. — Irrigator, liquid manure pump, fire and garden engine, with hose and hose reel. A draining level.

123A Usher, J. Edinburgh, Inv.—Model of locomotive steam-plough; the ploughs revolving behind the carriage act as propellers: patent.

123B Jones, P. High St. Fulham, Prop.—Portable hand garden engine, forces the water in a continuous stream upwards of forty feet.

124 Ransomes & May, Ipswich, Inv. and Manu.—Patent iron ploughs; double breast or moulding ploughs; West Indian, double furrow, universal, broad share, and subsoil ploughs; trussed whippletrees; Biddell's scarifier; Indian cultivator; corn and seed-dropping machine; portable steam engine; fixed steam engine; thrashing machines; cane-top cutter; crushing mill; oil-cake breaker; barley awner; chicory cutter; Scotch cart, &c.

124A Dufour and Co. 21 Red Lion Sq. Prop. Dr. S. Newington Inv.—Agricultural implements: eight-depositor hand dibble, hand cultivator and drill hoe, subsoil plough and pulverizer, horse dibble drill, single horse cultivator, &c.

124B Cowan, H. Corstorphine, Edinburgh, Inv. and Manu.—Self-cleansing two-horse grubber.

125 Paxton, J. Ealing, near Brentford, Inv.—Improvement on water-power, for grinding corn, &c. Registered.

126 Robinson, W. Halsham, Inv. and Manu.—Corn-dressing machine, for dressing, blowing, hariffing, and blowing and hariffing combined. Hariff machine. Patent straw-shaker, &c.

127 Wedlake, Mary, & Co. Fairkytes Works, and 118 Fenchurch St. London, Manu. — Patent improved hay-making-machine, rake, winnowing-machine, ploughs, horse-hoe, and scarifiers. Improved machine for bruising oats. Machine to bruise gorse or furze. Oil-cake mill. Turnip and chaff-cutting machine, &c. A chaff-cutter and oat-bruiser, combined.

128 Barrett, Exall, & Andrews, Reading.—Portable farm steam-engine, with expansive movements. Patent portable and other thrashing machines for horse power.

Patent hand-power thrashing machine. Improved corn grinding mill. Two varieties of one-horse carts. Registered haymaking machine. Cavalry forge, with tools, and specimens of horses feet and shoeing. Patent safety horse gears. Norwegian harrow. Ducie cultivator. Circular and patent iron harrows. Crushing mills. Oil-cake mill. Patent paragon chaff-cutters. Iron lifting crab. Read's patent sub-pulveriser. Improved ploughs. Barley hummeller. Model of engine and machine house for a farm of 400 to 800 acres, with machines as arranged for work.

129 GIBSON, M. Newcastle, Inv. and Manu.—Northumberland clod-crusher, for wet land, &c.; also used on young wheat for the wireworm, and for making drills for clover and other seeds.

130 LAMPITT, C. Banbury, Inv. and Manu.—A horse seed dibler, patented.

131 MAPPLEBECK & LOWE, Birmingham, Warwick.—Weighing machines, mills, and draining tools.

132 BALL, W. Rothwell, near Kettering, Northamptonshire, Inv. and Manu.—Criterion prize ploughs made of iron, with steel or cast-iron furrow-turner. Two-horse waggon, either with pole or shafts.

133 JONES, E. Great College St. Camden Town, Inv.—Machine for moulding bricks and tiles, with pug-mill attached. Model of the exhibitor's patent, with important additions and improvements.

134 LAYCOCK, J. Winlaton, Newcastle-on-Tyne.—Subsoiler and plough.

135 CROSSKILL, W. Iron Works, Beverley, Pat and Manu.—Mills (for steam power) for grinding vegetable and mineral substances, clod crushers, drills, horse-hoes, thrashing machines, chaff-cutters, crushers, ploughs, harrows, waggons, carts, Farm railways, turnip cutters, and various other agricultural implements.

136 GRIMSLEY, T. of Oxford, and RANDALL & SAUNDERS, of Bath, Inv.—Brick and tile presses. Model of kiln and drying-room. Patent draining tiles. Hollow bricks and tiles. Model of fire-proof cottages, &c.

137 RICHMOND & CHANDLER, Manchester, Inv. and Manu.—Corn-crusher, chaff-cutting machine, grain-crusher, chaff-machines, &c.

138 GILLAM, J. Woodstock, Inv.—Seed-cleaner and separator.

139 TAYLOR, G. Bury, Lancashire, Inv.—Locomotive shearing and mowing machine, worked by hand.

139A ROBINSON & SON, Coventry, Manu.—Model churn.

140 HILL, E. & Co Brierley Hill Works, Dudley, Inv. and Manu.—Skim for paring stubbles, turf, &c. Expanding horse-hoe. Wrought-iron gates and posts. Continuous iron fencing, hurdles, &c.

141 LYDES, —.—Improved mode of boxing horses for railway conveyance.

142 GARRETT & SONS, Leiston Works, Suffolk, Inv. and Manu.—Drills, horse-hoes, thrashing machines, portable steam-engines, hummelling and corn-dressing machines, chaff-cutters, crushers, ploughs, corn-reaping, harrows, and other agricultural machinery.

143 COMINS, J. South Molton, Inv. and Manu.—Wrought iron horse-hoes. Oneway turnovers or turnrest plough for hilly land. Subsoil pulverizer. Harrows, &c.

144 SQUIRES, W. March, Cambridgeshire, Manu.—Road waggon, and improved plough.

144A ELLIOTT, G. Farnham, Inv. and Manu.—Hop bagging-machine, for bagging hops when dried, of a new construction : will bag two tons of hops in a day.

145 TROTTER, W. Bywell, Stocksfield, near Gateshead, Inv.—Model of reaping machine for cutting corn with revolving knives.

146 PONDER, W. R. Goldhanger, near Maldon, Essex, Inv.—Bee-house, or hive.

148 GROUNSELL, W. Louth, Lincolnshire, Manu.—Improved patent drop drill. Registered corn-dressing machine. Registered corn and turnip hoe.

149 HENSMAN & SON, Castle Works, Woburn, Inv. and Manu.—Four-horse power portable steam-engine. Patent bolting thrashing-machine, complete. Eight-row patent cup-drill, with independent steerage. Patent Vandyke hand thrashing-machine. Patent iron ploughs.

150 GRAY & SONS, Uddingston, Manu.—Farm cart; ploughs. Subsoil pulverizer. Drill grubber. Parallel horseshoe. Canadian chaff cutter. Scotch thrashing machine.

151 WILLIAMS, W. Bedford, Inv. and Manu.—Patent four-beam iron harrows. Patent wrought-iron ploughs. Chaff-engine. A machine for making drain pipes, tiles, &c.

152 ROME, R. M. Langholm, Des. and Manu.—Sheep-dipping machine, for applying sheep-washing compositions.

152A MOREWOOD & ROGERS, Steel Yd. Wharf, Upper Thames St. Inv.—Model of farm-yard and buildings, agricultural implements, &c. chiefly of galvanized tinned iron.

154 BLYTH, R. J. Norwich, Inv. and Manu.—Portable horse works. Registered portable bolting thrashing machine, for steam or horse power.

154A COODE, G. 473 Oxford St. Inv.—An irrigator for grass land, or low crops, applicable also for watering roads. Irrigator for highstanding crops. Patented.

155 FAIRLESS, T. Corbridge, near Hexham, Northumberland.—Reaping machine for cutting corn and hay. Improved pump.

156 SADLER, W. J. Bentham, near Swindon, Wilts, Inv.—Agricultural chimney filter drain and draining tools.

157 RUDD, T. 16 Ebury Sq. Pimlico, Inv. and Manu.—Improved patent hand-thrashing machine; mounted upon carriage wheels, and remains so when at work. Working model of improved machinery, for working marble, stone, &c.

158 HALL, A. Bank Buildings, Manchester.—Garden net. Substitute for glass houses.

160 CRUMP, T. Derby, Inv. and Manu.—Garden-engine, or portable fire-engine. Liquid manure pump. Instrument for singeing horses with gas.

161 NIXON T. Kettering, Inv. and Manu.—A garden light or sky-light.

170 WILMOT, E. W. Congleton, Des.—Model of farm buildings for a farm of about 300 acres.

180 DEANE, DRAY, & DEANE, Swan Lane, Upper Thames St. London Bridge. — Grindstones, mills, corn-crushers, chaff-cutter, portable forge, churn, seats, pump, pig-trough, crane, and various other agricultural implements.

181 WHITE, J. 266 High Holborn, Inv. and Manu.—Machine for converting gorse into nutritious food for cattle, crushing corn and linseed, and rasping beet-root for sugar making. Patent cider mill. Wheat mill and dressing machine.

182 TURNER, E. R. Ipswich, Inv. and Manu.—Four-horse power portable steam-engine, for agricultural purposes. Apparatus for regulating the supply of water to a high-pressure steam-boiler. Mill for crushing corn and seeds, and grinding beans, peas, maize, &c.

183 ROGERS, J. W. 88 St. James St.—A deodorizing chamber.

185 SAMUELSON, B. Banbury, Manu.—Patent double-action turnip-cutter. Chaff-cutter. Universal mill. Improved bean mill. Oil-cake breaker. Registered atmospheric churn. Ploughs. Horse-hoe. Ornamental cast-iron table, and stool. Self-acting kitchen range.

186 BATES, F. Summertown, Oxford.—Implement to facilitate the removal of plants in pots.

190 WINDER, R. 2 Ingram Court, Fenchurch St. Inv.—Model of a machine for mowing corn or grass by rotatory horizontal knives.

191 HENTON, J. Inv.—Hand roller; object, lightness of draught.

192 SMITH, H. 12 Rufford's Row, near the Church, Islington, Inv. and Manu.—Registered horticultural hot-water gas stove.

193 KEENE, W. 42 Cornhill.—Beehive. Mode of preparing seeds for sowing.

195 WILLOUGHBY DE ERESBY, Lord, 142 Piccadilly, Inv.—Machinery to plough land, with stationary engine.

196 TEBBUTT, C. P. Bluntisham, near St. Ives, Huntingdonshire, Des.—Model farmstead, for 250 or 300 acres.

197 BELL, F. & Co. 7 Noble St. City, Manu.—Patent ventilating waterproof cloths for stacks, ricks, &c.

197A FUSSELL, SON & Co., Mill Iron Works, Somerset.—Scythes, rip-hooks, sickles, hay and chaff knives.

198 ALEXANDER, E. Taylorton, Stirling, Scotland, Inv. and Manu.—Models of draining ploughs: First furrow plough, which cuts a depth of from fifteen to eighteen inches. Second, or finishing plough, which cuts a further depth of from ten to twelve inches.

199 BOYD, J. E. 70 Lower Thames St. Inv. and Manu.—Patent self-adjusting sythe, can be put together without the assistance of a blacksmith, and shuts up like a knife.

200 CABORN, J. Denton, near Grantham.—Portable seven-horse power steam-engine for agricultural purposes. Portable thrashing-machine, with straw shaker. A corn-dressing machine.

202 DE PORQUET FENWICK, 11 Tavistock St. Covent Garden.—Models: haymaker's horse hay rake, skim plough, dressing machine, turnip cutters, light ploughs, &c.

204 PANNELL, J. Feltham, Hounslow.—Working model of registered heating apparatus for hothouses, pineries, &c., whereby a moist bottom heat and a dry top heat can be obtained from the same boiler.

205 BLAND, J. G. Market Harborough, Inv. and Des.—A two-knife hand-power chaff-cutter, by Cornes, of Barbridge. Model of a farmstead.

208 RESTELL, R. 35 High St. Croydon, Inv. and Manu.—Garden and conservatory metallic labels and tree supporters.

208A HAYES, M. Enfield Highway, Inv. and Manu.—Beehive.

208B BEADON, Capt. R.N. Taunton, Inv.—Model cart. Improved apparatus for drawing off liquor from casks. Frame for tilting casks.

208C KENNEDY, Dr. Dublin.—Machine for watering plants.

210 TOBY & SON, King's Rd. Chelsea.—Model of a greenhouse, with potting shed and fruit-room, showing the boiler and hot-water-pipes, with improved ventilation, &c.

211 THORNTON, D. Ratho, by Edinburgh, Des.—Design for an arrangement of farm building, the grain crops under cover, &c. Model of a cheap form of field-drain.

212 TYTHERLEIGH, W. 350 Coventry Rd. Birmingham, Inv. and Manu.—Winter and summer, or self-temperature butter churn.

213 STEWART, C. & Co. 22 Charing Cross, Prop.—Patent potato-germ extractor. Anti-putrescent preparation to preserve the germs.

214 FERGUSON, J. Bridge of Allan, Stirling.—Model of a draining-plough.

215 PADWICK, W. F. Manor House, Hayling Island, Hampshire, Inv.—Hand-drill, for garden and other seeds. Improved planting line, and dibbler or transplanter.

215A TYSON, I. Selby, Yorkshire, Des.—Model of farmstead and buildings where steam power is used.

216 COLEMAN, R. Chelmsford, Inv. and Manu.—Patent drag harrows and scarifiers. Patent subsoil harrow. Patent expanding lever harrow, &c.

216A WHEELER, E. 16 Faulkner St. Manchester, Inv.—Machines for bagging hops, wool, or cotton; pressing the hops without breaking the leaf.

217 BENTALL, E. H. Heybridge, near Maldon, Essex, Inv. and Manu.—Patent broad-share and subsoil plough. Patent mangel or ridge hoe. Patent double tom, with wrought-iron beam. Patent N G H plough. The original gold hanger plough. Patent dynamometer, &c.

218 NUNN, J. P. & E. B 17 Stratford Pl. Oxford St. Inv.—Instruments for securing a swarm of bees.

219 SMITH, G. 3 Francis Ct. Berkeley St. Clerkenwell, Prod.—Registered enamelled garden labels.

220 WILKINSON, T. 309 Oxford St. Manu.—Improved Baker's patent mangle. Improved patent box churn.

221 FARLOW, J. K. 5 Crooked Lane, London Bridge.—Netting for protecting fruit and flowers.

222 SMITH, T. Hamor Cottage, Hornsey Rd. Islington, Inv.—Hyacinth glass, and glass support. Earthenware enclosure, and support for the fruit and foliage of the strawberry. Prov. Reg.

224 RITCHIE, W. & J. Ardee, Ireland, Manu. Improved drill and subsoil ploughs.

226 ROBERTS, J. 34 Eastcheap.—Strawberry, melon, and grape tiles. Celery sockets. Ventilating and transplanting flower-pots. Flower supporters. Cylindrical bricks.

227 VIVIAN.—Model machine for drying corn.

228 SCRAGG, T. Tarporley, Chester, Inv. and Manu. A double-action machine for making draining tiles and pipes.

230 BARKER, J. Dunnington, near York, Inv. and Manu.—Iron wheel plough. Wood swing plough. Expanding parallel horse-hoe, with a Norwegian harrow attached. Iron sliding horse hoe, &c. One-horse Yorkshire cart, &c.

232 ENNISKILLEN, Earl of, Manu.—Draining pipes and collars. Draining tiles. Water pipes. Roofing tiles. Flooring tiles.

233 HORNSBY & SON, Spittlegate Iron Works, near Grantham, Inv. Des. and Manu.—Patent drills. Six-horse power patent portable steam-engine. Improved portable thrashing-machine. Patent corn-dressing or winnowing machine. Double cake-breaking or crushing machine.

234 SMITH & Co. Stamford, Lincolnshire, Inv. and Manu.—Hay-making machine: patent. Litter and chaff-cutting machine: patent. Balance-lever; horse and hand rake: patent. Lever cultivator or scarifier. Fat-cutting machine. Park or luggage cart, &c. Patent iron wrought wheels.

235 CHARD & MUNRO, Bristol, Manu.—Light one-horse harvest cart. Light errand or market cart.

237 BURGESS & KEY, 103 Newgate St. Prop. or Agents.—Patent American churn (English) made by C. J. Anthony, of Pittsburgh, U. S. Kase's force and suction pumps. Turnip-cutter. Hose for fire-engines, &c. made of canvas, lined and coated with gutta percha. Lift-pump, made entirely of gutta percha. Davy's patent India-rubber saddles and collars.

238 CAMBRIDGE, W. Temple Gate, Bristol, Inv. and Pat.—Patent press-wheel roller, or clod-crusher.

239 WHITEHEAD, J Preston, Lancashire, Inv. and Manu.—Machines for the manufacture of draining pipes and tiles. New machine for making and pressing bricks.

240 HOWARD, T. & F. Bedford, Inv. and Manu.—Patent iron ploughs. Swing-plough, and double breast or moulding-plough. Subsoil-plough. Double-furrow plough. Iron harrows. Patent horse rake. Improved double-action corn-mill, horse-power gear-work, &c.

241 HOLMES & SONS, Prospect Pl. Norwich, Inv. and Manu.—Machine for thrashing, &c. Drilling and sowing machines. Registered horse-lever rake. Barley aveller. Corn-dressing, or winnowing machine. Hand barrow drill. Turnip and mangelwurzel-cutter, &c.

242 CLAYTON, SHUTTLEWORTH, & Co. Lincoln.—Improved

portable steam-engine for agricultural and contractor's purposes. Improved registered grinding mill suitable for all grain. Improved combined threshing, shaking, riddling, and blowing machine. (Also at Class 5, No. 39.)

243 MARRIOTT, J. 74 Gracechurch St. Des. and Manu. —New cottage bee-hive. Specimens of finished and unfinished comb.

246 WEST, W. Leicester, Inv. and Manu.—Drill, for sowing corn and turnips. Hand seed-drill, to work with cups, &c.

248 M'CARTNEY & DRUMMOND, Cumnock, Des. and Manu.—Threshing-machine, in cast-iron framing, with riddles, fans, and elevators. Improved construction of horse-wheel, and other parts of gearing. A peg-hummeller, for thrashing barley.

248A WEEKS, J. & Co. King's Rd. Chelsea, Inv. and Manu. —Cylindrical revolving furnace bars. Model of a conservatory, glazed light, &c. Pedestal, and stack of pipes for warming buildings by hot water, &c.

248B THOMPSON, H. A. Lewes, Manu.—Set of entrance gates, constructed upon improved principles. Steam cooking apparatus. Cast-steel measures for corn, &c. Forcing-pumps, &c.

249 WILSON, J. Kelso, Roxburghshire, Des.—Model of an improved seed-box for a turnip-sowing machine.

250 BROWN & ARCHBOLD, Horsley, Tyne Side, Newcastle-upon-Tyne, Inv. and Manu.—Miniature model machine for cleaning corn and grain.

252 PHILLIPS, C. & Co. Baptist Mills Foundry, Bristol, Manu.—Patent turnip-cutter, with reversing motion.

253 FLEMING, G. Trentham, Newcastle-under-Lyme, Inv. —Machine for destroying weeds, moss, lichens, &c. on gravel-walks, court-yards, &c.

254 RALSTON, W. Malletsheugh, Newton, Mearns, Renfrewshire, Scotland, Inv. and Manu.—Winnowing-machine, with cloth and revolving brush, for separating the grain from burrs.

255 STOKES, W. Dean, near Shepton Mallet, Somerset, Inv.—Treble cheese-press, and curd-mill.

255A SIEBE, A. 5 Denmark St. Soho.—A patent rotatory garden or house fire-engine, with improved hose and jet.

256 SMITH, J. Albert Iron Works, Uxbridge.—Chaff-cutter, cylindrical-sifter, thrashing-machine, oat and bean mill, plough, winnowing machine, turnip-cutter, &c.

257 WARREN, J. Heybridge, near Maldon, Essex, Inv. and Manu.—Turn-wrist and other ploughs. Revolving calendar-roll. Vegetation-hoe. Alarum guns, &c. Skim plough, for hoeing and cleaning land.

257A JOHNSON, T. (with Mr. Kinnear), Newcastle-upon-Tyne, Inv.—Model of a machine for sowing wheat and barley, with harrow attached.

258 MCPHERSON, P. Norton Pl. Edinburgh, Imp.—Improved mill for breaking, skutching, and preparing flax, and adapting it for hacking.

259 SPURGIN, J. M.D. Guildford St. Russell Sq.— Double hoc. Shark's-tooth-shaped hoe and spud.

259A WINTON, H. Birmingham.—Spades and other tools.

259B BURCHAM, C. Heacham, near Lynn, Inv. and Manu. —Model of a steam and human-power cultivator, or universal tillage machine and irrigator.

259C HAY, J. Florabank, Haddington, Inv.—Implement for cutting turnips for sheep and cattle.

262 SEAL, S. Wakefield, Manu.—Scythe-stones. Grind-stones.

262A CRAIG, J. & Co. Paisley, Manu.—Drain pipes and tiles, for field drainage, made from common clay.

262B ROWBOTTOM, J. Halifax.—Beehive, or bees'-skip, for taking honey without destroying the hive or bees.

263 DIGGES LA TOUCHE, Rev. T. Killenaule, Ireland, Inv.—Models of a cart, of an under carriage with high forewheels, of a grubber, harrow, and turnip-dibbler. Machine for making butter without handling. A ball-iron, for horses.

264 LOW, A. 72 Overgate, Dundee, Scotland.—A mouth-bag for horses, with gauze-wire front. Double water-furrow roller plough.

265 DANIELL, J. C. Simpley Stoke, near Bath.— Samples of manure.

266 SMITH, A. & W. & Co. Woodside Works, Paisley. Inv. and Manu.—Registered centrifugal churn for making butter. Steam apparatus, for cattle food. Corn and bean bruising, and hay and straw-cutting machines. Weighing-machines. Model of water-wheel and sugar-mill.

267 GRANT, J. C. Stamford, Inv. and Manu.—Patent lever horse-rake. Patent harrows. Improved haymaking, chaff, and weighing machines. Improved iron ploughs, whippletrees, garden drill, mill for grinding beans, Uley cultivator, Norfolk dock or thistle extractor, &c.

268 STUART, J. Aberdeen, Des. and Manu.—Two-horse plough, with double or single mould-board, and shifting coulter; subsoil plough, &c.

269 JONES, C. E., B.A. Birt House, Huddersfield.— 1 The cottager's double beehive, with regulating doorway in the floor-board. 2 Rim for enlarging the hive.

269A FORBES, R. B. Glasgow.—A Scotch farm cart.

269B SANDERS, S. Birmingham, Manu.—Improved garden spades, draining tools, and shovels.

270 SMITH, W. Kettering, Northamptonshire, Inv. and Manu.—Improved double-blast winnowing-machine. Newly-invented horse-hoes.

271 TUXFORD & SONS, Iron Works, Boston, Lincolnshire, Manu.—Patent portable housed steam-engine.

272 PLENTY, J. & E. Newbury, Berks.—Four-horse portable machine. Machine for pressing or bagging hops.

274 FERRABEE & SONS, Phœnix Iron Works, Stroud, Manu.—Chaff-cutter. Patent grass-cutter. Set of registered screw-wrenches.

275 LOMAX, W. R. Birmingham, Warwick.—Chaff and turnip-cutter. Universal cutter for vegetable substances.

277 UFFILL, E. Birmingham, Warwick.—Wrought-iron sheep-fold. Hay-rack for feeding sheep. Improved apparatus for melting pitch and tar. Tree guard.

278 RICKMAN, W. C. 21 Park Side, Hyde Park Corner Inv.—Farmer's level.

—— In North Transept Gallery.——

290 NEIGHBOUR & SON, 127 High Holborn.—Ventilating box beehive of Appleyard's. Payne's and Nutt's patent hives.

291 MILTON J. 10 Great Marylebone St.—British birds in cases; bee-hives, and bees at work in glass hives.

Proceed to Class 22, page 109.

Class 10. PHILOSOPHICAL, MUSICAL, HOROLOGICAL, AND SURGICAL INSTRUMENTS.

—— North, North Central, West, and South Central Galleries. ——

1 BENNETT, J. 65 Cheapside, Inv. and Manu.—An economical regulator beating half-seconds, with mercurial pendulum for compensation. Hall clock. Marine chronometer. Bennett's model watch, on a magnified scale; constructed to show the most compact form of the modern watch, with all the recent improvements. Bennett's time-keeper, for railway guards. Cathedral clock, dial of plate glass, new design, with a movement in action. Standard thermometers, &c. A wind dial in action from a vane above the roof of the Exhibition Building, with a self-recording machine for registering the wind's force.

2 ADAMS & SONS, 21 St. John's Sq. Clerkenwell, Manu.—Watches and watch movements.

3 OLORENSHAW, J. & Co. 8 Charles St. Northampton Sq. and Oxford Ter. Coventry, Manu.—Marine chronometer, gold and silver watches, and watch movements, &c.

4 ORDNANCE SURVEY DEPARTMENT, by Lieut.-Col. Hall.—Two compensation bars and microscopes, used with measurement of the base lines of the triangulation of the United Kingdom.

6 VEITCH, J. 6 Ovington Sq. Brompton, Inv.—An invention denominated the medico-chirurgical ambulance, devoted to the preservation of the life of the wounded warrior.

7 HUTTON, J. 9 Lucas Pl. Commercial Rd. East, Inv. and Manu.—Watches with patent single compensation stud. Clock, with patent compensation pendulum and barometric regulator. Marine chronometer, with patent pneumatic auxiliary compensation. Hutton's patent lever chronometer, &c.

8 CRAGG, J. 8 Northampton Sq. Clerkenwell, Manu. —Varieties of gold and silver watches, and a model of lever movement.

9 YATES, T. Preston, Manu.—Patent clock, on the detached dead-beat principle. Gold watch, beating dead half seconds.

10 LOWRY, S. 3 Lower Charles St. Northampton Sq. Clerkenwell, Inv. and Manu.—Lever watch; marine chronometers, &c. to show dead and complete seconds on the ordinary train; gold chronometer, and other watch work.

11 CONNELL, W. 83 Cheapside, Manu. — Two 2-day marine chronometers, Earnshaw's detached escapements; compound balance adjusted for high temperatures.

12 LOSEBY, E. T. 44 Gerrard St. Islington, Inv.— Mercurial compensation-balance, exhibiting four modifications. An arc compensation. Improved form of mercurial pendulum.

13 HOLL, F. R. 8 Weymouth Ter. City Rd. Inv. Pat. and Manu.—Gold centre seconds 8-day chronometer; 30-hour pocket chronometer. Gold compensated duplex, and other index watches.

14 ADAMS, T. 36 Lombard St. Manu.—Timepiece of chronometrical movement. Black and white marble, oak, and imitation time pieces.

16 HOWELL, JAMES, & Co. Regent St. Manu.—Or-molu clocks, ornamented with figures illustrative of day and night, &c. Des. and mod. by G. G. Adams, Esq.

17 WEBSTER, R. jun. 74 Cornhill, Inv. and Manu.— Train remontoir clock, combination of magnetism with clockwork, and black marble Egyptian clock.

18 VENTURA, A. B. 17 Charles St. Mortimer St. Cavendish Sq. Inv.—The patent harp Ventura, Ventura's new

English cetra, the British Ventura, the Venturina, and the lyra Ventura.

19 DELOLME, H. 48 Rathbone Pl. Oxford St. Des. and Manu.—Gold watches, manufactured entirely in England Stethometer. Marine chronometer.

20 NEWINGTON, S. Hastings, Inv.—Patent tell-tale clock, or servants' regulator.

21 GIBBS, H. 2 Nelson St. City Rd. Maker.—Watch, showing double time, with improved stop-work.

23 CHEVALIER, B. 41 Brunswick St. Stamford St. Manu.—Chronometer cases.

25 BROOKES, J. 5 Berkley Ct. Clerkenwell, Manu.— Main-spring for a two-day marine chronometer.

26 FUNNELL, E. 2 Clarence Pl. Brighton —Very small lever watch.

27 GOWLAND, J. 52 London Wall, Inv. and Manu.— Free pendulum regulator, tourbillon remontoir chronometer; anemometer, electric clock, watches, &c.

28 TANNER, W. 83 Upper St. Islington, Inv.—The polyhorion clock, showing local time, the time at Dublin, Paris, and Edinburgh. Lever watch, shows the times of any two places.

30 DAVIS, W. 37 Gracechurch St.—Horizontal and duplex watches, made by hand, by H. A. Davis, Birmingham.

31 COLE, T. 2 Upper Vernon St. Lloyd Sq. Clerkenwell, Inv. Des. and Manu.—Inkstand, with eight-day clock, and elaborate fittings. Designs for timepiece, clock, horological lantern, &c.

32 JACKSON, W. H. & S. Red Lion St. Clerkenwell, Inv. and Manu.—Soliclave lever watches, duplex timepiece, and pocket and marine chronometer, with a new compensation for extreme temperatures, &c.

33 MOORE & SONS, 38 Clerkenwell Close, Manu.— Chiming skeleton clock to go a month, &c.

34 BARRAUD & LUND, 41 Cornhill, Inv. and Manu.— Marine chronometer, with a model of a newly-invented compensation balance. Common marine chronometer. Small gold pocket chronometer.

35 PARKINSON & FRODSHAM, 4 Change Alley, Cornhill, Manu.—Astronomical clock, with mercurial pendulum, eight-day chronometer, lever watches, pocket chronometers, &c.

36 FAIRER, J. 17 Bishopsgate St. Without. Inv. and Manu.—Railway guards' time-keepers.

37 ROBINSON, P. Bishop Auckland, Des. and Manu.— Skeleton spring clock, representing the clock tower at the palace of the Bishop of Durham.

39 ELISHA, C. 13 New Bond St. Inv. and Manu.—An eight-day timepiece (regulator) to go by weight, with a compensating pendulum. Two silver lever watches, with the radii compensating apparatus. Registered.

40 BROCKBANK & ATKINS, 6 Cowper's Ct. Cornhill, Inv.—Marine chronometer, on spring gimbals, enclosed in improved box.

41 WALTER, F. 9 Devonshire Pl.—New design for giving a moral and religious application to the dial of a clock.

42 LAMB, J. Bicester, Oxfordshire, Manu.—Skeleton clock, to go 400 days.

43 THORNELOE, C. Lichfield, Des. and Manu.—Clock, strikes quarters and goes 32 days. Design, Lichfield cathedral. Gothic skeleton clock.

46 GRANT, P. 29 Lower William St. St. John's wood, Des.—Timepiece stand, of ivory, tulip-wood, and ebony.

46A COPLAND, C. M.A. Prop. South Villa, Kennington Oval.—A watch once the property of Henry VIII. Two antique watches, one silver and one gilt, chased.

47 HARVEY, W. Stirling, Scotland, Inv. and Manu.— Improvement in clocks, dispensing with striking work.

49 BENNETT, G. W. Blackheath, Kent, Manu.—A timepiece, adapted for public thoroughfares.

52 DONEGAN, J. Upper Ormond Quay, Dublin, Manu. —Watches, of Dublin manufacture. Specimens of Irish gold and silver, from Ballycorus works.

52A AUBERT & KLAFTENBERGER, 157 Regent St. Manu. —Upright regulator, with new escapement, and mercurial pendulum chronometers, watches, &c.

53 PENNINGTON, J. High St. Camberwell, Inv. and Manu.—Marine chronometer, with improved compensating balance weight.

54 TAFFINDER, —. Rotherham, Des. and Manu.— Skeleton clock.

55 DENT, E. J. 61 Strand, 33 Cockspur St. and 34 Royal Exchange, Manu.—Large assortment of ladies and gentlemen's superior watches. Marine chronometer, with a glass balance-spring, glass balance, and compensation, for variation of temperature, of platina and silver. Azimuth and altitude compass. Dipleidoscope. Astronomical and other clocks, &c. Large church clock. (Main Avenue.)

56 DRURY, J. 16 North Avenue, North St. Pentonville, Des. and Manu.—Clock dial-case in brass, adapted for hot climates, bakers' shops, &c.

57 FRODSHAM, C. 84 Strand, Manu.—Astronomical clock. Marine chronometers. Gold pocket chronometers and lever watches. The double rotary escapement. Day of the month watch. Specimen of gold lever watches, with the split-centre second's-hand movement. Railway watches. Portable chime and other clocks, &c.

60 HALL, G. F Norfolk St. Fitzroy Sq. Inv.—An astronomical and meteorological clock.

62 HINTON, C. 10 Corporation Lane, Clerkenwell, Des. and Manu.—English hard white enamel watch dial, with sunk centre and seconds, with low glass.

64 JONES, JOHN, 338 Strand.—Gold and silver watches of peculiar construction.

66 KAISER, J. 30 Park Ter. Regent's Park, Inv. and Manu.—Improved detector clock, indicating the days of the week and of the month, &c.

66A MOORE, Major W. 3 Cornish Ter. Rathmines, Dublin.—A surgical instrument for use previous to operation for lithotrity, &c.

67 MACDOUAL, E. J. 12 Dorset Pl. Pall Mall East, Inv. and Manu.—Escapement for chronometers, watches, and clocks, without escape-wheel: patented. The same spring by India-rubber. Centrifugal Archimedean, vibrating, and other drill-stocks. A new decomposition cell, and medals made by the process.

68 MACDOWALL, C. 4 Hyde St. Bloomsbury, Inv.— Clock-movement, with a dead escapement of a new construction: E. J. Dent, Manu. and Pat. by assignment.

69 MAPPLE, D. D. 17 Hull's Pl. John's Row, St. Luke's, Prod. and Des.—Registered skeleton timepiece, with improved lever escapement. Improved clock winder.

71 MARCHAND, L. 1 Red Lion St. Holborn, Manu.— Small gold lever watch. Musical clock.

73 PAYNE, W. & Co. 163 New Bond St. Inv. and Manu. —Quarter clock, on eight bells, in Amboyna wood, and ormolu case, made for the Sultan of Turkey. Timepieces, Chime clocks. Astronomical clock. Patent pedometer, and odometer, for measuring distances.

74 RIX, I. 21 Conduit St. Westbourne Ter. Inv.— Skeleton chronometer time-piece, slow motion.

78 TOBIAS & Co. Liverpool, Manu.—Watches, with registered compound seconds' movement, &c. Silver lever watch, as used in Turkey. Horizontal movement, extra chronometer-balance, adapted to all climates. Railway guards' timepiece.

79 GILLETT, W. S. Upper Harley St. Inv.—Models of a system of thin rings or discs, which being conical, may by pressure be made to extend inwards or outwards. Applicable to pistons, stuffing boxes, &c.

80 THOMSON, A. 25 New Bond St. Inv. and Manu.— Autochronograph, for the instantaneous marking or printing of time, giving the month, day, and hour (night and day), with the minutes and portions of minutes.

81 PETTIT, W. & Co. 2 Crombie's Row, Commercial Rd. East.—A watch, performing, suspended in a glass globe, filled with water. The object of the invention is to secure the protection of time-keeping and other instruments from water, sea-damp, &c.

85 HARDY, G. 5 Wellington Rd. St John's Wood, Inv. —Electro-magnetic motive engine.

85A WATKINS, A. 7 Weymouth Ter. City Road, Inv. and Manu.—Eight-day self-acting repeating chronometer, comprising 200 pieces of mechanism. Small three-quarter plate chronometers, with hard cylindrical springs, jewelled in every hole.

86 COUSENS & WHITESIDE, 27 Davies St. Berkeley Sq. Inv. and Manu.—A sporting watch, which shows the time to one-sixth of a second.

87 ALLIS, J. H. Bristol, Inv. and Manu.—Bracket-regulator timepiece, with a new description of compound pendulum.

90 BARLING, J. 90 High St. Maidstone, Kent, Des.— Dial of a clock, exhibiting a new pattern figure. Table and desert spoons and forks, ornamented in a novel manner, with enamel.

91 VIEYRES & REFINGON, 129 Regent St. Manu.—Two-day marine chronometer. Watches, of various fashions, for the home and South American markets.

92 BLAYLOCK, J. Long Island, Carlisle, Inv. and Manu. —Motion-work for the hour and minute hands of a turret-clock with four dials. Apparatus for illuminating dials, self-acting and self-regulating.

94 BOLTON, T. Coventry, Manu.—German silver watches, plated with silver. Gold plated watch.

95 MOUILLIARD, PIERRE FORTIME VICTOR, 71 Albany St. Regent's Park, Inv.—The artificial leech.

95A BRISCALL, J. 48 Constitution Hill, Birmingham, Des. and Manu.—Self-correcting clock, with a detached lever escapement ; goes a month.

96 BRUTTON, C. Exeter, Prop.—Clock in a case, which occupied 34 years in completing it, with astronomical, chronological, and other movements, bird organ, &c.

99 CHURCHILL, G. Downton, near Salisbury, Manu.— Clock, with music attached, playing a tune every three hours : the whole made by a blacksmith.

100 DELL BROTHERS, Bristol, Inv. and Manu.—Specimens of ordinary clock-work. Transparent timepiece. Specimens of iron and brass wheel-cutting, &c.

102 DRIVER, J. Silver St. Wakefield, Des. and Manu.— Chime-clock, showing the time in any part of the world.

103 EDWARDS, J. T. Dudley, Manu.—Portable spring time-keeper, to go 426 days.

104 EDWARDS, J. Stourbridge.—Large transparent skeleton spring timepiece, made of glass and brass.

104A GRAY, Dr. J. Perth, Inv.—Medical walking-staff, containing instruments, medicines, &c.

105 ———.—Clock, on carved mahogany pillar.

106 EVANS, W. F. Soho St. Handsworth, near Birmingham, Manu.—Gothic skeleton clock ; Elizabethan timepiece ; skeleton lever clock ; Sir Walter Scott's monument, Edinburgh ; and dial.

109 GERARD, A. Gordon's Hospital, Aberdeen, Inv.—
An instrument for the solution of problems in spherical
trigonometry, &c. Portable, or field transit instrument.
Clock, with conical pendulum. Marine clock, with two
pendulums. A centrifugal, or conical pendulum clock.

113 HART, W. & Co. Christchurch, Hants, Manu.—
Chronometer and watch fusee chains, of different sizes.

115 LAWRENCE, I. North Curry, near Taunton, Inv.—
Sun-dial for any latitude, on a new plan. Spring screw-
wrench. Dividers. Hand-drill. Turner's centre, with friction rollers.

117 PACE, J. Bury St. Edmunds, Inv. Des. and Manu.
—Skeleton clock, which goes three years. Pyramidical
skeleton timepiece, which goes three months. Barometer, &c.

119 RADFORD, J. 339 High St. Cheltenham, Inv. and
Des.—Diagrams of a geographical clock or watch, and a
working model of the design. Prov. reg.

121 WRIGHT, W. Exchequer Row, Aberdeen, Des. and
Manu.—A clock, showing the days of the month, months of
the year, the motions of the sun and moon, and the state of
tide at some of the principal seaports of Great Britain,
Ireland, France, America, Spain, Portugal, Holland, and
Germany : it goes twelve months.

122 BROADBENT, J. Ashton-under-Lyne.—Peal of small
bells to ring changes. Scale for pitching wheels.

123 ROSKELI, J. Church St. Liverpool, Des. and Manu.
—Watch and clock machinery.

124 ROTHERHAM & SONS, Coventry, Manu.—Gold and
silver watches: the various parts of a lever watch in the
progressive stages of manufacture.

126 MAPPLE, H. Child's Hill, Hampstead, Inv.—Machine used in America for saving life on railways. Fire
alarm, clock work, electric telegraphs, &c.

127 EINSLE, E. 46 St. Martin's Lane, Manu.—Syphon
douche, invented by Dr. C. Jones. Model of an improved
syphon, for brewers, &c. Stomach-pump. Amputating and
other instruments. Double-action enema pump, &c.

127A TAYLOR, G. Wolverhampton, Inv. and Manu.—
Registered self-correcting eight-day date clock, showing the
day of week, day of month, &c.

128 SHEPHERD, C. 53 Leadenhall St. Inv. and Pat.—
Patent electro-magnetic striking clocks, in connection with
the large clock in the transept.

129 SMITH & SONS, St. John's Square, Clerkenwell,
Manu.—Regulator suited to any temperature. Detector
clock, or watchman's timepiece. Church and turret clocks.
Skeleton timepiece and almanac for twelve months. Whishaw's uniformity of time clock and telegraph instruments.

130 ROBERTS, R. Globe Works, Manchester, Prop.—The
patent alpha (church or turret) clock, with compensation
pendulum and remontoire escapement. Patent normal
drill, for watch and clock work. Patent wheel sector. Watch
which beats dead (centre) seconds, with only one train of
wheels, &c. Recorder watch, with double hands. Pat.

131 YOUNG, J. Knaresborough, Manu.—Skeleton timepiece.

137 RUSH, G. Elsenharn Hall, Bishop Stortford, Inv.—
Design for the improvement of the dial-plate and registering
of the Aneroid barometer.

138 GRAY & KEEN, Liverpool, Des. and Manu.—Wheel
barometer, applicable for naval establishments, &c.

140 ABRAHAM, J. A. 87 Bold St. Liverpool, Inv.—Barometer, designed to show, without adjustment, the true
height of the mercurial column.

141 JONES, W. & S. 30 Holborn.—A mountain thermometer.

144 BROOKE, C. 29 Keppel St. Inv. and Des.—Photographic, self-registering, magnetic, and meteorological apparatus, comprising the barometer, the wet and dry bulb ther-

mometers, and photographic apparatus for registering their
variations.

145 DOLLOND, G. St. Paul's Churchyard, Inv.—Atmospheric recorder, for registering the changes of the atmosphere.

146 GOOD, S. A., H. M. Dockyard, Pembroke, Inv.—
New method of transmitting motion.

148 SCHOLEFIELD, D. Freeman's Sq. Huddersfield, Manu.
—Portable metronome, for denoting time in music.

149 HARRIS & SON, 50 High Holborn, Manu.—Patent
compensating portable barometers for the pocket, for marine service and for mountain purposes. New self-registering thermometer. Patent micrometrical and double-
image telescope, and " coming-up-glass."

151 MERRYWEATHER, G. Whitby Des. and Inv.—Tempest prognosticator, for the protection of life and property.

152 HEWITSON, J. Newcastle-upon-Tyne, Inv. and
Manu.—Self-acting and self-registering tide gauge and tidal
indicator.

154 BRYSON & SONS, Edinburgh, Inv. and Manu.—Five
models exhibiting the various escapements of watches at
present in general use. Self-registering barometer clock.

157 Ross, A. H. 25 Bridge St. Sunderland, Inv.—A
barometer, self-compensating, with newly arranged scale, &c.

157A CASELLO, L. P. & Co. 23 Hatton Garden, Des. and
Manu.—Combined comparative barometer, exhibiting the
torricellian, the cartesian, and wheel barometers, and sympiesometer acting in combination, with varying scales of
1, 11, 4, and 2 inches respectively. Improved pocket barometer ; improved window thermometer, &c.

158 LOVEJOY, G. Reading, Prop.—Timepiece with invisible mechanism, goes twenty-one days.

159 GRIMOLDI, H. 31 Brooke St. Holborn, Manu.—Improved pediment barometer in carved gilt frame.

160 SANDERSON, G. Mansfield, Nottingham, Des.—Map
of the country twenty miles round Mansfield.

160A NEGRETTI & ZAMBRA, 11 Hatton Garden, Inv. and
Manu.—Standard open cistern barometer. Self-registering
barometer. Pocket sympiesometer. Rutherford's thermometer. Sixes' self-registering thermometer. Hygrometers.
pressing gauge, &c.

161 ORCHARD, J. Kensington, Manu. and Des.—Standard barometer. Slides for magic lanterns, to show the
planets, air pumps, &c.

162 PIZZALA, F. A. 19 Hatton Garden, London, Des.
and Manu.—Wheel barometer or weather glass, with rack-
work motion to supersede the use of ordinary weights.

163 TREMLETT, R. 9 Albemarle St. St. John's Sq. Clerkenwell, Inv. and Manu.—Marine barometer, &c.

166 DOBBIE, W. Falkirk, Scotland, Manu.—Barometer,
showing the thousandth of an inch in the rise and fall of the
mercury.

168 COLLARD & COLLARD, Manu.—Grand, bichord, and
square semi-pianoforte, with the patent repeater action;
grand cabinet pianoforte, with the patent check and repeater
action. Pianoforte for the people. A grand pianoforte (in
main avenue).

175 LIST, G. B. Southampton, Inv.—An apparatus for
setting fractures, and a rest for the treatment of other accidents and diseases: manu. by J. R. Stebbing, Southampton.

181 MATTHEWS, W. 10 Portugal St. Lincoln's Inn,
Manu.—Inhalers, for medicines requiring the aid of heat.
Inhaler, for administering chloroform in surgical operations.
Inhaler, for hydrocyanic acid, conicine, &c. Improved
stethoscope. Specula for the ear, &c. Gilbert's patent ful-
crum and chair, for extracting teeth New swinging apparatus for fractured legs. Table knives.

187 BATEMAN, J. LL.D. F.R.A.S. East India Rd. and
Inland Revenue Office.—Centrifugal machine, illustrating
planetary motion.

188 RICHARDS, N. 3 Somerset St. Aldgate, Prop.— Globe with an endless rotary action, named the geographical instructor.

189 MORRISON, J. D. 6 Rankeillor St Edinburgh, Manu. —Artificial teeth. Set of carved teeth from the hippopotamus's tusk.

190 RYLES, M. Cobridge, Staffordshire Potteries, Inv.— An apparatus, of a peculiar construction, showing the ebb and flow of the tides.

191 PAXON, W. Hampstead, Prop.—Lunarian, with improved contrivance for showing the phases of the moon.

193 MATHEWS, MARY, 16 Westbourne St. Hyde Park Gardens, Inv.—Astrorama. A concave representation of the heavens.

194 ASHE, W. A. 15 Brompton Cres. Prop.—Great circle course indicator; inv. Lieut. E. D. Ashe.

195 FACY, R. Wapping Wall, Des. and Manu.—A vertical orrery.

196 LITTLE, Major R. J. Woolwich Common, Des.— Apparatus and tools contrived to meet the loss of the right hand; manufactured by Gaze, 14 Beresford St. Woolwich.

197 ROPER, W. Bath, Manu.—The reclinia, invented by H. Lawson, Esq. for assisting astronomers in using large telescopes.

198 JOHNSTON, W. & A. K. Edinburgh, Manu.—A terrestrial globe, 30 inches in diameter, showing the geological structure of the earth, the currents of air and of the ocean, trade winds, trade routes, monsoons, and isothermal lines, or lines of equal temperature. The stand by W. Davidson.

200 FLETCHER, P. 11 South St. Andrew St. Edinburgh, Manu.—Pair of globes and case, showing the various stages in globe making.

201 ALLAN, T. 20 St. Andrew's Sq. Edinburgh, Inv.— Two pairs of patent electric telegraphs.

202 MURDOCH, J. Rothes, Fochabers, Elgin, Scotland, Inv.—Mechanical indicator of eclipses.

204 STOKER, John, Doncaster. — Angular terrestrial globe, to show the motion of the earth of 23¼ deg. Spherical geographical clock.

205 SAUNDERS & SON, 278 Strand.—Metallic tablet razor strops. Mechanical revolving pictorial kaleidescope.

207 EDKINS & SON, 16 Salisbury Sq. Manu.—Pair of 18-inch globes.

208 MALLOCH, P. 18 Market St. Edinburgh.—Mechanical indicator for teaching geography, designed and manufactured by the exhibitor.

209 WILLIS, H. London.—An organ consisting of three rows of keys and two octaves and a fifth of pedals. This instrument is built upon the German plan, viz., 8 feet manuals, and 32 feet pedals; altogether it contains, in 77 stops, nearly 4,500 pipes, the largest being CCCC 32 feet, the smallest C ⅜ of an inch. The great and swell organs are played by means of the pneumatic lever, exhibited in a vertical position, and worked without the aid of additional pressure of air. In the choir and pedal organs are introduced two newly-invented patent valves, over which the pressure of the air has but little influence. There is also introduced a patent movement in connexion with a compound application of the pneumatic lever, which brings the command of the instrument completely under the thumbs of the performer, enabling him to draw stops in combination of which there are 24 changes, thus rendering it, though elaborate, perfectly manageable. The mechanism includes several novel arrangements, and in the various bellows there are five different pressures of air.

210 DUNIN, Mx. E. de, London.—Piece of mechanism intended to represent the proportions of the human figure; it admits of being expanded from the standard size of Apollo Belvidere to that of a colossal statue. Composed of more than 7000 pieces of steel.

212 NEWTON & SON, 66 Chancery Lane, and 3 Fleet St. Manu.—Large manuscript celestial globe, 6 feet in diameter. Pair of 25-inch globes; other globes. Complete orrery, or planetarium. Orreries, for educational purposes. Armillary sphere.

213 BENTLEY, J. 13 Paternoster Row, Inv. — Plano globe.

215 PLANT, F. Nottingham, Inv.—Mechanical orrery. Model of self-regulating feeding apparatus, a substitute for the force-pump, regulating float, &c.

218 ADORNO, J. N. 6 Golden Sq.—A machine to measure and demonstrate the aliquot proportions of the periphery and diameter of the circle. A machine or instrument to draw ellipses, parabolas, and hyperbolas. A terrestrial and celestial globe combined. Globe and map in sections.

220 HORNE, THORNTHWAITE & WOOD, 123 Newgate St. —Dissolving views. Transparency of the moon. Electrogalvanic machine, &c. for medical galvinism. Oxy-hydrogen microscope. Daguerreotype and calotype apparatus and chemicals. Agricultural drainage-levels, galvanometer, &c.

233 GRAHAM, G. 8 Liverpool St. Walworth, Inv.—Invention for directing an aerial machine.

234 GILBERT, G. M. Ealing, Prop.—Globes, inflated with atmospheric air. Char-volant or carriage drawn by kites.

237 LUNTLEY, J. New Broad St. Court, Inv. and Manu. —Self-propelling rotatory balloon. Prov. reg.

248 PRITCHARD, A. 162 Fleet St. Inv. and Manu.— Achromatic microscope.

249 HETT, A. 24 Bridge St. Southwark, Preparer.—Injected microscopic objects, for displaying the structure of parts and organs, and illustrating the utility of the microscope to physiology and pathology.

250 FIELD & SON, 113 New St. Birmingham, Manu.— Achromatic microscopes, dissecting microscope, with Wollaston's magnifiers, compound achromatic lenses for photographic purposes. Calotype pictures.

252 POULTON, C. Southern Hill, Reading, Manu.—Objects prepared for the microscope, with drawings by M. S. Legg.

253 SMITH & BECK, 6 Coleman St. Manu.—Compound achromatic microscopes and apparatus. Cabinet for objects. Revolving tables for microscope, &c.

254 ROSS, A. 2 Featherstone Buildings, Inv. and Manu. —Astronomical telescope, the object-glass 11½ inches diameter, mounted on a stand, having equatorial movements and complete adjustments. The optical part wrought by Ross's improved system and machinery. Astronomical telescopes. Improved microscopes, and photographic camera obscura. (Main Avenue West.)

254A READE, Rev. J. B. Stone Vicarage. Aylesbury, Inv. —Solid eyepieces for telescopes, micrometers, &c. (Main Avenue West.)

256 HUDSON, F. T. Greenwich, Prod. and Des.—Animal, vegetable, and mineral tissues, and structures, prepared for the microscope.

257 VARLEY & SON, 1 Charles St. Clarendon Sq. Inv. and Manu.—Graphic telescopes. Reversing camera. Microscope. Reflecting telescopes. Apparatus for changing the small speculums of Gregorian telescopes. Air-pumps, &c.

258 JACKSON, E. & W. 315 Oxford St. Inv.—Microscopic apparatus, &c.

259 CHADBURN BROTHERS, Sheffield and Liverpool, Manu. —Spectacle glasses and lenses. Telescopes, microscopes, spectacles, reading glasses, agricultural and surveyors' levels, magnets, steam and vacuum gauges, barometers, syringes, galvano-electric machines. Craig's charactograph, &c. Portable barometer. Prov. reg.

263 ABRAHAM, A. & Co. 20 Lord St. Liverpool, Manu. —Trinoptric prismatic lantern, with apparatus for making oxygen gas. (Rev. St. V. Beechy, inv.) Dioptric prismatic lantern. Compound microscope. Portable sketching camera obscura.

264 RICHARDSON, T. W. Brede, near Northam, Sussex.— A reflecting telescope, for observing the sun's surface: the reflector, made of crown glass, is part of a paraboloid of revolution. Improved screw for straining wire fences. Hop-tallies. Specimens of the prismatic colour on glass, &c.

265 WILLATS, T. & R. 28 Ironmonger Lane, Cheapside, Inv. and Man.—Portable photographic camera and stand. Registering thread counter, or linen prover.

266 SALMON, W. J. 254 Whitechapel Rd. Manu.—Day or night telescopes for ships' use.

267 CRICKITT, R. E. Doctors' Commons, Des.—Universal equatorial telescope-stand.

268 CALLAGHAN, W. 45 Gt. Russell St. Bloomsbury, Manu.—An improved deer-stalking telescope. A pair of portable steel spectacles.

269 PILLISCHER, M. 398 Oxford St. Des. and Manu.— Achromatic microscopes. Students' microscope. Opera glasses and portable telescopes.

270 CARPENTER & WESTLEY, 24 Regent St. Manu.— Phantasmagoria lanterns, with a set of sections to show the optical principle. Series of astronomical diagrams, adapted to dissolving lanterns.

271 DIXEY, C. W. 3 New Bond St. Manu.—Barometers. Improved nautical sextant. Spectacles. Opera-glasses. Thermometers. Telescopes. Drawing instruments, &c.

273 BAYLEY, R. 18 Half Moon Cres. White Conduit House, Manu.—Gold and steel spectacles.

274 GODDARD, J. T. 35 Goswell St. Manu.—Achromatic object glass for a telescope of 9in. aperture, about 16ft. focus.

274A EVANS, W. Brecknock, South Wales, Inv. and Manu.—Artificial leg, to enable persons who have lost the knee either to walk or ride.

276 CLARK, F. 13 Park Side, Knightsbridge, Inv. and Manu.—New invented adjusting spectacles.

278 HYAMS, H. 59 Cornhill, Inv. and Manu.—Objectglass, consisting of a single piece of glass. Stanhope lens.

279 WEABER, H. 129 Oxford St. Manu.—Invisible steel spectacles, and other spectacles and hand-glasses.

280 WHITEHOUSE, N. 2 Cranbourn St. Prop. and Manu. —Artificial eye. artificial silver nose; opera-glass, &c.

281 WOODMAN, J. T. 6 Commercial Pl. Commercial Rd. Peckham, Inv. and Manu.—Portable self-adjusting foot-rest.

283 BRAITHWAITE, S. 169 Kirkgate, Wakefield, Inv. and Manu.—Registered ventilating eye-shades.

284 STARK, R. M. 1 Hope St. Edinburgh, Inv. and Manu. —Microscopic objects, in gutta percha cells, intended as a substitute for glass cells, being equally durable, and much cheaper. Slides for opaque objects.

285 JORDAN, C. 37 Chapman St. Manchester, Inv. and Manu.—Illuminative instrument, for inspecting the ear, &c. Instrument for the inspection of the eye. Instrument for illuminating moulds in iron-founding, &c.

286 SOLOMON, J. 22 Red Lion Sq. Manu.—Registered papier-maché opera glasses, eye protectors, &c.

287 KING, T. D. Bristol, Des. and Manu.—Compound achromatic microscope, &c. Improved spherical prismatic illuminator.

289 BRAHAM, J. St. Augustine's Parade, Bristol, Inv. and Manu.—Spectacles from their earliest invention: various modes adopted by Sir Isaac Newton, Drs. Kitchiner, Wollaston, and Herschell. Lenses, &c.: registered. Trigonometer. Herapath's registered blow-pipe.

290 ROWLEY, J. Wolverhampton, Manu.—Improved spectacles. Spectacles worked out of best cast-steel; weight,

2 pennyweights. Wire-gauze eye preservers. Hand-spectacles, eye-glasses, &c.

291 MAYALL, J. E. 433 West Strand, Prod.—Daguerreotype panorama.

291A LADD, W. 29 Penton Pl. Walworth, Manu. Case of instruments for pneumatic experiments. Compound microscope, with chain and spindle in lieu of rack and pinion, now in use. Registered.

292 BEARD, R. 85 King Wm. St. City, Pat.—Photographic pictures by a new process, whereby daguerreotypes are enamelled.

294 KILBURN, W. E. 234 Regent St. Prod.—Photographic miniatures.

295 PAINE, W. 5 Trinity Row, Islington, Prod.—Photographic pictures, showing the progress of the art.

296 CLAUDET, A. F. J. 18 King Wm. St. Charing Cross, Inv.—Photographic plates and pictures, and apparatus for photographic purposes.

297 HENNEMAN & MALONE, 122 Regent St. Westminster, Des.—Talbotype apparatus of improved design, made by J. Newman. Talbotype pictures. Talbotypes tinted by means of caustic potash and a lead salt. Specimens of Sir J. Herschel's cyanotype and chrysotype, and of Mr. Robert Hunt's chromatype pictures.

298 HAYWARD, E. L. & W. 196 Blackfriars Rd. Inv. and Manu.—A gauge, for ascertaining the thicknesses and weights of plates and rods of metal, &c.

299 TYREE BROTHERS, 44 Regent's Circus, Piccadilly, Inv.—Daguerreotypes.

301 SADD, W. Wandsworth, Inv. and Prop.—Ærial machine.

302 BINGHAM, R. J.—Photograph from paper negatives.

303 COLLS, R. & L. 168 New Bond St. Prod.—Sun pictures, on paper.

306 LEONARD, S. W. 11 Upper Stamford St. Des —Illustrations of the use of the microscope for detecting adulterations, and for discoveries in minute anatomy.

308 SHARP, S. New George St. Sheffield, Manu.—Set of ten lenses for a single microscope, from 1-10th to 1-100th of an inch focal length.

309 WRAY, W. 43 Havering St. Commercial Rd. East. Inv. and Manu.—A seven-feet achromatic telescope, into which a solid substitute is used in place of flint glass.

317 DENTON, J. B. Gray's Inn Sq. Inv.—Specimens of model or relief mapping. Workman's draining-levels.

318 PENROSE, F. C. 4 Trafalgar Sq. Inv. and Prop.— Spiral compasses. Sliding helicograph.

320 ELLIOTT & SONS, 56 Strand, Manu.—Drawing instruments. Dumpy-level. Theodolites. Transit instrument. New instrument for measuring distance. Telescopes. Opera-glasses. Standard English yard. Slide-rule. Azimuth and altitude instrument, &c.

322 LLOYD, Lieut.-Col. J. A.—Typhodeictor, or storm pointer, an instrument for obtaining, by inspection, the bearing and relative position of a revolving storm or hurricane, by Lieut.-Colonel Lloyd, constructed in accordance with the theory, commonly called the Law of Storms, as made known in several publications by Colonel Reid. Manufactured by Elliott & Sons.

323 DOBSON, J. 268 High Holborn, Manu.—Complete magazine set of drawing instruments in electrum or British metal. A variety of smaller sets.

324 TREE & Co. 22 Charlotte St. Blackfriars Rd. Manu. —Ewart's improved gauge for computing the carcase weight of live cattle, &c. Rules, scales, &c.

325 PURVIS, J. Newcastle-upon-Tyne, Inv.—Mechanical square, containing a plumb-rule, a spirit-level, square-level, foot-rule, and slide-rule.

326 MOREAU, F. 4 South St. Finsbury.—Aneroid barometer.

327 Towns, W. 19 Stangate St. Lambeth, Inv.—Spirit meter on a new principle.

328 Haggard, W. Bank of England, Inv.—A double protractor, three inches square.

329 Sinclair & Hockley, 42 Gerard St. Soho. Des. and Manu.—Artificial teeth, &c.

330 Best, T. Oldham.—Measuring and dividing machine. Rules, marked and divided by the machine.

331 Griffith, J. Darley Parsonage, near Derby, Des. —Standard barometer, manufactured by J. Davis, Derby.

332 Yeates, G. 2 Grafton St. Dublin, part Des. and Manu.—Barometers, theodolites, simple and effective air-pump, improved prismatic compasses, optic square, spectacles, &c.

333 De Grave, Short, & Fanner, 59 St. Martin's-le-Grand, Manu.—Assay balances and weights. Hydrostatic balances and weights. Diamond balances. Weights and measures, &c.

334 Oertling, L. 13 Store St. Bedford Sq. Manu.—Chemical and other balances of delicate construction.

335 Brown, S. 6 Marlborough Pl. Kennington Cross, Inv.—Patent power-engine and water-meter, and water and spirit meters.

336 Langlands, J. Chesterfield, Inv.—Patent compound tap with meter.

337 Park, S. H. Kingswood, Wootton-under-Edge, Gloucestershire.—Set of improved spanners, and centripetal punch and gauge, to find the centre in round or square iron.

338 Sang, J. Kirkaldy, Scotland, Inv. and Manu.—Pianometer, or self-acting calculator of surface.

339 Bridges, G. Hampton Wick, Kingston, Inv.—Instrument for ascertaining distances of objects, by day or night.

340 Rooker, J. & A. 26 East St. Foundling, Manu.—Sliding rule of involution. Specimen of hand dividing.

341 Marriott, M. Montpelier Sq. Inv.—Delicate balance for chemical analysis, made of pine.

342 Ross, W. Strathsteven, Golspie, Sutherland, Inv.—Graduator. An instrument for the approximate determination of heights and distances of objects; and it shows the time of day by the sun in any part of the globe.

343 William, B. H. Waterfoot, Ireland.—An instrument designed to take angles and bearings in the field, and transfer them mechanically to paper without reading off.

344 Dover, J. 14 Little New St. Prod.—Delicate balance for chemical analysis and assaying.

346 Dobbs, G. 37 St. Alban's St. Lambeth.—Universal spirit level, for all kinds of machinery.

347 Cox, G. 5 Barbican, Manu.—Instrument for ascertaining correct time. The periphan, for the study of astronomy, &c. Beam draining-levels and angle metre.

348 Hardy, J. 5 Wellington Rd. St. John's Wood, Inv. —Metrograph, an instrument to enable a person to draw any object from nature, by actual measurement.

349 Barrett, R. M. 4 Jamaica Ter. Limehouse, Manu. —Improved lunar sextants. Plain sextant. Improved brass quadrant, divided to half minutes.

350 Taylor, J. 104 Minories, Manu.—Sextant for measuring angular distances between the heavenly bodies.

351 Heath, G. Erith, Kent.—Solid bell-metal ivory-arched sextant, divided to ten seconds. Improved action magnifier. Improved spring hollow leg. Improved ivory-arch metal quadrant.

352 Williams, W. 47 Johnson St. Somers Town, Inv. and Manu.—Instrument to draw lines radiating from a centre.

353 Adcock, J. 4 Marlborough Rd. Dalston, Inv.—Model of a new machine for measuring and mapping, &c.

354 Baker, R. Glastonbury, Somersetshire, Inv.—Model of an instrument called the Periphan, by which the

ordinary solar and lunar phenomena are elucidated in a clear, simple, and unique manner.

355 Graham, J. High Row, Darlington, Durham, Inv. —A rule for showing the circumference of a circle; also the side of the square equal in area to a circle whose diameter or circumference is given.

356 Cameron, P. 87 London St. Glasgow, Inv.—Azimuth compass. Engineer's improved indicating level. Mathematical and nautical slide rule. Improved thermometer, steam and vacuum gauge.

357 Macdonald, Dr. 4 Coburg Pl. Upper Kennington Lane, Inv.—Instrument to facilitate finding the longitude at sea.

358 Siebe, A. 5 Denmark Street, Soho, Inv. and Manu. —Dial weighing-machine, with measuring apparatus. Steam-boiler feeder, with patent joint.

359 Smith, W. 6 Wyatt St. Maidstone.—Early-calling machine.

361 Miller, J. Jun. 30 Thomas St. Woolwich, Inv.—Miller's radiator for drawing lines to a point or centre.

362 Liddell, J. J. Edinburgh, Des. and Manu.—Spirit levels used in draining, road levelling, &c.

363 Thompson, J. 4 Wellington Pl. West India Dock Rd. Limehouse, Inv.—Trigonometrical machine for marking out clothing.

364 Adcock, J. Teignmouth, Inv. and Des.—Registered scale of the diameter and quadrant of the circle, for measuring standing timber. Drawing of improved paddle-wheel. Drawings of an invention for determining and registering the courses of the wind, of a new water-wheel, &c.

365 Gardner & Co. 21 Buchanan St. Glasgow.—Optical instruments.

366 Young & Son, 5 Bear St. and 46 Cranbourn St. Inv. and Manu.—A seat scale weighing machine.

367 Blyth, R 2 Cheltenham Pl. Westminster Rd. Lambeth.—Patent indicating level, for carpenters, masons, &c.

368 Ackland, W. 19 Dorset St. Portman Sq. Inv.—Machine for the graduation of hydro-meters, thermometers, &c. Scales for an hydrometer, showing specific gravities and per centages.

369 Besant, —, Wiltshire.—Music stands.

371 Nunn, R. M. Wexford, Ireland, Inv.—Hydrometer, for ascertaining the specific gravity of liquids from 0·600 to 2·000. Double reverse-action pump. Door-spring, &c.

372 Blunt, H. Shrewsbury.—Model of a lunar crater (Eratosthenes), diameter of the crater about 28 miles.

376 Hay, W. 113 Union St. Aberdeen, Des.—Foot gauge, by which the measurements are taken at once.

377 Fox, R. W. Falmouth, Inv.—Fox's magnetized balance, weighing to the ten thousandth part of a grain.

378 Yates, Emma Jane, 9 Portland Pl. Wandsworth Rd. Inv.—An instrument for the approximate determination of the problem of squaring the circle.

379 Dyer, H. Gt. Western Railway, Hungerford, Inv. —Registered office index and tablet memento, intended to assist the memory.

382 Tolputt, W. B. Folkestone. — Instrument to teach the blind to write.

383 Darnell, J. 3 King Edward Ter. Liverpool Rd. Islington, Inv.—Portable house alarm, for the detection of fire and robbery. Universal sun-dial.

385 Davidson, A. Nairne.—Tree measurer, to take the girth of a tree.

386 Weare, R. Princes Rd. Plumstead Common.—A fire annihilator.

387 Wertheimer, D. J. 5 Charing Cross, Pat. and Manu.—Calculating machine, adapted to Indian, American, Russian, Prussian, Brazilian, Portuguese, Neapolitan, Roman, French, Turkish, Chinese, and English money, &c.

D

Counting machine, for showing the number of strokes made by a steam engine, &c.

389 DARVELL, W. J. Chesham, Inv.—Improved refrigerator for cooling malt liquors, &c.

392 BOYLE, —.—Reflecting telescope.

395 MATTHIAS, J. H. 47 Hatton Garden, and 1 Dorset St. Ball's Pond, Inv. and Manu.— New invention for dividing lines, upon a geometrical principle.

396 BAKER, H. 90 Hatton Garden, Inv. and Manu.— Vacuum gauge. Steam gauge. Alarums and rain gauges. Thermometers, barometers, hydrometers, &c.

399 CHAMBERLAIN, W. jun. St. Leonards-on-Sea, Inv.— Models of machines to record votes. Patented.

401 HUGHES, W. Governor of the Blind Asylum, Manchester, Inv.—Typograph for the blind, enabling them to express their thoughts upon paper: registered. A similar instrument for embossing or printing in relief.

402 WILTON, W. St. Day, Truro, Manu.—Fox's magnetic dip and intensity instruments. Miner's theodolite, or improved dial and quadrant, for underground and surface surveying.

403 ANDERSON, J. Queensferry South, Edinburgh, Inv. —Perspective drawing machine.

404 GRIFFITHS & LE BEAU, 15 Coborn Rd. Mile End.— Daguerreotype portraits and pictures, with electrotype copies taken from them.

404 HEYWOOD, W. 95 Duke St. Manchester.—Experimental air-pump, with self-acting exhaust-tap.

406 BEAUFORD, R. Hastings, Inv. and Prov. Reg.—Improved photographic instrument, called the Daguerreotype accelerator.

407 GOGERTY, R. 72 Fleet St. Model of a pair of direct-acting steam-engines, with paddle-wheels. Plate electrical machine, air-pump, galvanometer, &c.

408 BRYAN, Rev. J. Norwich, Inv.—Improved air-pump without valves.

409 MARRATT, J. S. 63 King William St. London Bridge.—A five-feet achromatic telescope, the vertical and horizontal motion produced by endless screws. A seven-inch transit theodolite.

411 PHILLIPS, J. F.R.S. St. Mary's Lodge, York, Inv. —An electrophorus; rain gauge; maximum thermometer; anemometer, for collieries, hospitals, &c.; and air barometer, of very cheap construction, suited to collieries. Block of stone, coloured by infiltration, as nature colours her marbles.

413 ALLEN, E. E. Steel Yard Wharf, Upper Thames St. Inv.—Electro-magnetic railway-train alarm, for communicating with the engine driver from any part of the train.

413A PARKS, W. J. 25 Newington Cres. Manu.—Artificial teeth, &c.

414 NICHOLS, W. Cambridge, Inv.—Electro-magnetic alarum, for the protection of property against robbery or fire.

417 CRESSWELL, J. Winchmore Hill, Edmonton, Inv.— Electro-magnetic motive engine.

419 WHISHAW, F. 9 John St. Adelphi, Des. and Inv.— Telekouphonon, or speaking telegraph. Gutta percha telephone. Railway trains communicator. Gutta percha tube and lathe-band, as first made at the Society of Arts in 1845. Subaqueous insulated electric telegraph conductors. Battery protector. Telegraphic private code box. Model to illustrate the hydraulic telegraph. Centrimetal chronometer, made by Johnston, Clerkenwell, indicating the speed of railway trains, &c. Patent glass pipes to insulate and protect the wires of electric telegraphs under ground. Patent multi-tubular pipes of glazed earthenware, manufactured by W. Northen, Vauxhall. Chess-board, of enamelled slate, executed by Mr. Magnus, Pimlico, the game may be played without men. Index electric and mechanical domestic

telegraphs. Wrought-iron chain pipes for submarine telegraph.

420 HARRISON, C. W. & J. J. Richmond, Inv.—Electro-magnetic engine, for producing a motive power on a new principle.

421 McNAIR, A. & Co. 33 Oswald St. Glasgow, Inv. and Manu.—Conductor for electric telegraphs, consisting of a copper wire insulated with gutta percha, and inclosed in a leaden tube.

422 BRETT, A. 138 Holborn Bars, Prop.—Brett and Little's patent electric telegraph, alarum bell, bell handle, and battery, with underground submarine arrangement of conductors. Hydraulic battery, insulator, &c.

423 WINTER, J. 44 Littlewood House, Leeds, Manu.— Walking-stick, containing an electro-galvanic machine and battery complete.

424 SMITH, G. R. 16 De Bouvoir Ter. Culford Rd. Inv. —Comic electric telegraph and key-board.

425 BURDETT, J. 28 Hanover Sq. Clapham Rd. Inv.— Domestic telegraph, requiring only one bell for any number of rooms.

426 ALEXANDER, W. 52 West Register St. Edinburgh, Inv.—Model of an electro-magnetic telegraph, worked by means of voltaic currents through metallic conductors.

427 REID, W. 25 University St. Inv. and Manu.—Electric-telegraph instruments, adapted for hotels. Specimens of insulated wire, for submarine electric telegraphs, &c.

428 HENLEY, W. T. 46 St. John's St. Rd. Clerkenwell, Inv. and Manu.—Large permanent horse-shoe magnet, weighing 6 cwt.; magneto-electric machine; patent electric telegraphs, worked by the magneto-electric current, &c.

429 BRETT, J. & J. W. 2 Hanover Sq. Pat. and Prop.— Electric printing telegraphs. Communicator or corresponding apparatus. Circuit regulator. A portion of the experimental wire passed along the bottom of the channel in August last, when messages were printed by this telegraph from England to France. Iron-protecting cable for enclosing the covered submarine wires, where great strength may be required. Inv. by T. W. B. Brett. Electric bells, &c. Pat. in Great Britain, America, France, Austria, Prussia, Belgium, Holland, Sardinia, and Spain.

430 WALKER, C. V. Tonbridge, Inv.—Modes of insulation of telegraph wires, compound needle, bell transferer, branch double turn-plate, lightning conductors, graphite battery, and other electric telegraph apparatus.

432 BRITISH ELECTRIC TELEGRAPH Co. — Highton's patent electric telegraphs and apparatus. Printing telegraph, adapted to one or two wires; another, by which any one of 26 symbolical characters is printed by a single touch of a key. Morse's arrangement of telegraph, worked by secondary power. Telegraph for showing the letters of the alphabet instantly, by the touch of a single key; with a revolving pointer; with a revolving disc. Series of indicating and pointing telegraphs, worked by various descriptions of coils and steel magnets, and by coils acting on soft iron. Series of telegraphic alarums, &c.

433 BAKEWELL, F. 6 Haverstock Ter. Hampstead, Inv. and Pat.—Electric copying telegraph.

434 BAIN, A. Beevor Lodge, Hammersmith, Inv.— Electric clocks. Electro-chemical telegraphs. Electro-chemical copying telegraph.

435 FRENCH, W. H. Cardiff, Wales, Inv.—Electric telegraph turn-plates, for changing wires from main to branch lines.

436 DERING, G. E. Lockley's Welwyn, Herts, Inv. and Pat.—Electric telegraph apparatus, illustrative of many improvements.

437 MEINIG, C. L. A. 103 Leadenhall St. Agent.— Portable galvanic battery of 120 elements. Clockwork, for making and breaking contact. Patent galvanic chain battery, to be worn on the human body. Invented by T. L. Pulvermacher.

438 EDWARDS, J. B. Liverpool, Prod. and Manu.—Series of glass retorts, heapers, evaporating basins, and other glass and porcelain vessels for chemical purpose.

438A ARUNDELL, W. W. Falmouth, Inv. and Manu.—Carbonized cast-iron magnet. Impressions and specimens of seals, executed by machinery.

439 HEARDER, J. N. 34 George St. Plymouth, Inv. and Manu.—Permanent compound cast iron and steel magnets of great power. Medico-galvanic apparatus.

440 JOULE, J. P. F.R.S. Acton Sq. Salford, Inv.—Electro-magnet, constructed of a plate of well-annealed wrought iron, tapered to the poles. Tapered armatures. Surface electro-magnet, and armature, &c.

441 WAITE, G. 2 Old Burlington St. Inv.—Electric galvanic apparatus used in dental surgery.

444 WESTMORELAND, J. Derby, Des.—Patent gutta percha electrical machine.

446 GREEN, S. 7 Helmet Row, Old St. Manu.—Various compasses and sun-dials. Damp detectors. Angle-meters. Ivory circular thermometers with compass or magnetic sun-dial. Miners' compass with sites, &c.

450 WEIGHT, S. 14 Burton St. Cheltenham, Inv.—Model of a machine for expelling fire-damp from mines.

451 PALMER, W. V. Somers Town.—Electrotypes and engravings from electrotypes.

452 CRICHTON, J. 112 Leadenhall St. Manu.—Solid arch sextant, double limb sextant, coast surveying sextant, quadrants, azimuth compasses, theodolites, levels, telescopes, grumers, callipers, &c.

453 KNIGHT & SONS, Foster Lane.—Chemical cabinets. Portable universal chemical furnace, on the principle of Dr. Black. Improved air-pump. Plate electric machines, and galvanic batteries. Working models of electro-magnetic motive engines. Lathe for cleansing and polishing daguerreotype plates: invented by G. Knight. Photographic apparatus, &c.

454 COFFEY, J. A. & SMITH, J. 4 Providence Row, Finsbury, Prop. and Manu.—Improved chemical apparatus, containing a still head, with pans for decoctions, &c.; a drying closet, a condenser for steam, &c.

456 STATHAM, W. E. 4 Rotherfield St. South, Lower Islington, Inv. and Manu.—Portable chemical cabinets and laboratories, for amusement, analysis, and chemical research. Hydro-pneumatic apparatus, combining a pneumatic trough gasometer, and an hydraulic blowpipe.

457 GRIFFIN, J. J. & Co. 53 Baker St. Manu.—Graduated glass instruments for chemical testing in the arts; decimal weights and measures; hydrometers; ammoniameter, or hydrometer for liquid ammonia; small chemical apparatus, &c.

458 ALLMAN, F. 12 Stanhope Pl. Hyde Park. Inv.—An electric table-lamp, suitable for a room, with another, illustrating the way in which the dynamic effect of the current is made to govern the lamp. Patented.

459 IBBETSON, Capt. B. Clifton House, Old Brompton.—A blowpipe, giving an uninterrupted and regular flame. Oxy-hydrogene microscope, with new safety tubes and adjustments. Manu. by C. W. Collins, Royal Polytechnic Institution, Regent St.

460 NEWBERRY, F. Stoke Newington Green.—Electrotypes.

464 HARRISON, J. 2 Chorlton Ter. Upper Brook St. Manchester, Inv. and Manu.—Electrical battery, a substitute for the Leyden jar. Galvanic battery, combining the inventions of Smee and Faraday, &c.

464A HARRISON, J. 45 Upper John St. Fitzroy Sq. Manu. and Inv.—Improved pianoforte action, and pianoforte with reg. action.

465 WELLWAY, J. S. 7 Denmark St. Bristol, Inv. and Manu.—Syphon trough, for galvanic battery, made of gutta percha and vulcanized India-rubber. Registered portable gas lamp.

466 TAYLOR, T. 17 Fleet St. Dublin.—Pneumatic battery, for igniting gunpowder in blasting operations, &c.

467 KIRKMAN & SON, 3 Soho Sq. and 9 Dean St.—Miniature model of grand pianoforte. Concert grand with repetition action. The Fonda semi-grand, and oblique pianofortes.

468 GREINER, G. F. 51 Upper Marylebone St. Portland Pl. Inv.—Semi-grand pianoforte, constructed on the principle of the speaking trumpet, with unison tuning-screws, and repeat tongue check action.

469 SOUTHALL, W. 16 Baker St. Oxford St. Manu.—Grand pianoforte.

470 STODART & SON, 1 Golden Sq. Manu.—Patent horizontal grand and compact-square pianoforte.

471 CADBY, C. Gray's Inn, Pianoforte Manufactory.—Grand and upright cottage pianofortes, on new patent suspension principle.

472 ROLFE, W. & SONS, 61 Cheapside, Manu.—Two-unison common cottage pianoforte, with check or double actions, &c.

473 DEACOCK, T.—A pianoforte.

474 BRINSMEAD, J. 15 Charlotte St. Fitzroy Sq. Manu.—Registered pianoforte, with improved joint.

475 METZLER, G. 37 Gt. Marlborough St. Manu.—Small size cottage pianoforte, made in pollard oak, O G or arched fall, with ornamental shell front.

476 MOORE & Co. 104 Bishopsgate St. Within, Des. and Manu.--Grand cottage pianoforte, of new design.

477 LUFF & SON, 103 Gt. Russell St. Bloomsbury, Manu.—Albert cottage pianoforte and harmonium.

477A HUNT, R. 22 Blake St. Inv.—The tavola pianoforte. A drawing-room table, upon a centre-block or pedestal; contains a pianoforte on a grand principle, and a music closet. Provisionally registered.

479 ENNEVER & STEEDMAN, 31 George St. Manu.—Elegant walnut marquetrie semi-cottage pianoforte, with double action, &c. with pearl and tortoiseshell keys, manufactured by T. & H. Brooks, 31 Cumberland Market, Regent's Park. Square-fall piccolo, or microchordian pianoforte.

480 ALLISON, R. 69 Regent S. Manu.—Walnut-wood registered cottage pianoforte; the keys alternated in colour, to show all the scales.

481 JONES, J. C. 21B Soho Sq. Inv. and Manu.—A double or twin semi-cottage pianoforte.

482 HOLDERNESSE, C. 444 New Oxford St. Manu.—Cottage grand pianoforte with repeating check action.

483 ALLISON, R. 108 Wardour St. Soho, and 34 Brook St. New Rd. Manu.—A walnut-tree cottage pianoforte, with carved figures, and inlaid with flowers in woods of natural colours.

484 JENKINS, W. & SON, 10 London St. Fitzroy Sq. Inv. and Manu.—Expanding pianoforte for yachts, &c. Cabinet pianoforte in the Elizabethan style.

486 HUND, F. & SON, 21 Ebury St. Pimlico, Inv. and Manu.—"The Lyra," a cottage pianoforte, in the form of a lyre, with long scale and a peculiarly constructed platform. The performer or vocalist enabled to face the audience.—Prov. reg.

487 ADDISON, R. 210 Regent St. Pat.—Royal Albert transposing pianoforte, with immoveable key-board, hammers, and strings.

488 AGGIO, G. H. Colchester, Des. and Manu.—Pianoforte, in plate-glass case, gold carvings, &c

489 DIMOLINE, A. Denmark St. Bristol, Des. and Manu.—Registered compensation pianoforte, seven octave.

490 AKERMAN, W. H. H. Bridgwater, Somerset, Inv. and Manu.—A pianoforte of improved construction, with bevel movement of the damper.

491 SMYTH & ROBERTS, Birmingham, Inv. and Manu.—Cottage pianoforte, with grand action and repeater, having a sounding-board and back on the principle of a violoncello, suited for hot climates.

493 WOOLLEY, T. Nottingham, Pat. and Man.—Equilibrium patent pianofortes for all climates. Cottage piano, and utiliton piano.

493A HARWAR, J. 28 Bloomsbury St. Manu.—Pianoforte with transposing mechanism, metallic equilibrium string frame, adjusting tension rods, and improved sound-board.

494 TOWNS & PACKER, 20 Oxford St. Manu.—Grand transposing pianoforte.   Microphonic cottage pianoforte of economic construction.

496 ERARD, P. O. 18 Great Marlborough St. Inv. Des. and Manu.—Harps. "Prince of Wales' harp," richly decorated.

498 MOTT, I. H. R. 76 Strand, Inv. and Manu.—Patent metallic cottage grand pianofortes, not liable to be affected by change of climate or weather.   Horizontal grand pianofortes, with metallic frames.

499 WORNUM, R. Store Str. Inv. and Manu.—Improved piccolo pianoforte.   Semi-bichord grand pianoforte, upon the patent overstruck principle.

500 HOPKINSON, J. & J. 18 Soho Sq. Manu.—Horizontal grand pianoforte with new patent action.   Boudoir pianoforte, and a rosewood cottage pianoforte.

500A TURNBULL, W. 6 Frederick St. Regent's Park, Manu.—Set of pianoforte keys.

502 PEACHEY, G. 73 Bishopsgate St. Within, Manu.—Improved pollard oak "Victoria" piccolo pianoforte. Improved rosewood "Albert" piccolo pianoforte.

503 GREAVES, E. 56 South St. Sheffield, Manu.—Æolian pitch pipes.   Æolian violin mute.   Chromatic æolian pitch pipe.   Sostenuto tuning-forks.   Pair of chromatic tuning-forks.   Registered portable metronomes.   Printers' counting-machines.

504 KOENIG & PASK, 441 Strand.—Brass horns with valves, French horn, trombones, trumpets, ophicleide, euphonion, cornet-à-pistons, clarionets, flutes, &c.

505 DODD, E. 112 Vauxhall Walk, Lambeth, Manu.—Violin, violoncello, double bass, and harp strings.

506 DRURY, J. F. Cheshunt, Herts, Manu.—Box of musical bells.

507 GISBORNE, J. 37 Suffolk St. Birmingham, Inv. and Manu.—Cornopeans, trombo cornuta, Sax horns, keyed bugle, long valve trumpet, &c.

508 HENRYS & Co, 2 Budge Row, Prop.—Newly-invented musical instrument, called "Flœtina."

509 FORSTER, SIMON A. 13 Macclesfield St. Soho Sq. Manu.—A violin, viola, violoncello, &c., made after the models of "Old Forster."

510 HEAPS, J. K. Leeds, Manu.—Violoncello constructed upon improved principles.

511 ANELLI, J. 76 Queen St. Edinburgh, Inv.—Centripetal regulating pegs and pins, for tuning instruments. Spring "capo-tasto," for the guitar, changing at once the diapason of the strings.

512 McNEILL, J. 140 Capel St. Dublin, Inv.—Cambridge cavalry field-trumpet bugle.   Bulb cornopean.

514 CHURCH, G. 12 Berkeley Pl. Bristol, Inv.—Wrist-supporter, for the piano-forte.   Improved guitar.   Improved finger-board for the violoncello, and other bowed instruments.

516 EDWARDS, J. & Son, Church St. Burslem, Inv.—An instrument to give strength and flexibility to the fingers of all instrumental performers.

517 PACE & SONS, 49 King St. Westminster, Inv. and

Manu.—Cornopeans, trumpet, and valve horn, with valves of small diameter, and without angular turnings.

518 BROADWOOD & SONS, 33 Gt. Pulteney St. Manu.—Grand pianofortes, of different constructions.   (Also Main Avenue, West.)

519 BETTS, A. 27 Royal Exchange, Manu.—Two violins.

520 OATES, J. P. Lichfield, Inv.—Improved brass musical instruments: Cornets, pista-cor, Sax-horn, trumpet, Staffordshire horn, &c.

522 PRINCE, MISS ABELINDE, 29 Norfolk Cres. Hyde Park, Inv.—Gioco di Euterpe; a new musical game.

523 JORDAN, J. 34 Manchester St. Liverpool, Inv. and Manu.—Newly-invented euphonic serpentcleide, euphonic horn, tenor-valve ophicleide, and improved cornopeans.

524 DOBROWOLSKI, B. W. 20 Norton St. Portland Pl.—The semibreve guitar, containing one octave and a half in the treble more than the Spanish guitar, and producing a more powerful tone.   Reg.

525 PANORMO, L. 31 High St. Bloomsbury, Manu.—Enharmonic guitar (inv. and prop. T. P. Thompson, M.P.), capable of being arranged in the perfect ratios for upwards of 20 keys.

526 WHEATSTONE & Co. 20 Conduit St. Regent St. Pat. and Manu.—Concertinas, treble, baritone, concert tenor, concert bass, double, &c.   Symphonion.   Portable harmoniums, &c.

527 WARD, C. 36 Gt. Titchfield St. Inv. and Manu.—Kettle, bass, and side or signal drums.   Patent flute.   Newly constructed bassoon.   Pat. and Prov. Reg.

528 SNELL, R. Ball's Pond. Inv. and Manu.—Seraphine, with bichromatic or double scale of notes.

529 STORER, J. 26 Piccadilly, Inv. Pat. and Manu.—Percussion Æolophon, with two sets of vibrators.   Portable Æolophon, for flutes or violoncello parts, &c.

530 FAULKNER, E. 11 York St. James's Sq. Des.—Accordion stand.   Prov. Reg.

531 BRAY, J. 26 Westmoreland St. Dublin, Manu.—Double-action harp, with additional notes, music-stool, desk, and stand.

532 SIMPSON, T. Sea Lion Hotel, Hanley-in-the-Potteries, Inv. — Norma Viriums, or musical accentuators, intended to supersede the metronome.

533 JONES, B. Cardiff, Wales, Des. and Manu.—Grand triple-strung Welch harp.

535 SICCAMA, A. 135 Fleet St. Inv. Pat. and Manu.—Diatonic flutes, retaining the old system of fingering while affording numerous additional fingerings, on a system strictly based upon acoustic principles.

536 RUDALL, ROSE, & Co. 38 Southampton St. Strand, Pro. and Manu.—Carte's patent flutes, in silver and wood. Boehm's patent flute.   Improved ordinary flute.

537 PURDY & FENDT, 74 Dean St. Soho, Manu.—Violins, violoncellos, double bass.   To exhibit oil varnish equal to that on the Cremona; an art supposed to have been lost.

538 POTTER, H. 2 Bridge St. Westminster, Manu.—Clinton's flute, on acoustical principles, being the only one with the old fingering throughout, with equality of tone and perfection of tune.

540 KOHLER, J. 35 Henrietta St. Covent Garden, Pat. and Manu.—Patent valved wind instruments.

541 GUINNESS, R. 58 East St. Manchester Sq. Inv.—Violin, with self-acting pegs for tuning violins, violoncellos, and tenors.

542 SPURGIN, T. Saffron Walden.— Violin made from a description of one invented by M. Savart, of Paris.

543 DODD, J. Image Cottage, Holloway, Manu.—Bows for the violin, tenor, and violoncello, mounted with gold and tortoiseshell.   Silver strings for the violin, violoncello and harp.

544 CHIDLEY, R. 135 High Holborn, Des. and Manu.—Concertinas, in ivory, with gold stops.

545 CASE, G. 32 New Bond St. Manu.—Concertina three octaves and a half compass.

546 CARD, W. 29 St. James's St. Des. and Manu.—Silver, gold, electro-silvered, and other flutes.

547 CALLCOTT, J. 31 Admiral Ter. Vauxhall Bridge Rd. Inv. and Manu.—Newly-invented French horn and cornet-à-piston without loose crooks.

548 ROOME, T. F. 67 John St. Fitzroy Sq. Manu.—Organ metal pipes—trumpet, hautboy, cremona, flute, open diapason, viol de gamba, and keraolophon.

549 GROOME, J. Watton, Norfolk, Inv. and Manu.—Transparent music, adapted for instructing large classes.

550 MATHEWS, W. 5 St. James St. Nottingham, Inv. and Manu.—Model, the string frame of an upright pianoforte with lever tuning apparatus. An upright pianoforte, with improvements.

551 ANDREWS, R. 4 Palatine Buildings, Manchester, and 84 Oxford St. Inv.—Apparatus for giving position and strength to the fingers in learning the piano.

553 BISHOP, J. C. 1 Lisson Grove South, Des. and Manu.—Cabinet organ, containing composition pedals, &c.

554 DAWSON, C. 395 Strand, Inv.—Autophon, the tunes being produced by means of perforated sheets of mill board.

555 GRAY & DAVISON, 9 New Road, Fitzroy Sq.—A grand church organ of the first class. A small church organ. A small church finger-organ, the stops contained in a swell.

556 HILL, W. & Co. Tottenham Ct. Rd. Des. and Manu.—Finger organ with two sets of channels, containing reed stop of immense power, &c.

557 HOLDICH, G. M. H. 4 Judd Pl. East, King's Cross, Manu.—Small choir organ, with peculiar stop, called the " diaocton."

558 NOLAN, W. H.—Artificial teeth.

559 ROBSON, T. J. F. 101 St. Martin's Lane, Manu.—Enharmonic organ (T. Perronet Thompson, M.P. inv. and prop.), capable of executing with the perfect ratios in 18 keys; or in 20 with the exchange of one or two pipes in the octave, for the keys of five and six flats.

560 HEWITT, D. C. Twickenham.—The musical ratiometer. (On South Wall.)

561 WALKER, J. W. 27 Francis St. Bedford Sq. Manu.—An organ (in the Tudor style, designed by Banks and Barry), adapted for a hall or music room.

562 FORSTER & ANDREWS, Hull, Manu.—Original model of transposing organ, which enables the performer to change the pitch of the instrument five semitones higher or lower from a given pitch: the manuals remaining stationary.

565 GROSSMITH, W. R. 175 Fleet St. Inv. and Manu.—Artificial legs, artificial eyes, spring braces, &c.

566 BOURGEAURD, P. 10 Davis St. Grosvenor Sq.—The spiral compression bandage.

567 EAGLAND, T. Leeds, Manu.—Teale's trusses. Bandage for prolapsus. Knee-joint extensor.

568 MILES, J. Street, near Glastonbury, Inv.—Improved double truss for hernia, invented by a labouring man.

569 MASTERS, M. 12 St. David St. Newington, Manu.—Artificial leg, for amputation above the knee.

570 CAPLIN, J. F. I. Strawberry Hill, Pendleton, Manchester, Inv. and Manu.—Gymnastic apparatus, and orthorachidic instruments, for deformity of the spine, &c.

570A CAPLIN, Madame R.A. 58 Berners St. London, and 55 Princes St. Manchester, Inv. Pat. and Manu.—Hygienic corsets, registered corporiform corset, and child's boddice.

571 SWITHENBANK, J. 100 Bridge St. Bradford, Yorkshire, Manu.—Artificial legs.

572 LONGDON & TUBBERER, Derby, Inv. and Manu.—Elastic surgical stockings, knee-caps, belts, &c.

573 SMITH, S. 1 High Holborn, Manu.—Trusses, bandages, belts, &c.

574 GHRIMES, S. 71 Baker St. Des.—Artificial teeth, &c.

575 HORNE, J. West Regent St. Glasgow, Des. and Manu.—Artificial teeth. Models of mouths, &c.

576 LAURIE, S. 36 Argyle St. New Rd. Des.—Artificial teeth, carved in hippopotamus ivory.

577 JAMES, J. H. F.R.C.S. Exeter, Inv.—Surgical instruments and apparatus. Model of an apparatus employed in the treatment of fractures of the thigh.

578 ASH & SONS, 8 and 9 Broad St. Golden Sq.—Artificial teeth, with gold tubes, &c.

579 PARKS, 25 Newington Crescent, Kennington. — Artificial teeth.

581 PERKINS, W. 175 Prospect Pl. Maida Hill, Paddington, Des. and Manu.—Artificial teeth, carved from Hippopotamus ivory.

582 ROBINSON, J. 7 Gower St. Bedford Sq. Inv.—Artificial teeth, and dental apparatus.

583 REID, R. 19 Heriot Row, Edinburgh, Inv.—Compress for alveolar hæmorrhage.

584 RANSOM, R. 3 Verulam Pl. Hastings, Manu.—Case of artificial teeth.

585 MOLLISON, J. 3 Grove Ter. St. John's Wood, Inv.—Mollison's pedestal planisphere.

587 WHITE, J. 228 Piccadilly, Manu.—Patent moc-main lever trusses.

589 TOD, D. 5 Upper Fitzroy St. Fitzroy Sq. Inv.—Single and double trusses.

590 THOMSON, H. Greenock, Scotland, Inv.—Apparatus intended for fractures of the thigh or leg.

591 SPARKS, J. & Co. 28 Conduit St. Regent's St. and 115 New Bond St. Manu.—Spinal machine. Instrument for contracted knees. Portable spring crutch. Trusses. Portable cloak boat, &c.

592 FULLER, J. 239 Whitechapel Rd.—Artificial leg, eyes, and nose. Surgical instruments, &c. Antique metal-gilt oval watch, made in the reign of Charles I., by Francois Nawe, at London.

594 SALMON, ODY, & Co. 292 Strand, Inv. and Manu.—Patent single and double self-adjusting trusses. New resisting, anti-pressure, self-adjusting truss, suggested by Dr. Arnott.

596 BRUNTON, J. Huddersfield, Manu.—Artificial leg.

597 L'ESTRANGE, F. 39 Dawson St. Dublin, Inv.—Patent trusses. Apparatus for the reduction of dislocations, and for the cure of fractures of the lower jaw. Lithotrite instruments, &c.

598 HUXLEY, E. 5 Vere St. Manu.—Stockings, knee caps, calf-pieces, and anclets, for varicose veins, weakness, sprains, fractured, &c.

601 MILES, E. 15 Liverpool St. Bishopsgate, Prop.—Mineral and curved teeth, and gold palates.

601C CHAPMAN, T. & ALDERMAN J. 8 Denmark St. Soho, Inv. and Manu.—Invalid's couch.

601D MACMAHON, C. Upper Camden St. Dublin, Inv.—Jaw-lever, for keeping open the mouth of any animal whilst administering medicine, &c. A temporary horse-shoe, to fasten on without nails.

602 FINZI, S. L. 6 Dalby Ter. City Rd. Islington, Inv. and Manu.—Universal drill, for removing decay from teeth. Artificial teeth.

604 HALFORD, H. 8 St. John Sq. Manu.—Artificial human eyes, eyes for figures, animals, dolls, and birds.

605 ATKINSON, B. F. 26 Strand, Inv.—Artificial limbs, trusses, and bandages.

606 BUNNEY, C. 27 Lower Eaton St. Pimlico.—Surgical belts, &c.

607 WHIBLEY, E. 12 Lloyd's Pl. Brompton—Surgical operating table.

609 PUCKRIDGE, F. L. 4 York Pl. Walworth, Inv. and Manu.—Transparent waterproof membrane plaisters. Tinted goldbeaters' skin and court plaister.

610 BINYON, A. 3 Gt. Marlborough St. Regent St. Inv. and Manu.—Elastic chest-expanders.

612 SPRATT, W. H. 2 Brook St. Hanover Sq. Manu.—Single and double trusses; new truss designed by Dr. Arnott; various pads, belts, and bandages. Elastic laced stocking. New spinal chair, designed by R. Druitt, Esq., which may be used on a bed, chair, sofa, or in a carriage.

613 LINDSEY, M. 264 High St. Borough, Inv. and Manu —Trusses for hernia, &c.

614 LEE, J. Bideford, Inv. and Manu.—Devonia invalid bedstead.

615 HEEPS, J. H. 46A Liverpool St. City, Inv. and Manu. —Spring-bandages and supports for prolapsus, belts, &c.

617 ROBINSON, R. 27 Cumberland St. Portsea, Inv.— An artificial leg; the foot constructed so as to dispense with steel springs.

619 ARNOTT, J. M.D. 34 Baker Str. Portman Sq. Inv.— Apparatus for regulating the temperature of morbid parts, and causing equal pressure. Apparatus for removing contractions or obstructions in the excretory canals, &c.

620 LEARED, A. Oulart, Wexford, Ireland, Inv.—Double stethoscope, made of gutta-percha.

624 SIMPSON, G. F.R.C.S. 6 Bedford St. Bedford Sq. Manu. and Inv.—Anatomical model of the human figure, in papier-maché and gutta percha. Vertical section in gutta percha of the human head and neck.

625 TOWNE, J Guy's Hospital. Prod.—Deep section of the head. Model of the neck, upper extremity, and chest. From dissections by John Hilton, F.R.S. Models illustrative of incubation.

627 BROWN & SON, Grey St. Newcastle-upon-Tyne, Manu. —The railway tourniquet. The aneurismal compress. Dilators for stricture. The ostracide, or oyster opener.

628 SALT & SON, 21 Bull St. Birmingham, Manu.—A large assortment of surgical instruments of all descriptions, trusses, fracture apparatus, &c.

629 REIN, C. 108 Strand, Inv.—New ear-trumpets. Acoustic chair, vases, telescopes, whispering tubes, domestic telegraph, &c.

630 GREENHOW, T. M. Newcastle-upon-Tyne, Inv. — Fracture-bed, for the treatment of patients having fractures of the thigh and leg.

631 FERGUSON & SONS, 21 Giltspur St.—Complete set of surgical instruments, for capital and minor operations. Apparatus used in orthopœdic surgery.

631A WEISS & SON, 62 Strand, Manu.—Cabinet of surgical instruments, for every operation in surgery. Avery's apparatus for examining the ear, throat, and different canals of the body. Weiss's invalid bed chair or couch.

631B ELLIS, J. 41 Spring St. Sheffield, Manu.—Amputating and post-mortem instruments. Pocket instruments, and scalpels. Lancets and trusses. Splint and belts.

633 HARNETT, W. 4 Francis St. Brewer St. Golden Sq. Manu.—Instruments, mineral teeth, and materials, used by dentists.

634 DOWNING, C. T. M.D. 42 Gt. Russell St. Inv.—The aneuralgicon, an apparatus for applying warm medicated vapour for tic douloureux, &c.

635 PRATT, J. 10A Charles St. Middlesex Hospital, Manu. —Cupping instruments

636 GODDARD, L. 6 Cres. Minories, Imp.—Patent instrument for extracting teeth, invented by E. Bourne, of New Bedford, Mass.

639 GORDON, J. Bristol.—Anatomical figure.

640 WEEDON, T. 41 Hart St. Bloomsbury, Manu.—Surgeons' instruments. Various patterns of small instruments used in minute dissections, for the microscope, &c.

Specimens of cutlery, mounted in the Haliotis pearl shell, plain pearl, and agate handles.

641 PHILP & WHICKER, 67 St. James's St.—Cutlery and surgical instruments, &c.

642 SIMPSON, H. 55 Strand, Manu.—Instruments for a surgeon in the navy, &c. Amputating and other surgical instruments. Cutlery, &c.

643 WOOD, W. R. German Pl. Brighton, Manu.—A series of mechanical adaptations for regulating and preventing the irregularities of the permanent teeth.

643A EVANS & Co. 10 Old Change, Manu.—Surgical instruments.

645 GOWING, T. W. Camden Tn. Inv.—Instruments for operations on the teeth of horses, &c. Apparatus for fractures. New rotatory scissors and knife for dividing nerves.

646 KIDSTON, W. & Co. 18 Bishopsgate Without, Inv. and Manu.—Mechanical leech.

647 EVRARD, J. Charles St. Middlesex Hospital.—Dentists' and surgical instruments, in the various stages of manufacture, &c.

648 HESS, R. 16 Little New St. Shoe Lane, Manu.—The registered osteotom, a surgical instrument for cutting bones.

649 BARKER, J. M.D. 45 Mountjoy St. Dublin, Inv.— "Thoracitone," a new medical instrument for rendering more efficient and certain the act of percussion in disease.

651 SMALL, T. Boston, Lincolnshire, Inv.—Apparatus for restoring suspended animation in persons apparently dead.

652 JONES, P. High St. Fulham.—Improved metallic shield for the nipple.

653 BLACKWELL, W. 3 Bedford Ct. Covent Garden, Inv. and Manu.—Registered guard razor and corn-knife.

654 MACHELL, T. Carlisle St. Soho—Improved method of raising fluids. Surgical instruments.

655 FARQUHARSON, J. Ealing, near Brentford.—Spring stump for a wooden leg.

656 JONES, T. 28 Lombard St. Inv.—Silent alarum bedstead to turn any one out of bed at a given hour.

657 BOTTOMLEY, G. Croydon, Surrey.—A splint for fractured thigh.

659 WATKINS & HILL, 5 Charing Cross, Manu.—Large plate electric machine. Electro magnetic engine. Sextants, theodolites, levels, &c.

660 COLES, W. 3 Charing Cross, Inv. and Manu.—Patent self-resisting spinal spring trusses, and medicated bands for the cure of rheumatism.

661 RENCZYNSKI, Capt. G. A. 31 Tonbridge Pl. New Rd. Portable telescope stand, with desk for artists, engineers, land surveyors, &c., with various useful improvements and apparatus.

663 SIMONS, W. V. South Shields, Des. and Manu.— Electro-magnetic machine, with an improved arrangement of the primary coil and contact breakers, &c.

664 WARD, N. B. 14 Clapham Rise, Inv.—Closed cases, by which plants may be grown in any locality, even in the centre of the most crowded cities, or conveyed from one country to another with complete success. Also improved closed cases for ferns, exotic and British, by E. W. Cooke.

665 BRYSON & SONS, Edinburgh, Inv. and Manu.—Five models, exhibiting the various escapements of watches at present in general use, and a self-registering barometer clock.

666 ROSS, A.—Bleeding instruments, as substitutes for leeches and cupping instruments, adapted to apply to any part of the body. Invented by Baron Heurteloup; manufactured by J. Scholl, Berwick Street, Soho.

667 TOPPING, C. M. 4 New Winchester St. Pentonville Hill.—Microscopic objects. Test objects and fossil earths. Fossil and recent vegetable structures. Dissections of insects. Bone, teeth, shell, &c. Injected preparations.

668 DURHAM, J. D. 16 Linton St. New North Road,

Islington.—Hydrometer, with all the recent improvements, with improved tube. Thermometer, and book of instructions.

670 OWEN, H. 3 Somerset Ter. Bristol.—Series of views in Somerset, Wilts, and Devon by the calotype process, from negatives on paper.

670AEVANS, S. Hungerford, Berks, Inv.—Self-acting instrument for testing the strength of oak bark, valonia and other tanning materials.

671 PARKES, J. & SON, 5 St. Mary's Row, Birmingham.—Mathematical drawing instruments; six-inch drawing instruments; portable sun-dial and compass combined; architects' and botanists' companion, &c.

671A WEBSTER, W. BULLOCK, 2 St. James's Pl. Hampstead Rd. Inv. and Manu.—Fire escape. Percussion carbine musket, with rotary primer. Omnibus passenger register. A mileometer. Small weighing machine. Cannon, with improved percussion-lock.

672 TAYLOR, T. Dublin, Inv.—Hydraulic safety-lamp, to prevent explosion in coal-mines, water being used to prevent its becoming heated, and mica to give an increase of light.

672ANEWCOMB, T. 12 Norfolk Pl. East Lane, Walworth, Inv. and Maker.—Brass model of machine, for rolling tanned hides. Brass model of patent furnace for marine or stationary steam-engines. Improved brass strings for pianofortes, of hard-drawn steel wire. Lamps, intended to burn common pale seal oil, without smell, smoke, or shadow.

673 MACFARLANE, G. 85 Newman St. Des.—Improved cornôpean (cornet à piston), with short action valves, direct passage of the air, and can be played with ease.

673ABURSILL, G. H. 9 York Ter. Hornsey Rd. Holloway, Inv. — Patent compensating cistern barometer. Artificial hand, possessing elastic properties, inv. by Sir G. Cayley, Bart.; imp. and manu. by J. Buckingham, 13 Judd Pl.

674 NEWMAN, J. 122 Regent St.—Standard barometer. Portable mountain barometer. A variety of thermometers, hygrometers, rain-gauges, safety-lamps. Air-pump. Rain and wind gauge. Self-registering tide-gauge.

674ASTEPHENSON, R. Great George St. Westminster.—Machine for tracing.

675 NEWSON, H. 18 Percy St. Tottenham Court Rd.—Patent wire-trusses, single and double, the latter passing round one hip only.

675AOAKEY, H. 81 Dean St. Soho, Inv.—Diagrams for teaching the theory of music.

676 BIGG, H. & SON, 29 Leicester Sq. and 9 St. Thomas's St. Southwark, Manu.—Artificial legs, crutches, hands, trusses, and various descriptions of surgical and anatomical instruments.

676ABROWN, D. S. Alexandrian House, Old Kent Rd.—A large barometer, 39 feet high, range of scale 27 feet. Manu. by Casella and Co. 23 Hatton Garden.

677 READHOUSE, CHARLOTTE, Newark-on-Trent, Des. and Prod.—A model of the moon, giving a general idea of the relative position of the mountains, valleys, and plains of our satellites, in relief. An original production, and said to be unique.

677ASHADBOLT, G. 2 Lime St. Sq. Inv.—Sphæro-annular condenser, for condensing light in a peculiar manner on transparent objects while under examination by the microscope. Diagrams and description, illustrative of the action and construction of the condenser.

678 JACK, W. 38 Devonshire St. Portland Pl. and 14 Ratcliff Row, St. Luke's.—A case of new and improved patterns of tooth-forceps.

678AMORTON, Prof. Royal Veterinary College, Camden Town, Inv.— Medicated cotton for setons. Galvano-arsenical apparatus.

679 BELL, T. 19 Homer St.—An assortment of watches and time-keepers. A turret-clock.

679ABETTLE, P. 11 Regent St. City Rd.—Model of a steam-engine.

680 OFFORD, D. Great Yarmouth, Inv.—The improved truss for hernia. Improved instruments for the treatment of uterine diseases.

681 RICKMAN, W. C. 21 Park Side, Hyde Park Corner.—Road level, for agricultural purposes.

681ASOMALVICO & Co. 2 Hatton Garden, Manu.—Wheel, pediment, marine, and mountain barometers; new designs. Improved engineers' guide gauges and vacuum steam pressure gauges. Steam-engine indicators. Improved sextants, &c.

682 COXETER, J. 23 Grafton St. East, Manu.—Surgical instruments.

683 OETZMANN and PLUMB, 56 Great Russell St. Bloomsbury, Inv. and Manu.—Cottage and cabinet pianofortes, with newly-invented tubular supporters, patent double repeating check action, and other improvements.

683AMUDIE, J. Dundee.—Salinometer.

684 HARNETT, J. 45 Museum St. Bloomsbury, Manu.—Instruments and materials used by dentists. Specimens of mineral teeth. Natural specimens, showing the growth of the teeth.

684AMACPHERSON, D. 7 Salisbury St. Edinburgh, Inv. and Manu.—A weighing-machine used in the same way as the common balance.

685 COOK and WILLIAMS, 10 Princes St. Hanover Sq.—Respiratory organ and chest protectors. Reg.

686 MARSHALL and Co. 4 Parkside, Hyde Park Corner.—"Corset à tous ressorts." An invisible sling for paralysis of leg and foot, with belt. An invention of improved means of supporting and sustaining various parts of the human body.

687 WHITE, J. 228 Piccadilly. — Trusses and lacing stockings, with M'Main patent lever truss.

687AGALL, J. Myrtle Bank, Edinburgh.—Triangular alphabet for the blind, &c.

688 NASMYTH, J. Manchester.—Map of the moon: exhibiting the relative positions and character of the most striking features of its surface, as they appear when seen under the most favourable circumstances in respect to light and shade, with drawings from nature of certain portions of the lunar surface, as seen by the aid of a very powerful telescope.

688ALEBIHAN, E. Gothic Cottage, Old Brompton.

689 OXLEY, W. Manchester.—Smith's patent steam indicator and water indicator.

689ADUNN, T. Edinburgh.—Electro-magnetic machine.

690 GORE, G. 31 New St. Birmingham.—Medical galvanic apparatus.

691 HUGHES, —, Queen St. Ratcliffe.—Compass.

692 No name or address.—Compass.

693 PERIGAL, H. jun.—Lunarian.

696 LOOT, —, —A galvanometer, with Brett and Little's patentees engraved on the dial.

697 WALKER, J. 48 Princes St. Leicester Sq.—Clock, watches, chronometers, &c.

698 TROTMAN, S. Notting Hill.—Night clock.

700 VULLIAMY, B. L. 68 Pall Mall.—Model of a new mode of suspending a pendulum upon the basis of four isosceles triangles.

702 EDGE, T. Gt. Peter St. Westminster.—Photometer.

703 LIPSCOMBE & Co. 233 Strand.—Two patent pneumatic fountains.

704 TUDSBURY, R. Edwinston.—A "volta-subito" turnover desk and stand.

705 BROOKS, G. jun. St. Alban's.—Clavic attachment to violin.

706 TOOTAL & BROWNE, 73 Piccadilly.—Pianoforte.

707 DEARLOVE, M. W. Leeds.—Miniature model of a violin, and a miniature double bass.

708 BARTON, H. W. the Waterfoot Pettigo, Ireland.—Military sketching compass.

709 BELOE, W. LINTON, Coldstream.—Copy of Antonius Straduarius' violin.

710 MOYLE, S. Truro.—Mountain barometer, for measuring heights by boiling water.

711 PETERMAN, A. 5 Camden St.—Drawings.

712 CLAFHAM, J. K. 6, Briggate, Leeds.—Map on gum elastic.

713 BROWN, J. 71 Leadenhall St.—Aerial machine.

714 MASON, E. 5 Brompton Post-office. —Model of navigable balloon.

715 BELL, H. Baltic Wharf, Millbank.—Balloon valve, parachute, and balloon.

716 PLUMMER, H. L. 112 Powis St. Woolwich.—Model of an aerial machine.

717 WATT, G. T. 2 William St. Albert Gate, Hyde Park.—Artificial palates. Models of the mouth. Complete and partial sets of teeth of hippopotamus tusk, porcelain, &c.

718 DINSDALE, C. Newcastle-on-Tyne, Manu. & Inv.—Anatomical drawings. Artificial teeth. Two casts of heads, and wax models of incubation.

719 ROSE, J. E. Mount Pleasant, Liverpool.—Artificial teeth.

720 TRUMAN, E. 40 Haymarket.—Artificial teeth in gutta percha.

721 HARRINGTON, G. F. 84 St. Thomas St. Portsmouth, Inv. and Pat.—A new description of artificial teeth, with improved dental instruments.

722 LAWRENCE & Co. Islington Pl. Park Rd. Islington.—Flesh-gloves, belts, &c.

723 BOSSINGHAM, B. Wisbech.—Artificial leg.

724 GRAY, PETER, 47 Hanover St. Edinburgh, Inv.—Model of an invalid bed, made by J. Sturrock, Duke St. Leith.

725 KENNEDY, Dr. E. Merrion Sq. North, Dublin.—Syphons.

726 SELTZER, SOPHIA, 7 Upper Ranelagh St. Pimlico.—Chair for spinal curvature.

727 HIGHLEY, S. 32 Fleet St.—Anatomical statuette, showing the muscles of the human body.

727A TITTERTON, —.—Instrument for slaughtering cattle.

728 LANAGAN, F. 12 Brownlow St. Bedford Row.—Apparatus, and shoes for the cure of bunions.

729 EWART, G. Zinc Works, New Rd.— Three spirometers of different constructions.

730 RITTERBANDT, L. A. M.D. 7 Northumberland St. Strand.—A galvanic bath of zinc and copper, separated by a non-metallic substance. By connecting two wires attached to the two metals, this bath becomes a perfect galvanic battery.

731 WOODHOUSE, J. T. 6 Commercial Rd. Peckham.—Leg rest.

732 BADCOCK, J. Brighton, Prod. — Photographic specimens of vaccine, produced by inoculating the cow with small-pox, showing the character of the vesicles in their different stages.

733 HAMILTON, H. G. R.N. 71 Eccleston Sq.—Collection of ancient Greek coins electrotyped.

734 BLACKWELL, W. 3 Bedford Ct. Covent Garden.—Apparatus for fractures, trusses, and surgical instruments.

735 BRYCESON, H. 5 Tottenham Court Rd. Manu.—Powerful church barrel-organ in gothic case.

736 GOWING, J. W. Camden Tn.—Instruments for operations on the teeth of horses. Apparatus for fractures, &c. Neurotomy knife, and scissors for dividing nerves.

737 WOOD, J. W. Manchester.—Trusses. Support for curvature of the spine, and surgical instruments.

739 A violin in a case.

740 TAYLOR, G. R. Sunderland.—A geographical clock. (South-east Corner, United States Department.)

741 SIMMS, W. (late Troughton & Simms) Manu.—Equatorial instruments. The Westbury circle. Transit circle and instruments. Airy's isometrical elliptograph. Sextants, theodolites, &c. (Main Avenue, West.)

742 PAXTON, J., M.D. Rugby, Des.—Pathological illustrations, consisting of cartoon paintings.

Proceed to Class 23, page 122.

SECTION III.—MANUFACTURES.

Class 11.　COTTON.

—— Areas I. J. 1 to 8. ——

1 JACKSON, J. 73 Adam Sq. Edinburgh, Manu.—Fine wool shawl, wove on the Spolino or loop principle, to show that this mode of weaving would be applicable for figured wool shawls of the finest description.

2 SANDEMAN, H. Tullochfield, Perth.—Coverlet and handkerchief printed on cotton, being dyed by the rubia munjit-ha, commonly called East India munjeet, with a specimen of the plant as imported.

3 WALKER, J. & R. Earlstown, Melrose, Manu.— Cotton ginghams for dresses, hand-loom wrought.

4 PULLAR & SONS, Perth, Manu.—Umbrella and fancy ginghams, handkerchiefs, and woollen derries.

5 AULD, BERRIE, & MATHIESON, Glasgow, Manu.— Book muslins; mull muslin; jaconet muslin; bishop lawn muslin; Saccharilla and Tarlatan book muslins. Saccharilla mull muslin, harness, and Leno book muslins.

6 M'BRIDE & Co. Glasgow, Inv. and Manu.—Cotton table-cloths; bird's-eye diaper and huckaback towelling; furniture and jean stripes; ginghams, &c.; all made by patent power-loom. Table-cloths and tartans, the weft being from hemp, prepared by E. Slock, of Renfrew, Scotland.

7 ANDERSON, J. & A. Glasgow, Manu.—Ginghams. Cravats, checked muslin. Handkerchiefs, Turkey-red ground. Tartan muffler. Saxonies.

8 FINLAYSON, F. & Co. 25 Dundas St. Glasgow, Manu.—Lappet muslins; tarlatan; and lappets. Lappet flounced muslin dresses, &c.

9 LETHEM, BLYTH, & LETHEM, Friday St. and Virginia St. Glasgow, Manu. — Specimens of various plain muslins, woven from the same quality of yarn. Tamboured muslins. Ginghams for dresses.

10 & **45** OSWALD, STEVENSON, & Co. Glasgow and Manchester.—Cotton yarns dyed and spun in the west of Scotland, arranged according to Manchester classification. Water twist. Mule twist. Fine yarns.

11 PATERSON, JAMIESON, & Co. 58 Dundas St. Glasgow, Manu.—Ginghams and handkerchiefs; fabric all cotton, hand-woven, or printed.

12 YOUNG, J. H. & Co. Glasgow, Manu.—Muslins, &c. for East India, home, American, and other markets.

13 HENRY & SONS, 81 Buchanan St. Glasgow, and 120 Cheapside, Manu. — Embroidered merino dresses. White tambour muslin dresses. Sprigged evening dresses, embroidered in the loom. Specimens of plain linen ginghams.

14 SYMINGTON, R. B. & Co. Glasgow, Manu.—Harness book muslin and harness leno muslin window-curtains, all woven in the Jacquard loom.

15 THOMSON J. & SON, Glasgow, Manu. — Cotton-wove handkerchiefs, in imitation of India handkerchiefs.

16 ANDERSON, D. & J. Glasgow, Manu. — Checked cotton ginghams and checked cotton cravats.

17 DAVIDSON W. & J. Glasgow, Manu. — Sacherella and tamboored book-muslin. Scotch tarlatan muslin.

18 FYFE, H. & SON, 62 Queen St. Glasgow, Manu.— Specimens of ginghams, hand-loom woven.

19 DIXON, P. & SONS, Carlisle.—Grey and dyed yarns. Cotton checks, ginghams, and shawls. Scarfs and Robes. Twilled stripes, &c. For home consumption and exportation.

20 McGIBBON, E. Carlisle.—Carlisle ginghams, of six qualities, made principally for the American trade.

21 PEARSON & Co. Carlisle.—Shirting stripes, and striped and checked fancy ginghams and Hungarians.

22 LOWTHIAN & PARKER, Carlisle, Manu.—Varieties of ginghams, checks, stripes, poplins, &c. for the home, foreign, and colonial markets. Samples of dyed yarn.

23 KING, R. & W. Bristol.—Three African cushions, and three specimens of African cotton manufacture, from the King of Dahomey.

24 BROOK, J. & BROTHERS, Meltham Mills, Huddersfield, Manu.—Specimens of raw cotton, carded cotton, rovings, throstle yarns, sewing threads, thread and crochet cotton, &c.

25 HAYTHORN, J. W. Nottingham and Trent Mills, Burton-on-Trent, Manu.—Samples of sewing, knitting, and mending cotton. Lille thread. Lace thread, and doubled yarns. Prepared cotton, &c.

26 WALSH & WINDLEY, Nottingham.—Specimens of thrown silk for lace and hosiery.

27 THACKERAY, J. & SONS, Nottingham, Manu. — Cotton-gusset; Lisle and dress cottons; double-spun or single cotton; salvage and warp-cotton; threads, &c.

28 GREENHALGH & SONS, Mansfield, Manu.—Samples of double cotton yarns, as used in the manufacture of lace, gloves, hosiery, ribbons, cloths, and for sewing and knitting.

29 HARRIS, W. F. Leicester, Pat. and Manu.—Reels exhibiting specimens of sewing cotton, and patent reels to prevent imposition in the length of cotton upon each.

30 RAWORTH & Co. Leicester.—Samples of six-cord and other sewing cotton.

31 O'CONNELL, J. 27 South Main St. Cork, Ireland, Manu.—Specimens of linen and cotton ginghams.

32 CLARKE, J. P. King St. Mill, Leicester, Manu.— Patent embossed wood, metallic and other reels, containing sewing cotton. Reels also shown in their different stages of manufacture.

33 EVANS & Co. Darley Abbey, Derby, Manu.— Sewing cotton of various kinds, made up in different forms.

34 RATCLIFF, Mrs. Waltham Abbey.—White knitted counterpanes.

35 BARLOW, GOODDY, & JONES, Bolton, Manu.—Figured quilting vesting; white and coloured quilting bedcover; and white welted bed-cover, welted quilts.

36 HOLLINS, W. & Co. Pleasley Works, near Mansfield, Nottingham, Manu.—Merino, Cashmere, and cotton hosiery yarns, used in the midland counties in the manufacture of hosiery, and on the Continent for knittings, and hosiery purposes.

37 MARTIN & SON, Bolton, Manu.—Damask diced and plain furniture dimity.

38 COOK, W. W. & J. Bolton. — Cut brocade mull, white, in the piece, and flounced dress for ladies. Plaited and welted brocade skirts, white brocade stripe.

39 MYERSCOUGH, STEEL, & Co. Bolton.—Counterpane and quilting bed-cover, or toilet-quilt. Fine diamond quilting, for waistcoats.

40 BARNES, T. Farnworth Cotton Mills, Bolton.— White Polynesian swandown. Moleskin in different stages, illustrating the method of manufacture. Pattern designed and registered by the exhibitor; printed by Jackson and Co., Manchester, and finished by Whitehead, of Elton.

41 CROSS, J. Bolton.—Twilled long cloth and shirting.

42 SUDWORTH, J. Bolton.—Woven counterpane.

43 WATERS, J. & Co. Fountain St. Manchester.—Small wares, knitting and reel cotton, ribbon wire, webbing tapes, fringes, cotton, laces, bindings, &c.

44 CHRISTY, Fairfield Mills, near Manchester.—Royal Turkish bath-towels, with a plush or looped surface on both sides.

46 WALKER, W. 13 Marsden's Sq. Manchester, Manu.—Cotton cloth, with specimens in imitation of woollen broad cloth, beavers, Witneys, &c.

47 CROSS, C. and Co. Corporation St. Manchester, Manu. and Joint Pat.—Very wide doeskins; lambskin; shoe inings; twill; cord, &c. Seamless articles of wearing apparel, produced by patent machinery.

48 JOHNSON, J. 44 Spring Gardens, Manchester.—White and coloured figured wove and white diamond quilting for vests. White and coloured bed and toilet covers.

49 MAJOR & GILL, 49 Cannon St. Manchester, Manu.—Patent double coutils and nankeen for stays, consisting of two cloths woven together, and stitched, during weaving.

50 GLOVER & DUNN, Manchester.—Calicoes, &c., with examples of cotton in various stages of manufacture.

51 WALMESLEY, H. Fir Mills, Failsworth, near Manchester, Prop.—Goose's patent Jacquard machine. Table-cloth manufactured by power materials, with view of the "Exhibition Building," 80 inches wide, 110 long, &c. Specimens of figured weaving, &c. by power.

52 SPENCER, J. & SON, Marriott's Ct. Manchester, Des. and Manu.—Bed-quilts white woven, quilted in the loom, coloured woven, &c. Figured quilting hangings, for beds or windows. Quilting waistcoats.

53 BAZLEY. T. Manchester, Manu.—Case, containing illustrations of the progress of the manufacture of cotton, from the raw material to the finished results, in the coarse and fine departments of the trade.

54 HOULDSWORTH, T. & Co. Little Lever St. Manches-

ter, Cotton Spinners.—Specimens of fine cotton yarn, and of double yarn, or fine cotton lace thread.

55 JOHNSON, R. & NEPHEW, 95 Watling St. Importer.—Book-muslin for curtains, figured in the Jacquard loom. Leno muslin, figured. Robes, embroidered, &c.

56 BRADBURY, GREATOREX, & BEALL, 6 Aldermanbury, Prop.—Specimens of window curtains.

57 LINCOLN & BENNETT, 2 Sackville St. Piccadilly, and 58 Union St. Borough, Inv. and Manu.—Hats, with calico foundation. Drab hats for India, &c. Chess-table, &c. made of prepared calico, turned, carved, japanned, &c. in imitation of grained wood.

58 ROGERS, LOWREY, HOLYLAND, & Co. 91 Watling St. Prop.—Muslins manufactured in Scotland, Books, Swiss, Tarlatan, Nainsook, Mull, and Scotch cambric.

59 MAIR, SON, & Co. 60 Friday St. London, and 163 Ingram St. Glasgow.—Muslin window curtains; leno window curtain; and muslin dresses, figured in the loom. Muslin, made from No. 5408 cotton yarn, spun by T. Houldsworth, Manchester; believed to be the finest ever made; bleached by John Wallace and Co. Scotch needle and tambour work. Printed flannels, twilled bandannas, and cambric handkerchiefs.

60 HORROCKSES, MILLER, & Co. 9 Bread St. Manu.—Long cloths and twilled shirtings.

61 CROCKER, J. & A. 51 Friday St.—Blind and curtains of harness woven muslin, &c. Printed cotton, for furniture.

62 OWTRAM & Co. 13 Watling St. Manu.—Brocaded cottons and cotton damasks. Satin brocades and flush sprigged muslins.

63 MARSLAND, SON, & Co. Bridge Mill, Blackfriars Manchester.—Crochet and sewing cotton.

64 DAILY & Co. 9 St. James's Pl. Hampstead Rd.—Specimens of soiled and faded satins, dyed and embossed.

65 ALLEN, R. Sackville St. Dublin.—Free labour cotton goods.

Proceed to Class 16, page 85.

Classes 12 and 15.   WOOLLEN AND WORSTED, MIXED FABRICS, INCLUDING SHAWLS.

—— Areas L. M. N. O. 10 to 17, and South Transept Gallery. ——

1 SCOTT & WRIGHT, Vigo St. Regent St. Prop. and Des.—Elastic doeskins, angola, and Scotch angolas for trousers, railway rugs, and travelling shawls.

2 EAST, LANDON, & HOLLAND, 10 Old Bond St. Des.—Fancy woollen trouserings and coatings.

3 SCHOFIELD, BROWN, DAVIS, & HALSE, 1 Gresham St.—Flannels in a variety of styles, comprising Royal Victoria flannels, manufactured from yarn spun from silk and wool; merino, flax, silk warp, Thibet, and in fancy dyes.

4 TWEEDALE & SONS, Healey Hall, near Rochdale, and 56 Wood St. London, Manu.—Superfine Saxony and fine twilled cricketer's flannel. Anti-rheumatic and imitation Welsh flannel.

5 LEACH & SONS, 83 Wood St. Manu.—Flannels from English and Australian wools. Coatings, swanskin, gauze Saxony, &c.

6 WILKS, J. 79 and 80 Watling St. Des. and Prop.—Striped woven, and Lancashire and Welsh flannels.

7 FOX BROTHERS & Co. 27 Tokenhouse Yard, and Wellington, Somerset, Manu.—Woollen serges. Woollen blanketing, and blankets. Hosiery yarns.

8 POWELL, S. 52 Regent St. Inv. and Pat.—Double-laced cloth, having a perfect finish on each side of two dis-

tinct colours, woven in one fabric. Specimens for coats, vests, trousers, ladies' paletots, and overcoats.

9 BROWN & FORSTER, 5 Vigo St. Regent St. Prop.—Doeskins and casiimeres, Scotch tweeds, and natural Cheviot wool for trousers. Waistcoating of wool and wool and silk, of silk, of cotton, of China grass. Embroidery on cloth and on silk. All of British manufacture.

10 MURLEY, W. & C. 4 Bow Churchyard, Cheapside, Inv.—Waistcoat lengths, cotton; silk and cotton; silk, wool, and cotton; silk and wool plush; silk and linen; wool and cotton.

11 GOODWIN, J. Lawrence Lane, Prop. — Vestings. Quiltings, all cotton. Livery valencias. Silk figured cashmeres and China grass lustres, mixed fabric.

12 BULL & WILSON, 52 St. Martin's Lane, Prop.—Fine blue cloth, manufactured at Bradford, Wilts, from Saxony wool. Fine scarlet cloth, manufactured at Stroud, Gloucestershire. Black beaver cloth, woven by a patent process, invented by Mr. Daniells, of Freshford Mills, Bath. Himalaya cloth, &c.

13 CLARK, J. & J. Basinghall St. London, and Trowbridge, Wiltshire.—Woaded black single cassimere; patent beaver, Venetian, and ladies' cloth. Satin-face, milled, and single doeskins. Fur Janus beaver.

14 SMITH, J. B. & Co. 38 Basinghall St. Prop.—Woollen cloth waterproof, but not impervious to air.

15 LOCKE, J. 119 and 127 Regent St. Manu.—Scotch tweeds. Cheviot wool tweeds. Military tartans. Scotch mauds. Ladies' clan-tartan shawls. Scotch linsey woolseys.

16 STANCOMB & SON, Trowbridge, Wilts, and 19 Basinghall St. London, Manu.—Doeskins, fancy moleskins, and fancy Angolas; twilled buckskins, imperial cloths, &c. for summer coats; and Venetian cloth.

17 STANCOMB, W. & J. juns. Trowbridge, Wilts, and 14 Basinghall St. London, Manu.—Fancy single elastic, and fancy single moleskin, all wool.

18 SHEPPARD, W. B. & G. Frome, Somerset, and 7 King St. Cheapside.—Woollen cloths, Venetian cloth, and fancy coatings. Single and milled, plain and fancy cassimeres.

19 BARBER, HOWSE, & MEAD, 19 St. Paul's Ch. Yd. Des. and Prop.—Super broad cloths Moscow and royal British beavers. Alpa Vicuna royal shawl.

20 BRETT BROTHERS & Co. Wood St. Des.—Black and rifle-green cloths, black cassimeres, black doeskins, fancy trouserings, &c.

21 HUDSON & BOUSFIELD, Leeds. — Llama, Venetian, and superfine cloths.

22 SLATER, E. Leeds.—Blackwool barathea cloth.

23 WALKER, J. & Co. Bedford St. Leeds, Manu.—Mohair cloths, various colours, for making and trimming ladies' paletots.

24 SNELL, J. Leeds.—Superfine twilled summer cloth.

25 HAGUES, COOK & WORMALD, Dewsbury.—Spanish stripe and drab beaver cloths; white, coloured, and horse blankets.

26 IRWIN, E. Leeds.—Woollen cloths.

27 EYRES, W. & SON, Leeds.—Woollen cloths.

28 HARGREAVE & NUSSEYS, Farnley Low Mills, near Leeds, Des. and Manu.—Royal chameleon, elastic; transferable cloth; Vicuna fur, with woollen back; dyed black cloth, from colonial wool.

29 SMITH & SON, Leeds, Prop.—Piece-dyed sound wool black cloths. Mohair cloths, best quality.

30 LAMBERT, J. Leeds. — Ladies' coatings; tweeds, Circassian, Venetian, and mohair cloths.

31 BINKS, B. Leeds.—Superfine woollen cloths.

32 THORNTON, FIRTH, & RAMSDEN, Leeds.—Superfine cloths, silk and cotton warp, cashmerettes, and blankets.

33 LUPTON, W. & Co. Leeds, Prop.—Olive cloth. Blue carriage lining, and blue cloth, indigo dye.

34 SYKES & SONS, Woodhouse Lane, Leeds—Woollens, fast, common, and woaded colours, wool-dyed and piece-dyed.

35 STOW BROTHERS, Leeds.—Superfine woollen cloths.

37 FIRTH & SONS, Heckmondwike, near Leeds, Manu.—Blankets, coatings of alpaca wool, mohair, and camel's hair. Cotton diaper rugs.

38 HENRY, A. & S. & Co. Leeds.—Woollen cloths and cotton warp cloths.

39 BATESON & Co. Leeds, Yorkshire, Manu.—Specimens of cloths, piece and wool dyed.

40 PAWSON, SON, & MARTIN, Stonebridge Mill, near Leeds, Yorkshire, Manu.—Specimens of cloths, piece-dyed, wool-dyed, woaded colours, &c.

41 SWAINE, J. & E. & Co. Gomersall, and Leeds, Manu.—Superfine wool-dyed indigo blue Witney duffils. Police and Canadian cloths.

42 COOPER, D. & J. Leeds.—Superfine woollen and doeskin cloths.

44 HOTHAM & WHITING, Leeds, Manu.—Yorkshire flannel.

45 CHEETHAM, G. C. & W. Calverley, near Leeds, Manu.—Specimens of superfine olive broad-cloths of Australian wool, bottle green broad cloths. Samples of Australian wool.

46 SAVILLE, J. Leeds.—Oxford, pilot, and army cloths.

47 GOTT & SONS, Leeds, Manu.—Woollen cloths for the home trade, and for the American, China, and Russian markets.

48 SMITHSON, T. Bramley, near Leeds, Manu.—Woollen cloths, piece-dyed. Wool-dyed and woaded colour, &c.

49 YORK & SHEEPSHANKS, Leeds, Manu. Dyers, and Finishers.—Woaded wool black; second woollen cloth. Piece-dyed black, and black medium, and fast dye.

50 GEORGE T. W. & Co. Leeds, Dyers and Finishers.—Worsted lastings in fast black, not woaded.

51 WILKINSON, J. St. Helen's Mills, Leeds, Inv. and Manu.—New ship sheathing. Patent padding and wadding. Medical cloth, backed with India-rubber, &c. Gun wadding.

52 WILKINSON, W. & E. Leeds, Manu.—Crape, all wool. Cord, all wool, for summer cloth, manufactured in the worsted manner.

54 ROBINSON, T. Dewsbury Moor, Dewsbury.—Three-points Mackinaw, super merino, merino bath, and rosed blankets.

55 CRABTREE, W. Dewsbury, Manu.—Bath blankets, fine, and striped with fancy colours at the ends.

56 WHITWORTH, J. & SON, Earlsheaton, Dewsbury.—Two horse blankets,

57 STEAD, W. & Co. Leeds, Manu.—Superfine broadcloth, and wool-dyed woaded black. Sample of fine German wool.

58 HALEY, J. & SONS, Bramley, near Leeds, Manu.—Woollen cloths, made in the white.

59 HALEY, A. & C. Bramley, near Leeds, Manu.—Woollen cloths, made in the white.

60 PEASE, HEATON, & Co. Leeds. — Barège-de-laine cloth, all wool. Saxe-Cobourg cloth. Super de-laine cloth. Satin twill, finish of a new description.

61 HARTLEY & SON, Wortley, near Leeds, Des. and Manu.—Heather tweeds for shooting-coats, made from Australian wool.

62 WEBSTER, T. 154 Park Lane, Leeds, Manu.—Superfine broad woollen cloth.

63 WEBSTER, D. Leeds.—Superfine wool-dyed black cloths.

64 BRAMLEY WOOLLEN CLOTH Co. near Leeds, Dyers and Manu. — Specimens of black cloth, wool-dyed, true and common colour.

65 GREEN & SONS, Leeds, Manu.—Orleans cloth, in blacks and various shades.

67 GRAY, S. Calverley, near Leeds, Manu.—Woollen cloths: drab and blue prunell livery cloth; Russian green prunell habit-cloth.

68 CROMACK. J. J. Leeds, Manu.—Woaded black cloth, and fast black cloth.

69 FENTON, W. Eccleshill, near Leeds, Manu.—Billiard cloths, green, crimson, and scarlet.

70 ELLIS, J. W. & Co. 12 Upper Albion St., Leeds, Manu.—Samples of cloth, saved list indigo blues, all wool, and a frieze with cotton warp and Australian wool.

71 WOODHOUSE, J. Holbeck Moor Side, near Leeds, Manu.—Cloth, woollen weft and cotton warp, fast colour blue. Cloth, common colour, black.

72 BEAUMONT, W. Crawshaw House, Pudsey, near Leeds, Manu.—Black cloths, made from Sydney and Saxony wool, piece dyed.

74 MIDDLEBROOK, J. Birstall, near Leeds.—Cloth flannel, of extra width, and of the natural colour of the wool.

75 SYKES D. & Co. Leeds.—Black milled cloth.

77 GILL & BISHOP, Leeds, Manu.—Brown, gentian, drab, and black mohair.

78 YEWDALL & SON, Rawden, near Leeds, Manu.—Woollen cloths of different qualities; milled hair-list and double milled hair-list cloths.

D 4

79 WALKER & SONS, Millshaw, near Leeds, Dyers and Finishers, Manu.—Single and milled cassimeres, figured and coloured.

80 SMITH, W. Batley, near Dewsbury. — Woollen fabrics.

81 SHEARD & SONS, Batley, near Dewsbury, Manu.—Lodged blue pilot cloth. Blue mixture, steel mixture, and Oxford mixture Petershams.

82 JUBB & SONS, Batley, near Dewsbury, Manu.—Wool dyed Witney and pilot cloth. Woollen fabric, with cotton lining. Blue pilot cloth, piece dyed.

83 WILSON, D. Batley, near Dewsbury, Manu.—Indigo blue pilot cloth.

84 WEBSTER, A. Abbey Mill, Kirkstall, Leeds. — Superfine woollen cloths.

85 HUDSWELL & SON, Batley, near Dewsbury, Manu. —Fancy wrapper for travelling, and fancy wrapper for overcoats, &c. of English wool.

86 BROOKE & SONS, Honley, near Huddersfield, Manu. —Specimens in each stage of the manufacture of broad woollen cloth. Assortment of broad woollen cloth.

87 WALKER & SONS, Huddersfield, Manu.—Buffalo, alpaca, mohair, and dog-hair cloth, for ladies' cloaks and men's overcoats; a new kind of material.

88 TAYLOR, J. Meltham, near Huddersfield, Manu.— Fancy woollens.

89 LEAROYD, E. Huddersfield, Manu.—Specimens of cashmere merinos, for ladies' boot tops.

90 SHAW, P. Lockwood, Huddersfield, Manu.—Woaded black broad woollen cloths.

91 PEACE, A. & Co. Clayton West, Huddersfield, Manu.—Silk chiné dress. Silk and wool dress.

92 GREEN, J. Huddersfield.—Various linseys.

93 HINCHLIFFE & SON, Newmill, near Huddersfield.— Woaded mixed doeskin, mixed durables, exhibited for cheapness and utility.

94 KENYON, J. & J. Dogley Mills, Huddersfield, Manu. —Woollen Silesian stripes for gentlemen's dress.

95 BENNETT, J. & A. Bradley Mills, near Huddersfield, Manu.—Cloths from Prussian and Cashmere wool. Double Napier cloths, of Vicuna wool, &c.

96 HEBBLETHWAITE & LISTER, Market Pl. Huddersfield, Des. and Manu.—Specimens of (all wool) elastic elephanta ribs, for trouserings, &c.

97 CROSLAND, W. & H. Huddersfield, Manu.—Woollen fancy pantaloon cloths, new designs and improved elasticity.

98 SHAW, J. W. & H. Victoria Mill, Huddersfield, Manu.—Woaded wool-dyed and piece-dyed black cloths, &c.

99 MIDGLEY BROTHERS, Huddersfield, Manu.—Super Angola mixture for trousers.

100 HASTINGS BROTHERS, Huddersfield, Manu.—Cloths, doeskins and cassimeres.

101 WRIGLEY & SONS, Huddersfield, Manu.—Livery cloth, and carriage linings.

102 VICKERMAN & BEAUMONT, Huddersfield, Manu.— Black broad cloths, cassimeres, and doeskins, piece-dyed.

103 ARMITAGE BROTHERS, Huddersfield, and 80 Basinghall St. Imp. and Manu.—Woaded black and blue elephant beavers, weighing 45 and 48 ounces to the yard, made entirely of Port Philip wool. Albert check and Albert cloth, the two sides being different colours. Exhibition cloths, 56 inches wide, weighing only 12 ounces to the yard.

104 LOCKWOOD & KEIGHLEY, Huddersfield, Manu.— Patent woollen cords, velvet and leather cloths, chiefly for trousers.

105 BARNICOT & HIRST, Huddersfield, Wilshaw, and Meltham, Manu.—Buckskin, Orleans, doeskins, and hair-line, for trowsers, made from middle-price Port Phillip wool.

106 BARBER & SONS, Holmfirth, near Huddersfield, Manu —Drab kersey for trousers or coats.

107 HOLMES & SONS, Scholes, near Holmfirth, Yorkshire, Manu.—Woaded black doeskin and Vienna.

108 MALLINSON & SONS, Huddersfield. — Wool-dyed black doeskins, exhibited as specimens of manufacture and finish.

109 BEARDSELL, I. & Co. Thongsbridge, near Huddersfield, Manu.—Woaded broad coating, made of Australian and Silesian wool. Fancy woollen trouserings.

110 SHAW, SON, & Co. Huddersfield, Manu.—Woollen cloths. Fancy trouserings; reversible cloth. Pattern cards of fancy goods.

111 TAYLOR & SON, Newsome Huddersfield, Manu.— Fancy waistcoatings; woollen trousers' goods; shawls and scarfs; ladies' and children's dresses.

112 JOHNSON, J. Lockwood, Huddersfield.—Floss-yarns, in various shades.

113 DAY & SON, Mold Green, Huddersfield, Manu.— Merinos, for the tops of ladies' boots, &c. Cashmerettes, cotton or silk shot with woollen.

114 WILLOTT, W. & Co. Huddersfield.—Drab livery-kersey, &c. Woaded wool-dyed black cassimere, and wool, dyed black doeskin.

115 SCHWANN, F. Huddersfield.—Fancy vesting and pantaloon stuffs. Cashmerettes and merinos. Beavers and pilot cloths. Tweeds. Plaids and checks. Buckskins, &c. of mohair, alpaca, and Vicuna. Elephant and rhinoceros skins. Shawls, carpets, blankets, &c.

116 TOLSON & SONS, Dalton, Huddersfield, Manu.— Waistcoatings; trouserings; challi wool plaids, for children's dresses.

117 WRIGLEY, J. & T. C. Huddersfield, Manu.—Moscow beaver; Moskitto; Janus; partridge mixture, for shooting-coats; cloth, finished on both sides; fancy trouserings, &c.

118 SYKES & OGDEN, Huddersfield.—Samples of burry and motey wool, clean and unclean.

119 HINCHLIFF, J. & G. Huddersfield, Manu.—Drab kersey; doeskins; fancy woollen trouserings.

120 BEARDSELL, C. & SON, Holmebridge, Des. and Manu.—Woollen pantaloons, plain and fancy.

121 STARKEY, J. & A. Sheepridge, Huddersfield, Manu. —Drab woollen cords. Drab thickset constitution. Fancy, plain, and woollen velveteens.

122 COWGILL, JESSOP, & Co. Huddersfield, Manu.—Cashmerettes for coats and ladies' boots.

123 HUTH & FISCHER, Huddersfield.—Plain and striped Franklin coatings, wool face. Mohair back. Reg.

124 CLAY, J. T. Rastrick, Huddersfield, Manu.—Woollen trouserings, from fine Saxony and from Australian wool. Waistcoatings, union cloth, and Vicuna cloth.

125 SCHOFIELD, J. Rastrick, near Huddersfield, — Fancy trouserings. Silk, woollen, and cotton waist-coatings. Patent British cashmeres, all wool. Fancy bed furniture.

126 NORTON, J. Clayton West, Huddersfield, Manu.— Summer shawls and coatings. Registered winter woollen shawls, waistcoatings, cloakings, glove-cloths, trouserings, &c.

127 OLDFIELD, ALLAN, & Co. Lockwood Mills, Huddersfield, Manu.—Specimens of the various stages of the fancy woollen mannfacture. Patterns of fancy woollen trouserings, and broadcloth for over-coats. Doeskin and crape trouserings, made from wool. Tweed made entirely from waste.

128 HOADLEY & PRIDIE, Halifax, Manu.—Damasks, for furniture purposes, manufactured of silk, cotton, and wool, either separately or in combination.

129 BROWN, W. Halifax.—Damasks and table covers, cotton and worsted, cotton, silk, and worsted, and worsted.

130 AKROYD & SON, Halifax, Manu.—Table-covers;

damasks; articles for ladies' dresses; plain goods, all worsted; plain goods, worsted and cotton; ponchos; yarns.

130A ECROYD, W. & SON, near Burnley, Manu.—Power-loom Coburg cloth wool; Orleans cloth; Saxony Orleans cloth; mousseline de laine; power-loom Saxe Coburg cloth; power-loom barège de laine, made from cotton and wool; buntin for colours, &c. Worsted Heald yarn; genappe cord; press bagging, &c.

131 SHEPARD & PERFECT, Cross Hills Mill, Halifax, Manu.—Cotton and worsted, all worsted, and silk and worsted damasks. Victoria velvet damasks. Table covers. Worsted ponchos, &c. Patterns, registered.

133 BARRACLOUGH, W. & SON, Halifax, Manu.—Specimens of striped lists, cloth, druggeting, padding, kerseys, linseys, tweed, house cloths, and table covers.

134 WARD, J. W. Halifax.—Cotton and worsted damasks, Jacquard wove. Worsted damask for draperies. Victoria table-cloth, from cotton and worsted, fast colours.

135 M'CREA, H. C. Halifax, Manu.—Furniture damasks, piece and yarn dyed. Table covers, all registered. Poncho stuffs, all worsted, used in South America.

136 CLAY & SONS, Halifax, Manu.—Linsey, for jackets; plaiding, for drawers; cricket jackets; raised and milled kersey; fearnought; blue flannel; ironing blanket, &c.

137 AKED & SONS, Halifax, Manu.—Pantaloons; fancy checks; mixture coatings; plain lastings, and super worsted crapes; cashmeres, &c.

138 WILSON, J. Forest Cottage, Ovenden, near Halifax, Manu.—Ponchos, Mantuas, and shawls; in woollen, cotton, and worsted.

139 SALT, T. Bradford, Yorkshire, Manu.—Alpaca manufactures. Specimens of British and American alpaca wool, &c. Mohair manufactures, and specimens of mohair. Moreens made from English and Russia wool, with specimens of Russia wool.

140 MILLIGAN & SON, Harden Mills, Bingley, Yorkshire, Manu.—Patent embroidered alpaca and silk furniture-cloths, satin striped dress goods, damasks, &c. Alpaca grogram coatings. Mohair mixtures. Specimens of alpaca and mohair, in the various stages of manufacture.

141 SCHWANN, KELL, & CO. Bradford, Prop.—Merinos, Cobourgs, lastings, alpacas. Silk and cotton dresses. Cotton and worsted checks. Cotton and wool plaids, &c.

142 ROGERS, G. Bradford.—Cobourg cloth of fine quality; silk and cotton warp.

143 FOSTER & SON, Black Dike Mills, near Bradford, Manu.—Goods made of cotton and alpaca; of cotton, silk, and alpaca; of silk and alpaca; and of cotton and mohair. Fancy coatings; vestings; Chiné; damasks. Alpaca mohair, and worsted yarns.

144 JOWETT, T. & CO. Bingley, near Bradford, Yorkshire.—Mixed fabrics, of cotton, alpaca, silk, and china grass, for vestings, dresses, &c. woven by power-looms.

145 HARRIS & FISON, Bradford, Manu.—Circassian cloth; the weft is a combination of the finest wool and silk. Cloth woven from the hair of the Angola rabbit.

146 ARMITAGE, G. & CO. Bradford, Dyers —Orleans, Cobourg, and Brazilian cloth; mohair, silk and mohair, and silk and alpaca figures. Exhibited as specimens of dyeing.

147 TREMEL, A. & CO. Bradford, Manu.—Plain alpaca lustres and chameleons; figured Orleans; twilled satteens; figured Circassians, &c. in cotton warps, and piece dyed. Madonnas, or mixed alpaca lustres; silk warp alpaca lustres, in natural colours, and piece dyed. Mixed alpaca coatings, &c.

148 RIPLEY & SON, Bradford, Yorkshire, Dyers.—Orleans cloths and Cobourg cloths. French de laines and merinos, ombré damasks, and alpaca and balzarine brocades. Damask table-cover. Plain balzarines; all exhibited as specimens of dyeing.

149 CRAVEN & SON, Prospect Mill, Thornton, near Bradford, Manu.—Lustre Orleans, in different qualities, blacks and colours.

150 DRUMMOND, J. Bradford.—Mixed fabrics composed of cotton, alpaca, and silk plain and figured, for vestings, dresses, &c.

151 CLOUGH, R. Bradford.—Specimens of merinos, all wool, various qualities.

152 DALBY, J. Bradford.—Cobourg cloths, silk stripes and checks, single and double twill; plain and figured alpacas, silk and cotton warps, and figured worsted chiné. Dyed by Messrs. Ripley and Son.

153 CRAVEN & HARROP, Bradford, Manu.— Cobourg and Paramatta cloths; full-twill cloths; shawl cloths; merino, Orleans, and alpaca cloths. Moreens. Union and worsted damasks. Canton cloths; lining and serge cloths, &c.

155 HAGGAS & SON, Bradford.—Samples of Orleans, lustreen, worsted lining, and mohair.

156 SHUTTLEWORTH, W. & CO. Bradford.—Plain and figured Orleans cloth.

157 CLAPHAM, J. Bradford, Manu.—Net, cotton and alpaca; net, cotton and worsted; Cobourg cloth, cotton and worsted; diagonal lining, cotton and alpaca.

158 CLAPHAM, W. Wilsden, near Bingley, Yorkshire, Manu.—Cobourg cloths, of various qualities and colours.

159 WALL, COCKSHOT, & WALL, Linton Mills, near Skipton, Yorkshire, Manu.—Shaded tapestry ground, with silk figure, shot and printed ground Orleans, &c. Preparations of worsted yarn.

160 MORTON, D. Baildon, near Bradford, Manu.—Ends of union tweeds. Cotton warp and woollen weft.

161 KERSHAW, S. & H. Laisterdyke, near Bradford.— Black Orleans cloth.

162 TOWNEND, Brothers, Cullingworth, near Bingley, Manu.—Worsted heald and worsted genappe yarns; mohair poplin; worsted and mohair and alpaca yarns; worsted weft and warp yarns.

163 SEMON, SILTZER, & CO. Bradford, Prop.—Orleans cloth, manufactured by Chapman and Whitaker, Baildon; by Lund, Keighley; and by Turner, Horton: all dyed by J. M. Kirk. Lastings, serges de Berry, and damasks, by Taylor and Sons, Ovendon: dyed by Smith, Halifax, and Holroyd and Co. Leeds. Carded worsted yarns, spun by Taylor and Sons.

164 PEEL, W. & CO. Bradford, Yorkshire, Manu.— Cobourg cloths. Silk warp paramattas, Brazilians, and silk warp double twills.

165 BOTTOMLEY & SONS, Shelf, near Halifax, Des. and Manu.—Figured Angora, and gauze lace, composed of mohair and silk. Figured mohair lustre, and Orleans of worsted and cotton. Mohair, and Orleans serge. Mohair lustre, &c.

165A HOLDSWORTH, J.—Orleans and mohair cloths, figured and plain, exhibited as specimens of dyeing.

166 HOLDSWORTH & CO. Halifax and Bradford, and 9 Goldsmith St. London, Manu.—Damasks, table-covers, plain and fancy stuffs, &c.

167 SUGDEN, J. & BROTHERS, Dockroyd Mills, near Keighley, Bradford, Manu.—Plain and striped calimancos; shalloons; merinos; cubicas; summer cloths; union princettas; bombazets, &c. 800 specimens of yarns used in the manufacture of poplins, &c.

168 MILNER, J. & CO. Clayton, near Bradford, Manu.— Orleans, worsted weft and cotton warp.

169 CLARK, J. 56 High St. Bradford. — Table-cloth embroidered with thread on crimson sarsenet.

170 SLATER, H. Yeadon, near Leeds, Manu.—Woollen netting, for the protection of the bloom of fruit-trees.

170A NICHOLSON, J. Bradford, Manu. —Specimens of pattern cards.

171 ROBERTS, H. Bradford.—Grogan coatings.

172 TETLEY, Mrs. Bradford.—Embroidered quilt.

173 RAND & SONS, Bradford, Manu.—Cobourg cloths, cotton and worsted; the same, with silk warp; merinos, moreens, single and double twill.

174 HORSFALL, J. G. & Co. Bradford, Manu.—Henrietta cloth, silk, and worsted. Fine Saxony cloth, all wool. Fine Cobourg cloth, cotton, and worsted. Cobourg cloth.

175 TOWNEND, S. Thornton, near Bradford.—Worsted, heald, and genappe yarns, spun from English wools; healds, for weaving; braids, poplins, &c. made from genappe yarn.

176 WHITLEY, J. Morton, near Bingley, Yorkshire. Manu.—Alpaca yarns prepared for weaving. Mixed alpaca and mohair yarns.

177 SHARP, D. W. Bingley.—Alpaca yarns, prepared by Ross's new process. Mohair yarn and slivers, combed. Worsted yarn.

178 QUITZOW, SCHLESINGER, & Co. Bradford, Prop.—Berlin wool, spun and dyed in England. Flax, produced by the new patent process of Mr. P. Claussen. Yarns, spun from the flax, alone, and mixed with cotton, wool, and silk.

179 CHEESEBOROUGH, W. Bradford.—Specimens of wool from each county in the United Kingdom.

180 BEHRENS, J. Bradford.—Figured Cobourg cloths and satteens, silk and cotton warp.

181 BOTTOMLEY, J. 6 Cheapside, Bradford, Manu.—Crape and plain and figured Orleans, embroidered with silk and alpaca. Silk and worsted mixed lustres, embroidered with two colours of silk. Saxony cloth embroidered with gold and silver.

182 GREGORY BROTHERS, Bradford.—Mixed fabrics of alpaca and mohair.

183 BAUGHEN BROTHERS, Banbury, Manu. — Mohair table-covers. Chinese prints. Livery plushes. Angora velvet plushes. Utrecht velvet. Mohair.

184 PEASE, H. & Co. Darlington, Manu.—Specimens of worsted manufacture from the fleece to the finished cloth. Pieces of Cobourg cloth, made of Lincolnshire, Cheviot, Southdown, Australian, and Saxony wool, &c.

185 BENNETT & Co. Abingdon St. Portland St. Manchester, and 46A Newgate St. London, Manu.—Utrecht velvet, for decorations, furniture, upholstery, and carriage linings.

186 KAY, RICHARDSON, & WROE, Chancery Lane, Manchester, Manu.—Brocade Chene, Chene Barège de Valenciennes. Chene Versailles. Barège robe de Verona.

187 DIXON R. & T. Galashiels, Scotland, Manu.—Saxon wool plaids. Specimens of Scotch tweed.

188 COCHRANE, J. & W. Galashiels, Scotland, Manu.—Specimens of Scotch tweed trouserings.

189 SANDERSON & SIBBALD, Galashiels, Scotland, Manu.—Scotch tweed trouserings.

190 GILL, R. Inverleithen, Scotland, Manu.—Regimental tartans, in a summer fabric, made of fine Saxony wool. Tartans, for ladies' dresses, made of Saxony lambs'-wool, &c.

191 INGLIS & BROWN, Galashiels, Scotland, Manu.—Specimens of Scotch tweeds.

192 LEES, R. & G. Galashiels, Scotland, Manu.—Plaids, shawls, and cloakings.

193 CLAPPERTON, T. & G. Galashiels, Scotland, Manu.—Scotch Stewart and fancy plaids. Scotch tweeds.

194 BALLANTYNE & SON, Galashiels, Scotland, Manu.—Ladies' woollen scarfs or shawls. Woollen tartans for ladies' dresses. Scotch tweeds.

195 SIME, J. & Co. Galashiels Scotland, Manu.—Plaids worn by the Scotch Highland regiments. Ladies' and gentlemen's plaids. Scotch tweed vestings, &c.

196 SANDERSON, R. & A. & Co. Galashiels, Scotland, Manu.—Scotch woollen clan and fancy plaids. Gentlemen's plaids.

197 FYFE, A. & Co. 77 Queen St. Glasgow, Manu.—New dress fabrics. Fancy cotton and union shawls.

197A KNOX, A. L. 9 Cochrane St. Glasgow, Manu.—Material for dressing gowns.

198 RAINEY, KNOX, & Co. Glasgow, Manu.—Shawl dresses for robes de chambre, wool and cotton.

199 LAIRD & THOMSON, Ingram St. Glasgow Manu.—Set of clan patterns in gala cloth.

200 WINGATE, SON, & Co. Glasgow.—Harness woven long and square shawls; printed Barège and Cashmere and woven woollen shawls. Woollen goods in the piece.

201 CAMPBELL & Co. 34 Candleriggs St. Glasgow, Prop.—Scotch printed cashmere d'écosse and other long shawls. Woven square shawls, Scotch printed, &c. Scotch printed mufflers. Barège and cashmere handkerchiefs, &c.

202 CROSS, W. 62 Queen St. Glasgow, and 45 Friday St. London, Manu.—Saxony wool shawls, clan, shepherdess, and fancy patterns, square, long Byzantine style, pure cashmere. Saxony wool plaid dresses.

203 GILMOUR, W. & Co. Glasgow, Manu.—Scotch woollen tweed trouserings; Scotch woollen Saxony tartans.

204 BLACK & WINGATE, Glasgow, Manu.—Samples of cotton yarn. Cotton lawn and cambric handkerchiefs. Fine cotton Scotch cambric. Fine bishop's lawn. Woven fancy shirt fronts. Fancy printed cotton and linen handkerchiefs.

205 LEADBETTER, J. & Co. Glasgow, Manu.—Pieces of fancy linen, entire; mixed and union. Linen listados. Fancy linen drills.

206 BAUMANN & WUNSCH, Glasgow, Agents and Manu.—Printed shawls of wool, worsted, and cotton. Printed cotton shawls and handkerchiefs. Linens, in various stages of manufacture. Mixed fabrics.

207 HELME, W. New Mills, Stroud, Manu.—Cassimere waistcoats, doeskins, cashmerette, silk warp, woollen wefts. Cassimeres. Sardinians for waistcoats.

208 GRIST, M. Capels Mills, Stroud, Manu.—Mattress-wools, woollen millpuffs, and flocks, &c. manufactured by improved machinery, and purified during the process.

209 MARLING, S. S. & Co. Ebley Mills, Stroud, Manu.—Superfine broad cloth, wool-dyed, woaded black, &c.; superfine doeskin, superfine cassimere, &c.

210 HOOPER, C. & Co. Eastington Mills, Stroud, Manu.—Cloths, wool-dyed, woaded, piece-dyed, &c. Single-milled cassimere. Patent elastic trousering, and gloving cloth.

211 PLAYNE, P. P. & C. Nailsworth, Manu.—Woaded wool-dyed cloths Illustrations of the process of manufacturing woollen cloth.

212 PARTRIDGE, N. Bowbridge, Stroud, Des.—Double-colour woollen cloth, for officers' cloaks, dividing saloons in the East, curtains, &c. Army cloth, improved red

213 PALLING, W. Lower Mills, Painswick, Manu.—Double-milled scarlet hunter, double-milled cloths. Fine single-milled scarlet, billiard cloths, &c.

214 DAVIES & SONS, Stonehouse Mills, Stroud, Manu.—Scarlet military cloth. White cloth for uniforms. Scarlet cloth, for foreign uniforms. Black cloth, cassimere, and doeskins.

215 SAMPSON, T. Lightpill Mills, Stroud, Inv.—Machine for twisting the fringe of wool shawls. Wool shawls. Twilled black flannel. Scarlet flannel.

216 OVERBURY, J. Nind and Monk Mills, near Wotton-under-Edge, Gloucestershire, Manu. — Superfine Saxony woollen cloths, wool-dyed woaded black, rifle and medley, and blue indigo-dyed.

217 PHILLIPS, SMITH, & PHILLIPS, Melksham, Manu.—Fine Saxony broad cloth, woaded olives, woaded rifle, and wool-dyed black.

218 EDMONDS & EDMONDS, Bradford, Wilts, Manu.—Superfine woollen wool-dyed cloths, made on a patent principle, and of superior dye. Superfine woollen cloth, water-proofed.

219 BARNES, E. Oxford, Des. and Manu.—Counterpane composed of 9,851 pieces.

220 PETERS, D. 44 College Green, Bristol.—Black single-milled kerseymere.

221 CHICK, R. Knapp Mills, near Chard, Somerset, Manu.—Samples of drab cloth, made of English wool by power-loom.

222 PHILLIPS, J. Knapp Mills, near Chard, Somerset, Manu.—Striped, plain blue, and white linsey, made from flax and wool.

223 BIRD, R. Crewkerne, Manu. — Linen, worsted, white and coloured linen and worsted; webs for girths, braces, &c.

224 STANTON & SON, Land's Mill, Fordington, near Dorchester, Manu.—Drab milled waterproofed cloths, made from English wool.

225 ALLEN, G. St. Stephen's St. Norwich. — Elastic cloths for trowsers, gloves, &c.

226 ALLEN & BANKS, Norwich.—East Anglian cloths manufactured from Norfolk wool.

227 GARVIE & DEAS, Perth, Manu.—Linsey-woolsey, or ladies' dresses. Hand-knitted hose. Hand-loom, grass-bleached, cotton shirting, &c.

228 CROMBIE, J. & Co. Cothal Mills, Aberdeen, Manu.—Scotch tweeds of various qualities.

229 THOMSON, W. Stonehaven, Scotland, Manu.—Specimen of a method of working up engine waste, into floor-cloth or carpeting.

230 BRUNTON, W. J. & Co. St. Leonard's Factory, Edinburgh, Des. and Manu.—A variety of fine wool scarf shawls. Superior gentlemen's plaids. German lambs' wool and yarn, of which the shawls are made.

231 BOWMAN & SON, Langholm.—Shepherd tweeds of Scotch and Austalian wool. Shepherd unions, cotton and wool. Gentlemen's shepherd plaid German wool.

232 BYERS & SON, Langholm, Manu.—Shepherd's tweed; railway plaid, &c.; and linsey, made of cotton and wool.

233 RENWICK, T. & A. Langholm, Manu.—Linsey-woolsey weft, Eskdale shepherd plaid, and Scotch hosiery yarn; Scotch tweed and marble yarn, of Australian wool.

234 DICKSONS & LAINGS, Hawick and Glasgow, Manu.—Scotch lambs'-wool hosiery, &c. Clan, shepherdess, and fancy tartan wool plaids. Cheviot, Australian, and Saxony wool trouserings.

235 SMITH, J. & SONS, Saddleworth, near Manchester. (Agents, Nield and Collander, London.)—Fine and superfine and silk warp and stout flannels. Fine and superfine and silk warp. Shawls and scarfs for printing.

236 HAIGH & SONS, 9 New Brown St. Manchester, Manu.—Black broad cloth. The same, wool and cotton.

237 BAMFORD, J. Rochdale, Lancashire, Manu.—Fine gauze flannel, manufactured from sheep's wool.

238 LEWIS, W. Llandilofawn, Wales —Welch woollen cloth.

239 PEARSON, J. Carlisle, Manu.—Woollen and cotton trouserings.

240 DALRYMPLE, W. Union Mills, Douglas, Isle of Man, Manu.—Shepherd plaid, made from Australian wool; and striped and tweed cloth and shepherd plaid, made from Isle of Man wool.

241 WHITMORE & Co. Leicester, Manu.—Worsted yarns for hosiery-fleecy, and for embroidery and soft knitting.

242 BREWIN & WHETSTONE, Leicester.—Worsted and merino yarns.

243 BURGESS, A. & Co. Leicester, Manu.—Berlin wool embroidery yarns. Soft and hard knitting yarns. Shetland embroidery, weft, hosiery. Alpaca, mohair, and other yarns,

single and doubled. Samples of the wools used in the manufacture in various stages of preparation.

244 POPPLETON, R. Westgate, Wakefield, Manu.—Manufactured knitting worsted and yarns.

245 WILSON, J. J. & W. Kendal, Manu.—Railway wrappers. Stout horse-clothing; also, fine and light, for race-horses.

246 GANDY, G. Kendal, Manu.—Brace, girth, and roller webs, in worsted and woollen. Horse sheetings, railway blankets, collar-checks, &c. for saddlers.

247 IRELAND, J. & Co. Kendal, Manu.—Railway-travelling and bed-rugs, horse blankets, Alpaca cloth, saddle-cloths, Prince's check and kersey, Saxony lining, flannel, plaiding, linsey drugget, gentlemen's scarfs, &c.

248 GOODS, Brecon.—A variety of woollen goods.

249 MARTIN, J. Cockermouth, Inv. — Improved ventilating waterproof cloth and paper; the paper made by I. Cropper, Burneside, near Kendal. Patented.

250 SALTER, S. & Co. Trowbridge, Wilts, Manu.—Specimens of fine woollen trouserings.

251 HUGHES, R. Tregarth, Bangor, Wales, Manu.—Gown pieces and apron woven in a loom, invented and made by the exhibitor.

252 WILSON, W. & SON, Hawick.—Scotch mauds and travelling wrappers.

253 MILLS, ELIZABETH, Dolgelly, Inv. and Manu.—Linsey dresses, mixed with silk. Linsey aprons. Waist-coat pieces, of Welsh wool. Welsh cloth, for gentlemen's shooting-clothes, &c.

254 LLOYD, W. & Co. Newtown, Montgomery, Wales, Manu.—Specimens of Welch flannel, all manufactured from sheep's wool.

255 PIM BROTHERS & Co. Dublin, Des. and Manu.—Irish poplins. Double tabbinet, &c.: registered designs. Brocaded poplin.

256 ATKINSON, R. & Co. 31 College Green, Dublin, Prop. — Irish poplin Jacquard loom at work (Main Avenue), with new brocading machine. Irish poplins brocaded and gold-barred; and gold tissue. Brocaded and tissued Irish poplin scarfs; striped furniture and figured tabourets, &c.

257 WILLANS BROTHERS & Co. Island Bridge Mills, near Dublin, Manu.—Super frieze, shepherd's plaids, military tartan, and woollen shawl yarn.

258 DILLON, L. 7 Parliament St. Dublin, Des.—Friezes and rumswizzles. The rumswizzle is made from undyed foreign wool.

259 ALLEN, R. 28 Lower Sackville St. Dublin, Prop.—Irish made heather tweeds. Irish frieze. Black cassimere Irish embroidered vests; the designs by J. Healy, a pupil of the Dublin School of Design; worked by Miss Hamilton and others. Irish linens, &c. Irish frieze wrappers, &c. Samples of figured and double-watered Irish tabinets, manufactured by E. Jones, of 3 St. Andrew Street, Dublin, &c.

260 MACDONA, G. 32 Molesworth St. Dublin.—Specimens of the "Albert frieze;" heather and black tweeds Patent drawers. Tabinet and cloth vesting, embroidered with gold.

261 NICOLLS, A. Cork, Ireland, Manu.—Blankets, flannels, swanskins, and friezes.

262 MURPHY, MARGARET, Ballysmutton, Blesinton, Ireland, Manu.—Home-made frieze, from wool grown and spun by the exhibitor.

263 NEILL, CATHERINE, & SONS, Tallaght, Dublin, Manu.—Brown mixed, and sheep's gray frieze. Blankets.

264 DALY, J. Cashel.—Specimens of plain friezes, chiefly used for men's clothing and horse sheeting. Manufactured at Rossmore Mills.

265 JONES, E. Dublin.—Tabinets and poplins.

266 REYNOLDS, W. 81 Grafton St. Dublin, Des. and

Manu.—Imperial blue and gold, and white and gold tissue poplin. Figured furniture. Corded, plaided, tartan, and checked poplins.

267 FRY, W. & Co. Dublin, Manu.—Plaid tartan, and brocaded poplins, &c. Patterns of coach laces.

268 EARLY, J. & Co. Witney, Manu.—A variety of Witney blankets.

269 EARLY, E. Witney, Manu.—Witney blankets, made from different descriptions of English wools. Crib blankets, girth and roller webs, &c.

270 BLISS, W. Chipping Norton, Oxfordshire, Manu.— Kersey check webbing, &c. for horse-clothing. Tweeds for trousers. Alpa Vicuna beaver cloth, and Royal shawl, Angola and beaver shawls. Coverlets for beds, &c.

271 WHEELER, W. S. 4 Ludgate St.—Samples of patent dress beavers, mohairs, fancy doeskins, &c.

272 FOX & Co. Devizes, Wilts.—Broad and narrow cloth, made entirely from British wool, the produce of Wiltshire. Specimens of the wool and yarns.

273 CARR, T. & W. Twerton Mills, Bath, Manu.—Cloths from German wool. Bath fur beaver, and dressed fur of fine Australian wool. Black beaver, and black Venetian, or summer cloth of German wool.

274 JOHNSTON, J. Newmill, Elgin, Scotland, Manu.— Mauds, or plaids, made of undyed or natural brown wool. Natural brown tweed, of different wools, waterproofed.

Nos. 275 to 313 in SOUTH TRANSEPT GALLERY.

275 KERR & SCOTT, 31 and 32 St. Paul's Churchyard.— Grenadines, all silk; and Barège, silk and wool. Crapes, printed in imitation of real China. Long floral Cashmeres, and soft silks, &c. Manu. by R. Kerr. Paisley.

276 LEWIS & ALLENBY, Regent St.—Registered Barège shawls.

277 WEBBER & HAIRS, 31 Milk St. City.—Printed Barège shawls: Cashmere and Grenadine. Printed handkerchiefs and Foulard dresses.

278 JAMESON & BANKS, Honey Lane Market, Cheapside, Manu.—Barège shawls, printed, wool texture; silk and mixed texture. Cachemire d'Ecosse, printed, wool texture. Crape shawls, printed, silk texture.

279 KEITH, SHOOBRIDGE, & Co. 124 Wood St. Prop.— Shawls: printed Barège; grenadine silk: Cashmere; mufflers; and satin, long and square.

280 HOLMES & Co. Regent Street, Des. Manu. and Reg. —Circular shawls.

281 STANDEN & Co. 112 Jermyn St. St. James's, Imp.— White Shetland knitted shawl, veil, stockings, gloves, hand spun.

282 LITTLER, MARY ANN, Merton Abbey, Surrey, Prod. —British Barège shawls and twilled bandanas, wax and chintz print, &c.

283 SWAISLAND, C. Crayford, Kent, Manu.—Printed Barège shawls. Printed Chinese velvet for furnitures, or " application plush." Printed flannels for dresses.

284 CLABBURN & SON, Norwich, Manu.—Registered figured Cashmere shawls. Spun-silk, fancy check, and Albanian silk shawls. Registered Jacquard figured poplins, and chiné poplins; and mixed fabrics, &c.

285 BLAKELY, E. T. River House Factory, Duke's Palace, Norwich, Manu.—Norwich Cashmere green scarf shawl, gold introduced. Shawls of Cashmere wool, design by John Funnell. Anglo-Indian scarfs, shawls, dresses, brocade, &c.

286 TOWLER, CAMPIN, & Co. Elm Hill, Norwich, and 46 Friday St. London, Manu.—Villover scarves; silk ground. Printed silk, and silk net shawls. Ladies' paletots, worked to fit the shape.

287 WHITEHILL, M. & Co. Paisley, Manu.—Scarfs, with tamboured ends; and shawls, handkerchiefs, and vests embroidered. Satin aprons, and babies' robes. Tamboured and embroidered dresses, &c. Silk dresses.

288 HOLMS BROTHERS, 7 St. Mirren's St. Paisley, and 21 Friday St. Cheapside, London, Manu.—Fine wool tartan long shawls. Fancy tartan and plain wool. Vicuna long shawl. Wool tartan cloaking.

289 BURGESS, C. Paisley, Manu.—Long woven shawls.

290 BAIRD, J. Paisley, Manu.—Embroidered French merino ladies' dresses. Embroidered Canton crape shawls.

291 FORBES & HUTCHISON, Paisley, Manu. — Paisley woven, printed, tartan wool, embroidered, and figured gauze shawls. Embroidered handkerchiefs. Wool mufflers. Embroidered vests and robe. Tartan and printed dresses.

292 ABERCROMBIE & YUILL, Paisley, Manu.—Printed long and square shawls.

293 CLARK, J. Jun. & Co. Causeyside, Paisley, Manu. —Printed Cashmere long and square shawls or plaids.

294 LAWSON, J. & Co. Caledonia Print Works, Paisley. —Barège printed shawls, in wool and in silk.

295 DICK & SONS, Paisley.—Printed Cashmere shawls.

296 ROXBURGH, J. & A. Paisley, Manu.—Woven long shawls.

297 MACFARLANE, SON, & Co. Paisley, Manu.—Spun silk fabrics for ladies' dresses, in tartan and fancy designs.

298 STEWART, R. Paisley.—Machine for inventing and displaying tartan and other patterns. Inv. by T. Hutchison.

299 MORGAN, J. & Co. Paisley, and St. Paul's Church yard, London, Manu.—Woven long shawls, of Cashmere yarn, of silk and wool; and of mosaic style. Woollen plaids. Printed Barège long shawls.

300 KERR, R. Paisley, Manu.—India long and square shawls. Printed and fancy wool long and square shawls.

301 ROBERTSON, J. & J. 3 Forbes Pl. Paisley, Manu.— Coloured woven harness. Wool plaids and shawls. Coloured printed plaids and shawls, in Barège, Cashmeres d'Ecosse, &c.

302 ROWAT, R. T. & J. Paisley, Manu.—Printed Barège and Cashmere long shawls. Printed wool square shawls.

303 MASON, W. & Co. Honey Lane, Cheapside, Prod. —Dress fabrics: printed Cashmere and lama wool texture; and embroidered Cashmeres, wool and cotton texture.

304 WELCH, MARGETSON & Co. Cheapside—Dressinggown fabrics.

305 SALOMONS & SONS, 42 Old Change, Prop.—Ladies' embroidered robes, &c. Irish and French cambric handkerchiefs. Muslin trimmings, flouncings, and insertions, &c.

306 PUGH, J. W. 163 and 165 Regent St.—Mixed fabrics.

307 SAYCE, J. & Co. 53 Cornhill, Manu.—Mixed fabrics.

308 GODEFROY, P. A. 3 King's Mead Cottage, New North Rd. Islington, Inv. and Manu.—Woven fabrics, finished by patent machinery and chemical agency.

309 FOWLER, CAMPIN, & Co.—Norwich challi. Satin striped de laines. Paramatta cloth and Barège for dresses.

310 WILLET, E. NEPHEW, & Co. Norwich.—Mixed fabrics for dresses, consisting of bombazines and paramattas; poplins, brocades, chinés, &c. A mixed fabric, composed of materials from nine different countries.

311 BOLINGBROKE, C. & F. Norwich, Manu.—Plain and watered poplins.

312 MIDDLETON & AINSWORTH, Norwich and London, Manu. — Poplins corded and brocaded, and black paramattas.

313 HINDE, E. & F. Norwich Manu.—Barèges, and brocaded poplins.

462, 463, 467, & 468, *placed on the North Wall with Class* 6.

432 CLARKE, T. Stephen St. Waterford, Ireland. Manu. —Blue cloak, of camlet stuff, made by Coleman, Stephen Street, Waterford; has been worn for twenty years. Samples of serge and carpeting.

459 SMITH & WHYTE, Glasgow, Manu.—Embroidered robes and lady's dress. (South Transept Gallery.)

460 ROBERTS, R. Llanberris Rd. Carnarvon, Wales, Manu.—Linsey-woolsey manufactures.

462 BRUNTON & NESBIT, Edinburgh.—Shawls and scarfs.

463 BRAYSHAM, G. 61A Park St. Camden Tn Manu.— Pictorial mosaic cloth-work table cover or quilt.

464 GIBSON, W. & Co. Tillicoultry, Alloa, Scotland, Manu.—M'Kenzie and M'Lean clan tartan woollen shawls. Fancy woollen shawls. Frazer and Forbes clan tartans, &c. (South Transept Gallery.)

465 ARCHIBALD & SONS, Tillicoultry, Alloa, Scotland, Manu.—Rob Roy, Colquhoun, and M'Donald of Staffa tartan long shawls. Malcolm and Bruce tartan wool shawls. Fancy wool shawls. Royal Stewart and Gordon tartans.

466 PATON, J. & D. Tillicoultry, Alloa, Scotland, Manu. —Fancy wool tartan, designed by Romanes and Paterson, Edinburgh. Long wool fancy shawls, des. by Mitchell, Miller, and Ogilvie, Glasgow, and Arthur and Frazer, Glasgow. (South Transept Gallery.)

467 SINCLAIR, J. jun. 49 South Bridge St. Edinburgh, Mann.—Scarf plaids, all wool.

468 WILSON & SON, Bannockburn, near Stirling, Scotland, Manu.—Specimens of the tartans of the Scottish clans.

469 BROWN, J. & H. & Co. Ettrick Mills, Selkirk, Scotland, Manu.—Scotch tweeds and fancy woollens.

470 HALLY, G. Perthshire.—Various plaids. (North Wall.)

472 HUGHES, W. Benygroes, near Carnarvon, Weaver. —Worsted and silk dresses. Aprons, of Welsh linsey. Table-cover, of wool and flax.

474 SCHOFIELD, A. Spring house, near Delph, Saddleworth, Manu.—Patterns of woollen goods manufactured in the years from 1780 to 1820. Fine doeskin, or satin-face, all wool. Cashmere and merino. Maude fabrics, with specimens of dyeing. Fine patent black broadcloth, and cassimeres.

475 HUGHES, W. Bethesda, near Bangor, Wales.—Durable bed covering. (North Wall.)

477 WATSON, J. & A. Galashiels, Scotland, Manu.— Scotch clan and fancy plaids. Ladies' woollen scarfs or shawls, and tartans. Scotch tweeds.

480 ROBERTS, W. & Co. Galashiels, Scotland, Manu.— Pieces of Scotch tweeds.

481 REID & SON, Langholm, Manu.—Cotton and Scotch wool hose; shepherd's plaid check, &c. made from Cheviot, Australian, and German wool.

486 KEISALL & BARTLEMORE, Rochdale.— Flannels: Lancashire and imitation Welch, swanskin, medium and gauze, made of English, Australian, and Saxony wool.

487 BROOK, J. & SON, Upper Thong, near Huddersfield. —Specimens of woaded black cassimere, doeskin, and cloth.

490 BURNLEY & SONS, Heckmondwicke, near Leeds, Manu.—English, Witney, and Irish blankets. American blankets for clothing, and Mackinnow and scarlet striped.

493 THOMAS, W. Haworth, Keighley, Bradford, Manu. —Dyed wool, combed; wool-dyed yarns, in hanks and on spools; died yarn, floated with silk.

496 STOWELL & SUGDEN, Bradford, Manu. — Crimson and white-fold mohair chair.

500 H.R.H. PRINCE ALBERT. Two brocaded dresses, two shawls, and a specimen of coarse cloth, the weft of the dresses and the shawls and cloth entirely of cashmere wool, from goats kept in Windsor Park. (In Main Avenue West).

501 UNDERWOOD, W. 1 Vere St. Oxford St.—Heraldic tapestry hangings. Cloth curtains in various colours. (In South Transept Gallery.)

Nos. 463, 467, & 468 Ground Floor, North Side, behind Western Refreshment Room.

Proceed to Class 14, page 83.

Class 13. SILK AND VELVET.

—— South Transept Gallery. ——

1 KEITH, D. & Co. 124 Wood St. Cheapside, Manu— Silk trophy. Rich tissues, brocades, brocatelles, silk damasks silk and worsted damask, carriage linings, diaphane, window blinds, &c. (Main Avenue West.)

1A REDMAYNE & Co. 20 New Bond St. Inv.—Taffets and glacé gros d'Afrique, &c. made by Stone and Kemp, Spitalfields Ribbon made by Cornell and Co. Nuneaton.

2 PUGH, J. W. 163 and 165 Regent St.—Bombazeen cloth, for mourning. Widow's silk.

3 SANDERSON & REID, 7 Gresham St. Manu. and Prop.—Specimen of silk weaving for a chair cover. New pattern for furniture. Samples for wainscotting, &c.

4 VANNER, J. & SON, 15 Spital Square. — Silk for umbrellas and parasols; vest satin.

5 ROBINSON, I. & R. & Co. 30 Milk St. Cheapside, Manu.—Velvets for pulpits and vestings. Armozines for robes. Figured silks and satins for dress and vests. Figured silk manufactures for fancy purposes, as a memento of the Exhibition. All registered patterns.

6 ROBINSON, J. & T. Fort St. Spitalfields, Manu.— Black and coloured velvets.

7 STILLWELL & SON, 7 White Lion St. Norton Folgate, Manu.—Brocatelle for curtains, &c. Damasks. Pattern of Dalmatia robe, worn by Her Majesty at her coronation.

8 WASHINGTON & DAVIES, 13 and 14 Milk St. Cheapside, Manu.—Waistcoatings, of Spitalfields manufacture, in imitation of foreign furs.

9 WALTERS & SONS, Wilson St. Finsbury, and Kettering, Manu.—Silk plush for hats.

10 WILSON & Co. 37 Wallbrook, Manu.—Silk plush.

11 SWAN & EDGAR, Piccadilly and Regent St. Prop. —Silks, &c., Spitalfields and other manufactures. Black gros-de-Naples, Ducape, gros-de-tour, glacé, satin, satin Grecian, barrathea, Balmoral, paraphanton, watered silk, velvet, coloured damask, striped, small check, and coloured Chenie silks, &c.

12 DUTHOIT, J. 26 Steward St. Spitalfields, Manu.— Brocade garment silks.

13 BOYD, I. Spital Sq. Des. and Manu.—Registered figured damask silk furniture. White watered figured and blue tissue and gold figure garment silk. Moiré antique.

14 GREGSON & BRIEN, Gresham St. West, Agents.— Irish poplin or tabinett, plain, plaids, ribbed, double Irish, watered, and moiré antique. Manu. by W. M. Geoghegan, 50 Francis St. Dublin.

15 SEAMER, T. 5 Milk St. Cheapside, Manu.—Thirty-six inch moiré antiques, English dye and crimson velvet.

16 LEWIS & ALLENBY, 193, 195, and 197 Regent St. Des.—Brocaded ribbons. Silk, brocaded with fifteen colours. Manu. in Spitalfields.

17 GRAHAM & SONS, 31 Spital Sq. Manu.—Velvet, satin, and watered silks.

18 STONE & KEMP, Spital Sq. Manu.—Velvets. Figured and chiné silks,

19 SEWELL, EVANS, HUBBARD, & BACON, 44, 45, and 46 Old Compton St. Prop.—Brocaded silk, and rich plain moire antique, made by Campbell & Co. Spitalfields. Figured damask, by Winkworth & Co. Manchester.

20 CLARKE, JANE, 170 Regent St. Des. and Manu.—Spitalfields enamelled silks.

21 LE MARE & SONS, 27 Spital Sq. Manu. Black and coloured satinette, woven by hand and power loom. Black ducape, watered; black coloured velvet.

22 CORNELL, LYELL, & WEBSTER, 15 St. Paul's Church-yard, and Nuneaton.—Chiné and brocaded sash, and other ribbons.

23 CASEY & PHILLIPS, 13 Spital Sq. Manu.—Silk, velvets, Algerias, gros-de-Naples, glace, gros, &c.

24 ROBINSON, J. & W. & Co. 3 and 4 Milk St. Cheapside, Manu.—Velvet for pulpits; and for waistcoats. Black amozines for robes. Figured silks and satins. &c.

25 HILL, J. & Co. 30 Spital Sq. Manu.—Registered oak and ivy brocaded silk, Jacquard woven. Silk velvets. Rich shot glacés, Spitalfields hand-loom woven, the colours all British dyes. Brocaded figures, &c.

26 BROOKS, T. 26 Spital Sq. Manu.—Brilliant black gros-de-Naples; Sutherland silks, and satins; velvets.

27 HOWELL, J. & Co. Regent St.—Two richly embroidered silks, manufactured by Campbell & Co. Spitalfields. Rich chiné, 12 inch, and rich brocaded sash ribbons.

28 VANNER & SON, 15 Spital Sq. Manu.—Vest satin. Silks for parasols, &c.

29 SOPER, H. 32 Spital Sq. Bishopsgate St. Manu.—Silk for parasols. Figured satin and damask rip and ducape. Silk for umbrellas.

30 CARTER, VAVASEUR, & RIX, 9 Trump St. Cheapside, Manu.—Figured poplin dress. Rich figured satin dress. Figured satin, richly brocaded. Maize moiré antique. Napoleon blue satin.

31 CAMPBELL, HARRISON, & LLOYD, 19 Friday St. Manu.—Rich figured moiré antique damask. Scotch tartan satins and velvets. Coloured moiré antique. Rich brocade figure for vestings.

32 CROSS, C. 19 Gutter Lane.—A specimen of Jacquard silk weaving, pattern 29 inches by 24, portraits of the Queen and Prince Albert, made by a 2,400 loom, and 20,000 cords. Black and fancy cravats, plain, checked, and figured.

33 MARSHALL & SNELGROVE, 11 & 15 Vere St. and 19 Henrietta St. Cavendish Sq.—Shaded silks in glace and moiré antique; and ribbons.

34 COURTAULD S. and Co. Manu.—Specimens of crape and aerophane.

35 MASON, G. Yateley, Hartford Bridge, Hants, Prod.—Damask silk and English cloth, embroidered with silk grown and wound at Yately. Manufactured by Messrs. Houldsworth, Manchester. Fishing gut from imperfect silkworms, waste silk, and cocoons.

36 GROUT, J. & Co. Foster Lane, Manu.—Folded and rolled black crape, aerophane crape, lisse gauze, gossamer, crêpe lisse, silk gauze grenadine, muslin scarfs, and brocaded silk muslin dress, &c.

37 DEAR, A. 37 Crispin St. Spitalfields, Agent.—Figured silks, designed and woven by the pupils of the Spitalfields School of Design.

38 BROCKLEHURST & SONS, Macclesfield.—Raw, thrown, and dyed silk. Sewing silk in raw and dyed state. Spun silk exhibiting the material and its stages in process. Velvets, satins, moire antiques, glacé gros de Naples, levantines, serges, vestings, sarsnets, Persians, ribbons, handkerchiefs, scarfs, shawls, gauze veils, &c.

39 ADSHEAD, W. & Co. Macclesfield.—Silk dyed in the skein, and prepared for the use of the manufacturer.

40 CRITCHLEY, BRINSLEY, & Co. Macclesfield, Manu.—Ladies' foulard dresses, aprons, neck-ties. Gentlemen's cravats, and boys' neck-handkerchiefs.—Designs reg.

41 WARDLE, H. & T. & Co. Macclesfield, Manu.—Ladies' silk handkerchiefs, plain and checked, figured and chiné. Handkerchiefs and cravats. Small silk shawls.

42 HADWEN & SONS, Kebroyd Mills, near Halifax.—Specimens of raw material: waste silk, in the dressed state and carded; the same in the slubbing and thick roving, and in the fine rovings. Single and double spun silk yarns.

43 STUBBS, P. Leek, Manu. — Needle-worked silk buttons.

44 BROUGH, J. & J. & Co. Leek, Manu.—Sewing silks. Purse or netting silk. Leger twist; silk twist.

45 HAMMERSLEY and BENTLEY, Leek, Manu.—Twist of various colours, for tailors. Italian sewings, for tailors and milliners. Purse twist.

46 WESTON & SON, Leek, Manu.—Buttons, including Florentine, brown Holland, real twist Italian, youths' dress silk, silk fancy vest, ladies' silk dress, &c.

47 DAVIDSON, J. & Co. Leek, Manu.—Tailors' sewing silks; silk twist; milliners' sewing, and stay, embroidering silk; saddlers' silk; tram; purse twist; and silk serge.

48 ALSOP, ROBINS, & Co. Leek, Manu.—Silk serges. Black silk handkerchiefs, 20 handfacing. Prussian bindings, and sewing silk. Rich twist, dyed by W. Hammersley & Co., Leek. Netting silk. Barber's twist. Silk whip-lashes, Needlework buttons, &c.

49 BRIDGETT, T. & Co. Derby, Manu.—Specimens of sewing silk for saddlers, bookbinders, staymakers, tailors, &c. netting or purse-twist, and plain sarsnet ribbon.

50 ALLEN & HOLMES, Derby, Manu.—Black silk ribbons and braids. Algerines. Black satin trimmings. Silk warp, prepared for the manufacturer.

51 SMITH, MARY, 3A Abbey St. Bethnal Green, Des. and Manu.—Chenille shawl, made of choice silk, and manufactured in a loom made for that purpose.

52 GROSVENOR, W. Kidderminster.—Silk brocade, brocatelle, and figured satinet damasks for upholstery.

53 PULLING, J. 6 Brudenell Pl. New North Rd.—Trains of crape tunics and tucks, &c. Mantle. Elizabethans. Berthas.

54 WRIGHT, P. & R. Edinburgh, Des. and Manu.—Duke of Wellington on horseback, in silk damask.

56 WILSON, J. 5 Church Passage, Spital Sq. Manu.—Mourning hat-band, circular and elastic.

57 BURRE, T. H. 6 Bull Head Ct. Newgate St.—Embossed silks, velvets, &c.; ladies' sashes, flounces, trimmings, &c. Model of the Exhibition, embossed. Victoria mounts for drawings and prints. Embossed lace papers, handscreens, ornaments for dining-tables, &c.

58 GREENSHIELDS, W. Whitburn, Linlithgowshire, Manu. — Specimens of ornamental work, accomplished without the aid of a needle.

59 PENFOLD, O. 4 Blackmoor St. Clare Market.—Gauze diaphane for covering looking-glass and picture frames, &c.
Lowndes Ter. Knightsbridge.

60 EVANS, S. Wirksworth, Derbyshire, Manu.—Specimens of silk plush for vestings.

61 HOLDFORTH & SON, Leeds, Inv. and Imp.—Specimens of the article known as silk waste; spun silk yarns, and samples of silk yarn, dyed and finished, spun by the exhibitors' patent process.

62 HARROP, TAYLOR, & PEARSON, Piccadilly, Manchester, Manu.—Gros de Naples. Black edged ducape. Tape edged armazine. Black velour. Glace silks. Gros d'Ecosse.

63 BOOTH & PIKE, 43 Oldham St. Manchester, Manu.— Imperial or carded plush for hats, bonnets, &c., in the various stages of manufacture. Galloons, hat-bands, hat-linings, &c.

64 HOULDSWORTH, J. & Co. Portland St. Mill, Manchester, Des. and Manu.—Rich figured silk fabrics for furniture. Patent machine embroideries. Silk banners, one composed of silk grown and manufactured in England.

65 WINKWORTH & PROCTERS, Manchester, Manu.— Figured silks. Chiné silk, striped watered, and plain silks.

66 COX, R. S. & Co. 7 St. Paul's Church Yard, and Coventry, Manu.—Rich sashes and other ribbons.

67 BRAY, C. & Co. Coventry.—Ribbons illustrative of the ordinary Coventry ribbon manufacture.

68 CALDICOTT, R. & R. Coventry, Manu.—Ribbons: specimens of Coventry manufacture.

69 SHARP, ODELL, & JURY, Coventry, Manu.—Ribbons,

illustrative of a medium quality of goods manufactured at Coventry.

70 COPE, HAMMERTON, & Co. Coventry, Prod.—General fancy ribbons.

72 COVENTRY RIBBONS COMMITTEE. Specimens of Coventry ribbons.

73 RATLIFF, J. & C. Coventry, Manu.—Ribbons illustrative of Coventry manufacture. Plain satin, striped or vellum satin, and plain and pure edged lutestring ribbons; simple fancy ribbons.

75 BERRY BROTHERS, Coventry. — Figured ribbons, &c., manufactured by steam power. Ribbon trimmings for dresses.

76 HART, J. Coventry, Manu.—Group of ribbons, illustrative of cheapness of production.

77 ROBINSON, T. Coventry. — Satin, lutestring, and figured ribbons; and rich brocaded ribbons, made by steam.

78 McRAE, J. Coventry, Manu.—Mourning gauze; crape, love, and rich figured lutestring ribbons.

79 STURDY & TURNER, Coventry, Manu.—Samples of ribbons, remarkable for beauty of design, manufactured by steam power. A peculiar quality of white ribbon, &c.

80 BROWETT, W. & H. Coventry, Manu.—Bullion, sewing silk, and mohair fringes. Silk brace webs. Gimp and fancy trimmings for dresses.

Proceed to Class 2, page 22.

Class 14.   FLAX AND HEMP.
—— Areas L. M. N. O. 6 to 8. ——

1 HOLDEN, J. & Co. Belfast, Ireland, Des. and Manu.—Sewed book muslin collar capes. Caps. Infants' frock bodies. Cambric and book insertion. Sewed cambric flouncings. Linen cambric handkerchiefs. Polka jackets.

2 BROWN, J. R. & W. Bangor, County Down, Ireland, Manu.—Lady's and baby's robes, embroidered muslin.

3 DUFFERIN's, Lord, School, Belfast.—Embroidered handkerchiefs, worked by peasant girls.

4 PELLING, C. Belfast, Manu.—Lady's robe, designed by M. M'Kinsie, Belfast. Embroidered linen shirt fronts.

5 ANDREWS, M. Royal Manufactory of Linen and Damask, Ardoyne, Belfast, Ireland, Manu.—Table cloth to be presented to the Earl of Clarendon by the Royal Society for the promotion and improvement of the growth of flax in Ireland. Table cloth of new pattern, designed by J. Mackenzie, Government School of Design.

6 BELL, T. & Co. Bellview, Lurgan, Belfast, Ireland.—Samples of cambric bordered handkerchiefs, clear lawn, and plain cambric.

7 RICHARDSON, SONS, & OWDEN, Belfast, Ireland, Manu.—Double damask table-cloths, des. by W. J. Magee, Lisburne. Double damask cloth. Samples of Irish linens.

8 FLETCHER, A. Glasgow, Manu. — Patent linen thread, various.

9 LEADBETTER, J. & Co. Belfast, Ireland, Manu.—Linen drill. Fancy drill, plain checks and stripes, all linen, and mixed. Linen creas, platillas, and hollands.

10 KIRK & SONS, Annvale, Keady, Ireland.—Specimens of linen.

11 BENNETT & ADAMS, Coleraine, Ireland, Manu.—Samples of fine linen.

12 ADAMS, JANE, Strabane, Ireland, Manu.—Needlework scarf, apron, collar, and cuffs, made of linen yarn in imitation of lace.

13 CRAWFORD & LINDSAYS, 3 Lawrence Lane, Cheapside, Manu. and Bleachers.—Linen sheeting, white and brown; damask table linen, &c.

14 CARSON, R. Randalstown, Manu.—Woad, bleached, and unbleached linens.

15 PINKERTON, J. & R. Ballymoney, Ireland, Manu.—Fine linens.

16 HENNING, J. Cambray House, Waringstown, Banbridge, County Down, Ireland.—Samples of handkerchiefs, embroidered, &c. Printed linen cambric dresses; and lawns, shirt frontings; satin damasks; napkins. Damask coronation cloth, &c.

17 BROWN & SONS, Waringstown, Banbridge, Ireland, Manu.—Double damask napkins and table cloths, various.

18 SADLER, FENTON, & Co. Belfast, Ireland, Manu.—Samples of Irish flax. Specimens of Irish linen. Slate linen. Linen and brown sheeting. Creas, brittanias, estopillas, silesias, platillas, and drill.

19 M'CAY, F. Lisnashanker, Dromore, Ireland. — Bleached linen and linen netting.

20 CLIBBORN, HILL, & Co. Banbridge, Ireland, Manu.—Bird-eye diapers, manufactured from linen yarn.

21 RICHARDSON, J. & T. & Co. Springfield, Lurgan, Ireland, Manu. — Irish cambric handkerchiefs, plain, hemstitched, printed, and wreathed.

22 MALCOLM, J. Lurgan, Ireland, Manu.—Linen cambric, clear lawn, and hemstitched handkerchiefs. Shirt frontings. Lawns. Handkerchiefs of fine hand-spun yarn.

23 RICHARDSON & Co. Lisburn, Ireland, Manu.—Samples of Irish linen.

24 CORRY, BLAIN, & Co. Belfast, Ireland, Des. and Manu.—New damask table-cloths. Specimens of steampower loom manufacture applied to damask table linen. Design for a table cloth. Linen damask vestings.

25 M'MURRAY, T. & Co. Dromore, County Down, Ireland, Manu.—Bleached and unbleached linen.

26 KINNIS, W. Dunfermline, Scotland, Manu.—Damask table-cloths made of mill-spun flax yarn. Table-cloths of yarns produced by Marshall & Co. Leeds, from China grass.

27 BIRRELL, D. Dunfermline, Scotland, Manu.—Table-cloth of fine Flemish flax yarn.

28 Hunt & Son, Dunfermline, Scotland, Manu.—Double-damask linen table-cloth, manufactured for the Queen. Linen and silk wefted show-cloth, of the same design. Double-damask table linen.

29 Beveridge, E. Dunfermline, Scotland (Agent in London, W. Manvell, 12 Bow Churchyard), Manu.—Table-cloths, napkins, and doyleys. Table cloths and dinner napkins, silk and linen. Nursery and towelling diapers. Stair carpeting and crumb cloth. Table covers, three-coloured brocade, coloured tapestry, &c. mixed fabrics.

30 Sadler, —, Ironmonger Lane.—Specimens of fine linen and cambric.

31 Wilks, J. 14 and 15 Bread St.—Specimens of linen.

32 Rogers & Wroe, 134 Cheapside, Prod.—Scotch embroidered handkerchief, on French lawn.

34 Devas, Minchener, & Routledge, 24 Lawrence Lane, Prop.—Damask table linen exhibited as good and cheap.

35 Dewar, Son, & Sons, King's Arms Buildings, Wood St. Prop.—Silk and linen table-cloths ; the same, bleached. A Communion napkin. All designed by James Balfour.

36 Canter, J. Carter Brothers, Fletcher, H. T. Hattersley, Parkinson, & Co., Haxworth & Carnley, Jackson & Matthewman, Pigott & Newton, Barnsley.—Dowlasses ; pillow linens ; towellings ; dusters ; cooks' cloths ; huckabacks ; diapers ; damasks ; crumb-cloths ; stair damasks ; ticks for beds, blinds, and marquees ; ducks ; drabbets ; horse-bandages ; and railway tarpauling cloth.

37 Tee & Son, Barnsley, Des. and Manu.—Linen drills. Linen and silk and linen vestings. Fancy vestings, mixed. Plain and fancy fabric for dresses. Toilet-cover. Linen saddle rug. Printed linen and cotton yarns.

38 Walton & Co. Knaresborough, Manu.—Sheeting woven in hand-loom. Knaresborough linen. Heavy watertwist cotton sheeting. Blue linen check. Huckaback. All made by hand-loom.

39 Hibbert, T. Knaresborough, Manu.—Diaper table-cloths, table-napkins, and pocket-handkerchiefs, all made by hand-loom.

40 Emshall, G. Knaresborough, Manu.—Linen-duck sheeting. Linen shirt without seam.

41 Leeming, J. Knaresborough, Manu.—Shirtings and ticking. Linen chemise, woven without seam. All made by hand-loom.

42 Wilford & Sons, Brompton, near Northallerton, Manu.—Bleached sheeting, made from China grass. White linen drills for military trousers. New drills—1. " Commodore ;" for naval. 2. " Wellington."

43 Pegler, C. Leeds, Manu.—Double damask table-cloths ; brown and bleached napkins ; bordered linen sheets. Communion cloth, design the Last Supper, and other appropriate emblems.

44 Hayward & Sons, West Chinnock, and 93 Minories, London, Manu.—Canvas for ships' sails, known as Coker canvas. Twines, used for sewing sails.

45 Row, J. Crewkerne, Manu.—Sail-cloth, and towelling, called medical rubbers, made of flax grown in the neighbourhood.

46 Poole, J. & C. South Petherton, Manu.—Canvas for ship and yacht sails. Seaming twine, made from English flax.

47 Withey & Smith, North Perrot, near Crewkerne, Somerset, Manu.—Twines, made of flax, hemp, and cotton, for crochet knitting, netting, carpet and silk weaving, &c.

48 Finlayson, Bousfield, & Co. Glasgow ; Manufactory at Johnstone.—Patent linen thread, common satin finish, in best and second quality, for tailoring purposes.

49 Morrison & Hurn, 25 Norton Folgate, Manu.—Rope, line, and twine. Model marquee, flags, rick-cloth, horse clothing. Netting. New portable fire-escape. Bed-sacking, cocoa-fibre matting. Sacks. Waterproof cloth, &c. All patented.

50 Houghton, Sarah, Ashford, Manu.—Superfine double damask table-cloths and napkins.

50A Schwann, F. Huddersfield and Leeds.—Specimens of yarn.

51 Titley, Tatham, & Walker, Leeds, Manu.—Patent linen sewing threads. Superior patent satin finish, or polished sewing threads. Shoe threads, closing and stitching flaxes or lines.

52 Grimshaw & Wilkinson. 13 Bridge-end, Leeds.—Oiled cloths and sack covers.

53 Holdsworth & Co. Leeds, Manu.—Linen thread, patent soft satin-finish, and old finish ; linen shoe thread.

54 Hawke, E. H. Scorrier, near Truro, Manu.—Ropes of Polish or Russian, China, and Manilla hemp.

55 Day, J. Market St. Oxford, Manu.—Church bell-ropes.

56 Yeates, H. Abingdon, Manu. and Des.—Cocoa-nut and Manilla matting ; fancy cocoa-nut matting ; superior jute carpeting, &c.

57 Lockhart & Sons, Kirkaldy, Scotland, Manu.—Fine feather-bed tick, made entirely from flax. Bleached diaper bed-room towels. Double huckaback. Bags for holding flour, grain, potatoes, &c. manufactured entirely from tow.

57A Falmouth Committee.—Fishing nets.

58 Wemyss, R. Kirkaldy, Scotland, Manu.—Piece of fine four-treadle bed-tick, made entirely of flax yarn. Taken from stock.

59 Jeffrey, Robert, Mary Hill, Glasgow, Kirkaldy, Forfar, and Brechin.—Specimens of huck, dowlas, ticks, loom sheeting, diaper, &c.

60 Jameson & Co. Hull, Importer and Manu.—Hemp and flax from Russia, and jute from the East Indies, in the raw and undressed state as imported, and in several stages of manufacture. Yarn, canvas, &c. from the same.

61 Hall, J. & Co. Hull, Yorkshire, Manu.—Patent made cordage, from Baltic hemp, and patent made cordage from Manilla hemp, tarred.

62 Spyvee & Coopers, Hull, Manu.—Patent cordage for the use of sailing and steam vessels, mines, and collieries, the whale fisheries, and deep-sea fisheries. Manufactured by steam and manual labour.

63 The Dundee Local Committee, Scotland, Prod.—Loom, or yarn bleached linens, manufactured by Smeeton & Son, Dundee. Duck and sheeting, manufactured by Laing, Dundee. Dowlas, sheeting, huckaback, ducks and drills, diapers, &c. manufactured by A. Lawson, King's Kettle. Common bleached canvas, and tailor's padding canvas, manufactured by J. Mori, Dundee. Hessian, or packing canvas, striped bedding, bed sacking, padding canvas, &c. manufactured by Cox, Dundee. Flour, coal and corn sacking, jute sacking, and navy canvas, manufactured by A. Easson, Dundee. Jute carpeting, and matting made from coir and Manilla fibre, manufactured by J. Neish, Dundee. Osnabergs, manufactured by Don Brothers & Co. Dundee. Brown sheeting, manufactured by W. & J. Don & Co. Forfar. Heavy floor-cloth, manufactured by T. Bell, Dundee. Jute stair-carpeting, jute bed-sacking, cotton, or coffee bagging, and hop pocketing, manufactured by A. J. Warden, Dundee. Strong bed-tick and twilled sheeting, manufactured by J. Brown, Dundee. Striped and checked fancy linens, manufactured by J. Leadbetter & Co. Dundee.

64 Soper, R. S. 4 Blossom St. Norton Folgate, Manu.—Patent lines, of various sizes, used for hanging window sashes. Fancy skipping-ropes, &c.

65 Smith, J. East Greenwich, Manu. Specimens of ropes, lines, twines, &c., manufactured by machinery from Russia, Manilla, and Italian hemp. Irish, Baltic, and Egyptian flax and tow.

66 ULLATHORNES & LONGSTAFFS, 12 Gate St. Lincoln's Inn Fields, Manu.—Shoemakers' and saddlers' threads, &c.

67 MOORE, W. F. Crinkbourne, Douglas, Isle of Man, Manu.—Sail canvas made from long Irish flax, woven by power, without starch or dressing. Twine-canvas. Twine for sewing canvas for sails.

68 HUDDART, Sir J. & Co. Limehouse, Manu.—Tarred and untarred cordage. Power loom-woven sailcloths.

69 TULL, S. 153 Fenchurch St. and Globe Fields, Mile End Rd. Manu.—Twine, fishing lines, cords, ropes, casting nets, &c., made of differens materials.

70 WALL, E. & T. Banbury, Manu.—Cords and twines; whipcords; sash and jack lines; clothes-lines; horse-hair clothes-lines. Horses' halters. Bed sackings. Horse-hair cloth. Door-mats, &c.

71 HARFORD, G. Gateshead, Inv.—Improved sail-cloth, made by Milvain and Harford.

72 GOUROCK ROPEWORK Co. Greenock, Manu. (Agent in London, Sadler, Ironmonger Lane.)—Sailcloth; tarred cordage; Manilla cordage.

73 THE BRIDPORT LOCAL COMMITTEE. Edwards, J.; Ewens, J. B. & Co.; Gundry, J. & Co.; Hounsell, J.; Hounsell, W. & Co.; Pymore Company; Rendall & Coombs; Stephens, J. P. & Co.; Tucker, T. & Co.; Whetham & Sons; Manu.—Specimens of the staple manufacture of the town. Hemp and flax in various stages of preparation. Twines, Canvas. Webs. Fishing Nets. Lines. Shoe-threads. Seaming-twines. Bags. Sacks. Sacking. Tarpaulin.

74 HOLLOWAY, T. J. Salisbury.—Hemp and flax twines.

74A BREMNER, J. Kirkaldy.—Samples of sail-cloth.

75 DIXON & LONGSTAFF, Stockton-on-Tees, Manu.—Sail-cloth, made from Baltic long flax; hand-loom woven.

76 HARRIS & SONS, Cockermouth, Manu.—Linen threads dyed and bleached.

* The fourteen following are placed in the North Wall, near the flax machinery in Class 5.

77 BEALE BROWN, T. Andover-ford, Gloucestershire.—Sacking, tubing, tarpaulin of hemp and flax, flax great coats, &c. (With Class 5.)

78 PLUMMER, R. Newcastle.—Specimens of canvas.

79 FRASER, D. Arbroath, Scotland, Manu.—Navy bleached and boiled canvas. Improved brown canvas flax warps, &c.

80 DUNCAN, D. & Co. Arbroath, Scotland, Manu.—Hemp sail-cloth.

81 RENNY, SONS, & Co. Arbroath, Scotland, Manu.—Navy sail-cloth made for British Government. Improved sail-cloth, for the British merchant navy.

82 GORDON, G. & A. Arbroath, Scotland, Manu.—Specimens of line and tow-yarn. Sail-twine.

83 SALMOND, W. Arbroath, Scotland, Manu.—Bleached unstarched sail-cloth; mill-washed long flax sail-cloth. Tarpaulin, unstarched. Single best tow vitrie. Best brown tow double canvas.

84 GARLAND, W. Arbroath.—Fine hop pocketting.

85 RAMSAY & SMART, Arbroath, Scotland, Manu.—Sacking. Brown canvas; brown single canvas.

86 ANDERSON, C. Arbroath, Scotland, Manu.—Imperial and Russia ducks. Ticklenburghs. Russia sheeting, canvas, hemp tarpaulins, &c.

87 NICOL, A. & Co. Arbroath, Scotland, Manu.—Towelling. Sheeting. Osnaburg. Mixed-hemp sacking. Flour sacks. Rye-grass, Coffee-bags. Twine, &c.

88 CURR & Co. Arbroath, Scotland, Manu.—Brown flax sheeting; brown tow sheeting. Loom dowlas; loom sheeting. Ticklenburghs. Ducks.

89 DAGNALL & Co. Little Chelsea, Manu.—Mats and matting. Coir yarn, junk, and fibre, from Cochin, Bombay, and Ceylon. Silk grass, jute, or paut hemp, from Calcutta. Manilla hemp.

90 EDGINGTON, T. F. 45 Botolph Lane.—Composition cloth, made from the best long flax, perfectly waterproof; for railway luggage, truck covers, &c.

* THE FOLLOWING ARE PLACED WITH CLASS 11.

91 SADLER, S. 24 Ironmonger Lane, Imp.—Bleached linen, Irish manufacture, a light ornamented fabric. Heavy bleached Irish linens. Medium and sheetings.

92 COULSON, J. Lisburn, Ireland, Manu.—Fine damask table-cloths, breakfast cloths, sideboard cloths, and dinner napkins. (In both Classes.)

93 COULSON, W. Lisburn, Ireland, Des. and Manu.—Fine damask table-cloths and napkins. (In both Classes.)

95 CAPPER & SON, 99 Gracechurch St. part Inv. and Makers.—Table-covers of linen damask, as manufactured for Her Majesty. Zittaw Baden towellings, registered. Other towellings, linens, and sheetings.

96 M'LEOWNAN, J. & Co. 3 Barge Yard, Bucklersbury, Manu.—Bleached sail canvas, made from Irish flax, by hand-loom.

97 BROWN & SON, Waringstown, Banbridge, Ireland.—Unbleached damask.

Proceed to Class 18, page 95.

Class 15.   MIXED FABRICS, INCLUDING SHAWLS. (See Class 12.)

Class 16.   LEATHER, SADDLERY, BOOTS AND SHOES, SKINS, FUR, AND HAIR.
——— Areas G. H. I. J. 10 to 14. ———

1 BEVINGTON & SONS, Neckinger Mill, Bermondsey, Manu.—Skins and leather, with varieties in tanning and leather-dressing. Morocco, Cape sheep seal, lamb and kid leather, coloured, for furniture, bookbinding, shoes, and gloves.

2 SQUIRE, T. Latchford, Warrington, Manu.—Sole leather, made from hides, the produce of Buenos Ayres, tanned with Belgian oak bark and valonia, from Smyrna. Sole leather, made from English hides, tanned with equal proportions of divi divi, gambier, and valonia.

3 LUPTON, J. Chapel Lane, Bradford, Manu.—Cemented leather strapping, used as driving-belts in weaving and spinning.

4 BUSE, N. Oxford St. Swansea, Manu.—Improved calf-skins for the upper-leather of boots.

5 NICHOLLS, H. 5 Stafford St. Bond St. and 4 and 5 Birchin Lane, City, Inv. and Manu.—Waterproof tanned leather, for sporting articles. Black buckskin trousers, &c.

6 HARTLY, ELIZABETH, Knaresborough.—Woollen rugs, bonnets, muffs, &c.

7 ROBINSON, J. Waterside, Knaresborough.—Carriage rugs, hearth rugs, boas, muffs, slippers, table mats, &c.

8 HILL, G. Knaresborough.—Woollen, rugs, mats, &c.

9 CLAPHAM, J. Knaresborough.—Hearth rugs, travelling shoes and boots, muffs, boa, victorine, &c.

LEATHER, SADDLERY, BOOTS and SHOES.

10 DEED, J. S. Little Newport St. Leicester Sq. Manu. —Specimens of leather. Dyed sheep and lamb skin wool rugs or mats.

11 WILSON, WALKER, & Co. Leeds, Manu.—Coloured sheep-leather skivers; coloured roans; roller leather, for silk and cotton spinning; chamois, or wash leather. Coloured calf and morocco.

12 BENSON, C. Leeds.—Oil cake han for extracting oil from seeds.

13 HOGARTY BROTHERS, Cork, Ireland, Manu.—Boot fronts and legs; black-grained calf; calf-skins, waxed and russet, and tanned in sumac.

14 WINSOR & SON, Gt. Russell St. Bermondsey, Manu. —Rugs. Skins for cavalry, ladies' boas, &c. French dog and lamb skins. Carriage and foot muffs.

15 RHEAM, E. Hull, Manu.—Specimens of boot and shoe leathers, of French and English calf-skin. Horse-hide from Spanish America, tanned and curried in England.

16 HOLMES, T. Anlaby Road, Hull, Importer and Manu. —Specimens of tanned hide of the walrus, or sea-horse. Polishing wheels covered with the same. Heads of male and female walrus or sea-horse, taken by Capt. Gravil at the Davis' Straits fisheries.

17 STOCKILL, W. 33 Long Lane, Southwark, Manu.— Wellington boot fronts and graft, waterproof.

18 EVANS & SON, 10 Silver St. Wood St.—Parchment and chamois leather.—Direction labels.

19 GLOVER, J. & T. 7 Wood St. Cheapside, Inv. and Manu.—Improved oil leather, and gloves manu. of it, and from Irish kid skins. Improved button, &c.

20 HEMSWORTH & LINLEY, 30 West Smithfield, Manu. —Boot fronts of English and foreign calf skins. Cordovan, from South American horse hides.

21 BRINDLEY, T. Paradise St. Finsbury.—Leather reticules, dressing case, &c.

22 TOMLIN, W. Canal Bridge, Old Kent Rd. Inv. and Manu.—Superior parchment, nearly resembling vellum.

23 BYAM, ELIZA, Bazaar, Soho Sq.—Compound stationery case. Travelling, writing, working, dressing, and refreshment case. Lady's carriage companion, &c.

24 LEVER, J. & J. 13 Sise Lane, Manu.—Writing, drawing, and binding vellum. Drum and tambourine heads, and parchment.

25 WOOD, W. & S. 32 Bow St. Manu.—Calf skin in the various stages of manufacture.

27 LENNY, J. T. 12 Market St. Manchester, Inv. and Manu.—Portmanteau for travelling, with improved frame.

28 JIMISON, C. 11 Smithson St. York St. Hulme, near Manchester, Des. and Manu.—Improved portmanteau.

29 FINNIGAN, J. Manchester.—Travelling trunk.

30 JONES, W. D. High Street, Shrewsbury, Des. and Manu.—Improved patent shot-belt, and other articles, in leather.

31 SMITH & SON, 136 Strand.—Despatch boxes. Travelling, dressing, writing, blotting, and card cases, &c.

32 GEORGE, C. 102 Dean St. Soho, Imp. and Manu.— Morocco and Russia leather.

33 LAST, J. 38 Haymarket, Inv. and Manu.—Portmanteau, with five compartments. Knapsack for pedestrians, &c.

34 EAST & SON, 214 Bermondsey St. Southwark, Inv. and Manu.—Velvet-napped, embossed, coloured leather. Embossed by Messrs. Cussons and Co. 51 Bunhill Row, London.

35 ALLIN, W. 126 Drummond St. Euston Sq. Inv.— Pair of bellows, with wooden sides.

36 ALLEN, J. M. 37 Wardour St. Soho, Manu.—Homœopathic medicine cases. Tooth-powder box, to prevent the escape of the powder.

37 MOTTE, A. 16 Southwark Bridge Rd. Inv. and Manu.—Patent waterproof leather portmanteau, in one piece.

38 LAST, S. 256 Oxford St. Inv. aud Manu.—Railway portmanteau, divided into four compartments.

39 EVERETT & Co. 51 Fetter Lane.—Blacking. Varnish for dress boots. Waterproof varnish for boots, harness, &c.

40 JAMES, J. 102 Oxford St. Manu.—Registered railway trunk. Patent wardrobe portfolio.

41 JUDGE, C. 6 Sion Pl. East St. Walworth, Des. and Manu.—Leather buttons of one piece.

42 WOODMAN, W. 13 Three Colt Ct. Worship St. Finsbury, Manu.—Leather backgammon table.

43 HARROWS, G. 38 Old Bond St.—Ladies improved waterproof travelling chest.

46 MAIBEN, C. North Cottage, Vicar's Hill, Lewisham, Inv.—Saddle on an improved principle of fixing and relieving the flaps and pannel by hand.

47 READ, J. B. Penryn, Cornwall, Manu.—A tanned shaved hide, for best bridle reins; a rough tanned cow-hide for saddle-skirts and stirrup-leathers. Specimen of the leather used for gearing the buckets of pumping engines.

48 CLARK, C. & J. Street, near Glastonbury, Inv. Des. and Manu.—Model of a rural factory. Urn-rugs, muffs, &c., made from English lamb-skin. Socks for shoes, goloshes, shoes, and gaiters; hearth and other rugs of sheep, lamb, and Angola skins.

49 ROOD, G. & Co. Boltons-borough, near Glastonbury, Somerset, Des. and Manu.—Hearth, carriage, and toilet rugs, of sheep-skin and Angola goat. Sheep and Angola goat-skins.

50 COOPER, M. 25 Swingate, York, Des. Inv. and Manu.—Improved side-saddle, with pilch of Berlin wool work, by Jancowski, York. Military saddle: improved light hunting and racing saddle; Somerset saddle.

51 SOUTHEY & Co. 16 Little Queen St. Lincoln's Inn Fields, Manu.—Seal, calf, and hog skins and hides. Hippopotamus hides, &c.

52 MAXWELL & Co. 161 Piccadilly, Manu.—Socket spurs, &c. in the several stages of manufacture

53 LUTWYCHE & GEORGE, Skinner St. Snow Hill, Manu. —Goat skins, manu. in England. English sheep skins.

54 MARLOW, J. Walsall, Manu.—Steel carriage and riding bits. Spenser's patent metallic saddles. Harness, with registered mountings. Stair balustrade in malleable cast iron, possessing strength of wrought iron.

55 COX, S. Walsall, Inv. and Manu.—Newly invented Albert stirrup and stirrup leather, and improved drawmouth clipper-bit. Prov. reg.

56 BANTON, E. Walsall, Inv.—Patent enamelled waterproof horse harness. Patent Hackney riding-bit, and bridle. Hunting breast-plate, and bits.

57 HAWKINS, J. Stafford St. Walsall, Manu. and Inv.— Registered carriage and hackney bits. Registered Chifney bit. Improved steel stirrup irons, &c.

58 BRACE, H. Walsall, Manu.—Bits, stirrups, and spurs, for the South American markets.

59 PIM, J. E. Mount Mellick, Queen's Co. Ireland, Manu.—Snaffles. Snake's-head bit. Plain riding bit. Pelham stirrup irons.

60 HUDSON, S. Dublin, Inv. Des. and Manu.—Improved side-saddle, with safety stirrup. Hunting saddle with elastic seat. Light form saddle with steel-plated tree.

61 LENNAN, W. 29 Dawson St. Dublin, Manu.—Full-chased, silver and brass-mounted harness. Quilted lady's side-saddle. Hunting and steeple-chase saddles. Double and single saddles for children.

62 KANE, G. Dublin.—Portmanteaus and camp furniture.

63 LAMBERT & SON, Bermondsey New Rd. Manu.—

Wellington boot-fronts. Grain and waxed calf hides. Cordovan hides, &c.

64 ASHFORD, W. & G. Birmingham, and Houndsditch, London, Des. and Manu.—Specimens of whip manufacture; whip-sockets, registered. New design for a lady's bridle and bit, &c.

65 BROWN & SON, 7 Moat Row, Birmingham, Manu.— Specimen of cut back-head saddle-tree, whalebone springs, galvanized plates, spring bars, and copper rivets, to prevent corroding, &c.

66 PEEL, A. R. 151 Strand, Des. and Manu.—Improved Cleveland and East India hunting saddles; lady's saddle. The Victoria bridle and stirrup. Improved shaft and trace tugs.

67 MIDDLEMORE, W. 31 Holloway Head, Birmingham, Des. and Manu.—Gig harness. Saddle, with elastic seat. Embroidered lady's saddle. A new mouthing-rein for unbroken horses. Shot-pouches, &c.

68 COLEMAN, T. G. Lilley Hoo Farm, Offley, near Hitchin, Herts, Inv. and Pat.—Expanding saddle; self-acting elastic spring roller; harness, with spring trace, &c.; safety rein.

69 GARNETT, W. Tarporley, Cheshire, Inv. and Des.— A saddle, with seat, skirt, and flap in one piece, with patent spring bars to release the rider if thrown from his horse.

70 VICK, R. Gloucester, Inv.—Improved registered harness hames.

71 MUSSELWHITE, T. Devizes, Inv.—Patent elastic collar for horses, formed of iron, cork, horse-hair, &c.

72 WEIR, J. Dumfries, Inv. and Manu.—Riding saddle, with elastic seat. Neck collar, to answer the double purpose of separate collar and hames. Portmanteau, containing hat case, drawers, umbrella, &c.

73 MELLER, C. C. 15 Riding House Lane, Langham Pl. —Enamelled leather travelling bag, with improved fittings.

74 RAMSEY, W. Hull, Inv. and Manu.—Registered elastic-seated saddle.

75 CLARK, W. Mill Hill, Leeds, Des. and Manu.—A quilted summerset saddle

76 THOMAS C. Stratford-on-Avon, Manu.—Registered flexible saddle, with metal cantle, yielding to the slightest pressure, constructed to cause a circulation of air between the seat of the saddle and the horse's back.

77 CAISTOR, A. B. 7 Baker St. Portman Sq. Des. and Manu.—Hussar saddle, and hunting saddle.

78 BLACKWELL, S. & R. 256 Oxford St. Inv. and Manu. —Cab or phaeton harness, of black patent leather. Improved fetlock leg, and speedy-cut boots, &c.

79 PASSMORE, W. 27 Little Windmill St. Golden Sq. Des. and Manu.—Single-horse harness, with improved hames and furniture.

80 ATKINSON & ELDRID, 185 Regent St. Manu. and Prop.—Whips, walking sticks, riding canes. Bottles and flasks. Whistles, &c.

81 MARTIN, W. H. 64 Burlington Arcade, Inv. and Manu.—Whips and canes, &c. Walking-stick, bottle with wine-glass. Inv. by F. Whishaw, Esq.

82 SHIPLEY, J. G. 181 Regent St.—Large quilted saddle improved stirrup leather. Prov. reg.

83 SKINNER, A. Camberwell Green, Inv. and Manu.— Air-filled horse-collar, to prevent galled shoulders and jibbing.

84 HICKS, H. 52 Davies St. Berkeley Sq. Inv. and Manu.—Lady's saddle, with elastic support for the left leg. Prov. reg,

85 GREEN, R. 8 Edward St. Portman Sq. Manu.— Ladies' saddle, hunting saddles, bridles, harness, &c.

——**86** WHITE, J. C. 29 Liverpool St. City, and 185 Regent St. Inv. and Manu.—Silver-mounted harness, with improved registered tugs. Light pony and tandem harness, &c.

87 BOWMAR, C. B. Leicester.—Lapland rugs, boas, muffs, &c.

88 TISDALE, E. 34 St. Broad Golden Sq. Manu.— Officer's Hussar saddle-tree. Side saddle-tree, with a leaping-head.

89 LANGDON, W. jun. 9 Duke St. Manchester Sq. Des. and Manu.—Light phaeton harness.

90 BLYTHE, R. 4 Park Lane, Manu.—Lady's saddle, and hunting or park saddle, with improved elastic seat. Harness pad, &c.

91 PENNY, J. 37 Union St. Middlesex Hospital, Manu. —State pony bridle for the Prince of Wales, des. by W. H. Rogers, made by W. Langdon, &c.

92 SWAINE & ADENEY, 185 Piccadilly, Manu.—Riding whip, mounted with gold, set with brilliants and rubies. Whips. Canes. Improved whip-socket. Horse and other brushes, with flexible backs.

93 BELL, C. 34 Wigmore St. Manu.—Improved lady's saddles. A dress single harness, &c.

94 BYWATER, W. M. 99 Piccadilly, Des. and Manu.— Harness, with patent silvered glass front, &c. Improved Russian cavalry and other bridles.

95 MORIARTY, D. 34 Berwick St. Oxford St. Manu.— Phaeton harness. Single-horse harness, &c.

96 CUFF, R. 18 Cockspur St. Des. and Manu.—Embroidered velvet saddle, riding bridle, and harness, with gilt ornaments. Hunting and other saddles and bridles.

97 COLEGRAVE, F. E. Round Hill House, Brighton.— A saddle, made by Bartley, of Old Quebec. It is fitted with a patent saddle-girth spring.

98 WILSON & SON, 18 and 19 Vere St. Oxford St. Manu. —New safety side-saddle, in case of a fall.

99 RUTLAND, W. 199 Sloane St. Chelsea, Manu.— Lady's saddle, with moveable leaping head. Gentleman's spring saddle.

100 PEARL, J. Old Kent Rd. Manu.—Harness. Painted canvas for harness fronts, &c.

101 CANAVAN, A. 7 Wyndham St. Bryanstone Sq. Prop. —Two saddles, made by Gibson and Co. Coventry Street; one with Canavan's registered safety panel; the other with Reed's patent girth regulator. Five brushes, made of elastic buff leather, by Kent, of Marlborough Street.

102 CLARKSON, I. C.—Harness straps, &c. manufactured by machinery.

103 STOKER, J. 49 Old St., St. Luke's, Inv. and Manu. —Ladies' saddle for riding either side. Pack saddle, &c.

104 MACKIE & SON, Maidenhead, Berks, and Beaconsfield, Bucks, Inv. and Manu.—Horse collar, for heavy draught, especially up hills. Improved pony harness.

106 HUGHES, R. 52 Clifton St. Finsbury Sq. Manu.— Heraldic mountings for harness.

107 EARNSHAW, H. 91 Wimpole St. Manu.—Blue Morocco bridle, hunting breastplate, and other harness. Improved dumb jockey. Reg. Victoria and hunting bridles.

111 KIRKBY W. Caistor, Lincolnshire.—Ladies' side saddle, of superior workmanship.

112 BOOTH, J. P. South Quay, or Union Quay, Cork, Ireland, Inv. and Manu.—Victorine, boa and muff, made of the Irish turkey feather side. Victorine, made of the Irish turkey wing feathers.

114 HOOK, J. 66 New Bond St. Manu.—Ladies' riding boots; dress boots and shoes; costume boots and shoes; slippers, clogs, &c.

115 BERRALL, W. & SON, 60 and 61 Marylebone Lane, Manu.—Top boots for racing. Wellington boots. Ladies' boots. Children's boots for weak ankles. Boot fronts from skins imported in a rough state. Bark tanned soles.

116 PARKER & SONS, Wood St. Northampton, Manu.— Boots and shoes.

117 LLOYD, J. P. Northampton, Manu. — Boots and shoes.

118 BEARN & JEFFS, Parade, Northampton, Manu.— Boots and shoes.

119 MOORE, G. Northampton, Manu.—Boots and shoes.

120 LINE, W. & J. Daventry, Northamptonshire, Manu. —Boots and shoes.

121 GROOM, J. & R. Northampton, Manu.—Policemen's boots and shoes; waterproof boots; regulation army Blucher boots.

122 GRAHAM, J. 109 Naylor St. Oldham Rd. Manchester.—Pair of clogs.

124 HUTCHINGS, J. 20 Green St. Bath, Somerset, Inv. and Manu.—Elastic boots and shoes, with noiseless heels, &c.

125 LOMAS & EVES, 155 Moor St. Birmingham.—Improved boot-trees and stretchers.

127 RAMSBOTTOM, E. Merton, Surrey, Inv.—Improved clog.

128 ROBARTS, G. Tavistock, Devon, Inv.—Patent clogs.

130 THOMPSON, S. Blackburn, Manu.—Clogs, as worn by the operatives of Lancashire and Yorkshire. The same, with steel-springs in the soles.

131 ATLOFF, J. G. 69 New Bond St. Inv.—Boots, shoes, and clogs with side spring. Dress boots, with steel spring waist. Military boots, &c.

132 WALLACE, T. Brandling Pl. Newcastle-upon-Tyne, Inv.—Improved boots for children having weak ankles.

133 HENSON, W. G. Chigwell Row, Essex.—Morocco boot designed without blocking.

134A PETTITT & SON, Birmingham, Des. and Manu.— Waterproof goloshes, compounded of caoutchouc, leather, and gutta percha.

135 SAUNDERS, C. Reading, Manu.—Red morocco leg patent goloshed vandyked button boot.

137 ATHENÆUM BOOT AND SHOE WAREHOUSE, Norwich. —Boots and shoes.

139 MATHER, J. Rochdale, Lancashire, Maker.—Wellington boots, with steel spring shanks.

141 CREAK, J. Wisbech, Inv. and Manu.—Improved waterproof button, buckle, and Blucher boots. Prov. reg.

142 COWLING, J. Richmond, Yorkshire, Inv. and Manu. —Gentlemen's safe and easy shooting boots, on a new principle.

145 DOE, W. Colchester, Manu.—Improved strong high shoes.

146 NEWMAN, G. 101 Gloster Lane, Brighton, Manu.— Wellington boot, exhibited for construction and workmanship.

147 McGIBBON, J. 30 North John St. Liverpool, Manu. —Dress military boots, with revolving heel, &c.

148 BARRACLOUGH, S. Tamworth, Inv. and Manu.— Dress boots impervious to water.

149 ALLEN & SON, Treffgarne Rocks, Pembroke, Wales, Manu.—Gentleman's waterproof shooting boot.

150 HEFFORD & EACER, Derby, Manu. — Boots and shoes, ornamental leather, and satin dress Wellington. Patent top-boots, and patent shoe without a seam.

151 HUDSON, A. Cranbrook, Manu.—Pair of top boots, the legs and tops seamless.

152 WRIGHT, R. Richmond, Yorkshire, Manu.—Patent boots and shoes, free from seam or roughness under the sole of the foot.

153 VINCENT, R. Glastonbury, Manu.—Suit of leather clothes, to imitate superfine black cloth.

154 CLARK, B. 57 Lowther St. Whitehaven Manu.— Ladies' Cumberland shoe.

155 BURGESS, G. South Bridge, Edinburgh, Des. and Manu.—Improved Balmoral shooting boots. Highland brogues, worn with the full Highland costume.

156 BAXTER, R. Thirsk, Yorkshire, Inv. and Manu.— Pair of walking boots, with clogs and springs. Pair of skating boots, with springs, &c.

157 PEPLOW, W. Browning St. Stafford, Manu.—Ladies' elastic button gaiter, side lace and cashmere boots, &c. Goloshed boots. Velvet carriage tie boots. Slippers. Silk elastic cloth and button shoes; design for registration.

160 DODGE, W. Sherborne, Dorset, Manu.—A pair of hunting boots.

162 MEDWIN & Co. 86 Regent St. Manu.—Registered elastic boots, top-boots for racing, &c.

163 HALL, J. S. 308 Regent St. Manu.—A series of imitations of ancient boots and shoes, to illustrate the history of costume in England. Elastic shoe soles, cut by machinery. Elastic gaiters. Vulcanized India-rubber goloshes.

164 HALL & Co. Wellington St. Strand, Pat. and Manu. —Boots and shoes, leather-cloth, or pannus-corium.

165 LEWEN, R. G. 22 Portman Pl. Edgware Rd. Inv. and Manu.—Mechanical lasts, made from models taken from nature.

166 HARTLEY, J. 11 King St. St. James's Sq. Manu.— Top-boots of English leather; boot polish.

168 GODFREY & HANCOCK, 3 Conduit St. Regent St. Inv. and Manu.—New ladies' boots, shoes, goloshes, &c.

169 CANT, G. W. 69 High Holborn, Manu.—Patent boot-tree for bootmaker's use.

170 M'DOWALL, W. 11 Mills Buildings, Knightsbridge. —Ankle-supporting boots, for ladies and children with weak ankles, also applicable to gentlemen's boots. Prov. reg.

171 DESMOND, M. Manu.—Pair of patent-leather gentleman's boots.

173 GUNDRY, W. 1 Soho Sq.—Ladies' and children's boots and shoes, &c. Boots made of elastic silk. Cork-soled boots, with Dowie's patent elastic waistpieces.

174 MARSH, F. 148 Oxford St. — An assortment of ladies' and children's boots and shoes.

176 GOODEVE, G. 16 John St. Crutched Friars.—Pair of top boots for horse racing, weight 3½ ounces.

177 GUPPY, J. W. 2 Prince's Ct. Dorset Pl. Pall Mall East. Manu.—Ladies' cloth button boots.

178 WINTER, C. Norwich, Manu.—Ladies' elegant boots and shoes.

179 GILBERT & Co. Old Bond St.—Jockey, hunting, Holderness, shooting, and dress boots. Ladies' riding boots. (Main Avenue, West)

180 DOWIE, J. 455 Strand, Inv. Pat. and Manu.—Boots and shoes. Military boots with India-rubber waists. Model of a machine for boot and shoemakers. (Main Avenue, West.)

181 TAYLOR & BOWLEY, 53 Charing Cross, and 25 Spring Gardens, Manu.—Boots and shoes, with patent elastic waists, &c. (Main Avenue, West.)

182 HALL, R. 97A Quadrant, Regent St. Inv. and Manu. —Boots and shoes of elastic enamelled cloth, for tender feet. India-rubber goloshes and fishing-boots.

182A DODSON, J. 79 Chiswell St. Manu.—Ladies' and gentlemen's boots, shoes, and slippers.

183 GATES, T. F. 5 Upper Eaton St. Pimlico, Des. and Manu.—Improved wigs.

184 HODGES, T. 316 Oxford St. Manu.—Self-adjusting shoe, composition for waterproofing, &c.

186 PATTISON, E. 74 Oxford St.—Ladies' boots and shoes.

188 BARKER, W. G. 18 Old Cavendish St. Inv. and Manu.—Shoes, closed by an invisible elastic fastening.

189 BIRD, W. 86 Oxford St. Inv. and Manu.—Ladies' elastic boots. Registered boots, without seam in the front.

190 WILDSMITH, M. 1 Sherrard St. Golden Sq. Inv. and Manu.—Flexible Wellington boots, with springs at the sides,

191 CLARKE, E. W. 12 Southampton Row, Bloomsbury,

Manu. and Inv.—Boots and shoes. Casts and lasts for deformed feet, &c.

192 HICKSON & SONS, 20 West Smithfield, Manu. or Des. —Boots and shoes of various sorts, with samples of the materials used in their manufacture. (Main Avenue, West.)

194 HUBERT, C. 292 Regent St. Manu.—Boots and shoes. A boot and a shoe made from a single piece of leather.

195 HEATH, S. H. 38 Poultry, and 17 St. Martin's-le-Grand, Des.—Boots and shoes of soft leather, &c.

196 CROW, T. 3 Maidenhead Ct. Cripplegate, Des. and Manu.—A patent leather boot, with shell heel, &c. Full-dress boots.

197 PEAL, N. 11 Duke St. Grosvenor Sq. Manu.— Hunting and fishing boots, of waterproof leather.

198 CREMER & Co. Old Kent Rd. Manu. and Inv.—Boots on a new principle, in a complete state, and in course of manufacture.

199 ROBOTHAM, S. 28 Newton St. Birmingham, Manu. —Clogs, made of gutta percha, leather, and wood, with patent fastening.

200 BROTCHIE, R. 3 Oxendon St. Haymarket, Inv.— Boots and shoes with vulcanized soles.

201 NORMAN, S. W. 4 Oakley St. Westminster Rd. Inv. and Manu.—Ladies' cork and leather boots and shoes.

202 HOBY, G. 48 St. James's St. Manu.—Napoleon and other boots made of waterproof leather. Specimens of the leather, and cleaning composition.

203 SCHALLER, J. 19 Charles St. Middlesex Hospital, Inv. and Manu.—Waterproof boots, shoes, and overshoes, clogs, elastic gaiters, &c.

204 RIDLEY, J. { St. Paul's Chyd.—Ladies' boots and shoes.

205 WILSHIN, S. B. 86 Albany Rd. Camberwell, Manu. —Skating-boots on a new principle.

206 WALKER, E. 19 Whitecross Pl. Wilson St Finsbury, Des. and Manu.—Ladies' elastic boots. Registered.

207 WALSH, W. 9 Clipstone St., Portland Rd. Manu. and Des.—Pair of shoes.

208 STANLEY, C. 238 High St. Borough.—Model of a shoe.

209 SALTER, G. 46 Windsor St. Islington, Inv. nd Manu —New invented cork boots, waterproof and ventilating.

210 POLLETT, T. Earl's Ct. Kensington, Inv. and Manu. —Boots, with revolving leather heels.

211 THOMAS & SON, 36 St. James's St. Manu.—Household cavalry jack-boot; other boots. Highland brogues. Regulation steel and gilt spurs. Model pump.

212 GORDON, E. 6A Prince's St. Leicester Sq. Inv. and Manu.—Screw clump-sole boots, with pegged waist.

213 MITCHELL, F. 8 Cartwright St. Royal Mint, Manu. —Ladies' cork sole boots, made of royal purple silk velvet.

215 CURRIE, J. 3 Panton St. Haymarket, Inv. and Manu. —Improved waterproof boots.

216 FAULKNER, O. 30 Wigmore St. Cavendish Sq. Inv. and Manu.—Waterproof fishing or shooting boots.

219 BRIDGES, C. H. 57 Charlotte St. Portland Pl. Inv. and Manu.—Registered rotatory heel for boots and shoes.

220 BECKETT, G. 41 Fenchurch St. Manu.—Various boots.

222 LANGDALE, H. 57 Mount St. Grosvenor Sq. Manu. —Children's boots and shoes, the needlework by Ann and Helen Langdale, &c.

224 ROBERT, A. 123 Regent St. Manu.—Boots.

227 GRUNDY, T. 44 St. Martin's Lane, and 133 Leadenhall St.—Boots made of leather, soft and pliable, having a fine polish, and requiring no blacking.

228 SCOTT, S. T. Union St. Southwark.—Reg. adjusting lasts, with metallic slides and moveable toes.

230 GARNER, D. 41 Finsbury Market, Manu. and Des.

—Portable boot-trees for five kinds of boots and shoes, containing blacking brushes, boot-lasts, &c.

235 GEARY, N. St. James' St.—Military boots and gauntlets.

236 BOWLER, J. 2 Little Portland St. Manu.—Lasts, trees, and stretchers, for boots.

237 SMITH, J. Bedford, Pat.—Sorcopedes elasticus. Ladies' boot.

238 HEWLETT, A. 5 Burlington Arcade.—Busts of Her Majesty, His Royal Highness Prince Albert, and the Prince of Wales; exhibited to display a new method of artificial hair without springs, elastics, or ribbons.

240 BUTTERWORTH and Co. 9 Great Dover St. and 4 Swan St.—The registered panelastic boot.

241 MARSHALL, C. 207 Oxford St.—Ladies' boots and shoes.

242 PARKER, J. 35 Dame St. Dublin, Manu.—Boots and shoes; all made of Irish materials.

243 WEBB, E. Worcester, Manu.—Coloured hair-cloth, and cloth composed of hair and silk. Horse-hair carpet, woven like Brussels carpet.

244 BURGESS, R. 15 and 16 Opera Arcade, Charles St. St. James's, Inv. and Manu.—Improved wig. New hairbrushes. Bandoline.

245 BROWNE, F. 47 Fenchurch St. Manu. and Des.— Head-dresses of ornamental hair.

246 BOUCHET, C. 74A New Bond St. Manu.—Specimens of the new improved crochet-work in wig-making, on skin and on net.

247 BECK, R. 79 Cheapside, Manu.—Specimens showing the improvements in wig-making during the last ten years.

248 ROSSI, L. 254 Regent St. Inv. and Manu.—Wigs of various kinds.

249 WINTER, W. 205 Oxford St. Inv.—Transparent wigs, head-dresses, &c.

250 PREVOST, M. 100 St. Martin's Lane, Westminster, Inv. and Manu.—Improved wig.

251 CARLES, H. R. 45 New Bond St. Inv. and Manu. —Wigs, head-dresses, &c.

253 ISIDORE & BRANDT, 217 Regent St. Inv. and Manu. —Wigs, perukes, and other works in hair.

255 WORN, R. 17 Dawson St. Dublin, Manu.—" Gossamer" transparent Temple spring wig.

256 MADDEN & BLACK, Capel St. Dublin, Manu.—Ladies' and gentlemen's perukes, bar wig, &c.

257 DOUGLAS, R. 34 North Audley St. Inv.—Specimen of joined hair, seven feet long. Circular hair-brushes.

259 CAUSSE, D. A. 267 Regent St. Manu.—Perukes, &c.

260 MUSSA, M. 4 Victoria Rd. Pimlico, Inv. and Manu. —Improved theatrical wigs and beards.

261 PIGOTT, J. Cork, Manu.—A lady's head-dress.

262 ROBEY, W. Richmond, Surrey.—Ladies' head dress.

264 TYZACK, W. V. Norwich, Manu.—Specimens of false hair.

265 O'LEARY, J. South Mall, Cork.—Improved wig.

266 KELSEY, J. T. Lingfield, East Grinstead, Manu.— Crop hide of North Wales runt, weighing 82 lbs., used for boot and shoe soles, &c., prepared at Batnor's tan-yard, Lingfield. The tanning occupied two years.

267 DUCIE, Earl, Tortworth Park, Wotton-under-Edge, Gloucestershire.—Cart-harness, for agricultural and other purposes, with improved registered hames, by R. Vick, Gloucester.

269 TAYLOR, T. Banbury.—Ladies' and gentlemen's riding saddles, inflated with air. Hunting saddles, with patent moveable panels. Registered bits, various webs, &c.

270 OAKLEY, Tom, Maidstone, Des. and Manu.—Light lady's saddle, quilted all over, with fancy wool-work introduced.

LEATHER, SADDLERY, BOOTS and SHOES, &c.

271 SAUNDERS, F. W. Thame, Oxon, Manu.—A four-horse cart harness, for agricultural and general purposes.

272 BLOWERS, W. R. High St. Maldon, Essex, Manu.—Variety of harness for draught horses.

273 COWAN, L. Barrhead, New Paisley, Prod.—Set of cart harness.

275 COX, T. Buff Coat Lane, Norwich, Des. and Manu.—Pony harness, and fancy baskets, woven from flax grown in Norfolk.

277 CHARGE, R. Horse Market, Darlington, Durham, Manu.—Saddle, of light weight, and a good hunting saddle.

278 DAX, R. High St. Welshpool, North Wales, Inv.—Harness and riding bridles, with noseband horse-stopper to stop horses when running away.

279 POLLOCK, J. 151 Stockwell Street, Glasgow, Manu.—Complete set of Scotch horse harness, &c.

283 COZENS & GREATREX, Walsall.—Tanned and curried leather for bridles, &c. Curried hog and seal-skins.

284 RANDALL & DICKS, 21 Greek St. Soho, Manu.—Skins for oil leather, in raw state and in various stages of manufacture.

285 PULLMAN, R. W. & J. 17 Greek St. Soho, Manu.—Specimens of oil leather in various stages of dressing.

286 OASTLER & PALMER, Grange Rd. Bermondsey, Manu.—Japanned enamelled hides. Calf skins and crop butts.

288 JACKSON, R. B. 9 Hampstead St. Fitzroy Sq. Inv.—New mode of restoring Morocco leather.

289 GEORGE, J. 81 Dean St. Soho, Manu.—Gilt and painted, embossed and gilt, and other ornamental leathers.

290 DIXON & WHITING, Bermondsey, Manu.—Samples of enamelled, japanned, and coloured hides. Extremely large hide split. Hide split into three, the grain enamelled, and the two splits japanned.

293 BOUTCHIER, MORTIMER, & Co. Bermondsey, Prop.—Hides, leather, and tanning materials.

294 BOSSARD, J. 7 Church St. Russel St. Bermondsey.—Leather. Boot fronts, &c.

297 TOMBS, E. Theberton St. Islington.—English calf skin.

298 BRANSCOMBE, S. Liverpool, Manu.—Tanned buffalo hides, imported from Cape of Good Hope in 1847, and tanned at Lynn, in Cheshire.

299 HEINTZE, L. 1 School Lane, Liverpool, Imp.—Black japanned calf-skins, tanned and prepared by Heintze and Freudenberg, Weinheim, near Mannheim, on the Rhine.

300 BROWN, A. Milsom St. Bath, Inv.—Peruke, manufactured without stitching.

301 HUDSON'S BAY Co.—An assortment of skins from the polar regions. (Main Avenue, West.)

301A NICHOLAY & Co. Oxford St. a large collection of skins from all parts of the world, and manufactured furs. (Main Avenue, West.) Hunting jacket from the skin of an English stag, the property of Major Neville.

302 POLAND, SON, & MEREDITH, 52 Bread St. Cheapside, Des. and Manu.—Leopard and other hearth-rugs.

303 SAMSON, P. 1 Little Knight Rider St.—Fur articles, embroidered in chenille, &c. in floral and figured designs. Fur collar. Fur and imitation fur elastic cuffs.

304 MEYER, S. & M. Bow Lane, City, Manu.—Dressed English rabbit skins, riding boas, muffs, gloves, &c.

305 ELLIS, G. 23 Fore St. Des. and Manu.—Boas, victorines, muffs, &c. in fur and velvet.

306 DRAKE, R. 25 Piccadilly, Manu.—Russia sable, spotted ermine, and grebe muffs. Coronation robes. Astracan lamb's skin.

307 CLARKE & SONS, 157 Cheapside, Manu.—Manufactured furs of ermine, mink, and musquash, natural and dyed.

308 CALLOW & SON, 8 Park Lane, Inv. and Manu.—Riding whips, of clarified rhinoceros hide. Riding and driving whips, with the handle of hippopotamus leather, enamelled green.

309 INCE, J. 75 Oxford St. Manu.—Royal tiger-skin rug, mounted with black bear. Two coronation ermine muffs, one inflated with air, the other folded up.

310 LUTGE & PARSONS, King Edward St. Manu.—Registered Russia sable, Princess Royal, American sable, mink, ermine, minevir, chinchilla, squirrel, and seal boas.

310A SMITH & SONS, 10 Watling St. Manu.—Fur muffs, cardinals, flat boas, riding boas, cuffs, &c.

311 DICK, A. 35 George St. Edinburgh, Manu.—Fur hearthrug, worked with upwards of 2,500 pieces of martin, sable, rabbit, ermine, squirrel, kolinsky, &c.

312 GARNER, D. 41 Finsbury Market, Manu. and Des.—Registered portable boot-tree, adapted for button-boots, shoes, &c.

313 HIDDEN, T. 88 London Rd. Southwark, Manu.—Leather buttons, with flexible shanks. New leather beads.

314 CORRY, J. & J. Queen Camel South, near Sherborne.—Specimens of kid and lamb leather curried.

315 CASE, C. 45 Wood St. Cheapside, Manu.—Riding whips, of black and white twisted whalebone. Walking sticks and gig whips, &c.

316 MARSDEN, C. Waterloo House, Kingsland Road, Inv.—Patent ventilating boots and shoes.

317 LEATHART, C. 15 John St. Waterloo Rd.—Liquid hair dye.

318 TAYLOR, T. Dublin, Inv. — Specimen of soluble leather.

319 PHIPPS, W. D. Cadogan House, Sloane St.—The Eupadian registered elastic spring boots.

320 HADLEY, R. High St. Worcester, Manu.—Ladies' ornamental hair.

321 MANTEL, W. Bedford.—Three improved wigs.

322 CARR, W. 10 Hatton Wall.—Improved premier blacking.

323 NEWCOME, J. Swinegate, Grantham.—Shoes made from a new material.

323A ADCOCK & Co. 3 Princes St. Cavendish Sq.—A choice collection of dyed feathers. (Main Avenue, West.)

324 NELSON, J. Holloway.—Boots warranted to wear in centre of sole.

325 CARRON, W. Birmingham.—Patent clogs.

326 ESSEX, J. 1 Charterhouse Lane, St. John St. Manu.—Fancy lamb and sheep-skin wool rugs for hearths, carriages, &c. Carriage feet muffs, and wool boots.

327 ALLIN, W. S. 1 Dorset Mews East, Baker St.—Pair of boots which have not been cleaned for two years.

328 LUTGE & Co., King Edward St. Manu.—Princess Royal boas in Russian and American sable, mink, ermine, mineva, seal, and chinchilla. Large rug, with rare skin in centre, surrounded by the Royal and other arms.

329 BOWER, M. Birmingham, Manu.—Patent screen saddle, by which a horse's loins can be covered while standing, by a pair of reins which lie over the dash-board.

330 LAYCOCK & SONS, Porto Bello Pl. Sheffield.—Plain satin and fancy hair seating, in black and coloured damasks. Samples of curled hair. Raw materials. (Placed in Class 11.)

331 McDOUGALL, D. Inverness.—Highland stalking-boots and dress shoes.

332 BEVINGTON & MORRIS, 67 King William St. City, Manu.—Sheep-wool and Angora goat mats for hearth rugs, carriages, &c. Furs, including cardinals, muffs, boas, &c.

333 LITTLEHALES, P. Sunderland.—Boot showing fine stitching. (South-east Corner, United States Department.)

Proceed to Class 27, page 137.

Class 17.   PAPER, PRINTING, AND BOOKBINDING.

—— **Areas F. 27 to 29; G. H. I. J. 26, 27.** ——

1 ACKERMAN & Co. 96 Strand.—Envelope case. Sea weeds. Pole screens. Ornamental colour box. Scrap book.

4 HUGHES, E. Greenwich Hospital Schools, Des.—An improved map of the British islands, physical, political, and industrial. Map of Palestine and adjacent countries.

5 REMNANT, EDMONDS, & REMNANT, 9 Lovell's Ct. Paternoster Row.—Specimens of binding in morocco, vellum, Russia, and calf, elegant, plain, and antique. Sheep and cloth, plain and elegant.

7 HAWTHORNE, J. 77 Charrington St. Manu.—Various descriptions of writing inks, and the materials from which they are made. Specimens of hair dyeing with ink. Nutgalls, fruit of the Terminalia Chebula, from Bengal. Inks.

8 EVANS, J. S. 64 Berwick St. Soho, Manu.—Bookbinding; and leather stained in imitation of woods.

9 FAIRBAIRN, R. 37 Gt. Cambridge St. Hackney Rd. Manu.—Specimens of wood type for printing, &c.

10 FISHER, J. H. New North Rd. Hoxton, Inv.—Specimen of bank note printed in chemical water-colour, in two colours at one operation.

11 GALLARD, W. 30 Lisson Grove, Des.—Portable frame for cases at the imposing stone, or for extra cases.

12 GILL, T. D. 27 Charlotte St. Fitzroy Sq. Inv.—Postage stamp expedient, for saving time, &c.

14 BINNS & GOODWIN, Bath. — Treatise on British grasses with natural illustrations.

17 HIDER, ELIZABETH, 15 Manor Pl. King's Road, Chelsea, Des. and Manu.—Fancy floral paper for valentines.

18 DEAN & SON, 35 Threadneedle St.—Ornamented and illustrated letter and note paper.

19 STIDOLPH, —, 2 New Bond St., Bath, Inv.—" The Chiragon," or hand-guide for blind and tremulous writers.

20 HUGHES, G. A. 9 Mount Row, Westminster Rd. Inv. (Blind)—Machines for enabling the blind to write, calculate, and copy music, &c.

21 HYDE & Co. 61 Fleet St. Manu.—Rider's new mode of taking impressions from intaglios. Solid India and other sealing-wax.

22 KING, T. & J. H. 4 Bartlett's Buildings, Holborn Hill, Des. and Manu.—Specimen of a new type-music. Original design of a series of letters called arabesques.

23 KIRBY, J. 103 Cornwall Rd. Lambeth.—Split paper, and improved method of mounting woodcuts.

24 LEIGHTON, J. & J. 40 Brewer St. Golden Sq.—Specimens of bookbinding and processes, designs by Luke Limner. Imitations of old printing, &c.

25 LLOYD, R. 26 Birchin Lane, Inv. Pat. and Manu.—Cork cut by machinery, to preserve books and paintings from damp.

26 MACOMIE & Co. 6 Percy St. Bedford Sq. Manu.—Specimens of pulpit, family Bible, and other binding. A clock case.

27 MANSELL, J. 35 Red Lion Sq. Des. and Manu.—Ornaments for decorating linens, cloths, &c. Embossed and perforated Bristol boards. Paper. Envelopes and cards, &c.

29 MARTIN, J. Pat.—Waterproof paper. The paper manufactured by Mr. Pearson, Branthwaite.

31 PARSONS, FLETCHER, & Co. 22 Bread St. Manu.—Printers' inks, black and coloured.

32 PENNY, H. 11 Old Bailey, Manu.—Metallic pocketbooks.

33 PINCHES & Co. 27 Oxendon St. Manu.—Illuminated note paper. Stamping in relief. Smith's improved stamping press. Medal, button, and other dies.

34 ROYSTON & BROWN, 40 & 41 Old Broad St. Manu.—Specimens of bank notes and bills of exchange, engraved by a patent process to prevent forgery. Various account books.

35 SAPSFORD, N. 17 Kirby St. Hatton Garden, Manu.—Specimen of bookbinding.

36 SAUNDERS, T. H. Queenhithe, and Dartford, Kent, Manu.—Parchment paper. Bank-note papers. Glass transparency to show the water mark. Safety paper for cheques, &c.

37 SAUNDERSON, C. Kilburn Lodge, Kilburn, Prop.—Map of Ireland, by J. Dower.

38 SCHLESINGER & Co. 8 Old Jewry—Registered metallic memorandum books. Pocket-books. Letter-clips. Parallel rulers.

40 SILVERLOCK, H. 3 Wardrobe Ter. Doctors' Commons, Des.—Letterpress printing from stereotype plates of medallion and machine engraving.

41 SMITH, J. 42 Rathbone Pl. Inv. and Manu.—Adhesive envelopes. &c.   Dowse's tracing and writing cloth.

42 SPICER BROTHERS, New Bridge St. London, Wholesale and Export Stationers, Prop.–Writing papers, Joynson's extra superfine quality. Large bank post. Imperial, royal, and demy. Foolscap, for account books. Superfine plate papers for engravings and lithograph printing. Superfine printing papers. Fine news. Fine long elephant, in a sheet of 750 yards in length. Fine double long elephant, in one sheet 46 inches wide and 2,500 yards in length, for paper staining, &c. Long elephant, for paper hangings. Brown papers from pure rope, very tough for packing. A sheet of brown paper, 93 inches wide, 420 feet long. Millboards, for bookbinding, &c.

42A JOYNSON, W. St. Mary Cray, Manu.—Specimens of writing paper. Large bank post, blue wove, blue laid, and cream laid post; cream laid and blue laid foolscap.

43 TARRANT, A. 190 High Holborn, Manu.—Specimens of bookbinding.

44 THOMAS & SONS, 20 Cornhill, Manu.—Ledgers in various sizes and bindings.

45 TURNBULL, J. L. & J. Holywell Mount, Shoreditch, Manu.—London drawing boards. Royal drawing boards. Coloured crayon boards, &c.

46 WATERLOW & SONS, 66 London Wall, Manu.—Account books, with patent backs, and general stationery.

47 WEDGWOOD, R. 84 Lombard St. Manu.—Patent manifold writer. Improved noctograph for the blind, &c. Registered desk clip.

48 WESTLEY, J. Playhouse Yard, Blackfriars—Specimens of bookbinding by hand and by machinery. Designs by Luke Limner.

49 WHITAKER, R. 13 & 14 Little Britain—Playing-cards, the backs ornamented in gold and colours.

51 WHITEMAN, F. J. 19 Little Queen St. Holborn, Manu.—Improved perforated plates for marking linen, &c. (In North Gallery, F. 18.)

52 WIDNALL, G. F. 6 Harrow Rd. Paddington, Inv.—Railway, omnibus, and toll-bar pocket-book and purse.

53 WILLIAMS, J. 29 Bucklersbury, Manu.—An assortment of ledgers.

55 ARLISS & TUCKER, 15 Frith St. Soho, Inv. and Manu.—Views of the Exhibition Building, printed on tinfoil, &c.

56 ATKINSON, W. Lambs' Passage, Finsbury, Manu.—Dyed and embossed calico, for bookbinding purposes.

59 BATTEN, D. Clapham Common, Manu. — Guard books, and specimens of bookbinding.

60 BENNER, Dr. W. Cheyne House, Collegiate School, Chelsea, Inv. — Complete phonological English alphabet. Mechanical syllabicator and instructor.

61 BINGLEY, M. 10 Lawrence Pountney Lane, Inv. and Manu.—Patent headbands for bookbinding, made by machine.

62 BONE & SON, 76 Fleet St.—Specimens of bookbinding, showing the present state of the art.

63 BOWDEN, G. 1 Little Queen St. Holborn, Inv. and Manu.—Registered artist's economical desideratum, containing seat, and the necessary requisites for sketching.

64 BRETNALL, T. D. Manu.—Patent paper cloth, in rolls of 100 yards, transparent and opaque.

65 CAHN, D. 16 Wilson St. Finsbury, Manu. and Imp. —Vine and ivory blacks for printers, dyers, japanners, paperstainers, and curriers.

66 CANDY, T. H. King's College, Strand, Inv.—Map of the globe, the meridians of equal length, and the parallels of latitude in their true proportion.

67 CHURTON, E. 26 Holles St. Des.—Specimens of bookbinding; each work ornamented according to the era or the subject of which it treats.

68 CLARKE, J. 61 Frith St. Scho—Various specimens of bookbinding.

69 CUSSONS & CO. 51 Bunhill Row.—Bookbinders' cloth dyed, embossed, and finished by the exhibitors.

71 CLEMENTS, J. 21 & 22 Little Pulteney St. Golden Sq. Inv.—Material for bookbinding, or other purposes where plain or ornamental surfaces are required.

73 COOKE & SONS, 84 Cannon St. Manu.—Coloured, embossed, and transparent sealing-wax.

74 CRUCHLEY, G. F. 81 Fleet St. Des.—Large map of England and Wales, consisting of 65 sheets, each 24 by 19 inches, at two miles to the inch; and other maps.

76 DE LA RUE & CO. 110 Bunhill Row, Manu.—Envelope folding and gumming machine, invented by E. Hill and W. De la Rue. Samples of stationery, and specimens of printing and bookbinding.

77 ARMSTRONG, J. 11 Gt. College St. North, Camden Town, Sculp.—Specimens of illustrated music printing.

78 CASLON & CO. Chiswell St.—Specimens of caligraphic type, engraved, &c. by E. Baileau. Colours for ornamental printing.

79 DOBBS, KIDD, & CO. 134 Fleet St. Des. and Manu. —Embossed drawing-boards, cards, and paper. Lace-bordered cards and paper. Application of embossing to the fine arts.

80 STOKES, R. Ivy Cottage, Kingsland, Inv.—New chemical ink for writing on paper or parchment besmeared with grease, for butchers, bakers, oilmen, conveyancers, &c.

83 HEYWOOD, J 170 Deansgate, Manchester, Manu.— Copy-books, with printed headings, and in two qualities of paper.

84 HAMER, A. Horsforth, near Leeds, Manu.—Cloth papers for pressing and finishing woollen cloths. Press papers for stuff goods. Gun wadding.

85 HASTINGS & MELLOR, Leeds, Manu.—Press papers, for woollen cloths. Brown papers, glazed and unglazed, for wrapping up, &c.

86 KNIGHT, J. Y. 39 Briggate, Leeds, Manu.—Ledgers and smaller account-books.

87 BAGSTER & SONS, 15 Paternoster Row, Prod.—Polyglot bible, printed in separate pocket volumes, which correspond, page for page, with each other. Other specimens of typography.

88 CROSS, G. New Coventry St. Inv. and Manu.—Print collector's improved scrap-book, without guards.

89 RIVIERE, R. 28 Gt. Queen St. Lincoln's Inn Fields, Des.—Specimens of bookbinding.

90 FERGUSON BROTHERS, Edinburgh, Manu.—Specimens of printing type.

91 NEIL, R. 13 North Bank St. Edinburgh, Des. and Manu.—Bookbinding. An imperial quarto Bible, splendidly bound, with case, &c.

92 SINCLAIR, DUNCAN, & SON, Whiteford House, Edinburgh, Des. and Manu.—Small founts of music type of different sizes and body, with specimen pages, &c.

93 WATERSTON, G. Edinburgh, Manu.—Specimens of sealing wax and wafers.

94 MACKENZIE, W. London St. Glasgow, Inv.—A volume printed in church text, illuminated with red capitals, both colours printed from the same form.

96 BANCKS BROTHERS, Weirhouse Mill, Chesham.— Writing-papers, with ornamental designs, and autograph signatures in the water-mark, &c.

97 BUDDEN, E. Cambridge, Des. and Manu.—Bookbinding:—Album, inlaid in colours; the leaves gilt, silvered, and painted with colours, &c. Bible in purple morocco, with gilt cover and joints.

98 WHITELEY & SONS, Stainland.—Press boards.

100 SMITH, E. Felling Shore, Gateshead, Prod.—Glazed brown paper, by Gallon and Co., paper brokers, Felling Shore. Glazed by improved process.

101 COWAN, A. & SONS, Valley Field Mills, near Edinburgh; and 45 Upper Thames St. Pat.—Specimens of paper: cream-laid and blue-laid post; bank post; demy and medium for account-books; demy for bank notes, banker's checks, &c.; letters and notes, with views in oil-colours; envelopes in packets, and account books in various bindings.

102 WILDES, W. Snodland, Rochester, Des. and Manu. —Specimens of writing paper ornamented by wreaths of various flowers in water-mark. Design registered.

103 WISEMAN, H. R. 9 Trinity St. Cambridge, Manu.— The King's Bible, printed at the Pitt Press, Cambridge, bound in royal scarlet morocco, illuminated vellum fly-leaves, tooled edges, &c.

104 BOWER, BROS. Sheffield.—Specimens of typography.

106 CUNDALL & ADDEY, 21 Old Bond St. Publishers.— Specimens of bookbinding: in gold paper, morocco, and cloth, by J. Hayday. Metal ornaments, by T. Burt & Sons.

107 KNIGHT & HAWKES, 13 Clerkenwell Close, Manu.— Stereotype casts, in English, German, Irish, Syriac, Hindostanee, Chaldee, Persian, and other type; from engravings in wood, steel, &c. Stereotype plates for surface printing in colours, and for embossing.

108 ROCK BROTHERS & PAYNE, 11 Walbrook, Manu.— Scrap books—views of England. Account books, &c.

109 ORR, W. S. & CO. Amen Corner.—Specimens of plain and ornamental binding. Series of maps, illustrating the physical features and phenomena of the globe.

110 PECKERD, J. P. Des.—Tate's exchequer ink.

111 WESTLEYS & CO. Friar St. Doctors' Commons, Manu.—Specimens of bookbinding, in plain and ornamental styles.

112 FOLKARD, W. J.—Specimens of printing from wood blocks, &c.

113 EVANS, E. Yorkshire St. Oldham, Des.—Specimens of typography.

117 MACNAIR, W. Glasgow. — Specimens of bookbinding.

118 STIRLING, W. Kenmure House, Glasgow, Prop.— Bible printed in Scotland in 1811; only 100 copies were printed on large paper; bound in white morocco, and gilt, as a specimen of bookbinding.

119 TODD, J. Perth, Manu.—Writing inks and ink powders, known as the Perth writing inks.

120 PARKER, J. H. Oxford, Prop.—Illustrated books.

121 PLOWMAN, J. St. Aldate's St. Oxford, Inv. and Manu.—Portable letter-case, for taking copies of letters, written in ink, by the mere pressure of the hand.

123 COCKS, R. & Co. New Burlington St. part Manu.—Dr. Boyce's collection of cathedral music, by J. Warren; a specimen of the art of engraving and stamping musical notes on plates of pewter; also of music, printing, and book-binding.

124 FIGGINS, V. & J. West St. Smithfield, Manu.—A form of pearl type, containing upwards of 220,000 pieces of moveable metal, and weighing 140 lbs. Supported only by the lateral pressure of locking-up. Exhibited to illustrate the truth of type manufacture. A type mould, polytypes, electrotypes, &c.

127 NOVELLO, J. A. 69 Dean St. Soho, and 24 Poultry, Prod.—Specimens of music type, and a sketch of the method of printing music from moveable types, &c.

128 MANCHIN & MOREL, 8 Wilson St. Gray's Inn Rd. Manu.—A wood-cut, bituminous stereotype plates, and engravings.

134 CLARK, W. Dunfermline, Scotland, Des.—Specimens of bookbinding.

135 CLARK & DAVIDSON, Mauchline, Scotland, Manu.—Specimens of bookbinding in wood boards, ornamented with arabesques, &c. Metallic books, with arabesques, &c. Ornamented wood flower-vases. Work-box. Crochet snuff-boxes, &c. of fancy wood, with imitation of tartan.

136 BRADBURY & EVANS, Whitefriars. — Specimen of letter-press and wood-cut printing.

137 DUDMAN, J. Camberwell Pl. New Rd. Inv.—Specimens of three sorts of self-sealing envelopes.

139 WRIGHT, J. 14 and 15 Noel St. Soho.—Various specimens of bookbinding, including the illuminated books of the middle ages, by H. Noel Humphrey and Owen Jones.

140 PICKERING, W. 177 Piccadilly.—The Victoria Book of Common Prayer. King Edward VIth's Book of Common Prayer, with musical notes by John Merbecke, 1550. Euclid, the first six books, with coloured diagrams and symbols. Specimens of the decorative art of the middle ages, by H. Shaw.

141 ELLIS, H. Hardwick Place, Dublin. — Original poems, by the exhibitor.

142 RALPH, F. W. 36 Throgmorton St. Manu.—Registered polychrest envelopes, combining the note and envelope.

143 DEWDNEY, J. Cullompton.—Specimens of paper.

144 BYAM, ELIZA, Bazaar, Soho Sq.—Compound stationery case; travelling, writing, working, dressing, and refreshment case; lady's carriage companion, &c.

147 LAMB, J. Newcastle-under-Lyme, Manu.—Pottery tissue papers, used for printing china and earthenware from copper rollers and plates. Specimens of old rope from which the paper is manufactured.

148 NEWBERY, J. & R.—Gold and coloured papers, for bookbinding, &c.

149 VENABLES, WILSON, & TYLER, 17 Queenhithe, Manu.—Specimens of the present state of the paper manufacture in Great Britain, classified and arranged in portfolios and reams. Specimens of the materials used.

150 MILLER & RICHARD, Edinburgh, Founders.—A specimen of the smallest types ever manufactured in this country, cut and cast expressly for the Great Exhibition. The whole of Gray's Elegy, consisting of thirty-two verses, is contained in two columns, 3¾ inches deep.

151 AUSTIN, W. 5 Furnival's Inn Pl. — Fancy boxes, &c.

152 BURKE, —.—Bull Head Ct. Newgate St.—Fancy stationery.

153 HAMPSON, B. 14 Fountain St. Manchester.—Labels, tickets, &c. used to ornament manufactured goods.

154 RELIGIOUS TRACT SOCIETY, 56 Paternoster Row, Prod.—Religious books and tracts, printed in the languages and dialects of Great Britain, Western, Northern, Central, and Southern Europe; Asia, Africa, North America, and Polynesia.

155 SWANN, T. F. 43 Southampton Buildings, Inv. and Manu.—Specimens of red marking-ink for linen, silk, &c.

156 WEBB, W. 34 Southampton Buildings, Chancery Lane.—An improved instrument for writing with pens and ink several copies simultaneously.

157 HOOD, J. H. 25 Red Lion Sq.—Improved portfolios. Illuminated vellum binding, &c.

158 LEIGHTON, JANE & ROB. Harp Alley, Shoe Lane.—Specimens of bookbinding by machinery, each book being ornamented at a blow by an engraved die. Designs by Luke Limner.

159 WODDERSPOON, J. 16 & 17 Portugal St. Lincoln's-Inn-Fields.—A specimen of ledger and index, showing the introduction of the registered vellum cloth bands, whereby the binding is strengthened, and the leaves secured from coming out by wear.

160 GILL, H. Dublin. — Various quarto and octavo volumes. Specimens of illustrated printing.

162 RAINS, T. 24 Gt. Ormond St. Queen's Sq.—Specimens of bookbinding.

163 LEWIS, Mrs. C. Duke St. St. James's.—Specimens of bookbinding.

164 WATTS, W. M. 12 Crown Ct. Temple Bar.—Oriental and other types in sixty-seven different languages or dialects. The Lord's prayer in Chinese, and in embossed characters for the blind.

165 ISAAC, J. R. 62 Castle St. Liverpool, Inv.—Registered cabinet, in oak, for containing maps, diagrams, &c. Registered music and reading desk. Bottles in earthenware and glass, with lip for holding ink.

166 HODSON, J. S.—Portugal St. Lincoln's Inn.—Specimens of letterpress printing in various colours.

167 CAFFRY, J. 18 Palace Row, Armagh, Ireland.—A copy of a one pound Ulster bank note, executed on Bristol board with a common pen.

168 LINES & Co.—Blue writing fluid, &c.

169 BRETTELL, T. Rupert St. Haymarket.—A hymn for all nations, by M. F. Tupper, D.C.L. F.R.S.; translated into thirty languages. The music composed by S. Sebastian Wesley, Mus. Doc.

170 EDINBURGH SCHOOL FOR THE BLIND, Abbey Hill, Edinburgh.—Dr. Foulis's tangible ink for the blind, producing raised characters on paper; manuscript music notation for the blind, &c. Mr. Gall's typhlograph, a simple apparatus to teach the blind to write; system of arithmetic for the blind, and types by which blind persons can correspond with one another, &c.

171 GALL, J Myrtle Bank, Edinburgh, Inv.—Gall's triangular alphabet for the blind; Gall's apparatus for writing by and to the blind.

172 BAXTER, —, Fromefield School, Frome, Somerset. —The national anthem, with music, copied on a large scale, for school teaching.

172A WEBB, ELIZ. Kirby Hall, Horton.—Church services, ornamented with needlework.

173 HARRIS & GALABIN, 142 Fenchurch St.—Account books, ledgers, &c.

174 MUIR, R. Dunlop St. Glasgow, Inv.—Electro-stereotype plate for letter-press printing, from a mould of gutta percha, taken from a page of diamond type in a screw-press.

175 WYLD, J. Charing Cross East, 454 West Strand,

2 Royal Exchange, and the Gt. Globe, Leicester Sq.—A General Atlas, containing 67 maps of the various parts of the world, describing their respective, physical, and political features, including all the recent discoveries. Other atlasses; maps and globes.

176 LOVEJOY, G. Reading, Berks.—Permanent or indelible black writing ink, not affected by age or any of the ordinary chemical agents.

177 SHEAN, W. J. Halsey Ter. Cadogan St. Chelsea.— Class roll, or school attendance register book.

178 WILSON, R. Whitehaven.—Specimen of penmanship.

179 GALBRAITH, W. 26 Bennett St. Blackfriars Rd.— Various samples of ink.

180 OWEN, H. Falcon Sq. Des.—A specimen of typography, being the speech of H. R. H. Prince Albert at the Mansion House banquet, in various languages.

181 KRONHEIM & Co.—A variety of fancy borders.

182 STEPHENSON, BLAKE & Co.—A varied assortment of printing type.

183 DAVIS, J. 1 Duke St. North Parade, Bath.—New system of music.

184 REED & PARDON, 1, 2, and 3 Lovell's Ct. Paternoster Row.—Various specimens of printing type.

185 TAIT, W. J. Church St. Rugby.—A variety of school outlines.

186 HUME, Rev. W. E. White Colne, Halstead.—The Jubilee almanack on vellum, with poetical illustrations.

187 RAMSAY, R. 2 Greenside Pl. Edinburgh.—Specimens of ornamental typography.

188 WASON, R. Esq. M.P. Corwar, Girvan, Ayrshire, Glasgow.—Plan of an estate.

189 BARKER, J.—Casts from wood matrices for the use of silk, cotton, and other printers.

190 MEEK, G. 2 Crane Ct. Fleet St. Manu.—Ornamental perforated papers, representing lace and crochet work.

191 TAPPERELL & INNES, 2 Winchester St. Old Broad St.; and Queen's Arms Hotel, Cheapside.—Ancient map of the Cities of London and Westminster, and the adjacent districts, as they appeared in the early part of Queen Elizabeth's reign. In this ancient map and drawing, the palace of Westminster, the government and public edifices, &c., are very clearly indicated.

192 WHITBREAD, J. 142 Oxford St.—A map of London.

193 RUFF & Co. 2 and 3 Hind Ct. Fleet St.—Map of London and its environs, on a scale of eight inches to the mile, showing the division of parishes, &c.

194 RICKMAN, W. C. 21 Park Side, Hyde Park Corner. —Portfolio bracket, opening and shutting.

195 BESLEY R. & Co. Fann St. Aldersgate St.—Specimens of printing types. A complete set of Elizabethan or church text, with initial letters of the Tudor period. Typographical ornaments, taken from the remains of Nineveh and Etruria. Court hands, Persian, Syriac, and Arabic. A type-founder's mould. Matrice, with types attached.

196 BARRITT & Co. 173 Fleet St.—Specimens of ecclesias-

tical binding, in carved wood and polished oak, with electrotype mountings; solid metal covers, &c.

197 PITMAN, T. 5 Nelson Pl. Bath.—Chart of the phonographic and phonotypic alphabets. The Bible, &c., printed phonetically, and the Testament in phonetic short-hand.

198 SOCIETY FOR TEACHING THE BLIND, Avenue Rd. Regent's Park.—Embossed books on the stenographic system. Cyphering boards. Raised maps. Embossed copies for writing. Geometrical boards. Apparatus for writing, musical characters, and chess-board, the inventions of Mr. Wood. Specimens of basket-work and knitting.

199 GARDNER, W. H. Troy House, Manningtree, Essex, Des. and Exec.—Specimen of penmanship.

200 ANDERSON, D. Glasgow, Prop.—Copies of engraving executed with a common pen, in China ink, by Joseph Lindsay, a deaf mute, and pupil of the Glasgow Deaf and Dumb Institution.

201 BRITISH AND FOREIGN BIBLE SOCIETY, Earl St. Blackfriars, Prod. — Specimens, containing 165 books, in different languages from the 170 versions of the Holy Scriptures, either in whole or in part, which have been published directly or indirectly by the Society, and of which 118 are from translations never before printed; and of which more than twenty-four millions of copies have been circulated since its institution in 1804. Eight specimens of four editions of the English Bible, showing the improvement made between the years 1816 and 1851, in reference to quality of paper, printing, and binding, at an average reduction of 62 per cent. in the cost price.

202 HARRISON, A. P. 190 Western Rd. Brighton, Des.— Arms, printed and stained in blazonry colours. Fac-simile of Magna Charta. Death-warrant of King Charles I., and of Mary Queen of Scots.

203 BELL, Major, 17 Cecil St. Strand.—A variety of charts, in illustration of the exhibitor's system and mechanism of historic memory. (In Class 1, wall space.)

204 STRANGEWAYS, J. 28 Harpur St. Red Lion Sq.—A new chart of British biography from the commencement of the 15th century.

206 WALTON, T. King Edward the Sixth's School, Birmingham.—Outline chart of general history. (In class 9.)

207 CLEAVER, W. J. 46 Piccadilly.—An assortment of bibles, prayer books, and other works, in modern and antique bindings.

208 SPIERS & SON, Oxford.—An assortment of envelopes and writing papers, ornamented, and a variety of fancy stationery.

210 WATSON, W. 8 George Street, Pocklington.—Plan of the town of Market Weighton. (In class 9.)

211 COMMITTEE OF THE NATIONAL SOCIETY FOR PROMOTING THE EDUCATION OF THE POOR. Depository, Sanctuary, Westminster, Prod.—Specimens of new maps of British geography, models of school apparatus, reading lessons, and school materials.

Proceed to Fine Art Court, page 147.

Class 18.   WOVEN, FELTED, AND LAID FABRICS, DYED AND PRINTED.

—— Areas L. M. N. O. 2 to 5. ——

1 EVANS, D. & Co. 121 Cheapside, Manu. and Printers —British and foreign silk handkerchiefs, dresses, and table-covers. Registered designs.

2 BAKER, TUCKERS, & Co. 30 and 31 Gresham St. Manu. and Printers.—British and East India silk handkerchiefs and dresses, printed in London. Registered designs.

3 LIDDIARD & Co. Friday Street.—Printed de-laines, bareges, &c.

4 INGLIS & WAKEFIELD, Busby Print Works, near Glasgow.—Printed mousselines-de-laine on cotton warp; printed Cashmeres, balzarines, cottons, and jaconets: designs registered.

5 ANDREWS, SONS, & GEE, 55 Friday St.—Printed cotton, muslin, woollen, and mixed fabrics.

6 DEVAS, MINCHENER, & ROUTLEDGE, 24 Laurence Lane, Prop.—Printed cambric and muslins.

7 WELCH, MARGETSON & Co. 17 Cheapside, Manu.— A selection of silk handkerchiefs manufactured from China silk, and India Corahs, printed by the exhibitors.

8 WILKINSON, W. 89 Watling St.—China cord " pongee" handkerchiefs, and China and grey twilled bandanas, British manufacture. India corahs, specimens of madder red, cochineal, crimson, &c. Specimens of printed and dyed work, in various stages.

9 SWAN & EDGAR, Piccadilly and Regent St. Prop.— Spitalfields silks, velvets, &c. manufactured by J. Balance and Sons, Stone and Kemp, and Winkworth and Proctor. Muslins, printed by Hargreaves, Brothers.

10 LAW, WM. & EDW. 37 Monkwell St. Manu.—Embossed silk and velvet. Specimen of cloth used for bookbinding. Embossed velvet and furniture-linings for decorations. Embossed grounds for paper-hangings.

11 CROCKER, J. & A. 51 Friday St.—Harness woven muslins, for curtains. Complete drapery, blind and curtains of harness woven muslin, showing its adaptation for window decoration. Printed cotton for furniture uses; the colours produced by machine, and by machine and blocks.

12 KEYMER, J. Lawrence Lane, Prod.—Silk bandana handkerchiefs, &c. a study, commemorative of the Great Exhibition. Printed by A. Applegath, Dartford.

13 MAIR, SON, & Co. 60 Friday St. London, and 163 Ingram St. Glasgow.—Twilled bandannas, and cambric handkerchiefs.

14 MCALPIN, STEAD, & Co. Cummersdale, Carlisle, Des. and Printers.—Machine and block chintz furnitures, upon cotton velvet, and upon calico.

15 HINDLEY & SONS, 134 Oxford St. Des. and Manu.— Printed chintz furniture: original designs, English production.

16 FOSTER, PORTER, & Co. 47 Wood St. Cheapside, Manu.—British and East India silk handkerchiefs, printed in London. Blocks employed in printing handkerchiefs.

17 WILSON, —.—Specimens of cloth for bookbinding.

18 WELCH, T. Merton Abbey, Merton, Manu.—Printed and embossed cloth drawing-room table-covers, different designs and colourings.

19 WALFORD, R. 27 Laurence Lane, Prop.—Printed silk handkerchiefs, East India silk manufacture, printed in England.

20 JOHNSON, R. J.—Specimens of dyed goods.

21 SWAINSON & DENNYS, 97 New Bond St. Des. and Printers.—Chintzes for dining-rooms, libraries, &c. Chintz, imitation of drapery, for wall-hangings, curtains, bed furniture, &c.

22 UNDERWOOD, W. 1 Vere St. Oxford St. Manu.— Printed cloth table cover, commemorative of the Great Exhibiton, exhibiting the arms of the principal nations ef the globe.

23 CLARKE, E. Neate St. Cobourg Rd. Old Kent Rd.— An assortment of printed and painted japanned table covers.

24 YATES & TAYLOR, 42 Gutter Lane, Cheapside, Manu. —Specimen of printed and embossed table covers, &c.

25 THOMSON BROTHERS & SONS, 1 Mosley St. Manchester, Prod.—Printed cambrics and de laines, cotton warps, shot silk, and worsted; printed cambrics, &c. silk warps, shot silk.

26 BURD & SONS, Manchester, Printers.—Machine-printed calicoes and muslins, madder and steam colours. Block-printed calicoes, steam colours. Block-printed window blinds. Printed quilts.

27 DALGLEISH, FALCONER, & Co. Lennox Mill, Lennox-town, Stirling, Scotland, Printers.—Calico prints and muslin prints.

28 THE STRINES PRINTING Co. Manchester, Prod.— Specimens of machine printing on cotton velvet; eight colours, produced by one operation, at the rate of sixty yards per minute. Specimens of madder work, &c.

29 NELSON, KNOWLES, & Co. 11 George St. Manchester, Printers.—Chintz furniture; chintzes and other prints: all the colours printed at once by cylinder.

30 POTTER, E. & Co. Dinting Vale, Glossop, and Manchester, Prod.—Variety of calico prints; moderate in cost, and produced by machine throughout.

31 SAMUELS, J. & Co. Manchester, Manu.—Velvets; velveteens; moleskins; satins; printed drills; Albert tweeds; Holsteins; Waldemars; mock quiltings and herring bones; diamond and welted quiltings and satins.

32 RAMSEY, C. & Co. Manchester, Prop.—Dyed and printed cotton trouser cloth, in imitation of woollen.

33 BANNERMAN & SONS, Manchester, Prod.—Dacian cloth. Patent cloth, used for curtains, &c. Cloth for ladies' dresses, coats, bindings for books, &c.

34 BAYLEY & CRAVEN, 61 Mosley St. Manchester.— Calico prints, fast lilacs, madder colours; and two and three coloured madder works. Sample of a new "resist" purple, &c.

35 SWANWICK & JOHNSON, Manchester, Prod.—Printed calico and printed muslin.

36 HOYLE & SONS, 58 Mosley Street, Manchester.— Printed calicoes. Printed cambrics, suitable for children, and large patterns for dresses. Printed muslins. Checked and plain jaconets. Printed mousseline-de-laines and Llamas, both mixed fabrics.

37 STEINER, T. & Co. Church, near Accrington, Manchester, Manu. and Inv.—Cotton fabrics, dyed Turkey-red and printed in various colours.

38 HARGREAVES, BROTHERS, & Co. Manchester; LEDDIARD & Co. London, Manu.—Chintzes and muslins, printed in permanent colours. A design of ore block printing, by Mercer's patent process, with the ordinary colours, &c.

39 SALE, J. N. Manchester, Prod.—Collection of shirtings and of cottons, printed by machine and block.

40 BRADWELL & ADAMS, Ardwick, Manchester, Prod. and Des.—Printed velveteens; a memento of the late Sir Robert Peel. Bart.

WOVEN, FELTED, and LAID FABRICS, DYED and PRINTED.

41 SALIS, SCHWABE, & Co. Manchester, Prod.—Printed cotton cambrics, or calicoes. Printed cotton muslins.

42 BENECKE, W. & Co. Manchester.—Printed calicoes, muslins, furnitures, and velvets; and warps, after printing, manufactured by T. Knight & Co. Manchester.

43 ANDREWS, W. & Co. Tipping Street, Ardwick, near Manchester.—Specimens of their dye, and Mellowdew's patent cotton velvet.

43A WORLEDGE, Manchester.

44 KESSELMEYER & MELLODEW, 23 Cooper St. Manchester, Inv. and Manu.—Patent velvets and velveteens, cotton, and cotton and linen, finished in imitation of silk velvet. Cotton velvet and velveteen of the old make.

45 WOODCROFT, J. & Co. Salford, Printers.—Velvet and velveteen. Beaverteens. Satintop. Diagonal tweed, cords, &c. grey and printed.

46 GREENWOOD & BARNES, Irwell Springs, Bacup, Dyers.—Fancy cotton muslins, dyed Turkey red.

47 SIMPSON & YOUNG, Foxhill Bank, Accrington, and 23 Mosley St. Manchester, Prod.—Balzarines, barèges, and mousseline-de-laines, cambrics, cotton velvets, &c., printed by machine.

48 MERCER, J. Accrington, Inv.—Cotton cloth, printed, dyed, &c., prepared by patent process.

49 MONTEITH, H. & Co. 11 George Sq. Glasgow, Manu.—Specimens of Turkey red yarns and cloths. Printed handkerchiefs, garments, furnitures, scarfs and shawls, in Turkey red.

49A CAIRNS, J. 9 Charlotte St. Manchester, Manu.—Fancy cotton muslins dyed Turkey red.

50 M'NAIR & BRAND, Glasgow, and 23 Friday St. Des. and Manu.—Printed shawls. Long and square woollen fabrics. Indian styles. Registered designs.

51 BLACK, J. & Co. Glasgow, Manu.—Printed cambrics, mousseline-de-laines, barèges, &c.

52 GOURLIE & SON, 8 South Frederick St. Glasgow, Des.—Printed muslins, on plain and fancy fabrics: designs registered.

53 MONTEITH, J. & Co. 51 Buchanan St. Glasgow, Manu.—Printed muslins and jaconets. Printed mixed fabrics.

54 KERR & McMILLAN, Glasgow.—Two printed silk pocket-handkerchiefs, exhibited for fabric and design.

55 CUSSONS & Co. 51 Bunhill Row, Manu.—Cotton velvets dyed and embossed by the exhibitors.

56 STIRLING & SONS, Glasgow, Manu.—Specimens of Turkey-red dyeing and printing, on cotton fabrics.

56A BLIND ASYLUM, Glasgow.—Specimens of work by the inmates.

57 EWING, ORR, & Co. Glasgow, Manu.—Turkey-red full chintz furniture printed by blocks. Turkey-red chintz print, printed by cylinder machine.

58 WALSHAW, J. & SONS, North Bridge, Halifax, Dyers.—Specimens of variously dyed two-fold thirties worsted warp.

59 HITCH, M. 47 High St. Cowes, Isle of Wight, Prod.—Hair, to show the effect of dye. Wools, showing different dyes applied without fire-heat. Horn, stained without the application of soda or potash, to imitate tortoiseshell.

60 LE LIEVRE, H. Cleveland St. Mile-end Road.—Specimens of black dyed silk.

61 JOURDAIN, W. D. 60 Milton St. Cripplegate.—Coloured and black specimens of silk dyeing.

62 CHABOT, P. J. Spitalfields, Prod.—English and foreign woollen yarns, English dyed.

63 REYNOLDS & SON, Temple St. Hackney Rd. Dyers.—Specimens of skein silk dyeing.

63A MAIR, SON, & Co. Friday St.—Printed flannels.

64 McCALLUM, Government School of Design, Manchester.—Panorama of calico printing, showing progress from 1765 to 1851.

64A BRADBURY, GREATOREX, & BEALE, Aldermanbury.—Specimens of wood-cut printing for pocket-handkerchiefs.

₊ DESIGNS with CLASSES 5 and 6 on NORTH WALL A. 28, 29, 30.

65 CARTER, —.—Designs for paper-hangings.

66 HUDSON, C. Merton, Surrey, Des.—Design for printed shawl.

67 WATERSON, J. A. 22 Ormond St. Chorlton-on-Medlock, Des.—Designs for printed muslins.

68 KAY, H. Rawlenstoll, Manchester, Des.—Designs for mousseline-de-laine and cotton muslin.

69 FLETCHER, J. Altrincham, Des.—Design, eleven colours, repeat of sketch; design, nine colours, repeat of sketch, intended for practicable work (block work).

70 GAUTHORP, —.—Design for ornamental panel.

70A GREEN, H. Melbury Park, Dorchester, Des.—Designs for printing on calico and mousseline-de-laine.

71 HAMMERSLEY, J. A. Government School of Design, Manchester.

72 WATERHOUSE, J. Manchester, Des. — Ornamental design for a dress skirt; adapted for machine printing on fabrics.

73 PERCIVAL, J. Manchester, Des.—Designs for muslin-de-laine.

74 CADMAN, —.—Designs for muslins.

76 WHITTAKER, J. Manchester, Des. — Design for muslin.

77 LENNON, R.—Various designs.

79 BRIDGES, —.—Designs for printed fabrics.

81 ROBERTS, T. New St. Altrincham, Des.—Six five-colour designs for de-laine; blockwork enclosed in the same frame.

82 JARVIE, —. Hulme, Manchester.—Designs for printing.

83 HOBBS, W. 33 Great Jackson St. Hulme, Des.—Design for printed chintz furniture.

84 BRAMLEY, —.—Various designs.

85 REES, MARY, School of Des. Somerset House.—Designs in various colours.

86 COLLINS, F. School of Des. Somerset House.—Various coloured designs.

87 ASHWORTH, S. A. Central Female Government School of Des.—Various designs in colours.

88 MANSBENDEL, F. 63 Bread St. City, and 34 Acton St. Gray's Inn Rd. Des.—Chintz furniture design, arranged for block printing.

89 SMITH, J. Sandiway, Altrincham, near Manchester, Des.—Designs for a portiere, or door-screen; and for machine and block printing on silk, de laine, and cambric.

90 HUNT, J. C.—Various designs.

91 HEAVISIDE, J. 30 Bedford Sq.—Designs for china and papier maché.

92 GLOVER, M. School of Design, Manchester.—Designs for wall decoration.

93 SANDWAY, —, Altrincham.—Various designs.

94 GANN, LOUISA.—Various designs.

Proceed to Class 11. page 73.

Class 19.   TAPESTRY, FLOOR CLOTHS, LACE, and EMBROIDERY.

—— South Central Gallery. ——

(Carpets, Table Covers, Tapestries, Oilcloths, &c., suspended from the Girders in the Galleries, and against the Walls of the Building.)

1 BIDDLE, D. 81 Oxford St. Prop.—Specimen of Honiton lace, des. by T. Sharp, and manu. by J. Tucker. Honiton guipure mantle. Bridal and guipure scarfs ; shawl ; double flounce. Flounce of point d'Angleterre.

2 FISHER & ROBINSON, 12 Watling St.—Black silk lace and piece goods, blonde machine-run curtains, tambour-flowerings, needlework, quiltings, &c.

3 GROUCOCK, COPESTAKE, MOORE, & Co. 5 Bow Chyd. Manu.—Lace from Honiton and Buckinghamshire, embroidered muslins, cotton lace, net, needlework, &c.

4 LAMBERT & BURY, Limerick, Ireland, Des. and Manu.—Lace : shaded lace flounce ; shawl ; and worked scarf, in imitation of Valenciennes, &c.

5 HOWELL, JAMES & Co. Regent St.—Honiton guipure lace shawl, mantle, and berthe. White silk dress and apron, embroidered with birds and flowers.

6 WEEDON, F. Goldsmith St. City, Manu.—A rich British point-lace square, and specimens of flouncing.

8 NERINCK, Mdlle. SŒURS, 10 New Cavendish St. —Lace.

10 LAUGHER & COSENS, 97 Oxford St. Prop.—Guipure lace half-shawl, manufactured at Honiton.

11 WEEDON, F. P. 29 Lower St. Islington, Des. and Manu.—A lace berthe of a description of work designated British point.

12 PULLAN, MATILDA, 126 Albany St. Regent's Park, Des. Inv. and Manu.—Modern point lace, worked with a common sewing needle.

13 TAWELL, S. 16 Gresham St. West, Manu.—Tamboured lace scarf, imitation of Honiton, manufactured in London.

14 GOULD, J. & F. 89 Watling St. Manu.—Registered Victoria lace work, produced entirely by hand.

15 URLING, G. F. 224 Regent St. Manu.—White lace scarf, in imitation of Brussels point, embroidered in gold, &c. and worked upon a fine clear patent net.

16 GARD, W. S. 268 Regent St. Des. and Manu.—British point lace scarf. British guipure lace berthe, a new manufacture.

17 RIEGO DE LA BRANCHARDIERE, ELENORE, New Bond St. Inv. and Manu.—Crochet work. Flounce, imitation of Spanish point lace. Design, in silk and gold, for Prayer-book covers.

18 CLARKE, J. 170 Regent St. Manu.—Royal Irish snow point lappet ; head dress of Irish rose point ; loop point scarf of Belfast ; Hibernian point collar, &c.

19 BALL, DUNNICLIFFE & Co. Nottingham, Manu.—Patent elastic velvet, plain and mixed pile ; silk elastic taffeta, elastic fabrics : Simla and lace shawls, &c. Des. by J. Wilkins.

20 BIRKIN, R. Nottingham.—Black silk flounces, falls, trimming-laces, white and coloured blonds, Valenciennes, laces, &c. all made and finished on the machine at once.

21 ADAMS & SONS, Nottingham, Manu.—Laces and edgings, made entirely by machinery.

25 HEYMANN & ALEXANDER, Nottingham.—Machine-wrought cotton lace curtains. Cotton extra twist Brussels net. Zephyr net, for embroidery. Mechlin net, and cotton Brussels linings. Black silk Jacquard lace, shawl, &c.

27 WHITLOCK & BILLIALD, Mary Gate, Nottingham, Manu.—Machine-wrought cotton Mechlin laces, needle embroidered. The groundwork made from No. 520 yarn, spun and doubled.

28 HERBERT & Co. Nottingham, Manu.—Lace of various kinds from the warp machine ; crotchet lace from the warp and twist machine. Blond edgings, from the twist machine.

29 MALLET & BARTON, Nottingham, and New Basford, Manu.—Silk lace ; silk lace fringes, imitation Valenciennes ; cotton laces, hand and machine-wrought.

30 HOLLINS, S. Nottingham, Manu.—Lace goods : Machine-made cotton Brussels nets and laces, figured by the needle. Various hosiery goods.

31 MOORE, S. W. Hockley Mill, Nottingham, Manu.—Lace and net made from No. 520 lace thread, and plain net made from No. 630.

32 RECKLESS & HICKLING, Nottingham, Manu.—White and black lace flounces, &c., falls, shawls, &c., embroidered partly by machinery, and partly by hand.

33 VICKERS, W. Nottingham, Manu.—Black silk lace shawls, scarfs, mantles, falls, &c., from the pusher bobbin-net machine, and embroidered.

34 GREASLEY & HOPCROFT, Nottingham, Manu.—Lace articles. Jacquard pusher silk shawl. Figured needlework shawls, falls, &c.

41 STEEGMANN & Co. Nottingham, Inv. and Manu.—Figured lace-curtains, made entirely on the lace machine by Jacquard application.

45 FORREST & SONS, 101 Grafton St. Dublin, and Abbey Ct. Factory, Limerick, Manu.—Laces : Royal Irish guipure, Irish appliqué ; Limerick ; lace dresses, flouncings, scarfs, &c.

47 VISCHI, A. M. J. 21 Greville St. Hatton Garden, Manu.—Artificial flowers in wool, green turf, &c.

47A MOORE, Mrs. Gt. Castle St.—An embroidered lace smoking cap.

48 JANCOWSKI, W. York, Des. and Manu.—State chair, of ruby-coloured silk velvet, embroidered with gold, silver, and jewels. Arms of the city of York, embroidered in gold, silver, and silk. Picture, embroidered with silk.

49 DAVIES, Mrs. 29 Harewood Sq. Des. and Exec.—Set of chessmen, draughtsmen, dice, and board in needle-work. The pawns representing Her Majesty's body-guard.

50 ROSE, ELIZABETH, Paulerspury, near Towcester, Des. and Manu.—Point lace flounce. Shawl. Scarf-shawl. Veil. Berthe, made of black pillow lace.

51 MEE, CORNELIA, Bath, Inv. Des. and Manu.—Banner screen, the flags of all nations, richly embroidered in fine silks. Embroidery applied to decorative furniture.

53 O'DONNELL, MARY, 69 London St. Reading, Des.—

E

Ornamental leather. Hand-screens in stamped gutta percha preserved real flowers and embroidery, &c.

55 TREADWIN, C. E. 27 Cathedral Yd. Exeter, Manu.—Devonshire, or Honiton, point lace. Designs from the Government School of Design, London.

56 ONION, E. 38 Broad St. Birmingham, Manu. — Velvet drapery valance, worked with gold silk braid. Crimson valance fringe. New drapery rope. New diamond valance fringe, in silk. Registered bell lever ornaments. Curtain-holder. Ornaments for valances. Coach and railway carriage lace and trimmings.

57 BROWNE, SHARPE, & Co. Paisley, and 18 Watling St. London, Manu.—Embroidered and tamboured book muslin dresses. Embroidered scollop and insertion trimmings, flounces, collars, &c.

58 BROWN, S R. & T. Glasgow, Manu.—Muslins embroidered by the peasantry of Scotland, and the north and west of Ireland, consisting of dresses, collars, caps, habit-shirts, trimmings, &c.

59 PARK & THOMSON, Glasgow, Manu.—Children's sewed robes; ladies' collars, handkerchiefs, fancy habits. Cambric and book flounces, sewed trimmings, &c.

60 MACARTHUR, D. & Co. Glasgow, Manu.—Hamilton lace goods:— Dresses, cloak or mantilla, capes, veils, sleeves, &c.

61 CONNAUGHT SCHOOLS, Glasgow. — Embroidered muslin.

62 ROBERTSON & SONS, Glasgow, Manu.—Sewed book-muslin and cambric squares for fancy table covers. Rich specimens of embroidery.

63 McFARLANE & PORTER, 38 Queen St. Glasgow, Manu.—Embroidered black and white muslin collars, chemisettes, habit shirts, &c. for mourning. Lace veils, cloaks, &c. Black lace flounced embroidered robe skirt.

64 BROWN, H. 100 & 104, Virginia Pl. Glasgow Manu.—Sewed book muslin collars, frilled chemisettes, fancy habits, cambric handkerchiefs, embroidered book-muslin dresses, &c.

65 MACQUARIE, FISHER, & Co. Glasgow, Manu.—Black and white silk, cotton, and linen lace. White silk and gold under sleeves. Coloured silk and gold apron and parasol cover.

66 MACDONALD, D. & J. & Co. Glasgow, Manu.—Embroidery on book-muslin, &c. Embroidered French cambric. Embroidered baby linen. Embroidered trimmings, insertions, flounces, &c.

67 SIMPSON, M. 5 Aldermanbury.—Sewing a ting silk, silk laces, specimens of raw silk.

68 FOOT & SONS, 38 Spital Sq. Manu.—Fringes, elastic ribbon trimming, combination of velvet and brocading, &c.

69 ARTHUR, ANN, Manu.—Silk, worsted, and cotton braids, for figuring. Netted buttons. Fringes, gimps, girdles, and tassels. Olivets. Braids and frogs.

70 GABRIEL, J. W. 135 Regent St. Manu.—English embroidery, on silk and woollen, for waistcoats.

71 DANBY, C. & T. 14 Coventry St. and 43 New Bond St. Manu.—A crochet silk gimp robing, resembling the rose leaves and flowers. Brandenburgh crochet silk gimp trimming, girdles, silk fringes, crochet head-dress, &c.

72 BRADBEE, G. W. 115 Newgate St. Manu.—Needlework by Mrs. Marsh, &c. A group of flowers, &c., made of leather. Fringes, gimps, tassels, trimmings, &c.

74 EVANS, R. & Co. 24 Watling St. Manu.—Silk ornament, bell-pulls, curtain-holders, cords, gimps, tassels, and rosettes, trimmings, &c.

75 BURGH, R. 42 Bartholomew Close, Manu.—Deep bullion fringe, woven to shape. Ornamental hangers, pendants, fringes, rosette medallions, &c.

76 BARRETT & CORNEY, 70 Little Britain, Manu.—Gold

and silver threads for lace, embroidery, headings of cloths, muslins, &c., gold and silver bullions, purls, plates, and spangles, cords, braids, gimps, and laces. Embroidery, des. and worked by R. Abraham, 5 Lisle St. Leicester Sq.

77 IRISH WORK SOCIETY, 233 Regent St.—Specimens of appliqué lace. Crochet work. Real guipure, from old models. Straw plait, made of Irish grasses. Tabinets or poplins. Black and white pillow lace. Fine knitting. Black silk mittens, knitted and netted. Bog oak carvings. Imitations of guipure. Embroidery, worked *au blanc*, &c. Knitted hosiery. Plain-work. Woven cotton hosiery, by Smyth of Balbriggan. White mats, made of Irish wool, &c.

79 LEES & Co. R. 36 King St. Cheapside, Manu.—Printed mohair tapestry; Utrecht mohair velvet; mohair velvets; printed Chinese velvets of mohair, &c.

80 SURR & SON, 12 King St. Cheapside, Manu.—Silk twist, manufactured at Leek, Staffordshire.

81 HART, G. 7 Market St. May Fair, Inv. and Manu.—Registered boxes, ornaments, &c. in muslin and cotton.

82 SMITH, ANDERSON, & Co. Cheapside, and South Hanover St. Glasgow, Prod. (Macdonald & Co.)—Bassinette quilt. Infant's long robe. Infant's caps, horse-shoe and round crowns.

83 LAMBERT, BROWN, & PATRICK, 236 Regent St. Manu.—Epaulettes and laces. Embroidered waistcoats. Masonic regalia. Church decorations. Fac-simile of Bible used by King Charles I.

84 JACKSON, C. 10 Curzon St. Mayfair.—An occasional table, mounted with *appliqueé* embroidery.

85 HARRISON, T. 21 Brownlow St. Bedford Row, Des. and Manu.—Altar cloth and cushions, of crimson Genoa velvet, embroidered in gold.

86 STIRLING, MARY ANNE, 29 John St. Bedford Row, Des. and Manu.—A fire-screen, worked in chenille, &c.

88 PURCELL, FRANCES, 3 New Burlington St. Prod.—A needle-worked table-cover.

90 STURMY, MARIA, 8 Wellington St. London Bridge, Des.—Table-cover, embroidered with the needle, without a pattern.

94 BARNARD, E. Little Bardfield Rectory, near Dunmow, Manu.—Two figures in Berlin wool work, for the purpose of holding open doors.

95 BARNES, R. Y. City Rd. Manu.—Specimens of decorative floor cloth.

96 BATTERS, MARTHA, 9 Rose Hill Ter. Brighton, Des.—Picture in tapestry.

97 BAYNES, R. AGNES, Cheshunt, Herts, near Waltham Cross, Inv.—Knitting designs.

100 BENBOW, Mrs. 11 Hanover Pl. Regent's Park.—Three specimens of tapestry embroidery, after the ancient Saxon style.

103 BLACKBURN, ANN MARIA, Beaumont Hill, Lincoln, Manu.—North-west view of Lincoln Cathedral, worked upon white silk, with the rovings of black lutestring, and manufacturer's silk.

106 BOTTOM, J. 65 Brook St. Derby, Des. and Manu.—A hearth-rug, with the border and ends formed of upwards of 20,000 shreds of cloth, and the centre of lamb's wool.

108 BRIDGES, W. Ensham, near Oxford. — Tapestry wool-work; worked during leisure hours.

110 BRINTON & SONS, Kidderminster, Manu.—Patent velvet tapestry. Super Wilton carpet. Registered designs. Patent Axminster velvet rugs.

111 ROGERS, —, Wilton, Wilts.—Embroidery, "Esther and Mordecai."

112 WILSON, CHARLOTTE, Guildhall, Broad Sanctuary, Westminster, Des.—Netted quilt or coverlid for summer use.

113 Brooks, E. 2 Chester Pl. Kennington, Manu.— Specimen of embroidery, descriptive of English history.

114 Brown, M'Laren, & Co, Kilmarnock, Scotland, Mann.—Velvet-pile, Threeply, & Kidderminster carpeting.

115 Burch, J. & Co. Carpet Print Works, Crag, near Macclesfield.—Velvet pile and Brussels carpets; tapestries, furniture covers, &c., woven by Sevier's patent power loom, and afterwards printed by patent machinery, by J. Burch.

117 Burton, M. Libberton Bank, Edinburgh, Prop.— A shawl, table-cover, rug, &c., knitted on wires by an aged person. Picture frame, in imitation of old carved oak, composed of leather and putty.

118 Burton, M. Sarah, Ospringe, near Feversham, Kent. Manu.—Italian girl, in fancy work. Berlin wool.

119 Caley, J. W. & F. G. Windsor, Des.—Diaphane transparent silk for blinds, manufactured for the use of Her Majesty at Windsor Castle.

122 Cardwell, C. & T. Northampton, Manu.—Pillow-lace; trimming for caps, collars, &c.

123 Kightley, J. Northampton.—Pillow-lace, trimmings, &c.

125 Caulfield, W. B. 54 Coal Harbour, Blackwall, imp.—Knitted lace-work, by children at the school of Bally-castle Quay, north of Ireland.

126 Chambers, Elizabeth Rebecca, Wilton, Sq. Dublin, Des.—Carpet worked for the benefit of the Society for Promoting the Scriptural Education of the Native Irish.

128 Chapman, Elizabeth Annie, Gt. Bowden, Market Harborough.—Tapestry copied from a painting by Leonardo da Vinci: The Last Supper.

129 Clarke, Eliza, Hackford, by Reepham, Norwich, Prod.—Collars in imitation of Marguerite Guipure lac., Brussels point lace, and ivory Guipure lace.

130 Clarke, Esther, 18a Margaret St., Cavendish Sq. Manu and Des.—Flounce of Honiton lace.

132 Cole & Son, 18 Newgate St. Prop.—Brussels, Venetian, and Kidderminster carpeting.

133 Collins & Rose, Kidderminster.—Various carpets.

134 Constable, Hannah, Clonmel, Ireland, Des. — Infant's crochet dress, made of white thread.

135 Cook, W. Causeway, Chippenham, Des. and Manu. —Table-cover, made with about 30,000 pieces of broad cloth.

136 Copeland, Fanny, 15, Charlotte St. Liverpool, Inv. —Sofa pillow, croched in imitation of tapestry.

138 Jones, L. V. 33 King William St. London Bridge, Prod.—An embroidered map of the United Kingdom : executed by a girl of 14. Framed in English pollard oak.

139 Coveney, Mrs., Munster, nr. Queensborough.— Carpet of thirty squares, worked in Berlin wool.

140 Crick, Ellen, Soham, Cambridgeshire, Des. and Maker.—A veil worked by the needle, in imitation of Honiton lace, and in the hope that it may be the means of giving employment to many poor needle-women.

141 Cross, Mary, Paul St. Bristol, Des.—Crochet counterpane.

142 Crossley & Sons, Halifax.—Large pattern mosaic tapestry. Patent mosaic carpet and table-covers. Patent mosaic rugs. Patent velvet carpets. Patent tapestry carpet. Kidderminster, Dutch, and other carpets.

144 Cunliffe, Sarah Ann, Saffron Walden, Inv.—An infant's knitted robe.

145 Daniel & Cossins, Mdlles., 55 Herbert St. New North Road, Hoxton.—Embroidery.

146 Conerding, Mrs. Ida Von, 12 Cambridge Row, Hackney.—Newly-invented knitting, the embroidery being only seen on one side.

147 Hardy, F. C. Miss, 9 Mount St. Crescent, Dublin. —Specimens of Knitting from Hackestown, County Carlow, Ireland.

148 Davidson, Lieut., Bombay Artillery, Haddington,

imp.—Embroidery from Hyderabad, for table-cloths, shawls, cushions, &c.

149 Dawson, Deborah, Newtownbarry, Ireland, Prop. —Cuffs, hand-spun and knitted, from the wool of French poodle dogs.

150 Dewar, Son, & Sons, King's Arms Buildings, Wood St. Prop.—Table covers, of elaborate design, the first mixed fabric of the kind made in Spitalfields, Designed and executed by Webb & Son. The number of cards used in the production are 3,000, the number of cards used in the Jacquard machine 40,000. Chintz printed woollen table covers, and embossed.

152 Ditl, Madame, 23 Charlotte St. Portland Pl.— Embroidery, in imitation of engraving. Embroidery in silk and gold on velvet. Embroidery in silk, chenille, and gold.

155 Dove, C. W. & Co. Leeds, Manu.—Velvet pil Brussels, Kidderminster, and Threeply carpets. Des. reg.

156 Dowbiggin & Co. 23 Mount St. Grosvenor Sq.— Carpet made at the patent Axminster carpet manufactory, Glasgow, for Her Majesty, designed by L. Gruner, Esq.

157 Downing, G. & J. H. Kings Rd. Chelsea.—Specimen of floorcloth.

158 Smith, Maria L., 24 Basing Lane, Des.—A design for a lace curtain.

159 Ellis, Sophie A. Kildemoc Rectory, Ardee, Louth, Ireland, Des.—Specimens of tatting or frivolité, for ladies.

160 Eustace, R. & J. 10 Weaver's Sq. Dublin, Manu.— Turkey rug; tufted hearth-rugs, girth, roller, and suspender web. Specimens of linen mill band.

161 Evans, S. A. 18 Charles St. Middlesex Hospital, Des. and Manu.—The Death of Douglas, after C. Landseer, in embroidery.

162 Evenden, Eliza Anne, 31 High St. Margate, Manu. —Berlin wool work; Mary Queen of Scots, mourning over the dying Douglas.

164 Flower, Ann, 25 Duke St. Grosvenor Sq. Des. and Manu.—Picture, "Flags of All Nations," worked in cross-stitch in silk, chenille, beads, and wool.

165 Faudel & Phillips, 38, 39, and 40 Newgate St. Des. and Manu.—State bed, in needlework; the bedstead of carved wood, richly gilt. Patterns for needlework and crochet. Worsted yarns, silks, &c.

168 Fortune, Eliza, 101 St. George's Rd. Southwark. —Hearth rug, knitted by hand.

169 Franklin, J. D. 14 Lower Ormond Quay, Dublin, Prod.—Printed floor-cloths 16 yards by 6, woven in one piece.

170 Frewen, Elizabeth, Marlow, Bucks, Des. and Manu.—Lace collar, cuff, lappets, and neck-tie, made entirely by hand on the pillow.

174 Gardner, M. A. 22 Gt. Leonard St. Finsbury, Manu.—Berlin wool-work by the exhibitor, who is blind.

175 George, C. 33 Oxford St. Prop.—Velvet pile carpeting.

176 Gilbert, J. 7 Charlotte St. Old Kent Rd. Des.— Design for Axminster centre carpet.

178 Heyn, Emma, 14 Gloucester Ter. Gloucester Rd. Old Kent Rd.—An ornamental vase of flowers made entirely of Berlin wool with the crochet stitch.

180 Greene, R., Lichfield.—Folding-screen, worked by a nun of the Convent of Mercy, at Birr, Ireland.

181 Greenwood, Anne Christiana, Brookwood Park, Alresford, Inv.—Panels for the walls of a room, painted with birds and flowers in the style of India paper.

182 Gregory, Thomsons, & Co. Kilmarnock, Scotland, Manu.—Specimens of royal Wilton, Brussels, and imperial carpeting.

183 Harris, Brothers, 87 Watling St. Manu.—Embroidered satin aprons and handkerchiefs, cambric flouncings and insertions, all needlework.

E 2

184 HARRISON, J. Halifax, Yorkshire, Manu.—White rug, all wool, used for bed-sides, door-mats, carriages, &c. ; may be washed and dyed any colour.

185 HALL, A. Manchester.—Canvas patterns, for embroidery.

186 HAMBURGER, ROGERS & Co. 30 King St. Covent Garden.—Helmets, epaulettes, and gold embroidery.

187 BLOOMFIELD, Miss, Poole, Dorset, Manu.—" Raphael in the Vatican," in Berlin wool.

188 HANSON, C. Fetter Lane, Des.—Design for an Axminster hearth rug, in the Italian style.

190 HARE, J. & Co. Bristol, Des. and Manu.—Floorcloth. Marble mosaic and oak and wood centres, &c.

191 HARMSWORTH, MARTHA, Twickenham, Embroiderer. Tapestry. The Last Supper, worked in French floss silk.

192 HARRIS, G. & Co. Stourport, Manu.—Brussels velvet pile carpets.

195 HARTTREE, E. & G. 11 Edgware Rd. Des. and Manu —Needlework, on a new silk canvas.

196 HARVEY & KNIGHT, Upper Marsh, Lambeth, Manu —Floor cloth, pattern copied from a Roman tessellated pavement.

197 HARVEY, J. K. 25 Ely Pl. Holborn, Des.—Designs for printed fabrics and for carpets.

198 HAYTER, F. S. Hull, Des. and Manu.—Carpet; needlework in Berlin wool.

199 HELBRONNER, R. 261 Regent St. Des. and Manu.—New style of needlework, new canvas for embroidery, patent elastic draught excluder, &c.

200 HENDERSON & Co. Durham, Manu.—Wilton or pile carpet. Brussels carpet. Wilton or pile stair carpet. Superfine ingrain carpet. Damask Venetian carpet. Venetian stair carpet.

201 HENDERSON & WIDNELL, Lasswade, Manu.—Portière, or door curtain of fine velvet, Whytock's patent, probably the largest piece ever manufactured on this principle. Rich patent velvet carpets and rugs.

202 HATCH, CAROLINE, Tunbridge Wells.—Specimens of embroidery.

203 HILL, B. Olney, Buckinghamshire, Manu.—Specimens of pillow-lace edging and insertion. Pillow lace, suitable for caps, dresses, and flouncing.

204 HILL & Co. Worcester and Gt. Malvern, Inv.—Needlework for ottomans, hanging for walls, table covers, &c. original in style and execution, not being copied from Berlin or coloured patterns, by the sisters E., P., S., and O. Rogers, of the above firm.

205 HINDHAUGH, Mrs. MARY, Newcastle-upon-Tyne, Prod.—Pictures: Tapestry work pictures.

206 HINDLEY & SONS, 134 Oxford St. Des. and Manu.—Rich velvet carpeting. English hand-wrought carpets, Turkish style. Oriental carpets.

207 HOLLOWAY, PHŒBE, Grove Buildings, Dorchester, Des.—Quilt knitted by hand, in one piece, with cotton.

208 HOLMES, J. Kidderminster, Manu.—Carpets, commonly called velvet.

209 HOPE, G. C. 17 Robertson St. Hastings, Des.—Hassocks of common rush for the church or closet ; needlework, &c.

210 HUMPHRIES, T. Vicar St. Kidderminster, Manu.—Super-velvet pile, and Brussels carpeting. Patent registered.

211 HURST, G. High St. Bedford, Des. and Inv.—Pillow-lace with glass introduced into the figure.

212 HALLING, PEARSE. & STONE, Regent St.—Velvet pile, and Brussels carpets, registered.

213 LADIES' INDUSTRIAL SOCIETY, 76 Grafton St. Dublin.—Limerick lace: shawls, handkerchiefs, and cazarees. Spanish point; old point, &c.; and embroidery. Horse-hair ornaments. Linens. Knitting. Hand-spun flannel. Appliqué: scarfs, caps, veils, &c.

213A SISTERS OF MERCY, Kinsale, Ireland.—Specimens of work, lace and embroidery.

214 Knitting by a blind person, "Prayer for the Houses of Parliament."

215 JAMES, H. 7 Ferdinand Ter. Pancras Vale, Inv. and Des.—Enamelled floor-cloth.

218 JOHNSTONE, J. 102 Graham St. Airdrie, Scotland, Inv.—Table-cover, consisting of 2,000 pieces of cloth, the sole work of the exhibitor, and has occupied his leisure hours for 18 years.

219 JONES, MARY, Abbey St. Chester.—Bible cushion, in fancy work, from a plan of the mosaic pavement in Canterbury cathedral.

220 COX, Miss, A., Blossom St. Norton Folgate.—A rug worked from waste silk.

221 KEDDELL, J.S. Sheerness, Prop.—Armorial bearings of the exhibitor, worked by himself in Berlin wool and silk.

222 BEACH & BARNICOTT, Bridport, Dorset.—Tapestry, a scriptural subject.

223 KETTLEWELL, MARY, Clonmel, Ireland, Prop.—Trimming lace, and lace berthes. Large knitted lace collar, and fine lace lappet. Small thread lace scarf, &c.

224 KING, Miss, 3 Bloomsbury Pl. Bloomsbury Sq. Des. and Manu.—Mediæval embroidery.

225 KINGSBURY, LOUISA, East St. Taunton, Somerset, Des. Inv. and Manu.—Basket of flowers, in Berlin wool.

226 KITELEY, J. Kidderminster, Manu.—Brussels and velvet pile carpets.

227 SCHOOL OF CHARITY, Cangort Park, King's County, Ireland.—Embroidered muslin, by the children.

228 MOWLAND, CHARLOTTE G. 23 Eaton Mews South, Eaton Sq. (aged 11), Manu.—Wreath on white satin, with chenille and crape; design for an ornament.

229 LAMBERT, ELIZABETH, Tunbridge, Des.—Embroidery, portrait of Her Majesty. A group of flowers, with vase.

230 LANCHENICK, JANE A. 5 Brompton Row, Brompton, Des. and Manu.—Table-cover, embroidered in silk.

231 MACKELLAR & HAMPSON, 50 Old Change.—Lace mantle figured by a patent process, silk texture.

232 LAPWORTH, A.—Axminster and patent carpets. Velvet pile and tapestry velvet carpets.

234 LA TOUCHE, DIGGES, Miss, Killmaule, Ireland, Inv.—Lace flounce, worked by the poor girls of Killmaule.

235 VICCARS, R. Padbury, Buckingham, Manu.—Insertion. Crowns and laces for bordering caps, &c.

236 LESTER, T. Bedford, Manu.—Specimen of Bedfordshire pillow-lace. Improved lace fall-piece. White and black trimming lace; flouncing lace, &c.

237 FRYER, Miss N., Barnsley.—Crochet counterpane.

238 WHELER, Mrs. John, 42 Dorset St. Portman Sq.—Table of mounted embroidery.

240 LOCKWOOD, GEORGIANA, 31 Great Titchfield St. Oxford St. Manu.—A child's fancy crochet frock.

241 LEE, J.—A specimen of lace made by a poor woman in Stone, Aylesbury.

242 MACDONALD, MARGARETTA, 105 South Portland St. Glasgow, Manu.—Fancy needlework, in Berlin wool and silk, Haddon Hall in the Olden Time, by F. Tayler.

243 McFARLANE BROTHERS, Glasgow, Manu.—Chenille hearth rugs and carpeting.

244 MALLALIEU, W. Agent of the Moravian Establishments at Fulneck, near Leeds, and Ockbrook, near Derby.—Handkerchiefs of embroidered needlework.

245 A crochet toilet-cover.

246 M'CARTEN, H. 97 Gt. Charles St. Birmingham, Manu.—Ancient funeral pall. Design from Mr. Pugin's "Glossary of Ecclesiastical Ornament and Costume."

247 M'DARMID, Miss, Bagthorpe House, Nottingham, Des.—Embroidered quilt.

248 MACLEAN, JANE, Tynan Rectory, Tynan, Co. Armagh, Ireland, Prop.—Imitation guipure lace flounce, worked by the children of Tynan Glebe school.

249 RICHMOND LUNATIC ASYLUM.—A quilt knitted by the inmates.

250 MELTON, ELIZA, 8 Peacock Ter. Walworth Rd. Manu.—Embroidery: The Last Supper, after Leonardo da Vinci.

251 MONKHOUSE & SON, Barnard Castle, and 75 Wood St. Cheapside, London, Manu.—Carpets, Kidderminster fabric, cumber and point styles. Dutch fabric carpets all wool, and Dutch fabric carpets, warp made from silk noils.

252 MORTON & SONS, Kidderminster, Manu.—Specimens of velvet pile carpets. Saxony and Brussels carpets.

253 NAIRN, M. Kirkaldy, Scotland, Des. and Manu.—Floor-cloth, used for halls, lobbies, &c.

255 LEY, F. Victoria cottage, Bickington, nr. Barnstaple, Devon.—A piece of needlework in floss silk, representing the Bible encircled with roses, &c.

256 BUTCHER ,Misses, 2 Clarendon Rd. Notting Hill.—A variety of Berlin wool-work.

257 NEWCOMB & JONES, Kidderminster, and 19 Skinner St. London, Manu.—Model carpet of superior velvet pile. Velvet pile carpet. Best Brussels. New material for ladies' dresses.

258 NEWTON, JONES, and WILLIS, Temple Row, Birmingham.—Episcopal robes, &c. embroidered in silk and gold. Satin damask hanging, &c. Velvet-pile carpets, for churches, &c.

259 OLVER, LYDIA, Liskeard, Manu.—Embroidered collar stomacher, and sleeves, for a lady: the exhibitor born without a right arm.

260 OSBORN, MATILDA, 4 Sydney Sq. Commercial Rd. East, Prod.—Mary, Queen of Scots, mourning over the Dying Douglas, in Berlin wool.

261 PADWICK, ANNE, Westbourne, Emsworth, Des. and Manu.—A crotchet table-cover in Berlin wool.

262 PALMER, HELEN, Dunse.—Panel for a pole-screen. Lady's dress. Cushion for a chair, embroidered in coloured silks upon a white satin.

263 PARDOE, HOOMANS, & PARDOE, Kidderminster, Manu.—Whytock's patent tapestry carpeting; the colours printed on the worsted before it is woven. Pat. Berlin rugs.

264 PATENT CAMPHINE COMPANY, Hull.—Rugs.

265 PATENT UTRECHT COMPANY, 36 Steward St. Spitalfields.—Lace curtains, patent silk lace dress and curtains, patent lace quilt, scarf, and curtains, Spanish mantilla.

266 PEARSE, CLARA, Broad St. Bath (fourteen years of age), Des.—Crotchet quilt; the Ten Commandments in the centre, with imitation of point lace border.

268 PERRY, E. Rev. 26 Portland Pl. Leamington.—Scarf of British silk the produce of 2,000 silk worms, kept at Goodrich, in Herefordshire. The silk was wound, spun, and made into the scarf by Mrs. Perry and her daughter.

270 HALLOWELL, Mrs. E., Limerick. — Knitted lace scarf.

271 PHILLIPS, EMILY, 166 Bermondsey St. Southwark.—Le Vendredi: a Catholic family eating meat on Friday.

272 PHILLIPS, REBECCA, Swanbourne, Winslow, Manu.—Ornamental linen-thread pillow-lace.

273 PICKTHORN, ESTHER, George St. Hockley, near Birmingham, Manu.—Hearth-rug, raised in needle work.

275 READ & HUMPHREYS, 21 Glare St. Bristol, Manu.—Folding screen on canvas, worked in cross and tent stitches.

276 RISDON, J. 194 High St. Exeter, Prop.—Fancy silk and velvet quilt.

278 ROBINSON, Miss, Newport Ter. Bolton, Lancashire, Des.—Group of flowers worked in a new style, from an oil painting by herself.

280 RODGERS & SON, Islington, near Birmingham, Manu.—Purses, embroidered in the weaving.

281 ROLLS & SON, Lower Kennington Lane, Manu.—Piece of floor-cloth.

282 ROLPH, J. Coggeshall, Essex, Manu.—A dress in imitation of Brussels point lace in tambour-work, &c.

283 ROOME, ANN EMPRINGHAM, Beaumont Hill, Lincoln, Des. and Manu.—South-west view of York Cathedral, worked upon white silk, with the rovings of black lutestring and manufacturer's silk.

284 ROYAL VICTORIA ASYLUM for the BLIND, Newcastle-upon-Tyne.—Shawl-veil, knitted in imitation of lace. Baskets, &c. made by the blind inmates of the asylum.

285 RUSSELL, SARAH ANN, Bromsgrove, near Worcester Manu.—Berlin wool work.

286 Crochet wool toys (a tea-service, &c.)

288 SEWELL, EVANS & Co. 44, 45, 46 Old Compton St. Prop.—Straw-work on crape, applicable to various other fabrics. A patent Axminster carpet. Specimens of knitting, &c. by poor Irish children.

289 SHAKELL, MARIA, FANNY, & EDW. Belle Vue Cottage, Shirley, near Southampton.—Needlework: Scripture subject, in a frame designed and executed by E. Shakell.

290 Two crochet caps.

291 MORANT, J., 91 New Bond St.—Various carpets.

293 SHEDDEN, H. 38 Stanhope St. Liverpool, Manu. Royal standard of England, made of bunting, the devices embroidered on the whole cloth of Berlin wool.

294 SHERIDAN, P. 22 and 23 Parliament St. Dublin, Manu.—Brussels and Kidderminster carpeting, manufactured at 23 Pimlico, Dublin. Hearth rugs.

296 SHIRER, A. Cheltenham, Des.—Cut-pile Brussels carpet: manufactured by Brinton and Sons, Kidderminster.

298 SHULDAM, HARRIET, Dunmanway, Ireland.—Lace scarf.

299 SIBTHORPE, FANNY LOUISA, Limerick, Ireland—Berlin wool, Haddon Hall in the days of yore; The Morning of the Chase.

301 SIM, C. J. High St. Bedford, Manu.—Bedfordshire pillow-lace.

302 SIMCOX, G. P. Kidderminster, Inv. and Manu.—Two large finger worsted rugs. Velvet carpet, made for the marriage of the late Princess Charlotte.

304 SMITH, Mrs. R. Rolvendon, Staplehurst, Kent, Manu.—Group in wool, Her Majesty, the Princess Royal, and the Prince of Wales.

306 FOSTER, RUTTY, & Co.—Embroidered lace curtains.

307 STOKES, S. Kevin St. Police Barrack, Dublin, Inv.—Table-cover of mosaic cloth-work, composed of pieces of cloth fine-drawn together.

308 SUTTON, ELIZA, Maidstone, Des. and Manu.—A fine white crochet bed-quilt, finished with a wide lace, and lined with pink cambric.

309 SUTHERLAND, JANET, Falkirk, Scotland, Des. and Manu.—Drawing-room table-cover, embroidered in a new style, and without the aid of drawings or patterns.

310 TARIN, M. L. A. 8 Nelson St. Mornington Ct. Camden Town, Des. and Inv.—Berlin wool needlework. Lamp pillar, &c.

313 TENNISON, Mrs. M. A. 8 Broughton Pl. Hackney Rd.—Chair of papier maché, inlaid with mother-o'-pearl, with cushion of needlework.

315 TEMPLETON, J. & Co. Glasgow, Manu. and Pat.—Patent Axminster carpets; hearth-rugs; stair carpeting; Tourney table-covers; and door or window curtains, &c.

316 JOHNSON, G. & Co. 11 Bow Church Yard, 84 Bow Lane.—Mourning collars, &c.

317 THWAITES, MARY, 4 Quadrant Rd. Lower Islington, Prop.—Knitted, embroidered, and lace work, manufactured by the poor children of Newry, &c.

318 TURBEVILLE, SMITH, BOYLE, & Co. 9 Gt. Marlborough St. Prod.—Axminster carpet. Velvet pile tapestry carpet. Brussels carpet.

320 TROLLOPE, ROSE, 6 Allen Ter. Kensington.—Folding screen of tapestry work.

321 CARDINAL & Co., St. Helen's Pl., Bishopsgate.—Persian and Turkey carpeting.

322 TURNER, AGNES, Sutton Rectory, Dartford, Manu.—Knitted lace scarf.

323 UPHILL, MARY ANN, Fonthill Bishop, Salisbury, Des. and Manu.—Toilet cushion, twist, a lace scarf, and a bassinette lace cradle-cover, made of thread and fine gold.

324 VEEVERS, Mrs. Mohill, Ireland.— Articles manufactured from the fibres of plants and flowers.

325 LAWSON, J. 4 Sidmouth St. Gray's Inn Rd. Des.—Axminster hearth-rug, manu. by Blackmore, Brothers, Wilton. Designs for carpets, &c.

327 THE VICTORIA FELT CARPET Co. 8 Love Lane, Wood St. Manu.—Patent felt carpeting. Printed and embossed table-covers, window curtains, &c.

328 VINCENT, S. Turvey, Beds, Manu.—Buckinghamshire pillow-lace, veils, &c., with lace pillow and bobbins.

329 VOKES, F. 9 Hope Cottage, Clapham Rise.—Braided table-cover on a new principle

330 HAYES, Miss E. J. 24 Richmond Ter. East St. Walworth, Des. and Manu.—Pictures composed of needlework and seed-beads, including "The Successful Deerstalkers," "The Chorister Boys," "The Royal Arms," "Country Girls," and "Our Saviour administering the Sacrament."

334 WARD, ANNE, Coleraine, Ireland, Des. and Maker.—Specimens of needlework, in imitation of line engraving, and the material employed, with cotton and silk thread, on linen and lutestring.

335 WASHBOURN, ANN, Great Marlow, Bucks, Manu.—Muslin dresses, embroidered.

336 WATERHOUSE, EMMA & MARIA, A. Claremont Cottage, Loughborough Rd. Brixton, Makers.—Crochet counterpane, 12 feet square, worked in Strutt's cotton. The patterns designed by Wilks, Regent Street.

337 WATSON, BELL, & Co. 35 and 36 Old Bond St. Manu. and Imp.—Axminster carpets, manufactured by Blackmore, Brothers, and velvet-bordered Brussels carpet, manufactured by Watson and Co. Kidderminster. Carpets, manufactured in Masulipatam. Real Turkey carpets.

339 WAUGH & SON, 3 & 4 Goodge St. Des.—Royal velvet pile carpet. Design for a carpet for a Royal palace.

341 WELLS, W. B. Windmill Lane, Camberwell, Manu.—Registered floor-cloth, an imitation of Berlin wool work.

343 WHITE, SON, & Co. 108 Cheapside, Prop.—Carpets. Printed cloth table-covers.

345 WHITWELL, J. & Co. Kendal, Des. and Manu.—Kidderminster carpeting. Twilled Venetian carpet, woven in a power-loom. Improved Brussels carpet. Berlin hearth-rug, new design and material.

347 WHITNEY, E. Cleveland Pl. Bath, Des.—Embroidered lady's apron. Coat of arms in needlework.

349 WILLIAMS, LADY GRIFFIES, Marlborough.—"The Last Supper," in German wool and floss silk.

350 WILSON, ANNE, Downpatrick, Ireland, Manu.—Fancy work in wool, in which new stitches are introduced.

352 WOOD, H. and T. 22 Watling St. Prop.—Printed and embossed cloth table-covers, &c. Brussels carpet.

354 WOODWARD, B. HIGGINS, Kidderminster, Manu.—Brussels and velvet pile carpeting, in various new styles.

355 WOODWARD, H. & Co. Church St. Kidderminster, Manu.—Carpets: Velvet pile; Brussels pile, and velvet pile for stairs and corridors. Registered designs.

356 WOOLCOCK, CATHERINE, 13 New Quebec St. Portman Sq. Manu.—Banner screen, crocheted with silk, in colours.

357 WRATISLAW, MATILDA EMILY, Rugby, Warwickshire, Des. and Manu.—Cap, worked in crochet in imitation of point lace.

358 WRIGHT, CRUMP, & CRANE, Kidderminster, Manu.—Velvet pile, bordered. Brussels carpets, and stair carpets.

365 ROBERTS, Mrs. Bexley.—Knitted counterpane.

367 CHAPLIN, —.—Versicolour patchwork table cover.

371 SMITH & BABER, Knightsbridge, Inv. Des. and Manu.—Floor-cloth, in imitation of tessellated Roman pavements discovered in England.

372 BERNARD, Hon. JANE G. Cork, Killrogan, Bandon, Ireland.—Knitted quilt for a baby's crib. Exhibited on behalf of the workers, the children of Killrogan school.

373 PRIOR, Rev. H. E. Lucan, Dublin—Specimens of Irish lace, the work of the Lucan Industrial School.

374 WEST, C. MARY, 1 Brougham Ter. Kingstown, Dublin, Des. and Manu.—Scarf of black lace, embroidered in a new style, in Deccan silk, interspersed with wings of the Indian beetle, &c.

375 BATES, JEMIMA, Gt. Dover St. Surrey, Des.—Specimens of needlework upon machine net.

377 DALRYMPLE MARY E. 5 Wilton St. Grosvenor Pl. Inv. and Prod.—Table-cover of fawn-coloured cloth, embroidered with chenille.

378 FANCOURT, CATHERINE, Grimsthorpe, near Bourne, Des. and Manu.—Fancy bed-quilt.

379 LADY MAYORESS (1850), and 150 LADIES of GREAT BRITAIN, the executants.—Part of the pattern for a carpet, presented to and exhibited by Her Majesty the Queen; design by J. W. Papworth; the patterns painted by and the work superintended by W. B. Simpson, West Strand.

381 GEORGE, J. B. 4 Wells St. Gray's Inn Rd. Des.—Design for an Axminster centre carpet, in the Italian style.

382 BRAYSHAW, J. 118 Church St. Lancaster.—Counterpane of mosaic needlework, in forty-four compartments, each representing a popular print.

384 KIDDLE, J. Norwich, Inv.—Woven cushion, completed in the loom without the aid of needlework.

386 GILL, W. L. Colyton, Axminster, Manu.—Honiton lace:—Portion of an original design for the flounce made for Her Majesty. Chromatic silk berthe, silk lappet, &c.

388 AYERS, W. Newport Pagnell, Bucks.—Specimens Buckinghamshire pillow lace pieces.

390 JACKSON & GRAHAM, 37 & 38 Oxford St.—London carpet. Carpets of moresque design. Velvet pile carpets. Patent tapestry velvet carpet and border. London rugs, &c Carpet-loom at work (in North Transept.)

391 TAWTON, MARY, 9 Union St. Plymouth, Manu. and Des.—Child's cloak, elaborately braided and embroidered.

392 PENLEY, E. A. Grove House, St. Peter's, Margate, Des. and Manu.—Silk patch-work table-cover, box pattern.

394 BENNOCH, TWENTYMANN & RIGG, 77 Wood St. Cheapside. — Ribbons. gimps, fringes, trimmings, silks, handkerchiefs, satin wire, bullion, and gimp, for manufacturing purposes.

395 BEAVIS, J. 27 Mint St. Borough.—A hearth-rug.

396 HEAL & SON, Tottenham Ct. Rd. Manu.—A crimson satin eider-down quilt, with white satin border, embroidered. Duvet in blue and gold silk, filled with eiderdown.

398 SZAFFELD, S. 4 Dean St. Finsbury, Prod.—Por-

trait of Her Majesty and His Royal Highness Prince Albert in Berlin wool work. Cartoon, in Berlin wool work.

400 BENTINCK, Col. H. for R. Palmer.—A table-cloth, embroidered with the royal arms and various other devices. Made by Robert Palmer, a private in the Coldstream uards.

401 BRIGHT & Co. 22 New Brown St. Manchester, and 20 Skinner St. London, Manu.—Velvet pile carpets woven in Sievier's patent loom, and printed by patent machinery, invented by Burch. Patent tapestries for curtains, &c.

403 UNDERWOOD, W. 1 Vere St. Oxford St. Manu.—Heraldic tapestry hanging.

VARIOUS DESIGNS.

173 NAYLOR, J. H. St. Mary's Pl. Nottingham.—Shawl centre.

179 TURTON, S. Radford, Nottingham.—Single tier lace curtain.

180 MOIR, McD. Clumber St. Nottingham.—Shawl centre.

183 MILFORD, J. Nottingham.—Lace scarf.

184 BOLLER, C. Nottingham.—Lace flouncing.

269 HEALD, B. Nottingham.—Flouncing in Honiton lace.

295 HEALD, H. Nottingham.—Black lace shawl.

Proceed to British Colonial Possessions, page 156.

Class 20. ARTICLES OF CLOTHING, FOR IMMEDIATE, PERSONAL, OR DOMESTIC USE.

—— South Transept Gallery. ——

1 BUCKMASTER, W. & Co. 3 New Burlington St. Des.—Proposed new court suit, in detail. Chaco. New head-dress for infantry of the line. Undress military coat.

2 FOSTER, PORTER, & Co. 47 Wood St. Cheapside, Manu.—Silk, thread, woollen, leather, and silk-plush gloves. Bandannas. Ribbons. Fancy hosiery, &c.

3 TAYLOR, W. G. 285 Regent St. Prop.—Balbriggan lace-stockings, lambs'-wool stockings, knitted by hand, and hosiery, knit by children at Ballindine.

4 HALL, J. S. 308 Regent St. Manu.—Elastic stock-ing-net boots, elastic webbing, and improved elastic mate-rials for boots and shoes.

5 PEART & DOSSETOR, 12 and 13 Poultry, Inv.—Cotton and silk glove half-hose; cotton and woollen drawers. Rail-road caps and protectors. Silk shirt fleeced, for rheumatism. Flannel. Silk and Segovia half-hose.

6 POPE & PLANTE, 4 Waterloo Pl. Pall Mall, Manu.—Specimens of hosiery. Beaver fur stockings, and scarf, made on the hosiery frame. Elastic netted corsets. Reg.

7 NEVELL & Co. 11 Gresham St. West, Manu.—Frame-worked knitted hosiery and other wearing apparel.

8 GREGORY, CUBITT, & Co. 15 Aldermanbury, Imp. and Manu.—Specimens of straw, chip, and horsehair manu-factures in the various stages. Flag-grass, from Cuba; hats from the same, called Brazilian hats.

9 PRICE & HARVEY, D. 6 Pilgrim St. Ludgate Hill, and Tottenham.—White bonnet, patented. Registered car-riage bonnet. Dress opera bonnet, &c.

10 FIELD & SONS, 114 Fore St. Cripplegate, and Har-penden, Herts, Manu.—Improved Dunstable bonnets. Chip bonnet, manufactured from the poplar-tree. Straw bonnets, in new designs and combination of materials.

11 VYSE & SONS, 76 Wood St. Manu.—Ladies' bonnets, of finest quality, produced from wheat-straw, plaited and made up by the hand. Fancy horse-hair and straw: the material made by the loom, and then sewn into bonnets by the hand. Leghorn: the material produced in Italy, the bonnet formed in London.

12 WELCH & SONS, 44 Gutter Lane.—Specimens of wheat straw, straw plaits, bonnets, &c.

13 ALLAN, J. 158 Cheapside, Manu. and Des.—Ladies' and children's straw bonnets and hats, of a peculiar com-bination of material.

14 SPURDEN, WOOLLEY, SANDERS & Co. 42 Friday St.

Manu.—Bonnets of split straw plait, made by hand of English plait, showing the inner side of the straw, &c.

15 WOODHOUSE & LUCKMAN, 33 Wood St. Cheapside, Des. and Manu.—Bonnets, made from the English willow.

16 WINGRAVE & SONS, 62 Wood St. and at 2 St. Albans.—A variety of bonnets.

16A LONG, G. Loudwater, Wycomb, Bucks. Inv. Des. & Manu.—Hats and bonnets made upon a lace pillow.

17 HOMAN & Co. late RODGERS & SON, 39 and 40 Chis-well St. Finsbury, Manu.—Printed handkerchiefs, and other shirts; flannel vests; braces; purses; riding belts, &c.

18 PHILLPOTTS, MARY ANNE, 37 North Audley St. Prop.—Figure of a lady in full court dress.

19 PATERSON, J. 104 Wood St. Cheapside, Manu.—Fancy cravats. Black satin stock. Improved braces. Belts. Collars. Shirt-front, plaited in the loom.

20 NEVILL & Co. 124 Wood St. and 1, 2, and 3 Gold-smith St.—A piece of Irish linen made from the finest flax. A shirt, shirt-front, and collars, made from the above piece of linen. Richly embroidered neck-tie.

21 CAPPER & WATERS, 26 Regent St. St. James's, Inv. and Manu.—Five Corazza dress shirts; court dress. Sotta-nello of silk. Registered frock dress. Fatigue shirt, trans-pirante. Sottanello tourist, registered. Tourist, weighing 3¾ ounces. Morning shirt.

22 WHEELER & ABLETT, 234 Regent St. and 28 Poultry, Manu.—The bachelor's shirt, of peculiar construction, without buttons. Child's jacket; pair of gaiters and pair of gloves as specimens of English embroidery.

23 REID, W. 51 Conduit St. Hanover Sq. Inv. and Manu.—The registered " sans-pli " shirt.

24 BRIE, J. & Co. 189 Regent St. Prod. and Des.—Shirt fronts. Shirts of an improved cut. Embroidered handker-chiefs and flannel waistcoats.

25 MARSHALL, W. 80 Regent St. Inv. and Manu.—Re-gistered improved shape shirt.

26 POWELL, S. 52 Regent St. Inv. and Pat.—Bisunique, or reversible garments, coats, vests, trousers, paletots, &c. The royal bisunique jacket, constructed of cloth which has two distinct faces of contrasting colours, in one fabric.

27 BARNES, T. & G. 9 New Ct. Goswell St. Des. and Manu.—Registered buckskin braces, of new and old designs. " Flexible " razor-strops.

28 HEMMING, E. 6 Piccadilly, Des.—A model shirt, of r fine Manchester long cloth and Irish linen.

29 SMITH, J. E. 3 Lawrence Lane, Manu—Shirt without seams or gathers. Moravian needlework, illustrating the growth of flax.

30 PORTER, T. 94 Strand, Manu.—Specimen of a shirt cut on mathematical principles.

31 WAGNER, LOUISA & MARIAN, 35 Doddington Grove, Des. and Manu.—Feathers and rosettes, in coloured mohair silk. Hand-netted head-dresses, in floss silk, &c. Fancy bracelets. Silk caps. Berthe caps, of gold, silver, and chenille, &c.

32 ATLOFF, J. G. 69 New Bond St. Inv.—Ladies' shoes of various materials; silk slippers, embroidered in gold; ladies' silk boots, and ladies' half boots.

33 WEATHERHEAD, H. 27 Panton St. Haymarket, Manu. —Silk and India-rubber braces. Gros-de-Naples belt, with silk and India-rubber springs.

34 NICOLL, B. 42 Regent Circus, and 46 Lombard St. Manu.—Shirt of a new material, in silk. Shirt of Irish linen. Hunting shirt.

35 CHRISTY & CO., Gracechurch St.—Specimens of hat manufacture.

36 FORD, R. 185 Strand, Manu.—Shirt, intended as a specimen of plain British needlework, &c.

37 GLENNY, C. 33 Lombard St. City, Prop.—Cotton hosiery, manufactured at Balbriggan, in Ireland.

38 SANDLAND & CRANE, 55 Quadrant, Regent St. Inv. and Manu.—Belt drawers and shirt exhibited on a statuette.

39 BRADSHAW, G. 103 Bishopsgate St. and 25 High St. Islington, Inv. and Pat.—Patent fastening, as applied to gentlemen's collars, stocks, &c. Gentlemen's anti-rheumatic belt and drawers.

40 JOUBERT, C. 8 Maddox St. Hanover Sq.—Self-adjusting white watered corset. Elastic corset belt for invalids. India-rubber tissue, of French manufacture.

40A ROBERTS, G. 183 Oxford St. Manu.—Corset made upon an expanding principle; corset, requiring no lacing, &c. measurement of the human body.

41 PIPER, T. F. 4 Bishopsgate St. Without, Inv. and Manu.—Mechanical spring-corset, scapular or contractr.

42 MARTIN, E. & E. H. 504 Oxford St. Des.—Elastic bodices, composed of vulcanized India-rubber and other materials. India-rubber belts.

43 SYKES, MARY E. 280 Regent St. Inv. and Manu.— Elastic corset, with new mode of fastening. Registered.

44 DEVY, ELIZA, 73 Grosvenor St. Inv. and Manu.— New registered riding stays. Nursing stays. Dress stays, &c.

45 CAPPER & SON, 69 Gracechurch St. part Inv. and Makers.—Registered bassinete pliante, trimmed with lace made in Ireland. Another, folded for carriage. Infant's basket, lace made in Ireland. Various clothing.

46 THOMAS, W. & BROTHERS, 128 and 129 Cheapside, Pat. and Manu.—Specimens of patent inventions; stays wove without seam. Elastic corsets. Webbing or tape for Venetian blinds, made in one fabric. Safety carpet and leather bags.

46A SHREEVE, Mrs. Charing Cross.—Elastic knitted corset.

48 JOHNSON & CO. 113 Regent St. Pat.—Patent ventilating hats. Military and naval cocked hats. Full-dress court hats. Her Majesty's royal state livery hats. Ladies' riding hats, &c.

49 GEARY, N. 61 St. James's St. Inv. and Manu.—Improved and elastic corsets, belts, spinal-supporting corset, perforated gossamer corset, hydropathic belt, &c.

50 DANDO, SONS. & CO. 42, 43, 44 Cheapside, Manu.— Specimens of a new description of patent light, net-work velvet hats, in various stages of manufacture.

51 WHITE, W. 68 Cheapside, Manu.—Ventilating velvet-nap and zephyr hats.

51A FELIX & CO. 10 Cheapside.—Hats of a peculiar construction, designed to render them elastic, waterproof, and ventilating.

52 ASHTON & SONS, 55 Cornwall Rd. Manu. and Inv.— Drab and black patent elastic beaver hat, on beaver body. Light elastic velvet hat; French plush, &c.

53 ASHMEAD & TYLER, J. T. 7 Mount St. Grosvenor Sq. Inv.—Patent folding hat, without springs. Soft velvet folding hat. Minerva hunting cap.

54 MELTON, H. 194 Regent St. Manu.—Hats made of English plush, by Walters and Son, Finsbury.

55 SMITH, GEORGE, & CO. Union Hall, Union St. Borough, Inv. and Manu.—Light silk hat; silk hat on soft felt body; lady's riding hat; a gossamer body japanned.

56 DIETRICH, F. A. 2 Bennett St. Blackfriars Rd. Inv. and Manu.—Patent elastic hat lining. Newly-invented silk hat; military cocked hat; court hat, and lady's riding hat, on horsehair body.

57 BARBER, S. Brentford, Inv. and Manu.—French silk hat, the body being made of Manilla grass, combining lightness, durability, and perfect ventilation, being waterproof, and resisting the grease.

58 STAINBURN & BAUGH, Gresham St. Manu.—Illustrations of the processes of felting beaver and silk hats.

59 ZOX, L. 84 Long Acre, Manu.—Registered Korychlamyd, or helmet cap. Patent aquatic naval life-cap. Folding college cap, &c.

60 GROSJEAN, F. 109 Regent St. Inv.—Invention for producing a red stripe on regimental trousers. Safety pockets, &c.

61 GARRARD, R. & J. Loman St. Southwark.—Japanned leather peaks for caps. Registered japanned felt hat. Fireman's japanned leather helmet, &c.

62 THOMPSON & SON, 11 Conduit St. Des.—Jackets, hunting coat, trousers, waistcoats, and ladies' polka, of elastic British webbing.

63 WALKER & BABB, 346 Strand, Inv.—Registered waterproof alpaca over-coat and case that can be carried in a coat pocket.

64 CODY, J. 6 Marshall St. Inv.—The "monomeroskiton," a dress coat of British manufacture, from one piece of cloth.

64A BRAUN, L. 65 Wood St.—Caps of various sizes.

65 KISCH, S. A. 250 Regent St. Inv.—Registered autocrematic gown, and Cossack waistcoat.

66 BRAUND, J. 26 Mount St. Grosvenor Sq.—Travelling cap, with transparent peak. Manufactured by Christy and Co., Gracechurch Street.

67 LYONS, J. 12 and 13 Artillery Pl. Woolwich.— Military caps.

68 PRICE, W. 115 Chancery Lane, Des. and Manu.— Flexible spring gowns: law, clerical, and civic.

69 CUTLER, W. 25 St. James's St. Inv.—The "duplexa," or morning and evening coat.

70 BAIN, W. 141 High Holborn, Inv.—Floatable life-preserving cape cloak.

71 SMITH & GIBBS, Wellingborough, Northamptonshire, and 84 Cheapside, London, Inv. and Manu.—Cloth and leather gaiters, with patent fastenings, &c.

72 GATES, LAURA CHARLOTTE, 5 Upper Eaton St. Pimlico.—Model of lady's dress, with elastic sides.

73 HURLEY, D. 10 Hare Ct. Aldersgate St. Inv. and Manu.—Lady's safety pocket. Model of a pair of trousers, with improvements, &c.

74 CAHAN, E. 371 Strand, Des.—The Anaxyridian trousers.

75 SHINTON, R. 29 Spencer St., St. George's East.—A pocket protector.

76 BETHEL, WARE, & CO. 62 Aldermanbury, Manu.—

Bonnets, hats, and ornamental work, in Devon, Luton, Italian, chip, and Dunstable plait.

77 ROBERTS, E. B. 239 Regent St. and 32 Moorgate.— The beaver (castor-fibre) applied to articles of clothing.

78 DENT, ALLCROFT, & Co. 97 Wood St. Manu.—An assortment of ladies' and gentlemen's gloves of various materials, colours, and styles, with plain and fancy sewing.

79 THRESHER & GLENNY, 152 Strand, Manu.—India gauze waistcoats. Silk and thread, silk and lambs'-wool, and improved spun-silk hosiery. Spun-silk for under clothing. Gauze merino waistcoats. Hosiery, made from waste silk.

80 BALL, W. Y. & Co. 32 Wood St. Cheapside, Manu. —Kid leather gloves, cut and made in England; manufactured from French-dressed kid skins.

81 LART & SON, 116 Wood St. and Rutland St. Nottingham, Inv. and Manu.—Ladies' Lisle thread hose and silk jacket, made in the stocking frame at Nottingham. Gentlemen's pantaloon drawers, with elastic washable gussets. Gentlemen's cotton and spun silk half-hose, and children's socks. Gentlemen's merino, kashmir, and spun-silk vests.

82 FOWNES BROTHERS, 41 Cheapside, Manu.—Ladies gloves, from kid skins, produced in Ireland and dressed in England. Gloves, from French-dressed kid skins. Silk, velvet, Lisle thread, beaver, Vicuna wool, and other gloves.

83 MACDOUGALL, D. Inverness, Scotland, Manu.— Tartan plaids. A Shetland knitted shawl. Highland carpet, made from first-class Sutherland Cheviot wool. Plaid and tweed manufactured at St. Kilda, the most remote of the British islands. Home-made gloves of wool, and of wool of the white mountain hare. A woman's shoulder plaid, &c., showing the state of industry in Lewis eighty-three years ago. Linsey-woolsey, made of Cheviot wool and bog cotton. Tweed, &c., made of Vicuna wool. Highland brooches, made of carved bog-oak, deer's teeth, and Cairngorms. Highland ornaments. Yarns, showing native dyes; native dye-stuffs. Specimens of rock crystal, or Cairngorm, from the mountain of that name in Inverness-shire.

84 HOLMES, J. & Co. 171 Regent St. Inv. and Manu.— Full-dress or opera cloak, composed of the finest white wool, and ornamented with 1,200 gold pendants. Registered shawl-cloak, woven in one piece. Cloak of cameleon cloth. Reg.

85 WIGHAM & Co. Edinburgh.—Tartan plaids or long shawls of various Highland clans, combined and separate.

86 SOLOMON, SARAH, 52 York Rd. Lambeth, Des. and Manu.—A lady's English costume ball dress, embroidered with gold and silk.

87 GWATKIN, EMILY & ELIZA, 37 Westminster Bridge Rd. Des.—Bonnet made from cotton, crochet, and bonnet made of satin, of new design and workmanship.

88 OLIVER, B. S. Nottingham.—Various boxes for containing lace, hosiery, &c.

89 MILES, S. Bunhill Row.—A variety of Berlin wool-work.

90 SAXTON, A. Nottingham, Manu.—Ladies' mitts, cuffs, and gloves, embroidered and made of silk; neck-ties and silk shawls, Jacquard pattern, &c.

91 SHAW, J. Radford, near Nottingham.—Berlin wool vest, made from the stocking frame, with the Jacquard. Piece for window curtains from the stocking frame, and "antimacassar" from the stocking frame (cotton).

92 THURMAN, PIGGOTT, & Co. Friar Lane, Nottingham, Manu. and Inv.—Thurman's patent silk hosiery.

93 GALLOWAY & SONS, Nottingham.—A variety of silk gloves.

94 FURLEY, J. Nottingham, Manu.—Merino vests, in wool and mixed materials.

96 HOLLINS, S. Nottingham, Manu.—Lace goods :— Machine-made cotton Brussels nets and laces, figured by the needle. Various hosiery goods.

97 MUSSON, R. & J. Nottingham, Manu.—Silk gloves, Lisle thread gloves. Patent Brayama gloves; a new material. Embroidered gloves.

98 CARVER & GILBERT, Nottingham, Prop. and Manu. —Cotton; Novi silk; spun silk; merino; cashmere. Gentlemen's and ladies' vests.

99 HURST & SONS, Nottingham, Manu.—Brown and white, plain, open work and embossed cotton hose and half-hose; cotton, and spun silk drawers and vests.

100 ALLEN & SOLLY, Nottingham and London, Manu.— Samples of hosiery, showing the progress of cotton-spinning for hosiery from an early period.

101 MORLEY, I. & R. London and Nottingham.— Specimens of cotton and lisle thread stockings; Balbriggan stockings; silk stockings; silk gloves and socks; Derby-ribbed socks; lisle thread socks; half-hose; merino half-hose; spun silk shirts, &c.

102 TRESS & Co. Blackfriars Rd. Manu.—Silk hats, &c.

103 BERNI & MELLIARD, 56 and 57 Gt. Guildford St. Southwark, and 203 Strand, Manu.—Military and court hats, new styles. Ladies' black napless beaver riding hats. Silk plush hats. Velvet folding opera hat.

104 EVELEIGH & SON, Manchester, Manu.—Various kinds of hats, in silk, felt, and cork.

105 SIMMONDS & WOODMAN, Oldham, Manu.—Beaver hatting materials, from the skin to the hat complete. Black silk hats, and patent reflectors.

106 STANDISH, ANNE, Kidderminster, Lace-worker.— Court dress of needle-work.

107 HILL, L. M. Whitby, Inv.—"Unique habit," cut out in one piece, and having few seams.

108 WATTS, W. Banbury, Inv.—Complete coat, trousers, and gaiters, in one piece, without any seam.

109 WALSH & Co. Bristol.— Embroidered over-coat.

110 GOULDING, J. Beverley, Inv. and Manu.—Novel full-dress coat, with two seams instead of nine.

110A LEE, J.—A quilted coat, and instrument for quilting.

111 HARRIS & TOMKINS, Abingdon, Berks, Manu.— White duck agricultural labourer's frocks, designed by T. Watson; worked by Hannah and Esther Stimpson, cottagers, Radley.

112 CAULCHER, J. D. Anstruther Villa, Boundary Rd. St. John's Wood, Inv.—Life-preserving elastic cork-jacket, capable of being worn unobserved under a coat.—Reg.

113 DOUDNEY, E. 17 Old Bond St. Inv. and Maker.—Waterproof Irish poplin registered cloak.

114 LEWIS & SON, 1 Quiet St. and 1 John St. Bath, Des. —Over-coat, of novel design and light texture.

115 DINGLEY, W. & S. Sherborne, Inv.—A new over-coat, combining a paletot, trousers, and wrapper. Reg.

115A CROSS, C. & Co. Corporation St. Manchester.— Articles of clothing made by power-loom.

116 FRY, J. L. Honiton, Devon, Inv. and Manu.— Dress coat: the body cut in one piece of cloth. New measure, registered.

117 GRIFFIN, B. High St. Leominster, Herefordshire, Inv.—Four systems of cutting coats, vests, trousers, &c.

118 M'GEE, J. G. & Co. Belfast, Manu.—Embroidered vests: the designs by pupils of the Belfast Government School of Design; the embroidery by poor girls.

119 SMITH, CHARLOTTE, Bedford, Inv.—Patent symmetrical corsets; patent elastic silk boots, made by Mr. Longdon, of Derby.

120 GALLAWAY, T. 43 Albion St. Leeds, Manu.—Three woven corsets.

E 3

121 ODDY, S. Armley, Leeds, Manu.—Coloured fine wool shawls, with rich embroidered corners, &c.

122 TINSLEY, J. & Co. Leeds, Manu.—Improved woven corsets for ladies' wear, without a seam; made of pine cotton yarn expressly prepared.

123 MIDDLEBROOK, T. Leeds, Manu.—Military officer's cap and cover

124 HALEY, W. Leeds, Inv. and Manu.—Protection travelling cap, adapted for cold climates.

125 MOLLADY & SONS, Warwick, Manu. — Stuff and silk hats and bonnets. Raw materials, in the different stages of manufacture. Cork hats, zephyr, and silk. Welsh lady's hat. Felt bonnet.

126 CARRINGTON, S. & T. Stockport, Manu.—Felt hats of various descriptions.

126A PEARSON, J. Gorse Brow, Stockport, Manu.— White beaver bonnet.

127 TAYLOR & Co. St. James St. Rochdale.—Specimens of hat silk plush.

127A LEES, A. Manchester, Manu.—Felt, velvet, and alpaca hats. Cloth caps.

128 M'RAE, J. J. Newark, Notts, Des. and Inv.—A triple stay, for those parts of male attire requiring additional strength. Waistcoats of novel form and arrangement, to supersede the use of braces: the fabric manufactured by Peace & Co. Clayton West, near Huddersfield.

128A JOHNSTON, J. Stirling.—Hose, showing improvements at different periods.

129 PATERSON, J. Dumfries, Des. and Manu.—A web of patterns, a vest, several vest-pieces, and half-hose. All off the common stocking-frame.

131 DARLING, G. 35 George St. Perth, Inv. and Manu.—Gentlemen's hats, thoroughly waterproof and ventilated, the mode of ventilation being quite novel. Highland bonnets.

132 GIBSON, C. Perthshire.—Shepherd's plaid of natural colour.

133 LAING, J. Hawick, Scotland.—Patterns of hosiery and under clothing knitted upon the stocking-frame, from Australian wools.

134 HADDEN & SONS, Aberdeen, Manu. — Knitting worsteds, spun from British wools. 1,000 colours, dyed on worsteds manufactured from British and Saxony wools. Knitted worsted shawl and hosiery.

135 SMART, R. 10 Upper Eaton St. Grosvenor Pl. Inv. —The "Subclavian sector," an apparatus for taking a more correct measurement of the body.

135A CATTANACH, B. Aberdeen, Inv.—Apparatus for measuring the human figure, and for transferring the measure to cloth.

136 ROY, JESSIE, Ferry Hill, Aberdeen, Inv.—A landscape, knitted in Berlin worsteds. A pair of stockings, with Cashmere pattern.

137 WOOD, JANET, Stonehaven, Scotland, Manu.—Pair of fancy knitten worsted gloves.

138 WEBB, Capt. THEODOSIUS, R. E. Woolwich, Prop.—Specimen of knitting from Shetland Isles.

139 WHITEHEAD & SON, 41 South Bridge St. Edinburgh Manu.—Tartan hose, each pair containing 1,300 diamonds.

140 KAYE, FINDLAY, & Co. Langholm and Glasgow, Manu.—Cheviot wool hose; Saxony wool; grey Shetland wool; and Vicuna wool hose. Gauze vests, and full dresses, of Cheviot wool; pantaloons, of Cheviot and Saxony wool, &c,

141 SCOTT, P. 9 South Bridge, Edinburgh, Des. and Manu.—The V-breasted and swivel-collared shirt.

142 MACKENZIE, W. B. 126 Princc's St. Edinburgh, Prop.—Articles knitted by the hand in the Shetland Islands, from the wool of their sheep. Stockings have been made from a very ancient period; but fanciful knitting is of recent introduction.

143 JOHNSTON, J. & G. Paisley, and 2 Chapter House Ct. St. Paul's, London.—Buckram and Paris net bonnet tops and crowns, manufactured by steam power.

144 LAUGHLAND, J. Kilmarnock, Scotland, Manu.—Australian sheep's wool. Officer's dress bonnet, showing the process of knitting. Bonnets of Australian wool, worn by the officers of the Highland regiments. Forage caps. Prince Charlie, Turkish, Balmoral, and Glengary bonnets.

145 RITCHIE, P. Kilmarnock, Scotland, Manu.—Regulation military forage caps: Scarlet Fez cap; Prince Charlie caps; Balmoral and Glengarry caps; Caledonian hats, &c.

146 COPLAND, MISS, Lerwick.—Specimens of Shetland hand-knitting.

147 LENNOX, F. M. K. Lennox Castle, Lennox Town, Glasgow, and 9 Arlington St. Piccadilly, Prop.—The needlewoman's shirts, cut and worked by one pair of hands.

147A RUTTENS, HELENE, 13 Charles St. Soho, Inv.—The fan bonnet. A bonnet in white silk, contained in a fan box.

148 HAYWOOD, MARY, 3 Dyer's Buildings, City Road, Des.—A shawl of white cashmere, worked in braid, ornamented and fringed with peacocks' feathers, &c.

149 JONES, J. 17 Duke St. Liverpool, Inv.—Tailor's symmetrometer, for cutting coats and waistcoats. Registered Trousers' rule.

149A ROBINSON, J.—Measuring apparatus for tailors.

150 CLOWES, F. St. Ann St. Birmingham.—Registered belt, vest, and braces. Elastic coat.

151 MINIFIE, C. Bristol, Inv. and Manu.—Registered coat-sleeve shirt.

152 M'CLINTOCK, J. & Co. Barnsley, Inv. and Manu.—Double silk elastic woven corsets, to fit the body and not impede respiration. Thread-wove corset, without seam.

153 BIRT, A. Shepton Mallet, near Wells, Somersetshire, Inv.—The Birtan transitional coat Surtout, with concealed hood for travelling, &c.

154 TOLLET, G. Besley Hall, near Newcastle, Staffordshire.—Tippets, cuffs, cloak, victorines, and muffs, composed of feathers and goose down, made by the needle.

155 HODGSON, T. Jun. 39 Iron Market, Newcastle-under-Lyme, Des. and Manu.—Elastic corset. Invisible spinal support.

156 CLEMES & SON, St. Austell, Manu.—Hats for Cornish miners, &c., for protection against falling stones, &c.

156A BEAUFORT, Miss, Cork.—Knitted child's pelisse.

157 MASON, W. Newcastle-under-Lyme, Manu.—Velvet-nap hats, on an improved body; waterproof beaver hat; Waterproof felt hat. Silk hat, on a body of Cashmere.

158 LAURENCE, ELIZABETH, 15 Montpelier Walk, Cheltenham, Manu.—White French merino dress, braided and trimmed with satin. Crimson velvet dress for boys, braided. White satin drawn-bonnet.

159 WHITE, E. Edgar Buildings, Bath. — Bassinette, completely furnished. Infant's frock and robe. Lady's chemise and night-dress. Gentleman's shirt.

160 HATHAWAY, Mrs. Brompton, near Chatham.—A baby's hat knitted in fine white silk.

161 FIRMIN & SONS, 153 Strand, and 13 Conduit St. Bond St. Manu.—Specimens of buttons. Stars of the Order of the Garter, the Thistle, and of St. Patrick. Swords.

162 HURST & REYNOLDS, 100 New St. Birmingham, Manu.—Lady's corset, to fasten, &c. without lacing.

162A BEESTON, J. S. Swaile's Cottages, Hammersmith.—Inflated railway travelling caps.

163 FIRKINS, J. & Co. Worcester, Manu. — Ladies' habits. French kid gloves; calf gloves; Cape-goat gloves. Lamb, buck, doe. Lisle, Berlin, and cloth gloves. Prov. reg.

164 REDGRAVE, J. Worcester.—Men's Cape gloves. Ladies' white Cape gauntlets. Habits made from lambskins and Cape sheep.

165 RIDLEY, J. St. Paul's Churchyard.—Ladies' boots and shoes.

166 THROGMORTON, Sir JOHN, for the NEWBURY LOCAL COMMITTEE.—An oil painting: instance of a coat made from the fleece in thirteen hours and a half.

167 NORMAN, S. W. 4 Oakley St. Lambeth, Inv. and Manu.—Ladies' cork and leather light waterproof boots. Ladies' shoes.

168 LONGDON & SONS, Derby, Manu.—Patent frame-work gloves, without any seam on one side. Smith's patent boot, which requires no lacing.

168A HELPS, Miss, London Rd. Liverpool.—Gutta percha articles.

169 POORE, J. B. 9 Princes Ct. Banner St. St. Luke's, Des. and Manu.—A lady's victorine, with two cuffs to match, made of feathers, ornamentally arranged. Original design and manufacture.

170 BARFORD, F. Market Pl. St. Albans, Hertfordshire, Inv.—Brazilian palm-leaf Wellington hats : registered. The "Princess Alice hat," and the "Chinese hat." Hats from the English willow tree.

171 ASHTON, A. George St. Portman Sq.—Registered bonnet and case.

172 ELLIOTT, W. Dunstable, Beds, Manu.—Straw hats, bonnets, plait, and fancy straw articles.

172A COOPER, J. J. & G. Dunstable, Manu.—Plait and fancy straw articles. Straw hats and bonnets.

173 MUIRS, CONNELL, & BRODIE, Luton, Bedfordshire, Manu.—Specimens of plaits and bonnets, made from wheat straw grown in Bedfordshire. Specimens of the straw in all stages of the work, &c.

174 LINKLATER, —, Shetland Isles. Specimens of knitting peculiar to the islands.

175 KEARSE, T. 40 George St. Limerick, Ireland, Des. —Winter and summer overcoat combined, composed of Irish frieze and tabinet, &c.

176 FARRANGE, Miss, Wicklow, Ireland. — Knitted stockings.

177 VINCENT, R. Glastonbury, Manu.—Suit of leather clothes, to imitate superfine black cloth.

177A STEWART, JANE, Templetrine Glebe, Bandon, Ireland, Prop.—Articles made at the Templetrine Industrial School by the poorest class of the peasantry.

178 KELLY, J. & Co. 98 High St. Kilkenny, Ireland.— Buckskin hunting breeches ; buckskin raw material, &c.

179 NAIRN, T. G. Limerick, Manu.—Irish uniform frock for the Royal Horse Artillery. Irish frieze national cape, and Irish frieze paletot jacket.

180 WOODHOUSE, 39 Lower Ormond Quay, Dublin, Manu.—Gilt and plated buttons. German silver letters and figures. Brass mountings for military accoutrements.

181 PEASANTS, FEMALE, of Wexford, Ireland.—Samples of traneen grass of Irish growth, plaited in the Leghorn and Tuscan style.

182 MAHER, LOUISA, Ballinkeele, Enniscortley, Ireland, Prop.—Samples of Cynosurus cristatus grass, or Traneen ; and of rye straw. Plait of these articles. Articles made of Traneen plait, and of rye straw plait.

183 WILSON & SON, Drogheda, Balbreggan.—Balbreggan stockings.

184 DICKS, W. Yeovil.—Lambs'-skin gloves.

185 ENSOR, T. Milborne Port, near Sherborne.—Fur Gloves. Gloves lined with silk plush, wool, &c. Kid, goat, calf, lamb, sheep, deer, and fawn gloves. Patent purse glove.

186 WHITBY, E. Yeovil. — Skin in various stages of manufacture, and gloves.

187 PITMAN, J. Milborne Port.—An assortment of gloves.

188 RAWLINGS, J. B. Abbey Silk Mills, Sherborne, Dor-set, Manu.—Gloving and sewing silks, for tambour. Scarf, half twist cloth, &c. of superior quality.

189 MONEY, ELIZABETH, Woodstock, Oxon, Manu.— Lamb-skin, as received from leather-dresser. Gloves made from lamb-skins. Fawn-skin riding-gloves for ladies.

190 CORRY, J. & J. Queen Camel, near Yeovil, Somerset. —Coloured and white lambskins. Coloured and black leather grain gloves.

191 MATHEISON, LADY.—School in the Hebrides.

192 THOMPSON, J. & Co. Kendal, Manu.—Hand-knit Guernsey frocks. Kilmarnock caps. Fancy Glengarry and plaid bonnets, mits, overalls, &c.

193 FRY, J. Godalming, Surrey, Manu.—Lisle thread hose embroidered. Fleecy breast-plates. Segovia shirts and pantaloons. Merino shirts and vests. Cotton pantaloons, drawers, and shirts.

194 HOLLAND, T. & Co. Langham Factory, Godalming, Inv. and Manu.—Under clothing, manufactured of a fleecy, superior, and peculiarly prepared wool. Segovia shirts, trousers, hose, &c. Outer clothing. Registered shirts.

195 WARD, STRUT, SHARP, & WARD, Belper, Derbyshire, & 89 Wood St. Cheapside, Manu.—Specimens of hosiery and glove manufactures ; lisle-thread, merino, cashmere, and silk.

196 CARTWRIGHT & WARNERS, Loughborough, Leicester, Manu.—Patent Angola and merino yarns. Hose. Shirts, drawers, ladies' vests and dresses, &c.

197 TAYLOR & BEALES, Leicester, Manu.—Worsted and woollen hose. Cotton stockings of all kinds.

198 HARRIS & SONS, Leicester, Manu.—Gloves, cuffs, and gaiters. Caps, hoods, hats, and bonnets. Mantillas and muffs. Worsted vests. Lambs'-wool pantaloons. Fancy cotton shirts. Children's dresses. Polkas and jackets.

199 HUDSON, J. Leicester, Manu.—Lambs'-wool, Cheviot Cashmere, Saxony, Victoria, and worsted hose.

200 BAINES, J. Bowling Green St. Leicester.—Wool, worsted, and Cashmere hose and half-hose.

201 BILLSON & HAMES, Leicester, Manu.—Children's socks and ¾ hose.

202 ANGRAVE BROTHERS, Leicester, Manu.—Lambs'-wool hose, shirts, and pantaloons. Royal ribbed and Cashmere shirts and pantaloons. Ladies' woollen vests and dresses.

203 WARD & SONS, Leicester—Patent fancy cravats, boas, and pelerines without seam. Alpaca coats and capes. Polka coats. Worsted and cotton hose. Wool frocks, &c.

204 BEALE, C. & LATCHMORE, 5 Belvoir St. Leicester, Manu. — Lambs'-wool shirts, pantaloons, drawers, vests, ladies' dresses, &c.

205 BIGGS & SONS, Leicester, Manu.—Worsted, lambs'-wool, royal ribbed, and cashmere shirts and drawers, hose, &c. Guernsey and Jersey frock. Fancy polka-coats. Lisle thread, silk mixed, cashmere, &c. gloves, &c.

206 WHEELER, T. & Co. Abbey Mills, Leicester, Manu. —Polka jackets, muffs, and mantillas of patent pile fabric. Elastic woven fabrics. Elastic braids, &c. Non-elastic webs for braces and belts.

207 BIDDLE, J. Leicester, Manu.—Gloves of hares'-fur cloth and Cashmere goats'-wool, cloth ; Vicuna and Saxony. Gloves of Lisle-thread web. Travelling rug ; Vicuna fleece.

208 CORAH & SONS, Granby St. Leicester, Manu.—An extensive assortment of hose. Wool vests and drawers. Fancy wool cuffs and sleeves, hoods, hats, and bonnets. Ladies' wool paletots.

209 ELLIS, F. & J. Leicester, Manu.—Silk, Lisle thread, and Cashmere gloves.

211 HARDING, T. 108 Regent St. — Vest buttons in lapis lazuli, malachite, coral, onyx, cornelian, &c., for gentlemen. Fancy pearl and other buttons for ladies.

211A CLARKSON, J. C., 31 Bennett St. Blackfriars.—Patent hat and hat bodies,

E 4

Class 21.

CUTLERY, EDGE, AND HAND TOOLS.

212 WELCH, MARGETSON, & Co. 17 Cheapside, Manu.—Robe-de-chambre, dress stock, dress full front stock; patent wove, and embroidered linen shirt fronts. Improved flannel shirt. Prince of Wales' belt. Cantab brace. Reg.

213 STANDON, ANN (widow), 23 Wood's Mews, Grosvenor Sq. Manu.—A quilted silk bed-quilt, elaborately worked.

213A LERWICK LOCAL COMMITTEE.—Specimens of knitting, from the Shetland Isles.

214 RAMSAY, P. & Co. 19 Lancefield St. Glasgow.—Waterproof leggings, caps, capes, &c.

215 MUIRS, CONNELL, & BRODIE, Glasgow.—Specimens of straw bonnets and plait, manufactured from rye straw grown in the Orkney Islands.

216 DAVIES, R. Shaw's Lane, Carmarthen.—A hat made of leather by a peculiar process.

217 THE MARCHIONESS OF WESTMINSTER.—Specimens of Shetland hand-knitting.

218 M'CRA, Western Highlands.—Specimen of hand-knitting, Berlin wool.

Proceed to Class 13, page 81.

Class 21.   CUTLERY, EDGE, AND HAND TOOLS.

—— North Gallery. ——

1 WEATHERLY, E. 3 Belmont Ter. Wandsworth Rd.—Tall's saw-set, being a patent for improvements in the apparatus for setting saws.

2 THORNHILL, W. 144 New Bond St.—Steel chatelaine, style of the old pierced steel work. Instrument, for pruning trees at any height. Flower-gatherer, cutlery, &c.

3 BRADFORD, R. & W. 72 Patrick St. Cork, Ireland, Manu.—Pearl, tortoiseshell, and ivory-handled razors, lock-joint knives, pruning and other knives, and cork-screws.

4 BLOFELD, T. G. & Co. 6 Middle Row, Holborn, Manu.—Table cutlery, made in London.

5 KING & PEACH, Hull.—A variety of planes.

6 DEANE, DRAY & DEANE, London Bridge.—A choice assortment of table cutlery.

7 MORTON, J. & G. 8 Gt. Turnstile Lincoln's Inn Fields, and 39 Cheapside, Manu.—Table cutlery.

8 WOOD, J. 28 Spurrier Gate, York, Cutler and Surgical Instrument Maker.—The York razor, showing the various stages of manufacture.

9 COWVAN, B. & S. 164 Fenchurch St. Inv.—Canton strop, or Chinese razor-sharpener.

10 SHARPE, J. & R. 5 Gough Sq. Manu.—Table-knife cutlery, made in London.

11 ADDIS, S. J. 20 Gravel Lane, Southwark—Tools used by carvers.

12 MECHI, J. J. 4 Leadenhall St.—Cutlery.

13 MOSELEY & SON, 17 & 18 New St. Covent Garden, Manu.—Planes and tools, with modern improvements. Tool-chests, cutlery, and needles.

14 LOY, W. 24 King St. Whitehall, Manu.—Club skates, ladies' skates, &c.

15 LOY, W. T. Jun. 60 St. Martin's Lane, Des. and Man.—Razors and other articles of cutlery.

16 FIELD, E. 17 Mary Ann St., St. George's, East, Inv.—A cabinet-maker's case of tools.

17 WALDRON, W. & SONS, Stourbridge.—Scythes, crown chaff knife, hay-knives, American grass-hook, English reaping-hooks; hedge brushing-hook, and pea bill-hook.

18 BUCK, J. 91 Waterloo Rd. Lambeth, Manu.—Circular and other saws, turning and other mechanical tools.

19 YEATES, F. G. 10 Winckworth Buildings, City Rd. Inv. and Manu.—Registered lever knives, for opening preserved provisions, &c. Registered twine or string boxes.

20 BAKER, W. Allen St. Goswell St.—Various awls, bodkins, &c., for shoemakers, carpenters, &c.

21 STEWART, C. & Co. 22 Charing Cross.—Patent Plantagenet guard razor. Improved razor-strops and paste. The process of cutlery in the manufacture of the razor.

22 TYZACKS, J. 7 Upper Berners St. Commercial Rd. East.—Double patent British razor.

23 ADDIS, J. B. jun. 17 Charlotte St. Blackfriars Rd. and 29 Lu.ns St. New Town, Deptford.—Carvers' tools, &c.

24 KNIGHT, G. & SONS, Foster Lane.—Cutlery suitable for lathes and tool-chests.

25 COLGAN & SON, Limerick, Manu.—Cutlery.

26 BRADFORD, S. Bagwell St. Clonmell, Ireland, Manu.—Razors. Razor-blades, from the bar of steel to the finished blade. Penknives, pocket, and sporting knives. Daggers. Cucumber-slicer. Tobacco-cutter.

27 IBBOTSON, —. Glasgow.—Panel or block plane, capable of being altered to a mitre plane.

28 OFFORD, D. Great Yarmouth, Inv.—Improved masticating knife and fork for dyspeptic persons, &c. Prov. reg.

31 HANNAH, A. Glasgow, Manu.—Thomson's augers, braces, bits, claw and clench hammers, scollops, for boring wood, &c.

32 MATHIESON, A. Glasgow, Manu.—Assortment of braces and bits; pianoforte-maker's key tools; turning and carving tools, &c. Flit ploughs. Sash and side fillisters, &c.

33 HILLIARD & CHAPMAN, Glasgow, Inv. and Manu.—Razors of various kinds and strops. Table cutlery; pocket knives, &c. Truss, for hernia.

34 SAUNDERS, G. Broadway, New York.—Four-sided metallic tablets and razor strops.

35 MATHIESON, T. A. & Co. 65 Nicholson St. Edinburgh, Manu.—Improved sash fillister plane, wood brace, and pattern bits.

36 MACPHERSON, C. & H. 1 Gilmore St. Paul's Works, Edinburgh, Manu.—A brace, with all kinds of bits used for boring, drilling, and countersinking.

37 BARKER, R. Easingwold, Yorkshire, Manu.—Butchers' and house steels.

38 TOMLIN & Co. Kettering, Northamptonshire, Manu.—Sickles for reaping corn. Shears for sheep-shearing, wool-sorters, thatching, and carpets.

39 STUBS, P. Warrington and Rotherham, Manu.—Blister and shear steel. Cast-steel. Coach-spring steel. Lancashire files and tools. Magnets, made according to the system of the Rev. W. Scoresby.

40 GRADWELL, G. 8 Market St. Manchester, Prop.—Knife with 300 blades, each having a separate spring.

42 BELCHER, I. Waterloo St. Wolverhampton, Manu.—Tools used by shipwrights, carpenters, coopers, pump-borers, and wheelwrights.

46 DURHAM, J. B. 456 New Oxford St. Manu.—Cutlery, with illustrations of manufacture. Cut steel chatelaine, in the antique style, with improved scissors and tablet.

47 HILL, J. V. 5 Chichester Pl. Gray's Inn Rd.—London made saws, and other tools.

48 BEACH. W. Salisbury.—An assortment of cutlery, including fox pad, fawns' feet, and sportsmen's knives. Carvers. Fine scissors. Pruning and paper knives.

49 EASTWOOD, G. 31 Walmgate, York, Inv. and Manu.—A panel-plane to answer the purpose of panel and mitre.

(For Sheffield goods, see Class 22, Nos. 102 to 235, &c.)

Proceed to Class 28, page 139.

Class 22. GENERAL HARDWARE, INCLUDING LOCKS AND GRATES.
—— L. M. N. O. 18 to 20, & 25 to 27 ; O 9, & P. 3 to 29. ——

1 HOOD, S. 81 Upper Thames St. Prop.—Stable stall with a cast and wrought-iron hay-rick, enamelled manger and cistern, &c.

2 SMALLMAN, SMITH & Co. Stourbridge.—A variety of glazed iron ware.

3 CLARKE, G. R. 2 Somerset Pl. Kennington, Des.— Designs for chairs in ornamental iron-work.

4 GUY, S.—A variety of horse-shoes.

4A BARROW, East St. Marylebone.—Patent window sash.

5 KING, C. 5 Tonbridge St. New Rd. St. Pancras, Des. —Designs for carriage-gates, and for stained glass window.

6 PHILLIPS, J. B. Battersea Fields, Des.—Design for ornamental iron gates for a park entrance.

7 STEVENS, H. R. Newmarket, Cambridgeshire, Manu. —Specimens of horse-shoes and plates for race horses.

8 WOODIN, D. 28 Shepherd St. Piccadilly.—Patent shoes for horses or other animals, to prevent slipping on wood, ice, or similar surfaces.

9 MILES, W.—Various horse-shoes.

10 WHITEHEAD, J. Oxford St. Manchester, Inv. and Prod.—Horse shoes.

11 CHOPPING & MAUND, 370 Oxford St. Pat. and Manu. —Rodway's improved patent concave horse-shoes. Patent machine-made, fullered, and seated horse-shoes

12 HOLMES, Captain.—Improved horse-shoes.

13 FOGARTHY, J. Adam St. West, Bryanstone Sq.— Horse-shoes.

15 HILLMAN, J. 4 Leaver's Buildings, Glasshouse Yd. Inv. and Manu.—Concave expansion horse-shoe.

16 COOK, W. Willesborough, Ashford, Kent, Manu.— Horse-shoes in most general use.

17 PLOMLEY, W. Maidstone, Inv.—Model of an improved horse-shoe.

18 PEIRCE, W. 38 Loyd St. Green Heys, Manchester, Inv. and Manu. — Registered letter-copying machines. Model of a window with registered sash-fasteners.

19 BAKER, E. B. 9 Walbrook, Des. and Inv.—Portable and cheap hand-pressure letter-copying machine, called a "manutype."

20 RUTHVEN, J. New St. Edinburgh, Inv. and Manu.— Letter-copying press, combining seal press and letter weigher.

21 Metal combs.

23 SYMES, W. 19 Victoria Rd. Pimlico, Inv. and Pat. —Lump-sugar chopping machines.

25 BARTRUM & PRETTYMAN, Brick Hill Lane, Upper Thames St. Manu.—Wrought copper nails, roves, rivets, and washers.

26 RICHARDSON, ROBT. 1 Tonbridge Pl. New Rd.— Wire-work.

27 COOMBES, —, Mank Lane.—Fine twilled wove wire.

29 WALKER, E. 6 Cardington St. Euston Sq. Manu.— Perforated brass.

30 WILKINS & WEATHERLY, 29 High St. Wapping, Manu.—Smith's patent galvanized and ungalvanized iron and copper wire ropes.

31 VERE, H. H. 2 Andover Pl. Kilburn, Des. and Manu.—Improved bird-cage.

32 KUPER, W. Surrey Canal, Camberwell, Manu.— Specimens of round and flat wire-rope for mining and railway purposes, suspension bridge, &c. Copper lightning conductors and sash-lines. Strands for fencing, &c.

33 WOODS, W. 1 Queen St. Southwark. Manu.—Hooks and eyes, for uniforms, and drapery purposes. Brass chains for lamps and scales.

34 BARNARD & BISHOP, Norwich, Manu.—Galvanized iron wire netting. Wrought-iron hinge.

35 FOX, T. H. 44 Skinner St. Manu.—Ornamental garden arch flower stands. Wire netting for aviaries, &c. Birdcages. Wove wire, and other wire work.

36 NEWALL, R. S.—Patent improved wire-rope.

37 REYNOLDS, JOHN, New Compton St.—Wire flower table.

38 FLAVEL, S. Leamington, Inv. and Manu.—Patent kitcheners, or cooking grates.

39 GREENING & SONS, Warrington, Manu. —Extrastrong wire cloth, woven by steam-power

40 GORRIE, T. Perth, Des. and Manu.—Malleable iron garden-chair. Wire netting. Land-measuring chains.

41 LINLEY & SONS, 34 Stanley St. Sheffield, Pat. and Manu.—Patent circular double-blast bellows. Improved circular bellows. Patent and improved portable forge, &c.

42 GREEN, A. 27 Upper George St. Edgeware Rd. Inv. and Manu.—Protective syphon chimney-pot.

43 DANNATT, J. Norfolk St. Sunderland, Inv. and Manu.—Domestic mangle of simple construction.

45 BRYDEN & SONS, Rose St. Edinburgh, Inv. and Manu.—A manifold bell-pull, to ring bells in any number of rooms. An air signal mouth-piece and bell. A bank safe lock. Bell furniture, blind rollers, &c.

46 STEWART, C. Bell St.—A playing ornamental fountain.

51 EDGE, J. Coalpool, Shropshire, Manu.—Model of a pair of pit frames, with barrel and flat chains. Wood and iron-keyed flat chains, for pits.

54 LAWRENCE, T. B. & J. 55 Parliament St. and 10 York Pl. Lambeth.—British zinc ores ; zinc in ingots, sheets, and plates. Perforated sheet zinc, zinc nails, &c. Various manufactured articles.

55 TREGGON, H. & W. 22 Jewin St. and 57 Gracechurch St. Manu.—Zinc window-blinds, mouldings, cornices, gutters, &c. Drawn and moulded zinc bars, for metal sashes, &c.

56 SAVAGE, R. W. 15 St. James' Sq.—An alarm bedstead. Bedstead for invalids. Door spring.

57 SMITH, T. Chelsea.—Portable folding iron bedstead.

58 TONKIN, J. 315 Oxford St. Des. and Manu.—Ornamented iron bedstead, of the Italian order, with registered spring lath bottom.

59 COTTAM, E. 76 Oxford St.—Metallic bedstead.

60 STEELE, W. & P. 61 George St. Edinburgh, Inv. Manu. and Pat.—Kitchen-range, including apparatus for heating water for a bath.

61 PERRY, E. Wolverhampton, Manu.—Specimens of iron ore, pig iron, bar and sheet iron, block tin, &c. Strong tin ware, planished tin ware, and japanned ware.

62 COWLEY & JAMES, Walsall, Manu.—Patent iron bedsteads. Child's cot. Wrought-iron gas and steam tubes and joints.

63 TYLOR & PACE, 313 Oxford St. and 3 Queen St. Cheapside, Manu.—Perforated metal. Patent iron bedsteads, steel folding portable bedsteads with wrought-iron joints, &c.

64 PERKES & Co. Emerson St. Southwark Bridge.— Patent folding metallic bedsteads, which can be used also as a crib, couch, &c. Registered.

65 HILL, E. & Co. Brierley Hill Iron Works, near Dudley, Manu.—Patent bedsteads, with pillars of taper iron tubing, richly japanned fancy bead and foot-rails, &c.

66 SHOOLBRED, LOVERIDGE, & SHOOLBRED, Wolverhampton, Des. and Manu.—Coal vase, baths, wine coolers

dish covers. Beart's patent coffee-pot, &c. Date dials for counting-houses, &c.

67 JOHNSON, E. Piccadilly.—Metallic bedsteads.

69 WALTON & Co. Wolverhampton.—Coal vase and scoop; enamelled foot bath, pail, and sponging and milk cans; block tin dish covers; bronzed kettles and stands.

74 STIRK. J. Wolverhampton.—Engineers and tinmen's anvils, smith's vice, &c.

75 WOOD BROTHERS, Stourbridge, Manu. — Chain cables, and all descriptions of chain. Anchors, scythes, shovels, nails, anvils, vices, windlass purchase, &c.

76 KEEP & WATKIN, Foster's Works, Stourbridge, Manu.—Spades and shovels. Improved cast-steel draining tools. Plough-share, beam, and coulter moulds, for foreign and home markets, frying-pans, ladles, and hand-bowls. Scythes; hay, chaff, and thatchers' knives. Specimens of crane and coal chain. Nails; anvils; vices; best faggoted axle arm moulds, for carts and wagons.

82 HANDYSIDE, A. Britannia Foundry Derby, Des. and Manu.—Cast-iron fountain. Vases, copied from the Warwick and Medici vases. Bacchanalian and other vases, from the antique, &c.

83 THE BOWLING IRON Co. Bradford, Yorkshire, Prod. and Manu.—Specimens of iron ore, coal, &c., and of smelted and manufactured iron.

84 BATEMAN, JAMES, Low Moor, near Bradford, Manu. —Bloom of iron H.C. produced at East Ries, Norway, of great toughness and strength; billet and wire rod rolled, and wire drawn from the same; cards manufactured with the wire, by D. Bateman and Sons.

85 HIRD, DAWSON, & HARDY, Low Moor Iron Works, Bradford, Prod. and Manu.—Minerals from the Low Moor Company's mines, near Bradford: Black ironstone; black bed coal. Specimens of Low Moor pig iron, and of wrought iron tested by tension, &c. Ten-inch gun, of 9 feet 4 inches, weighing 85 cwt. used with hollow shot, shells, grape, and canister shot; mounted on a carriage made by C. A. and F. Ferguson, Mast House, Mill Wall, London. Thirty-two pound gun, of 6 feet, weighing 25 cwt. used with solid shot, shells, grape, and canister shot. Sugar-cane mill; cylinders or crushing rolls, 24 inches diameter by 48 inches in length. Olive mill. Wilson's elliptograph, for drawing ellipses of any proportion from a straight line to a circle.

86 ELLIS, W. 136 High St. Isle of Wight, Manu.—Kitchen-range, with hot-plate, oven, &c. Boiler, steam-closet, and baths.

87 NICHOLSON, W. N. Newark-on-Trent, Inv. and Manu.—Cottage cooking and other grates, with improvements under Leslie's patent. Various other cooking stoves for cottages, farmhouses, &c. Gas brackets, and ornamental iron work.

88 COLLINS, J. Leominster, Herefordshire, Inv. — Stoves for warming and ventilating buildings, kiln for drying malt, hops, &c. Machine for separating hops, &c.

89 DULEY, J. Northampton, Inv. and Manu.—Registered self-acting effluvia-trap. Patent cooking-stove.

90 SHAVE, W. J. 74 Watling St. Manu.—Patent oven, for baking bread, pastry, meats, &c. with great economy of fuel and time.

92 KERSLAKE, T. Exeter, Manu.—Registered boiler for heating churches, mansions, &c.

93 HALSTEAD & SONS, Chichester, Sussex, Manu.—Kitchen-range, combining all the conveniences of a close range, with the advantages of a large open roasting fire, &c.

94 KEENE, W. 42 Cornhill.—The conducting leaf stove.

95 POWELL, W.—Portable economical oven.

96 HARPER & SONS, Dudley, Des. and Manu.—Fender, or-molu mounted. Pierced fire-guard. Kitchen fender. Best steel fire-irons.

96A FIRTH, T. Eliza St. Belfast, Ireland, Prop.—Registered model fire-box, with hollow fire bars, for locomotive and other furnaces.

97 HAYWOOD, J. Derby, Manu. — Burnished steel drawing-room stove, with porcelain hearth. Radiating hall stove, with hearth-plate. Church stove.

98 BENHAM & SONS, 19 Wigmore St. Manu.—Roasting range with radiating back. Smoke jack. Hot-plate and broiling stove. Bain-Marie pan. Vegetable steamer, &c. Copper warm and shower-bath.

99 GREGORY, T.—Dining-room fire-screen.

100 COLLIER, SON, & SNOWDEN, 10 Foster St. Bishopsgate, Pat. and Inv.—Coffee-roasting apparatus.

101 LESLIE, J. 59 Conduit St. Inv. Pat. and Manu.—Patent fire-brick grates. Patent domestic gas purifying apparatus. Patent gas regulating apparatus. Patent gas burners, &c.

102 STUART & SMITH, Sheffield, Manu.—Sylvester's patent grates. Register grate, with a revolving canopy; a French invention, patented in England. The marble chimney pieces manufactured by Messrs. Nelson, Carlisle. Fenders, fire irons, &c. Air-stoves. Three miniature steam-engines, made by W. Hurst, watchmaker, Sheffield.

103 EVANS, SON & Co. 33 King William St. and 10 Arthur St. West, Manu.—Register and warm-air stoves for drawing rooms, cabins, &c. Kitchen-ranges, including the exhibitors' improved cooking apparatus. A classic pedestal lamp, &c.

104 MORTON, J. 32 Eyre St. Sheffield.—A cast-iron table, with marble top, and an or-molu fender. Berlin and bronze fenders.

105 LONGDEN & Co. Sheffield, Des. and Manu.—Improved cooking apparatus. Ornamental warm-air gas stove. Specimen stair balusters, &c. Gallery front for entrance hall, &c. Perforated pedestals for hot-water pipes.

106 JOBSON & Co. Sheffield, Manu.—Patent light and heat reflecting stove-grate and marble chimney-piece. A burnished steel register-stove, ornamented with twisted steel mouldings, gilt coronet, and silver feathers. (Main Avenue, West.) Patent air-stove.

107 PIERCE, W. 5 Jermyn St. Des. and Manu.—Chimney-pieces of enamelled iron and alabaster. Pyro-pneumatic ventilating stove-grate, &c. Stove-grates and fenders with or-molu and silver ornaments. Reg. cottage grates.

108 CARR, J. & RILEY, Bailey Lane Works, Sheffield, Manu. — Patent double-edge Lewis and spiral machine knives, for dressing cloth. Circular, frame, and pit saws. Files, &c.

109 JOHNSON, CAMMILL, & Co. Cyclops' Steel Works, Sheffield, Yorkshire.—Model of the Cyclops' Works. Specimens of iron and steel suitable for engineering, tool making, &c. An assortment of specimens of files and rasps, from one to forty-six inches in length. Specimens of locomotive engine and tender, railway-carriage, horse box, bearing, buffer, draw springs, &c.

110 DEAKIN, G. & Co. 48 Eyre St. Sheffield, Manu.—Ivory carvers; plated fish carvers. Silver and silver-plated dessert-knives. Ivory, silver, and plated table-knives. Silver knife, fork, and spoon. Silver cake-knife.

110A BROOKES, WM. & SONS, Sheffield, Manu. of emigrants, horticultural and gentlemen's tool-chests, wedge axes. felling, siding, squaring, and various other axes, adzes, &c.; Brazil tools, mattocks, stone-picks, &c.; hatchets, cleavers, choppers, hedging bills; horticultural and other shears; engineers' and carpenters' edge tools; coach and locomotive wrenches; screw stocks, taps, and dies, pincers, pliers, compasses, hammers of all kinds; table cutlery, &c.

111 ——, Sheffield.—Two drawing-room grates.

112 MAKIN, W. Attercliffe Steel Works, near Sheffield, Manu.—Paper-mill, rag-engine, roller-bars, and bottom-plates, for grinding ropes, rags, and other materials into pulp. Knives for rope and rag-cutting machines. Tobacco and snuff knives. Miller's best refined cast-steel chisels and picks, &c. Samples of steel, used in the various branches of the manufactures of Sheffield.

113 SPEAR & JACKSON, Sheffield, Manu.—Cast steel circular saw, 5 feet diameter; spring steel handsaw, 30 inches long, and a collection of other saws. Knives, for machinery, and other purposes. Files and rasps. American wedge axe, and edge tools of all sorts. Cast steel plate for engravers, and specimens of cast steel in bars.

114 FENNEY, F. Sheffield, Manu.—Razors, including specimens of the best work; new in pattern and design. Specimen, showing the different stages of the manufacture of the blade.

115 COCKER, S. & SON, Porter Steel Works, Sheffield, Manu.—Steel suitable for all purposes. Cast steel files used by every trade or profession. The various stages of file and needle manufacture. Edge tools, saws, and other articles.

116 HARGREAVES, W. & Co. Sheffield, Manu.—Table knives; dessert knives; carvers; game carvers; elaborately-carved ivory-handled bread knife.

117 TURNER, T. & Co. Suffolk Works, Sheffield, Manu. —Pair of Albert venison carvers, with stag antlers. Carved table cutlery. The Prince of Wales's sailor's knife. Gardeners' cutlery; sportsmen's knives; razors; pocket and penknives. Stone, circular, hand, and back saws. Files, &c.

118 ALGOR, J. 105 Eldon St. Sheffield, Manu.—Knives for shoemakers, clickers, and curriers, farriers, saddlers, joiners and cabinetmakers, coopers, painters, and glaziers, plumbers, butchers, basket-makers, and cooks. Newfoundland fish-knives.

119 PARKIN & MARSHALL, Telegraph Works, Sheffield, Manu.—Table and dessert knives; carvers; fish-carvers; mellon-carvers; bread-knives, with carved handles. Large slicers.

120 ELLIN, T. & Co. Sheffield, Manu.—Shoemakers', glaziers', painters', and furriers' knives. Table knives in common use A.D. 1800. Sheffield whittle. Carving and table knives and forks, &c.

121 OLIVER, W. Sheffield, Manu.—Forty pieces of miniature cutlery. Silver pistol. Table-knives, as manufactured in 1750 and 1800. Venison-carvers, and steel. Jones's patent game-carvers, and steel.

122 WILKINSON & SON, Grimesthorpe, Sheffield, Manu. —Sheep and horse shears; shears for glovers, thatchers, and weavers.

123 GILBERT BROTHERS, Sheffield, Manu.—A variety of superior razors.

124 STEER & WEBSTER, Castle Hill Works, Sheffield. —Nippers; gold and silver scissors; surgeons' scissors; tailors' shears; garden-shears, and slide pruning shears, &c.

125 WOSTENHOLM, G. Sheffield.—A variety of cutlery.

126 WHITELEY, ELIZABETH, 12 Norwich St. Sheffield Park, Manu.—Cast steel scissors.

127 SHEARER, J. Eldon St. Sheffield, Manu.—Sheep-shears; shears as used in the glove trade; horse-shears; pair of best polished bronzed trowel shank sheep-shears, in miniature, containing a variety of small articles; weavers' shears, knife, and nippers.

128 MARPLES, R. Sheffield, Manu.—Braces and bits; squares; mitre-square; turnscrews; improved sliding T bevil; saw-pads; spirit-level; screw-slide mortice-gauge; saw and frame; spokeshaves; shell-gimlet; improved auger-gimlets, &c.

129 TAYLOR, H. 105 Fitzwilliam St. Sheffield, Manu.— Tools for engravers, carvers, and print-cutters. Hand-drawn steel. Sculptors' chisels. Screw-tools, &c.

130 HOLMES, C. 90 Wellington St. Sheffield, Des. and Manu.—New registered bolster. Specimens of table-knives.

131 HARDY, R. E. Burnhall St. Sheffield, Manu.— Carved bread and plated dessert knives. Nut-picks, and instruments for ladies' work. Boxes, and gentlemen's dressing-cases.

132 MARTIN, S. 29 Norfolk St. Sheffield, Manu.—Specimens of various kinds of razors, manufactured from Sheffield steel.

133 NEWBOULD & BAILDON, Surrey Works, Sheffield, Manu.—Specimens of Roberts' patent table cutlery. Table cutlery, with ivory and silver handles, &c.

133A NEWBOLD & OWEN, Sheffield, Manu.—Samples of best steel polished goods, including new and improved forms and varieties of scissors.

134 WINKS & SONS, Sheffield, Manu.—Samples of razors and table knives.

135 HAWCROFT & SONS, Sheffield, Manu.—Ivory, pearl, and tortoiseshell razors. Articles illustrative of the processes of manufacture, &c.

136 JONES, J. West Field Ter. Sheffield, Inv. Pat. and Manu.—Improved dinner-knife and carvers. Rust-preventive composition.

137 NICHOLSON, W. 17 Sycamore St. Sheffield, Manu.— Pocket and pen knives. American dagger and spear knives. American cotton and hunting knives, &c.

138 The productions of the united journeymen file-makers of Sheffield.

139 MAPPIN & BROTHERS, Sheffield and London, Manu. —Assortment of cutlery, including sporting and pocket knives; pen-making machines; gardeners' knives; table cutlery; razors and scissors in great variety.

140 HOOLE, ROBSON, & HOOLE, Green Lane Works, Sheffield, Manu.—Drawing-room, dining-room, and other register grates. Burnished steel, bronzed, and cast-iron fenders. Cast-iron chimney pieces, with natural fixed colours.

142 CLAYTON, G. 5 Love St. Sheffield, Manu.—Specimens of table cutlery. The same plated on steel in ivory and pearl. A large bread-knife.

143 BAGSHAW, W. 37 Spring St. Sheffield, Manu.— Assortment of fine penknives.

144 BARGE, H. Low St. Sheffield, Manu.—Pocket-knives American hunting-knives, &c.

145 BRIGGS, S. 186 Solly St. Sheffield, Manu.—Needles and awls for basket, mattress, and staymakers, saddlers, &c. Bookbinders' or printers' bodkins. Punches. Packing-needles. Curriers' steel-blades. Nut-pickers. American socket-vice, &c.

146 HARDY, T. 9 Moore St. Sheffield, Manu.—Stilletoes, crotchet-needles, button-hooks, nail-files, corkscrews, tweezers, boot-hooks, &c.

147 SELLERS, J. Sheffield, Manu.—Razors. Pocket and sportsmen's knives. Fine Penknives. Surgeons' cutting instruments. Engravers' tools. Pen-making machines.

148 WALTERS, J. & Co. Sheffield.

149 NOWILL, J. & SONS, Sheffield, Manu.—Assortment of knives for the Levant trade, other cutlery, razors, dressing-cases, &c.

150 ARMITAGE, M. & H. Sheffield.—Anvils, vices, and hammers.

151 ELLIOTT, J. Townhead St. Sheffield, Manu.—Sample razor, manufactured of the best steel. Frame-back razor. Pearl-tang razor. Razors, with hollow-ground blades. Scales with registering dial.

154 WEBSTER, G. Howard St. Sheffield, Manu.—Razors of superior finish and quality. Double-edged razor, provisionally registered.

155 LEDGER, C. 83 Carver St. Sheffield, Inv. and Manu. —Various razors; curiosity razor; barbers' razors. Table

knives; silver-plated dessert knives, with chased blades; pearl-handled plated dessert knife, with emblematical ferrule.

156 ELLIS, I. 188 West St. Glossop Rd. Sheffield, Manu.—Card of razors. Table knives. Butchers', pallet, putty, and stopping knives.

157 DEAKIN, G. 83 Arundel St. Sheffield, Inv. and Manu.—Scissors for clipping horses. Elastic metallic combs. Lamps for singeing horses. Tailors' shears.

158 SLAGG, H. W. Ford, near Chesterfield.—Reaping-hooks, sickles, scythes, &c.

159 UNWIN & ROGERS, Rockingham Works, 124 Rockingham St. Sheffield, Manu.—Sporting knives; pistol, pencil, and cigar knives; desk, garden, pen-machine, scissors, sailors', and pocket knives. Razors, lancets, farriers' knives, fleams for bleeding cattle. Nail-files, button-hooks, &c.

160 MARRIOTT & ATKINSON, Fitzalan Works, Sheffield, Manu.—Files and rasps, for various purposes, and in various stages of manufacture. Specimens of steel, for coach springs, chisels, spindles, and tools. Model for locomotive engines, springs, drays, railway waggons and carriages, elliptic carriage-spring, gig or light cart-spring.

160A FEARNCOMBE, H. Wolverhampton.—Portable wash-stands, coal vases, oval dish-covers, tea-trays, copper bronze kettles, tea caddies, hot-water dish and cover, dressing-case, &c. (Placed in Class 21.)

161 KIRK & WARREN, 11 Coalpit Lane, Sheffield, Manu.—Files and rasps, suitable for mechanics, engineers, &c. Large file, 54 inches long, to show the various forms of cutting. Designed and executed by H. Younge, of Sheffield.

162 MARSH, BROTHERS, & Co. Sheffield, Manu.—Specimens of steel used for tools, cutlery, &c. Table and small cutlery. Butchers' knives; razors; edge tools; files; scythes; hay-knife; straw-knife. Spring for railway trucks, waggons &c.

163 BROOKSBANK, A. Malinda Works, Sheffield, Manu.—Files and rasps, manufactured from the best cast-steel.

164 WORRALL, HALLAM, & Co. Sheffield, Manu.—Hackles and gills for flax-dressing. Cast-steel wire and spiral springs. Needles in process of manufacturing. Brushmakers' engine-combs. Cast-steel broaches for wool-combing.

165 COUSINS & SONS, Garden St. Sheffield, Manu.—Tailors' and horse-trimming scissors. Ladies' cutting-out and fancy scissors. Grape scissors, and flower-gatherers. Left-handed scissors, &c.

166 HUTTON, J. Ridgeway, Sheffield.—Specimens of iron and cast steel, welded together under a water or steam-power hammer, for scythes, &c. Street door and window protection, of cast steel and iron. Berkshire hook, for cutting down the harvest. Pair of cart axles, with revolving spherical bushes, to reduce friction. Cutting instruments, with cast-steel edges.

167 FLATHER, —, Sheffield. — Bits, screw drivers, skates, &c.

168 MACHON, J. Sheffield, Manu.—A variety of scissors and slide pruning shears.

169 MARSDEN BROTHERS, & SILVERWOOD, Bridge St. Works, Sheffield, Manu.—The Royal Albert and other skates. Joiners', carpenters', and cabinet-makers' tools, of the best manufacture. Botanical and horticultural tools.

170 JOWETT, J. Arundel Lane, Sheffield, Manu.—Edge tools and sheep-shears. Horse, rag, and weavers' shears.

171 BROOKES, J. Dorset St. Spring Lane, Sheffield.—Articles suitable for ladies' work-boxes and gentlemen's dressing-cases.

172 HALL, T. H. Leecroft, Sheffield.—Taps, saw, screws, &c.

173 WILLOUGHBY, T. Sheffield.—Secret dial pen-knives.

174 TURNER, H. & W. Sheffield, Manu.—Fire-irons of

various descriptions, elaborately cut and ornamented, including the "Cyma Recta." Reg.

175 WILKINSON, T. & G. 17 New Church St. Sheffield, Manu.—Duplicate specimen of scissors, manufactured for the Queen, with the ornamental work filed out of solid steel. Large assortment of scissors and shears.

176 BLOOMER & PHILIPPS, Albert Works, Sheffield, Manu.—Braces and bits, spirit levels, chisels, &c.

177 WRIGHT, J. New George St. Sheffield, Manu. and Inv.—Ladies' and gentlemen's skates. Truss. Horse-scraper. Shoe-lift. Horse trimmings, in cast-steel. Ladies' steel busks. Combs for graining oak, &c.

178 UNWIN, W. Sheffield.—Knife, with various blades, scissors, cork-screws, &c.

179 MORRISON & PARKER, Rockinghamshire St. Sheffield, Manu.—Carpenters' braces and centre bits; spirit levels, gauges, saw pads, augers, and other tools.

180 MAPPINS, J. Sheffield.—Engraved razor, and knife handles.

181 HOWARTH, J. Sheffield, Manu.—Tools for engravers and print-cutters; mariners' compass; needles; gunsmiths' stocking tools; turning and carving and other tools; tool-chest.

182 BROWN & SONS, Western Works, Sheffield, Manu.—Braces and bits. Squares, bevil, gauges, twinscrews, spoke-shaves, saw-pads, saw-set, spirit-levels, saw-frame, pricker-pads, and augurs. Skates of ebony inlaid.

183 SKIDMORE & Co. Enema Works, Sheffield.—Surgical instruments.

184 DONCASTER, D. Sheffield, Manu.—Patterns of steel.

186 DEANE, DRAY, & DEANE, London Bridge, Inv.—Five lump stoves. Yacht stoves. Model of kitchen range, &c.

187 WARBURTON, C. 60 Eyre Lane, Sheffield, Manu.—Bright Scotch screw-auger, 7 feet long. A variety of Scotch screws, four-twisted, and other augers. Improved shell-auger.

187A JOWITT & BATTIE, Saville Works, Sheffield, Manu.—Specimens of forged, tilted, rolled, and hand-drawn, cast, shear, and spring steel. Engineers' and machine-makers' cast-steel files.

188 HIGGINBOTHAM, G. & W. Sheffield, Manu.—Assortment of scissors, ornamented and mounted with gold, &c. Fine scissors, forged from refined steel, hardened and tempered upon a peculiar principle. Razors, ivory, tortoiseshell, and mother-o'-pearl handles, gold and silver mountings, &c.

190 TURTON & SONS, Sheffield, Manu.—Illustrations of steel manufacture from Swedish bar-iron. A large assortment of files, edge-tools, and cutlery. Springs for locomotive engines, railway carriages, &c.

191 IBBOTSON, BROTHERS, & Co. Sheffield, Manu.—Collection of cast-steel circular saws, polished. Segment of a circular veneering saw. A large collection of mill and hand saws. Cast-steel patent scythes. An assortment of files. Table, hunting, and other cutlery.

192 BUTCHER, W. & S. Sheffield, Manu.—Specimen, and other razors; edge tools and files. Superior saws.

193 BLAKE & PARKIN, Meadow Works, Sheffield, Manu.—Improved cast-steel files and rasps. Improved cast-steel saws. Knives, &c., for paper-makers, cloth manufacturers, tobacco manufacturers, cork-cutters, tanners, curriers, &c.

194 GIBBINS & SONS, Sheffield, Manu.—A pair of scissors nineteen inches long, produced as a specimen of workmanship. A pair of scissors in a forged state. An assortment of nail-nippers. Champagne nippers. Pruning-shears. Sets of scissors, assorted sizes, &c.

195 WILSON & SON, Sycamore St. Sheffield, Manu.—Knives for shoemakers, butchers, cooks, curriers, farriers, glaziers, and weavers; palette knives, bread knives, butchers' steels, &c.

196 WARD & PAYNE, Sheffield, Manu.—Edge tools in

every variety, for various trades. Burnishers, braces, bits, turnscrews, spokeshares, &c.

197 MARSHALL, S. 25 Eyre Street, Sheffield, Des. and Manu.—Specimens of illustrated Sheffield cutlery, consisting of razors, carved in mother-o'-pearl, &c. Pocket combs, &c.

198 SAYNOR & SONS, 13 Edward St. Sheffield, Manu.—Pruning and budding-knives, of superior workmanship and material.

199 NAYLOR, VICKERS, & Co. Sheffield, Manu. Illustrations of cast steel by models of furnaces, rolling mills and forge. Manufactured articles.

200 WHITE, T. jun. Thorpe Heeley, Sheffield, Inv. and Manu.—Improved hooks for fixing gas and water-pipe. Improved horse-nails. New wrought-iron nails for shipbuilders, carpenters, &c. Improved rivets.

203 EYRE, WARD, & Co. Sheffield, Manu.—Table-knives, commencing with the cheapest and commonest manufactured for export. Ivory, silver, and other descriptions of table cutlery. Razors, including the cheapest serviceable razor to the most costly. Pocket and penknives. Dagger and Bowie knives. Scissors, scythes, and sickles.

204 SORBY, R. & SONS, Carver St. Sheffield.—Carpenters' and other tools. Every variety of axes, adzes, hedging bills, and garden tools. Circular saw, 5 ft. diameter. Hand, pit, frame, and cross cut saws. Sheep shears, scythes, reaping-hooks, hay and chaff knives, &c.

204A LUCAS & SON, Dranfield, near Sheffield, Manu.—Malleable steel cart naves and axles, coach-naves and axles, and carriage-naves and axles. Spindles used for spinning flax, worsted, cotton, and silk. Railway wheels cast in one piece, and left hard on the face, the inner part malleable.

205 TASKER, H. Sheffield, Manu.—Cast steel saws, polished and etched with silver and gold

206 FISHER & BRAMALL, Hoyle St. Works, Sheffield.—Files and rasps. Ironstone, pig and bar-iron. Bar, ingot, and other steel. Engineers' and masons' tools. Circular saw, for cutting railway bars when in a heated or cold state.

207 EARL, SMITH, & Co. Sheffield, Manu.—Files and rasps, of all shapes, kinds, and sizes. Samples of steel, from blister to the smallest watch-spring.

208 SLACK, SELLERS, & GRAYSON, Sheffield, Manu.—A large assortment of all descriptions of pit, frame, and hand saws. Straw or chaff-knife. Ledger blade and cylinder of spiral cutters for shearing woollen cloth, &c.

209 IBBOTSON, R. Shoreham Works, 7 Shoreham St. Sheffield, Manu.—Improved bill-pruning saw. London pattern hand and back saws, &c.

210 MATKIN, T. Hawley Croft, Sheffield.—Shears.

211 TAYLOR BROTHERS, Burnt-tree Lane, Sheffield, Manu.—Circular, pit, and hand-saws, in great variety.

212 BIGGIN & SONS, Sheffield, Manu.—Ripping-saws, hand-saws, and back-saws, plain and ornamental.

213 WHITTLES & FROGGART, Sheffield.—Surgical instruments and penknives.

214 STANIFORTH, T. Hackenthorp, Sheffield, Manu.—Sickles and hooks ; scythes and hay-knives.

215 HUTTON & NEWTON, Highlane, near Sheffield, Manu.—Patent and crown hay and straw knives. Scythes, reaping hooks, and sickles, suitable for New South Wales, Australia, Canada, the Indies, the Cape of Good Hope, Russia, and the United States of America.

216 SHAW & SON, Sheffield.—Magnets.

217 CUTLER, J. Sheffield.—Edge tools.

218 MARPLES, W. Sheffield.—Braces and bits.

219 CARFITT & SON, Sheffield, Manu.—A collection of scythes. Knives for chaff, rag, and turnip machines. Elbowed, Irish, and bagging hook. Cast-steel Kendal hook. Cheshire and Kendall sickles, &c.

220 SKELTONS, S. & R. Sheffield and Attercliffe, Manu.—Shovels and spades for various uses. Draining-tools.

221 TASKER, JOHN, Sheffield.—Gutta percha soled cricketing shoes.

222 BURROWS, S. 94 Spring St. Sheffield.—Specimens of table cutlery, blades all steel, with an ornamental shank.

223 COOPER, G. Sheffield.—Models of venetian chimneypots.

224 HINCHCLIFFE, J. 8 Hermitage St. Sheffield, Manu —Flambeau dagger, hunting clasp knife, 10½ inch, haft carved in pearl and ornamented. Pocket-knives in pearl, ivory, &c. American hunting knives, &c.

225 LEON, A. Sheffield, Manu.—American hunters and dagger knives, in ornamental sheaths.

226 SANDERSON, T. J. Sheffield, Manu.—Anvils and vices for engineers', blacksmiths', and farriers' use.

226A HAGUE, S. Devonshire Lane, Sheffield, Manu.—Fancy penknives, with corkscrews, silver pencils, &c.

228 HUNTER, E. Broomhall St. Sheffield, Manu.—Scissors and shears of every variety, with specimens from the rough steel to the finished article.

229 NELSON, J. Sheffield, Inv.—Set of parturition forceps, for domesticated animals. Pair of forceps for giving balls to horses.

230 JONES, J. Sheffield, Inv. — Glass sash bars and columns for plate-glass windows.

231 LINLEY, G. A. F. 43 Regent St. Sheffield, Yorkshire, Des. and Manu.—Horse-shears, sheep-shears, wool-sorters' or thatchers' shears, grass shears, glovers', belting or dragging, and rag shears.

232 BELL, J. Sheffield.—Silver fruit knives.

233 PEACE, J. Sheffield, Manu.—Saws ornamented in a new style, large circular saw, &c.

234 COCKER & SONS, Hathersage, Derbyshire.—Specimens of needles in every stage of manufacture.

235 BROWN, J. Sheffield. — Patent conical railway buffer and draw-springs.

236 HUXLEY & HERIOT, Inv. and Manu.—Cook's patent self-regulating stoves. Economic gas stove. Hydraulic stove, heated by gas. Gas chandelier, designed by Mair, &c.

237 JEAKES, W. 51 Gt. Russell St. Inv. Des. and Manu.—Improved ventilating stove grate, the heating surfaces of which are composed entirely of pure fire loam. (Main Avenue, West.) Improved grate, to be fixed in the chimney-piece, exhibited by Mr. Thomas, of Paddington.

238 GLENTON & CHAPMAN, 147 New Bond St.—Marble chimney-piece. Polished steel register stove, fender, &c. Vapour bath.

239 PRIDEAUX, T. S. 2 Garden Road, St. John's Wood, Inv.—Dwelling-house grate, feeding at the bottom. Model of a patent steam-engine boiler. Model of a patent machine for cutting agricultural drains in clay soils.

240 BUTTERLEY, R. Sheffield.—Elastic sickles and hooks.

241 EDWARDS, D. O. 5 Sydney Pl. Brompton, Inv.—Patent " atmopyre " hoods, or artificial embers for gas fires. Kitchen range of porcelain and furnaces, adapted thereto. Regulators of gaseous and aerial currents. Prov. reg.

242 WHITMEE & CHAPMAN, 18 Fenchurch B. 70 St. John St. and 11 Ray St. Clerkenwell—Coffee-mills, corn-crushers, machine for grinding and dressing flour at one operation; smoke-jack, &c.

243 POPE & SON, 80 & 81 Edgware Rd. and Grove Foundry, Lisson Grove, Inv. and Manu.—Patent double-action rarefying stoves, ornamented. Section, showing the internal arrangements.

243A SHERWIN, J. 21 Norton Folgate, Manu.—Economic range and supply cistern, hot closet steam kettle, bath stove, &c.

244 CROOK, W. 5 Carnaby St. Inv. and Manu.—Improved open fire hot plate, oven and boiler, kitchen range for steam, warm baths, &c. by one fire, and improved smoke-jack. Improved tailor's stove for heating a larger number of irons.

245 CORNELL, T. Messrs. Feetham's, Clifford St. Bond St. Inv. and Manu.—Model of a cooking apparatus to be used either with coal or gas, and suitable for large establishments.

247 BURTON, W. S. 39 Oxford St. Inv. and Manu.—New nautilus register stove, fender, and chimney-piece. Ornamental fenders, and metal wares.

248 WARRINER, G. 16 Arundel St. Haymarket.—A gas oven of fire-clay, glazed. Gas bath heater.

249 ONIONS, J. C. 63 Bradford St. Birmingham, Manu.—Smith's bellows. Improved portable forge, vice, &c. Fancy satin-wood. Japanned and other bellows.

250 CARTWRIGHT & HIRONS, 138 and 139 Gt. Charles St. Birmingham, Des. and Manu.—Electro-plate on German silver: waiter, liqueur and cruet-frames, salad or fruit-stands, sugar, cake, fruit and card-baskets, &c.

251 TAYLOR, S. 117 New Canal St. Birmingham, Manu.—Specimens of ordinary and ornamental bellows.

252 STOKES, J. C. Monmouth St. Birmingham, Inv.—Registered water-closet. Cabinet water-closet, made of china and earthenware, by Ridgway and Co. Registered brass tap. Improved shoe and round valves.

253 ALLDAY, W. 32½ Constitution Hill, Birmingham, Manu.—Assortment of bellows, plain and ornamental. Improved portable forge, with hearth attached.

254 GRIFFITHS, T. F. Bradford St. Birmingham, Manu.—Tin goods, and block tin ware. Cooking utensils coated with glass. Iron stampings, of various shapes.

255 COPE & COLLINSON, Birmingham and London, Manu.—Specimens of improved castors for furniture. Patent globular blind mountings, &c. Patent bedstead-brace. Registered music-stool screw. Horne's patent butt hinges. Locks, hinges, springs, &c. for pianofortes.

257 HARCOURT, W. & J. Bristol St. Birmingham, Manu.—Specimens of brass foundry used by bell-hangers. Door-handles, tea-bells, cornice-poles and ornaments, &c.

258 SOLLY, J. Leabrook Iron and Steel Works, Tipton, near Birmingham, Manu.—Specimens of English iron for conversion into steel, and of various kinds of steel; and articles of hardware and cutlery made from the said steel.

261 MALINS & SON, Birmingham, Manu.—Brass window-cornices and poles. Pole ends and ornaments, curtain bands and pins. Finger-plates for doors, &c.

262 GRAY & SON, 9 Wenman St. Birmingham, Manu.—Polished steel fire irons and standards. Coal vase, tongs, &c.

263 HANDS, J. Prospect Row, Birmingham, Manu.—Specimens of ornamental stamped brass foundry, cornice pole ends, curtain bands, finger plates, frames for miniatures or pictures, coffin furniture, &c.

264 LINGARD, G. Snow Hill, Birmingham, Manu.—Patent dovetail lock. Registered air-vent cock. Coffin furniture; medal and button dies; patent table fastener; glass movements, &c.

265 ABATE, F. 3 Ernest St. Albany St. Inv.—Specimens of a new art, called metallography; consists in printing on, and ornamenting, metallic surfaces. Provisionally registered.

267 BIRD, A. Birmingham, Inv.—Hydrostatic syphon water-purifier. The Victoria night-light.

268 WINTON & SONS, Birmingham.—Patent electro-plated spoons and forks. Tinned iron spoons, ivory and pearl spoons, knives, &c.

269 SMITH, T. H. 20 Brewer St. Golden Sq. Des. and Manu.—Stove ornament. Design for a centre ornament for a ceiling, composed of 5,000 postage stamps.

270 SIMONITE, J. Pope St. Birmingham, Manu.—Tinned wrought-iron culinary utensils. Copper coal-shovel. Wrought-iron melting ladle for plumbers, pitch, or seaming ladle &c. Japanned iron and galvanized sail thimbles, and

ship's hooks and thimbles. Tinned wrought-iron tinmen's furniture.

271 HICKMAN & CLIVE, 34½ William St. North, Birmingham, Manu.—Coffin furniture produced by pressure from thin plates of metal in dies of cast iron or steel.

273 SHENSTONE & MILLS, 25 Mary Ann St. Birmingham, Prop.—Polished fire-irons, locks, &c. exhibited for cheapness. Metallic tokens, labels, &c. Vesta and other boxes. Knives, forks, paper-knives, &c.

274 MOORE & Co. Gt. Lister St. Birmingham, Manu.—Brass, German silver, and embossed electro-plated hinges. Process of making plain and embossed brass wires. Tube and wire of brass, copper, tin, &c. Brass rolled latten. Polished and sash bars.

275 HORNE, T. Birmingham, Manu. —Curtain poles, curtain pole ends, curtain pole rings, &c. Variety of hinges.

276 WOLVERSON, E. 2 Ashton Ter. Birmingham, Inv. and Manu.—Secure lock, with an improved detector.

276A FEETHAM & Co.—A polished steel stove, or-molu mountings. (Main Avenue, West.)

277 JONES, R. & SONS, Birmingham. — Specimens of cork-screws.

278 ROWLEY, CHARLES, Newhall St. Birmingham—Patent and registered shawl pins, studs, brooches, &c. buttons, belt-plates and sword furniture. Wire-loop brace-buttons and eyelet-holes. Whip and stick handles.

279 TWIGG, G. & W. Summer Hill, Birmingham, Manu.—Buttons, livery, military, naval, and sporting. Glove and brace, glass and pearl buttons. Steel brooches. Shirt studs registered fasteners, &c.

280 WILLIAMS, T. Helstone, Inv.—Model of iron safe, with water between the inner and outer cases. Model of axle for carriage, with hollow perforated arm for oil-box.

281 PIGGOTT & Co. St. Paul's Sq. Birmingham, Manu.—Naval, military, and livery buttons. Bronzed sporting and other buttons. Glass buttons. Chased and enamelled studs. Medals. Coat links. Fasteners and slides for dresses.

282 HAMMOND, TURNER, & SONS, Snow Hill, Birmingham, Manu.—Various naval, military, sporting, and club buttons, gilt, plated, bronzed, &c.

283 ASTON, W. Prinsep St. Works, Birmingham, Manu.—Buttons, Florentine, linen, and Holland, covered in silk, satin, &c. Upholstery buttons. Shell suspender gaiter, great coat buttons. Polished cut steel buttons, &c. Steel dress-fasteners and ornaments. Series, illustrating the manufacture of buttons.

284 HARDMAN & ILIFFE, 38 Newhall St. Birmingham, Manu.—Buttons, medals, hooks and eyes, &c.

285 NEAL & TONKS, 13 Gt. Charles St. Birmingham, Manu.—Real stone and fancy glass buttons. Shirt studs. Coat loops. Glove bands and bracelets. Horses' bridle rosettes in fancy cut glass.

286 CHATWIN & SONS, 92 & 93 Gt. Charles St. Birmingham, Manu.—Illustrations of button manufacture, covered nails.

287 BANKS, E. Birmingham, Manu.—Mother-of pearl shells used in the manufacture of buttons. Mother-of-pearl buttons.

289 KNOWLES, H. Howard St. Birmingham, Manu.—Gold-plated enamelled buttons.

290 WELLS, J. T. Birmingham.—Patent horn-buttons.

290A LONG, J. & J. & Co. Little Tower St.—Curvilinear window blind pulley.

292 SHELDON, J. 55 Gt. Hampton St. Birmingham, and 33 Bucklersbury, London, Inv. and Manu.—Gold pencil case, gold-pens, penholders, pocket escritoires, snuff-boxes, &c.

293 ALLEN, F. Birmingham, Manu.—Silver and gilt filigree work.

294 GOODE & BOLAND, 24 St. Paul's Sq. Birmingham, Manu.—Specimens of jewellery, chains, &c.; and samples in the rough and subsequent stages. Specimens of blood-stones, slit by a self-acting machine.

295 SMITH, KEMP, & WRIGHT, 165 Brearley St. West, Birmingham, Manu.—Buttons of gold, silver, brass, gilt, papier-maché, mother-of-pearl, &c. Registered shirt studs of gold, silver, gilt, pearl chased, enamelled, and engraved.

296 WALTERS & STONE, 28 Ludgate Hill, Birmingham, Manu.—Black ornaments. Chatelaine, containing devices formed with hair. Brilliant finger-rings, pins, and studs.

297 BIDDLE, J. 23 Victoria St. Birmingham.—Seals, pen-holders, letter-clips, book-clasps, and mountings.

298 PARKER & ACOTT, 54 Brierly St. West, Birmingham Manu.—Gold and silver pencils and pen-holders. Gold tooth-picks, seals, and keys.

299 BALLENY, J. Birmingham, Manu.—Gold jewellery. Gilt and Black ornaments. Spectacles. Monument, in black glass, " to the late Sir Robert Peel."

300 ALLEN & MOORE, 35 and 36 Gt. Hampton Row, Birmingham, Des and Manu.—Vesta match-boxes ; cigar boxes ; taper-stands ; lamps ; and other fancy articles in metal. Case of medals. Metal buttons.

301 ASTON, J, 41 St. Paul's Sq. Birmingham, Manu.—Ornamental silk, satin, and velvet buttons, dress ornaments, and patent linen buttons.

302 ELLIOTT & SONS, Regent St. Works, Birmingham, Manu.—Fancy buttons for ladies' dresses. Gilt and plated, buttons. Patent silk, velvet, satin, Florentine, and linen buttons. Pearl buttons with metallic rims.

303 AVERN, E. 72 Newhall St. Birmingham, Manu.—Patent shoe-scraper.

304 INGRAM, T. W. 85 Bradford St. Birmingham, Des. and Manu.—Horn buttons, illustrations of the manufacture prior to the patent, and the improvements made since.

305 HEELEY & SONS, Mount St. Birmingham, Manu.—Chatelaines ; sword hilts ; buttons ; snuffers ; stirrups ; watch-guards ; invalid tongs ; and other ornamental steel wares.

306 OTTLEY, T. Birmingham.—An assortment of medals.

307 COTTERILL, E. 101 Henry St. Ashted, near Birmingham, Inv. and Manu.—Patent climax detector locks, made to the keys. Two locks cannot be made alike, unless formed from the keys cut at the same time.

308 A fire escape.

309 EYKYN & MILLICHAP, 50 George St. Parade, Birmingham.—Patent safety and other improvements to car-riage axle-trees.

310 NASH, R. 20 Russell St. Birmingham, Prop.—Spoon and collar dies ; medal dies ; coin, and office desk dies ; button dies.

311 JACKSON, W. Birmingham, Manu.—Model of a raising machine, for raising dish covers. Tools used in the manufacture of tin and copper ware, &c.

312 TIMMINS & SONS, Pershore St. Birmingham, Manu.—Carpenters' and farriers' tools. Shoemakers' tools. Vices, coach wrenches, saddlers' and upholsterers' tools, &c.

313 MANLY, J. jun. 55 Bread St. Birmingham, Pat. and Manu.—Patent ornamental nails.

314 TYE, G. P.—Hyacinth glasses and supports, (Reg.)

315 REYNOLDS, J. Crown Nail Works, Newton Row, Birmingham, Manu.—Cut nails, consisting of upwards of 200 distinct varieties of the most useful sizes, made of iron, zinc, brass, and copper.

316 HENN & BRADLEY, Cheapside, Birmingham, Manu.—Taper wood screws in iron, brass, and copper. Iron thread screws. Taper hand-rail screws, for pianoforte-makers, &c.

317 JAMES, J. Bedditch, near Worcester, Manu.—Needle-boxes, furnished. Needles and fish-hooks in the various processes of manufacture.

318 HAWKINS, J. 22 Prinsep St. Birmingham, Manu.—Screws in iron, brass, and copper ; railway, coach, grate, machine screws, and bolts

319 BAKER & Co. 68 Cecil St. Birmingham, Manu.—Flower-stands. Plate and dish covers. Wire-gauze fire-guards. Squirrel-cage, with bells. Fancy window-blind patterns. Gauze Davy lamp. Mattress and sofa springs. Brass and iron weaving, &c.

320 COOKSEY, H. R. 148 High St. Bordsley, near Birmingham, Manu.—Coffin furniture, in plated gold and silver and brass and tin japanned.

321 SIMCOX, PEMBERTON, & SONS, Birmingham, Manu.—Curtain decorations. Lock furniture, finger plates, bell pulls, &c. Door-knockers and chains. Gothic and Eliza-bethan work for churches, &c. Letter clips, letter balances, &c. Sconces. Stair and curtain rods ; miniature and picture frames. Butt and other hinges, bolts, castors, &c.

322 CORNFORTH, J. Berkeley St. Wire Mills, Birmingham, Manu.—Specimens illustrative of the manufacture of iron and other wires. Steel-wire. Soft and hard tinned wire Coppered iron-wire. Wire nails of various sizes and forms.

323 POTTS, W. 16 Easy Row, Birmingham, Manu.—Bronzed and lacquered gas lamps, chandeliers, lanterns, candelabra, girandoles, glass frame, clock stands, epergnes, &c. Potts' patent picture supporting moulding.

324 GILLOTT, J. Victoria Works, Birmingham, Inv. and Manu.—Specimens of metallic pens

325 WILEY, & Co. 34 Gt. Hampton St. Birmingham. Manu.—Gold, paladium, gold and silver, and silver pens, pointed with the native alloys of iridium and osmium, the hardest of known metals.

326 HINCKS, WELLS, & Co. Buckingham St. Birmingham, Manu.—Patent self-acting steam cutting, piercing, and raising pen machine. Illustrations of the manufacture of steel-pens and specimens of finished pens.

327 KELL, A. & Co. 28 Summer Row, Birmingham, Manu.—Steel pens, showing their different forms and qualities, with improvements.

328 MITCHELL, W. 6 St. Paul's Sq. Birmingham, Manu.—Metallic pens and pen-holders.

329 BARTLEET, W. & SONS, Redditch, near Birmingham, and 37 Gresham St. London, Manu.—Needles and fish-hooks of every description, with specimens exhibiting the different stages in the process of manufacture.

330 BOULTON & SON, Redditch, near Birmingham, Manu.—Needles ; steel meshes ; surgeons' needles ; sail hooks ; bodkins ; harpoons ; spears and grains for whale fishing ; fish-hooks, &c.

331 HEMMING, H. Redditch, near Birmingham. Manu.—A general assortment of sea and river fish-hooks.

332 NICKLIN & SNEATH, 57 Bradford St. Birmingham. Manu.—Copper, brass, and iron weaving ; fine drawn brass and copper wire ; strong iron weaving ; brass wire cloth, as used for paper-making machines.

332A MARTIN & GRAY, Berkeley St. Birmingham, and Gough Sq. Manu.—Gas chandelier, finished in gold colour and artistic bronze. Pattern, finished in artistic bronze and gold colour, relief. Gas brackets, carriage lamps, &c.

333 MORRALL, A. Birmingham. — An assortment of needles.

334 HORSFALL, J. Oxford St. Birmingham, Manu. and Prop.—Highly-finished steel wire. Annealed wire. Hitch and bridge pins. Spun brass strings, &c. for pianofortes and other instruments. Steel wire, for needles, fish-hooks, &c.

335 GOODMAN, G. Caroline St. Birmingham, Manu.—Patent fine-pointed pins, black, purple, and dress. Brass pins, and needles.

336 EDELSTEN & WILLIAMS, New Hall Works, Birmingham, Manu.—Pins, the heads and shafts in one solid piece, made by improved machinery. Elastic hair-pins. Iron wire, &c

337 WAKEFIELD, J. T. Lichfield St. Birmingham, Manu —Specimens of iron and brass wire. Sofa chair, and mattress springs. Brass, copper, and iron wove wire. Iron and brass chain, made by machinery. Wire gauze work.

338 MYERS & SON, Newhall St. Birmingham, Manu.—Specimens of steel pens, and improved steel pen and quill pen-holders in gold, silver, and other metals.

339 MITCHELL, J. 48 New Hall St. Birmingham, Manu. and Pat.—Patent self-adapting pens and holder, and steel-pens in great varieties.

340 MESSENGER & SONS, Broad St. Birmingham, Manu.—Domestic groups of the Queen and the Prince of Wales, in or-molu and bronze: modelled by John Bell. Portion of a chandelier in bronze, as designed by Mr. Gruner, for the Pavilion in Buckingham Palace gardens. Ornamental designs in or-molu and bronze. Registered station-signal, and tail-lamps; hand signal lamps; roof lamp for carriages; carriage lamps; gas fittings; engine cocks, &c.

341 STURGES, R. F. 46 Broad St. Birmingham, Manu. and Pat.—Electro-plated articles on hard white metal, cast in metal moulds in a heated state; a stream of water is made to play upon the moulds, which causes them to contract, and thus produce great sharpness in the casting: the metal used expands in cooling.

342 PRIME & SON, North Wood St. Birmingham, Des. and Manu.—Specimens of magneto-plate salver. Liqueur frame with grotesque handle. Knives, forks, and spoons.

343 SALT & LLOYD, 17 Edmund St. Birmingham, Des. and Manu.—Lamps and stands, candelabra, &c. Cast brass from Bankart's patent copper, English's patent camphine.

345 EDWARDS, E. Birmingham, Manu.—Inkstands in glass and cast-iron, and bronzed. Glass screws, showing the method of manufacturing twelve at once by pressure.

346 LOWE, J. & H. Birmingham, Manu.—Axletrees, and a variety of ironmongery for saddlers, including carriage-lamps, harness-mountings, &c.

347 WOOLDRIDGE, J. 38 St. Paul's Sq. Birmingham, Manu.—Or-molu door lock and bell lever. Brass bell levers, door handles, hat and coat hooks, and door fittings, castors, ventilators, &c.

348 HOLDEN, H. A. 96 Suffolk St. Birmingham, Manu.—Door-handles, carriage-door hinges, mouldings and beadings, harness-buckles, &c. Chariot lamps and railway signal lamps.

349 BLEWS & SONS, Bartholomew St. Birmingham, and 55 Bartholomew Close, London, Manu.—Brass candle and ship lamps; candlesticks; imperial measures and weights; bells, scuttles, &c.

350 DUGARD, W. & H. Upper Priory, Birmingham, Inv. and Manu.—Carriage-lamps. Registered horse-collar, &c. Improved pattern of hair horse-saddles. Registered thiller cart-horse collar, &c.

351 HETHERINGTON, T. & Co. 28 Cannon St. Birmingham, Manu.—Carriage lamps full silver mounted, engraved and stained glasses, gilt, enamelled, and chased.

352 EVERITT & SON, Birmingham, Manu.—Copper and brass tubes, for locomotive and marine boilers, gas, steam, &c. Specimens, showing process of manufacture of rolled metals, and of brass and copper wire.

353 BOLTON, T. Broad St. Metal Works, Birmingham, Manu.—Specimens of the process of manufacture of wire and tubing; locomotive and mandril drawn tubing; brass solder, &c.

354 SOUTTER, W. 10 New Market St. Birmingham, Manu.—Copper bronzed tea-urns and swing kettles. Bright copper fluted coal-vase, and round or oval kettles.

355 HILL, J. Broad St. Birmingham, Manu.—Stamped ornaments, for lamps, chandeliers, &c. Six-light chandelier body and arms. Lamps, &c.

356 WHITFIELD, S. Oxford St. Birmingham, Manu.—Window cornices, in stamped brass-foundry, with velvet,

wainscot, and knotted oak, rosewood, and white enamel ground. Wrought-iron fire-proof safes.

357 LLOYD, G. B. Berkeley St. Tube Works, Birmingham, Manu.—Lapwelded iron tubes, for steam boilers; the same with fittings for conveying gas and water; and for hydraulic presses.

358 THOMAS, R. Icknield Works, Birmingham, Manu.—An assortment of axes, hatchets, and adzes, augurs, plane-irons, chisels, trowel, gun and hand harpoons, and garden tools.

359 TAYLOR, W. 13 Sheepcote St. Birmingham, Inv. and Manu.—Original designs for nut-crackers, sugar tongs, door knocker, and improved inside shutter bar.

360 WORDSWORTH, J. Birmingham, Des. and Manu.—Model of an economical kitchen range, for a close or open fire.

360A KENRICK & SONS, West Bromwich, Staffordshire, Manu.—Model of an enamelled tank or cistern with gutta percha joint. Enamelled water or gas-pipes, troughs, &c. Pulleys, castors, &c. Nail casting, &c.

361 TONKS, W. & SON, Cheapside, Birmingham, Manu.—Brass foundry, consisting of hinges, ventilators, bolts, bell-cranks, pulleys, castors, chair-arms, stair rods, desk rails, window fittings, &c.

362 KIMBERLEY, J. 56 and 57 Inge St. Birmingham, Factor and Des.—Stamped brass foundry, consisting of curtain bands, cornice pole ends, letter clips, door furniture, &c.

363 MARRIAN, J. P. Birmingham, Manu.—Specimens of bronzed scroll ornaments. Naval brass foundry, consisting of ship-scuttles. Glass deck lights. Gun-hole screw valves. Ordnance metal pulleys, with anti-friction rollers, &c.

364 BRISBAND, H. Howard St. Birmingham, Manu.—Mother-of-pearl studs and buttons, black pearl ditto. Slides, and ornaments for dresses, &c.

365 ATKIN & SON, Birmingham.—Large circular saw and edge tools.

366 WRIGHT, P. Constitution Hill, Dudley, Manu. and Pat.—Vice, with patent solid box.

367 ASTON, J. 20 Dale End, Birmingham.—A variety of brushes for all purposes, some tastefully worked in various devices.

367A ALCOCK, S. Redditch, near Birmingham.—Fishing tackle.

368 WARDEN, J. jun. Old Church Works, Birmingham, Manu.—Springs, axles, &c. Engineers' vice. Patent vice, with spherical washers. Vice, with solid brass box. Smith's anvil. Specimens of fagotted iron.

370 MAPPLEBECK & LOWE, Birmingham, Prop.—Chimney-piece, grates, fire-irons, &c. Brown's patent economical cooking apparatus. Open fire cooking range. Scales, weighing-machines, iron bedsteads, &c. Stocks and dies for iron gas tubing, and for engineers' and whitesmiths' work. Model of a steam-engine furnace, with Bedington's patent smoke consumer.

371 PEYTON & HARLOW, Birmingham, Inv. and Manu.—Patent improved metallic bedsteads, japanned to correspond with papier-maché furniture exhibited by Jennens and Bettridge, &c.

372 POWELL, J. New Windsor, Inv. and Manu.—Windsor portable economical oven, baking over the top of the fire, leaving the front for other purposes, &c.

373 WINFIELD, R. W. Cambridge St. Works, Birmingham, and 141 Fleet St. London, Pat. and Manu.—Plain and ornamental cased and patent tubes. Wire and rolled metals. Cornice-pole. Patent curtain-bands and rings. Stamped brass window-cornices. Brass and iron bedsteads and furniture. Chandeliers, bracket, gas-fittings, &c.

374 GORTON, G. Birmingham, Inv. and Manu.—Drawing-room grate, &c. with or-molu ornaments. Dining-room grate. Cast-iron fender, with fire irons. Registered designs.

378 KEED, G. F. 100 Crawford St. Marylebone—Improved kitchen cooking apparatus.

379 ANDREWES, H. P. 2 North St. Mews, Tottenham Court Rd. Inv. and Manu.—Emigrant's stove and general cooking apparatus. Meat screen and reflector.

380 GODDARD, H. Nottingham. Manu.—Patent cooking apparatus, for culinary and other purposes.

381 WAKEFIELD, F. Sherwood Iron-Works, Mansfield. Des. and Manu.—Great Western cooking apparatus. Sherwood range. Artizan's cooking stove &c. Wrought-iron palisading. Iron casting of antique bronze statuette of Bacchus.

382 LOVE, J. 20 St. Andrew's Sq. Glasgow, Inv.—Gas-machines for heating, cooking, and lighting hotels and taverns, &c. Newly-constructed grate. Machine for generating gas, and illuminating locomotive engines and carriages.

383 PETERSON, T. Water Lane.—Economical Stove.

384 YATES, HAYWOOD, & Co. Effingham Works, Rotherham, and 200 Upper Thames St.—Drawing-room and iron register stove grates, in or-molu and burnished steel, &c. Dining-room, cottage, and other grates. Warm air and other stoves. Self-acting cooking stoves, &c.

386 SLATE, J. 14 Belmont Pl. Wandsworth Road, Inv. and Pat.—Patent stove, for the cure of smoky chimneys. Improved smoke guards, &c.

387 EDWARDS, F. 42 Poland St. Manu.—Circular corrugated and oblong Dr. Arnott's stoves, for warming churches, halls, &c. Dr. Arnott's ventilating valves and wind guards.

388 NETTLETON & SON, 4 Sloane Sq. Chelsea, Inv. and Manu.—Gothic ventilating church-stove. Gothic stoves. Portable bed-room and conservatory stove.

389 COURT, J. 18 Queen St. Grosvenor Sq. Inv. and Manu.—Improved hot-air stove, composed of two earthen cylinders. The same for gas.

390 TOZER, T. 55 Dean St. Soho. Inv. and Manu.—Ventilating gas stove for halls, shops, &c. Bachelor's kitchen. Registered calorifere, or hot-water vessel.

391 NORMAN, G. 5 St. Ann's Pl. Limehouse, Inv.—Improved cooking stove for private families.

393 FROST, H. 17 Rathbone Pl. Inv. and Manu.—Model kitchen fire-place and cooking apparatus.

395 HEWETT, H. B. 308 High Holborn, Inv.—Apparatus for speedily cooling or warming liquids.

396 KENT, J. 8 Elizabeth St. South, Pimlico, Des. Inv. and Manu.—Improved vegetable cullender. New potato steamer.

397 PRICE, V. 33 Wardour St. Soho, Inv. and Manu.—New patent washing machine. Chopping machine. Ventilator. Letter copying machine. Patent knife and fork cleaning machines. Stove for heating irons. Patent snuffers.

399 ROPER & SON, 68 Snow Hill, Manu.—Patent japanned plate-warmer.

400 REEKES, J. 50 Hasker St. Chelsea, Inv.—Nautical cap. Safety swimming belt. Portable oven, on a new principle, which can be used in the open air.

401 TYLOR & SON, Warwick Lane.—Improved baths, tea urns, garden engines, and syringes, standard weights and measures and copper goods.

402 WARREN, G. 15 Lower Market St. Woolwich, Manu. —Models of register and thermometer stoves.

403 ALDERTON & SHREWSBURY, Hastings, Des. and Manu.—Open fire hot-air stove, made from iron ore obtained and smelted in Sussex.

404 ARGALL, J. & W. St. Agnes, Cornwall, Inv. and Manu.—Cooking apparatus, by which saving of fuel is said to be effected.

405 GRAY, J. & A. 85 George St. Edinburgh, Inv. and Manu.—A new radiating and reflecting stove grate, with flue passing up the back of the concave front, and thus transmitting a large amount of heat into the apartment.

406 HUXHAM & BROWN, Exeter.—Kitchen stove, with large cast oven and steaming boiler. Shutting-up cooking stove with novel flue, and may be used as a range. Emigrant's or cottage stove.

407 KING, S. 1 South Hays, Bath, Inv.—Registered ventilating and smoke-consuming register stove grate, with King's octangular wedge bricks, &c.

408 McSHERRY, M. 3 James St. Limerick, Ireland, Inv. —Model of registered stove, for heating conservatories, hot-houses, and buildings.

409 BLAIR, J. Scotland.—Portable couch or bedstead.

410 REDGATE, J. Nottingham. Manu.—Register stove grates, with registered fire-brick backs.

411 RIGBY, P. 167 Grove St. Liverpool, Inv.—Portable cooking-stove, for cooking with gas generated from heated spirits. Emigrant's kitchen, &c.

412 TIPPEN, J. Chichester, Inv.—Model of a novel invalid bedstead. Model of an improved kitchen range.

413 WALLACE & SON, Leith, Inv.—Model of a patent safety cooking apparatus, for ships, and of improved ventilator, for warm climates.

414 STOCKER, —.—Metal castings.

416 MASSEY, W. & Co. 58 Baker St. Manu.—Stands for flowers, of different sizes, made of brass, by hand.

418 M'KENZIE, A. 38 De Beauvoir Sq. Kingsland, Manu. —Model of condensing engine, with coffer valves under cylinder, &c. Instrument for registering the speed of paddle-wheels, printing-presses, gun-carriages, &c.

421 HASLAM, W. St. Helen's, Derby, Des. and Manu.— Specimen of hammered iron church-door hinges, with branches of scroll-work, after the early English style.

422 BOTT & ALLEN, Manchester, Manu.—Fenton's patent anti-friction metal, for the bearings of machinery. Plumbers' work, steam-engine valves, ship nails and fastenings, blocks, pulleys, &c. Dickenson and Falkou's patent equitable gas-meter.

424 PADDON & FORD, Brownlow Mews, Gray's Inn Rd. Manu.—Patent wet gas meter.

426 BOTTEN, C. Crawford Passage, Clerkenwell, Inv. and Manu.—Patent protector gas-meter, for preventing fire-damp, &c.

430 SPARKS, J. 12 King St. Tower Hill, Inv.—Cash-box for railways. India-rubber door hinge.

431 GRANT, D. Luton Pl. Greenwich, Inv.—Patent gas-light, perfectly ventilated. Gas stove for baking and cooking. Stove heated by either gas or coal.

432 HALDANE & RAE, George St. Edinburgh, Des. and Manu.—Gas lustre and branches; wash-hand basin; patent water-closets; spiral taps, &c.

433 RICKETS, C. 5 Agar St. Strand, Inv. and Manu.— Apparatus for cooking, &c. by jets of coal-gas mixed with air, for chemists' use, &c.

434 COCHRANE, J. Greenside Lane, Edinburgh, Manu. —Gas-meter, 10 inches diameter.

435 SIEBE, A. 5 Denmark St. Soho.—Patent rotatory universal syringe to keep up a continual flow of water.

436 RYAN, J. 13 Stafford St. Dublin, Inv. and Manu.— Transparent gas meter.

437 ROPER, J. Wigan, Lancashire, Manu.—Transparent gas meter, to register the consumption of gas.

438 BIDDELL, G. A. 22 Montpelier Sq. Knightsbridge, Inv. and Pat.—Gas burners, which regulate themselves to the pressure, keeping the flame at any desired height.

438 SHEARS & SONS, 27 Bankside.—Inv. and Manu.— Patent dry gas meter.

439 LOCKERBY & STEPHENSON, Glasgow, Des. and Manu. —Six-light chandelier, for gas.

440 HARVEY, G. Great Yarmouth.—Ship's stove.

441 EDGE, T. Westminster, Manu.—Patent wet gas-meter. Patent dry gas-meter. Photometer to ascertain the illuminating power of gas.

442 YOUNG, W. 18 and 33 Queen St. Cheapside, Inv. and Manu.—Vesta lamps, lanterns and burners, to burn rectified turpentine. Spirit cases, with air-tight stopper.

443 STRODE, W. 16 St. Martin's-le-Grand.—Gas cooking range, boiler, stoves, and signal lamps.

444 FARADAY & SON, 114 Wardour St. Manu—Gas chandelier, upon Professor Faraday's principle, by which all noxious products are carried off.

445 DEBAUFER, H. 10 and 11 Creed Lane, Des. and Manu.—Concentrating gas-lamp, for externally illuminating shop-windows, on the parabolic construction.

446 CLARK, R. & RESTELL, T. 447 Strand, Des. and Inv.— Lamps and gas burners. New locks. Railway passengers' communications. A new principle in clockwork; gravitating clock without pendulum.

447 PALMER & Co. Sutton St. Clerkenwell, Manu.—Candle lamps. Weather lamps, to burn candles, for warehouses, stables, and out-buildings.

448 HOLLIDAY, R. Huddersfield, and 128 Holborn Hill, London, Manu. — Self-generating gas lamps. Patented. Sulphate, muriate, carbonate and liquor of ammonia, &c.

449 RETTIE & SONS, Aberdeen, Manu.—Patent signal lamps for vessels in distress. R. Rettie, inv. and pat.

450 HOLGATE, J. 6 Arthur St. East, Inv. and part Des.—Signal lamps for railways, &c. Hardware fittings for railway carriages.

451 SQUIRE, R. 16 South St. Manchester Sq. Manu.—Plated basterna and other carriage lamps; railway tail lamp; hand signal; improved magic lantern; travelling Etna; improved lamp for singeing horses.

452 SMITHS & Co. Blair St. Edinburgh, Des. and Manu.—Stationary railway-signal, lantern, and lamp. A lantern and lamp for a railway train. A railway-carriage roof lamp. A stage-coach lantern and lamp. Hand signal-lamp for a railway.

453 BIGGS, —, Frome, Somerset.—Tin pastry moulds.

455 SAUNDERS, W. J. 11 Polygon, Clarendon Sq. Inv. and Manu.—Pneumatic solar lamp for railways, lighthouses, &c. adapted for common animal or vegetable oil.

458 BRIGHT, R. 37 Bruton St. Inv. and Manu.—Lamps. Patent lamp wicks, &c.

459 CHILDS, J. Brentford, Manu.—Brass fountain lamp, with adjusting concentric burner, for a lighthouse lantern.

461 HUGHES, J. G. 158 Strand, Prop.—New designs for candle lamps, candelabra, and for spirit and oil lamps. Gas chandelier. Hall lantern. Flower-stand. Model of tent, &c.

462 BARLOW, J. 14 King William St. City, Inv. and Manu. An illuminator, or vault light. Self-acting syphon tap.

464 BLACK, B. 49 South Molton St.—Ornamented carriage lamp.

465 PYRKE & SONS, Dorrington St. Manu.—Bronze tea urns and swing tea-kettle, of new designs.

470 SARSON, T. F. Leicester, Manu.—Gas lamp, with ornamental construction for ventilation.

472 NIBBS, J. S. Baslow, Blakewell, Inv.—Forms of the oxidate condensing lamp. Improved weather lantern, for out-door purposes, cellars, &c.

474 HAWKINS, J. 42 Bow St. Dublin, Manu.—Circular silver-mounted Clarence carriage lamps.

476 DOWSON, J. E. 123 Oxford St. Manu.—Cundy's patent hot-air ventilating stove.

477 BROWN & REDPATH, Commercial Rd. near West India Docks, Pat. and Manu.—Fire hearth, or cooking apparatus, as used on board H.M. steam ships. Lanterns for marine purposes.

479 CALLAM, T. 56 Shore, Leith.—Ship's cooking apparatus, for baking, boiling, roasting, and steaming at the same time.

480 SEARLE, C. M.D. 51 Weymouth St. Inv. and Pat.—Tubulated solid fire-brick stove or heat condenser, for libraries, schools, passages, shops, &c.

481 GOODBEHERE, G. T. 9 Wellclose Sq. Manu.—Improved ship's hearth, to cook for fifty men.

482 DEFRIES, N. Regent St. Inv. and Pat.—Gas works. Gas stoves. Patent gas bath heater. Dry gas-meters. Conservator, heated, lighted, and ventilated by gas. New mode of melting and distilling, &c.

483 GARTON & JARVIS, Exeter, Inv. and Manu.—Improved universal cooking apparatus, or range-stove. Exonian cooking apparatus. Hot-house boilers, &c. Model hot-water apparatus. Double-action hydraulic cider-press.

486 HALE, T. & Co. Bristol, Des. and Manu.—Gas brackets, chandeliers, &c. Improved plunge and beer-cocks. Musical-clock bells. Kettles; coal-scoops; registered copper bath. Brass figures, bronzed, and lackered.

487 HODGES & SONS, Dublin. — Copper kettles and lamps.

488 LOYSEL, E. 34 Essex St. Strand, Inv.—New coffee filters. Potato roaster of a new description.

489 KEPP & Co. 40, 41, & 42 Chandos St. Manu.—Copper bath. Steamers, hot-water pipes, and skylight frame. Copper covering for roofs, casement, clock-hands, &c.

490 WILSON, R. & W. 49 Wardour St. Soho, Des. and Manu.—Baths of various descriptions.

491 NOIRSAINS, —, 131 Regent St.—Ventilating grates and stoves.

493 GILLESPIE & SON, 62 Broughton St. Edinburgh, Inv. and Manu.—Model of the Victoria shower-bath.

494 GILBERT, S. Ironmonger St. Stamford, Lincolnshire, Inv. and Manu.—Somapantic bath: registered.

495 MOGGRIDGE, M. The Willows, Swansea, Inv.—Model of a sponging bath.

496 HARDWICKE, W. 32 Hatton Garden.—A portable domestic bath-room.

498 MOSS, R. Bartholomew Sq. Inv. and Manu.—Registered copper vapour bath, worked by a spirit lamp.

499 DAWBEE & DUMBLETON, South Town, Yarmouth, Inv.—Working model of a stone filter, in a slate cistern.

500 BRAY, C. 14 Cranbourne St. Leicester Sq. Inv.—Pedestal wash-stands of papier-maché, &c. japanned and ornamented with gold mouldings. Bath, and cooking utensils.

501 DALE, R. 195 Upper Thames St. Manu.—Model of an improved warm bath and heating apparatus.

502 FAULDING, J. Edward St. Hampstead Rd. Inv. and Prod—Registered portable vapour bath.

503 LONGFIELD, W. Otley, Near Yorkshire, Inv. and Manu.—Ornamented wrought-iron safe or chest, with patent positive security lock: patented.

504 MATHER, J. Chelsea. — Bath of improved construction.

506 LEADBEATER, J. 125 Aldersgate St. Manu.—Fire-proof safes, secure against burglars and injury from fire.

507 TANN & SONS, Pat. and Manu.—Fire-proof iron safes, with hollow chambers filled with chemical salts.

508 FISHER, J. N. 10 Charles St. Manchester Sq.—Safety boxes for collecting money bags from railway stations, applicable also for counting-houses, &c.

509 BAKER, C. Jireh Cottage, Rotherfield St. Islington, Inv.—Fire-proof safe.

510 MARR, W. 52 Cheapside, Manu.—Wrought-iron patent fire-proof strong room, secured with the double chamber wheel-action detector lock.

516 ROSINDALE, C. High St. Hull, Inv.—Service-box, applicable to every description of water-closet.

517 CLARK, C. C. Reading, Inv. and Manu.—Self-acting sanitary water-closet. Self-acting valve-trap.

518 GRAY, T. W. 79 King William St. City.—Cabin window apparatus. Bull's eyes, &c.

519 HODGES, T. Dublin, Manu.—Church, farm, and altar bells. Brass force and lift pumps, and metal pump. Patent composition pipes for liquids or gas.

520 TURNER, E. W. K. 31 Praed St. Paddington, Inv.—Model to illustrate the application of centrifugal force to the purification of water, for the supply of cities, towns, &c.

522 DAVIS, C. 12 Walcot St. Bath.—Portable waterfall.

523 McCULLUM, J. 79 George St. Edinburgh, Inv.—Spirit-meter, for measuring liquids by index.

524 GUEST & CHRIMES, Rotherham Brass Works, Manu. and Pat.—Tubular water-closet: inv. and registered by W. Kirkwood, of Edinburgh. Hydrant, or fire-cock, for extinguishing fires, and for street cleansing : High-pressure bib, ball, stop, and double-valve cock.

524A GUEST, J. & W. Little Hampton St. Birmingham, Manu.—Gilt ware: Cornelian and onyx tazzas, inkstands, chanticleer bell, candlestick, chatelaines, &c.

525 WISS, R. 38 Charing Cross, Inv. and Manu.—Patent, self-acting, portable water-closet.

529 ABERRY, J. 29 North St. Hackney, Inv. and Manu.—Improved water-closet, fitted up on improved principles, and fixed without nails, screws, or brads.

530 DOWNTON, J. 4 Conant Pl., Commercial Rd., Limehouse.—Patent water closet.

531 MARSDEN, C. Waterloo House, Kingsland, Inv. and Manu.—Patent ventilated thimbles. Registered funnels for naphtha, spirits, &c. Propelling apparatus, &c.

532 GREEN & Co. Princes St. Lambeth.—Registered syphon flushing basin, with self-acting closet connections. Henry & Co.'s. water filter by ascension. Registered beer and spirit preservers.

533 CHAMBERS & ROBBINS, 47 Carey St. Lincoln's Inn Fields, Manu.—Portable water-closet, with improvements.

534 LAMBERT, T. New Cut, Lambeth, Inv.—Diaphragm valve and stop cocks. High-pressure ball or cistern valve. Self-closing valve-cocks. Economic lamp. Hydrant water closet, &c.

535 PRICE, —.—Patent washing machine.

536 DAVIS, J. B. 63 Roupell St. Lambeth, Inv.—A clear-way valve or cock: registered.

538 ADAMS, J. Selby, Manu.—Improved washing, wringing and mangling machine.

539 TASKER, W. St. James's Rd. Halifax, Des. and Manu.—Machine for washing, wringing, and mangling.

540 WILKINSON, —.—Improved patent mangle.

541 PEARSON, Leeds.—Washing, wringing, and mangling machine.

542 TINDALL, E. O. D. L. Scarborough, Inv.—Imperial mangle, with horizontal spring pressure : registered. Napkin press. Kitchen range.

543 REID, J. 10 Thornton Pl. Aberdeen, Des. and Inv.—Model of a bathing, washing, wringing, and mangling machine. Self-acting cradle.

544 TARIN, M. L. A.—Nelson St. Mornington Crescent.—Cartridge cases, dust-pan, &c.

545 STUTTERD, J. Banbury, Inv. and Manu.—New lever mangle, with elastic band pressure. Improved portable mangle, &c.

546 FRYER, R. 4 Wood St. Spitalfields, Inv. and Manu.—Washing, wringing, and mangling machine. Double-acting washing machine. Models to illustrate the same.

547 BAKER & Co. 65 Fore St. Cripplegate, Inv. and Manu.—A revolving mangle.

548 MACALPINE, W. Hammersmith, Inv.—Machine for washing linen or cleaning rags for making paper. Patent vessel, with steam apparatus for washing heavy goods.

550 TUPPER & CARR, 3 Mansion House Pl. City, Pat. & Manu.—Patent galvanized iron. Specimens of corrugated

sheets for roofing purposes. Electric telegraph and fencing wire. Cast iron seats, stands, &c.

551 STANLEY, C. 238 High St. Borough.—Model of coal scales for ships, with regulating lever.

552 ORPWOOD, G. 82 Bishopsgate St.—Patent self-acting coffee roaster.

553 KENT, G. 329 Strand, Inv. Pat. and Manu.—Rotary knife-cleaning machine. Triturating strainers. Rotary cinder-sifter.

554 MORETON, J. New Vauxhall, Wolverhampton.—Mangling machine.

555 HARRISON, W. Fisher St. Birmingham, Manu.—Bright and tinned, round and oval, frying-pans and bakepans. Havannah sugar-moulds, &c. for refining sugar, coated with patent glass enamel, &c. Sugar bowls and skimmers.

556 GIDNEY, J. W. East Dereham, Norfolk, Inv. and Manu.—Models of improved wire fence, and portable iron sheepfold. Ornamental castings, for gates, palisading, &c. Door, with lever spring-drop, to exclude the draught: inv. and reg. by M. Gardiner, of Ashill, Norfolk. Hemispherical stove: des., reg., and manu. by Barwell & Co. of Northampton. Model of greenhouse.

557 WATTS & HARTON, 61 Shoe Lane, Holborn, Manu.—Pewter articles, moulds. Warmer and cooler for confectioner's counter. Plates for printing music. Dishes, plates, and drinking-cups. Brass castings, &c.

559 BAKER, W. 14 Allen St. Goswell St. Manu. -Awls, bodkins, steels, &c. for shoemakers, carpenters, &c.

560 FARROW, C. 18 Gt. Tower St. Manu.—Machines, &c. used in the management of wines and other liquors.

563 HALE, J. Walsall, Manu.—Spring curb hooks, for bridle-bits. Steel spring swivels. Polished steel pole and trace-chains, for pair-horse carriage. Buckles. Fancy chain dog-collars.

565 ROBERTSON, H. Milngavie, Scotland, Inv.—Cutter gauge, for cutting a square. Machine for washing yarn. Trap for shooting pigeons. Rat-trap.

566 POPE, W. Bridge St. Exeter, Manu.—Felt, for pump valves and for shoeing horses; also for polishing marble and for back collars of carriage-wheels, &c. Furnace for consuming smoke, with apparatus for producing naphtha.

568 M'CLURE, J. Galloway House, Garlieston, Scotland, Inv.—Model of a swing door, without the use of springs or pulleys.

570 GREEN, C. 2 Portland St. Brighton, Inv.—Machine for cutting bread, and a letter-box.

571 GRAY, J. Dunbar, Scotland, Manu.—Pattern of traps for killing rabbits, &c.

572 ENGLISH, J. Epping, Essex, Manu.—Fumigating apparatus for killing and capturing insects.

573 COLLINGE, C. & Co., Lambeth.—Hinges and models of carriage gates.

574 PINDER, W. & SONS, Sheffield Works, Manchester.—Steel and composition doctors. Engravers' steel plates, files, &c.

575 BRADNACK, I. R. Gt. Yarmouth, Inv.—Summer skates, adapted for a macadamised road, &c. Improved knocker, letter-plate, &c. for a door.

576 BURROWS, T. Barnsley, Inv.—Bed-joint, to supersede the use of the screw.

577 HEDLEY, G. Ireland.—Gas cooking apparatus.

578 LEARWOOD, T. Truro. — Walking-stick stool and novel screw driver.

579 COOK, T. Ann St. Plumstead, Inv. and Manu.—House alarum for doors or windows, and gardens or shrubberies.

580 ARMSTRONG, J. jun. 10 Pollen St. Maddox St. Regent St.—Dressing and other combs.

Class 22.

GENERAL HARDWARE, including LOCKS and GRATES.

581 HUGHES, H. 72 Charles St. City Rd. Inv.—Patent gauffering machine.

582 HAYWARD BROTHERS, 196 Blackfriars Rd.—Sherringham's registered ventilator.

583 LEAVER, J. C. Maidenhead.—A chandelier.

584 HAYNES, J. 88 St. James's St. Inv.—Apparatus for extracting corks.

587 KNIGHT, T. W. 33 Regent Ter. Widcomb, Bath, Inv.—Bolt for folding doors, which fastens on closing the right-hand door.

591 BISHOPP, Rev. J. M.A. 11 Canterbury Row, Kennington Rd. Inv.—A rotatory cinder-sifter, by which cinders are thoroughly sifted, and, without opening the machine, are made to fall down instantly into the coal-scuttle.

592 HOCKIN, C. 38 Duke St. Manchester Sq. part Owner and Agent.—Carson's patent meat preserver, to salt a joint in ten minutes.

594 JENKINSON, J. 21 President St. Goswell St. Inv.—Improved blind roller and spring bracket.

595 MOORE, J. 38 Clerkenwell Close, Prop.—Patent lever ventilator for windows.

597 AZULAY, B. Rotherhithe, Inv.—Improved patterns for Berlin work, &c. Hot water bath, gas-stoves, copper, &c. Window-roller bracket spring.

600 WENHAM LAKE ICE Co. 164A Strand, Manu.—Ice safe or refrigerator, lined with the patent glass enamel. Syphon water filter, inv. by Alfred Bird.

601 KEITH, G. 36 Piccadilly.—Ling's patent ice-safes Gablen's ice-box. Registered ice-plane. Coffee or chestnut roaster. "Magic mirror." Liquid meter.

602 HOLLAND, —.—40 South Audley St.—Improved brass cock for kitchen boiler.

604 HELY, A. A. 16 Manchester Buildings, Westminster, Inv.—Patent cork driving apparatus and vent bottle. Sliding candle lamp. Chemical vase.

606 BENTLEY, W. H. Bedford, Inv. and Manu.—Garden irrigator; Cooking apparatus; self-acting kitchen-range; apparatus for sweeping chimneys; tea-kettle; alarm lock; reg. stove; improved coffee-pot; and filtering cistern.

607 DANIELL, J. C. Limpley Stoke, near Bath.—Piece of ordnance, to be loaded at the breach instead of the muzzle, and affording greater protection to the gunners.

609 HUGHES & KIMBER, 106 & 107 Shoe Lane, Fleet St. Manu.—Copper-plate for line engraving, hard and polished. Steel-plate for mezzotinto engraving, invented by R. Hughes.

610 MOREWOOD & ROGERS, Steel Yard Wharf, Manu. Inv. and Prop.—Galvanized tinned iron for gutters, pipes, mouldings, wire for telegraphs, fencing, &c.

611 MITCHELL, J. Stonehaven, Scotland.—Pipe fittings in tin-plate, German silver, and sterling silver. Malleable iron tobacco pipe, invented by the exhibitor.

612 HAMPDEN, J. 448 West Strand, Co-Prop. and Agent. —Fire escape, &c. Williams's temporary rudder. Scott's door spring. Nash's air-tight jar. Joysel's tea-urn. Enamelled zinc.

614 DURHAM, T. D. 16 Linton St. New North Road, Islington.—Registered hot air funnel kettle, for boiling water on a common fire in a few minutes.

615 GRAY, J. 11 Inverleith Row, Edinburgh, Inv.—Registered gravy-dish, for separating the liquid fat of roasted or boiled meat from the gravy at table.

616 HANSON, J. Huddersfield, Inv. Pat. and Manu.—Samples of patent manufactured lead.

619 DOWSTON, J.—Machine for setting the teeth of saws.

620 SEARS, R. 2 York St. Middlesex Hospital, Des. and Manu.—Coffee filterer and small cooking apparatus.

621 RIDLEY & EDSER, Vincent Sq. Westminster, and St. James's Ter. Vauxhall Bridge Rd.—Working mode, showing patent safety doors and apparatus.

622 TAYLOR, J. Wolverhampton, Inv. and Manu.— Bramah locks. Improved balance detector lever locks. Barron's chest and latch till-lock.

626 CUNNINGHAM, A. R. Addison Rd. Kensington, Inv. —Registered knife-cleaner and sharpener.

627 FARRAR, W. Leicester.—Zinc fountain, made by hand, and without the aid of casting or stamping. Improvement for sash windows. Cylindrical bed-warmer, &c.

628 FITCH.— Patent oven for baking bread, pastry, meats, &c.

630 COMMON, J. Melrose, Scotland, Inv. and Manu.— Slide ball-cock, capable of standing a great pressure.

633 BURNEY & BELLAMY, Mill Wall, Poplar—Des. and Manu.—Tanks for water, biscuits, oil, and paint. Cistern and barrel for oil, tar, spirit, &c.

634 MASTERS, T. 309 Regent St. Inv. and Manu.—Freezing, heating, and cooling apparatus. Knife-cleaning and aerating machines. Anti-corrosive self-acting taps, &c.

636 HART & SONS, 53, 54, & 55 Wych St. Strand, Manu. —Door-knobs and finger-plates in brass, china, glass, &c. Dr. Arnott's ventilating chimney valves, improved.

637 RIDDLE, W. East Temple Chambers, Inv.—Everpointed pencils. Apparatus for extinguishing fires in ships. Railway carriage, lighted by compressed coal gas. Signal lamps, stoppered canisters, latch and bolt-union, suspensory couch, detector bolt, railway buffer, &c. Pat. and Prov. reg.

638 NAYLOR, J. 121 Radnor St. Hulme, Inv.—Lamps for pillars on the ground; and for brackets to the wall.

639 MACHELL, J. C. Carlisle St. Soho Sq.—Patent portable shower-bath.

640 NIXEY, W. G. 22 Moor St. Soho, Inv.—Patent till, to prevent fraud, &c. Fire escape. Flexible cement, to fasten metal, marble, glass, &c. to wood, or to each other.

641 COALBROOK DALE Co. Coalbrook Dale, Inv. Des. and Manu.—Iron and bronze castings. Ornamental park entrance of cast-iron, bronzed, consisting of a pair of principal gates, and two side gates, hung on iron pillars of new construction: each of the four gates was cast in one piece. Ornamental rustic dome of cast-iron, bronzed, 20 feet in diameter by 30 feet high; adapted for glazing, as a greenhouse, &c.; it contains an iron casting of the Eagle-slayer, a statuette of Æolus, by J. Bell. (Main Avenue, West) with ornamental fountain of cast-iron, bronzed, seven feet wide by eight feet high, of Cupid and the Swan: the group forms the jet, and occupies the centre of a tazza, decorated with an ornamentation of the white and yellow water-lily: English design; John Bell. Ornamental chimney-piece and grate, with decorations illustrative of deer-stalking, boar-hunting, and hawking; enriched with a bronze group of the Death of the Stag, modelled and chased by B. W. Hawkins, general designer. Bright ornamental grate, composed of burnished and sprung steel front, with electro-gilt ornaments, novel panels and mouldings, and a marble mantel-piece: English design: C. Crookes. A large collection of stoves, grates, ranges, fenders, &c. Ornamental work. Collection of small works in foreign design; and groups and statuettes of English design, by B. W. Hawkins and John Bell.

642 MILNER & SON, Liverpool, Manchester, and 47A Moorgate St. Pat. and Manu.—Milner's patent holdfast and fire-resisting safes.

643 HULETT, D. 55 High Holborn, Manu.—Cut chandeliers. Rutter's ventilating gas chandeliers. Gas meter. Antique candelabra. Gas cooking stove, &c.

644 SEDGWICK & TAYLOR.—Various lamps and chandaliers.

645 MILLER & SONS, 179 Piccadilly, and 370 Oxford St. Inv. and Manu.—Patent Admiralty regulation lights. Ship, carriage, railway, police, and reading lamps.

646 CHUBB & SON, 57 St. Paul's Churchyard, Inv. Pat.

GENERAL HARDWARE, including LOCKS and GRATES.

and Manu.—Patent detector locks and latches, quadruple and rim locks; and fire-proof safes.

647 HAYWOOD & SON, 20 St. James's Walk, and Suffolk St. Clerkenwell. Manu.—Locks; specimens of gilding and engraving applicable to fancy brass foundry.

648 MAYO & BATES, Wolverhampton, Manu.—Door-lock keys, in different stages of manufacture.

649 The PATENT POINTED SCREW Co. Wolverhampton, Manu.—Patent pointed screws, cast out of malleable iron, which can be driven into wood without boring holes.

649A HUFFER, J. 20 Wilderness Row, Clerkenwell, Inv. and Manu.—Detector and chest lock, secret action. Locks for desks, trunks, portfolios, drawers, and carpet bags.

650 BIGFORD, H. Wolverhampton, Inv. and Manu.—Improved detector-lock.

650A FOSTER, R. 1 York Pl. St. George's East, Inv.—Self-acting detector lock.

651 GOLLOP, J. Wellington Foundry, Charles St. City Rd. Manu.—Patent rising and not-rising spring, swing, and other hinges for doors or gates. (In North Gallery.)

652 GERISH, F. W. East Rd. City Rd. Inv. and Manu. —Safety and other locks. A simple and cheap spring hinge.

653 BRAMAH & Co. 124 Piccadilly, Inv. and Manu.—Assortment of patent locks, with illustrations of their construction. Very fine ornamental iron castings.

654 GIBBONS, J. jun. Wolverhampton, Manu.—Improved locks, for doors, drawers, park gates, &c.

655 CARPENTER & TILDESLEY, Willenhall, near Wolverhampton, Manu.—Carpenter and Co.'s, Sanders', Tildesley's, and Brillies' patent locks. Rock's patent Gothic case locks. Curry-combs, horse-scrapers, &c.

656 WHITLEY, J. Ashton, near Warrington, Manu.—Case of wrought-iron hinges.

657 CLARK, T. & C. & Co. Shakespeare Foundry, Wolverhampton.—Enamelled cast-iron hollow ware.

658 OSMOND, G. 19 Somers Pl. East, New Rd. St. Pancras, Inv.—Improved fittings for roller blinds, &c. Spring latch. Bolts. Sash-fastener. Patent centres for swing-glasses.

659 PARKES, H.W. 110 Strand, Manu.—Shand lock.

660 HARLEY, G. Warwick St. Wolverhampton.—Patent detector locks.

661 CARTWRIGHT, D. Leek, Prop.—Alarm lock; on an attempt being made to pick it, a bell rings, and when the bolt is shot a pistol is fired.

663 AUBIN, C. Wolverhampton, Inv. and Manu.—Specimens to illustrate the rise and progress of the art of making locks. Miniature specimens, by H. and F. Aubin. Original method of ornamenting tin goods and panes of glass.

664 YATES, H. St. John's Sq. Wolverhampton, Inv. and Manu.—Locks for trunks, drawers, &c.

665 LEA, W. & J. Wolverhampton, Manu.—Fasteners for sashes; alarm bells; Gothic hinge; handles for locks; latches; locks, bolts, &c.

666 STIRK, J. Salop Street, Wolverhampton. — Engineer's anvil, smith's vice, and tinman's anvil.

667 WHITEHOUSE, C. & Co. Wolverhampton, Inv. and Manu.—Tubes and fittings for steam, gas, and water. Amalgamated Swedish iron, for gun-barrels.

668 WINDLE & BLYTH, Walsall, Pat. and Manu.—Model of Strutt's patent door-lock. Registered locks. Corkscrews. Patent compensating and other steel pens. (In North Gallery).

668A TUCKER, W. H. Taunton.—A double-action detector lock, that can only be opened by its own distinctive key.

669 MORETON & LANGLEY, 22 Bush Lane, City, and Wolverhampton, Prop.—General hardware, for home, colonial, and foreign markets, with imitations of foreign goods.

670 WALTERS, B. & P. 100 North St. Wolverhampton, Manu.—Patent locks, for furniture, doors, &c.

671 PEARCE, W. 50 High St. Dumfries, Scotland, Inv. —Safety lock.

672 MITCHELL, J. Redruth, Cornwall.—Improved pistol, Newly-invented safe lock.

673 LEWIS, G. High Cross St. Leicester, Inv. and Manu. —Lock, with newly-invented circular levers and self-dividing bitted keys.

674 HORTON, A. Ashburton, Devon, Inv.—Locks on a new principle, applicable for all doors, dock gates, &c.

675 DOWNS, W. Long Melford, near Sudbury, Suffolk, Inv. and Manu.—Improved twelve-bolt lock.

676 THRUPP, H. J. 5 George St. Grosvenor Sq.—Hinges.

676A GREENFIELD, J. Broad St. Golden Sq.—Model of door, with new safety fastenings.

677 BOULTER, B. Hull, Inv.—New backfasteners, for window-shutters.

678 BARNWELL & SON, 46 Bishop St. Dublin, Manu.—Wrought-iron double-cased safe, with secret lock. Hall-door and desk lock. Iron-rim lock, for prisons, &c.

679 WISSON, R. 5 Coburg St. Inv. and Manu.—Secret drawn lock. Padlock, with key. Secret padlock.

680 BOOBBYER, J. H. 14 Stanhope St. Clare Market—Venetian ventilators. Three-bolt mortice and rim locks. Various other locks, fastenings, &c.

681 BAMBER & SON, 27 Wood St. Westminster, Inv. and Manu.—Improved mortice night bolt for bed, dressing, and bath rooms.

682 TAYLOR & SON, Loughborough, Leicestershire, Manu.—Improved bells and bell-framing. (North Transept.)

683 MURPHY, J. 15 Thomas St. Dublin, Manu.—Two church bells, cast in tune from the furnace without any artificial tuning or chipping. (Main Avenue, West.)

684 MEARS, C. & G. 267 Whitechapel Rd. Manu.—Hemispherical bell. (Main Avenue, West.)

685 SOBEY, W. R. Exeter.—Case of plated goods.

686 FEATHAM, MILLER, & SAYER, 9 Clifford St. Bond St. Des. and Manu.—Fire grates, stoves, fenders, &c. Locks, finger-plates, fire-irons, &c.

687 ALDRIDGE, J. M. 20 Nelson St. City Road, Inv.—Double-action spring centre and top pivot for doors.

688 PERRY & Co. 37 Red Lion Sq.—Various specimens of steel pens. (In North Gallery.)

689 KNIGHT & FOSTER, 5 Eastcheap.—A variety of steel pens. (In North Gallery.)

690 RODGERS & SONS, Sheffield, Manu.—Sportsman's knife, containing eighty blades and other instruments. Sportsman's knife, three-quarters of an inch long, containing fifty-six blades and other instruments. Specimens of table and pocket knives of all descriptions, scissors, razors, &c. showing the several stages of manufacture, from the raw material to the finished goods. (Main Avenue, West.)

691 MOTTRAM & HAWKINS, 15 Carr Lane, Sheffield, Manu.—An assortment of shoe, butchers', cooks', weavers', bread, palette, putty, glaziers', and farriers' knives, &c.

691A PERRY, R. & SON, Temple St. Wolverhampton, Manu.—Copper, tin, and japanned wares.

692 LORKIN, J. 68 Basinghall St. Inv.—Patent egg-beater.

693A LEE, G. 90 Church St. Paddington, Inv. and Manu. —Spring-shank self-adjusting button. Embossing iron, to finish woollens, linens, cottons, silks, velvets, &c.

694 KNIGHT & FOSTER, 5 Eastcheap, Inv.—Paxton steel pens; Bank of England pens; swan pens; correspondence pens; anti-corrosive pens.

695 BARRON & SON, Prop.—A variety of locks for doors, drawers, safes, &c., on various principles. Fancy keys.

697 BOAKE, J. F. 11 and 12 Wellington Quay, Dublin.

GENERAL HARDWARE, including LOCKS and GRATES.

Inv.—Model of signal post; signal lanthorn and lamps; lighting case, &c. Table lamps, aerometric.

698 COTTAM & HALLEN, 2 Winsley St. Inv. and Manu. Enamelled manger, rack, and water trough, for horses. Park gates. Designs in iron for staircase railing, &c.

700 HARDMAN, J. & Co. Gt. Charles St. Birmingham, Manu.—Specimens of wrought-iron work, &c.

700A LLOYD & SUMMERFIELD, Birmingham.—Chandeliers and lamps.

701 WALTON, F. Wolverhampton.—Papier-maché, tin, japan, and patent enamelled goods, in wrought iron.

702 HANSON, G. Huddersfield.—Water-closet.

703 NUNN, Miss A. Welbeck St.—Domestic laundry in one machine. New method of warming several apartments from one fire.

705 THOMPSON, T. H.—A sewer trap.

754 CULVERWELL, W. 16 Charlotte St. Blackfriars Rd. Inv.—Registered portable domestic vapour bath.

755 JEFFCOAT, F. L. 26 Strand, Inv. and Manu.—Improved bedsteads, and bed for invalids, &c. Apparatus for heating laundry irons.

792 MAUND, E. 370 Oxford St. Prop.—Cast-iron vase stove, radiating vertically; smoke descending.

793 MURRAY, W. 20, John St. Adelphi, Inv. & Manu.—Tubular filter and a compensating ball tap.

794 LANE, W. R. 226 Strand, Inv. and Manu.—Economic percolator or improved registered coffee-pots.

795 MARRIOTT, W. 89 Fleet St. Manu.—Platform weighing machine, showing the weight of various European countries, dial weighing machine, domestic telegraph, &c.

796 LOSEBY, E. T. 44 Gerrard St. Islington, Inv.—Portable crane shower bath, reg.

797 DIXON, J. & SONS, Sheffield.—Powder and pistol flasks, shot pouches, drinking flasks, &c. in precious and other metals.

798 WARNER, J. & SONS, 8 Crescent, Jewin St.—Water, steam, and gas cocks, valves, sluice cocks, &c. Various lamps. Standard weights and measures. A set on the decimal system, Reg. Pat. Check indicators. Musical hand-bells. Beer and cider engines. Tea urns and coffee pots of novel patterns. Improved water-closets, self-supplying pans, &c. Three church bells. (North Transept.)

799 WHEELER, C. Birmingham.—Specimens of pearl buttons.

800 DE LA FONS, J. P. Carlton Hill, St. John's Wood. —Safety locks and bolts for windows and doors.

801 JONES, J. & Co. Sheffield.—Rust preventive composition. Samples of steel goods which have been exposed to the weather, the bright parts having been preserved.

802 ROBERTSON, CARR, & STEEL, Chantrey Works, Sheffield. —Ornamental cast-iron mantel pieces, drawing-room and other grates, fenders, and sets of polished fire-irons.

804 KENNARD & Co. 67 Upper Thames St. and Falkirk Ironworks, Scotland, Manu.—Four coats of arms, varied designs and sizes. Self-acting and cottage ranges; register grates, ornamental castings, &c.

805 BAILY, W. & SONS, 71 Gracechurch St. Des. & Manu. —A Gothic church stove. Saloon grate, with dogs and fender. Gothic stoves, with brass dogs, &c. Gothic chandelier. Old English door-handles, locks, &c. Cast-iron staircase work. Metal panels, &c. Improved pedestal stove, with candelabrum. (Main Avenue, West.)

806 OXLEY, W. & Co. Park Gate Steel Works, Rotherham, Manu.—Specimens of steel suitable for engineering, tool-making, spindles, &c.; also for carriage springs.

807 CHAMBERS, W. Brunswick Foundry, Birmingham.—Steel snuffers, showing the principal processes of manufacture. Carpenters' planes made of malleable iron and other metals. Patent metallic bed sacking.

808 THOMPSON, F. Westfield Ter. Sheffield, Inv. and Manu.—Patent gutta percha skates of various colours.

810 JENNINGS, G. Great Charlotte St. Blackfriars Rd.—India-rubber tube water-closets. India-rubber tube cocks. Pat. Improved cistern valve. Patent shop-shutter shoe. Patent joint for connecting pipes without solder, &c.

Proceed to Mediæval Court, page 136.

Class 23.   WORKS IN PRECIOUS METALS, JEWELLERY, ETC.
—— South Central Gallery. ——

1 ELKINGTON, MASON, & Co., Birmingham.—Specimens of electro-plated candelabra, tazzas, vases, table-ware, &c. And a variety of electro deposited sideboard and other plate from the antique. Electro deposited figures, &c. in bronze, from the Arts Manufactory of Mr. H. Elkington. (See also Main Avenue, West, Nos 92, 93, 94.)

2 MARTIN, BASKETT, & MARTIN, Cheltenham, Manu. and Des.—Centre-piece, with figures. Milton inkstand; toilet-stand. Tea and coffee service. Large model of a Great Western steam-engine. Rich Bohemian glass claret jug. Chatelaine in gold and enamel. Pearls, ornaments, gold chains and jewellery, manufactured by C. Sparrow, London. Chronometer and other watches in their different stages of manufacture. Time-keeper, newly-invented alarum, &c., invented by E. Burgess, Clerkenwell Green.

3 REID & SONS, 14 Grey St. Newcastle-upon-Tyne, Manu.—Silver goods: Chased claret jug, basket, and tea and coffee service; pierced and engraved basket, centre-piece, &c.

4 PAYNE & SONS, 21 Old Bond St. Bath, Prod.—Vase in silver, after a marble antique in the Capitoline Museum.

5 WALL, T. Stokes Croft, Bristol, Des. and Manu.—Original design in hair-work. Ladies' guard; bracelets, &c.

7 GREENWELL, J. Whitby, Manu.—Silver tea-pot, coffee-pot, and tea-kettle, weighing, together, only 140 grains.

8 GREENBURY, I. Whitby, Manu.—Jet necklaces, bracelets, brooches, candlesticks, pincushion, likeness-stand, earring. Rough jet, &c.

10 TUCKER, J. T. Exeter, Inv.—Registered universal brooch protector.

11 HARDING, J. St. David's, Exeter, Des. and Inv.—Gold and silver bracelets, with secure snap.

12 ELLIS & SON, Exeter, Des. and Manu.—Eight-day carriage time-piece, with duplex escapement and compensating balance. Safety chain brooches. Silver-wire gauze card-basket, &c. Silver plate, spoons, forks, &c. Devonshire granite knife-handles.

13 MORTIMER, W. Edinburgh.—Scotch pebble inkstand.

14 MAYER, J. 68 Lord St. Liverpool, Des. and Manu. —Silver waiters, inkstand, cradle, epergne, candelabrum, Mersey Yacht Club Plate, &c. Jewellery. Black Diamond.

15 WEST & SON, J. Dublin, Manu.—Jewellery, embellished with Irish pearls and other gems.

16 CONNELL, D. 10 Nassau St. Dublin.—Cup, carved, with designs from scenes at Donnybrook fair. Brooches, bracelets, &c., of Irish bog oak, mounted in Wicklow gold and Irish diamonds. Book-stands, card-cases, &c.

17 MOSLEY, 46 Wicklow St. Dublin, Des.— Carved casket, in white and red Irish bog yew, with subjects in alto-relievo.

18 BENNETT, T. Dublin.—Ark of the covenant in silver. Silver services. Irish bog oak ornaments.

20 WATERHOUSE, G. & S. 25 Dame St. Dublin.—Registered brooches, adapted to cloaks and shawls.

21 NICOLL, W. Prince's St. Edinburgh, Manu.—Gold pens, pointed with iridium.

23 MARSHALL & SONS, 87 Gt. George St. Edinburgh, Manu.—Accoutrements for a Highland dress. Silver claret jugs, of antique shape and figure. Scotch pebble trinkets and jewellery.

24 RETTIE & SONS, Aberdeen, Manu.—Gold and silver mounted granite, porphyry, and topaz bracelets, brooches, pins, &c.

25 THOMPSON, F. H. 10 Brandon Pl. Glasgow, Manu.—Decanter stand. Coffee-urns. Large centre-piece, with flower-basket, &c.

26 BAIRD, W. 72 Argyle St. Glasgow.—Scotch ram's-head, mounted as a snuff-box and cigar-case.

27 LISTER & SONS, Newcastle-upon-Tyne, Manu.—Snuff-boxes, card-cases, jewellery, and Highland ornaments. Silver claret jugs. Coffee and tea-pots, &c. Eight-day spring clock, and chronometer timepiece.

28 SPURRIER, Birmingham.—Silver and plated coffee-pots, dishes, candlesticks, &c.

29 HILLIARD & THOMASON, Birmingham, Manu.—Silver fish-knives and forks, taper-stands, brooches, bracelets, corals. card-baskets, snuff-boxes, paper knives, &c.

30 CARTWRIGHT & HIRON, Birmingham.—Plated and silver gilt cruets, inkstands, baskets, &c.

31 MARRIAN, F. Cannon St. Birmingham, Manu.—An épergne, or centre-piece. Etruscan jugs. Antique coffee-pot. Chased salvers. Candlesticks. Chalice. Antique castor frames. Tea and coffee service, &c.

32 WILKINSON & Co. 15 Gt. Hampton St. Birmingham, and 41 Tavistock St. Covent Garden, London, Manu.—Electro-silver plate upon German silver :—Centre-piece, candelabrum, flower vase, tea-urn, venison-dish and cover, &c.

33 GOUGH, W. 11 Parade, Birmingham, Manu.—Electro-plated articles :—Epergnes, candelabra. Fruit and flower stands. Piano candlestick. Waiters, Plateau, &c.

34 COLLIS, G. R. Church St. Birmingham, Manu.—A solid silver table-top. Solid silver salver ; centre ornaments ; branches ; tripod candelabra ; and a large number of specimens of silver work.

35 HAWKSWORTH, EYRE, & Co. Sheffield, Des. and Manu.—A silver centre piece, with tripod stand. An assortment of articles, plated on German silver, and electro plated.

36 BRADBURY & SON, Sheffield, Manu.—Coffee and tea services. Kettles and pitchers, plated and engraved. Plateau. Tea-urn. Antique bread-basket. Candelabrum, &c.

37 HARRISON, J. Sheffield, Manu.—A large collection of articles in electro-plate on imperial metal and nickel silver.

38 DIXON & SONS, Sheffield.—Sculptured silver candelabra and épergne, with crystal glass, weighing about 750 ounces ; designed by V. Nicholson. Silver and gilt coffee and tea service, with silver salver modelled from a leaf of the Victoria Regia ; and other articles in silver, in best Sheffield plate and in Britannia metal.

39 SCHOOL OF DESIGN, Sheffield.—Carved oak cabinet, and sideboard.

40 ROBERTS & HALL, Sheffield, Manu.—Electro-plated tea-trays, urns, kettles, and tea services ; liquor and cruet frames ; salvers ; baskets, candlesticks, &c.

41 OWEN & LEVICK, Sheffield. — Silver-plated and Britannia metal ware.

42 PADLEY, PARKIN, & STANIFORTH, Sheffield, Manu. Silver plated goods plated upon German silver in the ingot, with illustrations of the mode of plating.

43 BROADHEAD & ATKINS, Sheffield.—Silver plate. Electro plate. Britannia metal goods. Mounted jugs, &c.

44 WILKINSON, H. & Co. Sheffield, Manu.—Epergnes, candelabra, tea-urn, coffee-trays, venison, and side-dishes, with covers, tureens, &c. Registered. Silver decanter-stands, bread-baskets, claret jugs, communion plate, cups, candlesticks, coolers, &c.

45 CRESWICK, T. J. & N. Sheffield, Manu. — Plated articles, with silver mountings. Candelabra. Epergne and plateau. Candlesticks, with branches. Venison dishes, &c.

46 M'GREGOR, M. Perth, Manu.—Ram's-head, mounted as a snuff-box and cigar-case.

47 MEYER & MORTIMER, George St. Edinburgh, Des. and Manu.—Ornaments of Highland regiments. Tartans and kilts. Dirks, purses, brooches, &c.

48 DURHAM, J. P. 456 New Oxford Street. — A steel chatelaine.

49 THORNHILL, W., 144 New Bond St.—A steel chatelaine.

51 BIDEN, J. & F. 37 Cheapside—Solid gold seals and signet rings. Library seal, fine cairngorm, engraved with the arms and badges of the Prince of Wales. Engraving on stone, steel, &c.—Drury Freeman, 41 Gee St. Goswell St. Superfine gold watch-key, set with two stones, red cornelian, and amethyst, weight of gold 1 oz. 12 dwts. 13 grs.

52 EATON, E. 16 Irvine Crescent, Cripplegate. — Silver forks, spoons, &c.

53 WOODBRIDGE, T. 4 Albion Rd. Holloway, Prop.—Chased silver design : Death on the pale horse, after West.

54 RAWLINGS, J. 85 Portland Rd. Regent's Park, Manu. —Specimens of miniature frames mounted and engraved : imitation of or-molu.

55 MILLS, M. 17 Ossulston St. Somers Town, Manu.—Embossed and chased salver — subject, Aurora, or the Hours, after Guido ; border, after the Tredacns shell.

56 INDERWICK, J. 58 Prince's St. Leicester Sq.—Carved meerschaum pipe. Registered pipe tube.

57 MORTIMER, W. H., 12 Harley St., Cavendish Sq., Inv. —Mechanism for the teeth, set in gold.

59 CLEAL, W. 53 Poland St. Oxford St. Manu.—Specimen of working in human hair.

. **60** WARRINER, W. 16 Charlotte St. Fitzroy Sq. Manu. —Or-molu miniature frame, set in crimson velvet.

62 LOEWENSTARK, A. D. 1 Devereux Court, Strand, Des. and Manu.—Silver filigree ancient incense urn, &c. Different specimens of filagree masonic jewels.

63 RESTALL, R. 35 High St. Croydon, Inv. and Manu. —The registered cylindrical brooch protector.

64 GOODWIN, C. Prop.—China vase, mounted in metal gilt. Bloodstone cup, mounted in silver gilt. Pastile burner.

65 WISEDILL, G. V. 1 Gloucester Pl. Prospect Row, Walworth Rd. Inv. and Manu.—Registered fastening for brooches, &c. self-acting double spring swivels.

66 ABBOTT, G. 4 Perry St. Bedford Square.—Various chased silver articles, and a cast, not chased.

67 MORLEY, P. 140 High Holborn, Prop.—Electro-gilding on soft metal.

68 WOLLFF, L. J. 45 Upper York St. Bryanston Sq. Des. and Manu.—Desk seal, mounted in gold, set with turquoise, surmounted with large pearl.

69 GOWLAND, T. Inv.—Spring catch fasteners for brooches and bracelets.

70 BAKEWELL, W. 25 Red Lion St. Clerkenwell, Artist in Hair.—Specimens for lockets, brooches. Inscriptions and initials of pearls. The Prince of Wales' feathers in hair, &c.

71 LEE, B. 41 Rathbone Pl. Manu.—Bracelets of human hair and gold. Brooches. Hair-guard chains, &c.

72 SEYMOUR, E. & J. 40 Gerrard St. Soho, Prop.—A small enamelled gold vase, with portraits of Her Majesty and Prince Albert (painted on enamel, in imitation of cameo, by T. Haslem). The vase designed, engraved, and enamelled by the exhibitors.

73 HOPE, H. T. M.P. 116 Piccadilly, Prop.—Casket, containing a blue diamond, weighing 177 grains, mounted as a medallion, surrounded by brilliants, and supposed, from its size and colour to be unique.

74 HARDING, DANDO, & Co. 23 Hatton Garden, Invs. and Manu.—Patent spiral fastening, adapted to buttons, studs, pins, brooches, &c.

75 BAYLEY, W. George St. Goswell St.—Specimens of electro-gilding on medals.

76 CAMPBELL, A. 43 Tottenham Court Rd. Inv. Des. and Manu.—Cornucopia, being a brooch, flower-holder, and watch protector.

77 FORSTER, E. 19 Queen St. Haymarket, Manu.—Silver-gilt table-spoon, representing Jenny Lind as Alice in Robert le Diable. Silver snuff-box.

78 EDWARDS, R. 26 Lisle St. Leicester Sq. Des. and Exec.—Specimens of different colours in enamel, and portraits in enamel of the Queen, Prince Albert, Shakspeare, and the Duke of Wellington.

79 BUSS, H. 13 Gt. Newport St. Leicester Sq. Des. and Executor—Medallion, displaying the heraldic devices in incised enamels, on gold and silver, of the nations whose works are shown in the Exhibition.

80 ZIMMERMAN, G. & S. 38 Old Bond St. Manu.—Porphyry and malachite casket, mounted in or-molu, corners set with gems. Silver statuettes of the Queen, and Prince Albert and of Charles the First.

81 STOCKEN, C. 53 Regent St.—A variety of dressing cases.

83 GASS, S. H. & D. 166 Regent St. Prop.—Silver dessert service, of novel character and design, modelled from nature from water plants in Kew Gardens. Centre pieces; vases; christening cup, with figures by Redgrave. Silvered jewelled dessert set, in Elizabethan style. Brooch, in the style of jewels of the cinquo-cento period. Carbuncle and diamond bracelet, with portraits of Her Majesty and H.R.H. the Prince of Wales, after Thornburn, executed in niello, engraved by J. J. Crew. Silver gauntlet niello bracelet, designed by Maclise; and other articles of jewellery. Large vase, composed of human hair: executed by J. Woodley, 31 Cursitor Street.

84 PARAVAGUA & CASELLA, 3 Brabant Court, Philpot Lane, Imp. and Manu.—Branch of natural rough coral, of great size and value. Carvings, bracelet, necklaces, and cameos, in coral.

85 BARLING, J. Maidstone and London.—Forks and spoons in silver and enamel.

86 NASH, E. (late J. Butler) 30 Coppice Row, Clerkenwell, Des. and Manu.—Silver and gold pencil cases and penholders, engraved and jewelled. A set of silver engraved and gilt instruments for ladies. Gold pens. Tortoiseshell and pearl snuff-boxes, &c. gold and silver, inlaid and mounted.

87 PHILLIPS, Brothers, 31 Cockspur St., Inv. and Prop.—Statuettes, &c. in oxidized silver and gold, &c.

Chronometer. Watches. Chessmen in gold and silver, enamel, precious stones and pearls, &c.

88 ADAMS, G. W. Hosier Lane, Manu.—Dessert service, silver gilt; the same, in silver. Knives, forks, spoons and various other articles in silver.

90 HERMANN, A. 4 Oxendon St. Haymarket, Des. and Manu.—Laurel wreath, with imitation of lace, cut with scissors. Bouquets of various coloured hair, in a new style.

91 WHEELER, G. & M., 28 Bartlett's Buildings, Holborn, Manu.—Jewellery and trinkets; specimens showing the progress of a gold bracelet from the pure metal to the complete article.

92 HARVEY & Co. 126 and 128 Regent St. Prop.—Silver candelabrum, claret and water-jug, from the antique, from designs by Flaxman, &c. Statuette of Mercury, designed by Woodington, &c. Gold watch, invented by S. Boreham, to beat seconds, and to strike at the minute or 60th second.

94 SMILY, W. R. 9 Camomile St. Manu.—Richly chased silver coffee-pot, designed by King, chased by Worster. Child's mug, with Wilkie's Blindman's Buff, chased by T. Edwards; another designed by Percy.

95 MATTHEWS, E. 46 Berwick St. Soho, Des. and Manu.—Royal arms, &c. of England since the Conquest, engraved on different metals, and emblazoned with sealing wax.

96 ROBINSON, W. 70 Wynyatt St. Clerkenwell, Manu. and Pat.—Gilt clock-case, made of electrotype deposited plates, electro-gilt. Other articles showing the uses of electrotype in manufactures.

97 HUNT & ROSKELL (late STORR & MORTIMER), 156 New Bond St. Manu. 26 Harrison St. Gray's Inn Rd. Inv. Des. and Manu.—A work in silver, showing its application to sculpture, combined with metallurgical art. A shield, embossed and chased in silver and iron. Vases, presentation plate, centre pieces, candelabra, dessert stands, cups, salvers, tazzas, caskets, &c. with designs, &c. by Alfred Brown, A. Vechte, Sir G. Hayter, Frank Howard, Sir F. Chantry, E. H. Bailey, J. G. Crace, H. Armstead, J. Haslem, and Winterhalter. Watches and chronometers, of extraordinary construction. Carriage and other clocks. Specimens of the various precious stones, in the rough and wrought state. Pearls, &c.

98 GARRARD, R. & S. Panton St. Haymarket.—Nautilus cup, tankards, ewers, tea and coffee services, candelabra, centre pieces, table ornaments, and other specimens of gold and silver plate. Jewellery: suites of opals and brilliants; sapphires, pearls, and brilliants; rubies and brilliants; tiaras, bracelets, &c.

99 FORRER, A. 136 Regent St. Prop. — Ornaments worked in hair and gold. Jewellery; ornamental frame, containing the miniatures of Her Majesty, H. R. H. Prince Albert, and the Royal Family, mounted in hair and gold.

100 WIDDOWSON & VEALE, 73 Strand, Manu.—In silver, a centre-piece plateau with candelabra and dessert stands. Equestrian statuette of the Duke of Wellington. Sacramental flagon and chalice, &c.

101 GRAY, J. 5 Billiter Sq.—Series, illustrative of the manufacture of plated articles from metal plated in the ingot.

102 LAMBERT & RAWLINGS, Coventry St. Prop.—Candelabrum and dessert centre in silver. Silver wine flagon. Soup tureen and stands. Ruby glass cups, after the antique, &c.

103 ANGELL, G. 51 Compton St. Clerkenwell, Manu.—Large vase, in the Etruscan style, illustrative of the progress of civilization. Candelabra, in eastern style. Tea-tray, illustrative of the purposes of the Exhibition, engraved by Donalds. Trifle stand, in the Italian style.

104 MARSHALL, E. S. 31 John St. Tottenham Court Rd. Manu.—Gold-leaf and dentist's gold leaf, various. Illustrations of the malleability of the various metals. Gold beaters' skin.

105 WATHERSTON & BROGDEN, 16 Henrietta St. Covent Garden, Manu.—A standard gold enamelled and jewelled vase, designed by Alfred Brown, surmounted by group emblematical of Great Britain, with reliefs and busts of celebrated men, &c. Gold brooches, bracelets, necklaces, chains, seals, and rings.

106 HOLT, J. 80 Pratt St. Camden Town.—A variety of chased medallions.

107 MOSLEY & Co. 8 Hatton Garden, Manu.—Gold pens tipped with iridium, and silver pencil-cases, pen-holders, &c.

108 FORREST, W. 54 Strand—Silver rose-water dish, by Wagner of Paris, being his last work.

109 EADY, H. J. 26 Red Lion St. Clerkenwell, Des. and Manu.—Chessmen. Henry VIII. and Francis I. at the field of the cloth of gold, after Holbein, Titian, &c.

110 SMITH, NICHOLSON, & Co. Duke St. Lincoln's Inn Fields, Manu.—Candelabrum, with figures, by W. Beattie. Testimonial to W. C. Macready, designed by B. Smith and C. Grant. Dessert service, with figures, by J. S. Archer. Summerley's art manufacture. Electro-plated goods.

111 ANGELL, J. 10 Strand, Des. and Manu.—Groups in silver, Arab merchants halting in the desert; Sir Roger de Coverley and the gipsies. Chased shields : The battle of Alexander and Darius. Salver: The Labours of Hercules, &c.

112 HANCOCK, C. F. 39 Bruton St. Berkeley Sq. Manu.—Ebony, inlaid silver table and vase. Group in massive silver, modelled by Baron Marochetti, the dogs by M'Carthy, &c. Cravatte de drapeau, embroidered in gold on Pompadour velvet, &c. ; designed and executed by J. Holbeck & Co. 3 Vigo St. Regent St.

113 ATTENBOROUGH, R. 19 Piccadilly, Prop. — Silver centre for the table. Card-tray of silver and enamel. A bachelor's tea set. An agricultural prize cup, &c. Jewellery.

115 HIGGINS, F. 40 Kirby St. Hatton Garden, Des. and Manu.—Table and dessert cutlery. Silver table and other spoons and forks.

116 MOTT, W. 36 Cheapside, Prop.—Gold and silver ever-pointed pencils, in various styles, set with jewels.

117 MOREL, J. V. & Co. 7 New Burlington St. Regent St. Manu. — Equestrian statue of Queen Elizabeth, embossed with the hammer, in silver. Centre-piece, in silver of elaborate design. Oriental agate cups. Lapis lazuli cup. Vase, in rock crystal, mounted in gold and enamel, &c. Bouquet, composed of diamonds and rubies, separating into several different ornaments, &c.

118 ROWLANDS, C. & W. 146 Regent St. Manu.—Brilliant and ruby bracelet, Holbein style. Brilliant and emerald stomacher brooch. Gold and enamel bracelet, with carbuncle and diamonds. Another, in same style, with figures, &c.

119 EMANUEL, M. 5 Hanover Sq. Manu.—Large silver clock, by Woodington. Dessert stands. Gilt candelabra. Gilt plateau, with china racks and medallions. Natural crystal candlesticks. Processes of gold manufacture.

120 SHARP, T. 27 Burton Crescent, Des. and Manu.—Shakspeare cup, with subjects from Lear, Julius Cæsar, The Tempest, Othello, Hamlet, and Macbeth, and the "Justice" cup, in silver. A variety of electro-plated ware.

121 KEITH, J. 59 Britannia Ter. City Rd. Manu.—Communion services, consisting of flagons, chalices, patens, and offertory basins.

122 DODD, P. G. 79 Cornhill, Prop.—Silver tea and coffee service, with basso-relievo figures. Etruscan silver tea and coffee service. Silver claret jugs. Silver inkstand emblematical of science. Silver bread and sugar baskets, ice dish, &c.

123 STONE & SON, 7 Myddleton St. Clerkenwell, Manu.—A gold guard. Nepaulese and other guard chains. Prince Arthur, Albert, and imperial chains. Carbuncle and diamond bracelets and gem rings.

124 HANSSEN & DE KONING, Soho Bazaar and 50 Dorset St. Portman Sq.—Portrait of the Prince of Wales, Kensall Green Cemetery, flowers, &c., in hair work.

125 TOWNLEY, R. 6 Cursitor St. Chancery Lane.—Specimens of hair, plaited by machinery.

126 LIAS & SON, Salisbury Court, Manu.—Silver claret jugs, coffee-pots, tea-pots, sugar-basins, cream-jugs, cruet-frames, saltcellars, &c.

127 DONNE & SON, 51 Cheapside, Sculp.—The Spirit of Religion, after Armitage and Calcott Horsley. Gilt spoons and sugar tongs, engravings, scriptural subjects.

128 MASON, J. W. 4 Gate St. Lincoln's-Inn-Fields, Manu.—Embossed rosewater dish, Elizabethan style. Gilt and plated communion cups and plates. Solid wrought German silver candlesticks, plated. Sacrament cups and plates in cases.

129 SKIDMORE & SON, Coventry, Manu.—Chalices, patines, &c. after examples of the eleventh to the fifteenth century. Ancient modes of binding in silver. Offertory dish ; centre from design by Overbeck.

131 HENRYS & Co. 2 Budge Row.—Imitation precious stones.

140 HER MAJESTY THE QUEEN.—The great diamond of Runjeet Singh, called "Koh-i-Noor," or mountain of light. Jewel-case, in cinque-cento style, designed by L. Gruner, Esq. (In Centre Avenue.)

Proceed to Class 19, page 97.

Class 24. GLASS.

—— Central North Gallery. ——

1 ROSS, O'CONNOR, & CARSON, Belfast. — Watch glasses in all stages of manufacture.

2 HETLEY, J. H. & Co. 35 Soho Square.—Glass shades.

3 KIDD, W. 12 Poland St. Oxford St. Inv. and Manu.—New process for illuminating, embroidering, and silvering flat surfaces in glass. The designs are engraved on the under side of the glass.

4 SWINBURNE, R. W. South Shields and Newcastle-on-Tyne, Manu.—Silvered, naked, rough, and Venetian plates of glass. Pressed and coloured and opaque glass. Perforated glass. Glass domes. Glass pipes. Chemical apparatus. Glass trays, &c. Plate-glass (North Transept.)

5 PINKERTON, J. 143 High St. Borough. Des.—Plated metal dessert plates, inlaid with ornamental cut glass. Globe on pedestal, ornamental cutting, plated metal reflector inside Vase and dishes for chandelier. Flower vase, &c.

6 THE AIRE AND CALDER BOTTLE Co. Breffit, Edgar, Castleford, near Pontefract, Manu.—Bottles for dispensing and general purposes, with patent hollow corks and combination stoppers. Glass tablets, with inscriptions in glass. Glass insulators, for electric telegraphs.

7 WOOD & PERKES, Worsbro' Dale, near Barnsley, Manu.—Glass taps. Ruby épergne, and stand forming a separate fruit and flower vase. Glass inkstand and wafer-box.

8 SHEPHARD, J. 5 Crawford's Passage, Coppice Row, Clerkenwell. — Screwed connexions for glass tubing for

Class 24.
GLASS.

water, gas, or acids. Air-tight glass taps with screwed nuts for acids. Specimens of inside screw-cutting in glass.

9 SANDERSON & SON, 9 Brooke St. Holborn, Inv. and Manu.—New partition glass, for Seidlitz and other effervescing powders.

10 OHLSON, J. 70 Union St. Southwark.—Glass dishes, showing glass-cutting in three different stages, viz. cutting, smoothing, and polishing.

11 JONES & SONS, 5 Ludgate Hill, Des. Inv. and Manu.—Mantle piece girandoles. Cut glass, door handles, and furniture. Cornucopias, &c. Ruby glass decanters, richly engraved. Massive and brilliant cut glass bowl. Superb candelabra, designed for a console table.

12 GATCHELL, G. Anne St. Waterford, Ireland, Manu.—Etagère, or ornamental centre stand for a banqueting table ; consisting of forty pieces of cut glass. Decanters. Vases and covers, designed and executed at the Waterford glass works.

13 MOLINEAUX, WEBB, & Co. Manchester, Manu.—Specimens of cut, engraved, and coloured glass, consisting of jugs, goblets, decanters, finger-basins, glasses, flower and other vases, dishes, centre pieces, &c.

14 RICHARDSON, W. H. B. & J. Stourbridge, Manu.—Cut and plain crystal glass ; crystal, cased with coloured glass. Opal, cornelian, chrysolite, and Turkey glass, ornamented in enamel colours, &c.

15 DAVIS, GREATHEAD, & GREEN, Stourbridge, Manu.—Cut glass decanters, water jugs and goblets, ruby centres and stands, lustres, with ruby and flint drops, cut and enamelled ; coloured hock, and other wine-glasses. A great variety of ornamental vases ; white, opal, frosted, Mazareen blue, and topaz ; painted, enamelled, cut, and engraved.

16 WOOD, T. Stourbridge, Eng.— Blue-cased dish. Champagne bottle ; stained ruby bottle ; flint decanter ; tumbler ; ruby hock glass, &c.

17 WEBB, T. Platt's Glass Works, near Stourbridge, Manu.—Various patterns of glass, consisting of bowls and pedestals, dishes, ice-pails, pine-stands, decanters, flower-vases, pedestal lamps, lustres, &c.

18 LLOYD & SUMMERFIELD, Heath, Birmingham, Manu.—Table and dessert service of cut, and engraved glass, &c. Illustrations of flint glass manufacture. Busts of Her Majesty, and H. R. H. Prince Albert, &c.

19 BACCHUS & SONS, Birmingham, Manu. — Glass flower-stand, with vase and cornucopias ; vases ; decanters ; tazzas ; wine glasses, champagne glasses, and goblets ; claret jug, &c. ; white, coloured, and cased ; cut, engraved, enamelled, &c.

20 OSLER, F. & C. 44 Oxford St. and Broad St. Birmingham, Manu.—Candelabra (a pair), in richly cut crystal glass, carrying fifteen lights, each eight feet ; the property of Her Majesty. Crystal glass candelabrum, supported on three griffins, in frosted glass. Large table candelabra, in crystal glass, with prismatic shaft. Large lustres, richly mounted, with crystal prisms. Busts of Her Majesty and H.R.H. Prince Albert. Shakspeare, Milton, Scott, and Sir Robert Peel, in frosted glass. Large fountain, in cut crystal glass, twenty-seven feet high (at the intersection of the Main Avenue and Transept). (Messrs. Con, Vanden, Maeren, & Co. agents in Brussels.)

21 HARRIS, R. & SON, Islington Glass Works, Birmingham, Des. and Manu.—Pressed and moulded glass tumblers, goblets, wine glasses, sugar basins, butter coolers, door knobs, &c. Specimens of various articles in flint glass, cut and engraved. Ornamental glass, of various colours. Specimens of colours, combined by casing or coating. Specimens of threaded or Venetian glass.

22 CHANCE BROTHERS & Co. Glass Works, near Birmingham, Manu.—Crown window glass, of various kinds. Sheet, or cylinder window glass : the building for the Great Exhibition is glazed with this glass. Patent plate glass, for pictures, looking-glasses, &c. Coloured window glass. Glass shades. Optical glass. Flint disc, 29 inches diameter, &c. Dioptric revolving lighthouse. (Main Avenue, West).

23 LOCHHEAD, J. 35 Royal Exchange.—Perforated plate and sheet glass, for ventilation, &c. Patent ships' ventilating side scuttles, in perforated plate, sheet, and flint glass, &c.

24 SHOVE & Co. 488 New Oxford St.—Patent detached glass letters.

25 CLAUDET & HOUGHTON, 89 High Holborn.—Glass shades, round, oval, and square, of various sizes. Painted glass for three compartments of a window, the figures of St. Peter, St. Paul, and the Saviour.

26 COGAN, R. Des. Inv. &c.—Model of the Great Exhibition Building. Patent portable glass verandah, adapted for the growth of flowers, &c. A variety of articles in glass, including patent glass pens, &c.

27 VARNISH, E. 48 Berners St. Pat.—Plateaux. Vases. Salvers, &c., in silvered glass. Glass globes, mounted on eagles, Atlases, and ornamental stands. Silvered glass reflectors, applicable for artificial illumination.

28 CONNE, A. 118 Wardour Street, Oxford St. Des.—Goblets with ornamental designs. Amber champagne glass, with fancy border. Ruby wine glass, with vine border.

29 VIZETELLY & BRANSTON, Fleet St. Manu.—Ornamented glass ware, for architectural purposes, furniture, lamps, gas fittings, &c.

30 NAYLOR, W. 7 Princes St. Cavendish Sq. Des. and Inv.—Antique claret jug, engraved.—Reg. Massive butter-basin, cover and stand. Antique claret decanter. Antique water-jugs, with richly-engraved goblets, &c.

31 POWELL & SONS, Whitefriars Glass Works, Manu.—Painted, and patent pressed glass for windows. Glass pipes with patent joint. Chandelier and Glass pump with the same joint. Epergne, glasses for scientific purposes.

32 GREEN, J. G. 19 St. James's St. Piccadilly, Des. and Manu.—Samples of services of glass, engraved in Greek style. Large Etruscan-shape jugs. Pole fire-screen, with glass screen and pedestal, gilt, &c. Or-molu and silvered glass chandelier, &c.

33 PELLATT & Co. Falcon Glass Works, Holland St. Blackfriars, and Baker St. Portman Sq. Manu.—A highly refractive cut glass centre chandelier, 24 ft. long ; also a large chandelier of white, ruby, and blue glass, in style of Alhambra, and nine other variously ornamented chandeliers. A group of candelabra, richly cut crystal dessert services, Anglo-Venetian gilt and frosted glass, engraved glass vases and plates, medical glass, cameo incrustations, and models and specimens of flint glass, with illustrative specimens.

34 BINNS, R. W. 58 Baker St. Portman Sq. Des.—Miniature fountain for conservatory, with group in Parian statuary. Bridal and birthday dejeûné services.

36 PERRY & Co. 72 New Bond St. Des. and Manu.—Large cut glass chandelier for 144 candles, showing the style of glass-cutting of the 18 century, and modern improvements.

37 DAVIES, G. 20 Wyndham St. Bryanstone Sq. Des.—Painted marbles, opaque, on glass. Adapted for interior decorations, as panelling church altar work, ceilings &c.

38 DAVIES, W. 7 Broadley St. Blandford Sq. Des.—Opaque paintings on glass : Flowers and vase, and Angel rising from the clouds.

39 KIDDLE, H. 4 Eldor St. Norton Folgate.—Specimens of marble on glass adapted for altar-pieces, facias, plinths, fancy cabinet, and other ornamental work.

40 FORD, D. 4 James St. St. Peter's, Islington. Des.—Variegated specimens of "vitrum marmoratum ;" for table tops, tablets, panelling, &c.

41 HALL, J. W. Bristol, Manu.—Ornamental cut-glass

window; embossed British plate, for ornamental doors; letters, &c.; ornamental leaded stained-glass window.

42 FORREST & BROMLEY, Liverpool, Manu.—Stained glass window, representing the figure of St. Winifred. Glass chimney piece.

43 PRICE, 7 Bridge Rd. Lambeth. Des. and Inv.—Painted glass door, a specimen of the application of painting on glass to ornamental decoration.

44 JONES, Z. 17 Park Pl. Clifton, near Bristol.—Des. and Manu.—Top of a table in vitrilapis, a new style of ornamental glass, for decorative purposes.

45 BENINGFIELD, W. Colchester, Essex, Des. and Manu.—Glass picture-frames, an original design; the gilding or other ornamental work being completely protected.

46 BRAUN, H. Old Fish St. Hill, Doctors' Commons.

46A HANCOCK, RIXON, & DUNT, 1 Cockspur St. Manu.—Chandelier of cut glass, carrying thirty-two candles.

47 COATHUPES & Co. Nicholas St. Bristol, Inv. and Manu.—Glass water-pipes, plain, jointed, and angular. Glass curtain-poles.

48 FREEMAN, Messrs. 3 Wigmore St. Cavendish Sq.—Registered model of a percolator.

49 BARNES, W. 15 Grafton St. Fitzroy Sq.—Pieces of glass combined for decorations, suitable for churches, libraries, halls, &c., being transparent and waterproof.

50 SINCLAIR, C. 69 Old St. St. Luke's.—A model, in glass, of a glass cutter's cutting tool.

51 TARIN, M. L. A. 8 Nelson St. Mornington.—Magnifying-glass lamp reflectors.

52 SKIDMORE, T. R. 19 Haymarket.—Glass model of a pump.

53 MOORE, J. 33 Clerkenwell Close.—Patent lever ventilator.

54 MASH, J. 93 Farringdon St.—Royal crystal Venetian blind.

55 PETTIT, R. Lewis. Inv.—A reliquary, or box for small articles, made of slips of glass.

₊ STAINED AND PAINTED GLASS IN THE NORTH-EAST GALLERY.

60 CHANCE BROTHERS & Co. Glass Works, near Birmingham, Manu.—Dioptric apparatus of the first order, for lighthouses, with revolving lenses and catadioptric zones; constructed according to the system of Fresnel. Painted windows: leaded work, with medallions and ornamental work of the early Gothic style, and in the style of the fourteenth century. Landscape for staircase-window, on a single plate of glass. Group of flowers, with sample sheets of enamelled glass.

61 BAILLIE, E. 12B Cumberland Market, and 118 Wardour St. Prop.—Ornamented stained glass lights, picture enamelled on glass, Shakspeare reading a play to Queen Elizabeth and court, &c.

62 POWELL & SONS, Temple St. Fleet St.

63 HOLLAND & SON, St. John's, Warwick, Des. and Prod.—Fine Specimens of stained glass, in the decorated, perpendicular, and Elizabethan style.

64 BURT, T. T. 50 Welbeck St. Cavendish Sq. Des. and Prod.—Stained glass. Compartments of a window for an ecclesiastical building of the second pointed period.

65 O'CONNOR, M. & A.

66 ST. HELEN'S PLATE AND SHEET GLASS WORKS, St. Helen's, Lancashire, Manu.—Ornamental window of national emblems. Statue windows. Subject window, in colours, Michael casting out the great Dragon, &c.; each on a single plate of glass.

67 HOWE, J. G. 4 Cumberland Pl. New Road St. Marylebone.

68 GAUNT, T. Springfield Pl. Leeds, Des.—A painted window; specimen of a cheap and durable method of producing windows for churches.

69 HEDGLAND, G. 2 Grove Pl. Lisson Grove.

70 HALL & SON, Bristol.

71 TOMS, J. High St. Wellington, Somerset, Manu.—Painted window: St. Mary Magdalen. Natural forms of plants, applied to the decorative portions of a mosaic glass painting.

72 GIBSON, J. 89 Clayton St. Newcastle-upon-Tyne, Des.—Painted window, in black and white (en Grisaille), of early Norman character; a free imitation of a decorated window in St. Martin's-cum-Gregory, York.

73 WAILES, W. Newcastle-upon-Tyne.

74 CLAUDET & HOUGHTON.

75 GIBBS, I. A. 2 Harwood Pl. Camden Town, Des. and Prod.—Norman window. Decorated gothic compartments. Four compartments of pictorial glass.

76 MAYER, G. 1 Blomfield Terrace, Harrow Rd. Paddington. Des.—Stained-glass window, Saint George and the Dragon, standing under a Gothic canopy of the decorated period.

77 JACKSON, E. & W. H. 315 Oxford St. Prop.—The Royal Arms of England, painted on glass.

78 BALLANTINE & ALLAN, George St. Edinburgh, Des. and Manu.—Stained Glass, Elizabethan, and decorated style. Panel of ornamental glass, decorated style.

79 NEWSHAM, S. J. 1 Hereford St. Oxford St. Des. and Prod.—Painted glass: Prince of Wales' feathers, rose, thistle, and shamrock, &c. encircled with a wreath of oak leaves.

80 BLAND, S. K. 15 Lisson Grove North, Marylebone, Des. and Manu.—Enamel painted windows; Roman foliated ornament, adapted to modern decoration.

81 TOBEY, J. D. 10 Henrietta St. Manchester Sq. Des. and Prod.—Stained glass. The royal arms with national emblems, &c.

82 HOADLEY, G. 6 St. James's Pl. Hampstead.

83 ROYAL PATENT DECORATIVE GLASS WORKS, 21 Castle St. Southwark Bridge Rd.—A stained window of vitrified glass, representing the Adoration of the Wise Men of Bethlehem. Composed and executed by Poussein Cartisser. Two large windows of ornamental lace-pattern glass, and three large squares for blinds, &c. The nine windows of the Royal Commission room, in a new style of vitrified decorative glass. Composed and executed by Joseph Cartisser.

84 SWINBURNE, R. W. & Co. (North-west Gallery).

85 JAMES, W. H. 7 Ferdinand Ter. Pancras Vale, Inv. and Des.—Window-glass, ornamented by machinery. (Side of No. 18 exit door.)

86 LONG, C. King St. Portman Sq.—Specimens of engine turning on glass. (Side of No. 18 Exit Door.)

87 BANKART & SONS, Red-Jacket Copper Works, near Neath, South Wales, and 9 Clements Lane, London.—Stained glass window, containing several small pieces, united upon plate glass by Mr. F. F. Bankhart.

88 DANBY, J. 14 Halsey St. Chelsea—Imitation of lace-work on glass, produced without fire, the white parts ground glass.

100 HARTLEY, J. & Co. Sunderland, Manu.—Patent rough plate glass for ridge and furrow roofing. Models, &c. illustrating the manufacture of crown and sheet glass. Specimen windows of patent rolled coloured glass. Specimen of stained glass borders. Glass for horticultural, dairy, and railway purposes, &c. (Main Avenue East, South Corner.)

Proceed to Class 10, page 60.

Class 25.   CHINA, PORCELAIN, EARTHENWARE, ETC.

—— North Transept Gallery. ——

1 MINTON, H. & Co. Stoke-upon-Trent, Staffordshire, Manu.—Tiles, terra cotta, and vases, &c. in imitation of majolica ware. Encaustic and other tiles. Large vase, designed by Baron Marochetti, in terra cotta. Flower-pots, in terra cotta, with Parian bas-reliefs, after Thorwaldsen. Statuettes and busts, after John Bell, H. J. Townsend, Sir R. Westmacott, Thorwaldsen, Daneker, and Cellini. Ornamental vases, table ware, &c. in porcelain. Chemical utensils, in hard porcelain. Raw materials used in the manufacture and ornamenting of porcelain and earthenware. Fired specimens of colours. Earthenware, in the different stages of its manufacture.

2 COPELAND, W. T. Stoke-upon-Trent, Staffordshire, and 160 New Bond St. London, Manu.—Works in porcelain statuary, after J. H. Foley, R.A. W. Theed, W. C. Marshall, R.A. J. R. Hyatt, R.A. John Gibson, R.A. the Baron Marochetti, Cumberworth, J. P. M'Bride, John Steel, R.S.A. Mrs. Thorneycroft, &c. with a large collection of vases, tazzas, and plateaux; trays and table-ware, in porcelain; samples of common printed earthenware; and specimens of fine crystal glass, cut and engraved.

3 MASON, C. Longton, Staffordshire, Des. Manu. and Pat.—Patent ironstone china. Garden seats. Mandarin jars. Large jars and covers. White patent ironstone china, as used in hotels in the United States of America, &c.

4 KENNEDY, W. S. Burslem, Staffordshire, Manu.— Articles in china and earthenware: Mortise-lock furniture for doors of drawing-rooms, &c.

5 RIDGWAY, J. & Co. Cauldon Pl. Staffordshire Potteries, Newcastle-under-Lyme, Manu.—English porcelain table-service, tea and coffee service, improved fine earthenware, lawn fountains, and conservatory fountains. Specimens of staircase. Drab stone pottery. Hollow bricks. Model kiln (Ridgway's patent), for burning pottery, &c.

6 WEDGWOOD & SONS, Etruria, near Newcastle-under-Lyne, Manu.—Carrara porcelain statuary. Copy of Portland, or Barberini vase, &c. Blue jasper vase, with white bas-reliefs from the antique. Set of chess-men; thirty-four pieces, by Flaxman. Jasper: Cameos of various colours, with white bas-reliefs from the antique. Red terra-cotta vases, with black bas-reliefs from the antique. Voltaic stone-ware trough. Cream-coloured, or Queen's ware. Coloured earthenware. Garden-pots and stands, &c.

7 ALCOCK, S. & Co. Burslem, Staffordshire, Manu.— Specimens of china, porcelain, &c. designed by Alfred Crowquill, S. W. Arnold, and San Giovanni.

8 CLEMENTSON, J. Shelton, Staffordshire Potteries.— Two plates, enamelled under glaze. Flowered damascene classical antiquities. Soup and sauce-tureens. Tea services bowls, earthenware plates, &c.

9 MAYER, T. J. & J. Dale Hall Pottery, Longport, Burslem, Staffordshire, Manu.—Earthenware table-ware. Toilette and dessert ware. Garden and rustic seats. Finger-plates and door furniture, enamelled and gilt. White stone ware. Parian ware. Bust of Wesley, &c.

10 MEIGH & SONS, Hanley, Staffordshire, Manu.—Lotus candlesticks and jugs. Flower-pots and stand. Vases, &c. in porcelain. Statuettes, candlesticks, &c. in Parian and terra cotta.

11 BOOTE, T. & R. Burslem, Staffordshire.—Portland vase, fawn ground, white figures, about three feet high: process patented. Vases, groups of flowers, and statuettes, in Parian. Parian bust of Sir Robert Peel, after Sir T. Lawrence. Doric mosaic vases. Azure Grecian, and fawn jugs, inlaid with white, traced in gold; patent process.

12 *DIMMOCK, T. Shelton Potteries, Staffordshire,

Manu.—Table-plates, tureens, dishes and dish-covers. Garden-seats, richly japanned and gilt. Wine-cooler, terra cotta ware.

13 BOWERS, G. F. Brownhills, Tunstall, Staffordshire, Manu.—Specimens of ornamental earthenware cornices, wash-board, and centre pieces for rooms. Ornamental bricks. J. H. Baddeley's patent. Specimens of china ware.

14 KEYS & MOUNTFORD, The Potteries, Newcastle-under-Lyne, Stafford, Des. Inv. and Manu.—Porcelain statuettes: Boys, with perforated baskets for desserts, centre piece. Setter and pointer, with game. Bacchanalian ewer from the antique, &c.

15 PINDER, BOURNE, & HOPE, Burslem, Staffordshire Potteries, Manu.—Mazarine blue grounded and richly gilt soup tureen and stand. Cover-dish. Dish, plates, ewers, &c.

16 ANDERSON & BETTANY, Longton, Staffordshire Potteries.—Series of china cups and saucers, and dessert plates.

17 HILDITCH & HOPWOOD, Longton, Staffordshire Potteries, Des. and Inv.—Specimens of tea-table ware. Centre piece on pillar, with embossed vine border; grapes suspended from the handles, &c.

18 DEAKIN, E. Longton, Manu.—Silver lustre articles.

19 SERJEANT & PEPPER, Hanley, Staffordshire—Specimens of engraved patterns for printing on earthenware.

20 TILL & SON, Burslem, Staffordshire, Manu.—Specimens of earthenware, chamber ware, dinner and tea services. Stone and earthenware jugs.

21 CORK & EDGE, Queen St. Burslem, Staffordshire.— Tea services in black, lustre, drab and lilac earthenware.

22 PRATT, F. & R. & Co. Fenton Potteries, Staffordshire, Manu.—Specimens of terra-cotta and other ware, printed after pictures in the Vernon Gallery, &c. Dessert ware, with designs from Mulready, Landseer, Wilkie, Webster, Witherington, and Gainsborough. Bread platter, H. Warren.

23 DANIELL, A. B. & R. P. 18 Wigmore St., and 129 New Bond St.—Dessert services, executed at the Coalbrook Dale china manufactory.

24 EARNSHAW & GREAVES, Masborough Pottery, Rotherham, Yorkshire, Manu.—Painted biura, exhibiting specimens of Yates' patent porcelain letters.

25 GLOVER & COLCLOUGH, Longton.—Gold and silver lustre earthenware, useful jugs, &c.

26 BELL & Co. Glasgow, Manu.—Dinner and toilet and tea services and jugs, in stoneware and porcelain. Fancy articles in stoneware, porcelain, and Parian. Wine-coolers. Articles in Parian, and specimens in terra cotta.

27 WHALLEY, T. Stockton-on-Tees.—New compositions for glazing earthenware.

28 FELL, T. & Co. St. Peter's Pottery, Newcastle-upon-Tyne, Manu.—Specimens of common earthenware.

29 SOUTHORN, W. & Co. Broseley, near Iron Bridge, Shropshire, Manu.—Tobacco-pipes, the superiority of which consists in the preparation of the clay, giving the article a more porous quality.

29A MICHELL, J. Calenich, Truro.—Cornish crucibles.

30 JULEFF, J. & J. Redruth. Cornwall.—Specimens of crucibles for jewellers, and assaying silver, copper, and lead. Refiners' pots, skittle pots, muffles, &c.

31 KAY, T. Holbeck, near Leeds, Inv. and Manu.— Pots for horticultural purposes, with feeders. Suspending pots for orchids. Bordering for garden walks.

32 MILLS, J. Leeds, Manu.—Rockingham coffee and teapots. Shell, and blue shell teapots. Shell jugs, and smear-black teapots.

33 SIMPSON, J. 28 Theobald's Rd.—Table, tea, and

dessert services in earthenware. Plug basins and toilet ware. Parian statuettes.

34 WOOD, G. Brentford, Des. Inv. and Manu.—Gigantic ornamental orange-tree garden-pots, largest dimensions made in England.

35 BOURNE, J. Derby Pottery, near Derby, Manu.—Articles manufactured from fine stoneware clay. Garden labels, &c.

36 SHARPE, BROTHERS, & Co. Swadlincote, near Burton-on-Trent, Manu.—Specimens of Derbyshire ironstone caneware, Rockingham ware, and printed earthenware.

37 EDWARDS, J. & SONS, Dale Hall, Staffordshire.—Large Parian vase, and large earthenware tray.

38 FINCH, J. 6 Pickard St. City Rd. Pat. with F. T. Rufford, of Stourbridge.—Baths and wash-tubs. Porcelain wash and steam-tubs. Glazed bricks and slabs. Porcelain tile-bath, &c.

39 LOWE, T. 40 Ely Pl. Holborn, Prod.—Table plates, painted with subjects, portrait of Her Majesty, after Ross, Infant John, after Correggio. Jew's harp, after Wilkie. English rustic, after Howard.

40 ALLEN, J. M. 14 Catharine St. Strand, Prod.—Painted and gilt China dessert plates.

41 SHARPUS & CULLUM, 13 Cockspur-street, Charing Cross—Dessert services, &c. in china and earthenware. Decanters, wine glasses, &c.

43 BRAMELD, J. W. 7 Coburg Pl. Bayswater, Manu.—Ice pail of Rockingham china, with enamel painting of Bird-trap, and Charity. Vase, subject: Champion, after Webster. Grape basket. Cup and saucer, of the original Rockingham glaze, &c.

44 CHAMBERLAIN & Co. Worcester, Des. & Manu.—Tea service of egg-shell china. Communion and dejeûné services, &c., of pierced or honeycomb china. Portfolio China slabs. Vases, gilt, &c. China bracelets, brooches, &c.

45 BROWN, T. & M. L. 47 St. Martin's Lane. Manu.—Dinner and dessert plates, specimens of enamelling and gilding on stone china. Specimens of painting and gilding on porcelain. Various articles in glass.

46 GRAINGER, G. & Co. Worcester, Inv. Design. and Manu.—Chemical capsules. New ware, called "Semi, or

chemical porcelain." Small cabinet tea service and tray. Mediæval font, coloured, &c.

47 ROSE, J. & Co. Coalbrook Dale, Ironbridge, Shropshire, Manu.—Porcelain embossed dinner-services, dessert services, tea-services, tripod épergne, flower-vase, small coffee sets, clock-case, and flower-vase. Group of figures, &c. in Parian. Large porcelain egg-shell bowl, &c.

48 LEE, J. Pottery, Rotherham, Yorkshire, Manu.—Sign-board, with porcelain letters.

49 POTTS, W. W. Burslem, Staffordshire.—Specimens of patent cylindrical steam-printing on tissue paper for transferring to china, glass, papier-maché, &c.

50 GREEN, J. 35 Upper Thames St. Half-Prop.—Papworth's registered fountain, manufactured in china or earthenware, for large saloons and conservatories, supplied by the high-water services.

51 SHERWIN, H. Wolstanton, Newcastle-under-Lyme. Des. and Engraver.—Specimens of the ordinary style of engraving, as applied to the decoration of earthenware manufactures. Plates printed by Josiah Wedgwood & Sons,

52 LORKIN, J. 68 Basinghall St.—Patent egg beater.

53 BATTAM, T. Manu. 2 and 3 Johnson's Court, Fleet St.—Collection of vases with subjects from the antique.

54 LIPSCOMBE, J. & Co. 93 Regent St. Des.—Fountain, the basin of cut glass, the pedestal of Carrara marble, with a Cupid in biscuit china supporting a marble cup. Filtering machines, &c.

55 LOCKETT, G. Bleak Hill, Colbridge, Staffordshire.—Various specimens of ware exhibiting samples of hand, kiln, and enamel colours.

56 DUDSON, J. Hope St. Shelton, Staffordshire, Manu.—Ornamental china figures.

57 EMERY, F. Colbridge, Staffordshire, Manu.—Colours for painting on glass and china.

58 MARSH, J. Longport, Staffordshire, Mod. and Des.—Wine-cooler and bust in terra-cotta.

59 LEITCH & HAMMOND, 11 Mortimer Ter. Kentish Town, Manu.—Registered respirator smoking pipe.

60 HUGHES, T. jun. Colbridge, Staffordshire, Mod. and Des.—Bust of Rev. John Wesley, in parian.

61 LIPSCOMBE, F. 233 Strand.—Two portable fountains and two scent jars.

Proceed to Class 29, page 142.

Class 26. FURNITURE, UPHOLSTERY, PAPER HANGINGS, PAPIER MACHE, AND JAPANNED GOODS.

—— Areas I. J. 19 to 25, L. to O. 21 to 24. ——

1 THORN & Co. 98 New Bond St. Des. and Manu.—Gutta percha manu.—Decorations; girandole; various specimens and patterns of frames, brackets, mouldings, &c.

2 WALLACE, ELIZABETH, 4 Russell Pl. Fitzroy Sq. Inv.—Imitation marble on glass, for the walls of rooms, ceilings, &c. Picture and looking-glass frames, composed of a surface of glass over metal.

2A TOWNSHEND, J. E. High St. Camberwell, Inv. and Manu.—Bedsteads for invalids, &c.

3 MELVILLE, J. 64 John St. Fitzroy Sq.—A portable self-supporting pulpit, with handrails for stair, platform &c.

4 BURROUGHES & WATTS, 19 Soho Sq. Des. and Manu.—Billiard table and marking-board, of English oak, in the Elizabethan style.

5 JACKSON & SONS, 49 and 50 Rathbone Pl. Des. and Manu.—Works in carton-pierre, papier-maché, and composition, for decoration and furniture. Compartment of decoration, in carton-pierre, in high relief, for a large saloon, &c.

6 WHITE & PARLBY, 4 Rathbone Pl. Des. and Manu.—Model of a room, in composition ornament, as prepared

for the gilder, painter, upholsterer, &c. Ladies' work-table as prepared for the gilder and upholsterer.

7 ENGLAND, G. W. Leeds, Des. and Manu.—Library inkstand in rosewood. Library chair in oak, and dining-room chair in mahogany, the grain of the wood running in one uniform direction.

7A BURSILL, G. H. 9 York Ter. Queen's Rd. Hornsey Rd. Holloway.—Telescopic lounge, forming a neat substitute for the sofa bedstead; made by J. Rubery, 1 Goldsmith's Pl. Hackney Rd.

8 RIDGE, B. M.D. Putney, Invent.—Invalid bed-carriage, for spinal and other complaints.

9 TAYLOR & SONS, 167 Gt. Dover St. Southwark. Des. and Manu.—Cabin-furniture. Walnut-tree wood couch, as a life-preserver, stuffed with their patent cork fibre.

10 JOHNSTONE & JEANES, 67 New Bond St. Manu.—Sideboard of mahogany. Patent circular dining-table. Patent expanding plateau for dining table. Carved library chair, &c.

F

FURNITURE, UPHOLSTERY, PAPER HANGINGS,

11 SIEBE, A. 5 Denmark St. Soho.—Vase of flowers. The wood carved from the Royal George.

13 EARP, E. 15 Chester Ter. Chester Sq.—Ornamental rustic oak chair. Miniature chair and stool.

14 RIDDLE, T. 54 Wells St. Oxford St. Manu.—Invalid wash-stand, for persons confined to bed, forming a small table.

15 BROWN, J. M. & T. 165 Piccadilly—Patented suspensory chair, for forming a couch or camp bed.

16 DIXCEE, T. 14 Salisbury Pl. New Rd. Inv.—Self-swinging cot, or cradle for infants (or invalids). Model of a fire-escape.

17 THURSTON & Co. Catherine St. Strand, Des. and Manu.—Slate-top billiard-table, made of Spanish mahogany with patent cushions. The legs and frame carved in the respective styles of Elizabeth and Francis I.

18 BLOTT, ESTHER, Wellesbourne, near Stratford-on-Avon, Des.—Cushions, with mottoes. The design of which is "England's choicest flower." Horse-radish sauce. *La sauce stomachique*, for game, meat, and made dishes.

19 WYNNE & LUMSDEN, 30 East St. Manchester Sq. Manu.—Carved oak chimney-piece, designed by H. Clutton, architect. Richly carved oak altar chair, designed by E. Christian, architect.

20 CATTLE, J. Beverley, Des. and Manu.—Elizabethan wash-stand. New pattern wash-hand stand, of English oak, &c.

21 THE GUTTA PERCHA COMPANY, Pat. 18 Wharf Rd. City Rd.—Table and pier glass in gutta percha ornament, in the natural colour.

22 HUTCHINSON, E. High Wycombe, Buckinghamshire. —Oak antique arm chair, with carved ornaments, stuffed seat and arms, silk velvet. The carved work by E. Hutchinson, jun. self-taught.

23 LOVEGROVE, H. jun. Slough, near Windsor, Inv.—Portable expanding chair, of English ash, with cane seat and back. Portable sofa chairs.

24 FLEET, J. Tenterden, Kent, Inv. and Manu.—Bedpost, specimen of spiral turning with a common lathe and sliding apparatus.

25 GRUBB, F. C. Banbury, Manu.—Carved bread platters. Ladies' work-table, with needlework frame of English walnut, &c.

26 STARKEY, T. Farthingoe, near Banbury, Manu.—Table, convertible into a bedstead wardrobe, suite of drawers, sponge bath, &c.

27 EVEREST, J. Tunbridge, Kent, Manu.—Ottoman, convertible into a chair, with commode. Invented and patented by Everest and Osborne, Tunbridge, Kent.

28 ROSE, ELIZABETH, Oxford.—Screen embossed on both sides, convertible into a chess table.

29 SHACKLOCK, G. Bolsover, near Chesterfield, Derbyshire, Des. and Manu.—Carved royal heraldic chair, of native oak; the artist self-taught.

30 LYON, W. Marlborough, Wiltshire.—Agricultural machine to plough, sow, manure, and roll the land in immediate succession. Stove, which will bake, roast, boil, broil, fry, heat plates, &c. at the same time. Iron compressed bedstead. Compressed chairs and table.

31 GEARE, T. Sherborne, Dorset, Des. and Manu.—Model of an extending dining-table on an improved principle.

32 HORNE, R. 41 Gracechurch St. Manu.—Registered room decoration. Paper-hangings in imitation of wood.

33 FOSTER, G. East Retford, Nottinghamshire, Des. and Painter.—Panels, painted in encaustic and in imitation of inlaid wood, for doors of drawing-rooms and decorated apartments.

34 HUDSON, J. East Retford, Notts, Prop.—Rustic chair, designed and made by W. Marsh, of Retford, a labouring bricklayer, of knots of wood from the far-famed Sherwood Forest.

35 LAMBERT, S. East Retford, Nottinghamshire, Inv. and Manu.—Mahogany easy chair, with new and simple method of adjustment.

36 FISHER, J. W. Calvert St. Norwich, Manu.—Loo-table, in veneer, of English growth, viz. walnut-tree curls, and intersected with laburnum tree.

37 GUSHLOW, T. 34 Newman St. Oxford St. Manu.—Imitation china, for table-tops, tea-trays on iron slate papier-maché, &c.

38 FREEMAN, W. & C. London St. Norwich, Des. and Manu.—An ornamental cabinet, secretary, and bookcase, carved in walnut wood and ebony.

39 PUXLEY, W. Norwich, Des. and Manu.—Ornamental flower-table, slate top, carved maple, and knotted oak-wood border, with dial affixed showing the time on the top of the table.

40 FONNEREAU, KATE G. Ipswich, Inv. and Des.—Octagon box, in imitation of inlaid wood, applicable to piano-fortes, &c.

41 HANBURY, LOUISA EMILY, Ipswich, Des.—Slab, in imitation of marble, supported by carving in wood.

42 RINGHAM, H. Gar St. Ipswich, Manu.—Rood screen, carved in oak for a church in Surrey, designed by J. Clarke, 13 Stratford Pl. London. Group of wheat and poppies, carved in lime wood.

43 WHYTE, W. Banffshire.—Table and work table.

44 BATES, T. H. St. Albans, Herts, Des. and Manu.—Rustic loo-table, the top composed of upwards of 4,000 pieces of English wood—oak, maple, hazel, willow, and crab. The exhibitor a labourer.

45 ABBOTT, J. Horse and Groom, Crouch St. Colchester. —Inlaid pentagon table. Inlaid table, with carved pedestal, the sole work of the exhibitor, a blacksmith.

46 CHEEK, W. Saffron Walden, Essex, Des. and Maker. —Ebony cabinets, inlaid with ivory, for coins, medals, jewels, &c.

48 GARTHWAITE, W. Darlington.—Imitations of various woods, in painting.

49 RIDDETT, G. Ryde, Isle of Wight, Inv. and Manu. —Patent reading-table; music-stand, table, or screen, for an invalid.

50 EYLES, H. 31 Broad St. Bath, Des. and Manu.—An English pollard-oak table, with porcelain star, manufactured by Chamberlain and Co. of Worcester. English walnut-tree easy chair, and English walnut-tree drawing-room chair, with porcelain panels.

52 HEASMAN, W. 60 Middle St. Brighton, Inv.—Model of a circular roller-blind of improved construction.

53 PALMER, R. Brighton, Manu.—Specimens of mahogany and oak staining on deal.

54 NYE, E. Mount Ephraim, Tunbridge Wells, Manu. —Two round tables, book-stand, and work-box, ornamented with devices in wood mosaic.

55 Calder, J. 4 James St. Bath, Des. and Manu.—Circular dining-table, of walnut; the centre part revolves while the outside portion remains stationary.

56 HORSFALL, Mrs. Hawksworth Hall, Bradford.—Group of flowers painted on marble in gilt frame.

57 ENGLISH, E. F. Bath, Des. and Manu.—Pedestal cabinets, composed of ebony and Italian marbles, ornamented with Florentine mosaic. Suspending cabinet, and cabinet nest of drawers, of English oak and ebony, &c.

59 PALMER, H. 5 and 6 James St. Bath, Des. and Manu.—Registered loo-table and occasional table, in walnut wood. Sideboard, in English dark oak.

60 Wine cooler in walnut, with crimson velvet cushion.

61 KING, C. Tonbridge St. City Road.—Decoration window.

PAPIER MACHE, and JAPANNED GOODS.

62 CLARKE & Co. 29 West St. New Rd. End, Leeds, Inv.—Covering for the walls of apartments, having the appearance of superfine cloth.

62A HOLLAND, W. & SONS, Stained Glass Works, St. John's, Warwick.—Imitations of inlaid marbles and wood decorations, and table tops.

63 HALL, THEODOSIA, Baring Pl. Exeter, Des. and Exec.—Cheval screen, with a group of flowers in a new style of working in Berlin wool.

64 AZULAY, B. Rotherhithe.—Child's puzzle dissected in geometrical figures, and model pattern for Berlin needlework of many colours.

65 TANNER, W. 3 Harrington Pl. Bath.—Carved rigo and pollard oak cabinet, style Francis I. adapted for a drawing-room.

66 STOPHER, T. Saxmundham, Des. and Manu.—Reading, writing, and dressing desks.

67 HERBERT, W. Market St. Oxford, Des. and Manu.—Oak tables and cabinet, of Stanton oak, combined with glass and or-molu, &c., made and carved by three deaf and dumb persons; the castings by Marsh, of Dudley. Cabinet, of Oxfordshire walnut. Lounging-chair.

69 HOCKENDON, J. 15 King St. Oxford, Inv. and Manu.—University telescope reading-table.

70 SPIERS & SON, Oxford, Des. and Manu.—Decorated papier maché tables, screens, cabinets, portfolios, desks, albums, &c., ornamented with views of Oxford and its neighbourhood. University inkstands.

71 HEYWOOD, HIGGINBOTTOMS, SMITH & Co. Hyde Rd. Works, Manchester, and 62 Watling St. London, Des. and Manu.—Registered paper-hangings, produced by machinery in which 14 cylinders are employed.

72 WARNER, M. R. Stanton Harcourt, Witney, Des. and Manu.—Rustic table, inlaid with 1851 pieces of ivy.

73 WOODMAN, H. G. Melksham, Inv.—Carpet strainer.

74 POTTER, C. H. & E. Over Darwen, Blackburn, and 30 Budge Row, London, Des. and Manu.—Patent paperhangings, with registered designs, in colours produced by machinery and blocks.

75 JOHNSTON & Co. Quay St. Bristol, Des. and Manu.—Improved straw mattress, for lath and iron bedsteads.

76 SPURRIER, C. Bristol, Des. and Manu.—Cabinet chiffonnière of walnut wood. A vase of flowers, of pearl, inlaid in ebony. Easy chair, &c.

77 BURTON, Miss, Edinburgh.—Picture-frame ornaments, made of embossed leather.

78 JONES, A. J. 135 Stephen's Green, Dublin, Des. and Manu.—Series of Irish bog-yew decorative furniture, designed to illustrate history, antiquities, animal and vegetable productions, &c., of Ireland.

79 MECHI, J. J. 4 Leadenhall St. Manu.—Articles in papier-maché, tables, and bagatelle tables.

80 MEDCALF, F. 98 Bride St. Dublin, Des. and Manu.—Cabinet of oak, from Coolatin Park, county Wicklow, with top of Connemara marble, from the quarries of Ballinahinch, county Galway.

81 MOLLOY, T. Dublin.—Rustic chair.

82 CALVERT, —, Huddersfield.—Painted decoration.

83 AGGIO, G. H. Colchester.—White and gold Ottoman, embossed wool and silk, in glass case.

84 FLETCHER, E. Royston, near Barnsley, Des. and Manu.—Washable paper-hangings.

85 HOLD, A. Ardsley, near Barnsley, Des.—Pine frame.

87 ALLAN, D. Sloane St. Chelsea.—The registered melior. An appendage for chairs, to hold gloves, fans, bouquets, &c. while ladies are at dinner.

88 GAUNT & SON, Wortley, near Leeds, Inv. and Manu.—Decoration for library, dining and drawing-rooms. Durable and fixed colours.

89 LAW & SONS, Monkwell St.—Decorative paper.

90 COLLINSON, G. C. Doncaster, Yorkshire, Manu.—Hall or library chair, of black oak, found near Doncaster, Yorkshire, presumed to have been buried there 2,000 years.

91 INNES, ELIZABETH & SUSANNA, Castle St. Montrose, Scotland, Des.—Screen of white watered silk, with wreaths and basket of flowers, worked in feathers from the county of Forfar, &c. The frame was made by F. J. and F. Japp, Montrose.

92 DINHAM, ANNIE, Camelford, Prop.—Fancy worktable, veneered with tulip-leaves.

93 CAMERON, G. 11 Shepherd's Market, Mayfair.—Decoratious.

95 HASELDEN, —. Chelsea.—Designs for paper.

96 CRAWFORD, J. 242 Stobcross St. Glasgow, Des. and Manu.—Mirror, composed of plane-tree, made by an amateur.

97 NEWTON, W. 226 Argyle St. Glasgow, Prop. Des. and Manu.—Loo-table, composed of nearly 7,000 pieces of foreign woods. Chiffonnière, composed of above 4,000 pieces. Tea-caddy, composed of 1,340 pieces, &c.

98 IMRIE, P. Perth, Manu.—Circular loo-table, made of the root of a larch-tree raised near Murthly Castle, Perth.

99 ALEXANDER, J. T. Maxwelltown, Dumfries.—Ornamental garden chair of natural roots and branches of the oak. Picture-frame of natural roots and laburnum-tree branches, for a Scotch romantic scene.

100 HAY, J. & J. Aberdeen, Des. and Manu.—Gilded and emblematic national picture-frame.

101 SCRYMGEOUR, H. George St. Edinburgh, Des. and Manu.—British state bed, with canopy, Elizabethan style, carved in pine and plane tree. Blankets of the finest Cheviot wool; and sheets of finest Tweed linen.

102 WARRACK, HARRIET, Dee St. Aberdeen, Des.—Ornamental fire-screen.

103 KER, W. New Inn Yard, Tottenham Ct. Rd.—Table and table top, inlaid.

104 BARRIE, J. Edinburgh, Des. and Prod.—Carved book-tray, executed by a ploughman, in the evening, by candle-light, without the aid of any model or design, and solely with a penknife.

105 WOOD, J. Collingwood St. Blackfriars.—Table-top, &c. in marqueterie.

106 LITHGOW & PURDIE, 60 Hanover St. Edinburgh, Des.—Specimens of panels, and tables in imitation of inlaid marbles and of or-molu.

107 ROSS, D. 11 Norton Pl. Edinburgh.—Carved oak sideboard.

108 BONNAR & CARFRAE, Edinburgh.—Painted decorations.

109 CARSON, W. Stirling, Scotland, Des.—Wood painted in imitation of mahogany, maple, and oak.

110 FRENCH, G. J. Bolton, Des. and Manu.—Velvet cover for communion-table, with cushions, service-books, carpets, &c. Altar vestments of crimson velvet. Episcopal chair, after an ancient example in York Minster. Ecclesiastical banners, &c.

111 TILLING, E. Bradshawgate, Bolton, Manu.—Ornaments made of a new combination of materials, for interior decorations; exhibited for tenacity and facility in working.

112 BLAND, M. 2 Broad St. Halifax, Des. and Manu.—Sideboard, ornamented in representation of the vine.

113 KING, W. A. Whitehaven, Des. Inv. and Manu. Aldobrand Oldenbuck's cabinet, from Sir Walter Scott's "Antiquary," made of oak grown in Cumberland.

114 CARMICHAEL, J. William St. Workington, Cumberland, Des. and Prod.—Carved oak chair of novel design, made out of the root of oak, embroidered by G. Haines, Grosvenor Row, Chelsea.

115 MILLS, T. Bradford Yorkshire, Des. and Manu.—

F 2

Hall table and hat and umbrella-stand combined. Drawing-room chair, carved in solid mahogany, and gilded.

116 DREW, D. Truro, Cornwall.—Rustic table and two stools.

117 HARROLD, T. Hinckley, Leicestershire. — Table made of curiously gnarled oak, grown in Warwickshire.

118 WOOD, J. Milk St. Bristol.—Ornamental table.

120 MATHIESON, R. R. Stirling, Scotland, Des.—Plain deal lobby-table top, painted in imitation of various marbles.

121 GRUNDY, J. C. 4 Exchange St. Manchester, Des. and Manu.—Picture frames, specially designed for certain drawings and engravings. Circular table, in gold, the top of which displays 74 landscapes, painted in oil by J. B. Pyne.

122 DOVESTON, G. 106 King St. Manchester, Des. and Manu.—Ebony bookcase, carved in relief : the frames made by Cope and Collinson, of Birmingham. Boudoir chair of carved ebony. Bijouterie cabinet in tulip and king woods, with Sèvres china panels, &c.

123 MOUSLEY, C. E. Haunton Hall, Tamworth.—Mahogany table-top 14 ft. 3 in. by 5 ft. 3 in. wide, in one slab.

124 STEEVENS, J. Taunton, Des. and Manu.—Cabinet, made of walnut-wood, grown near Taunton, Somerset, carved with panels of raised embroidery, &c. by Miss Kingsbury.

125 BAMPTON, J. A. 49 Union Passage, Birmingham, Des. and Inv.—Specimens of material produced from moss or peat, to be called moss-wood. Specimens of a plastic material made from moss and lime. Specimens of pressed moss fibre.

127 CLARKE, J. Birmingham, Des. and Painter.—Designs of armorial bearings, including seventy-four coats of arms and crests.

128 LANE, T. 91 Gt. Hampton St. Birmingham.—Articles chiefly in royal patent pearl glass ; papier-maché table ; work-table ; cheval screen ; pole-screens ; reading-table ; cabinets ; chess-table, &c. Specimens of patent gem painting on glass, inv. by Miss E. Tonge, Boston, Lincolnshire.

129 DAVIES, G. C. 7 Brearly St. West Birmingham, Des. and Prod.—Papier-maché work-box, decorated in the Elizabethan style. Japanned papier-maché box. Glass tapestry panel, a decoration for rooms, furniture, &c.

130 GILBERT & Co. 114 Kingsland Road and Fleming St.—Invalid bedstead on an entirely new and simple principle. Quills and feathers, illustrative of Gilbert & Co's. chemical process.

131 HALBEARD & WELLINGS, 45 St. Paul's Sq. Birmingham, Manu. — Papier-maché toilet table of Elizebethan design. Large cabinets, &c. Series, illustrating the manufacture from the raw material to the finished article.

132 FOOTHORAPE, SHOWELL, & SHENTON, Birmingham, Manu.—Ladies' work-tables, drawing-room ornament-stand, small cabinet, writing-desks, jewel-boxes, folios, tea-caddy, ladies' reticule, hand-screens, trays, &c.

133 LEE, L. 118 Bedford St. South, Liverpool, Prod.—Fancy table, painted in enamel, on prepared wood.

134 THOMPSON & WORTHY, Durham.—Ladies' writing desk.

135 DAWES, B. 20 Carlisle St. Soho Sq. Manu. — Loo and chess tables of cedar, inlaid. Circular table with antediluvian top. Carved mahogany stand and cupboard. Lady's toilet-table and chair of tulip-wood, inlaid with purple wood, mounted in or-molu. Patent sun shades.

136 McCALLUM & HODSON, 147 Brearley St. Birmingham, Manu.—Papier-maché tables. Multiformia music-stand. Cabinet on stand. Ladies' portfolio and work-table. Bracket-glass, with branch lights. Tea-caddy, trays, &c.

137 SUTCLIFFE, I. 27 Gt. Hampton St. Birmingham Manu.—Ornamental papier-maché trays, loo-table, work-tables, vases, folios, caddies, work-boxes, inkstands, &c.

138 TURLEY, R. Birmingham, Manu.—Large folding

screen ; loo-table ; oval and gothic tables ; sexagon table ; cabinets ; trays ; chairs ; work-tables ; dressing cases, &c.

139 HOPKINS, R. P. Wimborne, Dorset.

140 BROWN, J. 71 Leadenhall St.—Ships' bedstead.

141 SMITH, G. F. March, Cambridgeshire, Des.—Specimens of painting, in imitation of various marbles. Painting, in imitation of oak, for interior or external decorations.

142 SCHOLEY, Misses, 36 Westbourne Ter.—Gilt chair and stool, embroidered in wool and silk.

143 DAVIS, G. Southampton, Des. and Manu.—Specimen of marbling, graining, and varnishing, on paper.

144 GORE, G. Speenhamland, Newbury, Des. and Painter.—Screen, painted in the old English illuminated style, and recording events of English history.

145 BELLEABY, W. York, Des.—Cabinet of oak, having ornamental panels of burnt white wood.

146 FINDLEY, C. V. 36 King St. Leicester, Des. and Manu.—Carved chair of Leicestershire oak.

147 BARKER, G. 2 Brook St. Bond St. Inv.—Perforated flexible screws, with nuts and hooks, for hanging pictures.

148 MEAKIN, J. F. Baker St. Portman Sq.—Registered chair.

149 COTTERELL BROTHERS, Bristol. — Paper-hanging, for a dining-room.

150 WELCH, T. Birmingham.—Ladies' cabinet and workbox in papier maché.

151 FLETCHER, R. Derby, Inv.—Crystal granite paper-hangings (washable).

152 RAMUZ, A. 17 Frith St. Soho. Prod.—Patent mechanical billiard table. Patent sofa, containing bedstead, &c. Models of bedstead, ottoman, &c.

153 RIVETT & SONS, 50 Crown St. Finsbury Sq. Des. and Manu.—Mahogany pedestal sideboard.

154 HOPKINS & SON, Birmingham, Manu.—Shade, with improved action.

155 MINTER & Co. Stoke-upon-Trent.—Two busts in marble.

157 BIELEFELD, C. F. 15 Wellington St. Inv. and Manu.— Articles, manufactured by patent machinery in a new material. Large dragon and eagle. Bust of Flaxman. Frame for glass, mouldings, architectural ornaments, &c. Corinthian capital in papier maché (Main Avenue, West).

159 GREIG & SON, 27 Farringdon St. Des. and Manu.— Winged wardrobe, of fine Spanish mahogany, with carved pediments, trusses, doors, &c.

160 WILLS & BARTLETT, Kingston-on-Thames.—Bookcase, of walnut-tree, combined with other woods in relief. Pair of candelabra, of three woods, in their natural colours.

161 HOLLAND & SONS, 19 Marylebone St. Ranelagh Works, Belgrave Sq., and 23 Mount St. Manu.—Bookcase, founded on the cinque-cento style, composed of British woods and marbles ; designs by Macquoid. Console table and glass. Water lily circular table.

162 TROLLOPE & SONS, 15 Parliament St. Westminster, Des. and Manu.—A sideboard in oak. A bed-room suite, consisting of bedstead, wardrobe, drapery table, toilette glass, and washing-stand, in satin wood, inlaid in marqueterie, worked with woods of their natural colours. A drawing-room chair, carved and gilt.

163 MOULIN, —Model of a pulpit.

164 MORANT, G. J. 91 New Bond St. Des. and Manu. —Specimen of rich decoration. Circular table, designed from a suggestion of the Duchess of Sutherland. Ornamental frame, made for Her Majesty. Cabinet of tulip-wood. Carpet, &c.

165 NUNN & SONS, 19 Great James St. Bedford Row.— Des.—Chess table, made of Italian walnut-wood, with bas-reliefs in electrotype silver. Chessmen, carved in ivory.

165A CUNNING, W. Edinburgh, Manu.—Improved drawing-room rocking-chair. Models of bedsteads, in brass and iron.

166 BANTING, W. & T. 27 St. James' St. Des. and Manu. —Circular marquetrie table. Sideboard made from oak grown in Windsor Forest. Satinwood china cabinet. Secretaire cabinet of kingwood, with English china inlaid. Oval table, Amboyna wood.

168 FOX, T. 93 Bishopsgate St. Within.—Bedstead of walnut tree, gilt, with lofty canopy and drapery of blue silk.

169 DURLEY & Co. 66 & 67 Oxford St. Manu.—Canopy bedstead of walnut-tree, in the Elizabethan style, with furniture of rich English brocatelle, &c.

170 SNELL & Co. 27 Albemarle St. Manu.—Chimney glass, the frame carved in walnut-tree. Walnut-tree cabinet. Sideboard. Satin-wood wardrobe. Oval-table, with marquetrie border. Library table. Carved fire-screen, &c.

171 WEBB, J. 8 Old Bond St.—Rock crystal vase and plateau, of the 16th century, with mountings of the present period, enamelled on gold by Morel. Chess table, &c.

172 BRAUN & Co. Old Fish St. Hill.—Pedestal glass ornament.

173 SANDEMAN, G. 9 Greenside St. Edinburgh, Des. and Manu.—The Holyrood seat. Design of an ottoman with rests, ornamented with thistle foliage, carved in dark oak.

174 SMEE & SON, 6 Finsbury Pavement, Des. and Manu. —Mahogany canopy bedstead, with hangings of crimson Spitalfields silk. Cabinets of walnut, king, and tulip wood, inlaid with marquetrie, &c.

175 WATSON, G. 42 Spring St. Paddington, Des. and Manu.—Octagon marquetrie table, with ebony moulding, elaborate design.

176 TOMASINI, D. 234 Tottenham Court Rd.—Chair, with rich figured satin.

177 WERTHEIMER, S. 35 Greek St. Soho.—Jewel caskets, work-boxes, candelabra, inkstands, and rich ornaments of various sorts, mounted in or-molu.

178 TOMS & LUSCOMBE.—A pair of pedestals in buhl and or-molu, and a pair of tulip-wood stands and cabinets, ornamented with china and or-molu.

179 CLARK, S. B. 14 Dean St. Soho, Des. and Manu.— Centre table of ebony, rosewood, and buhl. Work-table of English walnut. Petrifaction-table on figures of carton-pierre.

180 BRUNSWICK, M. 26 Newman St. Oxford St. Des. and Manu.—Shaped marquetrie chiffonnière, inlaid in walnut, king, tulip, and veneered inside with satin wood, &c.

181 LE MERCIER, SARAH S. A. Elm-tree House, Hammersmith, Inv.—Reg. chair, in honour of H.R.H. Prince of Wales; the tapestry work from a drawing by Mogford.

182 NICOLL, T. 39 Gt. Tichfield St. Des. and Manu.— Frames for water-colour drawings, &c. A cheval screen, convertible into a candelabra of five lights, a vase for flowers, music stand, and coffee table.

183 LECAND, S. 246 Tottenham Ct. Rd. Des. and Manu. —Console frame and table, carved in American pine and lime-tree, and double gilt in mat and burnished gold.

184 WILKINSON, W. & C. 14 Ludgate Hill, Des. and Manu.—Carved four-post bedstead, of walnut-wood. Improved spring mattress, &c. · Wardrobe veneered with fine walnut-wood on mahogany. Pedestal dressing-table, &c.

185 CARTER, MARY, 40 Mary St. Hampstead Rd. Des. and Prod.—Altar-piece, emblematical of evangelical faith, painted in the early English style.

186 GILLOW & Co. 176 Oxford St. and Lancaster, Des. and Manu.—Sideboard. Wine cooler. Albuera chiffonnière. Walnut tables. Library chair. Wanstead sofa. English yew cabinet secretaire. Marquetrie sofa table by G. Watson. Table, English porcelain, with painted landscapes, figures, &c. by W. T. Copeland. Mahogany picture frame. Gothic style, design by Pugin.

187 JENNENS & BETTRIDGE, 6 Halkin St. West, Belgrave Sq. and at Birmingham, Manu.—The Victoria Regia cot, designed by Bell. Pianoforte, the instrumental parts by Dimoline. Reg. Chairs, inkstands, tables, trays, and other works in papier maché. "Multum in uno." (Main Avenue, West.)

188 ELOURE, W. W. 12 Poland St. Oxford St. Manu.— Imitations of japan work. Fancy table, imitation of Persian work, &c.

189 CLAY & Co. 17 & 18 King St. Covent Garden.— Chiffoniere, in papier-maché, ornamented in mother-of-pearl, gold, and colours. Toilet-table and glass. Table fire-screens. Pot-pourri jars, &c.

190 DIXON, J. 18 Brownlow St. Holborn. Manu.—Papier-maché table, inlaid with pearl, &c. Paper trays, blotting-book, &c.

190A HOWELL, J. & Co. Regent St.—Large buhl and chased gilt inkstand for library table.

191 CHAPMAN, J. East St. Lambeth.—Pier glass, ornamental carved frame.

192 SOWERBY & CASTLE, 29 Albert St. Camden New Town, Inv.—Geometrical ottoman couch, constructed so as to assume various forms of drawing-room seating.

193 BOADELLA, J. 72 Charlotte St. Fitzroy Sq. Manu. —Marquetrie table; artists' colour box and easel, &c. Buhl cabinet.

194 WAKELING & SONS, 36 Gerrard St. Soho. Manu.— Carved Arabian bedstead, in white and gold, with silk hangings.

195 ROGERS, W. G. 10 Carlisle St. Soho.—Large pier glasses, with rich carvings.

196 PRATT, S. New Bond St. Manu.—Carved sideboard, of English walnut, the marquetrie and fretwork cut by machinery. Saloon commode of English buhl. Gothic altar-chair, &c., carved by machinery.

197 HANSON & SONS, 16 John St. Oxford St. Manu.— Ornamental walnut-wood cabinet, for china, bronzes, &c. Oval carved frame for a mirror, &c.

198 DONNE, G. J. 155 Leadenhall St. Manu.—Looking-glass; plate-glass, manu. at South Shields.

199 PONSONBY, T. Regent Circus, Piccadilly, Des. and Manu.—Large chimney-glass. Large antiqué girandole. Altar triptich Gothic Pierced and engraved picture-frames.

200 STOCKEN, C. 53 Regent St. Manu.—Ebony envelope-case, ornamented with imitation iron-work, in rich metal; gilt mountings. Dressing-cases, writing-desks, &c.

201 GOODISON, 14 Cullum St. Fenchurch St.—Various decorations.

202 HUNTER, W. J. R. & E. 30 Moorgate St. Manu.— Walnut-tree sideboards, showing the capabilities of English wood. The marble slab, from the quarry of Galway, Ireland. Two chairs, of studied structure and varied design.

203 LEVIEN, J. M. 10 Davies St. Grosvenor Sq. Des. and Manu.—Carved sideboard of New Zealand wood. Escritoire of satin-wood with tulip-wood. Jewel-case of tulip and king-wood.

204 POOLE & MACGILLIVRAY, 25 Prince's St. Cavendish Sq. Des. and Manu.—Sideboard in walnut-tree, with carved and bronze enrichments; bronze panels: Baucis and Philemon, and the Judgment of Midas.

205 HERRING & SONS, 109 Fleet St.—Cheval dressing-glass, carved in wood. Writing table, with marquetrie top. Centre table, of walnut-wood, inlaid with metals, ivory and pearl. Des. by Flaxman: "The opening of Pandora's box."

206 CALDECOTT, Messrs. 53 & 54 Gt. Russell St. Bloomsbury, Des. and Manu.—Sideboard of English oak, in the renaissance style. Octagon table, in Amboyna wood, inlaid.

207 RICHARDSON, C. J. 2 Keppel St. Russell Sq. Architect.—Carved oak frame and picture cornice. Table and stool, Learmouth, Ranelagh Rd. carver. Designs for Elizabethan furniture, wall papers, mounted horn. Chromolithographic prints.

208 BAILES, H. 29 Tottenham St. Des. and Manu.—Inlaid marquetrie door. Pair of therms inlaid with marquetrie, and mounted with or-molu. Fruit and flower pieces, &c.

209 HARDING & SON.—Walnut table, inlaid with marquetrie, of French manufacture.

210 WOOLLAMS & CO. 110 High St. Marylebone, Manu.—Decorative paper hangings in various styles. Alhambra. Pompeiian, arabesque pilasters, and raised gold mouldings. (East Gallery.)

211 MINTER, G. 51 Frith St. Soho. Inv. and Manu.—Invalid couch, or bed.

211A WHITCOMBE, A. Cheltenham, Des. and Manu.—Portrait frames and toilet-glass, in carved and gilt frame.

212 BELL, D. 10 Ann St. Belfast, Ireland, Manu.—Carved devotional-chair, of bog oak, ornamented with two crystals, termed " Irish diamonds;" the needlework on the panel designed by the exhibitor, and executed in Belfast.

213 ASPINWALL & SON, 70 Grosvenor St. Inv. and Manu.—Registered card-table, and dining-room chair.

214 CHAPLIN, T. Rose Tun St. Kilkenny, Ireland, Manu.—Ornamental circular oak table, with top veneered in figures, &c.

215 CURRAN & SONS, Lisburn, Co. Antrim, Ireland, Des. and Manu.—Sculptured and perforated arm-chair, from the antique; made by three poor working men, expressly for the Great Exhibition, of Irish black bog oak, found in Moyntagh's Moss; the crimson silk velvet manu. by E. Jones, 3 St. Andrew Street, Dublin. Oriental pencil designs, by the makers.

217 VERRINDER, J. Lincoln.—Sofa bedstead or couch.

218 BACON, W. 65 Wells St. Oxford St. Inv. and Manu.—Folding spring mattress.

219 BUDGE, —, Wells, Somerset, Bath.—Pollard oak chair, copy of the celebrated Abbot Whytney, of Glastonbury Abbey.

220 BRITTAN, W. Butleigh, near Glastonbury.—Carved chair and rustic flower basket.

222 HARRISON'S WOOD CARVING CO. Ranelagh Rd. Thames Bank, Pimlico.—Cabinet, in carved oak.

224 EVANS, F. 18 Albert St. Deptford, Inv.—Improved music stand. Model of improved chair.

225 CAWLEY, J. 1 Michael's Pl. Brompton, Des. and Manu.—A three-post bedstead in Spanish mahogany, the rod forms a part of the cornice.

228 NUNN, J. 7 Upper Vernon St. Lloyd Sq. Des.—Picture frame, to answer the purpose of a portfolio, &c.

229 PAGE, H. M. Coventry St. Manu.—Novel adaptation of a dressing glass and dressing case. Reg.

230 BILLAMORE, Mrs.—A newly invented chair.

231 GARDNER, J. H. 19½ Poppin's Court, Fleet St.—A satinwood toilet glass in carved frame, &c. containing secret jewel drawers. A mahogany table, combining in a small compass all the requisites for a gentleman's toilet.

232 WELLS, E. 310 Regent St. Prod.—Landscape transparent blind.

233 SANG, F. 58 Pall Mall.—Interior decorations.

234 HOPKINS, H. 13 Westmoreland St. Manu.—Table-top, painted in imitation of marble.

235 COOPER, W. M. Derby, Manu.—Pulpit for a church at Holbeck, Leeds; the figures by John Philip, from a design by G. G. Scott, of London.

236 WETHERELL, F. S. 13 Shepherd St. Oxford St. Des. and Manu.—Carved oak Gothic cheval fire-screen, with glass panel.

237 HAWKINS, S. 54 Bishopsgate St. Without, Pat. and Manu.—Expanding dining-table, with patent screw movement. Expanding round-table, with patent cog-wheel, and screw movement.

238 HOWARD & SON, 22 Berners St. Oxford St. Des. and Manu.—A cabinet of walnut-wood, the top of patent mosaic, and the whole ornamented with flowers drawn and modelled from specimens at Kew Gardens, by the designer, assisted by Mesdames Peachey and Strickland, wax and floral artists.

239 HANCOCK, N. 6 Bartlet Ct. Bow St. Inv.—Invalid and drawing-room easy reclining chair.

240 BOARD, C. 28 Swindon St. Gray's Inn Rd. Manu.—Spring pillows made of spiral steel springs and whalebone. Model of a quilt made of an article imported from Russia. White goose feathers.

241 ISAACS & CAMPBELL, 21 St. James' St. Inv and Manu.—Patent portable barrack, college, camp, and cabin furniture.

242 JACKSON, G. 4 Russell Mews, Fitzroy Sq. Manu.—Walnut-tree richly carved cabriole settee, representing three backs of chairs, covered.

246 KENDALL, C. H. 24 Mark Lane, Inv.—Decanting and corking machines, wine-fining wisp, and champagne capsule.

247 EDWARDS, S. 13 Cannon St. Rd. Manu.—Octagon revolving library table, containing 14,000 pieces of English and foreign woods.

251 LATHAM & DIGHTON, 1 Bateman's Buildings, Soho Sq. Des. and Manu.—Metal gilt vase and cover for flowers, ornamented with amethyst, garnets, turqnoise, &c.

252 MOXON, C. 33 High St. Marylebone.—Decorations for a drawing room, being imitations of inlaid marbles, panels, &c. Chimney-piece and glass frame, by J. Thomas.

253 MARCHANT, W.—Lady's work-table, consisting of a chess-table, with drawers, &c.

254 MARTIN, W. 6 Rutland St. Hampstead Rd. Inv.—Registered ornamental flower-pot cases.

255 GREVERIE, A. S. Farmington Cottage, Park Lane, Brompton, Manu.—Oval table; vases; basket, ornamented with flowers, &c.; made of mixed woods.

256 MILES, H. 16 Seabright Pl. Hackney Rd. Inv. and Manu.—Rosewood loo-table, inlaid on top and bottom block, containing a secret cash-box.

257 NORTH, D. 23 Gt. Windmill St. Haymarket. Des. and Manu.—Rose-wood oval tea caddy, with flowers carved in satin-wood. Two satin-wood sugar-basins. Oval vase ebony inkstand.

258 NUTCHEY, J. 5 West St. Soho, Des. and Manu.—Pair of candelabra, in ebony and ivory. Flower-stand in English yew-tree.

259 NORTH, C. 1 Queen's Head Ct. Gt. Windmill St. Haymarket, Des. and Manu.—Reading-stand. Bed-chair for invalids.

260 PINNELL, T. D. 5 Warren St. Camden Town, Des. and Manu.—Gilt zinc frame, with trellis-work border, and silk velvet lining.

261 JACKSON & GRAHAM, 37 and 38 Oxford St. Manu.—Sideboards, book-cases, chairs, sofa, cheval-screens, &c.; London carpet, carpet of moresque design, velvet-pile carpets, patent tapestry velvet carpet and border, London rugs, &c.

262 REYNOLDS, J. 57 New Compton St. Soho. Manu.—Wire table for flowers.

263 ROBINSON, C. 6 and 7 Greenland Pl. Gray's Inn Rd. Inv. and Manu.—Portable metal bedstead, which will form also half tester bedstead, chair-couch, and ottoman, &c.

264 ROGERS & DEAR, 23 and 4 St. George's Pl. Hyde Park Corner—Renaissance bedstead in walnut-tree, carved. Ottoman coal sarcophagus. Des. by F. Whishaw, Esq. Mahogany bedstead with washing apparatus.

265 ARCHER, E. T. 451 Oxford St.—Paper decorations.

266 HINDLEY & CO. 134 Oxford St.—Sideboard with pier glass chiffonnière, Devonport. Three chairs, portfolio stand, &c.

267 SIMPSON, G. 12 Eldon St. Finsbury. Des. and Manu. —Improved ornamental library table, reg. pattern.

270 SIMPSON, W. B. 456 West Strand.—Decoration papers, washable.

271 SCROXTON, J. H., 137 Bishopsgate St.—Show goods, used by tea dealers and grocers, for decorating shops. Vases in tin, ornamented and japanned, &c.

273 SQUIRE, C. 20 Old Fish St. Inv.—Apparatus for baking wood, for veneering, &c. Looking-glass, with ball and socket movement. Composition and wood picture frames, &c.

276 THOMAS, J. 9 Old Church St. Paddington, and New Palace, Westminster. Des. and Sculp.—Chimney-piece, imitation of inlaid marbles and decorations by Moxon. Des. for Preston Hall, modelled by T. Dighton. Model of fountain. Marble chimney piece and ornaments.

279 WARD (late GRIFFIN & WARD) 5 and 6 Leicester Sq.—Improved recumbent chair for invalids; a self-propelling chair, made portable for travelling, vulcanized India-rubber wheels.

287 JONES, W. Dolgelly, Wales, Inv. and Manu.— Portfolio table, and ebony tripod.

288 WARREN, T. 371 Oxford St. Inv.—Patent reading-stand, carved in rosewood, and enriched with gold and ormolu ornaments.

289 CREASER, Mrs. 18 Melton St. Euston Square— Ladies' writing table, with drawers, on an entirely new principle.

291 COOPER, G. Kingston, Surrey.—Rustic chair.

292 MUMMERY, F. H. 5 Railway Place, Holloway Road. —Pianoforte-case bedstead.

293 WILSON & Sons, 18A Wigmore St. Cavendish Sq. Inv. and Manu.—New oval centre table with a revolving top, table, with a circular bagatelle-board. New work-table. Chess table, library table, &c.

300 SCOTT, CUTHBERTSON, & Co.—Paper decorations.

301 D'ALMAINE, W. F. 8 Percy St. Bedford Sq. Des. and Manu.—Decorative panel, style of Edward I.

303 ARTHUR, T. 3 Sackville St. Prod.—Screen, painted by hand, in oil colours. Registered damask paper-hangings. Specimens of graining. Imitation marbles, &c.

304 ASCROFT, T. 35 Queen's Rd. Chelsea, Des. and Prop. —Original design for paper-hangings, being a new combination of damask and chintz work.

305 BARRETT, J. 246 Bethnal Green Rd. Des.—Drawings for paper hangings.

307 COOMBER, J. 66 Brand St. Blandford Sq.—Painted table-top, in imitation of inlaid woods. Slab, in imitation of inlaid marbles.

308 GODDARD, J. 21 Walcot Pl. East, Lambeth.—Design for paper hangings, of British and exotic flowers, air plants of the torrid zone, &c.

309 WOOLLAMS, W. & Co. 110 High St. Marylebone, Manu. — Decorative paper-hangings. Paper-hanging, designed at the Government School of Design.

310 HINCHLIFF & Co. 123 Wardour St. Oxford St. Manu. —Registered paper-hangings. Panel decorations, and an arabesque panel decoration, des. by Mr. J. Crane.

312 PRICE, J. Gateshead.—Table, with jaspar glass top.

312A TRAPNELL & SON, 2 St. James Barton, Bristol.— Console chiffonnière in walnut, with pier glass, &c.

313 NEWBERY, J. & R. 2 and 3 Hemlock Ct. Carey St. Lincoln's Inn Fields, Manu.—Gold, silver, and coloured tissues. Vulcanized, washable, enamel coloured papers.

314 NORWOOD, C. De Beauvoir Factory, Rosemary Branch Bridge, Hoxton, Manu.—An architectural decoration, composed of printed mouldings, figures, &c.

315 PURKISS & SON, 29 Old Change, Des. and Manu.— Imitations of marbles in water-colours on paper, and imita-

tion of Sienna, porphyry, Devonshire dove, and Brocatella marble, for skirting.

316 SOPWITH, T. & J. 15 Northumberland St. Newcastle-upon-Tyne, Inv. and Manu.—Monocleid writing cabinet, for collecting and arranging a great number and variety of papers, so as to be readily accessible.

317 TURNELL, I. 32 Pinstone St. Sheffield.—Ladies' work-table, a specimen of English elm.

318 TOWNSEND, PARKER & TOWNSEND, 132 Goswell St. Des. and Manu.—Paper-hanging decorations.

320 TURNER & Co. Elizabeth St. Pimlico, Manu.—Paper-hangings, including damasks, panels, and chintzes, from designs by Javet and Marchand, Paris; W. Draper and H. Turner, jun. (In South-east Gallery.)

321 WILLIAMS, COOPERS, BOYLE, & Co. 85 West Smithfield, Manu.—Drawing-room decorations. Damasks for dining-rooms. New mode of combining metal and flock, &c.

322 WOOLLAMS, J. & Co. 69 Marylebone Lane, Oxford St. Manu.—Paper hangings and decorations from block printing:—Panel decoration from drawings by Miss Palmer. Paper hangings printed by machinery. (East end of Nave, and East Gallery.)

326 JEFFREY, ALLEN, & Co. Kent and Essex Yd. White-chapel, Manu.—Paper printed by blocks in distemper. Specimens of a many-coloured chintz wall-paper, and of cylinder-printed wall-papers.

329 DAVIS, C. 26 Blackfriars Rd. Des. and Painter.— Design for the decoration of a ceiling, in imitation of inlaid woods.

336 JONES & Co. 214 Piccadilly, Inv. and Manu.—New method of decoration for the side of a room. Coloured decorations for ceilings, and other specimens.

337 M'LACHLAN, J. 35 St. James' St. Piccadilly, Prop. —Arabesque painting on glass, imitations of inlaid marbles on glass. Arabesque painting for the decoration of rooms, &c

340 SEWELL, C. & F. 13 Charles St. Westbourne Ter. Des. and Manu.—Elizabethan ornamental screen, in imitation of various marbles and woods.

341 SMITH, C. 43 Upper Baker St.—Imitations of marbles, in paint, on slate and wood. Arabesque decoration for drawing-rooms, boudoirs, &c.

342 SOUTHALL & Co. 157 Kingsland Rd. Manu.—Half top of table in imitation marble, inlaid. Slab, in imitation rouge royal marble. Imitation marble and woods, on paper, &c.

343 STRUGNELL, H. 25 Kirby St. Hatton Garden. Des. and Manu.—Lady's writing-desk, in ebony and buhl-inlaid.

344 HAYBALL, A. Government School of Design, Sheffield.—Cabinet carved in walnut.

345 HOYLES, H. Government School of Design, Sheffield.—Sideboard carved in walnut.

346 STEEDMAN, C. Charles St. Hampstead Rd.—Slate tablets, japanned and ornamented, adapted for churches and other buildings. (In Class 1.)

347 PICKERING, J. 39 Little Moorfields, Prod.—Specimen of drawing-room panel decoration, in colours and gold.

361 BURKE, J. H. 75 Castle St. East, Oxford St. Des. and Manu.—Fancy mounts and spandrils for drawings, prints, &c., in cardboard and gold paper.

364 FOLLIT, G. 67 Gt. Titchfield St. Marylebone, Manu. —Specimen of an imitation or-molu gilt mat flat, made of paper, and not liable to split.

365 NEWNHAM, B. 22 Princes St. Leicester Sq. Inv. and Manu.—Miniature frames in imitation of or-molu.

369 FURSE, C. & S. 4 Hanway St. Oxford St. Manu.— Washable gilding, applicable to looking-glasses, picture frames, cornices.

Class 26.
FURNITURE, UPHOLSTERY, PAPER HANGINGS, &c.

379 HERRING, C. 177 High Holborn.—Oriental silk down, from the Bombax tree of India.

380 BAXTER, R. 12 George St. Foley Pl. Des. and Manu. —Illustration of the art of gilding, as applied to picture and glass frames, cornices, &c.

382 VIGERS, E. jun. Union Mills, Upper Lisson St. Paddington, Manu.—Mouldings, architraves, skirtings, and sash-bars, prepared by machinery.

384 JORDANS, —, Belvedere Rd. Lambeth.—Circular table of walnut tree, and two Devonports and three chairs, all richly carved.

385 ARROWSMITH, H. & A. 80 New Bond St. Des. and Manu.—A decorated cabinet in zebra wood and gold, richly carved. Patent lace curtains, and patent damask curtains, &c. New dry process of cleaning carpets, &c.

386 M'LEAN, Fleet St.—Large looking glass and console table, ornamented and gilt. (Main Avenue, West.)

389 AVERY & DANGAR, 11 Great Portland St. Manu.— Shutter-blind for the Ambassador's new palace at Constantinople. Improved Venetian and bonnet blinds, &c.

390 BURT H. 238 Blackfriars Rd. Inv.—Improved patent window-blinds, entirely of metal, applicable for out-door use, and especially for warm climates.

391 AUSTIN, J. 8 Princess St. Finsbury—Patent sash and clock, blind, lamp, and picture lines, manufactured from flax, silk cotton, and worsted.

392 WELLS & Co. Bedfordshire.—Table-tops made of English oak. (South Wall.)

395 HARRIS, H. G. 528 New Oxford St. Manu.—Patent perforated transparent roller blind, made of the common prepared muslin.

396 KOBELT & SONS, 22 Newcastle St. Strand, and 17 Cross St. Blackfriar's Rd. Inv. and Manu.—Improved ornamental spring-roller blind.

397 LUCAS, P. jun. 19 Hyde Park Gardens, Inv.—Rotatory shop-blind.

399 THAMES PLATE GLASS Co. — Large specimens of plate glass. (Centre Avenue.)

400 NOEL, H. W. 37 High St. Camden Town, Des. and Manu.—Painted transparent window blinds, in imitation of stained glass; Chinese bird blinds, &c.

401 GRIGG, J. Banwell, Somersetshire, Manu.—Ornamental rustic chair, with picture of the Exhibition building inlaid. Mechanical pictures, all inlaid.

402 LEE, G. L. 245 High Holborn.—Imitation stained glass and marbling on surfaces by the water bath.

403 PRATT, H. 123 New Bond St.—Ladies and gentlemen's travelling wardrobes in scarlet morocco, lined with satin. Portable brass bedsteads and chairs.

404 DOWBIGGIN & Co. 23 Mount St. Grosvenor Sq.— A commode of various woods, the panels ornamented with marqueterie and carvings, and painted china in the centre; the whole finished with richly gilt mouldings, &c. A walnut carved bedstead and cornice with temporary hangings.

406 MARTIN, J. 45 Southampton Row, Russell Sq.— Walnut-tree chair, with the portrait of Dennis Affré, the late Archbishop of Paris, killed during the insurrection.

407 HOLLAND, W. St. John's, Warwick.—Specimens of ornamental painting and decorating in various styles, adapted for dining and drawing rooms. libraries, &c. Imitation inlaid woods and marble. Newly-invented flocking machine for decorating walls, &c.

408 BRITISH PLATE GLASS Co.—Two looking-glasses, each upwards of 12 feet high. (Main Avenue, West.)

526 COWELL & THOMAS, 103 High St. Marylebone. Des. and Manu.—Specimen of solid inlaying, by hand, for floors.

527 MARSDEN, C.—Specimens of marble and other paper hangings for halls, staircases, &c.

528 ENGLAND, G. W. Leeds, Des. and Manu.—Mahogany dining-room chair, showing novel mode of construction. Oak library chair of similar construction. Library inkstand in rosewood.

Proceed to Classes 12 and 15, page 74.

Mediæval Court.
—— South Areas N., O., 28, 29. ——

529 PUGIN, Messrs.—Various articles for the ornament and decoration of churches, &c.

530 CRACE, J. G. 14 Wigmore St. — Furniture and decorations in the mediæval style, piano, &c. Tapestry, damasks. Silk brocatelles. Woollen stuffs for hangings. Chintzes and carpets.

531 MINTON, H. & Co. Stoke-upon-Trent, Staffordshire. —Ornamental tiles, porcelain, and painted ware.

532 HARDMAN, J. & Co. Gt. Charles St. Birmingham, Manu.—Silver metal gilt, parcel gilt, and brass vessels used in churches; enamelled, set with stones, plated, pierced, and engraved. Casket of jewellery, girdles, brooches, crosses, earrings, &c. Painted glass windows. Embroidered robes, hoods, capes, girdles, &c., des. by A. W. Pugin.

533 MYERS.—Stone and wood carving.

534 BIELEFIELD, CAROLINE, 6 Canonbury Pl. Islington, Des.—Screen, St. George and the Dragon, with national arms and emblems, the Royal arms, &c.

535 DU CANE, A. Witham, Des.—Casket to contain a lock of hair.

536 TUCKER, F. & Co. Kensington, Manu. An assortment of candles.

Proceed to Class 26, page 129.

Decorative Ceilings.—*South of Nave.*
Bay M. 21 Messrs. TROLLOPE & SON.
  M. 22 Messrs. JACKSON & SONS.
  M. 23 Messrs. JACKSON & GRAHAM.
  M. 24 Messrs. CALLI & COTTI.

Under South Gallery.
P. 15 Messrs. JONES & Co. (late Robson & Jones.)
P. 1 Messrs. LITHGOW & PURDIE.

North of Nave.
I. 19 Messrs. JACKSON & SONS.
I. 20 Mr. A. HERVIEU, 10 Portugal St. Grosvenor Square.
I. 21 Mr. CROUGHTON, 100 Upper St. Islington.
I. 22 Mr. THOMAS, St. John's Wood.
I. 23 } SCHOOL OF DESIGN.
I. 24 }
I. 25 Mr. C. F. BIELEFIELD.

Proceed to Class 17, page 91.

[The wall decorations, imitation marbles and woods, blinds, &c., are placed against the principal walls and partitions of the building at the south side, east and west ends, north-east corner, and in the locomotive avenue.]

Class 27. MANUFACTURES IN MINERAL SUBSTANCES, FOR BUILDING OR DECORATIONS.
—— Areas G. H. 14 to 17, I. J. 16, 17. ——

1 KERSHAW, T. 35 John St. Fitzroy Sq. Painter.— Imitation of foreign and English marbles and woods, for house decorations; made of wood and slate.

3 BRENDON, W. S. Yeolm Bridge, near Launceston, Prop. Chimney-piece, pavement and skirting, for an entrance hall, designed by W. Damant, architect, of Plymouth, and executed by James Bovey, in Yeolm Bridge slate and polyphant freestone.

4 BOVEY, J. Plymouth, Devon, Manu.—A chimney-piece, designed by O. C. Arthur, architect; and a font, in the perpendicular style, designed by W. Damant, architect; executed in marbles, &c. found in the neighbourhood.

5 FREWER, J. Woolbridge Rd. Ipswich, Des. and Manu.—A Caen stone carved chimney-piece.

6 CHAMPERNOWNE, H. Dartington House, Totnes, Prop.—Table, manufactured of Devonshire limestone.

7 MAYO & Co. 17 Silver St. Wood St. Cheapside, Inv. — Patent syphon vases for containing aërated mineral waters.

8 WILLOCK, E. P. 10 Exchange Arcade, Manchester. —Specimen of Ladyshore terra cotta.

9 HUMBLE, W. 35 University St. London.—An octagon inlaid marble table.

10 KEENE, R. W.—Ionic capital, Parian.

11 WILSON, J. Stratford, Essex.—Chess-table, painted in imitation of marble.

12 HARTLEY, T. H. Westminster Marble Works, Earl St. Millbank, Prop.—Gothic stone mural monument.

13 EKINS, G. Ware, Herts, Manu.—Slate coffin, with copper screws, perfectly air-tight.

14 WILSON, S. Grimley, Notts.—Slab painted in imitation of marble.

17 THE LONDON MARBLE & STONE WORKING Co. Esher St. near Milbank, Westminster, Imp. Des. and Manu. —Grecian column chimney piece, and hexagon and octagon Gothic fonts, of white Carrara marble. Model of a bracketted staircase, worked and polished by the Company's machinery; inv. and pat. by James Tullock, F.R.S.

18 MIRROR MARBLE Co. 17 Castle St. Southwark Bridge Rd. Licenses under Pat.—New patent mantelpiece, made entirely of iron and glass.

19 COATES, E. J. 13 Bread St. Watling St. Prop.— Chimney-pieces, made exclusively of iron and glass. Pat.

20 VAUGHAN, J. Bath, Prop — Vase and pedestal, showing the quality of Bath stone.

21 BLACKBURN, B. Island of Valentia, Kerry, Ireland, Manu.—Specimens of slate slabs, from the island of Valentia. Sash bars. Roof ridge made and designed by B. Woodward. Park or garden seat. Table of slate.

22 BETTS, E. L. Aylesford, near Maidstone, Prop.— Products and manufactures from the Preston Hall estate. Cement. Terra cotta vase, designed by J. Thomas. Terra cotta bricks; registered. Stone-ware and agricultural pipes. Hollow bricks, Roberts' and Beart's patent.

23 DOULTON & Co. Lambeth, Manu.—Glazed stone ware drain and water-pipes. Terra cotta vases, garden pots, and architectural ornaments.

24 STEVENS & SONS, 186 Drury Lane, Manu.—Martin's cement, for internal walls, plain and coloured decorations, &c. Designed by J. T. Knowles (On South Wall, S. 21.)

25 MOORE, A. 19 Arthur St. Belfast, Ireland, Manu.— Table, painted in imitation of marble, inlaid or mosaic work.

26 PAGE, H. C. 28 Commercial Rd. South, Pimlico.— Marble prepared to resist the ill effects of grease and dirt.

27 KEENE, R. W. 124 Vauxhall Walk, Lambeth.— Samples of Parian for architecture. Ionic capital, des. by C. Barry, Esq.

28 ILES, C. & C. Bradford St. Birmingham.—Pedestals and slabs of a new material imitating marble.

29 Small scagliola table, with minerals.

30 VOKINS, C. Pimlico Wharf, Wilton Rd.—Chessboard and men, made from coal and gypsum.

32 READ, W. 28 Dorset St. Portman Sq. Des. and Executor.—Imitations of various kinds of marbles in paint, on slabs.

33 STEWART, W. Rhodeswell Rd. Limehouse, Prop.— Slab of Agra marble, inlaid with agate, cornelian, and other stones. From the palace of Akbar Khan, Cabool.

34 PLOWS, W. Foss Bridge, York, Des. and Sculp.— Small figure of David, carved in stone.

35 BRADLEY, J. Fore St. Exeter, Des.—Table painted on slate, in imitation of Devonshire marbles.

36 ORSI & ARMANI, 6 Guildhall Chambers, Basinghall St. Pat. and Manu.—Patent metallic lava pavement, ornamental slabs, and table in the Moorish style. Patent modern Venetian stucco. Stone, with marble-like polish.

37 & 38 HALL, J. & T. Marble Works, Derby, Manu. TENNANT, J. Strand.—Specimens of articles, manufactured by aid of steam machinery, at the Derby Marble and Spar Works : of black marble ; Derbyshire mottled alabaster, Derbyshire rosewood marble ; stalactite (Oriental alabaster) ; and variegated alabaster (gypsum) ; fluor spar.

39 WOODLEY, J. Torquay, Des. and Manu.—Circular marble table, small table and slab, inlaid with specimens of marbles and madrepores, found in Devon.

40 VALLANCE, J. Matlock, Bath, Derbyshire, Des. and Manu.—Tables, vases, and other articles composed of or inlaid with fluor-spar, and marbles from Castleton, Ashford, &c., Derbyshire.

41 OLIVER, 52 Upper John St. Fitzroy Sq. Des.— Imitations of Sienna, Mona, and rouge royale marble.

42 HALL, W. 5 Prospect Row, Walworth, Des. and Prod.—Writing on enamelled slate in imitation of glass.

43 WRIGHT, J. Aberdeen, Manu.—Polished granite ornamental head-stone.

44 BUCKLEY, G. Bayswater, Prod.—Column and two slabs, painted in imitation of Sienna marble.

45 DOLAN, D. 27 Blackfriars St. Salford, Manu.— Scagliola gothic columns, illustrating a new method of working, &c. in scagliola.

46 MAGNUS, G. E. Pimlico, Inv.—Manufactures in slate : Enamelled slate ; representing various marbles inlaid after Florentine mosaic, &c.

47 FRANCIS & SONS, Nine Elms, Manu.—Specimens of Parian cement of various qualities. Medina cement. Cement for railway-cutting drainage.

48 THORNHILL, J. 7 Windmill Pl. High St. Camberwell.—Two tables, the tops in imitation of marble.

49 LIPSCOMBE, J. & Co. 93 Regent St.—Two drawing fountains in glass and marble.

50 PLOWS, W. Foss Bridge, York, Des. and Sculp.— Table, inlaid with petrified woods (found in Yorkshire) on a pedestal of Yorkshire marble. Black marble table, with masonic symbols, found in the crypt of York Minster.

51 DUPPA, —.—A painting on tiles.

F 3

Class 27.

MANUFACTURES in MINERAL SUBSTANCES for BUILDING, &c.

52 BROWN, R. 58 Gt. Russell St. Bloomsbury, Des. and Sculp.—Sepulchral monument of the decorative period, in Caen stone.

53 LANE & LEWIS, Clifton, near Bristol, Des. and Executors.—Statue of St. Peter in canopied niche of Caen stone.

54 BAKER, R. C. 33 Above Bar, Southampton, Des.—Original symbolical model of a cemetery memorial.

55 STUART, W. Mem. Inst. C.E. Superindent of H. M. breakwater, Plymouth.—Polished marble slab on two pedestals, composed of limestone from the breakwater quarries, Plymouth.

56 MOON, G. Godalming, Surrey, Des.—Octagon table, made of several kinds of marble.

57 BELD, J. 25 Buckingham Pl. Fitzroy Sq. Des. and Manu.—A pair of obelisks in polished oolite.

58 HOBAN, M. 41 Bolton St. Dublin, Manu.—Conglomerate marble table top. Table top of red and white Irish marble, from Churchtown, county Cork.

59 RUMLEY, —, Essex St. King's Cross.—Two small table ornaments, cut in marble.

60 NEWMAN, W. H. Bathford, near Bath, Prod.—Bust in Bath freestone: The poet Milton.

61 WHISHAW, —.—A chess table of novel construction.

63 ROWLANDS, I. Llandegai, near Bangor, Wales, Manu.—Giant ink-stand, sculptured from a block of slate stones, from Penrhyn quarry, near Bangor.

64 CUMMING, Rev. J. G. Isle of Man.—Obelisk constructed in Isle of Man marble.

65 PEARSON, W. P. Harrogate, Yorkshire, Prod. and Des.—Octagon table of stalactites, principally from the Dropping Well, Knaresborough, and its neighbourhood.

66 PORTER, W. H. 3 Pembroke Road, Dublin, Prop. (in trust).—Specimens of ware, manufactured by Murray & Cowper, of Glasgow, from Irish clays. Ornamental specimens of Irish marble, from Clifden, county Galway, worked by A. M'Donald, a self-taught artist.

67 GRIFFITHS & STRONG, Eastrow, near Whitby, Manu. —Cement stone. Model of an agricultural cottage. Cement tiles for facing houses.

68 ALLEN, C. B. London.—Model of a labourer's cottage, and encaustic and improved drain tiles.

69 NICOL & ALLEN, 57 Upper Marylebone St. Des. and Painters.—Imitations of marbles; designs for table-tops, imitation of inlaid marbles.

70 LAMBERT, A. C. Cong Abbey, Ireland, Prop.—Dark green Connemara marble tables, serpentine tables from Ballynahinch quarry, Galway; on pedestals of black Galway marble.

71 ROYAL DUBLIN SOCIETY.—Bust pedestals of white statuary and green Connemara marble, from quarries in Donegal.

72 MONTEAGLE, Lord, Mount Trenchard, Co. Limerick, Ireland, Prop.—Specimen of statuary marble, from Dunluvey Quarries, Donegal. Statue of the late Henry Grattan, M.P.

73 FRANKLIN, P. L. Galway, Ireland, Prop.—Bust pedestal of black marble from Lough Corrib near Galway.

74 M'DONALD & LESLIE, Aberdeen, Manu.—Granite vases, pedestals, and a slab for table top.

75 PEARCE, W. Truro, Manu.—Tables, candelabra, vases, pedestals, tazzas, &c., of Cornish granites, porphyry, steatites, and serpentines.

76 OLDFIELD & Co. Ashford, Manu.—Column of black marble, from the Arrock Hill quarry, Ashford. Column of laminated rosewood marble, from Nettle-Dale, near Ashford. Column of russet grey marble, from High-Low, near Sheldon. Column of light entrochal marble, from Ricklow-Dale, near Monyash.

77 WOODRUFFE, T. Bakewell, Manu.—Black marble chess-table, inlaid border. Round table, inlaid. A black marble vase and a blue fluor vase.

78 REDFERN, G. Ashford, near Bakewell, Manu.—Marble mosaic table.

79 TOMLINSON, J. Ashford, Manu.—Mosaic tables of Derbyshire and Staffordshire marbles. Derbyshire black marble table, inlaid. Specimens of mosaic work.

80 BRIGHT, S. Buxton, Derbyshire, Manu.—Black marble vases; the material from the Duke of Devonshire's quarries. Mosaic octagon table, &c. "Blue John," or amethystone fluor spar chalice, from Castleton.

81 LOMAS, J. Bakewell, Manu.—Pedestals and chimney-piece of Derbyshire marble, the frieze inlaid.

82 TURNER, J. Buxton, Derbyshire, Manu.—Two jugs, made of black marble, found at Ashford, Derbyshire.

83 BIRD, E. Matlock Bath, Derbyshire, Manu.—Models of the obelisk at Heliopolis and of the Philœ obelisk, in black marble, etched. Black marble slab, engraved after a picture. Card plates, etched, &c.

85 ORGAN, J. Penzance, Cornwall, Manu.—Baptismal font, obelisks, vases, cabinet of specimens, &c. of serpentine stone from Lizard, Penzance.

86 MINTON, H. & Co. Stoke-upon-Trent, Staffordshire, Mann.—Tiles, terra cotta, and vases, &c. in imitation of majolica ware. Encaustic and other tiles. Porcelain bath. Stove in ornamental brick. Friezes in porcelain.

87 THE EARL OF LOVELACE.—Ornamental bricks and tiles, designed and manufactured at Ockham, in Surrey.

88 SINGER & Co. Vauxhall Pottery, Manu.—Specimen of patent mosaic pavement, of vitrified coloured clays.

89 RUFFORD, F. T. Stourbridge, Manu. and Pat. with J. Finch, 6 Pickard St. City Rd.—Bath, adult size, in one piece, made with fire-clay plated with porcelain, and glazed. Bricks for waterproof walls, &c.

90 RAMSAY, G. H. Derwent Haugh, Newcastle.—A wine-cooler in cannel coal.

91 MARGETTS, T. K. & EYLES, H. Oxford.—Sculptured baptismal font in Caen stone. Des. by T. K. Margetts and sculp. by H. Eyles.

92 BLANCHARD, M. H. King Edward St. Westmr. Rd. Manu.—Terra cotta: Ionic capital, des. by and under C. Barry, Esq. Gothic pinnacle, des. by and under F. Pouget, Esq. Model of the Yarborough testimonial, P. Rolt, Esq.

93 FERGUSON, MILLER, & Co. Heathfield, near Glasgow. —Fire-clay Warwick vase, with flower vase, and glazed stoneware pipes of the same.

94 BOWEN, J. Bridgwater.—Two figures in artificial stone—a Nymph, and Fidelity.

95 DOULTON & WATTS, Lambeth, Manu.—Flower vases, ornamented with ferns in terra cotta.

96 BELL, J. & Co. Glasgow, Manu.—Vases in terra cotta.

97 RANSOM & PARSONS, Flint Wharf, Ipswich, Inv. and Manu.—Artificial stone and marble in its various stages of manufacture, and its applications.

98 SPROT, M. & T. Garnkirk Works, near Glasgow, Manu.—Jet d'eau, vases, pedestals, and fire-bricks, manufactured from fire clay.

99 GRANGEMOUTH COAL Co. Grangemouth, Scotland, Manu.—Two large vases and pedestals, by Mr. Wornell. Fire-bricks, fire-clay, pipes, &c.

100 TOMPSON, L. Church Ter. Wisbech, Des. and Manu. —Moulded architectural bricks. Equilateral triangular quarterfoil brick window.

101 LAURIE, W. Downham Market, Suffolk, Sculp.—Models of Christian memorials, &c.

102 FERNLEY IRON WORKS.—Sundry articles in terra cotta.

103 ROBINS, ASPDIN, & COX, Northfleet, and Gt. Scotland Yd. Whitehall, Manu.—Illustrations Portland cement, to show the strength, for making landings, cills, paving, &c. illustrations of its comparative strength.

104 Bowers, Challinor, & Wooliscroft, Brownhills, Tunstall, Staffordshire.—Imitations of oak carved cornice, rosewood Gothic cornice, &c. in pottery.

105 Jones, W. Springfield Tile Works, Newcastle-under-Lyme.—Model roof material, of plain and ornamental tiles, &c. Paving-quarries, tile, chimney-pipe, terro-metallic plain and socket-pipes, &c.

106 Beswick, R. Stafford.—Bricks of new construction.

107 Hickman, R. & Co. Stourbridge, Manu. — Gas retort, made of Stourbridge fire-clay.

108 Pulham, J.—Window and architectural ornaments, in terra cotta and artificial stone. Polished column of Madrepore marble, the property of H. Champernowne, Esq. Dartington, Totness.

109 Hunt, C. Inv. and Manu.—Enamelled slate filter.

110 Ramsay, G. H. Herwent Haugh, Newcastle, Inv.—Fire-clay goods, gas retorts.

111 Luff, J. Tuddenham, Ipswich, Manu.—Ornamental chimney shafts, and red bricks; red and white ornamental bricks, ridge-tiles, paving-tiles, malt-kiln tiles, &c.

112 Cowen & Co. Blaydon Burn, Newcastle-upon-Tyne, Manu.—Patent fire-clay gas retorts; fire-bricks; rough fire-clay; and cannel coal.

113 Westwood & Moore, Stourbridge, Manu.—Specimens of glass bottles and improved stoneware.

114 Haddon, J. C. 29 Bloomsbury Sq.—Rhomboidal bricks.

115 Potter, A. Newcastle.—Two gas-retorts and a vase in fine clay.

116 Workman, J. Stamford Hill, Inv.—Waterproof bricks, &c.

117 Brown, R. Surbiton Hill, Kingston, Surrey, Inv. and Manu.—Grooved ridge tile. Ornamental and plain tiles for Gothic buildings. Curved Italian tiles.

118 Fordham & Son, Royston, Herts, Manu.—Improved bricks, from clay found upon the estate.

119 Harper & Moore, Stourbridge, Manu. — Glass-house pots. Crucibles. Stourbridge fire-bricks, &c. used in the manufacture of plate and flint glass.

120 Stirling, T. sen. Bow Bridge Slate Works, and 473 New Oxford St. Inv. and Manu.—Patent rapid ascension and other filters. Enamelled slate chimney-piece. Chess-table tops, &c. Patent steam fuel.

121 Skinner & Whalley, Stockton-on-Tees, Inv — Vitreous, white, and coloured marble pastes, for mosaics, buildings, &c. Patented.

122 Kent, A. Chichester.—Small piece of a new kind of glazing for greenhouses.

123 Peake, T. Tunstall, and 4 Wharf, City Road Basin, London, Manu.—Terro-metallic roof tiles, bricks, paving tiles, drain pipes, &c. Imitation of the Warwick vase, in terro-metallic, &c.

124 Soc. for Improving the Condition of the Labouring Classes.—Building contrivances, adopted in the construction of their model dwellings for the labouring-classes, particularly that of hollow brickwork. Drawings and models of buildings erected, and designs.

125 Green, S. & Co. Prince's St. Lambeth, Manu.—Chemical stone-ware apparatus. Salt glazed stone-ware. Imp. stone-ware glazed, without salt or lead in the composition. Drainage requisites. Vitreous stone-ware pumps.

126 Key, E. S. Bale, Dereham, Norfolk, Inv.—White and red brick window frames; prov. reg. Glazed valley tiles, manufactured by W. Colman, Swanton Novers.

127 Haywood, H. & R. Brownhill's Tileries, near Burslem, and 15 South Wharf, Paddington, Manu.—Superior metallic clay, from mines at Brownhill's, near Burslem, with samples of manufactures, ornamental pavements, &c.

128 Ambrose, J. Copford, near Colchester, Manu.—Gothic chimneys of red and white bricks. Specimens of white bricks and unmanufactured clay.

130 Sealy, J. Bridgwater, Inv. and Manu.—Patent roofing tiles. Corn and malt kiln tiles, paving tiles, &c. Bridgwater scouring bricks, Bridgwater clays, &c.

131 Brannam, T. Barnstaple, Devon.—Sample of Devonshire clay, in its untempered state, from Fremington, near Barnstaple. An oven for baking bread and meat. Jugs, pitcher, and milkpan, of the same clay.

132 Jepson, W. Edensor, Derbyshire.—A Blue John vase of extraordinary dimensions.

140 H. R. H. Prince Albert.—A block of Parrot coal from West Wemyss colliery, Kirkaldy, Fifeshire, partly polished; and garden seat, designed by L, Gruner, Esq. and executed in Fifeshire by Thomas Williams Waun, of parrot or cannel coal, from the estate of Rear-Admiral Wemyss.

141 Emery, J. 14 North St. Westminster.—Gothic door.

142 Cabanic Patent Co. 29 Marylebone St. Regent St.—Decorations in various devices. (South Wall.)

144 White, T. B. & Sons.—Wall decorations in plaster and cements, in various devices. Also a chimney-piece in Keene's cement. (South Wall.)

Proceed to Ceilings, page 136.

Class 28.   **MANUFACTURES FROM ANIMAL AND VEGETABLE SUBSTANCES, NOT BEING WOVEN OR FELTED.**
—— **North Gallery.** ——

3 Hastings, S. Limerick, Ireland, Manu.—Brushes, for shoes, horses, stoves, grates, &c.

7 Jones, D. Hay, Wales, Des. and Manu.—Welsh rustic picture-frame, of the excrescences of the apple-tree.

8 Wallis, S. Halifax, York, Des and Manu.—Ornamental carvings in mahogany for a sideboard.

9 Scaling, W. 37 George St. Edinburgh, Manu.—Flower-pot stand; a new combination of iron and willow.

10 Wippel, J. jun. 219 High St. Exeter.—Church furniture. viz., alms' basins, sacramental bread-cutter, &c.

11 Duthoit D. & Co. 6 Finsbury Pl. South, Des. and Manu.—Aerial tent. Reg. portable umberella tent.

12 Ramsey, J. Berwick-on-Tweed, Inv. and Manu.—Bee-hive, with moveable bottom and screw; with a moveable crown; and with glass crown, &c.

13 Cundall & Addy, 21 Old Bond St.—Bread platter and knife.

14 Chatwin, H. 30 Darwin St. Birmingham.—Work boxes, caddies, &c. in tortoiseshell, mother of pearl, &c.

15 Johnson, P. Wigan, Manu.—A quantity of fancy turned articles in ivory, wood, and cannel coal.

16 Farrar & Son, Chapel Lane, Bradford, Manu.—Twine made from hemp, flax, and cotton.

18 Crummack, E. York, Prop. and Manu.—Tortoise-shell, ivory, and horn dressing-combs, made by hand.

20 McClintock, G. York, Manu. and Des.—Chain cut from a solid block of wood.

21 Jackson, T. 3 Pinstone St. Sheffield, Manu.—Brushes, used by cutlers, silversmiths, &c.

F 4

22 SMITH, J. 79 Sidney St. Sheffield.—Door furniture, &c. in ivory and fancy woods. Carved bread-platters, &c.

28 MAUNDER, J. Launceston, Cornwall, Manu.—Small wood table, with miniature dessert set, turned in ivory.

29 Dow, A. Liverpool, Manu. — Plate, watch, and jewel brushes.

30 SCHOOL OF INDUSTRY FOR THE BLIND, Bristol, Manu. —Worsted hearth-rugs; worsted and cocoa-nut fibre door-mats; fire-screens; basket; dish-mats, &c. Made entirely by blind persons.

34 COOK, J. Bradford St. Walsall. — A variety of brushes.

35 LEE, F. Shipdham, Norfolk.—Carved oak lectern, of flamboyant, or late decorated style.

36 CRESPIN, E. Esq. Cheshunt, Hertfordshire.—Model carvings of church ornaments, &c.

38 BEVINGTONS & MORRIS, 67 King Wm. St. City, Manu. —Cocoa-nut fibre matting and mats. Manilla-hemp and worsted door-mats.

39 TRELOAR, T. 42 Ludgate Hill, Manu.—Matting, rug, mattress, brushes, &c. of cocoa fibre and Manilla hemp.

40 WILDEY & Co. 7 Holland St. Blackfriars Rd. Southwark, Pat. and Manu.—Cocoa-nut fibre, floor-mattings, door-mats, netting, &c. Cocoa-nut husk, fibre, &c.

41 KING, J. 49 Tufton St. Westminster, Des. Inv. and Manu.—Baskets and chandelier of coloured straw.

42 ROBINSON & Co. 38 Welbeck St. Cavendish Sq. Imp. and Inv.—Specimen of China matting, stained in pattern by a new process.

43 ARMSTRONG, J. 9 Chad's Pl. Gray's Inn Rd. Des. and Manu.—Carriage rugs. Mats. Rugs and mat of worsted, with hemp and jute, and cocoa fibre.

45 KAIN, J. F. 27 Brownlow Rd. Dalston, Inv. and Manu.—Bird cage, made principally of ivory.

47 TAYLOR, B. 169 St. John St..Road Clerkenwell.—A tower, with minarets, composed of upwards of 1,000 pieces, manufactured entirely of vegetable ivory.

48 FENTUM, M. 8 Hemming's Row, Charing Cross, Manu.—Improved ivory chessmen and board.

49 BROWN, H. 187 Whitechapel Rd. Inv.—" British ivory (not a composition)."

51 COATE, J. & Co. 5 Brewer St. Golden Sq. St. James's, Des. and Manu.—Concave tooth-brush. Hair-brush, &c.

53 TITTERTON, G. 70 Margaret St. Cavendish Sq.—A case of brushes.

55 GOSNELL & Co. 12 Three Kings Ct. Lombard St. Manu.—Extracts and perfumery. Fancy toilet soaps of various kinds. Fancy brushes and combs.

55A SMITH, A. 8 and 9 Osborn St. Whitechapel, Inv. and Manu.—Painting brushes, for heavy or fine work.

58 RIGBY, E. R. 80 Gracechurch St. Pat and Manu.— Specimens of brushes manufactured from quills, as useful and durable as bristles.

60 GREEN, —, Webber St. Blackfriars Rd.—Specimens of workmanship in hair.

61 CHILD, W. H. 21 Providence Row, Finsbury Sq. Prod.—Improved stock brush, bound with copper. Improved flexible flesh brushes. Hair brushes. Improved nutcrackers.

62 TRUEFITT, H. P. 20 and 21 Burlington Arcade, and 114 Piccadilly, Inv. and Manu.—Wigs, head-dresses, hair-dyes, brushes, combs, &c.

64 ROSS & SONS, 119 and 120 Bishopsgate St. Within, Inv. and Manu.—Ornamental hair. Specimens of dyed hair. Brushes, ornamental perfumery, &c.

65 TRUEFITT, W. 1 New Bond St. Inv. and Manu.— Carved ivory brushes and comb. Tortoiseshell combs. Head-dresses of natural hair.

67 SLAPE, G. 7 Brook St. New Rd. Des. and Manu.— Fancy feather brush, carved in English walnut.

68 NASH, T. jun. 19 Swan St. Dover Rd. Southwark, Inv. and Manu.—Registered copper-bound painters' brushes.

70 TALLERMAN, REBECCA, & SON, 20 White Lion St. Norton Folgate, Inv. and Manu. —Waterproof Cachmere for boots and shoes. Silk, satin, and velvet boots and shoes. Ventilating waterproof boot.

72 HODGES, R. E. 44 Southampton Row, Russell Sq. Inv. and Manu.—Mechanical purchases; highly elastic tackle, made of India rubber, &c. Travellers' staffs. A hand-carriage to convey bundles or packages, &c. Application of India rubber to guns, bows, &c.

73 SANDERS, J. 11 Fore St. Cripplegate, Reg.—India-rubber waterproof umbrella tent.

75 WANSBOROUGH, J. 52 Little Britain, Inv. Pat. and Manu.—A waterproof cloth in imitation of velvet, suited for upholsterers, binding of books, caps, &c.

76 MACKINTOSH & Co. 73 Aldermanbury, and at Manchester, Imp. Manu. and Pat.—India-rubber specimens, illustrative of its manufacture, and collection of manufactured articles, vulcanized and unvulcanized.

77 BUNN, LOCKINGTON, & Co. 19 and 20 Walbrook, Imp. —Specimens of the various descriptions of native Para India-rubber, or caoutchouc, and of gutta percha, with samples illustrative of the various stages of manufacture, and of the purposes to which each description is applied.

78 NICKELS, C. & Co. 13 Goldsmith St. Cheapside, Manu.—Various articles manufactured from India-rubber.

81 MATTHEWS, S. 58 Charing Cross, Manu.—Large-sized India-rubber portable boat, and India-rubber cloak boat, designed by Lieut. Halkett, R.N. India-rubber portable bath. (In East Gallery.)

82 CORDING, J. C. 231 Strand, Prod.—Waterproof coats, capable of being used with either side outwards. Waterproof capes. Ladies' waterproof silk capes and hoods, made of silk, &c.

83 HANCOCK, J. L. Goswell Mews, Goswell Rd. Manu. —Portable India-rubber shower-bath, vulcanized India-rubber tubing, hose reel, and inflated air-tight bed chair, &c.

84 BAKER C. Jireh Cottage, Rotherfield St. Islington. —New hair-brush and pocket tooth brush. Model writing-desk. A new fire-escape. New pattern tooth-brushes.

85 The GUTTA PERCHA Co. 18 Wharf Rd. City Rd. Imp. Pat. and Manu.—Gutta percha: collection of specimens illustrative of its various applications.

86 THORN & Co. Gutta Percha Manufacturers.—Looking-glass frames and console tables, and decorations; some richly gilt, and various specimens.

87 WALKER, T. 1 Conduit St. Regent St. Inv. and Manu.—Gutta percha hat-bodies. Ventilated velvet hats, &c. Hat-case, answering for a life-buoy float, foot-bath, &c.

90 HANCOCK, C. 48 Milner Sq. Islington, Manu.— Gutta percha tubes, picture frames, machinery belts, &c. and metallo-thionised gutta percha.

91 FAULDING, J. 11 Edward St. Hampstead Rd.— Fretwork cuttings.

95 SMITH, O. 21 King St. Covent Garden, Manu.— Specimen of ivory turning and carving, &c. by George A. Smith, 22 May's Buildings, St. Martin's Lane.

96 CLAYTON, B. 54 Mansfield St. Kingsland Road.—A newly-invented method of making calico printers' blocks and rollers. New methods of inlaying wood, gutta percha, papier maché, &c.

97 GRUGEON, A. 24 Thomas St. Hackney Rd. Des. and Manu.—Fish and flower-stand, bird's-eye maple, and dyed to imitate nature.

98 TURNBULL, T. William St. Portland Town, Prod.— Specimens of improved wood sawing.

99 MINNS, J. 40 Luard St. Caledonian Rd. Maker.— Model of the choragic monument of Lysicrates, at Athen

MANUFACTURES from ANIMAL and VEGETABLE SUBSTANCES.

Lantern of Demosthenes, B.C. 334 ; scale 7-8ths of an inch to the foot.   Carved in chesnut.

100 SCHOOL FOR THE INDIGENT BLIND, St. George's Fields, Southwark, Manu.—Articles manufactured by the blind. Worsted hearth-rug and fire-screen. Baskets. Knitted and netted work.   Hair brooches, bracelets, &c.   Paper cuttings, &c.

101 CRIPER, R. 18 Artillery Lane, Bishopsgate St. Without, Inv. and Manu.—New willow drawing-room chair. Willow sofa-bed chair.

102 WILLIAMS, J. 40 Exeter St. Strand, Manu.—Basket of superior fineness, for the use of soiled linen.

103 BODE, H. 11 Portsea Pl. Connaught Sq. Inv. and Manu.—Varieties in basket work.

104 POTTS, D. 18 St. Dunstall's Hill, Tower St. Inv. Des. and Manu.—Figured vase, for flowers, in basket work, with water-proof lining.

106 McRAE, J. & Co. 17 Ave Maria Lane, Manu.— Scotch wood articles, of new design, ornamented with paintings, tartan plaids, &c.

108 MALLANDAIN & Co. 5 James St. St. Luke's, Manu. —Table inkstands, with one stoppered ink glass made from English sycamore, stained black and polished.

109 WHEATLEY, W. 2 Clipstone St. Des. and Manu.— Blocks or lasts for the feet.

110 BEGENT, T. J. 8 York St. St. James's Sq. Inv.— Registered peg to secure linen whilst drying ; also applicable to holding papers together.

111 SHEPPARD, F. 125 Kingsland Rd. Prop.—Articles of fancy woodwork, manufactured in Ayrshire, consisting of needle, card, envelope and cigar cases, snuff-boxes, &c.

112 SANDY & POWELL, 76 George St. New Road, Des. and Manu.—Specimens of ornamental sawing or fretwork, cut by improved machinery, capable of executing from the thickest to the finest of detail.

113 TAYLOR, C. & A. 30 Berner's Mews, Oxford St. Des. and Manu.—Specimen of fret-work, cut by improved machinery, used in the decoration of piano-fortes, organs, cabinet-work, &c.

116 ROUSSEAU, A. 352 Strand, Manu.—Shawl boxes. Velvet embroidery.   Lace-cases, writing-paper, and other ornamental cases.

117 HARRIS, S. & H. 41 and 27 Mansell St. Imp.—Specimens of sponges, with description of their different uses. Samples of harness polishes, dye, and polishing pastes, with specimens of their effects.

118 BARBER, C. A. (aged 10 years) Counter, 440 Soho Bazaar, Des.—Landscapes and figures, cut from paper with scissors, without copy or outline.

119 BURGESS, J. 1 Johnson St. Horseferry Rd. Westminster, Manu.—Flower vase, cut from paper with scissors.

120 COLLINGS, J. 14 Gt. Ormond St. Bloomsbury, Inv. and Maker.—Arm-pad for journeymen tailors, abolishing cross-legged sitting.

121 WALLER, F. 49 Fleet St. Manu.—Commercial and diplomatic despatch writing-desk, in rosewood ; small, rosewood, open desk for ladies.

122 JONES, J. 25 John St. Cannon St. St. George's East. —Shoe pegs, to make boots or shoes without welts or stitches, cut by hand and by machine. Shoes made with pegs, and in the different stages of manufacture.

124 BASS, J. H. 6 Featherstone St. City Rd. Inv. and Manu.—Corks cut by machinery : the machinery originally patented in 1830, but has since been much altered.

125 ESDAILES & MARGRAVE, City Saw Mills, Regent's Canal.—Specimens of novel uses of cork and of preparations of cork, by steam machinery ; applicable to the making of hats, mattresses, bolsters, &c.

126 FRENCH & BUTLER, 28 Piccadilly, Manu. and Imp.

—Specimens of different qualities of ready-made corks of English and Spanish manufacture.

127 BLIZARD, J. Cheltenham, Manu.—Moulded panels and mouldings, cut by machinery ; with the tools employed in the process, &c.

128 FRANKS, C. Wolverhampton, Manu.—Basket, for clothes.

131 PETERS & SON, Birmingham, Manu. — Articles covered and inlaid with tortoiseshell, mother-of-pearl, gold, silver, garnets, &c.

132 HAYDEN, J. 35 Northwood St. Birmingham, Des. and Manu.—Lady's cabinet, and small cases ; tortoiseshell, and pearl.

137 WHITAKER, H. W. 20 Charlotte St. Manu.—Ornamental bird-cage.

138 SPRINGFIELD, W. Wisbech, Des. and Manu.— Models of wine pipes, casks, tubs, churns, and other articles of coopery.

141 GARRETT, 1 Victoria Ter. Woodbridge Rd. Ipswich, Manu.—Ornamental turned snuff-boxes, in ivory, and fancy foreign woods.

143 GOULD, J. Tottenham Park, Marlborough, Des.— Bible, with carved oak cover, silver plated clasps ; the carving and clasps hand worked.

144 RENDALL, J. Stromness, Orkney, Scotland, Manu. —Various samples of Tuscan plait, for bonnets : the straw grown and dressed in Orkney, and plaited by the females.

145 STILL, C. S. Smoogrow House, near Kirkwall, Scotland, Prop.—Specimens of the straw plait, for making bonnets, hats, &c., by the women of Orkney.

146 MacGREGOR, J. W. 28 Jamaica St. Glasgow, Manu. —Ship's harness cask, brass hooped and mounted ; deck buckets, &c. Imperial bushel measures. Ten-gallon cask, made out of red oak staves, prepared with melted tallow.

151 COOPER, J. M. Derby.—Pulpit, with carved figures, &c.

152 STEVENSON, J. & J. Sheffield, and 9 Cripplegate Buildings, Wood St. London.—Ladies' ornamental, dress, and other combs, manufactured from ox and buffalo horns.

154 TOPLIS & SONS, Ashby-de-la-Zouch, Des. and Manu. —Improved royal letter-basket ; fancy knitting-basket ; work-basket, and dog-kennel.

155 DUNLOP, J. Lauder, Scotland, Inv.—Fishing or trout basket.

156 ADAMSON, R. Colingsburgh, Fifeshire, Scotland, Des. and Manu.—Scotch willow basket for carrying fruits.

157 HALLIDAY, W. Chilton-super-Polden, near Bridgwater.—Piece of carving in solid English oak : " The Canterbury pilgrims setting out from the Tabard," by a self-taught artist.

158 HEMPHILL, W. D. Clonmel, Ireland, Des. and Exec.—Plain and ornamental ivory turning.

159 CANNINGS, MARY JANE, 9 Walcot Parade, Bath, Manu.—A variety of miscellaneous articles. The exhibitor being blind, deaf, and dumb.

160 HORNE, W. 54 Montague St. Spitalfields, Des. and Manu.—Work-box, composed of 1,500 pieces of wood.

161 HAWLEY, J. & T. 181 Bromsgrove St. Birmingham, Manu.—Specimens of bone tooth, nail, shaving, hair and hat brushes.

162 TATE, F. 18 Percy St. Bedford Sq.—A gilt casket symbolical of the Great Exhibition of Industry of all Nations. Plastic casts in imitation of metal.

163 WILLIAM, H. Dublin.—Eccentric ivory turning without eccentric chuck.

164 SHAW, C. Lower Mount St. Dublin.—Specimens of mechanical sculpture, reduced from models in plaster and bronze by machinery, adapted to a turning lathe.

165 MEADOWS, J. 71 Prince's St. Leicester Sq. Inv. Pat. and Manu.—New method of veneering. Picture frames.

MANUFACTURES from ANIMAL and VEGETABLE SUBSTANCES.

Specimens of patent builders' work, without joining at the angles or edges.

166 Howton, G. W. 34 Thayer St. Manu.—Decorative panel, carved out of lime-wood.

167 Mitford, B. Cheltenham, Maker and Inv.—Concentric balls, made of solid spheres of box-wood, like those made by the Chinese.

168 Winterborn, J. Hackney Rd. Inv. and Des.—Self-acting index, in case of spontaneous combustion; fire extinguisher and fire escape; warm bath. Carving in Italian walnut-tree.

169 Day, Miss, 4 Oakley Ter. Old Kent Rd.—A caddy formed of rare and valuable shells to the number of 100,000, the interior of the lid displays a bouquet of flowers worked in beads.

171 Bevan, C. Metropolitan Buildings. — Tea-caddy ornamentally carved.

172 Smith, T. Hurstmonceux, near Hailsham, Manu.—A set of Sussex truck-baskets, made of willow wood.

173 Wolstenholme, J. 12 Lord Mayor's Walk, York, Des. and Manu.—Six stall finials, or poppy-heads, of decorated Gothic architecture, and various designs, carved in Norway oak.

174 Strugnell, H. 25 Kirby St. Hatton Garden.—Ornamental writing desk.

175 Peel, J. Prospect Pl. Pudsey. — Specimens of cuttings in relief with the lathe. Fac-similes of medals, coins, flowers, &c.

176 Moore, G. W. Huddersfield, Yorkshire. — Wood carvings.

177 Hamilton, C. F. 15 Greek St. Soho, Inv. and Manu. —Shaving brushes.

178 Forster, —, Streatham, Surrey.—Inhaber Eines patent and other fabrics.

179 Rogers, M. Abbey St. Derby—A bracket being a specimen of ornamental carving in wood.

181 Frinneby, F. R. 63 Cannon St. City, Inv. and Manu. —Registered and other brushes for painting and graining.

182 Bushell, G. 222 Whitechapel Rd. Inv.—An economical substitute for stained glass, suitable for all kinds of ornamental and transparent devices.

183 Godfrey, W. Romford.—Ornamental window, and model of a life-boat.

184 Hall, J. S. 308 Regent St. Manu.—Improved elastic over-shoes, with leather soles and plush heels, to prevent slipping.

185 Tarbutt, W. Cranbrook, Kent, Des. and Manu.—Cradle, made of osiers, ornamented and moved by a weight and springs.

188 Horsey, J. 5 Sutton St. Soho Sq. Inv. and Manu. —India-rubber articles in original colour, prepared to resist heat and cold, and specimens in sheet in various colours.

191 Woodhead, J. Leeds, Yorkshire. — Hempen and bell ropes, netting for fruit trees.

192 Griffith, W. 29 Grofton St. Dublin.—Bog oak bracelets, brooches, and ornaments.

193 Cawley, J. 21 Bridgwater Gardens, Bridgwater Sq. Barbican, City.—Various mats and rugs.

194 Curtis & Brothers, 29 Green St. Friar St. Blackfriars Rd.—Gut bands for driving steam engines.

195 Hewens, N. J. Hayes, Middlesex.—Horse's hoof shod with gutta percha.

196 Hinde, J. G. Broad St. Birmingham.—A variety of brushes.

197 Clarkson, —, 111 Strand.—Patent cork hats.

198 Stevens, J. 4, Penton Row, Queen's Row.—View of the Exhibition on composition.

199 Dewsnap, J. St. Thomas St. Sheffield.—Razor-strops, &c.

200 Hawkins, T. Inverness Rd. Bayswater.—A case of brushes.

Proceed to Class 25, page 128.

Class 29.   MISCELLANEOUS MANUFACTURES AND SMALL WARES.
—— North Transept Gallery. ——

1 Rowland & Sons, 20 Hatton Garden, Prop.—Articles of perfumery and for the toilet; oils, cosmetics, dentifrices, &c.

2 Yardley & Statham, 7 Vine St. Bloomsbury, Manu.—Specimens of refined scented soaps.

3 Rimmel, E. 39 Gerrard St. Soho, and 19 Boulevard de la Gare d'Ivry, Paris.—Artificial hair. Scent fountain, for cooling and perfuming apartments, &c. Scented winter bouquets. Perfumery, &c.

4 Williams & Son, 28 Compton St. Clerkenwell, Manu.—Soaps used by cloth manufacturers, lace-bleachers, and woollen-manufacturers. Scouring soap. Mottled and yellow soap. Fancy soaps, perfumed.

5 Taylor, Humphrey, & Co. King's Rd. Chelsea.—British liqueurs distilled from foreign and English fruits, &c. Distilled waters, extracted from flowers, herbs, &c. Fancy scented soaps.

6 Lloyd, A. 10 Beak St. Manu.—The Euxesis, for shaving without soap or water.

8 Knight, J. Old Gravel Lane, St. George's, Middlesex, Manu.—Extra pale-yellow soap, of pure and harmless composition. Soft soap, used in the manufacture of cloth, silk, &c. for machinery, &c.

9 Warner, W. Eastbourne, Sussex.—Models of two casks and a filter.

10 Hendrie, R. 12 & 13 Tichborne St. Quadrant, Manu.—Toilet soaps. British perfumes. Perfumed essences. Cosmetics. Improved spirituous acetine, or toilet vinegar. Moelline, a peculiar oleaginous compound, &c.

11 Boully, Mrs. P., 6 Grove Ter., Queen's Rd., Bayswater. –A block perspective patchwork quilt. composed of silks and velvet.

13 Grossmith, J. 39 Friday St.—Summer and other fancy soaps; pomade, essences, perfumery, and essential oils

14 Clarne, W. R. 27 Compton St. Clerkenwell.—Walking stick.

15 Barnes, J. & W. Poyle, near Colnbrook.—A variety of whipthongs.

16 Carrick, J. 127 Crawford St. Inv.—Elder-flower toilet-soap.

17 Galbraith, W. J. T. 26 Bennett St. Blackfriars Rd. Inv. and Manu.—Writing fluids. Seidlitz powders. Marking ink. Culinary essences. Hair oils, perfumes, &c.

18 Ede & Co. 47 Ludgate Hill, Manu.—Perfumery Waithman's patent ink.

19 Cowan & Sons, 139 New Gravel Lane, Shadwell, Manu. —Specimens of pale-yellow, mottled, curd, and marine soap.

20 Cleaver, F. S. 18 Red Lion Sq. Inv. and Manu.—Honey toilet soap; winter soap; brown and white Windsor; white almond, and other soaps.

21 Farina, Jean Marie, Cologne and 1 Salters' Hall Ct. Manu.—A new extract of Eau de Cologne.

22 Fisher, T. W. and Co., King's Head-ct. Barbican, Manu. and Pat.—Perfumery and Chemicals.

23 STEVENSON, D. 4 Carlton St. Regent St. Manu.—Eau de Cologne, of British manufacture.
24 PEARS, A. & F. 91 Gt. Russell St. Bloomsbury, Inv. and Manu.—Transparent soap.
25 KENDALL & Co. Dublin, and 8 Harp Lane, Great Tower St. London, Manu.—Various fancy soaps manufactured without any deleterious ingredient.
26 FAIERS, J. 154 High St. Colchester.—Vegetable oil, for perfumery.
27 WHARRY, J. Market Pl. Chippenham, Manu.—Distilled lavender-water.
28 MACKEAN, W. Paisley, Manu.—White oil and other soaps. Palm-oil bleached by a cheap and simple plan. Ammoniacal soft soap made by a novel process. Purified American baking lard. Lard-oil, for machinery, freed from fat acids.
29 PAYNE, G. Cowes, Isle of Wight, Prop.—Royal Osborne bouquet, a superior perfume. Isle of Wight sand-soap, made with the coloured sands of the island. Royal Osborne sauce, an exquisite condiment.
30 Low & Co. 330 Strand, Manu.—Hair brushes in ivory, satinwood, and rosewood. Embossed perfumed soaps. Bottles of perfumery.
31 GOULD, A. 36 Great Marylebone St.—An assortment of fishing tackle.
32 WARRELL, J. Dofford St. Bath.—Cottage baskets and ladies' bridal baskets.
33 ADAMS, S. Nottingham.—Needlethreader for the blind.
34 FROST, H. 17 Rathbone Pl. Oxford St.—Steam and hot-water articles.
35 STIVENS & SONS, Aberdeen.—Snuff boxes, &c.
36 AUSTIN, G. 6 and 7 St. Andrew St. Dublin, Manu.—Dressing-cases, made of Irish bog-yew; the silver fittings from the Sugenure mines, county Wicklow.
37 BEST, T. 9 St. Mary's Row, Birmingham, Manu.—Dressing-cases. Writing case and desks. Ladies' reticules, &c. Note cases. Card cases. Cigar cases. Pocket books. Spectacle cases, &c.
38 HAYWOOD, M. Birmingham.—Fishing tackle, in great variety.
39 PURDON, T. 68 Whitefriar-gate, Hull, Inv. and Manu.—Registered travelling bureau. The Hull safety oil-lamp, combining lantern and lamp. Iron skate, made by Wm. Grantham.
40 RUSSELL, R. Tunbridge Wells, Kent, Inv. and Manu.—Tunbridge ware marquetrie inlaid lady's work-box.
41 HOLLAMBY, H. Tonbridge Wells, Manu.—Work-box and writing-desk; of mosaic inlaid Tunbridge ware, with specimens of the woods.
42 STRUDWICK, T. 14 New Bond St. Manu.—Yew-tree writing-box and dressing-case. Cedar of Lebanon dressing-case. Ebony box and library ink-stand, with silver taper-stand and ink-glasses.
43 STOCKEN, 53 Regent St.—Envelope cases, blotting books, &c.
44 LEUCHARS, W. 38 Piccadilly, Inv. and Man.—Lady's dressing-case of walnut-wood, mounted in the mediæval style, in pierced solid silver, &c. Gentleman's dressing case. Travelling tea-equipage &c.
45 MECHI, J. J. 4 Leadenhall St.—Dressing cases, workboxes, writing desks, tea-chests, and elegancies for presentation.
46 HURRELL, W. 66 Houndsditch.—Models of English oak vats.
47 HINE, J. 5 Skinner Pl. Holloway, Des. and Manu.—Cabinet work of ebony, inlaid with various coloured pearls, tortoiseshell, &c.
48 DALTON, T. 85 Regent St. Inv.—Combined writing-desk, dressing-case, and dispatch box, &c.

49 LUCAS, F. 9 St. John's St. Rd. Clerkenwell, Manu.—Solid rosewood improved folding wing medicine chest.
50 ASPREY, C. 166 New Bond St. Inv. Des. and Manu.—Ladies' dressing-cases, writing-desks, blotting-books, caskets, tazzas candlesticks, &c. and taper stand, en suite.
51 JOHNS, G. E. 3 Aldermanbury, Des. and Manu.—Toilet-box and work-box, paper and embroidered satin, of English design, materials, and workmanship.
52 TURRILL, J. 52 New Bond St. Manu.—Portable writing-desk and receptacle for private papers and money.
53 STURGEON, HARRIETT, 180 High Holborn.—Vase of flowers, made from feathers by an amateur.
54 CLIVE, J. H. Tunstall, Staffordshire.—A ballistina and chest expander.
55 LANGDALE, E. F. 83 Upper Thames St.—A variety of oils.
56 DOWN, J. Moat Row, Birmingham, Des. and Manu.—Wax fruit. Table of original design and manufacture.
57 STIRLING, C. M. Kippenross, Dunblane, Scotland, Des.—Impressions of leaves, representing, on a large scale, the peculiar growths of forest trees.
58 ARTHUR M. S. Glasgow.—Vase of artificial flowers.
59 JACKSON, ELIZABETH, Southport, Prod.—Vase of artificial flowers.
60 PERRY, J. 1 and 2 Victoria Pl. Ramsgate.—Vase of shell flowers.
61 TEMPLE, EMILY, 46 Connaught Ter.—Wax flowers and foliage modelled from nature.
62 SUGDEN, BORRAS, & Co. 22 Aldermanbury, Manu.—Artificial flowers. Feathers for ladies' bonnets, and head-dresses of British manufacture.
63 STRICKLAND, MARIA, 8 New Bond St. Manu.—The "Victoria Regia," in its various stages of development, with each side of leaf modelled to nature. Roses, night-blowing cercus and other cacti. Orchidaceous plants, &c.
64 SLAUGHAN, ELIZABETH.—Vase of artificial flowers.
65 RIDDIFORD, JANE, 14 Cowley St. Westminster, Des. and Manu.—Group of hand-cut rice-paper flowers.
66 RANDOLPH, WILHELMINA, 55 Marsham St. Westminster, Prod.—Specimens of plants and cut flowers, composed of feathers of various hues, without dye or tinting, by an amateur.
67 PURSEY, W. H. 14 Spring St. Sussex Gardens, Paddington.—Imitations of flowers cut in vegetables, and chemically preserved for garnish.
68 COX, J. Gorgie Mills, Edinburgh.—Patent swimming stockings and life preservers.
69 BURCH & SON, 32 Platt Ter. St. Pancras.—An assortment of lead pencils.
70 MINTORN, J. H. H. ELIZ. & REBEC. 36 Soho Sq. Des. and Manu.—Rare and curious botanical specimens, modelled in wax from life, showing their growing state, and exhibiting the varieties and phases of their existence, &c.
71 MAGUIRE, W. J. 5 Chenies St. Bedford Sq. Manu.—Flowers made from dyed feathers.
72 HOSKINGS, ANN, 7 Langthorn Pl. Stratford, Manu.—Basket of wax fruit. Dishes of wax pastry and vegetables.
73 GATTI, A. & G. 28 Westminster Rd. Lambeth, Des. and Manu.—Artificial peas, made from white muslin and velvet Flowers made of paper and preparations for the same. Articles used in making artificial flowers, both before and after being made up into flowers.
74 FOSTER, SON, & DUNCUM, 16 Wigmore St. Manu.—Artificial flowers, ostrich feathers, marabou muffs and boas, and articles used by artificial flower-makers.
75 EWART, H. Bath Pl. New Rd. and Ampthill Sq. Hampstead Rd. Manu.—Vases of wax flowers and plants.
76 POPE, W. Bridge St. Exeter.—Various specimens of felt, &c.

MISCELLANEOUS MANUFACTURES and SMALL WARES.

77 DORVELL, ELIZABETH, 199 Oxford St. Inv.—Wax flowers.

78 CHISHOLME, EMMA, 29 Edward St. Hampstead Rd. Manu.—Wax flowers.

79 LEMARE, JANE CLARA, 11 Cowley Ter. North Brixton, Manu.—Sheet wax for modelling flowers.

80 FISHER, J. 3 Cripplegate Buildings, Manu.—Hawthorn or May-tree and other artificial flowers.

81 HARDING & STANDFAST, 83 Hatton Garden.—Vase of flowers.

82 JONES, ISABELLA B. 22 St George's Rd. Notting Hill, Mod.—Group of wax flowers, from nature.

83 CALLOW & SON, Park Lane.—Various gig whips.

84 SKILL, REBECCA, 79 Warwick St. Pimlico, Inv. and Manu.—Infrangible wax flowers. Specimens of the materials employed.

85 MIERS, W. J. 15 Lamb's Conduit Passage, Red Lion Sq.—Specimens of ornamental letters.

86 FIELDER, W. Upper Portland Place, Wandsworth Rd.—Group of wax fruit.

87 HOOL, MARY.—Flowers made of feathers.

87A GOING J. & Co. Clonmel, Ireland, Manu. — Pale yellow and white soap, exhibited for quality.

88 STANTON, MARY, 19 Noel St. Islington, Manu.—Wax flowers.

89 EDWARDS, —, 21 King St. Holborn. — Various dressing cases.

90 BRIEN, C. Dublin.—Clarified tallow candles.

91 DIXON, G. 1 and 2 Upper Erne St. Dublin, Manu. —Improved composite and mould candles. Household soap.

92 MORRELL, J. Darlington High Row, Durham, Inv. and Manu.—Tallow candles, which burn without snuffing, marbled and perfumed.

93 GALTON, MARY ANN, 56 Upper Charlotte St. Fitzroy Sq. and 26 Hermes St. Pentonville, Des. and Manu.—Sofrano standard rose tree, mignionette; modelled in wax.

94 MITCHELL, G. A. Whitburn, N.B. Prod. and Inv.— Vinegar plant and samples of vinegar, mineral candles, and of a composition for preserving houses from damp.

95 JONES, Rev. W. H. Chailey, near Lewes, Sussex, Inv. and Pat.—The Acolyte or patent safety candle-cap.

96 KIRBY, BEARD & Co. Depôt, Cannon St.—An assortment of needles and pins.

97 SANDELL, E. Putney, Inv. and Manu.—Odoriferous lighters, for igniting tapers, lamps, &c.

98 LEWIS, Miss, Waithamstow, Essex.—Paper-cuttings executed with scissors.

99 HALE, W. S. 73 Queen St. Manu.—Stearine, and stearine and composite candles, &c.

100 ROGERS & Co., 137 Strand.—Baby jumper.

101 BELL, R. 16 Basing Lane.—Samples of improved fusees.

102 GOWER, T. Gun Lane, St. Stephen's, Norwich, Inv. and Manu.—Lemonade, prepared from vegetable substances.

103 GRAHAM, LEMON, & Co. Ireland.—The process of the manufacture of lozenges and comfits, with samples.

104 BOLAND, P. 138 Capel St. Dublin, Manu.—Various sorts of biscuits and cakes.

105 THWAITES, A. & R. & Co. 57 Upper Sackville St. Dublin, and 17 St. Alban's Pl. Haymarket, London, Inv. and Manu.—Soda water, of two degrees of strength, introduced to the public in 1800 by the late R. Perceval, M.D. of Dublin.

106 WOTHERSPOON, J. & Co. Glasgow, Manu.—Lozenges, made by patent steam machinery.

107 HUNTLEY & PALMER, King's Rd. Reading, Manu.— Sweet fancy biscuits, made by steam machinery.

108 LEALE & ALBRECHT.—Confectioners' cake moulds.

109 BEGG, W. G. 20 Market St. Edinburgh, Inv. and Manu.—Samples of lozenges and other confections, &c.

110 WILKEN, A. 6 Little Winchester St. London Wall. —Savoy cake, ornamented with sugar.

110A LUCAS, G.—Lozenges and other comfits.

111 TIDMARSH, R. 3 Jamaica Row, Bermondsey. — Cachous aromatic, fumigating and aromatic pastiles.

112 GUNTER, R. Motcomb and Lowndes St. Belgrave Sq. Inv.—Two bride-cakes.

113 HUBBARD, H. B. Baker St. Enfield, Manu.—Gingerbread nuts and gingerbread, which will keep for 20 years.

114 SCHOOLING, H. 7 North Side, Bethnal Green, Manu. —Pate de jujubes; chocolate, sticks, drops, and in cake; and other confectionery. Gelatine, for printing, &c.

115 WARRICK BROTHERS 3 Garlick Hill, Manu.— Jujubes, lozenges, and other confectionery.

116 VINE, R. 10 King St. Borough, Des. and Manu.— A bride-cake, ornamented with sugar icing by piping.

117 BURTON, H. Hampstead. — British insects, preserved.

118 RICHARDS, R. 21 Tonbridge Pl. New Rd.—Various fishing nets.

119 KEOGH, H. 22 Gilbert St. Grosvenor Sq. Des. and Manu.—Composition set of dessert ornaments of eight pieces, and centre table ornaments, in white and gold.

120 FARRELL, R. H. 35 Lambs' Conduit St. Des. and Manu.—Table ornaments for confectioners, in plaster of Paris, gilt. Models in wax and sugar.

121 SPRATT, I. 1 Brook St. Hanover Sq.—The game of "cockamaroo," improved. Model hay-cart.

122 MONTANARI, A. 29 Upper Charlotte St. Fitzroy Sq. Manu.—Model wax dolls, the hair being inserted into the head. Model rag dolls.

123 LASCELLES, J. W. Liverpool.—Model of Mansion-house. Flies for fishing.

124 BOUCHET, A. 74 Baker St. Portman Sq.—Animated and musical tableau, representing the Great Exhibition and people of all nations. Panoptic polyrama. Armorial trophies and Saracen armour, &c.

125 BLACKMORE, MARY, 1 Rosoman's Buildings, Islington Green, Inv. and Manu.—Artificial flower-plant, formed of beads.

126 SPURIN, E. C. 37 New Bond St. Des.—Mechanical toy model of an English farm, with figures, threshing-machine, windmill, &c. in action. Gulliver in Lilliput, modelled by A. Fleischmann, of Sonneberg.

127 LUCAS, H. 8 Broad Ct. Long Acre.—Progressive garden rocking-horse.

128 DEAR, J. C. 191 Bishopsgate Without, Manu.— Rocking-horse; and walking-sticks, carved.

129 SHORT, J. Wallington, Surrey.—Essential oils of peppermint and lavender.

130 BEANEY, T. St. Leonards-on-Sea, Manu.—Arrows, inlaid by machinery. Reg.

131 HOLLAND, H. Darwin St. Birmingham, Inv. and Manu.—Umbrellas and parasols, with metallic frames, illustrations of processes of manufacture.

132 STEARS, S. Briggate, Leeds, Manu.—The Princess Royal parasol.

133 WILSON & MATHESON, Candleriggs St. Glasgow, Manu.—New portable umbrellas.

134 WADDINGTON & SONS, 1 Coleman St.—Patent perlevis parasols and umbrellas.

135 SLARK, W. 67 Burlington Arcade.—Improved umbrellas. Parasols, driving and riding whip. Penang sword-cane. Steel foil, covered with leather. Improved railway calls and dog whips.

136 SANGSTER, W. & J. 140 Regent St. Manu. and Pat. —New patent parasol. Application of feathers as an ornament to parasols. Alpaca parasols and umbrellas. Holland's patent light silk umbrella.

137 RUTTER, J. & W. 122 Cheapside, Manu.—Brown walking parasol. Brown glace silk parasol, with jointed handle. Satin registered parasol, &c.

138 MITCHELL, J. Stonehaven, Scotland.—A variety of small wares.

139 OGLEBY, & Co. Lambeth.—Spermaceti and stearine specimens.

140 MEYERS, B. 18 Crutched Friars, Inv. and Manu.— Specimens of English sticks, rough and manufactured. Rattans, from India, &c. rough, and manufactured. Canes; bamboos; rattans; Spanish, Chinese, and American reeds; sticks from West Indies; and articles made of the same.

141 LEWIS & ALLENBY, 193, 195, and 197 Regent St. Des.—Parasols of new construction.

142 LINTON, W. Belae.—An assortment of fishing tackle.

143 CARPENTER, J. 59 Church St. Old Kent Rd. Prod.— Walking-sticks, carved and engraved by an aged gardener with his pruning-knife, and a file for finishing off.

144 PORTER, W. Northampton.—Rocking boat.

145 PRESTON, R. 37 Highbury Vale, Islington, Manu.— Walking-stick, manufactured from root of hornbeam.

146 BOSS, I. A. 6 Bury St. Inv. Pat. and Manu.—A new patent parasol. Travelling umbrella, with folding handle. Stiletto or defensive umbrella, &c. with metallic ribs, German silver, and other tubing.

147 HARGRAVE, HARRISON & Co. 13 Wood St. Cheapside. Inv. and Manu.—Registered cycloidal parasols.

148 EVANS, T. & Co.—Parasols.

149 FOSTER, PORTER, & Co.—Parasols.

150 MUIR, P. Archer's Hall, Edinburgh, Manu.—Specimens of bows, arrows, &c.

151 HORE, W. Harperstown, Taghmon, Co. Wexford, Ireland, Inv.—Trigger to a long bow, &c.

152 PARKINS, T. Carlisle, Manu.—Fish-hooks, artificial flies, minnows, &c.

153 ROWELL, J. Carlisle, Manu.—Fishing tackle in the various stages of manufacture, with materials.

154 NICHOLAS, MARTHA, 58 Castle St. Carlisle, Inv. and Manu.—Artificial flies and baits used in angling.

155 THE NORTHUMBERLAND PATENT TWINE, ROPE, and NET Co. Newcastle-upon-Tyne, Manu.—Samples of herring, trout, and mackerel nets, braided or meshed by machinery; of twines, fishing strings, and lines, rope, spun-yarn, marline, &c.

156 FLYNN, W. Worcester, Inv.—Flexible baits, for salmon, trout, &c.

157 ALLIES, F. Worcester, Inv. and Manu.—Various artificial baits, for salmon, trout, &c.

158 DAVIDSON, G. & W. 17 Quay, Aberdeen, Manu.— Aberdeen salmon bag-net.

159 KELLY & SON, 56 Lower Sackville St. Dublin, Manu. —Fishing tackle; artificial flies, &c.

160 BANIM, M. Kilkenny, Ireland, Inv. and Manu.— Amateur fly-angler's cabinet, made of Irish bog-yew.

161 DENNIS, Rev. J. B. P. Bury St. Edmunds.—Peacock with train spread (copy from nature). Small gull.

162 M'NAIR, J. Tillicoultry, Alloa, Scotland, Manu.— Fishing-rods, exhibited for superiority of execution.

163 PULMAN, G. P. R. Crewkerne, Manu.—Artificial flies, for river fishing.

164 NICHOLLS, W. Chippenham.—Samples of Beaufort Hunt sauce, &c.

165 MORLEY, J. Nottingham, Prod.—Fishing tackle.

166 HARDING, J. P. 83 Hatton Garden.—Feather bonnets of novel manufacture, and in various colours.

167 REMMIE, Misses, 20 New Ormond St. Bloomsbury, Des. and Manu.—Bride cake and other ornaments for table or cabinet, composed of gum.

168 HARMER, H. R. Gt. Yarmouth, Prod.—Net for keeping fish alive.

169 HARVEY, H. King's Head Court, Barbican.—Samples of sauce.

170 DANIEL, T. Burslem.—Subjects cut in paper, by Mrs. Thomas Daniel.

171 GOULD, A. 36 St. Marylebone St. Manu.—Fishing rods and tackle, on improved principles.

172 USTONSON & PETERS, 48 Bell Yd. Temple Bar, Inv. —Bamboo cane fly and salmon fishing-rod. Artificial angling baits, including flies and insects, silkworm gut, taper fly line, &c.

173 PEARCE, T. B.—Fishing tackle.

174 LITTLE & Co. 15 Fetter Lane, Fleet St. Inv.—Superior fly-fishing rod. Improved cane boat or punt-rod. Salmon rods; winches; fly and dubbing books, with tackle and flies.

175 BUCHANAN, J. 191 Piccadilly, Manu.—Three bows of yew wood, cut from the Alps, the first brought to this country. A variety of bows and arrows.

176 FARLOW, C. 221 Strand, Manu.—Fishing rods, tackle, and cases; with various artificial baits and insects.

177 BERNARD, J. 4 Church Pl. Piccadilly, Manu.—A variety of fishing rods and tackle.

178 BAZIN, G. 110 Old St. St. Luke's, Manu.—Assortment of taper quill floats for angling.

179 ALFRED, W. H. 54 Moorgate St. Manu.—Complete set of highly finished fishing tackle.

180 AINGE & ALDRED, 126 Oxford St. Manu.—Bows, arrows, and archery accoutrements. Fishing rods and tackle.

181 FARLOW, J. K. 5 Crooked Lane, City, Manu.—Tackle for salmon fishing, &c.

182 JONES, J. 111 Jermyn St. St. James's—Fishing-rods and tackle.

183 JACOBS, G. 32 Cockspur St. Inv. and Manu.—English and Flemish long bows, arrows, quivers, and accoutrements. The registered protector umbrella. Strangers' guide map of London. Malacca cane. Dragon canes and tortoiseshell walking-stick mounted in gold. Rhinoceros horn and sea-horse's tooth. English sticks, in rough and finished state.

184 JEFFRIES, I. 40 Mulgrave Pl. Woolwich, Manu.— Improved tennis racquets. Irish and English shaped racquets. Racquet and fives balls.

185 LOCAL COMMITTEE, FALMOUTH and PENRYN. — Preserved pilchards. Model of pilot-boat, built by R. Lee, Falmouth. Model of Falmouth river barge, and of the new Mevagissey drift and fishing-boat, made by Richard Treginza. Model of Seine boat, built by P. Lelean, Mevagissey. Nets used in the Cornish fisheries. Apparatus for extracting pumps from mines which are filled with water; inv. by Arthur and Edey. Reversing apparatus, &c. Inv. Mr. R. Hosking, of Perron Foundry.

186 CLAPSHAW, M. High St. Eton.—Bats, stumps, balls, gloves, &c. for cricket.

187 GILBERT, W. Rugby, Manu.—Footballs of leather dressed expressly for the purpose.

188 LAMBERT, ELEANOR, 89 Leman St. Goodman's Fields, Whitechapel, Manu.—Artificial flies, for angling.

189 CLEMENTS, J. Leicester, Inv. and Manu.—Newly invented cricket bat, with flexible handle.

190 MASSEY, W. A. 41 Sir Thomas's Buildings, Liverpool.—Pair of bowls and jack, representing the English game of bowling.

191 DUKE & SON, Penshurst, near Tonbridge, Kent, Manu.—Articles used for the game of cricket.

192 GOURLAY, J. Edinburgh.—Golf balls.

193 PEACOCK, A. 2 Cumberland Row, Islington, Inv.— Board and pieces, for playing the game of Agon, or the Queen's guards; with book of instructions.

194 PAGE, ELEANOR & W. Kennington Common, Manu

—Cricket bats. Gauntlets, India-rubber gloves, leg guards, balls, stumps, &c.

195 MEDWAY, J. 134 St. John St. West Smithfield. Des. and Manu.—Cricket stumps constructed on a novel and simple principle. Reg.

196 LILLYWHITE & SONS, 10 Prince's Ter. Islington, Inv. and Manu.—Cricket bats and balls. Wickham's trap balls. Allen's stumps. Leg-guards, new design. India-rubber gloves, flannel dress, &c.

197 DARK, MATILDA, & SONS, Lord's Cricket Ground, St. Marylebone, Manu.—Cricket bats and wickets.

198 DARK, R. Lord's Cricket Ground, Inv. and Manu.— Tubular India-rubber gloves; gauntlet gloves; leg guards; spiked soles for shoes; and cricket balls.

199 CALDECOURT, W. H. 14 Townsend Rd. St. John's Wood, Marylebone, Manu.—Cricket catapulta, a machine for propelling the ball. Bats and stumps.

200 TREBECK, T. F. 3 Sun St. Bishopsgate.—A variety of rocking-horses, dolls, and miscellaneous toys.

201 GOING, J. Clonmel.—Various soaps.

202 GORDON, C. Museum, Dover, Manu.—A group of stuffed British birds, an owl surrounded by small birds.

203 HARBOR, T. Reading.—Stuffed animals and birds.

204 BEEVOR, J. M.D. Newark.—Forester, a member of the Rufford Hunt.

206 RATTERAY & THOMPSON.—Fishing nets.

207 WALFORD, C. sen. Witham, Essex, Preserver.—A series of preserved British birds.

208 YERBURY, J. 114 Bishopsgate St. Within, Prop.— Staite's patent diaphragm tobacco-pipe bowl, manufactured in stone china by Messrs. Wedgwood and Sons.

209 THOMPSON, H. Weybridge Common, Chertsey, Inv. and Manu.—Imitative cameos, and gold and silver wafers.

210 BRINDLEY, J. Milk St. Bristol.—Small cask, of peculiar construction.

211 REED, J. W. 11 Peel Pl. Kensington.—A stick of a peculiar construction.

212 WALFORD, J. Witham, Essex.—Stuffed birds.

213 BARSHAM, SON & CO. London and Stratford.—Specimen of pulped cloth, a combination of paper with a woven fabric. Emery cloth, glass cloth, and glass paper. Emery, and black-lead. Patent framed door-mat.

214 SACKER, F. C. 7 Epping Pl. Mile End, Des.—Razor-strop, formed of a composition of wool.

215 ROGERS, R. & H. Prospect Row, Walworth, Manu.— Specimens of glass, emery, and sand papers and cloths.

216 BURSELL E. & CLARA, 9 York Ter. Queen's Rd. Hornsey Rd.—Compressible toys.

217 AUSTIN, W. Crowhurst.—A footstool.

218 SHARP, J. Halton, Bucks.—Specimens of carvings.

219 WILLIAMS, T. M.—Case of stuffed birds.

220 FISHER, J. Blandford.—Wire buttons.

221 LEADBEATER, J. Brewer St. Golden Sq.—Stuffed Indian game birds, &c.

222 SPENCER, T. 7 Gt. Portland St. Inv. and Prod.— Preserved birds, on artificial frost and snow.

223 GARDNER, J. 426 Oxford St.—Various specimens of stuffed birds, indigenous to Britain.

224 ANDERSON, R. Dunkeld, Scotland, Manu.—Artificial salmon and trout-flies, for the lakes and rivers of Scotland.

225 FISHER, E. St. Mar's, Wisbech, Inv. and Prod.— Models of stacks, to show a new mode of covering them.

226 SLATER, J. Cheadle, Staffordshire, Inv. and Manu. —Twine reel for drapers, druggists, grocers, &c.

228 DAUBARN, W. Wisbech.—Specimens of reel and ball sewing cottons.

230 QUIN, J. Kidderminster, Inv. Des. and Manu.— Combed wool, in white and various colours. Gothic bird-

cage, cut out of the wood. Lathe, on a new plan, for sitting to work. Improved carpet-shuttles. Novel parasol-frame.

231 CHAMBERLAIN, T. Ashby-de-la-Zouch, Leicester-shire, Manu.—Stones for burnishing plate and gilded work.

232 MOORE & MURPHY, Holborn Hill, Inv. and Manu.— Rich wedding cake, with removeable ornament.

234 DUNBAR, W. Loch Inver, Golspie, Scotland, Preserver.—Two cases of Sutherlandshire wild birds and animals.

237 BROWN & SON, Leeds, Manu.—Bobbins and skewers used in its preparing, spinning, and twisting of cotton; flax bobbins, creel pins, and bosses; worsted bobbins, spools, and carrying rollers; silk bobbins, &c.

239 STANDING, J. & BROTHER, Manchester, Manu.— Braids, in gold, silk, mohair, worsted, and cotton. Laces, and platted lines. Cord for dresses. Bindings, figured and plain; and fringes for trimmings.

240 FLETCHER, H. Manchester, Inv. and Manu.—Brass lettering on glass.

242 HALL, J. Green Gate St. Oldham, Des. and Manu. —A bird-cage, containing 2,522 pieces, and composed of 21 different kinds of wood.

243 BELL & BLACK, 15 Bow Lane, Manu.—Vestas and congreves matches, with machine for cutting them, &c.

244 FLETCHER, W. Burnham, near Bridgwater.—Working models of filtering vessels. Model of Burnham Lighthouse. Specimens of amber, jets, &c., found on the coast of Norfolk, polished.

245 COWPER, E. A. Kensington.—Models for the use of schools.

248 MORELL, H. 149 Fleet St.—Manufacture of lead pencils.

250 WRIGHT, H. Belview Steam Mills, Dublin, Manu.— Buttons, knives and forks, &c. made from bone and horn. Neats-foot oil. Cow hair, used in blanket making, and by felt-makers. Gelatine and portable soup. Farina from potatoes. Indian corn meal. Beet-root sugar.

252 STAIGHT & SONS.—Manufactures from ivory.

253 ILIFF, W. T. Newington.—"London street scenes," "May day," &c., modelled (by the hand) from gutta percha, by Miss E. Moorsom, of Kennington, aged 13.

257 BRISON, R. Bristol, Inv. and Manu.—Models of feet, of a material that will bear nailing or hammering.

259 RITCHIE, J. 2 South back of Canongate, Edinburgh, Manu.—Sash-line, with metallic centre. Metallic cord, for lustres, pictures, and bell-pulls.

261 EARNSHAW, R. J. Doncaster, Manu.—Wool sheets, or top sheets, for packing fine combed wool, called "tops."

262 NAPIER, J. 14 East Seienn St. Edinburgh, Inv.— Printing cases, taking one-third less space than those in general use. Model of a heating or cooling apparatus for rooms. A quick method of finding any place in books. A method of ornamenting end wood in joinery, &c.

266 WANLESS, T. Rock, near Alnwick, Newcastle, Manu. —Lady's pincushion and piercers, made by a working blacksmith.

267 DOWN, S. Ivythorn, near Glastonbury, Des.—Model of a decoy pool, for taking wild fowl.

270 LOCAL COMMITTEE LIVERPOOL.—Specimens of the various productions imported into Liverpool.

272 ALCOCK, S. B. & Co. Dublin Blacking Works, Manu.—Sample of liquid blacking.

274 MITCHELL, Rev. W. Woolwich, Inv.—Horn of a bull, with iron-frame and stuffed buffer attached, to prevent goring. Motto in eleven different languages. Somniferous electric brush, to ensure repose.

275 WESTHEAD & Co. Manchester.—Various small wares, including bell ropes, fringe, curtain holders, tapes, cotton, &c.

277 Lucas, G. 42 Kennedy St. Manchester, Inv. and Manu.—Brass and zinc door, window, and sign-plates, engraved by machinery, the letters filled with a composition which does not crack or decompose.

278 Esdaile, J. Elm Pl. Hulme, Inv. and Manu.—Hat-felt, used by printers of calicoes, silks, woollens, &c. Woollen-felt, for polishing plate-glass, marble, &c. Felted gloves, used by glass-blowers, iron-founders, and others, &c.

280 Smith, W. & A. Mauchline, Ayrshire, and 61 Charlotte St. Birmingham, Manu.—Articles of Scotch fancy wood-work, made chiefly of sycamore, ornamented with Tartan checking, and in the Arabesque and Scoto-Russian styles.

281 Cockerill, R. Banbury, Oxon.—Blacking.

282 Easterling, J.—Anchovy and other sauces.

285 Wood, P. H. 20 Redman's Row, and Assembly Pl Mile End.—Refining powder for coffee, and colouring for soups, gravies, &c.

286 Cocks, E. Reading.—Reading and other sauces.

287 Dutton & Co. Runcorn, Cheshire, Manu.—School, slates manufactured by machinery, framed in mahogany and bird-eye maple.

289 Mallalieu, W. 97 Hatton Garden, Imp.—Models of dwellings and implements made by the Christian Esquimaux, at the Moravian settlements on the coast of Labrador, North America.

290 Local Committee, Hull.—Specimens of the staple imported articles of the port of Hull, accompanied with descriptions and statistical information.

291 Bartlett, A. D. 16a Great College St. Camden Town.—Specimens of taxidermy. Life size models of the dodo, &c.

292 Withers, W. Devizes, Wilts, Prop.—Case of stuffed partridges.

293 Bessent, Maria, 5 Union St. New Bond St. Manu.—Fancy pincushions, match boxes, &c. manufactured from common egg shells.

295 James, J. Redditch, Worcester.—Pins and needles, fish-hooks, needle boxes, and needle books.

297 Chambers, R.—Pins and needles.

301 Herbert, Mrs. F. 20 Royal Avenue Terrace, Chelsea, Inv. amateur. — Chepstow Castle, Monmouthshire, by moonlight. Specimen of Papyrography: a novel method of representing landscapes in tissue-paper, simply by the use of knife and scissors, without the aid of colouring.

302 Rankin, Emily, & Lear, Ellen, South St. Wandsworth, Des. and Manu.—Picture frames of ornamental leather work.

303 Prideaux, Miss, Wellington, Somerset.—A small basket of rice-paper flowers, cut out with scissors.

304 Harrison, Margaret, 19 Bromley St. Commercial Road East.—Victoria Regina, and orchiderus, in wax.

305 Barling & Sons, 142 High St. Camden Town, Des. and Manu.—Silver-mounted meerschaum smoking pipes.

305A Gibbs, D. & W. City Soap Works, Inv. and Manu.—Perfumed patent exhibition, and inlaid cameo soaps. Naples shaving tablets. Naples and inlaid tablets. Samples of patent soft soaps for medical and manufacturing purposes.

306 Morland, J. & Son, 50 Eastcheap, London Bridge.—Umbrellas and parasols.

307 Adair, B. Workington.—Specimens of hair watch guards.

308 Barrett & Son, Beech St. Barbican.—Glass's patent machine for sweeping chimneys.

309 Burch, C. & Son, 32 Pratt Ter. St. Pancras Rd.—Rosewood box, glass top for ornamented pencils, with brass ornaments and screws of the Elizabethan style.

311 Pearce, T. B. Newman St. Oxford St.—Self-acting fishing-rod, by which many lines can be used at the same time, with a variety of newly-invented fishing tackle, &c.

312 Aggio, G. H. Colchester, Des. and Manu.—Ottoman of novel description, &c.

313 Hodge, W. 34 Great Marlborough St. Des. and Manu.—A cabinet writing-case, in ornamented morocco leather, and containing every requisite for correspondence.

315 Stirling, T. Bow Bridge Slate Works, Stratford, Essex, and 38 New Bread St. City.—Patent rapid ascension and royal Albert filters. Chimney piece, table tops, &c. of enamelled slate.

316 Lucas Brothers, 113 Aldersgate St.—Forty-nine different kinds of lozenges, ornamentally stamped, with the quantity of medicine each lozenge contains.

317 Cocks, J. & C. 6 Duke St. Reading, Manu.—Samples of genuine Reading and Old England sauces.

318 Walker, J. 56 Shaftesbury St. New North Rd.—Dried London flowers retaining their natural colours.

319 Schrader, Miss H. 4 Windsor Ter. Old Kent Rd.—Beaded purses, head dresses, &c.

320 Hancock, J. A.—Collection of stuffed birds and animals. (In North Transept.)

Proceed to Class 24, page 125.

Section IV.—FINE ARTS.

Class 30. SCULPTURE, MODELS, AND PLASTIC ART, MOSAICS, ENAMELS, ETC.

—— Areas F. 30 to 32, G. & H. 28 to 32, and I. & J. 28, 29, & 32. ——

FINE ART COURT.

1 Miller, T. 56 Long Acre, Inv. and Manu.—Paintings with silica colours and glass medium, with assortment of materials.

2 Concanen, E. 427 Oxford St. Inv. and Prod.—A marine piece, executed in the new style of aerial tinting.

3 Rowney & Co. 51 Rathbone Pl. Manu.—Artists' Colours brushes, pencils, crayons. Mathematical instruments. Specimens of typo-chromatic printing, inv. by F. W. Rowney, &c.

5 Kearney, W. H. Marlborough Cottage, Brompton, Inv.—Crayon painting, executed with Kearney's Venetian pastils; impervious to damp, and for internal decorations.

6 Robertson & Co. 51 Long Acre, Manu.—Canvas, prepared for painting brushes and pencils. Water colours.

7 Reeves & Sons, 113 Cheapside, Inv. and Manu.—Drawing pencils. Water colours, prepared with wax, &c.

8 Green & Fahey, 62 Charlotte St. Portland Pl. and 15 York Pl. Brompton, Inv.—Folding drawing models, in three series, illustrating the application of perspective, and the principles of light and shade.

9 COOK, J. E. Railway Office, Greenock, Scotland, Inv.—Prepared panel, for amateur painting.

10 GOVERNMENT SCHOOL OF DESIGN, SOMERSET HOUSE. —Designs for carpets, drapery, &c.

11 BURROWS, MARY L. 1 Park St. Islington.—Table top, painted on slate.

12 FARREN, M. 32 Dorset Sq. Des.—Original design for a bracelet. Strap of forget-me-nots.

12A GANN, LOUISA, 31 Norfolk St. Strand, Des.— Model of a flower vase.

13 SEAGER, W. Tavistock. — Model of geometrical staircase.

14 JIBB, J. 12 London St. Fitzroy Sq.—Model for an under-spring state carriage.

15 KEPP & Co. 40, 41, & 42 Chandos St. Charing Cross. —Model of the ball and cross of St. Paul's.

16 OLIVER, G. T. Victoria Ter. St. John's Wood, Des. —Device showing the arrangement and combination of colours of flowers, &c.

17 PAPERA, J. P. Clarendon St. Cambridge, Sculptor. —Queen Elizabeth, Sir Robert Peel, the Saviour, Rubens, Vandyke, Oliver Cromwell, and King Charles I.

18 LASCELLES, E. Wavertree, Des. and Prod.—Models of Wavertree Church and Hall, Whitechapel, &c.

19 JOHNSTON, G. J. Newmarket, Prod. and Des.— Boss, frieze, and tablet for a church ; bracket of flowers.

20 SHARF, G. 16 Wentworth Pl. Dublin, Inv.—Models for the study of elementary drawing.

21 BURNS & PALMER, Manchester, Prod.—Models, in plaster, of windows designed by J. E. Gregan, architect.

22 UNWIN, W. H. Sawbridgeworth, Herts.—A tournament of the time of Queen Elizabeth's reign, cut entirely out of plain paper with scissors.

22A PAPWORTH, W. & J. W. 14A Gt. Marlborough St. Des.—Ornamental pavements. Designs for house decoration and for works in gold and silver, papier-maché, and marble, and for stones, painted glass, &c.

23 BURY, R. 9 Durham St. Southsea, Portsmouth, Pro.— Group of horses, carved in cork. Subject : Story of Mazeppa.

25 COSSENS, E. J. 15 Little Queen St. Holborn, Inv. and Maker.—Model, in elder pith.

26 SILLETT, J. Kelsale, Saxmundham, Suffolk, Des.— Model of ground-floor cottage.

27 WITHERS, W. Devizes, Wilts.—Group of stuffed partridges.

28 BOND, C. Edinburgh, and 53 Parliament St. London —Model of Highland cottage, combining simplicity of construction, comfort, warmth, ventilation, and economy.

29 FOX, C. Brighton, Des. and Mod.—Design for a pediment.

29A FOX, E. Brighton, Prop.—Statuettes in plaster: Chaucer and Spenser.

30 WYATT, M. DIGBY, 77 Great Russell St. Bloomsbury, Des.—Designs for manufactures and decoration, and for bookbinding. New combinations, mosaics, and encaustic paving. Frontispiece for works, published for the designer by Mr. Day, of Gate Street, Lincoln's Inn Fields. Stained glass memorial window, &c.

31 HARVEY, F. 1 Oriel St. Oxford, Inv.—Easel, for artists sketching out of doors, containing everything required by the artist.

31A SMITH, H. E. Saffron Walden, Prop.—Sheets of ancient designs, reproduced for modern ornamental floors.

32 PEARCE, E. E. Nailsea, near Bristol, Des.—Model, in glass, of a house, showing plain brickwork. Another, showing freestone work.

33 CALDWELL, G. Lichfield, Des. and Prod.—Bas-relief, from Burns' poem of Tam o' Shanter, in plaster.

34 BROWN, J. 71 Herbert St. New North Rd. Des.— Drawing-book, for elementary schools.

35 LIMNER, L.—Shaksperian shield.

36 CORNS, W. Waterloo Pl. Edinburgh, Manu.—Model of modern Jerusalem, for illustrating biblical history.

37 STANDIDGE, HARRIET, & Co. 36 Old Jewry, Prod. —Illuminated Kalendar. Specimens of printing in colours and tints, by lithography.

38 COWELL, S. H. Ipswich, Suffolk.—Specimens of anastatic printing, as applied to original drawings in chalk or ink, ancient deeds, wood engravings, archæological illustrations, &c.

40 KRONHEIM, J. M. 32 Paternoster Row, Eng. and Printer.—Colour printing. The Descent from the Cross, after Rubens, &c.

41 DONALDS, W. J. & C. 29 Artillery Pl. West, Bunhill Row, Des. and Eng.—Silver waiters; glass dessert plates, &c., elaborately ornamented.

42 BURKE, Bull Head Ct. Newgate St.—Model of Exhibition, fancy stationery, paper ornaments, &c.

43 WARD, M. & Co. Corn Market, Belfast.—Specimen of chromo-lithography; five plates, printed in gold and colours, representing St. Patrick's bell and its elaborate shrine.

44 WILSON, H. Glasgow.—Ornamental printing.

46 VOKINS, J. & W. 5 John St. Oxford St. Inv. and Manu.—Registered, revolving, double-standard folio-frame.

47 RAYNER, Mrs. 15 Berners St. Oxford St.—Diamond engraving on black marble.

48 WOOD, J. York, York.—Kegs for carrying wine, spirits, &c.

49 EARLE, J. H. 50 Upper Marylebone St.—Painted screen and table top.

50 HUMPHREYS, N. H. Dorchester Pl. Blandford Sq. Des. and Prod.—Specimens of decorative printing, and bookbinding.

52 BRETT, G. 21 Tysoe St. Wilmington, Sq. Des.— Onyx gem cameos: Cupid and Doves ; heads of Ariadne, Bacchantes, Goddess of Youth, and Medusa.

53 ABBOTT, G. 4 Percy St. Bedford Sq.—1. Alexander the Great crossing the Granicus. 2. Death of William Rufus.

54 JONES, O. 9 Argyll Pl. Regent St.—Printing in colours from stone for illustrated works.

55 WILSON, A. 17 Queenhithe.—Design for a book cover, carved with a penknife ; executed in cardboard by Walter Blackett, architect.

56 HARMER, J. jun. 10 Thornhill Bridge Pl. Pentonville, Des. and Sculp.—Sculptured frieze in plaster.

57 CROOK, F. 5 Carnaby St. Manu.—Large white lily, in wrought-iron.

58 DUELIN, M. 41 Tottenham Court Rd. Manu.— Coloured lithographic labels by a new process.

59 LEIGHTON, J. 40 Brewer St. Golden Sq. and 19 High St. Camden Town, Des.—The Seven Ages of Man ; des. for bas-relief, illuminated and mounted as a table top. Monograms, &c. Des. for medals, a chandelier, book covers, &c. Specimens of ink-lithography.

60 BURSILL, G. H. & H. 9 York Terr. Queen's Rd. Hornsey Rd. Inv.—Models in infrangible wax.

61 HELLYER & SON, Northumberland Wharf, Blackwall, Des.—Group of seventeen figures, carved in wood, on a pedestal.

62 FRENCH, C. College, Eton, Bucks, Des. and Manu. —Two candlesticks, carved of walnut-tree wood.

63 JULLIEN, & Co. 214 Regent St. Prop.—Ornamental printed music, in oil colours and from stone. The music engraved on pewter, transferred and printed from stone.

63A LEAKE, F. 9 Warwick St. Regent St. Des. and Manu.—Patent relievo leather tapestry hangings, in gold, silver, and colours. Oak bookcase, with relievo-leather carvings, designs in bookbinding, medallions, ornaments, &c.

64 HANHART, M. & N. 64 Charlotte St. Rathbone Pl. Prod.—Chromolithography, in graduated tints.

65 DAVIS, W. 13 Osnaburgh St. Regent's Pk. Des.—Ascent and Descent of Sabrina, from Comus. Titania and Oberon, "Come, trip we under the night-shade."

66 CHAPPELL & Co. 50 New Bond St. Prop.—Specimens of lithographic music printing,

67 EDWARDS, J. 40 Robert St. Hampstead Rd. Des. and Sculp.—Bas-reliefs: The last Dream ; Daughter of the Dawn, &c.

68 DICKES, W. 5½ Old Fish St. Doctors' Commons, Inv. &c.—Oil colour printing.

69 SOLOMONS, A. 22 Cambridge Sq. Hyde Park, Manu.—An ivory pagoda, after Sir Wm. Chambers, turned octagon, on a base of cannel coal. Fine specimens of old engine turning, &c., from the south of France.

70 JONES, A. J. 135 Stephen's Green, Dublin, Des. and Manu.—Series of Irish bog-yew decorative furniture, designed to illustrate history, antiquities, animal and vegetable productions, &c., of Ireland.

71 HULLMANDEL & WALTON, 51 Gt. Marlborough St. Inv. and Prod.—Drawing on stone with the stump. Combination of the stump style and lithographic chalk. Lithotint (patent), drawn on the stone with liquid ink and a brush.

72 DEACOCK, E. 26 Union St. Middlesex Hospital.—Working model of a newly invented mat machine, for wiping shoes.

73 TRUNDLE, Mrs. Cambridge.—Wax figures of Her Majesty and Prince Albert.

74 ROGERS, W. G. 10 Carlisle St. Soho.—A model in wood for a crozier head, intended to be worked in gold. Historical cup, in memory of William III. A boldly carved trophy on a gilt ground. Two brackets of wood carved and gilt, with porcelain figures, by Chamberlain from models, by W. G. Rogers. A toilet-glass suggested by the Duchess of Sutherland. A bust of Sir Walter Scott, carved by J. Engel, &c.

75 TRUEFITT, G. 6 Bloomsbury Sq. Des.—Design for a wrought-iron canopied tomb ; the roof and coloured parts to be of porcelain, and the figure of alabaster.

76 GRAF, C. 1 Great Castle St. Regent St. Manu.—Lithographic engravings, tinted and coloured. Illuminated prayers, ancient missal style, &c.

77 UNDERWOOD, T. Union Passage, Birmingham.—Lithographic print, exhibiting a new process of producing imitations of water-colour drawings and oil-paintings.

78 LAYARD, CAROLINE, M. Bird's Grove, Coventry, Mod.—Models of the Nineveh marbles now in the British Museum, by a relative of Dr. Layard, self-taught.

79 ALLEN, C. B. 12 Lower Porchester St. Hyde Park.—Vase in red clay. Design for a monumental cross to the memory of William Caxton, suggested by the Dean of St. Paul's.

80 DAY & SON, 17 Gate St. Lincoln's Inn Flds.—Specimens of tinted and chromo-lithography, by and after L. Haghe, G. Hawkins, E. Walker, M. Digby Wyatt, and F. Bedford.

81 GORDON, J. 46 Park St. Bristol, Carver.—Carvings in box-wood. Vase, from the antique ; and Belisarius.

82 WILLIAMS, J. 14 Alpha Rd. Regent's Park, Prop.—A Doric column, in various woods, in imitation of marble, ornamented with portraits of Raphael, Michael Angelo, and Vitruvio, and a statue of Minerva, by Bonzanigo.

83 SANGIOVANNI, B. 13 Clarence Pl. Brighton.—Terra cotta models of a wild boar, of a group of dogs, and of a stag hunted by dogs.

84 PULLEN, R. Farnham, Surrey, Des.—Carvings in

wood : The Village Dance, the Wearied Pedlar, and The Gipsy Fiddler.

85 MARTIN & HOOD, Great Newport St. London.—Specimen of lithographic drawing and printing.

86 HARVEY, A. Penzance, Prod.—Carvings in box wood : Peter the Great, and Laocoon ; Wild Sports of the East ; Attack of the Lion.

87 MITCHELL, J. T. Percy Pl. Clapham Rd. Prod.—Specimen of charred chesnut-wood engravings: The execution of Saint John. Chapeau de Brigand, by T. Uwins, R.A.

88 RINGHAM, H. Car St. Ipswich, Manu.—Group of wheat and poppies, carved in lime-wood.

89 WALLIS, T. W. Louth, Lincolnshire, Des. and Sculp.—Spring, represented by grape-buds, apple-blossoms, &c. Group of dead game. The golden plover. Group of fruit, flowers, and corn, &c., all carved in lime-tree wood.

90 KEHOE, J. Wexford, Ireland.—Frame, carved in bog oak.

92 DE GROOT, C. 1 Swift's Row, Dublin, Des. and Manu. (Agent in London, J. Kendall, 8 Harp Lane, Great Tower St.)—Basket of fruit, flowers, and ornaments, carved in sycamore ; oval picture frame, in lime-tree.

93 CARRICK, C. Canterbury, Des. and Manu.—Loo table slab, inlaid with variously-coloured woods, whalebone, cane, ebony, &c. Another, with 253 different kinds of woods, British and Foreign, representing geometrical figures, &c.

95 LONGLEY, W. H. 1 Eaton Pl. Park St. Oxford St. Manu.—Wood carving: basket of flowers, and two horns of plenty.

96 MILLS, ISABELLA, F. Little Paxton, St. Neots, Hunts. Inv. and Prod.—Copies of engravings etched with hot irons. The instruments invented by the exhibitor.

97 CALVERT, Rev. W. 3 Gt. College St. Westminster, Des. and Artist.—Specimen of pyrography, executed upon lime-tree, with a common poker, heated to a red heat.

98 WRIGHT, F. 23 Cirencester Pl. Fitzroy Sq. Des. and Sculp.—Bracket for an oratory, in mahogany.

99 MILLBANK, D. 10 Cumberland Pl. New Rd.—Two inlaid table tops.

100 NEWHAM, R. 15 Blackheath Hill, Kent.—Carved writing desk and work box.

101 PERRY, W. Bridge St. Taunton, Des. and Executor.—Vase of roses, &c., carved in boxwood.

102 TWELTIDGE, —. Mansfield, Notts.—Carved panel, "Othello."

102 WALKER, J. Gt. Market, Newcastle-upon-Tyne, Prod.—Carved oak panel, stained as old oak: Christ blessing little Children.

103 ESQUILANT, F. 346 and 541 Oxford St. Manu.—Leather flowers and fruit, adapted for upholstery and decorations.

104 COOK, G. Hyde Park Lodge.—Carvings in lime-tree wood,

105 SUTTON, H. 93 Vauxhall St. Vauxhall, Manu.—Picture frame, inlaid with tortoiseshell and mother-of-pearl.

108 STALON, J. 42 Berwick St. Soho, Des. and Mann.—Inkstand carved in English walnut.

109 BROOKER, S. Trinity St. Cambridge, Des.—Model of a 120-gun ship, in cork. Design of the great quadrangle of Trinity College.

110 COOKES & SONS, Warwick, Des. and Manu.—The Kenilworth oak buffet, with sculptured relievos, illustrative of events at Kenilworth Castle, from a celebrated oak tree grown upon its domain.

111 FLETCHER, J. 71 Patrick St. Cork, Ireland, Des. and Mauu.—Table ; the pillar represents a fighting gladiator, carved in solid Irish oak ; the top, a shield in fancy pollard oak.

111A BEESON, J. Wilmot St. Derby.—The Lord's Prayer

in illuminated characters, consisting of twenty-six different styles of lettering, executed with a sable pencil.

112 CUNDALL & ADDEY, 21 Old Bond St. Pub.—Colour printing, by Leighton, Lamb's Conduit St. Wood-cut-printing, by Robson, Levy, and Franklin.

113 KING, T. R., 5 Church Row, Islington, Inv. and Des.—New style of painting, consisting in the application of finely-pulverized colour to a granulated oil-ground.

114 LEITH, S. 9 South St. Andrew St. Edinburgh, Inv.—Specimens of a substitute for the use of India paper in plate printing.

115 BAXTER, G. 11 & 12 Northampton Sq. Inv. Manu. and Pat.—Specimens of oil-colour picture-printing : historical, portraits, architectural, and landscapes.

116 NISBET, J. & Co. 21 Berners St. Oxford St.—Bible, with carved boxwood cover by W. G. Rogers.

117 MYERS, —.   Specimen of patent printing, &c.

118 HAMER, M. J. 6 Kennington Row, Des.—Chemical drawing.

119 HARVEY, J. K. 25 Ely Pl. Holborn Hill.—Designs for carpet, chintz, &c.

120 ROBINSON, F. K. Whitby, Yorkshire, Maker.-Model of the ruins of Whitby Abbey before the fall of the great western window in 1780, and of the tower in 1830.

121 COLLEY, G. 8 Upper Dorset St. Belgrave Rd. Pimlico.—Plaster model, representing "The Peaceful Arts triumphant over War," with a medallion of Prince Albert in the centre.

123 WHITING, C. Beaufort House, Strand, Prop.—Specimens of compound plate printing, cameo embossing, and relief engravings.

124 MITCHELL, Mrs. 50 Wigmore St. Cavendish Sq.—Model of a lady in the Court costume of the reign of Queen Victoria.

125 LUMSDEN, Miss I. 8 Trevor Ter. Knightsbridge, Des. and Manu.—Tableau of flowers, modelled in wax, festooned with acorns and leaves.

126 SIMMONS, J. 6 Portobello Ter. Kensington Park, Notting Hill, Manu.—Statuary marble work-box, carved in bold relief.

129 WOLFF & SON, 23 Church St. Spitalfields, Manu.—Creta Laevis, or permanent coloured chalks, in cedar. Athenian crayons. Sketch book: reg. Cumberland, East India, and Spanish black lead. Drawing pencils, &c.

130 WATSON, E. F. 201 Piccadilly.—Specimens of gilding, bronzing, &c.

131 BARKER, T. J. 101 Stanhope St. Hampstead Rd. Des.—The Dying Troubadour. Vide Sir Walter Scott.

132 HAWKINS, B. W. 57 Cambridge St. Hyde Park Gate, Des.—Group in bronze of the European bison or aurochs.

133 RICHARDSON, E. 7 Melbury Ter. Mod.—William Marshall, Earl of Pembroke; temp. Henry the Third.—Bronze. John Gower reciting his poems to Richard the Second.—Bronze. Horse in full action.—Bronze. Youthful Athletæ, in plaster of Paris.

135 HATFIELD, J. A. 21 Cumberland St. Middlesex Hospital, Manu.—Bronze bust of Her Majesty, after Chantrey. Bronze figure, Youth at the Stream. The Gladiator. Napoleon. Venus at the Bath. Mercury.

136 COPLAND, C. South Villas, Kennington Oval, Prop.—Fac-simile of Portland vase.

137 CHRISTIE, A. Royal Institution, Edinburgh, Des.—Twine-holder.

138 SHERWOOD IRON WORKS.—Casting from an antique statuette of Bacchus.

139 BOOTE, T. & R. Burslem, Staffordshire.—Portland vase, fawn ground, white figures, about three feet high : process patented. Vases, groups of flowers, and statuettes, in Parian.

140 CONTE, —, 454 New Oxford St.—Statuary marble.

140A MASSEY & Co. Panklabanon, 58 Baker St.—Ornamental flower-stand.

141 MABEY, J. 26 Paradise St. Lambeth, Mod.—Model of a testimonial to the memory of H. Handley, Esq., M.P. Erected at Sleaford, from the des. of W. Boyle, Esq.

142 FOWLER, C. 1 Gordon Sq.—Model of St. John's church, Paddington, executed in card-board by Mr. T. Dighton.

143 LEWIS, D. Ragland, Maker.—The remains of the Cistercian Abbey of St. Mary, at Tintern, Monmouthshire.

144 PEAKE, C. C. 5 Grosvenor Pl. Camberwell New Rd. Des.—Model in wax of the Stephanotus plant, in flower, forming an ornament for a plateau, &c.

145 GILL, G. New Buildings, Ludlow, Prod.—Model of the chapel in Ludlow Castle, a copy of the Holy Sepulchre at Jerusalem.

146 CRIBB, T. J. Kilburn, Manu.—Working model landscape.

147 COCK, H. 6 Brewer St. Manu.—Etching ground. Bordering wax for etching.   Leo Nino and abbess, in silk.

148 POWELL, J. Trentham, Newcastle-nnder-Lyme.—Model of Shakspeare's house as it now exists.

149 WEBBER, J. Corfe Castle, Mason.—Design for a tomb in Purbeck stone, on a slab of Purbeck marble.

151 WEIR, J. 56 High St. Edinburgh, Maker.—Model of John Knox's house and part of High Street, Edinburgh.

152 ASHTON, W. 154 Sloane St. Chelsea, Prod.—Model of St. James's church, Louth, Lincolnshire. Executed in Bristol card-board, with a penknife.

153 WEBBER & BARTLETT, Bridge St. and St. James's St. Taunton, Prop.—Model of a cathedral, carved in oak.

154 MALING, —.—Design for a font.

156 BEAUCLERC, G. 23A Grosvenor St. West.—Specimens of sculpture. Statuettes in Irish clay.

157 BALL, R. LL.D. University Museum, Dublin, Des.—Model of the ancient harp, commonly called the harp of Brien Boroihme (Brien Boru), king of Ireland.

158 STEVENS, G. H. 14 Stafford Row, Pimlico, Des. and Manu. — Candelabra, in Keen's cement, in imitation of marble, lable tops, &c. inlaid with glass mosaic.

159 BRODIE, W. North St. Andrew St. Edinburgh, Des.—Group in plaster : Little Nell and her Grandfather.

160 DIGHTON, T. D.—Model of part of the Record Office.

161 MONTEFIORE, Sir M. B. Grosvenor Gate, Park Lane, Prop.—Two vases carved out of a species of sandstone of Jerusalem, with a penknife, by M. Schnitzer, of that city.

161A DAY, R. 1 Rockingham Pl. New Kent Rd. Mod.—Portico of the Parthenon at Athens ; Temple Church, Fleet St. ; portico of the Pantheon at Rome ; the Martyrs' Memorial at Oxford ; a chancel in decorated Gothic, the window from Herne Church, Kent.

162 WILBY, T. St. Bartholomew's Hospital, Maker.—Model of St. Paul's cathedral, in cardboard.

163 BAINBRIDGE, J. Gilling, Richmond, Yorkshire.—Model of Clumber House, the seat of the Duke of Newcastle, in cardboard.

164 GORRINGE, W. Chichester, Manu.—Architectural models in paper.

165 GRAINGER, R. Newcastle-upon-Tyne, Des.—Models of proposed Town and County Courts, and of the Central Exchange Buildings, Newcastle-upon-Tyne.

166 MIDDLETON, J. Bondgate, Darlington, Prod.—Model of York Minster, to a scale of 15 feet to the inch.

167 SMITH, T. jun. 49 Eastcheap, Manu.—Models in cork: Royal Exchange and Monument of London.

168 HOARE, M. Langport, Somerset, Manu. — Cork

model of the abbey church, Bath, to a scale of 1-18th of an inch to the foot.

169 FULTON, H. Stillorgan, Dublin, Des.—Model of a temple.

170 SMITH, F. S. Stourbridge, Des.—Model, in plaister, of a column, from a design for a building for the Exhibition.

171 TOBIN, Ballincollig, near Cork, Ireland, Inv.—Models, in ivory, of Roman and other temples. Bust of Her Majesty, &c., cut out of the solid ivory with a lathe.

172 MERRETT, H. S. 82 Fetter Lane, Des. and Manu.—Model for a general hospital.

173 BALLY, W. 54 King St. Manchester, Inv. and Manu. —Busts in miniatnre, in imitation of phrenology.

174 WOOD, C. 31 Paternoster Row.—Trophy of War, and the Four Seasons, in gum paste.

175 BARDWELL, W. 4 Gt. Queen St. Westminster.—Models for architectural designs. Model, Labourers' Friend Society's cottages. Design for improvement of Westminster in 1832.

176 SWAIN, T.—Model of church and stage coach, in cardboard.

177 COTTON. D. Longwood, near Huddersfield.—Model of the Leeds Industrial Training School.

178 SCOLLICK, H. C. Highgate Lane, Balsall Lane, near Birmingham, Manu.—Model of St. Paul's Cathedral made from card-board by a penknife.

179 LIMEUSE, CHARLOTTE, Delganey, Ireland, Prod.—Models, in elder pith, of Great Cross, and cross of Muiredach, Monasterboice; cross at Clonmacnoise, &c.

180 HARRISON, W.—Model of a house built on Putney Heath.

181 DICKENSON, J. 1 Waterloo Pl. Commercial Rd.—Model of York Minster, executed with a penknife.

182 TITE, W. F.R.S. 42 Lowndes Sq. Des.—Model of Portico and west front of the Royal Exchange, London.

183 WYATT, J. 33 Dudley Grove, Paddington, and 33 Spital Sq. Sculp.—Model of a Quadriga, with allegorica. figures of Britannia, attended by Peace and Industry. Designed for a triumphal arch.

184 MILNES, T. Judd Pl. East. Euston Squ. Des. and Sculp.—Design for monument to the memory of Lord G. Bentinck. Groups of animals, &c.

185 MAKEPEACE, ELIZA, 7 Manor St. Clapham, Surrey, Mod.—Models in wax:—the *Lilium lancifolium speciosum. Gloxinia perryana. Cymbidium eburneum, and Phalænopsis amabilis. Rhododendron cunninghamii,* and improved method of preparing wax for modelling flowers, &c.

186 STIRLING, ELIZABETH, Mrs. Pinn's, St. Thomas, Exeter, Des.—Statuette of Waverley, in ivory. Carved by a self-taught artist, 20 years of age.

187 WATKINS, H. Newport, Monmouthshire, Des. and Sculptor.—Group in marble: Death of Llewellin, the last Prince of Wales.

188 CHRISTIE, J. Carmylie, Arbroath, Des.—Groups in burnt clay, characteristie of the Scottish peasantry.

189 ANDERSON, W. County Pl. Perth, Des. and Mod.—A Highlander throwing the "putting-stone," with figures in relief, illustrative of highland games.

190 FRANCHI, G. J. 15 Myddleton St. Manu.—Statuettes in imitation of ivory. Designed by C. Grant.

191 ROSS, H. 15A Douro Pl. Kennington.—Statuette of Sir R. Peel (in wax).

192 DAYMOND, J. 5 Regent Pl. Westmer. Des. and Sculp.—Vase and flowers, in marble.

193 RITCHIE, J. 92 Princes St. Edinburgh, Des.—Statue in marble, of His Grace the Duke of Wellington.

194 CHEVERTON, B. 38 Camden St. Camden Town, Inv.—Carvings by machinery. Those in ivory and marble not finished by hand.

195 LEES, J. Hinckley, Maker.—Model of the stocking-

frame introduced into Hinckley, by W. Iliffe, in the 17th century, which, with some improvements is still in use.

196 WORRALL, C. 20 Little Drummond St. Euston Sq. Des. and Mod.—Specimens of modelling and casting. Tomb of Edward the Black Prince in Canterbury Cathedral, &c.

197 PALMER, W. 144 Western Rd. Brighton, Inv.—Revolving table for modellers, &c. Callipers, for reducing or enlarging to three different scales.

199 ALLIN, J. 26 Cannon St. Rd. East.—Group in wax: Sir Robert Peel and the Duke of Wellington, des. and mod. by J. G. Bullock.

200 WILSON, G. at Hime and Addison's, St. Ann's Sq. Manchester.—Cribbage-board inlaid with the nacre of a species of Pinna from the Pacific.

201 HINE, E. Orchard St. Kensington, Mod.—Model of a carriage in card-board. Every part made to act.

202 EVANS, J. 2 Kender St. New Cross.—Models of St. Mary's church, Whitechapel, and Swiss cottage.

203 WRIGHT, C. 8 Torriano Ter. Kentish Town, Des. and Mod.—Statuette of a sleeping baby, modelled from life, and cast in composition, to imitate marble.

204 MOSSMAN, W. 17 Rodney St. Pentonville, Des. and Manu.—Exhibition building in perforated paper. Lace and perforated papers. Decoration of rooms. Candelabra.

205 VINN, T. 6 Union Walk, Kingsland Rd. Des.—Specimen of single-leaf gilding, imitation or-molu on plaster.

206 RUSSELL, G. 4 Dee St. Aberdeen.—Snow-ball fight at school, in relief. Boy with dog.

208 JORDAN, C. Manchester.—Ivory balls, turned.

208A FOOTS, Mrs. 2 Little Chapel St. Westminster.—Feather flowers.

209 WOOD, C. H. 2 High St. Poplar.—Engraving on shell.

210 JACOT, H. L. Coventry St. Des.—Egg-shells carved with views inside, and others engraved on.

211 SMITH, H. A. 2 Caroline Pl. Hampstead Rd. Haverstock Hill, Des. and Exec.—Gothic ceiling of the fifteenth century, and a group in plaster, relief book-cover, designed by L. Limner.

212 BAETENS, MISS, 18 Oxendon St. Haymarket. —Miniature pack of playing cards, painted by hand, size half an inch, and other miniature articles.

213 SMITH, MARY A. P. Des. and Manu.—Model of an English villa home, furnished throughout.

214 LUNTLEY, J. & Co. New Broad Ct.—Specimen of machine engraving.

215 MORGAN, H. K. G. M.P. Johnstown Castle, Wexford, Ireland, Prop.—Model of Johnstown Castle, county Wexford, Ireland, the seat of Mr. Grogan Morgan, M.P.

216 PULHAM, J. Waltham Cross, Broxbourn, Des. and Manu.—A rich pale red terra-cotta Gothic vase on a granulated pedestal. Specimens of stone-like cement (at the basin of the crystal fountain).

217 HOLDING, MRS. SYBELLA, 31 Mount Pleasant, Liverpool, Des. and Maker.—Pair of wax figures, fancy costume; wax figure of Her Majesty, the drapery and gold trimmings in wax; groups of flowers; and shells in wax.

218 SEAL, J. Worship St. Shoreditch.—Model of Crosby Hall, Bishopsgate; built about 1470, by Sir John Crosby, Sheriff of London, and inhabited by Richard III.

219 FREWER, J. R. 105 Upper Thames St. Des. and Manu.—Model of a Gothic conservatory or fern-house.

220 MECHI, J. J. Tiptree Hall farmery, near Kelvedon, Essex, Des.—Working model of Tiptree Hall farmery, near Kelvedon; the model by H. S. Merrett, 83 Fetter Lane, London; the machinery of the model by G. F. Campbell, 17 Addington Street, York Road, Lambeth. The models of animals by Vincenzo Ruffoni, and Forzano, 4 Greville Street, Hatton Garden.

221 CAPLIN, J. H. I. Strawberry Hill, Pendleton, Manchester, Des. and Executor.—Topographical oil painting: Bird's-eye view of the gulf of Naples. An illustrative expression of the laws by which the surface of the earth assumes particular forms.

222 CLIFFORD, W. Exeter, Prop.—Models made of the pith of the common green rush, used in making rushlights.

223 GUSHLOW, G. 34 Newman St. Oxford St. Inv.— Composition table and plaster casts, in imitation of bronze, steel, and gold. Portland vase, the Nero cup, &c. in frosted silver.

224 MONTANARI, N. 29 Upper Charlotte St. Fitzroy Sq. Mod.—Figures, illustrative of Mexican town and savage life.

225 PIDGLEY, F. J. Conniger Cottage, Torre, Teignmouth Rd. near Torquay, Prop.—A plateau in Florentine marble, representing the fall of Troy, and the Greeks celebrating their victory.

226 BINGLEY, H. 17½ Kensington Pl. Holywell St. Westmr. Des. and Manu.—Enamelled slate tables. Imitations of marbles, and specimens of enamelled slate, for casing walls.

227 CRADDOCK, T. Wisbech, Prod.—Photographic copy of Holloway's print of Raphael's Elymas ; of Vandyke's St. Ambrose refusing Theodosius admittance into the church, &c.

228 CALVERT, W. 43 Clerkenwell-green.—Ornamental engraved zinc plate inlaid with different metals.

228A BULMAN, J. Kelso, Roxburghshire, Scotland, Des. —Model of a farm steading, erected at Wark, in the county of Northumberland, in the year 1850.

229 CRICHTON, G. North Bridge, Edinburgh, Des. and Manu.—Specimens of Scotch pebble mosaic work. Chatelains of silver scrolls, &c., ornamented with enamel of various colours. Silver claret jug, enriched enamelled scroll. Ornaments entirely new design.

230 RUSSELL, S. 3 Darnley Ter. Gravesend, Inv.—Specimen of a new process for producing from a print of a line engraving a fac-simile on steel.

230A DOWSE, HENRIETTA, 39 Upper Charlotte St. Fitzroy Sq. Inv. and Des.—Painting on vellum, in gold, silver, and colours, with raised work.

231 HOLMER, S.—Fragments of the Portland vase.

231A HUMPHREYS, J. 13 Howard St. Strand, Inv. and Manu.—Portable metallic letters, to be fixed on glass.

232 ROCHEAD, J. T. Glasgow, Des.—Model of the arch at Dundee, erected to commemorate Her Majesty's landing there in 1844.

232A WHISHAW, F. 1 St. John St. Adelphi.—Map of London.

233 GREEN, J. 109 Gt. Portland St. Des. and Eng.—A military trophy engraved on zinc.

234 ETHERINGTON, H. 2 West St. Pimlico.—Two enamelled table-tops, in imitation of glass mosaic.

235 ALDRED, S. working printer, 38 Fetter Lane, Sculp. —The Shakspeare Jubilee.

235A THOMAS, J. 9 Old Church St. Paddington.—Design for Preston Hall, modelled by T. Dighton.

236 THOMSON, J. 57 Devonshire St. Portland Pl.— Design for a colossal time-piece adapted for silver or bronze manufacture.

237 HASLEM, J. 1 Wilton Pl. West, Regent's Park, Prod. —Enamel paintings on gold. The Queen in her bridal dress ; the Prince of Wales and Prince Alfred, after Winterhalter, &c. from the collection of H.R.H. Prince Albert. Three enamels on porcelain: The Good Shepherd, after Murillo ; the Infant Samuel, after Reynolds ; and Sibilla Eritrea, after Domenichino.

238 BONE, H. P. 22 Percy St. Prod.—Enamel paintings on gold. Landscape after Morlu. Mater Dolorosa after Guido. Frances, Marchioness Camden, after Reynolds. Frank Hals. Peter the Great. Christ and Judas, after

Guido. Pastoral, infant Saviour sleeping on the Cross, after Murillo, &c.

239 CHABOT, C. 9A Skinner St. Snow Hill, Des. and Eng.—Specimens of transfer zincography, medallion, and sculpture engraving, by machinery.

240 LAING, J. Calton Hill, Edinburgh, Des. and Manu. —Glass chess or draught board.

241 ESSEX, W. 3 Osnaburgh St. Regent's Park.—An extensive collection of enamel paintings, from the collections of Her Majesty, H.R.H. Prince Albert, the Duke of Richmond, H. S. Hope, Esq. the Marchioness of Douro, Lord Overston, the Countess of Elgin, the Duke of Northumberland, and the Duke of Buccleuch.

242 CARRICK, T. 10 Montague St. Portman Sq. Inv.— Application of white marble to miniature painting. The frame by H. Vine, 2 Albion Place, Little Chelsea.

243 DE LARA, D. 3 Alfred Pl. Bedford Sq. Des. and Inv.—Illuminated design on vellum, in colours and gold, forming a chess-table with arabesque borderings, &c.

244 HARRIS, J. 40 Sidmouth St. Regent's Sq. Prod.— Imitations of ancient typography, by Caxton, Wynkyn de Worde, Pynson, &c. Italian illuminated painting of the 16th cent. Holbein's Dance of Death.

245 GEAR, J. W. 5 Charlotte St. Fitzroy Sq. Inv.— Specimens of a composition to supersede ivory, for large water-colour paintings. Two paintings executed on the material illustrating the effect.

246 CHESTERS, S. 1 Blomfield Rd. Maida Hill, Prod.— The Holy Family: a specimen of enamel painting on porcelain, after the picture in the National Gallery by Murillo.

247 GOULD, J. 20 Broad St. Golden Sq. Inv.—A new mode of representing the luminous and metallic colouring of the Trochilidæ, or humming birds.

248 COX, G. J. Polytechnic Inst. Inv.—Specimens of transfer of delicate copper and steel-plate engravings to lithographic stone.

249 BELL, W. C. 44 Dean St. Soho Sq. Prod.—Enamel painting: Ecce Homo, after Correggio.

250 NEWTON, Sir W. J. 6 Argyle St.—Pictures painted on ivory, joined together by the artist by a process of his own invention. The Homage. The marriage of Her Majesty, and the christening of the Prince of Wales, containing portraits of Her Majesty, Prince Albert. &c.

251 NICHOLS, MARY ANN, 7 St. Michael's Ter. Pimlico, Inv. and Des.—Imitation cameos.

252 LAROCHE, M. 65 Oxford St. Des. and Prod.—The Bath. The Evening Star. Daguerreotype.

253 DOE, E. High St. Worcester, Des.—Specimens of enamelling upon porcelain plates. Scene from Shakspeare's Richard the Second, &c.

254 VOIGTLANDER, EVANS, & Co. 3 Lowndes Ter. Knightsbridge, Pro —Daguerreotype portraits, by an improved instantaneous process. Artist, E. T. Pickering.

255 TROTMAN, S. Clarendon Rd. Notting Hill, Inv.— Printing on glass for ornamental purposes, such as glazing conservatories, windows, &c., and for philosophical purposes, such as dissolving views, &c.

256 PRING, Dr. J. H. Weston-super-Mare, Inv. and Des. —Specimens of ornamental engraving on polished steel, effected by means of voltaic electricity.

257 BYRN, O. 9 Monmouth Rd. Westbourne Grove, Des. &c.—Ornamental framework in cork.

258 BREMNER, J. James Ct. Edinburgh, Des. and Chaser. —Specimens of silver embossed chasing in heraldic and other styles of ornament, intended chiefly to be used for brooches.

259 HASSE, E. Leeds.—Ornamental frame and flowers.

260 YEO, D. D. Ashburton, Devonshire, Prop.—Specimen of oil painting on white velvet ; adapted for the coverings of chairs, ottomans, sofas, &c.

261 GARDIE, L. 59 Westbourne Green, Hyde Park Gardens, Sculp.—Bronze bust of Sir Robert Peel, and the Marquis de la Roche Jacquelin.

262 BATSFORD, J. 22 Stafford Place South, Pimlico, Sculp.—The kestrel hawk and butcher bird.

263 STAVELEY, T. K. late R. E. Old Steiningford, Ripon.—Relief map of Linz, Upper Austria, showing the entrenched camp of Maximilian Towers Des. by T. Firth.

264 BROWN, G. 25 Newman St. Oxford St. Des. and Manu. — Figure candelabra for the drawing-room, with figures and dolphins of carton-pierre.

265 PULLAN, R. P. 65 Higher Temple St. Manchester, Des.—Designs for polychromatic decorations, after the manner of the middle ages.

266 MORGAN, E. St. Helen's, Swansea, Des.—Topographical model of Tynemouth Castle. Model of Tintern Abbey.

267 PLACE, G. G. Nottingham.—Drawings illustrating the art of Church building in the United Kingdom.

268 BENNETT, E. C.E. 10 Great College St. Westminster.—Proposed national monument to H.R.H. Prince Albert, in commemoration of the Great Exhibition.

269 DRIVER, C. H. 46 West Sq. Southwark, Des.—Architectural design for a baptistry and font.

270 STOCKER, N. B. 7 Charles Pl. Kentish Town, Des.—Designs for church windows.

271 DICKSEE, J. R. 27 Holland St. Fitzroy Sq. Prod.—A chromo-lithograph, in six colours.

272 NICHOLL, S. J. 11 Argyll Pl. Des.—Design for a screen to enclose a chapel. An attempt to adapt the forms of mediæval architecture to cast iron.

273 TENNENT, Mrs. R. N. Vale of Health, Hampstead.—Miniature of Pope Pius IX. by the exhibitor, a self-taught artist. Miniature painting : the Grape Gatherer.

274 APPEL, R. 43 Gerrard St. Soho, Inv.—Prints by Albert Durer ; plates taken by the Anastatic process with impressions ; specimens of Appelotype printing.

275 WARNER, W. 44 Gerrard St. Soho.—Impressions and casts from intaglios, portraits, figures, seal of the Art-Union, &c.

276 MORISON, D. 31 Arlington St. Mornington Crescent.—Medallic portraits in wax.

277 SOUNES, J. 49 Rupert St. Haymarket, Manu.—Reduced model in wax : Group of animals.

278 BISHOP, J. North Audley St. Inv.—Engravings by clockwork, for the prevention of forgery. Oval medallion of Her Majesty, produced by a single line of equal thickness, and 229 feet in length.

279 RUNDELL, W. W. Falmouth.—Seals engraved by machine.

280 GIFFORD, J. Royal Polytechnic Inst. Sculp.—Lion, tiger, elephant, and Alpine goat, engraved in cornelian.

281 ADAMS, G.—Medals, dies, &c.

282 MARTIN, T. Newton Abbot, Inv. and Manu.—Wax impressions of seals engraved by machinery, by a process called "Tornography."

283 COX, H. 6 Upper Southampton St. Pentonville.—Model, Death on the Pale Horse: Rev. chap. vi. v. 8 to end.

284 WYON, W. R.A. Royal Mint, Des. and Mod.—Portraits of Her Majesty and H.R.H. Prince Albert, being the model for the obverses of the GREAT EXHIBITION PRIZE MEDALS. Proof coins of the present reign, &c.

285 BARCLAY, G. 22 Gerrard St.—Designs for visiting cards. Specimens of die-sinking and engraving on gems. Imitation coins in paper, by Miss P. S. Barclay.

286 WYON, L. C. Medallist, Royal Mint.—Portraits of the Royal Children, modelled by command of Her Majesty Model adopted by the Royal Commissioners as the second size Great Exhibition PRIZE MEDAL.

287 WYON, B. 287 Regent St. Des. and Sculp.—Impres-

sion of the great seals of England, Scotland, and Ireland ; the courts of law ; the British colonial governments, &c.

288 LONGMAN, —, Waterloo Pl. Des.and Manu.—Impressions from seals, engraved by J. and R. Longman.

289 KITCHENER, T. 3 Little Compton St. Soho, Des. and Eng.—Seals and dies. Initial letters from the eighth to the sixteenth centuries, &c.

289A WOODHOUSE, W. 23 Molesworth St. Dublin, Engraver.—Medals in bronze, &c. Medal dies made on a new principle in pure cast steel.

290 BUTTERS, L. 41 George St. Edinburgh, Engraver.—Intaglios, heads of Scott and other eminent men.

291 WILBUD, J. 6 King St. Snow Hill, Prod.—Profile bust of Shakspeare, in plaster of Paris, made to imitate ivory, and being equal to it in hardness.

292 WESTWOOD, J. O. Hammersmith, Prop.—Electrotype casts. Small frame of buhl work, in imitation of the chased work of the Louis XIV. period, &c.

293 GRAY, ELIZA MARIA, 5 Charles Sq. Hoxton, Des. and Manu.—Group of flowers, made of human hair.

294 ROUW, P. 13 Denmark Ter. Islington, Mod.—Medallic portraits in wax.

295 SELLERS, J. Sheffield, Manu.—Steel-plate machineruled, suitable for etchers and engravers.

296 HOPLEY, E. 16 University St. Inv.—Design for a simple scale to enable the statuary or painter to realize, with speed and certainty, the facial proportions.

297 MELTON, —, Edinburgh.—Printing in colours.

298 HARMER, H. R. Gt. Yarmouth, Prod.—Four "sun" pictures.

299 ROSS & THOMSON, Edinburgh, Prod.—Frames containing Talbotype pictures from albuminised glass.

300 HILL, D. O. Calton Hill Stairs, Edinburgh, Prod. and Des.—Calotypes of the fishermen and women of Newhaven, near Edinburgh ; groups, portraits, and studies from nature : produced by the Exhibitor and the late R. Adamson.

301 BUCKLE, S. Peterborough, Prod.—A series of pictures from nature, taken by Talbot's photographic process, called calotype, and printed from paper negatives. (Main Avenue, West.)

302 BURNARD, N. 36 High St. Eccleston Sq. Des. and Sculp.—The Prince of Peace, Isaiah ix. 6.

303 FOSTER, E. R. 1 Prince's St. Bank, Imp.—An ornamental stone vase, carved out of the rock of Malta, by a native of the island.

304 WILLSON, T. Crescent Buildings, Leicester, Mod.—Model of the Victoria pyramid for the British Metropolitan Necropolis. Designed by J. Willson, senr. architect.

305 CARRUTHERS, W. Reigate, Sculp.—Model, in Reigate stone, of the village church at Southwater, Sussex. Architect, J. P. Harrison.

306 LUCAS, R. C. The Firs, Otterbourne, near Winchester, Des. and Manu.—Ivory carvings ; and imitation bronzes.

307 BISS, J. Bradninch, Cullompton, Des. and Manu.—Carved Tudor bed-posts, made of walnut-tree, by a thatcher.

308 BAILY & SONS, 71 Gracechurch St. Manu.—Ornamental castings in iron, bronzed. Cast of a fly in bronze, from nature, by W. Midworth, of Mansfield.

309 NORCHI, E. 18 King William St. Strand, Manu.—Warwick vase and Rape of the Sabines, after John Belognar, in serpentine marble. Copies in scarce agate marble, from a very ancient jug in bronze, at the Museum at Volterra.

310 AITKEN & ALLEN, 102 Princes St. Edinburgh.—Emblematical carved pier-table and mirror-frame.

311 DE LA BOND, Count.—Specimens of wood-carving by machinery.

312 CUFF, R. P. 7 Owen's Row, Goswell Rd.—Design for a pendant hall lamp for gas.

313 AUSTIN, W. Limehouse.—Sculp. "The Crucifixion," carved in wood, life size.

314 CASTLE, J. Cowley Rd. Oxford, Des. and Sculp.—Baptismal font, in Caen stone, with four compositions in alto-relievo, and symbolical decorations of fruits, foliage, &c.

315 WILSON, J. 20 Leicester Sq. Des. and Eng.—The parting of Hector and Andromache, on red cornelian onyx.

316 KAULBACH, E. 5 Duke St. Grosvenor Sq.—Satan apostrophising the sun.

317 HALL, R. Rotherhithe, Des. and Carver.—Figure of Her Majesty, designed for a ship's figure head.

318 SMITH, Capt. R.N.—Design for monument to Nelson.

319 WILKINSON, Sir G. Portman Sq.—Small table, of original design, partly constructed from a piece of one of the great cedars of Lebanon.

320 PEACHEY. J. jun. 10 George St. Hanover Sq. Prop.—Bronze bust of Sir T. Lawrence, by S. Parker.

321 INGRAM, J. W. 120 Islington, Birmingham, Inv. and Des.—Cabinet, or commode, of wood decorated by the enamel process, with electro-gilt metal mouldings. Specimens of imitation marbles, &c.

322 GRAVES, D. King's Langley, Des and Manu.—Life of Christ, illustrated with a variety of original designs.

323 IBBETSON, Capt. L. L. B. Clifton House, Old Brompton, Manu. and Inv.—Electrotypes from the animal and vegetable kingdom. Ornamental castings in various metals, &c. (Also Main Avenue, No. 91.)

324 HULL, D. Royal Polytechnic Institution, Regent St., Manu.—Specimen of wire-work, executed by hand without tools, by the exhibitor, who is blind, and self-taught.

325 M'HARDY, —, Gardener.—Models of gardens, &c.

326 WEST, ALICE.—Fresco painting.

327 RUSSELL, H. H. C.E.—Model of the Royal Victoria Tower, proposed to be erected at Kingstown Harbour, Dublin, to commemorate Her Majesty's visit to Ireland. Design for the Peel Testimonial, proposed to be erected in Salford.

328 ADSHEAD, J. 45 George St. Manchester, Des.—Illustrated plan of the township of Manchester.

329 MILLS, ELIZA.—Fresco painting.

330 LITCHFIELD, J. Ridley, Huntingdonshire.—Model of cottage, composed of 2,000 pieces of willow wood.

331 CHANCELLOR, F. Chelmsford, Des. & Mod.—Model of a covered homestall for a farm of from 300 to 500 acres.

332 BEECHAM, —, Model of shop front.

333 PARTRIDGE, W. 28 Newman St. Des. and Prod.—King John's great Charter, with 57 shields of the Barons and Clergy, emblazoned on vellum.

334 BAXTER, J. Lewes and Ringmer, Sussex, Des.—Two models of improved farm-yard and buildings.

335 GRISSELL, H. & M. D. Regent's Canal Works.—Guerin's steering apparatus.

335A RUFF, E. Hind Ct. Fleet St.—Map of London.

336 PIKE, T. J. Cheltenham.—The royal arms, &c. emblazoned on glass.

337 HAYWARD, R. J. Danes Pl. Kentish Town, Inv.—New process of tinting steel plates for printing.

338 BELFAST GOV. SCHOOL OF DES. Ireland, Prod.—Designs for embroidery, &c. by pupils of the school.

339 BARRITT, J. L. 173 Fleet St. Des. and Manu.—Model of a picture: The water mill, summer evening.

340 WHAITE, H. C. 85 & 87 Bridge St. Manchester, Inv. and Prod.—Flag painted on silk; with an elastic preparation, to prevent the cracking of the silk.

341 LEE, J. G. Holborn.—Imitation of marble, &c., on glass.

342 COULTON, J. D.—Designs for decorations.

342A CLARKE, T. C. 9 Percy Circus, Lloyd Sq. Des.—Design for a national gallery for sculpture.

343 THOMPSON, T. J.—God save the Queen, in wood.

343A HERDMAN, W. G. Liverpool. — Illustrations of perspective.

344 BONNAR & CARFRAE, Castle St. Edinburgh, Des. and Executors.—Design, in imitation of fresco painting and of inlaid wood. Designs, in imitation of inlaid marble.

345 SALTMARSH, G. Southampton House, Kentish Town.—Specimen of penmanship.

346 NORTON, J. Clayton West, Huddersfield.—Model of manufactory.

347 HERWITZ, B. 1 Brydges St. Strand.—Emblematical decoration for drawing-room, and emblazoned glass tablet.

348 ZUCCANI, B. 40 and 41 Brick Lane, Spitalfields.—An aviary.

349 BURY, T. 50 Welbeck St. Cavendish Sq. — Design for a palace of arts, and national gallery.

350 His ROYAL HIGHNESS PRINCE ALBERT.—Two slabs for tables, designed by L. Gruner, Esq. in the cinque-cento style, executed by Mr. Thomas Woodruff, at Bakewell, in Derbyshire stones, in imitation of the Florentine mosaic.

351 Candelabrum in the cinque cento style, designed by L. Gruner, Esq. modelled by Ant. Trentanove, and executed in scagliola in imitation of giallo antico, by L. Romoli.

352 DREW, T. Troy Town, Rochester.—Model of the Holy Temple.

353 HER MAJESTY.—A cradle, carved in Turkey box-wood by W. G. Rogers, and designed by his son, symbolising the union of the Royal House of England with that of Saxe Coburg and Gotha. (See page 5.)

354 HILLIER, G. Lambeth.—Illuminated vellum.

356 PEPPERCORN, —, Various statuettes.

357 LAWSON, J.—Design for a carpet.

358 MARSHALL, Lieut. R.—Four specimens of Xulo-pyrography, or charred wood engraving.

359 SOUNES, W. 49 Rupert St. Haymarket.—Impressions from dies (cut in steel) for stamping metal.

360 FIELD, G.—A specimen of wood carving in the middle of the last century by Demontreuil.

361 SPIERS & SON, Oxford, Des. and Manu.—Various models in card-board. Fancy articles.

362 SKINNER, —, Sheffield.—Fac-simile of chasing and engraving on metals, done by means of printing.

363 WILSON, CHARLOTTE E. 19 Howland St. Fitzroy Sq. Des. and Manu. — Blotting-book, ornamented with pearl and lined with satin.

363A STEEDMAN & Co. Charles St. Hampstead Rd.—Specimens of japanning on slate and other decorations. (South Wall.)

364 WILLS, W. J. Harrison St. Gray's Inn Rd.—Models of table lamp and lock furniture.

364A HORNER, G. 53 Rathbone Pl.—Painted decorations. (South Wall.)

SCULPTURE COURT.
—— AREAS Q. to S. 28, 29. ——
(Behind the Mediæval Court.)

1 BROWN, A. 4 Red Cross Sq. Des.—David before Saul, a statue in plaster.

2 KIRK, J. R. A.R.H.A. Jervis St. Dublin, Sculp.—An original group, in plaster: The creation of the Dimple.

3 HUGHES, T. 28 Long Acre, Des.—Plaster figure of Eve: "The serpent me beguiled, and I did eat."

4 FOLEY, J. H. A.R.A.—The Wanderer.

5 DURANT, SUSAN, 14 Conduit St. West, Des. and Sculp.—Group in plaster: Belisarius.

6 JENNINGS, B. Hereford, and 17 Lower Eaton Sq. Grosvenor Pl. London, Des. and Sculp.—Marble bust of the Madonna.

7 THOMAS, I. E. 7 Lower Belgrave Pl. Sculp.—The spirit of Science unveiling Ignorance and Prejudice.

8 LEGREW, J. 1 St. Alban's Rd. Kensington, Des. and Prop.—Group: Cupid stung by a Bee, complains to Venus.

9 CAREW, J. E. 40 Cambridge St. Hyde Park, Des. and Sculp.—Baptism of Christ : the model of the altar piece in the Catholic chapel, Brighton.

10 Whittington, original model.—*Carew.*

11 Design in relief for a temple in Suffolk.—*Carew.*

12 THOMAS, J.—Nymph and sea-horse.

13 THEED, W. 12A Henrietta St. Cavendish Sq. Des. and Sculp.—Statue of Prometheus.

14 HOGAN, J.—A drunken Faun.

15 MARSHALL, W. A.R.A. 47 Ebury St. Eaton Sq. Sculp.—Sabrina. *Vide* Milton's Comus.

16 EARLE, T.—Ophelia.

17 MILLER, F. M. 24 Bloomfield Ter Pimlico, Sculp.—Group : Childhood.

18 FARRELL, T. 132 Lower Gloucester St. Dublin, Des.—Early Sorrow, sculptured in marble.

19 FOLEY, J. H. A.R.A. 19 Osnaburgh St. Regent's Park, Des. and Sculp.—Ino and the Infant Bacchus.

20 SHARP, T. 27 Burton Crescent, Des. and Sculp.—Statue, in marble : Boy and Lizard.

21 Pastorella.—*Earle.*

22 LAWLOR, J. 30 Wyndham St. Bryanstone Sq. Des.—A Bather, statue in plaster.

23 CAMPBELL, T.—Portrait of a lady as a Muse.

24 BELL, J. 15 Douro Pl. Victoria Rd. Kensington, Sculp.—Purity, or Una and the Lion.

25 KIRK, W. B. A.R.H.A. Jervis St. Dublin, Sculp.—Original group, in plaster : Pastoral Age.

26 SHARP, T.—Model in plaster : Christ's charge to Peter.

27 PAPWORTH, E. G. 17 Newman St. Oxford St. Sculp.—Cupid in disguise.

28 Cupid and a swan.

29 RITCHIE, J. 62 Princes St. Edinburgh, Des.—Statuette in marble of a poetess.

30 McDONNELL, London.—Mother and child, by a deaf and dumb artist.

31 FARMER, P.—Bas-relief of boys.

32 SUMMERS, C. 86 Warwick St. Pimlico, Des. and Mod.—Statue, in plaster, of boy playing with shell.

33 FRANCIS, J. 56 Albany St. Regent's Park, Sculp.—Statue of Her Majesty, in Carrara marble.

34 THORNYCROFT, T. & MARY, 30 Stanhope St. Hampstead Rd. Sculp.—The Prince of Wales, and royal children as a young Shepherd, a young Gleaner, &c.

35 NELSON, G. 30 Bidborough St. Burton Crescent, Sculp.—Victory, to the memory of the officers and men of the 50th reg. who fell on the banks of the Sutlej.

36 STEPHENS, E. B. 27 Upper Belgrave Pl. Pimlico, Des. and Inv.—Eve offering to Adam the Forbidden Fruit. The Expulsion from Paradise. The Curse. The death of Abel.

37 ADAMS, G. G.—Murder of the Innocents.

38 Bas-relief : Brothers and sisters in Comus.—*Miller.*

39 THRUPP, E. 30 Gloucester Pl. New Rd. Des. and Sculp.—The Maid and the mischievous Boy.

40 JONES, J. E. 41 Upper Charlotte St. Fitzroy Sq. Des. and Sculp.—Children and animals, portraits.

41 MUNRO, A. 33 Brewer St. Golden Sq. Sculp.—Paolo e Francesca ; Dante.

42 TAYLOR, F. Ramsey, Hampshire, Des. and Sculptor.—Life-sized figure of our Saviour bearing his cross.

43 GALLAGHER, J. 10 King St. Regent St. Des. and Prod.—Design for a fountain in plaster : Ariadne disconsolate at the loss of Theseus.

44 SMITH, C. R. 37 Gloucester Pl. New Rd. Sculp.—Statue in mediæval costume : Lady Danberry.

45 JONES, J. E. The Favorite.

46 KIRK, J. School of Design, Birmingham, Des. and

Manu.—Bas-relief, in plaster : " Spiritless, afflicted, fallen," Milton's Paradise Lost.

47 PHYSICK, E. J. 6 Gloucester Pl. New Rd. Des. and Sculp.—Pluto carrying off Proserpine.

48 ADAMS, G. G.—Bas-relief, combat of Centaurs and Lapithæ.

49 Bas-relief, Titania.—*Miller.*

50 Ariel.—*Miller.*

51 BEAUCLERC, Capt. G.—Sleeping Nymph.

52 FARRELL, J. 123 Lower Gloucester St. Dublin, Des.—The pet dove's return, a group in marble.

53 Original model, Descent from the Cross.—*Carew.*

54 BEHNES, W. 13 Osnaburgh St. Sculp.—Statue, in marble, of a Startled Nymph.

55 Boy, child, and goat.

56 Boy catching a butterfly.—*Thrupp.*

57 MANNING, S. 3 Union Pl. Regent's Park, and 61A York Ter. Regent's Park, Sculp.—A model of statue of Prometheus, now being executed in marble.

58 Arethusa.—*Thrupp.*

59 THEED, W.—The Prodigal's return.

60 FRANKS, J. 50 Bazing Pl. Waterloo Rd.—Portrait statue of John Flaxman, by the late M. L. Watson. Executed in marble by Nelson.

61 M'DOWELL, P. R.A.—Early sorrow.

62 ADAMS, G. G. of Rome.—Contest between minstrel and nightingale. Strada.

63 BEAUCLERK, Capt. G.—Female figure on a couch.

64 GIBSON, J. R.A. of Rome.—Bas-relief in plaster, representing the Hours and the Horses of the Sun.

65 THORNYCROFT.—Group of children, bas-relief.

66 MILLER, F. M.—Bas-relief, spirit of Calm.

67 The attendant spirit in Comus descending on a glancing star, in bas-relief.—*Miller.*

68 Bas-relief, Lycidas.—*Miller.*

69 PHYSICK, E. G.—Head in marble : the dying Saviour.

70 FOLEY, T. H. A.R.A.—Innocence.

71 Dorothea, from Don Quixote.—*Bell.*

72 The Babes in the Wood.—*Bell.*

73 MANNING, S. 3 Union Pl. Regent's Park, and 61A York Ter. Regent's Park, Sculp.—Model of a statue of John Wesley, executed in marble, and presented to the Wesleyan Theological Institution, by T. Farmer, Esq.

74 WESTMACOTT, J. 1 St. John's Pl. Lisson Grove, Des.—Model of Saher de Quincy, Earl of Winchester, A.D. 1215, to be executed in bronze, for the House of Lords.

75 DURHAM, J.—L'Allegro.

76 La Penserosa.—*Durham.*

77 BEHNES, W. 13 Osnaburgh St. Sculp.—Statuette : Lady Godiva.

78 Statue of a girl : a study from nature.—*Durant, Susan.*

79 THEED, W.—Narcissus.

80 YARBOROUGH, Earl of.—Statue in marble, a Greek hunter and dog, by J. Gibson, R.A. of Rome.

81 Statue of Cupid.—*Jennings.*

82 Nature's mirror.—*Earle.*

83 SMITH, C. R.—Statue of Michael Angelo, in mediæval costume.

84 JONES, J. E.—Mother and child.

85 Art Union Statuettes, submitted to competition for the premiums of 100*l.* and 50*l.*

86 ART UNION OF LONDON.—Tazza, modelled from a Greek design, by E. W. Wyon.

87 MILLER, F. M.—Miseries of War, bas-relief.

** For other Sculpture, *see Transept and Main Avenue.*—Pages 8 to 11.

Proceed to Class 9, page 54.

Colonial Possessions.

INDIA.

RAW MATERIALS.

CLASS I.—*Mineral Products.*

Iron stone, iron, and iron ores, of many varieties, from various parts of India and of Central Asia.

INDIAN IRON & STEEL COMPANY, Beypore, near Calicut, Malabar, and at Porto Novo, near Cuddalore, Carnatic. Office in London, 10A King's Arms Yard, Moorgate St. Prod. Manu. and Imp.

Specimens of the ores and charcoal used, &c.: as magnetic oxide; crystals of the magnetic ore; ore as prepared for the blast furnace; argillaceous iron-stone; charcoal used in the manufacture; pig-iron from the blast furnace, and refined; annealed castings made from the pig; chain 5-16ths, cast entire in links; round bar to show surface and polish; flier used in worsted spinning, hitherto made only of wrought iron; springs of sorts, all of the cast-iron.

Specimens of the wrought-iron: of bars and rods fractured; of worked and twisted cold; iron drawn into wire.

Bar-iron for steel purposes: bar-steel; cast-steel ingot, showing its colour and crystallization; cast-steel drawn to sizes; files, saws, chisels, gouges, and plane-irons.

Table knives and carvers; razors, scissors, and knives, fine cutlery; sword blade.

From these magnetic ores of iron the "Wootz," or Indian steel, is made by the natives; also malleable iron by the direct process.

Specimens of chrome ore; of the chromate and bichromate of potash manufactured from this ore.

Saltpetre of Maganore and Errode; corundum chromate of iron; carbonate of magnesia; iron ore; cutties, or blooms of iron; palms, or bars of iron; vuttoms, or pieces of cast steel, as it came from the clay crucible; ollies, or bars, drawn out from clay crucibles; small bag of iron beads which ooze out from the blooms in the blast furnaces; steel made from the blooms in the same kind of blast furnace, and used in making edged tools—from Salem. —G. F. Fischer, Esq.

Primitive marble; serpentine marble; primitive lime-stone; red and yellow jasper; pudding stone; jasper; brown jasper; fossil woods; plastic, yellow, and slate-coloured clays; white Kaolin earth; soap-stone for stills; white Kaolin earth; fossil wood; Kashning garnets in serpentine, used for making pots and pans; goldwasher's sand; petroleum, and Meharnet oil; iron sand; iron-sand clay.— Major Hannay, from Assam.

Strings of Nimluck beads; plain and diamond-cut cornelian; greenstone and mother-of-pearl beads; mother-of-pearl buckle; black stone earring drops; large and small pieces of crystal; cornelians for brooches; stones for clasps; bloodstones; gowries; large and small amethysts; large and small emeralds; rajawahs; assorted stones; ferozahs; sapphires; cat's-eyes; garnets; romarooks, salemon stone; blue-stone; turquoises.—From the Lapidaries of Calcutta.

Mergui coal; limestone; iron ore; manganese; tremen, herite; alabaster; petroleum; lead and copper ore; agate cornelian, and calcedony; Ava gem sand; tin ore, first and second washing; antimony ore—from Tenasserim Province.

Iron ore, two sorts; limestone, two sorts; specimens of iron ore, smelted iron, and pig iron—from Mirzapore.

Sulphuret of antimony; pearl ash prepared from nitre and charcoal, two sorts.—Madras.

Carbonate of soda, nearly pure, prepared from Dhoby's or Washerman's earth.

Iron ore, the bisulphuret embedded in stone; soda—from Cuddapah.

Marble slabs from Bellary; bricks made of white clay; marble mortar, rough—from the Ceded District.

Hone stone from Toongbudra River—from Kurnool.

Lithographic stones—from Kurnool, Juggiapettah, and Datchapilly.

Silver box of gold-dust, villages of Kapoo and Nelamboor in Ernaak.—from Calicut, and Wynaad.

Iron ore, magnetic; salt Nowpadah pans—from Vizagapatum.

Copper ore; bell metal; soda, carbonate of—from Bellary.

Salt produced by periodical inundation of sea over a sandy plain, collected into heaps after evaporation—from Coombaconum.—Madras.

Potash, from Lahore. Bottle containing Bootan rock salt.

Antimony, calamine, pyrites, copper, and copper ores.

Copper ore and raw copper, and lead and lead ores, from Nepal. Lead, superior, from Shockpoor. Plumbum; tin ore; tin; gold dust.—Singapore.

Chromate of iron. Specimens of bell metal and pewter from Bellary and Nepal. Moss and other agates, from the Nerbudda, Kane, Soane, and other rivers. Pebbles, from Soane River. Blood stones; chitta hindnee, piebald or spotted; Grass stone; lapis lazuli; cornelian and onyx; jasper and marble—from Bombay and Bengal.

Coal of various kinds; lignite; petroleum; resinous earths; chalcedony; sulphur; salt; and other minerals; serpentine, from various localities in the peninsula of India, and the Presidency of Bengal, &c.; soda and its carbonates; nitrate of potash; pearl-ash; magnesia; salt-petre; steatite; lithographic slates; alum; corundum (from Malabar); talc; pipe-clay; talc, petrifactions and petrified woods; magnesia, and other earths; a plate of stonelike jasper, three of agate, two of green marble; two cups jasper agate, two of brecciated agate; two pestles and mortars, and two of jasper agate; six squares of the above, three stones, and three rough blocks—from Jesselmere; six varieties, including rock and rose crystals, quartz, amethysts, flint, white and pink sandstone; soapstones; potstones; corundum; white felspar; calcareous, icy, cube, and other spars, and felspar; gypsum; selenite; iron flint; pipe-clay; yellow and other clays; light and red marls; lithomarge; hyalite; green stone; Venetian talc; salt, raw and refined; car-bonate of potash; marbles—yellow, white, green, pink, grey lavender, wax, and purplish coloured; dolomite limestone; porphyritic rocks; granites—white, flesh-coloured, pink, and grey; micaceous rocks, silex, basalts, slates, about 160 varieties in all; together with specimens of hyacinth, white and blue sapphires, garnets, and other stones; diamond breccia; beryl; schorl; jasper; cat's-eye; agates, and amethysts; rock crystal; opals; calcedonies; cornelians; onyxes; bloodstones, &c.; Black, grey, and green copper; purple copper ore, and malachite; tin; umber, or oxide of manganese; galena (sulphuret of lead); chromate of iron; iron sand; compact black and sherry ironstone, and brown limestone; oolite, pure stone coloured; lapis lazuli and Bombay preparations of ultra-marine from it; ochres of various kinds; plumbago; alumine.

CLASS II.—*Pharmaceutical Products and Medicinal Substances.*

From Bengal.—Jabrang (Xanthoxylum) fruits used in medicine; Nux vomica—from Assam.

From East India Company's Dispensary, Calcutta.—Cannab, Ind. ext. and tinct.; Nux vomica; Nux vomica bark; Aconitum ferox; Aconitum ferox (tincture of); Castor-oil seeds; Cassia fistula; Senna leaves; gamboge; Ipomea cærulea; Cheretta; Cheretta extract and tincture; Colycynth; Colycynth extract; Catechu; Assafœtida; Calotropis gigantea; Calotropis powdered; Hemidesmus indicus (Anantomool); Borax, refined; Acid, nitric; Acid, benzöic; Meloe trianthemæ (Native blister fly).

Hill honey; Gall nuts; Arsenious acid; Realgar; Orpiment; Mineral carbonate of soda; Sulphate of soda; Saltpetre; Sulphate of copper; Carbonate of lead; Litharge; Minium; Cinnabar, respectively from Singapore, Malacca, the Malayan Peninsula, Nepal, Salem, Surat, and other places. Corrosive sublimate; Magnesite; Magnesiæ sulphas; Hydrochlorate of ammonia; Oil of cubebs and of croton; Mustard oil; Grass oil; Gurjun oil; Medicinal opium; Morphia; M. Hydrochloras el Acetas; Hyoscyami fol.; Hyoscyamus, extract and tincture; Stramonii sem.; Cannabis indica; Malkungnee, or Celastrus nutans; Myrica sapida (bark of the); Annutamool, or substitute for sarsaparilla; Momordica, sp.; Mishmee bitter and tita.

From Bombay.—Oondee oil (Tanna). *Calophyllum inophyllum*, oil expressed from the nut, used as a stimulant externally and internally. Imported from Somali Coast.

Kurunj oil (Tanna). *Pongamia glabra*, oil expressed from nut; used externally as a stimulant.

Napaula oil (Croton Tiglium)—from Vizagapatam and Ganjam.

Calabunda (*Aloe perfoliata*)—from Vizagapatam.

Hemidesmus indicus; Convolvolus turpethum root and powder; Clitoria ternatea seed and powder; Cannabis indicas (flowering tops).

Specimens of mylabaris cichorei; Pulvis mylabaris cichorei; Tinctura cannabis sativæ; Hoya viridiflora (*Asclepias vomitoria*); Hymenodictyon utile; Soymida febrifuga; Dry bark of the mullay or jungle margosa; Dry bark of the vapum or margosa tree.

Justicia paniculata; creyat; specimens of salt—from Nellore.

Gamboge—from Wynaad and Canara.

Collection of mineral, vegetable, and animal substances, useful as medicines and in the arts, from the bazaars of India, by J. Forbes Royle, M.D.

CLASS III.—*Substances used as Food.*

Vegetable Kingdom.

Wheat :—Pissee, sohalya, jullalya, kutya, varieties of *Triticum sativum*, from the Valley of the Nerbudda.

Flour; three qualities, produced by native mills, from Calcutta.

Oats (*Avena sativa*), from Patna.

Banaful rice, and some of its straw, from Hooghley.

Rice, and rice straw, from various parts of India. Paddy, or rice in the husk. Indian corn; Indian millet; Buckwheat; Green grain (Moong); Black grain; Esculent vegetables, seeds, &c., from Nepaul and other countries.

Substances used in the preparation of Drinks.—Pekoe, Souchong, and gunpowder teas, from the East India Company's tea nurseries in Kemaon in the Himalayas. Pekoe, Congo teas, and others from Assam. Coffee.

Intoxicating, &c. Drugs.—Tobacco, from Arrakan, Gwalior, &c.; Cheroots; Opium; Cigars; Hemp plant, &c.

Spices and Condiments.—Cinnamon; Nutmegs; Mace; Cloves; Cassia; Round pepper and black; White and wild pepper; Cayenne pepper, and Chillies; Betel nuts; Ginger.

Starch Series.—Starch series, including arrow roots, pearl sago, tapioca, &c.

Sugar Series.

Sugar manufactured after European and native method, in district of Rohilkund.

(*Saccharum officinale*), from Ganjam, Cossipore, &c.

Sugar, manufactured in Dutch high-pressure vacuum pans, and by a new process not generally known, made in common open battery; other sorts, manufactured in low-pressure vacuum pans, from Sourabaya, Java.

Sugars from the cane; from juices of spathe of date (Dacca) from butter tree, and from neepah.

CLASS IV.—*Vegetable Substances, chiefly used in Manufactures.*

Gum and Resin Series, including products of Arabia, Bengal, Vizagapatam, &c.

MACKINTOSH & Co. Cambridge St. Manchester, and 73 Aldermanbury, London, Imp. Manu. and Pat.—Specimens of East India rubber; of India rubber in process of cleaning, in masticated block, and in thin cut sheets; in laid sheets, in colours, and in solution; laid on various fabrics as material for making waterproof articles; embossings for making up various fancy articles; thread for weaving into various elastic articles; and of India rubber thread for ladies' knitting and crochet work.

Gutta percha (*Isonandra gutta*), from Johore, Malay Peninsula. Gutta trap used for birdlime (*Artocarpus*), from Singapore. Birdlime bor attock, from Assam.

Oil Series.—Volatile Oils.

Atto of roses, from Ghazeepore.

Oil of roses, from Rajpootana.

Rose water, from Ghazeepore.

Grass oil, from Malwa; together with the grass and seed from which it is extracted.

Lemon grass, siri oil.

Cajaputi oil, Kayer pateh, from Malacca.

Sandal, aloes, saffron and other oils. Camphor.

Fatty Oils.

Linseed and linseed oil, from Moorshedabad, and specimens of between 30 and 40 other oleaginous products from various regions of India and the Archipelago.

Dyes and Colours.

Indigo (*Indigofera tinctoria*), from English factories, and Cuddapah market, Kotah, Sindh, and Madras.

Pala indigo, from Salem, F. Fischer, Esq.

Madder, and lichens, from Assam, Meerut, &c.

Mangrove bark, and bark and wood, both used for dyeing, from Arracan; Sagah bark, Samak bark, and other barks, from Singapore and Celebes.

Various woods, &c., for dyeing, from Bengal, Celebes and Java, Assam, Dacca, and Tanna.

Annatto, from Assam. Hursinghar flowers, from Cuttack.

Nutgalls, and various vegetable dyeing substances, berries, barks, &c., from Malacca, Lahore, Madras, Assam, Moorshedabad, Rajpootana, &c.

Tanning Substances.—Varieties of barks, catechu, kino, gambir, from the several Presidencies, &c.

Fibrous substances (including materials for cordage and clothing).

Cotton, both indigenous and the American kinds, cultivated in India during the several experiments made by the East India Company, from Broach, Khandeish, Belgaum, Coimbatora, Tinnevelly, Bengal, Agra, and Jellundrea Doab.

Numerous specimens of pine-apple, plantain, nettle fibre, &c.

Flax, dressed and raw, from Java, Assam, Singapore, &c. Specimens of sun, jute and other tropical substitutes for hemp and flax; also of Indian cordage, &c.

Cellular substances, as pith-like stem of *shola* or *noona* plant (*Æschynonum Aspera*).

Timber and fancy woods.—A great variety from all parts of India.

Animal Kingdom.

Animal Substances used as Food.—Isinglass; fish-maws; shark fins; edible birds'-nests.

Skins of leopards, tigers, spotted deer, white or tawed deer, fawns, Bengal buffalos, goats, cows, and sheep. Cowries or shells. Stick-lac; seed-lac; lac-dye; from Bengal.

Blistering beetle. Wild boar, elephant, and porcupine bristles. Raw and tanned skins of elk, buffalo, bull, tiger, cheeta, wild cat, goat, sheep, deer, elephant, bison, and wild boar. Feathers of paddy-bird and sarus. Beetles' wings. Tusks of elephant. White ivory. Horns of bison, buffalo, elk, antelope, and deer. From Madras.

Horn tips. Deer and buffalo horns, with and without skulls. Wild Mithon cow's head, complete. Mountain sheep's and takin's heads. Mishmee ring pohoos. Ring pahoos without skulls. Skins of deer, otter, jowomalah, squirrel, and kooteah. Musk in bamboo bottle. Squirrel. Lizards. Lac peepul (*Ficus religiosa*). Ber lac, or of Indian fig-tree. White and black twisted and untwisted wool. Jesselmere wool. Brown bear skin. Tails of the bos gruniens. Bees'-wax. Seed-lac. Tusseh or Tussur Cocoons. Raw Tusseh, best Tusseh silk. Areah cocoons.—From Bengal.

Sharks' fins, fish-maws, ostrich and paddy bird feathers, elephant's tusks and teeth, from Bombay, Zanzibar, &c.

Silk and cocoons.

Sheeps' wool from Ladak, Tibbit Yarkhandi, Khotani, and Turfani; goats' down, from Yarkend, Khoten, and Turfan, Chinese Turkey.—Lieut. Strachey, B.C.

Kulu, yak's down. Isos-kul, down of the Tsos antelope, and a piece of the animal's skin.

Eggs, and caterpillar. Cocoons and silk of Tussur. Eri, Moonga, and Pat silks. *Saturnia mylitta* (Tussur) *Bombyx Saturnia* (Moonga). *Phalæma cynthia* (Eri). *Bombyx mori* (pat.)—Ch. Huffnagle, Esq., of Calcutta.

Class V.—*Machines for direct use, including Carriages.*

Models of a coin-sorting machine, from the Mint at Madras.

An eka, or native carriage, and a bamboo hackery.

Model of carriage for ladies; models of Mahratta carriages; bullock carriage and two carts—from Lahore.

Model of state palankeen, made for the Rajah of Travancore, by Messrs. Simpson, of Madras.

Country cart for bullocks, and basket complete, manufactured at Chicacole.

Wooden ruth of Muchhunder Nath (a god); another, of Kumaree (a goddess); another, of Juggunnatte (a god)—from Nepaul.

Iron balance and weights: dharnee, bisowlee, seer, tin-paw, and ek paw—from Nepaul.

Class VI.—*Manufacturing Machines and Tools.*

Models of various spinning-wheels, from Lahore.

Spinning-wheel for making pine-apple thread.

Models of a machine for twisting together silk threads, used in weaving, and of a hand machine for spinning cotton.

Weaver's looms, and implements for manufacturing Dacca muslins.—Dr. Wise and J. Taylor, Esq.

Model of a weaver's loom, and of various looms and other machines connected with weaving; preparation of flax and silk threads, carpets, and all works in cottons and silks. Gins for cleaning cotton, &c.; implements of mining; tools for making filigree works; millwork, carpenter's, ard mason's tools; wooden dairy; farming utensils; instruments

and tools employed by native artificers in the works of black and white smiths, goldsmiths, plate-workers, and copper-pot makers, and implements of bricklayers, stone-cutters, and other labourers.

Class VII.—*Civil Engineering, Architectural, and Building Contrivances.*

Model of a Persian wheel, from Lahore.

Piccotah model, for drawing water from a well, from Madras.

Models of iron bridge in Doottee, bridges on the Britawti, Trisool Gunga, Bishnomuti, and Bagmuti rivers, and of common bridges in Nepaul; from Nepaul.

Models of a tank, or soan dhara, and of a house, from Nepaul.

Breakwater, adapted to Madras surf.

Class VIII.—*Naval Architecture, Military Engineering, Ordnance Arms and Accoutrements.*

Models of vessels navigating the Indian seas.

Buglo, naodee, gungo, koteo, and muchoo, from Cutch.

Snake-boat of Cochin, catamaran of Madras, Bombay fishing-boat, ferry-boat of Cochin, bumboat of Bombay, Point de Galle canoe, batelle of Bombay, Arab batelle (Capt. Hawkins), Arab dow, Cutch dingee, Cutch coteyah, Ceylon doni, Arab bugalow, pattamar of Bombay, and Kurrachee bugalo, from Bombay.

A large cargo boat and dingey, from the Ganges.

Model of a pleasure-boat of a Sikh chief, from Lahore.

Massulah boat, with oars, from Madras.

Model of a boat and of an oar, from Nepaul.

Models of Lanun pirate prahus; the first class carries a crew of 100 men, and the second class a crew of about 60 men; from Mindanao.

Model of Padewakhan or Bugis trading prahu. The Bugis trade and the Trepang fishery is carried on in these vessels.

Models of Sampan boats, peculiar to Singapore; three classes; first class very swift: from Singapore.

Models of the East India Company's artillery, from the three Presidencies. Military accoutrements, from the same.

Shako topee, silver moons, and chain used by Nepaul non-commissioned officers, from Nepaul.

Accoutrements used by Gorkha battalion, from Nepaul.

Nepaul captain's coat, worked with gold thread.

Powder-flasks and powder and shot belts, from Lahore.

Powder-flask, with girdle and pouches, used by Gorkhas, from Nepaul.

Matchlock, from Boondie.

Matchlocks, and matchlock rifles, with rests, and some with powder-flasks, &c., from Jeypore, Bejnour, Nugeena, and also Dhampoor, Rohilkund and Lahore; some also from the collection of the Rao of Cutch.

Guns, swords, and pistols, respectively from Lahore, Rampore, Rohilkund, Malwa, &c.

Swords of many kinds, battle-axes, single and double barrelled percussion guns, daggers, hatchet-knives, rhinoceros' shields, bows and arrows, with quivers and slings.

The following articles are used by Indian athletæ:—Bamboo bow, with iron chain in place of string; wooden clubs of Sissoo wood; two-handed sword, made at Saugor, Central India; shields for practising sword-play; foils, or sham swords.

Suit of armour; two pieces of horse armour; suit of armour, nine pieces; two locks; blunderbuss (Sikh); cannon (model); double cannon (model); mortar (model); howitzer.

Camel-gun and saddle; hill-gun, complete—from Lahore.

Two 3-pounder brass ornamented guns, with carriage complete, from Kurnool.

Two brass guns and carriages, from Mysore.

Two oriental brass guns—models.

Tent, manufactured at the Jubulpore School of Industry. The fact of this being throughout the work of reclaimed Thugs, and of their progeny, who, but for the measures of a benevolent government, would assuredly have followed their hereditary trade, will, it is hoped, obtain for it an interest which neither the materials or construction would otherwise have done.

CLASS IX.—*Agricultural and Horticultural Machines and Implements.*

Wooden models of two kinds of ploughs and carts, with agricultural implements used in the Tenasserim Province;—plough, harrow, hoe, spade, sickle, rake, and bamboo stick, covered on one end, used in Kemaon, North-west Provinces; —plough, yoke, whip, mattock, hoe, rake, muzzle, shovel, reaping-hook, chopper, axe, and cotton-cleaner: as used in Hooghly, Lower Bengal;—plough, yoke, harrow, ladder used as a harrow, weeding instrument, plank on which paddy is beaten out, tripod stand for the same, and broom for sweeping the grain.

A variety of models of native agricultural implements, from Nepaul, Kurnool, Broach, and other places.

CLASS X.—*Musical Instruments.*

Guitar, kettle-drum, sarindah or fiddle, tomtom, trumpet, flute, cymbals, &c.

Various stringed and wind instruments, used by natives of Benares, and of others used by the natives of Nepaul.

Kind of kettle-drum, and toogna, from Bhotan.

Others, as guitars, &c., contributed by H.H. the Rajah of Jodhpore.

Model of a tsigu wigu ; tsoung, or harp, &c. from Moulmein.

CLASS XI.—*Manufactures.—Cotton.*

Pieces of fine muslins, from Dacca.

Bordered, flowered, and embroidered muslins, chintzes, and printed cloths.

Cloth sent by the Resident at Nagpore.

Towelling, table-napkins, cotton cloth, diaper, chintzes, and muslins, from Lahore, &c.

Cotton cloth, striped and chintz pattern, from Scinde.

Fine punjum long-cloth, from Jugginpettah, manufactured in the Northern Circars.—Mr. Masters.

Muslins, from Arnee, the Northern Circars, Oopada.

Close-wove muslin, plain and crossed-barred, from Bengal.

Ginghams, Nepalese check, white cloth, Dorca cloth, cloths, bales of canvass, Sumatra cloth, &c., from different parts of Hindostan.

CLASS XII.—*Woollen.*

Cloth shawl worn by natives, from Rampore.

Pieces of cloth.

Woollens, striped and checked, Cashmere and shawl cloths, from Lucknow, Scinde, and South Arcot.

Cumlees, blankets, &c., from the Ceded District, and from Hoonsoor in Mysore.

Wool thread of shawls, from Bootan, &c.

CLASS XIII.—*Silk and Velvet.*

Silk thread and twine; coloured silk; pieces of silk cloths; Cossimbazar silk corahs; skeins of raw silk ; and pieces of silk handkerchiefs; from Moorshedabad. Various specimens and qualities of the raw material and the manufactured article, from Mysore, Poona, Tanna, Lahore, &c.

Pieces of ribbon and velvet, from Ahmedabad, &c.

CLASS XIV.—*Manufactures from Substitutes for Flax, Hemp, &c.*

Two coils of Jute rope; bolt of Chandernagore hemp canvas; bolt of hemp and cotton canvas; Bombay hemp rigging; warm and cold register coir rigging (first manufactured in India); Jubbulpore hemp; Dhanchee hemp rope ; and pine apple flax rope—presented by the manufacturers, Messrs. W. H. Harlon & Co. of Calcutta.

Gunny and other cloths from plantain fibre, from Madras.

Canvas from Wackanoor or Wackoonar fibre from Travancore.

Bark cloth, manufactured by the Semangs or Oriental negro tribes, from Kedah, Malay Peninsula.

Bark cloth, made from the bark of the paper mulberry from Kailli, west coast of Celebes.

Bark cloth, made from Papyrus bark, from Java,

Cloth manufactured by Arafuras from native fibres.

CLASS XV.—*Mixed Fabrics, including Shawls and Embroidered Works.*

Silver enwrapped, plain gilt, and silvered turbans, from Calcutta.

Fine cloths for dresses, shawls, and turbans; gold embroidered cloths worn by Rajpoots, and used for turbans, sent by Maha Rajah Rao Scindiah.

Two varieties of cloth, with the raw material and thread, from Azimghur.

Several pairs of sheets, embroidered with gold and silver, and gold and silk, and a turban with gold ends from Bengal.

Piece of gold cloth; silver tinsel stamped; gold edging; and silver edging, rose coloured, from Benares.

Head covering worked with gold and silver tinsel; the same, with gold dyed purple tinsel; the same with sky-blue bobbinet spangled tinsel, from Benares.

Gold embroidered manufactures, from Benares.

Silk dress-piece, worked with gold and silver; scarlet silk dress-piece, worked up with silk in needle in imitation of China work ; embroidered flowered silk ; and silk, from Agra.

Gold embroidered velvet carpet, with a long and two square pillows, forming a sort of throne for native princes, from Moorshadabad.

Embroidered shawls and embroidered scarfs, from Dacca.

Embroidered and net scarfs ; net square and three-cornered ; neck scarfs ; muslin, embroidered in gold and in silver ; net scarf, embroidered in gold for head-dresses ; net scarf, embroidered in silver, from Dacca.

Gold embroidered muslin and net scarfs ; net scarf, embroidered in silver ; Jamdanee scarfs, from Dacca.

Rich kincob or brocade, &c. from Benares.

Cashmere shawl, worked in green, crimson, blue, and scarlet, and embroidered in gold and silver.

Gold chundarree selah or dopatta, intended for a marriage present for Sindia, but was not ready, from the Resident at Indore.

Boorhanpoor fabrics.

Musnud cover or shawl, very richly gold embroidered.

Long shawls, red and green, and worked with needle square Cashmere shawls, from Loodianah.

Long shawls, from Lahore.

Long shawls, white; square black shawl, black, blue, and figured, Maha Rajah Goolab Singh from Cashmere.

Tinsel tape, ribbon, and thread, from Lahore.

Caps, embroidered with gold and pearls ; with other fabrics, from Benares.

Long, square, and small shawls, green, blue, and black : worked shawls, red, with pearls ; shawls, white and red ; shawl scarf, from Lahore.

Large and small broad-cloth table-covers, embroidered with silver and gold thread; broad-cloth table-cover, embroidered with silver thread; velvet chair-covers, embroidered, from Sindh.

Figured cloth, from Khyrpoor.

Fabrics of silk and gold, from Ahmedabad.

Waistcoat piece; cap pieces; tinsel ribbons; bed strings; strings for the hair, from Lahore.

Mixed silk and cotton, imitation Suttaree silk.

Mooltan tambour work; Mooltan busmedans.

Borhanpore fabric brocade, and pattern of same, from Indore.

Brocades, silk and gold, from Ahmedabad.

Loongee, with gold thread border, and gold thread, green, red, white, and yellow; the same, red, black, and yellow; large and small table-cloths, embroidered with gold and silver thread; small table-cloth, embroidered with silver thread; chair cushion covers, with gold—from Scinde.

Pattern green and orange silk, with gold thread; piece green silk, with gold thread—from Ahmednuggur.

Silk scarf from China produce, and raw pine-apple silk, chickoned, and worked by Mussulmen; worked muslin dresses; beetle-wing dresses; lace scarf—from Madras.

Fine cottar muslin, with gold lace border; cottar muslin, unwashed, with gold lace border—from Travancore.

Kincob silk, from Trichinopoly.

Cloths woven, plain red, with silk; cloths woven, purple and black; cloths woven, red, with lace—from Guntoor.

Scarfs, embroidered with gold thread, from Tringanee and Pabang, Malay Peninsula.

Silk handkerchiefs and shawls, from Tringanee, Sing, and Timor.

Scarfs, cotton, and dyes of native growth; raw silk from the continent of Asia—from Sumatra.

Embroidered cloth, from China.

Embroidered tape, from Celebes.

Infant's robe, embroidered grass cloth, from Serampore.

Muslin mantillas, jackets, and collars; pine-apple cloth and collars; muslin caps; pine-apple cloth caps; frock bodies and sleeves—embroidered; worked by natives.

Waistcoat dhoottee, cotton and munga mixed; chupean or overall coat; scarfs, gold bordered, and embroidered in gold—from Assam.

A pulla doputta for dresses, &c. from Benares.

Straw-coloured, lilac, red, and crimson kincobs; red and white mundrils; striped, green, red, and saree red lailahs; maymoodee; and dhoties, with silk border—from Benares.

Turbans and lailahs—from Tonk.

CLASS XVI.—*Leather; including Saddlery and Harness; Skins; Furs; Feathers; and Hair.*

Embroidered elephant trappings in velvet, awning in velvet, and cloth carpet; saddle-cloth in green velvet; head-stall to match, and rein, all embroidered in gold—from Moorshedabad.

Mahratta saddle, embroidered with gold and silver thread, and accoutrements complete, as used by the Mahratta nobility—from Maha Rajah Rao Scindia.

Horses' bits; reins for a bridle; saddle-cloth stall and crupper.

Saddle and cloth (floss silk and woollen)—from Kotah.

Mahratta leather and water-bag.

Bengalee made horsewhips.

Buffalo leather, manufactured for the purpose of army accoutrements; Bengal cow-hide, and a calf-skin, both tanned with the bark of the Babool tree, dressed and patent enamelled, for the purposes of carriages, and boot and shoe makers; specimens of Bengal cow-hide, similarly tanned with the same substance, the former dressed black, the two latter brown; half a buffalo-hide, tanned with Babool bark, suited for boot and shoe makers, and machinery; half a Bengal buffalo-hide, similarly tanned, and suited for harness and other purposes; half a buffalo-hide, together with other hides; calf-skins, variously tanned, dressed, and prepared, and adapted for various objects, from Messrs. Teil of Calcutta.

Leather of various kinds, from Honsoor and Trichinopoly. Camels' and other saddles.

Raw feathers; boas; artificial flowers; tippets, manufactured by natives; grey, white, black, and swan's-down boas; grey and white muffs; Commercolly muffs; fur muffs for the neck; victorines—from Commercolly.

CLASS XVII.—*Paper, Stationery, Bookbinding, Printing, &c.*

Paper made from Daphne cannabina, Nepalee Kagujj, from Nepaul and Lahore.

Paper, from Madras and Ahmedabad.

Specimens of bookbinding by natives of India.

Sealing-wax sticks, from Guntoor.

Sealing-wax, red, green, gold, yellow, and black, from Madras.

CLASS XVIII.—*Printed and Dyed Goods.*

Printed and dyed silks. Corahs. Printed and dyed calicoes from Bengal, Lahore, Cutch, Bombay, Singapore, and the Indian Islands.

CLASS XIX.—*Tapestry, including Carpets and Floor-cloth, Lace and Embroidery.*

Bengal and Sasseram cotton carpets of different sizes.

Woollen carpets and rugs, and Hookah carpets, from Mirzapore, Moorshedabad, Goruckpore, Ellore, &c.

Blankets, white, coloured, and striped.

Richly embroidered carpets in gold; gold embroidered velvet carpet; embroidered velvet carpet—from Benares.

Cashmere carpet, silk, and silk-embroidered carpets—from Lahore, Cashmere, Mooltan, &c.

Carpet for silver bed to stand on; and other fabrics in silks and woollens, plain and embroidered.

Also gold, silver, blonde, and other lace, of India manufacture.

CLASS XX.—*Articles of Clothing, &c.*

Wrappers worn by both sexes; dresses for nobility; and numerous suits, habits, clothing, and clothes, from the several Presidencies.

A Kamptee dotee or male dress. Patdhootees, male dresses. Poosoong, Pat silk, a female dress. Silk meghankshore.

CLASS XXI.—*Cutlery and Edge Tools.*

Silver-mounted carving knife and fork, in silver-mounted velvet case—from Trichinopoly.

Knives, betel-nut cutters, and other cutlery; instruments used by men of rank, as well as a wood-cutter's tools.

Carving knife and fork, and dessert knives, from Trichinopoly.

CLASS XXII.—*Iron and General Hardware.*

Metal goblet, used by natives of Malabar—from Calicut.

Wire—from Cuttack.

Brass peacock lamp, and other manufactures, as plates cups, vessels, and cooking utensils—from Agra, &c.

Cooking utensils—from Bengal.

Numerous utensils in inlaid metal, or bedry work.

Miscellaneous collection of articles used in worshipping, and for domestic use—from Nepaul.

CLASS XXIII.—*Jewellery.*

The Durria-i-Noor, or Sea of Light, Diamond set as an armlet, with ten smaller diamonds surrounding it.

A pearl necklace, consisting of 224 large pearls.

Shorter one, of 104 pearls.

Short necklace, of four very large spinelle rubies.

Pair of emerald armlets, three large stones in each.

Carved emerald and diamond turban ornament.

Set diamond and emerald bridle and martingal.

Gold-mounted saddle set with diamonds, emeralds, and rubies.

Pearl robe and emerald girdle of a Sikh chief.

Silver filigree ornaments; head ornaments; bracelets; brooches; umbrella; elephants' hair bracelets; hair pins; neck chain; girdle; flower holders—from Cuttack.

Enamelled lutchkas; garlands; gold and silver lutchkas; gold and silver gothas.

Glass bracelets; beads of silver, hollow; small globes of glass, silvered inside.

Buddha necklace; ornaments worn in turbans; gold and silver wire; silver toys, viz., Deer fighting, ram fighting, combat with tiger, wrestlers.

Armlet, engraved, iron gilt; gold thread.

Silver golabas, or rose-water bottles, embossed in gold.

Silver filigree, worked uterdan, or uter holder, in glass case; silver filigree flower-basket; baskets, &c., in the same metal and work; gold ear-rings.

Gold and silver thread from Moorshedabad.

Chain ornaments for the head; ear, nose, and thumb rings; ear and neck ornaments; pendant; armlets; ornaments for the feet; neck-chains of gold and silver—from Delhi.

Bangles of white ivory and red, worked with gold; buffalo horn, brass mounted clasp; lac gilt and plain bangles; bracelets, gilt.

Hookah bottom in silver; cocoa-nut and silver mounted; silver flower-cases, gilt; silver filigree-worked spice-box.

Diamond armlet, necklace, and ear-ring; necklace, with a star and work emeralds; string of gold moorkee; gold armlet and wristlet, &c.

Gold necklaces, bracelets, silver box, and other articles; necklace of pearls, with diamonds and emeralds.

Diamond ring, bangles set with jewels; gallow bund, with jewels and pearls; necklace of pearls; garland of pearls; armlets; ear-rings; bracelets; utter bottle; golab dan, or rosewater; pawndan.

CLASS XXIV — Glass.

Glass, plain goblets, mug, glass cup, tumblers, hydraulic toy, large phial, and pickle-pot—from Mizapore.

CLASS XXV — Ceramic Manufactures.

Jars of glazed pottery.

Assortment of Pegu jars, as used in the H. C.'s Dispensary.

Drinking cups, with covers; tumblers, with handles; vessels for sprinkling rosewater and distributing pan; cups, hookah, called Ever-fresh; large hookah, for placing on the ground; specimens of earth from which the above are manufactured.—Manufactured at Almona, district of Moradabad, in Rohilkund.

Complete assortment of native pottery for domestic purposes, from Moorshedabad and Azunghur.

Bread pot; dessert plate; goblet, &c., from Mirzapore, division Benares.

Specimens of painted pottery, from Kotah.

Specimens of painted pottery, and of earthenware, from Lahore, &c.

Improved pottery, from Madras, made by natives under the superintendence of Dr. Hunter.

CLASS XXVI.—Furniture and Upholstery.

Royal bed, with silk and velvet covering, and velvet mattress for the same.

Bedstead and cover; bedstead complete; furniture, bed pillows, two pads, &c., from Deo Narain Sing, of Benares.

Ivory chairs, from Maha Rajah Golab Sing, of Cashmere, the Rajah of Vizianagrum.

Carved couches; chiffonniers, chairs; pier tables, in black wood; sandal and ebony wood-work, &c., from Bombay.

Candelabra, bookcase, work-box, and tea-caddy, from Madras.—Exhibited by D. Pugh, Esq.

Two marble couches and chairs, of Rajpootana marble, presented by Rajah Anund Nath Roy of Nattore, in Rajpootana.

Agate, and cornelian chessmen, exhibited by Lieut.-Colonel Sykes.

CLASS XXVII.—Manufactures in Mineral Substances.

Polished variegated marble specimens; lattice-work in black and white marble, from Ajmeer, Bengal.

Stone screens, from North-west India.

Stone figures, from Gya.

Floating swans and fish, cups, bottles, and plates, in white marble, from Rajah of Joudpore.

CLASS XXVIII.—Manufactures from Animal or Vegetable Substances.

Shell bracelets; chankshell entire, cut, and partially cut; half-moon saw for cutting the shells, and complete set of apparatus used by the bracelet makers, from Dacca.

Carved cocoa-nut shells, silver mounted, black; and without silver mounting, black and brown, from Travancore.

Ivory elephant; ivory horses from Travancore.

Ivory camelleopard; bison-horn lizard; ivory images of Kistna; very small ivory elephant; and a great variety of other subjects—fruits; flowers; spices, &c.; all carved out of ivory.

Shell of a pea containing an ivory elephant, from Calicut.

Small polished cocoa-nut snuff-box; bilva-fruit snuff-box.

Sandal-wood whisk, from Calicut. Ivory whisks.

Palghat mats, of different patterns, from South Malabar.

Straw mats; reed mat; lotus flower made of sandal-wood from Calicut.

Articles cut out of ivory, of various kinds.

Hats; life-preservers, made from pith-like stem of Aschynomena aspern (Hedysarum lagenarium).

Toys; various sorts of mats—from Midnapore.

Lac ware:—Goblet, varnished; large and small pots; a kind of mug. Wood ware:—Bottle pot; large and small cups; small water-pot; pot for vermillion; plates and toys —from Mirzapore.

Baskets, inkstands, pipes, hookahs, &c., various cocoa-nut and lac hookahs.

Lacquered toys.

CLASS XXIX.—Miscellaneous Manufactures.

Boxes and other ware, in ivory, buffalo-horn, sandal-wood, porcupine-quill, and cornelian work; gold-worked shoes, and slippers and red and yellow leather shoes; and buffalo-horn combs. Furs; boxes of beads; mats.

State umbrella, and a state fan with silver sticks, from Moorshadabad. Chattahs.

Marine soap, made of cocoa-nut oil and soda.

Porcupine pen-holder, from Vizianagrum.

Sandal-wood box, from Mangalore.

Ornaments made from dried fruits.

Ivory backgammon-board; fluted envelope-case, and knitting-box; sandal-wood and ivory box; porcupine-quill box; white and black elk-horn inkstands.

Porcupine-quill baskets; box made of bison-horn, containing chains made of lac.

Specimens of sand with which lac grindstones are made; corundum stones, which being pulverized, are used in making lac grindstones; lac grindstone—from Coimbatore.

Red cotton for ink, and bottle of red ink, from Madras.

Seal cut in stone, General Munro's statue at Madras; ditto, lighthouse at Madras, from Madras.

Combs, from Scinde.

Merry-go-round.

CLASS XXX.

Clay figures, manufactured in Kishnaghur, and representing the various castes and professions of the Hindoos, viz.:—Sheristadar, sirdar-bearer; chaprassee; and many others.

G

162 JERSEY AND GUERNSEY.

Model of a collector of revenue making his settlement with the cultivators.

Model of an European and a native court of justice in the provinces, made by a native modeller; musjid wood, from Ahmedabad; beautiful style of model—from Madras.

Stone sewalla, or Hindoo temple; and model of Hindoo temple, from Bengal.

Model of unfinished roygoporum, or entrance to the pagoda at Streerungum; model of Nagasoorum pagoda, at Combaconum—from Trichinopoly.

Plaster casts, in pith white clay, from Poona, and plaster models, from Ahmednugger.

Carving in wood, " Cutch," from Rao of Cutch

Two portraits, Nabah Rajah and his father.

Pair of pith-like figures, from Trichinopoly.

JERSEY AND GUERNSEY.
—— North Areas I. J. 30. ——

Commissioners—Captain W. Walbanke Childers, Terrace House, St. Helier, Jersey, and Thomas Clugas, jun. Esq. New Grand Terrace, Guernsey.)

1 White, H. C. F.G.S. Regent Road.—Geological specimens of the granites of Jersey.

2 Le Couteur, Col. (Q: A. D. C.) Jersey.—Specimens of wheat, grown in the island of Jersey.

3 Dunlevie, Mrs. Belmont Place. — A richly knit silk purse: worked by a lady 83 years of age.

4 Berland, J. Great Union Road.—A machine to stop railway carriages instantaneously.

5 Le Moyne, H. St. Helier. Inv.—Diagrams to elucidate the method of tri-secting any angle.

6 Chevalier, J. Don St. Inv.—Model of a swinging beacon, for marking the situation of rocks. Not liable to be damaged, or carried away by sea or shipping.

7 De la Conde, M. Broad Street, Manu.—Specimens of artificial teeth of novel construction, and with double hinges.

8 Feltham, R. D, 1 Oxford Pl. St. Mark's, Jersey, Dentist.—Spring skeleton regulator, a clock which goes 500 days without winding up; its new principle being the adaptation of a pendulum, making but one complete vibration in sixteen seconds.

9 Dupre, W. H. Charing Cross, Inv.—Defiance wind guards, for the prevention of down-draught, or the descent of smoke in chimneys.—Patented. Roof light of glass.

10 Le Feuvre, P. St. Clement Academy, Inv.—Orrery, for school use.

11 Le Feuvre, Mrs. F. Edward P worked in tapestry by the exhibitor.

12 White, G. St. Mark School, Prop.—Class box and illustration board, to exhibit writing, &c. Door governor. Chimney-pot or ventilator: to prevent " down-draught." Registered. Illuminated clock: to show the hour after dark. Pump and blower, for the conveyance of water or air. (Door governor, and pump and blower, all intended for registration.)

13 Brohier, H. New Street, Prop. — Specimens of Jersey knitting.

14 De Faye, T. Seale Street, Prop.—Twelve pairs of knit stockings.

15 Vibert, S. St. Mary, Manu.—A pair of knit stockings.

16 Marie, M. King St. Manu.—Richly knitted silk jacket.

17 Scarfe, G. Beresford St. Prop.—Chaise harness.

18 Carmalt, J. David Pl. Manu.—A pair of scissors and a knife, the two less than one grain in weight.

19 Jouraud, P. Peter St. Inv. and Manu.—Carriage-gun: takes readily to pieces, and can be used as a rifle, a fowling-piece, or a pistol.

20 Le Feuvre, G. C. Edward Pl. Manu.—Chiffonnière, composed of oak, a portion the produce of the Island of Jersey.

21 Stead, W. Hill St. Manu.—A piece of furniture, applicable as a celeret or font.

22 Collie, W. Belmont House.—Specimens of calotypes, done from life.

23 Saunders, George, Bath St. — A model in paper, representing Her Majesty landing at Victoria Pier, Jersey, 3rd September, 1846.

24 Simon, Miss, Elizabeth Pl.—Basket-work, in paper; an heirloom from her progenitor, Madame Manger, in 1728.

25 Clugas, Thomas, jun. — Specimens of Guernsey granites.

26 Martin, Peter, St. Peter's Port. Prod.—Raw Silk, the produce of the Island of Guernsey. Arrowroot fecula.

27 Alleond, Emanuel, St. Peter's Port. Inv.—Model of a machine to determine the distance run by a ship, and at the same time to determine the ship's place on the chart.

28 Harris, P. G. Inv.—A corking machine.

29 MacDonald, Sophia, Woodland. Inv. Des. and Manu.—Tulle dress, embroidered with groups of floss silk flowers, copied from natural flowers.

30 Dobree, Harriet, De Beauvoir, Des. & Inv.—Table-top, ornamented with shells found in the Island of Herm. Group of poultry.

31 Hutchinson, Elizabeth, Queen's Road, Des. Inv. & Manu.—Vases, with shell flowers. Octagon table slabs in rosewood cases.

32 Sarchet, J. Victoria Road, Inv.—Model of a machine for welding chain-cable and other links.

33 Arnold, A. 11 Commercial Arcade, Manu.—Manufacture of iodine and hydriodate of potash. Specimens of the fuci and algæ which grow abundantly on the north and west coasts of the island of Guernsey. Fused mass, consisting of the ashes of these marine plants, and containing salts of soda, potash, lime, and magnesia. Iodine in the rough state. Iodine (commercial). Crystals of iodine of potassium. Residuary product, containing the salts of potash, soda, lime, and magnesia, as chlorides and sulphates.

34 Gould, T. Manu.—Salts, similar to those commonly called "Epsom."

35 Dobree, D. Forest Rectory, Prop. — Original Guernsey frock. Frock of Guernsey wool. Drawers, men's and women's stockings, nightcaps, gloves, fishermen and labourers' cravats, and slippers.

36 Le Beir, N. St. Peter's Port, Prop.—Guernsey farm-saddle. Mat and foot-stool of "han." Bullock's and horse's collar of "han." Coil of "han" rope. Shackles of "han." "Han," a hank of the raw material.

37 Dorey, D. St. Mary de Castro, Prop.—Guernsey osier crab-pot. Osier fish-basket. Large osier bait-pot. Small bait-pot.

38 Guernsey home-knitting work by cottagers.

39 Goodridge, J. jun. (of the Express steamer, running to Jersey.—Model of a life boat.

40 Valpy, Mrs. King St. St. Helier.—Specimens of conchology of Jersey, collected, classified, prepared, and arranged by exhibitor during a twenty-two years' residence in Jersey. Leather frame. Large knitted quilt.

41 Bertrams, Mrs. St. Helier, Manu.—Pair of socks knit without glasses by exhibitor, aged 93.

42 Marquard, P. Blacksmith, North Pier, Inv. and Prod.—Model of a patent truss for the yards of ships, of "Muntz" metal.

43 Pope, Mrs. Halket Pl. St. Helier, Confectioner.—Various descriptions of confectionary in sugar.

44 ELLIS, Miss (daughter of General Ellis), Prop.— Specimen of fine workmanship in leather, shown in a pier-glass frame and stand, with brackets.

45 DRAKE, FRANCIS.—Model of collapsing life boat.

46 RANDELL, MISS, Guernsey. — Two mats worked in wool.

47 LETOUREL, J. H.—Acts of the Martyrs, in French.

48 MANUEL, H. L. Jersey.—Two pair of Newfoundland fishing boats.

49 STAFFORD, MRS. B. A. Guernsey. — Stand of wax fruit.

CEYLON.
—— North Area I. J. 31. ——
(Commissioner, JOHN CAPPER, Esq.)

COLLECTION OF NATURAL PRODUCTIONS AND MANUFACTURES OF THE ISLAND OF CEYLON.

GREY, The Countess.—A gilt sprinkler under a glass shade from Ceylon.

Cocoa-nuts, from the South and West Province. Rice, general. Arrow-root, from the South Province. Manioca, from the West and South Province. Hill paddy, from the Central Province. Curugan, general. Maize, millet, and Tinne, from the South and Central Provinces.

Coffee, from the Central Province, chiefly.

Cinnamon, from the Western Province.

Talipot leaves, from the Central Province.

Manioca flour, from the West and South Province. Arrow-root flour, from the Southern Province. Sago, from the Northern Province. Vinegar, general.

Cotton, native, Bourbon, and Sea Island; from Batticaloa and Jaffna.

Coir fibre, from the South and Western Province.

Gamboge, from the West and East Province. Areca nuts, from Four Korles. Copperas, from the East and West Province.

Aloe fibre, cardamum, plantain, and hibiscus fibre, from Kandy and Colombo.

Ivory and buffalo horns, from the North and East Province. Deer horns, from the Central and North Province.

Honey and wax, from Bintenne. Hides, from Colombo. Turmeric and myrobolans, from the East Coast. Pearls. Bèche de mer, or sea snail, a radiated animal of the Holothuria tribe, from the Northern Province.

Oils:—cocoa nut, cinnamon, clove, citron, lemon grass, and cajeputi, from Colombo and Galle. Margoas oil, from Kandy. Croton and castor oils, from Colombo. Kekuna and gingelly oils, from Kandy. Citronella, meomel, and spearmint oils, from Gallee. Mee oil, from Colombo.

Models of carriages and palanquins, from Colombo.

Chekoos from the Western Province. Looms; medical stills, from the North, North-west, and South Provinces.

Forges; smelting furnaces, from the Central and South Provinces. Models of boats; guns; weapons, general, from Kandy, &c. Agricultural tools.

Cotton fabrics, plain and dyed, from the North, East, and South Provinces. Cotton painted fabrics, from Kandy.

Lace, from Galle. Cutlery, general.

Crockery, plain, and painted; and four toms, from Kandy and Matura. Matting, from Kandy and Caltura. Coir cordage, from the Southern Provinces. Coir webbing and bagging, from the Southern and Northern Provinces.

Aloe bagging, from Kandy. Hibiscus bagging, and cordage. Sansera bagging, from Colombo. Tortoiseshell and Chank ornaments, from Kandy, Matura, and Galle. Fishing lines and nets. Kandy painted baskets and boxes; umbrellas; punkahs, from Kandy.

Ornamented olas soap, from Kandy and Matura, Galle.

Carved work, ebony, from Galle and Caltura; ivory, from Four Korles; woods, from Galle and Caltura; steel, from the Central Provinces; cocoa-nut shells, from Galle

PARLETT, O'HALLORAN & Co. Colombo. — Specimens of cinnamon, with essential oils extracted therefrom, with implements for cutting and peeling.

KITCHIN, J. 42 Commercial Sale Rooms, Mincing Lane.—An ebony table, inlaid with 50 different woods; a fair specimen of Cingalese cabinet work.

Model of coffee works and apparatus used in Ceylon.

Model of patent stove and apparatus for curing coffee, by M. CLERIHEW, of Rathnagon.

Thirty specimens of medicinal oils, from T. A. PIERIS, of Kandy.

Gums and resins, from T. A PIERIS, of Kandy.

Forty specimens of ornamental and housebuilding timber Desk of porcupine quills. Ebony carved flower vase. Painted ivory fan handle.

Buffalo horns mounted in silver.

IONIAN ISLANDS.
—— North Area I. J. 30. ——

1 WOODFORD, Lady.—A Greek dress, made in Corfu. A pair of silver-bracelets, made in Corfu; the one with the motto "ΣΦΙΓΓΩ ΑΔΟΛΟΝ ΦΙΛΙΑΝ." "My pressure is that of friendship without guile;" the other, "'Ο ΦΕΡΩΝ ΑΓΑΠΗΝ." "He who feels affection" (offers it to you).

A silver brooch of elegant pierced work, formed by a garland of grapes and vine-leaves, surrounding the emblem of the Seven Islands.

A brooch in silver filigree-work, with the head of Corcyra on the one side, for Corfu; the winged horse of Bellerophon on the reverse, for Zante.

A Greek cap, made at Lefchimo, a village of Corfu, forming part of a lady's costume.

Memorial clasp in gold, made at Corfu, and of remarkable workmanship; the gold filigree being placed on a plate of polished gold, which reflects it as from a mirror.

2 MAVROIANNI, Madame.—A gold bracelet, made at Corfu, of filigree-work, surrounding the emblem of the islands.

Two silk handkerchiefs, of fine fabric, of Zante manufacture.

An apron of muslin, made in Corfu, with a border worked on linen with the needle; somewhat similar to Dresden-work, but of larger stitch, on a very elegant and classical pattern, of grapes, vine-leaves, and butterflies.

An apron of crochet-work, remarkable for the beauty of the pattern and execution, and showing that what has but recently appeared in England as an accomplishment, has been for ages the common needlework of the Ionian peasant-girls. The border is of deep Dresden-work, of magnificent effect, with emblematical designs of lions, cupids, flowers, &c.

These aprons are the ordinary work and every-day wear of the peasant-girls of Corfu. The dress of the Greek peasant women, in general, being of an extraordinary richness, so that a peasant-bride's dress is often her dowry, being not unfrequently worth 400 or 500 dollars.

3 MAVROIANNI, —.—Samples of Cephalonia currants. The island of Cephalonia, though not so rich in currants as Zante, nevertheless supplies a great part of the quantity consumed in Great Britain.

Olive-oil, the growth of Corfu.

4 FITZROY, Lord C.—Three Zante silk scarfs. A Zante handkerchief.

5 Lord SEATON. (Articles exhibited by).—1. Specimen of Cephalonian stone. 2. Three specimens of olive

wood. 3. Two large specimens of raw silk. 4. Six small specimens of raw silk. 5. Five Zante scarfs. 6. Embroidered gold bag, from Santa Maria. 7. Gold embroi dered handkerchief, from Santa Maria. 8. Large, and two small, embroidered bags, from Corfu. 9. Four specimens of samples, worked by Greek girls. 10. Gold bracelet, made after the model of an ancient one found in a tomb. 11 Silver-gilt bracelet. 12. Silver seal. 13. Ten silver bracelets. 14. Three gold rings. 15. Two silver brooches. 16. Small pocket-book, Corfu work. A silver inkstand by Anastasio Florias, of Corfu, silversmith. A wooden lamp of olive-tree wood, common in the island of Corfu, and used in the Greek churches. A knife by Antonio Arlionoli, peasant, from Prinilla, in the district of Giri, Corfu.—(Sent by Sir Henry Ward).

GIBRALTAR.

Box containing manufactured specimens of aloe and rock stone.

MALTA.
—— North Areas I. J. 32. ——

(Commissioner C. J. Gingell, Esq. of Valletta, and 66 Cornhill, London.)

1 Tonna, J. Strada Forni, Valletta, Manu.—Double-bass fiddle, made of bird's-eye maple.

2 Bonavia, C. Casal Naxaro.—Cotton sail cloth: One piece of four threads of 70 canes; one piece of five threads, containing 69 canes; one piece of six threads, containing 70 canes; one piece of seven threads, containing 70 canes. Chequered cotton cloth for carpeting: One piece of seven canes; two pieces of ten canes.

3 Schembri, G. Valletta, Manu. — Cotton tissues: Pieces of natural Malta nankeen, white, narrow, and wide squares. Piece of light colour, and damasked square.

4 Pulis, G. Montebello. — Cotton tissues: Natural nankeen, plain; striped, with Malta raw silk; and superfine plain nankeen. Sample of common Maltese cotton. Common Maltese nankeen cotton. Indian nankeen cotton. Sea-island cotton. Mastodon American cotton. Sample of cummin seed. Aniseed. Sesame seed. Sample of Maltese hard wheat (called tomnia). Soft wheat. Samples of cotton thread, from four kinds of cotton. Cotton thread, from common Maltese cotton. Maltese cotton. Sample of Maltese silk and cocoons.

5 Villa, Fratelli, Strada Mercanti, Valletta, Manu. —Cotton fabrics: White and red cotton blankets; figured counterpanes. An assortment of straw hats.

6 Fenech, V. Floriana.—Specimens of Maltese bookbinding. Collection of ancient and modern costumes of Malta.

7 Gravagna, Maria, Valletta.—Several pieces of broad lace.

8 Naudi, Rosina, Valletta.—Velvet bags, embroidered; plain embroidered muslin dress; plain embroidered baby's dress. Toilet-cover (lace, Greek style). Embroidered handkerchief. Various specimens of lace and mittens.

9 Enriquez, Maria, Valletta.—Variety of black silk mittens. Habit-shirts, plain embroidered.

10 Shembri, Antonia.—Specimens of lace with gold ʒead. Collars. Two lace collars.

11 Gozo, Salvo del.—Specimens of black silk lace.

12 Casha, Costanza, Valletta.—Piece of lace of Greek pattern.

13 Polito, Canonico, Vittoriosa.—Specimen of lace (Greek pattern).

14 Camilleri, E. Valletta.—Specimen of broad lace, with pieces for sleeves for a clerical dress. Various specimens of lace.

15 Vella, Paolo, & Co. Valletta.—Specimen of lace.

16 Camilleri, Fortunata, Valletta.—Specimen of lace.

17 Grech, Giuseppina, Valletta.—Baby's plain embroidered muslin dress.

18 Lagrestiz, Elena Nuzzo, Valletta.—Sample of embroidery with silks: Top of a pincushion.

19 Fenech, Antonia, Valletta.—Paper envelopes, embroidered with silks and gold.

20 Azzopardi, J. M. Valletta.—Pair of mittens, with beads.

21 Dimech, Mrs. Valletta. — Various specimens of long and short mittens. Long mittens with beads. A breadth of black tulle, embroidered. Black lace. Flounce and breadth of broad lace. Numerous specimens of lace. Collar and two cuffs. Maltese nankeen dresses, embroidered with wool and silk. Two pieces of Maltese nankeen.

22 The Conservatorio of San Giuseppe.—Knitted collars. Knitted fronts of habit-shirts. Specimens of knitted broad and narrow lace; knitted caps; knitted thread stockings.

23 Portelli, A. Strada Strella, Valletta. — Silver filigree reticule.

24 Cretien, E. Strada Forni, Valletta, Manu.—Gold filigree: Bracelets; rose-chain bracelets; cross and knot brooches. Double pin for hair. Rose chains. Flat and rose rings, &c.
Silver filigree: Basin. Oval plates, with flowers. Round plates. Card-cases. Candlesticks. Tea-spoons. Cups. Wreath for the head. Bead bracelets. Pins. An arrow for the hair. Bouquet-holder brooches. Stars. Knot, tie, and shawl brooches. Rose chain, &c.
Gold articles: Gold rose chain for waistcoat. Broad flat rings.

25 Falson, S. Strada Reale, Valletta, Manu.—Gold articles: Maltese rose chain. Bracelets, with scales, cameo, coral, oriental cameo, &c. Brooches, with bunch of flowers, in the form of a knot, and with a rose and flowers. Chain, imitation of Venice work. Large-sized pins. Bracelet, lace pattern. Pair of hair-pins. Various pins, with coral, mosaic work, cameo, &c. Shirt-studs. Chain rings. Rose chain rings. Small rose chain necklaces, &c.
Silver ornaments: Filigree flower-stands. Flower ornaments for the hair. Hair-pins. Plates and small cups. Bead bracelets; rose bracelets; and bracelets of Gothic pattern; rose chain bracelets. Breast-pins and chatelaines. Arrows for the hair. Large and small flowers. Shawl-pins and pincushions. Pins for necklaces, &c.
Money-bag and card-cases. Bead buttons, various sizes. Butterfly of gold and silver. Pins in the form of a cornucopium. Small pins.

26 Darmanin, J. & Sons, Strada Levante, Valletta.—Inlaid marble table-top, with the Royal arms, 4 feet long, 3 feet broad. Inlaid marble table-top, with fancy scroll and Maltese cross in the centre, 3 feet square. Inlaid marble table-top, with Etruscan vase in the centre, 2 feet 6 inches in diameter. Inlaid marble table-top, with the emblem of Carthage in the centre, 2 feet 2 inches in diameter. Pieces of Malta stone, oiled and prepared for pavement. Drip stone of Malta stone. Specimens of Malta and Gozo stone and stalactite. Vase, with pedestal of red Gozo marble. Wax and cloth figures.

27 Decesare, P. P. Strada San Giovanni, Valletta, Sculp.—Very large jugs, with pedestals, 7 feet in height, and 1 foot 11 inches in breadth. Large vases, 5 feet 2 inches in height, and 2 feet 10 inches in breadth. Jugs, 1 foot 6 inches in height, and 1 foot 2 inches in breadth.

28 Dimech, F. Strada Teatro, Valletta, Sculp.—Stone carvings: Candelabrum, 6 feet high, and 2 feet 8 inches in breadth. Large vase, 4 feet high, and 3 feet 9 inches in breadth.

29 Soler, J. (Foreman to Mr. G. Muir), Strada Reale, Valletta, Sculp.—Stone carvings: Vase with handles, 1 foot

8 inches high, 2 feet 10 inches broad. Jug, adorned with vine-leaves, 2 feet 3 inches in height, 1 foot 2 inches wide. Oval vase, 1 foot 4 inches in width. Small basket.

30 TESTA, S. Strado San Giovanni, Valletta, Sculp.— Vase, with satyrs and flowers, 4 feet 8 inches in height, and 2 feet 9 inches in breadth. Vase, with eagles, 1 foot 9 inches high, and 1 foot 3 inches broad.

31 BUTTIGIEG, M. Birchircara. — Manufactures in straw: Straw mats, hats, caps, and samples of straw plaits. Waterproof hats: two oil-skin pliable hats; two oil-skin strong hats.

32 GERADA, A. & DAUGHTERS, Strada Mercanti, Valletta.—Basket of artificial flowers, with shells.

33 TESTA, F. Strada Santa Lucia, Valletta, Sculp.— Vase of antique form, with satyrs, wreaths of flowers and vine-leaves, 5 feet 4 inches in height, and 2 feet 4 inches in breadth. Vase of antique form, with vine-leaves, 4 feet in height, and 1 foot 9 inches in breadth. Common vase, 1 foot 6 inches high, and 1 foot 4 inches broad.

34 THE CANONICO POLITO, Vittoriosa, Manu.—Figures in wax: The grand master Valletta; the grand master Lonzadari; knight of the order of Malta; grand master in warlike costume.

CAPE OF GOOD HOPE
—— South Areas L. M. 30. ——

(Agent, Mr. H. WATSON, St. Peter's Chambers, Cornhill.)

1 MAITLAND MINES, Port Elizabeth.—Lead ore, from Port Elizabeth. Iron ore, from Uitenhage. Graphite, from Cape Town. Coral, from Caledon. Oyster shells, from Uitenhage.

2 DE VILLIERS, P. I. Cape Town, Paarl.—Argol, white and red.

3 THALWITZER, M. Cape Town.—Medicinal plants and drugs; "klipsweet." Bark for tanning. Tamboukie wood.

4 JEPPE, H. Swellendam.—Medicinal plants and drugs. Specimens of soda. Mustard seed, and walnut oil.

5 BAYLEY, J. B. Caledon.—Preserved fruits; gold of pleasure.

6 VOLSTEEDT, J. P. Caledon.—Samples of maize.

7 PAARDEBERG, J. S. C. Malmesbury.—Samples of honey.

8 TRUTOR, H. A. O. Cape Town and Caledon.—Flour. Ostrich eggs.

10 BOTANIC GARDEN, Cape Town.—Samples of cotton.

11 MANUEL, C. Cape Town.—Samples of Natal cotton.

13 CLARENCE, RICHARD, Cape Town.—Sea elephant oil; sheep's tail oil.

14 KUNHARDT & Co. Cape Town.—Sheep's tail oil.

15 THOMSON, G. Cape Town.—Sea-cow teeth.

16 MEESER, F. Cape Town.—Ox horns, polished and rough.

17 WATERMEYER, C. Green Point.—Specimens of hemp (aloe).

18 BLACKBURN, J. Cape Town.—Karosses. Specimens of wild cats and jackals' paws.

19 DEANE & JOHNSON, Cape Town.—Karosses, or cloaks, such as are worn by the Kaffirs, made of the skins of wild animals. Ivory, elephants' teeth. Three Malay hats.

20 HANBURY, E. Cape Town.—Skins of wild animals.

21 BRIDGES, C. Cape Town.—Skins of wild animals. Kaffir chair, battle-axe, hoe. Buffalo, and other horns. Rhinoceros'-hide—sticks and whips. Stone box, &c.

22 CLUAPPINI, A. & Co. Cape Town.—Skins of wild animals. Twelve goat skins, weighing 65 lbs. each.

23 RUTHERFOORD, H. E. Cape Town.—Specimens of wheat. Ostrich feathers.

26 WOODMAN, J. C. Cape Town.—Manufactured olive wood. A cabinet, composed of seven species of wood, and of stinkwood.

27 THALWITZER, M. Cape Town.—Bark for tanning. Curiosities; bows and arrows; Bushman's blanket.

28 HANBURY, E. J. Cape Town.—Rhinoceros horn sticks and whips. Leopard skin.

29 MOAG, W. Cape Town.—Kaffir warrior's head-dress.

30 FOORD, R. Cape Town.—Model in clay.

30A SUTHERLAND, J. 17 Great Saint Helen's, London, (Agent to Twist Niet Steam Mills, of Messrs. J. F. Fredericksen and Thomas Sutherland, jun.)—Wheat flour, the produce of the Cape Colony.

30B BAZLEY, T.—Three bales of cotton, from Port Natal.

SOUTH AFRICAN PRODUCTIONS, forwarded by the AGRICULTURAL SOCIETY OF THE CAPE OF GOOD HOPE.

31 REITZ, RIEDA, & Co.—Samples of fine wool.

32 BREDA, D. J. VAN, Hatch river.—Samples of fine wool.

34 PRINCE, COLLISON, & Co.—A barrel of fine flour.

35 VOLSTEEDT, J. P.—Preserved fruits.

36 Moss, N. Cigars and kanaster tobacco.

37 SEARIGHT, J.—Two tins Malagas guano.

38 SMITHERS, J.—Tallow and soap.

39 SCHLUSSLER, H.—Cask of salt beef.

40 MARTIN, W.—Cask of salt pork.

41 Mossos, T.—A roll of sole leather.

42 SCHMIETERLOEW, C.—A tippet made from the feathers of various Cape birds. Samples of sole leather. Sea elephant oil.

43 MISSIONARY STATION, GROENKLOOF. — Quince walking-sticks, stained; riding whip, stained; and olive wood work-box.

44 MORAVIAN MISSIONARY STATION at GENADENDAL.— Double chopping knife, bread cutting and hunting knives, vine cutter, pocket knives, and boschlemmer knife. Box composed of thirty specimens of various woods, in the rough and polished state; olive wood box.

45 LINDENBERG, J. Worcester district.—Specimen of berry wax; specimens of bees'-wax.

46 BARN, T. A.—Sack of wheat.

47 DUMBLETON, H. George district.—Box, containing forty-three specimens of Cape woods, in the bark, rough and polished.

48 SCHEUBLE, J. H. & Co.—Forty packages and fifty-one bottles of medicinal herbs and drugs.

49 SEPPE, H.—Impure carbonate of soda, prepared from gunna ashes.

50 PASS, A. DE.—Samples of guano.

51 WATERMEYER, C.—Orchilla weed.

52 JOUBERT, J. G.—Honey.

53 BUCHANAN & LAW.—An elephant's tusk, weighing 103 lbs. another weighing 97 lbs.

54 CLARENCE, R.—Oil. Dried fruits, viz.: Almonds, peaches, raisins, apricots, pears, currants, and walnuts.

55 CALF, J.—Specimens of plumbago, Fuller's-earth, &c. Box of oyster shells, from Uiterhage.

56 GREIG, G. & Co.—Specimens of iron-ore.

57 A library chair, presented to C. B. Adderley, Esq. M.P. by the inhabitants of the Eastern province of the colony of the Cape of Good Hope. Designed by T. Baines, and carved by J. Hart, of Graham's Town.

58 Pair of polished ox horns, (with head complete,) measuring from tip to tip 8 feet 4 inches, and 21 inches in circumference—from Port Natal; and stone slab, from Natal mounted as a table.

58A CROUCH, —.—A model of machinery of H. M. S. "Dee."

59 A slab of coloured marble, from the district of Natal, mounted on a stand of oak grown on the estate of Lord Willoughby D'Eresby; carved by Messrs. Jno. Wells & Co. of Regent Street.

60 BUSH, C. J. 12 Pancras Lane, London.—Specimen of red ebony, from Natal, with fourteen engine-turned draughtsmen, made from part of the same. The wood has not been dyed, but merely oiled and polished.

WESTERN AFRICA.
— South Areas L. M. 32. —

1 WESTON, WARWICK, 73 Gracechurch St. Imp.—
1 Teak timber or African oak, for ship building, &c. 2 Iron stone. 3 Cotton, with the seed. 4 Cotton cleaned without the seed. 5 Palm oil. 6, 7 Bennie seed and ground nuts, from which oil is extracted. 8 Arrow-root. 9 The root of arrow-root. 10 Shea butter. 11 Ginger. 12 Coffee. 13 Pod pepper. 14 Cayenne pepper. 15 Gum colpa. 16 African mats and small baskets made there from dried grass. 17 African country cloths made there from their own cotton. All the produce of the Western Coast of Africa.

2 Messrs. FORSTER & SMITH.—Zobes, or cotton robes, from Sierra Leone. Pagnes, or cotton cloths, from Gambia. Knife from Gambia. Grass cloth from Sierra Leone. Table mats from Gambia. Leather pouch, containing MS. extracts from the Koran. Leather pouches worn as charms in Gambia. Ashantee glass armlets; the glass obtained by melting European beads.

3 BROWN, J. PETER, Cape Coast Castle, Gold Coast, West Africa.—A large silk-cotton horse-cloth, manufactured at Dahomey, Africa; worn by the king's favourite son.

4 ROTHERY, Miss, 10 Stratford Pl. London.—Two large wrought-cotton counterpanes, manufactured in the Cape de Verd Islands. Three silk pangs, or mantles, manufactured in the island of San Nicolas, Cape de Verd Islands; worn by the ladies of the island.

5 TROTTER, Capt. H. D. (R.N.)—Various articles of African growth and manufacture, chiefly from Egga and other places on or near the banks of the Niger, between 300 and 400 miles from its mouth; brought to England by the exhibitor.

1 Samia Aduga raw silk, can be had at Brini Cauna-town, in the Haussa country.

2 Samia Augu, manufactured at Kattam Karafi. This yellow dye is a species of arrow-root, which grows wild in some places on the banks of the Niger, and also on the coast.

3 Specimen of raw cotton, grows spontaneously on the banks of the Niger, and often cultivated by the natives.

4 Lime, material made of bones burnt into ashes, mixed with water, and dried in the sun. Used by those who spin thread to keep their fingers dry.

5 Poisoned arrows, used by the Felatahs, or Fulas, as well as by the people of Yoruba.

6 Cotton thread, including white and blue.

7 Ropes made of native hemp. Also a specimen of linspun hemp.

8 Female country cloth, worn by the higher classes; manufactured at Yabotchy. The woollen that is woven with the cotton is of European manufacture.

9 Goat or sheep skin.

10 Female dresses of country cloth, worn by the higher classes; manufactured at Illoryn, Yoruba country, and at Moko, in the Haussa country.

11 Female fashionable dress of country cloth, worn by the higher classes; manufactured at Nikij or Bahuh, in the Yoruba country. The brown cotton is taken from the silk cotton tree, which grows on the Gold Coast, and most other parts of the west coast of Africa. The natives make their canoes by hollowing it to the required size. The green leaves just budding are very wholesome, and used as vegetables.

12 Female dresses of country cloth, manufactured at Seluh, a town nine days' journey on foot from Nubba, a town on the left bank of the Niger.

13 Female dress of country cloth, generally worn, after it has been dyed, by the higher classes as a shawl; manufactured at Yabotchy.

14 Female dresses of country cloth, manufactured at Ki-lamij and in Yoruba country.

15 Female dresses of country cloth, worn by all classes, by young females of respectable birth, and by the higher classes; manufactured at Yabotchy and Yoruba.

16 Female dresses of country cloth, worn by the higher classes. The red silk to be had only at Brini Canu.

17 A variety of other country cloths, worn by different classes; manufactured at Yoruba, Abuna, and Egga.

18 Full-size country cloth, worn by the respectable people, and also used as a counterpane; manufactured at Little Popo, in the Bight of Benin. The red thread is of European manufacture.

19 Female head-bands, worn by the higher and lower classes; manufactured at Yabotchy and Egga.

20 Female fine dress head-band, worn by the higher class of people. The red silk brought by the Arabs through the desert from Tripoli into Haussa country, and amongst other towns to Birmi or Brini Canu.

21 Female head-band; length 4 ft. 1 in. The brown cotton is taken from the silk cotton tree.

22 Fine and blue-glazed tobes, worn by the higher class. The manner in which the tobe is glazed is as follows:—After the cloth has been well dyed, it is taken out of the indigo dye, and hung up until it is thoroughly dry; then it is spread on a wooden roller, well rubbed with the shell of a snail as hard as the force of the wrist can bear, which gives the gloss.

23 Fine plain and dyed unbleached cotton tobe.

24 Fine dress striped tobe, worn by the higher class of people. The yellow colour is dyed at Kattam Karafi, a town on the left bank of the Niger, a short distance above its confluence with the Chadda. The red silk is brought by the Arabs into the Haussa country.

25 Fine checked short tobe, wove with raw silk, worn by the higher class of people.

26 Fine checked long tobe, and Haussa trousers, braided with red silk about the ankles, made after the Turkish fashion; worn by the higher class of people.

27 Strainer or sieve, made out of the slips of bamboo; manufactured at Brini Canu.

28 Small earthen cooking pot and cover, earthen dishes, and stands for lamps; used by the higher class of people.

29 Cushion. The red baize of European manufacture; the yellow skin dyed by the natives of Kattam Karafi.

30 Strings of fancy palm nut beads, made out of burnt kernels; worn round the waist and neck by respectable females.

31 Coloured basket, made out of bamboo; manufactured at Birmi or Brini, in the Haussa country.

32 Basket to hold provisions, rice, corn, &c.

33 Calabash bowl; wooden bowl carved out of solid wood; and calabashes, various sizes. Used by both high and low class of people either to eat or drink out of.

N.B. Calabashes are made out of a species of pumpkin, which is not eatable, and which has a bitter taste similar to that of quassie. The largest sizes are between twelve and thirty inches diameter. They are used to convey provisions from one place to another.

34 Wooden carved ladles or spoons.

35 Bag to hold corn or articles of commerce.

36 Netted bag, for exposing articles of commerce in the market-place.

37 Dahomian leather bag.

38 Carved ivory bracelet, from Egga.

39 Two mats from Egga, brought there by Richard Lander in 1833.

5A Articles brought to England, and now exhibited by

J. O. M'WILLIAM, M.D. F.R.S. Principal Medical Officer of the late Expedition to the Niger.

1 Shea butter (fat of the Bassia Parkia), from Egga, River Niger.

2 Camwood dye ball, from the confluence of Niger and Tchadda.

3 Bow and arrows, with iron barbs, from the Icari market, River Niger.

4 Filatah spear, from Kakundah.

5 Small musical instrument from Kakundah, River Niger.

6 Cloth made at confluence of Niger and Tchadda.

7 Cloths from Egga and Kakundah, River Niger.

8 Horn ornamented on silk, worn by the females at Iddah, River Niger.

9 Small leathern bottles, for galena to dye the eyelids. Confluence of Niger and Tchadda.

10 Tobe, embroidered in front with needlework; worn by the Mallams at Rabbah (Filatah-town), River Niger.

11 Breeches of the same. (These articles 10 and 11 are the property of Sir James Clark, Bart. Physician to Her Majesty.)

12 Knitted and small scarfs from Egga.

13 Broad-brimmed straw-hat, from Kinee, or Icari Market, River Niger.

14 Earthenware, from Icari Market, River Niger.

15 Ropes of vegetable fibre, by which the Africans ascend the naked trunks of the palm trees.

16 Calabash workmanship, comprehending a series of dishes of various kinds and sizes, and platter spoons, bottles, cups, &c.

17 Pipe, from confluence of Niger and Tchadda.

18 Staff of honor, carried before the African chiefs.

18A Fetische from the River Congo, in the garb of a slave travelling through the country. Bag made by one of the wives of Obi, the king of Eboe: River Niger. Phosphate of lime from bones, used by the cotton-spinners to dry the tips of their fingers: at the confluence of the Niger and the Tchadda.

5B JAMIESON, J., Custom House Agent, London.
Mandingo cup, sword, and dagger, from the River Gambia. Calabash and spears, brought from the Gambia.

6 HUTTON, W. B. & SONS.—Dahomey cloth or dress, manufactured at Abomey. Dahomey chief's throne and cushion, made at Abomey. Tusk of the Queen elephant, worshipped by the natives of Dahomey. Grass hat, made and worn by the natives of Dahomey. Popo cloth or dress, manufactured at Popo on the Oil Coast. Basket, manufactured by the natives of Little Popo. Ashantee chief's cloth or dress, manufactured at Coomassie, capital of Ashantee. Copper weights, used by the Ashantees for weighing gold: cast in clay moulds. Powder and shot belts, made of leather in the neighbourhood of Cape Coast. Specimen of the intergrowth of two branches of different trees from Cape Coast. Dagger, made at Grand Bassam. Grass cloth, the only article of clothing worn by the natives. St. Andrew's drum, made of monkey-skin. Mandingo cloth, manufactured by the Mandingoes on the River Gambia. War dress and sword, made and worn by the Mandingoes. Fiddle, made and used by the Mandingoes. Specimens of palm fruit, kernels, oil, and kernel oil soap. Ground nut, nut oil and soap.

7 KING, R. & W. Bristol.—Three cushions from the king of Dahomey. Two pieces of cotton cloth of same country.

8 FORBES, Commander F. G. (R.N.)—Two weavers' looms, chief's stool and footstool, and two lamps, from Dahomey. Dress worn by the Amazons of the king of Dahomey. Bag manufactured at Wydah, on the west coast of Africa.

9 MATSON, Capt. (R.N.)—Cap worn by the chiefs of Kabenda (Congo) Musical instrument, with a gourd as a

sounding-board (River Congo). Fetisches, from the same river.

10 MILLER, T. Esq. Ireland, and also of San Nicolas, Cape de Verd Islands.—Door lock, used at the Cape de Verd Islands. This lock is nearly the same as that which has been in use with the Egyptians for some forty centuries.

11 TOWNSEND, G. Esq. Exeter.—From Abbrokuta; cloth; market-basket iron bracelets; native dress; and drum.

12 BEECHAM, Rev. Dr.—Hat and messenger's bag of Mandingo manufacture, from the Gambia. Large Ashantee cloths. Pipes from Coomassie. Brass figures used as weights. Chief's stool and large round cushion, from Ashantee. Cartouche box of Dahomey manufacture. Two market baskets; water pot; market bags made of grass, from Badagry. Specimen of raw indigo from Abbrokutu.

13 TOWNSEND, G. Exeter. — Various articles from Abberkutu, a town of 50,000 inhabitants in the Yoruba country.

14 ACLAND, Lady.—Two pieces of native cloth from Abbrokuta.

15 FORBES, Commander F. G. Royal Navy.—Various articles from Dahomey.

16 SUTHERLAND, Her Grace the Duchess of.—Various birds from the River Niger.

17 ACLAND, Sir T. D. Bart. M.P.—A sword or hatchet from Abbrokuta.

18 STRAITH, Major H.—Two grass cloths from Abbrokuta.

19 FADDY, Col. P. (R.A.), Woolwich, Prop. — A koodoo, a harte-feest, and a water-boc (a male), killed by Captain Faddy, R.A., nearly 2400 miles from Cape Town, in Kaffirland. The water-boc (a male) is the only specimen that has ever been brought to Europe.

20 Mrs. Col. FADDY, Pro.—Gold aresbesque scarf of Fez manufacture. Pair of Barbary ladies slippers. Vase of Barbary ware.

21 HUTTON, J. F. 25 Watling St. Imp.—African produce :—Cotton cloth, made by the slaves of the King of Dahomey, at Aboney, 90 miles in the interior of Africa. Cushion for a seat, made at the same place, and by the same people. Cotton cloths, made at Popoe, on the slave coast of Africa; and at St. Andrew's, West. Grass cloths, for wearing round the loins. Cotton cloths, from the banks of the river Gambia. Baskets, from Popoe. The cotton of these manufactures is grown and spun in Africa by the natives—all the dyes are native, except the red.

22 JAMIESON, R. Esq. Liverpool.—Articles from the Niger and other parts of Western Africa: 1—4 Copper jug, &c. 7 Earthenware pot. 10—15 Calabashes, with rings and with spoon. 18 Basket. 27—29 Three combs. 32 Rings. 34—38 Five fans. 39—41 Grass fan; antimony ore; and pepper. 33 Tablet. 42—63 Two grass bags; pein sandals; boots; flask; brass case, earthenware, and kid skin, for antimony; spurs; tin case for papers; leather knife; reaping-hook; small arms; leather wallet; string of beads; leather threads; beads. 65, 66 Two knives. 67—69 Calabash handles; leather; nuts. 79 Spear-head.

23 SWANZY, A. Esq.—Specimens of rock gold, from Ashantee.

24 Specimens of Dahomain cloth, from Porto Rico.

GOLD COAST AND ASHANTEE.

1 FORSTER & SMITH, Messrs.—Ashantee glass armlets, composed of glass obtained by melting down European beads. Cotton cloth prepared with native dyes. Silk cloth woven from silk threads obtained by unravelling European silk goods. Copper figures, used as gold weights by the natives,—all from Ashantee. Weaving and spinning instruments; cotton cloths; gold ornaments; pottery used for

cooking; pipe heads and pipe stem; native leather; grass and mixed grass and cotton cloths, all from the Gold Coast.

CANADA.
—— South Areas L. M. 31, N. O. 31 32. ——
(Commissioner, HENRY HOUGHTON, Esq.)

1 LOGAN, W. E. Director of Provincial Geological Survey, Montreal.—A collection of minerals from various parts of the province, consisting of ores of iron, zinc, lead, and copper; native silver and stream gold; earthy manganese, cobalt bloom; uran ochre, molybdenite, chromic iron, dolomite, magnesite; barytes, iron ochre; lithographic stone; agates; sandstone for glass making; soap-stone, asbestus; millstone rock, whetstones, tripoli earth; gypsum; white and red bricks, roofing slates, granite and limestone for building; hydraulic limestone, marbles, serpentine; asphalt.

2 WILSON, Dr. J. Perth.—Magnetic iron ore, from South Sherbrooke. Phosphate of lime, from Burgess. Dolomite, from Dalhousie. Serpentine, from Burgess. Perthite, peristerite, and graphic granite, from Bathurst.

3 DICKSON, Mr. Sheriff, A. Packenham.— Specular iron ore from Macnab.

4 MARMORA IRON COMPANY, Marmora.—Pig-iron, smelted at their furnace, from the magnetic ore of the township.

5 FERRIER, Hon. J. Montreal.—Specimens of iron, bog-iron ore, and refractory sandstone.

6 LANCASTER, —, Vaudreuil.—Specimens of bog-iron ore, and phosphate of iron.

7 PROULX, J. St. Eustache.—Specimens of bog-iron ore, from Rivière du Chêne.

8 MARCOTTE, F. Portneuf.—Specimens of bog-iron ore.

9 MORIN, Capt. St. Vallier.—Specimens of bog-iron ore.

10 MONTREAL MINING COMPANY.—Copper ore, from Bruce mines, Lake Huron, and tough cake copper, smelted there from the same. Native copper and silver, from St. Ignace Island, Lake Superior.

11 BADGLEY, J. F. Montreal.—Silver ore, from Prince's Location, Lake Superior; and smelted silver from the same.

12 CHAUDIERE MINING COMPANY, Quebec.—Specimens of native gold.

13 CLAUSEN, CHEVALLIER, London.—Labradorite, from Labradore, &c.

14 HARWOOD, Hon. —, Vaudreuil.—Specimens of black-lead from Grenville.

15 BOUDOIN & LEBERE, Vaudreuil. — Specimens of white quartzose sandstone for glass making.

16 SEER, L. M. St. Eustache.—Specimens of iron ochre.

17 LA BARRE, D. G. Point du Lac.—Specimens of iron ochre.

18 HALL, J. Melbourne.—Specimens of iron ochre, and roofing slates.

18A HERBERT, J. W. Montreal, Manu.—A pianoforte. Case of type. Indian dress.

19 CARON, E. St. Ann, Montmorency.—Specimens of iron ochre.

19ARAHU, C. Toronto.—A set of dentistry.

20 QUIGLEY, M. Frampton.—Specimens of slates.

21 DUBERGER, G. Murray Bay.—Specimens of iron ochre, from Iberville.

22 KELLY, R. W. Gaspé.—Specimens of iron ocre and shell marl.

23 YEOMENS, A. Belleville.—Specimen of shell marl.

24 DE LESDERNIERES, P. T. C. Vaudreuil.—Specimen f shell marl.

25 BOSTON, Mr. Sheriff, Montreal.—Shell marl.

26 BOUTILLIER, Dr. St. Hyacinthe.—Samples of peat.

27 LOGAN, J. Montreal.—Three bushels fall wheat.

28 ALLAN, J. Longpoint.—Three barrels of wheat.

29 WEESE, W. F. Ameliasburgh.—Three barrels of spring wheat.

30 DESJARDINS, P. Terrebonne. — Three barrels of spring wheat.

31 LAURENT, D. Varennes.—Three barrels of spring wheat.

32 DRUMMOND, J. Petite Coté.—Three barrels of spring wheat.

33 PROVINCIAL AGRICULTURAL ASSOCIATION, Canada, W.—Three barrels of fall wheat.

34 GRAHAM, J. Sydney.—Three barrels of fall wheat.

35 PROVINCIAL AGRICULTURAL ASSOCIATION, Canada, W.—Three barrels of fall wheat, raised by Mr. Christie of Dumfries, C. W.

36 TITTEMORE, G.—Barrel of oats.

37 MUIR, A. Hinchinbrooke.—Barrel of oats.

38 WATTS, R. M. Grantham.—Barrel of oats.

39 BOA, W. St. Lawrent.—Barrel of peas.

40 LIMOGES, D. Terrebonne.—Barrel of peas.

41 JONES, D. Sydney.—Barrel of peas.

42 LAMERE, Madame, Montreal.—Barrel of beans.

43 FISHER, J. Riviere du Prairie.—Barrel of horse-beans.

44 BRIEN, J. St. Martin's.—Barrel of yellow beans.

45 FOURNIER, C. Longueuil.—Barrel of beans.

46 BOA, W. St. Lawrent.—Barrel of barley.

47 DESJARDINS, P. St. Rose.—Barrel of buckwheat.

48 SIMPSON, J. and Co. Bowmanville.—Barrel of flour.

49 LINGHAM, T. Thurlow.—Two barrels of flour.

50 TAILEY, V. P. Thurlow.—Barrel of flour.

51 SQUAIR, R. Bowmanville.—Two barrels of oatmeal.

52 FRENHOLM, E. Kingsey, E. T.—Barrel of buckwheat flour.

53 CANIFF, F. and T. Thurlow.—Barrel of buckwheat flour.

54 TRENHOLM, E. E. T. Kingsey.—Barrel of Indian meal.

55 RICHER, A. St. Lawrent.—Barrel of Indian meal.

56 SHAW, A. Toronto.—Specimens of corn in the ear.

57 LOGAN, J. Montreal.—Specimens of corn in the ear.

58 DESJARDINS, B. St. Rose.—Barrel of flax seed.

59 FISHER, J. Riviere du Prairie.—Specimens of Siberian oil-seed.

60 UBARDEAU, S. St. Anne.—Barrel of timothy seed.

61 M'GINN, T. Montreal.—Barrel of timothy seed.

62 JEFFRIES, J. Burodan.—Specimens of red clover seed, and garden seeds.

63 SHEPHERD, G. Montreal.—Various samples of garden seeds.

64 SMITH, B., Stanstead.—Bale of hops.

65 PENNER, J. Lachine.—Bale of hops.

66 CENTRAL COMMISSION, Montreal.—Samples of double refined and unrefined maple sugar.

67 BALES, J. York.—Specimen of double refined maple sugar.

68 PARKER, J. Hatley.—Specimen of maple sugar.

69 FISHER, A. Ascott.—Specimen of maple sugar.

70 BASTIEN, M. St. Rose.—Specimens of flax.

71 GRICE, F. Montreal.—Specimens of hemp and of seed.

72 MACCULLOCH, Dr. J. Montreal.—A fungus from the pine-tree, used in Canada as a bitter tonic.

73 LEVEY, J. Montreal.—Roll of tobacco.

74 EGAN, J. Ottawa.—Plank of bird's-eye maple.

75 REED & MEAKINS, Montreal.—Planks of birch, cherry, pine, bird's-eye and curled maples, and butternut.

76 PARISAULT, J. St. Martin.—Plank of chesnut.

77 PARISAULT, F. St. Martin.—Planks of soft maple and beech.

78 DAVIS, J. Simcoe.—Plank of black walnut croch.

79 HENSON, J. Dawn.—Black walnut plank. Indian corn in the ear.

80 CENTRAL COMMISSION, Montreal.—Shipbuilding crooks and futtocks, planks of pine, spruce, tamarack, bird's-eye maple, soft maple, basswood, ash, curled ash, birch, red rock elm, butternut, black walnut, white oak, and ironwood.

81 CENTRAL COMMISSION, Montreal. — Specimens of maple veneer. Cross of oak veneer. Black walnut veneer.

82 BRAINERD, O. N. Hamilton, Canada West.—Corn-whisps and dusters.

83 BRAINERD, O. M. Hamilton.—Corn-brooms.

84 NELSON & BUTTERS, Montreal.—Corn-brooms and whisps.

85 WEESE, W. F. Ameliasburgh.—A churn.

86 BAILEY, J. Sherbrooke.—Several pails.

87 DODD, R. S. Ayr.—A tub.

88 SKINNER & MCCULLOCH, Brookville. — Several pronged hay-forks. Two and four-pronged hay-forks. Manure-fork. Scythe snaiths.

89 GLASSFORD, —, Brookville.—A grain cradle.

90 SKINNER & MCCULLOCH, Brookville.—Grain cradles.

91 HULBERT, S. Prescott.—A plough.

92 FLECK, A. Montreal.—A light plough.

93 CENTRAL COMMISSION, Montreal.—A turnip cutter.

94 ALLO, J. Montreal.—Specimens of calf leather, upper, and harness leather. Tanning materials.

95 M'LEAN & CUMMINGS, Chippewa.—Sides of sole leather.

96 MURRAY, H. Montreal.—Calf skins. Sides of upper leather.

97 TEONGATHASEA, P. Quebec.—Specimen of moose skin.

98 TOURANGEAN, P.—Specimen of tanned moose hide.

99 THOMPSON, T. Three Rivers.—Pair of moose horns.

100 ALLON, J. Montreal.—Tanning materials.

101 HOLWELL, —, Quebec.—A duplex safety rein.

102 DEAN, R. Montreal.—A patent leather travelling trunk.

103 BELL, P. W. St. Catherine.—An Indian saddle.

104 WARDLE, M. Montreal.—Shoe-lasts.

105 MCGILLAN & SULLIVAN, Hamilton. — Hunting saddle.

107 HENDERSON, J. Montreal.—Bear, wolf, and fox-skin sleigh robes.

108 WILLOCK, J.

109 JETU, C. A. Quebec.— Dressed porpoise-skin and whale-skin leather.

110 BARBEAU, J. Quebec.—Fishing boots of deer-skin leather, with whalebone stiffeners

111 DANGERFIELD, —, Montreal.—Pair of ladies' shoes.

112 CENTRAL COMMISSION, Montreal.—Long and short Canadian boots.

113 MORRIS, R. Montreal. — Set of double sleigh-harness.

114 MORRIS, J. Montreal.—A black walnut bedstead.

115 PATERSON, G. Dundas.—Blankets and assortments of cloths

115A REED & MEAKINS, Montreal.—Chairs, sofas, chiffonnière, and black walnut centre table.

116 LAFLAMME, M. A. Montreal.—Patterns of oil-cloth, and table-cloths.

117 RAMSAY & MCARTHUR, Montreal.—Tables of painted mahogany, and of imitation oak and marble.

118 HAMMOND, R. Montreal.—A stone centre-table.

119 DUNN, W. Quebec.—Embroidered chairs.

120 REDHEAD, T. Montreal.—Black walnut chairs. An office chair.

121 ALLAN, W. Montreal.—Drawing-room chair.

123 HILTON, J. & W. Montreal.—Walnut centre and pier-tables. Spring-back sewing-chair. Various chairs. Two tête-à-têtes.

124 M'FARLANE, A. Côte des Nieges.—Specimens of glue.

125 PRENDERGAST, J. Montreal.—Samples of starch.

126 ROBB, J. Montreal.—Box of biscuits.

127 FLETCHER, J. Montreal.—"Maiden hair" syrup. Raspberry vinegar.

128 BRUNSDEN & SHIPTON, St. Hilaire. — Preserved potatoes, particularly adapted for ships' stores on long voyages. Potato starch.

129 PARISAULT, J. St. Martin.—Bees'-wax.

130 LEVEY, J. Montreal.—Samples of snuff.

131 LYNAM, H. Montreal.—Samples of honey.

132 PENNER, J. Lachine.—Bottled cider.

133 GILLESPIE & Co. Montreal.—Barrel of vinegar made from wood.

134 STEWART, W. Toronto.—Barrel of fine ship biscuit. Set of single sleigh harness, made of patent leather.

135 FITTS, A. Montreal.—Fancy biscuits.

136 FLETCHER, J. Montreal.—Samples of candy.

137 BEAN, S. HATLEY, C.E. — Woollen counterpane; table-cloths.

138 DIXON, T. Toronto.—Woollen counterpane.

139 GAMBLE, W. Milton Mills.—Horse-blanket. Pieces of carpeting. Assortment of blankets.

140 BARBER, Messrs. Esquesing.—Piece of carpeting.

141 FORTIER, M. St. David.—Piece of linen.

142 BEAN, S. E. T.—Table-cloths.

143 WILLET, Messrs. Chambly.—Piece of grey cloth.

144 McKAY & Co. New Edinburgh.—Pieces of grey cloth and of satinette, of various kinds.

145 HENDERSON, H. Montreal.—Embroidered table-cloth.

146 PATTERSON, J. Dundas Mills.—Six pair of blankets. An assortment of woollen cloths.

147 WALLACE, A. Montreal.—Bench and moulding-planes.

148 SCOTT & GLASSFORD.—A chopping-axe.

149 SHAW, S. Toronto.—Hunting, chopping, and broad axes. Coopers' tools. Framing chisels.

150 LEAVITT, G. Dundas.—Chopping and broad axes.

150A RICE, W. H. Montreal.—Wire cloth.

151 CHENEY, G. H. Toronto.—A cooking-stove.

151A LADD, C. P. Montreal.—Patent balance scales to weigh 20 cwt. Various chopping axes.

152 HOLLAND & DUNN, Montreal.—Cut nails, assorted.

154 MOLSON, G. E. Montreal.—A church bell.

155 CHENEY, G. H. Toronto.—A sad-iron plate.

156 CHENEY, G. H. Toronto.—A parlour-stove.

157 PERRY, J. Montreal.—A copying-press.

158 GARTH, C. Montreal.—A steamboat engine-gong. A steam-boiler gauge-cock of improved construction. A 1-inch water-cock or valve.

159 CHENEY, G. H. Toronto.—Copper furniture for a stove.

160 BOYD, F. J. Montreal.—A cut rifle gun.

161 ASHFIELD, J. Toronto.—A cut rifle gun.

162 BARTRAM, A. Montreal.—Model cannon, &c.

163 DE MONTENAC, Madam.—City arms.

164 FERGUSON, W. Montreal.—Flexible branch-pipes.

165 CLARKE, J. Montreal.—Ship-blocks, of various kinds.

166 THRELKELD, —, Toronto.—An assortment of whips.

167 WHEELER, T. Toronto.—Various brushes.

168 HENDERSON, —. Quebec.—Coils of rope.

169 SPOONER, A. Montreal.—Box of twine, assorted.

170 DIXON, T. Toronto.—Specimens of cordage.

171 CENTRAL COMMISSION, Montreal.—A bark canoe.

172 ONDAGAHOUT, P.—Pair of snow-shoes; also mocassins.

173 BELL, P. W. St. Catherine.—Indian dress, viz. coat, pair of leggins, cap, gun-case, knife-case, bracelet, and pair of small belts.

174 HENDERSON, T. Montreal.—Embroidered slippers, cigar-cases, purses, and fan.

175 ROCHELEAU, HELEN, Three Rivers.—Bark box and fan.

176 CAMPBELL, Major, St. Hilaire.—Bark tray and box.

177 INDIANS OF LORETTE.—Indian curiosities.

178 McLEAN & WRIGHT, Montreal.—Single sleigh, with pole and shafts.

179 O'MEARA, M. Montreal.—A double sleigh.

180 LAURIN, J. J. Quebec.—A single sleigh. A light carriage and wheels.

181 PERRY, G. J. Montreal.—Fire-engine and hose-reel.

182 JOSEPH, J. G. Toronto.—A theodolite and stand.

183 McPHERSON, J. and Sons, Montreal.—A clarionet and a cornopean.

185 HIGGINS, P. H.—Violin and case.

186 PARKES BROTHERS, Toronto.—Various specimens of turning.

187 HENDERSON, —. Montreal. Case of pipes, assorted.

188 MATTHEWS, C. Montreal.—A lithotype.

189 PALSGRAVE, J. T. Montreal.—Case of type.

190 MEYER, H. Toronto.—A lithographic drawing.

191 STARKE & Co. Montreal.—Ornamental letter-press printing.

192 BUREAU & MARCOTTE, QUEBEC.—Specimens of plain and ornamental typography.

193 DICKINSON, C. M. Montreal.—Specimens of dentistry.

196 IRWIN, J. Montreal.—Travelling trunk.

244 LEWIS, R. Melbourne.—Model bridges.

301 CENTRAL COMMISSION, Montreal.—Wooden snow-shovels. Ornamental stool, with moose feet.

324 MANN, A. Montreal.—Mineral waters.

326 NICHOLSON, R. Montreal.—Barrel of beef.

329 MATTHEWSON & SON, Montreal. — Case of fancy soaps. Case of common soaps and candles.

331 ADAMS, W. H. F. Montreal.—*Etoffe du pays* suit of clothes. A fancy double coat.

333A STEWART, —. Toronto. — Set of single sleigh harness, lined with red morocco, showing a self-adjusting pad.

334 MORRIS, R. Montreal.—Military helmet. Proposed helmet of the Rangers, made for Sir James Alexander, A.D.C.

339 COMMISSIONERS, Quebec.—Straw-hats.

340 SAVAGE, G. & SON, Montreal.—A silver embossed tea-kettle. Silver table-spoon and fork. Silver dessert and tea-spoon.

341 LEGGATT, H., Montreal. — Gold cable-chain and other articles of jewellery.

346 RODIER, P. St. Hyacinthe.—A model locomotive.

351 DUNCAN, J. Montreal.—Designs for coinage.

353 WHEELER, T. Toronto.—Medallion in gutta percha of the Earl of Elgin, Governor-General of Canada, and the die from which the same was struck.

354 PERRY, J. Secretary, Canada Company, London.— A case of Canadian stuffed birds.

355 ASHTON, J. P. St. Laurent.—Specimens of the cottonia plant, or wild cotton.

NOVA SCOTIA.
—— South Area P. 30, 31, 32. ——

1 ACADIAN IRON MINING ASSOCIATION.—Iron, steel, tin plates, wire, cutlery, bars of iron and steel polished, pig and cast iron.

2 ARCHIBALD, C. D. (F.R.S.) 15 Portland Place.—

A collection of specimens intended by the exhibitor to prove the capacity of Nova Scotia to produce steel and charcoal iron, in quantities sufficient for the supply of the whole British Empire, and in quality equal to the best foreign articles, but at greatly reduced prices. Iron, cast and pig; grey, nettled, bar, and rod. Steel iron; horse nails, &c. Steel; bars, polished; and wire. Manufactured articles, as fenders, sword blades, knives, scissors, edge tools, surgical instruments, &c. Magneto-electric machines, steam engines, and working models.

ARTICLES exhibited by the CENTRAL COMMITTEE in NOVA SCOTIA, consigned to the care of C. D. ARCHIBALD, Esq. Portland Place. (Agent, Mr. MACLEAN, Lobby, Custom-house.)

Geological prints on clay. Specimens of freestone. Yellow and burnt ochre. Mineral paints. Coal. A fossil-tree. Shell, marl, and lime. Iron ore, and other mineral specimens. Samples of cod-liver oil. Chemical preparations. Maple sugar in crystals; pulverized; and in syrup. Samples of wheat grown by Indians, and grown by the farmers; weight 64 lbs. 11 oz. per bushel. Sample of maple sugar. Preserved fish. Digby herrings. Barley, wheat, straw, and oats. Indian corn. Beef and ham, 90 lbs. Bacon, &c. Specimens of woods: Curled maple, bird's-eye maple, veneered birch, grey and white oak, and lepidodendron stem. Young seal-skins. Specimen of human bones (Indian). Samples of hay-seed, moose heads, and horns; carriboo. Collection of botanical specimens. Specimens of preserved animals, birds, and insects. The birds stuffed by Mr. Andrew Downs, of Halifax.

Skins of wild cat (*Felis catus*); lynx (*Felis lynx*); red, cross, black, silver, and white fox (varieties of *Vulpes communis* and *Vulpes lagopus*); American hare (*Lepus americanus*); martin (*Mustela marites*); minx (*Mustela lutreola*); raccoon (*Procyon lator*); otter (*Lutra vulgaris*); beaver (*Castor canadensis*); bear (*Ursus americanus*); wolf (*Canis lupus*) weasel (*Mustela erminea*); squirrel (*Sciurus*); flying squirrel (*Pteromys volucella*); silver-grey fox, martin, musquash (*Nasua socialis*); raccoon, and cat-skin sleigh-robes. Two iron castings One Indian canoe and three paddles. Sample of French home-spun grey, green, striped, and plaid cloth. Check home-spun plaid cloth and brown cloth. Two shawls. Quilts, blankets, woollen hearth-rugs, &c. Woollen vest. Socks and mitts, assorted. Pairs of fine and coarse pegged boots. Shoe-lasts. Snow-shoes with mocassins. Grass bonnets and hats. Down hat, muff, victorine, and cuffs. An Indian dress, cradle, chairs, seats, mats, cigar-cases, and other Indian work. Map of Nova Scotia, and hand-book. Book of music. Piano, in case of bird's-eye maple. Soap and candles. Eel-spear and fishing-rods. Indian fan, reticule, hood, purse, and mocassins. Indian and negro bones and baskets. Reticules of grass.

NEWFOUNDLAND
—— South Area Q. 32. ——

1 STABB, EWEN, Liverpool St. London.—Samples of cod-liver oil purified (of much efficacy in pulmonary complaints), from the manufactory of W. L. M'Kay, St. John's, Newfoundland.

NEW BRUNSWICK.
—— South Area Q. 32. ——

Specimens of forest and other trees; as Bird's-eye, Carly Maple, Black birch, &c.

Wheats, white and blad; oats; beans, and other pulse and grain of many varieties; Italian maize.

Turquoise, cornelian, and other stones. Seeds: carrot, parsley, onion, &c.

Iron ores; muriates; grindstones.

Preserved salmon, and fresh codfish.

1 GREY, The Dowager Lady.—A canoe, with three figures, representing Joseph Jamar, the chief of the Melicite tribe of Indians, his squaw and her popoose, in their state costume. Sent by the Misses Close, two aged ladies who reside in the vicinity of the tribe.

2 GIBBS, BRIGHT, & Co. Liverpool—A figure head of an Indian chief.

3 GOULD, N. 4 Tavistock Sq. Imp.—Specimens of jet coal, or asphalte, recently discovered on the banks of the river Peticodiac, Albert County, New Brunswick, and not hitherto been discovered in any other part of British America. This coal has been found to produce gas of the purest colour, and in greater quantity than any other coal hitherto used for the purpose. (The property of Edward Allison, Esq. of St. John's.)

1. Lump of Plumbago.

ST. HELENA.
—— South Area Q. 32. ——

1 MASSANS, S.—Sample of coffee grown in St. Helena.

2 AGRICULTURAL SOCIETY of ST. HELENA, per Capt. BOLTON, 18 Wilton St. Belgrave Sq.—Box of raw cotton. Box of alkali, made from the Salsola plant. Bar of rock salt.

3 MAGNUS, SAMUEL, 127 Fenchurch St.—A bag of St. Helena coffee.

MAURITIUS.
—— South Area Q. 31. ——

1 GREY, The Countess.—Basket and wreath of flowers from the Sechelles Islands, made from the leaves of the palm of the Sechelles (*Nipa fruticaus*). A nest of baskets.

2 DUPONT, EVENOR, Esq., Port Louis.—A packet containing seven pounds of white silk, the produce of the Island of Mauritius, from silkworms reared in the district of Tamarin. The quality of the silk must not be taken as a criterion of what Mauritius will produce, as the manufacture is in its infancy, and has only lately been commenced.

About 300 acres of ground have been planted in the cooler districts of Mauritius with mulberry trees, which have rapidly grown up, and are now fit for use. A company has been formed in Mauritius by the exertions of Mr. Evenor Dupont, a barrister and planter there, and called the "Filature Evenor Centrale." An experienced "fileuse," Madame Boildieu has been engaged from the neighbouring island of Bourbon, and is now giving instruction to various proprietors. Some ten persons rear worms and send to the Company regular supplies of cocoons, and eighty-seven other proprietors have received cocoons and mulberry cuttings from the Company. It is considered that this manufacture will flourish and increase rapidly in the island, and form eventually an important branch of trade, the climate and the soil being peculiarly suitable to the profitable rearing of the silkworm. From Bourbon it is stated by the correspondent, Mr. Dupont, that silk was sent to Paris of such fine quality as to fetch 111 francs per kilogramme, or about 2l. 4s. the pound.

3 WEBB, CHARLES J. Imp.—A bag of Mauritius sugar, product of manufacture of the Phœnix estate, obtained direct from the cane, expressed by a horizontal mill, and clarified by steam.

4 THE ROYAL SOCIETY OF NATURAL HISTORY OF MAURITIUS, (Imported by A. Steele, 107 Leadenhall St.)— Cases of straw baskets, rice, liquors, and cocoa-nut oil; a bag of cloves, a dial, and a cask of cocoa nuts.

5 BALKFIELD & Co. Mauritius, on behalf of Mad. E.

Chapon, and Mdlles. Gancourt, (Importers Messrs. S. Baker & Co. London).—Works and ornaments in straw, made on the Séchelles. Bouquets in shell-work; baskets made of leaves of the cocoa; vases, dials, &c.

6 MELLON, M. Mauritius, Exhib.—Small cask of cocoa-nut oil. Woods found on the Séchelles. Specimens of sea cocoa nuts. A case of very choice liquers, in 12 bottles, from the manufactory of M. Eug. Bérichon.

7 READER, J. S.—A case containing samples of Mauritius rice, grown on the "Champ de Mars," Port Louis, raised without any irrigation or other watering. The sack containing the sample is made of the leaves of the Vacona tree (*Cayza Satira*), the ordinary package of the colony for sugar. A variety of ornamental basket work from the Seychelles.. A *Coco-de-mer*. Sample of cloves, &c.

GRENADA.
—— South Area R. 30. ——

1 GROSE, H. 12 Coleman St. Imp.—Tapioca and nutmegs (first imported into this island, by Mr. Kennedy, in 1827.)

MONTSERRAT.
—— South Area Q. 10. ——

A box of maize or Indian corn. A box of arrow-root.

JAMAICA.
—— South Area Q. 10. ——

1 NASH, Mrs. Manchester.—Ten varieties of tropical flowers, made from the film of the "yucca," or dagger-plant.

ST. KITT'S.
—— South Area R. 30. ——

A West Indian fish-pot, made by John Morris, a black labourer, in the Island of St. Christopher, from the inner bark of a tree. It is usually baited and weighted, and then sunk to the depth of eight or ten fathoms. A buoy marks the spot, and it remains about twelve hours in the water.

BARBADOES.
—— South Area Q. 30. ——

SPECIMENS OF NATURAL PRODUCTIONS.—*Fruits, Spices, &c.*

Cactus (*Cereus trigonus*). Dunks (*Ziziphus jujuba*). Purple peppers (*Capsicum purpureum*). Finger peppers (*Capsicum purpureum*). Sea-side grapes (*Coccoloba uvifera*). Otaheite gooseberry (*Cicca disticha*). Golden apple (*Spondias dulcis*). Pig plum (*Spondias lucea*). Water lemon (*Passiflora laurifolia*). Rose apple (*Passiflora laurifolia*). Chili peppers (*Capsicum*). Cherry peppers (*Capsicum cerasiforme*). Cashew (*Anacardium occidentale*). Red bell pepper (*Capsicum annuum*). Green bonnet pepper (*Capsicum tetragonum*). Yellow Carib pepper (*Capsicum Caribæum*). Mango (*Mangifera indica*). Peach mango. Jamaica plum. Red bonnet pepper (*Capsicum tetragonum*). Star plum-(*Chrysophyllum monospermum*). Green sugar apple (*Anona squamosa*). Purple sugar apple (*Anona squamosa*). Tamarinds. Cream-coloured peppers. Guavas. Green bell pepper (*Capsicum annuum*). Sapodilla (*Achras sapota*). Cacao (*Theobroma cacao*). Limes (*Citrus acida*). Star apple (*Chrysophyllum Cainito*). Red banana (*Musa sapientum*). Yellow banana (*Musa sapientum*). Avocado pear (*Persea gratissima*). Citron (*Citrus*). Pomegranate. Custard apple

(*Anona reticulata*). Bread-fruit (*Artocarpus incisa*). Sour sop (*Anona muricata*). Green plantain (*Musa Paradisiaca*). Yellow plantain (*Musa Paradisiaca*). Papaw (*Carica Papaya*). Grape fruit (*Citrus*). Sugar-cane (*Sauporum officinarum*). Specimens of bituminous coal and selenite. Bale of cotton. Gourd of aloes. Bundle of Spanish needles. Specimens of transparent and Bourbon cane. Flower of transparent and Bourbon cane. Bottle of seeds of *Guilandina Bonduc*. Samples of Gadesden pan sugar and oscillation-sugar. Specimen of starch made from the "tous les mois" (*Canna coccinea*). Wax model of flower of "tous les mois" (*Canna corinicæ*). Bulb of the "tous les mois" (*Canna coccainea*). Fibre of "Agave Americana," "Agave Viripara," used in Central America for hammocks. Fibre of Spanish needles. Persian or green seed cotton. Vine cotton. Demerara cotton grown in Barbadoes chalk. Petroleum, or green tar.

1 READE, A. Exhib.—Explanatory list of vegetables and roots contained in a basket, and modelled in wax by Mr. and Mrs. Braithwaite, of Barbados: Guinea corn, pigeon peas, bananas, ochroe, sugar bean, moonshine bonasis, plaintain, ginger, egg fruit, arrow root, corn (Indian) Chrystophine, cucumber (Moonshine), purple egg plant, cabbage, turnip, carrot, green Indian corn, roasting eddoes, cucumber, green egg plant, lime bean, turnip beet root, pumpkin, white yam, red potato, scratching eddoes, cabbage cassava, yellow potato, bread fruit, red yam, white potato, Madeira eddoes, squashes, Borneo pepper, Carib pepper, Bell pepper.

2 ELWELL, H. Esq., Birmingham and Barbadoes, Imp.—Sixty models in wax, executed by Mrs. and Mr. Henry Braithwaite, of Barbadoes, of as many varieties of flowers and fruits, contained respectively in the vase and basket exhibited.

ANTIGUA.
—— South Area Q. 30. ——

1 GREY, The Countess.—Fossil wood from Antigua. Sent home by Governor Higginson.

ST. VINCENT.
—— South Area Q. 30. ——

1 BULLOCK, G. Saint Vincent, Exhib.—A selection of supple jacks. Arooma, as it grows. The same, prepared by the Charibs for making baskets. Mahaut, as it grows, the bark being the part used. The bark of the same unprepared. The same, prepared for twisting into fishing-lines, and in the raw state. The same, prepared to be worked. The same, in fine and coarse lines, which are wonderfully strong for fishing.

BRITISH GUIANA.
—— South Area R. 32. ——

(CATALOGUE of ARTICLES, the Produce of BRITISH GUIANA, a colony on the coast of SOUTH AMERICA, comprising the counties of DEMARARA, BERBICE, and ESSEQUIBO, exhibited by ALEXANDER F. RIDGWAY, 42 Leicester Square, London, agent to the Royal Agricultural and Commercial Society of the Colony,)

1 & 2 POLLARD, T. M.—White sand, from Mount Pleasant, Warratilla Creek, River Demerara. Red sand, from Waratilla Creek, River Demerara.

3 & 4 DUGGIN, T. B.—White sand, from Monte Video, River Berbice, about 200 miles above its estuary. Oreala, a decomposed rock, from River Berbice, supposed to be valuable in the manufacture of pottery.

5 BEE, J. F.—Clays and sands, obtained from an Artesian boring, obtained at various depths.

6 NETSCHER, A. D. VAN DER GON.—Rice, from Plantation Klein Pouderoyen, River Demerara.

7 DUGGIN, T. B.—Rice, from Monte Video, River Berbice.

8—11 NETSCHER, A. D. VAN DER GON.—Maize, or Indian corn. Meal from maize, or Indian corn. Plantains, unripe, sliced and dried without the aid of fire. Plantain meal, or konkin tay, from Plantation Klein Pouderoyen, River Demerara.

12 DAVISON, W.—Plantain meal, from Plantation Vigilance, East Sea Coast, Demerara.

13, 14 GARNETT, H. T.—Plantain meal; meal from the bitter cassava, baked into bread, from Plantation Herstelling, River Demerara.

15 & 15A & B DE PURTRON, J.—Bananas, dried without aid of fire, from Plantation Vigilance, East Sea Coast, Demerara.

16 NETSCHER, A. D. VAN DER GON.—Coffee, from Plantation Klein Pouderoyen. River Demerara.

16A & 16B KENNEDY, J.—Pearl coffee, from Plantation Nooit Gedacht, Canal No. 1, River Demerara.

17 & 18 BEE, J. F.—17, 18 Coffee, in the husk and in the berry, from Georgetown, Demerara.

19 NETSCHER, A. D. VAN DER GON.—Cacao, or Cocoa seeds, from Klein Pouderoyen, River Demerara.

20 DUGGIN, T. B.—Saouari nuts, from River Berbice.

20A OUTRIDGE, J. Esq.—Seed-vessel of the "monkey pot," from the River Demerara. It contains a large number of oleaginous kernels.

21, 22 (A, B, C), 23, 24 SHIER, D.—Capsicums, dried capsules. Capsicums, preserved in dilute acetic acid. Capsicums, active principle extracted by olive oil and by vinegar; all from Plantation Kitty, East Sea Coast, Demerara.

25 STUTCHBURY, J. S.—Capsicums, preserved in dilute acetic acid, from Georgetown, Demerara.

26 DUGGIN, T. B.—Fruit of a shrub, called birambi, from River Berbice, preserved in pickle.

27 NETSCHER, A. D. VAN DER GON.—Lines, from Plantation Klein Pouderoyen, River Demerara, preserved in pickle.

28, 30 STUTCHBURY, J. S.—Kasareep, the inspissate juice of the bitter cassava, from Georgetown, Demerara. Turmeric root, also from Georgetown, preserved in dilute acetic acid.

29 BEE, J. F.—Kasareep, the inspissated juice of the bitter cassava, from Georgetown.

29A DE PATRON, J.—Saline ash; in appearance like a black cinder, but used by the Indians as a substitute for salt. The ash is obtained by burning various plants growing on the rocks near the rapids.

31 & 32 GARNETT, H. T.—Arrow root. Starch, from the bitter cassava, from Plantation Herstelling, River Demerara.

33—35 SHIER, D.—Starch, from the sweet cassava, plantain, Buckyam, from Plantation Kitty, East Sea Coast, Demerara.

36 ANDERSON, G. & Co.—Vacuum pan-sugar, from Plantation Ogle, East Sea Coast, Demerara.

37 & 38 JONES, J. — Vacuum pan-sugar, from Plantation Hope, East Sea Coast, Demerara.

39 STUTCHBURY, J. S.—Vacuum pan-sugar, from Plantation Emnore, East Sea Coast, Demerara.

40 LAING, J.—Sugar, from Plantation Friends, River Berbice, manufactured in Gadsden and Evans's pan.

41—44 SHIER, D.—Muscovado and molasses, from the Colonial Laboratory, Georgetown, Demerara.

45 & 46 STUTCHBURY, J. S.—Muscovado, from Plantation Fellowship, Mahaicong, East Coast, Demerara. Copaiba, balsam of, from River Pomeroon, Essequebo.

47 & 48 OUTRIDGE, J.—Caoutchouc, from River Demerara, near the Falls. Milk from the cow-tree, from River Demerara.

49 DUGGIN, T. B.— Gum resin, from the simiri or locust tree, from River Berbice.

50 BONYUN, G. R.—Karman, from River Essequebo.

51 OUTRIDGE, J.—Hyawai gum or incense, from River Demerara.

52 & 53 STUTCHBURY, J. S.—Laurel oil, from River Pomeroon, Essequebo. Crab-oil, from River Essequebo.

54, 56, 57 DUGGIN, T. B.—Seeds of the Dari tree; bark of the Mora tree; bark of Hog-plum tree; from River Berbice.

55 & 58 SHIER, D.—Sandbox tree, seeds of, from George-town, Demerara. Courida tree, bark of, from Plantation Kitty, East Sea Coast, Demerara.

55A & 55B KOCK, H. A. — Fruit of the Lana-tree, and Lana dye, from the River Berbice.

55C OUTRIDGE, J.—Indian paint, from the River Demerara.

59—61 STUTCHBURY, J. S.—Hy-yarri or Hai-ari, fish poison, from River Demerara. Angustora bark, from River Pomeroon, Essequebo. Rhizophora racemosa, bark of, from East Sea Coast, Demerara.

59A KOCK, H. A.—Fruit of Yarrisara, from River Berbice.

62 OUTRIDGE, J.—Trysale bark, from River Demerara.

63, 65, 66 STUTCHBURY, J. S.—Greenheart tree, bark of, from River Demerara. Guinea pepper, or grains of Paradise, from River Demerara. Alpinea nutans, seeds of, from Demerara.

64 DUGGIN, T. B.—Greenheart tree, seeds of from River Berbice.

67 SHIER, D.—Physic nuts, seeds of, from George-town, Demerara.

68 MAUGET, Mrs.—Physic nuts, seeds of, from George-town, Demerara.

69 ARRINDELL, Mrs.—Quassia amara, from Plantation Zeelandia, Wakenaam, River Essequebo.

70 STUTCHBURY, J. S.—Boeiari, bushrope, from River Demerara.

71 & 72 BLAIR, D.—Cotton, cleaned and uncleaned, from Plantation Batavier, Mahaica River.

73 NETSCHER, A. D. VAN DER GON. — Cotton, uncleaned, from Plantation Klein Pouderoyen, River Demerara.

74—76 BEE, J. F.—Cotton, hard and loose seed, cleaned and uncleaned, from Plantation Woodlands, River Mahaica, Demerara.

74A—74B HUGHES, P. — Mexican white seed. Large and small green seed; large and small kidney; loose black seed. All from plantation, Anna Regina, Essequebo.

76A & 76B ROSS, E. C.—Silk cotton loose and in pod, and bale of silk cotton. Both from George-town, Demerara.

77 DAVISON, W.—Plantain fibre, from Plantation Vigilance, East Sea Coast, Demerara.

78 NETSCHER, A. D. VAN DER GON.—Plantain fibre, from Plantation Klein, Pouderoyen, River Demerara.

79 DE BURTON, J.—Silk grass fibre, from Plantation Vigilance, East Sea Coast, Demerara.

80 & 81 DUGGIN, T. B.—Silk grass fibre, and fibre of Fibisiri, from River Berbice.

82 & 83 BEE, J. F.—Fibre of Mahoe, from Demerara. Table-top, including 84 specimens of different woods, the growth of the colony.

84, 84A, 85 OUTRIDGE, J.—Mora, transverse and vertical sections, both from River Demerara. Greenheart transverse section.

85A STUTCHBURY, J. S.—Greenheart, vertical section, from River Demerara.

85B & 85C OUTRIDGE, J.—Specimens of black green-heart; transverse and vertical sections.

86 & 86A BUCHANAN, A.—Purpleheart, transverse and vertical sections, both from River Essequebo.

87 & 87A—88, 88A, 89, 89A OUTRIDGE, J.—Kakarilli, vertical and transverse sections; wamara, or brown ebony, wooroballi, from Essequebo River, &c.

90 & 90A BUCHANAN, A.—Wallaba, transverse and vertical sections, both from River Essequebo.

90B DUGGIN, T. B.—Wallaba, tecuba, or hart, River Berbice.

91, 91A, 92, & 92A OUTRIDGE, J.—Bully and silver-balli, yellow trees, transverse and vertical sections, from River Demerara.

93 & 94 FAUSET, T.—Silverballi, portion of the planking of a drogher and punt.

95, 95A, 96, 96A BUCHANAN, A.—Camara, or tonquin bean, and saouri, transverse and vertical sections, from River Essequebo.

97, 97A, 97B, 98, 98A OUTRIDGE, J.—Yaruri, or pad-dlewood. Hackia, or lignum vitæ, transverse and vertical sections of trees, both from River Demerara.

99—102A DUGGIN, T. B.—Lana, mammee apple, hyawa, and corkwood trees, transverse and vertical sections, from River Berbice.

102B PONTIFEX, G.—Corkwood tree, abutment near the root, from Troolie Island, River Essequebo.

102C, 103A BEE, J. F.—Courida, tree-wood transverse and vertical sections, from Plantation Woodlands, River Mahaica.

104, 105A OUTRIDGE, J.—Itikiriburaballi; white cedar, or warracoori, transverse and vertical sections, both from River Demerara.

105B, 105C BEE, J. F.—White cedar, or warracoori, transverse and vertical sections, from River Mahaica, East Sea Coast, Demerara.

106—115A OUTRIDGE, J.—Suradanni, determa, crab-wood, koquerettaballi, coutabally, blackheart, cabacalli, yarri yarri, or lancewood, torchwood, tooroo, transverse and vertical sections from River Demerara.

116—117A BEE, J. F.—Coffee tree, portion of the trunk, and vertical section, from Canal, No. 2, River Demerara. Tigerwood, transverse and vertical sections, both from River Demerara.

117B—117C STUTCHBURY, J. S.—Transverse and vertical sections of lelter wood, from the River Corentyne.

117D—117E OUTRIDGE, J.—Transverse and vertical sections of the saka or bastard purple heart-wood; of the ita-balli; of the wadadwei or monkey-pot tree; of the hyaeo-aballi (or zebra wood); of the hilbaderi; of the simiri (a locust tree); of the towroneroo, or bastard bully-tree; of the Marisiballi:—all from the banks of the Demerara River, and most of them furniture woods.

MISCELLANEOUS ARTICLES.

118—118A STUTCHBURY, J. S.—Tonkin bean, and in capsule, from River Demerara.

119 DUGGIN, T. B.—Job's tears (bud-like seeds), from River Berbice.

120 ROSS, G.—Soap berries from Plantation Ruminveld, River Demerara; used for ornamental purposes.

121 MANGET, Mrs.—Barricarri seeds, from George-town. Demerara.

122 SHIER, D.—Buck or canna shoots, or seeds of the "Tous les mois," from Georgetown, Demerara.

123 MORISON & KNOX.—Isinglass, from Gilbagre, coast of Demerara.

124 BEE, J. F.—Honey, from Plantation Woodlands, River Mahaica.

125, 128, 129 BARKLY, Mrs.—Ornamented hammock. Hat, made of the bark of the eta palm. Indian hats.

126, 127 STUTCHBURY, J. S. — Eta palm hammock. Ropes to the same from silk.

130—132 HOLMES, W. H.—Case of packalls. Shaak-haak, from River Demerara. Fans, made of the eta palm.

133 SHIER, D.—Matpai, or cassava squeezer, made of the eta palm.

134 BEE, J. F.—Etami, or cassava sifter, made of the eta palm.

135 BARKLY, Mrs. — Model of Indian house, with native furniture, implements, &c. (articles numbered 1 to 28 inclusive).

136 ROSE, Miss.—Cotton hammock.

137 RIES, B.—Spun cotton, from River Pomeroon.

138, 139 STUTCHBURY, J. S.—Fishing nets of silk grass.

140 DENNIS, G.—Basket, for carrying young "bocks." Entire wardrobe of a female Indian of the Warrow tribe.

141 DUGGIN, T. B.—Indian war club, from River Berbice.

142—144, 145A ARNOTT, R.—Indian war clubs, from River Demerara. Blowpipe and quiver, with poisoned arrows. Bows and arrows, bows made of washiba.

146—148A DUGGIN, T. B.—Winna, made of the rind of the fruit of the Manicola palm, used by the Indians for enclosing tobacco for smoking, from River Berbice. Buck pots, used in preparing pepper pot. Indian fly brush. Walking-stick carved by the Indians.

148B to **153** OUTRIDGE, J.—Wadada, or wood-skin, employed by the Indians as the material for their bark canoes. Quaick, or covered basket, negro manufacture, made of moucourou. Basket, such as is used in coffee picking. Hand basket. Two baskets, negro manufacture, made of the leaf of the cabbage palm. Calabashes.

154, 155B STEELE, M. — Doorlocks, made of green-heart and crabwood of the growth of the colony.

156 BEE, J. F.—Two walking-sticks, made from the outer rind of the tooroo palm, from River Demerara. A box containing eighty small specimens of the woods of the colony.

157, 157A Diagrams showing the course of temperature at Georgetown, Demerara, during the five years 1846 to 1850, and the mean range thereof, &c.

158 Round table, composed of many woods, the growth of the colony.

159 Japanned cup and plate, made from the fig-tree. Contributed by Jonathan Hopkinson, Esq.

160, 161 RIDGWAY, A. F. Esq. — Stuffed birds :— Toucan; blue parrot, from the Essequibo; yellow-bellied trojan. Skins of monkey, panther, &c.

162 Model of a Birch Indian's house and family. Contributed by John Colling, Esq.

163 Cotton grown by W. Finlaison, Esq., Fullerswood Park, Blacknow, Jamaica. Contributed by A. T. Ridgway, Esq.

164 Specimens of the Snake-nut of the colony. A native bag of coloured beads.

BAHAMAS.
—— South Area R. 31. ——

BARNETT, Mrs. EDWARD, of Nassau, and 14 Woburn Sq. London.—Specimens of fruits in wax :—1 Bread-fruit (*Artocarpus incisa*). 2 Plantain (*Musa sapientium*). 3 Coco plum (*Chrysobalanus Icaco*). 4 Prickly pears (*Cactus Opuntia*). 5 Banana (*Musa paradisiaca*). 6 Cashew (*Anacardium occidentale*). 7 Spanish pepper (*Capsicum annuum*). 8 Star-apple, showing the interior (*Chrysophyllum Cainito*). 9 Papaw (*Carica Papaya*). 10 Spanish plum (*Spondias Chrysobalanus*). 11 Gooseberry (*Cicca disticha*). 12 Water-lemon (*Passiflora laurifolia*). 13 Aqui. 14 Sugar-apple (*Anona squamosa*). 15 Balsam (*Impatiens noli tangere*). 16 Star-apple (*Chrysophyllum Cainito*). 17 Fig (*Ficus Carica*). 18 Sugar-cane (*Saccharum officinarum*). 19 Banana, showing the interior (*Musa paradisiaca*). 20 Sour sop (*Anona mu-*

ricata). 21 Guava (*Psidium pyriferum*). 22 Custard-apple (*Anona reticulata*). 23 Cherry (*Cordia collococca*). 24 Guava, showing the interior (*Psidium pyriferum*). 25 Sapodilla, showing the interior (*Achras sapodilla*). 26 Hog-plum (*Spondias Myrobalanus*). 27 Bread-fruit, showing the interior (*Artocarpus incisa*). 28 Mango (*Mangifera indica*). 29 Avocado pear, cut to show the interior (*Persea gratissima*). 30 Banana, red (*Musa paradisiaca*). 31 Fig banana (*Musa coccinea*). 32 Sapodilla (*Achras sapodilla*).

Specimens prepared by JOHN THOMAS THOMPSON, Nassau.—Specimens of Yucca hemp :—A One leaf of the Yucca (*Serrulata*). B The billets between which they are packed are cut from the flower-shaft. This cork-like material (B) is of use where softness and elasticity are required in bedding, or stuffing, or packing different sorts of work; in bodies of razor-strops : in thick or thin sheets, it is very convenient for purposes where points have to be fixed and withdrawn easily, such as cases for entomological purposes. C Hemp prepared from the Yucca leaf. D Rope prepared from the hemp, but stained in soaking. E The same, but of the natural colour.

Specimens of Palmetto stuff :—1 Leaves of the Palmetto. 2 Fibre prepared from the leaves. 3 Rope completed.

BAINES, F. & Co. 109 Fenchurch St. Imp. and Agents.

NICOLLS, Miss, Caroline, Nassau.—Crown and pedestal of shell work.

GRANT, Miss, Nassau.—Vase manufactured of the Mimosa bean.

BARNES & Co. Nassau.—Case of specimens of different varieties of West India sponge.

Specimens of woods of many kinds : satinwood, horse flesh, cedar, crab, box, stopper, and lignum vitæ (woods).

GREIG, The Misses, Nassau, Manu.—An epergne composed entirely of shells, forming cornucopias fillled with flowers, in great variety of colour and beauty : the whole of the shells were gathered from the shores of the Bahamas. (Consignees, Messrs. Daniell, 18 Wigmore Street, London.) A large vase, with group of flowers, composed entirely of pure white shells. A figure in a fancy costume of shell work. Forwarded by Governor Gregory to J. B. Cameron, Esq.

TRINIDAD.
—— South Area R. 31. ——

ARTICLES sent to the EXHIBITION from TRINIDAD, by order of the Governor Lord HARRIS. (LIGHTLY & SIMON, 123 Fenchurch St. London, & Messrs. Daniell, of Wigmore St.)

MINERAL KINGDOM.

1 Pitch, from the springs in the centre of the pitch lake. 2 Petroleum, from springs in the Guapo Hills, near the pitch lake. 3 Cellular pitch, of which the surface of the lake principally consists. 4 Compact pitch, which crops out through other strata in the lands around the pitch lake. 5 Glance pitch, found in small detached masses, in the same. 6 Pitch turf, from a pitch bog, in the same. 7, 8 Pitch, mixed with organic matter. 9 Mineral charcoal, prepared by Mr. H. Warner, from Trinidad pitch; and used as a substitute for animal charcoal in the manufacture of sugar; it can be produced at about one-fifth of the price of the latter. 10—14 Petroleum, mineral oil, naptha, ammoniacal water and coke,—prepared from Trinidad pitch, and illustrating the process of making naphtha from pitch. 15 Pitch seam, found between strata of sandstone. 16 Sandstone, impregnated with mineral oils and naphtha. 17—20 Ochres, from the Guapo Hills. 21, 22 Sandstone, with specular iron, from the Guapo Hills. 23 Black sand, from the sea-shore at Guapo. 24 Hematite, from Gaspari Island. 25 Magnetic iron-ore, from Maraccas valley. 26 Iron pyrites, from

the mud volcanos. 27 Lignite, from Irois. It occurs in immense quantity, near the surface. 28 Coal, supposed to be anthracitic, from Manzanilla. 29 Slate, from St. Ann's hills; taken from the surface. 30 Hone-stone, from near Tamana. 31 Ochre, from Arima. 32 Clay, from Arima, used for making water-jugs. 33 White earth, from Arima, used for white-washing houses, &c. 34 Yellow earth, from St. Ann's river. 35 Sulphureous earth, from near the pitch lake.

ANIMAL KINGDOM.

Tortoiseshell : the hawk's-bill turtle is caught on all the coasts of Trinidad and the Gulph of Paria ; the shell forms an article of export.

Whale oil : the whale is caught in the Gulph of Paria ; it usually makes its appearance about January, when the fishing season begins, and lasts till June ; from 12 to 18 fish are caught annually, each giving from 60 to 80 barrels of oil.

VEGETABLE KINGDOM.—(*Oils and Fatty Substances.*)

Cocoa-nut-oil : a large quantity of this oil is made in the island, chiefly on the east coast.

Carap oil : this oil is made from the seeds of a common indigenous tree, called *Carapa Guianensis*.

Cocoa fat : this butter-like substance is obtained from the seeds of *Theobroma Cacao*, and is esteemed as an emollient.

Spices.

Nutmegs : the nutmegs grown in Trinidad are equal to any from the East. The annual produce per tree varies from 10 to 15 lbs.

Cloves : this tree bears an abundant crop twice in the year ; the produce is of good quality.

Black pepper : which thrives well, and is very prolific.

Cayenne pepper : the smaller kinds of capsicum (bird pepper) are like weeds in point of abundance, and when dried and ground, make good cayenne pepper.

Vanilla : there are three different species of vanilla, all producing this pod, and all indigenous to the colony.

Fibres.

Cotton, although not cultivated for many years, readily suits itself to the soil and climate ; the specimen sent is grown from that variety called sea island cotton, a few seeds of which were imported from Jamaica.

Bromelia (*Karata*) : this plant is indigenous to the island, and, like all the pine-apple tribe, furnishes a strong and soft fibre.

Sterculia (*Caribæa or Majagua*) : the bark of this tree furnishes the country people with cordage, and is strong.

Agave (*Vivipara or Langue bœuf*) : all the species of agave furnish a white, but somewhat harsh or brittle fibre.

AGRICULTURAL PRODUCTS.

Sugar (*Muscovado*) : this is the chief staple product of the colony, and great exertions are being made to improve its quality.

Rice : this article is productive in any part of the island, whether the land be high or low.

Cassava starch : is the produce of Jatropha manihot (or bitter cassava). This plant is extensively cultivated.

Arrowroot : the produce of Maranta arundinacea, and other species.

Tous-les-mois, or tulema : gives also a large return of starch ; it is said that the produce per acre, in good soil, is equal to that of sugar from the sugar-cane, viz., from one to two tons per acre.

Brazil nuts : the produce of Bertholettia excelsa. The tree has been introduced from South America, and is ornamental and useful.

Tonquin bean : from the tree Dipterix odorata, which was introduced from British Guiana.

Indian corn, or maize.

Coffee (Mocha) : this variety of coffee has been introduced some years, and preserves, in cultivation, its peculiarly small round grain.

Theobroma, cacao, or cocoa : this tree is extensively cultivated ; its produce forms a large article of export.

Cocoa, or chocolate manufactured.

Tobacco, in the leaf, from Siparia.

Tobacco, manufactured, from the same place.

Gums and Resins.

Gum-anime : from Arima, the produce of Hymenæa Courbaril, or locust-tree.

Incense : the produce of Trichilia trinitensis.

Medicinal Products.

Sarsaparilla : the root of a species of Smilax, and abundant. Ginger.

Tanning and Dyeing Materials.

Turmeric, logwood, and fustic.

Woods for Ornamental and other Purposes.

Hymenæa courbaril, or locust : a valuable timber, and abundant, which grows from two to six feet in diameter.

Yoke : a handsome wood, analogous to mahogany, usually from two to three feet diameter.

Cedrela odorata cedar : West Indian cedar ; a useful and ornamental timber, from three to twelve feet in diameter.

Rhopala montana (*Aguatapana*) : a very durable wood, and taking a fine polish ; from 18 inches to three feet in diameter.

Tapana : used for felloes of wheels, and where strength and toughness is required.

Cordia (or *Sepe*) : a useful light wood, analogous to English elm in texture, and possessing a bitter principle, which deters insects ; from one to two feet in diameter.

Acaras (*Balata*) : a timber much used ; from two to six feet in diameter.

Achras (*Acoma or Mastic*) : like the timber of the whole family of Sapotaclæ, much valued ; from two to four feet in diameter.

Achras (*Zapotilla or Zapodilla*).

Astrocaryum aculeatum (*Gri Gri*) : this, like most of the palm tribe, furnishes good material for veneering.

Acrocomia sclerocarpa (*Gru Gru*) : a wood similar to the last.

Carapa guianensis (or *Carapa*) : a useful timber, analogous to cedar ; from two to three feet in diameter.

Bucida buceras (or *Olivia*) : a strong useful wood, used for making shingles ; from two to four feet in diameter.

Purple heart : an abundant and useful timber ; from two to four feet in diameter.

Fustic : used for all purposes where strength is required, and as a dye wood ; from one to three feet in diameter.

Lecythis (*Idatamon or Aguatacaro*) : commonly used as shafts for carts, &c. ; a tough wood, of large size, and very common.

Tecoma serratifolia (*grey poui*) Tecoma (*black poui*) : Tecoma (*green poui*).

Brosimum guianense (*Letter wood*) : the heart wood is the only part used, and is never of any great size.

Crescentia cujete (or *Calabash*) : common tree, which furnishes timber applicable to the same purposes as that of the ash in England.

Geoffroya inermis (or *l'Angeline*) : a timber much employed as naves for wheels and other purposes.

Paltivia. Bois gri (or *Iron wood*).

Mimosa juliflora (*Yoke savan*) : a hard and useful wood.

Roble : a common and excellent wood ; from two to three feet in diameter.

Copaifera officinalis (*Copai*), is an ornamental and lasting wood.

Vitex capitata : this tree is reckoned durable timber, and is very common.

Bois lizard, Guaiacum officinale (*Lignum vitæ*) : very hard wood, about one foot in diameter.

MANUFACTURES, ORNAMENTAL SEEDS, &c.

A nest of baskets.

Sieves, made of a species of maranta, for sifting casava meal.

Culebra, for expressing the casava pulp, and separating the casava starch.

Carved calabashes.

Fans, for ladies.

Fish-basket, as used by the Indians.

Model of Indian house.

Seeds used as beads, viz., Adenanthera pavonina, Coix lachryma, Erythrina corallodendron, Ormosia dasycarpa.

An Indian hut, in the village of Arima, 16 miles from the town of Port of Spain, made by Manuel Sorzano.

FALKLAND ISLANDS.

1 WHITTINGTON, G. T. Woking, Surrey, Prop.—Portfolio of fourteen sketches of remarkable places, geological structures, plants, &c. of these islands. Portfolio, containing 27 sheets : specimens of grasses, sheep's wool, &c. produce of these islands. Box, with specimens of coal, copper, sandstone, quartz, spar, pebbles, rock, peat, lichens, Orchilla weed, &c. from the same.

BERMUDAS.

—— South Area R. 32. ——

1 GRAY, —.—Specimen of arrow-root.

2 JACKSON, H. H. Bermudas, Cabinet-maker.—Chess-board of remarkable workmanship, and exhibiting specimens of the Bermudas wood.

SPECIMENS OF NATURAL PRODUCTIONS, &c.

Pumice-stone.

Bermuda arrow-root.

Collection of marine productions.

Model of Bermuda sailing-boat.

Model of a hoop for a mast, for the boom to work in, in stead of a "goose-neck."

Specimens of Bermuda palmetto plait.

NEW SOUTH WALES.

—— South Area S. 31. ——

1 ARMITAGE BROTHERS, Huddersfield, Imp.—A bale of scoured Sydney skin-wool, grown in New South Wales, and washed by Armitage and Co. of Sydney.

1A BIDWELL, J. G. Government Commissioner of Lands, Zinana, Wide Bay, Australia.—A log of wood from the interior of Wide Bay district, north-east coast of Australia, the *Briggalo* of the squatters (Bricklow of Leichardt's Journey), a species of Acacia, probably undescribed.

2 BOGUE, A. manufactured and forwarded by Messrs. J. and W. DAY, boat-builders and oar-makers, New South Wales.—Two beef hams spiced and cured by Mr. J. Briears, Sydney. Specimens of colonial timber. Pair of ash oar and a pair of paddles manufactured of colonial wood.

3 BURCHETT, J. R. 15 Edmonton Cres. Edmonton.— A desk and a chess-board, of polished woods.

4 CALLAGHAN, —, Crown Prosecutor, Attorney-General.—Two volumes of statutes, printed from types made in Sydney, and the books bound in Sydney.

5 CLINCH, J. 31 Abchurch Lane, Imp.—A set of bag-pipes, made by George Sherrer, Sydney.

6 DUNBAR, D. Limehouse.—Samples of wheat flour from Port Phillip, New South Wales. Agent, N. Tweeddale.

7 DANGAR, R. C. Billiter St.—Preserved fresh beef and mutton, a substitute for salt meats.

8 LEARMOUTH, T. 40 Royal Crescent, Notting Hill, Imp.—Merino wool, from Port Philip.

9 MOTLEY, T. Leeds, Prop. — Wool, from Sydney New South Wales.

10 DEVITT & MOORE, 9 Billiter St.—A coach wrench, made at Sydney.

11 DUDGEON & Co. 1 New Bank buildings.—Ores and specimens of woods from Sydney. Cured hams. Various samples of cotton grown near Maitland.

12 LEARMOUTH, T. 40 Royal Cres. Notting Hill.— Four samples of Australian sheep's wool from New South Wales.

13 MACARTHUR, Lieut.-Col. E.—Case, containing 132 specimens of Merino wool, derived from the late Mr. Macarthur's original flock. In 1807 the first importation into England of this wool was 245 lbs. In the year 1848 it was 23,000,000 lbs. from New South Wales alone (valued at more than 1,200,000*l.*) ; and from the whole of the Australian colonies 36,000,000 lbs. — Four views in N. S. Wales, one being of Camden (46 miles S.W. of Sydney), the original seat of Australian sheep husbandry, and now becoming celebrated for its vineyards.

15 MOSES, SON & DAVIS, 14 & 15 Aldgate High St.— Cask of Australian mutton tallow, and another of beef tallow, from the boiling establishment of Messrs. Benjamin and Moses, Sydney.

16 WATSON, YOUNG & Co. 2 Abchurch Lane, City.— Orchilla maroon roans ; red roans. Enamelled hides, enamelled kangaroo skins, patent kangaroo skins, prepared by Thomas Hall and Co.

17 BLAND, Dr. Sydney.—Model of his invention for extinguishing fire arising from spontaneous combustion in wool ships.

18 SHIELDS, FRANCIS W. (C.E.)—1. Model of a railway lattice bridge, with original construction of details, suitable for colonial work. 2. Model of iron plate and longitudinal timber rail of a New South Wales hard wood, with original construction and details. 3. Model of trestle frame to carry railway. 4. About 15 specimens of New South Wales hard wood, suitable for the above purpose.

19 MITCHELL, Lieut.-Col. Sir T. L. Surveyor-General of New South Wales.—1. A close cylinder for testing the action of different screw propellers. 2. Original Bomareng propeller. 3. Rope made from the *Doryanthes excelsa*, with specimens of leaf and flax. 4. Cone of the *Bidwellia araucaria*. 5. New map of New South Wales, and original three-sheet map of the colony. 6. School-book, written, printed, and published at Sydney. 7. Specimens of native copper and galena from Canobolas, New South Wales.

20 BOGUE, Mr. A.—List of articles exhibited by, and forwarded by the following parties from Sydney, New South Wales, for the Grand National Exhibition, London :—

Case No. 1. Box containing two specimens of doe skin-cloth, 20 yards of each, sent by A. and G. Ragner.

Case No. 4. One package of cabbage-tree hats, from Capt. Webster, of Darlinghurst Gaol. These hats are manufactured by the prisoners, and are sent to the Exhibition to exemplify the industry and discipline of the prisoners in the Australian gaols.

Case 5. Small case containing neatsfoot oil, forwarded by Colonel Gibbs, Sydney.

Case 6. Small parcel, containing stockings and mits, knitted by an old Scotch woman (Mrs. Morrison) from a thread made of the opossum fur.

21 THE AUSTRALIAN AGRICULTURAL COMPANY, 62

King's Arms Yard, Moorgate St.—Specimens of coals from the Company's mines at Newcastle, New South Wales.

22 Leon, L. 65 Hatton Garden, London.—A block of spermaceti.

SOUTH AUSTRALIA.

—— South Area R. 31. ——

1 South Australian Company, New Broad St.—Mineral specimens from Ranmantoo.

2 The Barossa Range Mining Co. by Messrs. Coode Browne, & Co. 10 King's Arms Yard, Moorgate St.—Stones of copper ore, as raised from the lodes. Sulphuret of copper, containing 40 per cent. of pure copper, raised in the Lyndoch valley, about thirty miles from Adelaide, South Australia.

3 Graham & Hallett, South Australia, Prop.—The following articles are from the mines of Burra Burra:—

1 Red oxide of copper.
2, 3 Green carbonate of copper.
4 Red oxide and carbonate combined.
5 Red oxide and blue carbonate.
6 Strata in which the minerals occur.
7 Native copper.
8 Malachite and red oxide of copper.
9 Fibrous malachite.
10 Cabinet specimens, arranged.
11 Views of Burra Burra mine and smelting-house, and of the township.

Burra Burra Mines, specimens of the ores from :—
The Burra Burra mines present one of the most striking examples of successful mining speculation with which we are acquainted. From indications which were regarded as the most favourable character, the mine was started on the 5th of September, 1845, with a capital of 12,320l., subscribed by a few merchants and traders at Adelaide. The following returns of ore raised from the commencement of the undertaking to September, 1850, will exhibit the extraordinary success of this undertaking:—

		Tons.	Cwt.
September 30, 1846	. . .	6,359	10
,, 1847	. . .	10,794	17
,, 1848	. . .	12,791	11
,, 1849	. . .	7,789	16
,, 1850	. . .	18,692	9

Making a total in 5 years of 56,428 2 of copper ore, varying in quality from ore containing 30 per cent. of copper to much that produces 70 per cent. of that metal. The money value of this is 738,108l.

Nearly all the copper ore raised at the South Australian mines has been hitherto sent to England, and smelted at Swansea; but there has been recently a smelting establishment introduced which promises to be of great advantage to the colony.

The number of people now employed at the Burra Burra mines are 1,003.

4 Moses, H. E. and M. 87 Tower Hill.—Fine sample of Australian wheat, weighing 64 lbs. per bushel; the produce of Adélaide, South Australia. Preserved fresh meats, prepared at the Camperdown establishments, Sydney, New South Wales. They are upwards of three years old, have undergone a voyage of 16,000 miles, are in a perfectly fresh state, and will keep so for any number of years.

5 Hallett, R. & Sons, Broad St. Ratcliff, London, Imp.—Articles from South Australia:—
1, 2 Wheat.
3 Hard soap.
4 Olive oil.

5 Five cases, containing specimens of opal and other rocks allied to precious stones.
6 Two samples of flour, and one of barley.
7 A dried bouquet of small native plants.
8 Specimens of stream gold, and gold in its matrix.
9 A case of polished stones, the produce of the colony.

6 Murray, Mrs.—Specimen of silk raised by exhibitor, at Adelaide, in 1850, the produce of 580 worms fed on white and black mulberry leaves.

7 Earl Grey, sent by.—Specimens of silk produced in South Australia, and showing the capabilities of that country for the production of this article.

9 Heath & Burrows, 6 New London St. Mark Lane, and Old Corn Exchange, Imp.—Specimens of South Australian grain.

10 Joseph, J. A. 7 Blomfield Crescent, Bayswater.—Ores, minerals, and geological specimens from South Australia, &c.

VAN DIEMEN'S LAND.

—— South Area S. 31. ——

Denison, His Excellency Sir W. T.
1 Blue gum timber of Van Diemen's Land (*Eucalyptus globulus*). Equal to oak as a ship-building timber, and may be obtained in any quantity and of any dimensions up to 200 ft. in length. The two sections exhibited were taken from one tree at a distance of 134 feet apart.

2 Stringy bark of Van Diemen's Land (*Eucalyptus robusta*). Squared log 20 ft. long, 12 ins. by 12 ins. Forms for the most part of a large tree; timber coarser than the last, but abundant, chiefly used for house-building and fencing.

3 Blackwood, or lightwood, of Tasmania (*Acacia melanoxylon*). Squared log 20 ft. long, 12 ins. by 12 ins. A very hard close-grained dark and richly-veined cabinet wood, obtainable in any quantity and of the largest size, requisite for furniture and fittings.

4 Sassafras of Tasmania (*Atherosperma moschatum*). Squared log 13 ft. long, 12 ins. by 12 ins. A soft, even, and close-grained timber, well adapted for turning and, probably, for the carver. Has been used for flooring-boards and in the inside work of houses, and for cabin fittings in ships. Obtainable in any quantity, of moderate dimensions.

5 Myrtle of Tasmania (*Fagus Cunninghamii*). Squared log 12 ft. long, 12 ins. by 12 ins. This timber is plentiful, and may be obtained of any size. It is hard and close-grained, with a lively red tint, streaked and mottled near the root; takes a beautiful polish.

Adcock, Mrs. Elizabeth St. Hobart Town.
6 Two canisters of preserved meat.

Hamilton, —, Elizabeth St. Hobart Town—Manu.
7 Hall chair of blackwood (*Acacia melanoxylon*). Has a raised shield cut on the back, with kangaroo and emu for supporters, &c. tastefully carved in relief and polished.
8 Small round table, of Huon pine, with chess-board in the centre, the pedestal of Huon pine (*Dacrydium Franklinii*). The chequers alternately of plain Huon pine, and wood of the she-oak of Tasmania (*Casuarina quadrivalvis*), with a border of blackwood, surrounded by a narrow string of myrtle, the whole enclosed with a band of figured pine.

Pierson, —, Manu.
9 Pier table or chiffonier, of polished blackwood. Intended to show the rich dark tints and veining of this wood, and the high polish of which it is susceptible.

Fraser, A. Collins St. Hobart Town—Manu.
10 One pair carriage wheels. The naves of the wheels are of blackwood, the spokes and felloes of blue gum, and

for these purposes the two sorts of timber have been found admirably suited.

REEVES, J. G. Elizabeth and Macquarie St. Hobart Town.

11 Specimens of leather, viz.:—
Hides of black and brown harness leather. Kip. Kip waxed on the grain, and black-grained kip. Kangaroo-skins, grained, brown, and waxed. Calf-skins, waxed and brown. Black bazils. Pair racks, cordovan horse hide. Sole leather.
These skins and hides are of Tasmanian production, and have been tanned and dressed at Mr. Reeves' establishment.

CHAMPION, —, Hobart Town.

12 Table of muskwood, eurybia, argophylla of Tasmania. Round turnover table, with brasswork and springs entirely of Tasmanian manufacture; the muskwood of which it is made possesses great beauty.

DOUGLAS RIVER COAL CO.

13 Coal, two bushels. Sample of the strong bituminous coal occurring on the east coast of Van Diemen's Land, traceable over a large area of country, in seams varying in thickness from a few inches to ten feet and upwards.

BROWN, JOHN, Launceston—Manu.

14 Sideboard of blackwood of Tasmania. The timber of *Acacia melanoxylon* is considered to be more deeply veined and tinted on the northern than the southern side of the colony. It is called blackwood in Launceston, and lightwood in Hobart Town.
15 Top of star loo table. Composed of alternate-pointed sections of figured Huon pine and blackwood veneered on cedar. 148 pedestal.
16 Lady's table of muskwood. An elaborately-finished article of highly-polished muskwood, the top resting upon an inverted arch, turning on a pivot, and supported by a slender pedestal, with a tastefully worked collar.

STRAHAN, R. Bonnington.

17 Box of salt: coarse, for pickling, and table, or basket salt. A sample from which the magnesian salts are said to be thoroughly separated.

MURRAY, W. Liverpool St. Hobart Town.

18 Box of starch: the box of Huon pine, figured. There are now several starch manufactories in Hobart Town.

DIXON, J. Skelton Castle, Isis.

19 Flax, dressed in 1850. The exhibitor is endeavouring to establish the cultivation of flax in Tasmania.
20 Box of dried apples. More fruits are dried in the northern than the southern side of Van Diemen's Land.

BUTTON, T. Launceston.

21 Samples of glue.
22 Concentrated solution of mimosa bark, extracted by cold water. This solution is considered in a great measure free from colouring matter, and from the principles which give a dark, uneven character to leather, rendering it brittle, and depreciating it in the English market.
23 Mimosa bark, ground. Bark of *Acacia mollissima*. Bark of the black wattle, said to be the best bark for tanning.

DENISON, Sir W. T. Norfolk Island.

24 Box of tobacco in leaf.
25 Box of arrow-root.
26 Box of maize.
27 Cayenne pepper.
28—35 Wheats: Farmer's friend, white velvet, James's Essex, Golden drop, white Kent, mother of plenty, velvet, and white Lammas.

MARSHALL, G. Noble Farm, Pittwater.

36—37 Samples of wheat and oats.

DENISON, Sir W. T.

38 Wheat (Chidham).

MILLIGAN, J. Oyster Cove.

39 Sassafras bark of Tasmania. Bark of *Atherosperma moschatum*. Used medicinally as a bitter and stomachic.

MURRAY, W. Liverpool St. Hobart Town.

40 Mould candles.

M'NAUGHTEN, A.

41 Cask of velvet wheat.

LIPSCOMBE, F.

42 Cask of white Lammas wheat.

M'NAUGHTEN, A.

43 Cask of white wheat.

WALKER, J. Barrack Street, Hobart Town.

44 Cask of white wheat. Cask made of silver wattle, with hoops of young wattle.

BROWN & CO. New Wharf.

45 Cask of white wheat. Cask of Huon pine, hooped with black wattle (*Acacia mollissima*).
46 Cask of white wheat. Cask made of black wood, with hoops of black wattle.

TOOTH, E. Bagdad.

47 Cask of malt.

PATTERSON, —; Liverpool St. Hobart Town.

48 Cask of small malt. Cask made of silver wattle, wattle hoops.

WALKER, J. Barrack St. Hobart Town.

49 Pearl barley. Cask made of silver wattle, wattle hoops.

CLAYTON H. Norfolk Plains.

50 Flour. Cask made of silver wattle, wattle hoops.

WALKER, J. Barrack St. Hobart Town.

51 Fine flour. Cask made of silver wattle, with hoops of young black wattle.

M'NAUGHTEN, —.

52 Superfine flour of Van Diemen's Land.

MILLIGAN, A. M. Launceston.

53 Small cask of biscuit, made of Tasmanian flour.

BROCK, —, Macquarie St. Hobart Town.

54 Common seamen's biscuits.
55 Fine ship biscuits.

DENISON, Sir W. T.

56—65 Muskwood (*Eurybia argophylla*), smoothed and polished on one side to show the grain. The muskwood of Tasmania is valuable for the purposes of the cabinet-maker, being variously veined, dotted, and marked upon a brown-ground colour. It is close and fine in the grain, takes a high polish, and harmonizes well with the gilding on picture-frames, into which it is often worked up. The musk-tree grows only in dense forests and damp situations; and though it does not attain the size of a forest tree of Van Diemen's Land, it yields slabs large enough for ordinary ornamental work.
66 Slab of myrtle, of Van Diemen's Land (*Fagus Cunninghamii*). The myrtle of Van Dieman's Land often composes dense forests of many miles, and the individual trees in such situations attain a girth of 30 to 40 feet with a proportionate elevation. The wood is of a fresh pink colour when newly hewn, and the wood part is often very beautifully veined and watered, fitting it admirably for showy picture-frames, and such like cabinet-work.
67—70 Cedar, or pencil pine, of Tasmania, Marlborough (*Athrotaxis selaginoides*), and Lake Country. Found in the ravines and gorges of the mountain, and on the high table-

land of the colony, in groups, or singly; sometimes in the forests, and not unfrequently in bare, unsightly groves; of dead, dry, and bleached stems, with a few large limbs attached, 3000 to 4000 feet above the level of the sea.

71—72 Sections, with bark.

73 Celery-topped pine of Tasmania (*Phyllocladus aspleniifolia*). The celery pine attains a height of 150 feet, and grows in all the cold and moist parts of Van Diemen's Land, in a handsome pyramidal form. The timber is beautifully white, and very close in the grain; useful for household purposes.

74, 75, & 76 Section with bark, 12 inches in diameter. The same, 12 inches in diameter. Rosewood or zebra-wood, of Tasmania. Said to be plentiful about Marlborough and Lake Country.

77 Muskwood log, from Tasman's Peninsula.

SMITH, C. T.

78 Hops, Tasmanian.

MILLIGAN, J. Mount Wellington, and Constitution Hill.

79 Hones for edged tools.

DENISON, His Excellency Sir W. T.

80 A drip-stone, from Norfolk Island. Filters made of this rock, which appears to be a raised beach of calcareous grit; are in general use here, and much approved.

MILLIGAN, J. Flinders' Island, in Bass's Straits.

81 Gum: gum resin of the grass tree (*Anthorrhæa australis*). The gum resin, or balsam, is highly inflammable, yielding, on combustion, a clear white flame and rich fragrant odour, said to be used in churches in place of frank-incense; dyes calico a nankin colour; is used in making sealing-wax, and may become the basis of a varnish. Very abundant on many of the meagre soils of clay and sand in this and the neighbouring islands and continent.

FOWLER, —, Maria Island.

82—85 Dogwood slabs (*Bedfordia?*).

86, 87 Muskwood slabs (*Eurybia, argophylla*).

88 He-oak.

89 Ironwood, or *Lignum vitæ* of Tasmania (*Notelæa ligustrina*.)

ROBINSON, —, Westbury.

90 A gun-stock of blackwood. Roughly cut into form, and polished on one side to show the grain of the wood.

WHITESIDES, —, Hobart Town.

91 Blackwood of Tasmania, polished on one side.

92 Myrtlewood.

93 Muskwood.

QUINN, —, Argyll St. Hobart Town.

94 Blue gum of Van Diemen's Land (*Eucalyptus globulus*). A piece taken near the root, squared and polished to show the grain.

QUINN, —, Norfolk Island.

95 Maple. Small piece of veneer, polished.

M'NAUGHTEN, —, Hobart Town.

96—102 Muskwood of Van Diemen's Land (*Eurybia argophylla*).

HADDEN, Capt. R.E.

103, 104 Muskwood of Van Diemen's Land.

EUSTON & MILLIGAN, Macquarie Harbour.

105, 106 Ironwood, or *Lignum vitæ* of Tasmania. Cross section of the trunk of the tree, being the largest ever met with. It rarely attains a diameter of more than 12 to 14 inches.

BROWNRIGG, —.

107, 108 Muskwood slabs.

BURGESS, Mrs. Davey St. Hobart Town.

109 Worsted work, representing a branch from a blue gum tree in flower (*Eucalyptus globulus*) with four birds of

Tasmania perched on the twigs. The birds represented are a red-breast, a small honey-sucker, a pardalote, and the blue-headed wren. The frames of this and the next are of the timber of the myrtle-tree of Van Diemen's Land, and made by Mr. Pearson, of Hobart Town.

110 Worsted work, representing a group of indigenous flowers of Tasmania. In the centre is the warratah (*Telopea truncata*); immediately over it is a head of the grass-tree of Mount Wellington in flower (*Richea distichophylla*); then in order, *Acacia verticillata*, *Billardiera longiflora*, *Acacia armata* (an exotic, *Richea sp.*, *Acacia mollissima*, *Acacia verniciflua*, *Casuarina quadrivalvis*, *Pomaderris*, *Boronia variabilis*, *Tetratheca sp.*, *Pultenea*, *sp.*, and *Solanum laciniat*).

HOOD, R. V. Liverpool St. Hobart Town.

111 Timber of silver wattle (*Acacia dealbata*). One side polished.

112, 113 Muskwood slabs.

114, 115 Blackwood slabs, squared (*Acacia melanoxylon*).

116 Cross section of small tree of Huon pine. One corner smoothed and polished.

117 Huon pine slab (*Dacrydium Franklinii*). Squared and polished.

118 Muskwood slab (*Eurybia argophyllia*). Squared and polished.

119 Myrtle-root slab (*Fagus Cunninghamii*).

120 Myrtle slab, from the stem of the tree.

DENISON, His Excellency Sir W. T.

121 Rosewood of Van Diemen's Land (*Acacia sp.*) Found in the Lake Country near Marlborough.

122, 123 Rosewood of Van Diemen's Land.

124 Celery pine slab, squared (*Phyllocladus aspleniifolia*).

125 Rosewood.

HOOD, R. V.

126,129 Huon pine picture-frame; gilt moulding, the gold-leaf made by Mr. Hood. Myrtlewood picture-frame.

127 Muskwood picture-frame.

MARRIOTT, Archdeacon.

128 Muskwood picture-frame.

WISEMAN, —, Hobart Town.

130 Whip. Thong of colonial leather, and the stick a young sassafras of Tasmania.

131 Ladies' riding whips. Of whalebone, tipped with silver, by Mr. Jones.

132 Stock-hunting whip. Thong of colonial leather, stick of she-oak.

133 Stock-hunter's-saddle, of colonial cow-hide, prepared in Hobart Town.

134 Stock-hunter's breastplate.

BUTTON, T. Launceston.

135 Dressed kangaroo skins.

DENISON, His Excellency Sir W. T.

136 Roll of Tweed. Colonial material, manufactured by the inmates of Cascades' establishment. 137 Hank of yarn.

QUEEN'S ORPHAN SCHOOLS.

138 Woollen gloves, knitted. Manufactured by the children.

139 Woollen socks, knitted.

140 The same, unbleached.

141 Woollen stockings, knitted.

142 Shawls, knitted.

BARNARD, J.

143 Swansdown, two skins.

CLEBURNE, R. Murray St. Hobart Town.

144 Samples of soap.

LUMSDEN, —, Brisbane St. Hobart Town.

145, 146 Loo-table top of Huon pine, and pedestal for the same.

WATCHORN, W. Liverpool St. Hobart Town.

147 Tallow. The exhibitor claims to have been the first to export tallow to England from the colony.

DENISON, Sir W. T.

149 Loo-table top, dogwood (*Bedfordia sp.*) The dogwood, or *Bedfordia* tree, is one of the richest-looking and most beautiful fancy woods of Van Diemen's Land. It attains to a larger size on Maria Island than elsewhere. In the vicinity of Hobart Town it is a mere shrub.

150 Pedestal for the same.

151 Top of a sofa-table, inlaid with chess-board in the middle.

ROUT, W.

152 Portmanteau. Made of colonial leather.

GUNN, W. Launceston.

153 Feathers of mutton-birds, or sooty petrel (*Puffinus brevicaudus*). Much used for pillows, bolsters, and mattresses. From the almost inconceivable numbers in which this bird resorts to the islands in Bass's Straits, and the profusion of feathers with which it is clothed, there is no difficulty in obtaining the commodity in any quantity.

ROUT, W. Elizabeth St. Hobart Town.

154 Small rope line.   155 Small lines of three sizes. 156 Best small rope of three sizes.   157 Cable-laid lines of three sizes.   158 Common lines of two sizes.

MARSHALL, —, Hobart Town.

159 Common riding-whip. Made entirely of colonial material.

160 Gig and hunting-whip thongs, made of horse-hide dressed in Hobart Town.

OAKDEN, P. Launceston.

161 Wool, two fleeces, Leicester improved. The produce of sheep imported from the best flocks in England in 1837, and now forwarded to show the improvement in softness and silky appearance, attributed to the superiority of climate.

HART, —, Hobart Town.

162 Glue.   163 Neat's foot oil.   164 Sheep's trotter oil.

HOOD, R. V.

165 Gold leaf. Manufactured from Californian gold, brought to Tasmania by colonial trading vessels.

166 Gold-beaters' skin.

M'KENZIE, Mrs. Blue Hills, Bothwell.

167, 170 Knitted gloves, made from opossum fur. Lady's cape of opossum fur.

SLIEGLITZ, Mrs. Killymoon, Break-o'-day.

168 Gloves, made from opossum fur.

TOOTH, E

169, 171 Gloves, made from opossum fur and lambs' wool.

BUTTON, T. Launceston.

172 Parchment.

ROUT, W.

173 Brushes, one set of four.

LIPSCOMBE, F.

174 Flax, dressed.

SHARLAND, W.

175 Carriage-rug. Made of skins of the black opossum, ined with skins of the native cat.

DENISON, Sir W. T.

176 Rug of various furs. Made of skins of the brush-kangaroo (*Hatmaturus Bennettei*), forest kangaroo (*Macropus major*), black opossum (*Phalangesta futiginosa*), native cat (*Dasyurus viverrinus*), tiger-cat (*D. macutatus*), well preserved, and amongst them some specimens of great rarity and beauty.

SHARLAND, Mrs. George Town.

177 Book of pressed algæ, collected by the exhibitor.

DAVIES, Archdeacon.

178 Rug of skins of black opossum (*Phalangista futiginosæ*).

179 Rug of tanned skins of brush-kangaroo.

MILLIGAN, J.

180 Carpenter's bench-screw.

181 Three pairs of shoe-lasts.

VALENTINE, Dr. Campbeltown.

182 Organ-pipes of Huon pine, bored in the solid, with stops, &c. Two of these are bored in solid pine, and are found to yield a softer and more mellow tone than those made of woods which are soft and spongy in the grain. It is considered that, being free from joints and glue, the tube will be less affected by atmospheric changes. The wood, too, of the Huon pine, is very durable, and, when properly seasoned, it is little influenced by atmospheric agencies. This pipe is therefore not likely to be often out of tune. The small pipe has a stopper, which being removed, the octave above will be produced. Mr. Valentine regards the stopped pipe as a novelty, and observes, " it gives a very soft note, well adapted for the treble half of the stop-diapason of a chamber-organ." No. 3 is but to show how an open pipe of the usual construction may be tuned by means of a stopper, without injury to its size.

WARD, C. Collins St. Hobart Town.

183 Stockman's ankle-boots, of colonial material.

REGAN, —, Liverpool St. Hobart Town.

184 Nine dressed kangaroo skins, tanned with wattle bark.

HARPER, —, Launceston.

185 Prepared groats.

WARD, C.

186 Blacking for shoes.

ROUT, W.

187 Thylacynus cyanocephalus: tanned skin with hair on. The hyena, or tiger of the colonists, which has become very scarce.

DENISON, Sir W. T.

188 Ornythorynchus paradoxus: six tanned skins. The platypus of colonists: the fine fur under the coat of long hairs upon its back is said to be equal to the fur of beaver for hat-making.

SMITH, M. C. T.

189 Sample of fine wool.

DUNN, —, Davey St.

190 Mylitta Australis, obtained on the Snug Estate, North West Bay, D'Entrecatteaux Channel. Native bread of Tasmania, grows under ground, like the truffle in England, and, like it, has a peculiar smell. Edible, having formed, in a half-roasted state, a portion of the diet of the aborigines. Has been tried with approval in soup and in puddings by Europeans. This specimen is unusually large, having weighed 14⅞ lbs. in 1846.

LOWES, T. Y.—191 Mylitta Australis, obtained at Glenorchy seventeen years ago.

M'NAUGHTEN, —.—192 Writing-desk, muskwood, inlaid with pine, blackwood, she-oak, and myrtle.   193 Dressing-case, or work-box, of the same materials.

MILLIGAN, J., Argyll St. Hobart Town.—194 Necklaces of shells, as worn by aborigines of Tasmania. The shell composing these necklaces seems closely allied to Phasianilla. It is very abundant in the various bays and sinuosities. It possesses anacreous brilliant lustre, which is disclosed by the removal of the cuticle, and this the aborigines effect by soaking in vinegar, and using friction. Various tints, black, blue, and green, are afterwards given by boiling with tea, charcoal, &c.

WALKER, ABM. Norfolk Plains.—195 Plumbago, black

lead. Found in a shaft sunk in pursuit of indications of galena and copper ore, in a seam or vein about 5 inches thick, traversing schistose clay, overlying an old quartzose and crystalline limestone, in which the lodes of lead and copper are expected to be realised.

ROLWEGAN, —, Collins St. Hobart Town.—196 Book, printed and published in Van Diemen's Land, bound in colonial calf, gilt and lettered with Californian gold, manufactured in Hobart Town into gold leaf.

MILLIGAN, J. Argyll St. Hobart Town.—197 Tasmanian Journal, three volumes, printed and published in Van Diemen's Land. 200 Snuff-box, turned of ironwood (*Olea apetala*). 201 Another, of muskwood of Tasmania (*Eurybia argophylla*). 202. Another, of Huon pine. 203. Another, globular, turned out of the tooth of the sperm whale. 204 Ladies thread-holder; 205 Ladies' puff-box; 206 Goblet.

ANDERSON, —, Liverpool St. Hobart Town.—198. Set of ladies' tortoiseshell combs.

BROWN, FIELDING, —, Hobart Town.—199 Candlestick, turned of ironwood of Norfolk Island, (*Olea apetala*). The tops of the root of the Norfolk Island pine (*Araucaria excelsa*).

MOSES, S. Liverpool St. Hobart Town.—207 Jaw of a sperm whale, with 48 teeth complete.

HULL, HUGH.—208 Half section of the trunk of the Tolosa tree (or *Pittosporum bicolor*). This is the wood of which the aborigines chiefly made their waddies or clubs.

M'NAUGHTEN, —.—209 Muskwood slab.

FREEMAN, Rev. E. Brown's River.—210, 211 Veneer, of the oak of Tasmania (*Casuarina quadrivalvis*). 212 Piece of a knot of myrtle-tree of Tasmania. 213 Veneer of he-oak of Tasmania (*Casuarina stricta*). 214 Two veneers, of native cherry-tree of Tasmania (*Exocarpus cupressiformis*). 215, 216 Veneers of Tasmanian honeysuckle-tree (*Banksia australis*).

DENISON, Sir W.—220, 221, 222, 223 Half sections of limb of honeysuckle tree, the same of she-oak.

MILLIGAN, J.—221 Section of a small stem of *Richea pandanifolia*, obtained at Macquarie Harbour. Specimen, sliced, bevelled, and French-polished, to show the pith, medullary rays, and beautiful markings of the wood. This plant grows like a palm, and attains the height of thirty and forty feet and ten inches diameter—confined to the dense wet forests on the western side of the island. 223 Specimen of pinkwood (*Carpodontos lucida*) obtained at Macquarie Harbour. Attains an elevation of 100 to 150 feet in height with a good clear barrel—grows chiefly on the western side of the island in dense myrtle-forests; the timber is fine grained and remarkably hard; has been used for making sheaves for ships' blocks. 227 Butter-print of Huon pine. 230 Seven baskets, made by the aborigines of Tasmania. 231 Model of water-pitcher, made by the aborigines of Van Diemen's Land, of the broad leaved kelp. Often made large enough to hold a quart or two of water. The only other vessel possessed by the aborigines for carrying a supply of water was a sea-shell—a large cymba—occasionally cast upon the northern shore of Van Diemen's Land, which would contain about a quart.

SMITH, P. Ross Reserve.—222 Small bale of wool.

PECK, GEORGE.—224, 225, 226 Cribbage boards, veneered on pine, inlaid, &c.

MOSES, CHAMPION & Co.—228 Eight ivory teeth of sperm whale.

DENISON, Sir W. T.—229 Maple of Norfolk Island—square specimen.

STRUTT, W. Bath St.—232 Marble, from Maria Island, partially dressed.

BOYD, J.—233 Marble, from Maria Island, cut and dressed as paper weights.

TIBBS, —, Goulbourn St. Hobart Town.—234 Specimens of crockery-ware, made from the clay found in the domain.

KERMODE, R. Q. Mona Vale.—235 Small bale of wool—very fine sample.

JENNINGS, J. D. Liverpool St.—236 Churn, made of Huon pine.

MOSES, S.—237 Bundle of whalebone; an important article of export.

SMITH, Lieut. R.N.—238, 239, 240, 241 Raspberry and currant, green gooseberry, red gooseberry, and quince jam.

ROUT, W.—242 Bundle of curled horse-hair.

SYMONDS, E.—243, 244 Corn and barley riddles, coarse. 245 Corn sieve, fine. 246 Fire-screen, for chair-back; made of willow, grown dressed, and dyed in Van Diemen's Land. 247 Bottle basket, flat ; 248 Bundle of willow rods ; 249 Fishing basket; 250 Three baskets with double lids ; 251 Book basket; 252 Knife basket; 253 Child's basket, round.

MILLIGAN, J.—254 Gum of Acacia (*Mucranata*). A shrubby tree on Flinders' Island, Bass's Straits. 255 Guano, from Babel Island. 256 Specimen of grey granite, from Flinders' Island. 257 Granite, from east coast of Van Diemen's Land. 258 Granite, from Hampshire Hills. 259 Porphyritic granite, from Webb's Harbour. 260 Limestone, from Fingal and Break-o'-day. 261, 262 Limestone, with galena, from Norfolk Plains. 263 Brown-clay iron ore, near Fingal. 264 Clay iron-stone. In beds, alternating with bituminous coal, near the Douglas river, on the east coast of Van Diemen's Land. 265 Reddle—red ochre or red chalk. Occurs in masses of uniform and determinate shape, imbedded in alluvium of loam and earth. 266 Ore of iron, from Hampshire Hills ; magnetic. Nearly pure iron ; seems crystalline ; highly magnetic with polarity; occurs in masses, at the line of contact between granite and basalt. 267 Ore of iron. Found in nodules with quartz, in granite soil, near the Housetop Mountain, north-west of Van Diemen's Land ; formerly used by the aborigines of Van Diemen's Land as a paint; first peroxidized by roasting, and then reduced to a fine powder by grinding between two stones. 268 Ore of manganese, from the vicinity of the French-man's-cap Mountain.

DENISON, Sir W. T.—269 Two cross sections of the barrel of the blue gum-tree. 270 Limestone, from Maria Island.

FLEGG, R. C.—271 Wellington boots of Kangaroo skin, dressed in Hobart Town.

DENISON, Sir W. T.—272 Specimen of calcareous grit, from Norfolk Island.

MILLIGAN, J.—273 Cake of bees'-wax, of Tasmania. 279 Four models of canoes of aborigines of Van Diemen's Land. These are exact models of the large catamarans in which the natives used to cross to Brune Island: the material is bark of the *Melaleuca squarrosa*.

SYMONDS, E.—274–278 Key basket; round basket, open; long basket; straw hat, from Norfolk Island; hoop for a sieve, made of Huon pine.

COX, F.—280 Case of Tasmanian insects.

BONNEY, —.—281 Case of Tasmanian birds

GUNN, W., & MILLIGAN, A. M., *Launceston*.—282 Oil of the mutton bird, or sooty-petrel (*Puffinus brevicaudis*). An oil of a deep-red colour, obtained by pressure from the stomach of the young bird. It is said to possess virtue as a liniment in rheumatism, and it burns with a clear bright light. The sooty-petrel frequents certain low sandy islands in Bass's Straits, in inconceivable numbers during the summer, burrowing to lay its solitary egg, and literally undermining the ground.

BROWN & Co.—283–285 Samples of oil of southern black whale, sperm whale, and black fish.

LOWES, T. Y.—286 Oil of the shark.

DENISON, Sir W. T.—287 Blood juice, obtained from a tree in Norfolk Island. Makes an indelible marking-ink, and is said to be used as a dye for calicoes, &c.

MILLIGAN, J. & HULL, H. 288 Gum-kino, from the blue

gum-tree, the stringy bark, and other eucalypti. Equal, as a medicinal agent, to the kino from the East Indies, and yielded very profusely by the eucalypti, after incision or injury.

BONNEY, —. —289 Manna. An exudation from the leaves and delicate succulent twigs of the white gum-trees of Van Diemen's Land, after a perforation by an insect in the summer. It soon exiccates, and falls in the form of irregular tears; and during December, January, February, and March is usually very abundant. Its properties are similar to, but less powerful, than those of the manna of the druggist.

ABBOTT, J.—290 Iron-sand, a fine emery-like substance, occurs in thin layers on the sea-shore at Long Bay in D'Entrecatteaux-Channel, a deposit from water passing through iron-stone beds, percolating the soil, and depositing the metallic matter where it comes in contact with the salt water.

ROUT W. —291 Honey of Tasmania. 1849 and 1850. 293 Bees'-wax, Tasmanian. Three cakes, unbleached. In no country in the world do bees thrive better than in Van Diemen's Land, or prove so productive with a trifling amount of attention; circumstances due, no doubt, to the mildness of the winter season, and the fact of many Tasmanian plants blooming throughout the winter months. The bee has now become naturalised in the forests, and many of the hollow trees are filled with the produce of their labour.

MILLIGAN, J.—292 Resin of Oyster Bay pine (*Callitris australis*); a delicately white resin, sometimes, but rarely, in tears of a bright amber tint, scarce. The Oyster Bay pine is only found along a narrow strip of country near the sea, on the east coast of Van Diemen's Land, and islands adjacent.

BICHENO, J. E.—294 Alum, from near Bridgewater; occurs as an efflorescence in caverns in the clayey rocks.

SMITH, Lieut., R.N.—295 Epsom salts, sulphate of magnesia, found in caverns on the side of the Dromedary Mountain, near the Derwent. 296 Gum of the wattle-tree; *Acacia mollissina* and *dealaita*. Wattle gum exudes in streams during the summer season from fissures and accidental injuries to the bark, soon hardening into tears and lumps of various size. It is equal to the gum-arabic of the shops, for all purposes to which the latter is applicable.

LIPSCOMBE, F.—297 Ham, cured by Mr. Marshall.

HAINES, J., *Murray St., Hobart Town.*—298—303 Pickles: —Red cabbage; walnuts; cauliflower; onion; mixed; tomata sauce.

DENISON, Sir W. T.—304 Walking stick, made of the solid side of the bone of a whale, the head turned out of the tooth of the sperm whale.

SCREEN, T.—305 Walking stick, made of the solid side of the bone of a whale.

MILLIGAN, J.—306 Iron ores, from Long Bay; occurs in a bed about 7 or 8 feet thick, over sandstone, and at the foot of green stone hills.

MARRIOTT, Arch.—307 Walking stick, of the oak of Tasmania (*Casuarina quadrivalvis*).

LIPSCOMB, F.—308 Small round table, Huon pine, inlaid.

DE LITTLE, R.—309 Galena, from the Tama River. 310 Iron ore, three specimens, found near York River, over limestone.

MILLIGAN, J.—311 Galena, from Macquarie Harbour, occurs in a vein of mountain limestone, in the channel of Franklin River. 313 Opal wood, salt-pan plains. 315 Rock crystal (sp. 25). 316 Beryl (*Aqua marine*), 30 specimens. 317 Straw-coloured topaz, 300 specimens. 318 Yellow topaz, 40 specimens. 319 Pink-coloured topaz, 30 specimens.

REEVES, —. —314 Wattle bark, chopped, as it is prepared for the tan-pits.

DENISON, Sir W. T.—312 Coffee, from Norfolk Island.

KEMP, GEORGE.—320 Cornelian, from the margin of Derwent, opposite Hobart Town.

SHARLAND, W. S.—321 Thread lace, made by a girl eleven years of age, at New Norfolk.

REEVES, —. 322 Wool. Sample of skin-wool. 323 Another, scoured.

MILLIGAN, J.—324 Jet, or lignite, from Macquarie Harbour. 325 Limestone, from the Gordon River.

BICHENO, J. E.—326 Limestone from the Mersey River. 327 Limestone from the foot of Mount Wellington range.

AKERS, Lieut., R. E.—328 Section of Norfolk Island pine (*Araucaria excelsa*).

SLY, J. Liverpool St. Hobart Town.—329 Pair of dress boots.

FENTON, Mrs.—330 Honey of 1850.

DOWLING, H.—331—333 Books:—Tasmanian Kalendar, 1848, 1849, 1850

DENISON, Sir W. T.—334 Potash from Tasmanian timbers. 336 Red ochre, Norfolk Island. 336 Yellow ochre, Norfolk Island. 337 Specimens of marle. 338 White oak timber of Norfolk Island. 339 Specimens of timber of pine of Norfolk Island (*Araucaria excelsa*). 340 Specimens of iron-wood timber (*Olea apetala*).

MILLIGAN, J. — 341 Specimen of timber of Oyster Bay pine (*Callitris australis*). 342 Specimen of greenstone, from Fingal, Van Diemen's Land.

BLACKBURN & THOMSON.—343 Model of bridge across the river Derwent, at Bridgewater, Van Diemen's Land, on the line of road between Hobart Town and Launceston.

THOMSON, JAMES.—344 Coloured sectional elevation of the bridge and cause-way at Bridgewater, Van Diemen's Land.

COUNCIL OF THE ROYAL SOCIETY OF VAN DIEMEN'S LAND. —345 Books and bookbinding; papers and proceedings of the Royal Society of Van Diemen's Land, printed by Messrs. Best, and bound by Mr. Rolwegan, Collins St. Hobart Town; the lithographs by Mr. T. Brown, Macquarie St. Bound in colonial calf-skins, tanned and dressed by Mr. Reeves. Gilt and lettered with gold leaf, manufactured from Californian gold, by Mr. R. V. Hood, Collins St. Hobart Town.

WATSON, JOHN, Hobart Town.—346 Plank of blue gum (*Eucalyptus globulus*); length, 146 ft. breadth 20 in. depth 6 in.

GRANT, J. Tulluchgorum, Fingal, Van Diemen's Land. Three ram fleeces—1 Fleece from a hogget ram, weighing, after being scoured, 3 lb. 10 oz. 2 Similar fleece weighing 3 lb. 11 oz. 3 Fleece from an older ram, weighing 4 lb.

RICHARDSON BROTHERS & Co. 17 St. Helen's Pl.—Specimens of two sorts of wool.

MCPHERSON & FRANCIS, Hobart Town, Agent, W. Francis, Corn Exchange, London.—Sample of wheat 65½ lbs. per bushel.

In Central Avenue.

MC. LACHLAN.

Specimen of silicized wood found about 32 miles from Hobart Town, embedded in two flows of scoriæ (probably thrown out with the tree by a volcanic eruption).

NEW ZEALAND.

—— Areas Q. R. & S. 30, 31, 32. ——

1 TYRREL, —.—Flax and wool.

2 MURCHISON, J. H. 10 Holles St. Cavendish Sq. Prop.—Copper ore from Kawan, a small island a few miles from Auckland, New Zealand.

3 COLLINSON, Rev. J. Gateshead, Prop.—Geological specimens from New Zealand. Specimen of iron sand from New Plymouth, in New Zealand. Small bag made from New Zealand flax, by a lady in New Zealand. Flax prepared by the natives; native pattern and native dyes. Mat made of New Zealand flax; made by the natives, being their usual clothing.

4 ROBERTSON, J.—Specimens of raw materials, New Zealand flax (*Phormium tenax*), of various qualities.

5 MCVAY, J.—Specimens of leather and skins

4 Kip leather. 5 Crop leather. 6 Half-dozen sheep-skins. 7 One good sheep-skin (not tanned). Specimens of tanning and black dyeing barks.

6 SMITH, J. A.—Specimen of soap, manufactured in Auckland, New Zealand.

7 ST. JOHN'S COLLEGE.—No. 1 Specimens of cloth and hat made by a native lad, aged 17 years, from wool grown, clean, carded, spun, and woven at St. John's College, and dyed with native woods. 2 Hat made by Nicholas Cod, pensioner, Howick, New Zealand. Specimens of basket work: made by J. Meagher, pensioner, Howick.

8 HARGREAVES, J.—Specimen of lignite, from the banks of the Tamaki.

9 GREENWOOD, W.—Specimens of coal.

10 CONNELL, W. (as Secretary of the Auckland and Waikato Coal Company.)—Specimens of Waikato coal.

11 TAYLOR, J.—Geological specimens of the copper series from the Kawau Company's mine, Kawau.

12 REEVE, J.—Specimens of copper ore from Whitaker & Heale's mine, Kawau:—1 Yellow ore. 2 Blue ore.

13 LEWIS, T.—Specimens of copper ore: Specimens from Great Barrier Island Mine, 35 miles N.N.E. of Auckland.

14 SMITH, J. A.—Two specimens from Brodie's mine, Mongonui, 100 miles to the northward of Auckland. Specimen of iron sand, obtained in large quantities in Cooper's Bay, Auckland. Specimen of sulphur, from White Island, Bay of Plenty, on the east coast of the Northern Island, New Zealand.

15 MEURANT, E.—Specimen of pumice stone, from the banks of the river Waikato.

16 BROWN, W.—Specimen of Kauri gum.

17 GREENWOOD, W.—Specimens of building stone.

18 BROWN, W.—Specimen of limestone, from Wangarei.

19 SMITH, J. A.—Specimens of Roman cement stone. Specimen of sharks' fin. Specimens of flax seed and orchilla weed.

20 BALNEAVIS, Lieut. H. C. H. M. 58th Regt.—Model of New Zealand war pah.

21 JOHNSON, J.—Fifteen specimens of New Zealand furniture woods.

22 THE WAIKATO COAL COMMITTEE, Auckland.—Specimen of coal.

23 PURCHAS, Rev. A.—Specimens of iron ore and limestone.

24 LOW & MOTION.—Specimen of native grown maize. Specimen of Maori wheat and flour.

25 CARADUS, J.—Specimens of New Zealand flax: twine and line.

26 KING, Miss, New Plymouth. — Reticule, made of New Zealand flax, dyed from New Zealand woods, the pattern and work copied from the mat of a New Zealander.

27 LIGAR, C.—Drawing of White Island by C. Heaphy.

28 TYRREL, J. Prof.—Specimens of native flax and wool.

29 SMITH, J. A.—Specimen of oil, from the humpbacked whale, caught at the Bay of Plenty.

30 MCLEOD, R.—Specimens of Manganese, from Brown and Campbell's land at Waihaka, 15 miles from Auckland.

31 Specimen of flour presented by the natives of Rangiarwhia, from wheat grown by Maories.

32 WHITELY, Rev. J.—Specimen of a native box of papa mahuara, in which the natives keep their head dresses.

33 TAYLOR, T. E.—The grub of "Sphinx" destroyed by a vegetable fungus found under the rata tree.

34 WHYTLAW & SON. — Specimen of flax (Phormum tenax) cleaned by machinery.

35 BOURNE, W.—Specimen of iron-casting. The first casting at Auckland Foundry, 18th Dec. 1850.

36 MCLEOD, R.—Specimen of salted mullet.

37 MOORE, P. G. 30 Arundel St. Strand, Prop.—Lithographic picture of a native village, or Pah, in New Zealand, situated in Cook's Straits;—after a large original, now in London, by Professor Gilfillan. Six water-colour drawings and six steel engravings of New Zealand subjects. Four native mats or garments. One greenstone Mari or chief's club. Three specimens of greenstone. One carved box. One war-club. Native fishing net and fishing hooks. Two bottles of insects. Specimens of native grasses. Large map of New Zealand.

38 Articles brought by the "Lord William Bentinck,' from Wellington :—Thirteen packages, containing table-top, composed of nineteen specimens of Taraseki woods. Five samples of Workan coals. Native basket, with four hanks of flax. Suviri or iron-wood. Earthy substance, collected at the town of New Plymouth, and supposed to be alum in a very pure state. New Plymouth iron-sand in its natural state. Unwased barley, from St. Vincent's, Nelson.

39 Malt and hops, made and grown by Hooper and Co. Coals from Massoere Bay, taken from an open pit on the beach. Sandstone, native fishfork and net. Specimens of dyed flax, tanned leather, canogreen moss, &c.

40 LUCAS, R. & Co., 35 South Audley St. — Specimens of New Zealand woods, comprising octagon table-top, veneered with eleven specimens; sofa table-top, veneered with three specimens; small circular inlaid table; a watnot, with twisted columns, veneered with three specimens; a papeterie, with hinged flap and sliding screet panels, fluted with green silk.

LABUAN, AND OTHER PARTS OF THE EASTERN ARCHIPELAGO.

1 GREY, The Countess.—Cloth manufactured by the Seribas, in Borneo. Cloth made by the Mellanoes, in Borneo; sent home by Governor Sir James Brooke. 29 drawings of Borneo plants.

2 HAMMOND, W. P. & Co. Merchants, London. Specimens of sugar; coffee; sago, pearl; sago, common; sago, flour; pepper, black; pepper, white; nutmegs; mace; cloves; gambier; cutch; gum gamboge; gum benjamin; gum lac; rice; tortoiseshell; turtleshell; M. O. P. shells; elephants' teeth; elephants' grinder; gutta percha; gum caoutchouc, or India-rubber; gum damma; isinglass, manufactured in the Archipelago from the interior membranes of fish, and valued on account of its highly glutinous character. A series of thirty-six paintings, by a Malay artist. A model made to scale of a sailing-boat used by the natives in the China Seas for smuggling and piracy. Specimens of rattans, bamboos, &c., grown in and imported from the Eastern Archipelago.

3 WOOLLEY, W. Sec. to the Eastern Archipelago Co. 34 Cornhill.—Bark cloth, manufactured by the Dyaks of Borneo. Specimens of hard wood from Borneo; and surface coal from Labuan.

Foreign States.

AMERICA, UNITED STATES OF.

EDWARD RIDDLE, Esq. Commissioner.
N. S. DODGE, Esq. Secretary.

1 BAKER, S. Inv. Portsmouth, New Hampshire.—Paying machine for vessels. Invention for tarring the seams of vessels.

2 AMOSKEAG MANUFACTURING COMPANY, Manchester, New Hampshire.—Cotton cloth, including ticking, sheeting, striped shirting, bleached flannel, and drilling.

3 EASTMAN, R. Concord, New Hampshire.—Stone-dressing machine.

4 HAUEL, J. Philadelphia, Pennsylvania.—Perfumery and fancy soaps.

5 SPRATT, JAMES, Cincinnati, Ohio.—Lightning-rods, points, and insulators.

6 HEATH, G. Prod. Delhi, Ohio.—Specimen of Indian corn.

7 LOUDERBACK, M. J. Cincinnati, Ohio.—Specimens of preserved peaches.

8 MOOKLAR & CHILDS, Cincinnati, Ohio.—Specimens of leaf and chewing tobacco.

9 HUNTER, W. M. Cincinnati, Ohio.—Artificial teeth on an improved principle.

10 SHEPHERD, R. A. J. Cincinnati, Ohio.—A shirt.

11 YEATMAN, T. H. Cincinnati, Ohio.—Specimens of American Catawba wine.

12 BUCHANAN, R. Cincinnati, Ohio.—Specimen of Catawba wine.

13 CORNEAR, J. B. T. & J. B. Cincinnati, Ohio.—Specimen of Catawba wine.

14 WILLIAMS, N. L. Cincinnati.—Hemp-dressing machines.

15 DUHME, H. Cincinnati, Ohio.—Specimen of Catawba wine.

16 HAZART, R. Cincinnati, Ohio.—Compound microscope.

17 BARNARD, J. Zanesville, Ohio.—Brushes, brooms, and whisks.

18 EMORY, T. Cincinnati, Ohio.—Lard-oil and adamantine candles.

19 FRANK, F. Cincinnati, Ohio.—Lard-oil.

20 M'GREGOR & LEE, Cincinnati. — Improved bank lock.

21 DOMINICK, G. Cincinnati, Ohio.—Specimen of beef tallow and lard.

22 SMITH, H. & D. Newark, Ohio.—Specimens of flour.

23 OTIS, B. H. Cincinnati, Ohio. — Mortising and boring machine.

24 OHIO STATE, BOARD OF AGRICULTURE, Prod. Columbus, Ohio.—Samples of Indian corn in the ear, illustrative of the different varieties raised in Ohio. Samples of corn on the stalk. Case of specimens, illustrative of the economic geology of Ohio. Box of malt from Indian corn.

25 MOYSTON, W. A. Columbus, Ohio.—Buck-eyed squirrel (stuffed).

26 THOMPSON, R. Columbus, Ohio.—Plough. Surgical instruments. Invention for teaching the blind to draw and write; said to be very simple, and to be applicable to the teaching of geography, geometry, mathematics, &c.

27 TILLINGHAST, J. B. Inv. Steubenville, Ohio.—Patent churn.

28 EATON, C. L. Columbus, Ohio. — Brooms and broom-corn.

29 STAFFORD, J. R. Cleveland, Ohio.—Specimens of steam-dried corn meal.

30 BARTLETT, R. M. Manu. Cincinnati, Ohio.—Commercial and banking tables.

31 GLOBE PRINT COMPANY—CHAPIN, W. G.—Fall River, Massachusetts.—Printed calicoes. These prints are on a cloth containing 60 by 64 picks, averaging about the same count as the British 66's.

32 POPE, J. Memphis, Tennessee.—Specimens of ginned cotton.

33 JONES, WHITE, & M'CURDY, Philadelphia, Pennsylvania.—Artificial teeth and gold foil. Exhibited for natural appearance, and other good qualities.

34 BILLINGS & AMBROSE, Inv. Claremont, New Hampshire.—Method of connecting hubs and axles.

35 LONSDALE Co., GODDARD BROTHERS, Providence, Rhode Island.—Cotton goods.

36 BAZIN XAVIER, Philadelphia. — Perfumery and soaps.

37 BOND, S. Memphis, Tennessee.—Specimen of ginned cotton.

38 LEARNED & REYNOLDS, Indianopolis, Indiana.—Flour extractor.

39 PALMER, FRANKLIN B. Philadelphia.—Artificial leg; made on a new principle; the tendo Achillis, flexor and extensor muscles.

40 BROWN, P. A. Philadelphia, Pennsylvania.—Specimens of fine wool.

41 LACEY & PHILLIPS, Philadelphia, Pennsylvania.—Harness.

42 ROOT, M. A. Philadelphia.—Daguerreotypes.

43 WETHERILL BROTHERS, Philadelphia, Pennsylvania.—Four bottles of chemicals and a sample of white lead.

44 MORRIS, JONES, & Co. Manu. Philadelphia, Pennsylvania.—Specimens of the best hanging boiler-plate iron. Specimens of the best hanging boiler-plate iron and hammered bar-iron. Specimens of the iron ore and limestone used at the furnace, and the pig-iron made from it by charcoal. Specimens of machine-made cut nails.

45 OAKFORD C. Philadelphia. — Moleskin hats, White Rocky Mountain beaver, and lady's riding-hat.

46 CORNELIUS & Co. Philadelphia, Pennsylvania.—Lamps, chandeliers, and gas fixtures.

47 WARDLE, S. Philadelphia.—Artificial block teeth.

48 HOWELL & BROTHERS, Philadelphia.—Paper-hangings.

49 HUSBAND, T. J. Manu. Philadelphia, Pennsylvania—Specimen of calcined magnesia.

50 MATTSON, T. W. Philadelphia.—Travelling trunk

51 CRAWFORD, H. M. Philadelphia, Pennsylvania.—Various calf-skins.

52 DUVAL, P. S. Philadelphia.—Chromo-lithographs and transfer from copper-plates to stone.

53 WATSON, G. W. Philadelphia, Pennsylvania. — A trotting sulkey.

54 ABBEY & SON, C. Philadelphia, Pennsylvania.— Fine gold foil. Exhibited for softness, toughness, and uniformity.

55 SAVERY, P. B. Philadelphia. — Enamelled hollow-ware.

56 YEAGER & ORD, Philadelphia, Pennsylvania.—Artificial leg.

57 LIPPINCOTT, GRAMBO, & Co. Philadelphia.—Various books, and specimens of bookbinding.

58 HICKEY & TULL, Philadelphia.—Two trunks.

59 MEYER, C. Philadelphia.—Pianofortes, constructed with iron-plate frames, particularly adapted to damp and warm climates.

60 SIMES, S. Manu. Philadelphia. — Samples of cod-liver oil.

61 REYNOLDS, R. J. Philadelphia.—Artificial teeth.

62 LANGENHEIM, W. F. Philadelphia, Pennsylvania. —Specimens of fine magic lantern slides.

63 BUCKINGHAM, T. L. Philadelphia.—Artificial teeth, mounted in silver, galvanised.

64 M'MULLEN, J. Baltimore, Maryland.—Specimens of netting machines.

65 HUSSEY O. Baltimore, Maryland.—Reaping and mowing machine.

66 DETMOLD, C. E. Prop. Lonacoming, Maryland.— Specimens of pig-iron, iron-ore, coal, and coke.

67 HYDE, F. Baltimore, Maryland.—Fancy soap.

68 CHAPMAN, J. L. Baltimore, Maryland.—Glass ware.

69 BARLOW, T. H. Lexington, Kentucky. — A planetarium.

70 McCULLOCH, S. D. Lexington, Kentucky. — Specimen of Burrow's mustard.

71 COLMAN, Mrs. C. Louisville, Kentucky.—Three bed quilts.

72 PERRY, J. Narragansett, Rhode Island.—Meat cutters, adapted to a variety of purposes.

73 M'CORMICK, C. H. Chicago, Illinois. — Virginia grain reaper.

74 PEALE, C. W. Hickscherville, Pennsylvania.—Specimens of Anthracite coal.

75 SENNEFF, J. Philadelphia, Pennsylvania.—Weaver's heddle.

76 AVERY, O. Honesdale, Pennsylvania.—Specimens of dentistry.

77 WRIGHT, W. B. & C. B. Rochester, New York.— Bevelled sawing machine.

78 LLOYD, L. J. Maker, Albany.—Harness exhibited for manufacture. Lady's whalebone trunk. Gentleman's whalebone trunk. The locks of these trunks are exhibited or novelty of invention.

79 DICK, D. Imp. and Inv. Buckingham Street, Adelphi.—Embossing press. Boiler plate, shears, and punch. Bailing press. Rail straightener. Saw-tooth cutter. Anti-friction machines. Designed and manufactured by J. E. Holmes, of New York.

80 HURST, J. A. Albany.—Prepared animals, birds, and fishes.

81 MOTT, C. A. Lansingburgh, New York.—Specimens of mineral paints.

82 GRANT, A. T. & Co. Schaghticoke, New York.— Fanning mill.

83 NEW YORK STATE AGRICULTURAL SOCIETY, Albany, New York.—Case of wheat. Jar of maple sugar.

84 KIRTLAND, B. B. Greenbush, New York.—Sample of Indian corn.

85 AMERICAN CHAIR Co. Manu. Troy, New York.— Chairs with patent centripetal springs and railroad-car seats.

86 SMITH, L. Troy, New York.—Smut machine.

87 MAWSON BROTHERS, New York.— Natural-colour American silver-martin muff, Victoria boa, and gauntlets, made from the skins of animals abounding in the State of North Carolina. The colours are considered to be very beautiful, the choice of each having been made out of 1,000 skins.

88 STARR, C. New York.—Two machines to be used in bookbinding; one for backing, the other for finishing the backs. These machines are intended to be kept in operation during the Exhibition. Books for the blind : two Bibles. Quarto Bible, to show the style of work effected by the above machine.

90 PIRSON, J. New York.—Patent double grand pianoforte. Patent square pianoforte.

91 STARBUCK, N. B. Troy, New York.—Fourteen ploughs.

92 PAGE, E. 20 West Street, New York, and 38 Eastern R. R. Wharf, Boston.—Two sweeps, of 36 feet each : made of one stick. Four oars, of common stock, in the finished state. Four oars, in the rough state, as left by the machinery. Pair of oars, decorated : intended as a present for His Royal Highness the Prince of Wales. Pair of model oars, with pens : intended to be offered to the Lords of the Admiralty.

93 MILWARD, J. & SON, New York.—White Parmela bonnets.

94 HOTCHKISS, G. Windsor, New York.—Noddle-iron, tram-block, and bridge-tree, for saw-mills.

95 ST. JOHN, J. R. Inv. Buffalo, New York.—Self-determining variation compass.

96 MIX & GARDINIER, Schoharie, New York.—Model of a waggon.

97 ALLEN, A. B. & Co. Manu. Water Street, New York. Agents in London, Charlwood & Cummins, 14 Tavistock Row.—Thermometer churn with a double zinc case, into which hot or cold water may be put to regulate the temperature of the cream. Specimens of the most improved kinds of handled axes for chopping, Hay-rakes used in connection with horse-rakes for gathering hay. Scythe and sneath. Two and three tine hay-forks, for pitching and handling hay. Shovel and spade. Manure-forks, 4, 5, 6 tine. Sausage-cutter, No. 1, for making fine mince or sausage meat. Sausage-cutter, No. 2 ; more efficient than No. 1 : it has mince knives and pins. Sausage-stuffer for filling sausages. Garden-hoe, made from solid steel without welding. Road-scraper, for levelling roads, cleansing ditches, digging cellars, excavating, &c. Post-hole auger, used for setting fences, making holes in the ground for posts, &c. Indian corn sheller, containing two fly-wheels and friction roller. Steel tooth, cast steel and universal cultivators. Different styles of cultivators. Fan-mill. Portable patent ladder. Subsoil plough. Ordinary plough, complete. Various other ploughs on approved constructions, chiefly for one horse.

98 GOULD, J. & Co. Manu. Albany, New York.—A pony sleigh.

99 CHASE, M. W. Chatham, New York.—An herbarium.

100 LEARNED & THATCHER, Albany, New York.—Chandelier stove for the parlour ; a " golden age " parlour-cooking stove.

101 DEAN, AMOS & Co. Albany, New York.—Argilla knobs, &c.

102 PRATT, Z. Prattsville, New York.—Samples of feather ; various specimens of lithography.

103 BELL, T. Morrisania, New York.—Farm products : —Spring wheat ; soule wheat ; Mediterranean wheat ; Baid white fliut wheat ; barley ; rye ; buckwheat ; oats ; Indian corn ; Indian corn in the ear ; broom corn ; flax, millet, clover, and timothy seeds. Groom brush.

104 Oswego Starch Factory, Oswego, New York.—Samples of starch manufactured from Indian corn.

105 Evans, O. B. Buffalo, New York.—Specimens of daguerreotyping.

106 Peters, T. C. Darien, New York.—Specimens of Saxony wool.

107 Wells, L. Rochester, New York.—Agricultural implements. Wheel cultivator, used to prepare land for wheat, by once ploughing only.

108 Leask, Mrs. J. Albany, New York.—Needlework:—Satin patchwork cradle-quilt; satin nursery-basket; merino embroidered under-shirt; linen stitched and corded slip; cambric shirt; infant's articles; mourning articles of various kinds; polka dress-cap, with narrow white satin piping.

109 Mead & Brothers, New York.—Daguerreotypes.

110 Brown, G. S. Inv. New York.—Specimens of body braces.

111 Fenn, J. New York.—Ivory articles:—One comb, having 150 teeth in the inch, was cut by manual labour. Exhibited for workmanship.

112 New York State Institute for Blind, New York.—Willow, bead, silk-work, &c., manufactured by the blind.

113 Brooklyn Flint Glass Co. Brooklyn, New York.—Specimens of flint glass.

114 Hecker & Brother, Croton Mills, New York.—Twenty boxes of farina, prepared from wheat. Samples of fine and coarse hominy. Samples of flour, from wheat grown in the Genessee Valley, in the state of New York. Sample of baker's flour, and of wheat. Glass jars containing samples of the grain.

115 Pell, R. J. Pelham, New York.—Specimens of American forest and other woods.

116 Jeffers, W. H. New York.—Cork-sole and well-stitched back-part gaiter-boots. Gaiters of various kinds. Red and embroidered morning satin slippers.

117 Tuckerman, E. G. Prop. New York.—Model of a machine for tempering saws.

118 Jennings & Co. New York.— Black dress-coat (American cloth). Black cassimere pantaloons (American doeskin).

119 Simmons & Co. New York.—Specimens of axes and edge tools.

120 Chevalier, J. D. New York.—Dental instruments.

121 Seabury, J. & J. L. Manu. New York.—Stove polish.

122 Putnam, G. P. New York.—Books, and specimens of binding.

123 Walker, Edward & Co. New York.—Specimens of printing and binding.

124 Herring, S. C. New York.—Salamander safe, Wilder's patent.

125 Gavit, D. E. New York.—Daguerreotypes.

126 Atlantic Dock Mills, Brooklyn, New York.—Specimens of flour and farina from Indian corn.

127 Rogers, J. New York.—Telegraph registers and keys.

128 Raymond & Schuyler, West Farms, New York.—Barrel of flour, made from pure Genessee wheat. Keg of pearl barley.

129 Commeford & Redgate, Prop. New York.—Four light chairs.

130 Leary & Co. New York.—Specimens of hats.

131 Blakeslee, J. Prod. North Castle, New York.—Samples of Merino wools.

132 D'Avignon, F. Des. New York.—Specimens of lithography.

133 Clirehugh, V. Manu. New York.—Two gossamer wigs. Two gossamer scalps.

134 Brown, L. Manu. Brooklyn, New York.—Six gold pens and cases.

135 Woodcock, F. Brooklyn, New York.—Specimen of oil floor-cloth.

136 Frisbie, M. J. New York.—Specimens of India-rubber shoes.

137 Brady, M. B. New York.—Daguerreotypes; likenesses of illustrious Americans.

138 Arrowsmith, G. A. Prop. New York.—Jenning's permutation locks.

139 Dix, E. R. Prod. Vernon, New York.—Specimen of North American guano, Indian corn, wheat, maple sugar, flax, hemp, &c.

140 Gwynne, J. S. Inv. and Manu. New York, and 1 Agar Street, Strand, London.—Gwynne's patent balanced centrifugal pumps. This pump has a rotary movement, and is without valves, excentrics, or other contrivances which consume power in friction.

141 Cochran, J. W. New York.—Brick machine.

142 Brady, D'Avignon & Lester, Prop. New York.—One volume, entitled "Gallery of Illustrious Americans," a specimen of lithography, letter-press, and binding.

143 Sherman & Smith, New York.—Map of the United States.

144 Griffin, D. New York.—Model of a water-wheel, furnaces, &c.

145 Bullock, S. W. & J. New York.—Self-operating oil-press.

146 Ericsson, J. New York.—Instrument for measuring distances at sea. Marine barometer. Instruments for taking soundings and for measuring fluids. Pyrometer. Model of a gas engine. Instrument for measuring the compressibility of water. Model of an equestrian statue of Washington, by Horace Kneeland, of New York.

147 Iron Bridge Co. New York.—Iron bridge.

148 Emory & Co. Albany, New York.—Railroad horse-power seed-planter.

149 Moore, D. D. T. Watervliet, New York.—Corn-brooms.

150 Jeffrey, A. Canandaguia, New York.—Oil-paintings of the wild flowers of Western New York.

151 Lawrence, M. M. New York.—Daguerreotypes

152 Benjamin, J. R. New York.—Elastic trusses.

153 Hawes, G. E. New York.—Specimens of dentistry.

154 Hotchkiss & Prescott, Manu. Phelps, New York.—Sample of kiln-dried Indian meal.

155 Leach, M. S. & H. J. Manu. Lyons, New York.—Sample of extra Genessee flour.

156 Hotchkiss, H. G. & L. B., Manu. Lyons, New York.—Sample of oil of peppermint.

157 Hill, C. J. & Son, Manu. Rochester, New York.—Sample of extra Genessee flour.

158 Harmon, A. Clifton, New York.—Sample of extra Genessee flour.

159 Leech, D. Leechburg, Pennsylvania.—Samples of wheat flour, the property of the exhibitor.

160 Tourey, Professor, Tuscaloosa, Alabama.—Specimens of minerals.

161 Inslee, J. A. Lafayette, Indiana.—Self-weighing grain scales.

162 Gating, R. J. Indianopolis, Indiana.—Grain-drill.

163 Missouri Iron Mountain Company, St. Louis, Missouri.—Specimens of iron ore.

164 Merriweather, J. B. Montgomery, Alabama.—Specimens of cotton, rice, hominy, flour, &c.

165 Gamble & Brothers, J. K. Manu. Philadelphia—Specimens of Morocco leather, made from goat-skins, of American manufacture.

166 New Jersey Exploring and Mining Company Prop. Newark, New Jersey. Agent in London, O. Mac Daniel, 36 Albert Street, Mornington Crescent.—Specimens of zinc, iron, and steel, and other minerals, &c., found near

them. Specimens of zinc ores. According to Thomson and Berthier, it is composed of 88 parts oxide of zinc and 12 parts sesquioxide of manganese. Franklinite: an iron ore from the same locality, the constituents of which, according to the above chemical authorities, are 67 parts peroxide of iron, 17 oxide of zinc, 16 sesquioxide of manganese. The iron and steel made from this are of good quality. Specimens of pure metallic zinc or spelter, the produce of the red oxide of zinc ore. Zinc white, or white oxide of zinc. This is superior to white lead or the carbonate of lead as a paint: it is free from its poisonous properties; it has no offensive smell, and its colour is durable. Specimens of painting, executed on wood with zinc paints.

167 TRENTON IRON COMPANY, Trenton, New Jersey.—Specimens of iron wire, rivets, &c.

168 HEINIZCH, R. Newark, New York.—Shears, trimmers, and scissors.

169 TREESE, T. Greensbury, Pennsylvania.—Shell propeller.

171 BRYANT, W. Nashville, Tennessee.—Brass model of subsoil plough. The improvements aimed at in this plough are, arrangement, cheapness, and utility.

172 JONES, J. V. Charleston, South Carolina.—Samples of Upland cotton.

172A JONES, J. R. Charleston, South Carolina.—Samples of Upland cotton.

172B HAMPTON, W. Charleston, South Carolina.—Sample of Upland cotton.

172C HERIOT, E. T. Charleston, South Carolina.—Sample of clean rice.

172D WARD, J. J. Charleston, South Carolina.—Specimens of sheaf rice.

172E M'LEOD, W. W. Charleston, South Carolina.—Specimens of Sea Island cotton.

172F SEABROOK, W. Charleston, South Carolina.—Specimens of Sea Island cotton.

173 JAMISON, V. D. V. Charleston, South Carolina.—Samples of spirits of turpentine.

174 CAPERS, C. B. St. Helena Island, South Carolina.—Cypress canoe-boat, cut out from a cypress tree—the common boat of the country.

174A ARTMAN, J. Charleston, South Carolina.—Phaeton carriage.

175 GRANITEVILLE FACTORY, Graniteville, South Carolina.—Specimens of shirting and drilling.

175A CHARLESTON FACTORY, Charleston, South Carolina.—Cotton cloth (shirtings and sheetings).

176 BELL, E. B. Charleston, South Carolina.—Specimens of Palmetto cedar, oak, and other woods.

176A DE SAUSSURE, J. B. Prod. Charleston, South Carolina.—Specimen of sweet gum wood.

177 SOUTH CAROLINA RAILROAD Co. Charleston, South Carolina.—A circular table.

177A MELLICHAMP, MARY H. Charleston, South Carolina.—A basket.

178 NAILOR, J. Vicsburgh, Missouri. — Specimens of cotton.

179 MITCHELL, G. D. Vicsburgh, Missouri.—Specimens of cotton.

180 MAYLAND SOAP-STONE COMPANY, Baltimore, Maryland.—Specimen of soap-stone. One bath tub. Sample of stone. One sizing roll. Three griddles.

181 JAMES & CHAPMAN, Crawford County, Missouri.—Specimens of iron ore and iron work.

182 STRATTON, W. J. Glasgow, Howard County, Missouri.—Specimens of manufactured tobacco.

183 ALBRO & HOYT, Elizabethtown, New Jersey.—Floor oil-cloth.

184 BRYANT, W. Nashville, Tennessee.—Cotton and wool cards.

185 WRIGHT, G. W. California.—Steam-engine quartz crusher.

186 WALBRIDGE, H.—Specimens of gold and other ores.

187 BURT, W. A. Mount Vernon, Macomb County, Michigan.—Burt's solar compass.

188 EWING, J. H. Prop. Washington, Pennsylvania.—Specimens of wools.

189 GEVELOT, —, Philadelphia.—A medal.

190 CLINTON, E. Prop. Philadelphia, Pennsylvania.—Hair and cloth brushes.

191 DARLING, W. Prod. Reading, Pennsylvania.—Specimen of iron, and iron ores.

192 HOPKINS, J. M. Brock, Pennsylvania.—Pig of iron.

193 RAGAN, W. Philadelphia.—Reclining chairs.

194 STAR, E. Philadelphia, Pennsylvania.—Forms of printing bank notes and stereotyping. Specimens of the note and of electrotyping.

195 DUNTON, J. H. Philadelphia, Pennsylvania.—Red cedar bedstead.

196 VINE & ASHMEAD, Hartford, Connecticut.—Gold-beating machine and gold foil.

197 SIBLEY, S. Hopkington, New Hampshire.—Sample of Saxony wool from the exhibitor's own flock.

198 WOOLMAN, E. Inv. Damascoville, Ohio.—Gate, so constructed as to be opened by a rider without getting off the carriage seat.

199 LONGWORTH, N. Cincinnati, Ohio.—Specimens of Catawba and other wines.

200 SCHOOLEY & HOUGH, Cincinnati, Ohio.—Samples of hams and shoulders.

201 PERKINS & BROWN, Akron, Ohio.—Sample of fine combing wool.

202 MORRELL, STEWART, & Co. Cincinnati, Ohio.—Sheet-iron made from iron ore, the produce of this State.

203 SALT & MEAR, East Liverpool, Ohio.—Water vase, manufactured from fine brick clay.

204 SCHUMANS, C. A. Cincinnati, Ohio.—Specimens of Catawba wine.

205 WISDOM, RUSSEL, & WHITMAN, Cleveland, Ohio.—Specimens of curled hair.

206 WESTERN FIRE COMPANY, Cincinnati, Ohio.—Hose carriage.

207 TROTMAN, J. Cincinnati, Ohio.—Saddle-trees.

208 HOLBROOK & STANLEY, Manu. Cincinnati, Ohio.—Winter strained lard oil, made from lard procured from the hog by the action of steam.

209 HUGGET, J. jun. Columbus, Ohio.—Joiner's panel or grooving plough.

210 DE BONNEVILLE, M. Providence, Rhode Island.—Autumnal leaves.

211 BRETTS, S. G. Gilmanton, New Hampshire.—Shoe-pegs.

212 READ, C. A. Oneida County, New York.—Model of a fluted fulling mill.

213 ROSS, C. Rochester, New York.—Improved portable mills.

214 AMBLER & AVERY, New York.—Articles for dentistry.

215 DISTURNELL, J. New York.—Maps of the United States and of the State of New York.

216 BROWN, S. New York.—Articles for dentistry.

217 GODWIN, T. New York.—Specimens of mechanical inventions.

218 HILER, S. New York.—Stair-rods, copper rivets, &c.

219 ARMSTRONG, S. T. New York.—India-rubber air pontoons.

220 ALCOCK, J. New York.—Articles for dentistry.

221 LYON, E. New York.—Magnetic powder for the destruction of insects.

222 BROOKS, W. T. New York.—Jackson's annunciator.

223 HARRISON, C. C. New York.—Camera obscura, and daguerreotypes.

224 THOMPSON, W. M. New York.—Pictorial bookbinders' stamps.

225 POOLEY, S. J. New York.—Two miniature dinner sets. Dinner set, mounted with pearl handles. Miscellaneous table knives, carvers, &c., mounted with gold, pearl, &c. Scissors. Pair of forceps. Razors. Surgical instruments in miniature, mounted with pearl, tortoiseshell, &c.

226 GRIFFITH, J. W. New York.—Model of an ocean steamer. Treatise on Marine and Naval Architecture.

227 THORNTON, FRANCES, New York.—Articles in shirt-making and laundry-work.

228 BARTON, C. D. Keesville, New York.—Magnetic oxide of iron from Peru Mine, Chirton, New York, weighing 600 lbs. Box of magnetic oxide of iron from Bowton Ore Bed, in Essex county, weighing 100 lbs.

229 TUCKERMAN, E. G. Prop. New York.—Air exhausted coffin, intended to preserve the dead from putrefaction. Air-exhausted fruit-box, for preserving fish, fruit, game, &c.

230 PEASE, R. H. Albany, New York.—Specimens of lithographed engravings.

231 HIGGINBOTHAM, L. C. Vernon, New York.—Miniature steam-engine, made by the exhibitor.

232 GENIN, J. N. Manu. New York.—Hats and caps.

233 BLAKE, W. Inv. New York.—Specimens of fireproof paint.

234 CLARK, R. New York.—Sample of oatmeal, manufactured at Clark's Mills, in Oneida County, New York.

235 PARKER & BROWN, Utica, New York.—Bale of fine wool.

236 ALLEN, G. F. Prop. Utica, New York.—Telescopic rifle.

237 SMEAD, C. New York.—House's printing telegraph.

238 THOMPSON, S. L. Setauket, Long Island.—Sample of wheat.

239 UBRICI, R. W. St. Louis, Missouri.—Specimens of lead ore. Found in Franklin County, in the State of Missouri.

240 WHITEMAN, E. jun. Baltimore, Maryland.—Railway, horse-power, and straw-cutter.

241 THOMPSON, Rev. Z. Burlington, Vermont.—Specimens of Vermont woods.

242 COOK, J. Burlington, Vermont.—Burlington mill cloths.

243 WILLIAMS, MARY, Woodstock, Vermont.—Vermont autumn leaves.

244 PARMENTER, E. Mechanicville, Vermont.—Specimens of bird's-eye maple veneers.

245 DEAN, L. Prod. Manchester, Vermont.—Sample of maple sugar, and jug of fine maple molasses.

246 BARNES, W. Rutland, Vermont.—Sample of maple sugar in a tin box.

247 CAIN, J. Manu. Rutland, Vermont.—Samples of slate pencils.

248 PECK, Mrs. C. P. Burlington, Vermont.—Silk hose.

248A PIERCE, Mrs. J. S. Burlington.—Two silk handkerchiefs. Two specimens of marble, black and white.

249 PENNIMAN, U. H. Colchester, Vermont.—Specimen of pure limestone.

250 CATLIN, H. W. Burlington, Vermont. —Sample of wheat flour.

251 BENJAMIN, J. R. St. Alban's, Vermont.—Specimens of brass spring trusses.

252 M'LENAN, E. Newbury, Vermont.—Sample of American polish, supposed to be superior to emery.

253 KITTERIDGE, F. O. Mount Vernon, New Hampshire. —Corn-husk mattrasses.

254 REMERS, P. Pittsburg, Pennsylvania.—A bust of Bishop Upfold.

255 HALL & SPEAR, Pittsburg, Pennsylvania.—Iron centre plough.

256 EAKINS, S. Pittsburg, Pennsylvania.—Galvanic plastic hydrometer.

257 BAKER, A. Honesdale, Pennsylvania.—Pump.

258 ROGERS, C. B. Philadelphia, Pennsylvania.—Plough.

259 BROWN & WELLS, Philadelphia, Pennsylvania.—Specimens of tools.

260 HART, MONTGOMERY, & Co. Philadelphia, Pennsylvania.—Paper-hangings.

261 PULSIFER, J. S. Osnaburg, Pennsylvania.—An alphabet.

262 POWER & WEIGHTMAN, Philadelphia, Pennsylvania.—Chemicals.

263 FISHER, T. Inv. Philadelphia. — 1. Mathematics simplified on geometrical principles. 2. Dial of the seasons, a chart illustrating the sun's declination at all seasons, with the effects of light and heat on animal and vegetable life in all climates. A book explanatory of the chart.

264 PRATT, W. A. & Co. Richmond, Virginia.—Daguerreotypes.

265 ROBINSON, P. Richmond, Virginia.—Specimens of manufactured tobacco.

266 MILES, G. C. Richmond, Virginia.—Specimens of ladies' and gentlemen's saddles.

267 SIMS, E. W. Buckingham County, Virginia.—Specimens of iron ore.

268 HARDGROVE, T. & S. Richmond, Virginia.—Sample of manufactured tobacco.

269 BRAXTON, C. Hanover County, Virginia.—Specimen of greensand marl.

270 INSTITUTE FOR THE BLIND, Stanton, Virginia.—Specimens of books, types, &c.

272 COCKE, Gen. J. H. Fluvanna County, Virginia.—Samples of iron ore, soap-stone, and other minerals.

273 DILL & MULCHAHEY, Prod. Richmond, Virginia.—Specimen of manufactured tobacco.

274 SIMS, E. H. Buckingham County, Virginia.—Specimens of roofing slate.

275 SIMS, E. H. Buckingham County, Virginia. —Slab of slate.

276 JENNINGS & CLAGHORN, Richmond, Virginia. —A gentleman's saddle.

277 HOBSON, F. Buckingham County, Virginia.—Specimens of gold ore.

278 PATTESON, R. S. Buckingham County, Virginia.—Specimens of iron ore.

279 FABER, W. Prop. Nelson County, Virginia. —Specimens of iron ore.

280 FAKER, W. Nelson County, Virginia.—Specimen of galena and silver combined.

281 ANDERSON, J. R. & Co. Richmond, Virginia.—Specimens of iron ore.

282 BELVIDERE MANUFACTURING Co. Richmond, Virginia.—Envelope paper.

283 BROWN, —, Buckingham County, Virginia.—Specimen of quartz rock.

284 GRANT, J. H. Manu. Richmond, Virginia.—Specimen of tobacco.

285 MAUPIN, S. Richmond, Virginia. — Specimens of minerals.

286 FARRINGTON, A. C. Prop. Newark, New Jersey.—Apatite. Some of the specimens exhibited are pure Franklinite iron.

287 DUMONT, J. S. Patterson, New Jersey.—Silk plush for hats.

288 MORGAN, J. S. Tuscumbia, Alabama. — Specimen of cotton.

289 COLLYER, Gov. H. W. Prop. Montgomery, Alabama.—Minerals, collected and forwarded under the direction of

the Governor of the State of Alabama, intended to illustrate the mineral wealth of that State.

290 STEERE, E. Providence, Rhode Island.—Blacking.

291 AMBLER & AVERY, Honesdale, Pennsylvania.—Specimens of mechanical dentistry.

292 TAYLOR, H. P. & W. C. Philadelphia, Pennsylvania.—Transparent soaps, intended to represent stained glass.

294 HAYWARD RUBBER Co. Colchester, Connecticut. — Specimens of India-rubber boots and shoes.

295 GOODYEAR RUBBER Co. Nangatuck.—India-rubber.

296 PENFIELD & CAMP, Middletown, Connecticut. — Judd's medicated liquid cuticle.

297 COCHRAN, J. W. Agent, New York. — Improved railway switch. Ship-timber sawing and stone-dressing machine.

298 DAY & NEWELL, New York.—Parautoptic permutating locks.

299 LATHROP, J. Le Roy, New York.—Samples of Genessee wheat.

300 FINCH, H. Manu. Honcoye, New York.—Specimen of Genessee wheat flour.

301 COLEGATE, W. & Co. New York.—Samples of pearl starch.

302 GRAY, Dr. J. New York.—Artificial human eyes.

303 SIMMONS, Mrs. W. New York.— Millinery.

304 GARDNER, J. N. Troy, New York. — Specimens of curry-combs.

305 OYLER & ANDERSON, Lynchburg, New York.—Samples of tobacco, manufactured out of natural honey-dew, bright sun-cured leaf, the growth of Roanoke County, Virginia.

306 MACY J. & SONS, New York.—Specimens of spermaceti and candles.

307 PECARE & SMITH, New York.—Self-locking and repeating pistols, with stocks of ivory, and rosewood, mounted with steel and gold.

308 DAY, H. H. New York. —India-rubber manufactures.

309 BOURGAIN, C. New York.—Hair work. Hair wig.

310 COLTON, J. W. New York.—Map of the World.

311 HANNINGTON, W. J. New York. — Stained glass; two window heads. Portraits of George the Fourth and William the Fourth. A Newfoundland dog. A pentography head, ornamented frames.

312 BOOLE, L. H. New York.—Model of a clipper ship.

313 SPAULDING, J. New York.—A silk quilt.

314 ROUSSEAU, A. J. Troy, New York. — Specimens of iron ore.

315 BASHAM, F. New York.—Plaster model of the Exchange, New York.

316 HOLMES, G. L. Memphis, Tennessee. — Samples of ginned cotton.

317 REMSBURGH, J. Frederick County, Maryland.—Specimens of Indian corn and wheat.

318 COOKE, W. & SONS, Baltimore, Maryland.—Samples of leaf tobacco.

319 OWENS, J. Ann Arundel County, Missouri.—Specimens of leaf tobacco.

320 GETSINGER, M. R. Charleston, South Carolina.—Raised embroidery. Needlework.

320A GOLDING, M. C. Spartanburgh, South Carolina.—Imitation Marseilles quilt ; a specimen of needle-work by Mrs. Golding.

320B PECKHAM, J. Columbia.—Gold-headed walking-stick, made from the curled hickory (Careja), a common forest wood.

320C SWEDISH IRON MANUFACTURING COMPANY.—Specimens of iron ore, nails, &c.—Magnetic iron ore, adapted for making steel.

320D SEABROOK, W. Charleston, South Carolina.—Sample of Sea-island cotton in seed, and of the long staple, or black-seed cotton.

320E HORRY, W. B. C. Charleston, South Carolina. Sample of Indian corn in the ear. Sample of tea (graminæ), commonly called flint corn, averaging about 30 bushels per acre.

320F TEW, H. S. Charleston.—A variety of brooms.

321 COLT, S. Hartford, Connecticut. — Specimens of fire-arms.

322 HAVENNER, T. H. & BROTHERS, Washington, D. C. —Pilot bread, water and soda crackers.

323 NORTH WAYNE SCYTHE COMPANY, South Wayne, Massachusetts.—Specimens of scythes.

324 VASSELBORO MANUFACTURING COMPANY, New Vasselborough, Maine.—Cashmeres from American wool.

325 WARWICK & OTEY, Lynchburgh, Virginia.—Samples of manufactured tobacco.

326 ROWE, M. & J. M. Philadelphia, Pennsylvania.—Brooms and whips.

327 PENNSYLVANIA RAILROAD COMPANY, Philadelphia, Pennsylvania.—Model of an aqueduct. Model of one span of a wooden viaduct, deposited by Elliott Cresson, 86 Bloomsbury Sq.

328 ROBBINS & LAWRENCE, Windsor, Vermont.—Rifles : with their various parts made to interchange.

329 BAGBY, Gov. A. P. Montgomery.—Sample of raw cotton.

330 LAK, D. Memphis, Tennessee.—Samples of ginned cotton.

331 HOLMES, J. E. New York.—Model of a ratchet hoisting machine.

332 LEE, W. New York.—Specimen of spathic iron ore.

333 TUCKERMAN, E. G. Prop. New York. — Butterworth's patent combination lock.

334 BROWNE & LAMBERT, Prop. New York. Two of Whitmarsh's patent portable extension beds.

335 BARTHOLOMEW, F. H. New York.—Safety-valve hydrant.

336 RYLE, J. Patterson, New Jersey.—Floss, and sewing silk.

337 CHATAIN, H. New York.—Patent machine mouldings.

338 EASTMAN, W. P. Newark, New Jersey.—Knitting machine, &c.

339 SIBELL & MOTT, New York.—Bank and account books. One set was made to order for the City Bank, New York.

340 HASKELL, MERRIT & BUEL, Manu. New York.—Samples of powdered drugs.

341 OLIVER, T. New York. — Tailor's transfer and patterns.

342 HOTCHKISS, W. Lewiston, Kentucky.—Samples of Soule's winter wheat.

343 HILLYER, V. New York.—Samples of wheat flour.

344 ADIRONDAC MANUFACTURING COMPANY, New York.—Specimens of iron and steel. Pigs of decarbonized metal. Bars of iron, and 500 lbs. of assorted cast steel.

345 SPERRY, H. New York.—Clock.

346 GIBSON, W. New York.—Stained glass.

347 PALMER, W. R. New York.—Specimens of two rifles.

348 WADSWORTH & SHELDON, New York.—Specimens of prime mess beef.

349 MONAHAN & BEERS, New York.—One box of tobacco.

350 BARLOW, E. New York.—Articles for dentistry.

351 BATTY, T. New York.—Improved serving mallets.

352 FOX & POLHEMUS, New York.—A bolt of cotton duck.

353 BARON, BROS, New York.—Fire ladder, escapes, &c.

354 WINSHIP, A. H. Choctaw Nation, Arkansas.—A book-mark.

355 ASHER, A. Manu. New Orleans, Louisiana.—Machine for manufacturing ice.

356 DENNINGTON, C. L. New York.—Model of a floating church.

357 RICHARDS, B. W. Philadelphia. — Specimens of plumbago.

358 CLINGMAN, T. L. Ashville, North Carolina.—Specimen of plumbago.

359 OLMSTED, Mrs. J. Hartford, Connecticut.—American forest autumn leaves, in their natural colours.

360 COWPERTHWAITE & Co. Philadelphia.—Maps.

361 WATSON, G. W. Philadelphia, Pennsylvania. — Trotting sulky.

362 M'ALISTER & TANNEHILL, Louisville, Kentucky.—Samples of mustard.

363 DUFFIELD, C. Prop. Louisville, Kentucky.—Specimens of smoked hams, in canvass.

364 HILL, J. New York.—A travelling trunk.

365 M'WEENEY, M. New York. — Portable parlour green-house.

366 LORD, LYNCH & Co. New York.—Soap.

367 STANTON, D. New York.—Specimens of penmanship, illustrating the portrait and character of Washington.

368 MACY, STANTON & Co New York.—Woollen cassimeres.

369 WHITLOCK, B. M. New York.—Sample of Henry County tobacco.

370 BARON BROTHERS, New York.—A blast-furnace.

371 STATE OF MARYLAND (by its Committee).—Cabinet made of Maryland woods.

372 FRYER, F. Baltimore, Maryland.—Ice-cream freezer.

373 ROY, W. L. New York. — Twelve Hebrew dictionaries.

374 NUNNS & CLARK, Des. and Manu. New York.—Two piano-fortes: A 7-octave rosewood pianoforte, carved. A 6½-octave rosewood pianoforte, with Coleman's patent Æolian attachment.

375 HANLEY, J. New York.—Model catcher and model key.

376 HITCHCOCK, W. L. New York.—Grass and corn scythes, manufactured from Norway iron, and Saunderson & Co.'s cast steel, by the North Wayne Scythe Company, in the State of Maine.

377 WHITEHURST, J. H. Baltimore, Massachusetts.—Daguerreotypes: Falls of Niagara.

378 GOODYEAR, C. New Haven, Connecticut.—India-rubber goods.

379 USHER, R. Louisville, Kentucky.—Plates and briskets of beef.

380 BRADY, W. N. New York.—"Kedge Anchor," a work on practical seamanship, with illustrations.

381 JACOT & COURVOIRIER, New York.—Gold magic hunting lever watch.

382 CHURCH & CHITTENDEN, New York.— India-rubber shoes.

383 TUPH, J. New York.—Cane chairs.

384 MAXWELL, Miss, New Jersey.—Autumn leaves.

385 HAIGHT, Mrs. E. New York.—An embroidered shirt. A stitched shirt.

386 HAYDEN, W. Willimantic, Connecticut.— Drawing frame for cotton, with an improvement for regulating the weight of the strand, called a drawing regulator.

387 NEWTON, I. Prod. Philadelphia.—Sample of Indian corn.

388 WILDER, A. A. Detroit, Michigan.—Revolving cylinder-engine and leeway indicator, with fog whistle for lighthouse stations.

389 LUDLAND, H. New York.—Sample of tobacco from Geo. T. Williams, Lynchburg, Virginia.

390 PHALON, E. Manu. New York.—Hair work, venting wigs, and toupee.

391 BACHMAN, J. New York.—Views of New York and Brooklyn.

392 STEPHENS, H. New York.—Two jars of preserved peaches.

393 STEWART & Co. J. J. New York — Sample of tobacco from D. H. London, Richmond, Virginia.

395 TOBIT, J. H. New York.—Combination type.

395A BACHE, Professor A. D. Washington. — Standard weights, measures, and balances.

396 WOOD & TOMLINSON, New York.—Sporting waggon

397 WHITE, M. New Orleans.—Sugar, pepper, and hemp.

398 RALLINGS, Mrs. W. New York.—Millinery.

399 HOBART & ROBINS, Boston. — Types, printing, and binding.

400 REED, CHADWICK, & DEXTER, Boston.—Specimens of printing cloths.

401 BAKER, W. R. Lowell, Massachusetts. —Liquid and paste shoe blacking.

402 NEWMAN, H. J. Andover, Massachusetts. —Imitation of wood.

403 UPHAM, APPLETON, & Co. Boston. — Ginghams, cassimeres, &c.

404 PROUTY & MEARS. Boston, Massachusetts.—Ploughs.

405 GRAY, T. & Co. Boston, Massachusetts. — Specimen of glassmakers' sand.

406 SAYLE, MERRIAM, & BREWER, Boston. — Samples of cotton cloths.

407 PARKER, WILDER, & Co. Boston, Massachusetts.—Wool blankets.

408 WARD, W. & J. W. Boston, Massachusetts.—Specimens of copper ore.

409 LAWRENCE, A. & A. & Co. Boston, Massachusetts.—Sheeting, woollens, and carpeting.

410 FOGG & BURBANK, Boston.—Pegged boots and shoes.

411 BREED, N. A. & Co. Lynn, Massachusetts.—Children's shoes.

412 SHATTUCK, W. G. Boston, Massachusetts. — School desks and chairs.

413 PROUTY & MEARS, Boston, Massachusetts. —Specimens of ploughs.

414 POND & Co. M. Boston.—Cooking ranges.

415 BLISS, R. & Co. Pawtucket, Massachusetts.— Hand-screws and other tools.

416 RUGGLES, G. H. Boston, Massachusetts. — Specimens of mica, or talc, for stove doors, &c.

417 CHILSON, RICHARDSON, & Co. Boston, Massachusetts.—Furnaces and stoves.

418 DOE, HAZELTON, & Co. Boston.—Centre tables.

419 BROWNE, C. A. Boston.—Specimens of teeth, for warded by Dr. Morton.

420 GASSETT, H. Boston.—Specimens of bookbinding.

421 WASHBURN, I. & Co. Worcester, Massachusetts.-Card wire.

422 THAYER, E. B. Boston.—Samples of shoe pegs.

423 GATES, W. East Lee, Massachusetts. — Hay an manure forks, and hoes.

424 LORING, G. Concord, Massachusetts.—Water pail

425 TORREY, T. Weymouth, Massachusetts.—Sample of edge blacking for boot and shoemakers.

426 ATWOOD, G. B. (for Phœnix Manufacturing Company), Taunton, Massachusetts.—Black-lead crucibles.

427 EVERETT, A. Middlefield, Massachusetts.—Wooden bowls.

428 LOMBARD & HALL, Boston, Grindstone.

429 ROBINSON, C. & Co. Lynn, Massachusetts.—mens of boots and shoes.

430 SUTTON, J. A. Boston, Massachusetts.—Specimens of purchase blocks.

431 WARNER, R. & Co. Boston.—Brooms, wooden ware, &c.

432 GILBERT, A. Boston.—A gossamer wig.

433 EMERSON, F. Boston, Massachusetts.—Ship ventilators.

434 POND, M. & Co. Boston. —Improved cooking ranges.

435 GILBERT & Co. Boston.—Pianofortes.

437 PAIGE, J. W. & Co. Boston, Massachusetts.—Samples of merrimac prints and calico.

438 HEWS, G. Boston, Massachusetts.—Pianofortes.

439 HOWE, S. G. Boston.—Specimens of books for the blind.

440 BATES, HYDE & Co. Bridgewater, Connecticut.—Cotton-gin.

441 JOHNSON, SEWALL & Co. Boston, Massachusetts.—A variety of flannels.

442 GEMUNDER, G. Boston.—Violins.

443 WOODBURY, J. P. Boston, Massachusetts.—Wood planing, tonguing, and grooving machine.

444 MILLS, J. K. & Co. Boston, Massachusetts.—Extra fine shirting.

445 MAYNARD & NOYES, Boston, Massachusetts.—Writing and copying inks.

446 POOK, S. M. Charlestown, Massachusetts.—Model of a clipper ship, frigate, &c.

447 LOWELL MACHINE SHOP, Lowell, Massachusetts.—Power-loom lathe, dresser, brush, &c.

448 SOWREL, A. Woburn.—Specimens of lithographic drawings.

449 DARTON, W. Boston.—Model of a clipper ship.

450 SKINNER, F. & Co. Boston.—Specimen of cassimere.

451 WHIPPLE, J. A. Boston.—Daguerreotypes.

452 CUMMINGS, J. A. Boston.—Tooth-wash and dentifrice.

453 LAWRENCE, A. & A. & Co. Boston.—Manufactures.

454 ALMY, PATTERSON & Co. Boston, Massachusetts.—Samples of cottons.

455 FIELD, A. Taunton, Massachusetts.—Iron and copper tacks and nails.

456 EARLE, T. K. & Co. Boston, Massachusetts.—Machine cards.

457 KIMBAL, D. Boston, Massachusetts.—Cotton duck.

458 CHICKERING, J. Boston, Massachusetts. — Pianofortes.

459 HOOPER, H. N. & Co. Boston, Massachusetts.—Epergnes, in or-molu, and castings.

460 MOREY, C. Boston, Massachusetts.—Machine for dressing, shaping, and ornamenting stone for architectural and other purposes. Invented by Robert Eastman, Esq. of Concord, State of New Hampshire, United States.

461 STIMPSON, G. jun. Boston. — Specimens of gold pens.

462 ADAMS, W. & Co. Boston. — Combination bank lock.

463 BOND, W. & SON, Boston, Massachusetts.—Electric clock, battery, &c.

464 LAWRENCE, STONE & Co. Boston.—Shawls and cassimeres.

465 BACON, S. F. Boston, Massachusetts. — Folding, pressing, and sewing machine.

466 RIDDLE, E. Boston, Massachusetts.—Specimens of an American coach, Prince Albert waggon, York waggon, and slide-top buggy.

467 STEPHENSON, P. Boston, Massachusetts.—Statue: the Wounded Indian.

468 GATCHEL, J. L. Elkton, Maryland.—Hydraulic ram.

469 FEUTCHWANGER, DR. L. New York.—A collection of gems, minerals, fresh-water shells, Indian relics, petrifac-

tions, &c., solely American productions. A mass of native copper, weighing 2,544 lbs., from the North West Mine, Lake Superior. A collection of crystalline arboreal native copper, from Isle Royal, Lake Superior. A cabinet of crystalline gems, native diamonds, gold, and copper. Two cabinets of small minerals.

470 UPFIELD, W. Lancaster.—Boot-trees and patterns.

471 ADDINGTON, W. H. Norfolk, Virginia. — Patent bellows. Leather California boots.

472 PERKINS, S. M. Athens, Pennsylvania.—Hot-air apparatus.

473 BRADLEY, B. & Co. Boston.—Specimens of bookbinding.

474 EVANS, H. Manu. New Bedford.—Sample of cordage from Manilla hemp.

475 STEVENS & Co. London, England. — Corrugated boiler, bridge, and excavator.

476 ADAMS, H. New York.—Portable saddle.

477 BIDWELL, Rev. W. H. New York.—Maps.

478 PATTERSON, New Brunswick, N. J.—Anthracite from Lehigh mountain.

479 FITCH, Dr. S. S. New York.—Plated abdominal supporters.

480 COCHRAN, J. W. New York.—Improved railroad scotch.

481 EISENBRANT, C. H. Baltimore, Maryland.—Flutes, &c. Printing machine for the blind.

482 M'ADAMS, J. & W. Boston.—Medium ledger, in Russia leather, with gilt sides and edges. Medium journal, in similar binding. Specimen-book of paper-ruling, Turkey morocco, with gilt edges.

483 DUNLOP, W. A. New Orleans, Louisiana.—Specimens of penmanship.

484 REED, I. & SON, Philadelphia, Pennsylvania.—Specimens of gold pens.

485 RODRIGUEZ, B. New Orleans, Louisiana.—Specimens of aerothermes, or hot-air ovens.

486 HOWLAND, C. New York.—Improved bell telegraph.

487 BORGNIS, Miss M. A. Boston, Massachusetts.—Embroidery: The Raising of Jairus' daughter.

488 SEARLE, G. Boston, Massachusetts.—Indian saddle and equipments.

489 MILES, PLINY, New York.—Gold and silver coins.

490 FULLER, J. E. Boston, Massachusetts. — Mathematical telegraph and model calculator. Computing telegraph. Pocket computer.

491 MAYALL, J. E. Philadelphia.—Daguerreotypes.

492 KIDDER, C. F. Boston.—Indian cap.

493 DALPHIN, J. E. Springfield, Otsego County, New York.—Self-adjusting churn.

494 TRUESDALE, JACOBS &. Co. New York.—Samples of cotton.

495 COMMIFORD & REDGATE, New York.—Four light chairs.

496 RODGERS, H. S. Prop. New York.—Two velocipedes.

497 HOWE, D. T. Prop. New York, and 355 Strand, London.—Dr. S. P. Townsend's extract of sarsaparilla.

498 BAKER, J. B. Maker, Boston. — Specimens of harness.

499 JEWETT, S. W. Middlebury, Vermont.—Sample of Indian corn, twelve-rowed variety, yellow; and a sample of Vermont products.

500 KIMBER, A. M. & Co. Philadelphia, Pennsylvania.—Specimens of fine wool.

501 M'HENRY, J. Philadelphia. — Specimen of soapstone.

502 HERRICK, J. K. New York.—An assortment of account books.

503 CLAWSON, H. N. Michigan.—"Excelsior" soap.

504 PINKUS, H. Inv. 17 North Audley Street, Gros-

venor Square.—The exemplification of processes, in the applications of philosophical principles, in combination with the progress of engineering developments, for their practical adaptations, as motive forces, to the purposes of safer, rapid transit, and economy on railways. Exhibiting stages of comparative improvements, from the year 1825 to 1851.

504A SANDERSON, A. Hatfield, Massachusetts.—Carpet-broom.

505 SIEBERT, S. Easton.—Maps of Germany.

507 HOUGH, R. M. Ohicheo.—Two tierces of beef.

508 HENRY, S. Charleston, South Carolina.—Brooms, made of the stalks of the broom corn.

509 SHATTUCK, W. F. Agent for G. W. EDDY and Co., Manu. Waterford, New York.—G. W. Eddy's patent tough-ened-metal railway-wheel.

510 ST JOHN, J. R. Prop. Buffalo. New York.—Cad-well, Payson, and Co.'s "excelsior" soap.

511 NEW YORK IRON BRIDGE COMPANY (RIDER, E. Manu. and Prop.) New York.—A reduced model of Rider's patent improved suspension truss bridge. A full-sized model of the same.

512 HARRIS, —, Waterville, New York.—Patent paint mills.

513 BURCH, S. D. New York. — Air-tight cooking stoves.

514 HOLLOWAY & Co. London, England.—Clocks.

515 ELIAS, A. Boston, Massachusetts.—Chairs.

516 LAWRENCE, Col. T. B. Boston, Massachusetts.— Iron flooring.

517 LAWRENCE, Col. T. B. Boston, Massachusetts.— Carving knife and fork.

518 HITCHCOCK, Dr. D. K. Boston, Massachusetts.— Mineral teeth.

519 SMITH, J. M. & Co. New York.—One barrel of beef.

520 TAPLING BROTHERS. London, England. — Six brooms.

521 LAWRENCE, Hon. A. Boston Massachusetts.—One map.

522 GRANT, J. London, England.—Statue of the Greek Slave.

523 EDDY & Co. Union Village, New York.—Horse power.

524 BORDEN, G. Galveston, Texas.—Meat biscuit.

525 WHITEHURST, J. Washington, D. C.—Daguerreo-types.

526 PFAFF, G. Philadelphia, Pennsylvania.—A flute.

527 KEREMERLE, M. Philadelphia, Pennsylvania.—Leaf turner for music.

528 DE FORD & Co. C. D. Baltimore, Maryland.— Tobacco.

529 WETHERED & BROTHER, Baltimore, Maryland.— Black doe-skin cloths.

530 LEE, J. & Co. Boston, Massachusetts.—Sample of thin linseed oil cake.

531 CATLIN, G. New York, Inv.—Model of the Falls of Niagara. (Main Avenue, East.)

532 ROGERS & Co. Newhaven Co.—Clocks.

533 HALE, J. P. Bachever, Vermont.—Piano-violino.

534 MOULTON, S. C. New York.—India-rubber goods.

535 ASMEAD & HARLBURT, Hertford County, Penns. —Gold foil leaf.

536 WILLARD, Mrs. EMMA, Troy County, Inv.—Chrono-logical maps.

537 GODDARD, L. 6 Crescent, America Sq. London.— Two blades of whalebone from the mouth of the polar whale. The horn of the sea unicorn. Rowing boat, built by T. Francis, of New York, of Spanish cedar.

538 SHOLL, J. Burlington County.—Beehives and bees.

539 FORREST, R. New York.—Shirts.

540 ANDREWS, H. Q. New York.—Sarsaparilla.

541 PERKINS, A. M. of London.—Hot water apparatus, hot water oven, blast-furnaces, hot water steam boiler steam gun, and cast-iron right and left screw-joint.

542 ST. JOHN, J. R. Inv. Buffalo, New York.—Aquatic velocimeter, for determining the velocity and the true dis-tance run by ships, steamers, &c.

543 DAWSON, G. Albany County.—Specimen of papers published in the State of New York.

544 BEACH BROTHERS, New York.—Cheap newspapers.

545 DELANOE, Capt. J. C. New Bedford, Massachusetts. —Sample of cotton cloth, with linen finish.

546 UPDEGRAFF, Dr. J. T. Wheeling, Virginia.—Silk handkerchiefs.

548 STEPHENSON, R. London.—Statue of the Fisher Boy, by Hiram Power.

549 NICHOLSON, A. New York.—Table-cover.

550 FONTAIN & PORTER, Cincinnati, Ohio.—Daguerreo-type of the city.

551 BLODGET, S. C. New York—Sewing machine.

552 BATJEMAN, H. C. Cincinnati, Ohio.—Patent bed-stead.

553 CAMPBELL, S. New York.—Lapping machine.

554 HOUSTON, J. D. Natural Bridge, Virginia.—Fire and water-proof paint.

555 CHICKERING, J. Boston, Massachusetts.—Plaster cast of Dan. Webster.

556 WHITING, C. London.—American specimens of bank-note printing.

557 BROWNING, W. New York.—Lithographic drawing of the engine of the American steamer Pacific.

558 PHILADELPHIA.—Samples of teeth filled with gold.

559 HICKS, G. London.—Samples of New Orleans moss.

560 NEW BRUNSWICK INDIA-RUBBER COMPANY, New York.—Shoes.

561 DAVIDSON, J. D. Virginia. — Specimens of alum rock; of Weir's cave; of petrified moss.

562 MEARS, G. Boston.—Four bottles of lard oil.

563 DAVIS, J. D. Pittsburg.—Indian ornaments.

564 MOORE, W. Boston, Massachusetts, Manu.—Soap.

565 SIMPSON, Professor, Edinburgh.— A silver cup, manufactured at New York.

566 SMITH, F. H. Baltimore.—Voting telegraph.

AUSTRIA.

(Commissioners : CHEVALIER DE BURG, and CHARLES BUSCHEK, Esq., 43 *Clarges St., Piccadilly.*)—Custom House Agent, C. J. MAJOR, 21 *Billiter St.*

1 MIESBACH, A. Vienna, Prop. (largest coal owner in Austria).—Coals, brown coals, and lignite, from Lower Austria, Upper Austria, Styria, Moravia, and Hungary. Alum.

2 IMPERIAL MINES, Vienna.—Mercury and cinnabar, and ores of the same, from Idria. Sulphur from Sworzowicz in Galicia, and Radoboj in Croatia. Rosette-copper, from Agordo in the province of Venice and Moldavia. Blistered copper, from Schmöllnitz in Hungary. Tin, from Schlaggenwald in Bohemia. Litharge, from Pribram in Bohemia. Zinc, antimony, and similar mining produce.

3 UPPER HUNGARIAN MINING ASSOCIATION, Schmöllnitz, Hungary.—Quicksilver, refined copper, block copper, and various other similar productions for smelting.

4 SZUMRAK, J. F. Neusohl, Hungary, Prop.—Cobalt and nickel ores, from Boiza, together with the residue obtained from the same. Calcareous slate, from Molisa in Hungary.

5 KOCHMEISTER, F. Pesth, Hungary, Prop.—Two kinds of spongy nickel from Hungarian ores; red and black oxide of cobalt. The varieties contain 97 and 98 per cent. of the pure metal.

6 SAPY, A. (Manager of the Philippi Jabobi Mine) Rosenau, Hungary.—Nickel ores.

7 ZEMBERG MINE, Dobschau, Hungary.—Ore of cobalt and nickel. Flower of cobalt, and nickel.

8 KENGYEL, J. (Manager of the Johannes Mine) Rosenau, Hungary.—Nickel ore.

9 BATKA, W. Prague, Bohemia, Manu.—Bohemian mineral produce. Ores of uranium, nickel, vanadium, and cobalt, oxide of iron, and various minerals.

10 SZEGÖ, S. (Manager of the Michaeli Mine) Rosenau, Hungary.—Antimony, and antimony ores.

11 GEISSBERGER, F. (the Francis Smelting-works) Metzenseifen, Hungary.—Regulus of antimony.

12 SZOLLENY, C. (Bisrtroer Smelting-works) Rosenberg, Hungary.—Regulus of antimony.

13 VOLDERAUER, G. Salzburg, Prop. — Arsenic ore. White and yellow arsenical glass.

14 HOCHBERGER, J. (St. Procopi Mineral Works) Kahn, Bohemia, Prop.—Sulphate of iron. Alum and sulphur.

15 SCHÖNBORN, E. Count of, Dlazhowic, Bohemia, Prop.—Rough Bohemian garnets (*Pyrope*).

16 LOBKOWITZ, Prince of, Duke of Raudnitz, Bilin, Bohemia, Prop.—Rough, cut and pierced Bohemian garnets (*Pyrope*).

17 IMPERIAL SALT WORKS, Galicia.—Samples of culinary salt.

18 WEBER, G. D. Venice, Manu.—Samples of fine cream of tartar.

19 WAGENMANN, SEYBEL & Co., Vienna, Manu.—Chemical productions, including tartaric acid, vinegar, acetic acid, acetate of sodium, arsenic acid, chloride of lime, arseniate, sulphate, and muriate of potassa.

20 BROSCHE, F. X. Prague, Bohemia, Manu.—Chemical productions, including succinic acid, tartaric acid, sesquioxide of cromium, sesquioxide of uranium, and mercurial compounds.

21 BRAUN, G. J. Prague, Bohemia, Manu.—Albunaim, stannate of soda, and ferrocyanide of potassium.

22 ENGELMANN, S. Karolinenthal, near Prague, Manu.—Albumen, dextrine, laiogome, and artificial gum.

23 SETZER, J. Weiteneggk on the Danube, Manu.—Ultramarine blue, in eight shades. Ultramarine green. Cadmium yellow. Red and rose madder.

24 KUTZER & LEHRER, Prague, Manu.—Ultramarine blue, in eight shades. Ultramarine, green and black. Various colours, including chrome yellow, chrome red, &c.

25 FIALA, W. Prague, Manu.—Indigo blue of three kinds.

26 HEINZEN BROTHERS, Tetschen on the Elbe, Bohemia, Manu.—Red and violet herb archil (*Orseille d'herbes*). Red and violet extract of archil (*Extrait d'orseille rouge et violet*).

27 KINZELBERGER & Co. Prague, Manu.—One hundred and eighty samples of colours.

28 PETZ, W. Pesth, Hungary, Manu.—Carmine of two kinds.

29 RATTICH, J. B. Atzgersdorf, near Vienna, Manu.—Black colour for copper-plate printing.

30 HERBERT, F. P. Klagenfurt and Wolfsberg, Carinthia, Manu.—White lead of different kinds.

31 EGGER, G. Count VON, St. Veit, Carinthia, Manu.—White lead of various kinds.

32 HERBERT, I. Klagenfurt, Carinthia, Manu.—Orange and bright red lead. Red and gold litharge.

33 DIEZ, E. Villach, Carinthia, Manu.—White lead of different kinds. Leaden shot and bullets.

34 BIGAGLIA, PIETRO, q'm. L. Venice, Manu. (Agents, Fordati, Coxhead, and Co. 13 Old Jury Chambers, London).—Selected samples of white lead, litharge, and verdigris.

35 HARDTMUTH, L. & C. Vienna, Manu. — Naples yellow. Artificial pumice stone.

36 SCHABAS, J. Ottercräng, near Vienna, Pat.—Patent artificial pumice stone of different kinds.

37 ROHLIK, L. Prague, Inv. and Pat.—Artificial stone : imitation of marble and lapis-lazuli.

38 CRISTOFOLI, A. Padua, Manu.—Eight samples of paving blocks, and columns of artificial marble.

39 STEARINE CANDLE (Apollo Candle) COMPANY, Vienna.—Stearine and stearine candles.

40 STEARINE CANDLE (Milly Candle) COMPANY, Vienna.—Stearine and stearine candles.

41 PFITZNER & BECKERS, Vienna, Manu. and Pat.—Candles, called palmatine candles (made by distilling palm oil).

42 STEARINE CANDLE COMPANY, Hermannstadt, Transylvania.—Stearine and stearine candles. Elaine soda soap.

43 CHIOZZA, C. A. & SON, Trieste, Manu.—Soap of different kinds.

44 MELZER, D. Hermannstadt, Transylvania, Manu.—Soap of different kinds, for bleaching, &c. Washing soap.

44A RICHTER, A. Königsaal, Bohemia.—Soap of various kinds.

45 CZEKELIUS, C. Hermannstadt, Transylvania, Manu.—Candles of Transylvanian tallow.

46 FURTH, B. Schüttenhofen and Goldenkron, Bohemia, Manu. (Agent, Julius Lippmann, 29 Nicholas lane, Lombard St. London).—Patent lucifer matches, of different kinds and forms.

47 POLLAK, M. Vienna, Manu.—Patent lucifer matches, of different kinds and forms.

48 PRESCHEL, F. Vienna, Manu. — Patent lucifer matches, of different kinds and forms.

49 HOFFMANN, G. Wisoczan, near Prague, Bohemia, Manu.—Patent lucifer matches of different kinds and forms.

50 DE MAJO, S. Trirsch, Moravia, Manu.—Patent lucifer matches of different kinds and forms.

51 DOLLESCHAL, J. Vienna. Pat.—Patent tincture for destroying vermin.

H

52 EDLER VON WURTH, W. Vienna, Inv. and Pat.—Material for stopping decayed teeth.

53 The DIRECTORS of the MINES of His HIGHNESS the PRINCE of LOBKOWITZ, Duke of Raudnitz, at Bilin, Bohemia.—Magnesia and digestive lozenges (pastilles digestives de Bilin). Prepared from the contents of the mineral waters of Bilin.

54 HALLA & Co. Prague, Manu.—Chemical powder, for making black writing ink instantaneously.

55 ROBERT & Co. Gross Sclowitz, Moravia, Manu.—Beet-root sugar.

56 MANUFACTORY OF THE BROTHERS CHEVALIERS DE NEUWALL, Klobauk, Moravia.—Beet-root sugar.

57 RICHTER & Co. Königsaal, Bohemia, Manu.—Beet-root sugar.

58 LODKOWITZ, Prince FERDINAND VON, Bilin, Bohemia, Manu.—Beet-root sugar.

59 LARISCH-MOENNICH, Count H. Karwin, Moravia, Manu.—Beet-root sugar.

60 BEET-ROOT SUGAR MANUFACTORY, Tlumacz, Galicia—Beet-root sugar.

61 REALI, G. (late A. Reali), Venice.—Four sugar loaves.

62 The PRIVILEGED STEAM FLOUR-MILL COMPANY, Vienna.—Flour from Austrian wheat. (Agent, M. Larstig, 31 Norfolk St. Strand, London.)

63 The PRIVILEGED STEAM FLOUR-MILL, Fiume.—Different kinds of flour from Hungarian wheat.

64 STEAM FLOUR-MILL, Smichow, near Prague—Different kinds of flour from Austrian wheat.

65 HAWRANCK, C. Troja, near Prague. — Different kinds of flour from Austrian wheat.

66 NOWOTNY, A. Prague. — Different kinds of flour from Austrian wheat.

67 THUN, COUNT F. Tetschen, Bohemia. — Different kinds of flour from Austrian wheat.

68 JORDAN & BARBER, Tetschen on the Elbe, Bohemia.—Different kinds of flour from Austrian wheat.

69 IMPERIAL TOBACCO MANUFACTORIES, Vienna.—Four kinds of snuff, produced in Galicia and Tyrol.

70 CARNIOLIAN AGRICULTURAL SOCIETY, Laibach.—Honey, chiefly collected by the bees from the blossoms of buck-wheat. Winter linseed, from Carniola white and red millet. Indian corn, grown in Upper Carniola, 400 fathoms above the level of the sea.

71 CHWALLA, ANT. C. Vienna, Manu.—Austrian trame of two and three filaments.

72 SCOLA, A. Linz.—Upper Austrian raw unspun silk.

73 SILK-WORM BREEDING ASSOCIATION, Gratz, Styria.—Styrian raw silk; illustration of the treatment of the silk-worms.

74 RADULOVITS BROTHERS, Weisskirchen, Hungary.—Hungarian silk.

75 LORENZ, ALOIS, Weisskirchen, Banak.—Raw unspun silk from the Banate.

76 HERZOG, E. Werschetz, Banate.—Raw unspun silk from the Banate.

76A HOFLER, HERMANN, & Co. Tyrol.—Various samples of floss silks.

77 MATTIUZZI, G. B. Varmo, Frionly.—Samples of raw silk.

78 SENIGAGLIA & CARMINATI, Palma, Frionly.—Silk

79 PAPPAFAVA, —, Zarra, Dalmatia.—Dalmatian silk.

80 SCHEIBLER & Co. Milan, Prod. (Agents, J. STONE, & Co. 53 Old Broad Street, London.)—1 Six specimens of cocoons: A, yellow, coarse fibre; B, yellow, delicate; C, yellow, satin; D, yellow, saffron; E, white, coarse fibre; F, white, fine fibre. 2 Specimens of raw silk, one thread; raw silk, yellow and white. 3 Specimens of tram silk, three threads. 4 Specimens of organzine silk, for velvet,

heavy and light satin and plush. 5 Specimens of Grenadine: Organzine Grenadine, four threads. 6 Two qualities of Grenadine manufactures. Looms, Messrs. Brevis Brothers.

81 SECCHI, F. Milan.—Samples of silk spun off with cold water.

82 RONCHETTI, A. Milan.—Samples of raw and spun silk.

83 GRASSI, Dr. G. Milan.—Diseased silk-worms, cured by Dr. Grassi's method.

84 OUERIM, G. Venice.—Samples of raw silk.

85 PARE, GERA DI, Canegliano, Province of Treviso.—Samples of raw silk.

86 CANOSSA, Marchioness ELEONORA, née MUSELLI, Verona.—Samples of raw silk.

87 STEINER, G. & Sons, Bergamo.—Samples of raw and spun silk.

87A VERZA BROTHERS (late Carlo Verza), Milan. — Cocoons, raw and spun silk, silk fabrics.

88 ROSSI, G. M. Sondrio.—Samples of raw and spun silk.

89 HUNYADY VON KETHELEY, Count J. H. Urmény, Hungary, Prop.—Sheep-wool in fleeces.

90 FIGDOR, T. & SONS, Vienna.—Hungarian and Austrian-Silesian sheep and lambs'-wool.

91 MITTROWSKY, VON, Count A. Grossherrlitz, Silesia, Prop.—Pure stock merino sheep-wool.

92 LARISCH MOENNICH, Count H. Karwin, Silesia, Prop.—Sheep-wool in fleeces.

93 WALLIS, O. Count VON, Kolleschowitz, Bohemia, Prop.—Washed and unwashed wool. Bohemian hops.

94 PANNA, N. & ALEXIS J. Cronstadt, Transylvania.—Washed and unwashed Transylvania Zackel-sheep and lambs'-wool, and washed and unwashed Transylvania Zigaja-sheep and lambs'-wool.

95 BIRNBAUM, J. Pesth, Hungary, Manu.—Prepared Hungarian hemp.

95A PRIVILEGED LINEN YARN SPINNING MILL, Schönberg, Moravia.—Raw flax, heckled flax, and flax made therefrom.

96 PATENT FLAX RAITING ESTABLISHMENT, Ullersdorf, near Schönberg, Moravia. — Raw and heckled flax of the year 1850. Water raitings.

97 TAMASSIA, L. Poggio, Lombardy.—Willow-straw for hats.

98 ROTSCH, & REICHEL, Gratz, Styria.—Styrian teazles, for the woollen manufacture.

99 SCHOEFEL, J. Saaz, Bohemia, Prod.—Hops from Saaz, Ausch, and Melnik, in Bohemia.

100 BATKA, WENZEL, Prague, Bohemia, Manu.—Bohemian vegetable produce. Medical plants and pharmaceutical productions.

101 REALI, G. (late Antonio Reali) Venice.—Bleached Venetian wax in grains.

102 MALVIEUX, C. T. Pesth, Hungary, Manu.—Refined and unrefined rape-oil.

105 SCHMIDT, H. D. Vienna, Engineer.—Steam-engine, with a paraboloidic regulator of new invention. Model of a patent scale-beam. Designs for beet-root sugar factories.

106 MILESI, A. Verona, Engineer.—Model of a double condensation steam-engine; has been erected in Verona, in full size, and is in use.

107 KNIERIM, F. Vienna.—A carriage.

108 LAURENZI, L. Vienna, Coachmaker.—A four-seated caleche, on nine steel springs and patent axles.

109 The HEIRS OF P. GAMBA, Milan, Engineers.—A Jacquard loom.

110 RIEDLER, F. Spital-on-the-Pyhrn, Upper Austria, Steel-worker.—Damascene steel. Damascened swords and sword-blades.

111 Perger, J. Gratz, Styria, Manu.—A pair of pistols.

112 Meyer & Co. Innspruck, Tyrol, Manu.—A Tyrolese rifle, exhibited for its superior qualities and cheapness.

113 Schoenhuber, J. Villach, Upper Carinthia, Manu.—An air-gun.

114 Lebeda, A. V. Prague, Manu.—A double gun. A rifle for target shooting. A pistol for target shooting.

115 Nowak, F. Prague, Manu.—A double gun. A pair of pistols for shooting at a target.

116 Kehlner's Nephew, A. C. Prague, Manu.—A pair of pistols for shooting at a target; the wood carvings by Mr. Warlinek, after drawings by Messrs. Marx and Seiberts.

117 Preis, A. Prague, Manu. — An assortment of weapons, hangers, &c.

118 Schamal, F. Prague, Manu.—An air pistol.

119 Micheloni, G. Milan, Manu. — Double-barrelled fowling-piece.

120 Bubenttick, J. Hermannstadt, Transylvania, Manu. —A travelling-pouch, containing a hunting-knife, a pistol, knives and forks.

121 Kirner, J. Pesth, Hungary, Manu.—A double gun.

122 Sellier & Bellot, Prague, Manu. (Agents, B. A. Grantoff & Co., 4 Lime Street Square, London.)—Patent percussion-caps.

123 Horsky, F. Libejic, Bohemia, Pat. and Inv.—A seed harrow, a potato cultivator, a drilling-machine, a turnip and weed eradicator, &c., the inventions of F. Horsky; manufactured at the iron-works of Count Stadion, at Josephs-thal, Bohemia. Provisionally registered.

124 Manufactory of Agricultural Implements of Prince F. von Lobkowitz, Eisenberg, Bohemia.—A seed harrow. A double marker. A seed coverer. A seed loosener. A weed destroyer. A sub-soil plough. The inventions of the Chevalier von Infeld, of Eisenberg, manager of the works.

125 Riesi-Stailburg, Baron W. F. von, Schlan, Bohemia, Prop.—A carrot driller.

126 Magni, G. Milan, Prop.—An iron harrow.

127 Carniolian Agricultural Society, Laibach. — Model of a Carniolian granary. Model of a Carniolian bee-hive.

128 Hoepfner, J. Grottenhof, Styria, Prop.—Model of an apparatus for silk-worms to spin in.

129 Proksch, A. Görkan, Bohemia, Inv.—An apparatus for assisting in carrying weights.

130 Mechanical Department of the Imperial Ly-technic Institute, Vienna. — A universal levelling instrument, patented by Professor Stampfer and M. Starke, Vienna. A levelling instrument measuring both height and distance, patented by Professor Stampfer and M. Starke, Vienna. Five different levelling instruments. A perspective ruler of novel construction. A perspective ruler, patented by Professor Stampfer and M. Starke. A theodolite. A dynamograph, for determining the average strength of draught. Invented by A. Chevalier de Burg, director of the Imperial Polytechnic Institute, Vienna.

131 Riedl, von, Leutenstein, Vienna, Inv.—Globe of the moon.

132 Zibermayr, M. Gratz, Styria, Inv.—Chronoglobium and planetarium.

133 Brandeis, R. W. Prague, Manu.—Saccharometrical apparatus for trying beer, designed by Mr. J. N. Balling, Professor of Chemistry, of Prague.

134 Jerak, F. Prague, Manu.—Philosophical, chemical, and medical apparatus and instruments. Works of art in glass.

135 Batka, W. Prague, Manu.—Chemical and philosophical apparatus. An electro-magnetic apparatus, by Professor Petrina, of Prague. An apparatus for trying beer, after the design of Dr. Steinheil, of Vienna.

136 Rocchetti, P. Padua, Engineer.—Geometrical instruments.

137 Wurm, F. X. Vienna, Engineer.—Pyrometer for discovering the degree of heat, a new invention. Patent furnace bar, new invention. Provisionally registered. Patent gridiron, new invention. Iron-wire rope.

138 Zwickl, J. Atzgersdorf, near Vienna, Inv.—A measure for concave surfaces.

139 Marchesi, G. B. Lodi, Inventor.—Writing apparatus for the blind.

140 Schneider, J. Vienna, Manu.—A pianoforte of American maple, with Viennese mechanism, ornamented with inlaid-work.

141 Vlasky, J. Prague, Manu.—A pianoforte of walnut-tree wood.

141a Pottje, J. Vienna, Manu.—Grand pianoforte of rosewood with carved ornaments, seven octaves; Vienna mechanism.

141b Scuffert, E. Vienna, Manu.—Piccolo pianoforte of rosewood, with buhl-work and transposition mechanism, from designs of the architect Bernardo de Bernardis, in Vienna. The bronze ornaments by A. Hollenbach, Vienna.

142 Wilhelm, A. Mödling, near Vienna, Manu.—Leather for covering the hammers of pianofortes.

143 Bienert, D. & Son, Maderhäuser, Bohemia (Agent, Mr. Holste, 76 Basinghall St. London), Manu.—Different kinds of prepared wood for musical instruments.

144 Bittner, D. Vienna, Manu.—A stringed quartett (two violins, tenor, and violoncello). A violin, a double bass, and a guitar.

145 Kosselt, J. Turnan, Bohemia, Manu.—A violoncello, inlaid with mother-o'-pearl.

146 Herzlieb, F. Gratz, Styria, Manu.—A stringed quartett (two violins, tenor, and violoncello).

147 Enrico, C. Cremona, Manu.—A violin.

148 Kiendl, A. Vienna, Manu.—Two zithers (stringed instruments).

149 Huther, M. Vienna, Manu.—A zither (a stringed instrument).

150 Callegari, A. (firm of Antonio Priali detto Re-manin & Co.), Padua, Manu.—An assortment of strings for musical instruments, including violin, violoncello, double bass, harps, &c. and specimens of cat-gut.

151 Indri, A. Venice, Manu.—Samples of strings for guitar, violin, violoncello, harp, and double bass.

152 Hell, F. Vienna, Manu.—Musical instruments: a clarionet, bugle, brass-tuba, trumpet, bass-instrument, a new invention, called Hell's-horn.

153 Riedl's Widow, J. F. Vienna Manu.—Various wind instruments of metal.

154 Stehle, J. Vienna, Manu.—Wind instruments of wood and metal.

155 Uhlmann, J. Vienna, Manu.—Various wind instruments of wood and metal.

156 Ziegler, J. Vienna, Manu.—Various wind instruments of wood.

157 Cerveny, W. F. Königgrätz, Bohemia, Pat.—Various wind instruments of metal; among them a horn called the phonikon, a new invention.

158 Rott, A. H. Prague Manu.—Various wind instruments of metal.

159 Rott, J. Prague, Manu.—Various wind and stringed instruments.

160 Stöhr, F. Prague, Manu.—Wind instruments of metal.

161 Pelitti, G. Milan, Manu.—Wind instruments of metal.

162 Rzebitschek, F. Prague, Manu.—Four musical boxes, playing two, three, four, and six tunes.

163 Reinisch, J. Vienna, Manu.—Different kinds concertinas, accordions, &c.

164 STEINKELLNER, C. Vienna, Manu.—Different kinds of accordions and concertinas.

165 LISZT, A. Vienna.—Two travelling clocks.

166 MARENZELLER, I. Vienna, Clockmaker.—A chronometer of novel construction.

167 RATZENHOFER, J. F. Vienna, Clockmaker.—A geogr aphical clock, showing the difference of mean time in all the capitals of Europe.

168 SCHUBERT, A. Vienna, Clockmaker. — Different kinds of clocks, including bracket, table, and small toilet clocks.

169 KRALIK, S. Pesth, Hungary, Clockmaker.—A travelling clock with 13 escapements. A pocket-watch.

170 ZELISKO, A. Prague, Clockmaker.—A pendulum clock, going a twelvemonth, jewelled socket and escapement.

170A ANDERWALT, PASQUALE, Trieste, Manu.—Three pendulum clocks, Nos. 1 and 2, moved by the disengagement of hydrogen gas, which renews, at stated times, their winding up. No. 1 will go for 30 years, and No. 2 for 20 years without ever requiring to be wound up. They may be wound up for a century, without alteration in dimensions or form. No. 3 constantly winds itself up by the pressure of the atmosphere on quicksilver applied to the clock itself, which goes, therefore, for an indefinite time.—Provisionally registered.

171 CHIACHICH, M. Fiume, Spinner.—Cotton yarns.

172 GRILLMAYER, J. Linz, Spinner.—Cotton yarn.

173 HIRSCHEL & MINERBI, Haidenschaft, Illyria.—White cotton yarn. Turkey-red yarn.

174 PERGER, J. Hirtenberg, Lower Austria, Spinner.—Cotton yarns.

175 COTTON MILL AND DYEING ESTABLISHMENT, Pordenone, near Venice.—Cotton twist, dyed Turkey red.

176 RICHTER, F. Smichow, near Prague, Bohemia, Spinner.—Cotton yarn.

177 FRÖHLICH's, G. & SONS, Warnsdorf, Manu.—Cotton velvet of different kinds, dyed and printed.

178 GROHMANN, C. Lindenau, Bohemia, Manu.—Cotton yarn, dyed Turkey red and pink. Cotton velvet and calico, dyed Turkey red.

179 LANGE, FRANZ, & SONS, St. Georgenthal, Bohemia, Manu.—Cotton velvets of different kinds.

180 WINTER, I. Vienna, Manu.—Piqué coverlids.

181 EHINGER, A. Oberlangenau, near Hoheneloe, Bohemia, Manu. and Bleacher.—Various cotton goods. Jaconets, &c.

182 FRIEDRICH, A. Vienna, Manu. — Various cotton goods, shirtings, muslins, thibets, &c.

183 JENNY & SCHINDLER, Hard, Vorarlberg, Manu.—Furnitures. Cloths. Ladies' dresses (all wool). Ladies' and children's scarfs.

184 KLAMER, J. Vienna, Manu.—Ladies' fancy cotton dresses of different descriptions.

185 LANG, J. Vienna, Manu.—Fancy cotton goods.

186 LEITENBERGER, E. Reichstadt, Bohemia, Manu.—Plain and assorted coloured cotton prints, printed by cylinder and hand. Jaconets, cambrics, muslins of different colours.

187 LEITENBERGER, F. Cosmanos, Bohemia, Manu.—Plain and variously-coloured cotton prints, printed by cylinder, hand, or perrotine. Coloured jaconets, cambrics, muslins. and printed shirtings.

188 LIEBISCH, J. Warnsdorf, Bohemia, Manu.—Printed piqués.

189 OSSBERGER's Successor, P. Zwetl, in Lower Austria, Manu.—Various cotton goods.

190 VOLKMANN, I. Vienna, Manu.—Ladies' fancy cotton dresses. A curtain.

191 KELLER, J. Brünn, Moravia, Spinner.—Woollen yarns.

192 LEIDENFROST, E. Brünn, Moravia, Spinner.—Woollen yarns.

193 SCHMIEGER, A. Neudeck, Bohemia, Manu. and Spinner.—Worsted and woollen yarns.—Woollen fabrics, including thibets, muslin, cloth, &c.

194 SOXHALET, H. F. & E. Brünn, Moravia, Spinner—Woollen yarns.

195 TETRNER, G. Gözkau, near Comotau, Bohemia, Spinner.—Woollen yarns. Vigogna yarns, spun of wool and cotton.

196 THOMAS, L. Graslitz, Bohemia, Manu.—Worsted and woollen yarn. Woollen stuffs: Thibet, ladies' cloth, half-wool tartans.

197 THUM, A. Reichenberg, Bohemia, Manu.—Worsted and woollen yarns. Woollen goods, including thibets, circases, Orleans, and waistcoats. Printed cashmere and circas shawls.

198 WORSTED YARN-SPINNING COMPANY, Vöslau, near Vienna.—Berlin worsted yarns and arras yarns.

199 KAMNER, G. T. Cronstadt, Transylvania.—Rugs. Black and white cloths (called Gujoratz cloth).

200 MAURER, V. Iglau, Bohemia, Manu. — Blankets, horse-cloths, and rugs.

201 MATSCHUKO, N. Cronstadt, Transylvania, Manu.—Long-haired winter rugs. Blankets.

202 TARTLER, M. Cronstadt, Transylvania, Manu.—Various druggets.

203 WOCHOVSZKY, J. R. Skalitz, Hungary, Manu.—Woollen bolting-cloth.

204 AUSPRITZ, L. Brünn, Moravia, Manu.—Fine cloths, cashmere, satins, and elastics.

205 BAUER, THEODOR, & Co. Brünn, Moravia, Manu.—Woollen cloths.

206 BIEDERMANN, M. L. & Co. Teltsch, Moravia, Manu. (Agent, S. Reuter, Moorgate St. Chambers, Moorgate, London.)—Fine cloths, cashmere, and doeskin.

207 BINDER, TRAUGOTT, Hermannstadt, Transylvania, Manu.—Cloths and doeskins.

208 FURLER, FRANZ, Gratz, Styria, Manu.—Broadcloths and Styrian beavers (Azors) of various colours.

209 CLOTH MANUFACTURING COMPANY, Gáes, Hungary.—A variety of cloths and doeskins.

210 GINZEL, R. C. Reichenberg, Bohemia, Manu.—Peruvian cloth.

211 GUERTLER, J. Brünn, Moravia, Manu.—Woollen trouserings.

212 HARTIG, J. Reichenberg, Bohemia, Manu. (Agent, Julius Mienerts, 43 Clarges St. Piccadilly.)—Cloths and Peruvians.

213 TRADE-UNION, Brünn, Moravia.—Woollens, cloths, summer buckskins and trouserings.

214 CLOTH-MAKERS' ASSOCIATION, Hermannstadt, Transylvania.—An assortment of cloths and flannels.

215 HONAUER, F. Linz, Upper Austria, Manu.—Woollens; velveteens; plush; camlets; harpins; buntings. Turkish and Wallachian belts.

216 ILLEK, F. Brünn, Moravia, Manu.—Samples of cloth and doeskin.

217 MIESS, G. Cronstadt, Transylvania.—White cloth, for Hallina cloaks.

218 MORO BROTHERS, Klagenfurt, Carinthia, Manu.—Cloth of the finest quality for uniforms.

219 MUELLER, A. L. Reichenberg, Bohemia, Manu.—An assortment of woollens.

220 CLOTH-MANUFACTURING COMPANY, Namiest, Moravia.—Fine cloths, Peruvians, doeskins, and cashmeres.

221 OFFERMANN, J. H. Brünn, Moravia, Manu.—Fine cloths and trouserings. Stuffs for summer and winter coats.

222 POPPER BROTHERS, Brünn, Moravia, Manu.—Fine cloths, Peruvians, doeskin, and zepherienne trouserings.

223 POSSELT, A. jun. Reichenberg, Bohemia, Manu. —Samples of cloth, doeskin, and cashmere.

224 SCHMIEGER, J. Brünn, Manu.—Woollens and stuffs for winter coats.

225 SCHMITT, F. Aicha, Bohemia, Manu.—Woollen cloths of different kinds.

226 SCHOELL, A. Brünn, Moravia, Manu.—Fine cloths, Brazilian, elastic cashmeres, doeskin, and winter stuffs.

227 SCHOELLER BROTHERS, Brünn, Moravia, Manu.— Fine cloths, Brazilians, elastics, Peruvians, and Americans. Winter and summer trouserings.

228 SEIDEL, C. & C. Kratzau, Bohemia, Manu.—Woollens, Cashmeres, Orleans, and Alpacas.

229 NEUHAEUSER, SIEGMUND, & Co. Reichenberg, Bohemia, Manu.—Fine cloths, Brazilian, Castorine, elastics, and Peruvians.

230 SIEGMUND, W. Reichenberg, Bohemia, Manu.— Fine cloths, beavers, and ladies' cloths. Woollen stuffs, including Orleans, mohairs, rips, mandarins, and Austrians. Woollen shawls. Shawls composed of wool and silk.

231 STEFPANEK, F. Bruck, on the Mur, Styria, Manu.— Cloths and Styrian beavers.

232 STEFFENS, P. Goldenkron, near Budweis, Bohemia, Manu.—Cloths, cassimeres, and buckskins.

233 STRAKOSCH, S. & Son, Brünn, Moravia, Manu.— Ladies' woollen cloakings. Trouserings.

234 TRENKLER, A. & Sons, Reichenberg, Bohemia, Manu.—Cloth and Peruvians.

235 TSCHOERNER, J. jun. Reichenberg, Bohemia, Manu. —Various samples of cloth.

236 ULLRICHT, A. jun. Reichenberg, Bohemia, Manu. —Cloths and Peruvians.

237 VONWILLER & Co. Senftenberg, Bohemia, Manu.— Cloth, Peruvians, and trouserings.

238 SCHMITT's, S. M. (Heirs of) & Co. Neugedein, Bohemia, Manu.—Thibets, Cashmeres, camlets, &c. Shawls, scarfs, &c.

239 BOSSI, J. St. Veit, near Vienna, Manu.—Printed shawls, scarfs, and dresses.

240 BRACHT, F. W. Vienna, Manu.—An assortment of woollen and half-woollen prints for ladies' dresses. Balzarines. Woollen and barege shawls, handkerchiefs, and scarfs.

241 LIEBIG, F. Reichenberg, Bohemia, Manu.—Printed Thibet and Circassian handkerchiefs and scarfs. Table-covers.

242 WINTER, J. Vienna; Tuppadl, Bohemia; and Trebitsch, Moravia, Manu.—Ladies' printed dresses; half-woollen stuffs.

243 HAAS, P. & SONS, near Vienna, Manu.—Velours d'Utrecht.

244 DIERZERS, J. (Heirs of), Kleinmünchen, near Linz. Manu.—Carpets of different sizes and colours.

244 A PROCHASKA, W. Prague, Tailor—Two patchwork table covers.

245 SALZER, C. Vienna, Dyer.—Samples of dyed silk.

246 MESSAT, A. Vienna, Manu.—Silk ribbons.

247 MOERING, C. Vienna, Manu.—Figured gros de Naples ribbons and satin ribbons.

248 PFENINGBERGER, J. Vienna, Manu.—Silk ribbons of various kinds.

249 BACKHAUSEN, C. & J. Vienna, Manu.—Half-silks for ladies' dresses.

250 BADER BROTHERS, Vienna, Manu.—Silks, ladies' scarfs, dresses, and handkerchiefs.

251 BLAHA & ROSENBERGER, Vienna, Manu.—Figured satin, white silk waistcoating, and velvet.

252 BUJATTI, F. Vienna, Manu.—Silk furnitures and damasks; carriage linings. Silk brocades for ecclesiastical vestments. Silk hangings, counterpanes, handkerchiefs, satin, &c.

253 DORFLEUTHNER, L. Vienna, Manu.—Half-silks and silks, ladies' dresses, satin, velvet, &c.

254 FLEMMICH, A. Vienna, Manu.—Figured silk dresses.

255 FRIES & ZEPPEZAUER, Vienna, Manu.—Silk dresses; ecclesiastical brocades; silk tapestry; damasks; satins; ladies' scarfs.

256 GANSER, J. Vienna, Manu.—Transparent silk gauze.

257 GIANI, J. Vienna, Manu.—Silks and half-silk; ecclesiastical brocades and damasks.

258 GRUBER & ENZINGER BROTHERS, Vienna, Manu.— Silks; satins; Gros de Naples; shawls.

259 HAAS, PHILLIP, & SONS, Vienna, Manu.—Silks and half-silks, damasks, furnitures, and lampas.

260 HELL, G. Vienna, Manu.—Silk furnitures, in brocatelle; lampas; satin and damasks. Velvet.

261 HERZIG, J. & SON, Vienna, Manu.—Figured silk dresses.

262 HORNBOSTEL, C. G. & Co. Vienna, Manu.—Silks; silk velvet Bayadere handkerchiefs; ladies' dresses; barege shawls. Printed foulards. The stuff made on self-acting water-looms, and printed by Gustav König in Vienna.

263 KRICKL, E. Vienna, Merch. and Manu.—Ecclesiastical vestments. Infula of real cloth of silver, richly embroidered with gold. Casuale of silk velvet, embroidered with gold and silver. Vestment of cloth of silver, embroidered with gold.

264 KOSTNER, A. Vienna, Manu.—Ecclesiastical brocades, embroidered in gold and silver, on silk and chenille.

265 LEMANN, J. & SON, Vienna, Manu.—Tapestry. Ecclesiastical brocades. Ecclesiastical vestments, richly embroidered with gold, silver, and imitation metal, on silk and chenille.

266 MAYER BROTHERS, Vienna, Manu.—Silk and velvet waistcoatings; satin scarfs and handkerchiefs.

267 MESTROZI, P. Vienna, Manu.—Ladies' silk handkerchiefs. Satin and velvet waistcoatings.

268 REICHERT, F. Vienna, Manu.—Silks; gros de Naples; gros grain; gros d'Afrique; Levantin and satin Turque.

269 SCHIPPER, C. Vienna, Manu.—Silk plush for hats.

270 SCHOPPER, M. A. Vienna, Manu.—An extensive selection of silk for furniture, in brocades, lampas, satins, and damasks. Carriage linings.

271 SIEBERT, F. Vienna, Manu. and Pat.—Chenille handkerchiefs and bayaderes.

272 SIGMUND, I. Vienna, Manu.—Silk lawn; transparent gauze; and bayaderes.

273 SPANRAFT, F. X. Vienna, Manu.—Plain and brocaded silk handkerchiefs; ladies' scarfs and shawls.

274 WOJTECH, F. Vienna, Manu.—Fancy silk goods waistcoatings, satin scarfs, &c.

275 HIELTEN, Sons of the late ELIAS, Schönlinde, Bohemia, Manu.—Sewing, crochet, and knitting thread. Linen.

276 TAUBER, F. Unter-Meidling, near Vienna, Manu.— Tow-thread, coloured, of various kinds.

277 ROPE-MAKERS' ASSOCIATION, Hermannstadt, Transylvania.—Manufactures of hemp and flax, including girths, cordage, &c.

278 JAGER, F. J. Prague. Bohemia, Manu.—Cordage. Carpet of Italian hemp, and of New Zealand hemp. Saddlegirths, halters, bridles, &c. Bell-ropes of New Zealand hemp (*Phormium tenax*).

279 PARSCH BROTHERS, Graupen, Bohemia, Manu.— Water-hose of Bohemian hemp, for fire-engines.

280 WEINBERGER, G. Linz. Manu.—Saddle-girths, halters, cordage, &c.

281 BUTSCHEK & GRAFF, Brünn, Moravia, Manu.—Sailcloth of different kinds, spun and wove in the same factory.

282 CHIACHIC, M. Fiume, Manu.—Sail-cloth of different kinds.

283 THE BENEVOLENT SOCIETY'S ESTABLISHMENT, Milan. —Three table-cloths and a piece of linen.

284 FERIL, W. Merklow, near Starkenbach, Bohemia.— Hand-spun linen thread. Fine cambric of linen thread, spun by inhabitants of the Riesengebirge, Bohemia. Pocket-handkerchiefs.

285 HARRACH, Count F. E. von, Janowitz, Moravia, and Starkenbach, Bohemia.—Linen damask furniture. Damask table-cloths and napkins. Linen towels. Linen handkerchiefs.

286 HAUPT, L. Brünn, Moravia, Manu.—Linens. Damasked coloured twills, &c., of various kinds.

287 MATHIE, J. Haslach, Upper Austria, Manu.—Linen table-cloths and towels.

288 PELDRIAN's HEIRS, Hohenelbe, Bohemia, Manu.— Linen yarns, hand-spun. Linen of different kinds, grass-bleached. Pocket handkerchiefs.

289 PETRAK, J. Branna, Bohemia, Manu.—Prepared flax. Linen yarn. Linen handkerchiefs.

290 SIEGL, J. & Co. Schönberg, Moravia, Manu. and Bleachers.—Bleached linen, of all widths and lengths, of the best hand-spun and machine yarn.

291 SIMONETTA, P. Helfenberg, near Linz, Manu.— Linen table-cloths. Dowlas, all linen. Damasks. Half-woollen-stuffs, lamas, wool and cotton. Rough, fine, and mixed drills.

292 VONWILLER & Co. Haslach, Upper Austria, Manu. —Mixed cotton and linen, drill, and rips.

293 WITSCHELL & REINISCH, Warnsdorf, Bohemia, Manu. —Figured linen trouserings. White waistcoats, of various patterns. Gambroon linings.

294 BLASCHKA & Co. Liebenau, Bohemia, Manu.—Woollens. Orleans' rips. Lastings. Thibet handkerchiefs. Printed shawls. Circas shawls.

295 BRUDER's Widow, RUDOLPH, Vienna, Manu.— Ladies figured dresses. Long shawls; woollen bayaderes. Cashmere waistcoatings; gentlemen's scarfs.

296 FURST, J. Vienna, Manu.—Fancy stuffs, including ladies' half-silk dresses. Fine, middling, and figured cotton dresses. Figured half-woollen cloaks. Scarfs, half and entirely of wool, for ladies and gentlemen. Printed cotton handkerchiefs.

297 KROITZSCH, M. Atssig on the Elbe, Bohemia, Manu. —Cloth of wool and cotton, alpacas, poil de chevre, &c.

298 LIEBIG, J. Reichenberg, Bohemia, Manu.—An assortment of plain and figured printed woollen stuffs, comprising Orleans, Thibet, lasting, mandarin, &c. Winter shawls, printed Thibets, &c.

299 NEUBERT, C. G. Georgswalde, Bohemia, Manu.— Ladies' dresses of silk, cotton, and wool, prepared for printing.

300 RAMEDE, I. Vienna, Manu.—Woollen shawls; petticoats; counterpanes.

301 WOLFRUM, C. Aussig on the Elbe, Bohemia, Manu. —Cotton and woollen stuffs, including victorines, poile de chèvres, imperials, alhambras, &c.

302 WURST, J. N. Freudenthal, Silesia, Manu.— Breakfast cloths of different colours, of linen, wool, and silk. Woollen coverlid.

303 BIENERT, F. Vienna, Manu.—A variety of waistcoatings.

304 ECHINGER BROTHERS, Vienna, Manu.—Waistcoatings and woollen scarfs for gentlemen.

305 KRAL, A. Vienna, Manu.—Waistcoatings of various kinds.

306 ROCKSTROH, H. Vienna, Manu.—Waistcoatings of wool and cotton.

307 TIAL, J. Vienna, Manu.—Waistcoatings of wool, and of wool and cotton mixed.

308 WESTHAUSTER, J. Vienna, Manu.—Waistcoatings of piqué and wool.

309 BERGER, J. Vienna, Manu.—Ramage, long, and a variety of other shawls.

310 BROTZMANN, A. Vienna, Manu.—Tapis and ramage shawls. Long shawls.

311 HAYDTER, S. Vienna, Manu.—Ramage and long shawls.

312 KUBO, J. & SON, Vienna, Manu.—Tapis and ramage shawls. Long and Thibet shawls.

313 MARTINEK, J. Vienna, Manu.—Tapis and ramage shawls. Long shawls.

314 MOGEL, N. Vienna, Manu.—An assortment of shawls.

315 REINHOLD, W. Vienna, Manu.—Tapis and ramage shawls. Long shawls.

316 RISS, J. Vienna, Manu.—Ramage and long shawls.

318 SCHINDL, A. Vienna, Manu.—Shawl-handkerchiefs and long shawls.

319 WENZEL, C. Vienna, Manu.—Fancy woollen and cotton shawls. Shawls for mourning.

320 ZJCISEL, J. & BLUMEL, J. & C. Vienna, Manu. —Large assortment of shawls, shawl-handkerchiefs, long shawls and scarfs.

321 MESSEENER, F. Reutte, Tyrol, Manu.—Brown calf-skin. Brown and black cow-leather, for waterproof boots.

322 POLLAR, J. J. & SONS, Prague, Bohemia, Pat. and Manu.—Brown, black, pressed, and grained calf-skin. Black japanned calf and sheep-skin. Black japanned grained sheep-skin. Chamois dressed sheep-skin.

324 SEYKORA, J. Alderkosteler, Bohemia, Manu.—Cow-leather, tanned with pine bark.

325 SUESS, A. H. Vienna, Manu.—Brown calf-skin, japanned calf-skin, calf and sheep-skin, and kid leather in various colours for fancy articles. Sheep-skin for furniture covering.

326 WOLFE, F. Hermannstadt, Transylvania, Currier. —Goat and sheep-skins of various colours. Calf-skins. Printed goat-skins.

327 CHRISTIL, J. Vienna, Manu.—Gentlemen's boots and shoes, waterproof-shooting-boots. Boots with cork and wood-pegged soles, and with hollow heels.

328 FRANK, J. Vienna, Pat.—Boots soled with a newly-invented material.

329 LANGDER, J. Vienna, Manu.—Gentlemen's boots and shoes.

330 SHOEMAKERS' ASSOCIATION, Hermannstadt, Transylvania.—Shoes and boots (called Tschiszmeń) belonging to the Saxon and Romanian national costume.

331 HELIA, J. Vienna, Manu.—Ladies' shoes, boots, and slippers.

332 FRIEDL, L. Vienna, Manu.—Ladies' shoes, over-shoes, and half-boots with pegged soles.

333 KUNERTH, A. Vienna, Manu.—Ladies shoes. Slippers with velvet and gold embroidery. Gentlemen's shoes. Over shoes.

334 BOULOGNE, P. Prague, Bohemia, Manu.—Kid and lamb-skins for glovers.

335 JAQUEMAR, F. Vienna, Manu.—Kid gloves for ladies and gentlemen.

336 GLOVERS' ASSOCIATION, Prague, Bohemia.—Ladies and gentlemen's gloves of kid, lamb, and sheep-skin. Gentlemen's gloves of rein-deér leather.

337 PORTSCHEST, —. Hermannstadt, Transylvania, Manu.—Sheep-skin and kid leather.

338 JELLINEK, J. Prague, Bohemia, Manu.—A variety of harness.

339 LÖFFLER, F. Prague, Bohemia, Manu.—Saddles of various kinds.

340 ZAPF, I. Vienna, Pat. and Manu.—Saddles, girths, bridles, and horse-rugs.

341 GRIESS, F. Vienna, Manu.—Riding and other whips, with buttons and handles of silver, ivory, whalebone, horn, &c.

342 MANSCHÖN, M. F. Pesth, Hungary, Manu.—Hungarian Csikós whip.

343 GROSHOFF, G. Vienna, Manu.—Travelling trunks, hunting-pouches, and carpet-bags.

344 EINHAUSER, J. Uderns, Tyrol, Leather-cutter.—Tyrolese hunting-pouches, gun-slings, and belts.

345 LEATHER-CUTTERS' ASSOCIATION, Hermannstadt, Transylvania.—A belt.

346 GEYER, J. Pesth, Hungary, Furrier (Agent Mr. J. G. Mayer, 58, Oxford-street, London).—Hungarian sheep-skin Bund (a cloak).

347 ASSOCIATED FURRIERS, Hermannstadt, Transylvania.—Black lamb-skins. Wallachian and Heltau furs.

348 DINZL, F. Vienna, Manu.—Gutta percha articles, including sticks, riding-whips, snuff-boxes, goblets, flower-pots, &c.

349 LANG, F. Stadt-Steyer, Upper Austria, Manu.—Artists' brushes of various kinds.

350 PATTAK, G. Hermannstadt, Transylvania, Manu.—Horse-brush. Cloth and hair-brushes.

351 BAYER, J. G. Hermannstadt, Transylvania, Hatter.—Felts, and materials for making felt.

352 HÜBSCH, J. Prague, Bohemia, Manu.—Bohemian silk and hair hats.

353 KRISE, C. Prague, Bohemia, Manu.—Felt and silk hats. Thibet mechanical hats.

354 MUCK, J. Prague, Bohemia, Manu.—Silk and felt hats and bonnets, of various kinds. Felt shoes and boots. Samples of coloured felt cloth.

355 SRBA, A. Prague, Bohemia, Manu.—Felt and silk hats; waterproof military hats; shooting hats of wool and hair.

HORSE-HAIR.—Sieve bottoms are made in Illyria in considerable quantities, at very moderate prices, and of good quality.

They are principally exported; and chiefly to Italy, France, the Netherlands, Spain, Gibraltar, Servia, Bosnia, &c.

356 BENEDIG, J. Strassisch, Krainburg, Illyria, Manu.—Horse-hair sieve bottoms, of various kinds. Cylindrical sieve-bottoms, for paper manufactories.

357 GLOBOTSCHNIG, A. Strassisch, Illyria, Manu.—Horse-hair seive bottoms of various kinds. Cylindrical sieve-bottoms, for paper manufactories.

358 LOCKER, D'ANTONIO, Krainburg, Illyria, Manu.—Horse-hair sieve bottoms of various kinds. Cylindrical sieve-bottoms, for paper manufactories.

359 PFENINGBERGER, J. Heiligenstadt, Vienna, Manu.—Oil-cloths. Figured fustians and cottons. Table-covers to resemble wood. Floor-cloths. Carriage carpets. Figured communion cloths.

360 SMITH & MEYNIER, Fiume, Manu.—White printing, drawing, writing, foolscap, and letter papers, of various kinds. Coloured paper.

361 EGGERTH, J. Stubenbach, Schüttenhofen, Bohemia, Manu.—Packing paper (flannel paper), of a peculiar kind, to be used in packing mirrors or glasses, by laying it between the same instead of strips of cloth.

362 IMPERIAL COURT AND GOVERNMENT PRINTING OFFICE, Vienna.—Specimens of typography and printing of all descriptions.

363 IMPERIAL MILITARY GEOGRAPHICAL INSTITUTE, Vienna.—A variety of maps.

364 CERRI, C. Officer in the Imperial Military Geographical Institute, Vienna.—Map of Italy, in eight sheets.

365 RAFFELSPERGER, F. Vienna, Pat. and Printer.—Maps, with the names in the German, Hungarian, Bohemian, Servian, Illyrian, Italian, French, and English languages, executed by the ordinary printing press.

366 BATTAGIA, G. Venice, Printer.—Specimens of typography, with simple and convenient binding.

367 HAASE, G. & SONS, Prague, Bohemia, Printers and Type-founders.—Type of various kinds. Specimens of typography, including a variety in gold, silver, and colours. A Missale Romanum, &c.

368 ARNETH, J. Director of the Imp. Numismatic and Antiquarian Cabinet, by W. Braumüller, Bookseller and Publisher, Vienna.—A work on gold and silver monuments, by the exhibitor (as a sample of the process of copper-plate engraving in Vienna).

368A KAYSER, Jos. Franz., Lithographer, Gratz, Styria, —Maps.

369 RAUH, J. Vienna, Lithographic Printer.—An album, containing lithographic copies from original drawings by Vienna artists. Specimens of the various styles of lithography and printing.

370 BERMANN, J. Vienna, Publisher.—Lithographs: Views on the banks of the Danube. The Austrian armies during the course of two centuries. Statistical maps of Austria.

371 MECHETTI (late Carlo Mechetti), Vienna, Publishers.—Portraits drawn from nature, by Krichuber. Music composed by Dessauer, Spohr, Willmers, Strauss, &c.

372 MULLER, H. F. Vienna, Publisher.—Map of Carniola. Illustrations to the History of Austria, by Professor Geiger. Album of the Vienna artists. Album of waltzes and national melodies.

373 NEUMANN, T. L. Vienna, Publisher.—Lithographs; Portraits, battle scenes, &c. Album, containing views of Vienna.

374 STEIGER, G. Vienna, Manu.—Playing-cards, of four sorts, exhibited in a frame. The frame by J. Griller, of Vienna. The metal ornaments by Gottochalk and Lamasch, Vienna.

374A GREINER, M. Vienna, Calligraphist.—A Lord's prayer, and three other specimens of calligraphy, executed entirely with the pen.

375 SCHUTZ, F. Vienna, Calligraphist.—A calligraphic tableau.

376 HABENICHT, A. Vienna, Manu.—Ladies' toilet-table, with ivory ornaments. A painter's easel. Fancy articles of leather, portfolios, cassets, pockets, ladies' and gentlemen's companions, travelling medicine chests, cigar-boxes, porte-monnaies, lucifer-match boxes, &c.

377 STIASNY, W. Prague, Bohemia, Bookbinder.—A bill casket. An album with a view of the royal residence at Prague, papeterie.

378 RENEL, A. Vienna, Manu.—Fancy-ware of wood and paper; paper baskets; screens; letter-weight; tableau. Samples of stamped-paper ornaments.

379 JOHNE & THIELE, Vienna, Manu.—Pasteboard ware: caskets, watch-stands, pincushions, goblets, &c. Stone pasteboard ware: cups, baskets, caskets, watch-stands, pincushions, &c.

380 BERGER, C. H. Vienna, Manu.—Wafers of paper and gelatine, of different kinds.

381 HARDTMUTH, L. & C. Vienna, Manu.—Black lead and red-chalk pencils of various kinds.

382 GROHMANN, A. Schönlinde, Bohemia, Manu.—Silk-lace, petinets, veils, &c.

383 MEINL'S, A. HEIRS, Baringen, near Carlsbad, Bohemia, and Vienna, Manu.—Silk-lace, woollen-lace, of different colours. Embroideries, including pocket-handkerchiefs, ladies' dresses, collars, &c.

384 RÖLZ, S. Graslitz, Bohemia, Manu.—Silk bayadere handkerchiefs. Embroidered cambric pocket-handkerchiefs. Embroidered chemisettes.

385 SCHLICK, F. Vienna, Manu.—A large assortment of silk-lace, petinet, and point-net-lace, bayadere, handkerchiefs veils, shawls, scarfs, &c.

386 Bossi, J. Vienna, Manu.—Embroidered shawls and scarfs.

387 Laporta, H. F. Vienna, Merchant and Manu.— Embroidered scarfs and handkerchiefs. Mantillas. Scarfs. Velvet and cashmere shawls.

388 Bauhofer, F. ·Vienna, Embroiderer.—A coat-of-arms, embroidered with gold, silver, and silk.

389 Benkowits, Marie, Vienna, Artistic Embroideress. —An embroidery of crape-thread on white gros de Naples, representing Beneficence. An embroidery of wool and silk, representing the grave of the fallen soldier.

390 Fusinata, Maria, Belluno. — An embroidered carpet.

390a Schreier, Susanna, Vienna, Manu.—Specimens of knitting.

391 Krach Brothers, Prague, Bohemia, Manu.—A dress coat of peculiar workmanship. A double coat, that can be worn on either side, made of a new material. A coat made of woollen stuff, of peculiar cheapness. Another made of a new woollen stuff.

392 Singer, J. Pest, Hungary, Manu.—Gentlemen's apparel.

393 Budinsky, A. Reichenberg, Bohemia, Manu.— Hosiery, including ladies' and gentlemen's vests, trousers, caps, shoes, &c.

394 Malatinszky, E. Miskolz, Hungary, Manu.—Hungarian national dresses, called szür.

395 Rigo & Kraetschmar, Rima Szombath, Hungary, Manu.—Various Hungarian coats (guba). Hungarian shooting coats.

395a Nessel, C. Tailor, Oedenburg, Hungary.—A coat and waistcoat.

396 Oestreicher, D. Mayk, Hungary, Manu.—A white and a grey Hungarian cloak (guba). Hungarian cloths (hallina) and rugs.

397 Schramm, S. Hermannstadt, Transylvania, Weaver. —Veils for the Romanian national costume.

398 Trade Union, Hermannstadt, Transylvania. — Szelistjan rugs. A Szarika, belonging to the Wallachian national costume (produce of the domestic industry of the Wallachian peasantry).

399 Seitter, A. Brünn Moravia, Manu.—Oriental caps (fez), of various kinds.

400 Radmeister Community, Vordernberg, Styria.— Soft pig-iron, sparry iron ore, gangue stone, slags. Bar-iron, prepared for making blistered steel.

401 Egger, Count G. Von, Knappenberg, Carinthia.— Heavy spar. Crystallized and efflorescent sparry iron-ore. Crystallized calcareous spar on brown iron-ore.

402 Egger, Count G. Von, Hüttenberg, Treibach, and Oberfellach, Carinthia.—Pig-iron, cast-steel, brescia, and die-steel. Nails for the Levant.

403 Rauscher's Co. Ironworks, St. Veis, Heft and Mocinity, Carinthia.—Pieces of iron-ore, white and refined scoriæ and sheet-iron.

404 Christalnigg's, Count Von, Mining Co. Eberstein, Carinthia.—Brown iron-stone. Brown and heavy spar. White cast-iron for making steel. Fine metal for puddling. Grey metal for casting.

405 Zois, Widow Carl, Ironworks, at Tauerburg, Freistritz and Wochin, Carniola.—Iron-ores, pig-iron, bar-iron, steel, and saw-steel.

406 Kossuch, J. Fzinobánga, Hungary.—Ankeris iron-ore, raw, half, and entirely efflorescent; also roasted. Samples of pig-iron produced from these ores.

407 Imperial Smelting Works, Pillersee and Zennbach, Tyrol.—Refined steel, spring-steel, and cast-steel. Cast-steel for scythe blades, refined steel and spring-steel from Zennbach. Sparry iron-ore. Pig-iron and steel from Pillersee.

408 Depôt of the Imperial Iron Mines and Iron Works, Vienna.—Cast-steel, from iron-ore, Styrian scoriæ, and slags from iron-ore. Raw-steel, wheel-tires, rails, angle-irons, and tools from Neuberg, in Styria. Sparry iron-ore and cast-iron from Mariazell.

409 Egger, Count Ferdinand Von, Lippitzbach, Carinthia.—Hoop, square, and cylindrical iron. Rolled saw-blades of raw steel. Plates of hard iron for cementing.

410 Egger, Count F. Von, Freibach, Carinthia.—A selection of Brescian steel, including cast, accialon, fir, and scythe steel.

411 Töpper, A. Scheibbs, Lower Austria.—Hoop and rod-iron. Sheet-iron. Ship, tender-roofing, and tubing sheet-iron. Welded tubes for manometers, and water and gas-pipes.

412 Furstenberg, Prince, Althütten, Neuhütten, Rostok and Neujoachimsthal, Bohemia.—Various samples of wrought and stretched iron, round and flat-angle iron, carriage-spring iron, plough-shares, spring-iron, sheet-iron for boilers, wrought lathe-spindles. Several cast-iron stoves and monuments. Colossal crucifix, chains, &c.

413 Metternich, Prince, Plas, Bohemia. — Cast-iron stove for a hunting-seat.

414 Bouquoi, Count, Kallich, Bohemia.—Hoop-iron, round bar-iron, sheet-iron, &c.

415 Andrassy, Count G. Dernö, Hungary.—Rod-iron stretched by charcoal-gas loops.

416 Ironworks of the Chapter of Gurk, St. Magdalena, Carinthia.—Various kinds of steel: Brescia steel. Steel for files and scythes

417 Schwarzenberg, Prince, Murau, Upper Styria.— Paal steel, Brescia steel, Styria steel, and hard iron. Refined steel. Soft iron for blistered steel.

418 Pfeiffer, J. Spitzenbach, Upper Styria.—Scharschach and Brescian steel. Steel for scythes aud mills.

419 Thurn, Count G. Von, Streiteben, Schwarzenbach, and Müss, Carinthia.—Various kinds of steel and iron for nails.

420 Fischer, A. St. Aegydi, Lower Austria.—Iron-ore and pig-iron. Spring-steel. Various samples of rolled bar-iron. An assortment of iron-wire. 285 samples of files.

421 Fischer, B. Traisen, Lower Austria, Manu.— Various articles of cast-steel, including spindles for spinning establishments, &c. Articles of malleable cast-iron, such as gun-locks; broken pieces, to show the grain, and its yielding nature.

422 Lindheim, H. D. Plan, Bohemia.—Railroad rails. Bar, hoop, and rod-iron.

423 Privileged Association of Manufacturers, Wöllersdorf, Lower Austria.—Tinned sheet-iron. Embossed and chased forms of tin.

424 Kleist, Baron Von, Neudeck, Bohemia.—Tinned sheet-iron. Thin sheet-iron, called iron-paper.

425 Egger, Count F. Von, Feistritz, Carinthia.— Musical string, cording, currying, bed-springs, and pit-rope wires. Fine, middle, and ordinary wire.

426 Fischer & Wurm, St. Ægidi, Lower Austria, Pat. & Manu.—Different iron-wire ropes.

427 Eberstaller & Schindler, Stadt Steyer, Upper Austria, Manu.—Ordinary and fine iron-wire. Wire for musical strings. Saws.

428 Hueber, F. Josefsthal, Styria.—Different kinds of iron and steel wire.

429 Schedl, C. Wasserlug and Frauenthal, Lower Austria.—Rolls of different kinds of iron-wire. Steel-wire. Ordinary, middling, and fine wire. Spring-wire.

430 Salm, Prince, Blansko, Moravia.—Cast-iron gas chandelier, from a drawing of Mr. Bernardis, in Vienna. Cast-iron statue: Field-marshal Count Radetzky, modelled by Fernkerna. Four cast-iron statues, representing heroes from the Nibelungenlied, also by Fernkerna.

431 Albrecht, Archduke, Trzinietz, Silesia.—Cast-iron cooking apparatus, with non-metallic enamelling.

432 BARTELMUS BROTHERS, & BERNHARDI, Neujoachimsthal, Bohemia, Manu.—Cast-iron cooking apparatus, with non-metallic enamelling. Horse-manger, &c.

433 PLEISCHL, A. Vienna, Pat. & Manu.—Sheet-iron saucepans, with non-metallic enamelling.

434 KITSCHELT, A. Vienna, Manu.—Various metal articles, viz. :—A vase, a cross, and two candlesticks, cast in iron, from the drawings of Mr. Stache, in Vienna. Table, cast in zinc. Flower-vase of bronze, cast in one piece. Toilet-table, fauteuils, and chairs of hollow wrought-iron tubes, with cast-iron ornaments.

435 EGGER, J. B. Villach, Carinthia, Manu.—A pressed leaden pipe, 900 feet long, in one piece. Two pieces of pressed leaden pipes (tinned). These leaden pipes are especially worthy of observation, on account of their great length, thinness, and equality ; they can be made of any length.

436 HIRSCHE, F. Brünn, Moravia. — Church-lamp, drawing-room service, writing materials, tea-pot, &c., of tin. Samples of ornaments and letters.

437 WAGNER, F. Prague, Manu.—Iron cash-box, weighing 270 lbs.

438 BEITL, F. Prague, Manu.—Two iron cash-boxes, weight 360 lbs. and 483 lbs.

439 DIETRICH, J. Baron, VON, Spital-on-the-Semmering, Styria, Manu.—An assortment of scythes.

440 GATT, A. Erl, near Kufstein, Tyrol, Manu.—A variety of scythes.

441 GRABER, J. Weer, Valley of the Lower Inn, Tyrol, Manu.—An assortment of scythes.

442 GRAUSS, J. Finsing, Tyrol, Manu.—An assortment of scythes.

443 HIERZENBERGER, G. Leonstein, near Stadt Steyer, Upper Austria, Manu.—Various scythes.

444 OFFNER BROTHERS, Wolfsberg, Carinthia, Manu.—Different kinds of scythes.

445 PAMMER, S. Schalchen, near Mattighofen, Manu.—Scythe, and chaff-cutter.

446 PENZ, J. Mühlerau, in the Zillerthal, Tyrol, Manu.—Different kinds of scythes.

447 PENZ, T. Kleinboden, Tyrol, Manu.—An assortment of scythes.

448 WEINMEISTER, G. Spital-on-the-Pyhrn, Upper Austria, Manu.—Various scythes, of Innerberg, and cast-steel.

449 WEINMEISTER, J. Brühthal, Upper Austria, Manu.—An assortment of scythes.

450 ZEITLINGER, J. Spital-on-the-Pyhrn, Upper Austria, Manu.—Different kinds of scythes.

451 ZEITLINGER, J. A. Eppenstein, Styria, Manu.—Different kinds of scythes.

452 ZIMMERMANN'S, B. HEIRS, Mairhofen in the Zillerthal, Tyrol, Manu.—An assortment of scythes.

453 FELDBAUMER, P. Trofajach, Styria, Manu.—Various kinds of pickaxes, hatchets, axes, saws, &c.

454 LOBKOWITZ, Prince F. VON, Miknitz, Styria.—Various kinds of shovels and hoes.

455 SCHMIDLEHNER, J. Neuzeug, near Stadt Steyer, Manu.—Various hatchets.

456 DUBSKY, Count, Eissitz, Moravia.—Various kinds of iron-wire tacks, and ornamental wire tacks for decoration, &c.

457 ERNST, P. Stadt Steyer, Upper Austria, Manu.—Brads (shoe-nails), assorted.

458 FALENT, M. Stadt Steyer, Manu.—Various kinds of forged nails.

459 SANDERL, L. Stadt Steyer, Manu.—Iron nails of different kinds, made by machinery.

460 VINGERT, A. Stadt Steyer, Manu.—Brads (shoe-nails), assorted.

461 WEIDL, M. Stadt Steyer, Manu.—An assortment of nails made by machinery.

462 HAILER, A. Neuzeug, near Stadt Steyer, Manu.—Brass rings of different kinds.

463 KRONOWITHER, J. Neuzeng, near Stadt Steyer, Manu.—Pinchbeck rings of different kinds.

464 POIGER, F. Stadt Steyer, Manu.—German-silver rings of different kinds.

465 KURG, C. Stadt Steyer, Manu.—Various iron chains for horses.

466 KOLLER, F. Steinbach, near Stadt Steyer, Manu.—Curry-combs of different kinds.

467 MITTERBERGER, J. Sierninghofen, near Stadt Steyer.—Shoe tips and heels.

468 RING, J. Neuzeug, near Stadt Steyer, Manu.—Steels for striking lights, of different kinds.

469 GRABNER, F. Molln, near Stadt Steyer, Manu.—Jew's harps, of brass and iron.

470 SCHWARZ, C. Molln, near Stadt Steyer, Manu.—Jew's harps.

471 SCHWARZ, F. sen. Molln, near Stadt Steyer, Manu.—Jew's harps.

472 SCHWARZ, F. jun. Molln, near Stadt Steyer, Manu.—Jew's harps.

473 SCHWARZ, I. Molln, near Stadt Steyer.—Jew's harps.

474 BLUMAUER, W. Stadt Steyer, Manu.—Bells for horses, of different kinds.

475 TOMASCHITZ, J. Veldes, Upper Carniola, Manu.—Bells of various kinds for cattle; used among the Alpine agriculturists of Tyrol, Styria, Carinthia, and Carniola.

476 PFLEIDERER, J. Stadt Steyer, Manu.—Scales (balances) of brass.

477 STRUNZ'S, J. Widow, Vienna, Manu.—Samples of pins and needles.

478 CASSEL, J. Vienna, Manu. — Shot-bags, powder-flasks, powder-measure, percussion-cap cases, hunting-pipe, fox-traps, lucifer-match boxes, travelling lucifer-match boxes, writing utensils, &c.

479 BUCHBERGER, J. Stadt Steyer, Manu.—Awls of different kinds.

480 DERFLER, J. Neuzeug, near Stadt Steyer, Manu.—Awls of different kinds.

481 DILTSCH, J. Stadt Steyer, Manu.—Awls of different kinds.

482 HANSER, J. Stadt Steyer, Manu.—Drills for wood, of different kinds.

483 KETTENHUBER, J. Stadt Steyer, Manu.—Awls of different kinds.

484 KOLM, J. Stadt Steyer, Manu.—Awls of different kinds.

485 METZ, G. Stadt Steyer, Manu.—Drills for wood, of different kinds.

486 MOLTERER, C. Sierninghofen, near Stadt Steyer. Manu.—Awls of different kinds.

487 MOLTERER, C. Neuzeug, near Stadt Steyer, Manu.—Awls of different kinds.

488 MOLTERER, G. Stadt Steyer, Manu.—Awls of different kinds.

490 MOLTERER, M. Taolmat, Stadt Steyer, Manu.—Awls for shoemakers and saddlers.

491 MOLTERER, V. Neuzeug, near Stadt Steyer, Manu.—Awls of different kinds.

492 NORTHHAFT, F. Neuzeug, near Stadt Steyer.—Awls of different kinds.

493 REINDL, J. Stadt Steyer, Manu.—Drills for wood, of different kinds.

494 TEUFLMAYER, C. Stadt Steyer, Manu.—A vice and a screw-plate.

495 BEYER, A. Stadt Steyer, Manu.—An assortment of files.

496 LECHNER, M. Stadt Steyer, Manu.—Files of different kinds.

497 NUSSBAUMER, L. Stadt Steyer, Manu.—Files, assorted.

498 PREITLER, M. Stadt Steyer, Manu.—Files of different kinds.

499 REICHEL, J. Stadt Steyer, Manu.—Files of different kinds.

500 SONNLEITHNER, A. Stadt Steyer, Manu.—Files of different kinds.

501 UNZEITIG, F. Stadt Steyer, Manu.—Files and rasps of various kinds.

502 VATER, F. Neuzeug, near Stadt Steyer, Manu.—Files of different kinds.

503 ALSTERBERGER, J. Stadt Steyer, Manu.—Knives and forks of different kinds.

504 BAUER, J. Steinbach, near Stadt Steyer, Manu.—Pocket-knives of different kinds.

505 BLEY, J. Stadt Steyer, Manu.—Razors of different kinds.

506 BRESILMAIER, J. Stadt Steyer, Manu.—Razors of different kinds.

507 BUBENITSCH, J. Hermannstadt, Transylvania, Manu.—Garden knives. Pistol and knife belonging to the Romanian national costume.

508 DAUCHER, S. Untergrünburg, near Stadt Steyer, Manu.—Knives and forks of different kinds.

509 DERNBERGER, F. Grunberg, near Stadt Steyer, Manu.—Garden-knives of different kinds.

510 DIETZL, M. Sierninghofen, near Stadt Steyer, Manu.—Table-knives of different kinds.

511 DOPPLER, A. Sierninghofen, near Stadt Steyer, Manu.—Knives and forks of different kinds.

512 FÖRSTER, L. Neuzeug, near Stadt Steyer, Manu.—Knives of different kinds.

513 FREUKNER, A. Sierninghofen, near Stadt Steyer, Manu.—Table-knives of different kinds.

514 FRÖHLICH, C. Steinbach, near Stadt Steyer, Manu.—Pocket-knives of different kinds.

515 FRÖHLICH, J. Steinbach, near Stadt Steyer, Manu.—Pocket-knives of various kinds.

516 GRUNWALD, J. Neuzeug, near Stadt Steyer, Manu.—Table-knives of different kinds.

517 HAINDL, A. Stadt Steyer, Manu.—Knives and forks of different kinds.

518 HELM, A. Sierninghofen, near Stadt Steyer, Manu.—Knives of different kinds.

519 HOFER, P. Sierninghofen, near Stadt Steyer, Manu.—Table knives of different kinds.

520 KALTENMARK, P. Linz, Manu.—Razors, and an assortment of knives and scissors.

521 KERBLER, J. Sierninghofen, near Stadt Steyer, Manu.—Table-knives of different kinds.

522 KRANAWETTER, J. Neuzeug, near Stadt Steyer, Manu.—Knives of various kinds.

523 LICHTL, J. Stadt Steyer, Manu.—Knives and forks of different kinds.

524 LIEDER, F. Stadt Steyer, Manu.—Knives and forks of different kinds.

525 LÖSCHENKOHL, C. Frattenbach, near Stadt Steyer, Manu.—Knives of different kinds.

526 LÖSCHENKOHL, J. Steinbach, near Stadt Steyer, Manu.—Pocket-knives of various kinds.

527 MADERBOECK, M. Steinbach, near Stadt Steyer, Manu.—Pocket-knives of various kinds.

528 MILLER, R. Steinbach, near Stadt Steyer, Manu.—Pocket-knives of various kinds.

529 MITTER, J. sen. Stadt Steyer, Manu.—Hunting knives and swords of different kinds.

530 MITTER, J. Stadt Steyer, Manu.—Knives and scissors of different kinds.

531 MOSER, A. Sierninghofen, near Stadt Steyer, Manu.—Pocket-knives of different kinds.

532 MOSER, A. Steinbach, near Stadt Steyer, Manu.—Penknives of different kinds.

533 MOSER, C. Steinbach, near Stadt Steyer, Manu.—Knives and forks of different kinds.

534 MOSER, F. Steinbach, near Stadt Steyer, Manu.—Knives of different kinds.

535 MOSER, G. Sierninghofen, near Stadt Steyer, Manu.—Pocket-knives of different kinds.

536 MOSER, J. Steinbach, near Stadt Steyer, Manu.—An assortment of knives.

537 MOSER, J. Sierninghofen, near Stadt Steyer, Manu.—Table-knives of different kinds.

538 OSTERBERGER, L. Stadt Steyer, Manu.—Knives of different kinds.

539 PIELER, J. Neuzeug, near Stadt Steyer, Manu.—Knives of different kinds.

540 PILSS, C. Neuzeug, near Stadt Steyer, Manu.—Knives and forks of different kinds.

541 PILLSS, F. Neuzeug, near Stadt Steyer, Manu.—Knives of different kinds.

542 PILSS, G. Sierninghofen, near Stadt Steyer, Manu.—Pocket-knives of different kinds.

543 PILSS, M. Neuzeug, near Stadt Steyer, Manu.—Knives and forks of different kinds.

544 PESSL, G. Sierninghofen, near Stadt Steyer, Manu.—Knives of different kinds.

545 PICHLER, J. Sierninghofen, near Stadt Steyer, Manu.—Table-knives of different kinds.

546 J. PFUSTERSMIDT, J. Neuzeug, near Stadt Steyer, Manu.—Table-knives of different kinds.

547 RAPP, M. Stadt Steyer, Manu.—Table-knives of different kinds.

548 RESSL, J. Steinbach, near Stadt Steyer, Manu.—Knives of various kinds.

549 RESSL, M. Steinbach, near Stadt Steyer, Manu.—Knives of different kinds.

550 RIEDLER, J. Neuzeug, near Stadt Steyer, Manu.—Knives and forks of different kinds.

551 RIEDLER, L. Stadt Steyer, Manu.—Knives and forks of different kinds.

552 RÖSLER, I. Nixdorf, Bohemia.—An extensive assortment of razors, knives, and scissors.

553 RUPPRECHT, S Stadt Steyer, Manu.—Razors of different kinds.

554 SALZWIMMER, P. Sierninghofen, near Stadt Steyer, Manu.—Table-knives of different kinds.

555 SCHINDLER, S. Steinbach, near Stadt Steyer, Manu.—Knives of different kinds.

556 SCHWINGHAMMER, S. T. Steinbach, near Stadt Steyer, Manu.—Pocket-knives of various kinds.

557 STIERHOFER, A. Stadt Steyer, Manu.—Knives and forks of different kinds.

558 STIERL, J. jun. Stadt Steyer, Manu.—Scissors of different kinds.

559 STUCKHART, J. Stadt Steyer, Manu.—Knives and forks of different kinds.

560 VOITH, A. Sierninghofen, near Stadt Steyer, Manu.—Cutlery of different kinds.

561 WACHTER, L. Stadt Steyer, Manu. — Razors of different kinds.

562 WEICHSELBAUMER, J. Neuzeug, near Stadt Steyer, Manu.—Knives and forks of different kinds.

563 WEICHSELBAUMER, M. Sierninghofen, near Stadt Steyer, Manu.—Knives of various kinds.

564 TEVFELMEYER, J. Untern Himmel, near Stadt Steyer, Manu.—A variety of surgical instruments.

565 BACHNER, F. Stadt Steyer, Manu.—An assortment of shoemakers' tools.

567 GROSSAVER, A. Stadt Steyer, Manu.—A variety of shoemakers' tools.

568 GROSSAVER, F. Stadt Steyer, Manu.—An assortment of shoemakers' tools.

569 KLEMENT, F. Stadt Steyer, Manu.—An assortment of tools of steel, for cabinet-makers, carriage-builders, carpenters, &c.

570 SAILER, J. Stadt Steyer, Manu.—Various tools of steel.

571 WELZIGBACH, K. Stadt Steyer, Manu.—Tools of steel, assorted.

572 WEISS, J. & SON, Vienna, Manu.—Assortment of cabinet-makers', coopers', and carriage-makers' tools.

573 WERTHEIM, F. Vienna and Scheibbs, Lower Austria, Manu.—An extensive variety of cabinet-maker's, cooper's, carriage-makers', leather-dressers', and turners' tools.

574 BRUNNER, A. Vienna, Manu.—Samples of compass saws.

575 BAECHER, A. B. Prague, Manu.—Embossed silver-ware: cups, goblets, saltcellars, bread-baskets, oil and vinegar-cruets, sets of knives, forks, and spoons; inkstands, &c.

576 GROHMANN, H. Prague, Manu.—Gold trinkets. Set of Bohemian garnets.

577 RATZERSDORFER, H. Vienna, Manu.—A toilet-glass of massive wrought and embossed silver, weighing 135 ounces.

578 WIEN, L., Prague, Manu.—Set of chessmen, wrought in fine silver.

579 BERG, F. Prague, Manu.—Various articles of bronze: group of horsemen; two candelabra; cups; centre-pieces; drawing-room lamps, &c.

580 BRÖSE, W., Vienna, Manu.—Two chandeliers of bronze, gilt, ornamented with porcelain.

581 HOLLENBACH, D. Vienna, Manu.—Two gilt bronze candelabra.

582 ABELE, F. Neuhurkenthal, Bohemia, Manu.—A mirror, cut in facets, 88 inches high, 43 inches wide.

583 THE MIRROR MANUFACTORY, Viehofen, in Lower Austria, and St. Vincez, in Carinthia.—A blown mirror, 84 inches high, and 42 inches wide.

584 BUQUOY, Count, Schwarzthal and Silberberg, Bohemia, Manu.—Flower vases and inkstands of red hyalite glass. Etrurian vases, pen-trays, and paper-weights of wavy hyalite glass. Vases, dinner service, jugs of ruby glass, flagons of chrome-green glass, bottles, coffee-cups, flower-glasses, goblets of white and enamelled porcelain glass.

585 CZERMAK, P. Prague, Manu.—Glass ware: Flower and chimney vases, fruit-dishes, bottles and flagons, sugar-basins, toilet-bottles.

586 GROHMANN, J. Kreibitz, Bohemia, Manu.—Glass ware: Alabaster flower-vases, centre-piece, flagons with gold ornaments, candlesticks.

587 HARRACH, F. E., Count VON, Neuwelt, Bohemia, Manu.—Glass ware: Vases, jugs, flagons. Wine bottles, goblets, cups. Large candelabra, lustres.

588 HEGENBARTH, A. Musterdorf, Bohemia, Manu.—Various glass goblets.

589 HELMICH, F. A. Wolfersdorf, Bohemia, Manu.—Glass vessels: Flower and chimney vases; butter-dishes; candlesticks; flagons; decanters; sugar-basins, &c. Samples of glass beads, artificial precious stones and bugles.

590 HOFMAN, N. W. Prague, Manu. (Agents, J. & R. McCRACKEN, 7 Old Jewry, London.)—Glass ware: Two large alabaster vases, 7 feet high; other vases, flagons, &c.

591 JANKE BROTHERS, Blottendorf, Bohemia, Manu.—Glass ware: Flower vases, goblets, centre-pieces, flagons, decanters, &c.

592 KITTL'S, HEIRS ANT., Kreibitz, Bohemia, Manu. (Agent, W. MIERSTEIN, 15 Watling St. London.)—Different kinds of glass. Flower vases, with various ornaments.

593 KUCHINKA, F. Katharinenthal, Hungary, Manu.—Goblets, decanters, national cups, liqueur-glasses, &c.

594 LÖTZ, Widow, & GERSTNER, Defferink, Bohemia, Manu.—Centre-pieces, flower vases, flagons, cups; wine and liqueur decanters, &c.

595 MEYR's NEPHEWS, Adolf and Leonorenhain, Bohemia, Manu.—Glass flower vases, of various kinds and sizes; centre-pieces, candelabra, sugar-basins, jewel-stands, milk-jugs, jugs, candlesticks, decanters, &c.

596 KÖNIG, F. P. Steinschönau-Bohemia, Manu.—Centre-piece, fruit-dishes, sugar-basins, dessert-plates, &c.

597 PELIKAN, I. Meisterdorf, Bohemia, Manu.—Glass goblets with cover.

598 VIVAT, B. Langerswald and Benedictthal, Styria, Manu.—Assortment of articles of crystal glass. Various coloured, cut, engraved, embossed, and gilt glasses.

599 ZAHN, J. sen. Steinschönau, Bohemia, Manu.—A centre-piece, glass goblets, flower-vases, flagons, &c.

600 BIGAGLIA, P. (late LORENZO BIGAGLIA), Venice. (Agents, Fordati, Coxhead, and Co. 13 Old Jewry Chambers, London.)—Cast-glass stained window frames. Enamelled stones, artificial precious stones, mosaics of artificial Aventurine for table-tops, and also in separate pieces.

601 BLASCHKA & SONS, Liebenan, Bohemia, Manu.—Paste, for artificial precious stones, beads, glass buttons, lustre pendants.

602 FRANKE, J. Kamnitz, Bohemia, Manu.—Hair ornaments: Breast-pins, brooches, and miscellaneous articles of glass.

603 PAZELT, A. Turnau, Bohemia, Manu.—Assortment of artificial stones of glass, cut.

604 PFEIFFER, A. F., Neudorf, near Mormenstern, Bohemia, Manu.—Paste for artificial precious stones, of different colours and designs.

606 PFEIFFER, J. & Co. Gablonzj, Bohemia, Manu. (Agent, O. FRAUENKNECHT, 80 Bishopsgate St. Within, London.)—Cut-glass buttons; glass breast-pins and brooches. Artificial stones. Beads, chandelier pendants, and fancy glass.

607 SANDER, P. Gablonz, Bohemia, Manu. — Assortment of beads, glass buttons, and artificial stones. Rings and ear-rings, breast-pins, hair-pins, brooches, flagons, &c.

608 SCHWEFEL, A. Vienna, Manu.—Artificial human eyes of glass.

609 SPIETSCHKA, V. Liebenau, Bohemia, Manu. (Agent, C. HOLLAND, 41 Finsbury Circus, London.)—Beads, pins and hair ornaments; bead necklaces, and other articles in glass and jewellery. Sample-book with drawings of chandelier drops, light rosettes, flagons, &c.

610 MIESBACH, A. Vienna and Pesth, Manu.—Bricks, roofing-tiles, and draining-tiles of clay, from Ingersdorf, near Vienna, and Rakos, near Pesth. Hollow bricks for building arches, made by machinery. C. M. Miesbach employs in his various establishments 4,220 persons, and manufactures annually, more than 107 millions of bricks.

611 PARTSCH, A. jun. Theresienstadt, Lower Austria, Manu.—Various samples of clay tobacco-pipes.

612 BAHR & MARESCH, Aussig on the Elbe, Bohemia, Manu.—Syderolite ware: Flower-vases, baskets, figures, fruit-dishes, pier tables, candlesticks, jugs, centre-pieces, &c. of clay.

613 HUFFZKY, VINCENZ (Widow), Hohenstein, near Teplitz, Bohemia, Manu.—Terralite ware: Flower-pots, centre-pieces, cups, milk-jugs, &c. of clay.

614 SCHILLER & GERBING, Bodenbach, near Tetschen on the Elbe, Bohemia, Manu.—Syderolite ware: Centre-pieces, flower-vases, hunting and wine jugs, inkstands, butter-dishes, tea and coffee pots, &c. of clay.

615 IMPERIAL PORCELAIN MANUFACTORY, Vienna.—Vases; dinner service; fruit, bread, and ice baskets, of porcelain. A table and various paintings.

616 BAGATTI-VALSEICHI, B. Milan.—Encaustic paintings on earthenware, porcelain, enamel, and glass.

617 FISCHER, C. Pirkenhammer, Bohemia, Manu.—Dinner, tea, and coffee services, vases, toilet service, inkstands, fruit-dishes, figures, &c. of porcelain.

H 4

618 FISCHER, M. Herend, Hungary, Manu. — Vases; dinner, tea, and coffee services; candlesticks, &c. of porcelain.

619 HAAS, A. Schlaggenwald, Bohemia, Manu.—Vases, tea and dinner services, fruit-baskets, &c. of porcelain.

620 HAIDINGER BROTHERS, Elbogen, Bohemia, Manu.— Dinner, coffee, and tea service, portable service, tea-caddy, bread-baskets, writing materials, milk-pots, &c. of porcelain. Chemical apparatus of porcelain.

621 HARDMUTH, L. & C. Budweis, Bohemia, Manu.— Dinner services; coffee and tea services of earthenware. Earthenware vessels, for chemical manufactories.

622 HUBNER, J. Gablonzj, Bohemia.—Porcelain pipe-bowls, painted. A painting: Varus, the Roman general, throwing himself upon his sword in the Teutonic forest.

623 KRIEGEL & Co. Prague, Manu.—Vases, dinner, tea and coffee service, figures, busts, inkstands, &c. of porcelain.

624 MINITZEK, Count S. VON, Frain, Moravia, Manu.— Vases, centre-pieces, coffee and tea pots, plates, chamber candlesticks, &c. of earthenware.

625 NOWOTNY, A. Alt-Rohlau, near Carlsbad, Bohemia, Manu.—Tea and coffee services of stoneware. Vases, flower-pots, dinner and coffee sets, and figures, of porcelain.

626 PORTHEIM, A. P. & SON, Unter Kodau, Bohemia, Manu.—Porcelain centre-piece and dinner service ; tea and coffee services, bread-baskets, dessert-plates, vases, and ink-stands. Assortment of figures, &c.

627 QUAST, J., Painter, Prague.—Painted porcelain vase and plate. A painting, The Last Judgment.

628 ZASCHA, J. Vienna, Painter.—Painting on porcelain: Madonna, after Carlo Dolce.

629 BATKA, W. Prague, Bohemia, Manu.—Two sets of chemists' and druggists' shelves and drawers.

630 COLOMBO, G. Milan, Manu.—A round inlaid table.

631 GRÖGER, F. Vienna, Manu.—Closet of ebony, with ornaments of stone mosaic. Work-box, with malachite and ivory ornaments.

632 KNILL, J. Vienna, Manu.—Billiard-table, with balls and cues.

633 LEISTLER, C. & SON, Vienna, Manu.—Four rooms, including dining-room, drawing-room, ladies' library, and bed room, with inlaid floorings and completely furnished, from drawings by Mr. Bernardo de Bernardis, the architect. The fringe, tassels, and gimp to the furniture made by Franz Huber, of Vienna. A Gothic bookcase presented to her Majesty the Queen by his Majesty the Emperor of Austria, designed by B. Bernardis and J. Kranner of Vienna.

634 LECHNER, F. Vienna, Manu.—Fauteuil of walnut. Oak balzac seat.

635 MENTASTI, B. Varese, Lombardy, Manu.—Oblong square table, with inlaid work representing Napoleon crossing Mount St. Gothard. A prie-Dieu, with inlaid work. Various specimens of cornices in marble.

636 MOSCHINI, P. Cremona, Manu.—A writing-desk and table. A lady's toilet-table, covered with leather, and inlaid. A small cabinet table.

637 PALHUEBER, V. Vienna, Manu.—Work-table. A wall basket, inlaid.

638 RIETSCH, F. G. Vienna, Inv.—Model of a ship-table.

639 ROSANI, P. Brescia, Manu.—A secretaire of American maple, with inlaid work. A small inlaid table.

640 STAUDINGER, A. Vienna, Manu.—Furniture : Buhl table of rosewood, book-shelves, sofa, chairs, &c.

641 THONET, M. Vienna, Manu. — Furniture: Sofas, easy-chairs, arm-chairs. Stand of rosewood and walnut wood. A small round inlaid table of rosewood. Specimens of inlaid floorings.

642 KLANNER, F. Vienna, Manu.—Different kinds of fancy cabinet work : Tea-caddies, sugar-boxes, work-boxes, reading-desks, travelling looking-glasses, candle-screens.

643 BECKER & KRONICK, Vienna, Manu.—Screen of japanned wood. Fire-screen covered with papier-maché. Papier-maché tables and cups. Cups of japanned tin. Two vases, designed by M. de Bernardis, architect.

644 HOFRICHTER, C. Reichenau, Bohemia, Manu. — Papier-maché tobacco-boxes; spice and sugar-boxes; sewing-cushions, &c.

645 BEHR, C. Prague, Bohemia, Pat. & Manu. — A column, a pedestal, and a box, as samples of artificial marble. Samples of gilt wood, which will bear washing.

645A KÖLBEL, B. Carv. & Gild. Vienna.—A gilt wooden frame for looking glass or picture. Specimens.

646 AFH, F. Vienna, Manu.—A flower-screen of bamboo and cane. A stand for a figure and flowers. Designed by M. de Bernardis.

647 FRANZONY, A. St. Wolfgang, Ischl, Upper Austria. —Flower-table.

648 MELZER, G. Krems on the Danube.—A wall-basket of various kinds of bark.

649 PAULLER, J. & SON, Vienna, Gilders. — Picture-frames ; sconces; gilt-wood.

650 POLT, A. Vienna, Gilder.—Prie-Dieu altar in old gothic style.

651 SPOERLIN & ZIMMERMANN, Vienna, Manu.—Paper-hangings, ceilings, and borders. Illustrations of machinery and parts of machinery, for the use of schools. Paper-hangings, prints.

652 HALLERS, J. Widow and Son-in-Law, Vienna, Manu. —Toys of paper, wood, metal, &c.

653 KIETAIBL, F. Vienna, Manu.—Toys of wood, metal, paper, &c. Musical boxes.

654 MULLER, C. A. Oberleutensdorf, Bohemia, Manu.— Toys of paper, wood, metal, &c.

655 PURGER, J. B. Gröden, Tyrol, Manu.—Carvings in pine, lime, maple, &c. such as lay figures, from the smallest to the largest size. Figures and toys.

656 FALLER, FRITSCHELLER, & Co. Vallonara, near Bassano, Manu.—Straw hats.

657 TANDLER, S. Zinnwald, Töplitz, Bohemia.—Specimens of straw plaiting and straw flowers.

658 KUMPF, I. Schluckenau, Bohemia, Manu.—Wicker table mats (spadrilles), hats, &c.

659 WUNSCHE, A. Altehrenberg, near Rumburg, Bohemia, Manu.—Wicker table-mats (spadrilles). Chip caps, &c.

660 BIONDEK, M. Baden, Vienna, Prod.—Scented agriot cherry-tubes for tobacco-pipes, sticks, &c.

661 LANG, F. Vienna, Prod.—Odoriferous cherry-tubes for tobacco-pipes, sticks, &c.

662 PARTSCH, A. jun. Theresienfeld, Lower Austria, Manu.—Odoriferous cherry-sticks for tobacco-pipe tubes.

663 TRENNER, J. Baden, Vienna, Prod.—Agriot cherry-sticks. Odoriferous cherry-sticks for pipe-tubes, sticks, &c.

664 ALBA, S. Vienna, Manu.—Cigar mouth-pieces of wood, bone, meerschaum and amber. Meerschaum tobacco-pipe bowls. Tobacco-pipe tubes and mouth-pieces. Amber mouth-pieces.

665 ARRER, J. Vienna, Manu.—Mother-o'-pearl buttons.

666 ASTRATH, C. Vienna, Manu.—Cigar-holders of meerschaum and amber.

667 BEISIEGEL, P. Vienna, Manu.—Fancy turnery: sticks. Tobacco-pipes and cigar-holders of meerschaum, amber, mother-o'-pearl and horn. Tobacco-pipe bowls of meerschaum.

668 DREHER, A. Vienna, Manu.—Ivory figures and chess-men. Tortoiseshell and horn snuff-boxes. Rosewood and horn ink-stands. Billiard balls. Set of salad-knives and forks of ivory, and similar turnery of mother-o'-pearl, horn, ivory, tortoiseshell, and wood. A crucifix, and various figures.

669 ENSTALLER, G. Stadt Steyer, Manu.—Styrian tobacco-pipe bowls of wood.

670 FLOGE, G. Vienna, Manu.—Wood, amber, and meerschaum cigar-holders, and tobacco-pipe tubes. Assortment of meerschaum tobacco-pipe bowls. Chess-board of ivory with figures.

671 FRIEDRICH, J. Vienna, Manu.—Cigar mouth-pieces of meerschaum and amber, with letters, figures, &c.

672 GRUNHUT, A. sen. Prague, Manu.—A meerschaum pipe; cigar mouth-piece; cigar-pipe.

673 GRUNHUT, J. jun. Prague, Manu.—A meerschaum tobacco-pipe. A cigar mouth-piece and a cigar-pipe.

674 GRUNHUT, W. Prague, Bohemia, Manu.—Meerschaum pipes and cigar mouth-pieces.

675 HARTMANN, L. Vienna, Manu.—Various kinds of walking-sticks, of wood, cane, &c. Stick-mountings. Tobacco-pipe tubes. Cigar-holders of wood, amber, meerschaum, and horn. Pipe mouth-pieces. Tobacco-pipe bowls of meerschaum, Turkish clay-pipes. Assortment of cut cameos. A tobacco-pipe of ivory. A cup of stag-horn. A large piece of amber.

676 INFANGER, M. Stadt Steyer, Upper Austria, Manu.—Styrian hunting tobacco-pipes, bowls of wood.

677 KRAFTL, J. Vienna, Manu.—Pocket ink-stands, of various kinds of wood. Pen-holders of bone and wood; and similar turnery.

678 LITSCHKE, C. Vienna, Manu. — Cigar-holders of meerschaum, amber, wood, horn, &c. Tobacco-pipe tubes and mouth-pieces.

679 FRANZ, L. Vienna, Manu.—Various kinds of walking-sticks, of wood and cane. Walking-stick pipes.

680 NAGL, L. Vienna, Manu.—Cigar mouth-pieces of meerschaum and amber. Tobacco-pipe tubes.

681 PFEIFFER, L. Vienna, Manu.—Different kinds of walking-sticks, of bone, walnut, cane, &c.

682 PFREGNER, F. A. Vienna, Manu.—Cigar-holders of various kinds of wood, horn, bone, and cocoa-nut.

683 SIEVERS, E. Vienna, Manu. — Meerschaum and amber cigar mouth-pieces.

684 SCHWARZ, J. Vienna, Manu. — Medallions, pen-holders, needle-cases, thimbles, paper-knives, ink-stands, screens, watch-stands, and similar articles of mother-of-pearl.

685 TANTZ, A. Vienna, Manu.—An assortment of walking-sticks, of bardin, whalebone, cane, snake-wood, with carved and engraved handles of stag-horn, ivory, silver, &c.

686 WOJTECH, J. Vienna, Manu.—Pipe-tubes of wood, of various kinds.

687 ZEITLER, J. Vienna, Manu. — Tobacco-pipe and cigar holders. Bowls of meerschaum. Cigar mouth-pieces of amber, cocoa-nut, &c.

688 PETSCHACHER, A. Vienna, Pat. & Manu.—Elastic tobacco-pipe tubes of various kinds, made by machinery.

689 BEGSTEIGER, M. Sierning, Stadt Steyer, Manu.—Rules, of various kinds.

690 BUCHBERGER, F. Stadt Steyer, Manu.—Rules, of various kinds.

691 TOBER, J. Prague, Bohemia, Manu. — Rules, of various kinds.

692 TIFFE, A. Vienna, Manu.—Sticks for umbrellas and parasols, and mountings for the same.

693 ZANDRA, J. Vienna, Manu.—Sticks for umbrellas and parasols, and mountings for the same.

694 HERDT, J. B. Vienna, Manu.—Silk umbrellas and parasols.

695 RADEMACHER, C. Vienna, Manu.—Silk umbrellas.

696 RITTER, N. Vienna, Manu.—Hair-powder, chignon combs and brushes of horn, tortoise-shell, and ivory.

697 KRATSCHSMANN, M. Vienna, Pat. & Manu.—Agent, M. L. Kanitz & Sons.—Horn buttons for coats, waistcoats, trousers, &c.

698 METZNER, W. Vienna, Manu.—Coat, waistcoat, and shirt buttons, of mother-of-pearl and hoof-horn, in various forms and colours.

699 BITTNER, F. Neudorf, Bohemia, Manu.—Planes for joiners. Rods of wood for making lucifer-matches.

700 BUERGER, J. Vienna, Manu.—Artificial flowers of various kinds. Export articles.

701 SCHLATER, H. Vienna, Modeller.—Various kinds of wax figures and artificial flowers. Export articles.

701A OPPENHEIMER, CAROLINE, Vienna, Manu. — A lamp screen, cut by hand.

702 SERAFINO, PALATINI, & Co. Venice, Manu.—Twenty-five specimens of assorted masks.

703 GASSER, J. Vienna, Sculptor.—Venus bathing, in bronze. Four smaller figures, in bronze. Model of a fountain. Flower vase, cast in bronze and zinc.

704 KAEHSZMANN, J. Vienna, Sculptor.—Three statues, of Carrara marble, representing: A Shepherd, a Flower-girl, and Hebe with the Eagle.

705 MAX, E. Prague, Sculptor. — A group, in white Carrara marble, representing: Hagar and Ishmael. A bas-relief in Carrara marble: an Amazon on horseback.

706 CACCIATORE, B. Carrara, Prof. Sculptor.—Boy in a flower-basket.

707 COCCHI, L. Milan, Sculptor.—Statue in marble: The Virgin.

708 CROFF, G. Milan, Sculptor.—Statues in marble: Leda and the Swan. Danae awaiting the golden Shower. A group, representing Hermes and Salmacis.

709 EMANUELI, G. Milan, Sculptor.—Statue in marble: A boy with a bird's nest.

710 FRACCAROLI, I. Milan, Sculptor.—Two statues in marble: The wounded Achilles, and David slinging the stone. A group in marble: Atala and Chactas.

711 GALLI, A. Milan, Sculptor. — Three statues in marble: Susanna at the Bath; Jephtha's Daughter; and A Youth on the Sea-shore.

712 GANDOLFI, D. Milan, Sculptor.—Group in marble: The Emigrant. Episode in the history of France, in the year 1793. Tomb with figures in marble, representing Grief and Faith. A statue in plaster. Italy.

713 STRAZZA, —, Milan, Sculptor.—Statue in marble: Ishmael in the Desert. (Property of P. Gonzales, Milan.)

714 MAGNI, P. Milan, Sculptor. — Group in marble: The first Step.

715 MANFREDINI, G. Milan, Sculptor.—Statue in marble: Narcissus at the Fountain.

716 MARCHESI, L. Milan, Sculptor.—Statue in marble: Eurydice.

717 MICOTTI, I. Milan, Sculptor.—A statue in marble: Candour.

718 MOTELLI, M. Milan, Sculptor.—Group in marble: Cupid's Vintage.

719 DAL NEGRO, P. Milan, Sculptor.—Statue in marble: Innocence.

720 PIEROTTI, G. Milan, Sculptor.—Group in plaster: Mazeppa bound to the Horse An Arabian Horse attacked by a Serpent, in Carrara marble.

721 PUTTINASI, A. Milan, Sculptor.—Statue in marble: Prayer.

722 SANGIORGIO, A. Milan, Sculptor.—Statue in marble: A soul ascending to Heaven. (Property of J. R. Jaffray, Esq.) Hermes, in marble. The Saviour. The Poet Monti.

723 SOMAJNI, F. Milan, Sculptor.—Group in marble representing Pan and Syrinxa.

724 GOTTL, B. Carlsbad, Bohemia.—Two vases of Carlsbad thermal tufa, executed by Knoll Brothers, of Carlsbad, each 2 ft. 9 in. high, and 1 ft. 7 in. diameter.

725 BENZONI, G. Milan, Sculptor.—A mantelpiece in marble, with eight figures.

726 BOTTINELLII, G. Milan, Sculptor.—Three marble mantelpieces richly ornamented:—one, the property of D. Sopransi, of Milan, and a mirror frame. Model, in plaster of a mantelpiece.

728 Motelli, G. Milan, Sculptor.—A mantelpiece in marble. A group in marble: Paolo and Francesca di Rimini. Nest of Cupids.

729 Szentpeetrij, J. Pesth, Hungary.—(Agents, R. and J. Garrard & Co. Gold & Silversmiths & Jewellers, 31 Panton Street, and 25 Haymarket.)—A copper embossed tableau (in the possession of Henry Kirk, Esq. of St. James's Square), representing the Battle of Arbela, after Lebrun. It contains hundreds of figures in a relief of 3 inches, produced from a single sheet of copper, about an eighth of an inch thick, hammered and punched up with punches of various forms and sizes; the sheet of copper being passed through the fire hundreds of times to soften it and make it malleable. The artist, who is self-taught, was occupied on this extraordinary work five years. A tableau representing the capture of King Porus; with 217 figures embossed by hand on a plate of silver weighing 18 marks 3 ounces.

730 Petrowits, D. Vienna, Inv. & Sculptor.—Fifty-three medallions cast in a metallic composition by a newly-discovered method.

731 Cesari, D. Milan, Sculptor.—Three portraits of S. Romagnosi, A. Rolla, and Bertini, chiselled in the style of Benvenuto Cellini.

732 Fraener, G. B. Milan, Engraver.—Medal in bronze.

733 Zapparelli, G. Brescia, Engraver. — Various medals and dies. Embossed work, rings; sample-book.

734 Borrini, L. Milan, Painter.—A lay figure.

735 Dinkler, C. Vienna, Engraver.—Specimens engraving on wood and metal.

736 Geyling, C. Vienna, Painter on Glass.—Paintings on glass, representing: A church; a winter landscape in Upper Austria; view of Johannisberg, on the Rhine; view of the town-gate of Kremnitz, in Hungary.

737 Bertini, G. Milan.—Great painted window, representing Dante and some of his Ideas.

738 Montanari, A. Milan, Decorator.—Decoration for a vaulted ceiling of a library.

739 Vogel, C. F. Milan.—Photographs.

740 Pucher, J. Veldes, Upper Carniola. Inven.—Photographs on glass, a new discovery.

741 Bongiovanni, B. Vienna, Sculptor.—Design for a candelabrum.

742 Hartmann, L. Prague, Pat. and Desig.—Various designs for prints.

746 Monti, Raffaelle, Milan & 45 Great Marlborough Street, London, Des. and Sculp.—Statues in Carrara marble: Eve after the Fall. A Veiled Vestal. (Property of his Grace the Duke of Devonshire.) Statuettes, Ancient and Modern Love. (Property of B. Cohen, Esq.) Group representing Innocence. Statue, a Circassian Slave in the market. Group. Angelica and Medoro. Group of two Girls. (Property of an English gentleman.) Statuette of a Boy catching a Grasshopper. (Property of Th. Baring, Esq. M.P.)

747 Thompson, Miss, 35 Euston Sq. Prop.—A carpet worked by the late Ex-empress Marie Louise, assisted by the late Queen of Wurtemburg, the late Queen of Naples, and Madlle. Beauharnois. Originally intended as a present to Napoleon, but not completed until after his death.

748 Farina, John Maria, Cologne, on the Rhine, opposite the New Market, and (London) 52 Mark Lane.—(In the furniture room).—Fountain which plays eau-de-Cologne.

BELGIUM.

(Custom House Agent, C. J. Major, 21 Billiter St. City.)

1 Guillaume, J. A. Bovigny (Luxembourg).—Sample of hones.

2 Otte, J. Vielsalm (Luxembourg).—Hones of different sizes.

3 Lamberty, C. Vielsalm.—Samples of hones.

4 Offergeld, F. J. Vielsalm.—Samples of hones.

5 Collette Doucet, F. J. Bertin (Luxembourg).—Slate pencil. Whet stones. Slates for roofs.

6 Societe Anonyme des Hauts Fourneaux de Pommerueil, Pommerueil. —Cast-iron for moulding, Nos. 1, 2, 3, 4. Grey, mottled, and white cast-iron for refining.

7 Societe de la Nouvelle Montagne, Verviers.—Oxide of zinc. Zinc tiles. Roofs covered with zinc tiles. Sheet zinc. Pigs of soft lead.

8 St. Hubert, E. de, Bouvignes.—A horizontal mill stone. A perpendicular mill-stone. Fragments, samples of mill-stones.

9 Morimont, J. B. Wierde (Namur).—Mill-stones.

10 Fallon Pirn, J. B. Namur.—A block of black marble from the quarries of Grand's Malades, near Namur.

11 Eloin, F. Namur.—Safety lamps (Eloin system), large and small models. Trimmed glasses for lamps. Apparatus serving for lamps.

12 Tombelle, —, Bonneville (Namur).—Samples of china clay.

13 Petit, F. & Co. Auvelais (Namur).—Various samples of coal.

14 Gaiffier, Baron E. de, Meallein (Namur).—Samples of china clay.

15 De Ferrare, F. Wierde (Namur)—Plastic earth.

16 Desmanet de Biesme, Viscount C. Golzines (Namur).—Gozynino black polished marble pilaster.

17 Societe de Vedrin, Namur.—Samples of pyrites (bisulphuret of iron). Samples of galena. Samples of nicolattic lead.

18 Perard & Mineur, Couvin, Bouillon, and Liège. —Specimens of iron and iron ores.

19 Dethier, A. Theux (Liege).—Specimens of marble. Specimen of zinc ore. Specimen of raw zinc produced by this ore.

20 Behr, F. L. Seraing (Liege).—Raw pig iron.

21 Societe de Corphalie, Director M. E. Brixhe, Antheit (Liege).— Zinc ore. Blende and galena. Pig of lead. Laminated zinc. Zinc nails. Grey oxide of zinc.

22 Compagnie des Mines et Fonderies de Blyberg (Liège).—Samples of galena and blende. Pigs of lead.

23 De Hanseh, Liege.—Iron ore.

24 Museler, B. L. Liege.—Two safety lamps for mines.

25 Lamberty Brothers, Stavelot—Eighty samples of whet stones, of different sizes.

26 La Societe des Mines et Fonderies de Zinc de la Vieille Montague, Liege.—Specimens of zinc and other ores, and metals, and chemicals.

27 Societe des Hautes Fourneaux, Usines et Charbonnages de Chatelineau, Chatelineau (Hainault).—Five samples of coals.

28 Compagnie des Charbonnages de Pont de Loup, Pont de Loup (Hainault).—Specimens of bituminous coals.

29 Compagnie du Charbonnage de Boubier, the firm L. J. Maulaz & Co. Chatelet.—Non-bituminous coals. Half fat coals.

30 Delcourt, A. Director de la Société du Poiras, Montigny-sur-Sambre.—A sample of bituminous coal.

31 Dianet, S. Gilly (Hainault). — Two samples of bituminous coal.

32 Charbonnage d'Oignie Coal Mines (Director, — Wautelet), Charleroi.—Samples of bright sparkling coals.

33 De Rasse, A. Mons.—Samples of copper ore, from the copper mine of Rouveroy (Hainault).

34 Societe des Charbonnages Pire et Violetto, La Chartreuse-lez-Liege.—Two samples of coals.

35 Wouvermans, —, jun. Brussels.—Azure and mineral blues; varnish and polish.

36 Vloebergs, —, Brussels.—Haeca and dyes.

37 Cappellemans, J. B., Deby, A. & Co. Brussels.—Chemical products, glass, bottles, &c.

38 SOCIETE DE FLOREFFE, Floreffe (Namur).—Vessel containing anhydrous sulphate of soda, and other chemical preparations.

39 DEBBAUDT, —, Courtrai.—Pure white lead; cakes of white lead.

40 SOCIETE DES CHARBONNAGES ET HAUTS FOURNAUX D'OUGRÉE, Ougrée (Liège).—Metallic colours for painting.

41 COLDTERS, VAN ROY, Antwerp.—Composition for preserving against damp. Sarangousty oil. Sheets of paper for the same object.

42 BRASSEUR, E. Ghent.—Two samples of white lead.

43 HERINCK, F. Uccle (Brabant).—Rye.

44 VANDEN PORRE, J. Uccle (Brabant). — Winter wheat.

45 VANDEN ELST, F. Uccle (Brabant).—Oats.

46 VERHEYDEN, E. Dilbeck (Brabant).—Brown winter wheat and rye.

47 LEGRAS, A. Nederovenheembeek (Brabant).—Winter wheat, barley, and rye.

48 D'HUART DE VILLEMONT, Luxembourg. — Oats, horse beans, and buck wheat.

49 VAN OPHEN, Uccle (Brabant).—Buck wheat and winter barley.

50 PEEMS, Mme. H. Corbeck Look (Brabant).—White winter wheat.

51 D'HOLLANDERS, Moeryeke (West Flanders).—White and brown wheat; rye.

52 VANDEN ABEELE, L. Appels (West Flanders).—Hay.

53 PERDICUS, J. Herent (Brabant).— Brown winter wheat.

54 MINTEN, A. Louvain.—Brown winter wheat.

55 BARON MERTENS, Ostin (Namur).—Wheat, barley, oats, rye, and vetches.

56 COOSEMANS, M. Kesseloo (Brabant).—Brown winter wheat.

57 DE MULDER, —, Poesele (East Flanders).—Wheat.

58 DE MATHELIEU, —, Messancy (Luxembourg).—Wheat, rye, and barley.

59 VYVENS, —, Huysse (East Flanders). — Brown wheat.

60 STOBBELAERS, —, Moerzeke (West Flanders).—Winter rye.

61 COLLE, —, Lootenhulle (West Flanders).—Wheat.

62 DE HEUNHEUSE, —, Aye (Luxembourg).—Spelt.

63 DEGRYSE, L. Poperinghe.—Hops and blue and white peas.

64 DE QUIDT, Madame, Poperinghe.—Hops.

65 VAN MERRIS, Madame, Poperinghe.—Hops.

66 DELBAERE, Madame, Poperinghe.—White winter wheat.

67 FONTAINE, G. Brussels.—Solidified milk.

68 DOCQUIR, P. J. & J. PARYS, St. Josse-ten-Noode, near Brussels.—Potato flour bolted and unbolted, made from diseased potatoes. Animal black.

69 CLAVEREAU, J. BROTHERS.—Dinant cake, called "Conque de Dinant."

70 BILLIARD, L. Menin (West Flanders).—Tobacco in leaf, called "Wervicq."

71 PLAIDEAU, J. P. Menin (West Flanders).—Parcels of snuff; parcels of tobacco.

72 BROVELLIO, J. B. & Co. Menin.—Samples of snuff, tobacco, and chewing tobacco.

73 BOCKEN, HUBERT & Co. Liege.—Blue starch and white starch.

74 VAN BUNEN, Miss, Bruges.—Bolted and unbolted potato flour.

75 PEERS, Le Chevalier E. Ostcamp (West Flanders).—Several species of wheat; samples of rye, summer barley, and buck wheat.

76 BEHEYT, —, Rumbeke (West Flanders).—Winter barley, rye, wheat, brown and white, oats, and buck wheat.

77 WILLEMS, —, Hasselt.—Samples of wheat grown in 1850, rye, spelt, barley, oats, and buck wheat.

78 BLYCKAERT, G. Tirlemont.—A sack of potato flour, farina.

79 VERSCHAEVE, L. Ypres.—Belgian tobacco, called "Wervicq."

80 LAHOUSSE, A. Wervicq (West Flanders).—Belgian tobacco, called "Wervicq."

81 CLAUS & CARON, Ghent.—Candied and other sugars.

82 VERCAUTEREN, J. L. Zèle (East Flanders).—Two cakes of native linseed.

83 ROELS & Co. Lokeren.—Samples of peeled flax.

84 VANDESTRAETEN, F. Brussels.—Vegetable oil purified for lamps; linseed oil purified for painting.

85 CLAUDE, L. Brussels.—Vegetable oil purified for burning.

86 DE MEVIUS, C. Forrest, near Brussels.—Samples of raw and floss silk.

87 BISSE, L. E. Anderlecht, near Brussels.—Animal and vegetable oleine,.

88 LECLERCQ, J. F. Longchamps (Namur).—Samples of flax steeped and refined.

89 JOBART, A. Dinant.—Glue.

90 DEGRAEVE, D. Gheluwe (West Flanders).—Samples of peeled and green flax.

91 VERCRUYSSE BROTHERS, Courtrai. — Oil cakes. Cakes of linseed.

92 DEBBAUST, DELA CROIX, Courtrai.—A bottle of cabbage oil. The same purified.

93 BIHET, H. Huy (Liège).—Five cakes of glue.

94 HANSOTTE-DELLOYE, H. G. Huy (Liege).—Samples of glue.

95 BORTIER, P. Adinkerke (West Flanders).—Mineral manures.

96 LAVIOLETTE, DE MOOR, Bruges.—Peeled flax, steeped green. English mark N.

97 STUBBE & BACYE, Bruges.—Oak bark. Bark of young oak near Bruges.

98 DE BOE, D. Antwerp.—Flemish flax.

99 BRIERS, J. sen. Antwerp.—Glue, made by steam.

100 REUSENS, P. T. Antwerp.—Samples of copal varnish.

101 VAN DER SCHRIECK BROTHERS, Antwerp.—Samples of artificial wool.

102 VERHELST, F. Grimbergen (East Flanders).—Raw hemp. Peeled hemp, grown in 1850.

103 VAN RIET, PIERRE JEAN, Moerzeke (East Flanders).—Samples of raw hemp, grown in 1850.

104 DESMEDT & Co. Zele (East Flanders).—Samples of peeled flax. Samples of flax, dried with its seed, grown in 1850.

105 GILTA, J. L. Appels (East Flanders). — Samples of raw hemp, grown in 1850.

106 VAN HOEY, S. P. Hamme (East Flanders).—Six plats of peeled flax.

107 VAN BOGAERT, J. B. Grimbergen (East Flanders).—Samples of peeled flax. Samples of hemp, grown in 1850.

108 VERSTRAETEN, E. Ghent.—Vessels containing animal black.

109 LE CHEVALIER SOENENS, E. Swynarde, near Ghent.—Five fleeces of raw wool. Twenty-eight skins of combed wool. Samples of wool, spun by hand.

110 SEGHERS, B. Ghent. — Natural animal black. Animal black, in reversed grains. Powdered natural bone black. Ivory and powdered peach black from colours.

111 DEPOTTER, A. Audenarde.—Skeins of raw silk and cocoons.

112 DECONINCK, A. Ghent.—White and yellow silk

cocooned. Raw silk reeled into skeins. Sample of parcel silk, corded by way of trial by the Société Linière of Ghent. Samples of forest silk.

113 VERBEEK, P. F. Grimbergen (East Flanders).— Samples of dried and peeled flax, with its seed; grown in 1850.

114 VAN WIELL, J. B. Grimbergen (East Flanders).— Samples of flax steeped in stagnant waters, and of scutched flax; grown in 1850.

115 HAESE, B. Zele (West Flanders).—Samples of flax steeped and dried, with its seed; grown in 1850.

116 DEMAN, T. Brussels. — A carriage, called cab-phaeton.

117 MONTHNY, A. Brussels.—Leather strap for steam-engines.

118 JONES BROTHERS, Brussels. — Four carriages—a calosh, a phaeton patent cab, pony break, and buggy.

119 COCKERILL, J. Seraing (Liege). — Sample of foundry pig-iron. An expansive and condensing marine steam-engine of 140 horse-power. A locomotive engine. A high-pressure steam-engine of 16 horse power, with vertical cylinder. A high-pressure steam-engine of 3 horse-power, with tubular boiler. Model (scale 3 inches to the foot) of a machine for lowering and lifting miners without danger or fatigue.

120 SOCIETE ANONYME DES HAUTES FOURNEAUX MINES ET CHARBONAGES DE MARCINELLE ET COUILLET, Couillet (Hainault).—A railway locomotive and tender on Stephenson's plan. A ventilator for airing mines, but qualified also for airing theatres, prisons, &c. A pair of rough locomotive cylinders. Three rails. A locomotive wheel-tire. Thirty-three bars of wrought-iron. A piece of sheet-iron. Iron railway sleepers. A round bar of iron for fluted cylinders. Samples of nails. Samples of coals.

121 VAN AKEN, C. B. Antwerp.—A four-wheeled carriage.

122 VAN AKEN, P. & SON, Antwerp.—A carriage, called "cabriolet chaise."

123 JOUVNE, L. H. F. Molenbeck St. Jean (Brussels).— A fire ladder. A circular loom, for knitting wool, worsted, thread, cotton, and silk. A force-pump.

124 VAN GOETHEM, V. Lembercq (Brabant).—Apparatus for purifying and whitening loaf sugar, worked by centrifugal force. A centrifugal force apparatus, for purifying raw and refined powdered sugar, patented.

125 HOUYET, A. Brussels.—Machine for peeling and polishing rice; patented. Model of a machine for grinding pearled barley; patent. Model of an air-mill. Machine for peeling raw coffee. Steam chimney with interior tube. Flours, rice, Italian paste, semolina ground and peeled, barley starch, sea-biscuits, &c.

126 VANDEVIN, F. Brussels.—New spinning machine.

127 KESSELS, H. Brussels.—Brick-making machine.

128 TROUPIN, J. H. & J. P. Verviers. — A shearing finishing-machine.

129 FETU, A. & DELIEGE, J. Liege.—Cards for spinning wool.

130 HOUTTHAVE, S. Roulers.—Metallic combs.

131 DEBAUNE, U. Antwerp. — Irrigating machine for corn and seeds: patented. Machine for corn grinding. Ventilating apparatus.

132 MERTENS. C. Ghent (Antwerp).—A parallel iron vice, for holding pieces of metal to be worked by the file, chisel, &c.

133 VAN MIERLO, A. Antwerp.—Machine for making combs, &c.

134 SOCIETE DU PHENIX, Ghent (East Flanders).—Spinning machine. Willow engine, invented by the Société du Phénix.

135 GOUDEAU, —. Alost. — New arrangement of spinning apparatus. Invented by the exhibitor.

136 ZAMAN & Co. St. Josse-ter-Noode (Brussels). —

Model of paving stones, made use of in New Orleans. Stones with channels for pavements and house entries. Parisian paving stones.

137 VAN ESSCHEN, N. G. Molenbeck St. Jean (Brussels).—Model of an iron bridge, 40 feet long and 3½ wide. Models of iron tubes, for bridges and tunnels.

138 SIOEN, J. Ghent. — Ceiling laths. Oak cut into veneers.

139 JANSEN, A. Brussels.—Guns, rifles, and pistols. A target.

140 HENRARD, M. Namur.—A percussion rifle.

141 RENKIN BROTHERS, Liege.—Fowling pieces, pistols, &c.

142 ROYAL CANNON FOUNDRY (Director, Mr. C. Fredric, Colonel of Artillery), Liège.—A cannon of cast-iron prepared with coke and wood. Light Netherland-fashioned piece, Short Belgian model piece. Battery piece, rough. Country, or light howitzer, Belgian model, wood, cast-iron wood. Mortar, cast-iron, Belgian model. Bombs. An eccentric howitzer, Prussian model. Shot.

143 ANCION & Co. Liege.—Guns, muskets, pistols, rifles, and other weapons.

144 THONET, J. Liege.—Gun, ornamented with gilt silver. A pair of Scotch pistols, incrustated.

145 LEPAGE, —. Liege.—Complete collection of fire arms: Double-barrelled guns, rifles, holster pistols, duelling pistols, pocket pistols.

146 PLOMDEUR, N. Liege.—Guns and pistols. Guard for a gun.

147 MALHERBE, L. Liege.—Double-barrelled and other guns. Rifles, pistols, &c.

148 LEDENT, M. Liege.—A lock for all sorts of guns, patented in Belgium.

149 DOUTREWE, F. J. Liege.—A "needle" gun.

150 BERNIMOLIN, N. & BROTHERS, Liege.—Double-barrelled guns and pistols.

151 LARDINOIS, N. C. Liege.—Rifle with accessories, Swiss style; double barrelled, with accessories, made, except the barrel and locks, by Mr. C. Lenders.

152 TINLOT, M. Liege.—A double-barrelled gun, with stock carved style Louis XI.

153 DEHOUSSE, L. Liege.—Guns and pistols.

154 FALISSE & RAPMANN, Liege.—Arms and percussion-caps. Fire-arms. Rifles, guns, and pistols.

155 TOUREY, H. Liege.—Collection of fire-arms.

156 GROETAERS, Captain J. B. Antwerp.—Instrument for measuring inaccessible distances. Invented by the exhibitor.

157 NEYT, A. Ghent.—Drawing showing the plan of an artillery battery for firing, at pleasure, either directly or obliquely, applicable to frigates and coast batteries.

158 MONTIGNY & FUSNOT, Brussels. — Three infantry guns (Montigny system).

159 DUFOUR, —, Neufville (Hainault).—A plough, patented.

160 DENIS, J. B. St. Leger (Luxembourg).—Ploughs with patent moulds.

161 LE DOCTE, H. Henge.—Gardening instruments.

162 VERBIST, E. Nivelles.—Plough, called "tourneroielle."

163 CLAES, P. Lembecq (Brabant).—A Scotch seed-bag. A cast-iron roller, for rolling arable lands.

164 SCHEIDWEILER, M. Brussels.—A mill for agricultural seeds on a movable waggon. Invented by the exhibitor.

165 ROMEDENNE, A. Eapent (Namur).—An improved plough, and movable harrow.

166 DUCHENE, J. J. Assche-en-Rifail (Namur). — Churns. Buckets.

167 TRAIN, B. Huy (Liege).—Winnowing-machine for corn.

168 VAN MACLE, —, Thielt (West Flanders).—Double ploughs, patented.

169 ODEURS, J. M. Marlinne.—Double and single ploughs.

170 BERCKMANS, J. Blaesvelt.—A Flemish plough.

171 D'OMALIUS, G. Anthisnes (Liege).—A Belgian and other ploughs, and agricultural implements.

172 VALERIUS, B. Author, Brussels.—A treatise on the manufacture of iron.

173 VAN SCHENDEL, P. Brussels.—A model of descriptive geometry.

174 BERDEN, F. & Co. Brussels.—Cabinet pianos of six and a half octaves.

175 MAHILLON, C. Brussels.—Counterbass, violoncello, bugles, bass ophicleide, trombone, horn, trumpets, bugle-horn, clarionets.

176 JASTRZEBSKI, F. Brussels.—Six and three quarters and seven octave-upright pianos.

177 DARCHE, C. F. Brussels.—Violins : violoncellos.

178 COLONEL DEMANET, Ixelles (Brabant).—Machine for converting rectilinear into curvilinear motion.

179 VERHASSELT, D'OULTRELEPONT, F. Brussels.—Patent harmonium for churches, and for drawing-rooms. Piano-harmonium.

180 STERNBERG, L. Brussels.—Cabinet piano.

181 VOGELSANGS, F. J. Brussels.—Grand and upright pianos. Patented.

182 GERARD, A. J. Liege.—Pair of compasses. Twelve small alarm bells. Pen and inkstand. Plan of an instrument for measuring distances.

183 DE HENNAULT, J. B. Fontaine L'Evêque.—Level for levelling roads, &c. Compasses. Anemometer.

184 LATINIE, A. Saignies.—Spectacle and other glasses.

185 LAMBERT, G. Mons.—Model of a ladder for mines, Patented. Compasses, patented.

186 AERTS, F. G. Antwerp.—Patent piano, rosewood,

187 CHAMPAGNE, —, Donstiennes (Hainault).—Mechanical hand and arm, invented and made by the exhibitor.

188 DEFFAUX, —, Brussels.—Three pianos.

189 DE BAST, C. Ghent.—Calicoes : unbleached and bleached.

190 CANFYN, N. Renaix (West Flanders).—Checks and strips ; cotton checks ; Romal and Madras handkerchiefs.

191 DE BEHAULT DU CARMOIS, A. Termonde. — Cotton blankets.

192 DE CUYPER, J. F. St. Nicholas.—Common cotton checks, tickings, plaids, and woollen shawls.

193 JANSSENS, D. St. Nicholas.—Worked cross barred flannels ; fancy flannels ; woollen stuffs called gala plaids.

194 SIMONIS, J. Verviers.—Seven pieces of smooth cloth. One piece of black satin-de-laine. Two pieces of light black cloth.

195 BIOLLEY, F. Verviers.—Several pieces of smooth cloth, casimere, tweed, satin Berry.

196 DUBOIS, G. & Co. Verviers.—Winter and summer stuffs for trowsers and paletots.

197 SIRTAINE, F. Verviers—Satin-de-laine ; double warped cloth ; light cloth ; coloured cloths.

198 LEONARD, D. Verviers.—Four pieces of cloth.

199 PIRENNE & DUESBERG, Verviers. —Satin-de-laine and beaver cloth.

200 PIRON, T. Francomont.—Satin-de-laine and zephyr cloth.

201 OLIVIER & Co. Verviers.—Silk cloth for livery ; double-warped black cloth ; blue and bronze cloth.

202 SNOECK, C. J. Herve (Liege).—Pieces of zephyr and smooth cloth, woollen Cashmere, and satin-de-laine.

203 DE HESELLE, A. J. Theniester, near Verviers.—Pieces of flannel and dumet.

204 XHOFFRAY, C. & Co. Dolhain-Limbourg (Liege).—Worsted yarn.

205 VANDERSTRAETEN, A. & C. Liege. — Pieces of woollen stuffs, called " Black Cashmere," "Satin-de-laine," and " Satin-de-laine Marengo."

206 D'HONT, J. Roulers.—Various pieces of satin.

207 METDEPENNINGEN, G. Antwerp.—Silk of various descriptions.

208 DOBBELAERE, H. Ghent.—Six pieces of unbleached linen.

209 AMEYE-BERTE, R. Ghent.—Flax sail-cloths ; tow linen ; flax linen for sheets ; ordinary and common linen. Linen for bleaching fine.

210 PYN & VAN PELT, Tamise.—Samples of hemp thread, and hemp specially made use of for shoemakers' thread.

211 WILFORD, W. Tamise.—Sail-cloths.

212 COOREMAN, A. J. Rebecq (Brabant).—Samples of flax thread, made use of for the groundwork of Brussels lace. Samples of thread for lace.

213 VERCRUYSSE, F. Deerbyck, near Courtrai.—Raw, retted and heckled flax and linen.

214 VERRIEST, P. Courtrai.—Pieces of mattress covers.

215 VAN ACKERE, J. C. Wevelghem (West Flanders).—Linen and handkerchiefs. Retted flax. A bundle of staked, steeped, and unbleached staked flax ; a bundle of unbleached flax with seed.

216 BERTHELOT & BONTE, Courtrai.—Flax thread made by hand, called " fil de mulquinerie."

217 DUJARDIN, C. Courtrai.—Unbleached and bleached damask napkins. A napkin with the portrait of H. M. the King of the Belgians.

218 DEBRABANDERE, P. F. Courtrai.—Flax thread of various kinds.

219 VAN OOST, P. Hooghlede.—A piece of linen.

220 THIBAN-ACCOU, Iseghen (West Flanders). — A piece of white linen spun and woven by hand, having 7,000 threads in the warp.

221 DECOCK, W. Roulers.—Bleached and unbleached linen, Orleans, alpaca, and paramatas.

222 PARMENTIER, P. Iseghem (West Flanders).—Pieces of unbleached flax linen manufacture. White cambric handkerchiefs.

223 DEMEULENACRE, E. Moorslede (West Flanders).—Skeins of flax thread spun by hand and above No. 500.

224 HARTOG BROTHERS, Mechlin. — Pieces of Russian linen.

225 VAN NUFFEL & COVELIERS, Antwerp.—Canvas for painting. Oil-cloth carpet.

226 BOARD OF DIRECTION OF THE HOUSE OF CORRECTION AT ST. BERNARD, Antwerp.—Pieces of white Russian and cream-coloured and other linen.

227 MARYNEN VUES, Turnhaut (Antwerp).—Tickings.

228 HAEGENS, C. Zele (East Flanders). — Sail-cloths made of hemp, thread, and waste hemp.

229 BONGAERTS, F. A. Antwerp.—Linen bags without seams ; shooting pouch without seams.

230 THE GHENT LINIERE COMPANY, Ghent.—Flax, tow, and thread.

231 MOERMAN, V. L. Ghent.—Unbleached flax linen.

232 DE SMEDT, B. Alost.—Unbleached linens.

233 DOMMER, T. Alost.—Cambric handkerchiefs, napkins, table-cloths, unbleached and bleached linen, blinds, and carpet.

234 ELIAERT, C. Alost.—Bundles of Lisle thread for sewing (divers colours), and a collection of knitting thread.

235 CUMONT, D. Alost.—A collection of sewing threads, white and coloured.

236 VAN OVERLOOP, J. C. Zele (East Flanders).—Sail-cloths for ships, made of hemp thread, spun by hand.

237 GOENS, L. Termonde.—Flat hemp cable ; flat wire cable.

238 BOSTEELS-GEERINCK, J. Zele (East Flanders). — Pieces of sail-cloth made of waste hemp, woven by hand.

239 DEROUBAIX, H. Courtray. — Pieces of worked ticking and unbleached linen.

240 LEMAIRE-DESCAMPS, & PLISSART, Tournay.—Stuffs for trousers.

241 GILSON & BOSSUT, Tournay. — Various pieces of cotton and flax thread stuffs (plain and fancy) for trousers. Woollen thread and cotton for trousers and paletots.

242 LIENART-CHAFFAUX, Madame, Tournay. — Stuffs for trousers, &c.

243 VERHULST, DE RONGE, & Co. Brussels.—Pieces of common cotton checks and jaconet.

244 CATTEAUX BROTHERS, Brussels.—Stuffs for trousers; cotton flax thread; cotton and flax thread, and cotton and wool.

245 CATTEAUX, G. Courtray.—Stuffs for trousers, fine and mixed cotton. Two pieces of swan-skin, wool and cotton. Cotton checks and stripes. Cambric handkerchiefs. White linens.

246—250 PETIT NOEL, LEROUGE, DEMYTTENACRE, L. DUJARDIN, J. B. TERREIN, & Co. Mouscron.—Various stuffs for trousers: wool and cotton; cotton; and flax thread and cotton.

251 SCHELSTRAETE, L. Courtray.—Fine cotton stuffs, and cotton and flax thread for trousers.

252 VANDENBERGHE, J. Courtray.—Cotton stuffs; wool and cotton stuffs; cotton and flax thread stuffs.

253 HOUDIN & LAMBERT, Brussels.—Varnished calves' leather for boots and shoes.

254 TAILLET, V. Brussels.—Boot and shoe leather.

255 VAN MOLLE, E. Assche.—A plough horse-collar.

256 LADOUBEE, L. Brussels.—Harness, saddles, &c.

257 HAUSSENS-HAP, B. Vilvorde, near Brussels. — Horse-hair and aloe-fibre stuffing for furniture. Aloe-fibre stuffs, both sides alike. Table-cloths and napkins, &c. Samples of pigs' bristles prepared and bleached for painting brushes.

258 WEBER, G. Brussels.—Leather purses and cigar-cases.

259 WEINKNECHT, T. Brussels. — Drawing-room fur carpets. Furred cloaks. Foxes stuffed so as to serve for stools.

260 FASBENDER, H. J. Brussels. — Patent varnished hides. Half black and yellow skins for harness and bridles.

261 LOMBAER, J. B. Jette St. Pierre (Brabant).—Varnished calf skins for boots and shoes; skins of different colours for boots and shoes.

262 BAUCHAU DE BARE, A. Namur.—Tanned skins for soles, and pump buckets.

263 CABU-FEVRIER, F. Namur.—Boots, buskins, shoes, &c.

264 VAN TROOSTENBERGHE, Bruges.—A pair of shoes without seams.

265 SOMZE-MAHY, H. Liege.—Brushes for waxing and washing floors; sweeping brushes, and horse brushes. Patented. Samples of pigs' bristles; horsehair, tails, and manes.

266 BOUVY, A. Liege.—Grey and polished calf skins.

267 MASSON, C. Huy (Liege).—Sole leather.

268 SOMZE, J. Liege.—Brush for cannons. Brushes of several sorts.

269 VANSTRAELEN, J. Hasselt (Limbourg).—Gentleman's and lady's saddle. Cab harness.

270 KISTEMAECKERS, H. Antwerp.—Horse-hair stuffs for sieves, and dyed horse-hair.

271 VAN ALLEYNNES, S. L. Ypres.—Leathers tanned and curried. Barks, for the manufacture of leathers.

272 DUSAUCHOIT, E. Ghent.—Natural and dyed skins. Drawing of a machine for preparing leather.

273 HESNAULT & BROTHER, Ghent.—Dyed and tanned rabbit and goats' skins; dyed and prepared dog's skin.

274 VANDENBOE-POELMAN, Ghent. — A pair of varnished calf leather top and other boots.

275 CASTERMAN, J. & SON, Tournay.—A collection of typographical works.

276 HAYEZ, M. Brussels.—Typographical works.

277 BRIARD, J. H. Ixelles.—Divers editions of the Bible and New Testament.

278 PARENT, T. J. F. Brussels.—Album of fruits.

279 LESIGNE, T. Brussels.—Typographical works: General statistics of the population of Belgium. Agricultural statistics of Belgium.

280 ZEGELAER, E. Brussels.—Sealing-wax.

281 TARDIF, E. Brussels.—Envelopes for letters.

282 WESMAEL-LEGROS, A. Namur.—Roman missals. Roman breviary, 2 vols. 4to. printed in black and red.

283 HENRY, P. Dinant.—Printing paste-boards.

284 GODIN, F. L. & SON, Huy (Liege).—Collection of paper for drawing, registers, writing, letter-paper, &c.

285 HANICQ, P. J. Mechlin.—Books of Roman Liturgy, printed in red and black.

286 GLENISSON & VANGENEHTEN, Turnhaut.—Marbled, plain, and coloured paper. Prints. Cards.

287 IDIERS, N. J. Brussels.— Dyed cotton threads, pink and lilac. Paliacos of different shades, Andrinople red, madder red, and bright red. Six pieces of calico dyed in Andrinople red.

288 DIETENS, J. B. Brussels.—Printed shawls.

289 VERHULST, C. & Co. Brussels.—Pieces of printed calico.

290 VERREYT, J. Brussels.—Pieces of silk handkerchiefs (called corahs). Pieces of printed handkerchiefs. Printed silk satin gown.

291 SERVAIS, J.B. Louvain.—Blue dyed cotton and linen.

292 THIBAU, S. Izeghem (West Flanders). — Coloured linen, for smock frocks and gowns.

293 DEWEWEIRNE, J. J. Ghent.—Pieces of stuffs for handkerchiefs. Pieces of dyed and printed calico. Skins dyed and printed.

294 VOORTMAN, A. Ghent.—Pieces of printed calico for shawls. Pieces of calico for handkerchiefs. Pieces of printed calico of different sorts.

295 SERVAES, M. T. Alost.—Printed cotton stuffs for handkerchiefs, cravats, gowns, &c.

296 VERDURE, B. C. Tournay.—Wilton carpet, representing the ancient coat of arms of the Netherlands and divers allegories.

297 ROYAL CARPET MANUFACTORY. Resident Directors Messrs. Overman & Delevigne, Tournai-Savonnerie.—Carpet worked by hand. Imitation of a "Smyrna" carpet, worked by hand. Wilton carpets. Velvet carpets.

298 POLAK, Mlle. F. Brussels.—Drawings for Brussels lace scarfs. Designs for black lace flounces.

299 VAN HAELEN, Madame, Brussels. — Imitations of Brussels lace: Scarfs, veils, mantle shawl, collars, &c.

300 LEMAIEUR, C. DETIGE, & Co. Brussels.—Laces for furniture and dresses, tassels and curtain bands, and ornaments for window curtains, &c.

301 ROY, C. F. Brussels.—Worked by needle: pocket-handkerchiefs, gothic flounce, part of a flounce, flowers, collar, and scarf.

302 MELOTTE, E. Brussels.—Embroidered flag.

303 VAN HALLE, J. Brussels. Church ornaments and Brussels lace.

304 ATELIER DE NOTRE DAME, Brussels.—Imitation of Brussels lace, gauze ground: Berthe, handkerchief, &c.

305 DELEHAYE, A. (successor to A. Ducpetiaux & Son), Brussels.—Brussels lace applied on real ground lace, comprising scarfs, veil, &c.

306 JOREZ, L. & SON, Brussels.—Oil-cloth and other fabrics. Tanned and curried hides. Varnished paper for packing.

307 STOCQUART BROTHERS, Grammont. — Shawls, half-shawls, and scarfs, of black silk lace. Mantilla. Veils. Berthe. Parasols. Head dresses, &c.

308 NAELTJENS, G. Brussels.—Three veils from Florence, one Cassaveka, and a half-shawl Brussels lace, application and needle point.

309 REALLIER, Miss, Brussels. — Brussels point lace handkerchief, flax thread, ground worked by needle.

310 HEUSSCHEN, VAN EECKHOUDT, & Co. Brussels.—Point-lace dress, worked by needle. Pillow lace dress, &c.

311 ROBYT, L. Brussels.—Real Brussels lace dress and imitation lace.

312 VANDERHAEGEN VAN OVERLOOP, Brussels.—Two Brussels lace pocket-handkerchiefs and one head-dress.

313 VANDER KELEN, B. Brussels.—Picture in embroidery. Pocket-handkerchiefs representing the arms of England. Flounces and berthes, &c.

314 DUHAJON-BRUNFAUT & Co. Brussels and Ypres.—Valenciennes and Brussels lace.

315 VANDERSMNISSEN, P. Brussels. — Imitation scarf, flounces, handkerchiefs, caps, head-dresses, specimens of lace, and berthes.

316 DEFRENNE, SOPHIE, Brussels.—Brussels lace handkerchief. Berthe and head-dresses and lace collars.

317 DUJARDIN, L. Brussels.—Tapestry cushions. Embroidered caps. Slippers, suspenders, caps, &c.

318 WASHER, F. Brussels.—Pieces of table ground work, for Brussels lace, the thread spun by Messrs. Nicholls & Ashton, Manchester, and doubled, gassed, and finished by Messrs. John Thackeray & Son, Nottingham

319 BELLONI-ANCE, L. Brussels.—Specimens of lace and embroidery. Basket of worsted flowers, worked by needle.

320 VIOLARD, G. Brussels.—New designs for lace.

321 EVERAERT, Misses, Brussels.—A square black lace shawl. Two flounces for a gown. A veil. A paletot, &c.

322 ESTABLISHMENT OF ST. JOSEPH, Verviers.—Collar and ruffle made of Flanders guipure. This lace is the reproduction of the old English guipure.

323 EMBROIDERY WORK-SHOP of SWEVEGHEM, Director, Mr. DESMEDT, Sweveghem (West Flanders).—Embroidered cambric handkerchiefs. Bands, &c.

324 BECK & SON, Courtray.—A collection of Valenciennes laces.

325 DEBLAUWE-PEEL, JEAN, Courtray.—Three small pieces of Valenciennes lace.

326 BEERNAERT & DE CUYPERE, H. Courtray.—Seven pieces of Valenciennes lace.

327 VAN STRAELEN, Director of the Poor School, Bruges.—Valenciennes lace. Two lace collars.

328 BOUSSON DE VLIEGHEER, Mrs. Bruges.—Two flounces for gowns made of lace.

329 DARTEVELLE & MOUNOURY, Brussels. — Embroidered tulle collars, head dresses, veils, handkerchiefs, laces, &c.

330 TOLLENAERS, THERESA, Miss, Bruges.—Seven pieces of lace.

331 PATERNOSTRE, J. Louvain.—Religious subjects embroidered in silk and gold. Picture (embroidery).

332 NOEL, F. Louvain. — Epaulets, cords, and tassels, sword-tassels, galloons, &c. A silk watch-cord without either knot or seam: patented. Gold vases with fruits, &c.

333 VAN KIEL, Miss, Mechlin.—A Mechlin lace headdress, collar, and veil.

334 BERENHARTS, A. & Co. Antwerp.—Flounce embroidered on fine ground. Scarf, berthe, head-dress, &c.

335 PAQUET, M. Antwerp.—Shawl on a foundation of lace tulle. Handkerchief and flounces on tulle.

336 WEIL-MEYER, & Co. Antwerp. — White cotton tulle dress, berthe, and scarf, with embroidered flounce.

337 HAMMELRATH, P. H. Ypres.—Assortment of Valenciennes lace.

338 SOENEN, F. Ypres. — Assortment of Ypres lace, called "Valenciennes."

339 VAN LOO, E. J. & F. Ghent.—A black lace shawl, needlework.

340 PLETTINCK, Madame MABILDE, Ghent.—Flounces, of Brussels application.

341 HAECK, J. T. Destelberghe, near Ghent.—Brussels application veil on real lace.

342 FRETIGNY, L. Wetteren (East Flanders).—Carpets, oriental style. Table-cover. Worsted rug, &c.

343 VAN NIEUVENBORG BROTHERS, Lokeren. — Silk and beaver hats, ordinary, military, for priests, &c.

344 ANCHIAUX, T. Lokeren.—Beaver hats.

345 VAN BENEDEN, B. Brussels.—Stays without seams.

346 VAN BENEDEN, Brussels.—Stays.

347 JACQUOT, F. Brussels. — Beaver hats. Brass moulds.

348 HEGLE, C. Brussels.—Leather gloves.

349 BERGER, Madame, Brussels.—Stays.

350 DE KETELAERE, —, Bruges.—Collection of wooden shoes of all sorts, elegant, for domestic use, &c.

351 LIEVAIN, L. Mechlin. — Ecclesiastical, military, and ordinary beaver hats. Silk hats.

352 MOUNOYER, P. J. Namur.—Table and dessert knives, and carving knife and fork, with silver ornaments.

353 DRION, E. Gosselies.—Samples of nails made by hand.

354 LEFEBVRE, V. & Co. Chercq-lez-Tournai.—Small wire nails, called "pin-nails." Nails for shoes, called "becquets." Iron pegs. Iron nails for glaziers. Rivets: iron and brass.

355 VANDERCAMER, J. A. Brussels.—Zinc vessels.

356 PUISSANT, F. Cour St. Etienne (Brabant).—A wrought-iron crucible, made use of in mints.

357 GOB, J. Brussels.—A strong box.

358 SIERON, L. Brussels.—Samples of nails, called "clous de Paris."

359 MATHYS, J. Brussels.—Strong box, cabinet shape. A double-cased iron scrutoire. Polished steel open fireplace, style Louis XV., and stove.

360 DU BOIS, A. & Co. Brussels. — A mantelpiece, groups for clocks, paper press, candlesticks, cigar-stand, &c.

361 DE BAVAY, P. Brussels.—Samples of nails, called "pointes de Paris," made of fine brass and copper wires.

362 MARCHAL, D. Brussels.—A laminated iron sleeper, with cast-iron chair, for railways; new model of chair. Patented.

363 DE LATOUR, A. Director of the firm of Van der Branden & Co. Brussels.—Cast-iron bust of the King of the Belgians. Cast-iron bust of the late Queen of the Belgians. Letter-boxes adopted by the Belgian Government.

364 DELAROCHE, F. T. Brussels.—Strong box. Chimney-pieces. Stove.

365 DE ROSEE, Baron A. Moulin (Namur).—Brass cauldrons, deep wide pans, "neploviacs," and saucepans.

366 MONCHEUR, F. A. Andennes (Namur).—Six ingots of cast iron for gun-barrels.

367 SEVRIN, E. Rochefort.—Nails for floors, slates, &c. and for the heels and soles of shoes. Espalier and other hooks.

368 AMAND, J. Emeton sur Biert (Namur).—Bars of iron for gun-barrels, war-arms, breeches, &c ; and cast iron.

369 BENOIT, F. Director of his Most Serene Highness the Duke of Arenberg's Establishment, Marche les Dames (Namur).—Samples of iron ore and cast-iron. Pieces of castings from A to AA.

370 THE PRINCE OF CHIMAY, Chimay.—Bars of wrought iron refined by charcoal, specially made use of for fire-arms and weapons.

371 REMACLE, J. & PERARD & SON, Liege.—Several sheets of polished sheet-iron, prepared with wood.

372 Orban, J. M. & Son, Liege.—Sheet-iron, whee tires and laminated bars of iron prepared with wood.

373 Lambert, T. Herstal.—Collection of bits for saddle and carriage-horses.

374 St. Leonard Company, Director, Mr. Regnier Poncelet, Liege.—Specimens of cast-steel. Bars of wrought iron. Various blades.

375 Peree, J. F. Liege.—Brass cock, with curved mouth-piece; the same, straight, with hidden spring.

376 Delloye, M. C. Huy (Liege).—Sheet-iron and sheet-steel for locks and hardwares.

377 Chaudoir, C. H. Liege.—Brass tubes, made without solder, for boilers of steam-vessels, &c.

378 Macquinay Brothers, & Nephew, Liege.—Samples of Belgian iron nails made by hand.

379 Giliay, J. J. Liege.—Spurs, nose-bands, bits, and stirrups.

380 Delire, Mad. F. Chatelet (Hainault).—Various sorts of nails wrought by hand.

381 Limelette, F. Gosselies (Hainault).—Samples of wrought iron nails.

382 Prins, L. & J. B. Brussels.—Collection of brooches, set in pearls, precious stones, &c. Bracelets. Chatelaines, &c. Model of a bench, with tools for cutting and polishing diamonds.

383 Julin, N. Liege.—Cameos.

384 Falloise, J. Liege.—Steel shield, iron and silver-gilt drinking-cups, steel bracelet, iron vase, steel pins, &c.

385 Michiels, J. Anvers.—A plaster statue, coated by electrotype process, representing H.R.H. the Princess Charlotte of Belgium.

386 Brodier, C. Brussels.—Cut glass pyramids for lamps.

387 Capellemans, J. B. Brussels. — Dinner-service, composed of vases, an ice-bowl, and fruit-dish, cut in large flat ribs, and other services.

388 Zoude & Co. Namur.—Specimens of cut glass, consisting of vases for pine-apples, drinking-cups, fruit-dishes, tumblers, &c.

389 Jonet, D.—Stained window-glass; imitations of old window-glass.

390 Bennert & Bivort, Jumet (Hainault).—Window-glass.

391 Dierckx, F. Antwerp.—Dinner-service, consisting of cut glass vase, fruit-baskets, fruit-dishes, sugar-bowls, wine-glasses, vases, decanters, plates, &c.

392 Frison, J. Dampremy. — Various specimens of glass and window-glass.

393 Cappellemans, J. B. & Daboust, Brussels.—Bust, and other specimens of biscuit porcelain. Dinner service made of embossed lace porcelain, and other services.

394 Temsonnet, G. & Dartet, Nameche and Samson (Namur).—Fire-clay for manufactures, glass-works, &c.

395 Pastor-Bertrand & Co. Audenne (Namur).—Gas retort fire-clay for high furnaces, and fire-bricks for lining the inside of high furnaces.

396 Communal Commission of Marchin, Marchin (Liege).—Plum-pudding stones for crucibles, high furnaces, &c. High furnace crucibles made of these stones.

397 Coste, F. Tilleur (Liege).—Plumbago crucibles.

398 Smal Werpin, A. Huy (Liege).—Fire bricks of reduced dimensions.

399 Boucher, T. Baudour.—Fire-clay retort for gas. Sagger for baking porcelain. Patented.

400 De Fuisseaux, N. Baudour.—Dessert service, porcelain, blue ground. Baskets, bowls, plates, &c.

401 Devis, E. Brussels.—Paper-hangings.

402 Demanet, C. Saint Josse-ten-Noode, Brabant.—An inlaid rosewood table. An inlaid rosewood shelved cabinet.

403 Lefevre, A. Molenbeek St. Jean (Brabant).—Collection of paper-hangings.

404 Couvert & Lucas, Brussels.—Mosaic floors. Table with mosaic shelf and carved foot.

405 Picard-Masy, E. Brussels. — Paper-hangings, glazed, velveted, gilt, &c.

406 De Keyn Brothers, St. Josse-ten-Noode, near Brussels.—A mosaic floor, made of natural wood of divers colours.

407 Dussaert, J. Brussels.—Holy-water vessel. Frame made of stone pasteboard.

408 Giron, Madame, Brussels.—Furniture made of lacquer. A screen, three tables, the shelf of a table, and two chairs.

409 Menge, A. G. Brussels.—Model of a fountain. Articles in carved oak. Tables and shelves of oak.

410 Jehin, H. J. Spa.—Spa wood table, tea chests, boxes, desk, &c.

411 Bruno, H. Spa.—Spa wood table, work-box, tea-chest, &c.

412 Misson, Emile & Louis, Spa.—Spa wood table, work-boxes, writing-cases, cigar and needle-cases, and various other articles.

413 Misson, A. Spa.—Spa wood writing-cases, work-box and other boxes; basket; music desk; book-case, &c.

414 Marin, J. E. Spa.—Spa wood tables; fire-fans; jewel-box; albums, &c.

415 Massardo, Madame J. Spa.—Spa wood work and jewel-boxes; writing-cases; table; screens, and baskets.

416 De Jonghe, A. Bruges, West Flanders.—Samples of ornaments on wood for furniture, pillars, &c.

417 Colfs, J. T. Antwerp.—Drawing-room chair and arm-chair; tête-à-tête.

418 De Raedt, J. G. Antwerp.—A wardrobe made of rosewood and deal.

419 Roule, A. F. Antwerp.—Furniture of dark wood. Gothic rosewood book-case, bedstead, and étagère. Oak and rosewood tables and chairs.

420 Judo, T. B. Berchem, Antwerp.—Chest of drawers of carved oak; carved mahogany and walnut chair; other mahogany chairs.

421 Delevoye, F. D. Ghent.—Library desk of carved wood.

422 Hooghstoel, Ghent.—Antique wardrobe.

423 Guislain, C. Hastière-Lavaux (Namur). — Four marble slabs for tables.

424 Soetens, C. St. Gilles, near Brussels.—Pillar, flags for pavements, and medallion portrait made of artificial stone, a fusible lava.

425 Leclercq, A. Brussels.—White and black marble chimney pieces. Basin. Marble toilet. Mosaic square, composed of Belgian marble.

426 Follet, Narcisse, Verviers.—Stucco or plaster of Paris column.

427 Vanderoost, M. Brussels.—Boots and shoes, boot-trees, and lasts.

428 Stainier S. Brussels.—Boot-trees; lasts, and shoes made on them.

429 Dosin, B. J. Hermalle-sous-Argenteau, Liege.—Platted willow table and arm chairs.

430 Loncke-Haeze, C. L. Roulers.—Brushes for clothes, hair, hat, sweeping, and other purposes.

431 Quanonne, C. & J. Cureghem, near Brussels.—88 parcels of stearic wax candles; lump of stearine.

432 Robert P. J. jun. Brussels.—36 silk and lace parasols.

433 Delstanche, R. & L. Molenbeck St. Jean, near Brussels.—Stearine and tallow candles.

434 Touche, G. E. St. Laurent, near Antwerp.—Soaps made of olive oil. Tallow, soap, hog's-lard, cocoa butter, &c.

435 BRENTA, D. Antwerp.—Belgian and foreign stuffed birds.

436 VANCAMPENHOUDT, C. & Co., Heusden, near Ghent.—Wax candles. Oleic acid.

437 VANDERMAELEN, P. Molenbeek-St.-Jean, near Brussels.—An atlas containing eight lithographs of the new map of Belgium.

438 CAPRONNIER, J. B. Brussels. — Church window. Stained glass, antique style.

439 BEERNAERT, A. Brussels.—A pile of five stones of Gobertange. Carved oak press for arms.

440 MAGNEE, F. Brussels.—Etchings.

441 HART, L. J. Brussels.—Collection of 39 medals.

442 WIENER, J. Brussels.—A collection of medals, representing the principal monuments in Belgium.

443 DUCHASTEL, Comte, Grimberghe (Brabant).—Models of xylopyrography.

444 JAMAR, A. Brussels.—Wood engravings. Illustrated books.

445 DEVILLE-THIRY, H. Liege. — Specimens of engraving on glass by a new process.

446 AVANZO, D. Liege.—Two lithographs, representing the Palace of Liege.

447 JEHOTTE, C. Liege.—Bronze medals.

448 DAVELUY, D. Bruges. — Lithography, in pencil drawing, etching, painting, and chromolithographic impressions. Patent playing cards.

449 ROSSEELS, E. Louvain.—Plan of a garden after the English style.

450 GEERTS, C. Louvain.—Groups, in oak. Model of a pulpit.

451 GEEFS, J. Antwerp.—Plaster statue: the Faithful Messenger.

452 VALERIUS-JOUAN, C. Antwerp.—Plan of the town of Antwerp.

453 VANHULLE, H. J. Rymenam (Antwerp).—Plan for the management of a kitchen garden.

454 VANHOOL, J. F. Antwerp.—A carving in palm-tree wood. Fragments of festoons and flowers, carved.

455 DE CUYPER, Antwerp.—Two marble statues: Canadian Woman and Moses.

456 TUERLINKX, J. Mechlin.—Marble statue: the Young Shepherd, Giotto.

457 JOOSTENS, G. J. Esten, near Dixmude (West Flanders).—An "Ordain stone" pinnacle, intended to be placed in the church of St. Nicolas at Dixmude.

458 VANDEMEERSCHE, C. Alost. — A carving commemorating the Exhibition of 1851.

459 JACQMAIN, G. Ghent. — Initial letters, with edge and flowered borders.

460 MARCHAND, E. Schaerbeek (Brabant).—Madonna (marble bust).

461 JACQUET, Schaerbeek (Brabant).—Three bronze groups: The Flood, the Murder of the Innocents, and the Death of Abel. Cupid disarmed (plaster).

462 JACQUET, jun. Schaerbeek (Brabrnt).—A plaster statue, the Top-player.

463 JEHOTTE, L. Josse-ten-Noode.—Statues: Madonna (marble); Cain (plaster); group (bronze); bas-relief (marble).

464 SIMONIS, E. Brussels.—Equestrian statue of Godfrey of Bouillon (plaster). Truth (plaster). Two small statues, the Happy Child and the Unhappy Child.

465 FRAIKIN, C. A. Schaerbeek, (Brabant).—Statues (plaster): Psyche, Cupid, &c. A small plaster statue.

466 GEEFS, G. Schaerbeek (Brabant).—A plaster group: The Lion in love; and a small marble statue, Cupid.

467 MALLET, E. C. Charleroy.—Nails, called "Pointes Paris."

468 KUMS, E. Antwerp.—Imitation pieces of various kinds of canvas, and strong sacking.

469 DUBOIS, G. Binche.—Two straps of cow's leather.

470 VERBERCKT, H. Antwerp.—A Gothic vase, style of Louis XIV.; basket, style of Louis XV. (all silver).

471 MACKINTOSH, T. Brussels.—Compositor's page-marker.

472 WYNANTS, C. Schaerbeek (Brabant).—Machine for carving wood, marble, stone, &c.

473 MUQUARDT, C. Brussels and Ghent.—A volume, containing specimens of divers illustrated publications.

474 POINT & SON, Mouscron.—Cast-iron kitchen stoves.

475 VANDER HECHT, Brussels.—Parachute for mines.

476 LUND, —, Brussels.—Valved funnel-pipe.

477 BERTANI, A. Brussels.—A mosaic straw table.

478 BEMAND & Co. Courtray.—Coloured parchment for binding. White parchment for writing and drawing. Yellow parchment for black lace. Green parchment for white lace.

479 LECHERF, —, Brussels.—Bronze statue, Rubens: after Geefs.

480 VAN HECKE, Dr. A. T. Brussels. — A ventilating apparatus. Ventilator for railway carriages. New system of counter-marking. New sounding-line. Alarm-bell.

481 FELHOEN-COUCKE, Madame, Courtray—Seven pieces of mattress covers, made of tow thread, flax thread, and cotton.

482 HUBERT, A. Brussels.—Gold watch-chains.

483 SAFFRE, Madame, Mouscron.—Cotton stuffs, wool and cotton, and flax thread, for trousers.

484 PASTEYNS, P. Louvain. — Scarf of Mechlin lace. Pieces of lace.

485 DE PAUW, —, Ghent.—Model of a new movable bridge. Combination of fixed and turning bridges.

486 LANTHEERE, F. & Co. Ghent.—Samples of flax-cards on combs.

487 ROBYNS, P. Louvain.—Brassica-arventis oil, purified, first quality, for carcel-lamps. Purified hemp-oil.

488 BOONE, A. J. Alost.—Leather for soles, and straps. Black leather for harness. Leather for uppers. Leather for carriages. Calf-skins. Boot-legs.

489 VANGEETERUYEN, C. Stamme (East Flanders).—Indian-wheat starch.

490 BROWNE, H. Brussels.—A globe.

491 PLUYS, J. F. Mechlin.—Historical church-windows, Coloured coats of arms. Coloured medals of the 17th century. Drawing, from Rubens.

492 WOOD, W. Antwerp.—French merinos of divers tints. Linen.

493 TIBERGHIEN, L. J. Binche (Hainault). — Calf-skins. Boot-legs. Boot uppers.

494 DUPIERRY, C. jun. Vielsalm (Luxembourg). — Whet-stones.

495 PONSEELE, E. Tournay.—Wooden shoes, of walnut-tree.

496 MERCHX, M. Kesselloo (Brabant).—Winter barley and rye.

497 SCHEPPERS, T. Loth (Brabant). —Combed wool. Woollen thread for warp and weft. Light woollen stuffs in the rough, dyed, and dressed. All made in the same establishment.

498 BRICHAUT, —, Schaerbeek (Brabant).—Crucifix in bronze gilt. The Lion of Waterloo reduced to one-sixth of its size. Statuette of Justus Lipsius. Statuette in bronze.

499 LACROIX, —, Molenbeek St. Jean (Brussels).—Wire strings for harps.

500 LAVA, K. Poperinghe.—Hops.

501 NOGGERATH, Dr. Brussels.—Instrument for introducing resinous vapours into the eustachian tube, through the nasal passages, or into the ear, in cases of obstruction of those parts. A pair of curved scissors for the excision of the elongated uvula. A pump for applying compressed air in cases of simple obstruction of the eustachian tube.

502 VAN BURKHOVEN, L. Moerbeke (East Flanders).—

Model of an Archimedean screw with double groove. An Archimedean screw with triple groove.

503 RENKIN, —, sen. Liege.—Four double-barrelled guns. Three pair of pistols. Both of a new system, invented by the exhibitor.

504 SACRE, E. Brussels.—Two pair of precision scales.

505 SUERMOND, —. Wauvre (Liege).—Coals.

506 ROMSEE, —, Thron (Liege).—Coals.

507 DANNEAU, —, Neufuilles (Hainault).—Cylinder for cleaning corn.

508 VAN LOY, F. Antwerp.—A cask divided into five compartments for containing five different liquors.

509 KENTEMOST, J. B. Brussels.—A brass suction and forcing pump, giving water continually. Patented in favour of the exhibitor.

510 DELSTANEHE, P. Marbais (Brabant).—A nineteen-fold artinlated roller. Patented. A triangular weeding machine for stubbles. Double plough. Plough (used in Brabant) with hinder share. Mole trap. Patented. Straw chopper. Patented. Oblique weeding machine, with six blades. A winnowing machine. Machine for clearing grains and seeds. Patented.

511 VAN DEN BRANDE, J. A. Mechlin.—One drawing-room table inlaid (natural wood). One chess-board.

512 VAN LINDEN, P. Antwerp. (86 Warwick St. Pimlico).—Virgin and Christ, in marble. Statuette. One vase in marble, sculptured, subject from Spenser's "Faery Queen."

BRAZIL.

1 ADAMSON, O. G.—A bouquet of flowers of Brazil, made of the birds' feathers of that country, with the exception of a few made of beetles' wings in their natural colours only. The bouquet comprises specimens of the coffee, cotton, and tobacco flowers.

2 COX, —.—Model of a native raft.

3 MORNAY, E. DE. Agent, Mr. Peat, Saddler, 14 Old Bond St. London.—Set of bridle reins. From the province of Rio Grande da Sul, Brazil. Made of raw bullock's hide, and linked with silver. Cap; the cap is made in the Sertaö (the interior) of the province of Pernambuco. The leather is made from the hide of the red deer of that country. Intended as specimens of the industry of the less civilized of the inhabitants of the Brazils.

4 MAJOR, C. T. Esq. 21 Billiter St. London.—Leaves and butterfly made of beetle's wings, by Henrique José da Silva, Rio de Janeiro.

CHILI.

1 Messrs. SCHNEIDER & Co. Broad St. Mews.—A lump of gold ore, weighing 3 cwt.

CHINA.

H. M. CONSUL SHANGHAE, Contributed through the BOARD of TRADE.

1 Gallingal, a Chinese root (*Leangkeang*). 2 A red colour. 3 Saffron (*Hunghwa*). 4 Camphor (*Chungnaon*). 5 Rhubarb (*Tahwang*). 6 Hemp (*Yuma*). 7 Uncleaned cotton (*Meenhwa*). 8 Cleared cotton (*Hwae*). 9 Hemp seed. Tobacco. 11 Coarse hemp. 12 Hemp twine. 13 A Chinese medicine root. 14 Coarsest raw silk, supposed to be the fibres of the cactus. 15 Turmeric. 16 White arsenic, from Hankow. 17 Arsenic, from Hankow. 18 Yellow arsenic.

19 Bees-wax, white and yellow. 20 Vegetable wax. 21 Sulphate of iron (green vitriol). 22 Three bottles of varnish. 23—27 Fused metal. 28 Japanese copper.

A complete collection of the various materials employed at the GREAT PORCELAIN WORKS of KIAING TIHT' CHIN, in the vicinity of the Poyang-lake, in the manufacture of porcelain.

1 Waukuh (literally skeleton of the cup). 2 Tseihe. Porcelain may be formed by a mixture of the above. 3 Material ready mixed. This made with water into clay will form porcelain. 4 Bedaubing powder, ready mixed. 5 Soap stone, very hard. Found in the districts of Luh siu and Kweihe, in Keangse province. 6 Bedaubing material. 7 White lead and other materials.

Various packages containing the colours.

Twenty-three packets, containing prepared colours of various kinds.

Forty-seven packets, containing colours for painting the best porcelain after baking.

Miscellaneous articles:—

1 A large cameo basso-relievo on yellow ground.

2, 3 Two large basso-relievos on blue ground.

4—7 Four basso-relievos on blue ground, representing flowers, shrubs, &c.

8 A lacquered table, with incrustations of mother-o'-pearl.

10—13 Four lacquered chairs, inlaid with mother-o'-pearl.

18 A square brazeiro and pedestal, for heating a room by charcoal ashes.

19 A censer, or perfume urn.

18, 19a Pedestals in sculptured wood.

20, 21 Two candelabra in bronze, enamelled in mosaic pattern.

22 A bronze vase, mosaic enamelled, with cover and pedestal in carved wood.

23—27 Ornaments of a Chinese table.

28 A Chinese sceptre, inlaid, silver-mounted, and carved.

29, 30 Two boxes of carved red lacquer-ware, from Sutchuen.

40 A tableau in carved wood.

41 Antique vase of enamelled and mosaic bronze, with pedestal of carved wood.

42, 43 Two vases of bronze inlaid with silver.

44 An armoire in carved wood, edged with ebony, and incrusted with ivory.

Contents of Box addressed to the Secretary of the HORTICULTURAL SOCIETY, London.

1 Specimen of indigo, the produce of plants in the north.

2 Specimens of the raw produce of the silk-worm, from Leotang in Manchouria.

3 Specimen of the fabric, manufactured in the same province for home consumption.

4 Another specimen of the same fabric.

Exhibited by the HON. EAST INDIA COMPANY.

Hemp-palm; its fibre, and the ropes prepared from it. Arrow-root. Tung-oil and seeds in spirits. The whi-mei of the Chinese, a green dye. Gardenia radicans (fruit), a yellow dye. Fortunæa Chinenses (fruit and flower). The ko-pal of the Chinese. Shang-hae indigo. Pith of the plant from which rice paper is cut. Wax tapers used at Peking. Brick tea (two samples). Green-tea dyes; articles used in the district of Hungchow to dye green tea for exportation; one bottle.

Articles exhibited by Captain SHEA, 31 Connaught-square, Hyde Park.

1 A snuff-box; specimen of Chinese carving on English cannel coal, the only specimen known.

2 A Chinese carved mother-of-pearl shell.

3 A saucer: Chinese specimen of enamel on copper.

4 A small saucer; specimen of Japanese lacquered ware.

5 A cup and saucer, specimen of Japanese lacquered ware.

6 A Chinese specimen of cloth made of paper.

7 A Burmese bamboo vase, elaborately carved.

8 Two japanned chairs of Chinese upholstery and lacquered ware.

9 A bamboo chair.

10 A Chinese lantern.

11 A specimen of green and another of crimson Chinese damask.

Articles exhibited by J. Reeves, Esq.

A tea-chest containing 8 silken cannisters of fancy tea; specimens in glass case.

Sixteen cases of China ink, exhibiting thirty-two views. Ten cups of white porcelain. Twelve upright china cups. Two metal tea-pots lined with earthenware and sundry-shaped china ornaments. Eight tin cups lined with porcelain. Two bamboo carvings of birds. Case containing a boat carved in bamboo. Two bamboo-carved penholders. Case with ten boxes of Fychow ware. Case with two boxes of the same. Chinese hooka. Four various-shaped tea-pots, metal lined with earthenware. Two carved steatite ornaments. Two carved cups. Three incense-burners in stone. Various Chinese tea-pots and tea-kettles in earthenware. Tea-kettle and fire-pan. Oven heated by the flame of a lamp passing into the centre. Oven to keep tea warm, being immersed in a vessel of hot water.

Reeves, J. R.

Bronze vases, &c., inlaid, three large and five small. Ink; one large box. Sale ornaments; case of three. Waistband buckle. Filigree silver necklace. Rolled paintings.

Articles exhibited by Hewett & Co., 18 Fenchurch Street, London, Importers.

China ware: Jars from 10 inches to 4 feet high. Sugar jars and covers. Sets of jars and beakers, five in a set. Plates, various designs. Curious jars, 24 inches high. Toilet set. Punch bowl. Flower pots and stands. Garden seats, tiles, and fountain. Figures for burning pastiles. Eggshell cups, covers and saucers; tea-pots; flower-boat.

Carved ivory ware: Work-box, a fine specimen of carving. Sets of chessmen or balls. Very large ball, carved, containing twenty smaller balls. Vases. Card-baskets, case, and racks. Cigar-box. Fan. Paper-knife. Work-basket, with handle. Model of a junk.

Lacquered ware, &c.: Pole-fire screens. Nest of four tables. Work table, with carved ivory fittings. Cabinet. Tea caddy. Cabinet, red lacquered, from Loo Chow. Reclining chair made of bamboo. Seats, marble tops, and wood frames. Panels for cabinets, wood, inlaid with wood. Tray for burning joss stick.

Japanese ware: Writing-desk. Box. Work-table and box. Cabinet. All inlaid with mother-of-pearl.

Miscellaneous articles: Skin rug. Model of Chinese summer-house. Swan pan, or calculator. Cane blinds. Umbrellas. Lady's shoes. Curious bamboo jacket. Embroidered satin apron. Embroidered satin counterpane. Printed glass lanterns, carved ebony frames. Paintings on glass. Oil paintings. Gongs. Box of toys. Paper and feather fans. Hand-screens, various, including painted feathers. Specimens of bronzes. Floor matting. Paperhangings. Specimens of soap stone. Screen, curious carved slate, in wood frame. Another, painted porcelain, in wood frame. Another, composition of rice, also in wood frame. Musical instrument. Mirror, in carved ebony stand. Beautifully-carved mother-of-pearl shells. Balloon and revolving lanterns. Carved tortoiseshell combs. Silver filigree card-case and needle-case. Carved wood summer-house. Chinese fruit, called lé ché, from the province of Fokien.

Enamelled copper: Jars, 3 feet high. Censer, cups, covers, and saucers. Toilet set, complete.

Painted glass screen.

Embroidered Mandarin's dress, &c. Mother-of-pearl temple. Large screens. Marble top table. Two Japanese

screens. Large Mandarin chair. Lacquered cabinet. Porcelain bath.

Produce of China: Manufacture of cotton. Samples of nankeens, yellow and white. Manufactures of grass or linen. Manufactures of silk. Pongee silk handkerchiefs, plain and figured. Pongee silk, plain white. Syechuen pongee, in various colours. Black silk handkerchief. Black silks and satins. Crape shawls, handkerchiefs, and scarfs, plain, damasked, and embroidered. Various silks, gauze, and embroidery.

Copland, Charles Matt. A. M. South Villa, Kennington Oval—Proprietor.

Chinese writing desk. Rice paper. Drawings, in five books in silk binding. Drawings on rice paper.

Chinese paintings in two silk frames. 12 desert plates, each formed from the mother o'-pearl oyster-shell, richly pierced border and finely engraved. Chinese screen, japanned, black, and gold. Chinese screen, of rosewood and painted marble panels. Japanese writing desk. Lady's tortoiseshell hair-comb, finely carved. Pair of bracelets, fine gold, filigree pattern. Chinese chopstick, bearing name of exhibitor in Chinese character.

Ladies' work-table. Box for playing-cards. Tea-caddies. Cigar-boxes. Round writers. Card case. Card counter boxes. Fan. Chess-men. Card-counters. Snuff-boxes. Fans. Chinese figures of soapstone. Chopstick and knife. Spoons. Chinese compass. China ink. Tissue paper. Writing and account books. Figured silk. Pith of a tree.

Lindsay, H. Hamilton, Berkeley Square—Importer.

Silk; damask; satin; and specimens of embroidery and embroidered chair-seats.

Flax:—seed, fibre, and yarn. Grass cloth, of various qualities. Cotton:—nankeen, cotton cloth.

Gaut Po. Gold and silver shoe. Specimens of sycee silver. Gold filigree. Silver filigree, ten specimens. Porcelain:—jars, punch-bowls, breakfast set, &c.

Bronze heong loo. Two carved rhinoceros' horns. Edible birds' nest. Beche de mer. Suy-hing Chinese wine. Two jugs for holding the same. Six silver cups. Two models of small feet of Chinese women. Three mariner's compasses. Model of a pump. Two pumps.

Parker, The Rev. Dr.

Box containing various seeds. Another containing various woods.

Astell & Co., Vigo Street, Piccadilly.

A Chinese printing press.

Palmer, Macelloch, & Co., 1 King's Arms Yard, City.

Some specimens of silks, made up especially from China for the Exhibition.

Dent, L.

A curious and elaborately finished Chinese bedstead, inlaid with ivory and mother-of-pearl.

Samples of silk.

Thoms, P. P., Printer, Warwick Square.

The original address, with the signatures of 776 merchants and tradesmen, presented to his Excellency Hwang, on his being appointed the deputy governor of the province of Canton, during the reign of the Emperor Kang He, about the year 1684.

The address measures in length seven feet nine inches, and in width six feet. It contains 2,328 Chinese characters, beautifully worked in gold, on silk, and is lined with Chinese embossed velvet, surrounded with a gold border. Accompanied with a translation of the address, by Mr. P. P. Thoms.

Dated during the reign of Kang He, whose reign closed about A.D. 1684.

2 Fifty Chinese engravings on wood.

3 A Chinese sceptre.

4 The Pa-sëen, or eight immortals, who confer benefits on mankind, carved in stone.

5 The goddess Kwan-yin, in stone, on a carved stand.
6 The god of wealth, and the god of longevity, carved in wood.
7 Chinese shells and insects.

RIPLEY, P. W., *Canton.*

A collection of the various teas exported from Canton, in chests, cases, and boxes.

BARING BROTHERS, *Bishopsgate Street.*

1 Carved ivory tree, with ball containing 24 others, all from one piece. 2 Two embroidered chair covers. 3 Card case, in ivory. 4 Another in sandalwood. 5 Four pieces rich satin, different colours. 6 Four paintings. 7 Four painted lanterns. 8 130 specimens of China ware. 9 Model of a cargo boat. 10 Model of a mandarin boat (revenue). 11 Curiously-carved stove and frame. 12 Carved wood chairs. 13 Six bronze and three carved wood figures. 14 Pair jars and stands, and pair wooden stools. 15 Case of small lacquered-ware articles. The above are all productions of Chinese, Nos. 5 and 10 being sent out by Houqua. 16 Twelve handkerchiefs, embroidered on pina (cloth made from fibres of the leaf of the pine).

BRAINE, C. T., *Way House, near Taunton.*

A feather painted and embroidered fan. Wooden furniture—Table, 3 ft. 3 in. square, 2 ft. 9 in. in height. Bookcase, 6 ft. high, 3 ft. 9 in. in breadth, 2 ft. 3 in. in depth. Hat-stand, 7 ft. high. Set of miniature furniture. Four earthenware flower-pots. All of Chinese manufacture.

BOWRING, EDGAR A., Acting Secretary to the Commission, Board of Trade.

Bas-relief specimen of Chinese costume, "a lady of rank reclining on a sofa." The whole formed of ash.

BOILEAU, Lieut.-Col. A. H. E., Bengal Engineers, *Gerston Terrace, Paignton, near Taunton.*

An illuminated missal.

DANIEL, J., 11 *Cumberland Place.*

Two embroidered Shang Hae dresses; and embroidered feather fan.

MONTEIRO, L. A., 2 *Upper Phillimore Pl. Kensington.*

Five cups and five saucers of Chinese or Oriental enamelled jewelled porcelain, with European landscape in the bottom.

BOWMAN, WM., 9 *Bread Street, London.*

A table made in the North of China,

RAWSON, CHRISTOPHER.

A japan cabinet. (26) Japan ware. (22)

RAWSON, T. S., Esq.

1 A Japanese inlaid mother-of-pearl cabinet.

RAWSON, C., Esq.

2 A Japanese red lacquered ware sweetmeat box, on wheels. 3, 4 Two Japanese red lacquered ware ornaments. 5 A Chinese ivory ball, containing 15 separate balls. 6 A specimen of bamboo carving. 7 A Chinese medicine cup. 8 A specimen of Chinese carving, representing the finger citron. 9 A Chinese figure with head and feet of cast-iron, and the mantle of the old cracked China ware.

RAWSON, Mrs.

10 A specimen of Chinese needlework, embroidery in silk. Specimens of grass cloth, or China linen, shipped by Messrs. WM. PUSTAN & Co., at Canton, to Messrs. JAMES BARBER & Co., Southampton, and Messrs. G. H. and J. F. Wulff, London,

Grass cloth. Bundles of flax yarn. Bundle of flax. Half-catty of flax seed.

SICHART & Co. (Importers of Chinese and other Fancy Goods), 169 *Fenchurch Street.*

1 to 8. A large Chinese vase, painted with 10,000 characters, each character a distinct word; the whole forming an ode on longevity. Carved ivory ornaments. Carved wood ornaments. Diminutive boxes, carved from peach stones, representing junks, baskets, &c. Glass screens and paintings on glass. A large censer, being a fine specimen of enamelling

on copper. Hand-screens, manufactured from the gelatine of the head of a fish. China-ware, of various descriptions.

W. WALKINSHAW, *Hong Kong.*

A Chinese temple or summer-house. By Patrick Dudgeon. The "Celestial Cup," presented at Hong Kong races 1850. Silver cup, presented at Hong Kong races. Nephrite or jadt stone cup.

TWINING, —. 13 *Bedford Place, Russell Square.*

Large copper tripod, with stand, and a marble stool for same.

Marble screen, large, and a smaller one.
1 Copper vessel, with wooden top and stand.
2 "Buffalo with Man." Stands for each.
Marble top and stand for the small articles.

CARPENTER, F. S., *Queen's Road, St. John's Wood,* Prop.

A carved bamboo walking-stick, from the north of China.

STANDISH & NOBLE, Importers.

Cupressus funebris, or weeping cypress, a new hardy tree, imported from the north of China. (Outside Eastern End.)

HAMMOMD, W. P. & Co. London, Importers.

Specimens of the various teas imported into this country from China, comprising the different qualities of congou, souchong, oolong, orange pekoe, twankay, hyson, young hyson, imperial, gunpowder, &c. Small bundles of tea leaves in an untwisted state, and also tightly twisted into rope: made from the large leaves which shoot from the plant after being cut down. 12 native paintings on rice paper illustrative of the tea-plant cultivation, &c. Specimens of the different qualities of China raw silk. A camphor work-box containing ivory carvings.

HAEMOND, WM. Merchant, London.

Model made to scale, of an opium smuggling-boat, used on the coast of China.

BERNCASTLE, DR. 80 *Albany Street, Regent's Park.* Exhib.

Chinese swords : a soldiers' : a man at arms' ; and a mandarin's (double in one scabbard). Sword made entirely of ash; pillow, razor, chopstick. Tea-plant, and articles of domestic use.

JAPAN.

No. 28, Red copper from Japan; No. 20, Vegetable wax; No. 22, Specimens of varnish; and No. 14, A product styled coarse silk in the list furnished, but supposed to be the fibre of a species of cactus.

DENMARK.

(Commissioner in London, REGNAR WESTENHOLZ, Esq., *Mark Lane.*)

Agent, C. J. MAJOR, 21 Billiter Street.

1 PUGGAARD H. & Co. Copenhagen, Prod.—Samples of barley, grown in the island of Möen, in 1850. Samples of wheat.

2 KOLBJÖRNSEN, K. Reikavik, Prop. — Sample of Iceland wool.

3 TOPP, A. L. Copenhagen, Manu.—Specimens of white lamb-skins for glovers, prepared with alum; exhibited for quality and dye. Goat-skins and white sheep-skins similarly prepared.

4 DREWSEN & SONS, Silkeborg, Jutland, Manu.—Specimens of paper, glazed by a machine constructed by the exhibitors.

5 WULFF, JENS, & SONS, Brede, Schleswig, Manu.—Specimens of thread lace and cotton stuffs.

6 MEYER, J. E. Copenhagen, Manu.—Specimens of japanned tea-trays, small trays, bread baskets. Oil-cloth mats for dishes, tureens, lamps, &c.; and floor-cloth.

7 WARMING, E. Copenhagen, Manu.—A carpet and foot-stool.

8 FJELRAD, Jutland, Prop.—Knitted worsted goods, viz., jackets, petticoats, stockings, &c., exhibited for firmness, cheapness, and warmth.

9 THOMSEN, —, Randers, Manu.—Randers' gloves.

10 MATTAT & SONS, Randers, Manu. — Gloves for gentlemen and ladies, exhibited for odour and softness. Specimens of Randers' skins.

11 PETERSEN, P. L. Copenhagen, Manu.—Patent goloshes, invented by the exhibitor. Gentlemen's dress and ordinary boots. A calfskin, prepared by the exhibitor. Ladies' black satin and prunella boots, with enamelled leather, and satin shoes.

12 LUNDE, P. F. Copenhagen, Manu.—Pump, which can be used as a fire-engine. Stove, for heating small or large rooms. A steam-gauge whistle, constructed in the workshop of the exhibitor, by Jacob Jacobsen.

13 SÖRENSEN, C. Copenhagen, Inv. and Manu.—A machine for composing, and re-sorting the types after printing.

14 JESSEN, N. S. Naval Arsenal, Copenhagen, Inv. and Manu.—A rifle, with an oval barrel, to discharge a conical ball. Specimen of cartridge.

15 ANDERSEN, P. Copenhagen, Manu.—A chaff-cutting machine, of simple construction.

16 FUNCH, A. Copenhagen, Inv. and Manu.—An astronomical clock, with an escapement which gives an impulse every ten seconds. The clock goes a month.

17 JURGENSENS, SONS, Copenhagen, Inv. and Manu. —Two box chronometers, with free escapement, &c. Gold watch adapted for observations. Metallic thermometers. A model of the detached escapement, usually employed in the chronometers of the exhibitors.

18 LANGGAARD, J. P. Copenhagen, Inv.—Model of patent surgical apparatus, for spinal curvature.

19 NYROP, C. Copenhagen, Manu.—Various artificial legs. Spinal apparatus. Osteotome, &c.

20 NISSEN, J. Copenhagen, Manu.—Double-acting air-pump with single cylinder. Scales for chemical analysis; for precious metals; and for affinities. Set of grain weights. Barometers. Psychrometer. Thermometers, &c. All exhibited for construction and cheapness.

21 WEILBACH, I. J. Copenhagen, Manu.—Azimuth compass. A transparent compass, with an improved balance. A storm compass. A new log-glass, invented by exhibitor.

22 NAYLOR, J. W. Copenhagen, Des. and Manu.—A series of twelve files made of cast-steel.

23 WULFF, Copenhagen, Manu.—Two brass tea-urns, executed by hand.

24 POTMAGER, H. Hjerting, Prop.—Specimens of common crockery, called black pots, made by peasants of Jutland.

25 HANSEN, C. B. Copenhagen, Des. and Manu.—A lady's rosewood writing-table; and a chair.

26 NIELSEN, N. Copenhagen, Des. and Manu.—Bookcase of oak, gothic style, veneered inside with candlewood (wood of the lemon-tree).

27 HOLMBLAD, L. P. Copenhagen, Manu.—Stearine candles. Playing cards. Glue of two different qualities.

28 TUTEIN, F. Copenhagen, Manu.—Samples of crystallized sugar-candy.

29 SMED, S. Copenhagen.—A carriage axle.

30 HORNUNG, C. C. Copenhagen, Inv. and Manu.—Cabinet and horizontal pianofortes, in rosewood cases, inlaid with metallic ornaments.

31 SELBOE, J. C. Copenhagen, Manu.—

Ebony flute, B flat, with eleven silver keys, and an Archimedean bore. Clarionet, in B flat, on J. Van Müller's construction, with two mouthpieces. Hautboy, with keys of German silver, on the older Dresden pattern.

32 MÖLLER, H. P. Copenhagen, Inv. and Manu.—An orthochord: A tuning-fork.

33 THE ROYAL PORCELAIN MANUFACTORY, Copenhagen.—Ornamented and decorated vases; decorated dessert-plates, and breakfast-cups and saucers; exhibited for style and cheapness. Figures, busts, and bas-reliefs, in biscuit, after Thorwaldsen, subjects sacred, allegorical, and mythical. Decorated Etruscan vases, modelled after the antique, exhibited for manufacture.

34 KLINGSEY, C. G. Copenhagen, Manu.—An ivory jewel casket, ornamented with bas-reliefs.

35 PETERSEN, P. Copenhagen, Des.—Four cameos, and a bronze medal.

36 CONRADSEN, N. Copenhagen, Des.—A reverse for a bronze medal, and two cameos.

37 SCHÖLER, P. C. Copenhagen, Inv.—Specimen of a graphic mode of representation called stylography, with plates showing the whole process,

38 BISSEN, H. W. Copenhagen, Sculp.—Eros or Love. A bust in marble. A Fisher-boy angling. Orestes.

39 JERICHAU, J. A. Copenhagen, Sculp.—Adam and Eve, a group in plaster. A group in marble, Hunter and panther. Two bas-reliefs in plaster. A bust in plaster.

40 DIRKSEN, G. Kiel.—Fire-buckets, engine, hose, &c.

41 HOLZAPFEL, C. Altona.—Fringe for curtains.

42 LANGÉ, H. Altona.—Hair-work.

43 MEYER, A. D. Altona.—Four tin jelly-moulds.

44 OWEN, J. Copenhagen, Manu. — Sulphuric and muriatic acids, oils, patent and bone manures, charcoal, soaps, &c.

45 BENZON, —, Laaland, Prod.—Sample of barley.

46 VOIGT, —, Fühmen, Prod.—Sample of oats.

47 HJORTH, S., Copenhagen, Inv. and Manu.—Working model of an electro-magnetic engine. Wooden diagram and plan of an improved arrangement, consisting only of one hollow electric magnet and a hollow piston, forming a moveable extension of either of the poles.

EGYPT.

THE EGYPTIAN GOVERNMENT. Commissioner, Captain ABDEL HAMID, ALEXANDRIA, and 54 Brompton Square. Agents, REDJEB HASSAN EFFENDI, Alexandria; HASSAN ALI EFFENDI, Alexandria. London Agents, CHARLES JOYCE and P. R. LAZZARI,. Customs' Agent, Mr. C. J. MAJOR, 21 Billiter Street, City.

1 Small top of a table in alabaster.
2 Square block of alabaster. 3 The same.
4 Large top of a round table in alabaster.
5 Square block of alabaster.
6 Piece of petrified wood.
7 A case containing plaster-stone.
8 Sample of mineral sulphur.
9 Case containing samples of yellow and grey earth.
10 Fardeh, large baskets.
11 Case containing different kinds of natron, viz. natron carnoudgi, from the lake of Harrara, and black and white sultani, from Terranch.
12 Two samples of potter's earth and clay.
13 Three cases containing different kinds of saltpetre.
14 One case containing a sample of hard red stone.
15 The same, of white stone.
16 Mineral natron.
17 Raw natron of Lower Egypt.
18 Refractory or stiff earth of Assouan.
19 Cassia. 20 Gum-ammoniac.
21 Mildew. 22 Coloquinto.
23 Opium of Upper Egypt.
24 Castor oil. 25 Senna. 26 Tombac.
27—33 Dates, sultani, from Siouah; from Ghazzal; sultani, from Oasis; pressed, from Cairo; from Amri; from Ibrim; sultani of Cairo.
34 Aqua, skinned and pressed dates of the province of Charkey.

35 Dates of Siouah.
36 Aqua, pressed dates of Ghizeh.
37 Tobacco of Upper Egypt.
38 Fruits of palm, Doum. 39 Mildew oil.
40 Rice, ordinary, of Damietta.
41 Rice, white, of Damietta.
42 Rice, red, of Damietta.
43 Pois chiches grillis.
44 Refined sugar from the manufactory at Minich.
45 Refined sugar of the steam manufactory.
46 Fenugru of Lower Egypt.
47 Raw sugar. 48 Half refined sugar.
49 Plant, good for eating, Habelaziz.
50 Liquorice paste. 51 Mustard seed.
52 Wheat of Upper Egypt, first choice.
53 Lettuce-oil. 54 Dates in preserve.
55 Carthame oil. 56 Honeycomb of Mehalech.
57 Large olives in oil.
58 Olives, ordinary quality.
59 White honey of Mehalech, first quality.
60 Dates in honey, from the province of Charkye.
61 White honey of Mansourah.
62 White honey of Charkyé.
63 Three vases of butter, different kinds.
64 Tamarinds. 65 Troêne.
66 Sugar candy. 67 Linseed.
68 Wheat of Upper Egypt. 69 Wheat of Lower Egypt.
70 White Indian corn.
71 Castor-oil seed. 72 Clover seed.
73 Barley of Upper Egypt.
74 Sessamum seed.
75 Rice of Rossetta, Fahl.
76 Cumin seed. 77 Fennel., 78 Anise seed.
79 Indigo of the country. 80 Poppy seed.
81 Clover seed of Meskaôui.
82 Boutargue of Damiette.
83 Rice of Rosetta, Aüselbent.
84 Beans of Lower Egypt.
85 Small Indian corn, yellow, Eouedgi.
86 Rice of Rosetta, first quality.
87 Small white Indian corn of Benisouet.
88 Harico of the country.
89 Beans of Upper Egypt.
90 Small red Indian corn, Eouedgi.
91 Yellow Indian corn.
92 Small white Indian corn of Lower Egypt.
93 Wheat of the province of Charkyé
94 Barley of Lower Egypt.
95 Pois chiches of Upper Egypt.
96 Lentils of Upper Egypt.
97 Pois chiches of Lower Egypt.
98 Lentils of Lower Egypt.
99 Yellow Indian corn of Turkey.
100 Saffron. 101 Peas. 102 Sesame oil.
103 Sugar for Turkish drink (sorbets).
104 Sugar-canes. 105 Flax combed by machine.
106 Makò cotton, first quality.
107 Flax of Fayoum. 108 Flax of Menauf.
109 Hemp seed. 110 Lupins. 111 Essence of mint.
112 Club of ebony of Sennar.
113, 114 Horns of antelopes and gazelle.
115 Elephant teeth of Soudan. 116 Virgin wax.
117—119 Horns of rhinoceros, wild bull, and capricorns.
120 Gum of Sennar, chosen. 121 Gum of Sennar.
122 Mimosa seeds. 123 Cardamomum.
124, 125 Horns of buffalo and of the ox.
126 Maps, ordinary, of Upper Egypt.
127 Skin of crocodile. 128 Mat for cheese.
129—131 Oil of cotton seed, turnip, and linseed.
132 Fibres of the date-tree.
133 Tray of date-leaves of Rosetta.

134 Sea island Cotton, cultivated by T. W. Larkins.
135 Rose-water of Fayrum.
136 Mint-water of Rosetta.
137 Orange-flower water.
138—140 Sample of alizier wood, of sycamore, and of palm, Doum.
141, 142 Trunk of date-tree; of ebony of Sennar.
143 Piece of ebony. 144 Rules of ebony, Sennar.
145 Piece of sweet palm-tree. 146 Acacia wood.
147—149 Sample of palm-tree, Doum; of date-tree; of azedarak.
150 Net of fibres of date-tree.
151 Cotton of second quality.
152 Hemp. 153 Coffee-mill.
154 Mill to be worked by the hands.
155 Trough for paste and bread.
156—158 Sieves for sesamum wheat and Indian corn.
159—161 Horse-hair sieve, and two silk sieves.
162 Measure in wood, bound in iron, Rouht.
163 Weight in brass. 164 Goat-skin bottle.
165 Steel-yard, with its appendages. 166 Flints.
167 Basket of dates. 168 Wooden locks.
169 Pick-axe. 170 Bill-hook. 171 Sickle for clover.
172 Hoe. 173 Egyptian plough.
174 Norez machine to sow seed.
175 Cotton cloth for cacatonas of a frigate.
176 Cotton cloth for topsail of a vessel or man-of-war.
177 Cotton cloth for cacatonas of a vessel or man-of-war.
178 Cotton cloth for topsail of a frigate.
179 Cambric printed in the manufactory, Shoulbrack.
180 Cotton cloth, unbleached, Bissa.
181 Cotton cloth, bleached, Bissa.
182 Cotton cloth, bleached, Settine.
183 Sail-cloth for the boats of the Nile.
184 Cotton cloth for soldiers' shirts.
185 Cambric, unbleached. 186 Cotton cloth, Borsato.
187 Cotton cloth for soldiers' pantaloons.
188 Woollen brown covering.
189 White woollen belts of Upper Egypt.
190 Coat in black wool.
191 Coat of fellah, in black wool.
192 Cap of fellah, in brown beaver.
193 Melayé, in silk, red ground, stripes worked in gold.
194 Habara veil, in black silk, for female.
195 Silk piece goods, violet colour, in four stripes.
196 Silk piece goods, dark green, in orange stripes.
197 Apron, in dark blue, with yellow and red border.
198—201 Silk piece goods: violet, with two stripes; dark blue, with four stripes; yellow striped; crossed in blue.
202 Table cloth, in silk, red ground, chiné in gold.
203 Silk piece goods, crossed in red.
204 Towel, with borders.
205—2 0 Silk piece goods: dark purple; crossed violet; green, with two stripes; violet, red, with two stripes; red, with green stripes.
211 Silk and gold fringe, for divans.
212 Sample of gold and silk fringe, for curtains.
213 Fringe in gold, to ornament divans.
214 Samples of gold fringe, for divans.
215 Crape, of red silk.
216 Plaited silk, of different colours.
217 Silk dark-blue cords, to suspend pistols.
218 Pair of garters, in silk and gold.
219 Tassel of dark-blue silk, for tarbuche.
220 Sample of plaited gold. 221 Sample of gold fringe.
222 Samples of fringe, in various colours.
223 Fringes of silk and gold, to ornament sword handles.
224 Cavalry sword, in blue and gold.
225 Samples of plaited silk and gold.
226 Linen cloth, for packing, from Lower Egypt.
227 Dromedary saddle, with its appendages.

228 Arab saddle, with the same.
229 Saddle of Cairo, worked in gold thread, appendages.
230 Saddle-cloth, in beaver.
231 (Marshaka) saddle, red cloth, embroidered in gold.
232—234 Skins of the ox : black ; bleached white ; red.
235 Skin of buffalo, bleached white.
236 Skin of buffalo, of Rosetta.
237 Skin of ox, for soles.
238 Skin of buffalo, bleached with oak bark.
239 Skin of calf, for boots.
240 Skin of calf, from Domanhour.
241 Skin of buffalo, for soles.
242 Skin of ox, bleached with mimosa seed.
243 Brushes for the use of stables, in date fibres.
244—246 Wallets, in wool, ornamented in leather, from de Bein Mezar, Ghizeh, and Upper Egypt.
247 Skin of camel.
248 One hundred and sixty-five volumes of works in Turkish, Arabic, and Persian, published at Boulac.
249 Carpet, in coloured beaver.
250 Sailcloth, of Broulos.
251 Holster for pistols, in skin, &c.
252 Sword of Damascus, ornamented in silver gilt, with gold belt.
253, 254 Gut cord, to clean cotton and wool.
255 Basket for cheese, in cane.
256 Scales, in date branches.
257 Little coloured basket, from Upper Egypt.
258, 259 Cord, of fibres of date, from Broulos and Ghizeh.
260 Wax candles, white and yellow.
261 Yellow shoes.
262—265 Red shoes: double and single soled, de citadin, and for grooms.
266 Narguilé, or water-pipe.
267 Donkey saddle.
268—270 Leather belts, of various sizes.
271 Red morocco tobacco bag.
272, 273 Mother-of-peal rows, large and small.
274 Chapelet, in nut of Dourn.
275 Bottle for antimony.
276 Ostrich eggs.
277 (Marghouna) basket, in date branches.
278, 279 Pipe bowls, of Assouan and Assiout.
280 Bag, in goat-skin.
281 (Tarka) veils, for women, red ground, with flowers.
282 The same, red ground, striped.
283 The same, in embroidered muslin.
284 (Kamar) belt, in silk, for grooms.
285—287 (Dekké) strings for pantaloons, embroidered.
288 (Yazma) kerchief, for women's head-dress.
289 Silk turbans, for Bedouins.
290 (Melayé Bassiouni) veil, for women, in silk.
291—293 (Bemoud) red silk strings.
294 (Zardakham) apron, for dress, in worked silk.
295, 296 Silk piece goods, with yellow and red grounds.
297 (Chaki) cotton and silk piece goods.
298 Silk piece goods, dark green.
299 Travelling belt.
300 (Derayé) thick silk, for lining.
301 Taftas, violet, changing.
302—304 Tarbouches of Touha, of various sizes.
305 (Cotné) silk and cotton piece goods.
306—309 Linens, from Lower Egypt, Mehallah, and d'Abiar.
310 Belt, in red silk.
311 Linen cloth, from Mehallah.
312 Linen cloth, ordinary, from Assiout.
313 Tassels in gold.
314 The same, for pipes.
315 Tassels in silk, blue and gold.

316 Tassels in silk, for pipes.
317 Tassels in silk, with the top in gold.
318 Crape, in black silk.
319 Handkerchief, in muslin, embroidered in Cairo.
320, 321 (Takié) white caps.
322, 323 Handkerchiefs, embroidered at Alexandria.
324 (Azbé) large head-dress, in black silk.
325 Silk piece goods, dark blue.
326 Taftas, red.
327 (Zardakham) apron, in silk, worked in gold.
328 Handkerchief, in muslin, worked at Alexandria.
329 Bag for a watch, embroidered in gold and silver.
330 Tobacco bag, embroidered in gold and silver.
331 Handkerchief, embroidered at Alexandria.
332 (Coufyé) veil of silk, with borders, for men.
333 (Azbé) hair dress, in black silk, from Cairo.
334 Taftas, red and green, changing.
335 Samples of taftas, different colours.
336 (Melazé) woman's veil, in silk.
337 (Cotin) silk and cotton piece goods.
338 Linen cloth, fine, from Assiout.
339 (Chaks) silk and cotton piece goods.
340 Lantern, in date branches.
341 Extinguisher, in Kench earth.
342 Jar, in the same.
343 Cover, of Indian cane.
344 Basket, containing a water jug.
345 Water jugs, of Kench earth.
346 Basket, containing a marghoune.
347 Water jugs, of Kench earth.
348 Writing case, in alizier wood.
349 Fans, &c.
350—352 Trays, in date branches, coloured.
353 Small baskets, in date branches, from Upper Egypt.
354 Piece of thick rope, in date branches.
355 (Leban) rope to tie boats.
356 (Salatch) rope to tie loads.
357 Large baskets, from Upper Egypt.
358—360 White baskets, of various sizes.
361 (Batta) butter-tub, for voyage, in leather.
362 Strings of date fibres, for carrying straw.
363 Pipes from Cairo.
364 Bowls of pipes.
365 Dromedary saddle, with complete appendages.
366 White and black wool.
367 Soda.
368 Narguile, in zinc, with the silver stand, &c.
369 Inkstand in silver.
370 Holster for pistols.
371 Raw and refined alum.
372 Saddle, in velvet, richly ornamented.
373 (Marchaha) saddle without the back.
374 Catalogue of the oriental books.
375 Silver tray for coffee.
376 Stoppers for jugs made in earth of assioul.
377 Box for holding the coffee.
378 Silver sieve for coffee.
379 Flask for antimony, in silver.
380 Silver coffee-pot.
381 Porcelain coffee cups.
382 Silver stands for the cups.
383 Large box, containing the coffee service.
384 Silk, first quality (imitation of Broussa) ; the same, ordinary, and six other qualities of silk.
385 Silver stoppers for jugs.
386 Flask for rose-water, and *cassolettes* for perfume.
387 Réchaud, coffee-stand, in silver.
388 Liquorice wood.
389 Rum, from Upper Egypt.
390 Oil.
391 Refined sugar, from Ibrahim Pasha's refinery.

FRANCE.

(General Commissioner of the French Government in London: M. SALLANDROUZE DE LAMORNAIX, 12 *George St.*
Hanover Sq.)   Agents, Lightly and Simon, *Fenchurch St.*

1 ADOLPHE, C. Manufactory, Mulhouse (Haut-Rhin), and at M. GUEBIN's, 8 Rue de la Bourse, Paris.—Pieces of silk and woollen damask, wrought by Jacquard looms.

2 AGOMBARD, P. Manufacturer, St. Quentin (Aisne).—Hydraulic lime reduced to powder (patented).

3 ALBOY, L. N. Manufacturer, Bois-Milan, Setz (Orne).—Elbow and broken axletree plough; back trains for a changel for various tilling purposes.—Patent.

4 ALCAN & LOCATELLI, Civil Engineers, 28 Rue d'Enghien, Paris.—Various files, patented in France, England, Belgium, and Germany.

5 ALCAN & LIMEY, Civil Engineers, 28 Rue d'Enghien, Paris.—Spun silk.   Calcutta silk cocoons.

6 ALLIX, A. J. Wax Modeller, 41 Rue Montmartre, Paris.—Figures for hair-dressers.   Stays and fancy articles.

7 ANGRAND, —, Manufacturer, 59 Rue Meslay, Paris.—Fancy papers and borders.   Boardings of all sorts.   China paper and cards.

8 ARDUIN & CHANCEL, Manufacturers, Briançon (Hautes-Alpes), Post Office.—White fancy combed floss silk, obtained by the preparation and the carding of spinning waste and throwing silk.

9 ARRAULT, Manufacturer, 96 Rue St. Denis, Paris.—Fancy papers; plate ornaments; shades made of lace-paper.

10 ANDREOLETI, W. C. Mechanician and Chimney Maker, at St. Lo (Manche).   Manufactory 167 Drury Lane, London.—Twenty-three models of different apparatus for cooking and distillation, bakehouses, &c.

11 AUDOT, E. J. Manufactory and Depôt, 81 Rue Richelieu, Paris.—Work-boxes of all sorts, for travelling and other purposes.

12 AUGAN, M. Manufacturer, 10 Rue de Latour d'Auvergne, Paris.—Artificial gum.

13 AUZOUX, L. M.D. 2 Rue de l'Observance, Paris.—Models in comparative anatomy.

14 ARMANGAND, sen. Professor at the Conservatoire des Arts et Métiers, Paris.—Drawings for manufactories: works relative to machinery, tools, and apparatus, both French and foreign, forming 7 vols., with Atlas.

15 BARANOWSKI, J. J. 3 Rue de Parme, Paris. (Agent in London, W. Lund, 24 Fleet Street, City).—Machine for printing, numbering, and registering tickets, &c—patented in England and France.   Gas-meter index; ballot box; and ready-reckoning machine.

16 BARRALLON & BROSSARD, J. St. Etienne (Loire).—Plain satin. Ribbons and fabrics made of raw silk. Patented. Dyed and printed after weaving.

17 BAHUET, A. Manufacturer, Beaumont (Marne).—Unbleached and coloured merino tissues.

18 DE BAJELAIRE, E. Ribbon Manufacturer, Moirans (Isère).—Satin and taffeta ribbons.

19 BARBEAUX LECUYER, J. L. Manufacturer, Bazancourt (Marne).—Pieces of merino, part unbleached, and part dyed.

20 BARRE-RUSSIN, —, China Manufacturer, Orchamps (Jura).—Hard description of china ware, fire-proof.

21 BARTH, MASSING, & PLICHON, Manufacturers, Sarreguemine (Moselle), and at 29 Rue du Temple, Paris.—Plush and silk velvets for hats.

22 BATHIER, V. Bootmaker, à la Souterraine (Creuse).—Wooden shoes of different shapes and sizes, a new invention.   Exported.

23 BEGUIN, A. Pasteboard Works Maker, 6 Rue du Marché St. Honoré, Paris.—Fine and common pasteboard.   Stationery, &c.

24 BENCRAFT, S. Saddler, 36 Rue de Ponthieu, Paris.—Horse-collars, harness, saddle, &c.

25 BERGER-WALTER, —, Watch Glass Manufacturer, 27 Rue de Paradis Poissonnière, Paris.—Spectacle glasses.   Crystal door-handles, mounted in glass or in metal.

26 BILLECOQ, A. Shawl Manufacturer, 25 Boulevard Poissonnière, Paris.—Fancy needlework on shawls, scarfs, and cashmere and crape fabrics.

27 BLANCHER, J.B. Manufacturer, St. Just-en-Chaussée (Oise).—Specimens of plain and embroidered net-work.   Plain and fancy silk stockings.

28 BLANZY, POURE, & Co., Metallic Pen Manufacturers, Boulogne-sur-Mer.—Steel pens of every shape.

29 BLECH, STEINBACH, & MANTZ, Manufacturers, Mulhouse (Haut-Rhin), and at 37 Rue de Sentier, Paris.—Printed cotton goods, for exportation.

30 BLERIOT & LEMAITRE, Manufacturers, 21 Rue de Cléry, Paris.—A piece of lawn kerchiefs and several pieces of linen.

31 BOILEAU, ROBERT, Manufacturer, Pontfaverger (Marne).—Pieces of unbleached merino.

32 BONIFACE & SONS, Linen Manufacturers, Cambray, (Nord).—Linen fabrics, cambric, and lawn.

33 BONTE, L. Manufacturer, Roubaix (Nord). -
Assortment of mixed fabrics of wool and cotton for trousers.

34 BOUCHEZ-POTHIER, —, Manufacturer, Warmeriville (Marne).—Dyed and unbleached merino fabrics.

35 BOYER, sen., LACOUR BROTHERS, Manufacturers, Limoges (Haute-Vienne).—Flannels and druggets.

36 BREAUTE, E. Fancy Paper Manufacturer, 11 Rue de la Monnaie, Paris.—" Aquarelle " cards, and embossed cards for drawings and frames.

37 BRUN, A. Glove Manufacturer, Grenoble (Isère).—Machine for cutting out gloves. Kid gloves, in process of manufacture.   Dressed leathers.

38 BRUNEAUX & SON, Machine Builders, Rethel (Ardennes).—Combed wool, spun by an apparatus of the exhibitors' construction.

39 BURGUN, WALTER, BERGER, & Co. Glassworks, Götzenbruck (Moselle). — Watch and pendulum glasses, watch cases, boxes, spirits of wine lamps, &c.

40 BARRERE, B. Engineer and Engraver, from LEMERCIER's, 62 Rue Mazarine, Paris.—Specimens produced by four new engraving and carving machines.

41 BARRES BROTHERS, St. Julien en St. Alban (Ardèche).—Specimens of cocoons, and silk winding. Organzine, for manufacturing silk fabrics, plush, satin, figured, and plain ribbons.

42 BATAILLE, V. Blangy-sur-Brest (Seine-Inférieure).—Pyroligneous and other acids. Chemical productions used in manufactures, principally for dyeing and printing of stuffs.

43 BAUDON, —, Wood-dyer, 6 Rue Neuve-St.-Laurent, Paris.—Black-wood, with patchwork of various colours, for fancy joiner's work, dressing-boxes, liquor-cases, &c.

44 BAUDOUIN, A. P. 12 Rue de Socrate, Rouen; and 74 Rue Richelieu, Paris.—Specimen of enamel painting.

45 DE BAY, —, Statuary, 5 Passage Colbert, Rotonde, Paris.—Artificial stone statues and ornaments. Patent baked clay.

46 DE BEAUFORT, —, 28 Rue de Bourgogne, Paris.—Artificial foot.

47 DE BEAUVOYS, CH., Surgeon, Seiches (Maine and Loire).—Beehives, pigeon-holes, &c. Apparatus for agricultural purposes, or for rearing bees.

48 BECHOT, jun., 3 Rue du Pont-Louis-Philippe, Paris.—Travelling-clocks.

49 BEGON BROTHERS, Italian Paste Manufacturers 6 Impasse des Argentiers, Bordeaux.—Vermicelli, starch, gluten, and vegetable meal of all descriptions.

50 BELVALETTE BROTHERS, Coach Makers, Boulogne-sur-mer.—Hunting and other carriages.

51 BERARD & Co. 44 Rue Blanche, Paris.—Small coals purified, and residue of the same. Patented in France, England, Belgium, and Germany.

52 BERLINER, A. 4 Rue de Provence, Paris.—Ornamental penmanship. Design in penmanship, representing Sir Robert Peel, Small ebony furniture.

53 BERLIOZ & Co. Plate Glass Manufacturers, Montluçon, and 16 Rue de la Douane, Paris.—Glasses unfinished, with gilt and carved frames.

54 BERR & Co. 17 Rue de Clery, Paris. Agents in London, Graetzer & Herman, 3 Huggin Lane, Wood St. Cheapside, City.—Net embroidery and muslin of all sorts.

55 BERRUS BROTHERS, 73 Rue Montmartre, Paris.—Designs of all kinds of cashmere shawls.

56 BERTHAULT, —, Manufacturer, Issoudun (Indre).—Parchments of various sorts for bookbinding, coverings, boxes, sheaths, printings, &c.

57 BERTHIOT, —, Currier, 5 Rue Oblin, Paris.—Paris and Milan leathers.

58 BERTONNET, —, Gunsmith, 56 Passage Choiseul, Paris. — Guns of several kinds: damasked and carved rifle gun; drawing-room pistol; pistol with carved barrel, &c.

59 BERTRAND, F. & Co. Ganges (Hérault).—Fish-net for sea-fishing, made by machinery with a single thread; patented.

60 BESCHER, R. F. 2 Rue Guénégaud, Hôtel des Monnaies, Paris.—Musical composing stick; patented. Apparatus representing the musical scale in relation with a set of pianoforte keys.

61 BESNARD, RICHOUX, & GENEST, Angers (Maine-et-Loire).—Various specimens of hemp ropes and cords of all sorts.

62 BIBER, L. 32 Rue Hautefeuille, Paris. — Clyster irrigator, or syphon irrigator; patented. Self-acting apparatus, easy to wind up.

63 BONDON, L. 5 Rue Grange-aux-Belles Impasse Ste. Opportune, Paris.—White and dyed porcelain paper and cards. Stucco-paper and cards. Damasked papers.

64 BONNASSIEUX, —, Carver, Paris.—Cupid cutting off his wings: a figure in bronze, by Messrs. Eck & Durand, founders, in Paris.

65 BLANK, —, 20 Rue du Roi de Sicile.—Mosaics, incrustation of ivory and tortoiseshell.

66 BLANVIN, —, Manufacturer, 23 Rue aux Ours, Paris.—Mirrors, looking glasses, &c.

67 BOURDALOUE, —, Civil Engineer.—Large drawings, representing the entire self-motive mechanism of the exhibitor.

68 BOAS BROTHERS & Co. 4 Rue Vide Gousset, Paris.—Brocaded cashmere and worsted shawls.

69 BOYER, P. J. Watch-maker, Dôle, Jura.—Patent watches going for eight days and for thirty-two days.

70 BOYER, —, Bronze Manufacturer, 38 Rue Saintonge, au Marias, Paris. — Various bronze articles: Clocks, candelabras, figures, cups, lustres, and bronze of art.

71 BOYER & Co. Chemists, 33 Rue de la Harpe, Paris.—Albumen of blood, called *Serum albumineux*. (Patent in France.)

72 BRAUN, C. Designer, 34 Boulevard Bonne Nouvelle, Paris.—Designs for ribbons, made by Vignat Brothers, of St. Etienne. Large drawings for silk fabric.

73 BREDIF BROTHERS, Manufactory, 5 Rue Colbert, Tours; Depot, 3 Rue Caumartin, Paris.—Improved boots, shoes, &c. with seams.

74 BROCCHIERI, P. 21 Rue Louis-le-Grand, Paris.—Human and animal prepared blood, in a healthy or unhealthy state; preserved by "Brocchieri's fluid." Patented.

75 BRUNIER, LENORMAND, & Co. 55 Rue Vivienne, Paris.—Aromatic vinegar for toilet purposes.

76 BRUNIER, —, 55 Rue Vivienne, Paris.—Specimens of gold plating upon copper.

77 BUDIN, —, Currier, 50 Rue du Fer-à-Moulin, Paris.—Tanned and curried horse hides: for shoe-tops and upper leather.

78 BUDIN-SIGNEZ, —, Manufacturer, Beauvais (Oise).—Woven felts of all sizes, for continuous machines for the manufacture of pasteboard and paper.

79 BURAT BROTHERS, Surgeons, 12 Rue Mandar, Paris.—Trusses, with eccentric pivot.

80 CAILLAUX, Madame A. 16 Passage du Saumon, Paris.—White satin stays. Moire stays, with mechanical busk.

81 CABRIT & ROUX, Silk Reelers, St. André de Valborgne (Gard). Agents in Paris, MM. A. Germain & Co. 30 Rue de l'Echiquier. In London, Fordati, Coxhead, & Co. 13 Old Jewry Chambers.—Raw silks: cocoons, white and yellow.

82 CAILLET, FRANQUEVILLE, Manufacturer, Bazancourt (Marne).—Unbleached and dyed merinos.

83 CASTEL, E. Manufacturer, Aubusson (Creuse).—Door-curtains, Aubusson tissue, and in the Gobelin style. Panels of the same description. Sofa, table-cover, and rug.

84 CERF & NAXARA, Paste-board Works Manufacturers, 17 Rue St. Rémy, Bordeaux (Gironde).—Fine pasteboard work for holding wedding-presents; toilet and perfume boxes, &c.

85 CHARTIER, P. Glass Manufacturer, Douai, Nord.—Glass demijohns, enclosed in white wicker. For exportation.

86 CHATELAIN & FORON, Cloth Manufacturers, Rheims (Marne). — Bolivart flannel. Cloaks. Sultana cloths. Zephyr cloths.

87 CHENARD BROTHERS, Hat Manufacturers, Rue du Puits-au-Marais, Paris.—Hare and beaver hats. Pieces of felt for waistcoats.

88 CHEROT & Co. Manufacturers, Nantes (Loire-Inférieure).—Specimens of threads, cloths, and cordings, of Loire hemp. Designs; a spinning-machine, and a machine for rope-manufacturing. Patented in England.

89 CHINARD, jun. Shawl Manufacturer, 9 Rue de Cléry Paris.—A variety of long and square shawls.

90 CHOCQUEEL, L. Printed Shawl Manufacturer, Labriche, near St. Denis (Seine).—Printed long shawls, and printed gowns and dresses.

91 CHRISTOPHE, L. A. Manufacturer, Leschelles (Aisne).—Various specimens of wood tissue.

92 CHAPELLE, —, Rue du Chemin Vert, Paris.—Machines; models of regulators for the foundry of wheel-work.

93 COLLET, F. C. Lace and Trimming Manufacturer, Rue des Vieilles Andriettes, Paris.—Various specimens of lace-work and trimmings.

94 CONSTANTIN, —, Manufacturer, 7 Rue d'Antin. Paris, and 135 Regent Street, London.—A variety of artificial flowers and branches, and a small tree, artificially perfumed, for head-dresses, and wreathes. Gilt-iron columns. Quick-silvered and other mirrors.

95 CORNILLON, J. H. Jeweller, 36 Rue du Temple, Paris.—Goblets. Dressing-case stand. Crystal flagons.

96 COUDERC & SOUCARET, jun. Silk-spinners, Montauban (Tarn and Garonne).—Raw silk. Raw silk tissues.

97 COURTEY BROTHERS & BAREZ, Manufacturers, Périgueux (Dordogne).—Woollen stuffs, called *Cadis.*

98 COUTURIER & RENAULT, Manufacturers, Sarguemines (Moselle), and 31 Rue St. Avoye, Paris.—Silk plush for hats. Bonnets.

99 CUGNOT, A. Locksmith, 177 Rue Montmartre, Paris. —Various articles of fine and ornamental locksmiths' work and ironmongery for buildings.

100 CAILLO, jun. & PRIN, Alimentary Preserve Manufacturers, Nantes (Loire-Inférieure). — Sardines preserved in pure olive oil. For exportation.

101 DE CALIGNY.—Hydraulic apparatus.

102 CANDLOT, —, Wadding Manufacturer, 6 Rue St. Pierre Popincourt, Paris.—Parisian waddings, made of one piece by a wadding-machine. Invented by M. Robertson 19 Boulevard Montmartre, Paris.

103 COLIN, —, Pianoforte Manufacturer, 30 Rue du Bac, Paris.—Pianos.

104 CARBONNEAU, J. B. C. — Wood engravings, for printing illustrations. Being a portion of a work named " History of the Painters of all Schools," edited by Mr. Armengaud.

105 CARNET, X. 1 Rue des Jeûneurs, Paris.—Designs for shawls, and of Cashmere for dresses, &c. Designs for printed fabrics.

106 CARRIERE BROTHERS, Curriers, Amiens (Somme).—Curried calf-skins and boot-legs. For exportation.

107 CASTELLE, H. 55 Rue de la Verrerie, Paris. — Waterproof gelatine in sheets. Glass-paper. Crystal-paper. Printed gelatine. Engraved gelatine.

108 CAZAL, 27 Boulevard des Italiens, Paris.—Self-opening umbrellas and parasols. Travelling-sticks and umbrellas.

109 DE CAVAILLON, —, Chemist, 30 Rue Taitbout, Paris.—Chemical productions, obtained by purifying gas.

110 COSNIER & LACHESE, Type-Founders, Angers (Maine a d Loire).—Type.

111 CHALEYER, J. 24 Rue du Roi de Sicile (Marais).—Beam and cutting-machine; for army equipments, jewellers, watchmakers, lamps, &c.

112 CHAMBON, F. Cheylard (Ardèche). — Printed and dyed fabrics. Bandannas of every description.

113 CHAMBON, C. Alais (Gard).—Raw silks, white and yellow, &c.

114 CHAMPANHET-SARGEAS, M. M. J. Vals, near Aubenas (Ardèche).—Cocoons of raw silk, applicable to the manufacture of various silks.

115 CHARBONNIER, —, Truss-maker, 347 Rue St. Honoré, Paris. — Shower-bath apparatus and syphons. Various trusses.

116 CHARDON & SON, 30 Rue Hautefeuille, Paris. — Various engravings, specimens of printing.

117 CHARLES & Co. 7 Rue Furstemberg, and 22 South Molton Street, Oxford Street, London.—Machines made of galvanized sheet-iron or copper, for washing linen, &c.

118 CHATEL, —, Designer, 2 Rue de Mulhouse, Paris.—Manufactured designs for silks, mousseline-de-laine, jaconet, printed cotton, and carpets.

119 CHENOT, A.—"Metallic sponges. Iron and steel, produced by means of the said sponges without smelting the ore." Patent.

120 CHENNEVIERE, D. Louviers (Eure).—Cloth, and other fancy articles.

121 CHEVET, J. Palais National, Paris.—Preserves of all sorts—complete dinners. Dishes prepared for cooking, with gravy and sauces ready for use.

122 CHOMEREAU, —, Drawing-master of the Lyceum at Laval (Mayenne).—Wax: relieve models of ornaments for jewel-boxes.

123 CHUARD, —, 6 Rue Carnot, Paris.—Safety lamps, without wire gauze; gasoscopes, &c. Apparatus used for preventing explosions of gas in pits and all places lit by gas.

124 COCHOIS & COLIN, 7 Rue des Déchargeurs, Paris (Manufactories at Troyes and Arcis (Aube). — Hosiery: Stockings, socks, gloves, trousers, waistcoats, and night-gowns.

125 COCU, A. 58 Faubourg du Temple, Paris.—Cash-mere texture: waistcoats of all descriptions.

126 COLLIN, C. E., 7 Quai Conti, Paris.—Hydrographic engravings, plans, charts; topographical and hydrographical studies. The above works are a portion of the publications of the Navy Depôt in Paris.

127 COUPIER & MELLIER, 20 Rue Gaillon, Paris.—Paper made of vegetable substances mixed with rag waste.

128 COPPIN, L. jun. Douai (Nord).—Improved hides for cards. Finished and unfinished linings and plates, for wool and cotton cards.

129 COULAUX, sen. & Co. Molsheim and Klingenthal (Bas-Rhin).—Side-arms and articles of hardware. Extensive manufactory—formerly a Royal arms manufactory.

130 COURTOIS, A. sen. 23 Rue des Vieux Augustins, Paris.—Curvilineal piston, for brass musical instruments, to replace into rectangular pistons. Patent.

131 CROPET, —, Piano-forte Manufacturer, Toulouse (Haute Garonne). — Cottage piano. Small mahogany model.

132 CROUTELLE, —, Rheims (Marne).—Spun yarn and sized yarn, for machine weaving.

133 CRUCIFIX, E. Crevecœur, near Beauvais (Oise).—Waterproof shoes, boots, &c. The sole is five-fold, made of leather, wood, and cork.

134 CUDRUE, F. 58 Rue du Faubourg du Temple, Paris.—Fasteners, for securing windows and doors.

135 CURMER, A. 13 Rue des Marais, St. Germain, Paris —Stereotype, made of papier-maché, of general use in French libraries.

136 DANJARD, L. F. A. Manufacturer, 40 Rue St. Germain, Paris.—Mechanical dolls for milliners.

137 DAUTREMER & Co. Flax Spinners, Lille (Nord).—Grey and yellow lawn threads.

138 DAVID-LABBEZ & Co. Woollen Manufacturers, Sains Richaumond (Aisne).—Unbleached and coloured merino fabrics.

139 DEBRAY, C. Basket-worker, 73 Rue Rambuteau, Paris.—Baskets of different shapes.

140 DEBUCHY, F. Manufacturer, Lille (Nord), Rue Basse.—Drills, and other tissues, for waistcoatings. New fancy materials for trousers.

141 DELAGE-MONTIGNAC, F. Net Manufacturer, 414 Rue St. Honoré, Paris.—Silk threads for fishing lines; fishing nets; sweeping nets.

142 DELATTRE & SON, Manufacturers, Roubaix (Nord).—Various fabrics for dresses, of long combed wool and combed merino wool.

143 DELEGUE & Co. Manufacturers, Saffres (Côte d'Or).—Woollen fabrics; combed wool; woollen threads of different kinds.

144 DELFOSSE BROTHERS, Manufacturers, Roubaix (Nord).—Woollen and other fabrics, in various qualities.

145 DERVAUX-LEFEBVRE, —, Hardware Manufacturer, Condé (Nord).—Chains, bolts, and other articles of hardware.

146 DIETSCH & Co. Cloth Manufacturers, Strasbourg (Bas-Rhin).—Kerseymere cloths. Zephyr cloths of various colours.

147 DOUCET & DUCLERC, A. Shirt-makers, 21 Rue de la Paix, Paris.—Shirting and various made-up articles.

148 DUBAR-DELESPAUL, —, Manufacturer, Roubaix. —Cotton textures for trousers, and other articles of apparel.

149 DUCROT & PETIT, Fan Maker, 11 Rue des Fontaines, Paris, and 133 Regent Street.—Various fans, and pasteboard moulds for folding fan leaves.

150 DUSSOL, —, Silk & Glove Manufacturer, Sumène (Gard).—Fine yellow and white raw silks; silk gloves of different colours.

151 DUVAL & PARIS, Lamp-makers, 1 Boulevard, St. Denis, Paris, and 57 King St. Golden Sq. London.—Bronze and porcelain lamps, with stand, shade, and glass; different objects in bronze.

152 DABARET-TAMPE, —, T. Precy-sur-Oise (Oise).— Silk buttons of all sorts.

153 DAMAINVILLE, —, Poudron, near Crépy (Oise), Depôt at Crepy.—Artificial honeycombs, for agriculture. New principle for feeding bees.

154 DAUCHEL, jun. Manufacturer, Amiens (Somme).— Various patent tissues for furniture, designed and manufactured by the exhibitor.

155 DAUDRIEU,—, Pontchartrain (Seine and Oise), and 4 Rue de Bussi, Paris.—Paper-hangings, painted by the hand, and capable of being washed.

156 DAUDVILLE, A. St. Quentin (Aisne). — Various stores and curtains, the designs of the exhibitor; patented. Pictures of Queen Victoria and Prince Albert, English colours, emblems of France.

157 DAVID BROTHERS & CO. St. Quentin (Aisne), Depôt at 20 Rue St. Fiacre, Paris.—Various woollen cloths, woven with yarn combed.

158 DELACRETAZ & FOURCADE, 18 Rue Croix de Nivert, Vaugirard, near Paris.—Stearine candles and stearine acids, Patented.

159 DAVID, —. Cable Manufacturer, Chaines, Havre.— Novel system of pulleys working friction.

160 DELEUIL, L. J. 8 Rue du Pont-de-Lodi, Paris.—Philosophical instruments and balances; coin-scales, air pumps, electric batteries, magneto-electric apparatus, &c.

161 DENIS, A. Dyer, Notre Dame de Boudeville, near Rouen (Seine-Inférieure).—Pink safflower dyed calicoes.

162 DERVILLE & CO. 36 Quai Jemmapes, Paris.—French marbles of various sorts.

163 DE HAUSSY, —.—Drawings for panels of hanging paper.

164 DESPREAUX, A. A. 6 Rue Neuve des Petits Champs, Paris.—Venetian leathers, silks, dresses, &c.; new patent process for manufacturing tissues.

165 DEUZY, P. Athies-les-Arras (Pas de Calais).—Pasteboard; linen pasteboard; straw pasteboard; for binding, packing, &c.

166 DEVISME, —, Gunsmith, 36 Boulevard des Italiens, Paris.—Muskets. Various fire and side-arms. Patented.

167 DEZAUX-LACOUR, —.—Tanner and Currier, Guise (Aisne).—Curried hides. Calf-skins for shoes. Calf-skins for spinning-mills and for harness-makers; exportation.

168 DILLENSEGER & PATRY, 8 Rue Frépillon, Paris.— Achromatic opera glasses. Gold, silver, tortoiseshell, buffalo, sham-gold, and steel spectacles. Hand, nose, and eye glasses of every description; patented.

169 DROUIN & BROSSIER, Chemical Production Manufacturers, Labriche, near St. Denis (Seine). — Various chemical productions.

170 DUBOIS & SON, Tanners and Curriers, 31 Rue Cheverus, Bordeaux, (Gironde)—Boot-legs; calf-skins, rough, white, and black.

171 DUCHENNE, —, M.D. 85 Rue Louis-le-Grand, Paris.—Volta-electric apparatus, and double-current magneto-electric apparatus. Invented by Messrs. Charrière and Deleuil, surgical instrument makers, Paris.

172 DUCHESNE, House Painter, 16 Rue Croix des Petits Champs, Paris.—Preparation for artistical and monumental painting; applicable upon flag-stones in damp places.

173 DUCROQUET, P. A. Organ-builder, Rue St. Maur St. Germain, Paris.—Church-organ, with 20 stops, two rows of keys, and one pedal stop. Patented.

174 DUFOUR, jun. Brushmakers, Lille (Nord), and 40 Rue de Paris. — Patent mechanical brush for rubbing floors.

175 DUMAINE, X. Silk-producer, Tournon (Rhône)— Yellow raw spun silk. Organzine, employed in manufacturing the rich stuffs, ribbons, crapes, and satins of Lyons and St. Etienne.

176 DUMERIL, SONS, & CO. St. Omer (Pas-de-Calais).—Clay pipes, patented; and clay figures. Samples of various sorts.

177 DUMORTIER, L. Bousbecque, near Lille (Nord).— Bunch of raw flax, French growth, retted in the river Lys (Nord) in 1849.

178 DUMOULIN, S. 44 Rue Basse du Rempart, Paris.— Stays without gussets. Patented invention.

179 DELVART, —, Clock Maker, Zougues, Pas-de-Calais. —Astronomical clock.

180 DUPONT, A. 3 and 5 Rue Neuve St. Augustins, Paris—Solid wrought and cast-iron ornamented bedsteads; spring mattresses. Patented.

181 DUPONT, P. 55 Rue de Grenelle St. Honoré, Paris. —Administrative printing office and library; lithography; litho-typography. Stereotype on stone, and stones for lithography.

182 DUPORT, V. 16 Rue des Francs-Bourgeois St. Marcel, Paris.—Hydes of large size, prepared by a new process, patented in France, for splitting hides.

183 DUPRE, J. F. Forges-les-Eaux (Seine-Inférieure). —Green copperas, or sulphate of iron.

184 DUPUIS, J. Marble-worker, 22 Petite rue St. Pierre Amelot, Paris.—Marble chimneys.

185 DERRIEY, —, Type-Founder and Music Printer, 12 Rue Notre Dame.—Impressions of music.

186 DURAND, —, La Sauvetat du Drob (Lot-et-Garonne).—Stove-oven: new principle, patented. Reduced model of the functioning apparatus, one-third of its size.

187 DU SEIGNEUR, J. B. Sculpt. 36 Rue de l'Ouest. —St. Michael and the dragon, colossal group, made of plaster.

188 DIETRICH & SONS, Hiederbonn.—Iron casting of the Saviour on the Cross. Sheet of cast-iron, 7 feet by 2 feet, and ½ inch thick. Ornamental iron casting with name of firm. Two boxes containing 11, and two others 24 specimens of iron casting. Dishes, stew-pans, and various pieces of wrought iron.

189 DUVAL, A. Caen (Calvados).—Yellow and white silk yarn, especially suitable to lace and blonde manufacturing.

190 EVROT, C. N. Manufacturer, Charmes (Voges).— Imitations of different marbles, prepared by means of oil-stucco.

192 ENGELMANN & GRAF, 12 Rue de l'Abbaye, Paris. —Patent mechanical process for lithographic colour printing.

193 BROTHER EUSTATE, of the Institution of Brothers of Christian Schools at Lille (Nord).—Dry and green herb mowing machine, invented by the exhibitor, and executed by Albert Dutreiz, his pupil.

194 FASSIN, —. jun. Rheims (Marne).—Worsted tissues, cachemire and Valencia waistcoatings.

195 FORGEOT, E. & CO. Saleux, Thil, near Amiens (Somme).—Goat hair spun. Skeins and reels of double-spun goat hair. Raw and combed goat hair.

197 FAYOLLE, L. T. 10 Galerie de Valois, Palais National, Paris.—Crosses for various French and foreign orders, made of gold silver, and imitation. Strass jewels, embroidered ribbons, and masonic decorations of all sorts for freemasons.

198 FEAU-BECHARD, V. A. Passy-les-Paris (Seine).—Woollens and cashmeres, dyed in various colours, for manufacturing cashmere shawls and fancy articles.

199 FELIX, A. Manufacturer, 40 Rue St. Honoré, Paris. Agents in London, M. M. Graetzer & Hermann, 8 Huggins Lane, Wood St. Cheapside, London.—Fans of all descriptions. Jewellery, and French skins for fans.

200 FEROUELLE & ROLLAND, Manufactory, St. Quentin and Tarare. Depot, 8 Rue du Sentier, Paris.—Stoves and broché for furniture. Plain and figured muslins, tartalanes. Fancy stuffs for dresses, &c.

201 FAUQUET-LEMAITRE, Flax Spinner, Bolbec (Seine-Inférieure).—Flax threads, lawn threads warp and woof for power-loom weaving; tissue of cotton waste.

202 FAUVELLE DELEBARRE, Comb Maker, 10 Boulevart Bonne Nouvelle, Paris.—Tortoiseshell and buffalo-horn combs.

204 FLAISSIER BROTHERS, Carpet Manufacturers, Nimes (Gard).—Carpets of various kinds; short-nap carpets, &c.

205 FONTANA, Mrs. Painter's Brush Manufacturer, 41 Rue des Marais, Paris.—Various paint brushes.

206 FORTEL, LARBRE & Co. Manufacturers, Reims (Marne).—Stuffs for waistcoats, dresses, cloaks, and paletots.

208 FROMENT, CLOLUS, Wooden Shoe Manufacturer, 15 Rue Neuve St. Méry, Paris.—Wooden shoes of different shapes.

209 FEYEUX, Manufacturer, 10 Rue Taranne, Paris.—Chocolate, alimentary flour, &c.

210 FIEUX, Son sen. & Co. Tanners and Curriers, Toulouse (Haute-Garonne).—Various sorts of leathers, for saddle, harness, shoemakers, &c.

211 FIOLET, LOUIS, St. Omer (Pas-des-Calais)—Various sorts of clay pipes.

212 FIRMIN DIDOT BROTHERS, Printers, Booksellers, and Paper Manufacturers, 56 Rue Jacob, Paris.—Books and various publications. Bibliotheca Scriptorum Græcorum; trade directory, &c.

213 FLAMET, —, jun. 87 Rue St. Martin, Paris.—Elastic stockings for varicose veins.

214 FLEURY, J. F. Chemist, La Teste de Buch, near Bordeaux (Gironde).—Purified marine turpentine. New principle for purifying raw turpentine, found in the wastes of Bordeaux. Patented. Exportation.

215 FLOBERT, —, Gunsmith, 3 Rue Racine, Paris.—Guns, muskets, and pistols: patented.

218 FROELY, A. 37 Rue Battant, Besançon (Doubs).—Various files made of French cast steel; some of which are cut by the hand, others by machinery.

219 FROMAGE, L. 5 Rue des Petites Eaux, Darnetal (Seine-Inférieure).—Power-looms, improved by the exhibitor. For weaving Rouen and Scotch articles.

220 FROMONT, —, Working Engineer, Chartres (Eure and Loir).—Improved model of a Turbine made after Fontaine's system.

220 FOUCAULT, P. (Blind), Aux Quinze Vingts, 28 Rue de Charenton, Paris.—Writing apparatus for the use of the blind. A new invention, adopted by the Institution for Blind Children, of Paris.

221 FOURNIVAL, SON, ALTMAYER & Co. Spinning-Mill Owners, Rethel (Ardennes), Manufactory of Merinos at Solesme (Nord).—Spun brown wool. Dyed merino

222 GOUDCHAUX-PICARD SONS, Cloth-Manufacturer, Nancy (Meurthe).—Fine woollen cloths, new patterns.

223 GESSON-MAZILLE, Wool-stuff Manufacturer, Rethel (Ardennes).—Pieces of merino fabric, unbleached and dyed.

224 GIGOT & BOISOTAU, Manufacturers, Reims (Marne). —Merino fabrics, unbleached and coloured.

225 GAILLARD, SON, 210 Rue de Faubourg St. Denis, Paris.—Copper, iron, and brass-wire gauze, &c.

226 GAILLARD, SON, sen. La Ferté-Sous-Jouarre (Seine and Marne).—Various grinding-stones. Grinding-stones, in pieces, manufactured and dressed with rays. Squares of grinding-stones for grinding all sorts of grain.

227 GAGNEAU BROTHERS, 25 Rue d'Enghien (Paris).—Lamps, bronze. Suspension mechanical lamps, for dining-rooms and other purposes.

228 GALIMARD, N. A. 4 Rue Honoré Chevalier, Paris.—Designs for manufactures: Epistle-writers writing their epistles. St. Apoline. St. Laurent; made on window-glass, for decorating the choir of St. Laurent's Church in Paris.

229 GALLICHER & Co. Iron-works, Bigny and Forge-neuve (Cher).—Best iron (called Berry iron); proper for agriculture, edge-tool making, ironmongery, machine and carriage building.

230 GANDILLOT & Co. 40 Rue Bellefond, Paris.—Bronze bedsteads. Hollow iron furniture, &c.

231 GERENTE, A. 13 Quai d'Anjore, Paris. — Stained glass.

232 GARACH, J. Roquemingarde (Hérault), near Montagnac.—Written compositions, for educational purposes, leaving blank the tenses of verbs.

233 GARNAUD, SON, 9 Rue St. Germain-des-Près, Paris, and Manufactory at Choisy-le-Roi (Seine).—Ornaments made of white baked clay, for ornamenting the outside of buildings.

234 GAUTHIER, SON, 14 Rue de la Parcheminerie, Paris. —Typographic prints, with bearing-blocks, vignettes, &c. a new invention, patented in France and in foreign countries.

235 GAVARD, A. 9 Quai de l'Horloge, Paris.—Diagraphs and pantographs, for reprinting maps and typographical charts, tableaus, and drawings of all descriptions.

236 GIDE & BAUDRY, Booksellers and Publishers, 5 Rue des Petits Augustins, Paris.—Volumes and various publications: Scientific Exploration of Algeria. Monument of Nineveh. Architecture from the fifth to the sixteenth century. Voyage in Persia. Voyage of Dumont D'Urville.

237 GILBERT, C. J. 63 Rue du Bac, Paris.—Painted and waterproof stores. Patented.

238 GILBERT & Co. Manufactory at Givet (Ardennes). Depôts, 18 Rue Quincampoix, Paris; and 105 Regent Street, London.—Various pencils for drawing, offices, &c.

239 GRATIA. —.—Pastel drawings. New system of the application of pastel.

240 GODARD & BONTEMPS, Manufactories at Cambrai and Valenciennes (Nord); Babpaume (Pas-de-Calais); Verviers (Aisne); Clermont (Oise): 40 Rue de Clery, Paris.—Lawn and cambric.

241 GOUIN, A. Painter, 37 Rue Louis-le-Grand, Paris.—Coloured daguerreotypes.

242 GERIMON, SON, St. Etienne (Loire).—Various ribbons.

243 GRANDJEAN, Mme. O. 8 Cité d'Antin, Paris.—Flowers made of spun glass. Patented in England.

244 GRANDBARBE, 48 Rue des Marais, St. Martin, Paris. —Design for manufacturing carpets.

245 GRAUX, J. L. Husbandman at the Ferm de Mauchamp, Commune de Juvincourt (Aisne).—Glazed and silk-like wool fleece, being a peculiar variety of merino sheep.

246 GREMAILLY SON, sen. Hotel du Sauvage, Gray (Haut-Saone).—Alimentary preserves (French cooking).

247 GRENET, L. F. Rouen (Seine-Inférieure).—Glue. Gelatine. Various sorts of gelatine and gelatine articles, &c.

248 GROS-ODIER-ROMAN & Co. Manufactory at Wesserling (Haut-Rhin): Depôts, 15 Boulevard Poissonnière, Paris

and SALOMONS & SONS, M. M. R. 42 Old Change, London.—Calico and woollen goods, bleached and printed with cylinder.

249 GROSSELIN, A. Geographer, 7 Rue du Battoir, St. André, Paris.—Celestial globe. Georamas and uranoramas, used also as lamp-shades. New sphere in the Copernican system. Terrestrial globe, with spherical covering, to represent the alternations of day and night.

250 GUESNU, —, 70 Rue du Temple, Paris.—Fancy papers. Stampings for boardings. Gold, silver, and coloured printing.

251 GUILLEMOT BROTHERS, Manufacturers, Meulan (Seine and Oise), Depôt 88 Rue Neuve des Mathurins, Paris.—Coach and livery lace.

252 GUINIER, T. 25 Rue Grenelle St. Honoré, Paris.—Water closets and cocks. New system, patented in France, in England, and in Belgium.

253 GUYOTIN-LORSIGNOL, Reims, 14 and 99 Rue du Borg, St. Denis (Marne).—Blankets, of various qualities.

254 GUYNET & BECQUET, 30 Rue du Sentier, Paris; houses at Valenciennes, Cambrai, and Nancy.—Printed and embroidered white cambric handerchiefs.

255 HADROT, —, jun. 37 Faubourg St. Martin, Paris; and 12 Castle St. Holborn; and 289 Regent St. London.—Patent moderator lamp, called hadrot.

256 HARTMANN & SONS, Munster (Haut-Rhin). Depôts at Lyons and 32 Rue du Sentier, Paris.—Spun cottons; white calicoes; cambric muslins; jaconet muslins; and printed woollen and cotton fabrics.

257 HARTMANN & Co. (Malmerspach, Haut-Rhin).—Fine raw and combed wool, and yarn for shawls and other articles.

258 HAYOT, J. J. Coachmaker, Caen (Calvados.)—Four-wheeled carriage: patented. Constructed so as to be divided into two separate parts.

259 HEILIGENTHAL & Co. Strasbourg (Bas-Rhin).—Ornaments made of putty-stone, for decorating the inside and outside of buildings.

260 HELBRONNER, G. 129 Rue Montmartre, Paris.—Needlework, and canvas for ornamental work.

261 HENOC, —, 1 Rue St. Sauveur, Paris.—Screens and feather-brooms, of various colours, made of ostrich, peacock, and other feathers.

262 HENRI, J. Oculist-optician, 21 Passage Delorme. and 12 Rue de Rivoli, Paris.—Glasses for persons affected with squinting. Sight-preservers

263 HESS, G. 6 Rue de la Villière, Paris. Agent, —, 1 Bread St. London.—Figured tissues in various styles.

264 HOEN, J. B. Nimes, (Gard).—New system of windows, blinds, and shutters. Patent for 15 years. An elegant and simple system, without machinery, springs, or gear.

265 HOSTIN, —, Flower-maker, Etel (Morbihan). — Flowers, leaves, and baskets made of shells.

266 HUARD BROTHERS, Versailles (Seine-et-Oise). — Nautical watch-works of various sorts.

267 DELAROCHE-DAIGREMONT, Manu. 17 Rue de la Paix, Paris ;—Depôt, London, 8 Maddox St. Hanover Sq.—Embroidery and nouveautés.

268 HUBERT, Madame JOSEPHINE, Mondeville, near Caen (Calvados) ; manufactory, 2 Rue du Grand Chantier, Paris.—Flowers, fruits, leaves, lace, and guipure, in relievo, embossed, and raised.

269 HUE, J. B. 76 Faubourg St. Martin's, Paris. — Various locks. Machine for cutting and bending at the same time hooks and eyes, made and invented by the exhibitor; patented. Hooks and eyes cut by the said machine.

270 HUET, Mme. Rouen (Seine-Inférieure), and 12 and 14 Rue du Cimetière, St. Nicolas, Paris. — India-rubber articles, braces, and twists.

271 JACOBBER, —, China-painter, 43 Rue du Faubourg, St. Denis, Paris.—One dozen painted plates, in porcelain of Sèvres. Two large paintings on porcelain, flowers and fruits, exhibited by the Sèvres National Manufactory.

272 JACQUEMART BROTHERS, Charleville (Ardennes).—Fire-arms. Patent articles of ironmongery, and hardware.

273 JAILLON, MOINIER, & Co. La Villette, near Paris (Seine).—Stearic acids. Stearine candles. Soaps. Patented in France and England.

274 JAPUIS & SON, Claye, near Paris (Seine and Marne).—Printed calicoes. Prints, articles for furniture; and muslins for dresses.

275 JAPY BROTHERS, Beaucourt (Haut-Rhin), and 108 Rue du Temple, Paris.—Watch-making: clock and watch works. Ironmongery, &c.

276 JOLLY, F. Mer (Loire and Cher).—Purified oil, for watchmakers, machinery, and fire-arms.

277 JOLY, —, Esternay (Marne) ; depôt, 24 Rue du Faubourg St. Denis, and at Mr. Lœullier's, Paris.—Two large vases in porcelain, all in one piece, ornamented.

278 JUHEL-DESMARES, J. Manufacturer, Vire (Calvados).—Cloth of various fabrics and colours : twilled beaver, double-milled and plain cloth, satin.

279 JULIEN, Miss MARGUERITE, Lace-maker, au Puy (Haute-Loire). — Blondes. Lace. Velvet-silk. Alençon silk. Florence shawl, collars, lappets, and veils.

280 KELLER, —, Hydrographic Engineer, 40 Rue du Bac, Paris.—Double planisphere for navigating on the great circle system.

281 KIRSTEIN, F. Chisler, Strasbourg (Bas-Rhin).—Silver alto-relievos, representing groupes of animals and hunting parties.

282 KNECHT, EMILE, Wood-carver, 45 Rue de Babylone, Paris.—Holy-water basin, carved in pear-tree wood, of a single piece. Oval frame, with the flowers and ribbons carved in oak wood, gilt by Picarel.

283 LACROIX & SON, Engine-workers, Rouen (Seine-Inférieure), and 23 and 27, Boulevard St. Hilaire.—Patent lithographic machine. Fulling machine, for cloths. Patented.

284 LAFAYE, P. 9 Rue de l'Empereur (Barrière Blanche), Paris.—Painted window-glass. The subjects chiefly composed by the exhibitor.

285 LAHURE, —, Havre (Seine-Inférieure).—Noncapsizable yawl.

286 LAINE-LAROCHE, & MAX, R. Angers, Maine-et-Loire.—Raw Angers hemp ; combed hemp for power-looms ; hemp yarns, for canvass warp and weft; and sail canvass made of hemp, woven without sizing, for the navy of France.

287 LANEUVILLE, V. 17 Rue Ste. Croix, de la Bretonnière, Paris.—Machine for making seamless purses ; machine for making watch-ribbons. Patented.

288 LANG, L. Schlestadt (Bas-Rhin).—Various specimens of wire gauze, for machine-made paper manufactory.

289 LANGLOIS & LECLERCQ, Booksellers, 81 Rue de la Harpe, Paris.—Various scientific and literary illustrated works.

290 LARIVIERE, C. Agent of the Slate Works, Angers (Maine and Loire).—Angers slate, the produce of eight quarries belonging to the Company.

291 LAROCHE, E. 10 Rue des Jeûneurs, Paris.—Manufacture designs, for printing on tissues, made use of by various houses in France and abroad.

292 LAUMAIN, C. Watchmaker, 15 Rue de la Truanderie, Paris.—Pocket chronometers.

293 LAUREAU, L. 12 Rue St. Gilles, au Marais, Paris.—Five figures made of a galvanized compound metal of bronze and pewter, representing the Republic, Europe, Asia, Africa, and América.

294 LAURENT GSELL, & Co. Glass-painters, 43 Rue St.

I

Sebastien, Paris.—Two armorial bearings, in the style of the 17th century. Two painted windows. One panel, style of the 16th century. Six panes of glass, with medallions, for ornamenting apartments.

295 Lautz, L. Ivory-carver, 40 Rue de Montmorency, Paris.—Ivory vase, representing the battle of the Franks against the Saxons, gained by Charlemagne.

296 Laydet Son, sen. & Co. Niort (Deux Sevres), and 37 Rue Grenelle St. Honoré, Paris. Agents—MM. Graetzer & Hermann, 3 Huggins Lane, Wood St. London.—Chamois leather; buckskin gloves; beaver and chamois gloves.

297 Leblanc, A. Miller, Mourroux, near Coulommières (Seine and Marne).—Wheat-flour, first quality, for making bread.

298 Lebrun, A. Optician, 3 Rue Chapon, Paris. Agent —Mr. Salomon, 22 Red Lion Sq. London.—Spectacles, telescopes, and optical-glasses.

299 Leclerc, H. Engine-worker, 105 Quai Valmy, Paris.—Hydraulic machines of different sorts. Pumps, jets, fountains, &c. Patented.

300 Lecoentre, —, Marine Officer, 52 Rue St. George, Paris.—Sounding-lead, nautical apparatus for soundings, adapted for the ships of the French fleet.

301 Lefrançois, —, 302 Rue St. Denis, and 7 Passage Basfour, Paris.—Sliding and other boxes for lucifer-matches. Patented.

302 Lehuby, —, Chemist, 78 Rue St. Lazare, Paris.— Medicamental envelopes, or lichen capsules (patented in France and England), for concealing the taste of medicines.

303 Lemolt, A. E. 42 Passage Jouffroy, Paris.—Galvanic battery, constructed in the workshops of M. Loyreau, optician, Paris. Choca. Patented in France and England.

304 Lemonnier, —, Jeweller, 6 Place Vendôme, Paris. —Set of emeralds belonging to Her Majesty the Queen of Spain, and various articles of jewellery.

305 Leon, —, Chemist, 7 Rue de Crussol, Paris.—Varnishes for bookbinding, pocket-books, &c.

306 Leon-Clement & Bourgeois, Morez (Jura). — Watch-making, called de comté. Clocks, watches, regulators, &c. Kitchen jacks. Exportation.

307 Leperdriel, —, Chemist and Druggist, 28 Rue des Martyrs, Paris.—Pharmaceutical articles. Elastic stockings, &c.

308 Leroux, —, Vitry le François (Marne).—Bark of willow-tree. Salicine, its active principle.

309 Leroux, —, Clockmaker, Cancale (Ile and Vilaine). —Clock with a new arrangement of striking mechanism.

310 Lapierre & Son, Vallerangue (Gard). — Raw and spun silk.

311 Lespinasse, —, 34 Quai de Billy, Paris.—Model of oven for bread-baking. New patented system.

312 Lethuillier-Pinel, Sotteville les Rouen (Seine-Inférieure).—New safety apparatus for steam-boilers and locomotive engines, patented. Steam-whistle, gauges, steam-gauges, &c.

313 Leunenschloss, M. Manufactory, Rouen (Seine-Inférieure); depôt, 19 Rue de la Fidélité, Paris.—Braces and trimmings for tailors, &c., for ladies' dresses.

314 Lorthiois - Desplanque, Tourcoing (Nord). — Carded wool yarn, for textures of three different qualities.

315 Louis, Blais Son, Letellier, & Co. Hâvre (Seine-Inférieure).—Various ropes for the navy, patented. Shrouds, foot-ropes, rigging, &c.

316 Louit Brothers & Co. Bordeaux (Gironde).— Chocolate and mustards, manufactured by steam.

317 Maire & Co. Chemical Manufacturers, Strasbourg (Bas-Rhin).—Acetate of lead, soda, lime, copper, acetate acid; white-lead, purified alcohol, vinegar. Patented.

318 Maitre, A. Bookseller and Bookbinder, Dijon (Côte d'Or).—Books, bound. Bound drawing-albums. Pocket-books of various forms, and for various purposes.

319 Malapert, —, Chemist, Poitiers (Vienne).—Sulphate of magnesia and sulphate of soda, obtained by new manufacturing processes.

320 Malo Dickson, & Co. Coudekerque Branche, near Dunkerque (Nord).—Flax-spinning mills, and manufacture of canvas for sails. Sail-cloth for merchant vessels and men-of-war.

321 Mame & Co. Booksellers, Printers, and Bookbinders, Tours (Indre-et-Loire).—Various illustrated works, bound or half-bound.

322 Malingie, —, Proprietor and Manager of the Agricultural School of La Charmoise, Pont Leroy (Loir-et-Cher).—Combed wool, the produce of sheep reared at La Charmoise.

323 Martin, W. Engine-maker, St. Pierre-les-Calais (Pas de Calais).—Jacquard machine for bobbin-net lace frame and weaving-looms. Patented in France and in England.

324 Montgolfier, —, Paper-maker, Annonay (Ardèche); depôt, 18 Rue de Seine, St. Germain, Paris.— Various sorts of paper and card-paper. Peculiar "natural vegetable paste copying-paper," and "animal parchment." The latter article is employed to make cartridges for the French navy.

325 Moreau, U. 3 Rue Drouot (Grange Bâtelière).— Lamp-oil. Essence for varnish. Oil for machinery. Grease. Soaps and pastes, from the bituminous mines of Schabwiller (Bas-Rhin).

326 Moreau, F. 88 Rue de la Glacière (Banlieue de Paris).—Newly-invented patent fuel, called French coals.

327 Mader Brothers, 1 Rue de Montreuil, Paris.— Stained hanging paper.

328 Moriceau & Cayeux, Engine-workers, Mouy (Oise).—Pendulum-regulator, for hydraulic movers, from one to a hundred-horse power. New invention, patented, suitable for all kinds of sluices.

329 Marechal & Guynon, Glass-Painters, Metz (Moselle).—Painted window-glasses:—1 St. Charles administering the communion to the plague-stricken. 2 A burgomaster. 3 A rose of the thirteenth century.

330 Mareschal, J. Engine-worker, 82 Rue du Faubourg St. Martin, Paris.—Machines for mincing and mixing meats, soaps, pastes, and vegetables Patented.

331 Marrel Brothers, Silversmiths and Jewellers, 27 Rue Choiseul, Paris.—Large gilt and oxidised vase. Dressing-case, cups, hunting-knives, dagger, and other gold and silver articles.

332 Marsaux & Legrand, P. 14 Rue de la Perle, Paris; and 27 Castle St. Holborn, London.—Articles of stamped copper, for decoration.

333 Massing Brothers, Manufactories at Luttelange (Moselle), Lyons, and Tarare (Rhône). Agents: Huber & Co. 2 Rue de Braque, Paris.—Silk plush, made use of by hat-makers.

334 Obry Son Jules Bernard & Co. Paper-manufacturers, Prouzel, near Amiens (Somme).—Various sorts of papers, and endless rollers; for envelopes, pamphlet-covers, &c.

335 Hardeng, —, Pianoforte Manu. Angers.—Two iron pianos of a new invention.

336 Opigez & Chazelle, late Gagelin, 83 Rue Richelieu, Paris.—Ready-made articles for ladies:—Rich Lyons silk embroidered fabrics, shawl, &c.

337 Paget, J. A. Clock-maker, Béziers, (Herault).— New "spring-box" watch.

338 Paillart Brothers, Tanners' Curriers, 17 Rue du Grand St. Michel, Paris. — Calf and sheep skins for leather manufactories. For wool and cotton cards. Straps, &c.

339 Papavoine & Chatel, Card Engineer, Rouen (Seine-

Inférieure).—Patent card-making machine, and cards of various sorts, in leather and felt cloth.

340 PARADIS, DE RUOLZ, & Co. 6 Faubourg Poissonière, Paris; and MM. DEVAUX & Co. 62 King William St. London.—Waterproof coating painting. Process of Ruolz, chemist. Patented in France and England.

341 PARDOUX, —, Engineer, Randon (Puy-de-Dôme). —Ploughs, with fore-carriage and fixed mould-boards; and ploughs with moveable mould-board. New inventions, patented.

342 PAUWELS, A. 179 Faubourg Poissonière, Paris.—Regulator and moderator; machines for regulating retort gas. Fireproof for gas-works. Patented in France, England, and other countries.

343 PERRON, Chocolate-manufacturer, 14 Rue Vivienne Paris.—Various sorts of decorated chocolate.

344 PESCHELOCHE - VAVIN, Clockmaker, Epernay (Marne).—Clocks, watches, and various clock-works, with new movements.

345 PETIT SON, sen. & Co. Nantes (Loire-Inférieure).—Millstones, suitable for wheat.

347 PICARD, E. Designer, 3 Rue de Lenôtre, Rouen (Seine-Inférieure).—Designs for woollen, cotton and other printing; white-ground design, chintz fashion, with portrait of Queen Victoria.

348 PICAULT, G. F. Cutler, 46 Rue Dauphine, Paris.—Oyster opener, saw-knife, shear-knife, and various articles of cutlery. Patented.

349 PICHOT, A. 20 Place d'Armes, Poitiers (Vienne).—Imitation of marquetrie, and inlaid work on thick or thin ivory.

350 PIERRET, —, Clockmaker, 21 Rue des Bons Enfants Paris.—Globe-clock, on Copernican system. New alarum, clocks and watches.

351 PILLAUT, Mrs. and Co. 8 Rue Vivienne, Paris.—Elastic and orthopedic dress, belt, and stays.

352 RENOUARD, JULES, & Co. Booksellers, 6 Rue de Tournon, Paris.—Various publications on history, science, fine arts, &c.

353 REYNIER-COUSINS, Silk Manufacturers, 19 Rue Puits Gaillot, Lyons (Rhône). — Neckerchiefs, shawls, scarfs, dresses, and parasols.

354 RICHER, F. Agriculturist and Feeder, Gouvix (Calvados).—Two fleeces of rams of a pure breed, two years old.

355 RIESS, M. Dieuze (Meurthe).—Gelatine and isinglass for preparation of textures, silk stuffs, clearing of wines, &c.

356 BIÉTRY & SON, Manu. 102 Rue Richelieu.—Broché and embroidered shawls; cachemire for dresses.

357 ROBERT, A. Clockmaker, Sancerre (Cher).—New repeating arrangements for watches and clocks. Patented.

358 ROJON, J. L. 51 Quai Valmy, Ruelle des Lias, Paris.—Prepared emery; colours ground by new mechanical process; tripoli, &c.

359 ROULET, GILLY, & CHAPONNIERE Marseille (Bouche du Rhône).—Palm-oil soap, for bleaching cloths, dyeing silk, &c.

360 ROUSSEAU, L. 12 Rue des Cinq Diamants, Paris.—Preserved fruits.

361 ROUSSEL, C. Typographic Carver, Besançon (Doubs). — Music composed with movable types and matrices of the types.

362 ROUXEL, F. Agriculturist, St. Brieux (Côtes du Nord).—Prepared flax, employed in hand and power looms.

363 RUEZ, L. Starch-makers, Cambrai (Nord).—Various sorts of starch.

364 SAGET, V. Lamp-maker, 17 Rue Sainte Elisabeth, Paris.—Lighthouse for the navy, with parabolical reflector; lantern for hydraulic crane, and other lighting apparatus.

365 DE SANDOVAL & Co. Chocolate Manufacturers, Tarbes (Hautes-Pyréenes).—Specimens of chocolate.

366 SANSON, E. Tick-manufacturer, Evreux (Eure).—Ticking for stays, feather-beds, and furniture.

367 SAURAUX, J. V. Manufacturers, 21 Rue du Faubourg du Temple, Paris.—Patent carved black-wood billiard table in buhl.

368 SAVARY & MOSBACH, Jewellers, 2 Rue Vaucanson, Paris.—Imitations of diamonds, precious stones, and pearls.

370 SCHMAUTZ, C. sen. 19 Rue du Cherche-Midi, Paris.—Rollers, frames, and straps for lithographic press.

371 SCHOENENBERGER, —, Music Editor, 28 Boulevard Poissonnière, Paris.—Index of the concerts of the National Conservatory of Music; classical catalogue for pianists and actors

372 SEGUY, —, Engineer, Thezan (Herault).—Wheelplough.

373 SENECHAL, —, Engineer, 41 Rue des Solitaires, Belleville, near Paris—Hemming machine, suitable to the sewing of coarse linen cloths. Machine for cutting gloves, made of skin or other materials. Patented.

374 SILBERMANN, G. Printer, Strasbourg (Bas-Rhin).—Letter-press of all descriptions, executed by a new process. Invented by the exhibitor.

375 SIMONET, Mlle. VIRGINIE, 161 Rue St. Jacques, Paris.—Copy, on porcelain, of Mr. Ingre's portrait of L. Cherubini.

376 BOUXWILLER MINES, JOINT STOCK COMPANY, Mr. SCHATTENMAN, Manager, Bouxwiller (Bas-Rhin).—Purified and common alum; sulphate of iron; Prussiate of potash; Prussian blue; gold size, &c.

377 JOINT STOCK COMPANY OF THE PAPER MILLS OF SOUCHE (Vosges), Mr. MAUBAN, Agent, 5 Rue du Pont de Lodi, Paris.—Various sorts of writing, painting, hanging, analysing, and flower papers; imitation of Indian paper.

378 SLATE WORKS OF RIMOGNE (Ardennes) JOINT STOCK COMPANY, A. MOREAUX, Agent.—Various samples of slates of Rimogne; grey slates of Deville (Meuse).

379 OURSCAMP SOCIETY (Oise), PEIGNE DELACOUR, Manager, 14 Boulevard Poissonnière, Paris.—Cotton spinning; weaving of thick calicoes (called *Cretonnes* and *Madapollams*).

380 SOEHNEE BROTHERS, Varnish Manufacturers, 17 Rue des Vinaigriers, Paris.—Various sorts of varnish, for leathers, wood, and metals, for oil and water-colour paintings. Natural flowers preserved by a chemical process.

381 SOINS & SON, Dyers, Esquermes-les-Lille (Nord).—Linen twists dyed and satined; cotton twists dyed and glazed, called Scottish and Irish linen. Patented.

382 STEINBACH, J. J. Petit Quevilly, near Rouen (Seine-Inférieure).—Starch fecula and gums, made use of in the manufactory of printed calicoes.

383 STEINER, C. Manufacturer, Ribeauvillé (Haut-Rhin).—Plain red dye; printings on Andrinophe red.

384 STURM, P. H. 28 Rue de l'Ancienne Comédie, Paris.—Eight paintings on enamel.

385 TAILBOUIS, E. Hosiery Manufacturer, 15 Rue des-Mauvaises-Paroles, Paris.—Silk gloves, scarfs, shawls, stockings, and other new and fancy articles. Patented.

386 TAILFER, J. B. and Co. Engine Builders, 4 Rue Notre Dame de Grâce, Paris.—Dynamometric apparatus, invented by Mr. Taurines, of Paris. Patented.

387 TAILLANDIER, L. H. Manufacturer of Tick, Evreux (Eure).—Various sorts of tick for bedding and stays.

388 TAMBOUR-LEDOYEN (Maison Privat) Glove-maker, 49 Rue Neuve St. Augustin, Paris.—Gloves cut by a new method.

389 TELLIER, —, Ivory Carver, 122 Grande Rue, Dieppe (Seine Inférieure).—Various articles made of carved ivory; a ship, a poor man, &c.

I 2

390 THOMAS, C. X. 13 Rue du Helder, Paris.—A calculating machine. Invented by the exhibitor, and patented in France and Great Britain.

391 THIERRY, C. A. Boot-maker, 301 Rue St. Honoré, Paris, and 278 Regent Street, London.—Revolving-heeled boots. Invented by Mr. Walker, of Birmingham, and patented in France and England.

393 TRANCART, A. A. 12 Rue Neuve St. Denis, Paris.—Tortoiseshell combs.

394 TREMAUX, P. Architect, Charcery, near Bourgneuf (Saône-et-Loire).—Patent improved harmonium.

395 DU TREMBLAY, A. 3 Rue de Milan, Paris.—Specimens of drawings reproduced, by means of *lithopony*, upon porcelain or crystal. Patented.

396 TRICOT BROTHERS, Texture Manufacturers, 25 Rue Stanislas-Girardin (Seine-Inférieure), Rouen.—Hand-loom fabrics of cotton, wool, thread, or silk.

397 TUDOT, —, Designer, Moulins (Allier).—Specimens of lithography.

398 TULOU, —, Flute-maker, 27 Rue des Martyrs, Paris. —Improved flute. New disposition of the keys.

399 ACKLIN, Machine-maker, 36 Rue Bourbon Villeneuve, Paris.—Jacquard loom, with an apparatus for the substitution of the paper or pasteboard (patented in France and England); with a diagram representing the details of the apparatus.

400 ALBINET SON, Blanket-manufacturer, 19 Rue de la Vieille-Estrapade, Paris. — Woollen, merino, and cotton blankets and counterpanes of every kind.

401 ARCHAMBAULT, A. Carver and Frame Maker, 124 Rue St. Lazare, Paris.—Mouldings. Frames of various kinds, fluted and plated.

402 ARNAVON, H. Soap Boiler, Marseille (Bouches-du-Rhône).—Various samples of soap for exportation.

403 AUBERT & NOEL, 265 Rue St. Honoré, Paris.—Fruit brandies; peaches, raspberries, apricots, strawberries.

404 AUCHER, —, Piano Maker, 44 Rue de Bondy, Paris. —Two upright pianos, the one with oblique strings and fixed finger-board, the other with vertical strings and moveable finger-board.

405 AMULLER, E. F. 51 Rue du Faubourg Poissonnière, Paris.—The model of a roof covered with improved tiles.

406 BAILLIERE, J. B. Bookseller, 19 Rue Hautefeuille, Paris.—Twelve works on anatomical and medical science, with coloured plates. Natural History of Molluscs, by Ferussac and Deshayes, with coloured plates.

407 BAILLY-COMTE, & SON, Morez du Jura (Jura).—A travelling-clock, striking the quarters, and going for thirty hours.

408 BALLY, P. Watch and Clockmaker, 25 Rue Notre Dame de Nazareth, Paris.—Clocks of various sizes and descriptions. Watch and clock works.

409 BAPTEROSSES, J. F. China Manufacturer, 27 Rue de la Muette, Paris.—Porcelain handles of every kind.

410 BARRAL, C. Silk Throwster, Ganges (Hérault).—Samples of raw and thrown silk, white and yellow.

411 BASELY, —, 11 Rue Constantine, Paris.—Stands for watch and clock works.

412 BATAILLER, A. P. E. au Château du Portail, près Montargis (Loiret).—Agricultural implements.

413 BAUCHET-VERLINDE, Paper Manufacturer, Lille —A machine for ruling paper. Account-books for commercial purposes.

414 BAYARD, H. 81 Rue de la Paix, Batignolles (Seine). —Photographic drawings, in frames.

415 BAYVET BROTHERS & Co. Choisy-le-Roi, depôt in Paris, 16 Rue Mauconseil.—Leather and morocco leather.

416 BAZIN, A. Mesnil St. Firmin (Oise).—A draining plough.

417 BORIE BROTHERS, Civil Engineers, 24 Boulevard Poissonnière, Paris.—Tubular bricks of whatever shape and size, and machines to manufacture them. French and English patents. (Agent in London, Mr. E. Elliott, 33 Bucklersbury.)

418 BERGER, F. St. Etienne (Loire).—Fancy fowling-pieces of various kinds.

419 CLESINGER, T. Sculptor, 32 Rue de Penthièvre, Paris.—A Bacchant, statue in marble.

420 BERNARD, —, Machine Maker, 34 Rue Constantine, Paris.—A filtering machine.

421 BERNARDEL, sen. 21 and 23 Rue Croix-des-Petits-Champs.—Violins, violoncelli, altos, fiddle-sticks, and strings for musical instruments.

422 BERTHELOT, N. Troye (Aube). — Two circular looms for the weaving of hosiery, and specimens of work.

424 BESSON, G. A. Manufacturer of Musical Instruments, 7 Rue des 3 Couronnes, Paris.—Cornet-à-piston, in brass and silver, ophicleide, &c.

425 BEZAULT, J. & Co. Machine Makers, 18 Rue des Vinaigriers, Paris.—Hydro extractor.

426 BODIN, J. Rennes (Ille and Vilaine).—Four ploughs and one harrow.

427 DE BOISSIMON, C. Earthenware Manufacturer, Langeais (Indre-et-Loire).—Ornamental vases. Stoneware articles. Fire bricks.

428 BOLAND, A. 52 Rue St. Louis, Paris.—A mechanical kneader, adapted to mixing and washing.

429 BONNAL, V. & Co. Silk Throwster, Montauban (Tarn-et-Garonne).—Raw silk, white and yellow. Pieces of unbleached silk for bolting flour.

430 BONTEMS, —, Manufacturer of Mechanical Objects of Decoration, 80 Rue de Cléry, Paris.—A bronze clock, surmounted with mechanical birds. Group of mechanical birds.

431 BOUCHON, L. A. Lafertè-sous-Jouarre, 16 Place de la Madeleine, Paris. — A hand-mill, with its bolting apparatus.

432 BOUDON DE ST. AMANS, China Manufacturer, Lamarque, near Agen (Lot-et-Garonne).—Specimens of a new process of enamelling china, &c.

433 BOULONNOIS, Manufacture of Bronze and Objects of Art, 48 Rue St. Sébastien, Paris. — Bronzes of various patterns, &c.

434 BOURGOGNE, J. Manufacturer, 2 Rue d'Arcole, Paris. —A series of microscopic preparations.

435 BRAQUENIE & Co. Carpet Manufacturers, 16 Rue Vivienne, Paris.—Carpets, door tapestry screens, and table-covers, patented.

436 BRETON BROTHERS & Co. Pont de Claix, Près Grenoble (Isère).—Two bundles of paper, with drawings.

437 BRICARD & GAUTHIER, Hardware Manufacturers, Woincourt (Somme), and 3 Rue Pavée St. Sauveur, Paris.—Various articles of locksmiths' work and rollers for spinning.

438 BRIERE, A. Arsenic Manufacturer, 24 Boulevard, Beaumarchais, Paris.—Arsenical acid; Scheele's green, &c.

439 BRIET, J. C. 22 Rue Neuve St. Jean, Paris.—Various apparatus, with a vessel for gaseous liquids.

440 BRISSET, E. Machine Maker, 13 Rue des Martyrs, Paris.—Iron lithographic press.

441 BROCOT, A. Bronze Manufacturer, 18 Rue Charlot, Paris.—Ornamental clocks, medallions, and various objects in bronze, marble, &c.

442 BUFFET, jun. Manufacturer of Musical Instruments, 4 Rue du Bouloi, Paris.—Clarionets, on a new plan; flutes, oboes, and bassoons, for military bands.

443 BURON, —, 8 Rue des Trois Pavillons, Paris.—Optical and mathematical instruments.

444 CAFFORT, J. Marble Cutter, Carcassonne (Aude), and at Rue Neuve, St. Jean, Paris.—Samples of marble from Languedoc.

445 CARRE, L. Bronze Manufacturer, 43 Rue Beaubourg, Paris. — Bronze, miniature, and daguerreotype frames.

447 LEROUX-MAINGUET, Nantes (Loire-Inférieure).—Distillation of salt water.

448 CHAPOT & PELON, Hyppolite, au Vigan (Gard).—Lithographic stones, from the quarries of Vigan.

449 CHAUVIN, G. Polished Steel Manufacturer, 10 Rue des Gravillers, Paris.—Purse, purse-trimmings, clasps, &c.; buckles, trinkets, and other polished steel articles.

450 CHAVIN, elder brother, Morez-du-Jura (Jura).—Clocks, &c. An enamelled dial. Varnished tin cases for clocks and regulators.

453 CHAVERONDIER, H. Lace Manufacturer, St. Germain, Laval (Loire).—Various specimens of lace and fancy articles.

454 CLAIR GODEFROY, sen. 63 Rue Montmartre, Paris. —Wood and silver flutes.

455 CLEMENT-BOURGEOIS, L. Morez (Jura).—Watch and clock works. Kitchen jacks.

456 CLOET, C. Manufacturer of Alimentary Pastes, Lille (Nord).—Pearl and unshelled barley. Vermicelli of various qualities. Macaroni (an imitation of the Neapolitan). Carolina rice. Wheat flour. Patented in England.

458 COLLETTA-LEFEBVRE, 9 Rue Mandar, Paris.—Snuffboxes, purses, needle-cases, &c.

459 COMBET, —, Violin-string Manufacturer, 6 Rue Grenetat, Paris.—Harmonic strings in silk and cat-gut for violins.

460 CORDIER, C. Sculptor, 5 Rue Carnot, Paris.—Bust in bronze, a negro from Timbuctoo on a column.

461 CORNIQUEL, C. Vannes, Morbihan.—Various kinds of leather.

462 COURNERIE & Co., Manufacturers of Chemical Produce, Cherbourg (Manche).—Iodide of potassium, sublimed iodine, chloride of potassium, sulphate of potash, &c.

463 COURTOIS, A. sen. 28 Rue des Vieux-Augustins, Paris —Brass musical instruments.

464 TOUSSAINT, E. N. 4 Rue de la Jusseine, Paris.—Design for lace scarf.

465 CRESPEL-DELISSE, Agriculturist, Arras (Pas-de-Calais).—Various samples of wheat. Sowing machine.

466 TROUILLIER, J. Designer, 31 Rue de Cléry, Paris.—Designs for stuff-paintings.

1468 CUSSON, POURCHER, & ROSSIGNOL, Armourers, Clermont Ferrand (Puy de Dôme).—Pistol, muskets, &c. Pat.

469 CUVILLIER, H. sen. 16 Rue de la Paix, Paris.—Preserved articles of food: mussels, oysters, mushrooms, peas, truffles.

470 DARRAS, P. Silk Manufacturer, Tixin (Côte d'or). —Substances employed in silk manufactories.

471 DAUPHINOT - PERARD, Manufacturer, Isles - sur-Suippes (Marne).—Merino fabrics of all colours.

472 DELACOUR, H. P. Tissue Manufacturer, 47 Rue Vieille-du-Temple, Paris.—Horse-hair and "vegetable silk" textures.

473 DELVIGNE, G. Machine-maker, 24 Rue du Bouloy, Paris.—Portable howitzer; priming-horn; and an apparatus for saving life.

474 DUVAL, —, Upholsterer, 17 Rue de Cléry.—Decorations for apartments, &c.; furniture.

475 DETIR & Co. (Piano Workmen Society), 162 Rue du Faubourg, St. Denis, Paris.—An upright piano, with semi-oblique strings. An upright piano with vertical strings.

476 DEYEUX, —, Liancourt (Oise), and at 7 Rue Garancière, Paris.—Crucibles for the melting of metals, and chemical utensils.

477 DOMENY, L. J. Musical Instrument Manufacturer, 101 Faubourg, St. Denis, Paris.—Harps; upright pianos.

478 DONNEAUD & Co. Wax Candle Manufacturers, 190 Quai de Jemmapes, Paris.—Stearic acid; oleic acid; lighthouse candles.

479 DOREY, J. Machine-maker, Hâvre (Seine-Inférieure).—Clock-dial, with its apparatus, applicable to a new system of lighting.

480 DUBREUILLE, DERVAUX, LEFEBVRE, & DE FITTE, Sugar Boilers, Wagnier le Grand (Nord).—Samples of beet-root sugar.

481 DUBUS, —, sen. 58 Route de Caen, à Rouen (Seine-Inférieure).—Four cylinders for grinding emery.

482 DUCOMMUN, —, 28 Boulevard Poissonniere, Paris. — A fountain; charcoal filter, with a new kind of tap. A box containing a pressure charcoal filter. Travelling canteen in pewter, with charcoal filter. Patented.

483 DUFOUR, L. Manufacturer, Boulevard Beaumarchais, Paris.—Machine-made gilt, silvered, and fancy paper. Burnishing stones and plates for every species of gilding.

484 FORTIN-BOUTELLIER, Manu. Beauvais.—Lengths of cloth, and cones of felted cloth for pianos.

485 DUFOUR, J. B. Saumur (Maine-et-Loire).—Samples of asphalte pavement. Mosaic work in natural stones, united together by asphalte.

486 DUMAS, A. 272 Rue St. Honoré.—Various gas-burners.

487 DUMEREY, —, 45 Rue des Petits Ecuries, Paris.—A machine employed in the manufacture of shoes, &c. Plates for engraving music.

488 DUMONT, F. L. H. Tanner, Rue des Wetz, Douaï (Nord).—Strong leather from Buenos Ayres.

489 MONTIGNAC, —, Goldsmith and Jeweller, 6 Rue Beauregard, Paris.—Jewellery.

490 DUNAIME, J. A. 18 Rue Lepelletier, Paris.—A four-wheeled carriage, of the description called town-Berline.

491 DANDOY-MAILLARDLUCQ & Co. Maubeuge (Nord). —Ironmongery. Tools and detached pieces for all kinds of spinning. Military weapons.

492 DUPRAT & Co. Cork Manufacturers, Castres (Tarn). Depôt, 1 Rue du Grand Chantier, Paris.—Corks and sheets cut by patent machinery.

492A FUNSTENHOFF, EMMA, 17 Rue de Choiseul, Paris.—Artificial flowers for the study of botany

493 DUPRE, A. G. Arcueil (Seine).—Metallic capsules for corking bottles.

494 DURANTON, J. B. Shirtmaker, 11 Rue St. Joseph, Paris.—Cotton and linen yarn fabrics for shirt-fronts. Patented in France and Great Britain.

495 DUVELLEROY, P. 17 Passage Panorama, Paris; Dépôt in London, 167 Regent St.—One hundred fans of various kinds, carved and painted, &c.

496 D'ENFERT BROTHERS, Plaine d'Ivry, Deux Moulins, near Paris (Seine).—Various sorts of gelatine.

497 ERARD, P. Piano Manufacturer, 13 and 21 Rue du Mail, Paris.—Pianos of various patterns. Harp, patented in England.

498 ERNOUX, C. H. Hatter, 9 Passage Ste. Avoye, Paris. —Fancy felt-hats, with or without ornaments—a new invention.

499 ESPRIT & NOYE, F. Manufacturers, 42 Quai de Retz, Lyon (Rhône).—Drawing of a regulating scale for hosiery. Gloves and stockings, manufactured by means of this regulator.

502 FAUQUIER, F. Brushmaker, 7 Rue Bourg Labbê, Paris.—Various articles of brushmaking, for all kinds of purposes.

503 FELIX, J. Manufacturer, 6 Rue Rambuteau, Paris. —Flat purses; cigar, blotting, and surgical-instrument cases, and embroidery, mounted in velvet and morocco.

504 FERON, J. F. 29 Rue de Clichy, Paris.—Bannisters, with "incrustated" handrails.

505 FERY, A. Agriculturist, La Teste, near Bordeaux (Gironde).—Samples of raw and shelled rice.

506 FISCHER BROTHERS, Manufacturers, St. Marie-aux-Mines (Haut-Rhin).—Tissues in cotton, wool, and dyed silk for gowns, cravats, and Madras fancy articles.

507 FLAUD, H. P. Engineer, 27 Rue Jean Goujon, Paris. —Steam-engine of twenty-five horse-power. Fire-engine with apparatus.

508 FONDET, sen. Architect, 11 Boulevard Poissonnière, Paris.—Apparatus for curing smoking chimneys. Warming apparatus. Prismatic warming pipes, which economize fuel, diffuse heat and ventilation, and preserving health.

509 FONTENAU, F. 8 Rue Dugommier, Nantes (Seine-Inférieure) —Percussion-gun, with under-box and a safety hammer.

510 FORTIER-BEAULIEU, Rue de la Lunette, Bercy.—Skins, hides, and leather.

511 FRANCOIS-GREGOIRE, Molasses Distiller, Haubour-din-les-Lille (Nord).—Spirit of molasses.

512 FRAY, M. Silversmith, 22 Rue Pastourelle, Paris.—A complete table service, including washing-stand, taper-stand, inkstand, and other articles of silversmith's work.

513 FUMET, C. F. Manufacturer of Chemical Produce, 25 Rue du Helder, Paris.—Apparatus for artificial ice.

515 GALIMARD, E. Silk Throwster, Vals (Ardèche). (Agents in London, Fordati, Coxhead, & Co. 13 Old Jewry Chambers.)—Samples of raw and thrown silk of various kinds.

516 GANNERY, V. St. Nicolas, d'Alihermont (Seine-Inférieure).—An astronomical clock.

518 GAYMARD & GERAULT, 10 Rue Montmorency, Paris. —Account-books for offices, counting-houses, &c. lithographed and ruled.

519 GEVELOT & LEMAIRE, 30 Notre-Dame-des-Victoires, Paris.—Percussion caps.

520 GERVAIS, 3 Rue des Fossés-St.-Jacques, Paris.—A copper boiler with a copper grate: patented.

521 GILLET, A. Manufacturer of preserved articles of food, Knevel (Morbihan).—Sardines preserved in oil.

522 GILLOT, —, Lithographic Printer, 8 & 10 Rue du Chevalier du Guet, Paris.—Three frames, containing typographical proofs with stereotypes. Patented in France and Belgium.

524 GOFFINET-SALLE, JEAN BAPTISTE, Rheims (Marne), Wool Spinner.—Carded wool-spinning. Hair; wool and cotton; all wool; woollen and cashmere, of various colours.

525 GOURDIN, —, Mayet (Sarthe).—A clock, striking the quarters.

526 GRASSOT & Co. Place du Collége, Lyons (Rhône), Manufacturers.—White damask thread table-napkins or cloths. Complete table-services.

527 GREY, M. Dijon (Côte-d'Or), Mustard Manufacturer—Various samples of mustard.

529 GROSSE BROTHERS, 29 Quai Napoléon, Paris.—Philosophical apparatus. Chemical utensils, such as crucibles, capsules, spoons, &c.

530 GROULT, —, jun. 16 Rue St. Apolline, Paris, Manu. —Pastes and flours for soups.

531 GROULT & Co. 7 and 9 Rue Frépillon, Paris.—Various kinds of copper tubes.

532 GUEUVIN-BOUCHON, & Co. Laferté-sous-Jouarre (Oise).—Mill-stones, whole and in pieces.

533 GUEROT, A. Elbeuf (Seine-Inférieure), Dyer.—Samples of wool dyed in various colours, and used in the manufacture of broad-cloths.

534 GUILLOT, J. J. A. 17 Rue du Bouloy, Paris.—Shoes, &c. and tanned leather.

536 HENRY, C. 21 Côte St. Sébastien, Lyons (Rhône), Machine Maker.—Steel combs for weaving silk and cotton stuffs.

537 HERME, —, Crest (Drôme), Silk Throwster.—Samples of raw and thrown silk.

538 HERRENSCHMIDT, G. F. Strasbourg. — Boot-legs. White and japanned calf leather. Calf-skins. Sewn straps.

539 HEYLER, Mdlle. MARY, 36 Rue de l'Echiquier, Paris, Silk Glove Manufacturer.—Silk-net mittens and gloves.

540 HILDEBRAND, A. 202 Rue St. Martin, Paris.—Chimes of bells for churches and belfreys. Tuning-forks for orchestras.

541 HUCK, —, 31 Rue Corbeau, Paris.—A complete apparatus for grinding alimentary substances, entirely in wrought or cast iron, or brass.

542 HUSSON, F. C. 13 Quai de la Tournelle, Paris.—Transparent cloths for the reproduction of drawings, maps, and plans.

543 IMLIN, F. Strasbourg (Bas-Rhin), Veterinary-Surgeon.—Plaster casts modelled from nature, representing club-feet of horses both before and after the operation.

544 NATIONAL PRINTING ESTABLISHMENT OF FRANCE, Paris.—One bound volume, typographic specimen; and three geographical maps. Copies of ancient missals and manuscripts.

545 JACQUET-ROBILLARD, Arras (Pas-de-Calais).—A double sowing machine.

546 JACQUIN, J. J. Troyes (Aube).—Circular looms. Samples of cotton and woollen and cotton weaving.

547 JACQUOT, —, Nancy (Meurthe).—Violins, one alto and one violoncello.

548 JAMIN, —, 71 Rue St. Martin, Paris.—Optical glasses, set and unset.

549 JEROME BROTHERS, Amiens (Somme), Machine Makers.—A machine for winnowing wheat.

550 JOURDAN, A. 3 Rue Neuve St. Eustache, Paris.—Brocaded worsted shawls, and cashmere shawls.

551 JOSSELIN, J. J. 37 Rue Louis-le-Grand, Paris, Stay Maker.—Stays of every kind.

552 JOUBERT-BONNAIRE, & Co. Angers (Maine-et-Loire), Manufacturers.—Raw and combed hemp and flax. Sail-cloths. Tent-cloths. Fireman's pail-cloths. White pantaloon cloths.

553 JOURNIAL, J. Cork Manufacturer, 46 Rue du Commerce, Grenelle (Seine).—Mechanical corks. Cylindrical capsules, for seltzer-water.

554 KISSEL, J. Cabinet-maker, 14 Rue Bonafoux, Bordeaux (Giroude). — Mechanical bed, on a new plan; patented in England.

555 KUHLMANN BROTHERS, Manufacturers of Chemical Produce, Lille (Nord).—Collection of samples of twenty different chemical products.

556 LABBAYE, —, Musical Instrument Manufacturer, 17 Rue du Caire, Paris.—Brass musical instruments.

557 LACOMBE, L. Enamelled Flower-maker, Calamane, Canton de Catus (Lot).—Artificial flowers, in enamel.

558 LEMERCIER, —, Rue de Seine, Paris.—Drawings.

559 LAILLER, E. H. L'Hotellerie (Calvados).—Heckled flax.

560 LAPORTE & DURAND, Toulouse, Haute-Garonne.—Bread and biscuits preserved since 1845.

562 LATACHE DE NEUVILLETTE, P. A. Ferme de Valbruant, near Arc (Haute-Marne).—Samples and fleeces of merino wool.

563 LAURENT, Mme. PAULINE, 44 Rue Richer, Paris.—Painting on porcelain.

564 LAURENT, F. Cabinet-maker, 5 Rue Chapon, Paris. —Dressing-cases, portfolios, liquor cellars, flower-stands, and other articles of cabinet-work.

565 LUSSON, A. Glass Painter, 21 bis Rue Laval, Paris.—Painted glass windows, in the style of the 13th, 15th, and 16th centuries, and modern style, with historical subjects.

566 LANTEIN & Co. Reims and Tinqueux (Marne).—Samples of dyed and undyed wool.

567 LAUR, J. A. 4 Rue St. Claude, au Marais, Paris.—Philosophical instruments.

568 LAURY, G. 29 Rue Tronchet, Paris.—Caloriferes in brass and cast-iron. Grates for chimneys. Fenders. Columns of various patterns. Various objects in bronze.

569 LEBERT, L. Manufacturer of Agricultural Implements, Pont-sous-Gallardon (Eure-et-Loire) — Ploughs, models of ploughs, and a machine for thrashing clover-seed.

570 LEBLEIS, H. Agriculturist, Pont l'Abbé (Finistère).—Wheat-flour, of various kinds. Potato-flour.

572 LEBRUN, J. A. jun. Marble-worker, 9 Boulevard du Temple, Paris.—Mantelpieces for chimneys, carved in various styles.

573 LESCHESNE, A. J. B. 37 and 30 Rue Fontaine St. Georges, Paris.—Pear-tree carved frame.

574 LECHESNE BROTHERS, 66 Rue des Martyrs, Paris.—Carvings: Bronze paper-presses; bookcase of carved oak; stone carved fountain; various articles in carton-pierre.

575 LECLERC, J. Manufacturer of Church Glass Windows, Mesnil St. Fermin (Oise).—Stained glass window, for churches.

576 LECLERC BROTHERS, Angers (Maine-et-Loire). — Hemp in a raw state. Heckled hemp and flax ropes.

577 LEFEBVRE, A. P. 4 Rue Jean Jacques Rousseau, Paris.—Sea and pocket chronometers. Watches, with cylinders and fusees. Various springs, for watch and clock making.

578 LEFEBURE, J. P. Shoemaker, 14 Rue du Paradis Poissonnière, Paris, and 27 Cranbourn St. Leicester Sq. London.—Ladies' and gentlemen's screw shoes; patented in France and England.

579 LEFEBVRE BROTHERS, Distillers of Molasses, Warguenel (Nord).—Various samples of alcohol and impure potash.

580 LEFEBVRE, T. & Co. Ceruse Manufacturers, Moulins-Lille (Nord).—Lamps.

581 LEFEVRE, sen. 53 Nantes-sur-la-Fosse (Loire-Inférieure).—Oxide of zinc.

582 LEFRANCOIS, Manu. 302 Rue St. Denis, Passage Barfour, Paris.—Metallic boxes for matches.

583 LEGAL, R. Chateaubriand, (Seine-Inférieure).—Calf leather.

584 LEGRAND, MARCELLIN, 99 Rue du Cherche-Midi, Paris.—Printing type, specimens of Chinese impressions. Composition plates of embossed type, for printing for the use of the blind.

585 LE GRAY, G. Chemin de Ronde de la Barrière de Clichy, Paris.—Specimens of photography.

586 LEMAIRE, P. H. Sculptor, 3 Rue Jean Bart, Paris.—Sculpture, a statue and a head.

587 LEMERCIER, R. J. 57 Rue de Seine, Paris.—Frames, with engravings.

588 LENORMAND, A. Manu. Vire, Calvados.—Various descriptions of woollen cloth, satin, beaver, &c.

589 LEONARD, C. 55 Boulevard St. Martin, Paris.—Ornamented iron bedsteads.

590 PAISANT, L. Agriculturist, Pont l'Abbé (Finistère).—Potato flour and gluten.

591 LERVILLES, J. Chicory Manufacturer, 21 Rue St. André, Lille (Nord).—Ground chicory, called powdered Mocha; Mocha in half beans; powdered Mocha.

592 LESECQ, H. Designer, 35 Quai Bourbon, Paris.—Two frames, with specimens of photography.

593 LESOURD-DELISLE, A. Angers (Maine and Loire).—The model of a vat for fermenting wines in a closed vessel.

594 LEVRAUD, P. J. Nantes and Belle Isle sur Mer.—Preserved soups, meats, truffled pasties, sardines, &c.

595 LEVY BROTHERS, Bronze Manufacturers, 76 Rue des Fossées du Temple, Paris.—Ornamented bronzed and porcelain. Clocks of various kinds. Vases. Cups. Chandeliers, &c.

596 MACHET-MAROTE, Manufacturer, Reims (Marne).—Zephyr cloths; superfine kerseymeres; satined merinos; smooth and double-milled valentias; cloaks; shawls; and sultana cloths.

597 MAILLOT, E. Manufacturer, 28 Rue Grenier St. Lazare, Paris.—Moulded, carved, and engraved smelling-bottles, with silver mountings.

598 MAISTRE BROTHERS, Manufacturers, Villeneuvette, near Clermont (Herault).—A piece of red and a piece of dark blue cloth for army clothing.

599 MALLET BROTHERS, Net Manufacturers, Calais (Pas-de-Calais).—Calais-Valenciennes, made by machinery; model of a lace machine.

600 MARGUERIE, —, 23 Rue Ménilmontant, Paris. — Painted and stained paper for hangings.

601 MONTANDON BROTHERS, Paris (Seine).—Springs for watch-work, lamps, and musical instruments; and various other springs.

602 MANTOIS, Mme. Rue du Pot-de-Fer, Paris.—Anatomical picture.

603 MAQUET-HERMEL, Manufacturer, Rethel (Ardennes).—Pieces of unbleached and dyed merinos, common description.

604 MAQUET, A. Manufacturer, Rethel (Ardennes).—Pieces of unbleached and dyed merino fabrics.

605 MARCELLE, S. Manufacturer, Bethenville (Marne).—Unbleached and dyed merino fabrics, of fine and strong descriptions.

606 MARCELIN, —, 40 Rue Basse-du-Rampart, Paris.—Mosaic table, carved; work-table; bookcase; Mosaic flooring; Mosaic backgammon board; vase, mounted with sphere.

607 MARCHAND, J. B. Bronze Manufacturer, 57 Rue Richelieu, Paris.—Gilt bronze candelabras and pendulums, with marble pedestals.

608 MARGA, E. 5 Boulevard des Filles-du-Calvaire, Paris.—Three chimney pieces carved in white marble.

609 MARION, A. Stationer, 14 Cité Bergère, Paris.—Fine and fancy papers. Machine for folding envelopes.

610 MARTENS, F. 6 Rue du Pot-de-Fer, Paris.—Three frames with daguerreotypes.

611 MARTI, S. 9 Rue d'Orléans, au Marais, Paris.—Various kinds of clock machinery.

612 MARTIN & CASIMIR, Plush Manufacturers, Tarare (Rhône), and Metz (Moselle). Depôts in Lyons and Paris.—Silk plush for gentlemen's hats.

613 MARTIN, C. A. sen. Trimming Maker, 18 Rue Mauconseil, Paris.—Lace, silk buttons, velvet trimmings, &c.

614 MARTIN, O. & VIRY, BROTHERS, Manufacturers, Sommevoire (Haute-Marne), and at 74 Quai de la Mégisserie, Paris.—Internal and external cast-iron house ornaments.

615 MASSUE, L. J. Comb Maker, 3 Rue Aumaire, Paris.—Ivory combs of every description.

616 MATAGRIN, STOLTZ, & Co. Manufacturers, Tarare (Rhône). Depôt, 13 Rue de Cléry, Paris.—White and coloured tarlatanes. Various muslins. For exportation.

617 MATHIEU-DANLOY, W. Buckle Manufacturer, Rethel (Ardennes).—Samples of iron and steel buckles.

618 MATHIEU, L. 28 Rue de l'Ancienne Comédie, Paris.—Various surgical instruments. Fire-arms.

619 MAUBAN & VINCENT JOURNET, Directors of the Paper Manufactory of Souche (Vosges), 5 Rue du Pont de Lodi, Paris.— Paper of various qualities; imitation of China paper.

620 MAUCOMBLE, —. 26 Rue de Grammont, Paris.—Five coloured daguerreotype portraits.

621 MAUREL, JAYET & Co. 43 Avenue de l'Observatoire, Paris.—Calculating-machines. Patented in England.

622 MAYER BROTHERS, 46 Rue Vivienne, Paris.—A

complete daguerreotype apparatus. A single camera-obscura on a new principle.

623 MASSE, V. 5 Faubourg St. Honoré, Paris; at London, 3 Goldsmith St. Gough Sq. Fleet. St.—Plans in relievo of all kinds of private landed property, country seats, parks, gardens, and tenements.

624 MAYER, Madame J. Fancy Paper Manufacturer, 22 Rue de la Vieille Monnaie, Paris.—Fancy papers, specimens of engraving and lithography, fans, pasteboard, and sweetmeat envelopes.

625 NAZE SON, & Co. 23 Rue du Sentier, Paris.—Designs for printing shawls, furniture, silk handkerchiefs, and dresses.

626 MAZARIN, J. G. 83 Passage du Havre, Paris.—An imitation of polished steel and oxidized silver. Patented, as a substitute for gilding.

627 MEHU, J. M. F. Engineer of the Mines of Anzin, Nord.—Apparatus (patented in France, England, and Belgium), for the extraction of ores, the free and safe ingress and egress of miners in and from the mines.

628 MASSON, VICTOR, Editor and Librarian, 1 Place de l'Ecole de Médicine, Paris.—Scientific works on nature.

629 MEILLET & PICHOT, Poitiers (Vienne).—Paper precluding the possibility of forgery. Postage stamps of different impressions.

630 MENE, P. J. 7 Faubourg du Temple, Paris.—Bronzes: boar hunting, stag hunting, mare and foal.

631 MERAUX, J. H. 7 Rue de la Jussienne, Paris.—Designs for lace manufacturers and fancy net.

632 MERCIER, A. & Co. Louviers (Eure), and 74 Faubourg Poissonnière, Paris.—Plaited card, roving card. Turninglathe, emery cylinder. A loom for spinning with 240 spindles.

633 MERCIER, S. 31 Boulevard Bonne-Nouvelle, Paris.—Diagonal stringed cottage pianos. For exportation.

634 MERLAUT, L. T. Rue des Catherinettes, Nantes.—Curried, japanned, and yellow calf leather.

635 MESNIER SON, & CARTIER, Engine Makers, Pontoise (Seine and Oise).—A portable mill on a new principle, for grinding corn and all sorts of grains, and capable of grinding hard substances.

636 MESTIVIERS & HAMOIR, Manufacturers, Valenciennes (Nord).—Linen fabrics, pieces of cambric and lawn.

637 MEYER, E. Typographic Printer, 2 Rue de l'Abbaye, Paris.—Printing in colours, in gold and silver.

638 MEYNIER, —. Designer, 1 Rue Hauteville, Paris.—Different designs for fabrics.

639 MEYRUEIS & SON, BROTHERS, Ganges (Hérault), Depôt in Paris, 18 Rue des Mauvaises Paroles.—Silk stockings, Scotch thread stockings. Silk and worsted gloves. Beaver gaiters for children.

640 MICHEL, A. Manufacturer of Chemical Products, Puteaux près Paris (Seine).—Bottles containing various extracts of the colouring matter of dye woods.

641 MICHELIN, T. Ribbon Manufacturer, 139 Rue Montmartre, Paris.—Silk and velvet ribbon.

642 MILON, M. Tissues Manufacturer, Beine (Marne).—Woollen fabrics, barege, &c.

643 MEISSONNIER, C. St. Denis (Seine).—Chemical products. Different species of salts; extracts of log-wood.

644 MILLY, DE —, Manufacture de l'Etoile, 52 Rue Rochechouart, Paris.—Stearine acids and candles, soaps.

645 MIROUDE BROTHERS, Card Makers, Rouen (Seine-Inférieure).—Cards made with machinery invented by M. A. Miroude, and patented.

646 MIROY BROTHERS, Bronze Manufacturers, Rue d'Angoulème du Temple, Paris.—Pendulums and chandeliers, representing different kings and great men of France and England; bronze statuettes. The same in imitation of bronze.

647 MOLINES, L. Silk Spinners, St. Jean-du-Gard. (Agents in London, Fordati, Coxhead, & Co. 13 Old Jewry Chambers.)—Samples of silks, silk waste, and cocoons.

648 MOLLET-WARME, BROTHERS, Manu. Amiens (Somme).—Fabrics in woollen and silk for dresses, shawls, &c.

649 MOLTENI & SIEGLER, Opticians, 62 Rue Neuve St. Nicolas, Paris.—Optical and mathematical instruments.

650 MONTCHARMONT, —, La Fermeté près Nevers (Nièvre). — Millstones from Nevers quarries.

651 MONTEBELLO, A. Lannes, de Château de Mareuil sur Ay (Marne).—Machine for corking bottles. Corks with annular incisions. New invention. Patented.

652 MOREAU & Co. Shirt Makers, 22 Rue d'Enghein, Paris.—Linen and cambric shirts, with stitched and embroidered fronts.

653 MOSER, —. Watch and Clock Maker, 15 Boulevard du Temple, Paris.—Clocks set in black marble. Travelling clocks of all descriptions.

654 MOTTE, BOSSUT & Co. Cotton Spinners, Roubaix (Nord).—Single and twisted cottons. A piece of cotton velvet. Patented in France and England.

655 MOULARD, Miss, Trimming Maker, 39 Rue Montmartre, Paris.—Lace head-dresses, caps, tobacco-bags, and net purses. Various fancy articles in chain-stitch work.

656 MAES, 9 Cour des Petites Ecuries, Paris.—White and coloured glass, optical glass, &c.

657 MOUSSARD, —. Coach Maker, 58 Allée des Veuves, Paris.—Four-wheeled carriage. Drawing of a new model of waggon.

658 MULOT & SON, 69 Rue Rochechouart, Paris.—A sample of sounding instruments.

659 NAST, H. J. China Manufacturer, 22 Place Royale, Paris.—Various articles of white and gilt or decorated china.

660 NAZET, B. Manufacturer, Reims (Marne).—Stuffs for waistcoats and cloaks. Fine light cloths for dresses. Double-milled cloths and kerseymere satin for paletots. Shawls.

661 NERAUDEAU, J. A. Ledger Maker, 16 Rue des Fossés-Montmartre, Paris.—Various ledgers for offices, &c.

662 NEUBURGER, —. Lamp Maker, 4 Rue Vivienne, Paris —Omnibus lamp with moveable burner. Convex glass lamps; night lamps. Patented.

663 NICOD, V. & SON, Annonay (Ardèche).—Twisted or platted wicks for stearine wax candles. For exportation.

664 NICOLAS, P. Cylinder Engraver, Thann (Haut-Rhin).—Machine, intended for cutting the bottom of enengraved rollers for printing fabrics. Patented.

665 NIEDREE, J. E. Bookbinder Gilder, Passage Dauphine, Escalier E. Paris.—Different books bound and gilt in a very rich style.

666 NOEL, Sen. 33 Rue de Lancry, Paris.—Ivory combs with hollow round teeth, in every variety.

667 NUMA-GRAR, & Co. Sugar Refiners, Valenciennes (Nord).—Samples of sugar extracted by the process of Mr. Dubrunfaut from molasses.

668 OCHS, J. Manufacturer of Fancy Articles, 28 and 30 Rue Notre-Dame-de-Nazareth.—Speciality of fancy articles in cornelian and agate, such as office articles, articles of jewellery, &c.

669 OUDIN-CORMY, Manufacturer, Bétheniville (Marne). —Unbleached and dyed merino fabrics.

670 OZOUF, H. 36 Rue de Chabrol, Paris.—An apparatus for gaseous liquids. Bottles with capsules. A machine for gaseous liquids.

671 PAILLARD, E. Manufacturer, 16 Rue de Grand Chantier, Paris.—Mirrors with copper and zinc frames. Various objects in zinc, in imitation of bronze.

672 PAILLARD, J. M Manufacturer, 21 Rue des Francs-Bourgeois, au Marais, Paris. — Artists' colours, crayons, and boxes.

673 PARNUIT, V. DAUTRESME, SONS, & Co. Clothiers, Elbeuf (Seine-Inférieure). — Gentlemen's superior fancy articles, such as trousers, waistcoats, paletots, for winter and summer, of various colours.

674 PATOUX-DRION, & Co. Plate Glass Manufacturers, Aniche (Nord). — Window glasses of every description. Blown glass. Chemical productions.

675 PAGNY, at Bayeux, Calvados. — Lace and embroidery.

676 PAUL, ULYSSE, Cotton Printer, Bourg-lès-Valence (Drôme).—Linen kerchiefs of different dyes. Fancy silk handkerchiefs. Maddered India silk pocket handkerchiefs.

677 PELTEREAU, A. Hide Manufacturer, Châteaurenault (Indre-et-Loire).—Raw hides. Smooth cow-skins. Smooth ox and cow-skin cuttings.

678 PESEL & MENUET, Manufacturers, 7 Rue Bourbon Villeneuve, Paris.—Samples of cashmere threads. Cashmere tissue cuttings.

679 PETIT-CLEMENT, Manufacturer, Boult (Marne).— Pieces of unbleached and dyed merino fabrics of fine quality.

680 PHILIP, —. Tortoiseshell Articles Manufacturer, 16 Passage Choiseul, Paris. — Tortoiseshell bracelets, brooches, ornaments, circlets, and ring.

681 PILOUT, —. Embroiderer, 21 Rue du Puits de l'Hermite, Paris.—An embroidered robe.

682 PIN-BAYARD, Manufacturer, Roubaix (Nord).— Woollen, satin, and satin-de-chine cuttings for dresses, merino, shawls, &c.

683 AUGUSTE, P. & BROTHERS, Paris.—Brazeros for Turkey.

684 PLICHON, V. Jeweller, 10 Rue des Filles-du-Calvaire, Paris.—Ornaments, bracelets, ear-rings, rings, and other articles of jewellery of gilt brass.

685 POITEVIN & SON, Manu., Louviers (Seine-Inférieure).—Fancy cloths for paletots (summer and winter materials).

686 POLLIART & CARPENTIER, Spinners and Tissue Manufacturers, Aubenton (Marne).—Samples of carded thread. Remnants of Reims cloths and flannels made by machinery.

687 POUYAT, J. China Manufacturer, Limoges, St. Leonards, and St. Yrieux (Haute-Vienne).—Raw materials for making china. Different samples of china.

688 PRAX & LAMBIN, Saddle Makers, 9 Passage Basfour, Rue St. Denis, Paris.—Various saddles. Harness. Apparatus intended for horse-riding. Patented.

689 PRESBOURG, P. Picture Brush Maker, 56 Rue Quincampoix, Paris.—Various brushes for all kinds of purposes, artistical and commercial.

690 SAUGRIN, —. 11 Boulevard Montmartre, Paris.— Daguerreotype miniatures.

691 SAINTIN, A. 8 Rue du Petit-Bourbon, Paris.— Frame with engravings.

692 SEGUIN, A. Rue d'Assas, Paris.—Chimney, carved in white marble, medal, basso-relievo, panel moulding, angel's head, &c.

693 SIMIER, J. Bookbinder, 38 Rue de l'Arbre Sec, Paris.—Bound books.

694 SLATE WORKS COMPANY OF RIMOGNE AND ST. LOUIS-sur-Meuse (Rimogne).—Slates of various kinds.

695 THIBIERGE, —, Wig Maker, 4 Rue Vide-Gousset, Paris.—Perukes and fronts.

696 THOUMIN, A. Manufacturer, 44 Boulevard Beaumarchais, Paris.—Stamped and cast-brass furniture ornaments.

697 DE TILLANCOURT, E. 85 Rue de Chaillot, Champs Elysées, Paris.—Factory for the spinning of raw silk from the North of France.

698 TILMAN, —, Artificial Flower Maker, 2 Rue Ménar, Paris.—Artificial flowers, ball dresses, wedding head-dresses. Patented.

699 TORDEUX, —, Bone Black Manufacturer, Cambrai, Nord.—Machine, used in the construction of factory chimneys. Bone black of various qualities.

700 TRELON, WELDON, & WEIL, Button Makers, Rue de Bercy, St. Antoine, Paris.—China knobs of every kind.

701 TROTTE, H. Hosier, 19 Rue Quincampoix, Paris.— Hosiery, network, &c.

702 TROUVE-CUTIVEL, & Co. Tanners and Curriers, La Suze (Sarthe).—White calf leather; Japanned calf leather; boot legs.

703 TRUC, Lamp Maker, 9 Rue Saintonge, Paris.— Porcelain lamps of all kinds, and appendages.

704 TUVÉE & Co. Fancy Article Manufacturers, 13 Rue de Choiseul, Paris.—Ribbons, silk-works, and fancy goods.

705 VACHON, SON & Co. Place Satonay, Lyons, Rhône. —Two machines, applicable to the cleansing of corn.

706 VALERIUS, P. Orthopedist, 7 Rue du Coq St. Honoré, Paris.—A surgical bed. Orthopedic belts and stays. Various bandages.

707 VALES, C. Artificial Pearl Manufacturer, 161 Rue St. Martin, Paris.—Various kinds of pearls; pearl head-dresses; statuettes mounted with pearl, &c.

708 VALIN, J. China Manufacturer, Faubourg Mont Jovis, Limoges, (Haute-Vienne).—Various objects in porcelain. Decanters. Lustres. Statues, &c.

709 VALTAT & ROUILLE, Shirt Makers, 70 Rue de Rambuteau, Paris.—Ready-made shirts. Shirt fronts of every kind made by machinery and by hand. Shirt collars. Stocks, flannel waistcoats, &c.

710 VAUCHER-PICARD. Manufacturer of Tissues, Rethel (Ardennes).—Pieces, merino fabric, grey and dyed.

711 VANDENBROUCKE, E. 16 Rue de Strasbourg, Paris. —Coffee-roasting machines. A newly-invented and patented process for preserving the fragrance of coffee.

712 VANDERDORPEL & SON, Fancy Paper Manufacturer, 3 Rue Chapon, Paris.—Gilt, lithographed, and coloured borders, corners, ornaments, and frames. Various kinds of fancy stationery. Embossing of all kinds.

713 VAN EECKHOUT & Co. Lace Manufacturers, 38 Rue Notre-Dame-des-Victoires, Paris.—White Alençon, Brussels, Binche, and Flanders lace. Black Chantilly, Bayeux, Caen, and Grammont lace.

714 VAN LEEMPOEL DE COLNET & Co. Quiquengrogne Glass Works, near Chapelle (Aisne).—Large and small-sized bottles for all kinds of purposes.

715 VANTROYEN & MALLET, Cotton Spinners, Lille (Nord), Rue Jemmapes.—Cotton-yarn for muslins; water-twist glazed for lace and bobbin-net; dyed and bleached yarns; glazed yarn (imitation of silk), &c.

716 VASSE DE ST. OUEN, Doctor of Sciences, Manufactory at Leribour's, Pont Neuf, Paris.—Universal gauge, comprising 17 different gauges, and indicating which to use in every particular case.

717 VARRALL, MIDDLETON, & ELWELL, 9 Avenue Trudaine, Paris.—A continuous process paper-machine, with a complementary machine to divide in sheets.

718 VAUGEOIS & TRUCHY, 1 Rue Mauconseil, Paris.— Gold and silver embroidery and lace-work; manufactured for exportation.

719 VEDY, F. Optician, 52 Rue de Bondy, Paris.— Astronomical instruments for the navy.

720 VEISSIERE, A. Woollen Stuffs Dyer, Puteaux, near Paris (Seine).—Dyed stuffs of merino wool.

721 VELIN BROTHERS, Manufacturers, Gerbeviller, (Meurthe).—Fabrics for trousers, made of unbleached yarn, plain, or with cotton mixture, of various shades.

722 VERGE, A. sen. 17 Chaussée Magdeleine, Nantes.— Oakwood arm-chair.

723 VERSTRAETE BROTHERS, Linen Spinner, Lille (Nord).—Twisted threads for sewing, and for the mounting of weaving-looms. Patented in France, England, & Belgium.

724 VAN-OVERBERGH, 9 Rue de Choiseuil, Paris.— Pianos.

I 3

725 VIAULT-ESTE, 17 Rue de la Paix, Paris. Depôt at MM. Thierry & Sons, 278 Regent Street.—Slippers, ladies' boots and ladies' foot coverings, of every description.

726 VIE, J. Caoutchouc Manufacturer, 161 Rue St. Jacques, Paris.—Caoutchouc tissues, elastic stockings, belts, knee-caps, &c.

727 VIDAL, R. Toulouse (Haute-Garonne). — Vermicellis, nutritive pastes, starch, &c.

728 VIGOUROUX, S. Spinner and Manufacturer, Reims (Marne).—Plain and printed fabrics in cotton, web, and fancy threads, for ladies' dresses and for waistcoats. Bobbin-machine: patented.

729 VIGUIER, B. 6 Boulevard Beaumarchais, Paris.— An hydraulic foot-warmer, or chafing-pan, adapted for day or night use: patented.

730 VINCENT & TISSERANT, Manufacturer, 21 Rue Michel le Comte, Paris.—Sealing-wax, wafers, gelatine-sheets, writing-inks, &c.

731 VIOLARD, G. Lace Manufacturer, 4 Rue de Choiseul, Paris.—Half a shawl and a piece of lace-work, made upon a new principle.

732 VIREBENT BROTHERS, Manufacturers, Toulouse (Haute-Garonne).—Artificial stone; capitals; monuments; ornamented chimneys in the Renaissance style, &c.

733 VISSIERE,—, Argenteuil (Seine-et-Oise).—Large and pocket chronometers, indicating minutes and seconds.

734 VIVET, E. T. Decorative Painter, 6 Rue des Petits Hôtels. Paris.—Patterns of hangings painted with wax.

735 VUILLAUME, J. B. 42 Rue Croix-des-Petits-Champs, Paris.—A complete set of string and bow musical instruments, with bows made by machinery: patented.

736 WAGNER, —, Clockmaker, 47 Rue Neuve des Petits-Champs, Paris.—Clocks of different structure and mechanism, a dynamometer, and other philosophical instruments.

737 WALWEIN, —, Designer, 24 Passage de l'Industrie, Paris.—Designs for cloth and Jacquard fabric printing establishments.

738 WATRELOT-DELESPAUL, Chocolate Manufacturer, 10 Rue Nationale, Lille (Nord).—Chocolate of various decriptions.

739 WEBER, J. Bookbinder, 2 Rue Hautefeuille, Paris. —A newly-invented binding process. Patented.

740 WEYGAND, A. Bronze Manufacturer, 138 Vieille Rue du Temple, Paris.—Clocks and candelabras in bronze; statuettes and groups in artistic bronze.

741 WHITAKER, SON, & Co. Charleville (Ardennes).— Plates and card-straps for wool or cotton.

742 WILLIAMS, H. Paper Manufacturer, 111 Rue de Charenton, Paris.—Three panels, in the Tuscan, Gothic, and Renaissance styles.

744 WOLF, —, 2 Rue St. Appoline, Paris. — Ivory carving.

745 YON, Mme. 110 Rue Vieille du Temple, Paris. —Eight carved wood medallions, representing religious subjects, executed by Messrs. Vechte, Gayrard, and Yon.

747 ZEIGER, A. Organ Maker, Lyons (Rhône), 8 Rue des Marronniers.—The gymnasium of the pianist: "Octavian" piano, a new invention.

749 AFFOURTIT, G. L. Valleraugne (Gard).—Silks and silk cocoons.

750 ALLARD & CLAYE, Perfumers, 317 Rue St. Denis, Paris.—Cakes and balls of soap; liquid or cream soaps, of various kinds; perfumes.

751 APPERT, —, Manufacturer of Alimentary Preserves, Paris.—Preserved, roasted, and stuffed mutton.

752 ARERA, N. G. 3 Rue de la Carillerie, Paris.—The machinery of a complicated clock with a new dial. A telltale clock, indicating the days of the month. Another, with simple movement. An hydrometer for liquids.

753 ARNHEITER, M. Manufacturer of Agricultural Implements, and various other Implements of Horticulture, 9 Place St. Germain-des-Près, Prieur, Paris. — Drying-frames, pruning-knives, fumigating apparatus, grafting-knives, hedging-knives, saws, and other horticultural implements.

754 AUBERGIER, P. H. Clermont Ferrand (Puy-de-Dôme).—French opium and syrup of lettuce.

755 AYNE BROTHERS, Silk Manufacturers, Lyons (Rhône), 26 Port St. Clair.—Dyed silks; silk for lace; finished edging for lace; edging for embroidery.

756 BARRANDE, J. B. 26 Rue du Fer à Moulin, Paris.— Tarring, tanning, and dyeing. Manufactured calf, kid, lamb, sheep, and goat skins, for boots and shoes, &c.

757 BARTHELATS, L. (DE), Logères, Commune de Châtel Allier.—Specimens of silk and silk cocoons.

758 BASIN, A. Agent of the Marsanne Mines, Drôme, and Rue d'Antin, Paris.—French Tripoli called Tellurine. Pink, yellow sifted, and native Tripoli.

759 BEARD, J. 20, Rue Jean Jacques Rousseau, Paris.— Copper-plate printing, with iridescent paper. New invention.

760 BENOUVILLE, M. Igny, Canton de Gray (Haute Saône).—Skeins of raw silk.

761 BERANGER, J. & Co. Manufacturer, Lyons (Rhône). —Scales, weighing-machines, and various other implements for weighing. Improved and patented.

762 BERNARD, D. F. Optician, 30 Rue des Marmouzets, Paris.—Microscope; camera lucida; and instruments for land surveying.

763 BERT, —, Silk Manufacturer, 7 Rue St. Marcel, Lyons (Rhône). — Silk fabrics of ancient manufacture; figured brocade and taffeta; chasuble cross; woven portraits of Louis the Fifteenth and Catherine the Second, &c.

764 BERTRAND, A. Silk Manufacturer, 26 Port St. Clair, Lyons (Rhône).—Fancy silk articles, Scotch poplin, chiné gros de Naples, chiné shawls, chiné parasols, &c.

765 BEYERLE, G. 44 Rue Mazarine, Paris.—Concave glasses; polyprisms; lenses; eye-glasses, &c.

766 BIONDETTI, H. 48 Rue Vivienne, Paris.—Hernia and orthopedic bandages.

767 BISLAUX, —, 54 Rue de la Victoire, Paris.—Painting in imitation of wood and marble.

768 BLANCHET BROTHERS, Manufacturers of Steel Articles, Fures, near Tullins (Isère). — Locomotive strap in natural and wrought-steel.

769 BOCHE, M. Manufacturer of Sporting Implements, 19 Rue des Vinaigriers, Paris.—Powder-flasks, and various sporting implements. Patented in England.

770 BOERINGER, & Co. Manufacturer, 6 and 8 Cour des Miracles, Paris.—A door with the application of a security bolt on a new system.

771 BONNETON, —, Silk Throwster, St. Vallier (Drôme). —Raw and thrown silks. Silk cocoons.

772 BONZE (Widow) & BROTHERS, White Lead Manufacturers, Haubourdin (Nord.)—Lumps of white lead; bottle of ultramarine blue.

773 BOSSI, J. B. 26 Rue St. Hyacinthe St. Michel, Paris.—Marble table in mosaic work.

774 BOUASSE (Widow), LEBEL & Co. Gelatine Makers, Rue du Petit Bourbon, Paris.—Gelatine figures, pinked and ornamented: a variety of specimens.

775 BOUCHARD-HUZARD, W. Mrs. Printer and Bookseller, 5 Rue de l'Eperon, Paris.—Natural history of the Mais, of golden birds. Description of machinery. The art of rearing silk-worms, &c.

776 BOUCHER, E. & Co. 15 Rue des Vinaigriers. Paris.— Culinary vases, hardware and trellis; tinned by electrochemical process.

777 BOUQUILLARD, —, Lithographer, 226 Rue St. Martin, Paris.—A frame representing a lithographic plan of Paris.

778 BOURGERY, Mrs. 24 Rue Hautefeuille, Paris.—Painting in relief. Paintings of fruit and detached fruit. Pathological anatomical subjects.

779 DE BRAUX-D'ANGLURE, 10 Rue de Castiglione, Paris.—Vases. Statues of galvanized zinc. Bronze busts.

780 BRIE & JEOFRIN, Milliner, Rue Richelieu, Paris.—Millinery articles; head-dresses, bonnets, caps, &c.

781 BRISON & SON, Rennes (Ile-et-Vilain). — Strong and smooth leathers. Crusted calf-skins for varnishing.

782 BRONSKI, Major Count DE BRONNO, Silk Throwster, Château de St. Selves, near Bordeaux (Gironde).—Unbleached silk and silk cocoons, the produce of the breed of Bronski silk-worms.

783 BUDY, J. P. A. 13 Rue de la Roquette, Paris.—Kitchen utensils and cast-iron stoves.

784 BUISSON, E. ROBERT & Co. Manosque (Basses-Alpes).—Three skeins of raw silk.

785 CABASSON, G. A. 12 Rue Taranne, St. Germain.—Drawings on wood for typographical engraving.

786 CABIROL, J. M. Surgical Instrument Maker, 6 Rue St. Marc, Paris.—Instruments and apparatus in gutta percha used in surgery. Electro-magnetic tissue and galvanic poultice, by Dr. Récamier. Patented in France and England, &c.

788 CALLAUX, BELISLENORIEL DE TINAN, & Co. Angoulême. Agents for the Veuze and Maumont Iron Works.—Specimens of papers for designs, ledgers, letter-writing, &c.

789 CAMUS, M. de la Rochelle (Charente-Inférieure).—Boxes of sardines preserved in oil.

790 CAMION-PIERRON, Mezières, Ardennes.—Iron and brass articles for buildings and furniture.

791 CARNET-SAUSSIER, 95 Rue Rambuteau, Paris.—Specimens of preserved food.

792 CARTEAUX & CHAILLOU, Physicians, 20 Rue Louis-le-Grand, Paris.—Anatomical models in embossed leather.

793 CERCEUIL, L. F. 33 Rue Traversière, Paris.—Dyed and milled goods, and paste colours for paper-hangings.

794 CHAMPOISEAU, N. Tours (Indre-et-Loire).—Raw silk, white and yellow. White and yellow hair weft. Sewing silk. Floss silk unbleached and dyed. Organzine silk, &c.

795 CHAPUS & RICHTER, Manufacturers of Ultramarine Blue, Wazemmes-les-Lille (Nord). Specimens of ultramarine of ten different qualities.

796 CHARTRON & SONS, Silk Spinners and Reelers, St. Vallier (Drôme).—Specimens of raw silk. Specimens of thrown silk. Specimens of silk cocoons.

797 CHATELAIN & BASSET, La Rochelle (Charente-Inférieure).—Specimens of preserved food.

798 CLAYE, J. Printer, 7 Rue St. Benoit, Paris.—Composing frames. Albums; illustrated volumes.

799 CLERGET, C. E. Ornamentist, 10 Rue Albouy, Paris.—Framed designs and proof engravings.

800 COINT-BAVARD & SON, Manufacturer of Combs for weaving, 26 Rue des Capucins, Lyons (Rhône).—Steel and brass weaving-combs of all descriptions.

801 COLLAS, M. A. C. 8 Rue Dauphine, Paris.—White and coloured essence of almonds and pine-apple. Digitaline.

802 COLVILLE, M. & Mlle. 22 Rue des Vinaigriers, Paris.—Specimens of coloured porcelain and enamelled plates. Portraits of the Queen of England and Prince Albert.

804 COSQUIN, J. 71 Rue de l'Université & 13 Rue Mayot, Paris.—Framed map of France executed for the French Government.

805 COUTEAUX, A. I. Tavaux-Ponsericourt (Aisne).—A noctograph, or instrument for writing in the dark.

806 COURTEPEE-DUCHESNAY, 11, Rue du Renard-St.-Sauveur, Paris.—Calf leather.

807 COURTIAL, —, Manufacturer of Ultramarine Blue, 9 Quai de Javel, Grenelle, Seine.—Bottles of ultra-marine blue.

808 COURTOIS, E. Chaussée de Clignancourt, Paris.—Leather for saddlery. Calf leather for boots and shoes.

809 CROCO, F. Stuff-Manufacturer, 163 Rue de Charonne, Paris.—Pieces of Cashmere, for waistcoats and scarfs.

810 CRUCHET, V. 58 Rue Notre-Dame-de-Lorette, Paris.—Wainscotting for rooms. Cartons Pierre: Figures of animals carved in oak. Consoles with basso-relievos.

811 DAGAND, —, Sculptor.—Heads: Spring, Summer, Harvest, Innocence. Statuettes: M. Dupin, M. D'Argout, and M. de Thury.

812 DAVID, C. 12 Rue Mauconseil, Paris. — Turkey leather. Shagreen morocco and sheep-skin.

813 DEADDE, —, Manufacturer, 18 Boulevard de Charonne, Charonne (Seine).—Patent leather.

814 DERAZEY, —, Mirecourt, (Vosges).—Musical instruments, &c.

815 DESCARTES, J. Cabinet-worker, 6 Rue du 29 Juillet, Paris.—Arm-chairs, chairs, sofas, and toilet-table. Ebony and lacquered articles.

816 DESPLANQUE, jun. Lizy-sur-Ourz (Seine-et-Marne).—Machines for washing, cleansing, and combing wool. Samples of washed and combed wool.

817 DESROSIERS, A. Printer, Moulins (Allier). — Six volumes: Ancient Bourbonnais, Ancient Auvergne, and Le Velay; four volumes in folio.

818 DEVERS, J. 32 Rue d'Enfer, Paris.—Terra cottas, painted with enamel-paste. Virgin, enamel-paste on lava. Painting with enamel-paste on china.

819 DEYDIER, Mme. 90 Rue de l'Ecole, Vaugirard.—Zinc vases. Roofing for belfry. Zinc dormer window, &c.

820 DIDIER, F. 40 Rue des Jeûneurs, Paris.—Design for printed shawl, &c.

821 DOUBLET & HUCHET, Typographic Engravers, 12 Rue des Moulins, Paris.—Vignettes, and ornamental letters for type-founding.

822 DOUMERC, E. Joint-Stock Company of Marais and St. Marie Paper-Mills, Jouy, St. Morin (Seine-et-Marne). Depôt, 3 Rue du Pont de Lodi, Paris. — Printing papers, drawing papers, writing paper, and card paper.

823 DOREY, J. F. Havre (Seine-Inférieure.)—A machine for manufacturing woollen stuffs.

824 DUCEL, S. J. Iron-Manufacturer, 26 Faubourg Poissonnière, Paris. — Statues with pedestals. Animals. Vases and portions of balustrade.

825 DUJARDIN, L. 18 Rue St. Sévérin, Paris.—Wood engraving. Framed engraving.

826 DUMONT-PETTRELLE, 12 Rue Thévenot, Paris.—Carving on wood: gilt and burnished by a process that resists damp.

829 DURAND & BAL, Manufacturers of Weaving-combs, 10 Rue St. Polycarpe, Lyons (Rhône).—Weaving-combs, with from 220 to 230 teeth in the space of 10 inches.

830 ENFER, —, 32 Rue de Malte, Paris.—Various blowing machines.

831 EYMIEU & SON, Saillans (Drôme).—Waste silk, and three fancy skeins.

832 FABREGUE-NOURRY, SON, HAROUIN & Co. Nîmes.—Silk waste and carded waste silk.

833 FAMIN, P. A. 13 Rue de Berlin, Paris.—Marble statue: Billiard player.

834 FAROCHON, E. 47 & 58 Rue d'Enfer, Paris.—Marble statue of a boy overloaded with fruit: Grasp all, lose all.

836 FLACHERON-HAYARD, Place d'Espagne, Ronne, and at M. DUBAN'S, Architect, 17 Rue de Lille, Paris.—Seven views of Rome and Albrun, with other views.

837 FOUCHER, —, Engineer, 8 Rue Salle-au-Comte, Paris.—Machine for weaving lace slippers. Slippers, with and without soles, made by it. Balls of lace used in the manufacture.

839 GAILLET - BARONNET, Wool - spinner, Sommepy (Marne).—Wool spun by hand, for the manufacture of veils barège dresses, and other light articles.

I 4

841 GATTIKER, G. 80 Rue des Marais St. Martin, Paris. —Designs for printed shawls. A dress, and fabrics for dresses.

842 GAUDET DU FRESNE, Artificial Flower Manufacturer, 41 Rue Richelieu, Paris.—Specimens of manufactured leaves for artificial flowers.

843 GAUME & Co. 4 Rue Cassette, Paris. — Books : Works of St. Chrysostom, St. Basil, St. Augustin, &c. Two volumes coloured paper, sewn.

844 GAUTROT, sen. 60 Rue St. Louis, au Marais, Paris. —Musical instruments : Harmony horns, cornets, nichorn, trumpets, clarions (chromatic), counter bombardons, ophicleids, trombones, &c.

845 GELLE, sen. & Co. 35 Rue des Vieux Augustins, Paris.—Perfumery. Toilet soaps.

846 GIBELIN & SON, Silk Spinners, La Salle (Gard).— Specimens of raw silk, white and yellow.

848 GILLE, J. M. China Manufacturer, 28 Rue Paradis Poissonnière, Paris.—Statuettes, vases, flagons, decanters, and various other articles in white and ornamented porcelain.

849 GILLOT, F. Bronze Manufacturer, 19 Rue du Pontaux-Choux, Paris.—Clocks and chandeliers, various compositions and groups in bronze.

850 GIRAUD BROTHERS, Tanners, 38 Rue du Fer-à-Moulin, Paris.—Morocco leather, real and imitation, for bookbinding, portfolios, furniture, and boot and shoemaking.

851 GOLDENBERG, G. & Co. Zornhoff, près Saverne (Bas-Rhin).—Hardware and edge-tools.

852 GOUBE - PHERACIE, Leather Manufacturer, Douai (Nord).—Leather for cards, spinning-machines, and military accoutrements.

853 GRAILLON, P. A. Dieppe (Seine - Inférieure).— Groups in terra cotta.

854 GRATIOT, A. Director of the Paper Mills at Essone, 8 Rue Vivienne, Paris.—White and coloured papers.

855 GRIMONPREZ & Co. Spinners and Manufacturers, Roubaix (Nord). —Woollen fabrics for dresses, shawls, aprons, and hangings.

856 GROSSMANN & WAGNER, Manufacturers, 11 Rue de Renard St. Sauveur, Paris.—Surgical instruments. Bandages and articles in caoutchouc.

857 GRUEL, —, 10 Rue de la Concorde, Paris.—Books in various bindings : Missal, mosaic volumes, bibles, prayerbooks, &c.

858 GUERRE, sen. —, Cutler, Langres (Haute-Marne). —Samples of cutlery.

859 GUESNU, —, 16 Rue Portefoin, and 14 Rue Aumaire, Paris.—Lithographic printing. Embossed papers.

860 GUILBERT & WATEAU, Manufacturers, Rue St. Fiacre, Paris.—Woollen fabrics, woollen and silk mixtures, unbleached and dyed.

861 HAMANN, E. F. 43 Quai des Augustins, Paris.— A calculating planimeter.

862 HAMM & Co. Surgical Instrument Maker, 6 Place de l'Ecole de Médecine, Paris.—Instruments for cataracts, amputations, trepanning, and lithotrity. Trusses, surgical instruments, &c.

863 HARAND, E. Artificial Flower Maker, 15 Rue de Choiseul, Paris.—Head-dresses, gown-trimmings, &c.

864 HARDING-COCKER, Manufacturer of Spinning Combs, 7 Rue de Metz, Lille (Nord).—The model of a machine for combing flax, wool, and silk, A machine for combing wool, articles used in spinning flax, wool and silk, such as gills, cylindrical combs, &c.

865 HARDOUIN, —. 26 Rue de Bréda, Paris. — Carved ornaments : lustre roses ; looking-glass frames.

866 HARO, E. F. Colour Manufacturer, 18 Rue des Petits Augustins, Paris.—Canvass for historical painting ; colours ; varnish ; new process for restoring pictures.

867 HARTWECK, E. Designer, 14 Rue de Mail, Paris.— Designs for long and square shawls.

868 HYPPOLITE, Madame, Stay Maker, 21 Rue de la Michodière, Paris.

869 HEBERT, L. A. 252 Rue St. Martin, Paris.—Varnish for boots and shoes.

870 HECKEL, sen. & Co. Silk Manufacturers, 14 Rue des Capucins, Lyons (Rhône).—Plain satin of different tints.

871 HENRI, P. Jeweller, 47 Rue du Vert Bois, Paris.— Boxes, cups, brooches, pins, &c. ; with imitations of jewels.

872 HERAULT, —, 22 Rue Neuve St. Eustache, Paris.— Designs for shawls.

873 HERMANN, G. Machine Maker, 92 Rue de Charenton, Paris.—Machine for grinding chocolate, colours, and drugs.

874 HERMANOWSKA, M. Troyes (Aube).—Stained glass in the style of Louis XV.

875 HOFER, H. & Co. Cotton Spinners, Kaysersberg (Haut-Rhin.)—Spun cottons, bobbins, skeins, wefts, and chains.

876 HOLSTEIN, J. P. St. Etienne (Loire).—Terra cotta mouldings.

877 HONORE, E. Porcelain Manufacturer, 6 Boulevard Poissonnière, Paris.—White and gilt porcelains.

878 HOUZEAU, E. 33 Rue de l'Arbre Sec, Paris. — Tracing paper.

879 HUBER, C. E. 29 Rue Bergère, Paris. —A door in the style of Louis XIV. ; niche and pilastre of a figured freize in renaissance style ; cariatides, medallion, vases, and capitals.

880 HUET, J. Polished Steel Manufacturer, Rue Pastourelle, au Marais, Paris.—Trimming for purses ; bead reticules ; buckles, brooches, bracelets, pins, &c.

881 HUGUES, J. J. SON, Grasse (Var).—Bottles of various essences.

882 HULOT, A. Assistant Engraver to the Mint, Hôtel des Monnaies, Paris.—Impressions from relievo engraved plates ; bank notes ; playing cards ; stamps, &c.

883 KUNZER, J. Cloth Manufacturer, Bischwiller (Bas-Rhin).—Various fabrics ; black satin, black cloth, china satin, twilled amazon, &c.

884 HURTREL & Co. Lille (Nord).—A ferule for generators, with its appendages.

885 HUSSON & BUTHOD, Manufacturers of Musical Instruments, 13 and 15 Rue Grénétat, Paris.—Violins, guitars, barrel organs, &c.

886 JACOBS & DUPUIS, Shoemakers, 32 Rue de la Paix, Paris.—Ladies' and children's boots and shoes.

887 JAUDIN, A. Manufacturer of Tinfoil for Mirrors, 15 Rue de la Croix St. Martin, Paris.—Tinfoil and coloured spangles.

888 JAVET, C. 10 Rue Geoffroy Marie, Paris.—Designs for fabrics.

889 JEANSELME, J. P. F. 93 Boulevard Beaumarchais, Paris.—Cabinet work : oak sideboard, dressing-room furniture, arm chairs, and chairs (Louis XV. style).

890 JOLLY-LECLERC, Cabinet-maker, 38 Faubourg St. Antoine, Paris.—Rosewood wardrobe, carved, with looking-glass, and small étagère.

891 JOLY, J. M. sen. Ropemaker, St. Malo (Ile-et-Vilaine).—Rope-work for shrouds.

892 JOLY, Mmes. Sisters, 45 Rue Neuve St. Augustin, Paris.—Fancy white satin, white drill, mohair, &c. Stays ; trimmings, &c.

893 JOUVIN, (Widow), XAVIER, Glove Manufacturer, Grenoble (Isère), and 18 Boulevard Poissonnière, Paris.— Glove-leather ; gloves ; patent machine for cutting out gloves.

894 KOPPELIN, E. 17 Quai Voltaire, Paris.—Lithographic printing.

895 LABOULAYE, C. & Co. Type-founder, 30 Rue Madame, Paris.—Specimens of various type-founts, and printing.

896 LAMORT, G. Merino Manufacturer, Rethel (Ardennes).—Unbleached and dyed merino fabrics.

897 LAUDE, A. 19 Rue de la Roquette, Paris.—Cast-iron bedstead ornamented with bronze, and having an elastic bottom.

898 LANGEVIN & Co. Floss-silk Thread-spinner, Laferté Aleps (Seine-et-Oise). — Floss-silk threads of various qualities.

900 LAPORTE, V. & SON, Cloth Manufacturers, Limoges (Haute-Vienne).—Double-milled cloths, light grey, plain Marengo, &c.

901 LAROQUE, SON, BROTHERS, & JAQUEMET, Manufacturers, Bordeaux (Gironde).—Assortment of spun wool for knitting woollen blankets. Short-napped carpets. Samples of manufactured hides.

902 LAURENT, J. B. Lace-maker, 40 Rue Rambuteau, Paris.—Twists, silk buttons, and other articles of trimmings.

903 LAURET BROTHERS, Hosier, 19 Rue des Mauvaises Paroles, Paris.—Stockings, gloves, and silk mittens. Scotch thread, silk poplin, and cashmere. Various other articles.

905 LAZARE, V. sen. & LACROIX, Silk-handkerchief manufacturers, Avignon (Vaucluse). — Thread, silk, and cotton kerchiefs. Flagon of garancine.

906 LEBRUN, L. J. 126 Rue de Grenelle St. Germain, Paris.—Specimens of binding; Lewis's Sketches; Napoleon in Egypt, &c.

907 LEFEBVRE, SON, & Co. Lille.—A glazed wardrobe of chesnut wood, with inside of oak, and pannels of cedar wood.

908 LEISTNER, G. L. 48 Rue de Chaillot, Paris.—Perfumery, tooth-powder, &c.

909 LEMONNIER &Co. Designer in Hair, 13 Rue du Coq St. Honoré, Paris.—Various trinkets set with hair ornaments.

910 LEPINE, F. D. Clasp Manufacturer, 12 Rue des Vinaigriers, Paris.—Clasps for gloves.

912 LHOEST, C. V. Manufacturer, 14 Rue Pastourelle, Paris.—Drawings from sculpture, effected by mechanical process.

913 LOMBARD, —, Ornamental Carver, 5 Rue Thorigny, Paris. — Ornamented looking-glass and picture-frames. Bronze articles. Furniture, &c.

914 LUNDY, J. A. V. 2 Rue Chapon, Paris.—Paleographic designs. Manuscript of the fifteenth century, on parchment.

915 MAEHLY, —, 69 Rue du Rocher, Paris.—Model of a machine for extracting oil from bituminous schistus.

916 MEISSONNIER, —, 8 Rue Meslay, Paris.—Colours and dyes.

917 MANSON, E. Nantes (Loire-Inférieure).—Japanned calf-leather.

918 MANTOIS, Mme. ELISA, Colourist, Rue du Pont de Fer, St. Sulpice.—Ceruse of zinc, for painting in water colours and in oil.

919 MARS, —, 20 Rue de la Cerisaie, Paris.—Screw-jack loading-machine.

920 MARSAT, SON, Iron Master, Angoulême (Charente). —Flat and squared iron refined. Cast-iron for artillery purposes.

921 MARTEL, GEOFFRAY & VALANSOT, Manu. Lyons (Rhône).—Fancy silk cravats and collars.

922 MARTIN DE LIGNAC, Agriculturist, Mont Levade, Commune de St. Sulpice (Creuse).—Patent concentrated milk.

923 MATIFAT, C. S. Manu. 9 Rue de la Perle, Paris.—Clocks, chandeliers, and various articles in bronze.

924 MAUZAIZE, J. N. 4 Impasse St. Michel, Chartres (Eure-et-Loire).—Machine applicable to flour-mills.

925 MENIER & Co. Chocolate Manufacturers, 37 Rue St. Croix de la Bretonnerie, Paris. Drugs prepared by steam. Chocolates. Pearl and shelled barley. Gruel.

926 MERLIE, LEFEBVRE, & Co. Ingouville (Seine-Inférieure).—Cables and cordage.

927 MERCIER, 100 Faubourg St. Antoine, Paris.—Drawing-room furniture. Cupboards with mirrors. A bed, chest of drawers, &c.

928 MEURISSE, —, Corset Maker, 1 Rue du 29 Juillet, Paris.—Two fancy corsets.

929 MILLIAU, —, jun. Soap maker, Marseille (Bouches-du-Rhône).—Various samples of soap.

930 MILON P. D. sen. 98 Rue St. Honoré, Paris.—Silk stockings. Trousers, babies' clothes, and various articles of hosiery.

931 MORISOT, —, Manufacturer, 12 Rue de la Cerisaie, Paris.—Art bronzes. Andirons, tongs, &c. Vases and statuettes.

932 MOTTET, C. Rue des Trois Bornes, Paris.—Orchil for dyeing and printing stuffs.

933 MOUSSILLAC, —, La Réole (Gironde).—A twelve circle mill of Acacia.

934 MUEHL-WAHL & Co. Tusey Iron Works, near Vaucouleurs.—Statues: Hebe; a Faun. Busts, candelabras, fountain, door panels, pilasters, table feet, &c.

935 NILUS, —, jun. Graville, near Havre (Seine-Inférieure).—A double pump.

936 NOEL, F. Filter Manufacturer, 14 Chemin de Ronde de la Barrière des Vertus.—Stone apparatus for filtering water.

937 NOGAREDE, J. L. St. Jean-du-Gard.—Skeins of raw silk.

938 ODENT X. SONS & Co. Courtalin (Seine-et-Marne). —Papers made by machine and by hand.

939 OGER, J. L. M. 17 Rue Culture St. Catherine, Paris.—Household and toilet soaps, and perfumery.

940 PAGNERRE, —, Bookseller and Publisher, 18 Rue de Seine, Paris.—Thirty-two volumes of various kinds.

941 PAIX DE BEAUVOY, C. Seiches (Maine-et-Loire).—Bee-hives in wood and straw.

942 PALMER, J. L. Wire Drawer, 16 Rue Montmorency, Paris.—Specimens of drawn wire, welding, &c.

943 PAPE, J. H. 19 Rue des Bons Enfans, Paris, and 310 Regent Street, London.- Square and patent console piano-fortes, console grand ditto; square and hexagonal table pianos; grand piano with patent action and improved sounding board.

944 PARENT, —, 33 Rue des Arcis, Paris.—Weighing scales, weights, and measures.

945 PAROISSIEN, A. Manufacturer, 12 Rue St. Appoline, Paris.—Waxen leaves. Ladies' head-dresses.

946 PAUBLAN, —, Locksmith and Machine Maker, 366 Rue St. Honoré, Paris.—Safes and locks of various kinds.

947 PEIGNE, V. J. Nort (Loire-Inférieure).—New self-priming gun.

948 PELLIER BROTHERS, Manufacturers of Preserves, Mans (Sarthe).—Bottles and boxes of preserves.

949 PELTEREAU, F. jun. Château Renaud (Indre-et-Loire).—Various kinds of leather.

950 PENEAU, J. Manufacturer of Preserves, La Musse, near Nantes (Loire-Inférieure).—Boxes of truffled game, sardines, green peas, and various preserved meats; bottles of fruits.

951 PEROT, G. J. sen. Engraver on Steel, 8 Rue Mandar, Paris.—Steel engravings of different descriptions.

952 PERROT, PETIT & Co. Manufacturers, 12 Rue de la Bourse, Paris.—Artificial flowers; fancy feathers for dress; gold, silver, and pearl embroidery, &c.

953 PETITCOLIN, J. Engraver, 2 Place Dauphine, Paris. —Copper-plate engravings of machinery.

954 PETITHOMME, L. A. Engineer and Founder, 283 Rue St. Jacques, Paris.—Patent system of suspension for bells, exemplified by a chime of four bells.

955 PEYRON, S. Sieve-hoop Manufacturer, Rumegnol, near Brest (Finistère).—Sieve-hoops; made of beech sawn and bent by steam machinery.

956 PHILIPPE & CANAUD, Manufacturers of Preserves, Ville-en-bois, Nantes (Loire-Inférieure).—Bottles and vessels of preserves, as meats, vegetables, fish, &c.

957 PIERON, —, Bronze Manufacturer, 13 Rue des Enfans Rouges, Paris.—Fenders, with shovels and tongs, gilt and oxidized, or gilt and bronzed. Patent screen.

958 PIERRET, J. B. 29 Rue de Breda, Paris.—A rotatory steam-engine of 10-horse power.

959 PITET, —, sen. Brush Maker, 305 Rue St. Martin, Paris.—Samples of brushes for painting.

960 PITOUX, V. Gelatine Flower Manufacturer, 24 Rue Parée, au Marais, Paris.—Gelatine flowers, ornaments and bouquets. Gelatine cylinders of various colours.

961 PÖELMAN, I. Moulins-lez-Lille; Agent, M. Gauthier-Bouchard, Rue du Cloître St. Méry, Paris.—Ceruse, or white lead.

962 POILLEU BROTHERS, Brest (Finistère).—Cenotaph of granite.

963 POIRIER, L. Machine Maker, 33 Rue du Faubourg St. Martin, Paris.—Patent copying-presses; presses for sealing letters; autographic presses; stamping-machine, &c.

964 POTONIE, 5 Rue Neuve St. François, Paris.—Clocks of various descriptions and patterns.

965 POULAT, A. Manufacturer, 6 Cours de Brosses, à la Guillotière, Lyons (Rhône).—Brass screw-plates, with holes set in rubies, for extracting all kinds of metals.

966 POULLOT, —. Optician, 85 Rue St. Louis, au Marais, Paris.—Eye glasses; spectacles, &c.

967 POUYER, Mechanist, Rouen (Seine-Inférieure).—Apparatus, available for a 40-horse power, by which any number of movers may be connected or disconnected at pleasure.

968 PECQUEUR, —.—Fishing-nets.

969 PROUTAT, MUTROT & THOMERET, Arnay-le-Duc (Côte d'Or).—Samples of tools and files.

970 BERTRAND PROVANCHER, Place du Château-Rouge, Montmartre.—A China plate, with portrait representing Queen Victoria and the Royal Family.

971 RAGOT, J. F. Designer, 89 Boulevard St. Martin, Paris.—Design for a white lace counterpane, Brussels application, without trimmings.

972 RAGOT-MAYEUX, Manufacturer Reims (Marne).—Unbleached and dyed merino fabrics, of different qualities.

973 RANDOING, J. Clothier, Abbeville (Somme).—Dyed cloths: beaver, cashmere, summer satin, &c.

974 RAPP, C. F. Bootmaker, 21 Rue Feydeau, Paris.—Various descriptions of shoes and boots.

975 REBERT, C. 25 Place du Dome, Strasbourg (Bas-Rhin)—Patterns of patent door fastenings, with single wires or with spiral rods.

976 REDELIX, C. H. 357 Rue St. Denis, Paris.—Flowermakers' tools.

977 REMOND, N. Rue du Foin St. Jacques, Paris.—Framed impressions, coloured, but not touched up with a pencil, and a painted sign-board.

978 RENARD, —. Cutler, 28 Rue des Gravilliers, Paris.—Tools for engraving.

979 REIGNIAUD, —, Hardware Manufacturer, 6 Rue Sainte Foy, Paris.—Metal foundry of all descriptions.

980 RICHARD BROTHERS, St. Chamon (Loire).—Silk gimp.

981 RENARD & SON, Plate Glass Makers, Fresnes, near Condé (Nord).—Window-glass: white, half-white, and common; and fluted glass.

982 RENODIER & SON, Cutlers, St. Etienne (Loire).—Steel-bladed knives, called Hustaches.

983 REPEYRE, S. Shawl Manufacturer, 9 Rue des Fossés, Montmartre, Paris.—Figured woollen shawls and scarfs.

984 REYDOR BROTHERS & COLIN, 17 Rue Jean-Robert, Paris.—Clocks. Regulators and kitchen-jacks.

985 RIBY, P. Angers (Maine-et-Loire)—Mill-stones.

986 RICROCH, C. & Co. (China Workmen Society), Limoges (Haut-Vienne).—Articles in China: white china table service.

987 RIVAUD, G. Petit Rochefort (Charente).—Fleeces of merino-wool.

988 ROBAUT, L. Tanner and Currier, Douai (Nord).—Leather for cards and military accoutrements.

989 GALLAND, ROBERT, Manufacturer, Pont-Faverger (Marne).—Merino fabrics unbleached and dyed.

990 ROCHE & DIME, Silk Manufacturers, 1 Place Romarin, Lyons (Rhône).—Three fancy silk shawls.

991 ROCHER, M. Nantes (Loire-Inférieure)—Patent apparatus for distillation. Submarine condenser.

992 ROEDEL & SON, Bordeaux (Gironde).—Preserved food.

993 ROTH, J. C. Strasbourg (Bas-Rhin).—Brass and wooden musical instruments.

994 ROUCHIER, F. & SON, Manufacturers of Preserves, Ruffec (Charente).—Rheims biscuits. Preserved green peas.

995 ROUX & FORTIN, Caster Makers, 21 Rue d'Anjou, au Marais, Paris.—Patent undulating castors.

996 SAINT JEAN, Artist, 2 Qui Futchiron, Lyons (Rhône).—Oil paintings.

997 SAVARESSE, H. 30 Avenue St. Charles, Grenelle (Seine).—Strings and musical instruments.

998 SAVARESSE, —. jun, Manufacturer of Strings, Grenelle, near Paris (Seine).—Strings in silk and catgut, with flowers of the same materials trimmed with lace, for harps, violins, violoncellos, and guitars.

999 SCHIERTZ, J. G. Cabinet Maker, 27 Rue de la Huchette, Paris.—Optical apparatus. Apparatus and stands for daguerreotyping. Stands for telescopes.

1000 SCHLUMBERGER GASPARD, & Co. Manufacturers, Mulhouse (Haut-Rhin)—Woollen and silk stuffs for furniture. Fabrics from the Jacquard-loom.

1001 SCHNEIDER, E. & A. & LEGRAND, Sédan (Ardennes).—A shearing-machine.

1002 SCHNEIDER BROTHERS, Merchants, 137 Rue Montmartre, Paris.—Silk ribbons manufactured by various houses at St. Etienne (Loire).

1003 SCHWARTZ & HUGUENIN, Calico Printers, Mulhouse, (Haut-Rhin). (Dép. in Paris, C. Muller, 3 Rue du Sentier; London, M. Sauphar, 9 Southampton St. Holborn.)—Printed woollen and cotton cloths. Printed lastings.

1004 SCHWARTZ, TRAPP, & Co. Wool Spinners, Mulhouse (Haut-Rhin).—Machine-combed woollen threads.

1005 SCRIVE BROTHERS, Manufacturer of Cards'-Straps, Lille (Nord).—Plates and card-straps for carding cotton, wool, and flax tow.

1006 SCRIVE BROTHERS, & DANSER, J. Tissue Manufacturers, Marguette and Halhein, near Lille (Nord).—Linen tissues. Various kinds of cloth. Ticks woven by power-looms.

1007 SCRIVE BROTHERS, Flax Spinners, Lille (Nord).—Flax and flax-tow thread, manufactured by new processes.

1008 SEGUIN, JOSEPH, Manufacturer, Puy (Haute Loire); and 40 Rue des Jeuneurs, Paris.—Silk lace.

1009 SEIB, J. A. Floor-cloth Manufacturer, Strasbourg, (Bas-Rhin).—Glazed cloths for floors, embroidery, cloaks, &c. of various qualities.

1010 SENGENWALD, —. Strasbourg (Bas-Rhin).—Samples of madder from Alsatia.

1011 SENTIS, SON & Co. Wool-spinners, Rheims (Marne).—Samples of woollen and worsted yarns.

1012 SERVAIS, J. B. Gilder and Ornamentist, 15 Rue St. Louis en l'Ile, Paris.—Gilt frames. Rustic ornaments of sculpture.

1013 SIGNORET ROCHAS, P. Woollen Cloth Manufacturer, Vienne (Isère) Rue du Chemin Neuf.—Woollen cloths of a new description; black cloth; grey twills, &c.

1014 SIMON, E. Strasbourg (Haut-Rhin). — Black and coloured prints. Lithographic aquarelle.

1015 SIMON, PAUL, 36 Boulevard du Temple, Paris.—Plastic art, a group.

1016 SIMON, J. 4 Rue Vide Gousset, Place des Victoires, Paris.—Marble clocks, goblets, inkstands, chimney-piece, &c.

1017 SIROT, Nail-maker, Valenciennes (Nord).—Samples of nails and pegs for shoes, in rut, copper, or steel.

1018 VIEILLE MONTAGNE, JOINT-STOCK COMPANY, Mr. A. GUYNEMER, Sen. Director, 19 Rue Richer, Paris.—Sheets of zinc, of various thickness and dimensions; samples of zinc products; statues, busts, and statuettes.

1019 LINEN JOINT-STOCK CO.—MM. RADIQUET, HOMON, GOUVY, & LEROUX, Managers, Landernau (Finistère).—Sail-cloth and yarn spun dry.

1020 SOREL, —, Civil Engineer and Oxide Manufacturer, Grenelle (Seine). Depôt, 6 Rue de Lancry, Paris.—Various qualities of oxide of zinc.

1021 STAMIN & CO. Thann (Haut-Rhin).—A spinning mule, with 120 spindles.

1022 SUSER, H. Tanner and Boot-maker, Nantes, and La Morinière (Loire-Inférieure).—Tanned leather. Curried leather. Boots and shoes. Exportation.

1023 SUSSE BROTHERS, Manufacturers, 31 Place de la Bourse, Paris.—Candelabras, statues in bronze and marble, clocks, statuettes, &c.

1024 TABORIN, P. F. 62 Rue Amelot, Paris.—Various kinds of files.

1025 TAILBOUIS, VERDIER & CO. Manufacturers, 17 Rue des Mauvaises Paroles, Paris.—New kind of silk gloves, &c.

1026 TAILFER, J. B. 9 Rue St. Etienne, Batignolles (Seine).—Dynamometric machines, patented.

1027 TALABOT, L. & CO. Toulouse (Haute-Garonne), and Sans-sur-Tarn, near Albi (Tarn).—Various kinds of scythes, cleavers, and files.

1028 TALBOT, BROTHERS, Mennetou Salon, near Bourges (Cher).—A plough.

1029 TAUTENSTEIN & CORDEL, 90 Rue de la Harpe, Paris.—Music, printed in types and lithographed printed volumes.

1030 TEILLARD, C. M. Silk Manufacturers, 25 and 27 Rue Nationale, Lyons (Rhône).—Silk, mohair, velvet, taffeta, and other stuffs.

1031 TEISSIER DU CROS, Silk Throwsters, Vallerangue (Gard).—Various samples of raw and thrown silk.

1032 TERRIER, J. & CO. Dyers and Finishers, Suresnes (Seine).—Various woollen stuffs; satin; damask; merino; muslin-de-laine, dyed and finished.

1033 TEXIER, T. jun. Glover, Niort (Deux Sèvres).—Gloves of deer, chamoy, castor, and sheep skins.

1034 TEXIER, V. 350 Rue St. Honoré, Paris.—Bound and stitched volumes. Museum of ancient and modern sculpture.

1035 THEIL, J. Millstone Manufacturer, St. Lucien, near Epernon (Eure-et-Loire).—Millstones.

1036 THEVENOT, ETIENNE, Clermont-Ferrand (Puy-de-Dome).—Patterns of painted glass for windows. Two painted glasses, representing two French queens.

1037 THIBERT & ADAM, Plush Manufacturers, Metz (Moselle).—Depôt, 10 Rue du Grand Chantier, Paris.—Silk plush, used in the manufacture of hats.

1038 THIERRY, J. Manufacturer, Rue Bat d' Argent, Hotel des Négociants, Lyons (Rhône).—A frame, containing nine photographic proofs.

1039 TAILLEFER & CO.—Manufacturers of pins and needles at L'Aigle (Orne).

1040 THOMAS BROTHERS, Silk Manufacturers, Avignon (Vaucluse). Depôt, Lyons (Rhône).—Florences from Avignon, various shades.

1041 THOREL, H. Manufacturer of Alimentary Preserves, Ruffec (Charente), Hotel des Postes.—Tureens of truffled ducks' livers; and of truffled red partridges. Patented in England.

1042 TIFFEREAU T. Watchmaker and Machine-maker,

10 Rue de Vaugirard, Paris.—Hydraulic clock, patented in France and England.

1043 TOULZA, F. St. Etienne (Loire).—Wrought iron. Locksmith's work. Shoemakers' tools, and small cleavers, &c.

1044 TRAVERS, P. L. 146 Faubourg Poissonnière, Paris.—A model of the upper part of the Custom-house. A model of the moveable cupola of the observatory. Various models the use of hothouses.

1045 TRUCHY, E. Jeweller, 18 Rue du Petit Lion St. Sauveur, Paris.—Imitation pearls. Imitation pieces, for of jewellers.

1046 TURPIN, F. A. 28 Rue Richelieu, Paris.—Chocolate, in lozenges and various forms. (Agent in London, J. Bissart, 5 King Street, Golden Square.)

1047 VIEL, —, Chemist, Tours (Indre-et-Loire).—Rotatory pill-making machine.

1048 WARMONT, V. E. Dyer, Neuilly-sur-Seine.—Chain arranged for weaving. Woollen scarfs. Wool in skeins.

1049 CHAMBER OF COMMERCE OF AVIGNON (Vaucluse).—Madder and madder extracts.

1050 ALCAN, M. 38 Rue d'Enghien, Silk Spinning Mill (Nimes), Paris.—Raw silks, &c.

1051 ALLUAUD, Sen. China Manufact. Limoges. (Haute-Vienne).—Specimens of china for the table and the toilet.

1052 AUCOC, —, Sen. Manufacturer, 6 Rue de la Paix, Paris.—Ladies and gentlemen's dressing-cases.

1053 ANDRE, J. P. V. Iron Master, Val d'Osme (Haute-Marne), and at 14 Rue Neuve Menilmontant, Paris.—Cast-iron beds; grates for chimneys; groups of animals; candelabras; statues and vases.

1054 ANDRE J. & Major Count DE BRONO-BRONSKI, Château de St. Silve, Arrondissement de Bordeaux, Gironde.—Two ploughs.

1055 AUBANEL, —, Bronze Manufacturer, 43 Rue de Trévise, Paris.—Bronze and marble chimney-piece. A door made of cast-iron, gilt, and carved, and gilt wood.

1058 AUBEUX, —, Stuffs Manufacturer, 6 Rue de l'Impasse, Paris.—Cashmere stuffs for waistcoats, a fashionable novelty.

1059 AUCLER, W. & P. Ledoux, au Fidèle Berger, 46 Rue des Lombards, Paris.—Confectionery, and articles for the use of confectioners.

1061 BACH-PERES, 99 Faubourg St. Denis, Paris.—Transparent painted blinds.

1062 BACOT, P. & SON, Sédan (Ardennes).—Satin cloths, and kerseymeres.

1063 BADIN, J. C. F. Manufacturer of Feather Tissues, 337 Rue St. Denis, Paris.—Basket-work, and hats of diamond-like feather tissues.

1064 BALAY, J.—Silk ribbons.

1065 BALLEIDIER, F. Manufacturer of Silks, 20 Rue des Capucins, Lyons, (Rhône).—Figured velvets, with or without embroidery; velvet waistcoats.

1066 BALNY, jun. J. P. 41 Rue de Charenton, Paris.—Furniture: Walnut-wood centre table, covered with silk, with bronze statue; elbow-chairs; chairs.

1067 BARBAT, —, Lithographer, Châlons-sur-Marne.—Illustrated volumes of the Gospel.

1068 BARBE, C. Designer, Mulhouse (Haut-Rhin). — Designs for stuff-printing.

1069 BATON, W. & SON, Lyons, 11 Rue Noire (Rhône).—Felt and silk hats.

1070 BATTENBERG, G. 20 Rue du Dragon, Paris.—Specimen of printing; one bound volume.

1071 BAUDRY, A. T. Athis, Mons (Seine and Oise).—Steel for springs and other purposes.

1072 BAUERKELLER & CO. (BERGER WALTER, successor), 7 Rue d'Enghien, Paris.—Geographical maps. Plans of towns in relievo, sacred paintings, and sky-lights.

1073 BAZIN, —, sen. Agriculturist, Mesnil, St. Germain (Oise).—Samples of wheat in the ear and in seed.

1074 BEAUFILS, —, Place des Quinconces, Bordeaux.—Writingtable, work-table, cupboard, sofa, causeuse or small sofa, arm-chairs, and chairs.

1075 BERNARD, A. 16 Avenue de la Mothe-Piquet, Paris.—Hunting-guns.

1076 BEAUVAIS, C. 18 Rue Notre-Dame-de-Nazareth, Paris.—Raw silk.

1077 BELLANGE, A. L. Rue de Marais St. Martin, Paris.—Articles of furniture in buhl.

1078 BELLEVILLE BROTHERS, Nancy (Meurthe).—A jug containing starch.

1079 BELLON, J. & Co. 2 Rue du Griffon, Lyons (Rhône).—Figured silks, &c.

1080 NATIONAL SHEEP FOLD OF RAMBOUILLET (Seine-et-Oise).—Four fleeces of real merinos.

1081 BERNARD, J. B. Valenciennes (Nord).—A panel of veneer work and inlaid floor.

1082 BERTECHE, CHESNON, & Co. Manufacturers, Sédan (Ardennes).—Cloths of all colours: Kerseymeres, satins, articles for paletots, fancy goods, &c. (29 Fossés St. Germain, Rue l'Auxerrois, Paris; and Agents in London, Vacossin, Bonet, and Fournier, 5 Wood St. Cheapside.)

1083 BARBOTIN & LEGOFF.—Capstans and iron rope-manœuvring apparatus, on board of vessels.

1084 BERTON, H. 13 Rue Faubourg, St. Martin, Paris.—Pasteboard boxes. Perfumed cases and bags. Envelopes.

1085 BERTRAND, GAYET & DUMONTAT, Manufacturers of silks, 27 Place de la Comédie, Lyons (Rhône).—Figured silks; shawls, neckerchiefs, scarfs.

1086 BETTIGNIES, M. China Manufacturer, St. Amand-les-Eaux (Nord).—Porcelain vases (soft biscuit), ornamented, and mounted in bronze; flower stands, &c.

1087 BIANCHI, J.& DUSEIGNEUR, Lyons (Rhône).—Various samples of raw and wrought silks.

1088 BISSON l. Jun. Broad-cloath Manufacturer, Bernay (Eure).—Cloth frocks. Bronzed waddings. Blue pilot cloth, &c.

1089 BLAIZE, H. Engraver, 3 Rue Tourraine St. Germain, Paris.—Embossed engraving on brass.

1090 BLANCHET BROTHERS & KLEBER, Rives (Isère).—White and coloured paper, sized and unsized.

1091 BLEUZE, H. 33 Rue des Lombards, Paris.—Divers specimens of soaps and essences.

1092 BOBEE (Widow) & LEMIRE, Choisy-le-Roi (Seine).—Chemical products.

1093 BOLLEE, E. Bell Founder, St. Croix-lès-le-Mans (Sarthe).—Three bells forming a perfect chime, and fixed in a two-storied belfry.

1094 BONFILS, MICHEL, SOUVRAZ, & Co. Shawl Manufacturers, 3 Rue des Fossés Montmartre, Paris.—Cashmere square shawls and scarfs.

1095 BONNET, J. B. Rousset.—A plough, with double subsoil action.

1096 BONNET, Jun. Earthenware Manufacturer, 5 Chemin de Ronde de la Barrière Ménilmontant, Paris.—Chemical apparatus and crucibles for casting in refractory earth.

1097 BONNET & Co. Manufacturers of silks, 2 Rue du Griffon, Lyons (Rhône).—Plain silks: taffeta and satin.

1098 BOQUET, MARIE VIRGINIE, Painter on Porcelain, 27 Rue Tronchet, Paris.—A portrait of Louis Philippe, painted on enamel.

1099 BORD, —, Pianoforte Manufacturer, 35 Boulevard Bonne Nouvelle, Paris.—Grand piano.

1100 BORSARY, —, Dijon (Cote d'Or).—Surgical apparatus: Instruments for various uses and bandages.

1101 BOTTIER, L. N. Engineer, 36 Rue St. Jean de Beauvais, Paris.—Machines for gold-beating; beaten gold, as specimens of the application.

1102 BOUASSE, V. LEBEL & Co. Rue du Petit Bourbon, Paris.—Samples of gelatine pictures.

1103 BOUCHARD, F. Tourcoing (Nord).—Satin, woollen, and cotton fabrics, &c.

1104 BOUCHERIE, J. A. 4 Rue Mondovi, Paris.—Various kinds of wood, dyed by a chemical process, which tends to their preservation.

1105 BOUDON, L. Silk Manufacturer, St. Jean du Gard. White and yellow silk for bolting cloth; weft and satin organzine, gauze and other articles.

1106 BOUHARDET, C. P. Maker of Billiard-tables, 70 Rue de Bondy, Paris.—Carved billiard-table, with appurtenances.

1107 BOUILLETTE, HYVELIN, & Co. Jewellers, 46 Rue St. Avoye, Paris.—Frontlet composed of seven brooches, stomachers, bracelets, brooches, and other articles of gold and silver jewellery set with stones.

1108 BOURDON, E. Machine-builder, 74 Faubourg du Temple, Paris.—Working model of a steam-engine; various instruments for measuring the pressure of steam and gases, the atmospheric pressure, the temperature, &c.

1109 FORTIN-BOUTELLIER, Woollen Fabric Manufacturer, 24 Rue du Moulin à l'Huile, Beauvais (Oise).—Manufacturing, spinning, and preparing of cloths.

1110 BOUVARD & LANÇON, Manufacturers of Silks, Lyons (Rhône). — Figured silks; satin, damask, lustring, brocatelle, &c.

1111 BRANDUS & Co. 87 Rue Richelieu, and 40 Rue Vivienne, Paris.—Printed music.

1112 BRETEAU, C. A. Artificial Flower Manufacturer.—34 Rue Notre Dame des Victoires, Paris.—Artificial flowers, and plumes of feathers for dresses and head-dresses; gown-trimmings, &c.

1113 BRETON BROTHERS, Mathematical Instrument-makers, 23 Rue Dauphine, Paris.—Rotatory air-pumps; electro-medical apparatus; electric locomotive.

1114 BENOIT, MALO, & VALBAUM, Rheims.—Merinos.

1115 BRIDARD, J. Boot-maker, 53 Rue Vivienne, Paris.—Japanned riding boots; hunting boots; various kinds of shoes and boots.

1116 BRIQUET & PERRIER, Tissue Manufacturers, 22 Rue Jean Robert, Paris.—Elastic caoutchouc tissues for braces, garters, &c., and specimens of that manufacture.

1117 BRISSON BROTHERS, Manufacturers, Lyons (Rhone), and 13 Rue du Griffon.—Silk and cotton plushes.

1118 BROSSE & Co. Manufacturers of Silks, Lyons (Rhône), and 1 Rue Lorette.—Plain velvets, in silk, of different colours.

1119 BRUNEAU, L. A. Silversmith, 40 Rue de Montmorency, Paris.—Silversmith works, and fancy jewellery, such as purses, seals, scent-bottles, snuff-boxes, jewel-cases, cash-boxes, &c.

1120 BRUNET, LECOMTE, GUICHARD, & Co. Manufacturers of Silks, Lyons (Rhône).—Silk prints: taffetas, satined muslins, damasked gauze, crape for shawls, scarfs and neckerchiefs.

1122 BUFFAULT & TRUCHON, Blanket Manufacturers, Essonne (Seine and Oise).—Wool and cotton blankets.

1123 BUGRE, A. Cane Manufacturer, 18 Rue Neuve St. Laurent, Paris.—Canes in tortoiseshells and ram's horn.

1124 BUIGNIER, G. S. F. 30 Rue des Vertus, Paris.—Matrices engraved on steel and artistic bronzes; battle of Brenneville; religious subjects; groups of animals and children, &c.

1125 BUISSON, —, sen. & Co. St. Etienne (Loire).—Silk ribbons.

1126 CABANES & RAMBIE, Bordeaux (Gironde), and 53 Quai de Paludate.—Grils flour; minots made with wheat from Bordeaux; and Egyptian flour.

1129 CAIN, J. Carver, 103 Faubourg St. Denis, Paris.—Bronzes: a nest with a group of birds fighting; a pair of goblets, &c.

1130 CANNEAUX & SONS, Wine Merchants, Reims (Marne), and 14 John St. Crutched Friars, London.—Apparatus for aerating and clarifying Champagne wines.

1131 CAVELAN & Co. Bagnères de Luchon (Hautes-Pyrénées).—Chemical products : Ore of argentiferous lead ; ore of oxide of manganese ; red litharge, and yellow litharge.

1132 CARLE, A. T. St. Maur-les-Fossés (Seine).—Specimens of brass foundry : candlesticks, clocks, flower-stands, &c.

1133 CARON, A. Passage de l'Opéra, Paris.—Gunsmith's work : A Parisian, and other guns and pistols.

1134 CARQUILLAT, Miss, MCH. CANDY & Co. Manufacturers of silks, à la Croix Rousse, Lyons (Rhône).—Pictures woven in silk.

1135 CARRIER-ROUGE, Candelabra Manufacturer, Rue de Puits d'Ainay, Lyons (Rhône).—Candelabras ; chandeliers ; bronze censers.

1136 CARRIERE, F. Silk Throwster, St. André de Valborgne (Gard).—Skeins of raw silk (white and yellow).

1137 CAUSSE & GARION, Silk Spinners, Lyons (Rhône).—Raw and thrown silks.

1138 CAUVET, C. Chantilly (Oise).—Manufactured produce : Wool combed and carded, and yarn.

1139 CHAGOT, sen. Feather and Fine Flower Manufacturer, 73 Rue Richelieu, Paris.—Feathers and bouquets of feathers—artificial flowers and vases.

1140 CHAMBELLAN & Co. Shawl Manufacturers, 8 Rue des Fossés Montmartre, Paris.—Square shawls and scarves in wool and cashmere.

1141 CHAMBER OF COMMERCE OF LYONS (Rhône).—Pictures woven in silk ; fashioned and broché silk stuffs for gowns ; broché and chiné gros-de-Tours ; lampas damask ; needle-brocatelle, &c.

1142 CHAMOUILLET, —, Looking-glass Manufacturer, 22 Rue de Cléry, Paris.—Oval glass and etched mirror glass.

1143 CHAMPAGNE & ROUGIER, Manufacturers of Silks, Lyons (Rhône).—Figured silks, divers specimens ; parasols and models of dresses, flounced.

1144 CHARAGEAT, E. Umbrella Maker, 268 Rue St. Denis, Cour des Bleus, Paris.—Umbrellas, parasols, &c. with handles of different materials.

1145 CHARRIERE, —, Rue de l'Ecole de Médecine, Paris.—Surgical apparatus and instruments of every kind. Cutlery, &c.

1146 CHEBEAUX, J. Manufacturer of Designs, 3 Rue St. Fiacre, Paris.—Designs for dresses and for Aubusson carpets.

1147 CARRIOL, BARON, Angers (Maine-et-Loire).—Combed wool.

1148 CHOCQUEEL, F. Shawl Manufacturer, Paris.—Scarfs in satinet barège ; with grounds of various colours, and cashmere designs.

1149 CHOQUART, C. 259 Rue St. Honoré, Paris.—Chocolate of different qualities.

1150 CHOSSON & Co. Glover, 63 Rue Montmartre, Paris.—Ladies' and gentlemen's kid gloves.

1151 CLAIR, P. 93 Rue du Cherche-Midi, Paris.—Rotary dynamometer. Model of a locomotive steam-engine, Clair's indicator. Lapointe's calculating machine.

1152 CLEMENÇON, Madame, Corset-maker, 8 Rue du Port-Mahon, Paris.—Fancy corsets in bleached silk.

1153 COIGNET & SON, Chemical Produce Manufacturer, La Guillotière, near Lyons (Rhône).—Chemicals : Glue, gelatine, phosphorus, prussiate of potash, &c.

1154 COLLIARD & COMTE, St. Etienne (Loire).—Silk ribbons.

1155 COLLOT BROTHERS, 4 Rue de l'Ecole de Médecine, Paris.—Scales and philosophical instruments.

1156 CONRAD, W. Manufacturer of Chemical Produce, 26 Rue Vieille du Temple, Paris.—Refined camphor blocks. Sublimed iodine and iodide of potassium.

1157 CORDERANT, A. Door-knob Manufacturer, 12 Rue de Paradis, Paris (Marais). — Porcelain door-knobs and plates. Hat-stands. Banisters, &c.

1158 CLAUDIN, —, 1 Rue Joquelet, Paris.—Guns and pistols of a new construction.

1159 CORDONNIER & Co. Furniture Makers, 5 Rue de Charonne, Paris.—Rosewood library. Drawing-room buffet. Flower stand.

1160 COUCHONNAL & Co. Embroidery Manufacturers, 79 Rue de Richelieu, Paris.—Silk embroidery on silk dresses and silk shawls.

1161 COUCHOUD, 11 Place St. Charles, St. Etienne, (Loire).—Silk ribbons.

1162 COUPIN J. Hatter, Aix (Bouches-du-Rhône).—Felt hats of various colours, without dressing.

1163 COURTOIS, A. Musical Instrument Maker, 21 Rue du Caire, Paris.—Trumpets, clarions, trombones, horns, ophicleids, and various other brass instruments.

1164 COURTE, P. Dyer, 47 Grande Rue, Lyons (Rhône).—Silks dyed black for plush.

1167 DAMIRON & Co. Shawl Manufacturers, 6 Rue des Capucins, Lyons (Rhône).—Long shawls of wool, and of wool and cashmere.

1168 DANIEL, —, jun. Jeweller in inferior articles, 33 Rue Michel-le-Comte, Paris. — Ornaments in steel, for purses ; steel jewellery.

1169 DARVIEU, sen. VALMALE, & Co. Silk-spinners, Laroque near Ganges (Hérault).—White and yellow silks.

1170 DAUDRE, A. St. Quentin (Aisne) and 17 Rue Bertin Poirée, Paris.—Fabrics, table-cloths, and napkins.

1171 DAUTHUILLE, A. T. Bookbinder, 84 Rue Montmartre, Paris.—Bindings on gilt and stamped cloth, relievo ; box covers in alto-relievo, gold, silver, and coloured, &c.

1172 DEBAIN, A. C. 15 Rue Vivienne, Paris.—A piano, an harmonium, and other musical instruments.

1173 DEBBELD, PELLERIN, & Co. Manufactory of Embroidery, Nancy (Meurthe), and 73 Rue Richelieu, Paris.—Embroidered bed-coverlet ; various cards of patterns.

1174. DEGARDIN, V. A. M. 62 Rue du Temple, Paris.—Burnishing stones, blood-stones, steel burnishing sticks for goldsmiths, &c.

1175 DELARBRE, —, sen. Lavalette, near Montpellier (Hérault).—Raw and thrown silk.

1176 DELARBRE, V. Silk-spinner, Ganges near Cazilhac (Hérault).—Raw and thrown silks.

1177 DUVAL, —, Paris.—A new system for railways.

1178 DELEUZE, A. St. Ambroix, arrd. d'Alais (Gard).—Raw silk.

1180 DELIGNON, V. Maker, 165 Rue Montmartre, Paris.—A hot-air stove, japanned tin lamps, flagons, &c.

1181 DELISLE & Co. Manufacturers of Printed Morocco Leather, Brié near Grenoble (Isère). — Printed morocco leather for slippers, &c.

1182 DENEIROUSE, E. BOIS-GLAVY & Co. Manufacturers, 16 Rue des Fossés Montmartre, Paris.—French cashmere shawl.

1183 DENUELLE, A. D. 43 Rue des Petites Ecuries, Paris.—Porcelain clay.

1184 DESAUGES, A. Tonnerre Stone, 57 Quai Valmy, Paris.—A carved mantelpiece ; two mangers ; two filterers.

1185 DESCHAMPS, N. 14 Galerie d'Orléans, Palais National, Paris.—Boots and shoes.

1186 LEROY & SON, Watchmakers, 13 and 15 Galerie Montpensier, Palais National, Paris.—Travelling and other clocks ; chronometers ; musical picture, &c.

1187 DEVIOLAINE BROTHERS, Glassmakers, Vauxrot (Aisne).—Samples of bells and bottles.

1188 DEVRANGE, B. B. 257 Rue St. Denis, Paris. — Pieces of lace-paper, for plates, &c. : cards.

1189 DIDA, A. Varnish-manufacturers, 11 Boulevard du

Temple, Paris.—Samples of varnish, samples of waterproof paper.

1190 DINANT & HUETTE, 8 Rue Levesque Nantes (Seine-Inférieure) —Fresh butter preserved without salt. Patented in England and France.

1191 DOLLFUS, MIEG, & Co. Printed Calico-manufacturers, Mulhouse (Haut-Rhin). Depôt: 9 Rue St. Fiacre, Paris; and 44 St. Paul's Churchyard, London.—Pieces of wool, muslin, jaconet, clear muslin, &c.

1192 DONAT, A. Manufacturer of Silks, Place Croix Paquet, Lyons (Rhône).—Waistcoats and dresses, fancy watered silk; grenadine, satin, poplin, &c.

1193 DONAT & Co. Manufacturers of Mixed Silks, Lyons (Rhône).—Silk plush for hats, in pieces. Plain hats.

1194 DOPTER, J. V. M. 58 Rue de la Harpe, Paris.—Specimens of black and coloured lace. Designs of screens, &c. with designs engraved on silk by chromo-lithography.

1195 DONZEL & MAUSSIER, St. Etienne (Loire).—Fancy ribbons.

1197 DUBOSCQ-SOLEIL, Optician, 35 Rue de l'Odéon, Paris. —Optical apparatus and instruments.

1198 DUCHENE, sen. Hatter, 7 Rue Geoffroy Langevin, Paris.—Silk and felt spring hats with boxes. Skeletons of mechanical hats.

1199 DUCOURTIOUX, C. L. Caoutchouc Stocking-manufacturer, 4 Rue Fontaine au Roi, Paris.—Machine-made caoutchouc stockings and belts.

1200 DUFOSSE, sen. 13 Rue St. Dominique, Faubourg St. Germain, Paris.—Waterproof hunting boots.

1201 DUFOSSEE, —, Shoe and Bootmaker, 20 Rue de la Paix, Paris; and 23 Old Bond Street, London.—Improved ladies' boots and shoes.

1202 DULUD, 27 Boulevard des Italiens, Paris.—Embossed leather for carving and ornamental hangings. Elbow chair and other articles of furniture.

1204 DUPAS, E. 6 Rue Folie Méricourt, Paris.—Articles of preserved food.

1205 DUPASQUIER, J. P. 20 Montée St. Barthélemy, Lyons (Rhône).—A coach seat with springs.

1206 DURAND, BONCOURT, & PITARD, Confectioners, 68 Rue des Carmes, Rouen.—Sugar of apples and cherries. Jellies. Sugar candy.

1207 DURAND, E. P. Cabinetmaker, 6 Rue St. Claude, au Marais, Paris.—Arm-chairs in mahogany and gilt. Chairs and sideboard. Bookcase.

1208 DURAND, G. Leather Manufacturer, 8 Rue Marie Stuart, Paris.—Tanned strong and calf leather.

1209 DUTROU, jun. Silk Ribbon Manufacturer, 345 Rue St. Denis, Paris.—Set of samples of silk ribbons for trimmings.

1210 DUVAL, M. Paris.—Cakes of onions, of coffee with milk, and of chocolate. Metal hangings, ivory, metallized horns and bones.

1211 ECK & DURAND, Artistic Bronze-Founders, 15 Rue des Trois Bornes, Paris. A statue of Cupid, by Bonnassieux. A fawn.

1212 EMMERICH, J. B. & GOERGER, M. jun. Manufacturers of Morocco, Strasbourg (Bas-Rhin).—Morocco leather of various colours. Gilt sheep-skins.

1213 ESSIQUE & DELAMARE, 5 Rue de Périgueux, Paris. —Metallic pearls.

1214 ESTIVANT BROTHERS, Brass-Founders and Tanners, Givet (Ardennes).—Brass plates and wire. Tanned leather from Buenos Ayres. Glue.

1215 ETEX, Á. Institute in Paris. Two groups in plaster.

1216 ERNEST, MADAME, 28 Rue de Bourgogne.—Stays without sewing.

1217 FARJON, H. Silk-Throwster, Roquemaure (Gard). —Raw silk and organzine.

1218 FAURE, M. Sculptor, 24 Place de Madeleine, Paris. —A figure carved on wood.

1219 FAURE, M. Furniture-maker, 14 Rue du Faubourg St. Denis, Paris; Depôt in London, 27 Gt. Russell St.— Ebony buffet with bronze ornaments. Chairs. Easy-chairs.

1220 FAVREL, A. Goldbeater, 27 Rue du Caire, Paris.— Gold and platina beaten into leaves. Samples of their application.

1221 FAYET-BARON, Locksmith, 269 Rue St. Honoré, Paris, at MM. Fontaine's.—Safety-lock.

1222 FORGES OF BIGNY.—Iron, casts, and wire.

1223 FLORANGE, —, jun. Furniture Maker, 20 Rue du Faubourg, St. Antoine, Paris.—Ebony and rosewood furniture.

1224 FLORIMOND, —, Artificial Flower Manufacturer, 8 Rue Montigny, Paris. — Artificial flowers; head-dresses; flowers and fruits.

1225 FONTAINE, F. Manufacturer of Silks, 16 Rue des Capucins, Lyons (Rhône).—Silk velvet of different shades.

1226 FONTAINE, FELIX, Lyons (Rhône).—Corsets of various fabrics.

1227 FONTAINE, P. L. 58 Faubourg St. Honoré, Paris.— Hydraulic apparatus of various kinds.

1228 FORTON, DUPONCEAU, & Co. Chattemoue (Mayenne). —Slate-billiard table.

1229 FOUCHE LE PELLETIER, E. E. F. Producers, Javel, near Paris.—Various chemicals and manures.

1230 FOUQUEAU, LECOMPTE, Orléans (Loiret). — Rich billiard table.

1231 FOURDINOIS, A. G. 46 Rue Amelot, Paris.—Sideboard, with dressing-table of carved walnut-wood.

1232 FOX, J. F. Tile Manufacturer, St. Génie Laval (Rhône).—Terra cotta and glass tiles.

1233 FRANC, A. & SON & MARTELIN, Silk Spinners, Lyons (Rhône).—Various samples of threads, combed wools, fancy twists.

1234 FRANCHE, C. Piano Manufacturer, 42 Rue de l'Université, Paris.—Two pianos.

1235 FRATIN, —, Sculptor, at M. Aubanel's, 43 Rue de Trévise, Paris.—Group of eagles, in bronze.

1237 FRIRY & RIGA, 124 Rue St. Jacques, Paris.—Typographic proof-sheets. Steel composing-pins and punches.

1238 GAAS D'AGNEN, V. Blind Children, National Asylum, Paris.—Geographical maps in relief. Two boards for raised letter-writing, with bodkins and gratings, &c.

1239 GALY CAZALAT, 14 Rue Charlot, Paris.—A new oscillating engine, patented. Manometers and safety apparatus in cases of boiler explosions, patented.

1241 GANTILLON, C. E. Manufacturer of Silks, 2 Rue des Capucins, Lyons (Rhône).—Pictures in silk, and silks for furnishing.

1242 GAUSSEN & Co. Shawl Manufacturers, 1 Rue de la Banque, Paris.—Cashmere scarves, &c.

1243 GAUSSEN, jun. FARGETON & Co. Shawl Manufacturers, 2 Place des Victoires, Paris.—Shawls: French cashmeres.

1244 GAUTHIER, J. Japanner 4 Faubourg Montmartre, Paris.—Lacquered morocco leather of all colours.

1245 GAUTIER, BOUCHARD, Colourman, 14 Rue du Cloître St. Merri. Paris.—Specimens of ochre, of different qualities.

1246 GERMAIN-SIMIER, M. Lithographic Printer, 20 Rue Poissonnière, Paris.—Papers for preventing forgery of bank notes, &c.

1247 GINDRE, L. Manufacturer of Silks, 23 Rue des Capucins, Lyons.—Plain silks. Satin, of various dyes.

1248 GIRARD, NEPHEW, & Co. 19 Port St. Clair, Lyons (Rhône).—Silk velvet of various shades.

1249 LE GENERAL, GIROD DE L'AIN, Chevry, près Gex, Ain.—Fleeces of Merino wool, from the flock at Nuz.

1250 GIRODON, A. Silk Manufacturer, 30 Quai de Retz, Lyons (Rhône).—Silk cravats, taffety, satin, silk, stuffs, &c.

1251 GODDET, A. Gun Barrel Maker, 130 Rue St. Lazare, Paris.—Pistol, and fowling-piece, with two and four barrels.

1252 GODEFROY, L. Tissue Manufacturer, 4 Quai National, Puteaux (Seine).—Printed tissues; square shawls and scarves; dresses, &c.

1253 GORSAS & PERIER, China Manufacturers, Limoges (Haute-Vienne).—Table services in China, and various other articles.

1254 GRADE, L. Furniture Maker, 9 Rue Castex, Paris.— Two bureaus with shelves; large shelf-stand; toilet-table; parlour-table of inlaid work; working table, &c.

1255 GRANDVAL, J. B. Chemist, Hôtel Dieu, Rheims (Marne).—Patented pharmaceutical products.

1256 GRANGOIR, J. M. Locksmith, 22 Rue Ste. Appoline, Paris.—Locks, for strong chests, pocket-books, room-doors, and other inventions of the exhibitor.

1257 GRASSOT & Co. Damasked Linen Manufacturers, 19 Port St. Clair, Lyons (Rhône).—Damask linen, napkins, table-cloths, &c. for tea, breakfast, and other table services.

1258 GRIFFON, BROTHERS & SISTERS, 99 Rue St. Honoré, Paris.—Specimens illustrating the dry scouring, and dyeing of silks, velvet, ribbon, &c.

1259 GRILLET, sen. & Co. Shawl Manufacturers, 11 Place Croix-Paquet, Lyons (Rhône).—Long white and black Cashmere shawls.

1260 GRISON, —, 15 Rue Bourg l'Abbé, Paris.—Different descriptions of lamp and lighthouse burners.

1261 GUERLIN-HOEL, Tanner and Currier, Grenelle (Seine).—Japanned smoothed and grained calf leather.

1262 GUIHERY, DESLANDELLES, & Co. Confectioners, &c. Nantes (Loire-Inférieure).—Pies, sardines, peas, and various other preserved meats.

1263 GUINON, N. P. Dyer of Stuffs, Lyons (Rhône).— Chromatic picture and circle. Specimens of silks and woollen stuffs dyed in various colours.

1264 GUYON, E. Blanket Manufacturer, 57 Rue Galande, Paris.—Woollen and cotton blankets.

1264A GONSE & MAGNEY, Bapaum (Pas-de-Calais).—Clarifying powder for beer, stout, ale, and porter, &c.

1265 HAYEM, —, sen. Shirt Maker, 38 Rue du Sentier, Paris.—Cambric shirts and fronts; collars of all descriptions. Patented.

1266 HENNECART, J. F. 30 Rue de l'Echiquier, Paris. —A bolting apparatus for sifting; samples of gauzes for bolters, of various qualities.

1267 HENRY, H. F. Designer for Fabrics, 69 Rue des Marais St. Martin, Paris.—Designs for prints and textures.

1268 HERZ, H. Piano Manufacturer, 48 Rue de la Victoire, Paris.—Piano organ, grand piano, semi-grand piano.

1269 HINDENLANG, —, sen. Wool Spinner, Cramoisy (Oise), and 24 Rue des Vinaigriers, Paris.—Woollen and Cashmere yarns and tissues.

1270 HOUDAILLE, F. N. Jeweller, 225 Rue St. Martin, Paris.—Jewellery in silver, gilt copper, silvered copper, &c.; specimens for books, furniture and ornaments, bookbinding.

1271 HOUETTE, A. & Co. 46 Rue de Fer à Moulin, Paris. —Japanned calf leather for boots and shoes.

1272 HUMBERT & Co. Dieuze (Meurthe).—Gelatine.

1273 JAME, BIANCHI, & DUSEIGNEUR, Silk Spinners, 4 Rue Désirée, Lyons (Rhône).—Raw and thrown silks; cocoons.

1274 JAULIN, J. Musical Instrument Maker, 11 Rue Albouy, Faubourg St. Martin, Paris. — A panorgue connected with a piano, and an organ upon a new principle.

1275 JEANNIN, 81 Rue de l'Ecole de Médecine, Paris.— Twelve billiard sticks.

1276 JEANSELME, —, jun. Cabinet Maker, 2 Impasse St. Claude, Au Marais, Paris.—Screens, window-cornices, easy-chairs, couches, chairs, &c.

1277 JEANTI, PREVOST, PERRAUD, & Co. Rue d'Isly, La Villette, near Paris.—Three loaves of refined sugar.

1279 JOUVIN & DOYON, Glovers, 8 Boulevard Bonne Nouvelle, Paris.—Skins; tools used in the manufacture of gloves; dyed skins; gloves.

1280 JULLIEN, —, Tours (Indre and Loire).—Trimmings for furniture.

1283 KRIEGER & Co. 79 Faubourg St. Antoine, Paris.— Several articles of furniture for drawing-rooms, dining-rooms, &c.

1284 LACARRIERE, A. 9 Rue Ste. Elizabeth, Paris.— Lustres, sconces, chandeliers, medallions, &c.

1285 LACHAPELLE & LEVARLET, Spinners, Rheims (Marne). — Spinning. Samples of combed and carded woollen yarn.

1286 LACHASSAGNE, A. China Manufacturer, 55 Rue Meslay, Paris, and at Limoges. — Vases and groups in biscuit china.

1287 LAHOCHE, P. I. Porcelain Manufacturer, 162 Palais National, Paris.—Gilt bronze-mounted ornamented porcelain articles. Engraved and gilt crystals, with similar mountings.

1288 LALANDE & CHEVALLIER, late MALLET, Mans (Sarthe).—Chemical products.

1289 LAMBERT & SON, Felt Cloth Manufacturer, Toulouse (Haute Garonne).—Paletots in felt cloths. Rabbit-hair hats; grey woollen hats.

1290 LANDON & Co. Perfumers, 67 Rue Montorgueil, Paris. —Aromatic vinegar, and essences.

1291 LANGE, DESMOULINS, 32 Rue du Roi-de-Sicile, Paris. —Carmine, lake, chrome yellow, vermilion, cinnaber, madder.

1292 LAPEYRE (Uncle) & DOLBEAU, Manufacturers of Silks, 1 Place Romarin, Lyons (Rhône). — Figured silks. Damask stuffs and shawls.

1293 LARCHER, FAURE, & Co. St. Etienne (Loire).— Silk ribbons.

1294 LARENAUDIERE, late GUYOT, 5 Rue du Mouton, Paris.—Inks of divers colours.

1295 LEFORT, —, sen. 12 Rue Mauconseil, Paris.—Artificial flowers and fruits.

1296 LAURENCOT, E. Brush Maker, 8 Rue Neuve-Bourg-l'Abbé, Paris.—Brushes of all descriptions in ivory, bone, and buffalo horn.

1297 LAURENT-FRANÇOIS, Carver, 98 Rue Ménilmontant, Paris.—Ornaments for framework, mosaic, and parquetrie work for floorings.

1298 LAVERNHE & MATHIEU, DIT VERGER, Silk Throwsters, Uzès (Gard).—Silk spun from cocoons on the system of Verger. The same silk, wrought and thrown.

1299 LAVOISY, A. D. 180 Rue Montmartre, Paris.— Three churns.

1300 LEEEL, L. Soissons (Aisne).—Tow-boat.

1301 LEBLOND, J. D. 5 Rue St. Louis, Au Marais, Paris. —Lay-figures of men and women, for artists.

1302 LECLERCQ, N. 17 Rue Chapon, Paris.—Gelatine in white and coloured leaves.

1303 LECOCQ-PREVILLE, Glove Maker, 50, 52 & 53 Passage du Saumon, Paris.—Kid gloves, of various colours.

1304 LECOQ & RIEDER, Manufacturers, Billom (Puy de Dôme).—Earthenware and various specimens of ceramic art.

1305 LE CROSNIER, M. L. Oil Cloth Manufacturer, 7 Rue Bourg-l'Abbé, Paris ; manufactory at Bourget (Seine). —Gummed silks and oil-cloth.

1306 LECUN & Co. Carpet Manufacturers, Nîmes (Gard). —Carpets of all descriptions.

1307 LEDRENEY, C. Looking Glass Manufacturers, 21 Rue de la Michaudière, Paris.—Mirrors, with gilt and carved frames.

1308 LEFAUCHEUX, 37 Rue Vivienne, Paris.—Different sorts of guns.

1309 LEFEBVRE DUCATTEAU, BROTHERS, Manufacturers, Roubaix (Nord).—Figured woollen textures for waistcoats. Fancy articles.

1310 LETESTUT, Fab. 118 rue du Temple, Paris.—Engines.

1311 LEFEVRE, —, 21 Rue Beaubourg, Paris. — Frame with fancy papers.

1312 LEFEVRE, E. Gevrolles (Côte d'Or).—Wool in tufts.

1313 LEGRAND, D. Manufacturer, Avesnes-les-Aubert (Nord).—Cambrics and lawn; samples of hand-spun thread.

1314 LEJEUNE, E. Hat Manufacturer, 251 Rue St. Honoré, Paris.—Felt and silk hats perfectly waterproof.

1315 LEMAIRE, —, Maker of Ornaments for Furniture, 2 Place du Caire, Paris.—Bed-stretcher; window ornaments; curtain-arms, &c.

1316 LEMAITRE, B. Manufacturer, Pontfaverger (Marne).—Merino textures, raw and dyed, of fine quality.

1317 LOUVET, —.—Dressed leather.

1318 LEROLLE BROTHERS, 3 Chaussée des Minimes, Paris. —Bronze clocks, chandeliers, cups, lamps, &c.

1320 LEROY SOYER, Mme. Glass Manufacturer, Masnières, near Cambrai (Nord).—Bottles of various shapes.

1321 LESSIEUX & SON, Manufacturers, Rethel (Ardennes).—Merino textures, raw and dyed.

1322 LETILLOIS, F. L. G. 47 Rue des Noyers, Paris.—Varnishing and ornamental painting. Painting in imitation of marble, &c.

1323 LEVEN & SON, 43 Rue de Loureine, Paris. — Tannery. Green calf-leather from the abattoirs, in Paris.

1324 LEVERT BROTHERS, Manufacturers, Rethel (Ardennes).—Merino textures, raw and dyed.

1325 L'HUILLIER, E. Feather Manufacturer, 86 Rue St. Martin, Paris.—Various kinds of feathers for mantel-pieces, head-dresses; clocks; screens in peacock feathers.

1326 LIENARD, M. J. Carver on Wood, Rue Plumet, Paris.—A carved walnut-wood clock, representing a boar-hunt. Basso-relievo.

1327 LION BROTHERS, & Co. Shawl Manufacturers, 9 Place des Petits Pères, Paris.—Brocaded woollen or cashmere scarf and square shawls.

1328 DU LISCOET, SON, & Co. Alimentary Producer, 42 Rue Barbet de Jouy, Paris.—Samples of biscuit-beef.

1329 LODDE, —, Feather Manufacturer, 50 Rue Bourg l'Abbé, Paris.—Plumes of feathers, and screens of all kinds. Various specimens of feathers.

1330 LOLAGNIER, —, 6 Rue St. Hippolyte, Paris.—Dressed calf, kid, lamb, and sheep-skins.

1331 LUCAS BROTHERS, Spinners and Manufacturers, Bazancourt (Marne).—Samples of spun yarn, and merinos.

1332 LUCE, P. N. Looking-glass Maker, Versailles (Seine-et-Oise).—A mantelpiece ornamented with mirrors.

1333 LUER, A. Surgical Instrument Maker, 19 Place de l'Ecole de Médecine, Paris.—Surgical instruments.

1334 MABIRE, SON, Agriculturist, Rouen (Seine-Inférieure).—Winter cerealia; red wheat (Spalding); red and white Russian wheats.

1335 MACE, J. M. Corset-maker, 5 Rue Neuve St. Augustin, Paris.—Tick corsets; silk corsets; tick belts.

1336 MATHIEU, —.—Sea maps.

1337 MAGNIN, J. V. Manu. Clermont Ferrand (Puy de Dôme).—French alimentary pastes, named *pâtes d'Italie*, and flours. Specimens of hard red wheat.

1338 MAILLARD, F. Furniture Manufacturer, 21 and 23 Rue Notre-Dame-de-Lorette, Paris.—Beds; mechanical sofa-bedsteads, &c.

1339 MAILLE & SEGOND, 14 Rue St. André-des-Arts, Paris.—Vinegars; mustards; fruits preserved in vinegar.

1340 MALLAT, J. B. Jeweller and Watchmaker, 5 Rue Neuve St. François, Paris.—Mechanical clock. Hoop-dancer. Everlasting pens.

1341 MANIGUET, N. Cloth, Leather, and Wool Manufacturer, Vienne (Isère). — Cloths, leather, wool, and fancy articles.

1342 MANSARD, Ceramic Manufacturer, 93 Rue Richelieu, Paris. —Ornamented stoneware.

1343 MINISTERE DE LA MARINE.—Plans of the coasts of France, by the Society of Hydrographers of the Navy.

1343A MINISTERE DE LA MARINE.—Maps of France, by the Staff.

1344 MARX & Co. au Vigan (Gard).—Two lithographic stones, one polished on both sides.

1345 MASSEMIN, C. L. Tanneur, 28 Rue de la Reynie, Paris.—Calf-skins, glazed calf-skins, pair of leggings, upper leather, and Clarence boots.

1346 MASSE, V. TRIBOUILLET, & Co. Chemical Producer, Neuilly-sur-Seine.—Stearic acids: Wax candles, &c. Patented in England.

1347 MASSEZ, 24 Rue Aubry-le-Boucher, Paris.—Boots, shoes, buskins, and slippers.

1348 MASSON, E. 8 Place St. Michel, Paris.—Preserved meats.

1349 MATHEVON & BOUVARD, Manufacturers, Lyons (Rhône).—Figured silks: for upholstery, dresses, and waistcoats.

1350 MATHIAS, L. A. Bookseller, 15 Quai Malaquais, Paris.—Objects appertaining to the Scientific Industrial Library.

1351 MATHIEU E. 132 Rue Montmartre, Paris.—Designs for manufactures. Designs for Cashmere shawls, brocaded and printed.

1352 MEIER, F. Shoe and Boot Maker, 17 Rue Tronchet, Paris.—Half boots, slippers, and shoes of various kinds.

1353 MEJEAN, A. Silk Spinner, Lyons (Rhône).—Zephyr and grenadine silks. Organzine mantles. White and yellow raw silks.

1354 MERCIER, Manufacturer of Passementery, 21 Rue d'Anjou, Au Marais, Paris.—Purses, cash boxes, reticules, and fancy articles.

1355 MERESSE, M. A. Noyon (Oise).—Four oil paintings, three of which were copied by a mechanical process from the fourth, which served as a model.

1356 MERO, D. Perfumer and Distiller, à Grasse (Var).—Various essential oils and perfumery.

1357 MEURER & JANDIN, Manufacturers of Silks, 29 Rue Nationale, Lyons (Rhône).—Pieces of printed silk handkerchiefs. Dresses and Indian tissues.

1358 MOISON, F. Apothecary, Mouy (Oise).—Model of a regulator for an hydraulic wheel.

1358A MIRAMOUT, Apothecary, Méru (Oise).—Horse and cattle medicines.

1359 MOLYN LESOUEF, Madame, Ribbon Manufacturer, 36 Rue Neuve-des-Petits-Champs, Paris.—Collars, cravats, rosettes, ribbons for orders, &c. Patented.

1360 MONTESSUY & CHOMER, Manufacturers of Silks, 25 Place de la Comédie, Lyons (Rhône).—Plain silks: tartan silk, muslin silk, crape, English crape, &c.

1361 MOREAU, A. U. Paris.—Lamp-oil soap; grease for railways; waterproof tissues.

1362 MORNIEUX, F. Button and Trimming Manufacturer, 31 Rue Mondétour, Paris.—Galloons and silk buttons.

1363 MOURGUE & BOUSQUET, Silk Throwster, St. Hippolyte du Fort (Gard).—A box containing four skeins of raw silk, and four samples of organzine.

1364 MOUTIER LE PAGE, Gunsmith, 11 Rue Richelieu, Paris.—Guns, carbines, pistols, swords, &c. Damascus sword blades, and shields.

1365 MULLER, T. A. Organ Builder, 42 Rue de la Ville l'Evêque, Paris.—Two travelling organs.

1366 MUZARD, L. Engine Maker, 22 Rue Buffault, Paris.—Machine for the preparation of silk.

1367 NATIONAL MANUFACTURE OF BEAUVAIS, Beauvais (Oise).—Furniture tapestry (for elbow chairs, chairs, sofas, screens). Carpets.

1368 NATIONAL MANUFACTURE OF GOBELINS, Paris; Depôt in London, 13 George St. Hanover Sq.—Tapestry known as de la Savonnerie. Carpets.

1369 NATIONAL MANUFACTURE AT SEVRES OF PORCELAIN AND STAINED GLASS, Depôt in London, 13 George St. Hanover Square.—Pictures and copies of pictures of the great masters done by various artists attached to the Sèvres manufactory. Vases, painted and ornamented. Artistical articles of china furniture. Complete services for tea and coffee. Various articles; enamels. Cups with paintings, in enamel.

1370 NACHET, 16 Rue Serpente, Paris.—Micrographic instruments.

1371 NILLUS, —, Engine Builder, Graville (Seine Inférieure).—Sugar-cane crushing machine.

1372 NOYE, F. Alimentary Preserver, 42 Quai de Retz, Lyon.—Ten jugs of vermicelli, chestnuts, and potatoes.

1373 NYSET & Co. 132 Faubourg du Temple, Paris.—Japanned calf leather for boots and shoes.

1374 OUDARD, L. SON, & BOUCHEROT, 42 Rue des Lombards. Paris.—Fruits preserved with steam, and confectionery.

1375 OUDIN & Co. St. Herblain, near Nantes (Loire-Inférieure).—Solidified milk.

1376 OUDIN, C. A. F. 29 Quai de la Fosse, Nantes.—Butter preserved with or without salt.

1377 PAILLETE, P. Brush-maker, 29 Rue du Grenier St. Lazare, Paris.—Hair and clothes brushes, in wood, buffalo, horn, and ivory; fancy brushes.

1378 PARET, M. Woollen-cloth Manufacturer, Sedan (Ardennes).—Broad cloths; kerseymere; satins.

1379 PARIS, C. E. 111 Rue de Bercy, Bercy.—Samples of galvanized iron sheets; enamels in a rough state.

1380 PATRIAU, C. Manufactory, Rheims. Depôt, Paris, 17 Rue des Mauvaises Paroles; London, 9 Wood St. Cheapside.—Woollen and cotton fabrics, for waistcoats, cloaks, &c.

1381 PATURLE-LUPIN, SEYDOUX, SIEBER, & Co. Manufacturers, Coteau; Depôt in Paris.—Pure wool and woollen and silk fabrics. Barège, muslins, merinos, summer materials.

1382 PAUWELS, A. 179 Faubourg Poissonnière, Paris.—Gas-meter for the public streets and roads. (Patented in England and France.)

1383 PELLERIN, C. A. 18 Cour des Petites Ecuries, Paris.—Melophones of various kinds.

1384 VENTUJOL & CHASSANG, 21 Rue des Gobelins, Paris.—Leather. Legs of boots; upper leather for shoes; black and japanned calf leather.

1385 PEROT, G. G. 13 Rue des Trois Portes.—Compositions and models of ornaments for jewel engravers.

1386 PICAREL, V. 11 Rue St. Jean, Paris.—Wood carving and gilding.

1386A PARREYRON, —.—Buttons, and systems of buttons.

1387 PEYRON, S. Quimperlé (Finistère).—Beech-sieve hoops.

1388 PICHARD, A. F. Jeweller, 26 Rue des Blancs Manteaux, Paris.—Ornaments for head-dresses; articles of jewellery; imitation of gold and precious stones.

1389 PICQUOT, E. Cotton-spinner, Monville (Seine-Inférieure).—Bundles and cops of unbleached mule yarn.

1390 PIEDAGNEL, Mlle. BLANCHE, 9 Quai Voltaire, Paris.—Copy on porcelain of the Virgin of Sasso Ferrato.

1391 PIMONT, —, Engine Builder, St. Léger-du-Bourg Denis (Seine-Inférieure).—Patent heating apparatus.

1392 PINSONNET, A. L. Wood-carver, 34 Rue Ste. Marguerite St. Germain, Paris.—A carved chair.

1393 PIQUES, —, Velars-sur-Ouche (Côte d'Or).—Articles of pasteboard.

1394 PLASSE, —, 67 Rue St. Honoré, Paris.—Patent water-jets.

1395 PLON BROTHERS, 36 Rue de Vaugirard, Paris.—Printed books, albums, plans, almanacks, and engravings.

1396 DE POILLY & Co. Folembray Glass-works, near Coucy (Aisne).—Various specimens of bottles, glasses, and glass-wares.

1397 POINSIGNON, —, 23 Rue Neuve St. Martin, Paris.—Imitation, tortoiseshell combs, &c.

1398 POIRIER, P. Shoemaker, Châteaubriand (Loire-Inférieure).—Watertight boots and shoes, and gaiters, for sportsmen.

1399 POISAT, UNCLE, & Co. 19 Rue d'Enghien, Manufactory, La Folie Nanterre (Seine).—Chemicals and models of apparatus, for distillation, with metallic bath. Patented in France and England.

1400 POMMIER, P. 22 Rue Neuve Coquenard, Paris—Chemical produce; varnish for carriages.

1401 POTONIE L. 5 Rue Neuve St. François, au Marais, Paris. Depôt in London, 20 Red Lion Sq.—Clocks of all descriptions.

1402 POTTON, RAMBAUT, & Co. Manufacturers, 18 Rue Lafont, Lyons (Rhône).—Figured silk stuffs; damask cravats; mounted parasols, &c.

1403 PONSON, —, Manufacturer, 21 Rue des Deux Angles, Lyons (Rhône).—Plain silks of various colours.

1404 POPELIN-DUCARRE, 137 Boulevard de l'Hôpital, Paris.—Artificial charcoal.

1405 POUSSIELGUE-RUSAND, P. Producer, 34 Rue Castelle, Paris.—Chandeliers, shrines for relics, lamps, monstrances, trays, ewers, chalices, &c.

1406 PRADIER, J. Silk-spinner, Annonay (Ardèche).—Raw white silks.

1407 PRADIER, J. Sculptor, Member of the Institute of Paris.—Marble and bronze statues.

1408 PRADINE & Co. Woollen yarn spinners, Rheims (Marne).—Specimens of woollen yarn combed and spun by machinery.

1409 PREINSLER, T. F. V. 20 Rue St. Fiacre, Paris.—Printing designs for handkerchiefs, dresses, &c.

1410 PRETOT, L. H. E. 3 Rue Harlay, Au Marais, Paris.—Articles of furniture, &c.

1411 PRIN, Son, sen. Tanner and Currier, Nantes Loire-Inférieure).—Black and yellow calf-skins, for exportation.

1412 PRUDENT, L. Optician, 29 Rue du Ponceau, Paris.—Tortoiseshell and horn opera-glasses.

1413 PUJADE, J. Physician, Amélie les Bains, near Arles-sur-Tech (Pyrenées Orientales).—Medical apparatus.

1414 PUZIN, —. Manufacturer, Beaumont (Seine and Oise), Depôt, 135 Rue St. Denis, Paris.—Lace and trimmings for coach-lining; lace for liveries, &c.

1415 QUERU, A. & Co Designer, 14 Boulevard Poissonnière, Paris.—Designs for all sorts of prints; woven carpets; embroidery.

1416 RABOURDIN, —. Manufacturer, 88 Rue des Marais-St. Martin, Paris.—Braces; garters; silk and India-rubber fabric.

1417 RAGUENET, R. 9 Rue des Capucins, Paris.—Cast-steel carding-combs; patented in France.

1418 BANCE, B 25 Rue Croix des Petits Champs, Paris.—Bound books: The Hotel de Ville (Town Hall) of Paris; Church of St. Eustace; Streets of Paris; Encyclopædia of Architecture.

1419 RAMUS, J. M. 33 Rue de l'Ouest, Paris.—Marble group.

1420 RABIOT, 2 Rue de l'Ecole de Medicine, Paris.—Models of beds for invalids.

1420A ROUSSY, C. Ganges (Hérault).—Cocoons and raw silk of all kinds.

1421 RASTOUIN, —. Engine-worker, Blois (Loire-et-Cher).—Patent regulating screw for carriages.

1422 RAUCHER, L. jun. Manufacturer of Animal Manure, Saumur (Maine and Loire).—Specimens of manure.

1423 RECY, C. M. H. St. Amour (Jura).—Opaque and transparent "tetrugeons porrographes."

1424 REDELIX, H. 29 Rue Notre-Dame-de-Nazareth, Paris.—Screw buttons, fastened without sewing.

1425 REDIER, A. Clock Maker, 2 Rue du Châtelet, Paris.—Clocks and other instruments; double chronometer used in the navy. Patented.

1426 REGARD BROTHERS, Silk Spinners, Darbres (Ardèche).—Cocoons, raw and wrought silk, for silk and plush stuffs.

1427 REGNY, L. & Co. Lime Works, Roquefort, La Nerthe (Arles); Depôt, Marseilles (Bouches du Rhône).—Hydraulic lime and cement.

1428 RIBERT, —.—Clyso irrigator.

1429 REICHMANN, A. Paper Manufacturer, 21 Rue St. Benoit, Paris.—Paper in rollers, divided into squares, for reducing designs. Patented.

1430 REIDON, E. St. Jean de Valériscles (Gard).—Raw silk, and twisted silk for satin.

1431 RENARD, L. 54 Rue des Gravilliers, Paris.—Black varnish and copa.

1432 REPIQUET & SILVENT, Manufacturer, Place de la Croix Paquet, Lyons (Rhone). Silks for waistcoats; galoons, velvets, and silk trimmings.

1433 REQUILLART, ROUSSEL, & CHOCQUEEL, Carpet Manufacturers, Tourcoing (Nord); and 20 Rue Vivienne, Paris. —Coarse and fine moquette, curtain and panel, &c. Specimens of combed wool merinos.

1434 REULOS, A. J. Tanner and Currier, 15 Rue Geoffroy St. Hilaire, Paris.—Curried horse-hide straps.

1435 REYNIER, COUSINS, Manu. 19 Rue Puits-Gaillot, Lyons (Rhone).—Scarfs, shawls, and various kinds of silk.

1436 RICHEZ, Madame, Corset Maker, 323 Rue St. Honoré, Paris.—Silk and tick corsets.

1437 RINGUET-LEPRINCE, A. E. 9 Rue Caumartin, Paris. —Medal cabinet of ebony and carved pear-tree wood. Decorative furniture.

1438 RISLER & SON, Cerney (Haut-Rhin).—New preparatory machine for the winding of cotton, called an "equivalent;" machine, called "a depurator," with a frame containing the produce of that machine.

1439 RIVART & ANDRIEUX, Manufacturer, 1 Rue de Normandie, Paris.—Furniture, inlaid with porcelain.

1440 ROBERT, A. & Co. Metal Refiners, La Villette, near Paris (Seine).—Plate, small ingots, pieces and ingots, forged in brass. Ingots of pure tin. Pewter box. Roll of tin-foil for looking-glasses, &c.

1441 ROBERT-GUERIN, Manufacturer, Pontfaverger (Marne).—Unbleached and dyed merino fabrics.

1442 ROBERT-FAURE, C. Lace Manufacturer, 27 Rue de Cléry, Paris.—Worsted lace of all colours; guipure silk lace, black and white worsted ribbons.

1443 ROBERT-MATHIEU, Manufacturer, Pontfaverger (Marne).—Unbleached and dyed merino fabrics.

1444 ROBERT-WERLY & Co. Stay Manufacturers, Barle-Duc (Meuse).—Seamless stays, a new system.

1445 ROBICHON, BROTHERS & Co. Window Glass Manufacturers, at Givors (Rhône).—Window glass of various colours.

1446 ROECK, L. Machine Maker, 10 Rue du Griffon, Lyons (Rhône).—Silk-meter, to ascertain the different qualities of raw and wrought silk.

1447 ROBIN, L. Bronze Manufacturer, 32 Rue Grénetat, Paris.—Various articles in bronze, cups, bells, &c.

1448 ROGER, Jun. Manufacturer of Millstones, La Ferté-sous-Jouarre (Seine-et-Marne).—Burr-stones. (G. Bailey, Toms, & Co., Agents.)

1449 ROGER BROTHERS, & Co. Wool Spinners, Trie-Château (Oise).—Assortment of woollen threads.

1450 ROISSARD, J. M. Cutler, 58 Grande Rue, Brest (Finistère).—Various specimens of cutlery; surgical instruments.

1451 RONCHARD-SIAUVE, Gunsmith, St. Etienne, (Loire). —Double barrel gun, fifteen shades.

1452 ROSSELET, C. P. 3 Rue de la Madeleine, Paris.—Gold reviving fluid for renovating gilding, lace-work, stuffs, &c.

1453 ROSSET & NORMAND, Cashmere Manufacturers. 32 Rue Feydeau, Paris.—French long and square cashmeres, Black Chantilly lace and Alençon point lace.

1455 ROUGET DE LISLE, T. A. 25 Rue des Vinaigriers, Paris.—Apparatus for the composition of designs for fabrics.

1456 ROUGET, SON & Co. Curriers, Chatenay near Nantes (Loire-Inférieure).—Two thick hides, and two shoulder belts.

1457 ROUSSEAU BROTHERS, Sugar Boilers, 9 Rue de l' Ecole de Medicine, Paris.—Sugar loaves (unrefined). Patented in England.

1458 ROUSSEL-DAZIN, Manufacturers, Roubaix, (Nord). —Woollen satin stuffs for dresses.

1459 ROUSSELET & BARONNET, Manufacturers, Betheniville (Marne).—Unbleached and dyed merino fabrics.

1460 ROUVENAT, L. Jeweller, 62 Rue Hauteville, Paris.— Ornaments, bracelets, head-dresses, swords, and other articles of jewellery, gold and diamonds.

1461 ROYER, J. C. A. 55 Quai de la Tournelle, Paris. —Gelatine leaves of all colours.

1462 ROYER, P. E. 6 Rue du Caire, Paris.—Artificial foliage.

1463 RUAUD, J. B. China Manufacturer, Limoges (Haute-Vienne).—Wrought specimens of earthenware, chinaware, statuettes, vases, &c.

1464 RUAS & Co. Silk Reelers, St. André de Valborgne (Gard).—White and yellow raw silk. (Agents in London, Fordati, Coxhead, and Co. 13 Old Jewry Chambers.)

1465 RUDOLPHI, —. Silversmith, 3 Rue Tronchet, Paris. —Various objects of silversmith work and jewellery; fancy works, &c.

1466 RUOLZ, Paints and Hydrofuge Coatings, 53 Rue de Verneuil, Paris.—Paints, oils, and other articles.

1467 SABATIER, H. 65 Palais National, Paris.—Daguerreotype portrait.

1468 SAGET, W. 17 Rue St. Elizabeth, Paris.—A sidereal light-house; a lantern with regular reflectors; various patterns of lanterns for locomotives, for signals, and hydraulic cranes, and reflecting hose. Sidereal lamp. Patented in England.

1469 SALLANDROUZE DE LAMORNAIX, Manufacturer, (formerly Royal Manufactory of Carpets at Aubusson), 23 Boulevard Poissonnière, Paris. Depôt, 13 George Street, Hanover Square, London. — Velvet carpets and tapestry; yarn combed at Felletin; carded woollen yarn, &c.

1470 SAMBUC, P. Silk Spinner, Vaison (Vaucluse).— White and yellow raw silk.

1471 SARRAN, H. & DUFOUR, Sauve (Gard).—Hames for horse-collars.

1472 SAUVAGE, R. & Co. 5 Rue St. Polycarpe, Lyons.— Stuffs of different shades, mohair, taffetas, &c.

1473 SAUTRET SON, Manufacturers, Betheniville (Marne). —Unbleached and coloured merinos.

1474 SAUTREUIL, —, jun. Manufacturer of Joiner's Work, Fécamp (Seine-Inférieure).—Planing and moulding machine.

1475 SCHWERBER, —, Ragolsheim (Haut-Rhin).—Vertical hammer to forge all kind of works with varying force, and capable of increase by the aid of springs.

1475A SCHNEIDER & Co.—Designs of machineries.

1476 SAVARD, —, Jeweller 22 Rue St. Gilles, Paris.— Lockets, chains, brooches, bracelets, &c. lined with gold; snuff-boxes, gorgets, and other ornaments, &c.

1477 SAVARESSE, P. 42 Rue des Marais, Paris.—Apparatus for gaseous waters.

1479 SCAMPS, P. Manufacturer, Roubaix (Nord).— Twilled pure cotton fabrics.

1480 SCHLOSS, WIDOW, & BROTHER, Portfolio Manufacturer, 15 Rue Chapon, Paris.—Portfolios, cash-boxes, cigarholders, and steels (patented in England). Baskets, knapsacks, and trusses.

1481 SCHLUMBERGER, jun. & Co. Cotton Printers, Thann (Haut-Rhin). — Printed cottons, and woollen and cotton prints.

1482 SCHOLTUS, —, Piano Manufacturer, 1 Rue Bleue, Paris.—Two upright pianos.

1483 DE SERIONNE, LOIN & Co. Manufacturers of Porcelain Knobs, 32 Boulevart du Combat, Belleville, near Paris.—Porcelain knobs, white and coloured. Patented in England.

1484 DE SERLAY, C. G. Gueurs (Seine-Inférieure).—Paper.

1485 SERRET, HAMOIR, DUQUESNE & Co. Sugar Manufacturers, Valenciennes (Nord).—Collection of beetroot products.

1486 FEYEUX, Preserver, 10 Rue Taranne, Paris.—Samples of preserved food, in flasks and packets.

1487 SIGAUT, —. Preserver, 23 and 25 Rue de la Vielle Monnaie, Paris.—Rheims biscuits, dried pastry and gingerbread.

1489 SIMON & HENRY, 179 Rue St. Honoré, Paris.—Fiddle-sticks for violins and violoncelli, in tortoiseshell or ebony, bordered with gold and silver.

1490 SOUBEYRAND, L. St. Jean du Gard.—Silk reeler and throwster. Specimens of cocoons. Raw and thrown silk. (Agents in London, Fordati, Coxhead, and Co. 13 Old Jewry Chambers.)

1491 SOUCHON, Jean Marie, Chemist, 111 Rue Montmartre, Paris.—Prussian blue, called Souchon.

1492 SOULES, Mme. Hyppolite, Corset Manufacturer.—21 Rue de la Michaudière, Paris. Two Corsets.

1493 SOURD, A. Wool Spinner, Tenay-l'Ain; Depôt, Lyons (Rhône).—Specimens of washed, combed, and reeled wool.

1494 STOLTZ, SON, Machine Maker, 10 Rue de Boulogne, Paris.—Models of steam-engines, rivetting, and hydraulic machines.

1495 St. UBERY, Tarbes (Haute-Pyrennées).—Specimens of indigenous woods, prepared for cabinet work.

1496 TABOURDEAU, P. Cutler, Moulins (Allier).—Knives with several blades; carving-knife; a flower-stand, &c.

1497 TACHY, A. & Co. Manufacturers, 24 Rue Dauphine, Paris.—Needles for blind people.

1498 TERRASSON DE MONTLEAU, J. A. St. Estèphe (Charente).—Wool in fleeces.

1499 THERET, J. Mosaic Manufacturer, 38 Rue des Saints Pères, Paris.—Articles of furniture, mantelpieces, clocks, pictures, &c.

1500 THEVENET, RAFFIN, & ROUX, Manufacturers of Silks 30 Rue Romarin, Lyons (Rhône).—Silk shawls; China crape; watered Pekin, figured.

1501 THIBAUD-DALLET, EMILE, Clermont-Ferrand (Puy-de-Dôme).—Church windows in different styles.

1502 THIBAULT BOILESVE, H. Cinq-Mars-la-Pile (Indre-et-Loire).—Mill-stones, floor-tiles, pannels, and drain-tiles.

1503 THIBERT, jun. 31 Rue Michel-le-Comte, Paris.—Opera glasses.

1503A TARRIDE, SON, & Co. Toulouse (Haute-Garonne).—Specimens of marbles used for the tomb of the Emperor Napoleon.

1504 TRIPET, —, Paris.—Collection of tulips.

1504A NURGAT, Madame, 28 Rue d'Enfer, Paris.—Painting on porcelain.

1505 THIER, —, Engineer and Machine-maker, 39 Passage Choiseul, Paris.—Surgical instruments. Patented in England.

1506 THIERRY-MIEG Manufacturer of Printed Stuffs, Mulhouse (Haut-Rhin).—Various kinds of printed cashmeres.

1508 TOUAILLON, C. 12 Rue Coquillière, Paris.—Mill-stones; and a dressing machine.

1509 TOURNEUR, —, 39 Rue Richelieu, Paris.—Specimens of coffee-roasting.

1510 TRIEBERT, F. Musical Instrument-maker, 132 Rue Montmartre, Paris.—Musical instruments.

1511 TROCCON, A. Manufacturer of Silks, 14 Rue des Capucins, Lyons (Rhône).—Shawls and cravats, of various silk stuffs.

1512 TRONCHON, N. Avenue St. Cloud, Passy, near Paris.—Iron articles of furniture for apartments and garden ornaments.

1513 TROUVE, A. Sculptor, 5 Passage Violet, Paris.—Frames decorated with ornaments in papier maché, ornaments in sulphur.

1514 VALANSOT, —, Manufacturer of Silks, Lyons (Rhône), and 4 Rue Puits Gaillot, Paris.—Plain silks: gros de Naples, and taffetas.

1515 VALANT, P. T. Stationer, 23 Rue de Seine, Paris.—Fancy stationery; envelopes cut by machinery, &c.

1516 VAN BALTHOVEN, P. 28 Faubourg St. Antoine, Paris.—A cupboard with mirrors; bedsteads: chests of drawers in rosewood with marbles.

1517 VANTILLARD & Co. Pin Manufacturers, Mérouvel, near L'Aigle (Orne).—Iron pins, tinned by a process patented in France and England.

1519 VERDET & Co. Avignon (Vaucluse).—Samples of wrought silk and organzine.

1520 VEZON BROTHERS, Ligugé (Poitiers), Vienne.—Specimens of gluten.

1521 VIARD, L. 54 Rue St. Martin, Paris.—Various samples of colours and varnish.

1522 VILLEROI, —, Civil Engineer and Musical Instrument-maker, 3 Rue Pavée St. André, Paris.—New musical instrument.

1523 VILPELLE, T. Montereau-sur-Yonne (Seine-et-Marne).—Steel dagger.

1524 VIGNAT BROTHERS, St. Etienne (Loire).—Silk ribbons.

1525 VINCENT, H. 14 Rue Neuve St. François (Marais), Paris.—Specimens of mouldings, &c.

1526 VINCENT, J. Silk Spinners, Valleraugue (Gard).—White and yellow raw silk.

1527 VINCENT, J. Quai des Tanneurs, Nantes (Loire-Inférieure).—Boot legs and upper leather for the feet of boots.

1528 VIOLETTE, J. H. M. St. Omer (Pas-de-Calais).—Ship-biscuits baked by immersing the stone or the dough in high pressure steam; charcoal obtained by immersing wood in the same; mercury distilled by the same process for amalgamating it with gold or silver.

1529 VIVIER & Co. Manufacturers of Silk, 1 Rue Croix Paquet, Lyon (Rhone).—Moire (watered) stuffs, velvets, &c., and nouveautés of all descriptions for waistcoats.

1530 VITTOZ, —, 10 Rue des Filles du Calvaire, Paris.—Artistic bronzes, chimney ornaments, clocks, chandeliers, vases; cups and lustres.

1531 VOIZOT, E. 32 Rue Bourg l'Abbé, Passage de l'Ancre, Paris.—Polished steel, and false stones for jewellery.

1532 VOLKERT, —, Cabinet-maker, 99 Rue du Faubourg, St. Antoine, Paris.—Veneering, on inlaid pannels.

1533 VORUZ, J. S. sen. Nantes (Loire Inférieure).—Railway carriage cushion.

1535 ZADIG, J. B. Fancy Silk Article Manufacturer, 28 Rue du Sentier, Paris.—Gauzes, barèges, shawls and scarfs; fancy silks.

1536 ZUBER, J. & Co. Rixheim (Haut Rhin).—White paper, paints, and artificial ultramarine.

1537 AGRICULTURAL SOCIETY OF LYONS (Rhône).—Spun silk and cocoons.

1538 ALLON, H. Manufacturer of Albumen, Annonay (Ardèche).—Natural produce; albumen from eggs.

1539 CHATEMONE SLATE COMPANY, Javron (Mayenne).—Slates for roofs, paving, and billiard tables.

1540 ANDELLE, G. & Co. Bottle Manufacturer, Epinac (Saône-et-Loire).—Various samples of bottles.

1541 ANTHELME, —, Andelin, (Aisne). — A lump of potash.

1542 ARNOUX, C. Coach-maker, 23 Rue du Mont Parnasse, Paris.—Coaches and carriages, on the scale of 1 inch to 5 inch. Patented.

1543 AVISSEAU, C. Tours (Indre and Loire).—Enamelled potteries, a large rustical goblet, &c.

1544 AUBRY BROTHERS, Lace Manufacturers, 33 Rue des Jeûneurs, Paris.—Dress, shawl, handkerchief, tippet, lace-lappets, piece of lace, application-lappets.

1545 AUDIAT, F. Lace Manufacturer, 22 Rue du Mail, Paris.—Embroidered tulles ; imitation of lace and applications.

1546 BERINGER, B. Gunsmith, 6 Rue du Coq St. Honoré, Paris.—Five fowling pieces of various prices.

1547 BERNARD, L. Gunsmith, 12 Rue Villejust, Passy (Seine).—Damascus gun and pistol barrels.

1548 BERNOVILLE, LARSONNIER. & CHENEST, Manufacturers of Woollen-tissues, 23 Rue des Jeûneurs, Paris.— Combed-wool; woollen-yarn; unbleached and dyed tissues ; printed and figured. Manufactured in four distinct establishments belonging to the expositors.

1549 BERTAUD, —. jun. Optician, 32 Rue de Bretagne, Paris.—Experimental crystals, spath, quartz, and crown prisms, achromatic objectives, &c.

1550 BILLIET & HUOT, 43 Rue du Sentier, Paris.—Combed-wool and woollen-yarn.

1551 BLANQUART, E. Lille (North).—A frame containing heliographic proofs.

1552 BLAQUIERE, J. M. Card Manufacturer, 6 Rue Neuve St. Augustin, Paris.—Parisian playing cards ; new kind of playing cards.

1553 BOURGOGNE, A. Lamp Manufacturer, 3 Rue du Havre, Paris.—Lamps, with moderator and warning chime.

1554 BOYER, V. P., 22 Rue de la Paix, Paris.—Vases, cups. pictures, and baskets of various kinds.

1555 BRETON, —. Musical Instrument Manufacturer, 28 Rue Jean Jacques Rousseau, Paris.—Crystal and wooden flutes, on Boemh's principle, and common flutes; wooden clarionet, on Boemh's principle.

1556 TAHAN, A. Manufacturer of Artistic Cabinet Work, 30 Rue de la Paix, Paris.—Furniture, book-cases, flower-stands, coffers, tea-caddies, cigars and whist cases, &c. ; canes. watch-stands, clocks, writing-desks, folding-stools, &c.

1557 CAIL & Co. Machine-maker, 46 Quai de Billy, Paris. —A locomotive engine for goods. Apparatus to take in the vacuum for sugar, with its steam-engine, a coining press, &c.

1558 CHAILLOUX, LEPAGE, & POCHON, Breeders of Bees, Puiseaux (Loiret).—A cask of honey, and a box of saffron.

1559 CHENNEVIERE, T. Cloth Manufacturer, Elbeuf and Louviers (Seine-Inférieure). — New fancy materials for trousers, gowns, cloaks, and linings. Plain, twilled, pilot, beaver cloths, and impermeable cloths.

1560 CHERIF BEN MIMOUN, Weaver, Beniabès, Constantine.—A white abessi bournous.

1561 CHRETIN, M. T. Mosaic Manufacturer, Amiens (Somme).—A mosaic representing a head of Christ.

1562 CHRISTOFLE & Co., Gold and Silversmiths, 56 Rue de Bondy, Paris.—Large tea urn, cup and saucer, milk-jug, and other articles of gilt and silvered ware.

1563 CLICQUOT, —. Courbevoie, près Paris (Seine).—A frame containing engravers' tools.

1564 COLIN, J. R. Marble-cutter, Epinal (Vosges).— Polished marbles, granites, and serpentine.

1565 COMMERCIAL CHAMBER of LYONS (Brosset, sen. President).—Damasks, gros de tours, brocatelles, droguets, and various other silk stuffs.

1566 COUDER, A. Designer, 67 Rue Rochechouart, Paris. —Designs for stained paper; portières for hangings of tapestry ; for printed shawls, and other industrial designs.

1567 CONNEROT, M. 37 Rue Bourbon Ville-Neuve, Paris. —Umbrellas and parasols.

1568 CONSERVATOIRE DES ARTS ET METIERS (Col. Morin, Director), Rue St. Martin, Paris.—Metrical measures. Flexible liquid, Troy, and long measures of various materials.

1569 COULBOIS, Leather Manufacturer, Avallon (Yonne). —Japanned leather, grained calf-skin, for boots and shoes and trimmings.

1570 COURTIN, R. Vinegar Manufacturer, 124 Route d'Oliver, Orleans (Loiret).—A barrel of vinegar, and various samples.

1571 COURTOIS, E. Currier, 13 Faubourg Montmartre, Paris.—Glazed calf-skins for boots and shoes, and all kinds of leather for saddlers, coach-makers, and harness-makers.

1572 COUSIN, —, 38 Grande Rue Verte, Paris.—Two frames containing proofs of lithographed drawings on paper.

1573 CREMER, J. Manufacturer of Checker Work, 29 Rue de l'Entrepôt, Paris.—A grand piece of furniture, with three doors, a writing-table, dressing-table, and pictures in mosaic and checker work.

1574 CROISAT, J. Hair-dresser, 76 Rue de Richelieu, Paris. —Perukes without toupees, and a machine to implant hairs in silk and other kinds of tissues.

1575 DAFRIQUE, F. Jeweller, 8 Rue Jean Jacques Rousseau, Paris.—Jewellery in gold, such as bracelets, leontines, chains, and cameo-brooches.

1576 DARBLAY, —. jun. Corn Dealer, 16 Rue des Vieilles-Etuves-St.-Honoré, Paris, and 37 Fenchurch St. London.— Two sacks and a barrel of wheaten flour.

1577 DARBO, F. Implements for Suckling and Injection Syringes Manufacturer, 86 Passage Choiseul, Paris.—Spiral suckling bottles; double pumps; artificial nipples; bidet for injections.

1578 DARNET, —. Rue Richelieu, Paris.—Ready-made linen for gentlemen, and shirts.

1579 DAUBET & DUMARET, Furniture-makers, Lyons (Rhône).—Various articles of furniture.

1580 DEYDIER, C. P. Cocoons Manufacturer, Ucel, près Aubenas (Ardèche).—Skeins of raw silk, and balls of organsin.

1581 BAUME, C. DE LA, Prop. Paris.—Machine for stamping and numbering, named Stamp-counter (provisionally registered), patented in France and in Belgium. Agents— in London, M. de Fontainemoreau, 4 South Street, Finsbury; at Paris, M. Féry, 20 Rue de Courcelles.

1582 DELACOUR, L. F. Side-arms Manufactures, Rue aux Fers, Paris.—Swords and sabres of various countries. Bronze and cast-iron articles : chandeliers, and irons, fenders, &c.

1583 DELAMORINIERE, GONIN, & MICHELET, Calico Printers, 12 Quai de Béthune, Paris (Isle St. Louis).— Satined barège dresses, mousseline de laine, Paris crape, &c. Long shawls. Fancy woollen and cotton fabrics.

1584 DELCAMBRE, A. Lace Manufacturer, 6 Rue de Choiseul, Paris.—Piece of black silk lace. Black silk lace scarf. Fine gold and natural-coloured silk lace.

1585 DELONGUEIL, H. Coachmaker, 8 Rue Nationale St. Honoré, Paris.—Closed calash, with vazistas, mounted on springs, pincer's fashion, grey lining, painted blue, with silver-plated ornaments.

1586 DEPOULLY, C. Silk Manufacturer and Printer, 7 Rue du Faubourg Poissonnière, Paris.—Dresses of various designs and fabrics. Various descriptions of silk handkerchiefs.

1587 DESBORDES, —, Manufacturer of Mathematical Instruments, 22 Rue des Fossés-du-Temple, Paris.—Scientific instruments ; indicators of water levels, with plain glasses ; monometers; barometer, &c.

1588 DESJARDINS-LIEUX, Manufacturer of Embossed Articles, 4 Passage St. Avoye, Paris.—Medallions; vases for holy water; small statuettes; lamps, and other embossed objects of all kinds.

1589 DETOUCHE & HOUDIN, Chronometer Makers, 158 and 160 Rue St. Martin, Paris.—Chronometers; large and small regulators; mathematical watch-work; watches, &c. Monographic apparatus, invented by Mr. Guenal.

1590 DIGEON, —, Manufacturer of Chemical Produce, 34 Route d'Ivry, near Paris.—Carbonate, nitrate, and sulphate of strontiane; sulphate of copper and ammoniac, &c.

1592 DUCHE, —, sen. & Co. Shawl Maker, 1 Rue des Petits Pères, Paris.—Long and square figured shawls of every kind.

1593 DUMORTIER & Co. Wax Candle Manufacturers, Lyons (Rhône).—A box of French wax candles.

1594 DUPES & Co. 21 Rue Fontaine au Roi, Paris.—Rods for curtains and apartments. Patented in France.

1595 DURAND, F. Goldsmith, 41 Rue du Bac, Paris.—Tea-service consisting of 17 pieces. Table centre-piece, accompanied with four crystal cups.

1596 DURAND, J. Alimentary Paste-maker, Grenade (Haute-Garonne).—Vermicellis, glutinous preparations, and various other sorts of alimentary pastes.

1597 ELOFFE, —, 10 Rue de l'Ecole de Medicine, Paris, and Boubée, Professor of Geology.—Various collections arranged for the study of geology, paleontology, and pure mineralogy, and applied to agriculture and to industry; synoptic and technological table, serving as a catalogue.

1598 FAUSSEMAGNE, J. M. Glue Manfacturer, Lyons (Rhône), and 6 Rue du Bœuf.—Isinglass.

1600 FELRAPPE BROTHERS, 144 Rue du Faubourg St. Denis, Paris.—A frame containing specimens of engraving on cylinders, for the printing of stuffs and the goffering of stuffs.

1601 FETU, J. Bronze Manufacturer, 10 Rue de Gravilliers, Paris.—Chandeliers; brackets; candlesticks; bed-room candlesticks; candelabras; clock; inkstand; statuettes.

1602 FOULQUES, H. Porcelain Manufacturer, St. Gaudens. —White and gilt porcelain.

1603 FOULQUIE, Mlle. & Co. Knitting-work Makers, 20 Rue Hauteville, Paris.—Collars, points, shawls, kerchiefs, and other articles of knitting-work; great novelty.

1604 FOURQUEMIN & GODET, 35 Rue Neuve-des-Bons-Enfants, Paris —Designs for shawls.

1605 FOURNEAUX, —, Organ Builder, 64 and 70 Galerie Vivienne, Paris.—An organ.

1606 FRAIGNEAU, A. Watch-maker, 114 and 115 Palais National, Paris.—Various watches, watch appendages, and alarms. Alarm clocks.

1607 FREY, SON, Engineer and Machine Maker, Belleville (Seine), 2 Inpasse St. Laurent.—A machine for nail making; a new system.

1608 FRINAULT, —, Brass Founder, Orleans (Loiret).—Hermetic taps; a new invention, destined to domestic economy.

1609 FROMENT, G. Manufacturer of Mathematical Instruments, 5 Rue Ménilmontant, Paris.—Scientific instruments; theodolite; and various models of electro-motive power.

1610 GASPARD, P. A. Engraver, 1 Rue Madame, Paris. —Frames containing engravings, religious subjects.

1611 GASTINNE-RENETTE, Gunsmith, 29 Allée d'Antin, Paris.—Guns; carabine; unfinished gun barrels; pistols for practice, in their cases; and small fancy pistols. Model of a machine to load pistols, and serving as a meter.

1612 GAUVAIN, J. Gunsmith, 93 Boulevard du Mont Parnasse, Paris. — Double-barrelled fowling-pieces, with engravings, and others.

1613 GEMINY, —, Manufacturer of Chemical Produce, Marseilles (Bouches de Rhône), 136 Rue de Paradis.—Cotton-seed oil, clarified and bleached; samples.

1614 GIUDICELLI & DELABARRE, Mathematical Instrument Makers, 154 Rue Montmartre, Paris. — Universal rulers, of various descriptions. New patented invention for precise measurements.

1615 GOCHT, F. Cabinet-maker, 10 Rue des Marais St. Martin, Paris.—A lady's writing-desk, in Courbary wood inside in rosewood and grey maple.

1616 GRANGOIR, E. Corset Manufacturer, 28 Rue de Bourgogne, Paris.—A satin fancy corset.

1617 GRIGNON, M. Rue d'Orleans, Paris.—Bronze clocks, candelabras, statuettes, &c.

1618 GROLLEAU & DEVILLE, Calico Printers, 33 Rue du Sentier, Paris.—Dresses (Foulard pattern), barège, silk, gauze, &c. Designs produced at the establishment of the exhibitors; printing executed by Messrs. Guillaume and Son, St. Denis (Seine).

1619 GUEYTON, —, Artistic Silversmith and Jeweller, 11 Rue Chapon, Paris.—Statuettes; cups; boxes; nosegays; pictures; sabres; swords; knives; bracelets; snuff-boxes; sweetmeats. Boxes; seals; cigar cases; cash boxes; rings; brooches; canes; riding-whips; plates in galvano-plastic.

1620 GUIMET, J. B. Manufacturer of Ultramarine Blue, Lyons (Rhône).—Flagons of artificial ultramarine blue, applicable to the industrial arts and to the fine arts.

1621 HEBERT & SON, Shawl Manufacturers, 13 Rue du Mail, Paris.—Long and square pure Cashmere shawls, various grounds.

1622 HENRY, F. Bronze Manufacturer, 8 Rue de Limoges, Paris.—Bronze chest, bronzed dagger; two keepsakes, fixed steel, inlaid with mother-of-pearl and bronze. Ladies' steel necessaries; bronze-framed glass, &c.

1623 HENNEQUIN, —, 17 Rue Chapon, Paris.—Jewels and caskets.

1624 HERVE BROTHERS, 127 Chemin Charenton, Bercy. —Gelatine and glue.

1625 HOOPER, G., CARROZ & TABOURIER, Manufacturers of Embroidery and Printed Stuffs, 6 Rue des Fossés Montmartre, Paris. Manufactory, Rohain (Aisne) and Lyons (Rhône).—Neckerchiefs and mittens in lace; shawls, dresses of various patterns, and embroidered and printed novelties.

1626 HOUSSARD, E. F. Manufacturer of French Alimentary Pastes, Persan (Seine and Oise), and 99 Rue St. Honoré, Paris.—French alimentary pastes.

1627 HOUBIGANT-CHARDIN, Glovers, 19 Rue de Faubourg, St. Honoré, Paris.—120 pairs of gloves made of skins matched in colour and quality.

1628 HOULLIER, B. Gunsmith, 36 Rue de Cléry, Paris.—A box of pistols.

1629 JACOB-PETIT, Porcelain Manufacturer, 32 Rue de Bondy, Paris.—A fountain in ornamental porcelain; porcelain biscuits, designs for patterns.

1630 JOUHANNEAUD & DUBOIS, China Manufacturers, 5 Rue de l'Entrepôt, Paris.—Vases, decanters, clocks, scent-bottles, tête-à-têtes, &c.

1631 JOURDAIN, X. Altkirch (Haut-Rhin). — Tissues, jaconets, organzins, muslius, &c.

1632 KARCHER & WESTERMANN, Manufacturers of Stamped Iron, Metz (Moselle).—Articles in stamped iron tinned or varnished.

1633 KLEINJASPER, J. F. Pianoforte Maker, 296 Rue St. Honoré, Paris.—A cottage piano.

1634 KOECHLIN BROTHERS, Mulhouse (Haut-Rhin).—Chintzes, printed cambrics, barèges, woollen, and half-woollen stuffs, &c.

1636 LACROIX BROTHERS, Paper Manufacturers, Angoulême (Charente)—Various sorts of stained and ornamental papers.

1637 LAIGNEL, J. B. Engineer, 13 Rue de la Harpe, Paris. —A model of drags for railways.

1638 LAMBERT, S. 34 Rue Verte, Paris.—Two globes of silvered crystals; two crystal vases; likewise silvered, and several other articles of the same kind.

1639 LANDRON BROTHERS, Tanners, Meung-sur-Loire

(Loiret).—Leather made from the skins of different animals, natives of France and of Buenos Ayres.

1640 LAUGIER, —, Ongle (Basses-Alpes).—Honey and wax.

1641 LANNE, E. Cutler, 130 Rue du Temple, Paris.—Scissors, razors, knives, and other articles of cutlery.

1642 LAPEYRE, KOB, & Co. 112 Rue de Charenton.—Stained paper, &c.

1643 LATELTIN & PAYEN, Place St. Nicholas-des-Champs, Paris.—Bracelets, brooches, seals, trinkets, and various articles of jewellery.

1644 LECOCQ, H. Manufacturer of Stamped Copper and Brass, Rue des Francs Bourgeois, au Marais.—Frames of ornaments in stamped brass; hot-air stoves, and various apparatus for warming houses.

1645 LEDUC, C. Rope Maker, Nantes (Loire-Inférieure). —Fishing rods, lines, and nets, and ship ropes exported.

1646 LEFEBURE, A. Lace Manufacturer, Bayeux (Calvados), and at 42 Rue de Cléry, Paris.—Thread lace counterpane; Alençon lace scarf and lappets; shawl, point scarf, veil, and black silk lace flounces; black silk blonde mantle.

1647 LE FEVRE, B. 109 Rue Montmartre, Paris.—Various kinds of varnish for the arts, buildings, and carriages, &c.

1648 LEFEVRE, —, Manufacturer of Galvano-plastic, 40 Rue Fontaine au Roi, Cité Holbacher, Paris.—Cash boxes, cigar cases, and other articles produced by the galvanoplastic. Patented in England.

1649 LEMIRE & SON, Silk Manufacturer, 1 Rue des Feuillants, Lyons (Rhône).—Silk stuffs for furniture and church ornaments. Velvets, damasks, brocade, &c.

1650 LEON LALANNE, Chief Civil Engineer, 18 Rue des Fleurus, Paris.—A calculating rule, with sliding rule. An abacus or universal arithmetician, and a tableau by which, by an easy combination of straight lines and figures, we can, at $\frac{1}{300}$ near, obtain the same results as by the sliding rule.

1650A LANGLADE, —, Paris.—Varnished cloth, invented by the exhibitor. Patented.

1651 LIEGARD, H. Saddler, 23 Val St. Catherine, Paris. —Framed designs representing specimens of saddles, harness, and articles of military accoutrements.

1652 LORTIC, P. M. Book Binder, 199 Rue St. Honoré, Paris.—Various publications. Fancy book-binding.

1653 MABRUN, P. Paper Hanging Manufacturer, 21 Place des Vosges, Paris.—Geographical maps of France and England; chronological tables of France and England.

1654 MAGNIN, J. M. Inventor, Villefranche (Rhône).—Sewing, embroidering, and cord making machine, called Cousobrodeur. New invention, patented in England. Samples of sewing on different stuffs.

1655 MALLET & BAILLY, 23 Rue de Rambuteau, Paris.—Artificial flowers in gauze.

1656 MAYER & Co. Painters on Porcelain, 64 Rue du Marais St. Martin.— A vase, imitation of China in gilt bronze, and other articles of China painted and decorated.

1657 MENET, J. Milled Silk Weaver, Beaulieu and Annonay (Ardèche).—Yellow and white organzines of different qualities and preparation; yellow and white woof; yellow and white spun raw silk skeins.

1658 MERCIER, C. V. 28 Rue des Gravilliers, Paris.—Tortoiseshell snuff-boxes; ditto, wood and ivory, rhinoceros, palm-tree wood, olive-tree wood, rose wood, &c.

1659 MEURANT BROTHERS & WILLEMIN, Machine Makers, Charleville (Ardennes), Depôt, 73 Faubourg St. Martin. (Director of the Factory, Mr. Willemin).—A press with an iron bucket and zinc basin ; a press of a different model.

1660 MICHEL, PASCAL, Sculptor, 27 Quai d'Anjou, Ile St. Louis Paris.—Marble groups of three figures, bearing as an epigraph: "Sinite parvulos venire ad me." A Carthusian monk at his prayers, a plaster cast.

1661 MITTELETTE, V. Engineer, Soissons (Seine and Oise). —Thrashing machines ; winnowing machines.

1662 MOHAMMED BEN ACHIR, Caid de Mascara (Oran).—A bournous in natural black wool.

1663 MOHAMED BEN SALAH, Weaver, Beni Abès, province of Constantine.—A white abessi Mouzaiah bournous.

1664 MONET, —, Manufacturer of Mathematical Instruments, 32 Rue Meslay, Paris.—Chronometers, giving several unusual indications, such as the days of the week, and of the month and year, &c.

1665 MONTAL, C. Musical Instrument Maker, 5 Boulevard Montmartre, Paris.—Three cottage pianos.

1666 MOREL BROTHERS, Manufacturers of Articles in Wrought and Cast Iron, Charleville (Ardennes).—Moulded cast iron, pottery, projectiles, mechanical nails, carved ironmongery, &c.

1667 MOUCHOT, —, Manufacturer of Joiner's Work by Machinery, Petit Montrouge (Seine).—A model of a machine to knead bread, and ten of these machines in full operation.

1668 MOURCEAU, —, 27 Rue du Mail, Paris.—Tissues for hangings and furniture, folding-doors, and table-covers.

1669 NOEL, —, Tinsel Ornament Maker, 16 Rue du Ponceau, Paris.—Gilt and oxidised eye-glass chains, neck-chains, leontines, watch appendages, and cornelian seals, &c.

1670 NOURRY BROTHERS, & MEYNARD COUSINS, Manufacturers of Silk Handkerchiefs, Lyons (Rhône).—Silk handkerchiefs, corahs, white damasks, and others.

1671 ODIOT,—Jeweller, 26 Rue Basse du Rempart, Paris. —Table-services in various styles, tea-services, and other articles of silversmiths' work.

1673 PARISOT, F. 192 Quai Jemmape, Paris.—Six burners for gas-lighting. A regulating apparatus for the pressure of the gas.

1674 PAYEN, A. R. 18 Boulevard St. Denis, Paris.—Gold jewellery for exportation.

1675 PEPIN-VIELLARD, Manufacturer of Woollen Blankets, Orleans (Loiret), and 14 Faubourg de la Madeleine, Paris.—Blankets wholly of wool.

1676 PEYROULX, H. Manufacturer of Cobalt Blue, Gouzon, Canton of Jarnages (Creuze).—Crystal flagon, filled with smalt or pure cobalt blue. Two vases of porcelain de Sèvres, coloured with smalt blue.

1678 PIVER, A. Soap Boiler, 103 Rue St. Martin, Paris. —Various kinds of soap, perfumed oils, grease, and alcohol.

1679 PLAGNIOL, —, Optician, 5 Rue Pastourel, Paris.—Spectacles. Ivory and polished opera-glasses. Daguerreotype pictures.

1680 POULET, J. F. Manufacturer of Spun Lead, 12 Rue Pierre Levée, Paris.—Spun lead, for horticulture and nurserymen.

1681 PRELAT, —, Gunsmith, 41 Rue de la Ferme, Paris. —Brace of pistols, with carved and chased gold mountings. Five-barrelled pistols, charges fired separately.

1682 PRAT, A. & AGARD, F. Aix, (Bouches-du-Rhône).—Productions of the liquid salines.

1683 QUENNESSEN, —, Platina Refiner, 4 Rue du Bouloi, Paris.—Platina crucibles, capsules, and various other platina chemical apparatuses, on a small scale.

1684 RANDON, L. Blonde Manufacturer, Caën (Calvados), and 9 Passage des Petits Pères, Paris.—White silk blondes scarf, overall, head-dress, and whiskers. Large gold and silk lappets.

1685 RIEUSSEC, N. Avenue du Bel Air, St. Mandé, near Paris.—Chronographers, or watches.

1686 RIGAULT, SON, Vinegar Manufacturer, Orléans (Loiret).—Various samples of vinegar.

1687 ROLLER & BLANCHET, SON, Piano Makers, 26 Rue Hauteville, Paris.—Four pianos of various descriptions.

1688 ROSWAG, A. & SON, Manufacturers of Metallic Cloths, Schlestadt (Haute-Rhin) ; Lyons (Rhône) ; and 321

Rue St. Denis, Paris.—A cylinder for continued laid paper. Metallic cloths and gauzes.

1689 Roucou, J. Manufacturer of Frosted Weapons, 21 Rue de Paris, Belleville (Seine).— Daggers, trophies, hangers, &c., with reproduction of ancient frosted work, inlaid work, and filigree.

1690 Roux, F. M. Trimming Manufacturer, St. Chamond (Loire)—Silk trimmings and lacing of various kinds.

1691 Saye, P. G. 9 Rue du Parc Royal, Paris.—Bronze clocks, statuettes, inkstands, and caskets.

1693 Seguin, —, Marble Cutter, 22 Rue d'Assas, Paris. —Samples of different marbles. Marble statuettes and statues, representing different incidents in the life of Napoleon. Quartz paper-presser.

1694 Si Amon ben Ouat, A. F. Weaver, Zamoura, Province of Constantine.—A zamouri bournous.

1695 Si Ali ben Lamouchi, Constantine.—A bournous zamouri.

1696 Si Hamida, Muphti of Oran.—A woollen common caban.

1697 Simon, S. Lyons (Rhône).—Japanned calf-leather.

1698 Soucin-Corbet, Chaumont (Haute Marne). — A dozen of dressed calf-hides.

1699 Soufleto, Piano Maker, 171 Rue Montmartre, Paris.—A long piano. Two cottage pianos.

1700 Suchel, J. D. 3 Rue St. Catherine, Lyons (Rhône). —Corsets without seams.

1701 Thollon, —, Manufacturer of Perfumery, Grenoble (Isère).—Flagons of various essences and perfumed liquids.

1702 Thouret, F. A. Silversmith, 31 Place de la Bourse, Paris.—Plated and electro-plated silver work. Patented in France and England.

1703 Troupeau, C M. Optician, 4 Rue Grange Batelière, Paris.—Diurnal reflectors.

1704 Vatin, —, jun. & Co. 13 Rue de Cléry, Paris.— Fancy gauze tissues, and woollen and silk tissues.

1705 Verstaen, L. N. 6 Rue Beaujolais, Paris.—Strong boxes or safes.

1706 Videcoq & Simon, Lace Manufacturer, 35 Rue des Jeûneurs, Paris.—Chantilly black lace shawls. Veil, lappets, and set of Alençon point lace.

1707 Villemsens, —, Bronze Manu. 71 Rue du Temple, Paris.—Bronze tabernacle candelabras, groups, lamps, &c.

1709 Barbedienne & Co. 30 Boulevart Poissonnière, Paris.—Sculpture, in reduced proportions, by mechanical processes; A. Collas, Inventor. Bronzes of art: Gate of the Baptistry at Florence, half the size of the original, &c.

1710 Lapeyriere, —, Iron Works at Bruniquel (Tarn-et-Garonne). (Represented by M. Detape, Paris).—Bars of iron. Charcoal made for conversion into steel; specimens for other purposes, after being subjected to torsion, punching, &c.; files and horse-rasps made from steel, converted from this iron by Messrs. Ibbetson Brothers, Sheffield.

1711 Martin, L. P. A. 13 Rue Fontaine-au-Roi, Paris (Agent in London, M. Frelon, 37 Piccadilly).—Percussion organ, with expression.

1712 Duclos, J. Gunsmith-worker, 47 Rue Richelieu, Paris.—Six guns and twelve pistols.

1713 Paillard, A. V. 8 Rue St. Claude, au Marais.— Bronzes, clocks, candelabra, &c.

1714 Genoux, F. 236 Rue du Faubourg St. Antoine, Paris. —Stained paper.

1715 Delicourt, E. 157 Rue de Charenton, Paris.— Seven panels of stained papers; rolls of stained paper; and a book (album) for showing the contrast of colours.

1717 De Bastard, A. 95 Rue St. Dominique, Paris.— Specimens of mediæval MS., illuminations, &c. Miniatures and ornaments in frames.

1718 Docagne, S. 3 Rue de Grammont, Paris.—Point d'Alençon lace

1719 Alexandre & Son, 39 Rue Meslay, Paris.—Two melodium organs. Organ on a new principle.

1720 Fromeut-Meurice, Orfèvre de la Ville de Paris.— Dressing-table of H. R. H. the Duchess of Parma. Milieu table, in embossed silver, the property of the Duc de Luynes.

1721 Festugiere, E. J. & Co. Aux Eyzies, Canton de Tayac (Dordogne).—Cast-iron and iron.

1722 Godefroy, —, Manager of the Society of Literary Men, 14 Cité Trevise, Paris.—Album of the society of literary men. Collection of drawings and autographs.

1723 Barbedienne, J. & Co. 30 Boulevart Poissonnière, Paris.—Art bronzes.

1724 Lagreze, —, Paris (Seine). — Gunsmith's work: Five guns.

1725 Sax, A. & Co. 50 Rue St. Georges, Paris.—Musical instruments, made of brass and wood.

1726 Morgant, E. Guines (Pas-de-Calais).—Two transparent water proof window-blinds.

1727 Rastouin, V. Carriage Maker, Blois (Loire-et-Cher).—Carriage axle, and nave boxes.

1728 Lemseigne, L. 72 Rue St. Jacques, Paris.—Engines, apparatus, mathematical instruments, tools, &c.

1729 Chevalier, C. Engineer Optician, 158 Palais National, Paris.—Magnifying glasses; improved camera chaira; photographs, with compound glasses; magnifying opera-glasses: improved telescopes; photograph proofs.

1730 Bourdin, C. Rhône.—Dyed thrown silk.

1734 Morel Brothers, Charleville (Ardennes).—Cast-iron; earthenware; projectiles; nails made by machinery: enamelled earthenware; cut hardware; rifle guns.

1735 Granger, J. M. F. L. 22 Rue St. Appoline.— Locksmith's work: Locks of all kinds, padlocks, &c.

1737 Goldenberg, G. & Co. Zornhoff, near Savern (Bas-Rhin).—Hard-ware, edge-tools, flattened saws, files, steel, &c.

1738 Zipelius, G. & Fuchs, Mülhausen, Des.—Design for a portière, executed by Roussel, Réquillart and Chocquel.

1739 Gregoire, F. Houbourdin, near Lille, Manu. (Agent, Mr. C. Sévin, 11 Catherine St. City.)—Three bottles spirit of molasses, and vinegar from corn; the former now, for the first time, so distilled as to be available as beverage.

1740 Mallet & Bailly, Artificial Florists, Rue de Rambuteau, Paris.—Glass case, containing an artificial tree, representing the "Sallow mourner," and other mourning flowers.

ALGERIA.

(Represented by Mr. Edmund Bouvy, Commissioner of Commercial Affairs for the Colony, and Delegate of the French Minister of War to the London Exhibition.)

1 Andre, Director of the Tobacco Service, Algiers. —Tobacco in leaves from the settlers of Sahel and Mitidja, and from the natives of those districts. Scaferlati hashed tobacco. Cigars made of Krachena tobacco.

2 Arnaud, Manu. Bonn (Constantine).—Samples of white soap.

3 Averseng & Co., Patented for Algiers and France; manufactory in Toulouse.—Vegetable hair, made of the leaves of the Algerian dwarf palm tree, &c.

4 Beauregard, Philippeville (Constantine). — Iron ore of Mount Filfilah.

5 Bedel, Grantee, Arzew (Oran).—Crystallised salt from the Salt Lake of Arzen.

6 Benes, Miss M. Philippeville (Constantine).— White cotton, called Naples Cotton, gathered in 1850.

7 Ben Zekri (the wife of the Caïd), Constantine.— A silk and woollen haïck.

8 Bernardon, H. A. a Soldier under confinement in the Military Prison of Bonn (Constantine).—Aloes thread cloak; by the exhibitor.

9 Borde, J. Manu. Philippeville (Constantine).— Oil of olives, gathered in 1850.

10 Boulanger, Pierre Honore, Saddler, — Crapeau saddle, full quilted leather saddlebow. Bauche saddle, leather saddlebow. Short-ride saddle, saddlebow, wooden band. Child's saddle ; a full quilted velvet. A bit upon a new principle.

11 Briqueler & Co., Grantee, Tenez.—Samples of brass pyrites from the Oued Allelah Mines.

12 Cabanillas, Widow, Saw-mill Works, Algiers.— Five specimens of veneering, adapted for cabinet-work.

13 Cailliez, A. L. J. Cabinet-maker, Mustapha.—A toilet table, and inlaid work-chest, made of native wood.

14 Canton, Merchant, President of the Chamber of Commerce, Algiers.—Samples of Bouçada and Medeah raw wool. Three samples of Upper Chilif wool, combed by machinery.

15 Casteiran, Colonist of the St. Louis' Agricultural Colony (Oran).—Boiled yellow silk and white silk hand-kerchiefs.

16 Chapel, Kouba.—Canna root flour (Canna discolor), a new article of food.

17 Chuffart, Agriculturist, Birmandreïs.—Hard and soft wheats of 1850. Cotton, called Louisiane, 1850. Silk in cocoons and spun silk.

18 Commission of the Mouzaie Mines.—Crystallized grey copper ores.

19 Ain Morka Mines Company, Constantine.—Steel made in France from iron ores of Ain Morka. Assortment of files. Set of scythes made of cast and refined steel.

20 Bonn Mines and Iron Works Company, Constantine.—Raw steel castings. Cast steel.

21 Converso, Bonn, Constantine.—Writing-desk, made of native woods.

22 Curtet, Jun. Manu. Bab-el-Oued.— Samples of olive oil ; oils of sesame, camelind, mustard, cotton, arachide, brassica, arvensis, ricinius, poppies, turnsol, lawn and madia saliva.

23 Dupre de St. Maur, Agriculturist Orbal, (Oran).— Soft wheat, tobacco leaves, Jumel cotton wool, madder-roots.

24 Flechey, J. B. Manu.—Patent paper and pasteboard made of the dwarf palm tree leaves.

25 Frederic, J. B. Agriculturist, Montpensier. — A sample of opium, accompanied with soumiferais ; white poppy capsules, 1850.

26 Grima, F. Agriculturist, Philippeville (Constantine).—White and nankean cottons, 1850.

27 Haloche, Agriculturist, Drariah.—Cotton, 1850.

28 Hardy, Manager of the Hamma Nursery, near Algiers.—Jumel, Louisiana, New York, Georgia long silk ; Macedonia and nankean cottons, 1849 and 1850. Raw silks of 1849 and 1850. Cochineal, opium, dry rice, oleaginous seeds. Varieties of maize. Eight and six months growth Bamboo shoots.

29 Jeantet, Agriculturist, (Constantine). — Hard wheat and barley of 1850.

30 Judas Moha, Manu. Oran.—Two gold embroidered silk dresses for Jewish ladies.

31 Julien, Manufacturer of preserves, Bougie (Constantine).—Pickled olives.

32 Laya & Co. Measures.—Sample of native wheat flour.

33 Lefelletier, Agriculturist, Fondouck—Soft wheat, 1850.

34 De Lutzow, Colonist, Bonn, Constantine.—Sample of saffron.

35 Maffre, E. F. Manu. Bougie, Constantine.—Olive oil.

36 Marchal, Agriculturist, Boudjaréah.—Soft wheat and brown oats, 1850.

37 Mercurin, H. J. Agriculturist, Cheragas.—Olive oil of 1850. Odoriferous essences.

38 Montigny, G. de, Agriculturist, St. Joseph, Oran. —Soft wheat and barley of 1850. Madder root ; saffron.

39 Morin, Agriculturist, El Biar.—Tobacco in leaves called Philippin. Hashed tobacco. Cigars. Jumel cotton, 1850. Silk in cocoons and spun silk.

40 Oxeda & Aqui, Cigar Manufacturers.—Samples of cigars of various qualities.

41 Fisheries of La Calle, Constantine.—Specimens of coral. Red chalkstone.

42 Pelissier, C. Agricul. Kaddous.—White cotton.

43 Piglia, J. Agricul. Constantine.—Madder-root.

44 Reverchon, H. Agriculturist, Birkadeny.—Tobacco in leaves and Jumel cotton, 1850.

45 Commission of Algiers Mines, (Province of Algiers). Samples of various ores.

46 Commission of the Mines, Bonn (Constantine.)— Samples of ores :—Geological specimens and minerals.

47 Commission of Wood and Forest.—Specimen of native woods and cork.

48 Si Ahmed-El-Hachemi, of the Amer Cheragas tribe, (Province of Constantine).—A hambel, a species of woollen blanket or carpet.

49 Si Amar-Smin, (his wife), Constantine.—Sample of hand-spun wool.

50 Si-El-Bey Ben-Bou-Ras, Manu. Constantine. — Arab saddle, gold and silver embroidered morocco covering, and every appendage forming an Arab horseman's equipment.

51 Simounet, P. Manu.— Perfumed essences of jasmine, geranium, &c.

52 Soual, Edge Tool-maker, Bonn, Constantine.—An iron axe.

53 Tribe of the Beni Abbes, Province of Constantine.—A white abessi burnou.

54 Tribe of the Bou Taleb, Province of Constantine. —A haïck boutalbi.

55 Tribe of the Drides, Province of Constantine.— Woollen burnou.

56 Tribe of the Haractas, Province of Constantine. —Specimen of raw wool. Two large woollen carpets. A woollen blanket.

57 Verrier, F. Manufacturer of Alimentary Preserves.—Oil-preserved Sardins.

58 The Delegate of Algiers.—Spun cottons, silks, woollens, carpets, blankets, belts, cloaks, scarfs, &c. Various articles of silversmith's work.

Various Articles.—Five hats, cotton felt of Algeria, with and without a mixture of hair, manufactured by Messrs. Ernoux Diolo at Paris. Three samples of felt made with Algerian cotton. A sample of paper manufactured in France with Aloës tow and Algerian banana tree.

59 Baruch Toledano, Embroiderer, Oran.—A tube of silk embroidered with gold for a Jewess.

60 Cherif Ben Mimoun, Spinner of the Beni Abbes, Constantine.—A white abessi mzouak burnous.

61 Caid Ben Zekie des Seignas (the wife of), Constantine.—A gandoura, made of wool and silk.

62 Mohamed Ben Achir (Caïd of Mascara), Oran.— A burnous in black wool.

63 Saad Ben Bartha, Bone (Constantine).—Basket made with the leaves of a palm-tree mixed with woollen.

64 Si Hamon Bel Onataf, Spinner, Zamenoua (Constantine).—A burnous made with a camel's hair.

65 Si Ali Bel Lamouchi, Merchant, Constantine.— A Zamouiri burnous, with red stripes, for a child.

66 Si El Medani, Spinner (tribe of the Ouled Taben of Bon Taleb), Constantine.

67 Beni Snous (Tribe of the), Oran.—A mat made of the bark of a palm-tree mixed with woollen.

68 Cox, E. & Co. Spinners, Louviére-lez-Lille—Cotton spun with the cotton grown in 1850. Series of samples from Nos. 200 to 360, single thread, and No. 400, double thread.

GERMANY. ZOLLVEREIN STATES.

Chief Commissioner in London, Mr. von Viebahn, 43 Albion Street, Hyde Park.
Prussia, Professor Dr. Schubarth; *Bavaria*, Professor Dr. Schaafhautl; *Saxony*, Dr. W. Seiffarth, L.L.D.; *Würtemberg*, Dr. Steinbeis; *Baden*, Professor Dr. Rau; *Electoral Hesse*, Mr. Schreiber; *Grand Duchy of Hess*, Mr. Rossler; *Thuringia*, Professor Dr. Schuler; *Brunswick*, Professor Dr. Varrentrapp; *Nassau*, M. Odernheimer; *Frankfort-on-the-Maine*, M. Philipp Ellissen.

1. PRUSSIA, BADEN, and UNITED STATES of NORTHERN GERMANY.

Agents in London, Messrs. Stein & Hall, 70 Newgate Street, City.

a. Provinces of BRANDENBURG, SILESIA, POSEN, and POMERANIA.

1 The Administration of the Royal Prussian Smelting Works and Iron Foundry, Gleiwitz, Prod.—Samples of wrought-iron, as used for rollers; sheet-iron and bar-iron rollers.

2 The Royal Prussian Iron Works, Malapane, near Opeln.—Pair of hard cast-iron cylinders. Samples of ores and other materials and products derived from them by charcoal furnaces at the Royal Iron Works at Malapane. Red and white calamine from the mines at Scharley, and the Calamine Works, near Beuthen, in High Silesia. Zinc in drops; white zinc (oxide of zinc); cadmium (metal).

3 Royal Works at Konighuette, Prod.—Sundry specimens of ores.

4 Elsner, von Gronow, & Co. Tarnowitz, Silesia, Prod.—Specimen of Roman cement found at a depth of 160 feet in a lead mine (Frederik's mine), near Tarnowitz, in Prussian-Silesia.

5 Stettiner Patent Bleiweiss Fabrik, Stettin, Manu. (Agent in London, C. Kekulé, 60 Mark Lane.)—Patent white lead.

6 Guettler, W. Reichenstein, in Silesia, Prod.—Arsenic ores, showing a process for extracting the gold from the residue of the arsenic ores. The process is founded upon experiments by M. Plattner, Professor of Chemistry, at Freiburg, in Saxony.

7 Du Bois, C. A. Hirschberg, Silesia, Prod.—Samples of cinnabar.

8 Lucas, M. Cunersdorf, near Hirschberg, Prod.—Samples of cinnabar.

9 Milch, A. Warmbrunn, and Cologne, Prod.—Samples of bricks, with drawing and description of a brick-press of a peculiar construction.

10 Rimann, E. Hirschberg, Silesia. — Rough and cut precious stones.

11 Ruffer & Co. Breslau, Manu.—An assortment of zinc-plates, including two as thin as a sheet of paper. Zinc-plates for tiles.

12 Cochius, E. E. Oranienburg, near Berlin, Manu.—Large specimen of crystallization, prussiate of potash.

13 Kunheim, L. A. H. Berlin, Prod.—A mass of crystals of sugar of lead. Acetate of lime. Nitrate of lead. Tinate of soda. Cyanate of potassium. Oxide of uran. Tungstanic acid, &c.

14 Bernhard von Sanden, Wiese and Marwitz, near Preuss. Holland, Prod.—Samples of raw and refined beet-root sugar from the growth of the estate of Marwitz, made at the first sugar-refinery erected in the province of Königsberg.

15 Christiani, C. H. Kerstenbruch, Prod.—Bottles of beer and extract of beer for ships' use, brewed without malt.

16 Farthmann, —, Klein-Schwein, Prod. — Dried " potato cuts," prepared in a peculiar manner, so as to keep for years. Potato flour. 100 lbs. of cut potatoes, prepared and dried by the exhibitor. Produce: 50 lbs. of fine; 14 lbs. of middling; 24 lbs. of black flour; and 6 lbs. of bran.

17 Gross, D. J. Berlin, Manu.—Vanille chocolates; santé chocolates, without spice; spiced chocolates.

18 Paetsch, G. Wrietzen on the Oder, Manu. — Potato-starch syrup. Much used by the German brewers.

19 Kruse, A. T. Stralsund, London agent, C. Jones, Manu.—Starch, prepared from the wheat of the country round Stralsund.

20 Weill, C. Berlin, Manu. — Fruits preserved in sugar. Vegetables preserved in butter, and in their natural state. Potted larks.

21 Uechtritz, L. Mühlraedtlitz, Silesia, Prod. — Specimen of potato-starch.

22 The Royal Remounting Depot, Treptow, Pomerania, Prod.—Carded wool, the fleece of an ewe four years old, of the Electoral breed, &c.

23 Thaer, A. P. Councillor, Moeglin, near Wrietzen on the Oder, Prod.—Washed and raw wool-fleeces, from the staple flock at Moeglin, intended to illustrate the richness of wool with fineness of hair in the merino breed.

24 Lübbert, E. Zweybrodt, near Breslau, Prod. — Specimens of wool.

25 Lipski, Von, Ludomy, near Obornick, Posen, Prod. —Specimens of wool, in glasses, &c.

26 Hey, High Administrator of the Royal Domain, Haynsburg, Sachsen, Prod.—Wool-fleeces.

27 Royal Administration of Frankenfelde, Wrietzen on the Oder, Prod.—Fleece of a ram and of ewes, sheared in spring 1850. Samples of wool.

28 Rothschild, Baron S. Von, Oderberg, Silesia Superior, Prod.—Fleeces of merino sheep and lambs. The flock from which these fleeces have been selected is said to be one of the most celebrated in Silesia; and out of it, sheep for breeding are sold to Silesia, Hungary, Galicia, and Posnania.

29 Küpfer, —, Councillor of Legation, Bromberg, Prod.—Merino fleeces of two-year-old ewes. Exhibited on account of the fineness and regularity of the wool-staple, and as an illustration of the advance of the production of wool in the Prussian countries of the Middle Vistula.

30 Nordmann, G. L. Liszkowô, near Inowraclaw, Prod.—Fleeces of wool, exhibiting great regularity in the staple.

31 Winkler, F. Berlin, Manu.—An assortment of prepared, bleached, and dyed figures, and Venetian sponges. The sponges cleared by chemical process, and dyed fast colours, by methods invented by the exhibitor.

32 Eckardstein, A. Baron of, Reichenow, Prod.—Fleece of wool exhibited on account of the regularity of the wool staple.

33 Schwerin, Count of, Wolfshagen, Ukermark, Prod.—Fleece of a ram and ewe of Saxon breed.

34 Rufin, A. Rûstern, Liegnitz, Prod.—Flax grown in Silesia, and "swingled" after the Belgian method, in the Royal Flax-cultivation School for Lower Silesia; heckled flax.

35 The Corporation of Millers, Lissa, Grand Duchy of Posen.—Samples of stamped millet, buckwheat, groats, and oatmeal.

36 Ziegler, Baron T. of, Dambrau in Silesia, Prod.—Three fleeces of wool, unwashed, from sheep of the genuine Spanish breed.

37 Lorenz, G. Wolgast, Manu.—Samples of glue.

38 BOLZANI, A. M. Berlin, Prod.—Spinning-hut with cocoons of silkworms.

39 KISZEWSKI, Meseritz, Posen, Prod.—Proofs of raw silk, made of 4, 5, 6, and 7 twisted threads. Produced upon the property of the seminaries of Paradies.

40 TESSLER, D. F. Stolp, Manu.—Two pieces of raw yellow amber, as cast up by the sea. Specimens of such dimensions are very rare; 100 dollars are often paid for one pound. Pieces of amber enclosing insects, &c.

41 TESSLER, C. L. Stolp, Manu.—Pieces of wood of the amber-tree; and of yellow amber as found under ground, and as cast out by the sea. Amber ornaments of milk-white colour. Snuff-box set in gold with the miniature of Frederic II. &c.

42 FREIHERR VON LUTTWITZ, Simmenau, near Oppeln, Prod.—Samples of unheckled flax; extensively cultivated at Simmenau. Fleeces of wool, from the flock of the exhibitor.

43 GRUENE, W. jun. Berlin, Manu.—Newly invented composition for dyeing wool; yarns dyed with it.

44 HEYL, J. F. & Co. Berlin, Manu.—Colours, in paste, for painters, and paper-hanging manufacturers; chemical substances and colours.

45 OBERBURGGRAF VON BRUNNECK, Trebnitz, Prod.—Fleece of a ram and of a ewe of the merino breed.

46 OBERBURGGRAF VON BRUNNECK, Bellschwitz, near Rosenberg, Prod.—Fleeces of wool indiscriminately taken.

47 LEHMANN, R. Nitsche, near Kosten, Prod.—Fleeces of fine raw-wool.

48 HOLTZSTAMM, F. Berlin, Prod.—Sample of silk-like vegetable fibres, exhibited to show that such parts of plants may be employed in designs for the manufacture of articles where silk is used.

49 FRIEDRICH, C. Potsdam, Manu.—Park carriage or phaeton.

50 GEVERS & SCHMIDT, Goerlitz, Manu.—Black and coloured broad cloths. Ladies' cloths, black and blue. Broad buckskin.

51 WURDEN, C. A. VON & Co. Grabow, near Stettin, Manu.—Steam-pump, complete.

52 HECKMANN, C. Berlin, Manu.—Vacuum boiling apparatus for sugar refining, 85 cubic feet English, sufficient for 245 loaves of sugar at 30 lbs. weight each; it boils these loaves in 1½ hours, out of clarified mixture of 30 "Beaumé," and employs steam of three atmospheres expansion, and from 4 to 5 cubic feet of condensation water per minute. Applicable for the manufacture of cane and beet sugars.

53 BONARDEL BROTHERS, Berlin, Manu.—Jacquard machines; machine for stamping patterns for jacquard work. Machine for cutting corks.

54 DOERFFEL, T. Berlin, Manu.—Frill machine.

55 LEONHARDT, J. E. Berlin, Manu.—Type-founding machine, a new invention. Zinc or copper moulds may be employed.

56 WINTER, F. Berlin, Manu.—Jacquard weaving-machines; improved by the exhibitor, the hooks being so placed that they cannot turn when the machine is at work.

57 THOMAS, H. Berlin, Prod. and Inv.—Shearing-machine, for shawls, for beating apparatus.

58 HAMANN, A. Berlin, Inv. and Manu.—A turning lathe.

59 RENNER, S. B. jun. Breslau, Manu.—Models of zinc-roofing, on a large and small scale.

60 GEHRMANN, T. Berlin, Manu.—Priming-pin rifle-gun. Rifle. Double-barrelled gun, with shooting implements.

61 LÜDLICH, W. Posen, Manu.—Rifle, with screw driver, powder measure, and bullet mould.

62 OHLE, E. F. (Heirs of) Breslau, Manu.—Samples of shot-tubes made by the hydraulic press, tinned inside and outside. Wire. Red lead and litharge. Bullets. Sheet-lead, tinned, &c. all of Silesian lead.

63 GRZYBOWSKI, H. Potsdam, Manu.—Rifle, in rose-wood; German silver mounted case.

64 KEHL, J. C. Berlin, Manu.—Pistols in box, with implements for cleaning, casting balls, &c.

65 STOLLE, Dr. E. Berlin, Inv.—Patent chaff-cutter, for cutting straw and other vegetable substances, containing a new application of vulcanized India-rubber. Manufactured by F. Thiele, Berlin.

66 BRUCKISCH, W. Koppitz, near Grotkau, Prop.—Erect double bee-hive; queen bee's basket, &c.

67 SPRENGEL, Dr. C. & Co. Regenwalde, Pomerania, Manu. — Sowing-machine; drill-machine; Indian corn thrashing-machine; Flander's plough, altered by Schwarz; Pomeranian vibrating plough; Mecklenburg hoe, with yoke; East Prussian zocke, with yoke; 16-share crooker; under-ground plough; water-furrow plough.

68 GUERLIN, P. Berlin, Manu.—Night clocks; cartel bronze clocks; regulator, &c.

69 KRUGER, A. Bromberg, Inv. — Electro-magnetic self-registering anemometer. A system of four electro-magnets. The galvanic circuit is completed by quicksilver every hour by means of clock-work.

70 KUNST, J. A. Berlin, Manu.—Specimens of artificial teeth. Samples of the material.

71 BESSALIE, H. P. Breslau, Manu.—Patent rosewood grand piano, with English mechanism and arrangement for easier tuning and tightening the wires.

72 THIEMKE, A. F. Berlin, Manu.—Brass travelling clock, in leather case.

73 GURICKE, B. Zossen, near Berlin, Inv. and Manu.—Grand piano, with powerful repeating mechanism, wholly constructed by the exhibitor himself.

74 SIEGERT, C. Stettin, Manu. — Complete vacuum-apparatus and air-pump.

75 SEEMANN, G. Warmbrunn, Manu.—House-clocks.

76 BAUMANN, T. Berlin, Inv.—A standard measure, after Bessel. An ordinary yard measure.

77 NOBERT, F. A. Barth, near Stralsund, Pomerania, Manu.—Glass plates, with divisions, applicable for observations with the microscope. Ocular micrometer for telescopes, with clear lines in the dark horizon.

78 THIEDE, F. Berlin, Manu. (Agent, Mr. Oertling, London.)—Astronomical regulator. Box chronometer.

79 POKORNY, J. A. Berlin, Manu.—Iron pill and other moulds and mortars. Improved Berzelius and other lamps. Gasometer, after Pepys. Belt rifle-gun and pistol.

80 WESTERMANN & Co. (Prop. of the firm, G. Willmanns) Berlin, Manu.—Rosewood grand piano.

81 LÜTTIG, C. Berlin, Manu.—Levelling instruments. Dioptric telescope. Ruling machine. Optometer. Ball and ring to demonstrate the expansion of metals by heat. Mathematical instruments. Camera obscura.

82 BALTZER, A. Frankfort, Inv.—Æolodion, an instrument with keys of six octaves, with metal springs or tongues put into vibration by means of bellows. Clocks striking and going for the space of a year. Pendulum clock, showing the variation of the time at twenty different places.

83 LUHME, J. F. & Co. Berlin, Manu.—Fluor-acid and apparatus made of platinum. Analytical weighing scales. Polarization apparatus for saccharine fluids. Sulphuretted hydrogen apparatus after Kipp. Berzelius and other chemical lamps, &c.

84 LUPPOLD, —, Stettin, Inv.—Instruments for accoucheurs, composed of steel, ivory, and German silver.

85 GOLDSCHMIDT, S. Berlin, Manu.—An assortment of surgical and physical instruments, bandages, artificial limbs, syringes, and a magnetic apparatus.

86 REIMANN, L. Berlin, Manu.—Balance, which weighs from one milligramme to one kilogramme; that is, from of a grain to 2¼ lbs. avoirdupois. Set of gramme-weights of brass, gilt by galvanic process, from one gramme to one milligramme, with ivory forks and pincettes.

87 OERTLING, A. Berlin, Inv. — Chemical balances, large and small, with weights. Hudley's sextants. Reflecting goniometer.

88 HOFFMANN & EBERHARDT, Berlin, Manu.—Complete assortment of apparatus and articles for chemical, physical, and pharmaceutical purposes.

89 BUSCH, E. Rathenow, Manu.—Spectacle-frames and glasses. Assortment of opera-glasses, &c. Daguerreotype portraits. Large telescope, with foot, and various others.

90 RUHMANN, A. Eulam, near Landsberg, on the Warthe, Manu.—A guitar.

91 VOELKEL, J. G. & Co. Langenbielau and Breslau, Manu.—Pieces of cotton stuffs—red inlet, jacquard ticks, and bed-ticks. Table-cover.

92 DIERIG, C. Langenbielau, near Reichenbach, Silesia, Manu.—Jacquard diaper, of double-cotton yarn and single-cotton twist, united with English machine yarn. Jacquard diaper, made of Chinese grass, and of blue fancy silk and English machine linen yarn. Pattern of bed-tick, warp of crimson organzine silk, united with bleached Chinese grass yarn. Glazed cotton shirtings.

93 NAUEN, LOEWE, & Co. Berlin, Manu.—Printed calicoes, woven by power-looms in Berberg and Marklissa in Silesia, and bleached and printed at Berlin.

94 MENTZEL, Royal Prussian Privy Councillor of the War Department, Berlin, Prop.—A variety of samples of blue and grey military cloths, such as are supplied for the clothing of the Royal Prussian army.

95 FABIAN, C. G. Humboldsau, near Breslau, Manu.—'Pine-needle wool" for upholstery, intended to guard against moths, and for wadding. " Pine-needle wool" wadding mattresses and bolster, &c. " Pine-needle wool " oil, used for medicinal purpose, &c.

96 WALD & SON, Zielenzig, Manu.—Woollen yarns, dyed and white, three and four fold.

97 ITZIGSOHN, M. Neudamm, Manu. — Broad-cloths. Grey mixture cloth, as used by the Prussian military for cloaks and trousers. Leather-coloured cloth for coaches

98 BEHREND & SCHMIDT, Berlin, Manu.—Woollen cloth.

99 HABERLAND, G. A. Finsterwalde, Manu. — Black cloth.

100 GEISSLER, C. S. Görlitz, Manu.—Woollen cloths, of various colours, dyed in the wool; manufactured out of Silesian wools.

101 RUFFER & SON, Liegnitz, Silesia, Manu.—Imperial woollen cloths, Segovia olive colour, and Cashmere, dyed in the wool; Electoral woollen cloth and Royal black, dyed in piece.

102 SCHEDER, F. & Co. Schweidnitz, Manu. — Buckskins and cloths for breeches, &c.

103 LUTZE BROTHERS, Cottbus, Manu.—Mulberry, olive, and black cloths.

104 COHN BROTHERS & HERMANN, Berlin, Manu.— Woollen, cotton, and silk mixed stuffs; woollen, plain, and fancy stuffs; fancy woollen, and woollen and cotton mixed stuffs.

105 COCKERILL, W. Guben and Cottbus, Manu.—Raw and coloured carded yarns, spun of Pomeranian wool.

106 BERGMANN & Co. Berlin, Manu.—Worsted zephyr yarns, best quality; the wools were manufactured by the United Spinning Company at Gotha.

107 FELLER & SON, Guben, Manu.—Black cloths, black royal, yarn, &c. exhibited for cheapness combined with quality; manufactured from wool of Silesian, Pomeranian, Marchian, Prussian, and Australian wools.

108 SCHLIEF, S. Guben, Manu.—Black cloth and satin, exhibited on account of beauty and cheapness.

109 FRIEDHEIM & SONS, Berlin, Manu.—Pieces of figured and plain Orleans and Gros-de-Berlin.

110 HOFFMANN, E. Sorau, Lusetia, Manu.—Coloured ladies' cloths. Black cloth.

111 MENDE & SON, Finsterwalde, Manu. — Pieces of black cloth, various; manufactured from Silesian wool.

112 BORMANN, F. A. Goldberg in Silesia, Manu.—Pieces of cloth, dyed in the wool, black and blue, dark green and red.

113 MARX & WEIGERT, Berlin, Manu. — Cashmere shawls, in sundry colours and designs. Mohair, woollen, and cotton velvets.

114 LEVIN, SONS, Berlin, Manu. — Cravats. Waistcoats, silk, worsted and silk, and embroidered. Silk and cotton plush. Patterns of sundry silk, and silk and cotton articles.

115 WEIGERT & Co. Schmiedeberg, Silesia, Manu.—Cashmere shawls: coloured and figured velours d'Utrecht; castorine: pallas; tallupp; transparent; leopard, &c.

116 OEHME, C. W. Berlin, Inv. and Manu.—Plush for hats, exhibited for colour and texture; manufactured of Italian and French silk, and of cotton spun in England. Silk plush for caps.

117 KAUFFMANN, H. Berlin (Agent in London, C. Schwebemeyer, 314 Oxford St.), Inv. and Manu.—Printed and other plush for furniture; livery plushes; plush for coats, shoes, caps, &c. Velours of cotton (castorine).

118 SCHAERFF, R. Brieg, Manu.—Silk and worsted borders, tassels, and gimps, for carriages. Bridles, gun-ribbons, girths, &c.

119 GABAIN, G. (GROPIUS BROTHERS), Berlin, Manu.—Various silk goods. Silk and cotton, silk and gold, and silk and silver goods, of original designs.

120 KIRSTEIN, C. Hirschberg, Silesia, Prop. — Linens, half linen, handkerchiefs, &c., manufactured by the weavers in the neighbourhood of Hirschberg.

120A Samples of drugs:—Lovage, hellebore, valerian, Iceland moss, angelica root, bilberries.

121 SEYLERS, G. (Heirs of) Wuestewaltersdorf, Silesia, Merchants.—Bleached linen, for the South American markets.

122 WEBSKY & SON, Wuestegiersdorf, Silesia, Manu.—White linen; No. 101 to 109 are exported to America under the name of platillas.

123 KAUFFMANN, M. Schweidnitz, Manu.—Half linen Jacquard diapers. Half worsted damask for furniture. Half linen and worsted stuff for apparel.

124 RIMANN & GEISLER, Hirschberg, Silesia, Prop.—Pieces of bleached linen.

125 ENGEL, E. jun. Goerlitz, Manu. — Hunting-bag made out of hemp pack-thread. Samples of two and three-cord extremely fine hemp-twine.

127 STILLER & SON, Sorau, Manu.—Linen and half linen damask ticking; table-cloth and napkins.

128 KRAMSTA & SONS, Freyburg, in Silesia, Manu.—Raw and bleached linens, creas and platilles royales. Dessert napkins. Linen handkerchiefs. Diaper, Jacquard, and damask table-cloths and napkins. Raw linen machine yarn. Sample of starch.

129 PRENTZEL, J. C. Greiffenberg, Silesia. — Linen pocket handkerchiefs.

130 TSCHORN & BÜRGEL, Wuestegiersdorf, Manu.—Raw and white household linen; Nos. 1 and 3; 2,400 warp threads; Nos. 2 and 4, 3,200 threads.

131 SCHILDKNECHT, C. F. Berlin, Manu.—Satin d'Amérique, manufactured out of the fibre of the American aloe for furniture. Shawls of various fabrics.

132 SUSSMANN & WIESENTHAL, Berlin, Manu. (Agent in London, C. Holland, 41 Finsbury Circus.)—Plaids, broché, fides, umbrella, and lucille, manufactured out of cotton and

woollen; Esmeralda and umbrella China, out of cotton, silk, and woollen; tartan, all wool.

133 MEYER, MAX, & Co. Berlin, Manu.—Coloured cotton and silk mixed plush, for export to North America.

134 OPDENHOFF & HARTUNG, Berlin, Manu.—Shawls of various kinds. Plaid, tartan, &c. The woollen yarns used are of German make, except two articles, which are worked partially with English yarns.

135 PINTUS, H. jun. & Co. Brandenburg, Manu. (Agent in London, A. Hurtzmann, 17 Ironmonger Lane.)—Embroidered Llama stuff; Cachemir mixed with silk; double Chiné; Chiné; ermin; Cachemir; and imperial. Manufactured from carded yarns.

136 LEHMANN, D. J. Berlin, Manu. Agents, Ullmann, Hirchhorn, & Co. 2 Wallbrook, London.—Velours d'Utrecht, for furniture, &c. Plush for caps, waistcoats, coats, manufactured partly of linen and partly of cotton, with mohair. Square and double long shawls; and stuff for cloaks of wool, and of cotton, with carded yarn.

137 COHN, PHILIPP, & Co. Berlin, Manu.—Shawls of woollen, half-woollen, and woollen with cotton & silk mixed.

138 LEHMANN, H. Berlin, Manu.—An assortment of deerskin, kid, and lambskin gloves.

139 KOENIG, L. Berlin, Manu.—Camaille from mink tails, with squirrel furs.

140 LUSK, A. Berlin, Manu.—Walking-sticks, riding-whips, life-preservers, &c.

141 BECHERER, J. Berlin, Manu.—Specimens of horse and other whips.

142 GRUTZMACHER & SONS, Stettin, Manu. — Brown calf-skins.

143 KOPPE, A. Berlin, Manu.—Assortment of cardboard, stone, wood, and leather fancy articles. Alarums; desks with mechanism. A Christmas-tree, the cupola can be transparently illuminated by the lamp inside of it, &c.

144 BEYERHAUS, A. Berlin, Manu.—A print in Chinese characters. 4,200 punches in these Chinese characters have been cut in steel for the American Missionary Society in New York. The types are divisible on a new perpendicular system; and form, by combination, 24,000 different characters.

145 EBART BROTHERS, Berlin, Manu.—Hand-papers for bank-notes, &c., and machine-papers from the paper-mill at Spechthausen; and glazing-boards and carton-pierre, for roofing, from the paper-mill of Weitlage, near Neustadt-Eberswalde.

146 GLANZ, P. Berlin, Manu.—An assortment of sealing-wax.

147 LIEPMANN, J. Berlin, Inv.—Mass of colour, for printing in oil, a substitute for ordinary printing ink. Specimens of various methods of printing, materials, &c.

148 DECKER, R. L. Berlin, Manu.—Specimens of printing and of printing types. The New Testament, in large folio. The paper is of Berlin manufacture. The types were cut in steel by J. Schilling. The drawings of the initials are by A. Muller. The wood-cuts were executed by Prof. Unzelmann, M. Vogel, and M. A. Vogel, &c. The illustrations were designed by Cornelius and Kaulbach, drawn on wood by M. L. Burger, and executed by the above-named engravers. The binding in velvet is by M. Vogt. The silver ornaments on the cover and the clasps were designed by M. A. Muller, and executed in embossed work by M. Netto. The steel punches of the types, &c.

149 LEISEGANG, W. Berlin, Manu.—Album of velvet, gilt. The method of gilding the velvet is patented.

150 OSTEN, L. V. D. Stralsund, Manu.—Carpets, table-covers, and pictures, printed upon cotton. Very rare copies of woodcuts, after Albert Durer. Packs of cards.

151 WUTTIG, G. L. Pulverkrug, near Frankfort on the Oder, Manu.—Machine-paper, coloured or stained, in sundry sizes and qualities.

152 KUEHN & SONS, Berlin, Manu.—Ledgers and ruled papers. Large red-morocco case, for keeping copper-plates, prints, &c. Portfolios, pocket-books, albums, cigar-cases, porte-monnaies, &c.

153 SCHAFFER, OTTO, & SCHEIBE, Berlin, Manu.—Samples of ornamental papers. The plates from which these impressions were taken are prepared by the electrotype process from papier-maché moulds.

154 SCHOENING, H. Berlin, Manu. — Album in dark velvet, gilt. Altar-bible, in morocco.

155 WAGNER, J. G. jun. Berlin, Manu.—Specimens executed by the lining and relief copying-machines of the exhibitor.

156 MOESER & KÜHN, Berlin, Manu. — Specimens of letter-press printing.

157 KARSCHELITZ, S. N. Berlin, Manu.—Printed table-covers.

158 TRAUTWEIN, T. Berlin, Publisher.—Map of the industry of Central Europe, drawn on linen.

159 STEPHAN, A. & Co. Berlin, Manu.—Pieces of cotton-twill dyed, partly without finish, partly glazed and embossed. Exhibited for the colours and the finishing.

160 SCHLEUSS, H. Berlin.—Assortment of embroideries.

161 STIEFF & HARRASS, Potsdam, Des. and Manu.—Specimens of embossed silk, representing the Neptune grotto, built by Frederick the Great, at Sans Souci. Gentlemen's silk cravats. Silk waistcoating. Embroidered waistcoats.

162 SEIFFERT & Co. Berlin, Manu.—Berlin paper pattern, for embroidery.

163 KOENIG, C. A. Berlin, Manu.—Large carpet, embroidered in cross-stitch. Bed-screen, embroidered after original drawings. Embroidery for a fire-screen, in the velours d'Utrecht fashion. Embroideries extra fine, petit-point in silk. Child's bed-cover, filet-work in silk.

164 BURCHARDT & SONS, Berlin, Manu.—Printed oil-cloth, table-covers, painted window-blinds, and double floor-cloths; hat-linings; oil-cloth for carriages; carpet.

165 LIPKE, W. Berlin, Manu.—Sofa and other carpets of machine-made felt, and of woven texture.

166 GRÜNTHAL, Berlin, Manu.—Paper patterns for embroidery.

167 LEHMANN, M. Berlin.—Manu. (Agents in London, Jonas Simonssen & Co. 46 Lime St.)—Oil-cloths; round table-covers. Painted window-blinds. Patterns of a new waterproof elastic cloth, for railway waggons, &c. Floor-cloths.

168 NEIE, F. W. Berlin, Manu.—Berlin paper patterns for embroidery, new composition.

169 PAREY, C. F. W. Berlin, Manu.—Embroidered carpet.

170 RUDLOFF BROTHERS (P. Trübe), Berlin, Manu.—Berlin paper patterns for embroidery, representing Cardinal Ximénes: Laban and Jacob; and Hagar in the desert.

171 TODT, A. Berlin, Manu.—Paper patterns for embroidery.

172 ADOLPHI, C. F. W. Berlin, Manu.—Ladies' boots and shoes, yellow morocco leather; ladies' slippers. Children's boots. Over-shoes, with metal springs.

173 SOMMERFELD, B. Berlin, Manu. — Embroidered altar-cloth, and other specimens of embroidery. Assortment of embroideries, on pocket-books, cigar-cases, porte-monnaies, &c.

174 BECKH BROTHERS, Berlin, Manu.—Carpet in Turkish style, flower pattern, and arabesque pattern, in one piece; and a variety of carpets with figures.

175 DINGLINGER, A. F. Berlin, Manu.—Velours carpets. Rugs. Velours for travelling-bags.

176 GLUER, L. Berlin Inv.—Patterns of paper used for embroidery.

177 ANDRESEN, P. Berlin, Manu.—Morning shoes, with embroidery in gold; riding boots; waterproof boots; cork boots, of varnished leather; ball boots for officers in the army, &c. Pegs made by Mr. Mielert, for fastening the soles of the boots instead of sewing them.

178 FREYSTADT BROTHERS, Berlin, Manu. (Agents in London, Krohn Brothers, 1 Bread St.)—Silk-shag hats, worked upon felt and chip; lady's riding hat, with veil.

179 PLESSNER, 'S. Berlin, Manu.—Doe-skin gloves. Washable kid gloves. Ornamented gloves, for ladies. Silk braces, &c.

180 WOLTER, G. C. Berlin, Manu.—Coloured kid gloves. Lambskin, deerskin, dress, and other gloves. All made of German leather.

181 SELDIS, C. Berlin, Manu. (Agent in London, C. SCHWEBEMEYER, 314 Oxford St.)—Assortment of felt hats, silk-shag hats; felt bonnets; imitation felt hats and bonnets. Several of these articles are made of new materials.

182 LIETZMANN, J. C. H. Rummelsburg, near Berlin, Manu.—Shoe vamps and legs: the leather from which these articles are cut is tanned by a patent process invented by the exhibitor, which renders it durable and waterproof.

183 MULLER, T. L. Berlin, Manu.—Boots for deformed feet. Feet and lasts modelled after nature.

184 PFEIFFER, C. Berlin, Manu.—Boots and over-shoes.

185 SCHNEIDER, F. Potsdam, Manu.—Lamb-skin and kid gloves.

186 VASSEL & Co. Berlin, Manu.—Silk hats. White and grey beaver hats. White, black, and natural beaver ladies' hats. Silk riding hats, for ladies.

186A MOHR, W. Berlin, Manu.—White satin boots. Boots of chamois and enamelled leather. Clogs. Calf-leather boots of ordinary appearance though fitted for a deformed foot.

187 HENKELS, J. A. Berlin and Solingen, Manu.—Cutlery manufactured of refined steel, the produce of the smelting works of Siegen.

188 BARDFELD, C. Posen, Manu. — Reindeer skin breeches. Doeskin gloves and braces. Leather braces. Knee girths.

189 ARNHEIM, S. T. Berlin (Agents, Krohn Brothers, 1 Bread St. London).—Iron-safe bureau: the large doors, cases, and locks open and shut, notwithstanding their great weight, with perfect ease. Exhibited for workmanship.

190 ZOBEL, W. Berlin, Manu.—Sliding and regulator lamps electro-plated. Brass lamps. Lamp with spring pressure. Lamp for cooking. Lanterns.

191 VON MINUTOLI, A. Councillor, Liegnitz, Prop.—Photographic copies of models for manufactories, executed by the photographer Birk, at Hirschberg. Phelloplastic model of the ruins of a Gothic church. Silesian marble slabs. Chimney-piece, brown glazed, to exhibit the application of clay formerly only used for pottery to finer objects. The designs and models by the exhibitor, and executed by Mr. Poehle. Crystal glass decanter, after a sketch by the exhibitor; executed by the glass-painter Finsch, at Warmbrum.

192 LOEFF, S. Berlin, Manu.—Porcelain coffee machines and teapots. Sliding and table-lamps. The porcelain made at the Royal Manufactory, Berlin.

193 GAERTNER, A. Stettin, Manu.—Cage for a parrot in Berlin silver.

194 KUMMER, K. W. Berlin, Inv.—Globe in relief, four feet diameter, on a pedestal.

195 ZOBEL, J. Berlin, Manu.—Varnished tin articles, representing Calla æthiopica, &c. in blossom. Embossed fruit-baskets. Bread-baskets, with pierced edges, and with fine network.

196 KOLESCH, D. Stettin, Manu.—Iron safe, the locks so constructed that they cannot be opened without the maker's explanations.

197 LEHMANN, A. F. Berlin, Manu.—Cast-iron balcony decoration, crucifix, and altar candlesticks. Various cast-iron large and small articles and ornaments.

198 LEWY BROTHERS, Frankfort-on-the-Oder, Manu.—A variety of tin and tin-plate articles.

199 STOBWASSER & Co. Berlin, Inv.—Japan articles, ornamented with paintings, &c. Lamps, in German silver, bronze, brass and composition, gilt, &c.

200 EGELLS, F. A. Berlin, Manu.—Cast-iron chimney piece, varnished; two side-pieces of cast-iron.

201 MUELLER, J. F. Müncheberg, Manu. — Leather bridles with steel bits and snaffles. Hunting-pocket, with a net.

202 SCHWARTZ, C. Berlin, Inv. and Manu.—Bracelets, a brooch, a pair of earrings, and a brooch, representing a combat between a lion and serpent, set with diamonds.

203 SCHNEIDER, F. Berlin, Inv.—Writing-stand, partly of gilt silver and partly of gold, under a glass cupola, upon a rosewood column. Daguerreotype plates, plated by galvanic process, and flattened without hammering.

204 WINTERFELD, J. A. Breslau, Manu.—Articles in yellow and white amber: vase of yellow amber; set of chess-men; set of ladies' ornaments; buttons for ladies' dresses; amber top with a meerschaum pipe, &c.

205 JANTZEN, G. E. Stolp.—A set of yellow amber ornaments chased with gold. Toilet table, bearing a tureen, two candlesticks, and six wine-glasses, all of yellow amber.

206 STRAHL, O. Frankfort-on-the-Oder, Manu. — Gilt and decorated fruit-vases. Coffee and tea-service. Cake-dishes, cabarets, &c. Assortment of white crockery ware of the best description.

207 WILLIAM BERGMANN, Warmbrunn, near Hirschberg, Silesia, Prod.—A collection of octagonal topazes. Large topaz seal-stamp. Topaz cane-heads.

208 THE GLASSWORKS OF THE COUNT OF SCHAFFGOTSCH, Josephinenhütte, near Warmbrunn, Silesia, Manu.—Flower decoration. Colossal ruby vases. Enamel-like flower vases. Aquamarin-enamel vases, with gilt decoration. Sugar-water set. Chalice-glasses, with carved arabesques, and with handles carved, &c.

209 WILLMANNS, C. W. Berlin, Manu.—Cut plate-glass, representing the theatre and the two turrets of the churches adjacent on the Gendarmes Square at Berlin.

210 COUNT SOLMS, Administration of his Glass-works, Baruth, near Berlin, Manu.—Samples of coloured glass. Lamp glasses; a variety of tumblers, wine, and champagne glasses. Coloured bottles; blue glass plate.

211 FINSCH, M. Warmbrunn, Silesia, Manu.—Punch-bowl, with cover, spoon, tray, and glasses. Vases of alabaster. Decanter, with glasses and tray. Wine-cup, with white opaque lines; and with deep and raised cut decorations upon a dull ground.

212 METZGER, U. & LUHME, J. F. Berlin, Manu.—Various glass articles for chemical or experimental purposes.

213 The ROYAL PRUSSIAN PORCELAIN MANUFACTORY, Berlin.—Vases, with paintings after Peter Vischer, Miéris, Slingeland, Von Klöber, and Bellermann. Chandeliers of a green mass, with biscuit-figures upon a bronze socket, and pedestal of gypsum-marble, with nineteen bronze candlesticks, and bronze lustres. Punch-bowl, with the painting of a drinking company, after Hogarth. Flower vessel, after Watteau. Octagonal dejeûner, of eight pieces, in lapis-lazuli ground, &c.

214 ACTIEN VEREIN, Wilhelmshütte, near Sprottau Manu.—An assortment of enamelled stoneware.

215 ALTMANN, J. G. Bunzlau, Manu.—Specimens of earthenware, including a coffee-pot to contain 200 cups.

216 FRANKENBERG, L. Count of, Tillowitz, near Oppeln, Manu. — Earthenware console, silvered. Fruit-baskets. Earthenware vases, silvered and gilt.

K

217 Mattschas, J. G. H. (Widow), and Son, Frankfort-on-the-Oder, Manu.—Crockery and earthenware, comprising consoles, lamps, vases, plateaus, and fruit shells, of clay in the vicinity of Frankfort.

218 Paetsch & Hintze, Frankfort-on-the-Oder, Manu. —A large assortment of earthenware crockery, manufactured from material found in Frankfort.

219 Tielsch. Ca⁻ ,and Co. Altwasser, Silesia, Manu.— Extensive assort ⌐n⌐ of painted and white porcelain china, made of the purest porcelain clay, and remarkable for its clear white and shining glaze. This china is known in all Germany, and is exported to Sweden, Denmark, Norw and North and South America.

220 Forster, F. Grueneberg, Silesia, Manu.—Woollen cloth. Spanish stripes. Ladies' cloth, lilac. Royal, or three-quarters and black fine cloth. Various samples of wool and yarn.

222 Bonge, A. L. Potsdam, Manu.—Figures and consoles, in stone and wood, carved, bronzed, and gilt.

223 Bauer, R. Schwerin-on-the-Warthe, Inv. and Manu. —Flower table, with a bird-cage of oak wood, in the gothic style.

224 Baumann, Louise, Berlin, Inv.—Fire-screen, with plush embroidery.

225 Zeisig, H. Breslau, Manu.—Bell-ropes of coloured silk, silk and gold, silk and silver.

226 Gropius, P. Berlin, Manu. (Agents, W. F. Sachse, 36 Trinity Sq. Bow, and Kingsford & Lay, London).—A wall ornament, consisting of figures upon brackets, looking-glasses, medallions, and sundry other articles in carton-pierre, with marble plate.

227 Muller, F. Berlin, Manu.—Samples of gilt frames, which have lasted seven years, and which were (with the exception of four corner pieces) gilt by a process that secures durability.

228 Stab, sen. C. G. Berlin, Manu. — Toilet-table of crown morocco leather and red velvet, exhibited for superior workmanship. Collection of fancy leather articles : exhibited for cheapness and solidity of workmanship.

229 Richt, G. Berlin, Manu. — Plate cabinet and étagère cabinet of rosewood richly carved: exhibited on account of their workmanship and the beauty of the wood.

230 Elsholz, F. Berlin, Manu.—Slabs of parquetted flooring.

231 Alberti Brothers, Waldenburg, Silesia, Prop.— Platilles royales, as exported to Mexico and the West Indies.

232 Becker, F. E. Berlin, Manu.—Easy chair, with mechanism, and a reading-desk attached.

233 Below, F. Berlin, Manu.—Pattern-card of papier-maché gilt cornices.

234 Bengen, D. Berlin, Manu.—Painted window-blinds in colours, and in sepia.

235 Cantian,—, Architect, Berlin.—Marble pedestal. Table-top of marble. Circular table-top of red granite. Large vase with pedestal.

236 Kuttner, A. Wolgast, Manu.—Linen press.

237 Schievelbein, J. F. E. Berlin, Manu.—Octagonal mosaic table of rare Indian woods. Samples of the wood. Easy chair capable of being taken asunder.

238 Sommerfeld & Hubner, Potsdam, Manu.—Round mahogany tables.

239 Wamp & Schroeder, Berlin, Manu.—Painted window-blinds.

240 March, E. Thiergartenfelde, near Charlottenburg, Manu.—A fountain, with group of children, &c. Gothic and Italian vases. Four figures of soldiers, at Berlin, with Gothic pedestal brackets manufactured out of highway dust. Mosaic slabs. Chemical apparatus.

241 Ungerer, C. Hirschberg, Manu.—Porcelain water-pipes.

242 Engeler & Son, H. M. Berlin, Manu.—An assort-ment of brushes of every kind and description. A plate with the royal Prussian arms, &c. formed of hair in the manner of brushwork.

243 Kersten, A. Berlin, Manu.—Papier-maché frames for daguerreotype pictures. Sundry articles, as pocket-books, cigar-cases, &c. used as frames for daguerreotype pictures.

244 D'Heureuse, C. Berlin, Manu.—Bonnets, of Brussels, Swiss, and Saxon straw; and Italian chip. Leghorn bonnet and table covers, the Prussian and Bavarian arms, embroidered with straw and Manilla hemp.

245 Dreusike, W. Neu Ruppin, Manu.—Writing-desk, with an iron safe and a clock. Ladies' casket. Work-table.

246 Koerner, M. Schönau, in Lower Silesia, Manu.— Basket, the mass of which is a composition of tin, lead, and glass, and consists of many thousand separate parts, which are soldered together and fastened upon wire rings.

247 Mess, L. & Co. Brandenburg, Manu.—Sample-card of wood lists-gilt.

248 Gebhardt, C. A. Berlin, Prod.—Portfolios and albums, in morocco and velvet. Pocket-books, cigar-cases, porte-monnaies, &c., with arabesques and medallions stamped upon the surface of the leather or velvet by a peculiar process.

249 Moniac, E. Berlin, Manu.—Samples of decorations in stamped paper. Gold-paper pressed objects. Sundry objects used in the cotillon dance. Wreaths, &c., composed of artificial paper flowers.

250 Wunder, L. Liegnitz, Manu. Inv. and Prop.— Sample of best tallow house-soap. Best palm-oil house-soap. Pine-apple soap, invented by the exhibitor.

251 Mossner, A. Berlin, Manu.—Purses, cigar-boxes, pocket-books, ladies' boxes, letter portfolios.

252 Gerlach, C. F. Naumburg on the Saal, Manu. (Agent in London, A. Heintzman, 17 Ironmonger Lane, Cheapside).—Paper boxes with tin toys.

253 Ringelhann, Hirschberg, Silesia, Manu. —Stuffed goat. ⁰ A stuffed colt, without a seam.

254 Daehmel, H. Quaritz, Province of Lower Silesia, Manu.—Specimens of soaps in various designs.

255 Sarre, H. jun. Berlin, Manu.—Green soap, with natural grain. White grain soap (Elain soap). Palm-oil soda soap. Tallow soap.

256 Bahn, A. E. Berlin, Manu.—Dolls of various kinds.

257 Wigdor, M. Berlin, Manu.—Umbrella and parasol sticks.

258 Tzitschke, Sorau, Manu.—Mother-o'-pearl buttons. Cocoa-nut, shell, and horn buttons.

259 Zeschke, L. Mullrose, near Frankfort-on-the-Oder, Manu.—Hunting and shooting bags. Hare and wildfowl bags. Large net bags.

260 Krebs, W. Berlin, Manu.—Purses, cigar and fuzee-boxes, pocket-books, spectacle-cases, ladies' boxes, card-cases, letter portfolios, and purses.

261 Krumteich, L. Schwiebus, Manu.—White wax baskets, with painted and gilt decorations. Coloured wax octagonal basket. Decorated wax tapers.

262 Motard, A. Berlin, Manu.—Samples of stearine from tallow, prepared in various modes. Stearine candles. Grease from palm-oil, and candles manufactured from the same, and with an exterior coat of stearine.

263 Palis, A. Berlin, Manu.—Tallow-oil and palm-soap. Tallow for candles, &c. The tallow used in these articles is of Prussian production; the palm-oil imported from Liverpool.

264 Schmerbauch, H. Berlin, Manu.—Cigar-cases, portfolios, embroidered card-holders, purses, pockets for keys, of straw and leather in combination.

265 Soehlke, G. Berlin, Manu.—Toys, an English regiment on parade in presence of Her Majesty Queen Victoria and of her royal suite, formed of painted pewter figures, &c.

266 FECHNER, F. Guben, Manu.—Gilt and ornamental borders. Artificial flowers and leaves. Gilt, silvered, and coloured paper. Articles used by bookbinders, leather-workers, confectioners, and perfume-makers.

267 GEISS, M. Berlin, Manu.—Statues cast in zinc: Eve, after Bailey. Boy with a Swan, after Kalide. Two stags, after Rauch. Niobe, after the antique. Hebe, after Canova, &c.

268 BERGMANN, L. Warmbrunn, Province of Silesia, Inv.—A landscape and several figures of animals, of very diminutive size, cut out of bone.

269 DAEHNS, A. Berlin, Inv. — Wreath of flowers, carved out of a solid piece of oak, applicable as a frame for a painting.

270 ALBERTY, J. Berlin, Inv.—Frame, carved in wood and gilt, after a drawing by Slüter; and Madonna, carved out of linden-wood; the property of H. M. the King of Prussia. Relief, carved in wood, representing Silenus inebriated, after the antique.

271 The ROYAL PRUSSIAN IRON FOUNDRY. Berlin—Group of figures in cast-iron. The Warwick vase, gilt inside. The Athenian vase, with figures and handles, and gilt inside. The Alexander vase, the border decorated with reliefs after Thorwaldsen, representing Alexander's entry into Babylon. Mounted with silver, and gilt inside.

272 EICHLER, G. Berlin, Inv. (Agents in London, Williams & Norgate, 14 Henrietta St. Covent Garden).—Bas-reliefs, in plaster of Paris, after Thorwaldsen. Plaster of Paris casts of antique and modern gems. Portraits and medallions, cast in plaster of Paris, after sculptures of German artists of the 16th century, &c.

273 DRAKE. PROF. F. Berlin, Inv.—Cast of size, of a part of the pedestal of the marble monument of Frederic William III. of Prussia, erected at Berlin. Boy reclining, in marble.

274 ENGEL, F. Berlin, Inv.—Model of Fresnil's undulating plain. Model of an ellipsoid.

275 MÖHRING, F. L. Berlin, Inv. — Electro-galvanic bust. Alto-relievo and table ornament, after Tieck, in two colours, electro silvered and gilt. Flower vases, &c.

276 LIEDEL, C. I. Warmbrunn, Inv.—Artificial compositions of moss and paper, representing Warmbrunn in Silesia, Kösen near Naumburg, the lead chambers at Venice, the Kochelfall, a mill on the hills. Chiefly made by the exhibitor himself.

277 KRUSE, C. B. Stettin, Inv.—Cork models of the gate at Basle; castle of Rheinstein on the Rhine; castle Langenau on the Lahn; ruin of the gate at Damascus; castle of Rhineck, &c.

278 KRAUSE, M. Berlin, Inv.—Casts of the Twelve Apostles, which were carved in onyx, and fixed in the shield, presented by the King of Prussia to the Prince of Wales. Bracelet of various pastes, with casts after gems in the Royal Prussian Collection, enchased in gold.

279 KISS, PROF. A. Berlin.—Group, in zinc, bronzed, representing an Amazon on horseback attacked by a tiger, after one cast in bronze in 1839, by a number of amateurs, and presented to the King of Prussia, and which was placed by his Majesty's command in front of the Royal Museum, Berlin, designed by the exhibitor, cast in zinc and bronzed over by M. Geiss, of Berlin, in his peculiar manner. Group in bronze, as above, on a small scale.

280 DEVARANNE & SON, Berlin, Inv.—Zinc casts:—Lion. Panther. Venus. Boy with a squirrel. Head of Paris. Stag's head, lion's heads. Assortment of fine cast-steel. Jewellery.

281 FISCHER. K. Berlin, Inv.—Portrait of Her Majesty the Empress of Russia (onyx). Various medals in bronze. Phrixus and Helle; relief in ivory. Original composition.

282 WINKELMANN, J. Berlin, Inv.—Statue of Frederick II., Elector of Brandenburg, produced by electrotype process. Trays; vine-bearer; large antique bowl; reliefs; chandeliers; candlesticks; candelabras, &c., all produced by the same process.

283 FRANZ, J. Berlin, Inv.—Model in plaster, a shepherd attacked by a leopard.

284 HAENEL, E. Berlin, Inv. (London agent, M. Kronheim, 32 Paternoster Row).—Specimens of bank-notes, labels, &c. in black, colours, and gold. Specimens of type. Brass types for bookbinders and gilders, and electro-types matrices for casting large types, &c.

285 KALIDE, T. Berlin, Inv.—Group: the Bacchants with the Panther. Cast of plaster of Paris from marble. A Boy with a Swan, in bronze, the property of H.M. the King of Prussia.

286 PFEUFFER, C. Berlin, Inv. — Various medals, in white and bronze metals.

287 MULLER, —. Berlin, Inv.—Ornamental castings in bronze: the Prince of Prussia, and Prince Albert of Prussia on horseback. A broken spider-web. These articles are unique, as the models did not admit of multiplication. The first two were finished in one casting, the others required two castings.

288 SONDERMANN, —, Artist of the Royal Academy, Berlin, Inv.—Stag's head, of plaster of Paris, saturated with wax and varnish. Buck's head, of stone.

289 FRIBEL, L. Berlin, Sculp.—Newfoundland dog in bronze, after the model of Moëller, and figure base, cast in one piece, and has not been retouched by the chisel. Bronze figure with pedestal representing Hope; after the model of Rauch, cast and chiselled by the artist.

290 HEYMANN, C. Berlin, Prop.— Architectural works. Map of Berlin, Potsdam, &c., exhibited as specimen of lithography.

291 SEELING, G. W. Berlin, Inv.—Front of the Royal Arsenal, Berlin, employed in 1844 as the emporium of the great German Exhibition. The principal material is paper; moulds for the bas-reliefs. &c., cut by the medalist Fischer.

292 MOELLER, C. Berlin, Inv.—Bronze groups: Boy with a Newfoundland dog; Girl with a bull-dog.

293 FRANZ, J. Berlin, Inv.—Bronze figures of Victory after the original of Rauch. Bronze figure: Victory recording her heroes.

294 FADDERJAHN, B. Berlin, Inv.—Casts from moulds used in the manufacture of ornamental paper and of embossed silver. Bronze cast of a gothic bas-relief, in commemorative of the union of the German Princes for the completion of the cathedral at Cologne, after a drawing by Prof. Hoffstadt of Munich.

295 BIANCONI, F. Berlin, Inv.—Marble busts; Shepherd after Thorwaldsen; Paris after Canova; Venus after Thorwaldsen.

296 FISCHER, C. H. Berlin, Inv.—Figures in bronze: Eagle; a Girl praying; a Danaïde.

297 DIETRICH, F. Berlin, Inv.—Two heads of children at play, in Carrara marble.

298 FRUH, G. Berlin, Inv. — The Butterfly catcher, cast in bronze.

299 KESSLER, C. Griefswald. — Bronze full length statue of the muse Polyhymnia, after the antique statue of the Royal Museum, Berlin.

300 KONARZEWSKI, A. Berlin, Sculp.—A bronze group representing a child with a clock, modelled by Albert Wolff, sculptor and member of the senate of the Academy of Fine Arts at Berlin.

301 MANSIS, H. Berlin, Inv.—Collection of models for gilders, in a composition of sulphur.

302 RUNGE, Dr. Oranienburg, Inv.—Paintings produced by chemical action; process applicable to the purposes of painters, designers, and calico printers. A new invention.

303 SCHROPP, SIMON, & Co. Berlin, Publishers.— Copper

K 2

plate printed maps. Lithographic printed and coloured maps, and geological maps by the most eminent artists of Berlin.

304 STETTER, C. G. Breslau, Prop.—Model of an old Greek theatre, made of paper.

305 SUSSMANN, L. Berlin, Inv.—Model of the obelisk of Luxor, at present on the Place de la Concorde, at Paris; electrotype and gilt. The electrotype art has here been employed to exhibit the plaster of Paris model with accuracy; this is difficult to attain in the ordinary process of casting, from the shrinking of both the mould and the metal

306 WINKELMANN & SONS, Berlin, Inv.—Lithographic prints; coloured and executed by the exhibitors.

307 WOLFF, A. Berlin, Des.—Marble statue: Girl with Lamb.

308 ZEBGER, F. W. Berlin, Glass-painter.—Ten panes of painted glass.

309 BERNHARD AFINGER, J. Berlin.—Bronze portraits: Prince of Prussia, Princess of Prussia, General Wrangel, and Professor Rauch. Bronze statuette: Virgin and Infant, invented and executed in bronze by the exhibitor, and chiselled by Mr. Mertens, the artist of the "Shield of Faith" (presented by the King of Prussia to the Prince of Wales).

310 BLAESER, G. Berlin, Inv. and Mod.—Statue of Louis van Beethoven, in bronze. Equestrian statue of the Empress of Russia, in bronze. The chasings by A. Konarzewski, academical artist.

310ASIEMENS & HALSKE, Berlin, Pro. and Pat.—Electric telegraphs in operation. Siemens' patent indicating telegraph in connexion with a pair of two printing instruments, and an intermediate excluding instrument with alarum. (These telegraphs are distinguished for requiring but one line wire; that each instrument breaks and recloses its own contact, and worked by the electric current only, without clock-work or other mechanical aid whatever.) Siemens' railway telegraphs. New single wire telegraph by Siemens and Halske. Improved Morse's telegraph, worked by secondary power. Single wire, and a magneto-electric telegraphs. Pair of electroscopes, &c.

b. Grand Duchy of BADEN; Southern parts of the West Provinces of PRUSSIA and ELECTORAL HESSE.

311 BIEGEL, J. Bliessen, near St. Wendel.—Manganese in masses and in powder.

312 BISCHOF & RHODIUS, Linz, on the Rhine.—White lead and white zinc; Kremserweiss pure carbonate of lead. Hard and soft ceruse.

313 BLEIBTREU, L. Bonn.—Two cylindrical blocks of alum, common and refined. The Rhenish alum is usually conveyed in crystallized cylindric blocks without any external case to protect them.

314 BRASSEUR & Co. Cologne, Inv. and Manu.—Oxidized plates of lead. The exhibitors state that, by adopting precautionary measures, they prevent the noxious effects of the manufacture.

315 BREDT & Co. Stolberg.—Ores of zinc and lead; Willemite and calamine, from the mine Bushbacherberg. Chlorophosphate of lead. White lead, carbonate of lead, and sulphuret of lead from the mines of Busbacher and Zufriedenheit, &c. Zinc from Steinfurth.

316 MEINERZHAGEN, & KREUSER BROTHERS, Mechernich and Commern.—Lead-ore, from the mines of the Count Lippe, and of the Messrs. Kreuser, on the Lead Mount in the Eiffel country. Metallic lead, shot, &c.

317 PORZELT & HARPERATH, Cologne, Manu.—Richly ornamented white marble chimney-piece, in renaissance style. Slab of coloured marble.

318 SOCIETE DES MINES ET FONDERIES D'ESCHWEILER, Stolberg—Samples of lead and zinc ore. Piece of silver, weight about 11 lbs. Spelter, and refined lead.

319 VON MULMANN, A. Plato Zeche, Prop.—Specimens of peat. Fire clay and fire brick. Crucible.

320 WALDTHAUSEN, O. W. Clarenburg.—White lead; exhibited for beauty and cheapness of manufacture.

321 LANDAU, S. Coblenz and Andernach, on the Rhine. —Lava millstones, from the lava quarries of Nieder Mendig, near Andernach on the Rhine. They can be procured as large as 6 feet in diameter, and 18 inches thick. The quarries are supposed to have been worked for twenty centuries.

322 HAGEN, F. Cologne.—Ores of zinc; calamine from Margaretha Josephe mine at Bergisch, Gladbach, near Mülheim on the Rhine; and spelter—fair average specimens of the produce of the mine.

323 KOENIG, G. Treves.—Sandstone for buildings and sculpture. Specimen from Udelfangen, very strong; from Aix, and of the same sort as that used by the Romans for the Porta Nigra, at Treves; from Lorich, Menningen, Wasserlisch, and Tawern.

324 STEELWORKS, Lohe, near Siegen.—Specular steel-iron, produced from carbonated iron ore. Pig-iron. Iron ore, to be used in the production of natural steel. Natural steel.

325 WEBER, C. Mannheim, Manu.—Rough pebbles, taken from the bed of the Rhine, cut as diamonds. Exhibited for the cutting, which caused the exhibitor a twelve-month's incessant labour.

326 ROYAL MINES AT LOHE, near Siegen.—Sparry and brown iron-stone from the blast-furnace. Hydrated oxide iron ore.

327 MARQUARDT, Dr. L. C. Bonn.—Chloroform, sulphuric ether, concentrated acetic acid, and other chemicals.

328 PAULI, O. Carlsruhe, Manu.—Specimens of prussiate of potash, sal-ammonia, muriate of ammonia, and phosphorous.

329 KOCH, C. A. Gladbach, near Mülheim on the Rhine. —Superfine post paper. Paper for mercantile books. Plate paper for copper-printing and lithography. Carton papers.

330 EIPENSCHLEID, L. Neuwied, Manu.—Potato flour.

331 WELCKER, A. C. Wallersheim, near Coblenz, Manu. —Farina, or improved potato flour; the same, ground. Extensively used for stiffening muslins, &c.

332 WAHL, F. Neuwied.—Sago and potato flour. Manufactured without the use of any chemical substance.

333 WEERTH, A. & Co. Bonn.—Samples of potato flour.

334 WIESMANN, A. & Co. Augustenhütte, near Bonn.— Mineral oil, bituminous paper coal, fossil black, paraffine, and fire-lac.

335 FLOCKENHAUS & Co. Cologne.—Coloured flock wool; printed half wool and silk; and merino wool. Nap tincture, used in the treatment of linen and cotton threads in all dark-coloured cloth.

336 LOOSEN, J. G. Cologne.—Samples of Cologne glue.

337 ROMER, C. Brühl, Manu.—Refined oil, obtained from bones and other animal substances, and which remains fluid till the thermometer sinks below zero.

338 GRUND, Karlsruhe.—Two pictures painted with new proceedings.

339 HOMBERG & SCHEIBLER, Eupen.—Specimens of buckskin and ladies' cloth.

340 MENGELBIER, J. Aix-la-Chapelle, Manu.—Carriage, called calash, with Collinge's patent springs of English steel; the body of mahogany panels, the inside lined with Lyons silk.

341 MIES, J. Cologne, Manu.—Various trusses and bandages, exhibited for their simplicity and cheapness.

342 RICHARD, L. Berlin & Locle Neufchatel, Inv. and Manu.—A ship's chronometer, and an explanatory plan, being a novel invention.

343 DORER, M. Baden, Manu.—A seconds-watch, made of ivory, with gold screws and steel moving power. It

works in ten rubies, and weighs, glass and vase included, only half an ounce. Another, weighing five-eighths of an ounce.

344 BAUNSCHEIDT, C. Endenich, near Bonn, Inv.—"Life-animators, new instruments for the medical art." Artificial leech.

345 ROLFFS & Co. Cologne, Manu. — Printed calicoes and handkerchiefs.

346 WAGNER & SON, Aix-la-Chapelle, Manu.—Twelve pieces of woollen cloth.

347 CHRISTOFFEL, L. Montjoie, near Aix-la-Chapelle, Manu.—Woollen buckskins for winter and summer.

348 ELBERS, J. H. Montjoie, near Aix-la-Chapelle, Manu.—Fancy cassimeres of 56 inches and 28 inches.

349 JANSEN, J. W. Montjoie, Manu.—Woollen stuff for summer paletots. Woollen summer buckskin, worked with silk. Woollen winter buckskin, manufactured chiefly from wools of Silesia.

350 OFFERMANN, F. W. Imgenbruch, near Aix-la-Chapelle, Manu.—Coloured buckskin.

351 MERKELBACH & SON, Montjoie, near Aix-la-Chapelle, Manu.—Winter, summer, and fancy buckskins.

352 MULLER, M. W. Montjoie, near Aix-la-Chapelle. Manu.—Winter and summer buckskin. Summer paletot of Australian wool.

353 SAUERBIER, J. A. Montjoie, Manu. — Winter, summer, and fancy buckskin.

354 SCHEIBLER, F. J. Montjoie, near Aix-la-Chapelle, Manu.— Summer buckskins. Flannel, made from yarn, which is a mixture of silk-waste and wool. Hitherto, silk and wool have only been used together twisted, or the warp was silk and the weft woollen. The peculiarities of this article are, that the silk and wool are more solidly united, and may be spun finer than when alone. Jacquard designs for winter goods.

355 ULLENBERG & SCHNITZLER, Opladen, near Cologne, Manu.—Woollen yarns, and knitting worsted yarns of various colours. Patterns of screws: the wire produced from Rhenish and Westphalian iron.

356 MENZERATH, J. Imgenbruch, near Aix-la-Chapelle, Manu. (Agents in London, Droin, Crüger, & Co., 47A Moorgate St.)—Black cassimeres (satin-de-laine) manufactured from Silesian wools.

357 HAAS & SONS, Borcette, near Aix-la-Chapelle, Manu. (Agent in London, H. Hoffman).—White cloth; white cassimere for court waistcoats; white satin for court dress; satins; and doeskins.

358 VISSEUR, P. Aix-la-Chapelle, Manu.—Doeskins and ladies' cloth.

359 ZAMBONA, J. & G. Burtscheid near Aix-la-Chapelle, Manu. (Agent in London, A. Heintzmann, 17 Ironmonger Lane, City.)—Winter Cashmeres; demi-saison and summer; black winter and summer tricots.

360 ANDREAE, C. Muelheim-on-the-Rhine, near Cologne, Manu.—Velvets: German, Lyons and Genoa styles; mantilla. Black figured velvet shawl. Worsted plush, for furniture &c.

361 VILLEROY & BOCH, Wallerfangen Mettlach, near Treves, and Mannheim, Manu.—Fine stone-wares, decorated with ornaments of the same material, but differently coloured with platina gold and paintings. Common and fine potterywares. Kitchen pottery of black material, with white enamel, called iron-ware.

362 BOEHME, C. L. Aix-la-Chapelle and Imgenbruch, Manu.—Cashmere cloth—Pensée, black, and olive.

363 BRUEGMANN & Co. Borcette, near Aix-la-Chapelle.—Thin and heavy fancy Cashmeres. Mohair headings. Mohair cloth of fine twisted yarns.

364 FEAUX & RIEDEL, Aix-la-Chapelle, Manu.—Russia cloth, bronze, for riding-coats. Piece of wool satinor; black croisé; and black royal Cashmere.

365 SCHOELLER, J. P. Düren, Manu.—Wool-dyed black superfine cloth; wool-dyed blue marine cloth. Black superfine satin-de-laine. Made and finished after the English methods.

366 HAAN, C. & SONS, Moselkern, near Coblenz, Manu.—Woollen coverlets, viz. :—White blanket, with red stripes. White and red check blanket. Horse-cover. Ordinary grey blanket, &c.

367 HENDRICHS, FRANCIS, Eupen, near Aix-la-Chapelle, Manu.—Specimens of fine and superfine cloths.

368 PAULI & BUCHHOLZ, Borcette, near Aix-la-Chapelle, Manu.—Black royal; croisé; Cashmere; satin; and satin tigre.

369 PEILL & Co. Düren, Manu.—Wool-dyed cloth: Blue Grecian, olive, and royal blue. Raw material. Silesian wool.

370 KAYSER, A. Aix-la-Chapelle, Manu.—Thin twilled cloth, and ladies' cloth.

371 KESSELKAUL, J. H. Aix-la-Chapelle, Manu. (Agent in London, A. Heintzmann, 17 Ironmonger Lane, City.)—Black twilled cloth, plain cloth, and doeskin.

372 KLEINSCHMIDT & VON HALFERN, Burstcheid, near Aix-la-Chapelle, Manu.—Drap croisé noir Electoral. D'Amazone Corinthe. All piece-coloured, and manufactured exclusively from German wool.

373 KNOPS BROTHERS, ALOYS, Aix-la-Chapelle, Manu.—Black cloth, plain and twilled; and black doeskin.

374 SCHOELLER & SONS, Düren, Manu.—Woollen cloths : Wool-dyed blue cloth; pomme de rhône; black. Sourier. Claret. Raisix de Corinthe. Crêpe de laine, broncé d'or, blue.

375 THYWISSEN BROTHERS, Aix-la-Chapelle, Manu.—Light twilled cloth; doeskin; paletot; tricot; fancy and silk twisted, and Cashmere.

376 STERNICKEL & GUELCHER, Eupen, near Aix-la-Chapelle, Manu.—Black twilled cloth.

377 PASS, C. G. Remscheid, Manu.—Silk ferret and floret twilled and silk ribbons. Coloured twilled; black shining; reddish twilled floret; white twilled; and coloured fine floret silk braid. Black shining Renforce silk laces.

378 ANTHONI, A. Aix-la-Chapelle, Manu. — Various specimens of black cloth

379 ANDREAE, C. Mülheim-on-the-Rhine, near Cologne Manu.—Velvet ribbons. Gilets velours, double stamped—a new article. Gilets velours chiné; figured velvet; and silk plush.

380 FELTEN & GUILLEAUME, Cologne, Manu.—Iron-wire ropes manufactured from German iron-wire. Ropes, cords, and threads, manufactured from Manilla, Rhenish, Russian, and Italian hemp. Samples of starch, manufactured of wheat.

381 FEDERER BROTHERS, Freyburg, in Baden, Manu. Black polished calf-skin leather. Boot leather. Boot-piece of calf-skins leather.

382 HEINTZE & FREUDENBERG, Weinheim, Manu. (Agent in Liverpool, Mr. L. Heintze, 1 School Lane).—Calf-skins, japanned black, and black polished, for boots and shoes.

383 OBERCONZ, H. Treves, Manu.—Skins of Morocco leather. The tanning has been effected by aspen and birch, till now not used in the department of Treves. German and Java upper leather; calf leather; leather for soles, tanned with the inner and smooth bark of the oak.

384 WEBER, W. St. Vith, Manu.—Hide of a Java black calf's skin, entirely tanned in five months.

385 BERRES, M. Treves, Manu.—Leather, consisting of hides tanned with bark from the environs of Triers.

386 BUSCHMANN, J. W. St. Vith, Manu.—Hide of leather for soles; tanned skin of a Buenos Ayres ox.

387 CAHEN LEUDERSDORFF, A. T. Mülheim.—Specimen of neat's leather and calf leather; and pair of boot legs.

388 WEILAND, Cassel, Manu.—Brace of pistols, with complete apparatus in a case.

389 ENGEL P. H. Hanau, Inv. and Manu.—Proof prints, by an improved printing press, with some original stamps.

390 Sommer, J. Heidelberg, Manu.—Portfolio and writing apparatus. Glove-case, velvet, and ivory. Small writing-desk, papier-maché. Ladies' work-box. Pocketbook, &c.

391 Karcher, F. Carlsruhe, Inv. and Manu.—Pouncepaper, or transparent tracing, drawing, and modelling paper, made by a peculiar and patent process.

392 Hoesch & Son, Duren, Manu.—Tissue paper in different colours. Coloured and white post, and other writing paper.

393 Schuell, L. Duren, Manu.—Thick and extra thick post-paper (glazed) in folio, &c.; large blue post; ribbed medium, &c.

394 Piette, L. Dillingen, Manu.—Post and other writing paper.

395 Flammersheim, W. Cologne, Manu.—Rolls of tapestry, copied from original paintings.

396 Meixel, A. Baden, Manu.—Knitted linen shawls, made with two needles, and of one thread.

397 Roessler, C. H. Hanau, in Hesse, Manu.—Felt and silk hats, particularly adapted for exportation.

398 Leimkueler, Aix-la-Chapelle, Manu.—Black felt hat; black soft short-haired hat; grey hat, double rings; black silk.

399 Shuetzendorff, H. F. Cologne, Manu.—Gentlemen's ball-room boots, with silken upper stuff; boots in buckskin stuff, without seam; and boots for children.

400 Kohlstadt, L. Cologne, Manu.—Braces and garters, of silk and caoutchouc.

401 Wahlen & Schmidt, Cologne, Manu.—Kid gloves, and card of patterns.

402 Schön, P. St. Goar, Manu.—Saws for goldsmiths, silversmiths, carpenters, and comb-makers; made of steel procured from watch-spring factories in Switzerland and France. The teeth of the compass-saws filed with English files, which only can be used for that purpose.

403 Ulrich, J. St. Goar, Manu. — Saws for the use of goldsmiths, silversmiths, girdlers, comb-makers, turners in ivory, and joiners. Those for sawing wood and horn are made of broad white spring-steel; and those for sawing metals of old watch-springs.

404 Reinecker & Co. Cologne, Manu.— Samples of pins, hooks and eyes, and elastic wires, representing Gothic arches, bearing the arms of the city of Cologne.

405 Schleicher, C. Bellevallée, near Aix-la-Chapelle, Manu.—Galvanized cast-steel wire. Various wire rings, and samples of unfinished and finished needles. The raw material is of English origin.

406 Assmann, J. Neuwied-on-the-Rhine, Manu.—Articles made of rolled sheet iron, and tinned with Banca tin.

407 Beissel (Widow) & Son, Aix-la-Chapelle, Manu.—Samples of needles, manufactured of cast-steel, from the works of Sanderson Brothers and Co. Sheffield, and rolled and drawn into wire in Germany. Fancy bodkins, knitting pins, &c.

408 Kaesen, J. Cologne, Manu.—Iron decorated mantle ovens.

409 Juenger, Jacob's Widow, Hanau, Manu. — An assortment of samples of enamel, in a great variety of colours.

410 Steinhaeuer & Bier, Hanau, Hesse, Inv. and Manu.—Jewellery, consisting of brooches, bracelets, and rings.

411 Backes, J. F. & Co. Hanau Hesse Inv. and Manu. (London Agent, T. Sachs, St. George's Ter. Hyde Park.) —A large assortment of jewellery.

412 Weishaupt, C. M. Sons, Hanau (Agent, R. Phillips, Messrs. Phillips & Son, 31 Cockspur St. London.)—Set of chess-men and board, in silver and gold in renaissance style, ornamented with enamel, precious stones, and pearls. The chief figures are portraits of the Emperor Charles V. and his daughter Margaretha of Parma, a stadt-

holder of the Netherlands, King Francis I. of France, and his sister Margaretha of Valois: the chess-board mother-of-pearl and turtoiseshell. Casket in silver, with a coral tree, various precious stones, and four malachite slabs.

413 Haulick, G. F. Hanau, Manu.—Flower, in brilliants and rubies, with leaves of emerald and enamel, in a vase of gold and enamel. The flower can be detached, and used as a brooch or hair-pin.

414 Wagner, A. Sulzbach, near Saarbrück, Prod.—Bottles, manufactured for Rhenish sparkling wine; for hock, with flat bottom and ribbed neck; and with concave bottom and smooth neck, &c.

415 Wiegandt, J. Cologne, Manu.—Circular tablet, of mosaic-work, composed of 24,700 pieces. Specimens of inlaid work for floors.

416 Kramer, C. A. Cologne, Inv.—Cornice, and ornaments in stucco.

417 Engelhard & Karth, Mannheim, Manu.—Several specimens of stained paper.

418 Noe, O. Hanau, Hesse, Manu.—A model of a chandelier, in gypsum.

419 Faller, Tritscheller, & Co. Lenzkirch in the Black Forest, Manu.—A variety of straw hats for gentlemen, youths, and children, of different styles. Round, flat, and square cigar-cases.

420 Neess, A. F. Cologne, Manu.—Samples of patent flat or curved wood mouldings, chiefly employed for making frames, and by upholsterers, decorators, &c.

421 Pallenberg, H. Cologne, Manu.—Lady's escritoire of rosewood, with carvings, containing secret drawers curiously arranged.

422 Kendall, H. Cologne, and Aix-la-Chapelle (Agent, Jos. Kendall, 8 Harp Lane, Great Tower St. London).—Cologne water, pomatum, sachets, assorted perfumes, samples of toilette soap, &c.

423 Leven, F. Heidelberg, Inv. and Manu.—A large collection of heads, &c. of animals.

424 Spendeck, P. & Co. 18 Grosse Neugasse, Cologne. —Samples of Eau de Cologne.

425 Martin, M C. Cologne.—Eau de Cologne. Carmelite spirit of melissa.

426 Farina, J. M. 4 Julich Pl. Cologne.—Various specimens of Eau de Cologne.

427 Herstatt & Co. Cologne.—Cologne water of different qualities.

428 Moosbrugger & Kobbe, Coblenz, Manu.—Table slabs of artificial marble (mosaic). Cash-box of the same.

429 Weygold, A. Eckelenz, Inv.—Tapestry: Ruth and Boaz; in 4,860 squares.

430 Heckel, C. F. Mannheim, Collector and Preserver of Plants.—Picturesque group of dried Alpine plants. A volume containing a collection of 25 specimens of Alpine plants. The pictures are formed solely of plants, as produced by nature, without colours or dyes.

431 Cauer, C. & Robert Brothers, Creuznach, Inv.—Statue: Arminius, prince of the Cheruskers, a hostage at Rome, full-length figure, a compound of plaster, copper deposited by galvanism, and Carrara marble. A faun, carrying a vine-branch, a compound of gypsum, copper, and Carrara marble.

432 Dickert, T. Bonn, Manu.—Relief maps of the Siebengebirge, on the Rhine, and of Mount Vesuvius. Intended to illustrate the geological and orographical relations of the respective regions.

---

c. Provinces of PRUSSIA and LITHUANIA.

433 Sauken, A. von, Julienfelde, Prod.—Two wool fleeces.

434 Waechter, J. Tilsit, Prod. and Manu. (Agent in

London, A. Gubba).—Linseed and rape-seed cake. Grained and powdered animal charcoal. Scum of sugar for manure.

435 HERMANN, C. Danzig, Manu.—A pair of bronze chandeliers.

436 LIECK, A. Marienwerder, Manu.—Coffee machine and teapots, particularly fitted for travelling, being of small size and easily heated. A machine for mashing almonds for marchpanes.

437 LOEWENSON, M. Tilsit, Manu.—A tower in filigree work set with garnets, similar to those used by the Russian Jews at the celebration of the Sabbath.

438 MANNHEIMER. W. Königsberg, Prop.—Two pieces of amber of 6 and 4½ pounds weight, exhibited on account of their size and beauty.

439 HOFFMANN, C. W. Danzig, Manu.—Sundry articles manufactured from amber; beads of the same, exhibited on account of their beauty and workmanship, and to show the difficulty of joining small pieces; the uniformity of colour is very difficult to obtain. The beads are sent to show the way in which they are prepared and packed for the trade.

440 HOFFMANN, G. I. Danzig, Manu.—Assortment of amber beads and sundry articles manufactured from amber.

441 ROY, W. VON, Danzig, Manu. and Collector.—A cabinet containing amber (raw) arranged according to natural history, which it has taken 25 years to collect. A tea-tray ornamented with the arms of Great Britain. Snuff-boxes. A hilt of a dagger. Brooches. Bracelets and seals. All manufactured from amber, and ornamented with silver.

442 REICHEL BROTHERS, Tilsit, Manu.—Various strings of musical instruments.

443 HEYDENREICH, Teacher at Tilsit, Prop.—A scene from sacred history carved in wood.

444 GRZYBOWSKI, Rev. Berent, Prop. — A carving of wood in a frame, representing a vase containing flowers, birds &c.

---

d. Northern Parts of Electoral HESSE, and of the PRUSSIAN WEST PROVINCES; Principality of LIPPE.

445 ROYAL PRUSSIAN SALT WORKS, Neusaltwerk, near Rehme.—Samples of salt, fine and middle grains, obtained from the soole (brine), gradually purified.

446 VORSTER, C. D. Eilpe, near Hagen, Prod. — Samples of rough or cast-iron, made malleable and decarbonised by a new process; stated to be rendered equal to steel. Adapted for cutlery.

447 LEHRKIND, FALKENROTH, & Co. Haspe, near Hagen, Manu. (Agent for London, E. Riepe, 38 Finsbury Sq.)—Rolled coops of steel, produced from German steel; bars of puddling and refined steel; patent waggon axle of refined steel.

448 STINNES, H. A. S. M. Muelheim on Ruhr, Prod.—Samples of coke, free from heterogeneous substances, manufactured from pit-coal of the Victoria Mathias Mine.

449 DRESLER, J. H. sen. Siegen, Manu. and Prod.—Samples of iron ore from Hohegrethe, Peterbach, St. Andreas, and Huth; all near Hamm. Laminated white cast-iron and mottled pig bar-iron.

450 THE UNITED COAL MINES (SAELZER and NEUACK), Essen, Prod.—Specimen of coal, considered to be more bituminous and to contain less sulphur than others of the district.

451 LAMBINON, ULRICH, & Co. Brilon, near Arnsberg.—Lead and silver ore; sulphuret of lead and zinc.

452 ROCHAZ & Co. Mulheim on Ruhr, Manu. (Agent in London, Rothschild).—White zinc, intended as a substitute for white lead. Samples of roasted zinc ore and spelter; of zinc ores and rolled zinc. The raw materials from native mines.

453 BOEING, ROEHR, & LEFSKY, Limburg, Prod.—Rolled and hammered pieces of puddling steel; round rolled and hammered samples of steel; made of German pig-iron, worked in puddling furnaces with pit-coal, and rolled or hammered as it comes out of the furnace. Exhibited in consequence of the assumed importance of the process.

454 HAMBLOCH, J. Crombach, near Siegen, Prop.—Iron ore, from the Müsen mines, with specimens of refined Müsen steel.

455 HANIEL, F. Ruhrort on the Ruhr.—Specimens of coal from Heinrich, Steingatt, Hagenbeck, Sälzer and Neuack, and Zollverein mines. Coke from Schölerpad, Sälzer, and Neuack.

456 HARKORT & SON, Wetter on the Ruhr, Manu.—Samples of German crude steel: best steel for knives; blister steel; common steel, for files; spring steel, and steel for hatchets.

457 KRIMMELBEIN & BREDT, Barmen.—Samples of red prussiate of potash; cyanide powder; extract of archil; safflower carmine; indigo; catechu; stannate of soda; tin powder, &c.

458 CURTIUS, J. Duisburg on Rhine.—Blue and green ultramarine, used by printers, painters, varnishers, and for tapestry; they resist alum, and improve by exposure to the air.

459 GUTHEIL & Co. Dusseldorf, Prod.—Specimen of prussiate of potash (ferrocyanide of potassium).

460 STOHMANN & WUSTENFELD, Neusalzwerk, near Minden, Manu.—Chemical products from the mother ley of the salt-works near Minden, chiefly combinations of bromine.

461 WESENFELD & Co. Barmen.—Samples of soda-ash, for glass manufacturers; caustic soda, from the red mother liquid of soda-ash, for soap-boilers; chloride of lime; antichlore, a preparation for neutralizing chloride of lime after bleaching, for paper-makers.

462 HORSTMANN & Co. Horst, near Steele, Manu.—Samples of azure-blue smalt. Samples of zaffre.

463 The ROYAL ALUM WORKS, Schwemsal, near Düben.—Refined and common potash-alum crystallized; containing only a small proportion of iron, and manufactured from native ores. Sulphuric acid clay, known in trade under the denomination of aluminas, which contains but little iron manufactured from native ores by exposure to the frost during the winter. Specimens of the alum schist, containing but little pyrites. Alum manufactured from alum schists, by simple exposure.

464 MATTHES & WEBER, Duisburg on Rhine, Manu.—Muriatic acid, exempt from iron and sulphurous acid. Bleaching powder. Sulphate of soda. Soda crystals, soda ash, carbonate of soda, caustic, soda, &c.

465 ELECTORAL MANUFACTORY, Schwarzenfels, Manu.—Blue colours, smalt; strewing blue; eschar and washing blue. Violet smalts; zaffres; nickel with ultramarine, &c.

466 SCHRAMM BROTHERS, Neuss on Rhine, Manu.—Dressing-starch, for fine linen, cotton, and silk wares.

467 ROCHOLL, T. Minden, Imp. and Manu.—Various samples of cigars.

468 CARSTANJEN, A. F. jun. Duisburg, near Duesseldorf, Manu.—Samples of tobacco, snuff, and cigars. Raw materials from the East and West Indies and Wurtemburg. (Agent for London, Mess & Co.)

469 JAEGER, C. Barmen, Manu.—Extract of safflower, drawn from the pigment of safflower, and used to give silk, cotton, linen, paper, and artificial flowers a fine rose colour.

470 ELMENDORF, E. F. Isselhorst, near Bielefeld.—Samples of flax yarn and raw flax.

471 BECKER, SAPP, & Co. Fredeburg, Manu.—Pieces of extraordinary-sized amadou; yellow and black amadou. Caps, with and without peak, the raw materials brought from Illyria.

472 DIEPERS, T. B. Crefeld.—A machine for spooling silk. Model machine, with 40 reels, for twisting silk.

473 PIEPENSTOCK & Co. Hoerde, near Dortmund, Inv. and Manu.—A tubular axle, with two disc wheels for railroad waggons.

474 ERDELEN, C. Elberfeld, Manu. — "Stays" for weavers; these stays are made of cast steel, and are preferable to reeds in their effect on the fabrics.

475 UHLHORN, C. & G. Grevenbruch, near Dusseldorf, Manu. — Cards for combing silk, cotton, wool, and tow. Card sheets for main cylinder. The leather of these cards is obtained chiefly from Belgium and Germany, the iron wire almost exclusively from England, but a small part from France and Germany.

476 UHLHORN, H. Grevenbruch, near Dusseldorf, Manu. —Three engines, for coining, punching, and milling, the raw materials from England and Germany; from 45 to 50 coins may be struck in a minute with a moving power equal to that of one horse.

477 SPANGENBERG, SAUER, & STURM, Suhl. — Finished double gun, with bronze damask barrels and percussion locks, revolving safety stop, silver mountings, inlaid with hunting scenes on gold, &c. German silver ornaments and a powder-flask of stag-horn, in style of the middle age.

478 SCHALLER, C. Suhl, Manu.—Rifle, with cast-steel barrel, iron trimming. Gold hunting-piece, engraved, with iron spring lid; it is loaded at the stock, and has a contrivance for pointed bullets (*Spitz-kugeln*).

479 SAUER & SON, Suhl, Manu. — A double gun and single rifle. A single rifle ornamented with silver, with all appurtenances, in case.

480 SCHNITZLER & KIRSCHBAUM, Solingen, Manu. — Infantry and cavalry swords, cutlasses, and sabres; officers' highly-finished swords, with German silver and gilt mountings.

481 PISTOR, G. & W. Schmalkalden, Kurhesse, Manu. —Rifle-gun, with barrel of German cast-steel, complete.

482 SUESS, W. Marburg, Electorate of Hesse, Manu.—A very large thermo-electric battery, with an electro-magnet, a heating apparatus, and an apparatus for producing a chemical reaction.

483 SEEL, H. jun. Elberfeld, Manu.—Pharmaceutical apparatus, and chemical utensils, including measures, &c., of various sizes.

484 SCHRÖDTER, E. Dusseldorf, Manu.—A silk-drying and weighing machine, and a machine for accurately ascertaining the weight of silk in bales, &c., by small samples, upon the Talabot system. This machine has a balance of extreme delicacy of adjustment. A 6-inch theodolite, with telescope magnifying 30 diameters, &c.

485 LAMPFERHOFF, F. & A. Essen.—Newly constructed solo clarionet. Solo flute. Military band clarionet.

486 HEITEMEYER, T. Muenster, Manu. and Inv.—A patent table pianoforte.

487 ADAM, G. Wesel-on-Rhine, Manu. (Agents in London, Mess & Co.)-Grand pianoforte; oblique pianoforte.

488 WIEDEMANN, PFERDMENGES, & SCHMOELDER, Rheidt, Manu. -Various samples of cotton twist.

489 KLÖPPER, H. Wellentrupp, near Oerlinghausen, Manu.—Piece of linen, made of hand-spun yarn, exhibited for durability, &c.

490 BOLTEN, WILL. & SON, Kettwich-on-Ruhr. — Samples of woollen cloths: Black doeskin, and drab doeskin, mixed grey, crossed-bar buckskin, doeskin, and black and white summer buckskin.

491 BRAUN BROTHERS, Hersfeld, Hesse. — Woollen clotns. Light blue; dark green; dark blue; bronze cloth; and black cloth, satin de laine.

492 TESCHENMACHER & KATTENBUSCH, N. E. Werden-on-Ruhr, Manu.—Woollen cloth, with and without gloss; the two materials from Silesia.

493 JOHANNY-ABHOE, A. W. A. Hückeswagen, Manu.—Woollen cloth of various colours.

494 BEECK (VAN DER), J. C. Dusseldorf, Manu.—Square shawls, all woollen; long shawls. Comforters. Woollen goods for ladies' dresses and cloakings; exhibited for quality and novelty.

495 WIESE BROTHERS, Werden-on-Rhur, Manu.—Woollen cloth, manufactured from Silesian wool.

496 SCHUERMANN & SCHRÖDER, Lennep, Manu.—Samples of black cloth; the same twilled; mulberry and blue cloth, dyed in the wool.

497 OELBERMANN, D. SONS, & Co. Lennep, Manu.—Specimens of black and invisible green woollen cloths.

498 HILGER BROTHERS, Lennep, near Dusseldorf, Manu. —Samples of twilled fine cloths, dyed in the wool, &c.

499 HUECK, D. & A. Herdecke-upon-Ruhr.—Various specimens of woollen cloth: Dahlia, blue, and black.

500 HUFFMANN BROTHERS, Werden-on-Ruhr.—Piece of woollen cloth, made of Silesian wool.

501 MOLL, C. Hagen. (Agent in London, J. H. Cohn, 3 Fenchurch Buildings.)—Samples of woollen cloth, black, indigo wool-dyed, marine blue, and mulberry. Raw materials from Saxony and Silesia.

502 MERTEN, J. F. Urdenbach, near Dusseldorf, Manu. —Striped flannels, and striped moltongs; made from German wools and English cotton yarn.

503 SCHNABEL BROTHERS, Hückeswagen, Manu. — Various specimens of blue and black woollen cloths.

504 SCHEIDT, GEBRUDER, & Co. Kettwig-on-Rhur, Manu. —Samples of black grey marengo, and striped woollen cloth.

505 SCHEIDT, J. W. Kettwig-on-Rhur.—Specimens of black satin de laine; black doeskin de laine; grey satin and blue doeskin de laine; all woollen.

506 CLARENBACH & SON, Hückerswagen.—Samples of carded woollen yarn. Patterns of iron screws. The screws exhibited for the clearness and sharpness of the worm, or thread.

507 FEULGEN BROTHERS, Werden-on-Ruhr, Manu.—Woollen cloth: Indigo blue cloth dyed in the wool; marine cloth; and black cloth; for the North German markets.

508 FORSTMANN & HUFFMANN, Werden-on-Ruhr, Manu. —Woollen cloths; black and green cloths.

509 DIERGARDT, F. Viersen, near Crefeld, Manu.—Specimens of black and coloured velvet, silk, and silk and cotton; moleskin, plush, waistcoat velvets, figured velvet ribbons, printed velvet collars, velvet scarfs, black satin stuff, &c.

510 DUYN, HIPP, & Co. Crefeld, Manu.—Silk for dresses and parasols. Patterns of silk parasol and dress stuffs.

511 STORK, P. Crefeld, Manu.—Silk wares: Coloured and black silk. Superior satin. Silk and satin cravats. Shawls and waistcoats.

512 KERKHOFF (VAN DEN) & KREITZ, Crefeld, Manu.—Various silk stuffs for parasols.

513 SIEBEL, C. W. & BRINCK, Elberfeld, Manu.—Patterns of ribbons and trimming.

514 SIMONS, J. (Heirs of), Eberfeld, Manu.—Silk shawls, scarfs. Ladies' neckerchiefs. Black sarcenet kerchiefs. Silk cravats. Waistcoats. Silk handkerchiefs (German web), (Indian web), and (imitation web). Silk velvet, and silk and half silk stuffs.

515 SCHROERS, G. & H. Crefeld, Manu.—Fancy silk, fancy velvet, and plain velvet waistcoating; exhibited for design and quality.

516 RAPPARD & Co., Crefeld, Manu.—Assortment of silk cravats.

517 RAPPARD & GOESMANN, Crefeld, Manu. — Velvet and silk goods: Jacquard velvet; levant; carré. Jacquard satin, &c.

518 PELTZER W. Rheydt, near Crefeld, Manu.—Velvet,

silk, and half-silk goods: Samples of velvet, satin waist-coating, and satin cravats.

519 HOENINGHAUS & SON, Crefeld, Manu.—An assortment of fancy silk velvet ribbons.

520 HERMES BROTHERS & WOLFFERS, Crefeld, Manu.— Silk wares: Silk for parasols; brocaded satin; figured satin; Jacquard figured satin; Jacquard satin, &c.

521 HEYDWEILLER & SONS, Crefeld, Manu.—Ribbons, silk, and silk and cotton; including black and coloured hat-bands, black and coloured edgings, and worsted braid.

522 NEUHAUS, H. T. Crefeld, Manu.—An assortment of coloured and printed silks.

523 NEVIANDT & PFLEIDERER, Mettmann, near Elberfeld, Manu.—Coloured silk aprons. Black and coloured silk fringed kerchiefs.

524 JACOBS & BERING, Crefeld, Manu.—Silk, satin, and damask umbrella stuffs. Silk parasol stuffs.

525 KAIBEL, J. Crefeld, Manu.—Silk and satin wares. Striped and printed gros de Naples; printed poult de soie, and satin de chiné, &c.

526 LINGENBRINK & VENNEMANN, Viersen (Agents in London, Walter & De Vos), Manu.—Specimens of black and coloured velvet, and velvet ribbons.

527 KRAUHAUS & KAUERTZ, Crefeld on the Rhine, Manu. —Satin for dresses; fine black satin. Black plain and fine satin, all silk. The plain satins, formerly made of silk, have of late been made of silk mixed with cotton, for the cheap markets.

528 KNUEPFER & STEINHAUSER, Greiz (Agent in London, C. Holland, 41 Finsbury Circus), Manu. — Specimens of Thibet, French blue, satin d'Espagne, grey satin herber, and satin rayé vent.

529 MEER & Co. Crefeld, Manu.—Silks for dresses, parasols, and umbrellas, with patterns.

530 MENGHIUS BROTHERS, Viersen, near Crefeld, Manu. —Silk and terry velvet, of different colours, and moleskin and stamped velvet. Silk ribbons.

531 LUMM & RUETTEN, J. W. Von, Crefeld, Manu.— Silk goods, of various descriptions.

532 MORGENROTH & KRUGMANN, Elberfeld, Manu.— Coloured velvets, including purple, royal blue, claret, green, crimson, embossed cérise, and violet.

533 GREEF, F. W. Viersen, Manu.—Silk for umbrellas and parasols. Patterns of silk and silk velvet and satin, for dresses and waistcoats, and cravats.

534 SCHEIBLER & Co. Crefeld, Manu.—Velvet ribbons; fancy ribbons, fringed; stamped velvet scarfs. Silk velvet. Plush for hats and caps. Watered silk. Striped and glazed silk. Black silk serge and lutestrings. Black silk for waistcoats.

535 BRUCK, H. VON, & SONS, Crefeld.—Fine black and coloured ribbon velvets, all silk. A variety of fancy and figured silk ribbon velvets. Plain silk broad velvets. Fancy silk velvet vestings.

536 BOVENSCHEN, H. & Co. Crefeld.—Silk fabrics used for ladies' dresses; exhibited for colour, design, and quality.

537 GERLICH & GREIFF, Elberfeld, Prod.—Spun silk buttons. Figured velvets. The stuff buttons woven of sewing silk and organzine. Tichleborn.

538 GROTE, H. G. Ronsdorf, near Elberfeld, Manu.— Silk ribbons. Silk and cotton hat-bands. Coat and other bindings. Tapes, braids, and cords of silk, silk and cotton, mohair, and wool.

539 BROCKMANN, F. Wellentrup, near Oerlinghausen, Lippe Detmold, Manu. — Piece of linen, exhibited for durability. Made by hand weavers, and bought from them at Oerlinghausen, and after being bleached is exported to almost all parts of the world.

540 VELHAGEN, W. R. Bielefeld.—Samples of bleached linen and handkerchiefs, made of hand-spun yarn.

541 MUELLER, J. G. Marl, near Recklinghausen, Manu. —Woven linen damask napkins, with the Counts of Westerhold, Wolf Metternich, Hompesk, and Baron Böselager.

542 WESSEL, F. W. Spenge, near Bielefeld, Manu.— Specimens of raw and bleached linen and handkerchiefs, made of hand-spun Westphalian flax.

543 WESTERMANN, A. H. & Co. Bielefeld and Cologne, Manu. (Agent in London, P. Amsel, 20 Providence Row, Finsbury Sq.)—Various samples of white bleached linen, manufactured from flax, spun by hand, woven on hand-looms, and bleached on grass.

544 WESTERMANN SONS, Bielefeld, Manu. — Samples of bleached and raw linen. Bleached cambric handkerchiefs. Damask table cloths with napkins; drilling and bleached table-cloths. Damask and drilling towels.

545 SCHWEMANN SONS, Lippstadt, Manu. — Various samples of twine, hand-spun. Exhibited for cheapness and quality.

546 The SPINNING SCHOOL, Heepen, Bielefeld.—Samples of flax yarn.

547 DOEBEL, H. J. Halle on the Saale, Manu.—Bell-ropes and ladies' pockets, of New Zealand hemp. Pressing-cloth, without seam, used in sugar manufactories. The raw machine-yarn is from Leeds.

548 DELIUS & SONS, E. A. Bielefeld, Manu.—An assortment of hand-spun linen and linen handkerchiefs: exhibited for the quality of the flax, the workmanship, and the bleaching.

549 EICKHOLT, A. HEIRS, Warendorf, Manu.— Brown and white linen table-cloths and napkins, with wreaths of flowers and views, viz.: Stolzenfels, Walter Scott's monument, the dome of Cologne, &c.

550 LANDWEHRMANN BROTHERS, Joellenbeck, near Bielefeld, Manu.—Specimens of bleached and raw linen made of hand-spun Westphalian flax: exhibited for durability and quality.

551 OLLERDISSEN, P. Urentrup, near Bielefeld, Teache for flax preparation.—Samples of flax.

552 KOENIGS & BUECKLERS, Duelken, near Dusseldorf, Manu.—Flax, thread, cord, staves for weavers. Samples of German flax. Patterns for paper, and imitation of oil-cloth, &c.

553 KISKER, W. Halle, near Bielefeld, Manu.—Samples of sail-cloth. Raw materials, both warp and web, of Westphalia. Spun hemp.

554 HOERKENS, H. I. Luebbecke, near Minden. — Samples of twine and cord for packing.

555 HEIDSICK, L. A. Bielefeld, Manu.—Specimens of bleached linen, and handkerchiefs, made of hand-spun yarn, and exhibited for fabric and durability.

556 KROENIG, FRIED. WILHELM, & SONS, Bielefeld, Manu.—Samples of raw linen, of best hand-spun flax yarn.

557 MEVISSEN, G. Dülken, near Dusseldorf, Manu.— Thread and raw flax. White embroidering yarn. Crochet thread, &c. The threads of German and English machine-spun and German hand-spun yarns. The flax from the Rhine Province, county of Dusseldorf, and Aix-la-Chapelle.

558 SCHNELL & SONS, Bielefeld, Manu.—Specimens of fine white linen, made of the best German flax, spun by hand; exhibited for strength and durability. Samples of threads of warp.

559 BRUENGER, A. Jöllenbeck, near Bielefeld, Manu.— Samples of bleached linen. Raw materials, hand-spun Westphalian flax. Linen, exhibited for fineness, fabric, and durability.

560 DELIUS, J. D. Bielefeld, Manu. — Samples of bleached linen and linen kerchiefs.

561 BLANKENBURG, F. & Co. Lippstadt, Manu.—Samples of twine and cord of various threads of hemp from the neighbourhood of Lippstadt and Italy. Hemp imported from

Italy is softer and of a lighter colour, but not stronger than the German.

562 Bolenius & Nolte, Bielefeld.—Samples of linen yarn, bleached linen, and bleached linen drill; linen pocket handkerchiefs.

563 Gante & Sons, Bielefeld, Manu.—Specimens of bleached linen, all home-woven, and made of hand-spun flax.

564 Trappmann & Spitz, Barmen, Manu. — Gimped buttons manufactured partly of twisted silk and trams from Italy and the East Indies, and partly of a mixture of silk, wool, and cotton.

565 Wuelfing & Windrath, Elberfeld, Manu.— Various sorts of cotton tapes, and cotton and worsted laces.

566 Zollmann & Steigerthal, Leichlingen near Oplaed, Manu.—Cotton and half-cotton and woollen goods, composed of wool and English twist. Jacquard dresses, of wool and English twist; and Jacquard Berlin dresses entirely of cotton.

567 Haarhaus, Söhne, T. C. Elberfeld, Manu.—Samples of shawls and ladies' dresses.

568 Pluecker, M. Gladbach, Manu.—Shawls of wool and silk; and of wool and cotton.

569 Weber & Metzges, Gladbach, Manu.—Specimens of pique waistcoating and waistcoating in wool and cotton. Raw materials for pique, from England; the other stuffs consist of fine wool and silk.

570 Weyerbusch, C. Elberfeld, Manu.—Patterns of silk and woollen stuffs and buttons.

571 Engelmann & Son, Crefeld, Manu.—Shawls and black silk.

572 Funke, I. H. Boeddinghaus, & Co. Elberfeld, Manu.—Silk and half-silk goods. Greek slips. Summer and other cravats. Atlas Jacquards. Taffetas. Arabic aprons. Shawls. Corahs. Fancy waistcoatings, &c.

573 Pferdmenges & Kleinjung, Viersen, Manu.—Stuffs for trousers and waistcoats; fancy cashmeres; satin checks; buckskin, wool and cotton. Stuff for trousers, linen and wool, and wool and cotton.

574 Pferdmenges Brothers, M. Gladbach, Manu.—Silk and half silk and cotton goods. Cassinets, elastiques, satin turk, and figure, Madras uni. Lutestring, watered and striped, and gros de Berlin.

575 Heymann, C. Crefeld, Manu.—An assortment of fancy waistcoatings and cravats.

576 Langenbeck & Martini, Elberfeld.—Specimens of buttons and braces of silk and lasting.

577 Neuhaus, L. Betterath, near Gladbach, Manu.— Cotton, and silk and cotton goods. Samples of cotton waistcoatings; dimity; silk; and cotton and silk.

578 Klein-Scheater, C. F. Barmen, Manu. (Agents in London, F. Huth & Co).—Cotton, and cotton and wool shawls.

579 Lamberts & May, M. Gladbach, Manu.—Specimens of cotton beaver and drill; cotton and wool cassinet; adapted for the working classes.

580 Rurmann & Meckel, Elberfeld, Manu.—Shawls, waistcoatings, and ladies' dresses, of cotton, cotton and worsted, silk, worsted, &c.

581 Mengen, C. Viersen, Manu.—Velvets and half-woollen stripes. Canvas for embroidery, silk and woollen. Furniture and carriage covering; horse-hair stuffs for the same, and for petticoats.

582 Meyer & Engelmann, Crefeld, Manu.—Silk scarfs and aprons, including satin checked, watered checked, and taffetas, of various qualities, from Italian silk.

583 Neitzer & Brabant, Viersen, near Crefeld, Manu. (Agent in London, G. Ems, 28 Swan Chambers, Gresham St.)—Stuffs made from silk, cotton, and linen, including union poplins, Turkish poplins, Persian handkerchiefs, plain and fringed, &c.

584 Luehdorff, J. & Co. Elberfeld, Manu.—Llama-wool shawls. Unions, with silk and barège; half-woollen

cloaking; waistcoat stuffs. Turkey-red and rose-coloured twist; red water twist. Yarns, spun in England, and dyed by the exhibitors.

585 Schmits & Holthaus, Elberfeld, Manu. (Agent, Gebhardt, Rottmann, & Co. 85 Hatton Garden, London.)— Stuff, in divers colours, for coverings of tables, coaches, furniture, &c.

586 Bockmuehl, P. E., Elberfeld, Manu. — Various specimens of silk and cotton neckcloths, ladies' shawls, and waistcoating.

587 Funke, R. M. Gladbach, Manu.—Samples of Victorias, China crape, and toile du nord; pocket handkerchiefs; diamond cotton; demilin; Germania and soie, cotton and silk; gloria, silk and wool, &c.

588 Lorentz, F. Gladbach, Manu. — Half wool and cotton wares. The half-cottons exhibited for cheapness and design; the waistcoats for cheapness and durability.

589 Schmidt & Co. Barmen, Manu. (Agents in London, Graetzer & Hamann, 9 Huggen Lane.)—Silk bands, and silk and wool laces and cords.

590 Greeff, Bredt, & Co. Barmen, Manu.—Silk, mohair, and gambroon buttons and button-stuff; plain and fancy silk buttons, and stuffs for covering buttons.

591 Grave & Neviandt, Elberfeld, Manu.—Various specimens of waistcoating.

592 Graff, P. Siegen, Prod.—Samples of cobalt ore and cobalt blue, from Philipp Hoffnung, near Siegen. Bright white cobalt, crystallized in microscopical forms, and diffused in slate, greywacke, quartz.

593 Schulz, C. Essen, Inv. and Manu. (Agents in London, S. Cahn & Co. 3 Copthall Chambers.)—Varnished leather for caps, shoes, and hats. Walking-sticks and sword-canes of whalebone. Dragon and Malacca canes, &c.

594 Reinecke, C. Horn, Lippe, Inv. and Manu.—Side-saddle, with arms, and two elastic stirrups, to allow the rider to move and turn about with ease.

595 Klems, J. B. Dusseldorf, Manu. (Agent in London, F. Klein, 38 Finsbury Sq.)—A grand pianoforte, after Erard's model: an additional iron spreading bar being placed above the strings in the lower bass, to give a greater counterpressure.

596 Fudickar, H. Elberfeld, Manu.—Horse-hair, with silk and cotton for upholstery. Coverings of horse-hair. Chair-cover, white horse-hair with red silk. Velours d'Utrecht.

597 Ruhl & Son, Cassel, Manu. — An assortment of pasteboard boxes. A series of embossed and printed envelopes. Patterns of coloured paper.

598 Hoddick, W. Langenberg.—Specimens of dyed jet-black silk, exhibited for brightness, purity, and colour.

599 Westhoff Brothers, Dusseldorf, Manu.—Specimens of printed calicoes: the raw materials are from England, and the madders from Holland.

600 Wolff, J. F. Elberfeld, Manu.—Samples of Turkey-red yarn.

601 Troost, C. & F. Luisenthal, Mülheim-on-the-Ruhr, Manu.- Specimens of prints: made from English yarn, on hand-looms in Westphalia, but printed and finished in Luisenthal. Exhibited for durability and colour.

602 Turkey-Red Dyeing Co. Hagen, near Elberfeld, Imp. and Manu. (Agent in London, J. H. Cohn, 3 Fenchurch Buildings.)—Turkey-red yarns. Printed calicoes. Raw materials, as warps and cops for cottons chiefly from England.

603 Neuhoff, J. H. Elberfeld, Dyer.—Turkey-red yarns. Good water and mule middle pink: spun partly in England and partly in Germany.

604 Lamberts, A. Christ. Son, M. Gladbach, Manu.— Specimens of brown cotton Kalmuck; black, green, buckskin, and mixture, Kalmuck Brown, black, and variegated beaver.

605 LUPP & SONS, Dusseldorf, Imp. and Manu.—Printed calico and coloured woven calico goods. Napolitaine, furniture, kerchiefs, plaids, &c. The raw materials from England and Germany, the cottons printed by machinery, the other articles woven and worked by hand.

606 BOCKMÜHL, SCHIEFER & HECKER, Elberfeld, Manu. —Patterns of printed calicoes, various colours, including rose, lilac, green, blue, orange, garamine, &c.

607 BRINCK, T. W. Gladbach, Manu.—Coloured cotton yarns. Turkey-red, of various shades. The raw material for spinning from England.

608 SCHOELLER, A. & F. Elberfeld, Manu.—Various samples of Turkey-red yarn. Specimen to show the process of dyeing in its various stages.

609 CROON BROTHERS, Gladbach, Manu. — Specimens of cotton bibers. Specimens of printed Kalmuck, beaverteen, cassinet, cotton and wool, and buckskin.

610 KRAMER, L. & G. Dusseldorf, Manu.—Printed cottons and stuffs. Gingham and twilled union. Twilled nankeen. Furniture, &c.

611 SARTORIUS, A. & Co. Dusseldorf, Manu.—Samples of Turkey-red yarn, for the Indian market.

612 DIECKMANN, W. C. Elberfeld, Manu. — Woven goods: portraits of the King and Queen of Prussia, woven in silk. Embroidered waistcoats. Cashmere and Valencia waistcoats.

613 RUPS, L. Crefeld.–Silk hats, with felt shape and form.

614 ERBSCHLOE SONS, Luttringhausen, near Elberfeld, Manu.—Steel tools: Cards, with fifteen samples of refined German steel; files and rasps; and planes and chisels.

615 POST, J. D. Wehringhausen, Manu.—Cutlass and sword blades; sabres. Table-knives and forks. Scythes. Hatchets and axes. Saws and other tools. Door and cupboard locks. Coffee-mills. Bolts. Sheep-shears, &c.

616 POST SONS, Eilpe, near Hagen, Manu. — Specimens of cast scissors.

617 MANNESMANN, A. Remscheid, Manu.—(Agent in London, Heirstmann, 8 Colebrook Row, Islington.)—Files, screws, and steel: Prime Siegen rough steel, manufactured in Remscheid.

618 PLUEMACHER, W. Solingen, Manu. — Scissors, in great variety.

619 PICKHARDT, G. Remscheid, Manu.—A variety of files and rasps, manufactured of cast, refined, and double-refined steel.

620 BRAND, P. W. Remscheid, Manu.—Specimens of saws, mill, crane, pit, cross-cut, "dwas," and "paunsch;" circular, tenon, and American blue-polished quellon, trunk, butcher, &c.

621 BRAUNSCHWEIG, F. A. Remscheid, Manu.— Various sorts of carpenters' tools, planes, chisels, &c.

622 REINSHAGEN, G. Remscheid, Manu.—Specimens of files of German steel.

623 BLECKMANN, J. E. Ronsdorf, Manu.—Specimens of scissors, shears, files, vices, hammers, brace-bits, compasses, gimblets, chisels, saws, locks, tools, skates &c.

624 THOMAS, C. Remscheid.—Augers and hardwares. Square rule. Various sorts of augers and saddlers' knives

625 FELDE, R. Feld near Solingen, Manu.—Specimens of polished steel saws: of unhardened sheet cast, best tempered, and of double sheet; and unhardened, of double refined, &c.

626 ARNS, A. Remscheid, Manu.—Various carpenters tools, including planes, chisels, &c.

627 ANTE, A. Zueschen, near Brilon, Manu.—Various axes and hatchets. Chaff-cutter. Raw materials: Syria steel, and cut steel, raised in the county of Siegen, Rhine-Prussia.

628 COPPEL, A. Solingen, Manu.—Various samples of cutlery, including pen, pocket, spring, clasp, and hunting knives.

629 LINDER, B. Solingen.—Assortment of pen and pocket knives.

630 LOHMANN, F. Witten on Ruhr, Manu.—Files and cast steel; pig-iron, employed in producing steel, &c. The bars of iron are decarbonized whole, without altering the shape; the invention is founded upon the experiments of Reaumure, and called by the inventor " steel adoucé."

631 HILGERS & SONS, LUCKHAUS & GUNTHER, LUCKHAUS & Co. and HASENCLEVER & SONS, Remscheid, Manu.—Hardwares, tools, and cutlery.

632 HUTH, FRIED. & Co. Hagen, Manu.—Samples of steel, ore, and hard wares; including cast-steel files, carpenters' tools, various vices, and anvils.

633 BOECKER, R. & H. Remscheid, Manu.—Hardwares and cutlery: Files, locks, scale-beams, skates, shears, saws, &c. Patterns of drawing, chopping, and coopers' knives, cleavers, saws, scythes, &c.

634 WESCHER BROTHERS, & STRASMANN Barmen, Manu. —Specimens of horn buttons; sporting and dress buttons, made from the hoofs of oxen.

635 NOTTEBOHM & Co. Lüdenscheid.—Samples of cast brass, and German silver articles.

636 TURK, (Widow), P. C. Lüdenscheid.—Specimens of metal buttons, buckles, and nails, for upholstery.

637 HOELLER, A. & E. Solingen.—Sword of honour, and court-sword. Foils and rapiers. Damask blades in the oriental style, &c. Scissors. Pen and pocket knives. Table cutlery. Razors, shears, saws, &c. Jewellers' tools, &c.

638 DREYSE & COLLENBUSCH, Sommerda, Manu.—Specimens of percussion-caps. Tin-plate, barrel, and copper rivets.

639 RITZEL (Widow), L. Lüdenscheid, Westphalia, Manu.—Various metallic buttons. Copper obtained from England, Sweden, and Germany. Zinc from Rhine provinces and Silesia.

640 SCHWARTE, J. D. Solingen.—Razors, pen-knives, and swivels.

641 DULTGEN, G. Dültgenthal, near Wald, Manu.—Umbrella and parasol frames. Cigar-boxes, porte-monnaie frames. Pad and portfolio locks, door-handles, &c.

642 ALTENLOH, BRINK & Co. Milspe, near Schwelm, Manu. (Agent in London, A. Heintzmann, 16 Colebrook row, Islington.)—Various specimens of screws, with round and flat heads.

643 SCHLEGELMILCH, C. Suhl, Manu.—Box made of rolled sheet-iron, to show its quality, toughness, and pliability. The lid opens by pressure.

644 SCHMIDT, C. Soest, Manu.—A middle-sized kitchen stove.

645 ASBECK, C. & Co. Hagen, Manu. — Locksmith's anvil, turning-lathe, and vices, exhibited for cheapness. Specimens of refined German steel, made of Siegen steel ore. Horse-shoes of half-hardened steel. Tools for shoeing horses. Padlocks and fodder knives.

646 SCHMIDT, P. L. Elberfeld, Manu.—Steel, iron, and brass wares, including screw-taps, files, gimblets, nippers, hammers, vices, shears, plane-irons, saws, locks, scales, hinges, taps, and skates, &c.

647 KISSING & MÖLLMANN, Iserlohn.—Brass and iron wares, including hand-bells, dial-plates, &c. Curtain cornices, ornaments, pins, and rings. Stamped brass candlesticks. Steel umbrella and parasol frames, &c. Iron, copper, and brass wire.

648 HOSTEREY, G. Barmen, Manu.—Samples of buttons, plated with gold, silver, and platina.

649 KRUPP, F. Essen, near Dusseldorf, Manu. and part Inv.—Rolling mill; the rollers exhibited for their equal hardness throughout. Forged cast-steel, exhibited for purity and toughness; used for axletrees, &c.

650 LUCAS, F. W. & Co. Elberfeld, Manu.—Hardwares, candlesticks, ink-stands, fire apparatus, paper-weights, lamp stands, and a statue of Guttenberg. K 4

651 SCHMIDT, T. D. Sprockhövel, Manu.—Hardwares, including locks; window-bolts, with appurtenances; iron and brass hinges; carpenters' and turners' tools; sugar-tongs, curling-tongs, nut-crackers, &c. Fox-traps. Scales, steelyards, and skates.

652 FUNKE & HUECK, Hagen, Manu.—Samples of hard-wares, including screws, with points and with nuts. Patent and common vice; screw wrench.

653 GREEFF & SON, J. P. Barmen, Manu.—Various metal buttons and boxes. Samples of snuff-boxes.

654 WOESTE, G. & Co. Solingen, Manu. (Agent in London, A. Heintzman, 16 Colebrook row, Islington.)—Cards of cast scissors, plain and ornamented. Samples of shears.

655 CARON, A. H. Barmen, Manu.—An assortment of gilt buttons and jewellery. Raw materials, British, Russian, and Swedish copper, and Bohemian glass-stones. The soldering done by means of hydro-oxygen apparatus.

656 WOLFF & ERBSLÖH, Barmen, Manu. (Agents in London, E. & H. Blank, 10 Trump St. King St.)—Various plated articles: raw materials, gold, platina, silver, and copper; principally manufactured by machinery.

657 SEEL, G. Elberfeld, Manu.—Ornamental articles in hair, for brooches, ear-rings, and rings. Album, with a landscape; album, with bouquet. Box, with braids of hair.

658 LIPP (VAN), FREDRICH, Dusseldorf, Manu.—Perfumery: Dusseldorf water, and Oriental pastil.

659 HILGERS, C. Dusseldorf, Inv. and Manu.—Lady's writing and work table, in ebony, with four views of the Rhine.

660 EICHELBERG, H. D. & Co. Iserlohn, Manu.—Window-curtain, with a frame of brass fixed on wood.

661 BIEFANG, C. Dusseldorf, Manu.—Paste and paste-board articles. Various frames for daguerreotypes and pictures, in velvet, bronze, and marble: étuis.

662 HOELTRING & HOEFFKEN, Barmen, Manu.—An assortment of India-rubber braces.

663 SCHELLER, WEBER, & WITTICH, Hesse-Cassel, Hesse.—Children's toys. Architectural apparatus. Garden and other tools; tools for emigrants: sold in Nuremberg and Sonnenberg, and exported to England, the East and West Indies, and America. Leather bags; railway and travelling bags, exhibited for appearance and cheapness; exported to Great Britain, America, and the Indies. Plate tools; a printing press; and pewter figures.

664 BASSE & FISCHER, Luedencheid, Westphalia, Manu.—Snuff-boxes, match-boxes, buckles, and lids for tobacco-pipes. Match-boxes of brass and metal, made by machinery, from one piece, &c.

665 KILIAN, H. Siegen, Prod.—Woodcut: The Lord's Supper, after picture of Leonardo da Vinci.

666 FELTHAUSS —, Wetzlar, Prod.—Fragments of ore, and samples of the cinnabar obtained from it.

667 PFEIFFERS & AX, Rheydt, Manu.—Cotton and cotton and wool, mixed. Buckskins.

668 SCHEEL, C. Cassel, Manu.—A pianoforte.

669 WIEDENMANN, T. Gladbach, Manu.—Damask table-cloth, napkins, and towels. Fine table-cloth and other coverings.

670 BREITHAUPT, F. W. & SON, Cassel.—Physical instruments of several descriptions.

671 VOGEL, Bookbinder in Tena, Saxe Weimar.—A highly-finished exemplar of F. von Schiller's works, under a glass cover and on a small table.

672 MECKLINGHAUS & WIX, Barmen, Manu.—Dressed hides.

673 SCHMOLZ, Wm. & Co. Solingen and Berlin. Manufacturers of German-silver wares, &c. (Agents in London, Bier Brothers, 2, St. Mary-at-Hill, City.—Swords and cutlery.

674 TACK, WM. & PELIZAEUS, Crefeld, Manu.—Silk and silk and cotton mixed stuffs for waistcoats.

675 SCHULTE, J. H. Barmen, Manu.—Silk and silk and cotton mixed stuffs for waistcoats.

676 SIEPERMANN & MOHLAU, Derendorff, near Dusseldorff, Manu.—Printed cottons.

677 KRUPP, F. Essen, near the Ruhr, Inv. and Manu.—Steel gun, 6-pounder, complete. Steel cuirass, and one tried by being fired at with six different bullets. Steel rollers, springs, and railway axle.

678 TEUTENBERG, L. Huesten, Kreis Arnsberg, Inv. and Manu.—Rifle with seven barrels, which can all be fired and loaded at once, particularly applicable for shooting wild-fowl, &c.

---

e. Grand Duchy of SAXONY, PRUSSIAN SAXONY, BRUNSWICK, ANHALT, and States of THURINGIA.

Commissioner, Dr. GUSTAV SCHUELER, from Tena.

679 BENNIGHAUSS, J. C.—Sparry ironstone, from the mines of Hoffnung and Segen Gottes. Brown iron ore, from the mine of Heiligenberg. Pig-iron, furnace slags, iron in bars, &c.

680 SCHADE, E. Breitenbach, Manu.—Picture on porcelain, representing Jubal, the inventor of music. Painted porcelain plate, after Raphael. Lady's portrait, in a costume of the time of Louis XVI.

681 ROYAL SALT WORKS at Artern, Manu.—Kitchen salt and mother-lye of salt.

682 WORKS at Maegdesprung, near Harzgerode, Anhalt, Bernburg.—Model of a wind instrument constructed by Lüdens. Sparry iron, raw and roasted, with magnetic iron-stone crystals. White pig-iron, &c. Axletree, puddled, and re-heated by gas. Waggon-boxes, and a sample of iron. Model of a gas-furnace, constructed by Bischof. Fluor-spar. Artificial lead-glance crystals. Crude antimony, three varieties. Litharge or protoxide of lead. Pure lead. Mixed vitriol.

683 ROYAL PRUSSIAN CHEMICAL MANUFACTORY, Schönenebeck.—Chemical preparations and specimens of common salt. White oxide of zinc, prepared in the dry way. Iron alum. Red prussiate of potash of Gmelin. Pure gallic acid. Salts of sodium, potassium, barytes, &c. Glacial phosphoric acid. Iodine. Chloroform. Bromine. Sulphuret of carbon. Preparations of tin, copper, and bismuth. Pure succinic acid. Caustic potash. Metallic cadmium. Biniodide of mercury.

684 WEISS, J. H. Mühlhausen, Manu.—Produce of plants: Madder lac-colours, for artistic painting. Madder covering-colours. Patterns coloured with the dyes.

685 BEHM T. Anhalt, Bernburg, Manu.—Sugar from red beet: one acre of ground will yield 120 cwts. of red beet, equal to 5½ cwts. of raw sugar.

686 BLEIBTREU, L. O. Brunswick, Manu.—Chicory-root, kiln-dried, in slices; roasted; and ground to powder. Prepared chicory-coffee.

687 BRUMME, A. F. W. & Co. Waldau, Anhalt-Bernburg, Manu.—Sugar, manufactured from red beet.

688 FEIGENSPAHN, A. Mühlhausen, Manu.—Samples of glue.

689 HABERLAND, W. Schoeningen, Brunswick.—Samples of dried fruit. Peeled apples, pears, plums, melons, cherries, &c.

690 HALLER, Halle, Manu. — Specimens of wheat starch produced by machinery, and by chemical processes.

691 HENNIGE & WIESE, Magdeburg, Manu. (Agent in London, J. Horstman, 26 Finsbury Sq.)—Sugar, made from red beet-root, and with the centrifugal machine. Loaves of sugar (purified). Refined beet-sugar.

692 SALOMON, J. A. & Co. Brunswick, Manu.—Dried chicory-root; the same powdered. Chicory-coffee.

693 TEICHMAN, C. Erfurt, Manu.—Samples of succory.

and powder; vermicelli, wheat-grits, pearl-barley, and mustard. Blacking.

694 The Loburg Manufactory, Magdeburg.—Brown and white sago; grape sugar; potato flour and starch; pearl barley: artificial gum; white and brown treacle; white sago-grits. Dry burnt starch, in three qualities, for factories; pipe starch; ringed and powdered starch, made of wheat of the first quality.

695 Wittekop & Co. Brunswick, Manu.—Samples of flour, groats, maccaroni, and chocolate, manufactured by hand and by steam.

696 Giessler, —, Tröchtelborn, near Erfurt.—Bale of woad, carefully prepared from pure woad leaves.

697 Hucke, —, Manager and Teacher of the School of Agriculture at Alach, near Erfurt.—Samples of hogs' bristles, taken from animals of different races. Canary and coriander seeds.

698 Anschutz, R. Zella, Duchy of Gotha, Manu.—Gun and rifle barrels of common wire, and flower-damask; of fine Paris and fine flower (Turkish) damask; of fine chain damask; of Laminette and Gotha damask; of fine steel-wire and iron damask. The iron for the steel is made in Zella of sparry iron-stone, obtained in the district of Schmalkalden.

699 Brecht, A. Weimar, Manu. (Agent in London, Consul S. Cahlman.)—Rifles with fine damask barrels and walnut-tree stock, ranged for pointed and round balls, &c. The iron employed is from Thuringia; the barrels from Lutsorh.

700 Hanau, W. Gera, Reuss, Manu.—Pair of pistols, with apparatus, in a case.

701 König, C. G. & Sons, Coburg, Manu. (Agent, Joseph Kendall, 8 Harp Lane, Great Tower St.)—Pair of octagon pistols, inlaid with gold in the Gothic style: the stocks of elm (*Ulmus campestris*) inlaid with silver. The above in a box, with instruments to correspond.

702 Sauerbrey, L. Zella Blasii, Duchy of Gotha, Manu.—Double rifle, of solid cast-steel. Both barrels are bored in a converging direction, to one aim, in such a manner as to direct the balls to the same mark. It carries pointed and also round balls, &c.

704 Ausfeld, A. Gotha, Duchy of Saxe Gotha.—Planimeter, an instrument invented by Dr. Flaussen, of the Observatory at Seeberg, for the purpose of measuring surfaces. Microscope.

705 Broemel, A. Arnstadt, Principality of Schwarzburg, Sonderhausen, Manu.—Decimal balance, to weigh from 10 to 15 cwts.; another in brass, to weigh 1 cwt.

706 Nietzchmann & Vaccani, Halle, Manu.—Sets of drawing instruments.

707 Schultze, J. F. Paulinzellà, Principality of Schwarzburg-Rudolstadt.—An organ: its pecularities consisting in great power of tone and simplicity of mechanism, with a contrivance for producing deeper tones, and an arrangement for accelerating the transmission of sound.

708 Wagner & Co. Gera, Reuss, Manu. (Agents, Elemenhorst Brothers, London.)—Accordions, inlaid with fine metal and mother-of-pearl. Glazed cupboard.

709 Zeitter & Winkelman, Brunswick.—A pianoforte, and a grand pianoforte.

710 Danneberg & Son, Eilenburg, Manu.—White and coloured furniture stuffs. Jaconets. Calicoes—millefleurs, light ground, pink, violet green, and madder.

711 Vogel & Carner, Gera, Reuss, Manu.—Cotton goods figured, coloured, and woven in the Jacquard loom, made of German and English cotton yarn; chiefly in demand in European Turkey, and in Persia.

712 Hagenbruch, C. G. Weimar, Grand Duchy of Saxe. Four-fold worsted yarns. Raw and dyed yarns, zephyr and castor, made partly from Silesian and West Prussian and partly from Saxon wools; dyed at the manufactory of Messrs. Schuster, of Berlin.

713 Haseloff & Co. Burg, Manu. (Agent in London, J. A. Seeger.)—Black, blue, and violet royal cloths, &c. of wools from Silesia, Posen, &c.

714 Walther, Hennig, & Co, Ronneburg, Manu.—Specimens of Thibet mousseline-de-laine, Cashmere d'Ecosse, and Napolitana. All woven of comb-yarn, and dyed in various colours.

715 Damsch & Muenzers Sons, Ronneburg, Duchy of Saxe Altenburg, Manu.—Pieces of doucet; plaid short flannel; gaze flannels; cashmere, all wool, short flannel, white; moltong, &c.

716 Weber, E. Gera, Reuss, Manu. (Agent in London, C. Holland, 41 Finsbury Circus).—Woollen plain unfulled stuff goods. Thibet: satin burbes and mousselaine-de-laine. Woollen stuffs, figured and printed. Chequered and plain table-covers.

717 Weiss, jun. & Co. Langensalza, Manu.—Specimens of worsted yarn spun from Prussian wool; used for Thibets, barèges, cashmeres, &c. Zephyr yarns for embroideries, shawls, and similar articles.

718 Zimmerman & Son, Apolda, Saxe Weimar, Manu.—Various cotton and woollen hosiery, and fancy articles.

719 Scheibe, G. Gera, Manu.—Tanned horse and calf skin for sole-leather.

720 Weissflog, E. F. Gera, Reuss, Manu. (Agent in London, B. Gous, 1 Sambrook Ct. Basinghall St.).—Specimens of Thibet, and satin-de-laine; the same figured. Piece of embroidery on velvet.

721 Directors of the Herford Prison, Westphalia, Manu.—Carpeting of cow-hair, &c., linen, furniture covering, and fancy works. String basket; hemp and string bags. Papier-maché case.

722 Hornig, C. E. Brunswick.—Samples of flax and tow.

723 Müller, A. F. Mühlhausen, Manu. — Ladies' working, crimson, blue, scarlet, green, grey, black, and white, and plain mixture, flag cloth. Ettamin for cantuches, sack-cloth, and plush caps, &c., all wool.

724 Urban, A. Gandersheim, Brunswick, Manu.—Damask table-linen, made of a hand-web, prepared from a yarn reaped and spun in the vicinity of Jandersheim. Sample of linen made of English machine-yarn.

725 Bauer & Furbringer, Gera, Reuss, Manu.—Woollen and half-silk goods; including Thibet, Cashmere, &c., handkerchiefs, shawls, and scarfs, in various colours.

726 Bodemer, J. jun. Eilenburg, Manu.—Half wool moussel; jaconet-de-laine, half wool; challis, all wool; moussel and cachemire d'Ecosse.

727 Broesel, Greiz, Reuss, Manu. (Agent in London, T. Kemp, 7a Basinghall St.)—Peruvian bordée. Carnation, light blue, and black Thibet. Isly Cashmere. Light green and light blue mousseline-de-laine. Pale Jacquard. Pensé Calabria. New atlas and dark green de-laine. Satin croisé.

728 Bauch, F. T. Greiz, Reuss, Manu. (Agents in London, Oppenheim & Co. 15 Addle St.) — Thibet, green and drab; Cashmere, nacarra; satin, nacarra; mousseline-de-laine shawls.

729 Lucius, J. C. & Co. Erfurt, Manu. (Agents in London, Schmuck, Souchay, & Co.) — Damasks, woollen, and silk, amaranthe, cotton, and silk. Scottish dresses, cotton and worsted fancy dresses. Tartan plaid; stranin hoods. &c.

730 Macht, H. W. Zeulenroda, Manu. (Agents in London, Gottschalk and Schroeder, 72 Basinghall St.)—Shoe-stuffs of cotton mixed with wool; woollen garments; garments of linen mixed with cotton, and of wool mixed with cotton.

731 Morand & Co. Gera, Reuss, Manu. (Agent in London, C. Holland, 41 Finsbury Circus.)—Half-silk goods; comb-wool stuffs; Cashmere; mousseline-de-laine; satin d'Espagne; Napolitaine: drap d'été, and cuir-de-laine.

732 SCHRAIDT & Co. Coburg, Manu.—Drills, half-linen, for trousers and stays; bed-ticking of cotton-warp and linen-shot; Turkey-red yarns dyed by the exhibitors.

733 SCHWEITZER & HELLER, Greitz, Reuss, Manu.—Specimens of Thibet black stuff; Cashmere, atlas-olive and black; mandarine, lilac and mode.

734 WIEGAND, E. Erfurt, Manu.—Double damask cover, with red silk fringe. On the right side a white cotton warp and silk shoot, on the other an orange cotton warp and blue wool shoot.

735 BUCHNER, A. Erfurt, Manu.—Large gaiter-boots, various; lilac velvet gaiter-boots; serge and cordovan shoes.

736 ENCKE, Gora Reuss, Manu.—Skins for light and black bridles. Pair of tops for boots. Ornamental table-cover.

737 KRAMER & BALDAMUS, Magdeburg. (Agent in London, Mr. Schoefer.)—Skin of smooth black leather. Brown and light bridle-skins, made of German skins, and curried with oak-tan.

738 KRETSCHMANN, H. W. E. Eisenberg, Duchy of Saxe Altenburg, Manu.—Shoe stuffs: Stramir cord and woollen shoe-cord. Ladies' and gentlemen's shoe tops, various.

739 LANGE, F. Halle, Manu.—Lady's saddle complete, with bridle, hind-piece, and fore part; gentleman's saddle; saddle-tree, complete, with the exception of the leather-work.

740 LANGETHAL, G. Erfurt, Manu.—Calf leather boots, enamelled boots, and button boots.

741 RANNIGER & SONS, Altenburg, Duchy of Saxe Altenburg, Manu. — Lamb-skins. Fine leather gloves. Dyed leather samples.

742 SCHEIBE, H. L. Gera Reuss, Manu.—Tanned calf-skins.

743 SONDERMANN, W. Erfurt, Manu.—Machine, or cylinder-parchment. Parchment skins, and drum calf-skins.

744 WEBER, C. F. Langensalze, Manu. — Smoothing-tree for kid leather.

745 WIEGAND, F. Erfurt, Manu.—Serge and brown leather shoes and serge boots. Varnished leather clogs. Stuff shoes with caoutchouc. The shoes are of English serge-de-Berry, varnished Mayence, calf leather, boonce leather from Paris, and vesite leather. The elastic caoutchouc material is manufactured by J. L. Raempler.

746 GRAF, H. Altenburg, Duchy of Saxe Altenburg.—Atar-Bible, with large steel-plate engravings, in violet leather, and cover and lining gilt.

747 KÖRNER, G. W. Erfurt.—Organ music by Bach, Friend, i. to vii.—Kühmstedt. Op. xxviii. Bruck, Fischer, Mendelssohn, Körner, &c.

748 REISSER, W. Manu.—Album of coloured drawing-paper, with violet margin, and gilt edge.

749 WESTERMAN, G. Brunswick.—European Gallery, a copper-plate work: the plates of English engraving. History of the Courts of Valkenstein: the printing, paper, and type of German manufacture.

750 EHRENBERG & RICHTER, Eilenburg, Manu.—Coloured calico:—Blue, orange, red, green, lilac, brown and red, pink and crimson. Coloured shirting.

751 ALBERTI, Miss FRIEDERIKE, Nauen, near Potsdam, Manu.—Table-cover, embroidered with silk, chenille, and gold.

752 GROSSMANN, AGNES, Weissenfels. — Embroidered carpet: principal design, The discovery of Moses in the ark of bulrushes.

753 GOTTSCHALK, J. A. Erfurt, Manu.—Gaiter-boots. Satin and japanned shoes. Brown kid-leather shoes. Japanned and lasting gentlemen's boots. Children's boots and shoes. Horse-leather gentlemen's boots.

754 ISRAEL, C. Erfurt, Manu.—Extra superfine four-seamed plush caps. Hand-knitting work. Tuck, plain, and pointed caps.

755 KROCKER & SON, Zeulenroda, Manu.—A variety of women's stockings and half-hose.

756 SCHMIDT & SONS, Zerbst, Manu.—Silk and beaver hats. The beaver hats are made of pure rupen hair; the white beaver hat of German white larin hair.

757 SCHOPPER, F. Zeulenroda, Manu. (Agent in London, W. Meyerstein, 15 Watling St.)—Specimens of ladies' stockings.

758 SCHOPPER, Henry Zeulenroda, Reuss, Manu. (Agents in London, Gottschalk & Schröder, 72 Basinghall St.)—Women's brown and white hose, and men's brown half-hose, made of English twist.

759 WEBENDÖRFER BROTHERS, Zeulenroda, Reuss, Manu.—Men and women's white and brown cotton hose, two and three threads.

760 BAUM, E. Coburg, Manu.—Stove of polished iron-plate, in the form of a "Knight in full armour," with a base of cast-iron.

761 BEYER & HEINTZE, Dobra, Manu. — Parquetrie squares, exhibited for workmanship.

762 EINSIEDEL, Count G. Iron Works, Lauchhammer.—Cast-iron goods. Ornamental bronze casts; bust of the Prince of Prussia, &c. Polar bears, monkeys, tigers &c. modelled from animals in the London Zoological Gardens.

763 FLEISCHMANN, A. Sonneberg, Saxe Meiningen, Manu. (Agent in London, J. Kendall, 8 Harp Lane, Gt. Tower St.)—An étagère, or specimen of Paxton furniture (provisionally registered), representing M Jullien and his band. Philharmonic chandelier (provisionally registered). Also, looking-glass frame, with looking-glass. Madonna and bracket, bronzed. Brackets. Roman and Greek, and Mazeppa and horse, all bronzed Byzantine and Gothic brackets in wood colour, and of the *renaissance* style. Dogs, &c. Candle screen. Architectural ornaments. An assortment of animals, in wood colour. Daguerreotype frames. Medallions in horn frames. Serpentine stone mug and a cup, with medallions.

764 MEYER & WRIED, successors to STOBWASSERS, Brunswick.—Japanned tea-trays, with pictures, after Nickoll and Mieris. Varnished paintings, after Füger, Wilkie, and Pfesffer.

765 PIEGLER, G. Schleiz, Manu.—Night-clocks. Dressing-glasses. Lamp. Candle-screens. Tinder-boxes. Match-boxes. Fumigating-machines. "Stalleur-lamps." Bottle-corks. Boot-jacks, &c.

766 STUBGEN & KLEEMAN, Erfurt, Manu. — Brass sliding or pillar lamp.

767 WALLACK, A. Weimar, Grand Duchy of Saxe Weimar, Manu. — Bronze jewel-box in the Byzantine style, partly gilt, and partly silvered.

768 RÖHRIG, C. Braunlage, near Brunswick, Manu. (Agents in London, A. & P. J. Meyers & Co. 144 Leadenhall St.)—Plate glass; with paintings, &c. Tiles and gutter-tiles of glass, made from white sand, quartz, and chalk found in the neighbourhood. Glass cylinders exhibiting the plate-glass in its half-finished state before opening out.

769 BOLM, C. Brunswick, Manu.—Tea-kettle, tea-pot, and milk-jug, manufactured and ornamented by hand.

770 HAGEN, VON, A. Erfurt, Manu.—Writing chiffonnière, of nut-tree wood, in the renaissance style, ornamented with carving, and marquetrie-work of silver, copper, brass, ivory, and mother-of-pearl.

771 HEINRICH, G. Zerbst, Manu.—Looking-glass, the frame of carton-pierre, with gilding and ivory medallions.

772 HENNEBERG, F. E. & Co. Gotha, Duchy of Saxe-Coburg, Manu.—A lady's work-table, with porcelain plates inserted, and painting. The carpenter's work and carving sketched by M. Amtker. A tea-tray, with a group, "The Fisherman's Family," after Riedel in Rome. Two vases. A statuette in biscuit. The materials for the manufacture of porcelain, all of inland produce.

773 HOFFMEISTER, T. & Co. Coburg, Duchy of Saxe-

Coburg, Manu. (Agent in London, J. Kendall, 8 Harp Lane, Gt. Tower St.)—Oak sideboard decorated with carved work, in the German-Gothic style of the middle age, and ornamented with brown plush ; four oak arm-chairs, to match.

774 HUPFER & WALFERMAN, Shmoelln, Saxe Altenburg, Manu.—Fancy and ornamental boxes, &c. in papier-maché.

775 PUFF, W. Coburg, Manu. (Agent, J. Kendall, 8 Harp Lane, Great Tower Street.)—Table in the old German style, with inlaid work, in the natural colours of the wood.

776 SCHARF, C. Bernburg, Duchy of Anhalt-Bernburg, Manu. — Ornamental draught-board, made of mahogany, chestnut, maple, rosewood, zebra, and keister woods.

777 SCHRADER, C. Bernburg, Duchy of Anhalt-Bernburg, Manu. — Ornamental draught-board, consisting of plum-tree, kingswood, rosewood, chestnut, molosse, mahogany, and maple-wood.

778 ARNOLDI, C E. F. Elgersburg, Duchy of Saxe-Gotha, Manu.—Pharmaceutical instruments, crucibles, measures, funnels, water-pipes, &c., made of earths and clay found in Thuringia Forest.

779 STOLBERG-WERNIGFRODE, Earl of, Ilsenburg Foundry.—A Gothic vase, intended for a fountain. A window-frame. A garden-table. A marble table ; the marble from the mines in the neighbourhood. A Corinthian and a Gothic stove, &c., exhibited as specimens of casting in iron.

780 THE DUCAL FOUNDRY INSPECTION, at Rübeland, Brunswick, Manu.—Slabs of marble found near Rübeland, principally black, grey, and red. Can be obtained in blocks of nine feet in length, and five feet in breadth.

781 ROMPLER, J. J. Erfurt, Manu. — India-rubber elastic braces and watch-guards. Silk and half-silk shoe stuffs, mixed with India-rubber: shoes made of the same material.

782 WALTER & SON, Brunswick, Manu.—Chairs, and paper-basket.

783 SCHREIBER, J. C. G. Merseburg, Manu.—A large dressing-case, inlaid with silver. A variety of dressing cases. Oval, round, seed, and sundry boxes. Visiting cards, albums, &c

784 ZIEGLER BROTHERS, Ruhla, Manu. (Agent in London, C. Holland, 41 Finsbury Circus.)—Real meerschaum pipe-bowls, and imitation meerschaum bowls. Wood and clay pipes and bowls, and china pipes. Real meerschaum bowls, coloured by being boiled in oil.

785 BOESCHE, C. J. Magdeburg, Prod.—Models: the cathedral at Magdeburg, made of limetree-wood ; the roof of the cathedral. The fine spring at Nüremberg, by Schönhofer. Original model of a spring.

786 JACOB, H. Schmoeln, Duchy of Saxe Altenburg (Agent in London, T. Wirkler, 16 Sidney St. Commercial Rd.)—Oil-paintings on iron plate, japanned and varnished, representing Idyl, after Nicholas Berchem, and the Magdalen, after Maes.

787 JACOBI, F. A. Brunswick (Agents in London, Jones, Simonson, & Co.)—Hunting-cup, with embossed and chased work. Lion's head (marble-plaster).

788 STOCKMAN, W. & Co. Brunswick.—Varnished paintings on tin-plates, in gilt frames, after Rubens, Raphael, Murillo, Ralisch, and André.

789 TRUMPELMANN, A. Ilsenburg.—Pictures and transparencies.

790 VEREIN, LANDWIRTHSCHAFTLICHER, Sangerhausen, Prod.—Samples of seed and hemp.

791 ZIRKENRACH, Raguhn, Duchy of Anhalt-Dessau, Manu.—Woollen cloth.

792 HAUCH, A. Halle, Manu.—Specimens of sundry articles manufactured from hemp.

793 BAUCH, J. F. Greitz, Manu.—Mousseline-de-laine, shawls, and handkerchiefs

794 KAUSCHE, G. Brunswick, Inv. and Manu.—Sundry fancy articles, embroidered with gold, silk, silver, pearls, &c.

795 KUENEMUND, J. G. Ronneburg, Manu.—A harrow.

796 LUX BROTHERS, Ruhla, Manu.—An assortment of different pipes.

797 WEIMARSSON, Fr. Iena, Manu. — Manufactures of wool, elastics.

798 HARRASS, P. Suhl, Manu.—Sundry articles made of wool.

799 BURBACH BROTHERS, Hoerselgau, near Gotha, Manu. (Agent, T. Peterson, Water Lane).—Woven fire-engine hose.

800 SELENKA, J. Braunschweig, Inv. & Manu.—Gilt and fancy leather and paper articles, portfolio.

801 BLANCKE, E. Naumburg, Manu.—Double-barrelled gun ; joint bullet rifle, with all appurtenances.

802 SOMMERMEYER & Co. Magdeburg, Inv. and Manu.—Iron fire-proof safe, of a novel construction.

803 GRAFF, W. Münchenhoff, Prod. — Stuffed sheep. Fleece of wool.

804 ASSOCIATION OF MANUFACTURES at Sonnenberg, Duchy of Saxe Coburg and Gotha.—Tableau of plastic work representing a rural fête, held at Castle Florence, the country palace of the Duke of Saxe Cobourg Gotha, the residence of H.M. the Queen, when on a visit to the Duke, and the place where H.R.H. Prince Albert was born. This tableau contains about 400 moving figures, bands of music, &c.

805 HUTSCHENREITHER, F. A. & SONS, Wallendorff, Manu.—Specimens of glass.

806 SCHRAMM, J. L. F. Dessau, Manu.—Samples of oil.

807 DIETRICH & SON, Poessneck, Manu.—Specimens of flannel.

808 GOEBEL, F. D. Wallendorff, Manu.—An assortment of articles in porcelian and glass.

809 SCHMIDT, C. & H. Poessneck Manu.—Transparent shades.

810 BURCKHARDT BROTHERS, Eisfeld, Inv. & Manu.—Paintings on glass.

811 SCHULZ, L. W. Meiningen, Inv. & Carver. — An assortment of sundry ivory cups, and other splendid works of art. The artist executed several elaborate specimens of his craft for the late King of Prussia.

812 HEINIG, J. G. & SONS, Altenburg, Manu.—Samples of string and twine.

813 FOESE, G. Halle, Prod.—Samples of bristles.

814 DAHLHEIM, F. Salzwedel, Manu.—An assortment of cotton goods.

815 CONTA & BOEHME, Poessneck, Inv. & Porcelain Manu. (Agent in London, J. Kendall, 8 Harp Lane, Great Tower Street.)—Sundry articles of glass, porcelain, &c. Assortment of china ornaments.

816 BRUHM & NAGLER, Gera, Manu.—Various woollen goods.

817 KUMMER, W. E. Widow, Weissensee, Manu.—Sundry toys and fancy articles.

818 SOMMER, C. J. Erfurth, Manu.—Money bags and porte-monnaies, &c.

819 WIRTH, F. E. Merseburg, Manu.—Variety of whips.

820 BODEMER & Co. Eilenburg, Manu.—Various cotton goods.

821 JANNASCH, H. Bernburg, Manu.—An assortment of earthenware.

822 VIEWEG & SON, Brunswick, Printer.—Sundry books.

823 JACOBI, F. A. Brunswick, Inv. & Manu.—Horse cast in iron ; sundry cast iron articles.

824 DIESEL & Co. Saalfeld.—Sundry colours.

825 COSACK, J. Arnsberg.—Lead and silver ore, sulphuret of lead, and sulphuret of zinc (black jack).

826 AUGUSTIN, H. F. L. Halberstadt. Manu.—Sugar of lead in crystals, bottom pieces, and in groups of crystals.

827 BARRE & KUSTER, Lübbecke, Manu.—Samples of wheat starch.

828 MAENNEL, F. Weissenfels, Manu.—A newspaper pocket or envelope.

830 BACHOVEN & VOLLSCHWITZ, Zerbst, Manu. (Agents in London, Brocklesby and Wessels, 4 Moscovy Court, Tower-hill.)—Samples of black plush, dyed in Germany.

831 SCHMIDT, J. C. Erfurt, Manu.—Wax baskets and flower-pots.

832 BADEKER, J. Elberfeld, Publisher.—The Holy Bible, for church and family use, in the German language, printed in very small type.

833 LANGNER, H. Halberstadt, Manu.—Paletot from nürz, with squirrel heads muff; and victorine, from pole-cat.

834 ROYAL SALT WORKS at Schoenebeck, near Magdeburg.—Kitchen salt.

835 ARNOLD, C. H. Hesse-Cassel, Manu.—Ornamental paper-hangings: sized-pattern papering; papering with representations of German sports; satin hangings, ditto, in velvet and gold, &c.

836 JANNASCH, O. Bernburg.—Samples of vinegar-spirit and medical vinegar.

837 DEVISSE, NAPOLEON, Berlin — Two columns; a sphere; two tables of Venetian and Florentine marble.

838 SPINN & MENKE, Berlin, Upholsterer. — A highly finished bookcase, with bowed glass doors.

839 GERHARDT, AL. Berlin, Cork-cutter.—Pictures and articles in cork-work; with gold and silver chasings.

840 WAGNER, J. & SON, Berlin, Jewellers.—Table ornament in shape of a fruit dish, 4 feet and a half in height, representing the degrees of civilization among mankind.

841 ZEITZ, J. F. Berlin, Furrier.—A blue-grey paletot, lined with the skin of the Virginian Altis.

842 BLANKENSTEIN, Potsdam, Inv.—Rosewood box for gloves.

843 SCHUER, Dr. & KOHRING, Brandenburg.—Chemical productions.

844 ZSCHILLE, J. C. & K. Frankfort-on-the-Oder (31 Finsbury Sq.), Manu.—Different samples of woollen cloths.

845 LAVERDURE, Breslau, Sculptor, and VON MINUTOLI, Leignitz.—22 patterns of various Silesian marbles.

846 FRIEDENTHAL, C. Giesmannsdorf.—Lasting dried powdered yeast.

847 KIELMAN, Posen, Mason: and VON MINUTOLI, Leignitz—Three mosaic floors in the old Roman style.

848 GEBAUHR, C. J. Königsberg, Pianoforte-maker.—Two rosewood pianofortes.

849 WESSELY in Klein-Nuhr.—Two specimens of elk-heads, modelled after nature.

850 THE COMBINED MINING WORKS OF MANSFELD.—Samples of the processes followed in the mining works for obtaining copper and silver. Samples of copper.

851 KRÖNING, Dr., at Stollberg.—Substances woven and unwoven, gilt or silvered by a mechanical process.

852 HANEL, T. Sculptor, and LAUCHHAMMER.—Ostrich, giraffe, dog, and tiger, in plaster ; full sized female tiger, in plaster (original is in the Zoological Gardens of London).

853 PRÆTORIUS, L., Weissenfels, Carpenter. — Tray bordered à la Ricocco, of ebony wood, ornamented with foliage, the plate of mosaic ; inlaid with mother-of-pearl.

854 GRESSLER, E. Erfurt, Manu.—Coal-zinc battery of 12 elements; 12 coal cylinders. A machine for spreading plasters. An economical furnace.

855 SCHILLING, Suhl, Manu.—Pair of fine target pistols.

856 ROYAL SALTERY at Duerrenberg.—Coarse grained, refined, common salt.

857 HEINRIGS, J. Cologne. — A calligraphic tableau, representing the Queen of England.

858 FARINA, JOHANN MARIA, Cologne, Manu. opposite the Julich Pl.—Eau de Cologne of the genuine sort, the first has existed since 1709.

859 ZONOLI, CARL ANTON, Cologne, Manu.—Samples of eau de Cologne.

860 GAMMERSBACH BROTHERS, Meckenheim, near Bonn, Manu.—Leather and varnish.

861 MOSER, A. & Co. Aix-la-Chappelle, Manu.—A double planing machine on a new construction.

862 SIEGFRIED & ED. WALDTHAUSEN, Burtscheid.—12 pieces of twilled cloth and satin-de-laine.

863 HÖSCH, EB. & SONS, Düren, Manu.—Rolled zinc-plates. Raw material from the Rhine provinces.

864 SCHEIBLER & SON, Montjoie. — Various woollen stripes, and loose carded woollen goods.

865 BÖTHCHER & ENGEL, Imgenbruch, Manu.—Fancy stuffs for common and winter trousers.

866 DELIUS, Imgenbruch, manu.—Woollen stuffs.

867 MERTINS, H. T. Imgenbruch.—Different stuffs for coats and trousers.

868 MARTENS, S. Imgenbruch, Manu.—Different stuffs for coats and trousers.

869 DEINHART & JORDAN, Coblentz.—Samples of Rhine and Mosel wine.

870 GEYGER, A. & Co. Creuznach.—Four bottles of Rhine and Mosel wine; "mousseux."

871 MICHELS, FR. H., Andernach.—Two small basaltic lava millstones.

872 GERRESHEIM & NEEF, Solingen.—An assortment of scissors, and a card with unfinished specimens. (Agent in London, H. & D. Sharpe, 26 Broad Street Buildings.)

873 BERG BROTHERS, Wald.—85 samples of scissors.

874 HILGER BROTHERS, Lennep, Manu.—Piece of fine violet cloth ; two pieces of fine black cachemere.

875 LEVERKUS, Wermelskirchen.—Different sorts of ultramarine.

876 HARKORT, CHR. Harkhorten.—Lumps of Cadmia, lead, sulphur, manganese, alum, cast and rolled zinc. A shamoy-tanned wild buffalo-skin. Russia leather.

877 KARCHER, FRED. Karlsruhe.—Tracing (or transparent drawing) paper, invented and patented by exhibitor.

878 SOMMER, F. Heidelberg —Writing case in velvet; glove boxes, writing desks ; shaving cases, &c.

879 KRAUSZ, Rodach.—Cast of a shield representing a Bacchanal.

880 SCHULZ, Jos. Meiningen, Carver in Ivory.—Ivory snuff-boxes, cigar-cases, walking-stick knops, knives, &c.

881 SCHULZ, Wilhelm, Meiningen, Carver in Ivory.—Various articles in ivory.

882 DIESEL & Co. Saalfeld. — Oil, water, and other colours, Indian ink, &c. &c.

883 HEIMBURGER, Sondershaussen.—Table of Jaccaranda wood, inlaid with mother-of-pearl, metal, and ivory, containing 12 scenes taken from Shakespeare.

884 SCHUTZE, ANDR. Frose near Aschersleben.—A fur of German marmot's skins, in squares.

885 ENGEL, PH., Hanau, Engraver. — Specimens of new productions for the printing press.

886 REIFFERT, T. C. Bockenheim, Coachmaker.—Various models of railway carriages.

887 GLEICHAUF, B. Bockenheim.—A needle pistol with 12 barrels.

888 KELLER & Co. Birkenfeld, Oberstein.—A service in red cornelian vases, boxes, caskets, jewels, case, and fancy articles in onyx, cornelian, and green moss-agate.

889 WILD & ROBINSON, Birkenfeld, Oberstein.—Bronzes, flower-vases, bracelets, &c., of agate.

890 GÖRLITZ, L. Idar Birkenfeld. — Box, necklace, plates, &c. of agate.

891 EIFLER, W. Idar and Oberstein. (Agents, Nestle & Hunstmann, 6 Great Trinity Lane.)—Samples of agate work

892 MEYERN, HOHENBERG LOUISE VON, Coburg.—A tabernacle in Serravezza marble.

893 SOMMER, F. Taur in Silesia, Inv.—The Sommero-

phone, a brass instrument with a compass of four octaves from E to E.

894 JANDA, J. Berlin.—Statuette of Shakespeare carved in wood.

895 STOLLE, Dr. E. Berlin.—Map of the beet-root sugar district in Europe.

896 KRIEG, J. Odelshofen.—Samples of Rhenish slit hemp.

2. BAVARIA.

(Agent in London, Dr. SCHAFHAEUTL, 5 Albion St. Hyde Park Terrace.)

1 BENDA, GEORGE, Fürth, Prod.—Bronze colours.

2 BIRKNER & HARTMANN, Nürnberg, Prod.—A series of ground, bronze, and hammered metals.

3A BRANDEIS, I. jun. Fürth, Prod.—Samples of bronze powder, of leaf-metal, and bars of molten lead.

3B MEIER, J. C. Fürth, Prod.—Metal, gold, and bronze colours.

4 FUCHS & SONS, Fürth, Prod.—Various specimens of metallic leaf; bronze powder; rolled orsedew (tinsel) and shavings (waste of leaf-metal).

5 LINZ, J. L. Fürth, Prod.—Specimens of white leaf-metal made of English tin.

6 LEPPER, G. Fürth, Prod.—Patterns of bronze colours. Fifty sorts of different colours. Metal-leaf.

7 STOEBER'S SON, L. Fürth, Prod.—Specimens of bronze colours.

8 BÖRER & PORZELIUS, Ratisbon, Prod.—Specimens of extract of nut of the quercus-cerris.

9 BENDA, G. Fürth, Prod.—Bronze powder, in a small case.

10 GERSTENDORFFER, J. J. & C. KUBLER, Jun. Fürth, Prod.—Samples of beaten metal (Dutch leaf).

11 KÜBLER, G. Fürth, Pro.—Samples of beaten metal (Dutch metal).

11A AMMON, J. P. Nürnberg, Prod.—Gold and silver wire.

11B FÜCHS, H. M. Nürnberg, Prod. (Agent in London, W. Meyerstein, 15 Watling St.)—1 lb. of soft and malleable brass wire for metallic cloth, length 76,000 feet. 1 lb. of extra fine chalybeate wire for lanterns, length 41,000 ft.

12 GADEMANN, H. Schweinfurt, Prod.—Specimens of blue, black, and green ultramarine.

13 RAU, I. Fürth, Prod.—Specimens of bronze powder and gold leaf metal.

14 SATTLER, W. Schweinfurt, Prod.—Specimens of varnish of colours in glass bottles. Extra fine printing ink.

15 SCHRUCK & UHLICH, Bamberg, Prod.—Pattern cards of various bronze colours.

16 STOEBER, J. J. Fürth, Prod.—Bronze.

17 WOLF & Co. Schweinfurt, Prod.—Specimens of ultramarine.

18 HAMMERSCHMIDT'S SON-IN-LAW, Ratisbon, Prod.—Samples of Bavarian wheat, bran, &c. wheat-meal, pollard, rye, rye-meal, provender meal.

19 ERICH, C. A. Munich, Millowner. — Bavarian wheat, wheaten grits, and meal and square barley.

20 HEINLEIN, C. V. Bamberg, Inv.—A rifle, highly finished, carved and ornamented in the old German style.

21 KUCHENREUTER, T. J. Regensburg, Inv. and Pro.—Two pair of rifle pistols, in rosewood cases, highly finished and carry 240 yards.

22 BAADER, J. A. & Co. Mittenwald. Pro. (Agents in London, E. Brandeis & Co. 5 St. Dunstan's Hill Chambers, Great Tower St).—Two violins; tenor; violoncello.

23 BOEHM, J. Munich, Inv. and Manu.—A key flute with silver and gold embrochures. A flute d'amour (in B flat), the same size and construction. Model of an oboe on same principle.

24 EISENMENGER, G. Fürth, Manu.—Collection of lorgnettes, spectacles, and eye-glasses.

25 ERTEL, TRAUGOTT, & SONS, Proprietors of the Reichenback Mathematical and Mechanics' Institute.—Astronomical universal instrument; constructed on most recent principle, with telescope.

26 ISSMAYER, I. M. Nürnberg, Prod.—Collection of magnetic toys.

27 JORDAN, J. F. Fürth, Manu.—Flexible syphon, ear-tubes, pipes, &c.

28 KAPELLER, L. & SON, Hafnerszell, near Passau, Manu.—Various sorts of black crucibles for melting gold, silver, iron, steel, &c.

29 KLINGER, C. A. Nürnberg, Prod.—Terrestrial and celestial globes, with stands and compasses.

30, 31 MERZ & SONS, Munich, Inv. and Manu.—Refractor, having 45′ apert., 48″ focal length, for variable latitude; equatorially mounted. Microscope, with various object-glasses and three eye-pieces, for nine magnifying powers, from 20 to 1,800 times. The instrument is provided with a screw micrometer and the necessary apparatus for holding and illuminating objects.

32 MECHANICAL SCHOOL, Zweybrücken, directed by Dr. H. Reinsch.—Electro-magnetic apparatus, and electromagnetic rotatory apparatus.

33 NEUNER & HORNSTEINER, Mittenwald, Prod.—Violoncello, tenor, and violins. Fernambuck violin and violoncello bows.

34 RIEFLER, C. Maria Rhine, near Nesselwang, Inv. and Prod.—Case of improved mathematical drawing instruments.

35 PFAFF, M. Kaiserslautern, Prod. —Bombardon ophocleide in C, with four valves and mouthpiece. Trumpet in B flat, with three valves, four crooks, and a mouthpiece.

36 BRENTANO, PELLOVZ & Co. Augsburg, Manu.—Patterns of silk cloth, with gold and silver, for furniture and church apparel. Patterns of various stuffs and cloths, manufactured from Bavarian silk. Specimens of said silk.

37 SIMON, H. Zweybrücken, Manu.—Silk plush.

38 KNORR, F. Zweybrücken, Manu. (Agents in London, Stahlschmidt & Co.)—Silk plush, for hats.

39 BRAUER, I. Wunsiedel, Manu.—Specimens of Manilla damask cotton and Manilla hemp, mixed.

40 SCHUTZMANN, A. Munich, Produc.—Canvas, prepared for paintings, twenty-three feet by thirteen feet four inches.

41 TRENDEL, J. J. & SONS, Culmbach, Manu.—Linen damask. Striped half-linen cloth for trousers. Fine white-linen satin; half-linen satin. Half-linen cloth for trousers; the same of half-linen thread.

42 GEBHART BROTHERS, Hof, Manu.—Shawls and handkerchiefs, cotton and wool, and woollen. Drawers, of cotton and caoutchouc.

43 LIENHART, F. Hof, Manu.—Cotton goods; cotton mixed with wool.

44 STEINHAUSER, H. Hof, Manu.—Shawls of wool, mixed with cotton. Tartans of mixed fabric.

45 GRIESS, L. Landau, Rope-maker.—Girths for horses of bleached hemp; girths unbleached. Halter, of red woollen thread; halter, of white hemp twist.

46 MAYER, I. Munich, Manu.—Enamelled coach hides. Enamelled calf-skins. Japanned shoe calf-skins. Curried bridle leather. Curried hog-skin for saddle seats.

47 HAENLE, L. Munich, Prod. (Agent in London, Mr. Schick, 56, High Holborn.)—Silver and gold paper, plain and ornamental. Bronze powder, and specimen of printing with bronze colours. Samples of gold paper borders, &c.

48 ESCHERICH, T. Munich, Manu.—Various portfolios and cases, in leather morocco, port-monnaies, cigar-cases, &c.

49 KOHN, M. T. Main-Bernheim, Prod.—Samples of sealing wax.

50 SAMMET, J. Marksteft, Prod.—Black ink for copper-plate printing.

51 PRAETZSCH, MINA, Hof, Prod.—Piece of embroidery in crape threads, representing the Madonna.

52 MAYER, EMILIE, Aschaffenburg, Prod.—Embroidery in silk, after a picture by Angelica Kauffmann.

53 FRANK, J. Ratisbon, Prod.—Ladies' boots of satin and of leather and black cloth. Embroidered slippers.

54 FEHR & EISENRING, Augsburg, Prod.—Metal plates, with letters and characters in relievo, for the instruction of the blind.

54A KALTENECKER, J. Munich, Manu.—1 Samples of textures of wires, hair, wood, and cane. 2 Sieve, with bottom and cover, of parchment. 3 Sieve, of parchment, for sifting gunpowder. 4 Triple sieve, for sorting. 5 Brass drum, with improved tuning screw. 6 Model of double gratings, for drying malt. 7 Vizors used in fencing.

55 GRADMAN, A. Erbacher, Fabrik, near Homburg, Prod.—Forty specimens of horse-shoes.

56 JANSEN & LUHDORF, Hof, Manu.—Ginghams.

57 KUHN, C. (E. Schmidner), Nürnberg, Prod.—Patterns of gold and silver-plated and copper wire, spangles, &c.

58 KULLRICH, F. Munich, Prod.—A casket with ornaments for ladies.

59 TROELTSCH & HANSELMANN, Weissenburg, Prod.—Gold and silver lace.

60 HECHINGER, H. Fürth, Manu.—Mirrors of tinted glass.

61 HEILBRONN, L. Fürth, Manu.—Mirrors.

62 NEFT, M. C. (O. Von Reder), Shleichach, near Eltmann, Prod.—Specimens of white crown glass, as half moon.

63 REINSCH, A. Kürnberg, Inv. and Prod.—Various objects of art, made of glass, and two damascened looking-glasses.

64 The ROYAL PORCELAIN MANUFACTORY, Nymphenburg, near Munich.—Porcelain and Biscuit: Vases, goblets, pitchers, and flower-vases, with pictures after various artists. Table services, for fruit. Plates, with views of Rens, and subjects from Goëthe's Reinecke Fuchs; white biscuit statues (the district of Bavaria, after Schwanthaler); busts and statues of celebrated men.

65 HELD, K. Kürnberg, Prod.—Tobacco pipes of Turkish clay, or in clay meerschaum; cigar tubes of the same material.

66 ADT BROTHERS, Ensheim, near Zweibrücken, Pro.—Various works in papier-maché.

67 BARTH BROTHERS, Würzburg, Prod. (Agent, C. Kendall, 8 Harp Lane, Great Tower Street.)—Lady's desk in renaissance style. Lady's work-table in rococo style.

68 DESSAUR, A. Aschaffenburgh, Manu.—Samples of coloured, and gold and silver papers.

69 FORTNER, F. X. Munich, Prod.—Marquetrie writing-table in old German or Gothic style, of rose-wood, inlaid with different metals, &c.; and portraits in the same style. Portfolio similarly executed. Portfolio in renaissance style; another in buhl style.

70 MAYER, J. Munich, Prod.—Two crucifixes. The Madonna. Flower-vase, of carton-pierre.

71 FLEISCHMANN, C. W. Nürnberg, Prod.—Anatomical pathologic casts in papier-maché.

72 PLEISCH, N. Enshiem, near Zweibrücken, Prod.—Snuff-boxes, needle and cigar cases in papier-maché.

73 HARTMANN, J. J. Munich, Prod.—Samples of parquetrie work for floors, of various woods; mirror frames, &c.

74 BAADER, I. Garmisch, Prod.—Candelabra of staghorn and wood, exhibited as a specimen of turnery.

75 FRANK, C. Fürth, Prod.—Goblet in carved ivory, with relievos from the "Lay of the Niebelungen," 14 inches high; chess-men cut in ivory, with chess-board and polished case. Spinning-wheel in ivory.

76 HENSTEH, J. Lindberg, near Zwisel, Manu.—Specimen of wood for sounding-boards.

77 LANG, G. (Heirs of), Oberammergau, Prod.—Ornaments and toys cut in wood, ivory, and alabaster.

78 JACOB, J. Würzburg.—Newly-constructed steam-extraction tea and coffee boiler.

79 BIRKMANN, M. Nürnberg, Prod. — Six-cornered blacklead pencils of various degrees of hardness.

80 EICHNER, G. L. Nürnberg, Prod.—Varnished toys of tinned iron plate.

81 FABER, A. W. Stein, near Nürnberg, Manu.—Patterns of black-lead pencils.

82 REHBACH, J. J. Ratisbon, Manu.—Black and red lead pencils. Boxes with crayons for drawing, &c.

83 HAGEN, M. Munich, Sculp. — Goblet of ivory, carved with figures and arabesques, representing a procession of Bacchanals; gilded silver inside.

84 HALBIG, J. Munich, Inv. and Prod.—Goblet cylinders, in plaster of Paris. A bust of Schlender's marble.

85 HANFSTAENGEL, J. Munich, Inv. and Prod.—Specimens of galvanography. Original copper-plate, with the drawing in relief. Secondary, or printing-plate, produced by galvanism. Print from the same.

86 KELLNER, S. Nürnberg, Prod.—Glass painting, a copy of the window by Volkanier, in St. Lorenz church, at Nürnberg.

87 OZANN, Dr. (Prof. at Univ. Würzburg).—Plate for printing, produced by the hydro-electric current, and samples of prints taken from it.

88 KNOLL, C. Munich, Sculp.—Model of a goblet, in plaster of Paris, to be cast in bronze, representing "Loving and Living on the Rhine."

89 LEEB, J. Munich, Sculp.—Young girl with a nest of hornets. Cupid sharpening his arrows; in Carrara marble.

90 MILLER, F. Munich, Prod.—Colossal lion, fifteen feet long and nine feet high. Two statues, seven feet high, modelled by Schwanthaler, cast in bronze and finished with the chisel. 1 Libussa, Queen of the Bohemians, anno 700. 2 George of Padiebrad, King of the Bohemians.

91 MUHR, J. Munich, Prod.—Stereochromic picture upon mortar-ground, plastered on wood; a new method for producing indestructible paintings on walls, invented by T. N. S. Fuchs.

92 SCHMIDT, C. Bamberg.—Paintings on porcelain, after Cornelius, Rembrandt, Lessing, Roekers, Van der Worft, Leonardo, and Waffers. An altar, with the Madonna del Sesto, after Raphael, with old German decorations.

93 ZEILER, F. Munich, Prod.—Silver fruit-plate in the form of a shell, in alto-relievo. Two alto-relievos in silver.

94 FOLTZ, L. Ratisbon, Sculp.—Model, in plaster, intended for a prize medal.

95 GRENANTH BROTHERS, Prop. Hockheim, Bavarien Rhene-Palat.—Iron for guns and railways. Rolled and wrought-iron, rasping-plate iron. and iron wire. Various kinds of steel, bronze, gilt, and silver fancy articles.

96 WEPPLER, C. L. Arsbach, Manu.—Fancy articles in straw mosaic.

97 NEUBRONNER, G. Frankenthal, in the Bavarian Rhine-Palatinate.—Six children's dolls, richly dressed.

98 BISCHOFF, C. A. & Co. Würzburg, Manu. (Agent, J. Kendall, 8 Harp Lane, Great Tower St.)—Writing portfolios, smaller portfolios, an album, cigar cases, portemonnaies, ladies' necessaires.

99 WAGNER and Co. Klingenberg-on-the-Mayne, Prod.—Samples of fire-clay.

100 KNOCKE, A. Munich.—Pair of kettle-drums.

102 REICHENBACH, C. Augsburg. (Agent, Mr. L. Bamberger, 20, King St. Snow Hill.)—Printng machine of a new construction.

3. SAXONY.

(DR. WOLDEMAR SEYFFARTH, LL.D. Commissioner for Royal Saxony, 91 Piccadilly.)

1 SOMMER, C. Sornzig, near Mügen, Prod.—Specimens of flax cultivated in the Belgian manner, water-retted and swingled, also swingled and heckled. Patterns of extra fine yarn, spun from the flax.

2 WATTEYNE, J. Lichtenberg, near Freiberg, Manu.—Patterns of swingled flax, cultivated in the Belgian manner, and water-retted.

3 GAETZSCHMANN, W. Zittau, Manu.—Flax, watered and swingled, also partly heckled, in five different qualities.

4 THIEME-WIEDTMARCKTER & PUESCHEL, Reudnitz, near Leipzic, Manu.—Bleached sponges, fine and common quality.

5 KUNZE, F. Rochlitz, Manu.—Varnished leather. Black varnished calves' leather, for the use of shoemakers and belt-makers; the same description, of sheeps' leather.

6 JORDAN & TIMAEUS, Dresden, Manu.—Assortment of dessert chocolates. Ornaments for dining-tables, nips, and Christmas presents. Chocolates and cocoa masses, in packets.

7 HARDEGEN, G. Leipzig, Manu.—Black printing-ink for hand presses and for machines.

8 JAGODZINSKY, A. Leipzic, Manu. — Strong oil-varnish. Calcined soot. Printing-ink for machines and presses.

9 THE ROYAL SAXON COBALT AND NICKEL WORKS Schneeberg (Agent, B. Biggs, 3 Lawrence Pountney Hill).—A series of twenty-eight specimens of cobalt blue, enamel blue, smalt and cobalt green. Metallic bismuth. Metallic nickel in cubes.

10 THE ROYAL SAXON CHINA MANUFACTORY, Meissen.—Complete series of ultramarine blue.

11 SCHMIDT & Co. Daubnitz, near Lommartzsch, Prop.—Safety fusees: No. 1, for common use in quarries, with black cover, 1,000 yards in one piece; No. 2, for working in mines, with grey cover; No. 3, for working under water. One box, with porcelain clay.

12 HOFFMANN, C. Leipzic, Manu. — Machine for planing printing types, with three different planing tools. Machine for boring corals.

13 BROCKHAUS, F. A. Leipzic, Prop.—Machine for casting types, with instruments for two different sizes of letters.

14 RICKBORN, C. H. T. Leipzig, Inv.—Machine for sweeping narrow chimneys.

15 STOEHRER, E. Leipzig, Inv. and Manu.—Electromagnetic telegraphing apparatus, with dial and hand: used on the telegraphic lines of Saxony and Bavaria.

16 LEYSER, M. L. Leipzig, Manu.—Electro dynamometer, with mirror and telescope: for measuring the intensity of galvanic currents.

17 LANGE, A. Glashütte, Manu.—Watches, manufactured as in Switzerland, by division of labour. A box with all parts of a watch, and watch movements in four different stages of manufacture. Watch cases, and engraved patterns Ten watches, lever escapements, chronometer balance. Six with eight stones.

18 KLEMM, G. A. Neukirchen (Agents, J. D. Kohler and Son), Manu.—Stringed instruments: Brescian counter, bass and violoncello. Violin; Paolo Albani; Amati, and Stainer. Cord-rims-violin. Violin in the antique style. Bass viol. Guitar. Violin bow, with silver ornaments. Pattern book of the appendages of the violin. Wind instruments: Chromatic horn in F, and trumpet in G.

19 HEROLD, C. G. Klingenthal, Manu.—Wind-instruments: Tenor-tuba, with three conic valves. Brass reed horn, with eight valves. Brass clarionet in E, with sixteen keys. Ivory piccolo, in D, with ten keys. Mouth-harmonica, or musical glasses. Combs of wood.

20 GLIER, F. & SON, Klingenthal (Agent, F. E. D. Hast, 18 Aldermanbury), Manu.—Wood-combs, and a book of patterns. Violins and fiddle-sticks. Guitar. Trumpet of German silver. Cornet of copper. Cornopean of brass

21 GLIER, G. Neukirchen, Manu.—Wind-instruments Saxe horns; bugle of copper, with eight keys of argentan; bugle of brass, with the same; D flute of ebony, with keys.

22 SCHUSTER, L. Neukirchen, Manu.—Musical instruments: Sackbut in B, with three cylinders; Packfong trumpet in G; cornet B alto.

23 SCHUSTER, jun. M. Neukirchen (Agent, C. Holland, 41 Finsbury Circus), Manu.—Wind-instruments: D clarionet, with all keys; B clarinet; B cornet, with three cylinders; bass clarinet, with all keys.

24 ZIMMERMANN, C. Carlsfeld, near Eibenstock, Manu.—Harmonicas and accordions: Chromatic concert harmonicas; bass and tenor harmonicas; accordions of forty and twenty tunes.

25 BREITKOPF & HAERTEL, Leipzig, Manu.—Concert pianoforte, in rosewood case.

26 THE ROYAL DIRECTION OF RAILWAYS, Dresden.—Models of the two great viaducts of the Saxo-Bavarian Railway, over the Elster and Goeltzsch valleys.

27 LATTERMANN & SONS, Morgenröthe, near Auerbach, Manu.—Tin goods. Culinary utensils used in Bavaria. Machines for making coffee. Iron spoons.

28 RECHSTEINER, J. B. Connewitz, near Leipzig, Inv.—Twenty-eight specimens of wood-screws.

29 WOLF, V. H. Burgstädt, near Chemnitz, Manu.—Iron wares. A pattern-book of nails, rivets, and tags.

30 KRUMBHOLZ & TRINKS, Neustadt, Manu.—Various pocket-knives, with from one to thirty-two blades, and with ornamented handles; knives for cutting the end of segars; champaign knives; table knives, &c. Hangers and daggers, with figured handles. Exhibited for execution and arrangement.

31 LEVY, H. Dresden, Manu.—Carving knife and fork, with handles of solid mother-of-pearl, and pins of silver.

32 THUERIGEN, F. T. Meissen, Manu.—A gun with double barrel, on a new percussion principle.

33 STRUBE & SON, Leipzig (Agents, Phillips Brothers, 31 Cockspur St.), Manu.—Silver works: a vase with fifteen silver flowers.

34 JAHN, A. Dresden, Manu.—Chess-boards of composition metal. Exhibited for cheapness and execution.

35 DE BUENAU, R. Reudnitz, near Leipzig (Agent, C. Holland, 41 Finsbury Circus), Manu.—Composition goods: playthings for children; sets of coffee and tea-things; millinery; toilets; caskets; segar-boxes, &c.

36 HOFFMANN, F. Sebnitz, Manu.—Parts of lamps for the trade, made of brass. Lamp-burners in different numbers. Regulating jacks. Tubes with screw thread.

37 GRUHL, F. Kleinwelka, near Bautzen (Agent, Mr. Mallalieu, 97 Hatton Garden, Holborn), Manu.—A bell of brass, 383 kilogr. weight, with iron clapper and tackle.

38 STRAUSS, E. W. E Chemnitz, Manu.—Cotton yarn of different numbers.

39 HEYMANN, G. F. Chemnitz, Manu.—Cotton yarn, Nos. 80, 70, 60, 50, 40, 24, 40, 30, single and medio, first quality. Nos. 10 and 24, six thread, knitting, first quality.

40 BODEMER, G. Zschopau, Manu.—Cotton yarn for stockings.

41 HOEFFER, C. F. Tannenberg, near Annaberg, Manu.—Specimens of twist, Nos. 30, 40, 50, spun from Georgia.

42 PANSA & HAUSCHILD, Chemnitz, Manu.—Knitting cotton yarn of various numbers and qualities.

43 MATTOCH, C. G. Chemnitz, Manu.—Cotton thread of different qualities and numbers.

44 THE SOCIETY OF WORSTED SPINNERS, Leipzig

(Pfaffendorf), Manu.—Illustrations of the process of worsted spinning, from the raw wool up to the finest yarn. Specimens of worsted yarns of different numbers.

45 Trinius & Sons, Leipzig, Manu.—An assortment of worsted yarns, raw and coloured, various threads.

46 Petzold & Ehret, Reichenbach, Manu.—Worsted yarns, of different numbers.

47 Solbrig, C. F. Chemnitz, Manu. —Woollen yarn, of different numbers.

48 Wolf, F. H. Burgstädt, near Chemnitz, Manu.— Woollen soft worsted yarn (raw), various Nos. each 5 lbs. weight; ½ lb. Nos. 24 and 26 on the reel.

49 Schmidt, J. G. jun. & Sons, Penig, Manu.—Knitting worsted yarn, in different colours, and a book of shades.

50 Behr & Schubert, Frankenberg, Manu.—Rich silk stuffs for tapestry, furniture, carriages, &c. Satin, damask, brocatelle, and côteline. Portrait woven in silk. A flag of double satin, with fringes.

50B Roehling & Co. Annaberg, Manu.—Rich silk stuffs, viz.: Lampas; damas lizeré; broderie Pompadour moiré à reserve: faconné, lancé, découpé; façonné glacé; armure.

51 Beyer's Widow & Co. Zittau (Agents, J. Wilson and Sons, 159 New Bond St.), Manu.—Linen damask table cloths; tray cloths, with napkins and doyleys—raw, white, and bleached.

52 Lieske & Haebler, Gross-Schönau, near Zittau (Agent, P. Amsel, 20 Providence Row, Finsbury Sq.), Manu.—Linen damasks, raw and bleached. Table cloths and napkins.

53 Waentig, D. & Sons, Gross-Schönau, near Zittau, Manu.—Manufactures in linen damask, viz.: A large table-cloth, unbleached; napkins, all linen, unbleached and white; half-silk, crimson, and chamois; half linen, red and white. Series of table-cloths, with napkins, of linen-bleached damask, including pieces executed in various years from 1770 to 1850, to show the historical progress of the art. Half-silk and silk damask napkins, partly with fringes.

54 Proelss, sen. seel. Sons, Dresden, Manu.—Table-cloths of brown and white linen damask. Napkins of the same with armorial bearings. Damask doyleys, with fringes.

55 Brandstetter, F. Leipzig, Manu.—Table-cloth of linen diaper, 24 feet long, 8 feet wide.

56 Boehler, F. L. & Son, Plauen, Manu.—White cotton fabrics and embroideries: Plain mull, figured cambric, plain and figured curtain-gaze. Curtains in figured mull, figured nainsoot stripes, embroidered jaconet stripes. Embroidered handkerchiefs of linen.

57 Heynig, J. G. & Co. Plauen, Manu.—Cotton goods for curtains: Gaze, with borders, figured. Gaze, with borders à jour. Figured damask. Plain mull. Cambric jaconet.

58 Krause, C. G. & Co. Plauen, Manu.—Embroideries: Figured jaconet; embroidered mulls; figured and coloured borders.

59 Mammen, F. A. & Co. Plauen, Manu.—Embroideries in mull, half cambric, jaconet, and linen cambric. Capes and handkerchiefs, tamboured, embroidered with the needle and with the loom.

60 Schmidt, G. F. & Co. Plauen (Agents, Ullmann, Hirschhorn & Co.), Manu.—Embroideries on jaconet, silk, and cambric, with cotton and silk. A set of furniture; easy chair, pillow and cushions embroidered à la Française; footstool; window curtains with fringes; wall basket; table-cover; shades; letter case; and pincushion, embroidered in the French style.

61 Meinhold & Stoffregen, Plauen, Manu.—Embroideries: Muslin curtains, rose and white (broché brode), new patterns worked with the Jacquard loom; gaze curtains, white (broché), worked with the Jacquard loom; embroidered (with the needle) linen handkerchiefs; mulls, plain and figured.

62 Schnorr & Steinhaeuser, Plauen, Manu.—Embroideries in mull, French, and Scotch cambric and net. Pair of sleeves of mull in the pagoda style; embroidered collars; cambric collars à l'Anglaise; guipures of net work; chemisettes of mull, à la Duchesse, à la Marie, à l'Amazone; cambric pocket handkerchiefs, English embroidery; pocket handkerchief of French cambric; morning dress of Scotch cambric; pillow of French cambric.

63 Glaeser, F. Lengenfeld, near Auerbach, Manu.— Cambrics, jaconets, and jaconets spotted, of different qualities. Exhibited for cheapness.

64 Hetzer, Ernst. & Son, Auerbach, Manu.—White fancy cotton goods: Gaze ramage for curtains, jaconet batist, and organdy.

65 Beck, G. F. Hohenstein, Manu.—Cotton woven goods (piqué): Coverlets, figured; red, plain, and rough. Piqué petticoats.

66 Stoelzel, G. F. & Son, Eibenstock, Manu.—Embroideries in mull jaconet, linen cambric, and cotton gaze. Capes: festooned of jaconet, mull and cambric, guiped of cotton gaze, of net work, black and white chemisettes. Bonnets, of thread; of white net work; white, black, and coloured with rosettes and fringes, with gold; double black with barbe, of net work. Visites, pelerines, mantillas, and shawls. Laces: Brussels and coloured woollen.

67 Priem, Emily, Eibenstock (Agent A. Heintzmann 17 Ironmonger Lane, Cheapside), Manu.—Laces: Bone laces; complete gown, volant. Embroidered: veil, corset, bertha of crape, fancheon of black net work, mixed with yellow; fancheon of white net work.

68 Foerster, F. Eibenstock (Agent, H. Kohnstamm, 7, Union Court, Broad St.), Manu.—Embroidered capes, ruffles, bonnets, barbes, veils, shawls, and pelerines. Laces: Zephyr bed laces, black bobbin, black silk laces, genuine blondes, and a long black barbe.

69 Doerffel, C. G. & Sons, Eibenstock (Agent, C. Holland, 41, Finsbury Circus), Manu.—Laces: White thread; black silk lace insertion; and black silk laces.

70 Koester & Uhlmann, Schneeberg (Agents E. and H. Blank, 10, Trump St. King St. Cheapside), Manu.—Laces: Imitation, Valenciennes and Brussels. Embroideries: Capes; Valenciennes; zephyr net work; ruffles, handkerchiefs of cambric; black silk half veils; berthas and barbes; mantillas; and shawl of zephyr net work.

71 Schreiber, F. A. Dresden, Manu.—Laces and embroideries, imitation Brussels. Volans; bertha; barbe écharpe. Embroidered scarfs in the ancient style; barbe bertha, &c. Embroideries: collars, ruffles, and pocket handkerchiefs.

72—83 The United Merchant Manufacturers: Friedrich & Son, Nacke & Gehrenbeck, Friedrich Neuber Franz Solbrig, Wex & Lindner, all in Chemnitz; Glaeser J. S. jun., in Schoenau, near Chemnitz; Haertel, H. C., in Waldenburg; Pester, August, in Limbach; Meinert Brothers, in Oelsnitz; Landgraff, Gottfried, in Hohenstein Webendoerffer, C. H. & Sons, in Lichtenstein; Sedlag Gustav, in Königsbrück (Agents. Nacke & Gehenbeck, Friedrich & Son, W. Meyerstein, 15 Watling St.; A. Heintzmann, 17 Ironmonger Lane, Cheapside; H. C. Härtel, G. Landgraff, D. Joshua, 34, King St. Cheapside).—Men's and women's hose; half hose; men's and women's gloves; children's and boys' hose; half hose and jackets; gloves; drawers, and caps; woollen and cotton amisols, amazons, &c., brown, white, and coloured. Women's hose; brown lace, white lace, and silk embroidered.

84 Becker & Schraps, Chemnitz, Spinners and Printers.—Printed calicos, fast colours. Ribbed cotton cloth, printed with eight steam colours. Cotton handkerchiefs, madder work. Cotton cravats and neckerchiefs, of various styles.

85 LOHSE, EDWARD, Chemnitz (Agent, W. Meyerstein, 15, Watling St.), Manu.—Damasks for furniture in half silk, all silk, half wool, and cotton, named Valentia, imperial, gobelin, berakan, president, rips, &c. ; foulard lustrine, half silk ; plain and figured cotton cameleons ; figured ginghams ; table covers and bed-cover of half silk, half wool, and cotton damask. Glazed gingham ; cravats, cotton jaconet ; atlas, and half silk satin.

86 HOESEL, R. & Co. Chemnitz.—Damasks: woollen, purple, green, crimson. Silk and wool, two and three coloured brown, striped gobelins, and two coloured green. Cotton and woollen, scarlet, light blue, brown, green, crimson, royal blue, nacarathe, &c., table-covers.

87 ROEHRIG & ALBRECHT, Chemnitz, Manu.—Damasks: cotton, cotton and wool, cotton and silk, wool and silk, in various colours.

88 SEYFFERT & BREYER, Chemnitz (Agents, Gottschalk & Schröder, 72, Basinghall St.), Manu.—Damask in different colours, named Victoria gobelin, coloured gobelin, coloured imperial ; silk-striped, woollen and cotton, woollen, silk, and cotton. Table-cover, named gobelin 'spis.

89 VOGEL, W. Chemnitz (Agent, D. Foshua, 34 King St. Cheapside), Manu.—Stuffs : woollen, cotton, and silk mixed. Fancy articles, named satin laine, satin laine rayé soie, satin cotton, &c. ; damas mi-soie velouté, royal mi-soie, royal coloured, woollen and silk mixed ; woollen, silk, and cotton ; woollen and cotton.

90 THUEMER & TOEPER, Chemnitz (Agents, Gebhardt, Rottman & Co. 29, Wood St. Cheapside), Manu.—Damasks: silk, cotton, and wool imperial ; cotton imperial ; furniture in cotton and wool. Table-covers : patent cotton and cotton and wool. Fancy stuffs : robes, satin laine façonné.

91 WINKLER & SON, Rochlitz, Manu.—Worsted stuffs from soft worsted yarn : Satin double ; maroquin laine ; cuir laine ; popeline laine ; velours laine ; velours rayé ; Cachemire electa.

92 ZIEGLER & HAUSSMANN, Glauchau (Agent, J. Borroughs, 18, Addle St.), Manu.—Woollen stuffs (made from soft worsted yarn, mixed with silk) ; fancy articles named poult de soie, Amienne, Cachemire, Thibet, satin imperial, satin de Saxe, Cachemire tissue, &c.

93 KOEHLER & SCHEDLICH, Glauchau (Agent, E. Buchler), Manu.—Stuffs, fancies, wool, cotton, and silk mixed, named Ecossais, Islyennes, Stradellas, Amiennes, Veloutés, Favoritas, printed Veloutés, &c.

94 GUENTHER & SIMON, Glauchau, Manu.—Worsted stuffs : Valentia, Estalla, Cachemirienne, and Armure.

95 FACILIDES & Co. (Agent, W. Meyerstein, 15, Watling St.), Manu.—Shawls : long, mosaic, teutonia, zephyr, Cachemire, Nancy, &c.

96 HECKER & TASCH, Glauchau (Agents, Cooper & Blagg, 44 Friday St. Cheapside), Manu.—Various fancy stuffs, woollen and cotton, named Lombard, Montpensier, Cachemires, tartan, and trisanna ; and woollen, named pure laine, first and second quality, sprinkled ; cameleon, woollen.

97 SCHIFFNER & ZIMMERMANN, Glauchau, Manu.— Worsted sluffs. Metaline ; Melpomene, all wool, and half silk ; Aqueline ; Castiglione ; Montauban ; Metaline, half silk.

98 TRINKS, E. Glauchau, Manu.—Stuffs : wool, and wool and cotton mixed. Robes, Florida, and façonnée. Lama for ladies' cloaks. Robes popeline ; faconnée, and striped ; imitée.

99 STAUSS & LEUSCHNER, Glauchau (Agents, Gebhardt, Rottmann, & Co. 29 Wood Street, Cheapside), Manu.—Fine worsted goods. All worsted, gros, mixed, Montpensier, thread warp, worsted weft. Lama, made with thread warp and woollen weft, and with silk warp and worsted weft.

100 THE WEAVERS' SCHOOL, Glauchau.—Stuffs ; wool, and wool and cotton ; robe Jacquard ; châles, or shawls, woollen and silk. Specimens worked by the pupils of the institution, which is supported by the manufacturers of Glauchau.

101 GRUENER, F.W. Glauchau.—Woollen stuffs (worsted stuff yarns) ; Thibets, superfine quality, different colours. Dyed by the exhibitor.

102 GRAEFE, J. F. & SON, Meerane, Manu.—Woollen and half-woollen fancy stuffs: Montpensier, Cachemiriennes. Plaids, first and second quality. Châles, damasés.

103 DIETRICH & STRAFF, Meerane, Manu.—Worsted woollen fancy stuffs ; and mixed tartan, Cachemirienne, Montpensier, Odéon checks, and satiné.

104 RICHTER, H. L. Meerana (Agent, A. Heintzmann, 17 Ironmonger Lane, Cheapside), Manu.—Half woollen stuffs: Angora, mixed with silk. Montpensier. Napolitaine, first and second quality. Muslin d'Ecosse.

105 GLAFEY & NEUBARTH, Reichenbach, Manu.—Woollen stuffs and printed covers. Table-cover of cloth and Circassienne, printed flannel. Atlas. Superfine woollen atlas, made from soft wool yarn, by Petzold and Ehret.

106 SEYFERTH, J. & Co. Reichenbach, Manu.—Woollen fancy stuffs and printed shawls ; Cachemire, Lama, Victoria shawls, printed in different colours and patterns.

107 LEHMANN, C. G. Boehrigen, near Rosswein (Agents, Gottschalk & Schroeder, 72 Basinghall St.), Manu.—Woollen and mixed stuffs : Llama flannels of different colours, and plaid patterns for mantles ; buckskin, entirely woollen ; molton, pepper and salt ; swan-skin for shirts and chemisettes, with cotton warp ; baize, with cotton warp, for petticoats, striped, quarried, and striped with borders.

108 BOETTIGER, H. G. F. Crimmitzschau, Manu.— Woollen stuffs, viz. cassinet, green, blue, brown, black, and mixed. Tricot cora. Double cassinet black ; and mixed. Cachemire.

109 BURKHART, H.T. Crimmitzschau, Manu.—Woollen stuffs. Winter and summer elastics, and cassinet.

110 COLLEL, F. Crimmitzschau, Manu.—Woollen stuffs: cassinet, summer satin, and winter buckskin.

111 HUEFFER, H. Crimmitzschau, Manu.—Woollen fancy stuffs for paletots and trousers. Buckskin of various qualities, for the summer. Grey and green cassinets.

112 HELLING, O. & Co. Crimmitzschau, Manu.—Woollen stuffs ; summer and winter elastics.

113 KIRSTEN, C W. Crimmitzschau, Manu.—Woollen stuffs : cassinet, and summer buckskin.

114 KAUFMANN, C. H. & SON, Crimmitzschau, Manu.— Woollen stuffs. Zephyr, deep scarlet ; Peruvienne ; paletot ; winter and summer elastics ; summer satin, and cassinet.

115 MUELLER & Co. Crimmitzschau, Manu.—Woollen stuffs ; summer and winter buckskin.

116 OEHLER, BROTHERS, Crimmitzschau, Manu.—Woollen stuffs. Cassinet of different colours ; back doeskin satinet, drab colour ; glacé.

117 SPENGLER, C. jun. Crimmitzschau, Manu.—Woollen stuffs. Winter buckskin.

118 MATTHESS, C. jun. Zschopau, Manu.—Cassinet, woven on power-looms. The manufacture of damask and figured woven goods, mixed of cotton, wool and silk, occupies many thousand hand and Jacquard looms in Chemnitz and neighbourhood.

119 ZSCHILLE, F. & Co. Grossenhain, Manu.—Buckskin, of various patterns. Satin, black, of different prices. Doeskin, light blue.

120 SCHROEER, F. H. Oschatz, Manu.—Woollen fancy stuffs : Satin grey, bronze, and green ; cassimer, bronze and olive ; Duffel cloth, black ; black satin. The pieces, No. 1267, 1250, and B 99, are made by C. F. Kunze, Oschatz.

121 BERNHARD, W Leisnig, Manu.—Woollen stuffs, buckskin for paletots and great coats, calmucs, great-coats, &c.

122 HERRMANN, F. G. & SON, Bischofswerda, Manu.—

Coloured cloths of finest quality. Black cloth of fine quality.

123 KOBLICH, H. M. Bischofswerda, Manu.—Cloths of thin quality: olive, bronze, and invisible.

124 GROSSMANN, C. G. Bischofswerda, Manu.—Superfine cloth: black, clare bronze, olive, dark bronze, dark green, clare green, and blue.

125 GROSSMAN, BROTHERS, Bischofswerda, Dresden, and New York, Manu.—Cloth for the United States market, in eleven different qualities and colours, woven by E. H. Bernhardt, at Leisnig, dressed and made up by the exhibitors.

126 MEISSNER, T. Bischofswerda, Manu.—Cloths of a fine black.

127 MOERBITZ, C. G. E. Bautzen, Manu. — Cloths, coloured and unfinished. A tableau showing the whole process of cloth manufacture, from the raw wool to the finished cloth.

128 FIELDER, A. D. G. Oederan (Agent, C. Holland, 41 Finsbury Circus), Manu.—Fine black cloth, and light cloth for summer coats.

129 MEISSNER, F. T. Grossenhain, Manu.—Cloths, thin black; coloured, olive and blue; thick, black and bronze.

130 MEISSNER, F. A. Grossenhain, Manu.—Cloth, black, brown, and green; best and middling qualities.

131 JUNGHANS, I. G. Grossenhain, Manu. — Cloths, black and coloured, of different prices.

132 CASPARI, I. F. Grossenhain, Manu.—Cloth: black, blue-green, wool-black, and bronze.

133 BUCHWALD, R. Grossenhain, Manu.—Black cloth, of middle quality.

134 JAEHNIG, W. Grossenhain, Manu.—Cloths: black, brown, and blue.

135 PRESSPRICH, ERNST, & SON, Grossenhain, Manu.—Various cloths: thick and thin black.

136 MEISSNER, E. Grossenhain, Manu.—Cloth, pensée and blue.

137 MEISSNER, M. Grossenhain, Manu.—Cloth, green and olive.

138 ZSCHILLE BROTHERS, Grossenhain, Manu.—Cloth, first quality, blue and black; second, green and black; thin cloth, for the United States market, black and coloured.

139 HERMANN, J. W. Leisnig, Manu.—Cloths of different qualities.

140 REICHEL, C. F. Rosswein, Manu.—Coloured cloths: dahlia, pensée, green, olive, bronze, scarlet, mineral blue, and black.

141 PETZOLDT, F. Lengenfeld, Manu.—Black cloth.

142 WOLF, C. A. Kirchberg, Manu.—Cloth of different qualities and prices: crimson, scarlet, blue, and black.

143 WOLF, J. G. sen. Kirchberg, Manu.—Cloths: black, scarlet, crimson, various qualities.

144 WOLFF, F. Kirchberg, Manu. — Woollen cloth: crimson, Turkey red, or deep scarlet, and chemic blue.

145 SINGER, C. F. Kirchberg, Manu.—Cloths: scarlet, black, mixed, indigo blue, dark green, kali blue.

146 UNGER, C. G. Kirchberg, Manu.—Cloths, of common quality, different prices.

147 KRAUSE, F. W. Grossenhain, Manu.—Printed woollen stuffs for waistcoats: chemic blue, scarlet with black, and printed on coloured ground.

148 BECK & HEYNIG, Glauchau, Manu.—Carpet articles: sofa-carpet with figures, carpet-bags, bow-pockets, and pockets with flaps and leather bottoms.

149 BECK, HENRY, Glauchau, Manu.—Tapestry and carpet goods: upper parts of shoes, cut in the Turkish fashion; pockets for children.

150 BATZ, P. Leipzig, Manu.—Ladies' bags. Velvet or velvetées, plain, embossed, with steel handles; with handles of mother-of-pearl. Hand-bags, embossed; velvet, with small artificial roses.

150A TEUBNER, C. Rosswein, Manu.—Ladies' pockets; interlaced work of zephyr worsted yarn.

151 EISENSTUCK & Co. Annaberg (Agent, C. H. Treibmann), Manu.—Bed-laces: white linen and black worsted. Belts: half silk; ribands with flattened gold and silver wire.

152 HAENEL, E. Annaberg (Agents, C. Ehrensperger and Co. 4 Lawrence Pountney Pl. Cannon St.) Manu.—Black silk laces, of different prices and qualities; thread laces, of modern and ancient patterns and style.

153 HAENEL BROTHERS, Annaberg (Agents, F. A. Hoffmann and Co.), Manu.—Various fringes: sewing fringes, black silk; black mohair and coloured mohair.

154 OEHMIG & SCHMIDT, Annaberg (Agents, J. Simonson and Co.), Manu.—Button-makers' productions. Strings for curtains. Curtain-holders of cotton, half silk and wool; loops for curtains; tassels for curtains.

155 UHLIG's Widow & JUNKER, Annaberg, Manu —Button-makers' productions: ladies' buttons, with and without tassels; strings for ladies' robes, with tassels; tassels for pipes; a garniture of insertion for ladies' robes; tassels for furniture; loops for cloaks and manteaux.

156 SCHUBERT, Mrs. Annaberg.—Worked table-cover, on net lace, after designs invented and drawn by Mrs. Schubert.

157 MUEHLENDERLEIN, C.F. Annaberg.—Button-makers' productions: twisted fringes of half silk, wool, and cotton; loops, half silk; chenille, all silk; mohair laces; India-rubber galloons, of silk, wool, and cotton.

158 BACH, G. F. & SON, Buchholz (Agent, C. H. Treibmann), Manu.—Fringes: white cotton, ball, coloured ball, half-silk bullion, half net, half sewing, sewing silk fringes; a large number of different patterns. Crêtes: half silk, worsted and cotton crêtes. Trimmings; half silk; sixty patterns. Exhibited for cheapness and execution.

159 HELWEG, HANS, Buchholz (Agents, Ullmann, Hirschhorn and Co.), Manu.—Fringes: white sewing and ball fringes.

160 HILLMANN, F. Sebnitz, Manu. — Button-makers' productions: silk and half-silk buttons; cords and galloons, of silk and Ispahan, and of silk and genappe; rich silk buttons.

161 ROELLER & HUSTE, Leipzig, Manu.—Oil cloths; floor cloths, partly varnished; and oiled fustian. The manufacture of oil cloths forms an important branch of Saxon industry, principally concentrated in Leipzig.

162 QUAST, F. Leipzig, Manu.—Oil cloth; oiled fustian; round table-covers; cornered table-covers; floor carpets double oiled.

163 TEUBNER & Co. Leipzig (Agents, Gottschalk & Schroeder, 72 Basinghall St.), Manu.—Oil cloth; floor cloth; piano-cover; table-covers; oil fustian, bronze, printed, and imitation of wood; table-mats; oil cloth, in imitation of marble and wood.

164 GOEHRING & BOEHME, Leipzig, Manu.—Oiled cloths, painted in gold and silver and in colours; round table-cover, of oiled fustian (tortoiseshell pattern); table-mats, floor cloth, linens and tickens for painters, and oiled cloths for hat-linings.

165 EINENKEL, J. C. C. Dresden, Manu.—Linens and tickens for painters, various lengths and colours. When extra width is wanted, the sewing is done in a way scarcely visible, and without injury to solidity.

166 WEICKERT, J. D. Leipzig (Agent, C. Holland, 41 Finsbury Circus), Manu.—Cloths for pianos; hammer cloth; damper cloth; red and green under-cloth.

167 MUEHLE, A. Pirna, Manu.—Articles made of felt: Ladies' woollen shoes, fine; gentlemen's shoes of plain felt; gentlemen's and ladies' slippers.

168 FISCHER, C. F. A. Bautzen, Manu.—Specimens of paper: Plate paper, for stone and steel plates: printing

paper; tissue paper, white and rose coloured; writing paper; drawing paper, worked on the endless machine, and sized with vegetable glue; vegetable paper, for counter-drawing; papers for documents, notes, and bank-notes. Gigantic millboard, for waggon manufactories.

168B HIETEL, J. A. Dresden, Manu.—Seven tableaus, embroidered with hair and silk, on silk ground; viz., the portraits of Her Majesty of England and His Majesty of Saxony, the flags of all navies, &c.

169 GOETZE, H. Leipzig, Manu.—Raw German hair, called Brabant hair, of various lengths and colours, including a weft of two yards and a half. Natural hair, completely purified and prepared for use, applicable for curls, &c. with specimens of the same hair dyed. Hair, artificially dressed. The exhibitor states that he employs more than seventy men in the preparation of human hair for sale.

170 KINDERMANN, A. Buchholz (Agent, C. H. Triebmann), Manu.—Papier-maché: Groups of animals, various sizes and execution.

171 FEISTEL & SON, Aue, near Schneeberg, Manu.— Snuff-boxes of tortoiseshell and metal, with paintings. Lady's box, with silver arabesques. Scottish boxes. Draughtboard. Ivory box, with paintings.

172 ROCKHAUSEN, W. Johanngeorgenstadt, Manu.— Fancy boxes, for toilet; travelling case, of rosewood; box for counters; boxes of mother-of-pearl; segar-boxes, &c.

173 PAPPERITZ, J. F. Dresden, Manu.—Saddlers' goods: Saddles in the English style, flat, wadded, and covered with hog's skin complete. Bridle: the leather being pierced, and the buckles covered with leather.

173B HAUSSMAN, L. Dresden, Manu.—A pair of complete horses' harness, with collars, brown round reins, counterholds, silver plated buckles, steel bridle. Three bridles, of different descriptions. Ten whips.

174 The ROYAL SAXON MANUFACTORY of CHINA, Meissen (Apply to Dr. Seyffarth, Royal Commissioner for Saxony).— China: Royal blue vases, with portraits of Her Majesty the Queen of England and H. R. H. Prince Albert. Chandelier, with nine girandoles, coloured and gilt. Camelia, in its natural state and colours, standing in a pot. Vase, after Mr. Semper's design. Vase, on a pedestal, with figures after Watteau, with similar figures, painted in colours, with flowers in relievo, richly gilt, with two girandoles. Vases, painted with flowers and bronzed. Figures: a flute-player and a girl playing the guitar, &c. Etagères. Dessert dishes and plates. Figure, a girl feeding doves. Fruit-basket. Tea-table appurtenances. Tableau, The Female Lace-worker. Six pieces with the armorial bearings of the kingdom of Saxony. Plate. Busts: Danaide, after Mr. Rauch; King of Saxony; King of Prussia; Madonna; Socrates. Figure, Ganymedes, after Thorwaldsen. Shades. China vessels, for the use of chemists and apothecaries.

175 ADLER, C. Königsbrück, Manu.—Vessels of clay: Soup tureen, coffee-pots, flower-vases, tea-pot, and milk-pots. Specimens of children's playthings.

176 BUCKER, H. Dresden, Des. and Painter.—Paintings on china: Brooches of painted china, enchased in bronze; small china paintings of various kinds, after classical pictures.

177 WALTHER, G. Dresden, Painter.—Enamel paintings on china, copies from classical originals.

178 BROCKHAUS, F. A. Leipzig, Manu.—Printed books: a collection of 356 volumes, all printed in the year 1850, in the office of the exhibitor; in elegant covers.

179 BARTH, J. A. Leipzig, Publisher.—Ornamental typographical works: Minstrels of Germany, edited by Herr Von der Hagen, printed on parchment; the vignettes, as well as the initials, painted in gold. Ancient Egypt, by Dr. Schwarze, printed in twenty-seven languages, being the first instance of Egyptian hieroglyphics having been ex-

ecuted in print; it has been done by means of more than 3,000 stamps cut for this purpose. Talmud Babli; Babylonian Talmud, in Hebrew, with German translation, and the commentaries of Raschi and Josephoth, by Dr. E. M. Pinner, vol. I. 1842.

180 HIRSCHFELD, J. B. Leipzig, Printer.—Products of the art of printing. A picture in polychromic print. Specimens of types.

181 MEINHOLD & SONS, Dresden, Manu.—Four specimens of coloured printing.

182 SCHELTER, G. Dresden, Inv. and Manu.—Products of a letter foundry: Complete set of the last specimens of printing types; music-book done with types cast and cut in English steel, in gilt frames; musical text-book, executed with types cast and cut in English steel, in a new style. Proof-sheet of printing with lately invented stenographic types, on Mr. Gabelsberger's principle, in gilt frame.

183 JAHN, F. H. Dresden, Sculp.—Engraving, with specimens of several engravers' work. Exhibited for execution.

184 The ROYAL SAXON MILITARY PLAN-OFFICE, Dresden.—The three first numbers of the engineers' map of the kingdom of Saxony. Exhibited for execution.

185 RIETSCHEL, ERNST, Prof. M.R.A.F.A. Dresden.— Sculptures: The Christangel, relievo, Carrarian marble; Cupid mounted on the back of a panther, relievo, Carrarian marble. Mary kneeling at the dead body of Jesus Christ, full-size group, in plaster of Paris.

185A KIETZ, T. Leipsic.—Portraits in ivory.

186 KUEGLER, H. Dresden.—Signet, in form of a vase, ground out of a piece of rock-crystal.

187 LUTHER, G. Plauen.—Lady's ball dress.

187A BUETHER, G. Dresden.—Galvanoplastic copies of shields.

188 SCHUETZE, —, Dresden.—Samples of wool.

---

4. WURTEMBURGH.

(Agents in London, Messrs. BRAND & SCHIEDMAYER, 6 Pinner's Hall, Old Broad St. City.)

1 ZELLER, F. Neckartenzlingen, Stuttgard.—Specimens of stone from the quarries of the exhibitor, adapted for millstones.

2 BONZ & SON, Boeblingen, Manu.—Kreosote. Hydroiodinic potash, &c.

3 BREUNINGER & SON, Kirchheim, Teck, Manu.—Ultramarine. Exhibited for colour and cheapness.

4 JOBST, F. Stuttgard, Manu.—Sulphate and other compounds of quinine; pure kali hydroiodinic.

5 LEUBE BROTHERS, Ulm, Manu.—Hydraulic chalk cement, which quickly hardens under water.

6 SIEGLE, H. Stuttgard, Manu.—Carmine, Munich carmine, lac, madder-lac, and azure colours; and a yellow innocuous colour for confectioners.

7 ABT, F. Esslingen, Manu.—Yellow colour, innocuous, and adapted for the use of confectioners.

8 BREUNING, F. Mohringen, Stuttgard, Prod.—Dried bilberries.

9 SCHMIDT, W. Calmbach, Prod.—Dried bilberries.

10 FRICKER, C. Kirchheim, Prod.—Dried plums, pears, apples, prunes, and cherries without stones.

11 NOERDLINGER, PROFESSOR, Hohenheim, Stuttgart.— Collection of various woods, showing the nature of their fibre. Collections of insects, especially those which infest the fields.

12 SCHOETTLE, G. J. Ebhausen, Nagold, Manu.—A heckle, or flax comb.

13 WOLFF, F. A. Heilbronn, Manu.—Steam-distilling apparatus for fluids, with new refrigerator. Distilling and

cooking apparatus, for the use of chemists and others. Apparatus for soldering lead by means of atmospheric air and hydrogen gas; with specimens. Graduated vessels, for measuring fluids.

14 KOHL, G. H. Stuttgard, Manu.—Gilt sabre, with modern ornaments. Roman sword. Gilt cutlasses and daggers, in various styles.

15 ROYAL GUN MANUFACTORY, Oberndorf.—Gun for infantry, rifle with bayonet, and common rifle, made of cast steel.

16 HALLER, F. Schwenningen, Manu —Dutch clocks with weights, of various sizes; alarum clocks, &c. Exhibited for cheapness.

17 BACHER, A. Stuttgard, Manu.—A novel escapement for watches, without a balance-wheel; a watch on this principle. Seconds watch, with compensating escapement and maintaining power, without distinct second-work. A week-going seconds watch, with five wheels only. Watch, of ivory. Watch with lever escapement, working on a plate of steel. Chronograph, on a new principle.

18 HOLCH, W. Hall, Manu.—Regulator, going eight days, in mahogany case, with silvered dial, and jewelled escapement.

19 STOSS, V. Ulm, Manu.—Patent small church-clock, striking hours and quarters, with a new escapement, intended to prevent wind and bad weather from injuring its hands. An eight-day clock.

20 DIEUDONNE & BLADEL, Stuttgard, Manu.—Grand pianoforte, with double action. Cottage pianoforte.

21 DOERNER, F. Stuttgard, Manu.—Grand pianoforte, in rosewood. Square pianoforte.

22 LIPP, R. R. Stuttgard, Manu.—Square pianoforte; the hammers are fitted up with a new and more durable kind of felt, intended to assist in producing greater clearness of sound.

23 SCHIEDMAYER & SONS, Stuttgard, Inv. and Manu.—Grand pianoforte, in rosewood, with newly-invented patent double action. Square pianoforte, in mahogany. Cottage pianoforte, in nut-wood, decorated and ornamented with original wood carvings.

24 HELWERT, J. Stuttgard, Manu.—Bassoon with nineteen keys, of improved construction.

25 REXER, C. Stuttgard, Manu. and Inv.—Pair of orchestra kettle-drums, tuned on a new plan. A large drum.

26 KINZELBACH, T. Stuttgard, Manu.—Improved diastimeter for the use of the army, with two parallel wires moveable at the same time, and at equal distances from the centre to the extent of the field of view, along a scale divided to minutes. Surveying cross, with a graduated limb and vernier reading to five minutes. Improved Wollaston's goniometer, with an auxiliary glass for measuring off the angles of prisms and crystals. Silver hydrometer. Telescope, mounted equatorially, with divided arcs, &c.

27 HECHT & ARNOLD, Reutlingen, Manu.—Toilinets and valentias, exhibited for cheapness and quality.

28 KOLB & SCHULE, Kirchheim, Manu.—Coloured cotton quiltings; green and blue cotton cameleon; coloured canvas, gingham, and dimity bed stuff; white cotton tricot; green cotton umbrella stuff, and grey cotton stuff.

29 WEIGLE, J. J. Ludwigsburg, Manu.—Quiltings and toilinets of various patterns.

30 SCHILL & WAGNER, Calw, Manu.—Woollen cloths; black satin cloth; flannels of various qualities and colours.

31 FINCKH, J. G. Reutlingen, Manu.—Several specimens of woollen cloth.

32 SCHÖNLEBER, A. Bietigheim, Manu. — Woollen trouser stuff, for summer and winter wear. Worsted yarn, dyed and undyed.

33 FABER, C. Stuttgard, Manu.—Damask linen table covers. Small desert napkins, with fringes. Brocaded tricoloured silk furniture stuffs, exhibited for quality.

34 LANG, A. F. Blaubeuren, Manu.—Bleached linen, and linen handkerchiefs.

35 MANUFACTORY OF LINEN YARN, Urach.—Samples of linen yarn.

36 SEEMANN, C. & H. Stuttgard, Manu.—Samples of bleached linen from machine yarn, made up in the Irish and Dutch style; unbleached linen drills; white linen drills and printed cambrics.

37 BANTLIN, C. D. Reutlingen, Tanner.—Specimens of calf leather; upper-leathers ready cut.

38 ECKHARDT, F. M. Ulm, Manu.—Black varnished leather, exhibited for quality and varnish.

39 REICHHOLD, G. Stuttgard, Manu.—Fancy leather goods: portfolios, books, albums, portmonnaies cigar and letter cases, &c.

40 SCHENCK & CO. E. G. Stuttgart, Manu.—Fancy leather portfolios; books: albums; card-cases, porte-monnaies, cigar cases, &c.

41 SCHAEUFFELEN, G. Heilbronn, Manu.—Coloured and white pasteboard. Tissue paper, white and coloured. Letter-paper, exhibited for quality. Post paper, white and coloured. The name of the manufacturer is inserted by a patent contrivance for machine paper.

42 KAEMMERER, C. Stuttgard, Manu.—Portfolio, containing pasteboard for the use of painters, of rough and smooth surface.

43 FAULHABER & LEUBE, Ulm, Chemical Factors.—Rheumatic pitch-plaister.

44 RAUCH BROTHERS, Heilbronn, Manu.—Fancy paper, which, by a process newly invented by the exhibitors, is coloured differently on the two sides of a single sheet.

45 VEIEL & CO. G. Stuttgard, Manu.—Fancy paper, and enamelled cardboard.

46 KOHLER, F. Goeppingen, Manu.—Printed woollen vestings. Printed linen handkerchiefs.

47 OTTO, H. Nurtingen, Manu.—First, second, and extra Turkey-red yarn.

48 ZAIS, W. Cannstadt, Manu.—Turkey-red printed cotton goods, of various patterns.

49 NEUBURGER & SONS, Dietenheim, near Ulm, Manu.—Embroidered curtains, in tasteful and elegant patterns.

50 ROBECK, C. Nurtingen, near Teck.—Cards, scollops, and " entre deux." Knitting work.

51 TANNER, T. Stuttgard, Des. and Inv.—Designs for tapestry; printed furniture materials; and large carpets.

52 VAN ZWERGER, DEFFNER, & WEISS, Ravensburg, Manu.—Curtains, white and red striped, and of embroidered net and muslin.

53 HILS, HAAS, & CO. Schramberg, Manu.—Knitted woollen hosiery, petticoats, hose, stockings, and shirts.

54 REHM, F. F. Reutlingen, Manu.—Woollen and cotton hosiery goods. Laces and collars, called " éternelles." Knitting work.

55 BOELSTERLI, C. & CO. Stuttgard, Manu.—Tools for the preparation and carving of wood.

56 GOEBEL, G. Stuttgard, Manu.—Tools for the preparation of wood.

57 DITTMAR BROTHERS, Heilbronn, Manu.—Patent razors and razor-strops. Penknives, paper-cutters. Wood, Circasian, Greek, and yataghan knives, daggers, hunting hangers, and stilettos. Garden knives and implements.

58 HAUEISEN & SON, Stuttgard, Manu.—Scythes, used in various countries.

59 BUHRER, F. Ludwigsburg, Manu.—Toys, representing various kinds of working utensils, in copper. Pastry moulds.

60 STOHRER, T. F. Stuttgard, Manu.—Brass and steel wire; metal wire for the manufacture of paper; metal wire gauze; brass wire and horse-hair sieves.

61 WAGNER, C. Esslingen, Brazier.—Coppersmiths' goods.

62 REXER, C. Stuttgard, Manu.—Brass and steel wire. Metal wire for the manufacture of paper. Metal wire gauze.

63 ERHARDT & SONS, Gmund, Manu.—Bronze chessmen. Game of chess, with fixable figures. Various useful and ornamental articles.

64 FAIST & STEINHAEUSER, Schramberg, Manu.—Garnets, cut in various sizes and shapes.

65 BRUCKMANN & SONS, Heilbronn, Manu.—Silver-plated tea-kettle, coffee and tea pots, cream jugs, sugar-basins, trays, tea canister, fruit baskets and plates, salvers, étagères, sauce-pot, chandeliers, candlesticks, cups, &c.

66 GROEBER, A. Riedlingen, Manu.—Fruit-basket in wrought silver.

67 LENZ, C. Gmund.—Silver spectacle frames.

68 UECHTRITZ & FAIST, Schramberg, Manu.—Crockery ware. Flower-pots in black enamel. Fruit baskets or plates in green enamel. Table service, in white earthenware. Several tea-services, with prints, in black and blue colours.

69 STAIB & WASSEROTT, Ravensburg, Inv. and Manu. —Gothic window. Gothic rosette, window, and monument, of terra cotta.

70 WIRTH, T. F. Stuttgard, Manu.—Dressing and writing table. Wardrobe, with carved ornaments, modelled by the exhibitor.

71 DEFFNER, C. Esslingen, Manu.—Iron flower table; cigar tray; writing case; thrift box; washing tubs; sugar box; working baskets; chess-board; fruit baskets; pictures; and coffee trays. Bird cages. Silver plated speaking trumpet; and miscellaneous articles of hardware.

72 RAU & Co. Göppingen, Inv. and Manu.—Various articles of japanned tin-plate and papier-maché, several inlaid with mother-of-pearl, by a new process. Plated metal articles.

73 ROMETSCH, C. Stuttgard, Inv. and Manu.—Patent metallic writing slates. Prepared after a new invention by the exhibitor.

74 VETTER & ERNO, Stuttgard, Manu.—New gilt frames.

75 LETTENMEYER, T. Stuttgard, Manu.—New gilt frames.

76 ABELE & Co. Stuttgard, Manu.—Snuff-boxes made of japanned papier-maché, with ornamental drawings, and inlaid with mother-of-pearl, gold, and silver.

77 HELLER, C. Stuttgard, Manu.—Gilt bas-relief of gypsum. Samples of gilt paper, &c.

78 SEEGER, E. Esslingen, Inv. and Manu.—New process for making bitumen mosaic work, exhibited for cheapness, resistance to damp, colour, and firmness.

79 HAAS, F. P. Schramberg, Prop.—Straw plaitings: hats, bonnets, baskets, bands, fringes, tassels, &c.

80 KLEIN, F. G. Tübingen, Manu.—Cloth, hair, velvet, and billiard brushes; large brush for cloth manufacturers.

81 KIESER & Co. Gaildorf, Manu.—Gothic tower, made of lignum vitæ; the same in bone. Match-box of lignum vitæ. Jewel-tray. Seals. Cane handles. Money-box. Bonbonière and napkin rings.

82 WITTICH, A. KEMMEL & Co. Geislingen, Manu.—Bone and ivory toys for children. Fancy goods: cane-handles, brooches, baskets.

83 SCHMIDT, F. Geislingen, Inv. and Manu.—Fancy goods in bone and ivory; cane-handles, brooches, baskets, &c.

84 WEBER, C. F. Esslingen, Manu. — Handles and buttons for carvers in ivory, deer-horn, wood, and lead, with ornaments.

85 STOLL, C. Ulm, Manu.—Ivory fan, carved; bone fans. Carved ivory snuff-boxes, inlaid with tortoiseshell.

86 WEEBER, G. & Co. Esslingen, Manu.—Fancy wooden boxes.

87 BAUR BROTHERS, Biberach, Manu. — Pastils, and confectionery goods, tragacanth-flowers, and birds with real feathers, &c.

88 GOLL BROTHERS, Biberach, Manu.—Confectionery, &c.

89 ROTH, W. jun. Stuttgard, Manu.—Specimens of comfits, sugar-plums, bonbons à liqueur, conserves, sugar devices, dragés, lozenges, chocolate.

90 RIESS, F. H. Gmund, Manu. — Wax ornaments, candles and tapers, baskets, flowers, cages, books, fruits, tea-cups, &c.

91 TROEGLEN, G. Ulm, Manu.—Lozenges and confectionery.

92 HEDINGER, C. Stuttgard, Manu. — Walking-sticks and canes, with engraved hooks and heads of ivory, buffalo, stag-horn, &c. Sticks and canes for umbrellas and parasols. Frames for umbrellas.

93 SCHUMACHER, Bietigheim, near Stuttgard, Manu.—Samples of artificial whet-stones, pumice-stones, and polishing powder, for the use of workers in wood, steel, &c. and for japanners.

94 BLUMHARDT, H. Stuttgard, Manu.—Toys made of japanned tin, lead, pewter, bronze, iron, and wood.

95 ROMINGER, J. Stuttgard, Manu.—Tin and glass toys.

96 DIETERICH, C. F. Ludwigsburg, Manu.—Kitchen, stable, and garden implements for children.

97 KNOSP & BACKE, Stuttgard, Inv. and Manu. —Dolls' houses, made of pasteboard.

98 ROCK & GRANER, Biberach, Manu.—Toys of tin and iron plate, brass, and papier-maché; carriages, countries, mountains, chapels, hermitages, mills, ships, &c.

99 REUSS, BROTHERS, Stuttgard, Manu.—Samples of stearine candles.

100 SUTORIUS, C. F. Gmund, Manu.—Samples of lucifer matches.

101 LINDAUER, Miss E. L. Stuttgard, Manu.—Artificial flowers.

102 KUHN, J. Ulm, Manu.—Lucifer-matches.

103 VIEHHAEUSER, G. Ludwigsburg, Manu.—Artificial flowers.

104 WAGNER, F. Stuttgard, Builder.—Samples of whet-stones.

105 VON HOFER, L. Stuttgard, Sculptor.—Models of two large groups, representing the breaking-in of horses. Executed in Carrara marble, in the royal park of Stuttgard

106 HOLDER, T. M. Stuttgard, Inv. and Painter.—Pictures in miniature, painted on ivory by a new method.

107 PLOUCQUET, H. Stuttgard, Prod.—Groups of stuffed animals and birds. A stag-hunt. Boar-baiting. Nests of birds of prey. Hawks pouncing upon owls, &c. Groups of domestic birds with their young, &c.

108 WAGNER, T. Stuttgard, Des. and Sculp.—Statue, Magdalen, in Carrara marble.

109 WETZEL, C. J. Stuttgard, Des. and Prod.—Glass paintings, after Begas, Murillo, &c.

110 BOELSTER, T. Eisbach—Machine for cutting bread.

5. FRANKFORT-ON-THE-MAINE.

1 BROENNER, F. I. Frankfort-on-the-Maine, Manu.—Creosote, pure, and refracting light powerfully. Pamphlet, containing specimens of printing inks.

2 BUSCH, P. A. Frankfort-on-the-Maine, Prod. — Rectified cognac oil, manufactured out of common gin, or thinned spirits.

3 ZIMMER, DR. C. Manu. (Agent, Roller & Co. 15 Union Ct. Old Broad St. London.)—Pure crystallized chinidine. The sulphate of this alkaloid is contained in the sul-

phate of quinine, manufactured from the ordinary sorts of yellow bark; but it is only lately that it has been produced separately as a salt, and its properties satisfactorily ascertained.

4 MINOPRIO & Co. Manu.—Samples of snuff: Rapé de Paris; Rapé de Holland. Marino Marocco, coarse and fine.

5 BARTHEL, J. C. Frankfort-on-the-Maine, Inv. — Models of apparatus for the use of the blind, and for houses of correction and punishment. Apparatus to facilitate twisting of straw or rope. Apparatus for making straw and list carpets. Lace apparatus and chair for a blind man. Apparatus for making and tarring tow mats. Articles manufactured with the apparatus by the blind, under the direction of the exhibitor.

6 WEBER & SCHULTHEIS, Frankfort-on-the-Maine, Prod.—Single and double-barrelled rifles.

7 ALBERT, J. W. Frankfort-on-the-Maine, Manu.— Daguerreotype apparatus, with double achromatic lenses $5\frac{1}{2}$ inches in diameter; with specimens produced by it.

8 MEYER & SCHWARTZE, Frankfort-on-the-Maine, Manu.—Specimen of coloured cottons.

9 ROTH, C. W. Manu.—Enamelled, waxed, and brown calves' skins.

10 ROTH & SONS, Frankfort-on-the-Maine.—Calf-skins, black on one side, brown, and varnished.

11 RUPP & BECHSTEIN, Frankfort-on-the-Maine, Prod. —Leather skins, soft and pliable.

12 BALDENECKER, T. B. jun.—Specimens of black printers' ink.

13 BAUER & KREBS, Manu.—Specimens of letter-press printing. The German-text types cut after the concordance system (proportional size of letters) extensively introduced into Germany.

14 WUEST, C. L. Frankfort-on-the-Maine, Inv.—Playing cards, of various kinds.

15 VACONIUS, J. J. Frankfort-on-the-Maine, Manu.— Sofa carpets, with border.

16 HOFFMAN, J. & SON, Frankfort-on-the-Maine.—Stove of Fayence, intended to combine the comforts of an open fire with the usual advantages of a stove.

17 JUNGE & WALTHER, Frankfort-on-the-Maine.—Gilt lustre, in the Grecian style.

18 RAAB, G. A. B. Frankfort-on-the-Maine, Prod.— Great key, exhibited for fine and difficult workmanship.

19 ZIMMERMANN, E. G. Frankfort-on-the-Maine, Manu. (Agent in London, F. Kellermann, 94 London Wall.)— Sundry articles in zinc and iron. Iron wire-work. Transparent plate. Watch, with white and red dials. Flower-pots.

20 GOLDSCHMIDT, M. jun. Frankfort-on-the-Maine.— Bracelet Brooch. Watch-hook. Ear-rings and chains of gold. Green in emerald with diamonds.

21 TACCHIS, P. A. & Co. Frankfort-on-the-Maine.— Fountain of alabaster; glass with ornaments of gilded bronze; and a carcel lamp, for dining-room or orangery. Vases, with gold decorations, &c.

22 VOGELSANG, I. & SONS, Frankfort-on-the-Maine, Inv. and Manu.—Glass wares, coloured, cut, and gilt, viz: Flower and candelabra ornaments; pink glass plated with layers of alabaster, cut and gilt. Vases in alabaster glass, &c. Hock bottle, wine glass, and champagne glass, cut with ruby Gothic pattern, spiral engravings, &c. Tazzas, candle lamps, scent bottles, &c.

23 ALBERT, J. V. jun. Frankfort-on-the-Maine, Manu. —Moor's head conjuring toy, and German dolls, glass eyes, &c. Optical objects for the polarization of light. Crystals, models of precious stones. Chemical apparatus. Thermometers. Phenakisticope, after Professor Müller, for explaining the theory of vibrations. Stereoscope, with drawings after Professor F. M. Hessemer, &c.

24 DRESLER, F. Frankfort-on-the-Maine, Inv. and Manu.—Specimens of types of the German, Gothic, English, French, Russian, and Hebrew languages; ornaments, borders, &c. Types and ornaments of a new metallic composition; used by bookbinders.

25 EHR, NICHOLAS, Frankfort-on-the-Maine, Manu.— Wood brushes. Hair brushes.

26 GOUDA, P. F. Frankfort-on-the-Maine, Manu.— Work-boxes, tea-caddies, knitting boxes, ink-stands, ladies' desks, &c.

27 KOEHLER, J. Frankfort-on-the-Maine, Prod.—Tea-caddy, made of wood in imitation of German needlework.

28 WOHLFARTH, I. E. Frankfort-on-the-Maine.—Show card. Writing desk. Diary; ruled paper.

29 DELKESKAMP, F. W. Frankfort-on-the-Maine.—Picturesque relief of the classical soil of Switzerland, and of the Alps of Switzerland and their boundaries. Incomplete specimens.

30 SCHMERBER, S. Frankfort-on-the-Maine.—Works and objects of the middle age, and renaissance, by C. Becker and S. von Hefner. Gothic A B C, or rules of the Gothic styles for artists and artisans, by Fred Hoffstadt. Monuments of Roman architecture on the Rhine, by Geier and Goertz.

31 VANNI, A. Frankfort-on-the-Maine. — Group, Ariadne, on pedestal.

32 KRESS, G. L. VON, Offenbach, near Frankfort-on-the-Maine, Prod.—Small statue of G. E. Lessing, produced in copper by electro-galvanism. The model by Professor Rietschel, of Dresden. Bas-relief, Amor upon a Panther. Cameos, lizard, snake, &c. moulded after nature.

33 STRAUCH, F. Prod. — Photography; and coloured photography.

---

6. GRAND DUCHY OF HESSE.

(Commissioner, M. HECTOR ROESSLER, 23 Southampton St. Strand.)

1 BUECHNER, W. Darmstadt, Manu.—Specimens of ultramarine.

2 ROSENBERG & Co. Giessen, Prop.—Specimens of manganese ore, exhibiting a very perfect crystalline structure.

3 SALT and LIGNITE WORKS at SALSHAUSEN.—Raw products: Earthy lignite, employed in the manufacture of salt; bituminous wood, employed in the manufacture of dressing-cases, &c.; and leaf lignite. Principal articles of manufacture: Lignite blocks (*Braunkohlenklœtze*); common salt; salt for manure (*Dungsalz*); salt scum (*Salzchaum*).

4 BRIEL, W. & Co. Giessen, Prop.—Specimens of manganese ore.

5 SALT WORKS at THEODORSHALLE, near KREUZNACH. —Salt crystals, remarkable for their size: bottle of concentrated mother-lye (*Mutterlauge*), containing bromine, iodine, and chloride of calcium and employed for baths.

6 JONGHAUS & VENATOR, Bauerkeller's Præganstalt, Darmstadt, Manu.—Maps in relief and maps printed in colours: Geological map, in relief, of the Grand Duchy and Electorate of Hesse, with the Duchy of Nassau and bordering countries, by L. Ewald, secretary of the Geographical Society of Darmstadt. Geological map, in relief, of Wurtemberg, Baden, and the neighbouring countries, including the Palatinate and Alsatia, tinted in 30 colours, by L. Ewald; upon the same scale as the preceding map. Bauerkeller's Hand-atlas, by L. Ewald.

7 KOCH, F. Oppenheim, Manu.—Alkaloids, from Peruvian bark, for medicinal purposes.

8 OEHLER, C. Offenbach, Manu.—Samples of chemically pure creosote, crystallized creosote, coal, naphtha, resin,

lamp black, Paris black, for copper-plate and lithographic printers, and for dyeing Spanish leather; pure crystallized sal-ammoniac.

9 BERNARD BROTHERS, Offenbach, Manu.—Samples of snuff.

10 MEYER & LINDT, Sprendlingen, Frankfort-on-Maine, Manu.—Samples of the finest wheat flour, meal groats, and rye flour.

11 MUELLER, J. P. Offenbach, Manu.—Specimens of tobacco and cigars.

12 ZAHN & VOLBRECHT, Ruesselsheim, near Mentz, Manu.—Samples of chicoré, or German coffee.

13 The CENTRAL BOARD of AGRICULTURE for the GRAND DUCHY of HESSE DARMSTADT.—Samples of agricultural products: Gommer, used in the preparation of soups; oak bark, used in the tanning of sole-leather. Tobacco leaves (Deckblätter), from Lorsch and Virnheim, near Mannheim. Models of agricultural implements, &c.:—The improved plough of the Bergstrasse; the Braunfels potato-mill, for crushing potatoes. Sluices of wood and stone, for irrigation.

14 HOFMANN, G. W. Ingenheim, near Darmstadt, Manu. —Specimens of starch from potatoes. Dextrine, two sorts: Gomelin in crystals, and in powder; glucose, used instead of gum-arabic; syrup of starch (Traubenzucker), employed in the manufacture of beer and vinegar; white and brown sago. Starch from wheat (Waitzenstärke), of four varieties.

15 APPEL, C. Griesheim, near Darmstadt.—Various sorts of forest, grass, and clover seeds.

16 MICHEL & MORELL, Mentz, Manu.— Black, for copper-plate printing, of different sorts. Lamp-black of various sorts, from pine, calcined. Varnish-black and real ivory-black. Paste-black, dissolved in liquid; vivid black. Paris black, black for blacking, Frankfort black, &c.

17 DICK & KIRSCHTEN, Offenbach, Manu.—Phaeton, built chiefly of iron, for one or two horses; and patterns of three different axletrees.

18 DICKORE, A. Giessen, Gun-maker.—Rifle, 4ft.10in. long, inlaid with gold and silver, with apparatus.

19 SCHUCHARD, H. Darmstadt, Manu.—Several patterns of hats; silk hats, with felt foundation; hat (and feather) of beaver and musk; glazed hats; officers' helmets, one being made out of a single piece of leather.

20 KUEHNST, G. Darmstadt, Manu.—Mahogany grand pianoforte, of 6½ octaves, with peculiar action.

21 MAURY, J. C. Offenbach, Manu.—Various helmets, military and other caps, in japanned felt and leather.

22 HUCH, H. C. Mentz, Manu.—Levelling instrument, with case and stand, furnished with an achromatic telescope, an object-glass of 1 inch diameter, and horizontal micrometer movement.

23 KLEIN, C. Mentz, Manu.—Alt vono, a small brass instrument; and an E flat clarionet; both with German-silver keys; F clarionet; B clarionet; B cornetto, of German-silver.

24 MUELLER, C. A. Mentz, Manu.—Brass cornet-à-piston.

25 SCHOTTS, B. & SONS, Mentz, Manu.—Semi-grand pianoforte, in zebra-wood, 6¾ octaves.

26 SEIDEL, J. Mentz, Manu.—Clarionets of box-wood, mounted with ivory, with brass keys. Flutes and piccolo, of the same materials.

27 ARZT, P. L. Michelstadt, Manu.—Specimens of woollen cloth.

28 MŒRSCHEL, WINZENRIED & Co. Herrenhag, near Büdingen, Manu.—An assortment of crochet woollen work, worsted gloves, &c.

29 LOHN, Steward of the Hospital of Schlitz, near Fulda, Manu.—Towels of different damask patterns, and damask table-cloths, with napkins.

30 STRUTH, V. sen. Lauterbach, Manu.—Table-cloth and napkins, from flax yarn, spun by hand, and grass bleached.

31 IHM, BOEHM & PFALTZ, Offenbach, Manu.—Specimens of japanned leather.

32 HEYL, C. Worms, Manu.—Black japanned leather for boots and shoes.

33 DOERR & REINHARD, Worms, Manu.—Japanned and enamelled calf-skins for shoemakers and furniture.

34 HELLMANN, J. Neckarsteinach, Inv. and Manu.— Patterns of leather for soles.

35 MAYER, PAUL, Mentz, Manu.—Half-brown hide, half-bridle hide, brown calf-skin, waxed calf-skin, and several boot legs and fore- shoes, manufactured from calf and horse hides.

36 MAYER, MICHEL, & DENINGER, Mentz, Manu.—Japanned and enamelled hides, black, and in various colours, for saddle and coach work. Dyed calf-skins, moroccos, roans, and split sheep-skins dyed. Black japanned calf-skins, enamelled goat and calf-skins, black and coloured. Japanned calf hides, hides for bridles, stirrups, and saddles.

37 MINOPRIO & HOHWIESNER, Bingen, Manu. (Agent, F. Kellermann, 94 London Wall, City.)—Black japanned calf-skins; calf-skins with the hair, and heifer-skin. Sheet nettle-cloth, japanned. Pair of boots of japanned calf-leather.

38 FREUND, E. A. Offenbach, Manu.—Specimens of ornamental labels, embossed and enamelled cards and paper.

39 FROMMANN, M. Darmstadt, Manu.—Specimens of playing cards.

40 REUTER, W. Darmstadt, Manu.—An assortment of various descriptions and qualities of playing cards.

41 PETRI, J. Mentz, Manu.—Specimens of black for copperplate printers.

42 SCHNAPPER, H. L. Offenbach, Manu.—Various specimens of playing cards.

43 WEBER, J. B. Offenbach, Manu.—Specimens of coloured and marble paper.

44 WUEST BROTHERS, Darmstadt, Manu.—Patterns of coloured and marble papers.

45 KERN, H., Mentz, Manu.—Various articles, ornamented with embroidery upon canvas.

46 IHM, F. Offenbach, Manu.—Several specimens of printed and painted oil-cloths for table covers, pianos, and the interior of railway carriages. Pieces of waxed oil-cloths.

47 SCHUMACHER, J. & SON, Shoemakers—Shoes, boots, slippers, &c.

48 WERNER, M. Mentz, Shoemaker—Assortment of gentlemen's boots.

49 REIS, G. & Co. Mentz, Manu.—Camphine lamps, and improved camphine.

50 SEEBASS, A. R. Offenbach, Manu.—Assortment of fine cast-iron articles, black varnished and bronzed, viz., inkstands; night clocks and night-lamps, candelabra, and other ornaments.

51 SCHREGER, B. Darmstadt, Manu.—Articles of jewellery, manufactured in oxidized silver, with solid gold ornaments. Paper weights; bracelets; brooches; chains, &c.; breast pins; ornament for a walking-stick, with horses.

52 WAGNER, J. Mentz, Manu.—Pattern of mock pearl and other beads in all colours, and several ornamental objects in beads.

53 BUETTNER, P. Darmstadt, Manu.—Oval looking-glass in gilt frame, the ornaments in composition; toilet-glass; the same, in velvet and gilt frame.

54 REINHARD, J. M. Mentz, Manu.—Various patterns of straw chairs, with walnut-tree wood frames.

55 WENDERLEIN, J. H. Darmstadt, Manu.—Several gilt picture frames, and an assortment of frame patterns.

56 ANDRE BROTHERS, Hirschhorn, near Heidelberg, Manu.—Patterns of walnut-tree veneers, from wood of the Odenwald.

57 Gick, J. G. Mentz, Manu.—An assortment of basket work.

58 Schmidt, E. Darmstadt, Manu.—Spun coat and waistcoat buttons, made by hand.

59 Anselm, F. C. Offenbach, Manu.—Specimens of purses, gold and silver lace, bullion, &c.

60 Berge Brothers, Offenbach, Manu.—Specimens of cigar cases, leather purses, pocket-books, dressing cases, &c.

61 Frank, J. G. Offenbach, Manu.—Varnished rattan walking canes, and snuff-boxes of papier-maché.

62 Haas & Co. Offenbach, Manu. (Agent in London, F. Kellermann, 94 London Wall.)—A variety of pocket-books, &c.

63 Klein, P. Offenbach, Manu.—Net purses, and other specimens of weaving, called "tricot."

64 Klein, J. G. sen. Offenbach, Manu.—Articles in leather, consisting of purses, cigar-cases, with or without steel bindings, paper and blotting-cases, &c.

65 Luettringhaus, A. Offenbach, Manu.—Specimens of pocket-books, cigar-cases, purses, &c.

66 Moench, J. & Co. Offenbach, Manu.—Various patterns of tea caddies; cigar, card, counter, and work-boxes, in yellow and white varnished wood, with steel mountings.

67 Naenny, H. Bingen, Manu.—Large portfolio, in red morocco leather, with lock and key.

69 Seeling & Becker, Offenbach, Manu. — Pocket-books of various descriptions, dressing-cases, albums, large writing portfolios, various leather purses and cigar-cases with steel bindings

70 Weintraud, C. jun., Offenbach, Manu.—Assortment of cotton, half-silk and silk purses, made partly by hand and partly by machinery, ornamented with beads and mounted in steel.

71 Birnstill, J. Darmstadt, Maker.—Specimens of wax flowers and fruit. Bunch of grapes with leaves, branches of apple trees; camelia branches.

72 Dulcius, C. Bingen, Worker.—Embroidery, imitating engravings, executed with fine black silk upon white silk, with portraits of Queen Victoria and Prince Albert.

73 Felsing, H. Darmstadt, Printer. — Impressions from two landscapes by Abbema of Düsseldorf. One proof shows the engraving, printed in the ordinary manner; the other, what may be accomplished by the taste of the printer.

74 Friedrich, F. H. Darmstadt, Carver.—Carvings in ivory and staghorn. Ivory goblet, sugar dish of cocoa nut, paper knives, cigar mouth pieces, brooches, &c.

75 Heyl, C. W. Darmstadt, Carver.—Carvings in ivory. A colossal goblet, composed of three principal portions, stand, body, and cover. Ivory carvings, for needle and ball books; paper weights, snuff-boxes, bracelets, paper knives, brooches, heads for walking-sticks, riding-whips, &c.

77 Schroeder, J. Darmstadt, Manu.—Geometrical and other models. Models of joinings in wood and of roof joinings. Patterns of roof and other mouldings. Models of crystals, according to Dr. Kopp. Model of a window frame, spiral staircase, several drawing instruments.

78 Zabern, T. Mentz, Printer.—Several specimens of typography, executed by the printing press.

79 Dunmich, P. Mentz, Manu.—Patterns of several articles manufactured of fur, and used for clothing.

80 Baron Klein, Mentz, Inv.—Choregraphical apparatus.

81 Stein & Schroeder, Mentz, Prod.—Several specimens of hops.

7. LUXEMBURG.

1 Godshaux Brothers, Schleifmühl, Manu.—Buckskins and lamas cloth.

2 Lamort, J. Luxembourg, Manu.—Paper hangings, variously coloured and gilded.

3 Wemmer, F. Luxembourg, Manu.—Hunting boots. Shoes and boots, with single and double soles.

4 Ganterie Française, De L'Union, Luxembourg, Manu.—Kid and lamb skin gloves. White and coloured kid and lamb skins. Gold, bronzed, and black glazed kid skins.

5 Boch, J. F. Luxembourg.—Mosaic pavements, composed of very small bricks of baked clay.

6 Metz, A. & Co. Eich.—Cast-iron stove. German eagle, as on the fortress of Luxemburg. Cog-wheels for machines.

8. NASSAU.

1 The Government Engineers of Mines—(in the Name of the Mining Proprietors).

Grey copper ore (*Fahlerz*), containing from 4 to 16 ounces of silver in the cwt. The grey copper ore is found united with lead ore in greater or less quantity, on which partly depends the quantity of silver contained in the smelted lead.

Lead ore; sulphuret of lead, containing from 1 to 2 ounces of silver in the cwt.; by the admixture of grey copper ore, a larger quantity of silver is obtained. The mines of lead ore in Nassau are in general of old date, but many veins are yet to be tried, or to be opened to a greater depth. Carbonate of lead, the result of oxidation in the upper and middle parts of the veins, containing sulphuret of lead. The quantity of silver in this carbonate of lead is not inconsiderable. The mines are near Oberlahnstein and Ems. Phosphate of lead, found in combination with carbonate of lead. Remarkable for its crystallization. From the lead mine near Ems.

Copper ore; from Dillenberg, *copper pyrites*, containing 30 per cent. of copper. The copper of Nassau is of the best quality, but the quantity produced is, at present, not considerable. Engines for draining the deeper mines are about being erected. (Kupferindig), sulphuret of copper (66 per cent.); found associated with copper pyrites. Ferruginous red oxyde of copper with malachite (green carbonate of copper); the produce of oxidation in the upper part of the copper veins.

Zinc ore, *sulphuret of zinc*. This ore fills part of the lead veins, and is used of late years for producing zinc metal only.

Manganese ore, pyrolusite (the greatest part) and psilomelane, *peroxyde of manganese*. District of Lahn. The mines of manganese ore in Nassau have been opened chiefly within the last 15 years, and yield a vast produce. The quantity raised every year is above 20,000 tons English, and is exported to all quarters of the world. 1,200 persons are employed in the mines and washing-mills. The manganese ore is used for extracting chlorine in the manufacture of soda from common salt; for glazing in potteries; for whitening glass, &c.

Iron ore, red hæmatite, red oxide of iron. The red hæmatite is raised in numerous mines, in very great quantity; it yields iron of superior quality, in the high furnaces of Nassau, worked with charcoal. This iron ore is also exported to the coal districts of Germany and to France, for the purpose of improving iron. From 1,500,000 to 2,000,000 cwts. of iron ore are raised every year, of which the half is smelted in Nassau. Part of the iron ore contains calcspar and is used in that state as the best admixture for smelting.

Magnetic iron ore, oxydulated iron. This ore is found united with red hæmatite. Hydrous oxide of iron, brown hæmatite—*stilxuosiderite*. This ore is found in Nassau in great quantities; it is chiefly worked for exportation, and is used especially for producing hard steel-iron. Spathose iron; from Hachenburg. There are only a few mines of spathose iron in Nassau, near the Prussian country of Siegen; the ore, and the steel produced from it are esteemed.

Bituminous coal; lignite—of remarkable wood-like character, covering a space of about 100 English square miles; used in Nassau and the neighbouring countries as the principal household fuel. For technical uses the lignite is valuable. At present the yearly produce amounts to 1,200,000 cwts. but the quantity which can be raised is incalculable.

Slate. The mines of slates in Nassau near the Rhine and Lahn are of good quality.

Heavy Spar, *sulphate of barytes*. Formely not worked in great quantities, but new discoveries of rich veins promise a considerable produce. The heavy spar is used as the basis for many sorts of colours, in order to give them more body. White lead is very commonly adulterated with heavy spar. The heavy spar is also used in potteries for glazing, and mixing with clay.

Fuller's earth. In some parts of the country worked for a long period. Extensive deposits have been recently found in other districts.

Potter's clay, and coloured earth; ochre. Nassau is very rich in potters' clay, of the best quality; it is partly exported in a raw state under the name of Valendar clay. The manufacture of earthenware in Nassau is susceptible of greater development; a great drawback hitherto having been the cost of fuel. These clays are manufactured into stone-ware cruets, pots, cans, jugs, and hydraulic pipes of great solidity. There are also some manufactories of Fayence and fine pottery ware, clay tobacco pipes; and common earthenware.

Samples of stone-ware, to show its mass. This stone-ware is extremely cheap, and is exported in great quantities.

2 Lossen, M. at the Iron Foundry of Michelbach.

Iron. Samples of pig, cast, and bar-iron. Grey tender pig, or cast-iron, with specimens of slags and artificial plumbago. White hard pig and cast-iron. Plate of cast-iron, direct from the high furnace. Samples of cast-iron bars, 3 feet long and 1 inch square, broken by bending them in the middle to an inch from the straight direction. Samples of bar-iron from the puddling process, once refined. The bars rolled and bent in right angles, and perforated by hammering, all in cold temperature. Samples 2½ inches broad, and ⅜ inch thick, worked on edge with hammers of 13 lbs. weight, without showing any cracks. Iron-bar, bent in right angle in warm temperature, the one end forged to show the sinew texture. Samples, bent till breaking. Iron axle (with box of cast-iron), bent in cold temperature.

3 The Isabellenhutte, Smelting Works, near Dillenzburg.

Nickel metal, and compositions of it. The nickel metal is found in combination with sulphur, and mixed with iron and copper pyrites. The separation of the metal is now performed, not by smelting, but by solution in acids. Nickel metal, in cubes, as it is brought to market, 97·5 per cent. of nickel, ·5 per cent. copper, ·9 per cent. of iron, 1·1 per cent. refuse and loss. German silver, bar, polished on one side, (composition, 8 copper, 3 nickel, 3½ zinc); and plate, polished on one side (composition, 8 copper, 3 nickel, 6½ zinc).

Combination of arsenic, nickel, and copper with sulphur and a small portion of iron, the produce of the smelting process.

In the mines 7,000 hands are occupied, and 2,000 more at the smelting works, or, in all, 9,000. The population existing immediately from the mining industry is, therefore, equal to 45,000, or the tenth part of the whole population of Nassau.

Specimens of clay tobacco-pipes: exhibited for the cheapness of produce, and to show the quality of the pipe-clay. Specimens of ochre and earth colours.

4 Von Rossler, Frederic, Westerburg. Cokes of bituminous coal.

5 Marble Manufactory at Diez.—Specimens of marble. The marble of Nassau forms part of the transition rocks of that country. This marble of different tints—red, black, yellow, and grey—is worked in manufactories and single workshops in the country near Lahn. Monuments, columns, vases, chimney pieces, &c. are made of it.

6 Leicher, A. Wiesbaden, Manu.—Samples of potters' clay. Articles manufactured of the clay. Column and vases, to show the quality of the material, and the style of workmanship.

7 Roehr, Friedrich, Wiesbaden, Manu.—Samples of ultra-marine, free from poison or any admixture of other colouring substances.

8 Heckel, T. A. Biebrich, Manu.—Clarionets and bassoon, of new and improved construction.

9 Wingender Brothers, Hochr. — Assortment of clay tobacco-pipes.

10 Mullenbach & Thewald, Hoehr.—Clay tobacco-pipes.

11 Montag, L. & C. Comb-maker, Wiesbaden, Manu.—Basket of black buffalo horn, inlaid with white Brazilian horn.

12 Beesten, J. van, Wiesbaden, Artist.—Models of fruit, embossed in wax.

13 Geismar, T. & Co. Wiesbaden, Manu.—Gun-press, overlaid with stag-horn, the ornaments in ivory, 7 ft. high, 4 ft. broad, and 1½ ft. deep. Cup in ivory, 1½ ft. high, 6 ft. diameter: "Christ blessing the children." Brooches in ivory, of various designs. Bracelets in ivory, of seven links, representing figures of game. Porte-monnaie; paper-knives; letter-case, and letter-weights.

GREECE.

(Commission in London, P. Ralli, Esq. President, and P. D. Scaramanga, Sectr. 25 Finsbury Circus; Agent, Mr. C. J. Major, 21 Billiter St.)

1 Zaphirakis, Z. Gythium, Laconia.—Valonia, the dried cups of the *Quercus Ægilops*, used for tanning.

2 Sophianos, A. Zea.—Valonia.

3 Malandrinus, A. Athens, Prod.—Madder root for dye.

4 Phillippos, G. Eubœa, Prod.—Madder root for dye.

5 Petropoulos, C. Tripolitza, Arcadia.—Kermes, used as a red dye, particularly for fezzes (red caps); gathered in different parts of Greece.

6 Londos, A. Patras, Prod.—Currants, the stock of which was not slit.

7 Inglessis, N. Santorin, Prod.—Raisins, light coloured, dipped in hot water and dried. The same simply dried.

8 Perotis, G. Messenia, Prod.—Five strings of figs. Figs in box.

9 Athanasiou, D. Lamia, Prod.—Tobacco.

10 Lapas, D. Livadia, Prod.—Sample of tobacco.

11 Cacoulidis, J. Ligouriou, Argolis, Prod.—Sample of tobacco.

12 Pavlides, B. Gulf of Nauplia.—Sponges.

13 Tsitzimbakos, A. Athens, Prod.—A jar of honey from Mount Hymettus. Honey in the comb.

14 Bishop of Eubœa, Carysto, Eubœa, Prod.—A jar of honey of Carysto, called rhodomeli.

THE GREEK GOVERNMENT.

15 *Milo.*—Two pieces of steatite or soapstone (French chalk); used for taking out spots of oil, grease, &c. from cloth, silks, and other fabrics.

16 Box of terra cimolia (*Cimolite*).

17 Box of iron ore, soft, and of a light-red colour, used as a pigment.

18 Three pieces of grinding-stone, or mill-stone. This stone is light and hard; being chiefly quartz.

19 Piece of native sulphur.

20 *Naxos.*—Box of emery; used in cutting, grinding, and polishing.

21 BOUDOURIS, B. Limni, Eubœa, Prop.—Carbonate of magnesia; white, and pure; it contains 44 per cent. magnesia, 46 per cent. carbonic acid, &c., is used for the manufacture of pure magnesia and Epsom salts; and in making bricks for furnaces.

THE GREEK GOVERNMENT.

22 *Santorin.*—Specimens of puzzolana. This material has the same properties as the Italian puzzolana; it is much used for building aqueducts, &c.

23 *Thebes.*—Meerschaum (écume de mer).

24 *Messenia.*—Piece of lithographic stone. Pieces are found as large as 6 ft. 6 in. cube.

25 MALAKATESI, J. Tinos, Prop.—Two pieces of marble; one white; one blackish.

26 *Sciros.*—Piece of white marble.

27 *Sparta.*—Piece of marble capable of receiving polish, and exhibiting a variety of colours

28 Piece of marble with reddish sky-blue green spots.

29 *Areopolis.*—Piece of grey marble from Cape Tenarus.

30 *Damaristica, South Maïna.*—A piece of marble with grey spots, having the appearance of white clouds.

31 *Perori.*—Piece of variegated marble; the ground is amethyst, with well-marked yellow veins.

32 *Pyrgaro.*—One piece of greyish-coloured marble.

33 *Nyphi.*—One piece of white marble.

34 *St. John.*—One piece of marble breccia; a variegated marble, the principal colour of which is violet.

35 One piece of marble, white, with yellow almond spots.

36 *St. Elias.*—One piece of greenish marble.

37 One piece of marble, with various shades of colour and veins.

38 *Carysto.*—One piece of Cipolino marble (Marmorum Carystium Cippolinum), from the quarry which produced the marble for the columns of Antoninus and Faustina, in Rome.

39 *Scutari.*—Three pieces of the marble called Rosso Antico, used by the ancients for sculpture and architecture.

CLEANTHES, S. Paros (island), Imp.

40 Piece of white marble.

41 Two pieces of marble, called Lichnites by the ancient Greeks. This marble is transparent, white and fine-grained.

42 Specimen of flesh-coloured marble, Lichnites.

THE GREEK GOVERNMENT.

43 *Crokea.*—One piece of marble, commonly called "porfido serpentino."

44 One piece of green marble, known under the name of "porfido verde."

45 The PRIOR of the MONASTERY, Pentelicon, Prop.—One piece of white marble of the kind used for the Parthenon and statues of old. Used also in modern building.

THE GREEK GOVERNMENT.

46 Piece of green porphyry; used in architecture.

47 *Tripolitza.*—Piece of black marble.

48 The PRIOR of the MONASTERY, Hymettus, Prop.—Piece of marble found near Athens in Mount Hymettus.

49 The GREEK GOVERNMENT, Psitalia (island).—Piece of marble alabaster.

50 RALLI, L. Piræus of Athens, Manu.—Specimens of yellow and white silk.

51 PANTAZOPOULUS, A. Calamata (Messenia), Manu.—Hank of silk, prepared according to the Italian method; the same, prepared according to the old method, used for fine woven silks; another, used for sewing and embroidery.

52 PITHOULIS, N. Sparta, Manu.—Hank of silk, prepared according to the Italian method.

53 COSTANTOULACHI, —, Hydra, Manu.—Silk sashes, worn by the seamen of Greece.

54 The NUNS of ST. CONSTANTINE, St. Constantine's Convent, Manu.—Silk musquito curtains. Silk handkerchiefs.

55 CALOTAS, P. Syra, Manu.—Leather, bullock hide.

56 SARIS & RENGOS, Athens, Manu.—Palicar dress, embroidered in gold, and consisting of doulama, fermeli (upper jacket); pair of gaiters; pair of silk garters; fez, with gold tassel; silk sash; fustenella; shirt; pair of trousers; and pair of red morocco shoes.

57 CONGOS, G. Patrass, Manu.—Liquorice juice.

58 JOHN, A. Cumi, Manu.—Ladies' scarfs.

59 TRIANDAPHYLOS, the Rev. Athens, Desig. and Artist.—The Cross, and the Annunciation of the Virgin. Both carved after the old Byzantine style.

60 VITALIS, L. Athens. — Bas-relief of Pentelicon marble, representing a small portion of the frieze of the Parthenon, in half scale of the original.

61 VITALIS, G. Athens.—Bas-relief of Parian marble, representing a small portion of the frieze of the Parthenon, in half scale of the original.

HAMBURGH.

(Commissioner, C. NOBACK, Esq. 20 Spring Gardens. Agent in London, M. PIGLHEIM, 14 Tavistock St.)

1 MEYER, T. W.—Specimens of manganese ore.

2 HILDEBRAND, C. G.—Glaziers' writing diamonds.

3 REESSING, H. B.—Samples of refined sugar.

4 WAGENER, J. C. L.—Samples of refined sugar.

5 PETERSON, JOHN (Agent, T. Peterson, Water Lane).—Oil-cakes.

6 REYNOLD, A. & G.—Fire-engine.

7 CROISSAN & LAUTENSTEIN.—Fashionable carriage.

8 FRIEDRICHSEN, K. A.—Blocks for ships.

9 BUFE, T. C. & SON, Cuxhaven.—A brig and barque, with drawings.

10 NIEBERG, J. L.—Constant pendulum clock.

11 BRÖCKING, W.—Electro-magnetical pendulum clock; clock with half-second pendulum.

12 BAUMGARDTEN & HAINS.—Horizontal pianoforte.

13 SCHÖRDER, C. H.—Horizontal pianoforte.

14 RUMMS, H.—Upright pianoforte (piccolo).

15 CELLIER, F. & SON.—Violoncello.

16 DE RODE, F.—Pair of kettle-drums.

17 KOHN, M. A.—A rose engine lathe.

18 PEPPER, OTTO.—Samples of curled hair.

19 WAMOSY, D.—Varnished calf-skins.

20 KRUGER, A.—Gentleman's riding saddle.

21 GERBERS, ED. — Chart on varnished linen cloth. Varnished double elephant paper for drawing.

22 MÖLLER, C. H. A.—Four ledgers.

23 LADE, ED.—Samples of corahs; designs and plates for corah-printing.

24 ARNDT & BEREND.—Table-cloth, printed on wool; piece of printed woollen furniture cloth.

25 DISSMAR & HARLOFF. — Pieces of printed and painted table-covers.

26 HEISER, F. L.—Coloured curtains.
27 MUCKENHEIM & ALPERS.—Coloured curtains.
28 VERHEIM, J.—Coloured curtains.
29 WINDMÜLLER, A.—Printed mousseline-de-laine cravats, shawls, &c.
30 REY, G. E.—Ladies' robes embroidered.
31 SCHELLE, J. G.—Embroidery.
32 GERSON, HENR.—Napkin darned; lace worked.
33 GOMPERTZ, B.—Hair-embroidered pictures of the Queen and the Prince of Wales, and of the Hamburgh Exchange.
34 CAHEN, T. J.—Sundry hats. A saddle-cloth.
35 CURJAR, TH.—Three hats.
36 SAHLBERG, C. F. G.—Gentlemen's and ladies' boots and shoes.
37 SCHOOST, J. N. C.—Gentlemen's and ladies' boots and shoes.
38 MAGDALINSKI, J.—Waterproof shooting boots, and gentlemen's dressing boots.
39 KINOL, A.—Jockey boots and gentlemen's dressing boots.
40 HENSEL, C. J.—Ladies' shoes.
41 KOPP & KROLL, F. W.—Gentleman's laced coat.
42 COHN, L. H.—Gentleman's cap, without seam, made of a new stuff.
43 RITTER, W.—Set of gimlets and augers, for metal and wood.
44 HÜNTEN, J. A. F.—Circular saw.
45 BEREND, W.—Engraved and engine-turned brass plates for bookbinders.
46 SCHULTZE, F.—Engraved music plates.
47 LEHRMANN, J. J. A.—Brass parrot's cage.
48 SCHULTZ, F. J.—Bird-cages, blue lackered, brown lackered, and brass.
49 SCHULTE & SCHEMANY.—Tea comforts; coal vases, coal bucket, and zinc bath; also a set of screw clabs, made by E. Rochlitz. A bathing vat, spelter-plated inside, coppered outside. Made by J. A. Lehmann.
50 RICHTER, J. M. S.—Brass parrot's cage.
51 HEINE, G. T.—Brass parrot and bird cages.
52 FLERSHEIM, J. M.—Fuel box; tea comfort and kettle.
53 KORLAN, G.—Frames for daguerreotypes.
54 BRAHMFELD & GUTRUP.—Silver writing stand.
55 MEYER, DIEDR.—Chimney-screen; wine-coolers; tea-plate; night-lamp, with two lithophanic plates, also a parrot cage of brass; and a lackered tray, with a picture on it.
56 HILDEBRAND, C. L.—Window glass; glass letters; and a glass box; also diamonds and planes for cutting glass, window-glass, and ivory; glaziers' diamonds and hammers.
57 WRIGHT, J. G.—Soda water bottles.
58 HANSA.—Various specimens of earthenware pottery.
59 ALBRECHT, A.—Varnished chimney-screen.
60 RAMPENDAHL, H. F. C.—Looking-glass, with hart's-horn frame.
61 HUEBENER & POHLE.—Sofa looking-glass, rococco style.
62 KORLAN, G.—Three looking-glasses. A window-blind representing a landscape.
63 BRUENING, C. D.—Writing bureau.
64 HAGEN, T. F.—Ebony sideboard.
65 ENGELS, H. W. M.—Sideboard of Jacaranda wood.
66 SENGLE, J. G.—Sideboard of rosewood.
67 ADIKES, J. D.—Sideboard of rosewood.
68 GESELLER, H.—Gentlemen's and lady's arm-chairs of rosewood.
69 PLAMBECK, C. F. H.—Round sofa-tables, with inlaid work.
70 RAMPENDAHL, H. F. C.—Writing bureau, inlaid with hart's-horn and ivory work.
71 FAULWASSER, C. E.—Lady's ebony working-table; sofa-table, with inlaid work; sundry boxes.

72 KÖHLER, J. H.—Sofa-table of rosewood, with inlaid work.
73 BEY, H.—Tables with inlaid work.
74 LOOSE, C. L.—Round table, with inlaid work; lady's work-table, with inlaid work; sundry boxes, with inlaid work.
75 LOOSE, J. R.—Round table, sundry boxes, with inlaid work.
76 MULLER, W. O.—Rosewood tables, with inlaid work.
77 KOPKE, C. J. C.—Lady's writing-table, in rococco style.
78 HEYMANN, J. D.—Rosewood sofa and chairs.
79 WERNER & PIGLHEIN.—Table with inlaid work; conversation sofa; arm-chair.
80 KRUGER, G. H.—Rocking chair; basket-work; and arm-chair.
81 MEHNE, PH.—Lady's rosewood work-table.
82 KOLL, J. N.—Rosewood sideboard, and four chairs.
83 JANTZEN, J. C. F.—Pattern card of turner's work.
84 ECKERT, J. C. H.—Pattern card, with mother-of-pearl and ivory articles, and pipe-tubes.
85 UMLAUFF, AUG.—Pattern card of tortoiseshell combs.
86 MEYER, H. C. Jun.—Large, small, and square pattern cards, containing—1 500 walking-sticks. 2 Samples of ivory, whalebone, rattins, &c., cut very fine. 3 Whips and rods. A glass case of stick buttons and caricatures cut out in bone, ivory, &c.
87 HARTER & HUBEN.—Samples of sticks, whips, whalebone, and ivory work.
88 ASPERN, W. M. V.—Lady's velvet box.
89 WÖBKE, H.—Tobacco pipes of Turkey clay.
90 OLSHARDSEN, F.—Artificial flowers, arranged in a frame.
91 LÖWENTHAL & Co.—Dolls' heads, in wax and papier-maché.
92 DOUGLAS, J. S. & SON.—Samples of soap.
93 ENGELHARD, F.—Statue of Richard Cœur de Leon, in bronze.
94 KLEFT, BR.—Marble figure of the Saviour, in relief. Two greyhounds in ivory.
95 SCHILLER, J.—Girl with a bunch of grapes. Model of Flora, plaster.
96 ENGELHARD, W.—Relief in plaster, illustrative of northern mythology; a series of designs. Model of the Lorley.
97 BOHM, AUG.—Engraved glass goblet.
98 RAMPENDAHL, H. F.—Engraved ivory goblet.
99 BOSTELMANN, A.—Coloured church window in miniature.
100 RÖSING, F. W.—Two coloured glass transparencies. Tops of tables in marble, stained and ornamented wood.
101 CORNIDES, LUDW.—Transparent horn paintings.
102 SCHUBERDH & Co.—Music of the Opera Lichtenstein, bound in velvet.
103 KOHNKE, F. J.—A daguerreotype painting, coloured; also a glass plate, with inlaid figures, blue on one side, brown on the other—subject: Cromwell at Marston Moor.
104 SCHNAUTZ, WM.—A sausage.
105 MEYER, Berlin.—Two green Orlean petticoats. Samples of prepared horse-hair, and horn.
106 BARTLELS, J. C. M.—Wood carvings.
107 ZUBER, J.—Carvings in ivory.
108 PRALE & BALLHEIMER.—Mahogany veneer, fifty-four plates to the inch.
109 THIELE, Jun.—A child's sofa.
110 CLASSEN, F. F.—A fender for a stove.
111 BUSS, W. H.—A bird-cage.
112 SCHULTZ, G. S.—Two bronze candelabra.
113 BOYE, C. T.—Spinning-wheel.

114 MIEOLCI, C. L.—Specimens of bookbinding.
115 HARTOG, C. H.—A needlework fire-screen.
116 BÖEKEL, A.—Painted window-blinds.
117 KAHLER, A.—Lithographic writings.
118 SEVERIN, E.—Needlework.
119 APPEL, J. C.—Needlework, carpet, and balls.
120 MEINKE, W. C.—Five flags.
121 BEINHAUER, C.—A stove.
122 BAHR, H. & Co.—Silk handkerchiefs.
123 HANSER-EISEN, & MESSING WEARNIN-FABRICK, VON CARL THIEL, Schledehaus.—Three iron forms for sugar refiners. Three cooking vessels. All tinned.

HANOVER.

(Commissioner, F. STAHLSCHMID, Esq. 14 Mark Lane.)

1 HENNING, —, Limmer, near Hanover.—Specimens of asphaltum stone and asphaltum earth; melted asphaltum; asphaltum prepared for roofs and pavements.
2 HOSTMANN, C. Celle.—Ink for typographic and lithographic printing, with specimens of soot and boiled oil.
3 TANNER, C. D. Hanover.—Brace of pistols, in case. Gun, with two double barrels, in case. Rifle, in case.
4 LOHDEFINK, W. A. Hanover. — Electro-magnetic apparatus, for telegraphs, on Morse's system, together with a subsidary apparatus ("Relais"), and a paper roller.
5 HANSEN, J. G. Hildesheim.—Piece of sail-cloth. Piece of linen, called "Franzleinen."
6 SCHULTZE, D. Bodenteich, Luneburgh.—Various samples of linen; some of raw or unbleached linen, and some of linen yarn and flax.
7 WAGNER, C. A. Hanover.—A hat, with felt body, covered with plush; of cotton cloth, covered with plush; another hat, covered with felt. Made upon a new principle.
8 BERNSTORFF & EICHWEDE, Hanover.—Gilt bronze lustre, for sixty candles. Bust in bronze of His Majesty the King of Hanover. Small bronze statue, the painter Holbein.
9 HERTING, C. Einbeck.—Specimen of paper-hanging.
10 FRIEDRICH, J. P. Norden.—Three calf skins.

LUBECK.

(Commissioner, Mr. F. STAHLSCHMIDT, 14 Mark Lane.)

1 PLATZMAN, CONRAD, Manu.—Oil-cakes.
2 CARSTENS, DANIEL HEINRICH, Manu.—Preserved vegetables, poultry, fish, fruits, and milk.
3 BEHRENS, JOHAN CHRISTIAN, Manu.—Skin of genuine black morocco leather. Specimen of glue.
4 BECKMANN, JOHANN, J. C. Manu.—Lamb's skin dressed with the wool.
5 FISCHER, CARL AUGUST, Manu.—Guns; double-barrelled rifle, with case; fowling-piece; and rifle.
7 BRUNSWIG, GEORG HEINRICH, Manu.—Japanned calf and sheep skin. Peaks of leather, and embossed pasteboard polished and ornamented.
8 SPIEGEL, WILHEIM ANTON CARL & Co. Des. and Manu.—Embroidery, on silk canvass, intended for a fire-screen. Embroidery in process, on perforated card-board, intended for a portfolio.
9 STOLLE, CARL, Manu.—Patterns of embroidery commenced, with the silk, wool, pearls, &c., necessary for its completion; on perforated card-board, and on cotton canvas and silk canvas. A fire-screen embroidered on cotton canvas.
10 BREYER, GEORG WILHELM, Manu.—A bed-screen of osiers.
11 ROEPER, FRIEDRICH, Manu.—A lady's work-box, decorated with embroidery, velvet, and bronze.

MECKLENBURG-STRELITZ.

(Commissioner in London, Mr. DE VIEBAHN, 43 Albion St. Hyde Park.)

1 BENECKE, W. Neustrelitz, Manu.—Tin-plate portable steam-producing apparatus. Brass stoves for heating rooms by steam.
2 LANGE, C. Neustrelitz, Manu.—Air-tight door to a stove for heating rooms. Drawing of a stove, constructed after the principle of the safety-lamp of Sir Humphry Davy.
3 SCHARENBERG, A. Neustrelitz, Inv. and Manu.—Finest madder extract, produced by a new and cheap method, for dyeing all sorts of stuffs.
4 GUNDLACH, C. Wesenberg, Manu.—Spinning-wheel with inlaid work, consisting in the whole of 450 pieces.

MECKLENBURG-SCHWERIN.

(Agent in London, M. PIGLHEIM, 14 Tavistock St.)

1 STOLZENBERG, J. Genoyen.—Apparatus for distillation.
2 SCHMIDT, J. Güstrow.—Three guns.
3 GERBER, C. H. A. Güstrow. — Two table-cloths, presenting, respectively, the arms of England and of Mecklenburg.
5 MEYNE, J. Schwerin.—A soup-tureen of German silver.
6 MEYER, W. 29 New Street, Spring Gardens, London.—Samples of charcoal, from the Warnemunde mines (Mecklenburg-Schwerin).
8 BEAR, H. Rostock, Manu.—An ornament of furniture, cut in linden-wood, carved in a fancy style called by the French "baroque."
9 BAHRT, H. Schwerin (City), Manu.—Seven concave razors, damasked.
10 YERBER, C. Güstrow, Mecklenburg, Manu.—Two half silk-damask table cloths, embroidered, the one with the arms of England, the other with those of Mecklenburg.

NUREMBURG.

FUCHS, MARIA, Nuremburg, Manu.—One pound extra fine brass wire, drawn to the length of 76,000 feet. One pound of extra fine chalybeate wire, for mining lanterns, drawn to the length of 41,000 feet.

MEXICO.

THE MEXICAN COMMISSIONER; through Messrs. Dunlop & Scherles, Southampton; and Messrs. Lightly & Sirren, London. — A landscape in a gilt frame of the material known by the name of Camalote: in relief. A frame of wax flowers. A collection of woods. Oil of coquillo in a small vessel. An etching in a frame. Three cakes of chittle. Designs of fruit and reptiles in wax.

NETHERLANDS.

(Commissioner, G. GOOSSENS, Union Hotel, Salisbury Sq.)

1 BLEEKRODE, Prof. S. Delft, and ENTHOVEN, L. Hague (Agents, Enthoven & Sons, Moorgate St. London), Inv.—Patent white paints from oxide of zinc. Yellow chromate of zinc. Green oxide of zinc. Chloride of zinc.
2 POORTMAN & VISSER, Schiedam, Manu.—White lead.

3 STRATINGH & Co. Groningen, Manu.—White lead white, soft, and pure.

4 MAAS, H. Doorn-Heg, nr. Amersfoort, Manu.—Hydraulic cement.

5 DUURA (VAN) & VERSTEEVEN, Rotterdam, Manu.—Prussian blue. Mineral blue. Chrome yellow. Chrome green. Water blue.

6 DIEDERICHS BROTHERS, Amsterdam, Manu.—Specimens of Dutch water-colours.

7 VIS, A. Wormerveer Manu.—Pearl barley, groats, dried starch, &c.

8 OOMEN, A. M. Ginneken, nr. Breda, Manu.—Oil-seed cakes. Oil-cakes. Glue and gelatine.

9 DE HAAN, A. Rotterdam, Manu.—Sample of rape-seed. Rape-oil.

10 DEYL (VAN DER), LEENDERT, & SON, Weesp, Manu.—Patent chocolate powder.

11 BOCKEN, C. Venlo, nr. Rotterdam, Manu.—Samples of starch. Starch, mixed with fine smalt.

12 PRINS, C. C. Wormerveer, Manu.—Starch, known in Holland under the name of Urling's patent starch. Best Dutch starch.

13 SCHONEVELD & WESTERBAAN, Gouda, Manu.—White and grey potato meal or farina. Potato gum. Sago, &c.

14 VOORST (VAN), DIRK, & SON, Zaandam, Manu.—Dutch wheat-flour.

15 VISSER & Co. Schiedam, Manu.—Potato-flour.

16 HEUVELDOP, H. Leeuwarden, Manu.—Specimens of chicory. Woollen manufactures.

17 VISSER, E. E. Amersfoort, Manu.—Yellow wax.

18 JORRITSMA, A. Dokkum, Inv.—Veterinary medicine for oxen, horses, and other cattle.

19 IANSSEN, N. H. A. S. Hertogenbosch, Manu.—Preserved provisions.

20 SMITS, P. Utrecht, Manu.—Polychromate, or chry-sammic acid, a new dye. Animal charcoal.

21 ROOSEGAARDE, G. J. Zutphen, Manu.—Sole leather, from Buenos Ayres skins. Glue.

22 BUYTEWEG, N. Delft, Manu.—Hides of Holland. Buenos Ayres; sheep-skin, dressed. Chamois leather, &c.

23 KOK, A. P. Apeldoorn, Manu.—Morocco leathers, "basils" and "splits." Calf-skins.

24 HOOP, VAN DER J. & Co. Rotterdam, Manu.—Java rattans, cleaned and prepared.

25 CRAP, H. J. L. Den Helder, Inv.—Mat, made of dried sea-grass.

26 HOOGEN, VAN DEN T. Dordrecht, Manu.—Patent standing-ropes.

27 BEEFTINGH (VAN), N. & Co. Katwyk, nr. Leyden, Inv. and Manu.—Rope, for ships' rigging; twisted in a con-centric manner.

28 LAFEBRE, A. Gouda, Manu.—Curtain cord. Strong twine and cord for fishing purposes, drum-cord, and forage of Dutch shell hemp.

29 DIRKS, H. J. Dort, Manu.—Brooms and brushes.

30 CATZ & Co, P. S. Amsterdam, Manu.—Specimens of horse-hair (drawn) for fiddle-sticks and stuffing.

31 HASE, J. H. The Hague, Manu.—A cloak, muff, and ruffles, made from the feathers of the Colymbus crystatus. Muff, made from the feathers of the marabou.

32 WARNAR, WILLINCK Amsterdam, Manu.—Utrecht velvet in different colours, for furniture and carriages.

33 VREEDE & Co. Tilburg, Manu.—Twilled duffe baize. Fine thin cloth, &c. Flannel, &c.

34 ZAALBERG, J. C. & SON, Leyden, Manu.—Blanket* for the markets of Holland, Belgium, Java, China, Japan, and France.

35 ZUURDEEG, J. & SON, Leyden, Manu.—Blankets of fine quality, made from Dutch wool, of a fast colour.

36 WYK (VAN) BROTHERS & Co. Leyden, Manu.—W o ollen coverlets, knitting-yarn, worsted stockings, &c.

37 HOOGEBOOM, J. J. & SON, Leyden, Manu.—Blankets of Dutch wool.

38 SCHELTEMA, J. & J. Leyden, Manu.—Blankets of various thicknesses, made of Dutch wool.

39 THEUNISSEN, J. Heppel—Manu.—Bed-tick, of linen thread, fine quality. Canvas, called "Meppeler everdoek."

40 KOOPMANS, K. Beverwyk, Manu. — Turkey-red cloth, dyed with Dutch madder.

41 ALPHEN (VAN), G. Breda, Manu.—Carpets of cow-hair, speckled, red, and black; and green, black, and striped.

42 HEUKENSFELDT, I. Delft, Manu.—Carpets: Velvet, new Brussels, and under-table, or "crumb-cloths."

43 KROONENBURG, W. F. Director of the Royal Smyrna or Turkey Carpet Manu. Deventer. — Carpets: Deventer carpet, woven in one piece.

44 VEN (VAN DE), P. C. Boxtel, Manu.—Napkins and table-cloths of fine damask. Cloths for communion-tables. Napkin with the weapons of Holland and Wurtemburg, &c.

45 VOORT (Van DER), H. Boxtel, Manu. — Damask table-cloth and napkins, linen, with the arms of Great Britain, of the Netherlands, of Russia, &c.

46 GEFFEN (VAN), J. H. Boxtel, Manu. — Nap. kins, table-cloth, altar-cloth of linen damask, and diaper linen.

47 GALLE, P. H. Kampen, Manu. — Table-cloth of linen damask, superfine. Napkins of linen damask.

48 TRAVAGLINO, J. A. Haarlem, Manu.—Sewing and other silk. Gold cloth. Silver damask. Black figured silk stuff, à la Jacquard. Satin de Chine. Gros de Naples. Silk lace. Ribbon, &c.

49 ENTHOVEN (VAN), A. J. Empe, near Zutphen, Prop.—Raw, Dutch, and other silks.

50 SWAAB, S. L. The Hague, Inv.—Flax, Dutch flax, and hemp. Cotton flax, &c.

51 KAISER, G. C. F. Amsterdam, Manu.—Chamois gloves.

52 ROOYACKERS & SON, Rotterdam, Makers.—Boots: Varnished boots, the leg without seam. A Chinese boot. Boots of vulcanized caoutchouc.

52A PILGER, L. Amsterdam, Manu.—Two safes.

53 LAFEBER, A. Gouda, Manu.—Twisted cotton reins, made by hand, for a set of four horses, in the English national colours. Twisted halters.

54 CATZ (VAN), J. B. Gouda, Manu.—Yarn and rope for fishing. Log lines and drum cords from Dutch hemp. Knitted reins, from English cotton.

55 POST & WENDT, Gouda, Manu.—Whalebone whips and walking-canes.

56 OTTO, F. H. Amsterdam, Maker.—Embroidery, representing an incident of Milton's youth.

57 COUCKE, C. Rotterdam, Manu.—Lady's head-dress. Periwig of grey hair.

58 ROOYEN (VAN), H. Utrecht, Des.—Specimens of dyed silk, coloured with newly-invented polychromate dye.

59 HONIG, B. C. & F. Zaandyk, Manu.—Fine parch-ment and double elephant paper.

60 HONIG & SON, Zaandyk, Manu.— Fine parchment, double elephant, large square folio, and other papers.

61 GELDER (VAN) & SONS, Wormerveer, Manu.—Paper for sugar refiners, white inside and purple outside.

62 GIESBERS, T. M. Roermond, Manu.—Iron fire-safes.

63 MARTIN, E. C. Zeyst, near Utrecht, Manu.—Queen's-ware stove. Patent architectural ornaments of clay. Con-soles, flower-vases, &c.

65 GRAAMANS, H. C. Rotterdam, Manu. — Patent kitchen stove, and two hearths.

66 HESSELINK, W. F. Gorssel, near Zutphen, Prop.—A seedlip and a cradle.

67 LANDKROON, J. Noordwold, near Dokkum, Maker.—Basket of willow twigs, painted with Frieslandish green, &c

L

68 DRAAISMA, D. Deventer, Manu.—Porous pots of earthenware, used in galvanic apparatus.

69 LINDEN (VAN DER), A. Rotterdam, Manu.—Cigars made of Dutch and East Indian tobacco.

70 BRANDON, N. D. Amsterdam, Manu.—Stearine candles and tapers. Lime soap. Stearic acid.

71 PERSELAERT & SON, Maastricht, Manu.—Marseilles, Limburg, Japan, odoriferous and other soaps.

72 SONDERMEYER, J. K. Rotterdam, Des.—Ground or earth-borer.

73 STAM, F. Bennebrock, near Haarlem, Inv. and Maker.—Liquid manure-machine, with arrangements to spread the manure.

74 JENKEN, W. Utrecht, Maker.—A swing plough of Flemish construction. A turnip and carrot-cutter of a new construction.

75 VAN VLISSINGEN, VAN HEEL, & DEROSNE CAIL & Co. Amsterdam, Makers.—Sugar-cane mill.

76 ENTHOVEN, C. L. at The Hague, Inv. and Manu.—An iron crane, for weighing and lifting.

77 GOOSSENS, G. Artificer at the Royal Manufactory of Percussion Caps, Delft, Inv.—A machine for the manufacture of percussion caps, and loading apparatus.

78 PETIT & FRITSEN, Aarlerixtel, near Helmond, Founders.—Cast bells for a chime, weighing about 2,500 kilogrammes, or 5,500 lbs. with a suspending apparatus.

79 ENSCHEDE & SONS, Haarlem, Manu.—Printing types, Javanese character. Stereotype plates.

80 NERING, BOGEL, & Co. Deventer, Manu.—Cast-iron flatting-roll, for calendering wool-velvet.

81 SOEDERS, G. Moorsien, near Utrecht, Inv. and Manu.—A moveable or double-acting safety-axle for carriages

82 BOSCH, C. G. Amsterdam, Inv. and Manu.—A case containing copper less oxidizable than ordinary copper, for shipping and other purposes.

83 BECKER, C. Arnhem.—A delicate balance, with weights. Two other balances. A levelling apparatus.

84 KAISER, A. The Hague, Inv. and Manu.—Regulator for clocks, a simplified astronomical clock, with some new arrangements.

85 UHLMAN, K. W. Zwolle, Inv.—Equatorial sun-dial.

86 HOHWU, A. Amsterdam, Manu.—An astronomical eight-day clock, chronometer and other articles.

87 LOGEMAN, W. M. Haarlem, Inv. and Manu.—Large permanent steel magnet. Electro-magnetic engine.

88 EDER, S. T. Rotterdam, Maker.—A clock.

89 CAZAUX, J. Valkenburg, near Leyden, Inv. and Prop.—A dynamostater, to be used as a dynamometer for ploughs, with a chronometric mediator or controller of the indications of the instrument affixed to it. Mechanical tuning-key for pianofortes, made by B. Van Beek, watchmaker, Leyden.

90 CONRAD, F. U. The Hague, Engineer-in-Chief, Inv.—Model of a crane-bridge on the Dutch railway, constructed over the river Schie, near Schiedam and Deefshaven. Model of a rolling-bridge on the Dutch railway, constructed over the old Rhine, a little below Leyde. Model of apparatus for shutting of sluice or dock-gates.

91 CLAASEN, P. C. Amsterdam, Inv.—Model of a patent railway waggon, with improved break. Model of a patent railway, with a third line of rails.

92 MAITLAND, R. T. The Hague, Inv.—Model of a self-acting preservative locomotive, with warning apparatus propelled in front.

93 VOLLENHOVEN (VAN), C. I. Rotterdam, Prop.—Models of a cutter, long boat, or launch, with a piece of cannon; gig; yawl and pinnace.

94 WAL (VAN DER), K. S. Heeg, near Sneek, Inv.—Model of a water-mill with two screws.

95 CUIJPERS, J. F. The Hague, Manu.—Small pianoforte, of purple wood.

96 ZEEGERS, F. Amsterdam, Manu.—A large folding screen, ornamented in Chinese or Japanese style. Wooden fire-screen and round table, varnished in red lacquer, &c.

97 HORRIX BROTHERS, M. & W. The Hague, Manu.—Ladder and staircase for the use of libraries.

98 SCHUTZ, L. W. Zeijst, near Utrecht, Des. and Manu.—Specimens of zinc casting. Stag, embossed by Mr. Bauch, at Berlin; flower table, &c. Flower tables; vases and baskets, in wood and twisted reed.

99 REGOUT, P. Maestricht, Manu.—Two large chandeliers; two smaller, in cut glass, supported by gilt metal. Vase of cut glass. Glasses, assorted. Glass conduit pipes.

100 LURASCO BROTHERS, Amsterdam, Manu.—Bronze statues, representing M. A de RUYTER, Prince William I., and Rembrandt van Ryn: all modelled by L. Royer.

101 KEMPEN (VAN), J. M. Utrecht, Manu.—Nineteen articles in silver, with a pamphlet.

102 GREBE, J. G. Rotterdam.—Specimen of embossing, in the form of a beaker, from a single piece of silver.

109A HEYNSBERGEN (VAN), W. J. The Hague, Manu.—Military ornaments, as epaulettes, sword, and shoulder knots, cords, scarfs, &c. Galloon, and gold and silver thread.

103 LUCARDIE, J. M. Rotterdam, Manu.—Silver ornamented tea-kettle, with embossed figures.

104 ROMAIN, D. Rotterdam, Manu.—Corsage or pointe, made of diamonds and pearls, in three parts.

105 VERSNEL, J. S. Rotterdam, Maker.—Flowers and butterflies, sculptured in Carrara marble, in various colours.

106 DIONISY, J. M. Roermond, Maker.—Cameos, among which is a figure of Her Majesty the Queen of England. Prints, from medals and stamps.

107 LEFEBRE, L. J. jun. The Hague, Des. and Manu.—Horn filled with artificial flowers in human hair, representing The Horn of Plenty.

108 HESS, T. A. Amsterdam, Maker.—An artificial eye.

109 ENSCHEDE & SONS, Haarlem, Letter-founders and Printers.—Bibles in quarto and folio, for the use of the Dutch Reformed Church, printed for the Dutch Bible Company, with stereotype plates.

110 NOORDENDORP, P. H. The Hague, Printer.—Specimens of Dutch printing.

111 ZWEESAARDT, ALBERTUS, Amsterdam, Printer and Binder.—Two books, in quarto, viz., Graduale Romanum; Antiphonarium Romanum.

112 REGEER, HENDRIKUS JOHANNES, Rotterdam, Bookbinder.—Works of Hogarth, specimen of binding.

113 FOON, Dr. H. Amsterdam, Inv.—Specimens of transparent writing.

114 SAUERBIER, J. C. Rotterdam, Manu.—A bracelet of diamonds, with a moveable rose and amethyst.

NEW GRANADA.

1 A bag of cocoa. Various emeralds.

2 GRUT, B.—A bag of cocoa Theobroma cacao), known in commerce as Caraccas cocoa; consumed chiefly in Spain and South America.

3 BALLERAS, G. E. Bogotá, Imp. A specimen of emerald, the property of the exhibitor, from the mine of Muzo in New Granada.

4 PARIS, E. Bogotá, Prod.—Specimens of emeralds, from the mine of Muzo in the republic of New Granada.

5 BONITO, Sir T.—Specimens of rough emeralds.

OLDENBURGH.

(Agent in London, M. PIGLHEIM, 14 Tavistock St.)

1 CASSEBOHM, M. T. H. Oldenburg.—A model of Heidelberg Castle, carved in corkwood, in exact proportion to its size on the scale of $\frac{1}{135}$.

2 BRAMLAGE, A. Lohne.—Manufactured quills.

3 SHARNHORST, C. Oldenburgh.—Thread spun by hand.

PERSIA.

ABBOT, F. 22 Jermyn St. Two Persian rugs. Two boxes carved pear-wood spoons. Three pair papier-maché book covers. Two looking-glass frames. Five kalemdans (pen-holders). Two Persian knives. Four purses.

ARAMAN, H. Woburn Pl. Russell Sq. (Agent, D. MULLER, 32 Lowndes Street, Belgrave Square). Three silk and gold embroidered scarfs. Two scarfs (all silk). Two dresses for ladies, in silk and cotton. A dress for a gentleman, in silk and cotton. A silk and gold embroidered cushion. Four silk and gold bags for ladies. Three pair silk and gold slippers for ladies. Two pair silk and gold slippers for gentlemen. Three silk and gold caps for gentlemen. A caffea (head-dress or turban). A silk girdle. Embroidered purses and sashes. Ornaments of various kinds.

THOMPSON, J. B. M.D. 5 Suffolk Pl. Pall Mall. Two pieces of Persian needle-work. Two handsome silk scarfs (new patterns). Four pieces of embroidered gold and silver (for slippers, caps, and reticules). A purse, scented wood. Two beads, scented wood. A mother-o'-pearl bead. A Persian khorapan dagger, with ivory carved handle, with female figure. A narghili or hooka, for smoking. A lady's amber mouth-piece. Three silk-purses. Two pair of lady's slippers, yellow. A silk and cotton under garment, of a peculiar manufacture. Cloak. Table cover. Silk samples. Four boxes. Persian tobacco, used as a medicine.

EDE, F. & SON.—Four Persian panels : 1 Agis. An old king of Persia, having no male issue, and an only daughter, is represented buying a neighbouring chief named Yussuff, to marry him to his daughter Zulika, thereby retaining the throne in his own family.

2 The old king Agis making a feast to his intended son-in-law, who stands on one side while the women dance.

3 The old king's daughter Zulika in her harem.

4 Yussuff becomes king by his marriage, and is represented at dinner with his courtiers.

WATSON, BELL & Co. Old Bond St.—Three Persian carpets.

COPELAND, Ald. M.P.—A carpet, 34 feet by 9 feet 6 inches.

BIDWELL, J. Esq.—A table cover.

MAJOR, C. T. Esq. 21 Billiter St. London.—Two Persian rifles, and a sabre.

MILLS, W. F. jun. Esq. King's Parade, Chelsea, Prop.—Various articles collected by Mr. Mills, sen. during a residence of some years in Persia.

HUDSON, J. 132 Oxford St.—Illustrations of Persian smoking, specimens of oriental pipes, tobacco, &c.

PORTUGAL.

(Agents, ANTONIO VALDEZ, Esq., and F. J. VAN ZELLER, Esq., 5 Jeffrey Square, St. Mary Axe.)

Mineral Kingdom.

1 to 17. Specimens of minerals. 18 and 19. Lignite—*J. J. Roque, Delgado.* 20 to 27. Specimens of minerals.

28. Muriatic acid. 29. Sulphurite acid. 30. Nitric acid —*Hirsch and Brother.* 31. Carbonate of potash. 32. Tartar of potash—*F. M. C. Leal.*

33. Tartar of potash. 34. Tartar of potash. 35. Red tartar (raw). 36. White tartar (raw)—*A. J. Ferreira.*

37. Brown tartar. 38. Tartar of potash—*Serzedello and Co.* 39. Cream of tartar. 40. Grey tartar. 41. Brown tartar —*Garland and Co.* 42. Refined nitre—*Serzedello and Co.*

43. Common salt in stone. 44. Common salt in powder —*Baron de Samora, Corrêa.*

45. Common salt in stone. 46. Common salt in lumps. 47. Common salt in powder—*From St. Ubes.*

48. Common salt in lumps—*Baron de Samora, Corrêa.*

49. Common salt in stone. 50. Sulphate of soda. 51. Carbonate of soda prepared with salt—*Serzedello and Co.*

52. Carbonate of soda prepared with salt. 53. Carbonate of soda prepared with salt—*Hirsch and Brother.*

54. Common white lime—*F. A. Machado.* 55. Brown lime. 56. Common white lime. 57. Common white lime— *From Minho.* 58, 59, 60. Specimens of minerals.

61. Nitrate of barytes. 62. Nitrate of strontia—*Serzedello and Co.* 63. Sulphate of iron—*From Algoza.*

64. Sulphate of iron—*Hirsch and Brother.* 65. Sulphate of iron. 66. Sulphate of copper. 67. Ammoniac sulphate of copper—*F. M. C. Leal.* 68. Sulphate of copper—*Hirsch and Brother.* 69. Sulphate of zinc. 70. Oxymuriate of tin— *Serzedello and Co.* 71. Carbonate of lead—*Maria Norziglia.* 72. Nitrate of lead—*Serzedello and Co.* 73. Chromate of lead. 74. Zodur of potash—*F. M. C. Leal.* 75. Acetate of potash. 76. Tartar of potash and soda—*Serzedello and Co.* 77. Chloride of lime—*Hirsch and Brother.* 78. Red oxide of mercury. 79. Corrosive sublimate—*F. M. C. Leal.*

80. Bisulphuret of mercury. 81. Emetic tartar—*Serzedello and Co.* 82 to 102. Specimens of minerals. 103. Granite.

104. Granite 105. Granite—*From Vianna do Minho.*

106 to 109. Specimens of minerals. 110. Lithographic stone. 111. Lithographic stone—*Mr Dejeant.*

112. Lithographic stone. 113. Lithographic stone, with a sketch of a window of Christ's Convent, at Thomar— *Royal Tobacco Contractors.* 114. Lithographic stone—*Duke de Palmella.* 115. Lithographic stone—*Mr. Dejeant.*

116. Hydraulic clay—*Marapez.* 117. Hydraulic clay— *Telim.* 118. Hydraulic volcanic skories—*Bagacina.*

119. A mineral specimen. 120 to 231. Specimens of marbles. 232 to 247. Marble slabs for tables, &c.—*Mr. Dejeant.* 248 and 249. Marble slabs—*J. J. de Figueiredo.*

250 and 251. Marble slabs—*Mr. Dejeant.*

252 to 257. Marble slabs—*J. J. de Figueiredo.*

258. Mosaic slab, made of 60 specimens of marbles from the province of Alemtejo—*C. Bonnet and Dejeant.*

259 to 274. Specimens of marbles—*Mr. Dejeant.*

275 to 278. Very refractive bricks—*Manufactory at Bulhoens.* 279 to 293. Porcelain bricks—*Ferreira Pinto and Sons.* 294. Flints—*From Rio Maior.*

295. Grindstone. 296. Grindstone—*From Braganza.*

Vegetable Kingdom.

297. Hard wheat, used for Italian paste.

298. Hard wheat (durazio rigo)—*From Lisbon.*

299. Hard wheat (rigo)—*Marquis de Ficalho.*

300. Hard wheat (rijo)—*J. J. R. Delgado.*

301. Hard wheat (rijo)—*Marquis de Ficalho.*

302. Hard wheat (rijo)—*From Figueira.*

303. Hard wheat (palhoca), Greek seed—*From Santarem.*

304. Hard wheat (rijo)—*From Alemtejo.*

305. Common hard wheat—*Viscount de Fonte Boa.*

306. Hard wheat black-bearded (anafil).

307. Hard grey wheat (rijo preto)—*Viscount de Benagazil.* 308. Giant wheat. 309. Giant wheat in the shell.

310. Wheat 4th quality (Ribeiro)—*J. R. de Azevedo.*

311. Soft wheat (Ribeiro)—*From Golegan.*

312. Wheat, 1st quality (Ribeiro)—*A. M. Xavier.*

313. Soft wheat (Ribeiro)—*From Benavente.*

314. Soft wheat (Ribeiro)—*From the banks of the Lado river.*

315. Soft wheat—*From Graciosa, one of the Azores Islands.*

316. Soft wheat—*From Flores, Azores Islands.*

317. White tender wheat (durazio mollar)—*Marquis de Ficalho.*

318. Wheat, 2nd quality (Ribeiro)—*J. V. d'Almeida.*

319. Wheat (Ribeiro)—*A. da Silva Junor.*

320. Soft wheat (Ribeiro)—*From Alcacer.*

321. Soft wheat—*From St. Michael's, Azores Islands.*

322. Soft wheat—*From Figueira.*

323. Hard wheat (muge).

L 2

324. Wheat (molle tremez)— *Viscount Benagazil.*
325. Hard wheat (tremez), 3 months' growth—*From Alcacer.* 326. Wheat (molle tremez)— *Viscount Benagazil.*
327. Wheat (tremez)—*Viscount Fonte Boa.*
328. Common hard wheat (durazio mollar)— *Viscount de Benegazil.* 329. Hard wheat (durazio mollar)—*From Lisbon.*
330. Flour from soft wheat.
331. Rye—*From Vianna do Minho.*
332, 333, and 334. Rye. 335. Rye—*Marquis de Ficalho.*
336. Rye. 337. Flour of rye. 338. Maize.
339. Maize—*Viscount de Benagazil.* 340. Maize.
341. White maize—*From Caminha.*
342. White maize—*R. C. Alvares, jun.*
343. Yellow maize—*From Vianna do Minho.*
344. White maize. 345. Yellow maize—*From Alemtejo.*
346. Yellow maize—*From St. Michael's (Azores).*
347. Yellow maize—*Marquis de Ficalho.*
348. Yellow maize—*From Caminha.*
349. Yellow maize—*J. P. da Silva.* 350. Yellow maize.
351. Barley—*Mocha.* 352. Barley— *Santa.*
353. Barley—*A. S. d'Albuquerque.*
354. Barley—*From Alemtejo.* 355. Barley—*From Lisbon.*
356. Barley. 357. Oats—*Marquis de Ficalho.*
358. Oats—*From Alemtejo.*
359. Yellow kidney beans—*A. F. Carvao.*
360. Yellow kidney beans—*V. C. V. Soares.*
361. Yellow kidney beans.
362 and 363. Red zebra kidney beans.
364. White kidney beans—*V. C. V. Soares.*
365. White kidney beans.
366. White kidney beans—*Viscount de Benagazil.*
367. White kidney beans. 368. Zebra kidney beans—*A. F. Corrêa.* 369. Zebra kidney beans.
370. Kidney beans (Fradinho)—*J. P. da Silva.*
371 and 372. Kidney beans (Fradinho).
373. Heat peas (grão de Bico)—*J. C. da Silveira.*
374. Heat peas (grão de Bico).
375. Heat peas (grão de Bico)—*Marquis de Ficalho.*
376. Heat peas (grão de Bico). 377. Large Windsor beans—*Viscount de Benagazil.*
378. Large Windsor beans—*Viscount de Fonte Boa.*
379. Lentils. 380. Peas. 381. Carob beans—*C. Bonnet.*
382. Lupines. 383. Lupines—*Viscount de Benagazil.*
384 and 385. Rice, from Carolina seed.
386 and 387. Rice (Carolina seed)—*Count de Belmonte.*
388 and 389. Rice in the shell—*From Evora.*
390 and 391. Millet—*D. C. V. Soares.*
392. Sweet almonds (mollares).
393. Hard almonds (durazias)—*M. T. Bretes.*
394. Filberts—*A. P. de Fonceca Vaz.* 395. Walnuts.
396. Walnuts—*A. P. da Fonceca Vaz.*
397 and 398. Walnuts. 399 and 400. Dried chestnuts and sweet acorns (cuercus bulato)—*Marquis de Ficalho.*
401. Arachide—*A. de Sá Nogueira.*
401 a. Bis-Arachide, from Angola—*F. R. Balatha.*
401b. Ter-Cyperus esculentus (shuffas) — *Marquis de Loulé.* 402. Ricinus (carapateire)—*Viscount Benagazil.*
403. Dried figs—*J. L. Gomes.*
404. Dried pears. 405. Dried plums.
406. Dried plums—*A. P. da Fonceca Vaz.*
407. Dried cherries—*E. J. da Silva Alves.*
408. Dried plums. 409. Raisins.
410. Drie peaches—*R. P. Mendes.*
411. Dried peaches—*A. P. de Fonceca Vaz.*
412. Preserved plums. 413. Preserved figs. 414. Preserved peaches. 415. Sweet dried pears. 416. Preserved apricots. 416. Bis-dried apricots—*From Villa Real.*
417. Different qualities of preserved fruits—*From the Nuns of Coimbra.* 418 to 420. Dried figs—*F. L. Gomes.*
421. Preserved peaches. 422. Preserved figs—*F. Castetto.*
423 and 424. Quince marmalade.

425. Sweet plums. 426. Preserved dried pears—*F. Castello.* 427. Preserved peaches.
428. Sweet plums. 429. Preserved apricots. 430. Preserved Tangerina oranges. 431. Preserved figs. 432. Preserved cherries. 433. Preserved peaches—*F. Castello.*
434. Sugar almonds. 435. Sugar crisp almonds.
436. Preserved citron—*From the Nuns of Sta. Clara, Pantarem.* ¹437. Preserved Seville oranges—*J. C. da Silveira.*
438. Preserved pears—*F. Castello.* 439. Chocolate crisp almonds. 440. Olives—*Marquis de Ficalho.*
441. Black olives—*Viscount de Fonte Boa.*
442. Black olives (Sevillanas)—*S. de Albuquerque.*
443. Black olives—*J. Martins.* 444. Olives, *from Elvas.*
445. Capsicums. 445a. Bis-guinea pepper.
446. Coffee, *from Madeira.* 447. Coffee, *from Angola.*
448. Coffee, *from Mozambique.* 449. Coffee, *from Timor Island.* 450. Coffee, *from Cape Verde Islands.*
451. Coffee, *from St. Thomas's Islands.* 452. Capers.
453. Starch, *from Evora.* 454. Starch—*M. M. Holbeche.*
455 to 457. Lump sugar in loaf—*F. Pinto Bastos and Co.*
458. Gum copal. 459. Pitch.
460 and 461. Olive oil—*J. L. de Catheiros e Menezes.*
462 to 464. Olive oil—*Almeida Praenca.*
465 and 466. Olive oil— *De Maudo.* 467 and 468. Olive oil—*Joao Larcher.* 469 and 470. Olive oil—*Count de Farrobo.*
471 and 472. Olive oil—*J. B. Pinto.*
473 to 477. Olive oil—*Almeida, Silva, and Co.*
478 and 479. Olive oil—*J. d'Albuquerque e Mello.*
480. Olive oil—*Almeida, Silva, and Co.*
481 and 482. Olive oil—*Marquis de Ficalho.*
483 and 484. Olive oil—*Count de Linhares.*
485 and 486. Olive oil. 487. Bitter almonds oil.
488 and 489. Sweet almonds oil. 490. Nut oil.
491 and 492. Castor oil. 493 and 494. Oil, *from Purgueira tree.* 495. Linseed oil. 495.a Bis-Arachide oil, *from Angola*—*F. R. Batalha.* 496. Linseed oil.
496.a Bis-palm oil, *from Angola*—*F. R. Batalha.*
497. Volatile oil of lavender. 498. Volatile oil of Romarine. 499. Volatile oil of Genevrier. 500. Volatile of lemon. 501. Citric acid. 502. Tartaric acid—*F. M. C. Seal.*
503. Oxalic acid—*Hirsch and Brother.*
504. Tartaric acid—*Serzedello and Co.*
505. Wood orchilla, *from Angola.* 506. Rock orchilla, *from Angola.* 506. Bis-wood orchilla, *from St. Thomas's Island.* Wood orchilla, *from Mozambique.* 507. Bis-rocks orchilla, *from Viannado Minho.* 508. Rocks orchilla, *from Cape Verde Islands.* 508.a Bis-rocks orchilla, *from Madeira.*
509. Wood orchilla, from Cape Rock—*F. R. Batalha.*
509.a Bis rock orchilla, from the Berlingues islands—*F. R. Batalha.* 510. Sumack—*M. B Ferreira, jun.* 511. Sumack.
512. Pounded sumack. 513. Sumack. 514. Ouse of cork-tree. 515. Absolute alkohol—*F. M. C. Seal.*
516. Sarsaparilla. 517. Capsules of copaiba—*P. F. Norberto.*
518. Mustard seeds—*Viscount de Fonte Boa.*
519. Macaroni. 520 to 527. Different sorts of Italian paste.
528. Vermicelli. 529. Biscuits of various qualities, for shipping—*A. Wheelhouse.*
530. Hemp of two months' growth, of 20 spars in height—*From the Duke de Palmella's estate at Calharig.*
531 and 532. Hemp, beaten—*Duke de Palmella.*
533. Raw flax. 534. Flax. 535. Thread of aloes—*Agave Americana—Marquis de Ficalho.* 536 and 537—Rush.
538. Raw cotton, grown near Lisbon—*A. Sa Nogueira.*
539 and 540. Raw cotton. 541. Manioca. 542. Manioca powder. 543. Tapioca, from Angola—*F. R. Batalha.*
544. Thistles—*M. M. Holbeche.* 545 to 551. Toothpicks of several qualities. 552. A box made of several species of woods—*Marquis de Ficalho.*
553 to 578. Woods of various trees, viz.: Pine-tree, plumtree, filbert-tree, wild olive, chesnut, wild pine, elm, mulberry, olive, pine, beech, ash, cherry, cypress, cork-tree,

holm, poplar, oak, cherry, platain, white acacia, olive, walnut, orange, box, and cratagus azarolus—*Marquis de Loulé*. 579. Carob-wood—*Marquis de Loulé*.

580. Arbutus unido—(*Medronheiro*) *A. P. F. Vaz*.

581 and 582. Wood—wild olive. Pine, from *Leiria* forests. 583. Pine, from *Leiria* forests. 584. Pine-wood, from *Caparica*. 585. Oak, from *Alcobaça*. 586. Wood from cork-tree, from *Alemtejo*. 587. Ash, from *Alemtejo*.

588. Wild mahogany. 589. Wood of Couta-tree, from the *Bissago's Islands*. 590. Tacula-wood, from *Angola*.

591. Teak-wood. 592. Sico-wood, from *Goa*.

Animal Kingdom.

593 and 594. Honey.—*T. P. de Maltos*.

595. Honey, from *Castello Branco*.

596. Honey—*Marquis de Ficalho*.

597. Honey, from *Bragança*. 598. Honey, from *Evora*.

599. Capsules of cod-liver—*P. T. Norberto*.

600. White merino wool, washed—*V. G. Cornêa*.

601. Black wool—*Marquis de Ficalho*.

602 and 603. Dark wool. White wool—*Marquis de Ficalho*. 604 to 610. Raw silk—*Duke de Palmella*.

611 to 615. Raw silk—*T. C. Gareez*.

616. Raw silk, from *Bragança*.

617. White wax—*M. L. de Carvalho*.

618 and 619. White wax. Bees-wax—*Marquis de Ficalho*. 620. White wax—*M. F. Bretes*.

621. White wax—*Marquis de Ficalho*.

622. Bees-wax—*M. T. Bretes*.

623 and 624. Bees-wax. Bees wax—*M. L. de Carvalho*.

625. Gelatine in lamina—*P. F. Norberto*.

626. Gelatine in filaments—*P. F. Norberto*.

627. Glue—*J. L. F. da Foncua*.

628. Glue—*J. L. Pairoto*. 629. Animal charcoal.

630. Animal charcoal, in powder—*J. F. Pinto Basto*.

Manufactures.

631. Decimal scales—*J. F. Pinto Basto*.

632. Agricultural instruments. 633. Surgeons' instrument-box—*A. Polycarpo*.

634. A set of scissors—*M. J. da Silva Cerqueira*.

635. Blunderbuss. 636. An old musket with gold and steel ornaments. 637. Musket of a curious construction. 638. Improved percussion musket. 639. A musket with covered locks. 640. Musket for percussion caps or flints—*Royal Military Arsenal*.

641 and 642. Leather covers for cannon locks. 643 and 644. Improved common locks for carronades. 645. Improved screw for the touch-hole of cannons—*D. J. Bobone*. 646. Regimental axe—*D. J. d'Azerado Bobone*.

647. Carding—*A. J. Loureiro*.

648. Mould for casting three letters. 649. Mould for improving type. 650. Moulding for measuring type. 651. Ditto for making type—*A. J. das Neves*.

652. A key—*From Santarem*.

653. Spun flax. 654. Linen weft and twist.

655. Strong canvas. 656. Strong canvas. 657. Striped brown ravens-ducks—*Manufactory of Janqueria*.

658. Canvas. 659. Common canvas. 660. Common canvas. 661. Fancy linen drills. 662. Fancy linen drills. 663. Fancy linen drill. 664. Fancy linen drills. 665. Fancy brown ducks. 666. Brown dowlas. 667. Linen bed tick. 668. Linen bed tick. 669. Brown linen—*Torres Novas Co.*

670. Fine hall canvas. 671. Brown raven-ducks.

672. Superfine linen sheeting. 673. Fine linen sheeting.

674. Fine linen sheeting.

675. Linen cloth—*From Vianna di Minho.*

676. Coarse linen sheeting. 677. Brownlinen.

678. Superfine linen sheeting. 679. Fine linen sheeting.

680. Brown linen drills—*J. Barboza*. 681. Brown drills.

682. Cotton and linen drills. 683. Cotton and linen drills—*J. Barboza*.

684 to 700. Fancy cotton drills—*Lisbon Weaving Co.*

701 to 704. Grey calico. 705. Bed and sofa tick. 706. Bed tick—*Scotch Linen Trade.*

707 to 712. Cotton shawls—*Lisbon Co.*

713 and 714. Cotton shawls—*J. S. Preira*.

715. Cotton blanket.

716 and 717. White tambour skeins—*A. G. Loureive*.

718 and 719. White tambour skeins. 720. Thread balls —*A. G. Loureive*.

721 and 722. Weft. 723. Twist—*Rio Vizello Co.*

724. Weft—*Rio Vezello Co.*

725. Blue and white skeins. 726. Blue tambour skeins—*Lisbon Weaving Co.*

727. Cotton stockings—*A. G. Loureive*.

728 to 747. Print for garments—*Miranda, Batatho, and Co.*

748 to 755. Printed cotton handkerchiefs—*Motter, Weyhe, and Co.*

756 to 760. Printed cotton handkerchiefs—*F. J. da Luz.*

761 to 769. Printed cotton shawls—*F. J. da Luz.*

770 to 774. Printed cottons—*Pinto and Co.*

775 and 776. Printed cottons—*F. J. da Luz.*

777 to 786. Printed cottons—*Pinto and Co.*

787. Fine cloth olive green. 788. Black woollen cloth. 789. Grey mixture fine cloth. 790. Brown woollen cloth. 791. Coarse brown woollen cloth. 792. Blue woollen cloth. 793. Coarse woollen cloth. 794. Fine black cashmere cloth. 795 to 797. Striped cashmere cloth—*Larchers and Brother.*

798. Dark woollen cloth. 799. Common dark blue cloth. 800. Blue cloth. 801. Green woollen cloth. 802. Common brown woollen cloth. 803. Brown mixture—*Correa and Brothers.*

804. Woollen cloth. 805. Striped cashmere cloth—*Mello and Brothers.* 806. Striped woolsey. 807. Linsey woolsey. 808. Strong woollen cloaking—*From Vianna do Minho.*

809. Blankets—*J. F. Loraine*.

810 to 813. Fine Blankets. 814 to 826. Woollen plaid shawls. 827 to 831. Woollen plaid shawls. 832 to 839, Printed woollen shawls. 840. Cotton and woollen tartan. 841 and 842. Ponchos. 843 to 850. Woollen caps. 851 and 852. Ponchos—*Lafourie and Co.*

853 to 855. Wool and cotton waistcoats. 856 to 859. Wool, cotton, and silk waistcoats. 860 to 865. Fancy wool and cotton checks. 866 to 871. Tartan and woollen shawls. 872 to 875. Figured woollen shawls. 876 to 881. Printed woollen shawls—*B. Daufrias and Co.*

882. Wide belts. 883. Narrow belts. 884. Cotton sash belts. 885 and 887. Woollen jackets for children. 887 to 889. Woollen comforters. 890 and 891. Silk and wool shawls. 892 and 893. Silk and wool table-covers. 894 and 895. Drugget carpet. 896. Kidderminster carpet. 897 and 898. Brussels carpets. 899 and 900. Hearth rugs. 901 to 904. Rugs—*Daufrias and Co.*

905 to 908. Silk tissue gold and silver. 909 to 917. Gold and silver stuffs—*J. M. S. Porto*.

918. Black satin velvet—*J. J. Moureira*.

919. Black satin velvet—*R. J. Martins*.

920 to 923. Check plaids in velvets for waistcoats. 924. Striped velvet—*T. M. Pimentel*.

925. Black velvet for waistcoats—*T. M. Pimentel*.

926. Black satin—*D. F. Carmiers*.

927. Black satin—*T. M. Pimentel*.

928. Light blue satin dress. 929. Fancy satin. 930. Fancy green satin. 931. Fancy satin for waistcoats. 932. Fancy embroidered satin—*M. J. Jorge*.

935. Gros de Naples with satin stripes. 936. Black watered Gros de Naples—*T. M. Pimetel*.

937 and 938. Gros de Naples striped and shot—*B. F. Carneiro*. 939. Gros de laine—*R. J. Martins*.

940 to 942. Fancy shot silk—*R. J. Martins*.

943 and 944. Fancy shot silk. 945. Fancy shot silk with satin lines—*B. F. Carneiro*.

946. Dark gros de Naples with satin lines. 947. Striped gros de Naples—*B. F. Corneiro.*

948. Strong black silk. 949 and 950. Fancy silks—*Joze Barboza.*

951 and 952. Blue corded silk for waistcoats—*T. M. Pimentel.* 953. Self-coloured silk for waistcoats—*M. J. Torge.*

954. Patterns of different silks—*T. A. Ramieres.*

955. Black and blue silk shawls—*J. J. da Silva.*

956. Black silk figured shawls—*M. C. Moreira.*

957. Fancy satin handkerchiefs—*R. J. Martin.*

958. Black silk cravats—*B. F. Carneiro.*

959. Satin neckerchiefs—*T. Barboza.*

960 to 962. Gentlemen's figured handkerchiefs—*B. F. Carneiro.* 963. Shot silk corded cravats—*M. J. Jorge.*

964. White watered silk—*T. M. Pimentel.*

965. Figured damask—*M. J. Jorge.*

966 and 967. Yellow and red damasks—*J. J. da Silva.*

968. Gentlemen's black and white silk stockings. 969. Fancy silk caps. 970 Silk hose or jacket. 971 Silk ribbons for orders. 972 Damask carriage hangings—*M. G. Jorge.*

973. Silk cocked hat. 974. Beaver cocked hat. 975. Silk hat. 976. Silk hat. 977. Black beaver hat—*Sottere Antonio Borges.*

978. White beaver hat. 979. Black beaver hat. 980. Boys' white felt caps. 981. Black silk hat. 982. French black silk hat. 983. Black silk hat. 984. Portuguese black silk hat—*F. C. Rocho.*

985. White silk hat. 986. Beaver hat. 987. *J. N. Kirsh.*

987.*a* Note paper. 988. Letter paper. 989. Red and white blotting-paper— *Count de Tojal.*

990. Samples of ropes—*J. F. Rodrigues.*

991 to 1014. Samples of shot—*M. da Silva.*

1015. Cast-iron garden bench. 1016. Black cast-iron vase. 1017 and 1018. Cast-iron vases. 1019 and 1020. Specimen of cast-iron ornaments—*T. Bacheley.*

1021. A diamond enamelled brooch—*Pinto e Sousa.*

1022. A set of amethysts in gold filigree work—*B. G. Mamede.*

1022*a* to 1022*c.* A silver snuff-box, a small gold chain, and one gold filigree—*A. de Franca.*

1023 to 1043. Different patterns of cut-glass decanters, tumblers, and wine-glasses—*M. J. Affonso.*

1044 to 1046. Sketched window-glass. 1047 to 1108. Porcelain of different patterns, comprising tureens, dishes, plates, tea and coffee services, night-lamps, washhand-jugs and basins, &c., made at Vista Alegre manufactory, near Aviero. 1109. Stoneware bottle. 1110. Earthenware olive-jar. 1111. Black earthenware kitchen-pots—*Pinto, Basto, & Co.* 1112 to 1115. Straw mats—*G. B. Ferreira.*

1116. Chest of drawers and slab. 1117. Mahogany wardrobe. 1118. Mahogany bedstead—*R. Fulcher.*

1119. Mahogany invalid chair—*Royal Military Arsenal.*

1120. Wine-cask—*A. P. Rangel.* 1121. Saddle—*J. J. Figueirado.* 1122. Sole-leather—*D. da Cunha Fialho.*

1122*a.* Sole-leather— *T. M. Breets.* 1123. Steer-skin—*D. C. Fialho.* 1123*a.* Calf-skin—*M. B. Monteiro, jun.*

1123*b.* Calf-skin—*F. T. Barroto.* 1123*c.* Calf-skin—*C. J. F. da Silva.* 1123*d.* Calf-skin—*J. Bollo.*

1124, 1124*a*, 1124*b.* Morocco leather of various colours.

1125. Steer-skin—*D. C. Fialho.*

1125*a.* Sheep-skin—*F. M. Bratts.*

1125*b.* Yellow sheep-skin. 1125*c.* White sheep-skin.

1126. Leather fire-bucket—*Royal Military Arsenal.*

1126*a.* Goat-skin—*J. G. Bollo.*

1126*b.* Wine pig-skin. 1126*c.* Leather peasant's wine-bottle—*C. A. Fragata.*

1127 to 1143. Ladies' parasols. 1144 to 1150. Umbrellas.

1151. Various qualities of sealing-wax—*M. R. Lassa.*

1152. Artificial passion-flower tree. 1153. Artificial camelia tree— *Vicente Ruball.*

1154. Various kinds of kid gloves—*F. Baron.*

1155 to 1157. Bell-ropes and tassels. 1158 to 1164. Various kinds of soap—*Royal Soap Contractors.*

1165. Fancy threadwork. 1166. Fancy threadwork—*From Guimarens.* 1167. Fine thread—*From Guimarens.*

1168. A tree made of thread—*M. J. da Costa Romão.*

1169 and 1170. Lace stockings—*M. Parreira.*

1171. Silk for sieves.

1172 to 1183. Various kinds of snuffs,—Princeza, Principe, and common. 1184 to 1195. Impalpable snuff. 1196 to 1209. Cigars, various kinds. 1210. Cut tobacco leaves. 1211. Cigarettes—*Royal Tobacco and Snuff Company.*

1212. Wax-candles. 1213. Painted candles. 1214 to 1221. Wax-baskets—*M. L. Carvalho.*

1222. A gilt spindle. 1223. Marble basket—*C. Bonnet.*

1224. Gilt round table and slab—*T. Caetano.*

1225. Arms of Portugal carved in wood—*Naval Arsenal.*

1226 and 1227. Capitals for columns, carved in wood—*Naval Arsenal.*

1228. Carving in wood. Prince Henry ordering Gonzalves Zargo and Tristan Vaz to discover new countries—*T. Caetano.* 1229 to 1231. Carvings in mahogany—*T. Caetano.*

1232. Wood-carving of St. Francis and Jesus Christ crucified—*H. T. Vieira.*

1233. Oil-skin table-cover—*Count Thomar.*

1234. Ivory carving. Prometheus—*M. T. Vieira.*

1235. Jesus Christ crucified. Ivory carving—*M. J. Vieira.* 1236. Ivory chain—*M. Mularinho.*

1237. Writing-desk, ebony-wood and ivory inlaid—*The King of Portugal.* 1238 to 1251. Lithographic sketches of Portuguese scenery. 1252. Panorama of history—*T. P. Monteiro.* 1253. Pen-drawing—*M. N. Godinho.*

1254. Drawing on a lithographic stone— *T. J. Lopes.*

1255 to 1264. White lace. 1265 to 1276. White lace—*F. A. Madeira.* 1277 to 1282. Broad white laces.

1283 to 1293. Broad white and black lace.

1294. An improved rudder—*Bicalho's Factory, Oporto.*

1295. A box of ten samples of lead ore—*From Bracal Mine.*

1296. Portrait of Queen Donna Maria II. (pen-and-ink drawing)—*A. S. P da Silva.*

1297. Genealogical tree of the Royal Family of Portugal (pen-and-ink drawing)—*A. S. P. da Silva.*

1298. An artificial orange-tree— *Vicente Russel.*

1299. A case of artificial flowers—*C. J. Marques.*

MADEIRA.

1 READ, J. (H.M. Consul), Terceira.- A variety of minerals and vegetable productions, peculiar to Madeira and the Western Islands. Cocoons, and samples of raw silk. Wool. Cochineal. Honey, &c. Specimens of manufactured articles, including linen cloth and lace, net shawls, and crochet articles. Artificial flowers, hair work, and straw plait. Tables, work-boxes, paper-knives, picture frames, &c.

2 FERRAZ, H. & SISTERS, Manu.—Wax copies of the blossoms of fruit produced on the islands.

ROME.

(Signor CARLO TREBBI, Commissioner for Roman Government. J. & R. M'CRACKEN, 7 Old Jewry, Agents in London.)

1 BIANCOUCINI, Count BIAGIO.—Samples of earth: Silicious quartz, with which, by means of a chemical process, vitrification is obtained for making bottles.

2 PASQUALI, DOMENICO RINALDI.—Samples of asphalte, natural and manufactured.

3 SNEIDER, PELLEGRINI.—Four blocks of natural alum.

4 BIANCOUCINI, Count.—Samples of the product of tow of the Bolognese hemp. Samples of several woods.

5 MORTI, Signor.—Sample of silk. Pine cones.

6 BERRETTA, DANIELE, Manu.—Samples of various silks, worked in the factory of the exhibitor.

7 THE FILANDA-BRACCI AL FANO.—Samples of silk.

8 RANUZZI, Count ANGELO.—Veils, partly craped, and partly striped with various colours.

9 THE CHAMBER OF COMMERCE OF THE CITY OF CENTO. —Sample of Centese hemp, from the province of Ferrara.

10 MINGHETTI, MARCO.—Samples of hemp, and of articles manufactured from it.

11 BIANCHINI, LUIGI, Inv.—A new spring bitt.

12 MILIANI, PIETRO.—Paper made of flax and hemp.

13 MARCHESI & OSSOLI.—Samples of bricks and tiles, in imitation of mosaic marble, manufactured of argillaceous earth from the vicinity of Rome.

14 LIVIZZANA, AVO ERCOLE.—Sample of a work in paper, cut by the exhibitor with scissors only.

15 BARBERI, The Cavaliere, Artist.—Mosaic table, invented and executed by the exhibitor.

16 LEYLAND, Capt.—Sculpture, consisting of three groups in marble, of figures the size of life.

17 BOSCHETTI, BENEDETTO, Artist.—Two mosaic tables.

18 MACDONALD, L. Sculp.—Ionic statue, in marble.

19 MODA, TOMMASO DELLA, Sculp.—Large tazza, of Egyptian alabaster, worked by the exhibitor.

20 MOGLIA, Cavaliere LUIGI.—Mosaics: Temples of Pestum; a circular table, &c.

21 MOGLIA, DOMENICO.—Mosaics: The Roman Forum the Colosseum; Temples of Pestum.

22 ROCCHIGIANI, ANTONIO, Artist.—Mosaic, representing the Temples of Pestum.

23 THE ROYAL MANUFACTORY AT ST. PETER'S.—Mosaic, copied from the celebrated "S. Gio. Battesta," by Guercino; and a medallion, the portrait of Pope Boniface II., copied from the picture by Sig. Roberto Bompiani; by Raffaele Castellini.

24 SAVALINI, THOMAS.—Cameos in Pietra Dura (onyx). Cameos executed in shell. Mount Roveto, from the fresco of Raphael, in the Vatican. Bellerophon receiving Pegasus from Minerva, from a bas-relief by Gibson, &c.

25 Small subject, in mosaic.

26 RAINERI, BISCIA, Count. London agents. Fordati & Coxhead, 13 Old Jewry Chambers.—Specimens of rough and refined sulphur.

27 PELLEGRINI, S. Rome, Exhibitor.—Pieces of natural alum from the mountains of Civita Vecchia.

28 GOTT, M.—Ceres, a statue.

29 RINALDI, R.—Rinaldo and Armida.

31 TRENTANOVE, A.—Dove; candelabra, in plaster.

32A MANLEY, GENERAL, Prop.—The celebrated cameo, on pietra dura (a fine onyx), of Jupiter vanquishing the Titans, engraved by Passamonti.

32B The Group of the Laocoon, executed at Rome. Exhibited by H. CASSIN, Esq.

33 View in mosaic, of the Pantheon, by Cavaliere Luiga Moglia.

34, 35 Two tables of the same material, by Dies.

36 Several small subjects, in mosaic.

37 Three portions of the Roman Forum, executed in yellow marble from the quarries of Sienna.

38 A table representing St. Peter's, the Campanile, &c.

39 A (mosaic), with two pigeons, and flowers.

40 Frame, representing two figures after Carlo Dolci (mosaic).

41 Frame—subject, a Wild Boar Hunt.

42 Frame—View of the Great Piazza of St. Peter's.

43 Frame—View of the Colliseum.

44 Frame—View of the Pantheon.

45 Frame—View of the Temple of the Sybil.

47 Frame—the Bridge of Lugano.

48 JONES, W. Esq. of Clytha, Rutland Gate.—A Bagnarola, of Oriental lapis-lazuli, by Signor Sybilio, of Rome.

49 Various shell cameos, carved by Guiseppe Deas.

50 DIES, F.—Four large folio volumes, in white vellum: —Canëna's Roman Edifices (*Edifizi de Roma*), 2 vol.; Canëna's Christian Epochs (*Tempi Cristiane*); Maritime Antiquities of Etruria (*Antichita d'Etruria Maritime*).

51 NORCHI, E. 13 King William St. Strand.—English vase, copied from the antique, in green Prato marble.

52 TRENTA NOVE. -Vase of white marble, in form of an Etruscan vase, executed in African stone.

RUSSIA.

(Commissioner in London, M. GABRIEL DE KAMENSKY, 34 Norland Square, Notting-hill.)

1 IMPERIAL BOGOSLOVSKY COPPER WORKS, Government of Perm.—Native copper, and copper ores. Vitreous ore, with copper pyrites, impregnated with quartz. Reniform malachite.

2 IMPERIAL ALEXANDROVSKY CANNON FOUNDRY, Government of Olonetz.—Iron ores. Limestone. Cast iron for heavy guns.

3 IMPERIAL ARTINSK WORKS, Zlataoust.—Cast steel.

4 IMPERIAL BARNAOULSK WORKS, Altaisk, Siberia.— Silver ores. Fine silver, &c. Limestone. Lake salt. Firebrick.

5 IMPERIAL CAST IRON WORKS OF KOUSHVINSK, Government of Perm.—Pig iron.

6 IMPERIAL COPPER WORKS OF PERM, Government of Perm.—Geological specimens of the rocks of the Permian system of Sir Roderick Murchison, &c.

7 IMPERIAL COROBLAGODATSK IRON WORKS, Government of Perm.—Magnetic iron ores and limestone.

8 IMPERIAL KAMENSK IRON WORKS, Government of Perm, district of Ekaterinburg.—Melnikovsk and other ores.

9 IMPERIAL KOUSSINSK IRON WORKS, Government of Perm, district of Zlataoust.—Fire-stone, brown iron-stones. Fibrous and wrought iron.

10 IMPERIAL IRON WORKS OF NIJNE-TOURINSK.—Bar and sheet iron.

11 IMPERIAL IRON WORKS OF VERKHNE-BARANTCHINSK. —Rolled iron of different forms and dimensions.

12 IMPERIAL IRON WORKS OF VERKHNE-TOURINSK.— Pig iron.

13 IMPERIAL IRON WORKS OF VOTKINSK, Government of Viatka.—Puddling and other iron.

14 IMPERIAL MANUFACTORY OF FIRE-ARMS OF ZLATAOUST, Government of Orenburg.—Cast steel.

15 IMPERIAL MINING WORKS OF POLAND.—Various geological specimens. Rails for railways, &c.

16 IMPERIAL NIJNE-ISSETSK WORKS, Government of Perm.—Scrap sheet; and boiler plate-iron.

17 IMPERIAL SATKINSK IRON WORKS, Zlataoust.— Wrought and soft cast-iron, and geological specimens, &c.

18 IMPERIAL WORKS, Government of Tomsk, district of Altaisk.—Samples of cast and Damasc steel.

19 IMPERIAL ALEXANDROVSK MANUFACTORY, near St. Petersburg.—Flax and tow.

20 IRON WORKS OF KHAMOUNITSKY VIATKA, Government of Viatka, district of Slobodsk.—Sheet, oxidized, and boiler plate-iron.

21; 120 DEMIDOFF, Nijne-Taghilsk, Siberia, Props.— Specimens of rocks, found in auriferous and in platina sands. Native gold. Pine-tree wood. Charcoal. (Agents, Henry Hall & Co. 34 Fenchurch Street.)

22 MINERALS found in NEW RUSSIA and BESSARABIA, and in the TRANS-CAUCASIAN PROVINCES.—Gneiss. Syenite. Syenite-Gneiss. Fine-grained syenite. Diorite. Feld-spar, &c.

23 PASHKOFF, A. Government of Orenbourg, district of Sterlitamatsk, Prop.—Copper in ingots.

24 PASHKOFF M. Government of Orenburg, district

of Sterlitamatsk, Prop.—Copper in ingots, in cakes, and in sheets.

25 JAKOLEFF, Madame C. Government of Riazan, estate of Grishino, Prop.—Samples of steel.

26 HIRSHMAN & KIJEVSKI, Warsaw, Manu.—Chemical productions.

27 SCHLIPPE, C. Government of Moscow, district of Vereisk, estate of Plesninsk, Manufacture.—Prussiate of potash. Alum. Muriate of tin. Oxalic acid; tartaric acid. Vinegar. Leiocome.

28 SANIN, —, Government of Kaluga, Manu.—Sugar of lead &c.

29 BRUSGHIN, A. Koselsk, Manu.—Prussiate of potash.

30 VERDAN & Co. Moscow, Manu.—Leiocome. Dextrine. Albumen. Starch.

31 KARNOVITCH, —, Government of Jaroslaff, Prop.—Flax, prepared after the Flemish method. Rape-seed.

32 KOUCHELEFF, Count, near St. Petersburg, estate of Ligovo, Prop.—Wheat and other agricultural produce.

33 LOSHKAREFF, (Peasant), Government of Simbirsk, Prod.—Wheat.

34 HIRSHMAN, —. Government of Lublinsk, district of Sedletsk, estate of Sokolovo, Prop.—New Zealand flax. Large-eared wheat. Rye.

35 KLEPATSKY, —. Government of Kharkoff, district of Koupiansk, Prop.—Spring wheat (called " arnaoutka").

36 DOKHTOUROFF, —. Government of Toula, district of Kashirsk, Prop.—Prepared manna. Buck-wheat. Pearl barley. Groats.

37 COSSACKS of the AZOFF SEA, Prod.—Blue and black-eared spring wheat.

38 MOROZOFF, —. (Peasant), Government of Kostroma, estate of Korobeinikoff, Prod.—Wheat (called " belotourka").

39 BAGUER, —. near the town of Kertch, Prop.—Hard wheat (called "arnaout").

40 MATVEIEFF (Peasant), Government of Orel, district of Eletz, Prod.—Prepared buck-wheat.

41 SCHOOL OF HORTICULTURE, Bessarabia.—Indian corn.

42 SHABELSKY, —. Government of Ekaterinoslaff, district of Rostoff. Prop.—Hard wheat (called "arnaout").

43 TRESKOFF, —. Government of Warsaw, district of Gostindsk, estate of Khodove, Prop.—Wheat (called " sandomirsk").

44 VIELHORSKY, Count MATTHEW, Government of Penza, estate of Znamensk, Prop.—Corn, Vielhorka.

45 N. N. Government of Kharkoff, district of Zmievsk.—Swedish and Himalayan barley.

46 BISTROM, Baron, Government of Courland, district of Mitaw, estate of Patzen, Prop.—Pearl barley.

47 ROPP, Baron, Government of Courland, estate of Bixten, Prop.—Pearl barley.

48 REKKE, A. Government of Courland, Prop.—Pearl barley.

49 RATSHINSKY, —. Government and district of Smolensk, Prop.—Groats.

50 VLADIMIRSKY (Peasant), Government of Novgorod, Prod.—Groats of unripe rye.

51 ZILFOOGAR-BECK, & ISKANDER-BECK-OGLI, Government and district of Shemakha, village of Matchakhi, Prod.—Chaltick. Groats.

52 SELIVANOFF, —. Government and district of Penza, estate of Koutchouk-Portch, Prop.—Oats.

53 VOLKONSKY, Prince, M. Government of Jaroslaff, district of Mologsk, Prop.—Oats.

54 OUNKOVSKY, —. Government of Novgorod, district of Tikhvinsk, estate of Paneff, Prop.—Oats.

55 SAFONOFF, A. E. Government of St. Petersburg, district of Shlisselburg, estate of Kiritsk, Prop.—Spring rye.

56 BOBRINSKY, Count A. Government of Toula, district of Bogorodsk, estate of Mikhailovsk, Prop.—Winter rye.

57 KHALIL-BECK-SAPHIEFF, Government of Erivan, district of Sharoor, village of Bashoorashen, Prod.—Rice and groats.

58 AGRICULTURAL SOCIETY of the CAUCASUS, district of Erivan.—Rice.

59 POUSANOFF, —. Government of Koursk, district of Stebigrovsk, estate of Nikitsk, Prop.—Millet, & black millet.

60 ERSHOFF, —. Government of Saratoff, district of Kamishinsk, Prop.—Wheat (called "koubanka"), and millet.

61 GOORIEL, Prince LEVAN, Government of Cootais, district of Ozerguet, Prop.—Caucasian millet (called "gomia").

62 MIAGKKOFF,—. (Peasant), Government of Jaroslaff, district of Rostoff, estate of Ugodino, Prod.—Green peas.

63 KHOKHOLKOFF & GREGORIEFF (Peasants), Government of Jaroslaff, Prod.—Green peas.

64 GOLOVANOFF (Peasant),Government of Olonetz, district of Poudojsk, estate of Sartchevsk, Prod.—Wheat flour.

65 MANIN, —. Government of Olonetz, district of Vitegorsk, Merchant.—Polish manna. Fine wheat flour.

66 ROUSSANOFF, Government of Orel, district of Eletz, Merchant.—Wheat flour.

67 SAPOJNIKOFF BROTHERS, Government of Saratoff, Merchants.—Wheat flour.

68 NIKITIN, —. Town of Smolensk, Confectioner.—Dried fruit.

69 SOROKIN, CATHERINE, Government of Jaroslaff, near the town of Rostoff, Prop.—Chicory.

70 VOLKONSKY, PRINCE V. Government of Tamboff, district of Shatzk, Prop.—Starch-gum.

71 ROTERMAN, C. Reval, Manu.—Wheat-starch.

72 YURGHENSON, Government and district of Novgorod, estate of Marieno, Prop.—Potato-starch.

73 MIKIRTITCHEFF, CARAPET, Government of Erivan, district of Soormaline, village of Amaret, Prod.—Castor-oil, lucerne, and sesamum seeds.

74 HEIRS OF TRESCOFF, Government of Warsaw, district of Gostindsk, estate of Streltze, Prop.—Turnip-seed.

75 EYDAROFF, M. Government of Tiflis, district of Bertchalin, Prod.—Turkish tobacco.

76 SPIGLAZOFF, A. St. Petersburg, Manu.—Tobacco,&c.

77 DOODINSKY, Government of Shemakha, district of Lencoran, Prop.—Tobacco.

78 SANGOUSHKO, PRINCESS MARY, Borough of Shepetovka, Government of Volhynia, district of Sasslaff, Prop.—Beet-root sugar.

79 HIRSHMANN, HIRSHENDORFF, & RAVITCH, Government of Lublinsk, district of Sedletsk, estate of Sokolovo, Sugar Refiners.—Refined and raw sugar.

80 EJOFF, J. Peasant, Government and district of Vologda, estate of Navoisk.—Portable soup.

81 MARIMANOFF & ARMAKOONA, Farmers of the Salyan Fishery, Government of Shemakha.—Isinglass fish, called *viaziga*.

82 FELKERSAM, Baron, Government of Courland, district of Grobinsk, estate of Papenhoff, Prop.—Madia. Sunflower seeds.

83 LISINSK FOREST INSTITUTION, Government of St. Petersburg, district of Ozarskoe Sielo.—Turpentine & resin.

84 RUDERT, H. Warsaw, Musical Instrument Maker.—Purified resin.

85 N. N. Government of Smolensk, district of Dorogobooj.—Wax.

86 BABAIEFF, A. Government and district of Derbent, Prod.—Madder-roots.

87 KERIM-RAGHIM-OGLI, Government of Derbent, district of Cubi. Prod.—Madder-roots.

88 N. N. Government of Shemakha, district of Shoosha.—Bark of the wild pomegranate tree.

89 N. N. Government of Stavropol, on the Banks of the Terek, and on the Plain of Coomack.—Dyewood (*Statice coriaria*).

90 KVAVILOFF, P. Government of Tiflis, di rict of Telaff, Prod.—Safflower.

91 AYVAZOFF, S. Government of Shemakha, district of Baki, Prod.—Saffron.

92 GOVERNMENT OF DERBENT, district of Cubi.—Yellow berries for dyeing.

93 GOVERNMENT OF SHEMAKHA, district of Nookha.—Sumach.

94 ABDOURZA-MARAM OGLI, Government of Erivan, district of Sharoor, Prod.—Native cotton.

95 DJIDJIVADZE, PRINCE NIKO, Imeretia, Prop.—Bourbon cotton.

96 BABARIKIN, M. Government of Pskoff, town of Kholm, Merchant.—Flax.

97 ARDAMATSKY, J. & T. Soletz, Government of Pskoff, Merchants.—Flax.

98 ARDAMATSKY, J. Government of Pskoff, town of Porkhoff, Merchant.—Flax-tow.

99 ARDAMATSKY BROTHERS, Government and district of Novgorod.—Flax and oakum.

100 KRASHENENEKOFF, Government of Orel, district of Sevsk, Prod.—Hemp.

101 KARNOVITCH, Government of Jaroslaff, Prod.—Flax, prepared after the Flemish method.

102 KAZALETT, A. St. Petersburg, Manu.—Oakum.

103 FILEMONOFF, K. Government of Jaroslaff, town of Rilsk, Merchant.—Hemp.

104 BUKHAREFF, Government of Pskoff, district of Porkhoff, estate of Idanovich, Prop.—Tow.

105 N. N. Government of Jaroslaff, estate of Velikoe.—Spread flax.

106 N. N. Government of Esthonia, district of Vinsk, estate of Valk.—Flax, sorted.

107 N. N. Government and district of Pskoff.—Flax, of two qualities.

108 ZAKHAROFF, S. Government of Pskoff, town of Kholm, Merchant.—Flax.

109 VOLKHONSKY, PRINCE, Government of Orel, district of Sevsk, Prop.—Hemp.

110 MILOKROSHETCHNOI, K. Pudoj, Merchant.—Korelsk flax.

111 MELNIKOFF, Government of Vladimir, district of Melenkoff, Merchant.—Flax.

112 VANIUKOFF, J. Soletz, Government of Pskoff, Merchant.—Flax.

113 VANIUKOFF, T. Soletz, Government of Pskoff, Merchant.—Flax.

114 CLARKE, MORGAN & Co. Government of Vologda.—Flax.

115 ZEMSKOFF, Government of Novgorod, town of Staraja Russa, Merchant.—Tow.

116 SABININ, —. Government of Toula, town of Beleff, Prod.—Oakum.

117 KAUFMANN, A. Governments of Grodno, Minsk, and Volhynia, Prop.—Specimens of woods.

118 GOVERNMENT OF COOTAIS, district of Ozoorget.—Plane-tree wood. Rhododendron wood.

119 GOVERNMENT OF TIFLIS, district of Djarobelocan.—Walnut-tree wood. Beech-tree wood.

121 GORIGORETZK FARM, Government of Mohileff.—Merino wool.

122 VASSAL, —. Government of the Tauride, district of the Dneiper, Prop.—Spanish wool (merino).

123 GAMALEY, T. Bessarabia, district of Ackerman, Prod.—Spanish wool (merino).

124 PHILIBERT, L. & F. Government of the Tauride, district of Melitopol, Prop.—Spanish wool (merino).

125 N. N. Esthonia, estates of Schloss Bargam, and Kaltenbrunn.—Merino wool.

126 AKHOONDOFF SHAH MIRZA, Government of Stavropol, district of Piatigorsk, Prod.—Unwashed wool, of the Caratchay sheep.

127 NARISHKIN, L. K. Government of Saratoff, district of Balasheffsk, estate of Serghievka, Prop.—Wool.

128 N. N. Schloss-Trikaten, Government of Livonia.—Wool.

129 YOUZBASH, MAHOMET KHAN, Government of Derbent. khanate of Kiurin, Prod.—White wool, unwashed.

130 GIGOLO, SHRVILI, district of Gorsk, Prod.—Black wool, unwashed.

131 ABRAMOFF, J. Government of Ekaterinoslaff, district of Rostoff, Prop.—Fine unwashed Cashmere goat's-hair.

132 COSSACK WOMEN, Government of Orenbourg.—Goat's hair.

133; 200 TRIBE OF THE BASHKIRS.—Camel's hair.

134 KORIAKIN & MOUGIKOFF (Peasants), Government of Vologda.—Bristles.

135 SEMENOFF & FALEYEFF BROTHERS, Government of Kalouga, Manu.—Bristles.

136 ZOLOTOREFF, J. Government of Kalouga, Manu.—Bristles.

137 JUDITSKY, —, Moscow, Prod.—Cocoons and silk.

138 RIER, Government of the Tauride, district of Molotchansk.—Raw silk.

139 REBROFF, A. Government of Stavropol, district of Piatigorsk, Prop.—Raw silk.

140 RAYKO, N. Odessa, Prod.—Raw silks and cocoons.

141 VIKOULIN, Government of Voronej, district of Zadonsk, Prop.—Raw silk and organzine.

142 OOSSEIN-OGLI, HADJI BABA KELBALAY, Government of Shemakha, Prop.—Dyed silks of various colours.

143 REBROFF, A. Government of Stavropol.—Cocoons, raw silks, and organzine.

144 POPOFF, A. Moscow, Merchant.—Fine down.

145 LAPSHIN, J. St. Petersburg, Manu.—Goose down. White Bejetsk feathers. Grey feathers.

146 N. N. Government of Erivan, District of Alexandropol.—Persian powder.

148 STAFFEL, I. A. Warsaw, Manu.—Calculating machine. A machine for weighing precious metals.

149 IMPERIAL ALEXANDROVSKY MANUFACTORY, near St. Petersburg.—Machines for trying the strength of sail-cloth, cotton twist, and cotton thread. A Jacquard loom.

150 GRAFF, H. St. Petersburg, Inv.—Silk-throwing machine.

151 MENTCHINSKY, A. Government of Kieff, Inv.—Patent machine for cutting files.

152 HEKE, D. Warsaw, Coppersmith.—A vacuum pan, for the evaporation of sugar syrup.

153 DEMIDOFF, Messrs. Nijni Taghilsk-Siberia, Prop.—A table for washing gold sand.

154 IMPERIAL COACH-MAKING ESTABLISHMENT, St. Petersburg.—Wheels without felloes. An oak wheel-ring.

156 IMPERIAL IRON WORKS OF VOTKINSK.—Iron work for gun-carriages. Girders for roofs.

157 IMPERIAL CAST-IRON WORKS OF KOUSHVINSK.—Shot.

158 IMPERIAL IRON WORKS OF BARANTCHINSK.—Shells, grenades, and bombs.

159 IMPERIAL NIJNE-ISSETSK IRON WORKS, Government of Perm.—Grenades.

160 ISMAEL-ABDOOL-RUGHIL-OGLI, Government of Shemakha, district of Lagitch.—Gun and pistol barrels.

161 IMPERIAL MANUFACTORY OF ARMS OF ZLATAOUST.—Sabres and lances. Broadswords, &c.

162 KHAMOFF, M. Fort of Temir-Khan-Shoori, North Daguestan.—Caucasian sabre (called *shashka*).

163 OOSTE-CATCHAY-OOSTE-ALI-BECK-OGLI, Government of Shemakha, district of Nookha, village of Gemzali. —Caucasian sabre.

164 BAZALAY, M. village of Cazanistch North, Daguestan.—Four Caucasian daggers.

165 OOSTE-SELIM-MOLLA-NOORI-OGLI, Government of Shemakha, district of Nookha, village of Gemzali.— A Caucasian dagger.

166 SHAH-WEDI-OGLI, Government and District of Derbent, Goldsmith of Coobatchin.—A Caucasian rifle.

167 IMPERIAL ARTINSK WORKS, District of Zlataoust.—Cast-steel scythes.

168 IMPERIAL EKATERINBURG ENGINE FACTORY, Government of Perm.—Mechanical tools.

169 IMPERIAL IJORSK WORKS, near St. Petersburg.—Drawing instruments. Sextants. Level and stand.

170 PICK, J. Warsaw, Manu.—Microscope, level, &c.

171 RUDERT, H. Warsaw, Manu.—A small violin.

172 LICHTENTAL, M. St. Petersburg, Manu.—Pianofortes.

173 VESOFFCHIKOFF, M. Nijne-Novgorod, Manu.—Iron scale-beam.

173A RABENECK, L. Government of Moscow, District of Bogorodsk, Estate of Sobolevo, Manu.—Twist cotton. Red twill (coumatch). Plain velveteen. Calico. Printed handkerchiefs.

174 POPOFF & SONS, T. Government of Vladimir, Shouia, Manu.—Long cloth.

175 PANTELEEFF, M. Government of Moscow, district of Bogorodsk, Prop.—Cotton velvet, of different colours.

176, 191, 199, 208 ROCHEFORT, J. Government of Moscow, Estate of Perovo, Manu.—Printed muslin dresses, shawls, lace, gauze, &c.

177 MAYER & ZINDELL, Moscow, Manu.—Chintz.

178 CZAREVSK CHINTZ MANUFACTORY, Government of Moscow, district of Dmitrovsk.—Chintz for furniture, &c.

179 LUTCH, J. St. Petersburg, Manu.—Chintz.

180 ZOUBOFF, D. & STEPOUNIN, A. Government of Tshernigoff, district of Sourajsk, Suburb of Klintz, Manu.—Dark blue cloth.

181 STUMPF, F. Government of Warsaw, town of Tomasheff, Manu.—Green and black cloth.

182 AKSENOFF, J. Government of Tshernigoff, district of Sourajsk, Suburb of Klintz, Manu.—Light grey cloth.

183 CACKI-SHVILLY, Government of Tiflis, district of Djarobelocan, Prod.—Ossetian cloth (called tiftick).

184 ISAIEFF, P. Government of Tshernigoff, district of Sourajsk, colony of Novi Meziritch, Manu.—Cloth of different colours.

185 ZAKHERT, W. Government of Grodno, town of Suprasl, Manu.—Cloth of different colours; doeskin.

186 TSCHARTI-OBDOOL OGLI, Government of Tiflis, district of Djarobelocau, Prod.—Cloth for Caucasian trousers. Lesghian cloth.

187 TCHETVERIKOFF, —, near Moscow, Manu.—Amazone made of wool from the flocks of Count Nesselrode.

188 TCHURILOFF, —, St. Petersburg, Manu.—Silk and wool mixed cloth. Checked Cashmere.

189 GOUTCHKOFF, E. & J. Moscow, Manu.—Cashmere and mousseline de laine. Table-covers. Poplin.

190 VOLNER, —, Moscow, Manu. — French merinos, Cashmeres, mousseline de laines, and satin de laines.

192 MOES & Co., Government of Grodno, near Belostok, Manu.—Doeskins. Patterns of doeskin. Woollen yarn, of Nos. 32—40.

193 NARIMOFF, O. Government of Shemakha, Town of Shoosha, Prod.—Woollen socks for men; ditto for women.

194 OOSTE, A. Government of Shemakha, Town of Nookha, Embroiderer.—Embroidered cushions of red and blue cloth.

195 FAVAR, C. District of Moscow, estate of Poushkino, Manu.—Woollen damask.

196 NOGAISK TARTARS, Prod.—Camel's hair-cloth.

197 DOURASSOFF, —, Government of Orenburg, district of Bougourousnalsk, Prop.—Cloth made of camel's hair.

198 COSSACK WOMEN, Government of Orenburg, Prods.—Spun goat's hair.

200 TRIBE OF BASHKIRS, Prod.—Spun camel's hair.

201 AYRAPET, TARAEFF, Government of Shemakha, town of Shemakha, Manu.—Taffeta, 54 yards; ditto, 7 yards.

202 SITOFF BROTHERS, Moscow, Manu. — Samples of brocade.

203 KOLOKOLNIKOFF, PAUL, Moscow, Manu.—Patterns of brocade.

204 LOKTEFF, J. Moscow, Manu.—Velvet. Ribbons. Plush. Waistcoats, in gros-gros. Neckerchiefs.

205 POLIAKOFF & ZAMIATIN, Moscow, Manu.—Silver glassett. Watered silk.

206 TEDJOOM-BECK-MELIK-SHAH-NAZAROFF, Government of Shemakha, town of Shemakha, Manu.—Caucasian silk stuff (called djidjim), and taffeta.

207 JRAF-OGLI, Pasha, Government of Shemakha, district of Nookha, village of Khatemar, Prods.—Taffeta of silk and cotton. Silk handkerchiefs. Caucasian silk stuffs.

209 ZALOGHIN, —, Moscow, Manu.—Gros de Naples glacé, and checked; gros-gros moirée, and satin.

210 & 219 IMPERIAL ALEXANDROVSK MANUFACTORY, near St. Petersburg. — Sail-cloths. Damask table-cloths. Silk portraits, &c.

211 PEASANT WOMEN, Government of Kherson, district of Tiraspol, Prods.—Ornamental head-dresses. Silk sheet, cloth, and towel.

212 MELNIKOFF-GLOUSHKOFF, PAUL, Rjeff, Merchant.—Hemp yarn.

213 MELNIKOFF-GLOUSHKOFF, PETER, Rjeff, Merchant.—Hemp yarn.

214 MELNIKOFF-GLOUSHKOFF, M. Rjeff, Government of Tver. Merchant.—Hemp yarn.

215 BISTROM, Madame, Government of Kalouga, district of Medinsk, Prop.—Sail-cloth.

216 BRUZGHIN, A. Government of Kalouga, Kozelsk Manu.—Sail-cloth.

217 BELIBIN, P. Government of Kalouga, Manu.—Sail-cloth.

218 ZOTOFF BROTHERS, Government of Kalouga, district of Kozelsk, Manu.—Sail-cloth.

220 KONOVNIZIN, Countess, Government of Kharkoff, district of Akhtirsk, Prop.—Linen.

221 JULENIUS, ANNA (peasant woman), Government of Abo, Finland, Prod.—Linen.

222 VON MENGDEN, M. Government of Kostroma, district of Keneshemsk, Prop.—Table-cloths; napkins; towelling; breakfast table-cloths.

223 CAZALETT, A. St. Petersburg, Manu.—Cordage, &c.

224 KOUSSOFF, J. & SONS, St. Petersburg, Manu.—Hides, half-tanned.

225 DIFFERENT MERCHANTS & PEASANTS, Nijne-Novgorod, Prod.—Sheep-skins.

226 LITKE, J. Warsaw, Manu. — Varnished leather. Russia leather. Calf leather, for shoes.

227 MAY, R. Warsaw, Manu.—Varnished leather, for shoes and carriages. Black oil-cloth.

228 OZEROV, T. Government of Koursk, district of Belgorod, village of Bessonovka, Prop.—Glazed leather, Russia leather, goat-skin, and white calf-skins.

229 PODSOSSOFF, P. & SONS, Government of Nijne-Novgorod, Arzamass, Manu.—Russia leather.

230 PEASANTS of the Government of Ekaterinoslaff, Prod.—Lamb-skins.

231 SHOUVALOFF & SON, —, Moscow, Manu.—Varnished leather.

232 Skvorzoff, —, Government of Moscow, district of Svenigorodsk, Manu.—Leather, and ladies' boots.

233 Satournin, M. (peasant), Government of Nijne-Novgorod, district of Balashinsk, Prod.—White and black leather.

234 Miller, M., jun. Warsaw, Manu.—Gentlemen's boots. Shoes, without seams, &c.

236 Jalovitzin, J. Government of Kalouga, Manu.—Sole-leather, tanned with extract of rye.

237 Gribanoff, P. Government of Kalouga, Manu.—Sole leather, tanned with extract of rye.

238 Boudelin, A. Government of Nijne-Novgorod Arzamass, Manu.—Russia leather.

239 Koteloff, P. Kasan, Manu.—Morocco leather, for exportation to China, and for home consumption.

240 Bakhroushin & Sons, Moscow, Manu.—Morocco leather of different colours; calf ditto.

241 Shouvaloff & Son, Moscow, Manu.—Ladies' waterproof boots and clogs.

242 Mahmet-Veli-Ogli, Shoosha, Prod.—A horse-rug.

243 Abdool-Mahomet-Ogli, Government of Shemakha, district of Nookha.—Skin of a wild goat.

244 Abass-Bak, Government of Shemakha, district of Lencoran.—Leopard, tiger, and pelican skins.

245 Mahomet-Ogli, Government of Shemakha, district of Nookha.—Skin and horns of the mountain sheep.

246 Ali-Mehemet, Government of Shemakha, district of Salyan, village of Saydan.—Antelope skins. Skins of martins.

247 Semenoff & Faleyeff Brothers, Government of Kalouga, Manu.—Trimming of eider-down.

248 Bezroukavnikoff-Sokoloff, A. St. Petersburg, Manu.—Prepared horse-hair for furniture and mattresses.

249 Cassim-Oussein-Cooli-Ogli, Shoosha, Government of Shemakha, Embroiderer.—Horse-trappings, embroidered with silk.

250 Dada, B. Shoosha, Government of Shemakha, Manu.—Caucasian saddle-tree.

251 Agadjan D. Shoosha, Government of Shemakha, Manu.—A Caucasian bit.

252 Arutin Tabanov, town of Shoosha, Prod.—A saddle-bag.

253 Hassan-Ooste-Neftali-Ogli, Shoosha, Prod.—Saddle-cloth.

254 Irza-Cooli-Hadji-Cagraman-Ogli, Nookha, Government of Shemakha, Prod.—Silk horse-cloth. Caucasian housing.

255 Raphi-Nuba-Ogli, Shoosha, Prod.—A saddle bag.

256 Roostam, C. Government of Shemakha, town of Shoosha, Manu.—Circassian stirrups.

257 Gambartzoomoff, Artem, town of Shemakha, Manu.—Caucasian steel stirrups, inlaid with gold.

258 Petit, A. Odessa, Inv. and Maker.—Wigs.

259 Ivanoff, P. St. Petersburg, Manu.—Horse and other hair, bleached, unbleached, and crimson-dyed.

260; 302 Vargounin Brothers, St. Petersburg, Manu.—Paper hangings; copying and writing paper.

261 Solenikoff, —, Government of Vladimir, district of Pokrovsk, estate of Serghievka, Manu.—Writing paper.

262 Fetter & Rahn, Warsaw. — Paper. Paper-hangings Table-covers in oil-cloth. Pencils.

263 Kerbalay-Khooda-Verdi-Aghali-Ogli, Government of Shemakha, Town of Baki, Prod.—Carpet.

264 Baba-Imam-Verdi-Ogli, town of Shoosha.—A felted carpet.

265 Bardoffsky, T. St. Petersburg, Manu.—Articles of furniture, and utensils, made of felt and hare's fur.

266 Levasheff, —, Government of Nijne-Novgorod, Prop.—Mats.

267 Ivanoff, Peasant, Government of Kostroma, district of Vetloujsk, estate of Starkovo, Prod.—Check mats.

268 Schultz, —, Government of Perm, District of Ekaterinbourg, Prop.—Mats made from the bark of the aspen-tree.

269 Hadji-Aga-Baba, Government of Shemakha, Town of Shoosha.—Blue woollen table-cloth, embroidered with silk.

270; 277 Lafont, P. Moscow, Manu.—Printed shawl, and silk gloves. Figured tulle.

271 Fitzner, C. St. Petersburg, Manu.—Folding hat, &c.

272 Lott, G. Warsaw, Manu.—Straw bonnets.

273 Benno-Niveta, Warsaw, Manu. — Russian kid gloves.

274 N. N. Town of Nakhitchevan, district of Taganrog.—Bracelets and other articles in silver. Sashes of gold ribbon. Fess cap. Embroidered shoes.

275 Shekhonin, Alexis, Government of Novgorod, Town of Novotorjok, Merchant.—Embroidered velvet boots. Silk and tinsel belts, &c.

276 Shekhonin, —, Torjok, Manu.—Boots, caps, and other articles embroidered with gold.

278 Khrghis, Prod.—Yergack, or cloak of horse-skins.

279 Kerbalay-Hoossein-Ogli, Government of Tiflis, district of Djarobelocan, Prod.—Caucasian felted cloak of the Lesghis.

280 N. N. Abasia.—Caucasian felted cloak.

281 Merlin, A & V. Government of Riasan, district of Jegorievsk, Prop.—A shawl.

282 A Cossack's Wife, Government of Orenburg, Prod.—Shawl of white goats' hair.

283 Ladighin, Madame, Government of Tamboff, Prop.—Articles made of goose-down:—a pillow-case, Turkish pattern. White woven muff, with borders. White neckerchief.

284 Albertzoom, S. Town of Shemakha, Manu.—Caucasian gallooned collars. Galloons of three qualities.

285 Imperial Alexandrovsky Cannon Foundry, Government of Olonetz.—Statue of Napoleon. Clock cases, &c.

286 Iakovleff, Madame Catherine, Government of Riazan, estate of Grishino, Prop.—Articles of hardware. Knives, &c.

287 Krumbigel, —, Moscow, Manu.—Two gilt bronze candelabra.

288 Imperial Mining Works, Poland.—Kitchen utensils, enamelled, and made of zinc.

289 Buch, —, St. Petersburg, Manu.—Metal buttons.

290 Aga-Melik-Mahomet-Hadji-Ussoof-Ogli, Government of Shemakha, town of Baki, Manu.—Enamelled gold trinkets.

291 Hadji Mahomet Oussein Hadji Ussof Ogli, town of Baki.—Enamelled gold trinkets.

292 Petz, C. Moscow, Manu.—Plated tea-urns.

294 Moussin, Poushkin, Government of Novgorod, district of Krestezk, Prop.—Window glass.

295 Kokhanoff, Government of St. Petersburg, district of Novoladojsk, Prop.—Window glass.

296 Ameloung & Son, Government of Livonia, near Dorpat, Manu.—A looking-glass.

297 Gambs, —, St. Petersburg, Cabinet-maker.—Cabinet in rose wood, ornamented with bronze and porcelain.

298 Imperial Polishing Manufactory, Peterhoff, near St. Petersburg.—A table inlaid with various stones in Florentine mosaic, on a bronze gilt pillar

299 Miller, G. jun. St. Petersburg, Pat. and Manu.—Coloured inlaid floors of various designs.

303 Beseke, —, St. Petersburg, Manu.—Cocoa-nut an oleine soap.

305 Matisen, A. & Co. St. Petersburg, Manu.—Stearine in lumps, and stearine candles.

306 Alftan, —, Government of Viborg, Finland, Parish of Kaklinsk, Manu.—Stearine candles.

307 Pitansier, —, Odessa, Manu.—Stearine candles.

308 Nilson & Junker, Moscow, Manu.—Stearine candles, &c. Soda soap, prepared from oleine.

309 SAPELKIN, V. Government of Moscow, estate of Vladimirovo, Manu.—Wax candles.

310 POPINOFF, SOPHIA, Tiflis, Embroideress.—Velvet cushions, embroidered. Lamp mats. Caucasian shoes.

311 LERKHE, —, St. Petersburg, Merchant.—India-rubber clogs. Waterproof morocco pillow.

312 BARSHAGHAN, Peasant, Archangel, Prod.—White felt boots.

313 STARIKOFF, —, Government of Nijne-Novogorod, district of Semenovsk, Prop.—Felt shoes for ladies.

314 DIFFERENT PEASANTS, Government of Nijne-Novgorod, Prod.—Felt shoes and boots, of white and grey colours; felt boots and shees for men and women.

315 TCHUPLATOFF, T. Rjeff, Manu.—Carmine and lake.

316 VOLOSKOFF, J. Rjeff, Manu.—Carmine.

317 VOLOSKOFF, A. St. Petersburg, Manu.—Samples of carmine; extract of carmine; carmine lake, and lake.

318 IMPERIAL CHINA MANUFACTORY, St. Petersburg.—Vases, ornamented with paintings. Slabs for tables.

319 LOUKUTIN P. & SON, Government and district of Moscow, estate of Danilkoff, Manu.—Snuff and cigar boxes. Other boxes.

320 FLEROVSKY, M. Tobolsk, Siberia, Manu.—Boxes of birch bark.

321 STARTCHIKOFF, N. St. Petersburg, Manu.—Specimen of a patented gold tissue.

322 BOLIN, C. and LAN, St. Petersburg, Jewellers.—Jewellery.

323 DEMIDOFF, Messrs. St. Petersburg, Props.—Articles made of malachite.

325 LIKHACHEFF, P. St. Petersburg, Manu.—Gold-plated and silver-plated epaulettes. Silver shoulder-knots.

326 IMPERIAL POLISHING MANUFACTORY OF EKATERINBURG, Government of Perm.—Bordered vase of greenish jasper, three feet high.

327 IMPERIAL POLISHING MANUFACTORY OF KOLYVAN, Government of Tomsk.—Jasper vases.

328 Count TOLSTOY, T. Vice-President of the Imperial Academy of Fine Arts, St. Petersburg, Sculp.—Electrotype and plastic medallions and casts. Medals in gutta percha, commemorative of the Turkish and Persian wars.

329 HEKE, D. Warsaw, Manu.—Copy of the Warwick vase in copper, hammered, not cast.

330 VSEVOLOSSKY, —, Government of Perm, District of Solikamsk.—Samples of sheet iron.

330A BELITCHEFF, M. St. Petersburg, Inv.—Hair dye.

331 ABASHEFF, N. Government of Smolensk.—Dried potatoes and potato flower.

332 DAVIDOFF, B. Government of Tamboff, District of Morschansk, Estate Kulevatovo, Prop.—Oat grits and rye flour.

333 PAVLOFF N. Government of Saratoff, Prop.—Wheat.

334 PROTASSOFF, A. St. Petersburg, Manu.—Cigars, cigarettes, and snuff.

335 KOUKELL JASNOPOLSKY, J. Government of Kharkoff.—Beet-root loaf sugar.

336 STCHEGLOFF, —, Government of Vladimir, district of Alexandrovsk, Manu.—Manufactured alum.

337 KONOVNITZIN, Count J. Government of Kharkoff, District of Akhtirsk, Estate Nikitoffka.—Fleece of three-year-old sheep.

338 NIKITA VSEVOLODOWITCH VSEVOLOJSKY'S, Government of Astrachan.—Dried fish and isinglass.

339 ERCHOFF A. Moscow, Manu.—Various bristles.

340 BAZILE KOUDRIAFFZEFF JADENOFFSKY, St. Petersburg, Manu.—Samples of horse-hair.

341 ROOCH, L. St. Petersburg, Manu.—Surgical instruments.

342 ROSINSKY, T. St. Petersburg.—Apparatus in lieu of leeches.

343 ZEITLER, M. Government of Radm, district of Olkoushsk, estate Dombrovo, Manu.—Samples of wire, nails, and screws.

344 IAKOLEFF, BROTHERS, St. Petersburg. — Droshki, sledge, and harness.

345 BABOUNOFF, B. St. Petersburg.—Droshki, sledge, and harness.

346 TOULIAKOFF, BROTHERS, St. Petersburg.—Droshki for two persons.

347 SKALKIN, — (Peasant), Government of Tver, district Rjeff, Estate Mouravievo.—An axe.

348 OBROUTCHEFF, —, Government of Orenburg Military Governor.—Rock salt from Iletz.

349 PROKHOROFF, Brothers, Moscow, Manu.—Wrappers, dressing-gowns, shawls, cashmere, cambric, chintz.

350 PEASANT OF THE ESTATE OF BEDLANO, Government of Radom, district of Opotchno.—Cloth usually worn by peasants.

351 FIEDLER, A. G. Upatovka, near Kalish, Manu.—Samples of cloth.

352 VAREN, A. Government of Tavasthousk, Parish of Tamel, Manu.—Cloth made of Finland wool.

353 KONDRASHEFF, —, Government of Moscow, district of Bogorodsk, Manu.—Fancy silks and damasks.

354 SOLOVIEFF, J. Government of Moscow, district of Bogorodsk, Manu.—Patterns of velvets.

355 DOMBROWITCH, C. Government of Angonstow, district of Mariampol, estate of Dobrowola, Manu.—Linen, table-cloths, and napkins.

356 DOLGOROUCKY, Prince N. Government of Smolensk, district of Gjatok, estate of Dmitrievsk, Prop.—Leather for boots and soles. Russia leather.

357 SHECHTEL, F. Saratoff, Merchant. — Embroidered carpet.

358 BONDAREVSKY, PRASCOVIA, OLGA, &c. Orenburg.—A shawl made of goat's-hair.

359 ARISTARKHOFF, —, Government of Kalouga, district of Borovsk, Manu.—Writing and coloured papers.

360 RABZEVITCH, —, St. Petersburg, Manu.—Samples of quills and pens.

361 REVILLION, —, St. Petersburg, Manu.—Specimens of type.

362 DREGGER, F. Moscow, Artist. — Chromo-lithographics of antiquities in Russia.

363 MANUFACTURING COMPANY, Moscow. — Stearine candles and samples of stearine.

364 STIER, H. Warsaw, Manu.—Toilet soap.

365 CHOPIN, F. St. Petersburg, Manu.— Bronze candelabrum, clock, &c.

366 SAZIKOFF, P. Moscow, Manu.—Large vase, candelabra, goblets, &c.

367 MATVIEFF, P. Moscow, Manu.—Figured cashmere and damask.

368 VARHOVZOFF, T. St. Petersburg. — Bas-reliefs in silver, chased by hand.

369 KOSHKOFF, M. Government of Vologda, Ustiug, Manu.—Silver articles in niello.

370 SHTANGE & VERFEL, St. Petersburg, Manu.—Bronze candelabrum.

371 LAPTEFF, N. Government of Moscow, district of Bogordsk, Manu.—Silks for cloaks, dresses, shawls, &c.

372 Heirs of SAPOGNIKOFF, —, Moscow, Manu.—Gold brocades.

373 MOLKEHANOFF, —, Moscow, Manu.—Cotton goods, usually worn by peasants.

374 CHARLOVETZ, —, Moscow, Manu.—Scotch cambrics, muslins, &c.

375 SCHOENFELDT, —, St. Petersburg, Manu.—Ladies' work-table.

376 KAEMMERER and ZEFTIGEN, St. Petersburg, Jewellers.—Diadem, bouquet, berthe, and brooch of diamonds.

SARDINIA.

(Royal Commissioner in London, CHEVALIER LENCISA, 124 Mount Street, Grosvenor Square; Messrs. LIGHTLY & SIMON, Fenchurch Street, Agents.)

1 GRANGE, F. Randens, nr. Aiguebelle (Savoy), Manu. —Specimens of spathic iron from the mines of St. Georges des Hurtières, and of white crystallized casting for the manufacture of steel.

2 ZOLESI, S. Chiavari. Slate table polished and varnished; polished writing slate; roofing slates.

3 PIANELLO, D. Chiavari. Rough slate fourteen decimetres (5 ft. 6 in.) square.

4 SELOPIS BROTHERS, Turin and Brozzo (Ivrée), Manu. Specimens of sulphuric, nitric, and hydrochloric acids. Sulphate of iron, copper, alumina, and potass. Pyrites, sulphur, &c

5 GIRARDI BROTHERS, Turin, Prop. Specimens of coleseed, castor, linseed, and walnut oil.

6 ROSSI & SCHIAPPARELLI Turin, Manu.—Stearine candles; soap made of oleic acid; stearic acid; sulphate and carbonate of magnesia.

7 ALBANI BROTHERS, Turin, Manu. Chemical matches. Gelatin and soda soap. Sulphuric acid, nitric acid, nitrate of barytes. Retort.

8 GIROD, M. and Co. Aiguebelle, Manu. Gallic acid, extracted from chesnut wood.

9 GARRISSINI, P. Toirano, Genoa. Samples of orange wine.

10 SALUCE, M. Manu.—Peppermint, crystallized; great absynthium, colourless; noyeau, crystallized. Mastic.

11 CALLOUD, F. Annecy, Manu.—Various chemicals.

12 BONJEAN, J. Chambery, Manu.—Chemicals and apparatus.

13 DUFOUR, L. Genoa, Manu.—Samples of sulphate and citrate of quinine.

14 PROFUMO, J. Genoa, Manu.—Specimens of white lead.

15 SIMONE MANCU, LE CHEVALIER, Sassari, Prop.— Olive oil, of two kinds.

16 SCOLA, B. Turin, Manu.—Gelatine capsules, filled with balsam of copaiba.

17 PALLESTRINI BROTHERS, Villabiscossi (Lomellina) Prop.—Specimens of rice cultivated in Piedmont.

18 BLONDEL GASTON, & Co. Turin, Prop.—Specimens of various qualities of rice.

19 BO, A. Turin, Manu. — Specimens of mineral colours, lakes and inks.

20 PREVER, J. J. Turin, Prop.—Specimens of raw Merino wool.

21 BRUN BROTHERS, Pignerol, Prop.—Specimens of washed Merino wool.

22 CALVI, J. Genoa.—Linseed oil and cakes.

23 GUISO, M. Nuoro, Prop.—Specimens of pure wax and white wax candles. Honey, sweet and bitter.

24 BRAVO, M. Pignerol, Prop.—Specimens of raw silks. Organzine with thrown silk.

25 SINIGAGLIA BROTHERS, Busea, Prop.—Specimens of raw and thrown silk.

26 JACQUET, H. and Co. Latour, Luzerne, Prop.— Specimens of raw and thrown silk.

27 CASISSA, & SONS, Novi, Prop.—Specimens of raw white silk.

28 VERTU BROTHERS, Turin, Manu.—Specimens of white thrown silk.

29 GALIMBERTI, C. Pella, Novara, Prop.—Specimens of raw silk.

30 RIGNON, F. & Co. Savigliano, Saluzzo, Prop.— Specimens of raw and thrown silk.

31 MESINA, S. Nuoro, Prop.—Black woollen yarn and raw wool. Coarse black woollen cloth. Olive oil.

32 ROCCA, J. Turin, Manu.—Two violins, after ancient models.

33 BENOIT, A. Cluses (Savoy, Faucigny, Manu.— Machines used in the manufacture of watches. Specimens of watch-work. High-pressure steam-engine. Measuring apparatus for railroads.

34 ANNECY & PONT, Manu. —Calicoes; handkerchiefs, Indian style; sarcenet percalina.

35 REY BROTHERS, Turin, Manu.—Woollen cloth for carpets.

36 The DIVISIONAL COMMITTEE of Nuoro.—Coarse woollen cloth for petticoats, spencers, stockings, and breeches; black.

37 FERMENTO, L. A la Rocca, Mondovi, Prop.—Specimen of thrown silk.

38 IMPERATORI, J. H. BROTHERS, Intra, Pallanza, Prop.—Specimen of organzine silk.

39 CHICHIZOLA, J. and Co. Turin and Genoa, Manu.— Plain and coloured velvets. Figured satins; silk gros; gros de Paris; glazed silk gros; and flowered damask.

40 SOLEY, B. Turin, Manu.—Specimens of silk of different colours; white and coloured taffetas.

41 GUILLOT, J. & Co. Turin and Genoa, Manu.—Silk plush for hats; piece of velvet, lace drawing; velvet for tapestry; a set of foulards for robes.

42 GUILLOT, J. & Co. Genoa.—Silk velvets—black, pensée, blue, crimson, spring-green, ruby, emerald-green, &c.

43 MOLINARI, A. Genoa.—Black silk-velvet pieces, antique style; silk velvet, silk damask, satin stuff, &c., for furniture and hangings.

44 DEFFERRARI BROTHERS, Genoa.—Fourteen patterns of silk stuffs and velvets.

45 BORZONE, J. Chiavari.—Two linen towels.

46 DURIO BROTHERS, Turin.—Samples of leather for soles and thongs.

47 FARINA, A. Turin.—Punches for small type; a set of punches for Roman, English, and German types.

48 BAYNO, J. Turin.—Various qualities of lace.

49 TESSADA, F. Genoa.—Embroidered cambric handkerchiefs; ladies' black-lace mantles; patterns of lace.

50 CROCCO BROTHERS, Genoa.—Embroidered cambric handkerchiefs; frame for embroidery; woollen waistcoats.

51 FORNO, J. Turin.—Evening dress; groom's dress.

52 GULLIA, J. B. Turin.—Boots, for postillions; boots made of leather prepared with the hair on; and of calf's leather, without seam, &c.

53 MANTAUT, L. Engraver, Turin.—Specimen of an engraved copper-plate.

54 ROPOLO, P. Turin.—A small gaufre-iron door mounted on mechanical pivots.

55 GRANZINI, J. Turin.—Iron-bed with elastic mattresses, enclosed in a buffet. Model of a "bomb à diaphragm."

56 BARBIE, J. Turin.—Lock for coffers, with pierced mounting, and a key of only one piece.

57 MONTEFIORI, C. Turin.—Silver plate with the portrait of the Queen of Sardinia, &c.; portraits of Victor Emanuel II., King of Sardinia, chased on a silver plate, &c.

58 LOLEO, J. Genoa.—Works in silver filigree. Column ornamented with emblems intended to celebrate the era of the great Exhibition of 1851.

59 BENNATI, J. Genoa.—Figure, with a pedestal, of Christopher Columbus, in silver filigree.

60 LENDY, N. Turin.—Dies for stamping Dorini, a kind of gold medal worn by the peasant-women in Piedmont.

61 BERTINETTI, P. Turin.—Carriage on a new principle veneered and inlaid.

62 MARTINOTTI, J. Turin.—A dressing-table, à étages, in rosewood.

63 MARTINOTTI, J. Turin.—Large wood frame, carved
and gilt, for a looking-glass or picture.

64 CAPELLO, G. Turin.—Cornice in pear-wood, carved.
A table, a curule chair, and a pedestal; the property of
H.M. the King of Sardinia. Mahogany round table on a
triangular stem, with carved figures and masks; the upper
part made of white wood, covered with velvet and fringed.
The property of His Royal Highness the Duke of Genoa.
A cabinet floor, inlaid with various foreign and indigenous
woods.

65 GRIVA, M. Turin.—A rosewood article of furniture,
forming a desk, a toilet, and a work-table for ladies.

66 PERELLI, A. Turin.—A table-sofa, in rosewood and
mahogany, carved and ornamented with Chinese marquetrie.

67 CUGLIERERO, R. Turin.—Two light chairs (trot-
teuses), made of indigenous woods.

68 CIAUDO, J. Nice.—An oblong drawing-room table
in olive-wood, with mosaic.

69 BISSO BROTHERS, Genoa.—Round table, inlaid.

70 MAGNI, F. Genoa.—Round table, with inlaid
drawers.

71 SPEICH, P. Genoa.—Ebony table, in the renaissance
style. A Prie-dieu stool of Indian walnut-tree, in a similar
style.

72 DESCALZI, J. Chiavari.—Round table, inlaid with
wood in imitation of marble. Round table, inlaid. Light
chiavari chairs. Looking-glass.

73 DA FIENO, J. B. and MONTECUCCO, A. Genoa.—
Console table, carved and gilt, with a marble slab.

74 CANEPA, J. B. Chiavari.—Chairs of white wood;
others, coloured yellow. Gothic chairs of black and white
wood.

75 BOURGOIN, B. Turin, Manu.—Specimen of blacking.

76 CASTAGNETO, E. Genoa, Manu.—White cream of
tartar.

77 FINO, J. Turin.—Specimens of various kinds of
brushes.

78 MONTU, J. & Co. Turin.—Specimens of Piedmontese
heath sprigs, for the manufacture of brushes; heath brushes
for various purposes.

79 BAFICO, J. L. F. Genoa.—Wooden vases, painted in
imitation of Japan wares.

80 STRAUSS, J. Turin.—A set of tobacco-pipes and
porte-cigares in white talc, carved and ornamented.

81 VALDETTARO, J. Genoa.—Fifty qualities of fine and
superfine paste or vermicelli.

82 ROMANENGO, G. Genoa.—Boxes, containing candied
fruits.

83 COMBA, F. Turin.—An elk (Cervus alces), from the
Zoological Museum of Turin.

84 ACQUARONE, J. B. Porto Maurizio.—Liquid citric
acid.

85 BOSIO, A. Turin.—The arms of the Royal House of
Savoy, carved in wood.

86 STEFANI, W. Turin, Prop.—Two large silk embroidery tableaux.

87 CAVIGIOLI, C. Turin.—Bronze medals cast with a
tenth proportion of pewter.

88 SPANNA, J. & Co. Turin, Manu.—Specimens of artificial marble, prepared with granite and wood.

89 CHIRIO & MINA, Turin.—A large volume, containing the history of Hautecombe Abbey.

90 RONDELLI, F. Nice.—An obelisk covered with shells
and other articles found on the sea-shore.

91 SCOTTO, The Chevalier, Genoa.—Steel engraving.

92 FRUMENTO, J. B. Genoa.—Marble statue, representing a Bacchante.

93 DE BARBIERI, Genoa.—Superfine paste of vermicelli.

94 GUELFI, —, Genoa.—Superfine paste of vermicelli.

95 GANDOLFI, —, Turin.—Military dress.

96 DOMENGET, —, Savoy.—Mineral water.

97 MASERA, —, Turin, Samples of machines, or surgical instruments.

SOCIETY ISLANDS.

HER MAJESTY POMARE, QUEEN OF THE SOCIETY ISLES.—
1 Eight fine mats, manufactured by women of the Society
Islands. The tissue is formed of the leaves of the Fara, a
variety of the Pandanus odoratissimus of Linnæus.

2 Five head-dresses (coronets), and eighteen pieces of tissue
for ladies' bonnets. These are also made by women. The
material used is the plant commonly known in these islands
by the name of pia, arrow-root by the English, Tacca puma-
lifida (?) by botanists.

3 Three pieces of white cloth, manufactured by the women
of the Society and neighbouring Islands. In this manufacture
they employ the bark of the young branches of the Artocarpus of Linnæus, commonly called the bread-fruit tree,
and known to the inhabitants by the name of Maiore, or
Uru. The yellow fringe to this is made from the inner bark
of the Hybiscus teleaceus, and is an article of dress worn by
the native chiefs of both sexes.

4 A hinai or Indian vase, in which are kept the utensils
which the Tahitians use during their repasts. The material
used is of a remarkable tenacity.

HURTELL, M. French Colonist. A specimen of native
coffee. A specimen of native cotton.

SPAIN.

(Commissioners in London, RAMON LA SAGRA, 34 Leicester Sq.; T. ALFONSO, 8 Hill St. Brompton; MANUEL DE
YSASI, 5 Water Lane, Tower St. City.)

1 CERAIN, J. B. Alava.—Ore from the Somo-rostro
mine, calcined. Slag and iron, in different states.

2 The INSPECTOR of MINES of the DISTRICT of BAR-
CELONA.—1 Galena, from the Government mines of Falset,
province of Tarragona. 2 Auriferous quartz, from Culera,
province of Gerona.

3 GUADALAJARA.—Silver ore from Hiendelaencina.

4 The INSPECTOR of MINES of the DISTRICT of GUI-
PUZCOA.—Ten specimens of minerals, from the Guipuzcoa,
including iron, galena, blende, lignite, &c.

5 The DIRECTOR of the MINES of LINARES.—1 Sulphuret of lead, from the Arrayanes mine. 2 Lead after the
first smelting from the above ore.

6 The INSPECTOR of MINES of the DISTRICT of CIU-
DAD REAL, Prod.—Thirty-two specimens of minerals from
La Mancha, including clay slate, sandstone, quicksilver,
iron pyrites, cinnabar, barytes, calcareous spar, &c.

7 The INSPECTOR of MINES of the DISTRICT of MUR-
CIA.—Specimens of eighty-four minerals, &c., found in the
district of Murcia, including galena, sulphuret of zinc, iron
pyrites, carbonate and sulphate of lead, litharge, alum, &c.

8 The DIRECTOR of MINES of RIO TINTO, Seville.—
1 Grey copper, from the Preciosa mine. 2 Raw mineral ore,
proceeding from the vein of double sulphuret of iron and
copper. 3 Ore prepared by slow roasting, and exposed to
the open air in piles, and worked by the damping process.
4, 5 Bar of forged iron, covered with a case of copper pre-

cipitated from the waters of the Rio Tinto. 6 Bars of fine copper, from the preceding.

9 The INSPECTOR of MINES of SANTANDER.—Copper pyrites, from the Constancia mine, town of Camaleno: the ore produces 20 per cent. of copper.

10 The MARTE MINING COMPANY, Losacio, Zamora.—Ore and regulus of antimony. Specimens of silver, lead, and other minerals.

11 The INSPECTOR of MINES of SARAGOSSA.—Specimens of argentiferous galena, copper, antimony, antimonial galena, sulphuret of lead and antimony, and argentiferous copper.

12 The DIRECTOR of the FACTORY of S. PEDRO DE ARAYA, Alava.—Specimens of sparry-iron, red amethysts, fire sandstone, coal, charcoal, iron, raw, refined, drawn, &c.

13 The INSPECTOR of MINES of the DISTRICT of ALMERIA.—A collection of forty specimens of ores and minerals from the district of Almeria, including silver, lead, mercury, copper, and iron ores, and products; alkalies; marbles and clays.

14 LINARES LEAD MINING ASSOCIATION.—Lead ore.

15 The INSPECTOR of MINES of the DISTRICT of ASTURIAS, Oviedo, Prod.—Twenty-eight specimens of minerals, from the district of Asturias, including copper, cinnabar, lead, calamine, iron, coal, and marbles.

16 The INSPECTOR of MINES of GRANADA.—Twenty-three specimens of mineral productions, including marbles, serpentine, cobalt ore, sulphuret of copper, ores of lead and zinc, magnesia, gold sand, &c

17 The INSPECTOR of MINES of the DISTRICT of LEON.—Eighteen specimens of minerals, from the district of Leon, including hydroxide and peroxide of iron, and chalk stone.

18 The INSPECTOR of MINES of LUGO.—1 Argentiferous ores. 2 Samples of lead. 3 Specimens of tin. 4 Specimens of Kaolin, fire-clay and fire-bricks. 5 Crucibles and fire-bricks. 6 Fire-bricks. 7 Nickel ore, with its products, to the pure metal.

19 The INSPECTOR of MINES of MALAGA.—Eleven specimens of minerals from Malaga: galena of various sorts, magnetic iron ore, nickel, graphite, or black lead, pyrites of iron and copper, plastic clay, serpentine, Fuller's earth, &c.

20 The MINING INSPECTOR of the DISTRICT of ZAMORA, Prod.—Specimens of carbonate and phosphate of lead, argentiferous lead, silicate of antimony, laminated regulus of antimony, ore of oxide of tin, fire-clay, &c., ores of hydro-oxide of iron, carbonate of iron, sulphuret of lead, and carbonate of lead, and yellow rock crystal.

21 The LEONES A ASTURIANA COMPANY, Asturias.—Specimens of steel.

22 AMOR, F. Cordova.—Iron from Villafranca. At this place the ore forms an entire mountain of considerable size.

23 GIRO, J. Malaga, Prod.—Specimens of iron, from the works of El Angel.

24 The PEDROSO IRON COMPANY, Seville.—Specimens of cast, rod, and plate iron, and mineral coal.

25 FERNANDEZ, V. F. Seville.—Specimen of fine copper.

26 IBARRA, J. M. Seville.—Mass of copper.

27 The INSPECTOR of MINES of the DISTRICT of PALENCIA, Province of Leon.—1 Coal, from the mines of the town of Barruelos. 2 Coke, from the same works: made in the open air.

28 The INSPECTOR of the MINES of SORIA.—Mineral asphalte, found in an extent of more than two leagues Spanish, impregnating sandstone layers of considerable thickness, which form the base of the mountain range of Picofrentes.

29 The INSPECTOR of MINES, CORDOVA.—Specrmens of marble: 1 Marble from Fuente de los Frailes. 2 Marble from the quarries of Acebuchal. 3 to 5 Marble from the same quarries, but differing in the colour. 4 Marble from the same, worked at the surface. 6 and 7 Marble from Lanchares. 8 and 9 Marble of the Cerro de Nuestra Senora.

30 HUELVA.—Samples of marble, from a quarry in the district of Fuente-heridos.

31 THE ROYAL LIBRARY at Madrid.—Marbles: Nos. 1—5 Different kinds. 6 From the River Pinzon, Asturias. 7, 8 Catalayud, Zaragoza. 9 Tortosa. 10 Biscay. 11 Anorve (Navarre). 12 Sierra de Moncayo (Aragon). 13, 14 Calatrau. 15 Puebla de Arbroton. 16, 17 Cuenca. 18, 19 Alcarria de Irriepar. 20, 21 Cogollundo. 22 Loronteras. 23 Cabrera (Siguerza). 24, 25 Unknown quarries. 26, 27 Caballar, Segovia. 28, 29 Montes de Toledo. 30 Banuela de Talavera de la Reina. 31 Montes Claos. 32 Buitragos (Castilla la Nueva). 33 Alabastro de Monasterio. 34—37 Valencia. 38 Murviedro, Valencia. 39 Calix, Valencia. 40 Almodovar. 41, 42 Murcia. 43—45 Granada. 46, 47 Malaga. 48, 49 Ronda, 50, 51, Cabra. 52, 58 Horon, 54 Baileu, 55 Estepa, 56 Ayamonte, 57 Sierra de Gao, 58 Cordoba.—Andalucia. 59 Sierra Morena. 60 —63 Consuegra (Mancha). 64—66 Orda, 67, 68 Villamayor, 69, 70 Puerto Lapiche, 71, 72 Salceda, 73 Manzanares. 74 Satander. 75—83 Espejon, 84, 85 Lastra de Cuellar, 86 Castro Mocho, 87 Leon.—Old Castille.

32 SARAGOSSA.—Marble, from Catalor; from Fuentes de Ebro; from Alhama; from Roden.

33 Oviedo, Asturias.—Jet, in the natural state, and polished, from the district of Villaviciosa. It is manufactured into various articles which are sold in the neighbourhood.

33A Canary Islands. — Carbonate of soda, extracted from the Salsola soda, which is produced in great abundance in these islands. Carbonate of soda (native mineral).

34 SANTOS Y DIAZ, Havannah.—Specimens of marbles.

35 The INSPECTOR of MINES of the DISTRICT of BURGOS.—1 Glauberite, from the mines of the town of Cerezo. 2 Crystallized sulphate of soda, and 8 Anhydrous, or calcined sulphate, from the glauberite.

36 The ANANA SALT WORKS, Alava.—Common salt. Native crystallized salt.

37 ALICANTE.—Barilla.

38 ANGULA, I. Barcelona.—Specimen of Barilla. Sulphate of soda extracted from running waters in the immediate neighbourhood of Cervera.

39 ELIAS, M. Barcelona.—Nitre: the "sal gem" of English commerce.

40 MAURAUDY, D. A. J. Cartagena.—Specimens of alum manufactured by the exhibitor.

41 SEMPEREDE, F. Elche.—A lump of sabior, from the plant of the same name cultivated in the province of Elcho.

42 GRANADA.—Seed and stone barilla.

42A CADIZ.—Crystallized sulphur, from the abandoned mine of Conil. Meerschaum, from San Lucar.

43 MAISTERRA, M. Lorca.—Native salt in crystals.

44 PAULO Y BARTOLINI, Saragossa.—Nitre.

45 MURCIA.—Barilla plant, very large specimen. Sulphurous earth and compact native sulphur, from the hills of Serrata, district of Lorca. Alum, refined. Selenite, from the Serrata hills. White lead. Stone barilla.

46 DURANGO Y TRIGO.—Sulphur, from the mines of Teruel, &c.

47 YUST & Co. Lorca.—Specimen of artificial sulphur.

48 PRATS, F. Alava, Prod.—Hydraulic lime.

49 CONCHA, A. Caceres.—Phosphorite of Estremadura.

49A CUESTA, A. DE LA, Santander.—Sulphate of lime.

51 YSASI, M. DE, Toboso, Manu. — Large earthen wine-jar, manufactured in the village of Toboso, in La Mancha.

53 THE AULENCIA Co. Madrid, Prod.—Fire-bricks.

54 TEGER & Co. Segovia, Manu.—Pavement-tiles.

55 GONZALEZ VALLS, R. Valencia, Manu.—Twenty-two frames, with 204 glazed tiles.

55A The APOLYTOMENE Co. Madrid, Manu.— Apolyzoo or artificial marble.

56 ALBACETE.—Samples of wheat.

57 BADILLO, J. M. Ciudad Real.—Wheat of Ciudad Real, of two kinds—macho and candeal—grown in the province.

58 GUZMAN, R. Ciudad Real.—Wheat of two kinds—ijona and candeal—grown in the province of Ciudad Real.

59 ALMERIA.—Fine and rough sedge.

60 HUELVA.—Specimens of the best kinds of wheat grown in the province, which constitutes its principal riches.

61 PINAN, J. Leon.—Wheat (called *mocho ó chamorro*), grown in the province of Leon.

62 NUNO, D. Guadalajara, Prod.—Wheat.

63 OVIEDO, ASTURIAS.—White wheat. White and yellow maize.

64 CEA, P. A. Leon—Wheat (called *del Blanquillo*) grown in the province of Leon.

65 MACORRA, F. Malaga, Prod.—Wheat grown in the same province ; the variety is known by the name of *recio ó claro*.

66 VALLADOLID.—Medina del Campo, Pedrosa, and Gomeznarro wheat.

67 TORRES, M. M. Seville.—Wheat (called *cerrado de color*), grown in the province of Seville, from Arahal.

68 TERNERO, J. Seville, Prod.—Wheat (called *pinton*). grown in the province of Seville, from Marchena.

69 FERNANDEZ DE CORDOBA, D. M. M. Constantina, Seville.—White wheat (known by the name of *papalina*).

70 GINOVES, J. Segovia.—Wheat (called *chamorra*) grown in the province of Segovia.

71 BECERRIL, A. Segovia.—Wheat, *candeal*, grown in the province of Segovia.

72 VALENCIA.—Rice: common in husk, and white moscado; long ; superior. Wheat: white ; from Alberique; canivano; red. Ears of nine varieties of rice. Four varieties of maize. Onions, white. Alubias del Pinet. Chufas Mani. Tares.

73 ENRIQUEZ, J. Alicante.—Sample of white maize.

74 CADIZ.—Barley, pearled, cultivated by D. Juan Colon, in San Lucar. Mustard seed, wild.

75 SALIDO, A. Ciudad Real, Prod.—Wheat (*candeal de raspa*), grown in the province of Ciudad Real. Guijas ó pitos, pulse. Yeros, a species of lentil. Rye.

76 CORPORATION OF CASTELLON.—Maize.

77 PENAFIEL, E. Ciudad Real, Prod.—Ceuchrus spicatus.

78 BENITO, M. Ciudad Real.—Panic grain, grown in the province of Ciudad Real.

79 GERONA.—Maize, of two kinds. Weld. Angelica. Valerian.

80 GRANADA.—Wheat, chamorro. Wheat, faufarrow lampino. Wheat, cuchareta. White maize. Sugar canes from Almunecar.

81 HUESCA.—Cereals, pulse, and fruits grown in the same province : White wheat, wheat, beans, round beans, almonds, walnuts, and dried peaches.

82 JAEN.—Dried peaches from Alcaudete and Bedmar. Wheat from Alcala la Real and Ubeda.

83 BARRIENTOS, Malaga.—Maize, grown in the province of Malaga.

84 PIEDROLA, M. Malaga, Prod.—Indian wheat, grown in the province of Malaga, cultivated in Churriana. Batatin, sweet potato.

85 CASADO, J. P. Malaga.—Wheat grown in the province of Malaga (of the kind called *chamorro*). Almonds (of the kind called *larga*). Vetches (*algarroba*).

86 MURCIA.—Beans (called *paniceras*). Capsicum pepper, ground (called *de flor*). Flour. Madder root. Root of *Anchusa tinctoria*. Weld.

87 MURCIA.—Wheat ; white wheat ; and Panic grain of two kinds.

88 MONFORT, F. Torrente del Cinca, Prod.—Wheat, rye, and beans. Different grains peculiar to the same province. Dried figs and peaches.

89 MARTINEZ Y PERIS, V. Valencia, Prod.—Rice grown in the province of Valencia.

90 FERNANDEZ VITORES, J. M. Valladolid.—Wheaten flour of first, second, and third qualities.

91 ZAMORA.—White wheat, from Hiniesta and Piedrahita de Casro. Beans, from Puebla de Sanabria. Flax, from Camarzana and Puebla de Sanabria. Weld, from Zamora. Lichen, from Puebla de Sanabria. Chamomile, from Villafáfila.

92 SARAGOSSA.—Amber wheat. Yellow maize. Amber. Alubias de Moncayo. Dried peaches, from Calatayud. Walnuts, from Calatayud. Figs, from Caspe. Treacle, from grape-sugar. Saffron.

93 HUELVA.—Beans. Large acorns, and branches of the oak which produces them.

94 AGRICULTURAL BOARD, MALAGA. — Chick-peas, from Alfamate. Walnuts. Chesnuts. Almonds. Drie peaches.

95 GIL, V. Segovia, Prod.—Chick-peas.

96 VALLADOLID.—Garbanzos chick-pea, grown in the province.

97 ALICANTE. — Almonds : pestaneta, p aneta, blanqueta, bitter, &c. Zahina (*Sorghum*).

98 VALGOMA, F. A. Cacabelos, Leon.—Dry chestnuts. Beans. Beans of superior quality. Various skeins of combed flax. Chestnuts.

99 THE AGRICULTURAL BOARD OF CORDOVA.—Dried figs. Olives. Zaragatona. Branches of olive. Mustard of Santaella.

100 ALBEAR, J. Cordova.—Prunes from Montilla.

101 ARAMBARRI, G. Cordova.—Sweet-smelling prunes.

103 ARAMBARRI, G. A. Cordova.—Dried figs.

104 LABAT, M. Cordova, Prod.—Giant walnuts, of peculiar kind, grown in the province of Cordova ; from Palma del Rio. Honey from orange-flowers.

105 CASADO, J. R. Malaga.—Muscatel raisins.

106 ENRIQUEZ, J. Malaga.—Dried figs.

107 OLMO, J. Malaga, Prod.—Prunes, cultivated at Priego. Dried figs.

108 MARQUEZ, J. Malaga, Prod.—Olives, cultivated in Alora and Casarabonella ; they are very mild, and easily separated from the stone.

109 THE BOARD OF TRADE OF REUS.—Almonds.

110 OVIEDO, Asturias. — Hazel nuts, chesnuts, and walnuts.

111 ZAMBRANO, J. Seville, Prod.—Olives (of the kind called *de figura*).

112 CARABE, M. Seville.—Olives (of the kind called *manzanillas á la reina*).

113 LESACA, J. J. Seville. — Giant olives from Padron.

114 BOARD OF AGRICULTURE, Tarragona, Prod.—Almonds. Hazel nuts.

115 BADAJOZ.—Sweet acorns.

116 PARDO Y BARTOLINI, Zaragoza.—Zaragatona, bryony, hound's tongue, viper's bugloss, melilot and liquorice.

117 ISERN, J. Barcelona.—Specimens of 105 indigenous

plants, the greater part growing at Monserrat, Mousen, and Monjuich, and many peculiar to Catalonia.

118 OVIEDO, ASTURIAS.—Extracts of aconite, belladona, lettuce, foxglove, orange-peel, and of sarsaparilla; honey of sarsaparilla; prepared sarsaparilla.

119 CANARY ISLANDS.—Euphorbia lathyris, known the islands as *tartaguillo*, and squills.

120 OVIEDO, ASTURIAS.—Prunus spinosa. Valeriana officinalis, root. Gentiana officinalis, root. Carqueja, flower. Digitalis purpurea, leaves. Carqueja, slips, with flower.

121 AMOR, J. Cordova.—Albarrana. Sarsaparilla.

122 GERONA.—Medicinal plants growing wild: Belladonna, pulsatilla, gentian, turbet, alchemilla vulgaris, digitalis purpurea, onosma echioides, polygonum bistorta, cynoglossum, saxifraga granulata, arnica montana, arbutus uva-ursi, aquilegia vulgaris, and tormentil.

123 HUESCA.—Herbs used in medicine, which grow wild in the province: Sage, foxglove, camomile, aristolochia, liquorice, zaragatona, aconite or monk's hood, lacines, wormwood.

124 PALENCIA, M. R. Leon.—Violet flowers. Arnica flowers. Lime flowers. Lichen.

125 MALAGA.—Artemisia arboresceus. Quercus torniglia. Atropa belladonna. Cotula aurea. Viola odorata.

126 BARTOLOME, M. Segovia.—Common sage.

126A GOMEZ, A. B. Havannah.—Various kinds of cigars.

126B GONZALEZ, C. M. Havannah.—Samples of cigars.

127 DURANGO Y TRIGO, Saragossa.—Lichen (*Cetraria islandica*). Wormwood. Sage. Arnica. Foxglove.

127BFERNANDEZ, D. F. Havannah.—Paper cigarettes.

128 MIRAT, G. Salamanca.—Two packets of superfine starch, in stick and powder.

128A ACADEMY OF MEDICINE AND SURGERY, Saragossa.— Lichen islandicus. Lichen pulmonalis. Salvia officinalis. Digitalis purpurea. Anthemis nobilis. Gentiana lutea. Valeriana officinalis. Aristolochia rotunda. Arnica montana. Atropa belladonna. Sarsaparilla. Liquorice.

129 ZABALA, P. V. Vitoria.—Extract of aconite.

130 ALMERIA.—Wheat from the Sierra de Filabres. Colocynth. Sage. Estacarocin, used as a spice, and for dyeing red.

131 PALMA.—"Majorca coralline."

132 THE AGRICULTURAL BOARD OF CASTELLON.— Branches of olive: varieties, called *Molvedrino, Morrudo, Fargo, Meno, Grosal, Blanco, Silvestre ó acebuche, Manzanillo, Colorado, Sevillano, Ulletrenco, Cuguello.*

133 MANSO, R. Logronno, Prod.—Preserved capsicums.

133A VAZQUEZ, J. Seville.—Liquorice.

134 BECK & Co. Seville.—Liquorice paste. Liquorice root.

136 HUELVA.—Grana lieres; cochineal dye.

137 GISBERT, J. Alicante.—Gualda dye or weld, a yellow dye.

138 CADIZ.—Madder root, from San Lucar.

139 CABELLO, D. E. Ciudad Real, Prod.—Samples of saffron.

139A CONTI, D. V. Corunna.—Beef, first and second quality. Bacon, best, with and without bone. Pork, cured in the American manner.

139B OVIEDO ASTURIAS.—Hams, from Aviles.

139C HUELVA.—Honey from Hinojos; chief produce of the place.

140 METESANZ, Z. Cuellar.—Madder.

141 CANARY ISLANDS.—Samples of madder, powder carmine, prepared from the same. Reseda luteola (Gualda).

142 VALLADOLID. — Madder, in plant, powder, and extract.

143 SEMOVILLA, R. Segovia.—Specimen of madder.

144 MATESANZ, A. Segovia.—Madder in powder.

145 MARTINEZ, D. Seville.—Weld.

146 TORRELOBATON.—Sumach (Rhus).

147 MARCOS, J. Vallodolid.—Extract of madder.

148 THE AGRICULTURAL BOARD OF ZARAGOZA.—Vegetable dyes, from cultivated and wild plants:—1 Alazor. 2 Madder. 3 Sumach. 4 "Pastal" blue. 5 "Gualda."

149 CRUZ, J. DE LA, Canary Islands.—Cochineal.

150 MERON, E. Malaga.—Specimens of cochineal.

151 ALCAIDE, D. M. G. Malaga.—Cochineal.

152 CALDERON, J. Granada.—Hemp, raw and combed. Flax and hemp seeds.

153 THE CORPORATION OF CASTELLON.—Raw hemp.

154 MURCIA.—Linseed. Cleaned hemp. Samples of hemp, unbroken and cleaned.

155 SARAGOSSA. — Hemp from Calatayud, raw and cleaned. Flax, from Borja.

156 MARTINEZ, P. Valencia, Manu.—Samples of hemp cordage, thread for sail-making, sail-cloth, and cotton stuff.

157 SAGRA (RAMON, DE LA).—Trunk of the plant Lagetta lintearia, showing the textile substance of the interior bark. Cord made from the fibres of the same. Cord and mat made from the textile fibres of the leaves of the palm and majagur. Yarn, extracted from the senegal hemp, and cord made from the same yarn.

158 HUESCA.—Vegetable productions used in manufactures:—11 Rush or grass, 12 flax, and 13 hemp.

159 PINAN, J Leon.—Flax, uncombed.

160 VINAS, A. Puerto Rico.—Fibre from the trunk of the plantain tree, in its raw state.

161 HERAS, DE LAS, Segovia.—Raw flax; flax combed.

162 VILLARS, J. B. Seville.—Raw cotton, growth of the province of Seville.

163 RIPALDA, COUNT, Valencia.—Combed hemp.

164 ALMERIA.—Common olive oil.

165 CORDOVA.—Olive oil, produced from the wild olive.

166 OVIEDO Asturias.—Nut oil.

167 MONTESINO, C. S. Estremadura.—Olive oil.

168 ZAYAS, J. Vega, Granada.—Olive oil, from the village of Niguëlas.

169 FERNANDEZ, M. Malaga.—Olive oil, filtered.

170 MURCIA, —.—Linseed oil, made in Lorca.

171 SEVILLE,—Olive oil, of the best quality made in the province.

172 DIEZ, DE RJBERA, Santa Fé, Granada.—Olive oil. Combed hemp.

173 THE BOARD OF AGRICULTURE, Valencia.—Olive oil of two qualities, produced by D. Vicente, Tortosa; olive oil, produced by D. José, Carrascosa.

174 THE COUNT OF SOBRADIEL, Saragossa.—Olive oil.

176 ENRIQUEZ, J. N. Velez Malaga.—Refined sugar, from the cane grown in the neighbourhood of Malaga. Made at the works of N. S. del Carmen, recently established at Torre del Mar, by M. R. dela Sagra.

177 OVIEDO, Asturias. — Preserved fruits and sweetmeats.

178 HUESCA, Manu.—Chocolate.

179 MARTINEZ, S. Vitoria, Manu.—Sweetmeats made from different fruits.

179A ZULUELA, J. DE, Havannah.—Samples of sugar.

180 MOLINA, A. Ciudad Real.—Virgin honey, from El Moral de Calatrava.

181 ABAD, M. Cordova.—Honey of orange flowers.

182 COLMENERO, F. Guadalajara, Prod.—Honey in the comb and clarified. White and yellow wax.

183 ESCUDERO, C. Guadalajara, Prod.—Honey in the comb.

184 CENTENERA, E. Guadalajara, Prod.—Honey in the comb.

185 BENJUMEA, J. M. Seville.—Honey from orange-flowers.

186 THE CABINET BOTANICAL GARDEN OF MADRID.—
Collection of specimens of woods employed in the Island
of Cuba for construction and other purposes. Sent from
Madrid. The list taken from the Botanical Section of
the Natural and Political History of the Island of Cuba, by
M. RAMON DE LA SAGRA.

187 The ECONOMICAL SOCIETY of MANILLA.—Collection
of 213 different species of wood growing in the Philippine
Islands. Collection of the different qualities of the tobacco-
leaf employed in the government factories in Manilla and
other places.

188 GUINART, J. Seville, Manu.—Corks and bungs.

189 GERONA.—Cork, in sheets.

189A BENJUMEA, J. M. Seville.—Honey from orange
flowers.

190 CASTELL, J. Esparraguera, Manu.—Specimens of
sail-cloth.

191 ROYAL ARSENAL, Carthagena, Manu. — Rigging.
Sail canvas.

192 ESCUDERO & ASZARA, Cervera del Rio, Manu.—
Sail-cloth.

192A BERENGUER, J. B. Valencia, Prod.—Cochineal.

193 MANUFACTORY OF ISABEL II. Ferrol, Manu. —
Linen. Canvas.

194 THE CORPORATION OF CASTELLON, Manu.—Hemp
socks. Mule furniture. Linens. Cables. Cordage. Lashings.
Pack thread.

195 EL BARON DE FINESTRAT, Alicante.—Skein of silk.

196 CANARY ISLANDS.—Silk from the *Marselles* and the
Trevoltino worm, and from the two varieties crossed.

197 PUJALS, F. Valencia, Prod.—Skeins of silk, of 4, 5,
6, and 7 cocoons.

198 GONZALEZ, S. Valencia, Prod.—Skeins of silk, of 4,
5, 6, 9, and 14 cocoons.

199 MURCIA. — Silk-worm gut, for fishing, first and
second qualities.

200 ALMANSA, D. Murcio.—Silk.

201 CRUZ, DE LA S. Sante Cruz de Tenerife.—Silk.
Cochineal.

202 MONFORT, F. Torrente de Cinca.—Silk produced in
the district. Silk from different worms, called *Trevoltinos,
de Raiko*, and *Turquia*.

203 MURCIA.—Skeins of spun silk. Chain of double
spun silk. Skein of spun silk, à la Piedmont, &c.

204 MARGUERIT, J. Barcelona, Manu.—Spun silk.

205 GARCIA, J. Murcia, Manu.—Specimens of spun
silk.

206 FERRER & Co. Roda, Manu.—Line flax and silk
thread.

207 REY & Co. Talavera, Manu.—Spun silk.

208 MONFORT, F. Torrento del Ciuco Huesca, Manu.—
Silk thread.

209 BOARD of AGRICULTURE, Valencia, Manu.—Spun
silk.

210 TRENOR, T. Valencia, Manu.—Specimens of spun
silk.

211 REINOSO, M. Valladolid, Manu.—Spun silk.

212 GINER, J. Villa Real, Manu.—Specimens of spun
silk.

213 ALCALA (the widow) & SON, Talavera, Manu.—
Silk thread. Silk stuffs.

214 ORDUNNA, V. Valencia, Manu.—Samples of silk
stuffs for draperies. Brocatel. Dress pieces of Chinese
and damasked gros. Velvet. Waistcoats of fancy velvet.
Damasks, velvets, square pattern.

215 DOTRES, GASPAR, & Co. Valencia, Manu.—Samples
of spun silk, white and yellow.

216 ROIG, J. Barcelona.—Picture in silk.

217 AMIGO, R. Barcelona, Manu.—Pieces of silk stuff
for umbrellas.

218 CASTILLO, M. Seville, Manu.—Specimens of silk
stuff.

219 MANUFACTURING Co. OF THE GUILDS, Talavera
and Ezcaray, Manu.—Silk and gold stuffs.

220 CALDERON, J. M. Granada, Manu.—Specimens of
spun silk.

221 FISTER, J. Barcelona, Manu.—Blonds: Large kerchief of black blonde with flowers; mantilla of black
blonde. Black and white blonde veils.

222 FISTER, —, Barcelona.—Dress and shawl of black
blonde, with coloured flowers.

223 MARGARIT & ENA, Barcelona, Manu.—Black lace
scarf. Dress, composed of skirt, body, sleeves, &c. White
blonde veil. Mantillas of black blonde, &c.

224 MUNICIO, V. Casla, Segovia.—Specimens of wool.

225 MONTERO, S. Seville.—Samples of fine wool, unwashed.

226 HUELVA.—Fine wool, from the flocks fed in the
Sierra de Audevalo.

227 The ECONOMICAL SOCIETY of TUDELA. — Wool
(called *churra*).

228 BARRASA, M. Valladolid.—1 White wool, washed·
2 The same, carded. 3 Brown wool, washed. 4 The same,
combed.

229 SARAGOSSA.—Black and white wool, and worsted,
from Ejea.

230 HERNANDEZ, J. Madrid, Prod.—Black and white
wool.

231 DELGADO, Zaragoza.—Hare and rabbit fur.

231A THE CORPORATION OF LUCENA, Castellon, Manu.—
A fulled cloth mantle.

232 THE CORPORATION OF MORELLA, Manu.—Travelling
bags of canvas. Travelling mantle. Two sashes.

233 The ALCALDE of Santa Maria de Nieva, Segovia,
Manu.—Coarse woollen cloth for winter clothing, of first
and second quality.

234 The ECONOMICAL SOCIETY (AMICOS DEL PAIS),
Bisayas Islands, Phillipine Isles.—Piece of "yloylo" stuff.
Various pieces, for a blouse. Piece of "jusi," and a shawl
of "jusi;" both worked.

235 ISLAND OF LUZON.— An apron; handkerchiefs;
camisets; collars and cuffs, embroidereed. Dresses and
shawls, with checks and stripes woven with "jusi." Cigar-
cases: crown of a hat, made of the filaments of "bejuco."

236 SMITH, CONSTABLE, & Co. Liverpool, per HAM-
MOND, W. P. & Co. London.—Embroidered Pinã muslin
dress from the Phillipine Islands, manufactured from the
fibre of the pine-apple, and embroidered by the Signora
Marguerita of Manilla. Pieces of striped Jusi dresses.

237 GILART, R. D. Madrid, Des. and Manu.—Shield of
the royal arms of Spain, in silk, gold, and silver. The baby-
linen made for the late Prince of Asturias.

238 ——, Mrs. G. M. Madrid.—Embroidered shirt.

239 BESCANZA, F. Corunna.—Cream of tartar. Bitar-
trate of potash.

240 ZABALA, P. V. Vitoria, Prod.—Schweinford green.
All the materials employed are of Spanish produce.

241 FLORES, CALDERON, & Co. Burgos.—Resins and
spirits of turpentine.

242 SANTO, D. C. Havannah.—Chemical products.

242A CANALES, J. Malaga.—Essence of lemons.

243 LEON Y RICO, E. DE, Madrid, Prod.—Hard soap,
made without the agency of heat.

244 GIRÓ, J. Malaga, Prod.—Variegated soap.

245 BERT, J. J. Madrid, Manu.—Various acids. Stearine
candles. Soaps.

246 BERT, J. DIRECTOR of the LIGHT MANUFACTORY.—
Wax-lights and vegetable wax candles, or stearine prepared
from oils. White oil-soap. Yellow oleine-soap.

247 GOLFERICHS & CUGAT, Barcelona. — Portable gas,
free from smell, and from smoke during combustion.

248 The Central Factory Philippine Islands, Manilla. —Specimens of cigars and cigarettes of the various kinds manufactured in the central factory of Manilla.

249 Jaren, J. A. Havannah.— Trusses of several sorts.

249a Vignaux, L. J. Barcelona, Manu.—Curried skins, for bootmakers. Enamelled leathers, for shoes. Glazed skins, for hatters. Leather, for saddlers, and coach and harness makers.

249b Roig, S. Barcelona, Manu.—Prepared fine skins, of various colours and gilt.

250 Economical Society of Manilla.— Samples of tobacco-leaf, and cases of cigars.

251 Partagas & Co. Havannah.—Case of cigars, imported by A. G. Wiltshire, 2 Lime Street Square, agent to Partagas & Co.

252 Carreras y Alberich, J. Barcelona.— Brass and steel combs for weaving.

253 Deu, G. Barcelona, Manu.—Cards for weaving.

253a Sastre, C. Lorca.—Woollen cloth.

253b Mendez, J. J. Lorca.— Woollen cloth.

253c Cruz De Arcas, D. Lorca.—Woollen cloth.

253d Moreno Brothers, Antequera, Mu.—Banaizes.

253e Trueba y Campo, Santander, Manu. — Woollen cloth, from the factory at Renedo.

254 Aleman, P. Ezcaray, Manu.—Cards for weaving.

255 Sastachs, J. Barcelona, Manu. — Wire cloth. Specimens of the various kinds manufactured by the exhibitor. Pair of paper moulds.

256 Belmonte, R. Navas Frias, Manu.—Two felt hats.

256a Ibarra, J. Plasencia, Manu.—Files.

257 Callejo, J. Madrid, Manu.—Locksmith's work.

258 Villardel & Callejas, Valladolid, Manu.—Kid gloves ; lambskin.

258a Baeches, A. Madrid, Manu.—Stirrups.

259 Sanches Pescador, and F. De Miguel, Madrid, Manu.—Bedstead of cast steel, with bronze ornaments, chased and gilt.

260 Miguel, F. De, Madrid, Manu.—Iron bedsteads and bed-room stand, with gilt and inlaid ornaments.

261 Moratilla, F. Madrid.—Tabernacle, silver-gilt, inlaid with precious stones.

262 Royal Ordnance Office, Onate, Manu.—1 Howitzer of wrought-iron, 16-inch calibre. 2 Mortar of wrought-iron, 9-inch calibre.

263 Royal Cannon Foundry, Seville.—A long howitzer, 9-inch calibre.

264 Zuloaga, E. Madrid, Manu.—Case, to contain a title nobility of Castille, of wrought-iron, with reliefs, incrustations, and Damascus-work of gold and silver.

264a Zuloaga, E. Madrid, Manu.—Two pairs of pistols and two hunting-knives, with their appurtenances, made of forged iron, with reliefs, incrustations, and damascenes. Cavalry sword damascened with gold and silver. Double-barrelled gun, mounted in the English fashion. Gun, mounted in the Spanish fashion.

265 Royal Ordnance, Placencia.—An infantry percussion musket and bayonet.

266 Royal Ordnance, Toledo.—Nine sword and sabre blades as used in the army. Ancient halberd, engraved and gilt. Dagger, enamelled and gilt. Case, with a silver blade, in form of a serpent.

267 Ysasi, M. De, Toledo.—Sword of extraordinary temper and flexibility, with metallic scabbard in the form of a serpent.

268 Ibarzabal, G. Biscay, Manu. — Two fowling-pieces.

269 Aretio, C. Biscay, Manu.—Two fowling-pieces.

270 Medina, M. Madrid, Prod.—Secretaire, with inlaid work.

270a Garate, M. de, Biscay, Manu.—A six-barrelled pistol.

271 Oppelt, E. Malaga, Manu.—Optical instruments.

271a Perez & Co. Barcelona, Inv. and Manu. — An octagonal table of inlaid wood, containing 3,000,000 pieces, the arms of England alone, in a space of 3 inches by 2, consisting of 53,000. This branch of industry has been introduced by the exhibitors.

272 Gallegos, J. Malaga, Inv. and Manu.—Guitarra harpa.

272a Settier, B. Valencia, Manu.—Thirty-three samples of straw-hats.

273 Cort y Marti, P. Madrid, Inv. and Manu.—Orthopedical apparatus. Lasts.

274 Leon, J. Madrid, Manu.—Artificial teeth.

274a Sena, Sorni F. de, Valencia, Manu.—Ribbons for decorations and fringes.

275 Yraburo, G. Madrid, Manu.—Decorations.

275a Island of Luzou.—Soap made from pure palm-oil.

276 Mir Brothers, Barcelona, Manu.— Lace trimmings.

280 Royal Ordnance, Trubia, Manu.—A bust, in iron, of H. M. the King of Spain, as taken from the mould.

281 Naury, J. B. Madrid, Prod.—1 Group of gilt bronze figures, representing an incident at a bull-fight. 2 Bronze group, representing the same. 3 Bronze figure, representing a Picador.

281a Gutierez de Leon, R. Malaga, Des. and Prod.—Three terra-cotta figures.

282 Pena, A. Madrid, Prod.—Terra-cotta figures.

283 Contreras, R. Aranjuez.—Arabesques, details from Alhambra.

284 Ysasi, M. de.—An original piece of the wall of the palace of the Alhambra at Granada.

285 Jimenez, M. Madrid.—Two wood mosaic pictures.

286 Pascual y Abad, A. Valencia, Prod.—Paintings for fans.

287 Mitjana, R. Malaga, Prod.—Fans, and paintings for fans.

289 Mata Aguilera, J. de, Madrid.—Model of one-half of the bull-fighting circus of Madrid, with 4,000 wooden figures, exhibiting various incidents in a bull-fight.

290 Carborell, M. Alcoy.—Travelling wrapper in the Jerezaro style, with wallet.

291 Portilla, —, Seville. — Samples of wheat and semouli.

292 Arrieda, —, Habana.—Samples of white sugar.

293 Bienaime, A. Rome, Sculp. (22 Newman Street).—Marble group : Love triumphant.

294 Portilla, —, Seville.—Wheat and semisole.

295 Arrieta, —, Havana.—White sugar.

ST. DOMINGO.
—— Area R. 30. ——

Transmitted by Sir R. Schomburgk, Her Majesty's Consul to the Dominican Republic.—Seventy-four specimens of mahogany and four of Espanillo or satin wood. Starch prepared from the plant, called Guayiga, found in great abundance in St. Domingo. Vegetable wax and "curiolis" prepared therefrom, the product of a shrief (probably the "*Myrica Ceriflora*" of Linnæus), indigenous to the northern parts of the Dominican Republic. A petrified mass of chanca, a wood used at St. Domingo for posts to construct huts, probably converted into stone after the hut had been burnt down, the wood still bearing the marks of fire.— (Received from St. Antonio Cotta, of the city of St. Domingo). Copper ore and allied rocks from the yet unexplored rocks of the interior of the island.

SWEDEN AND NORWAY.

1 LAGERHJELM, P. Christinehamn and Boforss, Sweden, Prod. and Prop.—Specimens of steel-iron and tough-iron; and also of the rock in which the mine is situated; the leading stone; the mineral intermixed with the ores; the ores and the analysis of them, showing their constituent parts, as to quantity and quality: the pig iron; the scoria; the blooms and the bars.

2 RETTIG, C. A. Gefle and Kihlaforss, Sweden, Prod. and Manu.—Iron ore from the Hammarin mines, in the district of Roslagen, near Stockholm; pig-iron from the same ore. Musket-barrels. Hardened steel, and polished work, from the same.

3 BLAST FURNACE OF GREKASAR, Orebro and Grekasar, Sweden, Prod.—Specimens of iron ore, in use at the blast furnace of Grekasar, province of Nerike. Pig-iron, and bar-iron, with specimen of the same bar-iron twisted into a spiral.

4 HELLEFORS IRON WORKS, Orebro and Hellefors, Sweden, Prod.—Specimens of iron ore in use at the blast furnace and foundry of Hellefors. Scoriæ and pig-iron from the same furnace.

5 OSTERBY IRON WORKS, Upsala and Osterby, Sweden, Prod. (Baron Tamm, Prop.)—Iron ore from Dannemora mines. Pig-iron, bar-iron, converted steel, and scoria from Osterby.

6 MOTALA IRON AND ENGINE WORKS, Motala, Ostergöthland, Sweden, Manu.—Round and square iron, tubes for steam-engine boilers, frames for iron vessels, edges for steam-engine boilers, plates from unballed and balled puddled iron; pig-iron for castings.

7 FLOOD, J. Porsgrund, Norway, Prod.—Specimens of iron ores and of bar-iron, from Bolvigs Ironworks, near Porsgrund.

8 HOE, H. Drontheim, Norway, Manu.—Specimens from the chrome manufactory, near Dromtheim.

9 TUNABERG COBALT WORKS, Sweden, Prod.—Crystals of cobalt, washed cobalt, oxide of cobalt, chaux metallique (calcinated).

10 ZETTERBERG, C. Eskilstuna, Sweden, Manu.—Specimens of sabres and swords.

11 IRONMONGERY from Eskilstuna, Sweden:—
HALLEBERG, L. J. Manu.— 1-26 Steel cutters. 27 Brace, with bits.
HELJESTRAND, C. V. Manu.—28 Razors.
LUNDQVIST, A. Manu.—29-33 Cutlery.
OESTERBERG, C. G. Manu.—34, 35 Cutlery.
SVALLING, F. Manu.—36-42. Cutlery.
OEBERG & Co. Manu.—43-50 Files and rasps.
RUDBERG, C. G. Manu.—51-56 Rasps.
THUNBERG, C. Manu.—57-62 Files and rasps.
HAGLUND, E. Manu.—63, 64 Files.
HEDLUND, J. Manu.—65-82 Padlocks.
BJÖRK, C. L. Manu.—83 Bench vice.
LUNDBERG, R. Manu.—84, 85 Locks.
ULANDER, F. Manu.—86, 87 Locks.
HALLENIUS & Co. Manu.—88-90 Locks. 91-106 Sundry ironware.
WALEN, J. Manu.—107, 108 Sundry ironware.
SPANGBERG & Co. Manu.—109-117 Sundry ironware.

12 STEELWARES, polished, etched, and gilt, by various makers at Eskilstuna :—
1 Paper scissors, polished.
2, 3 Rules, etched and gilt.
4, 5 Paper knives, gilt.
6 Paper scissors, gilt.
7 Steel plate, with a view of the Royal Palace at Stockholm.

12A STILLE, A. Stockholm, Manu.—Razors and paper knives, etched and gilt.

13 GODGARD FORGES, Norrköping and Godgärd, Sweden, Manu.—Box containing brads.

14 VIBERG, A. P. Falun, Sweden, Manu.—a Chemist's balance, with gramme weights. b Universal compasses. c, d, e Drawing instruments.

15 LITTMAN, E. Stockholm, Sweden, Manu.—1 Instrument for examining the bore of guns, and determining the amount of its elevation, when found deficient. 2 Chemist's balance, with gramme weights. 3 Universal compass. 4 Drawing instruments. 5 Miners' quadrant. 6 Levelling instrument, with stand. 7 Microscope.

16 GULDSMEDSHYTTAN MINES, Linde and Guldsmedshyttan, Sweden, Prod.—Specimens of silver and lead ores.

17 JOHANSSON, J. Stockholm, Sweden, Manu.—Specimens of stearine, and of stearine candles. Specimens of moulds for casting.

18 LAMM, S. L. Stockholm, Sweden, Manu.—Two large spermaceti candles.

19 WOOLLENS from Norköping, Sweden :—
BERGEWALL, F. Manu.—1 Specimens of broad-cloth. 2 Specimens of duffel.
SÖDERBERG & AROSENIUS, Manu.—3 Blue cloth dyed in the wool.
LANDMARK, T. Manu.—4 Specimens of brown cloth.
MALMGREN, C. T. Manu.—5 Specimen of mixed cloth.

20 Various samples of Swedish wool.

21 Specimens of flax, water-retted; broken by hand, and unhackled. From Angermaland in the north of Sweden.

22 Specimen of flaxen thread, spun by a girl thirteen years of age, in Angermanland.

23 Piece of linen, such as is made in hand-looms by the peasantry in Angermanland.

24 CASPARSSON & SCHMIDT, Stockholm, Sweden, Manu.—Specimens of silk, viz.: a Satin. b, c Moire façonné. d gros de Naples. e Black gros de Naples. f A shawl. g A neck-handkerchief.

25 MEYERSON, L. Stockholm, Sweden, Manu.—Specimens of silk, viz.: h Brocatelle, from silk produced in Sweden. i, k Taffetas quadrillé. l Gros de Naples. m Four shawlettes.

26 Samples of cotton goods, made in hand-looms, by the peasantry of the province of Westergöthland, without any dressing.

27 FURSTENHOFF, EMMA, Stockholm, Sweden, Manu.—Specimens of artificial flowers, executed in wax and other materials, for the purposes of ornament as well as botanical study.

28 HAMRÉN, SOPHIE, Halmstad, Sweden, Manu.—Needlework embroidery on muslin, representing the royal palace of Ulriksdal, near Stockholm.

29 HORN, Mrs. Halmstad, Sweden, Des. and Manu.—An embroidered pocket-handkerchief.

30 ALMGREN, K. A. Stockholm, Sweden, Manu.—A portrait of King Oscar, woven in silk.

31 HILLMAN, ADOLPH, Gefle, Sweden, Prop.—Statue in marble, representing a shepherd boy. Executed at Rome by Mr. Molin, a Swedish sculptor.

32 DE LIEWEN, Madlle. Sweden.—Portrait of Jenny Lind, sculptured in pasteboard by exhibitor.

33 JOHNSDOTTER, CHRISTINA M. Hernosaud and Sidensjo, Manu.—A skein of flaxen thread, 4,000 Swedish ells in length, and weighing less than half an ounce, woven by a peasant's daughter.

34 KONGSBERG SILVER WORKS, Norway, Prod.—Thirty-two specimens of silver in its different stages from the mine.

35 LOVENSKIOLD, —. Skein and Fossune, Norway, Prod. and Manu.—Specimens of iron ore and wrought iron.

36 TRESCHOW,—.Laurvig and Tritzoe, Norway, Manu.

.—Three iron bars knotted when cold, to exhibit their toughness, &c.

37 RORAAS COPPER WORKS, Norway, Prod.—Specimens of copper.

38 GARMANN, H. C. Drontheim, Norway, Prod.—Chromate of iron, raw, and purified by stamping and washing.

39 LEEREN MANUFACTORY, Drontheim and Leeren, Norway, Manu.—Bicromate of potash.

40 KONGSBERG MANUFACTORY OF ARMS, Norway.—A musket as made for the soldiers of the Norwegian army.

41 TORSTRUP, —. Christiania, Norway.—Specimens of pearls found on the coast of Norway, collected by the exhibitor.

42 ALNER, ANNA Madlle. Soderhaum, Sweden. — A portrait, in needlework, of Her Majesty the Queen of Great Britain.

44 THESEN, J. P. Christiania.—Various objects, carved by Norwegian peasantry, in wood, as bucket, coal tub and cover, tobacco and other boxes, jugs, spears, &c.

43 HJULA QUARRY, Christianea and Hjula (Norway). —Stone vase, boxes, &c.

45 ROSENKILDE, Christopher Stadshauptmand (Major), Christiansand, Norway.—Safety spring window, requiring no lines or weights.

For Nos. 46 to 117, *see* Addenda to Sweden and Norway, pp. 321, 322.

118 KULLGRIN, C. A. Uddewalla (Sweden), Manu.— Colossal monument of granite, in form of a cross, cut out of a single block. The stone remarkably fine grained, and exhibited as a sample both of quality, of material, and of workmanship. (See Objects outside the Building, Eastern End, p. 8.)

SWITZERLAND.

(Commissioners in London, Professor BOLLEY and Professor COLLADON, 39 Finsbury Square.)

1 NEUHAUS and BLÖSCH, Bienne, Manu.—Iron wire for making cards.

2 SUCHARD, P. Neuchâtel, Inv. and Manu.—Specimens of chocolate.

3 KEIGEL, F. A. Couvet, Canton of Neuchâtel, Inv. and Manu.—Pivot and depthning tool.

4 ERBRAU, J. Travers, Canton of Neuchâtel, Manu. —Turning, pivoting, depthning, and other tools.

5 JEANNET, F. Locle, Canton of Neuchâtel, Manu.— A rifle, with steel barrel.

6 BANDELIER, P. F. Locle, Canton of Neuchâtel, Inv. —Four watch-springs.

7 IUNOD BROTHERS, Canton of Vaud, Manu.—A repeating watch.

8 GRANDJEAN, H. Locle, Canton of Neuchâtel, Inv. and Manu.—Pocket chronometers. Gold hunting and other watches.

9 DUBOIS, F. W. Locle, Canton of Neuchâtel, Inv. and Manu.—An astronomical clock, with lever escapement. A marine chronometer, on a new calibre.

10 FAVRE-BRAND, F. E., Locle, Canton of Neuchâtel, Manu.—A pocket chronometer, with thermometer.

11 FAVRE-BRAND, A. Locle, Canton of Neuchâtel, Inv. and Manu.—Instrument for determining the epicycloidal curve of the teeth of wheels and pinions.

12 VUILLEUMIER, De LA R. Tramelan, Canton of Berne, Manu.—A repeating watch and clock. An eight-day watch. Ladies' and other watches, &c.

13 BOVET, F. Waldenbourg, Canton of Bâle, Inv.—A watch, going one year. A gold watch, *l'épine* movement.

14 RAUSS & COLOMB, Chauxdefonds, Canton of Neuchâtel, Manu.—Gold engine-turned watches.

15 MERMOD BROTHERS, Sainte Croix, Canton of Vaud, Manu.— A gold watch, size about one inch, &c. Gold watch

to go eight days. A chronometer. Gold and other watches.

16 DELY, M. Sonvilliers, Canton of Berne, Manu.— Two gold watches.

17 KOPP, H. F. J. Travers, Canton of Neuchâtel, Manu. —A repeating watch, &c.

18 PERRET, A. Brenets, Canton of Neuchâtel, Inv. and Prop.—Improved pocket-clock.

19 BOREL, H. J. Chauxdefonds, Canton of Neuchâtel, Manu.—Two travelling clocks, called imperials.

20 MOSER, F. jun. Bienne, Canton of Berne, Manu.— A gold watch.

21 PERRET & SON, Locle, Canton of Neuchâtel, Manu. —Several watches, in gold and silver cases.

22 AUDEMARS, L. Brassus, Canton of Vaud, Manu.— A watch with two dials, showing the phases of the moon, &c. A clock watch. Repeating watches. A pocket chronometer, and other watches. A pistol.

23 FAVRE, H. A. Locle, Canton of Neuchâtel, Inv. and Manu.—Pocket chronometers. A chronograph for taking the time of observations. Seconds watch.

24 GROSCLAUDE, C. H. Fleurier, Canton of Neuchâtel, Inv. and Manu.—Two open-faced watches.

25 LECOULTRE, A. Sentier, Canton of Vaud and Geneva, Inv. and Manu.—Pocket chronometers. Watch movements and pinions.

26 PAILLARD, E. & A. BROTHERS, Sainte Croix, Canton of Vaud, Manu.—A musical box; mandoline. Musical snuff-boxes.

27 JACCARD BROTHERS, Sainte Croix, Canton of Vaud, Manu.—Musical snuff-boxes.

28 VAUCHER, C. Fleurier, Canton of Neuchâtel, Manu. —A watch, with equations of time, &c.

29 EVARD, E. P. St. Blaise, Canton of Neuchâtel, Manu.—A gold watch.

30 GIRARD, P. Chauxdefonds, Canton of Neuchâtel, Manu.—A travelling clock.

31 BOCK, H. Locle, Canton of Neuchâtel, Manu.— Watches in silver cases.

32 LECOULTRE & SON, Brassus, Canton of Vaud, Manu. —A large musical box.

33 JAQUES & SON, St. Croix, Canton of Vaud, Manu.— Musical boxes; mandoline. Other boxes.

34 COURVOISIER, F. Chauxdefonds, Canton of Neuchâtel, Manu.—A gold pocket-chronometer. A gold hunting-watch. Gold watches of various descriptions.

35 BOVET & Co. Neuchâtel, Manu.—Cylinder prints. Handkerchiefs, jaconots, dress and furniture prints.

36 VAUCHER, DU PASQUIER & Co. Cortaillod, Canton of Neuchâtel, Manu.—Cotton prints, jaconots and muslins. (Agent, G. Bahud, 20 Bread Street, City.)

37 BOREL, BOYER, & Co. Neuchâtel, Inv. and Manu.— Mixed fabrics of thread and wool, &c.

38 JEANNERET BROTHERS, Neuchâtel, Inv. and Manu. —Basket. Hats and caps. Ladies' bonnets, &c.

39 PERRET, CHARLOTTE, Locle, Canton of Neuchâtel, Manu.—A piece of wide lace.

40 BESSON, A. D. Couvet, Canton of Neuchâtel, Manu. —White blonde.

41 MATHEY & SON, Locle, Canton of Neuchâtel, Manu. —A cylinder of rolled steel, for watch springs.

42 SCHNEITER, J. D. Tavannes, Canton of Berne, Inv. and Prod.—Map of Switzerland in relief.

43 DUBOIS, A. Chauxdefonds, Neuchâtel, Des. and Eng.—Gold plate, exhibiting ornamental designs for watchmaking, jewellery, &c.

44 PATTON, J. Chauxdefonds, Neuchâtel, Artist.—A gold plate, exhibiting letter-engraving in a new style.

45 KUNDERT, F. Chauxdefonds, Neuchâtel, Artist.— Engraved gold plates, representing Swiss subjects.

46 GRANDJEAN, P. H. Chauxdefonds, Artist.—Engraving on gold, applicable for watches, jewellery, &c.

47 FISCHER, J. Schaffhausen.—Ingots of meteor steel, and articles made of the same.

48 LAUTERBURG, F. 16 Rue de l'Arsenal, Berne, Prod.—Mineral waterproof composition, for linen, pasteboard, iron, &c.

49 PEDOLIN, P. Chur, Manu.—Soap-stone, or steatite, Polishing stone. Marbles.

50 GWINNER, J. Berne, Manu.—Water-colours. Tin pallet, with soft colours.

51 SOUTTER, G. Campagne des Lugeon, near Morges.—Tooth-powder.

52 BAUP, H. Vevey, Canton of Vaud, Inv.—Beef, mutton, veal, and fish, preserved in their natural state.

53 ROTH, J. Wangen, Canton of Berne, Prop.—Horse-hair and bullock's-hair.

54 FOGLIARDI, G. B. Melano, Canton of Tessin, Prop.—Raw silk.

55 LAUE, ELIZA, Wildegg, Canton of Argovie, Prod.—Raw silk; cocoons of silk.

56 LENDENMANN, T. C. Trub, near St. Gall, Canton of Appenzell, Manu.—Gelatine, for stiffening silks, &c.

57 STERN, A. Gunten, near Thoune, Canton of Berne, Prod.—Wood, for musical instruments.

58 LEDOUX, A. Geneva, Inv.—Frame of a double litho-graphic press.

59 SCHILT, V. Soleure, Inv. and Manu.—Calculating machine.

60 BOELSTLER, J. Arau, Canton of Argovie, Manu.—Improved machine for cutting bread.

61 DARIER, H. Geneva.—Press for cutting out and stamping watch hands.

62 SCHELLING & Co. Horgen, Canton of Zurich, Manu.—Sheets for cotton carding, and for sheep wool. Pillets. Leather cards.

63 STOTZER, F. Buren, Canton of Berne, Manu.—Files used for clock-making, and polishing instruments.

64 PAGAN, F. Geneva.—Tools for engraving on watch-cases and gold dials.

65 LAUE, F. Wildegg, Canton of Argovie, Inv. and Manu.—Patent boring apparatus for artesian wells.

66 KAPP, C. H. Lausanne.—Long bows of laburnum (or cytisus tree) of the Jura, with arrows.

67 PETER, J. Geneva.—Double shot gun.

68 SAUERBREY, V. Bâle, Manu.—Swiss rifle, and walnut case, with necessary apparatus.

69 VANNOD, J. Lausanne, Manu.—Improved fowling-piece, with apparatus.

70 CHOLLET, S. Mondon, Prop.—Aromatic cachou pitchfork; rakes; scythes; pruning-knife.

71 DESTRAZ, L. Mondon, Manu.—American fowling-piece, with apparatus. Barrel-churn. Bee-hive.

72 GISIN, J. Liestal, Bâle, Inv. and Manu.—Patent iron plough.

73 AUBERT, L. A. Lausanne, Manu.—Gold watch.

74 BARON & UHLMAN, Geneva. — Cylinder watches. Patent watches.

75 DAGUET, T. Soleure, Manu.—Flint-glass and crown-glass in rectangular prisms. Unpolished flint and crown-glass for optical uses.

76 DARIER, H. Geneva.—Samples of watch-hands and key-pipes.

77 DU COMMUN GIROD, Geneva, Manu. — Musical-boxes, carved and inlaid.

78 ELFROTH, D. H. Geneva, Manu.—Pen-holder watch.

79 FATIO, J. A. Geneva, Manu.—Gold watches.

80 FELCHLIN, C. Berne, Manu.—Bass clarionet. Box-wood clarionet. Ebony flute.

81 HOMMEL-ESSER, F. Aarau, Canton of Argovie, Manu.—Case of mathematical instruments. Pocket compasses.

82 FREY, A. J. G. Geneva, Manu.—Two upright tri-chord rosewood pianofortes.

83 GAY & LUQUIN, Geneva, Inv.—Musical box, imi-tating a military band.

84 GOLDSCHMID, J. Zurich, Manu.—Planimeter, by M. Wettli, for calculating the area of plane figures.

85 GYSI, F. Aarau, Canton of Argovie, Manu.—Case of mathematical instruments.

86 HUEBSCHER, C. Schaffhausen, Manu.—Bugle and other trumpets.

87 HUENI & HUBERT, Zurich, Inv. and Manu.—Patent harpsichord pianoforte.

88 KERN, J. Aarau, Canton of Argovie, Manu.—Ma-thematical instruments.

89 KUETZING, C. Berne, Manu.—A grand pianoforte.

90 LECOULTRE BROTHERS, Brassus, Canton of Vaud.—Musical box and pianoforte.

91 LEUBA, H. sen. Bâle, Manu.—Travelling clocks,

92 GOLAY-LERECHE, A. — Pocket chronometer with repeater and thermometer.

93 LOMBARD-JANPEAU, C. A. Geneva.—Wooden leg, used for amputation either below or above the knee.

94 LUTZ, —, sen. Geneva, Inv. and Manu.—Hair-springs suited to marine and other chronometers.

95 MASSET, L. Yverdon, Canton de Vaud, Inv. and Manu.—Patent planetarium.

96 MERCIER, S. Geneva, Manu.—A chronometer. Half chronometer for the use of the deaf and blind. Watch.

97 METERT & LANGDORF, Geneva, Manu.—Musical boxes. Mandoline, in black case.

98 MEYLAN-GOLAY, H. Geneva.—Gold repeating watch.

99 PATEK, PHILLIP, & Co. Geneva, Inv. and Manu.—Chrometers, watches, repeaters, &c. new winding-up by the pendant.

100 PUPINNAT, F. H. Lausanne, Manu.—Two violins and a violoncello; two violin bows.

101 RETOR, F. Geneva. — Chronometer. Strong de-tached lever escapement.

102 SCHNEIDER, F. Berne, Prop.—Relief, representing a view of the Jungfrau. Artificial teeth.

103 SPRECHER & BAER, Zurich, Manu.—Pianoforte.

104 JACCARD, L. Lausanne. — Biconcave, periscopic, convex, and concave glasses. Magnifying glasses.

105 PAQUET-FAZY, Mde. Geneva.—Watch spiral springs.

106 JUNOD, T. Lausanne, M.D.—Apparatus to super-sede, in many instances, bleeding, leeches, and cupping, without the loss of blood.

107 WERMUTH, J. Signau, Canton of Berne, Prod. and Prop.—Osteotome (a chirurgical instrument).

108 ZIEGLER, H. Winterthur, Canton of Zurich, Prop.—Machine for measuring the distance of gun-balls from the centre.

109 ALDER & MEYER, Herisau, near St. Gall, Canton of Appenzell, Manu.—White embroidered muslin for ladies' dresses. Embroidered curtains and bed-cover. Cravats, &c.

110 ALTHER, J. C. Speicher, near St. Gall, Canton of Appenzell, Manu.—Embroidered muslin.

111 ANDEREGG, T. St. Gall, Manu.—Ginghams; jaconet; cambric; cotton; and cottonade. Shawls; tartans; chinés; handkerchiefs. Nainzooks.

112 BAENZIGER & Co. St. Gall, Imp.—Muslins; bal-zorines; cravats; shawls. Ladies' dresses and handker-chiefs.

113 BEUGGER, J. Wülflingen, Canton of Zurich, Manu.—Ropes of cotton-yarns, bobbins, warp, and woof.

114 BLUM, T. G. Winterthur, Canton of Zurich, Manu.—Parcel of cotton-yarn.

115 BOESCH & SONS, Ebnat, Canton of St. Gall, Manu.—Muslin ginghams; shawls; handkerchiefs; cravats; scarfs; Barège, &c.

116 BLUMER & IENNY, Schwanden, Canton of Glarcis, Manu.—Cotton, muslin, and jaconet tasmas printed hand-kerchiefs. Chintz cotton damask.

117 Breitenstein, J. & Co. Zofingen, Canton of Argovie, Manu.—Cotton for ladies' dresses and aprons. Table-cloths, handkerchiefs, &c.

118 Bruderer. J. Teufen, near St. Gall, Canton of Appenzell, Manu.—Robes; aprons; violas; plis.

119 Braendlin Brothers, Rapperschwyl, and Hurlimmann, J. Richterschwyl-Uznach, Canton of St. Gall, Manu.—Three large ropes of cotton warp, spun from Egyptian mats.

120 Buchler & Sons, Rollbruner, Winterthur, Canton of Zurich, Manu.—Cotton-yarn.

121 Clais (Von), C. S. Winterthur, Canton of Zurich. —Specimens of cotton yarn warp.

122 Fehr, J. C. St. Gall, Manu.—Jaconet. Gauze; figured muslin; bobbinet shawl; muslin dress.

123 Greuter & Riester Brothers, Winterthur, Canton of Zurich, Manu.—Turkey-red printed calicoes; and union check. Hankerchiefs.

124 Heiniger, J. Berthoud, near Berne, Manu.—Cotton canvas and fine Java, coloured and striped. New canvas.

125 Huerlimann, J. Richterswyl, Canton of Zurich, Manu.—Red and brown printed chintz. Jaconets, for ladies' dresses. Muslin.

126 Imhoof, B Winterthur, Canton of Zurich, Manu. —Specimens of cotton yarn warp.

127 Imhoof, Brunner, & Co. Winterthur, Zurich, Manu.—Muslins.

128 Kunz, A. Uster, Canton of Zurich, Manu.—Yarns, twists, &c. Thread for ribbons; sewing thread; woollen cloth.

129 Lauterburg, J. & Co. Langnau, Canton of Berne, Manu.—White drill, cotton and thread; cotton; and mixed coloured.

130 Leumann Brothers, Mattweil, Canton of Thurgovie, Manu.—Turkey-red and rose-dyed cotton yarns of different numbers.

131 Naef, M. Niederuzwyl, Canton of St. Gall, Manu. —Moreas, half cotton; luting, satined; hakirs; gingham, &c.

132 Rieter, T. J. & Co. Winterthur, Canton of Zurich, Manu.—Cotton yarn.

133 Rikli, A. F. Wangen, near Berne, Prod.—Spun cotton, dyed red.

134 Schiesser, G. Hard, near Zurich, Manu.—Handkerchiefs printed on both sides.

135 Schlaepfer, J. Herisau, Canton of Appenzell, Manu. and Imp.—Plain muslin.

136 Schmid, H. Gattickon, Canton of Zurich, Manu.— Cotton yarn warp and woof.

137 Schwarz, H. Rickon, near Winterthur, Zurich, Manu.—Specimens of cotton yarn.

138 Springer, J. J. Schaffhausen, Imp.—Hand-spun yarn.

139 Sturzenneger-Nef, L. St. Gall, Manu.—Printed cravats on jaconets; jaconets, steam-dyed, &c.

140 Vonwiller, U. de G. St. Gall, Imp.—Plain white tarlatan and muslin. Fancy muslin dresses; figured muslins; spotted jaconets, &c. Collars and pocket handkerchiefs. Embroidered collars and veils.

141 Walty Brothers, Schöftland, Canton of Argovie, Manu.- Silk handkerchiefs, cravats, cords, &c.

142 Winkler, T. C. Friedthall, Canton of Zurich, Manu —Cotton yarn chain.

143 Zaehner & Schiess, Herisau, Canton of Appenzell, Manu.—Tarlatan, croched; muslin curtains and nets; batiste handkerchiefs, embroidered.

144 Zeller, H. Zurich, Dyer.—Spun cotton, Turkey-red dyed.

145 Zellweger, S. Trogen, Canton of Appenzell, Imp. —Glazed jaconets, woven from Swiss-twist.

146 Ziegler, T. & Co. Winterthur, Manu.—Merinos, prints, cottons, and yarns red dyed.

147 Billeter, Z. Herzogenmulle, Zurich, Manu.— Specimens of cotton yarn.

148 Custer & Schachtler, Altstädten, Canton of St. Gall, Manu. and Imp. Orleans quadrillé; façonné, and broché; half silk broché.

149 Ernst, F. Winterthur, Canton of Zurich, Manu.— Mixed coloured cassinets.

150 Kelly, J. J. of Mettendorf, near St. Gall, Manu. —Turkey-red cloth and prints.

151 Mueller, Pluess, & Co. Zofingen, Canton of Argovie, Manu.—Merinos, tartans, and poil de chevre, half wool; and various mixed fabrics.

152 Manufacturers of Silk Ribbons.—Twenty-one glass cases, containing 2,814 specimens of ribbons, from the following houses:—

Koechlin & Sons, Bâle;
H. A. Senn & Suter, Zofingud;
Jean Franç. Sarasin, Bâle;
B. di B. Straehelin, Bâle;
Sulger & Stucelckelbe rger, Bâle;
Buxtorf & Bischoff, Bâle;
Freres Bischoff, Bâle;
T. F. & T. Frey, Arau;
Charles Ryhiner, Bâle;
Lui. Preiswerck, Bâle;
Siber Bischoff, Bâle;
Richter Linder, Bâle;
T. De Bary & Bischoff, Bâle;

F. Feer & Co. Arau.
Waldner & Staehelin, Bâle;
Dietrich Burckhardt, Bâle;
Goetz & Ecklin, Bâle;
T. T. Bakofen & Sons, Bâle;
Freyvogel & Heussler, Bâle;
Emanuel Hoffman, Bâle;
M. Oswald & Co. Bâle;
Frey Thurneisen & Christ, Bâle;
T. B. Burckhard & Sons, Bâle;
D. Preiswerck & Co. Bâle;
Soller & Co. Bâle;
Sarasin & Co. Bâle.

153 Forty-two Manufacturers of Silk Stuffs, Canton of Zurich.—Silk stuffs. Velvet for waistcoats, aprons, handkerchiefs. Exhibited for cheapness and quality.

154 Alioth, T. S. & Co. Basle, Inv.—Samples of spun silk for foulards; and damask silk, and wool, made of silk wastes.

155 Lotz, F.; Wegner, T. R.; Muller, F.; Romain, jun. Bâle. Silk-dyers.—Specimens of silk.

156 Baenziger, Kolp, & Co. Ebnat, St. Gall, Prod.— Madras handkerchiefs. Saxonies. Checks and stripes. Ginghams.

157 Bischoff, C. J. Manu.—Black satin. Gros du Rhin. Serge.

158 Boelger, M. Bâle, Manu.—Specimens of spun silk warp for furniture stuffs; woof for half-silk stuffs.

159 Cuendet, Adeline, Geneva.—Scarf (points de Genève).

160 Mueller, T. B. & Co. Wyl, near St. Gall, Manu. —Handkerchiefs; romals; shawls, damasked; tartans; scarfs; ginghams; satins; Moreas; demi-cottons, &c.

161 Ryhiner & Sons, Bâle, Manu.—Machine-spun silk for silk and worsted damask, handkerchiefs, gloves, &c.

162 Von der Muehl Brothers, Basle, Manu.—Gros de Naples, four qualities. Serge. Taffetas. Gros de Rhine.

163 Beck & Sons, Miescher & Sons, Fankhauser Brothers, Schmid Brothers, Berne, Berthoud, and Eriswyl, Canton of Berne, Manu.—White linen handkerchiefs; table linen; towels. Drill tick, cotton and linen tick.

164 Haag & Son, Libefeld, near Berne, Manu.—Samples of linen.

165 Hanselmann, J. Güttingen, Canton of Thurgovie, Manu.—Morning jacket of fine Thurgovie linen.

166 Hunziker & Co. Aarau, Canton of Argovie, Manu —Coutils; toiles du nord, linen and cotton; cotonades; ginghams; handkerchiefs.

167 Miescher & Co. Berthoud, Canton of Berne, Manu. —Sewing thread.

168 Raschle & Co. Wattwill, Canton of St. Gall, Manu.—Handkerchiefs: Veronas, Madras, Indian, paillacats, mazzulipatams. Cottonets, ginghams, cambrics, &c.

169 Roethlisberger & Sons, Walkringen, near Berne,

Manu.—Towels, table cloth, table linen, and table napkins. Bleached linen for shirts, &c. Handkerchiefs, drill, &c.

170 REYMOND, jun. Morges, Manu.—Diapered skins: Calf-skin in different states.

171 GISSIGER, V. Laufen, near Bâle, Manu.—Dressed hides for harness and coaches; calf-skins, &c.

172 HAUSER, J. de J. Waedenschwyl, Canton of Zurich, Manu.—Leather for soles.

173 IMHOF & SONS, Bâle, Manu.—Sole leather. Calf-skins. Goat-skins.

174 KAPPELER, F. Frauenfeld, Canton of Thurgovie, Manu.—Sole leather.

175 MERCIER, J. J. Lausanne, Canton of Vaud, Manu. —Calf and morocco leathers: boot-legs, fronts, and backs. Chamois, calf, and sheep-skins.

176 MEYER & AMMANN, Winterthur, Zurich, Manu.— Calf-skins. Morocco. Sheep-skins.

177 MUELLER & Co. Aarau, Canton of Argovie, Manu. —Calf-skins in different states.

178 RAICHLEN, L. Geneva, Manu.—Strong sole leather, and strong white leather, for bands. Calf boot-fronts.

179 RESSEGUEIRE, C. Geneva, Manu. — Calf-leather. Cordovan, dyed. Kid leather, for gloves.

180 SCHALCH, A. Schaffhausen, Manu.—Leather for ladies' shoes. Goat-skins, for bookbinders. Fine parchment and calf-skins.

181 SPENGLER, H. Hasli, Canton of Thurgovie, Manu. —Sole leather.

182 THURNEISEN, —, Bâle, Manu.—Superfine paper, for prints and lithography.

183 STEINLIN, F. on the Sihl, city of Zurich, Manu.— Pasteboard. Silk paper. Paper of various kinds. Writing books and music paper.

184 BONTEMS, C. Geneva.—Black silk for sewing.

185 HUG-ITH, Schaffhausen, Imp.—Scarlet cloth dyed at Schaffhausen.

186 SULZER, G. Winterthur, Canton of Zurich.— "Moreas à flamines. Coutnys à flames satiné."

187 SULZER, H. Adorf, Canton of Thurgovie, Manu.— Calicoes of various descriptions.

188 BAENZIGER, J. Thal, near St. Gall, Manu.—Specimens of needlework and embroidery. Handkerchief with lace border. Plain muslins and jaconet.

189 DEPIERRE BROTHERS, Heiden, Canton of Appenzell, near St. Gall, Manu.—Specimens of embroidery on tulle. Veils, on white and black tulle. Cambric handkerchief.

190 EUGSTER BROTHERS, Speicher, Canton of Appenzell, Manu.—Muslin curtains. Curtains, embroidered, with net appliqué.

191 EHRENZELLER, F. St. Gall, Imp.—Embroidered curtains of various kinds.

192 FISCH BROTHERS, Buehler, Canton of Appenzell, Manu.—Muslin dress and curtains embroidered.

193 FORSTER, J. B. Ober-Utzwyl, St. Gall, Manu.— Muslin robes. Gauze and jaconet. Gauze and muslin shawl.

194 HERMANN, F. Diessenhosen, Thurgovie, Manu.— American carpet stuffs. Piece of printed calicoes.

195 HOLDEREGGER, C. St. Gall, Canton of St. Gall, Manu.—Curtains, embroidered on muslin and tulle; guipure appliqué, and long point, and other embroidered goods.

196 KOELLREUTTER, F. St. Gall, Manu.—Specimens of cotton embroidery on muslin, ornamented with flowers. Handkerchief.

197 METTLER & SON, Hemberg, Canton of St. Gall, Manu.—Ginghams. Jaconets. Robes. Muslins. Cravats. Handkerchiefs. Shawls.

198 NEF, J. J. Herisau, Canton of Appenzell, Manu.— Swiss muslin. Tamboured gauze balzorine, and nainzook. Striped gauze, Figured muslin.

199 PAULY, G. & A. Canton St. Gall, Manu.—Embroidered collar, and chemisette. Pelerine.

200 SCHIESS, E. Herisau, Canton of Appenzell, Manu.— Veil of cambric needlework.

201 SCHLAEPFER, SCHLATTER, & KURSTEINER, St. Gall, Manu.—Lace and muslin curtains. Muslin dress Tarlatan. White Jacquard muslin. Shawls with needlework and fringes, &c.

202 SCHOCH, SCHIESS, & SON, Herisau, Canton of Appenzell, Manu.—Embroidered handkerchiefs, and collar.

203 SUTTER, J. J. Bühler, Canton of Appenzell, Manu. —Curtains. Ladies' dresses and handkerchiefs, embroidered. Pelerine mantelets.

204 TANNER, B. St. Gall, Manu.—Embroidered muslins.

205 TANNER, J. U. Bühler, Canton of Appenzell, Manu. —Silk pocket-handkerchiefs. Curtain and bed-cover, muslin and silk, embroidered. Pictures of silk.

206 TANNER & KOLLER, Herisau, Canton of Appenzell, Manu.—Muslin scarfs, dresses, and shawls. Embroidered muslin curtain, and robes.

207 WALDBURGER & LANGENEGGER, Bühler, Canton of Appenzell, Manu.—Embroidered robes of silk.

208 STAEHELI-WILD, C. St. Gall, Manu.—Embroidered table-cloths. Curtains, and handkerchief, French cambric.

209 ZUPPINGER, T. Maennedorf, Canton of Zurich, Inv.—Carpet of new velvet, woven.

210 BALLY & Co. Schoenenwerd, Canton of Soleure, Manu.—Braces, elastic and non-elastic.

211 DIETIKER, J. Berne, Manu.—Japanned leather boots, red morocco legs.

212 FREY, T. F. & T. Aarau, Canton of Argovie, Manu. —Elastic braces and garters. Elastic cotton belts.

213 ISLER & OTTO, Wildegg, Canton of Argovie, Manu. —Laces, a new application of straw, for ladies' bonnets, &c.

214 LECOULTRE BROTHERS, Brassus, Vaud.—Razors à sonnettes. Razors with several blades.

215 LECOULTRE, J. Sentier, Canton of Vaud.—Razors of various kinds.

216 GRAESER & SCHWEIZER, Rheinau, Canton of Zurich, Manu.—Metallic cloth. Iron wire flower-pot.

217 SCHEITLIN, H. & D. Canton of St. Gall, Manu.— Buttons for coats and ladies' dresses. Umbrella, curtain, and boddice rings.

218 SCHOPFER, S. Gessnay, Canton of Berne, Founder. —Cow bells.

219 DUTERTRE, A. Geneva.—Gold pocket-book. Gold cigar-case, with watch. Gold purse, ring, and bracelet. Walking-stick head, &c.

220 GOLAY, L. Geneva.—Gold souvenir, with watch.

221 FRIES, H. Canton of Zurich, Des. and Manu.— Embossed drinking cup.

222 MASSY, J. F. Sentier, Canton of Vaud.—Imitative gems.

223 VERET, J. Nyon, Canton of Vaud.—Crystal of quartz. Imitation topaz.

224 FLUEKK, J. Brienz, Canton of Berne, Manu.— Table of maple-wood.

225 MEYSTRE, E. Lausanne.—Two turned cups and a watch-stand, made by a pupil of the Asylum for the Blind.

226 VOGEL, A. Thoune, Canton of Berne, Manu.— Round table, made of 28 different kinds of wood, inlaid with 38,000 pieces.

227 ABT BROTHERS, Buenzen, BRUGGISSER & Co., DUBLER & SONS, GEISSMANN & Co.; ISLER, J. jun.; ISLER, J. & Co.; ISLER, J. & SON; MEYER BROTHERS; WOHLER & Co. Wohlen, Canton of Argovie, Manu.—Twisted straw, willow chip, and plaits. Horsehair and manilla plaits. Plaited trimmings. Feathers. Flowers. Bags. Slippers. Carpet, &c.

228 CLARAZ, A. Fribourg, Manu.—Flowers, plumes, and wreaths, made of straw, for bonnets. Straw bonnets, plaits, trimmings, &c.

229 Faessler, J. A. Appenzell, Manu.—Milk tubs in miniature.

230 Hartmann, L. & Co. Fribourg, Manu.—Stalks of wheat grown in the Canton of Fribourg, prepared for straw plaiting. Specimens of plaiting. Ladies bonnets.

231 Hurter & Buholzer, Lucerne, Manu.—Horse-hair, double and single tress.

232 Lendenmann, J. C. Grub, Canton of Appenzell, Inv. and Manu.—Printers' rollers, made of "Swiss imitation caoutchouc;" it is elastic, tough, soluble in water, and capable of adaptation to different temperatures.

233 Piece, Louisa, Geneva.—Caoutchouc knit-stockings for invalids.

234 Sulzberger & Akermann, Meisterschwanden, Manu.—Horse-hair and silk lace. Lace made of Ostindian hemp, horse-hair and silk. Specimen of cabas, cigar-cases, tassels, and straw ornaments. Straw rope. Tresses of Indian hemp and silk. Bleached straw, bleached wood.

235 Baatard, J. A. Lausanne.—Plated work-box, with mahogany wood and steps.

236 Bautte, T. F. Geneva, Manu.—Presse-papier, in gold-enamelled rococo style; the base ornamented with painted views; groups of flowers, painted in enamel upon gold, with a mechanical singing bird.

237 Wettli, M. L. Berne, Manu.—Lady's mechanical escrutoire, of white wood, can be used for writing in a sitting or standing posture. Carved work, representing the rustic economy and Alpine life of the inhabitants of Switzerland.

238 Flueck, Elizabeth, Brienz, Canton of Berne, Manu.—Lady's work-basket, carved in maple-wood.

239 Baumann, A. Brienz, Canton of Berne, Carver.—A box, in white wood; the carving on the cover, represents the Alpine rose. Box of yew-tree wood, ornamented in carving with the garden rose and a garland of flowers. Small box, made of yew-tree wood, inlaid, &c.

240 Chenevard, L. Geneva.—Enamelled map of the islands of Great Britain: illustrating an application of enamelled painting to the improvements of maps.

241 Hess, L. Au Jeu de l'Arc, Geneva, Painter.—Enamels: Young Beggar, after Murillo. The Card-player, after Julius David. Jane of Arragon, after Raphael. The Bride of Lammermoor, after Tony Johanot. The Guardian Angel after Decaisne. Venus and Cupid, after Titian, &c.

242 Kehrli Brothers, Schwendi, near Meyringen, Canton of Berne.—Box-wood salad spoon and fork, ruler, drinking-cup for children, nut-crackers, folder, handle of chamois-horns, &c. Painted plate, sculptured by Daniel Wœgelin, of Thoune.

243 Kessler, N. Fribourg, Des. and Carver.—Statue representing Father Girard, a Franciscan friar.

244 Klarer, J. A. Appenzell, Canton of Appenzell.—Ornament, or jewel-case, of nut-tree wood, ornamented with figures, in the costume of the Canton of Appenzell, William Tell's shot, and other representations of Swiss characters and events.

245 Lombard, A. C. Geneva, Inv. and Prod.—Five enamels: Minature pocket-compass, with portrait of Admiral Nelson. Mourning dial, Turkisk calendar-dial, Chinese dial, and Romish dial.

246 Hallmeyer-Appenzeller, A. St. Gall, Manu.—Chimney-screen, with a view of Meyringen, Canton of Berne. The composition is a combination of the plastic art with that of the maker of artificial flowers.

247 Mezener, J. Jaun, near Meyringen, Canton of Berne.—Group of ten chamois and huntsmen, on a hill.

248 Michel, G. Brienz, Canton of Berne, Carver.—Peasant's farm-house in the Bernese Oberland, with its dependencies. By removing the roof, the interior, even to the cellar, is exposed to view, with the furniture, &c.

249 Dufaux, O. Geneva.—Full-length portrait of Her Majesty Queen Victoria, painted in enamel after Chalon. Painted with new colours, made in Geneva, by L. Dufaux, sen.

250 Schild, J. Brienz, Canton of Berne, Carver.—Carved table. Bernese peasant's habitation.

251 Schæck, Madame, Geneva. Paintings on alabaster, whitened and hardened for brooches and other articles of jewellery, covers of chests, boxes, and paper weights.

252 Schoell, C. A. St. Gall, Inv. and Mod.—Model in relief of the mountains of Appenzell, including a surface of about 130 square miles. The apparatus and the plastic substance of the relief are the exhibitor's own invention.

253 Spalinger, J. Schaffhausen.—Album, with several woodcuts, executed by the exhibitor. The drawings were executed by several Swiss artists.

254 Stoetzner, C. F. & Co. Schaffhausen, Prod.—Galvano-typic plates, subjects composed and drawn by M. Bendel, Munich, &c. The object of the galvano-typic plates is, to supply the place of woodcuts at a cheaper rate.

255 Jaun, T. Meyringen, Canton of Berne, Carver.—A group of nine chamois and huntsmen, carved in maple wood.

256 Ueltschi, J. Oberwyl, Canton of Berne, Manu.—Brooches, watch-keys, shirt buttons, and rings, made of chamois horns, &c.

257 Wyttenbach, C. Berne, Prop.—Model in relief of the cathedral of Strasburg, executed in card-paper, by J. Leemann, Zurich, executed with a penknife by a working bookbinder, who was employed on it incessantly for three years.

258 Leemann, J. Berne, Carver.—A model, representing a fountain erected on the market-place of Nuremberg, in Bavaria, by the celebrated masons George and Frederic Rupruht; the figures were executed by Sebald Schonhofes.

259 Wirtz, J. Berne, Painter.—A table in white wood, with view of Tell's chapel, and the costumes of the twenty-two Cantons. A table, with the view of the Bandekfall. A desk, with a view of the Siessbach, and other articles in painted wood. Letter-back, with the view of the Wengeralp.

260 Ziegler-Pellis, J. Winterthur, Canton of Zurich, Manu.—Divers articles of pottery ware, raw and glazed. The large pieces are exhibited for fineness and exactness in the expression of the medallions, &c.

261 Geilinger Brothers, Winterthur, Canton of Zurich.—Yasmas, dyed and printed.

262 Lecoultre, G. Canton of Vaud, Manu.—Razor with seven blades. Razors with three, two, and one blade, buffalo handle, &c.

263 Lecoultre & Golay, Canton of Vaud, Watch-maker.—Large pinion with twenty teeth; others with sixteen, twelve, eight, seven, and six teeth, fixed on a wheel.

264 Schuchmann, W. Canton of Neufchâtel, Engraver.—Two coins, engraved in steel; the one representing a group of two persons, the other the head of a warrior.

265 Fischer, E. Chur, Canton of Granbudten, Manu.—A double American rifle with two barrels and only one trigger; the right barrel straight, the left with a half winding.

266 Piguet Brothers, Sentier, Canton of Vaud, Manu.—A gold watch, enamel dial, duplex escapement, five rubies, maroquin case.

267 Paillard Brothers, E. A. St. Croix, Canton of Vaud, Manu.—A gold watch, five rubies, portrait of the Queen of Holland, with diamonds. A gold watch, five rubies, to wind up by the pendant.

268 Kramer, A. Locle, Canton of Neufchâtel, Manu.—A gold watch, independent seconds, and metal thermometer; twenty holes in rubies, compensation balance.

269 Schmid Brothers, Thalweil, Canton of Zurich, Manu.—Silk handkerchiefs; the weaving, printing, finishing, and entire manufacture by the exhibitors: warp silk, woof samples of spun silk, called shappe sublime.

270 BURKHARDT, J. Zurzach, Canton of Argovie. An assortment of improved razors and razor-strops.

271 PERRET, C. Chaux de Fonds, Canton Neufchâtel.—Thread lace.

272 GIMPER, G. Zurich.—Toothpowder, &c.

273 PIQUET BROTHERS, Sentier, Canton de Vaud.—Gold watch.

274 PATEK, PHILIPPE, & Co. (late PATEK & Co.), Geneva, Manu. & Inv.—Assortment of watches, highly finished, with all the modern improvements, and various species of ornaments.

TUNIS.

TUNISIAN PRODUCTIONS, sent for exhibition by order of His Highness MUSHIR BASHA, Bey of Tunis, under care of SY HAMDA ELMKADDEN, Pro-Commissary appointed for the occasion, and MOSES SANTILLANA, Interpreter to his Excellency General SIDY MAHMOUD BENYAD, the Bey's Commissioner, 9 China Terrace, Kennington Road.

1 Small blankets, manufactured at Gafsa. Mantles, wool and silk.

2 Small blankets, with silk, &c. Mantles, with stripes.

3 and 4 Gafsa blankets, with silk, &c. Mantles, with stripes.

5 Gafsa blankets, wool. Mantles, with stripes, good.

6 Bornuses, manufactured at Gerid and Gafsa, and at Kaff. Bornuses, woven with silk.

7 Pieces for making bornuses, with silk. Shawls, white and coloured. Joubbas, white and coloured. Mantles, white and coloured, with silk. Shawls, all wool. Coloured Gerby joubbas. Joubbas, with crimson ornaments, and mantles, woven with silk, of Gerby manufacture. White, light blue, and light crimson girth. Waist girths. Woollen Joubbas, Gerby manufacture. Men's white shawls. Taled, used by Jews. Joubbas of Gerid, with silk. Mantles, woven with silk. Small blankets, Touzer manufacture. Bornuses, with silk.

8 Blankets, made at Touzer. Blankets of Gerby manufacture. Mantles, of Gerby and Gafsa manufacture.

9 Mantles, common, Bedween style, &c. Jerby shawls. Shawls, Tunisian style. Pieces of common Tunisian-manufactured wool. Six complete woollen dresses and six long jackets, used by seamen, &c. Blankets, of Gerby manufacture. Common mantles, used by the Bedwenees of Sahel. Blankets, made at Sahel.

10 Red caps, called Calabash. Caps, called Orta. Caps, called Sakes. Ottoman court uniform caps, called Majidia. Caps, called Kaleb-shed. Small size, called Hramy sakes. Long shaped, Arab style. Smaller size, called Zenna. Caps, called Orta. Silken stuff, called Garmasud, imitation of India. Silk waist girth. Face coverings. Blue cotton fabrics. Silk mantles, used by Arabs. Silk girth, used by town people. Silken shawls and coloured girths, made at Kirwan. Arab veils. Handkerchiefs. Curtains. Silk girth, Algerine style. Head girths, Kirwan style. Light veil, made at Kirwan, &c. Silk aprons, Algerine style. Gaze dresses. Ladies' small waist girths. Ribbon. Gaze scarfs. Head coverings. Small girths. Kerchiefs, and neckerchiefs, and small handkerchiefs. Striped silk, for men's dresses. Head coverings, imitation of Morea. Fancy silk turbans. Jewish men's girths. Aprons, Algerine style, &c. Joubbas, Gerbine manufacture. Silk mantles. Jewish religious dresses. Pieces of silken manufacture. Gentlemen's girths. Head dresses, used by Tunis and Kirwan ladies. Coloured handkerchiefs. Silk scarfs. Silk curtain. Fancy silk scarf. Piece of yellow silk manufacture. Gaze veil. Cotton head coverings. Biserta aprons and towels.

The same, used for bathing, with silk. Linen stuff, made in Tunis, and at Susa.

11 Woollen blankets, made at the Gala, a province of Sahel. Joubbas, manufactured by the Hmamma tribe. Joubba, manufactured at Kirwan. Mantles, manufactured at Kirwan. Strong stuff for making bornuses. Black bornuses. Black bornuses, imitation of Tsbessa, made at Gafsa. Pieces for making bornuses. Red bags, used for feeding horses. Red bags, or purses, for putting on horseback. Red girths. Complete joubbas, silk and wool, made in Kirwan.

12 Men's shoes, Algerine style. Men's slippers. Slippers, called Yamany and Telemsany. Men's Arab slippers, made at Tunis and Kirwan. Ladies' shoes and slippers. Boots, yellow and red. Ladies' coloured shoes. Ladies' short coloured slippers. Arab and children's shoes. Red, black, yellow, and chocolate goat skins. Red and yellow sheep's skins. Light blue goat skins. White sheep's skins. Leather bag, Persian style. Leather bag, Kaff style. Powder and shot bag. Leather powder bag. Pair of pistol holders. Single pistol holder. Set of forehead ornaments, used by Arabs for horses.

13 Models of carved arabesque gypsum ornaments, used for decorating the interior of Moorish rooms.

14 Box of saffron.

15 Box of indigo.

16 Box of indigo, of another sort.

17 Box of the same.

18 Box of unwoven linen.

19 Large carpet. Small carpets, used in tents. Bags, for feeding horses. Horse coverings.

20 Carpets, used in tents and for wall tapestry. Carpet bags. Horse bandages.

21 Red thin skins and hides. White thin hides, for shoemaking. Forks, used for the wool manufacture. Copper stirrups, used by the Arabs of Derna, &c. Undressed goats' skins. Leather bags, for carrying water. Hair cords, for tying horses' feet, &c. Martingales. Hair girths, used for tying up loads on mules. Horse brushes.

22 Bornuses, woven with red silk and wool.

23 Jewish garments. Mantles, with silk and wool, made at Gerby. Mantles, with silk. Woollen thread, made at Gerby, for various manufacturing purposes. Spun thread, made at Gerby. Girths. Pieces for making joubbas, with silk, Gerby manufacture. White piece, with silk. Gerby shawls, with silk. Men's shawls. Complete silk mantles. Coloured shawls. Mantle. Bornuses, silk and wool. Bornuse, of Gerid, silk and wool. Tunisian carpets. Horse bandages, manufactured by the tribe of Awlad-Un.

24 Earth extracted from the mine of the Mountain of Slata.

25 Minerals of the same place.

26 and 27 Mineral lead from the Mountains of Gerisa.

28 and 29 Mineral lead from the Mountains of Wargha and Gerisa.

30 Lead from Slata.

31 Iron from same place.

32 Lead from the Ragba Mountains.

33 and 34 Copper and iron from the Mountain of Gerisa.

35 Piece of jujube wood. Untanned hides.

36 Mule saddle, complete. Horse saddles, complete. Horse leather bags. Stilettoes, manufactured at Biserta. Fans. Leather round waiters. Silk horse-neck ornaments. Cord bridles. Copper candlesticks. Pieces of coloured coarse cloth. Horse coverings, with stripes.

37 Parasols, with leather and silk. Parasols, with ostrich feathers. Parasols. Dry pommegranade, used for colouring yellow. Gall. Lion skin. Leopard skins. Weight for scales.

38 Sample of lime.

39 Bale of wool, weighing 581 lbs.
40 Bale of wool, weighing 504 lbs.
41 Shirts, with silver embroidery, various colours and patterns. Shirt, crimson and pearl coloured. Shirt, pearl coloured. Shirt, crimson coloured. Shirt, silk, with silver. Head coverings, gaze, with silver. Pair of trousers, embroidered. Silk scarfs, with silver. Curtain, with silver. Girth, with silver. Scarfs, with silver. Light-blue joubba, embroidered with gold and silver. Pair of trousers, with silk. Pair of trousers, silk, with mixed ornaments and silver. Pair of trousers, with silver. Silk shirts, with gaze, embroidered. Silk shirts, with gaze, without embroidery. Trousers, shirts, joubbas, and women's jackets, all embroidered with gold. Damask jackets, with silver. Complete gentleman's velvet dress. Small cloak, fully ornamented with silver. Long hair ornaments, with gold. Specimens of yellow and white silver; and of silver thread, yellow and white. Girths for ladies' trousers. Head covering, with silver. Head covering, gaze, embroidered with silver.
42 Mule saddle, fully embroidered, without stirrups. Gentlemen's cloth dresses, with ornaments, in the Algerine style, silver and silk. Gold-embroidered ladies' shoes. Slippers. Ladies' head ornaments, embroidered. Embroidered trousers' girths. Ladies' caps, with silver embroidery. Embroidered silk handkerchiefs. Kerchiefs. Arm ornaments, with stripes. Ladies' caps. Jew's waist girth. Trousers. Head ornaments. Silk leg girths, all with silver. Silk guards for watches. Silk watch ornaments. Chaplet ornaments. Kerchiefs and tobacco bags, with silver. Silk bags, ornamented with silk and coral. Jewish lady's girth, with silver. Mule saddle, fully embroidered, without stirrups. Head girths, with gold thread. Complete gentlemen's dresses, various designs, Algerine style. Breast embroideries, for ladies' dresses. Silk shawls, with gold. Ladies' dresses, with silver. Waist girths. Large scarf, with silver. Large waist girth, with silver. Curtains, with silver, &c. Piece of silk stuff. Tobacco purses, with silk and coral embroidery.
43 Saddles, embroidered with gold. Coral chaplets, with gold ornaments. Cloth bornuses. Cloth joubbas, with gold and silk embroidery.
44 Complete Algerine men's dresses, with silk. Long jackets, with silver and silk. Crimson and light-blue girth, of Gerby manufacture. Short jackets, with silk.
45 Lead from Dgebba, and one stone, called keddal, used for making lime, &c.
46 Saltpetre.
47 Jewish religious garments. Girths. Mantles, silk and wool, Gerby manufacture.
48 Pieces for making bornuses. Gerbine mantles, with silk. Pieces for making joubbas. Coloured and white joubbas. Joubbas, yellow. Bornuses, complete. Gafsa and Gerby, all of Gerid manufacture. Pieces for joubbas. Gerbine blankets.
49 Weeds for smoking pipes.
50 Gypsum, of various qualities.
51 Domestic implements, viz. : — Copper jugs and waiters. Fish casserole. Large boilers. Bucket. Arab wash-hand basins. Earthen cups. Soap boxes. Vases, used for throwing water upon the head in bathing. Covered casserolles.
52 Large copper boiler. Bucket. Casserolles. Wash-hand basins. Buckets. Basket, with dried raisins. A sample of a material used for tanning.
53 to 57 Ninety bottles of different sorts of scented waters.
58 Arm-holder, to hold up guns.
59 Carved door, with a curious key.
60 Wheat, called Hemira.
61 The same, called Azyzy.
62 The same, called Nigida.

63 The same, called Sbihy.
64 The same, lightly roasted when new, used for soups.
65 A jar containing prepared barley, for soups.
66 A jar containing hoskossoo, a dry preparation of the Semola.
67 A jar with barley.
68 A jar containing preserved olives.
69 A jar with wheat, called Mahmovdy.
70 A jar with mohammes, a dry preparation of the semola.
71 A jar with koskossoo. 72 A jar with barley.
73 Sponges. 74 The same. 75 The same.
76 Dry apricots. 77 Two pieces of white cloth.
78 Dates, produced at Gabes.
79 The same, in leather bags.
80 Gerby blankets. Arab mantles. Shawls. Blankets of Tunisian manufacture, &c.
81 Begia snuff. Bottle of ink.
82 Arab tents. Bags for feeding horses, used by Arabs.
83 Velvet saddles, embroidered with gold and silver. Plated stirrups, used by Bedween Arabs. Iron bridle-pieces, of different sorts. Holders for water, used on horseback, embroidered with gold. Gun-locks, with silver and copper. Gold foot-rings. Bracelets. Lizard skins. Complete Arab belt, &c. Smoking pipe-guards, embroidered. Leather cushions. Hatchet. Scythe. Arab bracelets, with silver. Foot-rings for girls. Ring, used by Arabs to tie up their waist-girths. Foot-rings, silver, and pins and ear-rings, Tripoline style. Pins and breast ornaments. Ear-rings. Pair of gun-locks. Silver breast-ring, with which Arab women tie their joubbas. Silver ornaments for the head. Boy's belt. Looking-glass, as used by Arabs, and other silver ornaments. Tunisian otto of roses. Otto of jasmin. Mixed essences. Essence of quince, of Benjamin, of oranges, of aloes, of apples, and of musk. Amber lozenges and necklaces. Pomatum, made with musk, aloes, and jasmin. Otto of jasmin. Saffron. Complete bornus, of Gerid.
84 Specimens of the Karouba tree. Dry figs.
85 Honna leaves, and powder.
86 A well-block. Sieves of different sorts. Turkish pike, or measure for cloth. Arab, of the same.
87 Parasols, with ostrich feathers, and in red silk. Ladies' shoes. Gentlemen's slippers. String. Thread. Sieves.
88 Ready-cut smoking tobacco. Tobacco in leaves. Begia, toborsook, korba, abidy, and aithy, for snuff. Hay seed.
89 Jars of pickled raisins and meat.
90 Jars of sausages, raisins, and meat.
91 Lime. Jar, with gunpowder.
92 Lion and leopard skins. A small black skin, in pieces. Ostrich feathers. Skin of a wild sheep.
93 Saddle, embroidered with gold and silver. Silver stirrups, for mules' saddles. Silver chains, for mules. Pair of home clogs, embroidered. Belts. Embroidered cushions.
94 Gentlemen's full dresses, embroidered with gold. Breast embroideries, for ladies' dresses. Tobacco bags and comb-guards, embroidered. Specimen of a complete Moorish belt. A general officer's belt. First-rank civil officer's belts. A major's belt. A lieutenant-colonel's belt. Under-caps. Woollen stockings. Slippers. K-hol, a collyrium, used for blackening the eyelids.
95 Piece of worked marble.
96 to 100 Various sorts of timber from Tabarca. Piece of cypress wood.
101 Garlic, and red and ground pepper.
102 Haricots. Droâ, a grain much cultivated at Tunis.
103 Fenugreek. Chick peas. Lentils. Black haricots.

104 Beans. Carroway. Gammam, much used for dyeing. Coriander.

105 Jistachiols. 106 Bamia, and other seeds.

107 Dry Muscatelle raisins. Hard almonds.

108 Another sort of almonds.

109 Dry raisins. A paste made with raisins.

110 Seeds of various sorts.

111 Mloukhia, used for cooking, in leaves.

112 to 134. 252 baskets of dates.

135 Pomegranates.

136 Medicinal herbs, produced in the Regency.

137 Box of tanning materials. Ground mloukhia and cotton. Scissors, used in the red cap manufacture. Spinning spindles. Hair sieves. Plate covers, made by the negroes. Junk waiter. Swak, used by Moorish women for whitening their teeth.

138 Small bundles of swak.

139 to 148. 627 pieces of common earthenware, Nabel and Gerby.

149 Red Gafsa pepper. The same, of Nabel manufacture. Common salt and natron.

150 Box, with sponges. 151 Box of the same.

152 Mineral waters of Hamman Ellen'f, near Tunis.

153 The same, of Korbus. 154 Preserved fish.

155 Four jugs of honey.

156 Two jugs of preserved olives.

157 Another sort of preserved fish.

158 Another sort of the same, and raisins.

159 The same, of olives.

160 The same. 161 The same.

162 Four jugs of salt butter, and ten smoking pipes.

163 Four jugs of honeycombs.

164 A comb and a well-block.

165 Common salt. 166 Gypsum. 167 One millstone.

168 Building and lime stones, and bricks.

169 Common dark gypsum, used for building.

170 Gypsum, not entirely macerated, used for building mills, &c. as a very strong cement.

171 Best gypsum, called Naksha, for making arabesques, and other ornaments.

172 Hard soap.

173 to 176. The same, of various sorts.

178, 179, 180. Junk and straw works, mats, bucket covers, straw saddles, bags for putting on camels, horses, &c., and agricultural instruments.

181 Goat's hair. 182 Cow's hair. 183 Yellow wax.

184 Junk mats. 185 Tallow. 186 An ostrich skin.

187 Samples of oil, called Beldy.

188 Samples of oil, called Darbma.

189 Soft soap. 190 A bale of camel's hair.

TURKEY.

(Commissioner, *Edward Zohrab*, Esq. Inspecting-Agent, Mr. *C. M. Major*, at the Turkish Collection in the Building)

PRODUCT and MANUFACTURES of the OTTOMAN EMPIRE, sent to the CENTRAL COMMITTEE OF CONSTANTINOPLE, by order of the SUBLIME PORTE.

This collection of upwards of three thousand three hundred objects is arranged under the several divisions of the Vegetable, Animal, and Mineral Kingdoms, and into two general classes, of Raw Materials and Manufactures. The numbers are not serial, but continuous, and each article is separately labelled.

RAW MATERIALS.

Woods (Dyeing and other).—49 varieties of woods, shrubs, and plants, herbs, roots, fruits, oil-yielding kernels, grains, and balsams—entering into the commerce of the Levant, &c.; or employed medicinally, as dyes, &c.; or for house-

hold and agricultural purposes—numerically arranged—from the Sendgiak of Jerusalem, Djibbe, Koniah, Egypt, Saide, and other divisions of Turkey (No. 65—170). Two specimens of gutta percha; seven specimens of yellow wax; one of sugar cane; specimen of saponiaca Egyptiaca, or "soda" (170—178 and 2,015—2063).

Cotton Wool.—Gosspium, or cotton wool (2,064—2,088). 25 varieties of cotton wool, including No. 2,082, a specimen of "Lana cardic" or "ocephala," contributed from Koniah, Cassabar. and several other districts of the empire in Asia and Africa.

Tobacco.—32 specimens, from about 25 provinces (2,089—2119).

Sponges of six kinds (2,126—2,131).

Wheats.—28 samples, from Salonica, Damascus, Koniah, Adrianople, Tripoli, &c. (2,132—2,159).

Pounded Wheat for making Pilauf.—Five samples (2,160—2,169).

Barley.—15 samples (2,165—69).

Oats.—Four samples (2,180—83).

Indian Corn or Maize.—15 samples (2,184—2,198).

Rice.—Nine samples (2,199—2,207).

Millet.

Pinicum-dani.—Seven varieties (2,208—15).

Sesamum.—11 samples of the seed (2,216—26).

Sample of Uskeep tobacco (2,227).

Flax.—Eight specimens of (2,228—2243).

Flax and Hemp.—Eight samples (2,228—2,243).

RAW MATERIAL, principally of the VEGETABLE KINGDOM.

Dyes.—Kinna weed for dyeing the fingers, toes, and beard. Vallonia acorns; shumac; madder-root; berries—yellow, white; galls—white, yellow, black, and green; leaves of the "Enbuch" flower; saffron flowers.

Balsams, Resins, and Drugs.—Absynth, resinous scammony; vegetable, pitch, and pure resin; white bird-lime (2,599—2,606); white resin; balsam of Mecca; Siam turpentine; storax or scented sennaar leaves; chamomile flowers; aloes-wood; cardamum; colocynth; hellebore; julep. A resin from Anatolia, used for making knife and fork handles (2,634). Myrrh; frankincense; calamite; prepared scammony; sassafras; opium (nine varieties); leaves of the Laurus nobilis; poppy-heads; poppy seeds and leaves; rose-leaves of the R. Damascenensis and R. Centifol; and other kinds.

Roots. — Gentian; valerian; liquorice; peppermint; angelica; saffron; varieties of lilliacum; wild thyme; asphodel (or King's spear), the prepared sort.

Other Grains.—Spring wheats; autumn wheats; maize; millet; sesame. Vetches.

Products, Medical and Alimentary.

Gums.—G. Arabicum, tragacantha, karamanicum, cirasorum, masticum, ladaneum (2,607—24).

Pepper.—Capsicums; long pepper.

Edible marsh mallows; grey peas (astragal foliac.); berries of the Mocha coffee plant; nasturtium; varieties of the cucumber; pumpkin; gourd; sweet potato; asparagus; spinach; turnip; cabbage (many varieties of "brassica)."

Seeds of coriander; mustard; annis; hemp; cummin.

Cotton, hemp, flax, errilac,; bamea; the castor-oil bean; "faba," larger and smaller; phœsiole (nine specimens), 2,254—2,262); fibres of the wild hemp.

Flowers and heads of the poppy; specimens of the heliotrope.

Fruits from all the dominions of Turkey. The "mahalet" and other varieties of the plum kind, as prunus persicus; P. Demascen, &c. Pears of many different varieties. 12 varieties of the almond — sweet, bitter, and soft-shelled (Amygdal; decorticatus), 2,648—59; tamarinds, cherries, mulberries, Egyptian jujube, orange, lime, lemon, &c.

Sugar-canes.—Grasses.

Nuts.—Common hazel, pistachio, cob, chesnut, walnut, &c.

Forest and Timber Trees.—50 or 60 varieties of the woods of the oak, ash, maple, hornbeam, willow, beech, plane, oriental lime, sycamore, &c. (2,947—85).

Plants.—Tobaccos, especially of the kinds called "nicotiana," "hosch," "Virginia."

Hemp-Flax of very numerous varieties.

Vines of 22 sorts, chiefly from Damascus, Smyrna, and Koniah.

Vegetable and Animal Products (Manufactured).

Sugars.—Raw and manufactured, or white; also sugar scented.

Oil of Olives.—Many varieties (2,757—65).

Other Oils.—Essential oils of cedar, sandars, and numerous other kinds; including oils of roses, almonds, laurel (expressed), terebinthus, compound of sesame oil, and water.

Sweet Waters.—Rose, honey, violet, jessamine, distilled water, laurel, violet, carmine, mertha, orange.

Syrups and Sweets.—Laurel, violets, almonds, inspissated juice of grapes.

Fermented Liquors.—Beer. Numerous white wines and red wines, the produce of Turkish Moldavia and other vineyards of the empire. Rosoglio and other liqueurs.

Wax, white, yellow, bleached, unbleached.

Snuff.—Six specimens of Turkey snuff (3,120—3,128).

ANIMAL KINGDOM.
Raw Vegetable and Animal Products.

Honey, common and wild.

Tallows of oxen, sheep, deer, &c.; ditto, produced from marrow-bones (2940).

Raw Silks and Cocoons.—Raw silk, in skeins, spun by household industry among the peasantry of Broussa, Adrianople, Ruga, Damascus, Smyrna, Wallachia (1590—1605). Also raw silks, in skeins and bundles, spun at the filanda of Torosoglio, by females of Tripoli, in Barbary; from the Djaniok of Philipopoli; by the steam filanda of Yussuck Bey Oglou, at Broussa (1705); by the peasantry of Damerdith (1592—1711); by the filanda of Paulakey, Broussa (1711); and by the filandas of Jossy (1970—1975). Numerous cocoons, and raw silks, from the filanda of Torosoglou, and the domestic spinning of the women of Tripoli.

Wool and Hair.—Camels' hair; sheeps' wool; goats' wool, called "Gillak;" ox hair; buffalo and buck leather.

Horns of buffalo, sheep, antelope, capricorn, stag, and rhinoceros.

Elephants' teeth, and other ivory.

Cantharides, shell of the cuttle or Pounce fish.

Skins of bear, lynx, tiger, deer, fox, jackall, wolf, wild cat, hare, badger, otter, beaver, marten, bear, goat, sheep, camel (999—1096).

Also 36 species of skins, stuffed fishes of several classes, ostrich wings, cocoons and silk worms, isinglass, botargo. Prepared fish-roes.

MINERAL KINGDOM.
Rocks, Minerals, Stones, &c.

Rocks.—Gypsum (prismaticoidal); helcrite with gypsum; limestone, in many forms—as carbonate of, calcinated, prismaticoidal, rhombohedral. Granite; quartz (uncleavable), and other varieties; gneis; jasper; porphyrh; serpentine (green); steatite, or soap-rock; volcanic whetstones.

Minerals.—Gold; silver; copper; lead; iron; sulphur, and sulphur as prepared; coal and brown coal. Salt—rock, glauber, grey, white, hexahedral, octohedral, ammoniacal. alum; vitriol, blue and green, used as copperas; mineral pitch and bitumen; iron and copper pyrites; natron; black mineral resin; black liquid naphtha, &c.

Stones.—Garnet (dodecahedral); opal jasper (uncleavable quartz); amethyst (rhombohedral), &c.

Ores.—Iron, red iron ochre (3111—3114, 3286—3434).

Earths and Clays.—White clay; pipe-clay; pipe bowl clay; potters' clay, used for the manufacture of fine china; other sorts for the glazing of china when made; chalcedony; potassium; earth nitre; aloysinum, or "meerschaum," or sea-foam. Natron earth; saltpetre (three varieties); fullers' earth; micassye earth; vitriolic earth; sulphurous earth; tufaceous and other volcanic earths; zeolite green earth, called "Verme," or Cyprus earth; silica sand mixed with silica and sandstone, used in Turkey for bleaching rice; marl—white, green, yellow; chalk—a species of marl used for grindstones.

MANUFACTURES.

The "articles of manufacture, the produce of Turkish industry, forwarded for exhibition by the Turkish Ministry of Commerce," comprises about 1,300 items; and the articles themselves illustrate, under the simple and intelligible conditions of this arrangement, the industrial progress, the arts, the costumes (and the varied materials of which these are composed) as they at present exist in some of the extensive dominions of the Sultan. Nos. 1 to 12 of this collection are silk manufactures; viz. a bridle and four pieces; black silk stuff used for the surtouts of resident Christians; silk, cotton, and cheque silk sashes; stuffs of silk and cotton, called "imitation Broussas," and "Abanches," for turbans; taffeta for dresses; mixed silk and cotton fabrics, called Guézy;" striped taffeta (silk) and silk and cotton satin, or "Eminick;" and cotton and silk stuffs, "Tehetari;" produced respectively by Seid Omer, (Tripoli); Tchertehy, of Beirout; Omer Kibery, of Tripoli; Eimen, of Tripoli; Yashari-Hosein, of Tripoli (13—24). Cotton and silk stuffs (Tchetari); cotton stuffs for dresses; men's jackets and under coats of cotton and silk; cotton twist; blue and other cotton cloths and sateens; gold threads of different qualities (manufactured by Yashari-Hosein, as above; Hadgi Mustaga Miher, of Zayakie; Hanonne, of Jerusalem; and by the household industry of families living on Mount Lebanon; also by Nameh, of Beirout (25). Caps of silk, cotton, and gold; silk sashes and cords; silk ribbons, coloured; gold and silk thread sabre-cords; silk gauze shirts, veils, and cloaks; sashes with silver fringes; sashes of silk and silver thread; cords of these materials; as also a cushion cover and cap; tobacco bag; braces; silk and gold ladies' slippers; mantle; silk purses; silver thread; antel chair; silk and silver thread garters; tassels for cap or "fez;" silk, cotton, and gold stuffs, called "Tchetari" (179), and "Talsiz Abani" (184). Crimson silk of Damascus for furniture, being a complete assortment of chair, arm chair, couches, sofa, and divan covers, with borders for the same, manufactured at Aleppo (192). Silk and cotton quiltings; silk and silk and gold stuff for turbans; dresses; silk gauze women's shirt with gilt fringes (203), and silk bed sheet, gilt fringes (207). Linen cloth, called "Riza Bezy;" silk and cotton and silk shirting; cotton sheeting; linen towels; embroidered towel (225). Goats' wool gloves and stockings; cloth of silk and gold, called "Fouzu," for the bath (232). Embroidered gloves, by household industry of the women of Argov (235). Silk and gold bed cover (234). Silk sedgada (or rug); assortment of clothes for the bath (250). Stuff of goats' wool, called "Soz" and "Shali;" silk gauze mosquito curtains; white cotton and silk stuff for trousers; silk and cotton towels and braces; camels' hair rug embroidered (274); and rug in felt (277). Silk stuff embroidered in gold, called "Katnariar" (280). Ladies' coat cloth embroidered in gold; silk braid; buttons in gold and silk thread; silk sashes and purse; embroidered napkins or Tcheieres; silk and gold stuff for furniture; in same combined materials — 3 pair of cushion covers, 2 large ditto, 1 divan, and 1 sofa cover (379); and other furniture stuffs embroidered in like manner, by Isaac Aga (395). Satins embroidered in gold (536). Scarf embroidered in gold (567). Goats' wool stuffs embroidered in silver and gold; silk crape or gauze skirting and sheeting (596). "Moshles" or cloaks assorted; red silk shawl of Damascus manufacture (617). Scarlet cloak embroidered in gold (1720). Turkish saddle, saddle cloth, bridle, holsters, and pistols; velvet and cloth embroidered in gold; white woollen sash, and stuff of same material (the former imitation of Tripoli, the latter of Merino (306, 307). Woollen l'hram for women, and cotton, silk, and gold ditto (397). Arab saddle cloth (392). Arab shirts, carpets (499), and rugs; cloaks; carpet, bed, and cushion cover, manufactured by the Arab women.

Shawl of stuff called "Shalaki" (544).

Felt, caps and jackets of, (387, 389); and for tents.

Linen sash, in imitation of Tripoli.

Cloth, Embroidered or Gold.—"Tcheure," or napkin; sash; covering for the head; ladies' caps (or fez), tassels and gear in gold thread (403).

Cotton cloths for turbans, called "Abane," for the bath; Arab shirt (391).

Muslins.—Flowered muslins for turbans, called "Abane" (318). Kerchiefs embroidered in gold, Tcherres (571, 572). Coffee-service cover embroidered at Constantinople, gold and spangles (573). Coffee covers embroidered in silk, and ditto scarf in gold (584). Head kerchief embroidered with gold and pearls and silver fringes.

Cotton and linen muslin covers, &c.

Velvet.—Tobacco bags, embroidered in gold and in beads and in silk; velvet jackets, called "Sattah," also worked in gold (see "Costumes").

Costumes.—Albanian (male) embroidered in gold (jacket, vest, gaiters, tastanelle garters, belt), ditto for arms three pieces; piece of shali; costume (female) ditto, one long, one short, gown; vest, jacket or mentar trousers or "shawan;" one shirt, sash, and slippers. Another lady's suit, all in silk, embroidered with silk and gold, complete (410, 411). Albanian deer skins (manufactured); morocco—red, yellow, and black; tanned and dyed sheep skins; tanned camels' skins (498). Riding boots in red morocco, embroidered in false gold: African shoes made by Tropoli shoemakers (707).

Silk and gold reins; gold and silk cords.

Miscellaneous.—Cup and spoons made of porphyrh, carved by Jacob Mislum, of Jerusalem; cup in bituminous stone found near the tomb of Moses, at Bethlehem, carved by Mordecai, a Jew of Bethlehem (108—111). Box cut from the stones of Jerusalem; inkstand made from roots of the olive trees of said city; piece of red porphyrh, cut by a poor self-taught Jew, and sent by H. B. Majesty's consul there; shell in mother-of-pearl, carved by Isaac, a Jew of Bethlehem; silver plates and anklets, soup bowls, looking-glass case, "Tarfs" or coffee cups, and cups of same metal; gold necklace, earrings, and silver bracelets, gilt silver ditto (121), &c. Ornaments for necks of beasts of burden, called "Kesrak" (740). Ostrich feathers; furs; thread of worsted, horse hair, and cotton; mohair, yarn, gold leaf, silver ditto, gold and silk thread, gold lace (807). Ramrod, silver and steel (821). Inkstand and pen case, silver and steel; sabre mounted in same metals; daggers, gold and steel mounted; pistols, steel and silver; rope made from bark of the lime tree (859); ditto from a plant called "Elbran;" gloves in gold and pearls, used as an ornament for the hand (874). Albanian cloaks (939). Slippers, called "Gilar," embroidered in gold and pearls; sheep skin cloak worn by the shepherds (1069). Silver bracelets, anklets, and ornaments; gold necklaces, earrings, bracelets (1102). Gold and silver scissors (1308). Perfumed soaps; book weights; dress embroidered in gold (1337). Various utensils—brass, copper, lacquered work, &c.; turners' work—spoons of wood, horn, coral, and mother-of-pearl (1384—1392). Copper dinner-service and gong, cymbals, &c.; pipe mouthpieces in amber (1441—1447). Glass and china porringers

and covers, saucers, &c.; various articles in china and glass (1448, 1524). Spoons in amber; chalcedony cups; Meerschaum cup; guns, carbines, pistols, sabre blades, knives, ramrods; silver gun, filigree work; pipe and pipe sticks of jessamine, ebony, cherry (1525—1678). Narguiles or water-pipes in silver, with amber mouth-pieces.

Models of a minister of state's caique, or boat; five pairs of oars, of passenger and private gentlemen's boats.

TUSCANY.

(Commissioner in London, Professor PHILIP CORRIDI, 7 Piccadilly.)

1 ROYAL TECHNOLOGICAL INSTITUTE.—Specimens of sandy stones for building purposes, from quarries existing in the various localities of Tuscany. Specimens of refractory stones, from quarries in Tuscany. Incrustations of the mineral waters of St. Philip baths. Ornamental stones, and stones used in the arts. Specimens of marbles, existing in the various localities of Tuscany. Specimens of lithographic stones, from various localities, and especially from the quarries of Ponte-a-Sieve, belonging to Mr. Pasqual Giovannini, of Florence. Specimens of chalcedony, and a variety of hard stones existing in Tuscany. Collection of every quality of alabastrides from the quarries known in Tuscany.

2 Produce of the ROYAL MANUFACTORY of SALT, VOLTERRA.—Rock-salt from the salt works of St. Leopold. Salt obtained from the evaporation of saliferous waters. Specimens of alum dug in Tuscany, and purified alum. Specimens of sulphur dug in Tuscany, and purified sulphur. Specimens of iron ore from the royal mines of the Elba island. Specimens of copper ore, dug in Tuscany, and from unwrought mines of a well-known produce. Specimens of (*Argentiferous*) lead ore, dug in Tuscany. Specimens of quicksilver, dug in Tuscany.

3 Specimens of colouring earth and Tripoli earth from Elba Island and other parts of Tuscany.

4 Specimen of sulphur, from the sulphur mines of Pereta, province of Grosseto; native and wrought sulphur.

5 Specimens of alum, from the Royal Alum Pit of Montioni, province of Massa Maritama. Crystallized alum, from the same alum pits.

6 Mine of quicksilver, of Levigliani, province of Pietrasanta.—Specimens of the ore and the metallic quicksilver.

7 Mine of cinnabar, of Ripa, province of Pietrasanta.—Specimens of the ore, the cinnabar, and quicksilver.

8 Mine of quicksilver, of Yane, province of Volterra.—Specimens of the ore and the quicksilver.

9 Mine of quicksilver, of Castellazzara.—Specimens of the ore and the quicksilver.

10 Mine of quicksilver, of Pian Castagnaio.—Specimens of the ore, the cinnabar, and quicksilver.

11 Mine of quicksilver, of Capita, near Capallio, province of Volserra.—Specimens of the ore and the native cinnabar.

12 HALL BROTHERS, SLOANE, & COPPI.—Specimens of their copper mine in Montecatini, in Val di Cecina.

13 VEGNI, Prof. ANGELO, of Siena.—Specimens of argentiferous lead from the mine of Serarerra.

14 METALLURGIC SOCIETY.—Specimens of argentiferous lead from the mine of Val di Castello (province of Pietrasanta).

15 MEJEAN, G. Florence.—Specimens of antimony of Montanto and Pereta (province of Grosseto).

16 FREDIANI, C. Lucca.—Quartz steaschist or refractory stone, for the building of melting furnaces; from a quarry in the neighbourhood of Camaiore (province of Lucca), which belongs to him

17 AMMANNIATI, GIOVANNI, Capt. of Florence.—Two fragments of tormaline from the Elba island.

18 A lady's collar, made of various stones from the Elba island, and mounted in gold.

19 CAILLOU, MAILLAN & FORMIGLI. — Specimens of coals from their coal-pit in Montebamboli.

20 SANTI, Dr. CLEMENTE, of Montalcino.—Fossil flour from Castel del Piano. Floating bricks made with the flour.

21 QUERCI, G. Florence, Manu.—Specimens of varnish.

22 CORRIDI, G. Leghorn, Manu.—Specimens of sulphate of quinina and of santonina.

23 CONTI & SON, Leghorn, Manu.—Specimens of soaps.

24 DE LARDEREL, Count F. Leghorn.—Alabasters and produce of the *suffioni* of boric acid, from the exhibitor's estates in Montecerboli, Castelnuovo, and Monterotondo.

25 RIDOLFI, Prof. M. Lucca.—Colours for encaustic painting, prepared by a peculiar process of the exhibitor's invention ; and paintings to show the effects of the colours.

26 MUSSINI, Prof. Florence. — Colours for painting after a new composition, and specimens of painting on a consistent body of terra-cotta, to show the effects.

27 BROCCHI, C. V. Florence.—Soft white wheat from the hills of Arecetri, near Florence.

28 SLOANE, F. Esq.—Soft white wheat from his estate at Carreggi, near Florence.

29 PAOLETTI, F.—Pondera stiff wheat for Italian pastes, from the plains of Pisa. Specimens of superfine Italian pastes.

30 RIDOLFI, Marquis C. Florence.—Fir-cones and fir-nuts, called *pinoli stiacciamanz*, from the exhibitor's estates.

31 ORSETTI, C. T. Lucca.—Olive oil, from the exhibitor's estates on the hills of Lucca.

32 RUSCHI BROTHERS, Pisa.—Olive oil, from the exhibitor's estates at Calci, near Pisa.

33 PACINI, D. Pisa.—Olive oil, from the exhibitor's estates at Buti, near Pisa.

34 SARACINI, C. A. Siena.—Olive oil, from the exhibitor's estate in Castelnuvo-berardenga, near Sienna.

35 PASTORELLI, D. Arcidosso.—Corn, called mazzuolo, supplying straw for bonnets.

35A ROYAL TECHNOLOGICAL INSTITUTE.—Madder-roots from the Maremmey, and other localities in Tuscany ; the same roots pounded and reduced to powder. Specimen of Indian-corn straw for brooms, from Campi, near Florence. Brooms. Specimens of Tuscany woods.

36 LAMBRUSCHINI, R. Florence.—Specimen of cocoons of silk-worms reared by the exhibitor from 1842 to 1850.

37 SCOTI BROTHERS, Florence.—Raw silk, from the exhibitor's spinning-mills.

38 DELLA RIPA, L. D. Florence.—Raw silk, from the exhibitor's spinning-mills.

39 POIDEBARD, N. Portico, near Florence.—Raw silk, from the exhibitor's spinning-mills.

40 PETRUCCI, C. C. Siena.—Raw silk, from the exhibitor's spinning mills.

41 PIERI, Count G. Siena.—Raw silk, from the exhibitor's spinning mills.

42 PANNILINI, C. A. C. Siena.—Raw silk, from the exhibitor's spinning mills.

42A RISTORI, M. Leghorn.— Potash from the exhibitor's manufactory in the Maremme of Grosseto.

43 FRANCESCHINI, G. Prato.—Raw silk, from the exhibitor's spinning mills.

44 RIMEDIOTTI, Signora A. Pistoia.—Raw silk, from the exhibitor's spinning mills.

45 MORDINI, C. G. Barga.—Raw silk, from the exhibitor's spinning mills.

46 DAVITTI, L. Loro.—Raw silk, from the exhibitor's spinning mills.

47 LEPORI, T. Modigliana.—Raw silk, from the exhibitor's spinning mills.

48 RAVAGLI, P. Marradi.—Raw silk, from the exhibitor's spinning mills.

49 ZAVAGLI, P. Palazzuolo.—Raw silk, from the exhibitor's spinning mills.

50 CASUCCINI, C. F. Chianciano.—Raw silk, from the exhibitor's spinning mills.

51 SAVI, Prof. P. Pisa.—Raw silk from silk worms, reared upon leaves of the Philippine mulberry.

52 COLLACCHIONI, G. Borgo San Sepolcro.—Three merino fleeces, from the flocks belonging to the exhibitor.

53 Estate of the Alberese, belonging to H. I. and R. H. the Grand Duke of Tuscany.—Three fleeces of cross-bred merino sheep, from the sheep-folds of the Alberese.

54 Estate of the Badiola, belonging to H. I. and R. H. the Grand Duke of Tuscany.—Three merino fleeces from the sheep-folds of the Badiola.

55 TURCHINI, L. Florence, Inv.—Machine for carrying heavy burthens, which the exhibitor has named a pemettoforo.

56 PELOSI, E. Lucca. Inv.—Model of a locomotive with an articulated system.

57 GONNELLA, Professor T. Florence. Inv.—Machine for measuring plane surfaces, executed under the exhibitor's direction by order of H. I. and R. H. the Grand Duke of Tuscany, to whom it belongs.

58 DUCCI, A. & M. Florence, Inv.—Organ of a new construction, enclosed in a box carved by M. A. Barbetti, of Siena, and gilt by Mr. Vincenzio Sbolgi, of Florence. Another organ, also constructed by the exhibitor.

59 CUYERE, Mrs. Florence.—Specimens of combs for silk weaving, from the exhibitor's manufactory in Florence.

60 PADREDDI, F. Visa, Manu. and Dyer.—Various tissues. Specimens of cotton dyed in red.

61 MANETTI BROTHERS, Navacchio, near Visa, Manu. —Various tissues.

62 FRANCESCHINI, F. Prato, Manu.—Blankets in floss silk tissued.

63 RIVA and MAFFEI, Florence, Manu.—Brocade of gold and silk.

64 CATANZARO, M. Florence, Manu.—Cotton and silk tissue for carriages.

65 CINI BROTHERS, S. Marcello, near Pistoia, Manu.— Endless felt for paper making.

66 VYSE & SONS, Prato, Manu.—Straw bonnets.

66A MARRETI, Mezzana, near Pisa.—A spring hedge-bill, of superior workmanship.

67 NANNUCCI, Florence, Manu.—Straw bonnets.

68 CINI BROTHERS, S. Marcello.—Specimens of papers.

68A MARIOTTI, S. Pontedera.—Sword, with the hilt and ornaments in gilt silver ; a well finished chiselled work.

69 REFFAELLI, P. & SON, Leghorn.—Pink marbled coral dress, consisting of collar, brooch, pin, and buckles.

69A CALAMIA, Prof. Florence.—Preparations from the male and female torpedo.

70 NARDI BROTHERS, Montelupo, near Empoli. Manu.—Chemical apparatus in glass, and other objects for domestic and commercial use.

71 CANTAGALLI, L. Florence.—Stove in terra-cotta.

72 GINORI, MARQUIS L. Florence.—Several objects in china, from the manufactory on the exhibitor's estate at Doccia, near Florence.

73 ROYAL FOUNDRY, Follonica.—Specimen of cast-iron of the first melting, a tabernacle. Another specimen of cast-iron of the first melting, a flower basket.

74 BARBETTI, A. Siena. Piece of furniture consisting of a console and a plate-glass, carved by the exhibitor.

75 LOMBARDI, A. Siena.—Frame in wood, carved by the exhibitor.

76 BARBETTI, RAFFAELE, Siena.— Frame in carved wood. by the exhibitor.

77 BARBETTI, RINALDI, Siena.—Basso-relievo, carved by the exhibitor.

78 BIGOTTI, L. Lucca. — Two basso-relievo in ivory, carved by the exhibitor.

79 MARCHETTI, L. Siena. — Frame for a glass-plate, in wood, carved by the exhibitor.

80 BARBETTI, A. Siena. — Dressing-table, carved in walnut, after the Greek style.

81 BONAIUTI, C. & SONS, Florence. — An arm-chair, carved and varnished to imitate china.

82 DUCCI, A. Florence.—Model executed by the exhibitor, to show the application in marquetrie of walnut sheets upon cornices. Joining of sliding-rules, with grooves.

83 PASQUI, R. Arezzo.—Frame in wood, carved by the exhibitor.

84 FALCINI BROTHERS, Florence.—A large chair, after the style of the 16th century, inlaid in woods of several colours, forming a rich design of flowers and ornaments.

85 BANAINTI, C. & SONS, Florence.—A desk inlaid in woods, of several colours, forming a splendid design of flowers of various kinds.

85A POLLI, F. Florence.—The top of a table inlaid in woods of several colours, with figures after Raffaele.

86 RAGNINI, E. Chiusi.—The top of a table, inlaid in woods of several colours, forming a design of flowers and various ornaments.

87 MAGGIORELLI BROTHERS, Florence.—Three table-tops, inlaid in Tuscany woods.

88 MARTINETTI, F. Leghorn.—A rectangular ebony table, supported by ornamented carved feet, with a top inlaid in various woods and mother-of-pearl.

89 CORRIDI, P. Leghorn.—A square table of angelica, with a top inlaid in woods of various colours.

90 MAZZETTI, A. Chiusi.—A frame inlaid in woods of various colours.

91 NOBILI, C. Lucca.—A fust of column in coloured marble, from the quarries of St. Maria del Giudice, near Lucca.

92 GUIDOTTI, G. Lucca.—Four fusts of columns in coloured marble, from the quarry of Pescaglia, near Lucca. Three tables, in coloured marble, from the same quarry.

93 GUIDO DE CONTI DELLA GHIRARDESCA, Florence. —Two tables in red marble, from a quarry belonging to the exhibitor in the Tuscan Maremme.

94 NANNI, L. Prato.—A round table in marble, called " Verde di Prato," from quarries belonging to the exhibitor near that town.

95 MAFFEI, C. G. Volterra.—A fust of a column from the quarry of Monte Rufoli, near Volterra, belonging to the exhibitor; the fust is the property of H. I. and R. H. the Grand Duke of Tuscany.

96 PANCIATICHI, MARQUIS, Florence. — A table of marble, called "lumachella," from the exhibitor's quarry near Florence. Two small tables in very hard marble, from the torrent Marnia, near Vallombrossa.

97 GIOVANNINI, P. Florence.—A specimen of sculpture in lithographic stone, from a quarry on the exhibitor's estate.

98 ROYAL TECHNOLOGICAL INSTITUTE. — A table of Cipollino marble, from the quarry of Elba Island. A broccatello table, from the quarry of Caldana, near Campiglia. A table of marble called "Porta Santa," from Caldana di Ravi. A table of eastern alabaster, from the quarry of Alberese. Two small columns of broccatello of Caldan'a with the capitals in yellow marble from Siena. A small column of light bardiglio, from the quarry of Campiglia.

89 GIOVANNINI, P. Florence.—Flag-stones in lithographic stones, inlaid in stucco, very hard, and resisting any kind of rubbing.

100 FERRIGINI, G. Leghorn. White cable, from the exhibitor's manufactory in Leghorn.

101 PARLANTI, E. of Borgo a Buggiano.—A very elaborate embroidery, framed in tapestry.

102 TONTI, L. Florence.—Five canes in small pieces of horn of various colours, with tops in gilt bronze.

103 CERU, C. Lucca. Manu.—A horse's bit.

104 CIONI, G. Empoli. Manu. —A lock of particular mechanism.

105 DUPRE, Prof. A. Florence, Sculptor.—The Death of Abel, and the Curse of Cain, marble statues by the exhibitor, and cast in bronze by Mr. C. Papi; the property of H. I. and R. H. the Grand Duke of Tuscany.

106 COSTOLI, Prof. A. Florence, Sculptor.—Columbus unveiling America to the three parts of the world then known, modelled in plaster by Prof. A. Costoli, and cast in bronze by Mr. C. Papi the property of H. I. and R. H. the Grand Duke of Tuscany.

107 VILLA, I. Florence, Sculptor.—Hagar and her son Ishmael, a group in marble.

108 NENCINI, Prof. L. Florence, Sculptor.—Bacchus reclining, a statue in marble of Seravezza, in Tuscany.

109 CHERICI, G. & SONS, Volterra.—A large alabaster vase, after the Etrurian style.

110 FRECCIA, P. Florence, Sculptor.—Psyche, a statue in marble, with a pedestal.

111 ROYAL MANUFACTORY, known under the name of the IMPERIAL AND ROYAL GALLERY OF HARD-STONE WORKS.—A mosaic table in hard pebbles, of a circular form, and a diameter of 1·75 meter, upon a ground of eastern *lapis lazuli*; the table belonging to H. I. and R. H. the Grand Duke of Tuscany.

112 BUONINSEGNI BROTHERS, Florence. Manu.—A round table in mosaic.

113 BIANCHINI, G. Florence. — A round table in mosaic, with the Florentine lily in the centre.

114 DELLA VALLE BROTHERS, Leghorn. — A rectangular table in scagliola, with various ornaments, and entirely inlaid A round table in scagliola, with several emblematic ornaments, partly inlaid. A vase in scagliola, entirely inlaid.

115 NAZZETTI, A., Chiensi.—A quadrilateral cornice, with the gorge reversed, in ebony, inlaid with various colours of wood.

116 PAPI, C. Florence.—Basket of flowers, taken from nature in one cast, with the stand also from nature, and in a single piece; the whole composed and cast by the exhibitor.

117 GIUSTI, P. Siena.—A medallion, in walnut-wood, carved by the exhibitor.

118, 119 ROMOLI, LUIGI, 6 York Terr. Chelsea.—A rectangular table of scagliola, the central group representing " The Sale of Loves." A round table in mosaic and plaster. A carved pipe-tube of ebony.

120 ROMOLI, LUIGI, Florence.—A cherry-stone, representing on one side a wild boar hunt, on the other 25 heads.

121 MARCHETTI, L. Siena.—A casket, carved in wood by the exhibitor.

122 FONTINA, ANDREA, Carrara, Inv. & Manu.—A clarionet and a German flute, of white marble. A painting on porcelain. enamelled, " Venus reposing." A large tazza, surmounting a truncated column, on coloured marble. A carved vase of white alabaster. A massive bust of Lorenzo il Magnifico, in white marble. A statuette of Galileo.

123 SERAFINO BUONAIUTO, Florence.—A fine plate mirror in a frame, of the 17th century, from a design by the exhibitor.

LONDON: Printed by WILLIAM CLOWES and SONS, Stamford-street, Printers of the Official Catalogues of the Exhibition.

ADDENDA TO SWEDEN AND NORWAY.

46 TOSTRUP, J. Christiania, Norway, Manu.—Ornamental box of chiselled silver, intended to hold consecrated wafers for the altar service.

47 ELFDAHL'S PORPHYRY WORKS, Sweden, Prod. and Manu.—(Capt. P. W. P. Wallis, R.N. Homebush, Southsea, Prop.)—Two porphyry vases on pediments of polished red granite, executed at the above works in Sweden.

48 DANCKWART, Lieut. Wernumo, Sweden, Artist.—Portrait of Jenny Lind carved in ivory.

49 PALMGREN, P. F. Stockholm, Sweden, Manu.—A silver drinking-can.

50 AHLBORN, C. Stockholm, Sweden, Des. and Manu. —A picture frame carved in wood, intended to surround a sculptured image of the Saviour, and representing in its principal parts, objects in connection with the subject of the sculpture, namely:—above, Flowers as an emblem of Patience. To the left, Angel with rose-branch, symbolical of Love. To the right, Angel with lilies, representing Innocence. Underneath, Ivy and palm-leaves, denoting Eternity and Peace.

51 HIS MAJESTY THE KING OF SWEDEN, Prop.—A colossal vase of porphyry, manufactured at the porphyry works of Elfdahl in Sweden. A table with inlaid top, composed of different descriptions of Swedish stone.

52 WAHRENDORFF, MARTIN VON, Baron, Akers Foundry, near Mariefred, Sweden, Manu.—Seventy-two-pound bomb cannon, with an invention for introducing the charge from behind, and its carriage, made of iron. This kind of ordnance has been selected to mount the fortress of Waxholm, at the entrance to Stockholm from the sea. The specimen exhibited has been duly tested. A six-pound field cannon, Swedish model. A six-pound field cannon, Danish model.

53 WEGELIN, J. Stockholm, Sweden, Inv. and Prop. —A coach, in the construction of which several new inventions have been adapted; such as the wheels being without naves, the axletrees moveable, and the turning effected in an eccentric curve by the fore-carriage. A gig, also with new inventions introduced in its construction. Seven spiral springs for carriages.

54 NORMAN, —, Stockholm, Sweden, Manu.—A sledge, with apron, covered in bearskin.

55 KREUGER, Admiral, Stockholm, Sweden, Inv.—A wind-meter, constructed by the admiral.

56 BOLINDER, J. & C. Stockholm, Sweden, Manu.— Two kitchen ranges of iron. A ship's cabouse of iron. An ironing oven, with flat irons appertaining.

57 BOHMAN, E. J. Stockholm, Sweden, Manu.—A whatnot of Jacaranda, with plate-glass back.

58 STENSTRÖM, P. A. Stockholm, Sweden, Manu.—A dressing-bureau, with polished ornaments on a ground.

59 MALMQVIST, A. Stockholm, Sweden, Manu.— A dressing-bureau, with inlaid zinc ornaments.

60 DUMRATH, H. Stockholm, Sweden, Manu.—A loo table, with inlaid ornaments in different metals.

61 EDBERG, C. K. Stockholm, Sweden, Manu.— A writing table of Jacaranda wood, ornamented. and with a novel contrivance for locking it up.

62 ROSENWALL, P. Stockholm, Sweden, Manu. — A grand piano-forte.

63 SJÖBLOM, C. G. Stockholm, Sweden, Manu. — A painted table, china pattern.

64 JOHNSON, A. Stockholm, Sweden, Manu.—A work table in papier mache.

65 EHRENBERG, J. F. Stockholm, Sweden, Manu.—A spinning-wheel, for double spinning, of measle birch.

66 MÖLLENBORG, G. Stockholm, Sweden, Manu.—A candlestick with two figures, in chiselled silver with glass painting.

67 FOLCKER, G. F. Stockholm, Sweden, Manu.— A salver (tea-tray), in chiselled silver. A flower vase in silver filigree work. A drinking can, in embossed silver, representing a scene from Bellman.

68 PALMGREN, P. J. Stockholm, Sweden, Manu.—An inkstand in embossed silver.

68 BERGSTRÖM, J. W. Stockholm, Sweden, Manu.—A chandelier, for 42 lights, of chiselled bronze, gilt. Two candelabras, with figures in the same material. for six lights each. Two candlesticks, with figures in the same material, for four lights each.

70 DJURSON, C., Stockholm, Sweden, Manu.—A lamp of embossed brass.

71 DAHLBOM, P. A., Stockholm, Sweden, Manu.—A tea-urn of embossed brass. Three lacquered tea-trays; three lacquered bread-baskets.

72 AHLBERG, O. Stockholm, Sweden, Manu.—A tenor-horn, of embossed brass.

73 AHLBECK, G. C. Stockholm, Sweden, Manu.—A sword of gilt, and damascened steel.

74 WARODELL, L. J. Stockholm, Sweden, Prop. — Sixteen different pieces of etched and gilt-steel ware, manufactured in Sweden, such as paper-scissors, knives, rules, &c.

75 KOCKUM, G. Malmo, Sweden, Prop.—Seven anvils, hammers, &c., of fine polished cast-steel.

76 LIDBERG, A. G. Stockholm, Sweden, Manu. — Twelve goldsmiths' and watch-makers' tools.

77 BERGSTRÖM, J. W. Stockholm, Sweden, Manu.— A bright-filed picklock, for double lock.

78 HOOK'S IRON WORKS, Smaland, Sweden.—A double-barrelled gun, with percussion lock, and engraving, made by a smith's apprentice, at the above place.

79 HAGSTRÖM, —, Stockholm, Sweden, Manu.—A brace of pistols, for mark-shooting.

80 BERGQUIST, —, Stockholm, Sweden, Manu.—Three models of the Swedish artillery's cannon.

81 HULTMAN, J. A. Stockholm, Sweden, Manu.—Two large lacquered balances.

82 NYSTRAND, —, Eskilstuna, Sweden, Manu.—A pair of skates, with their straps, &c.

83 EKMAN, G. Lessjöforss, Sweden, Manu.—Ten bundles of different kinds of iron wire.

M

84 STAHLBERG, —, Eskilstuna, Sweden, Manu. — Twenty-four carpenters' tools.

85 BERGSTRÖM, J. W. Stockholm, Sweden, Manu.— A chemical balance, with a load of 500 gram. It will give a decided indication of an excess of one-half of a milligram, in either of the scales. A hydro-electric induction apparatus, with pile.

86 LINDEROTH, G. W., Stockholm, Manu.—A time-piece, striking the hours, in carved and gilt frame-work. Fine cog-wheels for watches.

87 BERNHARDT, G. Nyköping and Torp, Sweden Manu. —Two carriage-wheels, and several parts of wheels, manufactured by machinery.

88 FOLCKER, J. P. & SON, Stockholm, Sweden, Manu.— Ten pieces of silk damask for furniture.

89 ALMGREN K. A. Stockholm, Sweden, Manu.—A piece of brocaded silk damask, for furniture.

90 MEYERSON, L. Stockholm, Sweden, Manu.—Two pieces of silk stuff, for covering furniture.

91 CASPARSSON & SCHMIDT, Stockholm, Sweden, Manu. —Two pieces of flowery gros de Naples.

92 HANEL, C. E. Stockholm, Sweden, Manu.— Two boxes, containing sundry cordwainers' trimmings.

93 ELIASSON, L. J. Norrköping, Sweden, Manu.—Six pieces of corduroy, for trousers.

94 STENBERG, G. Jönköping, Sweden, Manu.—Three table-cloths and three dozen finger-napkins, made in hand-loom by exhibitor.

95 HAGA SILKWORM PLANTATION, near Stockholm.— Specimens of Swedish silk and cocoons.

96 LINDGREN, CONSTANCE, Stockholm, Sweden, Manu.— Three pieces of embroidery, one of them being a portrait of King Oscar.

97 HASSELGREN, L. C. Stockholm, Sweden, Manu.— A writing-case and a box of water-colours.

98 JOHANSSON, J. Stockholm, Sweden, Manu.—A case containing stearine candles; stearine in cakes; a case containing impressions in plaster.

99 HIERTA, L. J., & MICHAELSON, J. Stockholm, Sweden, Manu.—Sixteen packages of stearine candles; a pot of clain soup; a bottle of sulphuric acid.

100 LUNDGREN, P. W., Stockholm, Sweden, Manu.— Grain, syrup, vinegar, &c., prepared from potatoes.

101 SEYBOLDT & Co. Stockholm, Sweden, Manu.— Three sugar-loaves, made with overturning-pan.

102 NORBERG & SATHER's, Iron Mines, Sweden, Pro.— A case containing specimens of ore.

103 BJÖRCKMAN, J. L. Stockholm, Sweden, Manu.— A case containing boxes, little trays, &c., made of birch bark.

104 BECK, F. Stockholm, Sweden, Manu.— Ten specimens of bookbinding.

105 SCHULDHEIS, A. E., Stockholm, Sweden, Manu.— A case containing combmakers' ware.

106 ERICSSON, A. & Co. Stockholm, Sweden, Manu.— Four various hats.

107 ISOZ, J. P. Stockholm, Sweden, Manu.—Twenty-one pairs of gloves, different kinds.

108 GULDA, J. Stockholm, Sweden, Manu.—A paletot, lining of Swedish martin-fur. A cloak, lining of Swedish squirrel skins. Three muffs, various. A fur cape.

109 FORSELL, D. Stockholm, Sweden, Manu.—A stuffed silver bear skin, suitable for a mat to place under the writing table. A fur coat, made of the skins of rein-deer calves, from Norrland.

110 CARLSSON, C. A. Stockholm, Sweden, Manu. — Twenty-nine various specimens of brushes.

111 ARONDAL's Manufactory, near Gothenburg, Sweden.—Seven rolls of paper-hangings.

112 M. STUBECKE, Stockholm, Sweden, Manu.—Five pairs of boots and shoes, &c.

113 HEURLIN, —, Stockholm, Sweden, Manu.—A quantity of playing cards.

114 WARODELL, L. J. Stockholm, Sweden, Prop.—Two pots, made of pot-stone, and mounted.

115 BROLING, J. Stockholm, Sweden, Des.—A proof-sheet of Swedish bank-notes, designed and executed by the exhibitor.

116 KULBERG, V. Stockholm, Sweden, Manu.—A chronometer.

117 UDDEHOLM'S COMPANY, Wermland, Sweden. — Three specimens of steel iron ore.

Great Exhibition of the Works of Industry of all Nations, 1851.

THE CATALOGUE'S ACCOUNT OF ITSELF.

Extracted from Dickens'. " Household Words," August 23rd, 1851.

I AM a Catalogue of the Great Exhibition You are the Public. I intend to have some private talk with you, and pour into your ear the story of my early life.

Of a class of celebrated men there is a common saying, that

"They learn in suffering what they teach in song."

I, as a celebrated Catalogue, had much to go through with ere I learnt that which I teach now in the Illustrated Edition, the Official Edition, the French Edition, the German Edition, and the Twopenny Edition. I call myself a celebrated Catalogue, and I consider myself a work of great importance. My father, the Exhibition, certainly begot in me an illustrious son, who shall hand down his name for the refreshment of posterity. My mother, the Committee, by whom I was brought forth, has, I think, been abundantly rewarded for her pains. There would have been a visible blank in the world's history if I had not been born.

On matters of business it is well known that my manner of speaking is extremely terse; I'm none of your diffuse Catalogues that quote poetry out of unpublished manuscripts or out of Scott, and have as many explanations to make as Ministers when Parliament is sitting, or as turtle-doves who have wounded one another's feelings, and desire to re-establish peace. I say a great deal, to be sure, but then there is a great deal in what I do say. This being my business habit, and which, as you know, fits me uncommonly tight, I feel it a relief now to throw off restraint, and wear something a little easier; something more flowing. In fact I mean to flow out now into a tide of gossip; to pour into your ear, confidentially, a stream of information on the subject of my early life, and to unbend—if I may say so, to un-catalogue myself; to loosen myself from the accustomed bondage by which I am compelled to travel only on a certain path. Still it is possible that a confirmed business character, like mine, may slip into the old train. Fond of arithmetic by nature, Walkingame is Byron to me, and my Wordsworth is De Morgan. Should these facts peep out, and should my figures be Arabic, with less entertainment in them than some other Arabian things that might be mentioned, you must shrug your shoulders, and say, It's his way; for, after all, what is he but a Catalogue?

What but a Catalogue? No, don't say that, because it sounds a little like depreciation. Now, I cannot afford to be depreciated, because, as it is, my greatness is not fairly understood. Mr. Dando's appetite for oysters was large; but what would you say about Mr. Dando when you reached home after dining with that Major Cartwright, whose own notion of a dinner you will find put down in one of Southey's common-place books? Said he to the young poet, "I make only two cuts at a leg of mutton. The first takes all that is on one side; the second all that is on the other. After that, I put the bone across my knife to get the marrow."

The epic grandeur of Major Cartwright's dinner, with its two sublime cuts, would put out of your mind the lesser lyric of a Dando, though nineteen dozen of natives should give *eclat* to his performance. The clatter going on about that horrid Exhibition Building keeps me, I fancy, too much unobserved. If I were to draw another parallel (the term is mathematical, but I am not yet in a state of De-Morganisation) —were I to draw another parallel, I should allude to the great mountain, Chimborazo, which is said in its first aspect to disappoint all travellers. The enormous magnitude of all surrounding features, dwarfs the chief feature to the mind; there are no Brighton Downs or Salisbury Plains at hand, as objects of comparison. Now, you have made a Chimborazo of the Exhibition, and it towers in Hyde Park, and you are astounded, and you do not look at the surrounding elevations. Call the peak Paxton, if you please; but I tell you that this peak is the centre of a mountain system which presents grand and bold heights to your view. Call me a mountain, and my peaks, if you will, you may call Ellis, Playfair, Yapp (my compilers), Clowes (my printer), and so forth. Never mind measuring comparative heights. Around Mont Blanc are many mountains; there are many large hills clustering round Snowdon. One fool makes many; one wise man makes more: and one great fact creates around it generally other facts great in themselves, although less lofty than the centre around which they are collected. In this way I am great, and what I want to talk to you for now, is this: I want to have my greatness understood.

I shall begin by quoting from a high authority, namely, myself; and when I say myself, I mean the Illustrated Catalogue. There I provide you with a little information, which I will repeat in a condensed form; and then, with as much modesty as is consistent with a proper self-respect, I shall have pride and pleasure in communicating to you some additional particulars. In the first place, you are aware that I am not one of your ordinary Catalogues; a list of books, or specimens already arranged and ticketed, made in a quiet way by a gentleman who walks among the articles in dressing-gown and slippers; then deliberately printed and revised in presence of the original articles which it is de-

signed to comprehend. No, nothing of the sort. I was a Catalogue before the Crystal Palace was an Exhibition. From the north and the south, from the east and the west, my fragments were brought together in ships and deposited by postmen at Hyde Park, in one parti-coloured heap. Tah-tsi here, Shah Tishoo there, 'Sharps over the water, John Smith at the Antipodes, Oaweehoitoo in the Sandwich Islands, Monsieur Tonson of Provence, Herr Grubstik of Heinefettersdorf, Ben Ismael, and Paskyvitchikoffsky, and fifteen thousand people more—deliberately I say, fifteen thousand people, of all climes, all tempers, and all manner of hands at literary composition, had to be written to, and from each had to be received his modicum of "copy." Before the articles described were sent, or when they were upon the road, each contributor was applied to for his description of the articles he meant to send. Overwhelming might have been the eloquence of Shah Tishoo, descanting on his carpet; stupifying might have been the account given by Meinherr Grubstik of his case of pipe-heads. If no precaution had been used, I should have been even a more wonderful thing than I now am; but there would have been a something fearful in my composition. I should have been a monster like that chronicled in Frankenstein. To obviate this inconvenience, printed forms were supplied to the contributors. These forms, which were to be to the Catalogue what the manuscript of an author is to his proposed work, were framed with care, and were accompanied with instructions for filling them up, which suggested those points on which interesting or important information might be supplied, together with the descriptive account. There were four varieties, each appropriated to one of the four great sections of Raw Materials, Machinery, Manufactures, and Fine Arts. The essential characters of these forms were similar in each section, but the instructions for filling them up differed necessarily with the peculiar differences suggested by each section. The subjoined form represents that used in sending in descriptions of machinery, and is a type of those used in the other sections:—

" List of Articles of MACHINERY to be Exhibited by
———— Exhibitor's Surname.———— Christian Name.
———— Country.———— Address, stating nearest Post Town.
———— Capacity in which the Exhibitor appears, whether as *Producer, Importer, Manufacturer, Designer, Inventor,* or *Proprietor.*

No. of Articles.	DESCRIPTIONS.

In order to facilitate their classification on being returned by exhibitors, the forms in the four different sections were printed in black, blue, red, and yellow, the latter applying to sculpture and fine art, the former to raw materials, and the intermediate ones respectively to machinery and manufactures. Every exhibitor was required to send in one of these forms, accompanied with a duplicate in every respect similar to it, and in so doing was supplied with a "Receipt for Catalogue Forms," which was a guarantee for the reception of his goods into the Building. A very large number of these forms were printed and supplied to local committees, and to all exhibitors who applied for them, together with instructions for filling them up. These I omit. They are well-articulated skeletons on which to construct a succinct and sufficient description; general forms like the "Rules for taking Cases," given to medical students in many of our hospitals.

Of the two copies sent in, one was held by the Executive Committee; the other placed in the hands of the compiler, Mr. Yapp. The directions above specified, of course, did give a certain uniformity and a reasonably manageable character to the separate flakes of the great storm of description. It is also to be understood that many of the exhibitors neglected altogether, or postponed to the last minute, their answers; many answered in their own rambling way, with a good deal of self-laudation; and many who endeavoured to comply with the desires of the Executive, made a sad mess of their descriptions, "unaccustomed as they were to public writing." These returned forms had then to be taken as they came, and referred to their respective classes. The classes were thirty in number, and the classifier was Dr. Lyon Playfair. The forms were then gone through in the compiler's office: all superfluous matter was as far as possible crossed out of them · knotty sentences were unravelled as far as time permitted, and bad grammar mended. The sending out of forms occupied several men for nearly a month, during which time they had folded, enclosed, and directed more than fifty thousand printed epistles. I am not quoting my Illustrated Edition now, but have begun to gossip, for I want to tell you a few odd things more in detail about my compilation. The most minute information, I know, is welcome, when it concerns any celebrated character. The office of my compiler was opened in the Building in Hyde Park, on the 21st of January, 1851, with a staff composed of the compiler-in-chief, and three *aides-de-plume*. After a lapse of a few weeks, this number was increased by one, and remained then fixed until the middle of April, when it was further increased. Six individuals then worked on with occasional aid until the end of May; when five or less, were found to be sufficient, and in the beginning of July, all compilation duty ceased.

The returns of exhibitors from divers parts began to meet each other in the compiler's office towards the end of January. As they came, they were sorted into sections and arranged alphabetically. Then they were re-examined to ascertain how many had neglected to bring duplicates; and duplicates were made in the office to supply all such deficiencies. For a third time, the returns were then examined, in order to compare them with a list of the proposed exhibitors; and not a few supernumerary papers, sent on speculation, were in this way detected and cast out. Then followed the grammatical revision; and finally, the packet in each class had its contents numbered, and the numbers registered, before it passed out of the compiler's office, and into the office of the printer.

The first parcel reached the printer's on the 31st of January, and on the 31st of March, six thousand and ten returns (from exhibitors in Great Britain and Ireland) had been sent to be set up in type After this time the printer was supplied at a more leisurely pace; and on the 22nd of April, the number of forms set up had advanced to six thousand two hundred and forty-one. The Colonial and Foreign returns were proceeded with simultaneously. Returns from the colonies were sent to press between the 6th of March and 21st of April · foreign returns between February 3rd and April 23rd, on which day the last fragment of my original manuscript was laid at the printer's door. The briskest of the foreign states, if we must judge by its promptitude in sending a return, was Tunis. The second parcel of foreign returns came from Lübeck, and the third from Switzerland. All the matter about which I have been speaking was first printed for the Illustrated Edition of the public's humble servant, and kept set up in a fragmentary manner, until that work was revised for publication. Proof impressions, taken from these fragments, were sent to the gentleman charged with the scientific revision of the work, Mr. Robert Ellis, who allotted the various portions to the scientific annotators. For a few remarks upon those annotators, I must refer once more to the information given by my Illustrated self.

Of course, among the returned forms there would not only be grammatical confusion to correct, but a large number of scientific blunders, Things would be falsely named; foreign scientific words would be inaccurately rendered, familiar objects of trade would be popularly expressed, and throughout the whole range of the Exhibition, a Catalogue supplied by thousands of people differently educated, would have no precision, uniformity or coherence. There was a German once, named Feuerstein (flint), who went to French Canada. The Frenchmen there could make nothing of his outlandish name, so they translated it, and called him Gun-flint. The English occupied, after a time, that part of Canada, and as Gun-flint remained among them, he was again translated into Peter Gun. So you would have had in your Catalogue here, Feuerstein; there, Peter Gun; and never could have known them both to represent one and the same name. To obtain uniformity, therefore, the plan was adopted which I now quote.

" A number of scientific gentlemen gave their consent to undertake the revision and correction of proofs of the returned forms in their peculiar departments, with a view to remove from them those errors which might present themselves, and to supply what might appear requisite to give prominence to their really important features. In addition to this, it appeared advisable, as critical observations were necessarily inadmissible, to relieve the tedium of mere description, and to assist in pointing out the leading features of interest in the objects described, or in direct relation with them, by appending, as the subjects of the proof suggested, such brief annotations as might appear best calculated to effect these objects.

" As a certain degree of harmony of procedure was considered absolutely necessary, in order to give a consistent character to such corrections and annotations, supplied as they would be from a variety of sources, a few suggestions of certain general principles were adopted, and, as far as possible, acted upon. It is not necessary to reproduce the whole of these suggestions in their original form; but since it is important that exhibitors should be informed of the principles which, to a great extent, guided and determined the corrections and annotations which are found in this work, they are here subjoined." Attention was particularly directed to the suggestion, under the head " annotations," by which critical notices were strictly excluded from the annotations appended to the descriptions.

In sending about slips, many of them consisting of three or four lines cut out of other proofs, of course there arose danger of inextricable confusion when the little slips, or snips, should all come back again, and have to be re-arranged.

A simple method of ascertaining not merely the place in the Catalogue, but its entire history, its destination, annotator, and return, was, however, contrived, and the history of every proof has thus been accurately recorded. The information thus obtained was so accurate and precise, that on the temporary delay of very small proofs, their original destination was instantly discovered, together with the date of transmission, and the name of the annotator to whom they had been sent. Much punctuality characterised the return of the dismembered portions of this large volume. Had not such been the case, the original plan of scientific and technical revision could not have been persisted in. But, while all this work was going on, I was being taught to speak in French and German, by gentlemen engaged especially for that purpose.

Furthermore, and finally, the slips of the large Catalogue, revised, annotated, and re-revised, were placed before the Compiler, that he might condense each description into an average of about three lines, for the shilling, or ' Official Catalogue." The reduction of the whole of the proofs of the British Exhibitors only occupied the Compiler, almost without any intermission, from the 24th of March to the 24th of April—just a month. The Foreign and Colonial portion was commenced on the 10th and finished on the 28th of April; so that the rough proof of the Catalogue was only completed two days before the opening of the Exhibition; fifty-two persons having been employed in the compiling and the annotating of these two English Catalogues.

It was not until all, or nearly all, the fragments were in the printer's hands that the final numbering and arrangement could take place; so that, at the last moment, all my inside was twisted up and down. Classification this was called. The Classification began at the printer's just before the arrival of the last corrected slips; and they came, as I told you, only two days before the Exhibition would be open, and the Catalogue would be demanded by the public. Woe be to the printer who should go to bed at such a crisis! The " Official Catalogue" was classified, made up, and printed, and bound in four days. The first perfect impression was only produced at ten o'clock at night upon the eve of the eventful opening. Ten thousand Catalogues, properly bound, were punctually delivered at the Building, on the morning of the 1st of May. The two copies presented to Her Majesty and to the Prince, that morning, elegantly bound in morocco, lined with silk, and with their edges gilt, had been bound, lined, and gilded in six hours. Now, perhaps, you do begin to wonder that you had a Catalogue at all upon the 1st of May, and are no longer surprised that, in that first edition, there were included descriptions of articles which the describers had neglected afterwards to send, or that the articles which had arrived of unexpected bulk, or otherwise exceptionally, could not be placed properly in the Building, according to the exact numerical order that had been established in the Catalogue Most of the errors of my first edition are corrected in my second. Now I mean to tell you a few more things about myself, well calculated to excite your admiration.

My " Official" self makes three hundred and twenty pages, or twenty sheets of double foolscap folded into eight. Two hundred and fifty thousand copies of this have been printed; one hundred and five tons of paper having been consumed therein; and, upon this paper, the duty paid is one thousand four hundred and seventy pounds. The publications connected with the Catalogues, and the number of pages in each, are as follows:—

English, French, and German Catalogues	960
Descriptive and Illustrated ditto	2,000
English and French Synopsis	192
Hunt's Handbooks	1,000
Penny and Twopenny English and French Plans and Guides	48
Priced Lists	500
Advertisements	160
Jury Reports	750
Pages	5,610

The new type of these publications is retained, set up for constant use and correction, and the weight of metal thus employed is sixty thousand pounds.

Up and down the courts of the Exhibition, I have been in the company of a good many people who have audibly voted me a bore I trust that I shall not again have to complain of this. I contain the composition of some fifteen thousand authors; most of them authors for the first time, who have had their excrescences pruned, and their diction occasionally mended. Now, the first production of an author, if only three lines long, is usually esteemed by himself as a sort of Prince Rupert's drop which is destroyed entirely if a person makes upon it but a single scratch. Some thousand authors, therefore, are dissatisfied with the attempts made to render me available for public use.

I say no more; having thus far indulged you with my confidence, I wrap myself in dignified reserve, conscious that I have told you quite enough to secure for myself your respect henceforward.

[60

MR. MURRAY'S ENGLISH HANDBOOKS.

Handbook of Modern London;
OR, LONDON AS IT IS IN 1851.

Among the Contents of this Work will be found a full Account and Description of the various

Palaces.	Railroads.	Theatres.
Public Buildings.	Places of Amusement.	River Thames.
Galleries of Art.	Streets.	Docks.
Churches.	Hospitals & Asylums.	Public Monuments.
Parks and Gardens.	Public Companies.	Excursions in the En-
Museums.	Clubs.	virons.
Private Mansions.	Exhibitions.	Conveyances, &c. &c.

With Hints about Hotels, Lodgings, &c. With Plans, &c. 18mo.

*** The aim of this Work is to describe to a stranger visiting London for the first time those features of the metropolis *best worth seeing*, and the way in which they may be seen to the best advantage : in other word, to make a "HANDBOOK OF MODERN LONDON" for the use of foreigners and strangers, on the plan of MURRAY'S CONTINENTAL HANDBOOKS.

Westminster Abbey.
ITS ART, ARCHITECTURE, AND ASSOCIATIONS.
New Edition. 16mo. 1s.

The British Museum.
A HANDBOOK TO THE ANTIQUITIES AND SCULPTURE.
Woodcuts. Post 8vo.

The Galleries of Art
IN AND NEAR LONDON, WITH CATALOGUES, AND BIOGRA-
PHICAL AND CRITICAL NOTICES, INCLUDING

The National Gallery.	Hampton Court.	Soane's Museum.
Windsor Castle.	Dulwich Gallery.	Barry's Pictures.

Post 8vo. 10s.

Windsor and Eton.
THE CASTLE, ST. GEORGE'S CHAPEL, AND ETON COLLEGE.
New Edition. 16mo. 1s.

Handbook for London;
PAST AND PRESENT.   BY PETER CUNNINGHAM, F.S.A.

Among the Contents of this Work will be found Descriptions of

Remarkable Old Inns, Coffee Houses, and Taverns.	Old London Prisons. Places referred to by Old Writers.
Town Houses of the Old Nobility.	The Wards of London.
Places of Public Entertainment.	The Churches.
Old London Sights.	Residences of Remarkable Men.
Ancient Theatres.	Streets Remarkable for some
Ancient Crosses.	Event.
The Hostels of Church Dignitaries.	Burial Places of Eminent Indi-
Privileged Places for Debtors.	viduals.

Second Edition. Post 8vo. 16s.

" We can conceive no companion more welcome to an enlightened foreigner visiting the metropolis than Mr. Cunningham, with his laborious research, his scrupulous exactness, his alphabetical arrangement, and his authorities."— *Times.*

Handbook of England & Wales.

Giving an account of the *Places and Objects* best worth visiting ; more especially those rendered interesting by Historical Associations, or likely to attract the notice of intelligent strangers and passing travellers ; arranged in connexion with the most frequented Roads and Railways in England.

With Maps and Plans. Post 8vo.   (*In preparation.*)

Part I.—The Eastern Counties ; including Essex, Suffolk, Norfolk
Cambridge, and Lincoln.   *Nearly ready.*

II.—Midland Counties ; Herts, Bedford, Northampton, Leicester, Bucks, Nottinghamshire.

III.—Derbyshire and Yorkshire.

IV.—Durham, Northumberland, Staffordshire, Cheshire, Lancashire, Cumberland, The Lakes.

V.—Berks, Bucks, Oxfordshire, Warwick, Gloucester, Worcester, Hereford, Shropshire, Cheshire.

VI.—North and South Wales.

VII.—Devon and Cornwall.   (*Ready.*)

VIII.—Somerset, Wilts, Dorset.

IX.—Hampshire, Isle of Wight Sussex, Surrey, Kent.

England as it is,
POLITICAL, SOCIAL, AND ECONOMICAL, IN 19TH CENTURY.
2 Vols. Post 8vo. 18s.

" We have directories for our streets, and we have essays without number written from every point of the political and religious compass upon every imaginable topic. But a manual which places before us, in a tone of sober and staid narrative, the whole of our being as a people, is what has not, that we are aware of, been thought of before." — *John Bull.*

The Manufacturing Districts
OF ENGLAND, SCOTLAND, IRELAND,
THE CHANNEL ISLANDS, AND ISLE OF MAN.
2 Vols. Post 8vo. 12s.

Travel Talk.
A SERIES OF SENTENCES, DIALOGUES, AND VOCABULARIES IN
THE ENGLISH, FRENCH, GERMAN, AND ITALIAN LANGUAGES.
18mo. 5s.

The Official Handbook.
A MANUAL OF HISTORICAL AND POLITICAL REFERENCE.
One Volume. Fcap. 8vo.

The object of this Work is to show concisely the machinery by which the GOVERNMENT of the country is carried on, including the RIGHTS, DUTIES, and AUTHORITIES OF THE QUEEN AND ROYAL FAMILY, with a succinct account of the duties, emoluments, authorities, and political relations of each DEPARTMENT, CIVIL, MILITARY, JUDICIAL, and ECCLESIASTICAL, as will, it is hoped, render the volume a useful manual of reference to all persons desirous to make themselves acquainted with British Institutions.

JOHN MURRAY, ALBEMARLE STREET.

LIST OF ARTICLES

SHOWN BY THE

Gutta Percha Company

AT THE

GREAT EXHIBITION OF 1851.

Waterproof Applications.

Specimens of covered canvas, and patent waterproof Gutta Percha cloth. Waterproof soles for boots and shoes. Piece of solutioned jean for insoles. Hydropathic bandages. Waterproof heels with metal tips.

For Agricultural Purposes.

Pumps for liquid manure. Stable bucket. Traces. Horse-shoe pad.

For Manufacturing Purposes.

Flat and round bands for machinery. Bucket. Pump bucket. Valves. Cutting board for glove-makers. Piece of felt edging for paper-makers. Flax holders (Plummer's patent). Specimens of packing for steam-engines. Washers for cold-water pipes. Bosses for flax manufacturers. Woven driving band, saturated with Gutta Percha. Specimens of Gutta Percha card cloth, of three and four plies; a substitute for leather for the backs of cards used in carding wool, cotton, and other fibrous substances.

For Maritime Purposes.

Anchor-floats. Buoys. Fishing-net floats. Life buoys, and air-tight life-boat cells. Pilot's hat. Sou'-wester hat. Coils of round band for signal halliards. Speaking trumpets.

Decorative Applications.

Brackets. Console tables. Cornices. Ceiling centres. Mirror and other frames. Picture frames. Friezes. Girandoles. An ornamental side-table, in panels, representing the Four Seasons, with glass frame, in three compartments; in the style of Gibbons. Chessmen and stand. Frame for print of the "Anti-Corn-Law League." Daguerreotype frames. Panels. Mouldings in imitation of carved oak, rosewood, &c. &c., for the decoration of rooms, ships' saloons, cabinet work, &c. Pattern Book of ditto. Specimens of gilded Gutta Percha.

LISTE DES OBJETS

envoyés à

L'EXPOSITION DE LONDRES

DE 1851

par la Compagnie fabriquant du

Gutta Percha.

Articles Imperméables.

Echantillons de tissus brevetés imperméables. Semelles de souliers et de bottes, imperméables. Tissu préparé imperméable pour les semelles intérieures. Bandages hydropathiques. Talons montés sur metal, imperméables.

Articles d' Usage Agricole.

Pompes pour engrais liquide. Seau d'écurie. Bourrelet de fer-à-cheval.

Articles employés dans les Manufactures.

Bandes plattes et circulaires pour les machines. Seau. Seau-de-pompe. Souspapes. Planchette pour la coupe des gants. Bordure à l'usage des fabriquants de papiers. Poignée brevetée par Plummer, pour le lin. Renfourage des pistons des machines-à-vapeur. Disques de tuyaux à eau froide. Bossettes employées dans les manufactures de lin. Bande tressée mécanique préparée avec solution de Gutta Percha. Morceau de toile cardée, en Gutta Percha, à trois et à quatre plis, employées au lieu de cuir pour la cardée des cotonlaines et autres tissus.

Articles employés dans la Marine.

Flotteurs d'ancres. Bouées. Flotteurs de filets. Bouées de sauvetage, et cellules imperméables pour bateaux de sauvetage. Chapeau de pilote. Chapeau "sud-wester" (de marin). Bandes circulaires pour signaliser. Porte-voix.

Objets de Luxe et de Décoration.

Tasseaux. Tables Consoles. Corniches. Centres de plafonds, Cadres divers. Cadres de tableaux. Frises. Girandoles. Une table élégante avec des panneaux ornees représentant les quatre Saisons avec un chassis de glaces en trois compartiments. Echecs et guéridon. Cadre pour la gravure de l' "Anti-Corn-Law League." Cadres pour daguerréotype. Panneaux. Moulures, imitations de chêne ciselé, de bois de rose, &c. &c., pour décorer les salons, l'intérieur des batiments, &c. &c. Livre d'échantillons de ces articles. Ornemens dorés en Gutta Percha.

Surgical and other Applications.

Bed straps. Ear cornets. Ear trumpets. Hearing apparatus for the deaf in churches, &c. Pessaries. Pieces of sheeting for splints. Pieces of thin sheeting for bandages, &c. Stethoscope. Dr. Foucart's clavicular splint. Set of Teeth in Gutta Percha Base or Bed.

Chemical and Electrical Applications.

Acid scoop. Vessels for acids. Carboys. Chemical bottles. Chemical flasks. Various specimens of submarine and other Electric Telegraph wire. Funnels. Insulating stool. Galvanic battery troughs, with 12 or 24 cells. Galvanic battery cell. Specimen of lining for acid tanks. Syphons.

Domestic Purposes.

Basins. Bowls. Baskets. Bread platter. Bouquet holder. Bottles. Bottling boot. Specimens of clothes line. Curtain rings. Decanter stands. Drinking cups. Finger cups. Inkstands. Ink cups. Lighter stands. Paper weights. Plates. Trays, ornamental, various patterns. Vases. Wafer holders. Watch stands. Specimens of lining for water tanks, &c. Specimens of window-blind cord.

Miscellaneous Applications.

Architects' plan cases. Bouncing balls. Golf ball. Cricket balls. Communion plate. Carriage tubes. Specimens of corrugated sheet for wine packing. Dolls. Fire bucket. Piece of fringe for mourning coaches. Fencing-stick guard. Cornish miner's hat. Northumberland miner's hat. Life preservers. Medallions. Music case. Discs for official seals. Specimens of paper for damp walls. Police staff. Powder flasks. Railway conversational tubes. Coil of sash line. Stop-cocks. Pairs of skates. Samples of thread. Tap ferrules. Whips. Specimens of welting cord for female dresses. Specimens of tubing of various sizes. Speaking tube. Union joints for Gutta Percha tubing.

Applications. Chirurgiques.

Sangles de lits Trompettes cornet pour les sourds. Trompett à l'usage des sourds. Appareil l'usage des sourds pour les église Pessaires. Morceaux de toile po éclipes. Morceaux de toile mince po bandages, &c. Stéthoscope. Ecli claviculaire du Dr. Foucart. Râteli complet monté sur Gutta Percha.

Applications Chimiques et Ele triques.

Ecope pour les acides. Vases po les acides. Carboys (cruches po préserver les acides). Bouteilles ch miques. Flasques chimiques. Pl sieurs especes de fil télégraphiq électrique sous-marin et autre Etonnoirs. Tabouret électriqu Auges de machines galvaniqu l'une à 12 et l'autre à 24 division Cercle galvanique simple. Manié de doubler les reservoirs à acide Siphons.

Articles Usuels.

Basins. Gamelles. Paniers. Pl teau pour le pain. Porte-bouqu Bouteilles. Bottes de remplissa de bouteilles. Cordes de blanch sage. Anneaux de rideaux. Port bouteilles. Gobelets. Doigtiers. Ec toires. Encriers. Portes-lumièr Presses papiers. Assiettes. Plates divers et de luxe. Vases. Port pains à cacheter. Portes-montr Echantillons de doublures pour reservoirs d'eau, &c. Echantill de cordes de jalousies.

Applications Diverses.

Boête à dessins d'architectu Balles élastiques. Balle. Ete Assiette pour aumônes dans églises. Tuyaux de voitures. Ech tillons de draps ridés d'emball pour les vins. Poupées. Seau d cendies. Morceau de frange p voitures de deuil. Garde porte-c d'escrime. Chapeau de mineur nouaillien. Chapeau de mineur Northumberland. Conserves. daillons. Etuis de musique. ques de cachets officiels. Echar lons de papiers pour les m humides. Bâtons de sergents police. Pulverins. Tubes de versation de chemin-de-fer. Rou de corde de jalousies. Robi d'arrêts. Patines. Echantillons fil. Viroles de robinets. Fou Echantillons de corde-à-border robes de dames. Echantillons tuyaux de dimensions dive Tuyau porte-voix. Jointures tubes en Gutta Percha.

GUTTA PERCHA COMPANY, Patentees, 18, Wharf-road, City-road, London.

J. & J. COLMAN,

MANUFACTURERS OF

MUSTARD, STARCH, BLUES, AND BRITISH GUM,

9, COLLEGE HILL UPPER THAMES STREET,

LONDON.

MUSTARD.—J. & J. COLMAN invite the attention of English and Foreign Merchants, and traders in general to the qualities of their Mustard, (manufactured from the best description of English Brown Seed,) and in so doing would observe that they have invariably directed their energies to the production of an article *warranted genuine in its character*, and which should combine the strength and pungency of the Seed with a certain pleasantness of flavour, whereby to render it one of the most agreeable of condiments—and it having ever been a source of complaint that Mustard when sent to Foreign Countries has, by the influence of climate and other causes, been considerably deteriorated, and at times so far damaged as to render it unfit for use, J. & J. COLMAN beg to announce that their DOUBLE SUPERFINE quality has stood the severest tests of climate and every contingency of transit; they have, therefore, the utmost confidence in recommending it for Foreign and Colonial supply as well as for Home Consumption. It is packed in bottles of 1 lb. and ½lb. of the largest sizes, for Foreign Markets.

In addition to the above, J. & J. COLMAN manufacture the three following kinds of Mustard, viz.—SUPERFINE, FINE and SECONDS, which qualities are warranted good, and will be found available for general purposes. These kinds are packed either in casks, tins, or jars, as well as in the usual sized bottles.

STARCH has been for a considerable time offered to the Public in qualities so various and dissimilar, that it has been found difficult to determine what to purchase, in order to secure at a low price an article of uniform good quality, which can be prepared by ladies and laundresses with the least possible trouble—and it having been discovered from experience that RICE STARCH is more to be depended upon in its application than any other, J. & J. COLMAN have devoted their best attention to the subject, and spared neither pains nor expense to bring the article to perfection. They have much pleasure to inform the trade that they have secured by Letters Patent a process for manufacturing a No. 1 PATENT RICE STARCH, and SATIN GLAZE RICE STARCH, of a quality superior to every other made from Rice, being quite free from all mucilaginous matter. It is SOLUBLE, and can be used with greater ease and facility than the common Starch. Sold in packets of 5 lb., 1 lb., ½ lb., and ¼ lb. each.

Ladies are especially invited to test the above SATIN GLAZE RICE STARCH. *Being used in a fluid state it imparts an equality of stiffness and gloss to the finer fabrics, and produces a finish unequalled by any other yet offered.*

As many persons, however, may still prefer the Wheaten Starches, J. & J. COLMAN continue to manufacture with the same care and attention their usual kinds, viz.—No. 1. London Starch. Patent White Starch. Soluble Satin Glaze Starch.

BLUE.—This article is manufactured of various shades of colour from Indigo and Prussian Blue, the former being used principally for Laundress purposes, the latter by the Manufacturers of Flannels, &c., &c., and when made genuine, they impart a colour which cannot be obtained from other ingredients. J. & J. COLMAN *warrant* the genuineness of their Blues, and the trade are respectfully invited to purchase them.

BRITISH GUM and GUM SUBSTITUTE, used by Silk and Calico Printers, in every variety of shade and colour, need only to be tried to insure satisfaction.

N. B.—The attention of English and Foreign Merchants, and the Trade in general is specially directed to the above articles, and all orders, addressed as above, will meet with prompt attention.

[201

JOHNSON, CAMMELL, & CO.,
CYCLOPS STEEL WORKS, SHEFFIELD.

EXTRACT FROM "THE TIMES."

"COMMENCING with the miscellaneous specimens contributed by various manufacturers, we then find last, though not least, a striking group from the Cyclops Works, the property of Messrs. JOHNSON, CAMMELL, & Co., comprising specimens of files and rasps from 1 to 46 inches long (some of them very remarkable in form, manufactured specially for use in the national dockyards), iron and steel suitable for engineering, tool-making, &c.; specimens of locomotive engine and tender, railway-carriage, horse-box, buffer and other springs, &c. Together with these specimens is displayed a large and beautifully executed model of the Cyclops Works, accurately representing all the ramifications of that extensive establishment. To this house is devoted not only a large portion of space at the end of the western wall and the counter beneath, but also the wall space at right angles with it as far as it extends. The name and address of the firm, together with the arms of royalty, are conspicuously blazoned, so as to attract the eye of visitors perambulating the principal avenue and the galleries in various directions. The large display of files in the compartment of Messrs. JOHNSON, CAMMELL, & Co. call for particular notice, inasmuch as, though of first-rate quality, they have not been made for exhibition, but taken from the ordinary stock. Of the larger descriptions of files it is well known that greater quantities are produced at the Cyclops Works than at any other house in the kingdom, while in the articles of springs it is equally certain that that establishment ranks first in the world in the extent of its productions; besides which, it stands amongst the foremost in the manufacture of steel. These facts sufficiently account for the great breadth of space assigned to Messrs. JOHNSON, CAMMELL, & Co. in the locality in which they exhibit."

EXTRACT FROM "THE WORLD IN ITS WORKSHOPS."

"WE now turn more immediately to the steel articles in the exhibition of British manufactures, many of them making an effective display. The most interesting contributions in this class are from the far-famed Cyclops Steel Works, Sheffield, the manufactory of Messrs. JOHNSON, CAMMELL, & Co., which enterprising firm were the inventors of the celebrated Patent Elastic Cast-steel Railway and other Springs, and, by their skilful manipulation of the metal, have vastly enlarged the consumption and improved the general quality and manufacture of steel. Here we have specimens of the different processes of making steel from the raw iron as imported from Sweden and Russia up to the most refined state of the metal, and, also, of manufactured articles in which the best quality of steel is an indispensable requisite. Follow that piece of iron through all its various stages, carbonized, converted, melted, and refined, until it terminates in one of the laminæ of those highly-finished carriage-springs, and you have a lesson in manufacturing art, few of which can be more useful or instructive. Then let your mind range over the fabrication of the metal—in the foreign department for instance—and trace in imagination the progressive stages of a similar piece of the raw material in the foundries of those countries described in a preceding page, and you will instantly recognise the cause of our superiority in the manufacture of steel: indeed the foreign metal in its most finished state is scarcely worth the name of steel, not having passed through the cementing ordeal to which it is subjected in England. The steel of Messrs. JOHNSON, CAMMELL, & Co., has acquired a high name for its superior quality, whether it be in the condition of 'cemented blister,' 'double sheer,' elastic spring, or double refined cast steel, all of which enter largely into the purposes of manufacture. In locomotive mechanical aids, such as springs, files, steel, &c. &c., Messrs. JOHNSON, CAMMELL, & Co. make a most interesting and important display; the 'curvilinear tanged file,' for instance, being a grand improvement upon the common form of that tool; so, also, the continuous tooth concave and convex file, which received the well-merited recognition of a medal from the Society of Arts. The steel, engineering, and machinists' files of Messrs. JOHNSON, CAMMELL, & Co., are used solely in Her Majesty's dockyards, the Honourable East India Company's workshops, and most of the public and private engineering establishments in this and other countries; and, from the great estimation in which they are held, bid fair to supersede all others. In mentioning one firm of real practical eminence, we mention, as it were, all that come within the range of their peculiar class of manufacture; therefore, by way of limiting our labours, we shall direct attention to the files of Messrs. JOHNSON, CAMMELL, & Co., whose careful finish will be immediately recognised; to their springs for railway carriages; and, above all, to their piston rod, weighing 16 cwt., the finest and largest piece of steel in the Exhibition. This rod is of cast steel, and has passed through the several processes of manufacture already enumerated, and, as regards its working qualities, it is fair to assume that they are very far more efficient than those of the ordinary pistons, which are generally made of greatly inferior metal.

[302